P9-AFT-451

PR
9619.3   SWEENEY, VERONICA
S936E4   GEOGHEGAN
1985   THE. EMANCIPIST

DATE DUE

PR
9619.3
S936E4
1985

RIVERSIDE CITY COLLEGE
LIBRARY
Riverside, California

DEMCO

THE
EMANCIPIST

AN UNFORGETTABLE EPIC OF AUSTRALIA

VERONICA GEOGHEGAN SWEENEY

SIMON AND SCHUSTER • NEW YORK

Riverside Community College
Library
4800 Magnolia Avenue
Riverside, CA 92506

PR9619.3.S936 E4 1985
Sweeney, Veronica Geoghegan
The emancipist : an
unforgettable epic of
Australia

, characters, places and incidents are either
or are used fictitiously. Any resemblance
iving or dead, is entirely coincidental.

Copyright © 1985 by Veronica Geoghegan Sweeney
All rights reserved
including the right of reproduction
in whole or in part in any form
Published by Simon & Schuster
A Division of Simon & Schuster, Inc.
Simon & Schuster Building
Rockefeller Center
1230 Avenue of the Americas
New York, New York 10020
Originally published in Great Britain by Pan Books Ltd.
SIMON AND SCHUSTER and colophon are registered trademarks of
Simon and Schuster, Inc.

Manufactured in the United States of America

1 2 3 4 5 6 7 8 9 10

Library of Congress Cataloging in Publication Data
Sweeney, Veronica Geoghegan.
    The emancipist: an unforgettable epic of Australia.
    I. Title.
PR9619.3.S936E4   1985   823   85-11947
ISBN: 0-671-60209-8

The extract from the poem The Old Prison (c) Judith Wright, which appears at the beginning of Part
Two, is reprinted by kind permission of the poet and Angus and Robertson Publishers.
    Máirín de Barra from a folk song by Seán O'Ciolean, which appears at the beginning of Part
Three, is translated by Riabárd O'Farachain, from a collection called Love Songs of the Irish,
edited by James N. Healy, and reproduced by kind permission of The Mercier Press.
    The extract at the beginning of Part Four from the poem Song of the Old Boundary Rider by
Vance Palmer, is reproduced by kind permission of the E.V. and J.G. Palmer Estates.
    The extract from The Lament of the Children of Lir, which appears at the beginning of Part
Five, is translated from the Irish by Eoin Neeson in The Second Book of Irish Myths and
Legends, and reproduced by kind permission of The Mercier Press.
    The extract from Dido's Lament for Aeneas, which appears at the beginning of Part Six, is taken
from Collected Poems (first published 1945) by Sidney Keyes, and is reproduced by kind permission
of Routledge & Kegan Paul plc.
    Will You Be As Hard? by Douglas Hyde (1862-1946), which appears at the beginning of Part
Seven, translated from the Irish by Lady Gregory, is taken from the anthology Love Poems of the
Irish, edited by Sean Lucy, published by The Mercier Press, and is reproduced by kind permission of
Mr. Douglas Sealy.

For my mother,
Elizabeth Sweeney
and for
James Brian Walpole
who never doubted.

Steadfast, serene, immovable, the same
Year after year, through all the silent night . . .

Longfellow: *The Lighthouse*

Acknowledgements

In Ireland: my thanks must go first and foremost to Sean Kierse, who honoured me by allowing me to read his then-unpublished manuscript, *The Famine Years in Killaloe*. Greater trust hath no writer . . .

My thanks also to his wife, Kathleen, and to Dolores and Jim McKeogh, all of whom helped so much in the early days of researching the Irish section, and with last minute checks for historical and idiomatic inaccuracies.

I am also indebted to the staff of the *Limerick Chronicle*, the *Clare Champion*, the staff of the Dublin State Paper Office, the librarians of Limerick, Nenagh and Killaloe libraries, the library of Trinity College, Dublin, the National Library of Ireland (with special thanks to Alf McLoughlin), and the librarians of the Law Library of Queen's University, Belfast.

In Australia: my thanks to Charles Tingwell and Shirley Wyndham, and all those connected with the Australian Film Commission who gave me help and encouragement during the early years; the librarians and staff of the State Library of New South Wales, State Archives, the library of the Australian National University, Canberra; the long-suffering staff of the Archives department, State Library of Tasmania, and the libraries of Bowral, Mittagong and Moss Vale; to Ian Brand, Chris Long, Merval Hoare and Milford McArthur for their kind assistance, and to Leslie and Betty Davidson for the long years of comradeship and encouragement.

A very special thanks must go to Colleen Clifford, my teacher, my godmother, and my friend.

Author's note

The characters of this novel are imaginary, but the background is factual, and all the crimes mentioned in Part One did, in fact, take place in County Clare during the Great Famine.

Tineranna is not based in any way upon the Killaloe property called Tinerana, except that I owe a debt to the Gleeson family for allowing me to use the name and change the spelling.

The pronunciation of Irish words differs, sometimes, from place to place within Ireland, and I have kept, as much as possible, to the pronunciation used in Killaloe.

The race of Tasmanian aboriginals numbered a tragic nineteen in the year 1849, when my central character, Aidan O'Brien, arrives in Van Diemen's Land. They were incarcerated at Oyster Bay, and it is quite possible that except for a glimpse in a Hobart street of the redoubtable Queen Trucaninni, Aidan would perhaps never have seen one of the dark people who had once lived at peace with the land that he, and other Europeans, claimed.

In the Southern Highlands of New South Wales, also, the surviving black Australians had long been driven from their park-like hunting grounds to the wilder bush areas or to settlements on the coast. For these reasons, the aboriginal people do not appear within the confines of this story. Much has been written of the tragedy of the lost tribes of Tasmania by knowledgeable and sympathetic writers. The story of the courage and dignity of the Southern Highlands tribes, also, deserves literature devoted to them alone.

There is some difficulty, when one is concerned with the conservation of Australia's forests and wildlife, to write dispassionately of one's characters' exploitation of their environment. It tends to rub the gloss of nostalgia from the word 'pioneer' to find, for example, that thousands upon thousands of koalas were slaughtered for their pelts – as late as the 1920s. I have tried in *The Emancipist* to write a story about men and women and events that have relevance today, for the nineteenth century gave its own challenge, less daunting only in retrospect. I coped with describing the energetic felling of Tasmania's Huon pine forests by reminding myself that Aidan O'Brien, Will Treloar and others like them, saw this country's resources as limitless. For us, today, there is no such excuse.

Veronica Geoghegan Sweeney
Bowral, New South Wales.

A guide to the Irish pronunciation
(Syllable to be emphasised is in italics)

Aidan	*Aid*'n
Ruadh (red)	*Ru*er
Killaloe	Killa*loo*
Ogonnelloe	O*gon*nelloh
Finlea	Fin*lay*
Beal Boru	Bale Bo*ru*
Samhradh (summer)	*Sow*rah
grá (love)	ḡraw
boreen (country lane)	*bor*een
ceili (cottage dance)	*cai*li
Seamus	*Shay*mus
Thady	*Tai*dy
Aoibheal	*Ae*vul
lough (lake)	loch
Tomás	Tom*aws*
Maicin (a spoilt child, a brat)	moc*keen*
Bean sidhe (fairy)	ban *shee*
balbhan	bolla*vawn*
ceolan	*kyo*lawn

Note: The Australian Aboriginal names Berrima, Mittagong and Bowral have their emphasis on the first syllable.

CONTENTS

Part 1
THE BIG HOUSE

For each man kills the thing he loves,
By each let this be heard,
Some do it with a bitter look,
Some with a flattering word.
The coward does it with a kiss,
The brave man with a sword . . .

OSCAR WILDE

1

If William Kelly had looked up towards the hill he would have seen the boy. For a moment he was silhouetted against the final glow of the sunset; an insect-like figure who scrambled over the rise and disappeared just as suddenly into the shadows on the slope. And the boy himself should have heard the horses' hoofs or William Kelly calling to his companion, would, perhaps, have heard, had he not been oblivious to everything but the damp bundle of fur that he held tightly in his arms.

He told himself the dog was not dead. 'Ruadh . . . ' he murmured into the icy coat, 'Y'r sick, that's all . . . Ma will make you right.' This was all that mattered, getting home to Ma. It was a long way from the brook above Finlea where he had finally discovered the puppy. All day he had been searching for her. Always in the week since he had brought her home she had come when he called her name. 'Ruadh . . . Ruadh . . . ' He stumbled on a stone. It was dark and his eyes were half-blind with crying. Before he could recover his balance there was a sharp cry to his left – a swoop of wings – a curlew, frightened from her nest, came swinging threateningly up at him through the dusk. He screeched, afraid, and dodged, and cried the harder in his shame. A curlew . . . Just a curlew . . .

The hedge, now, rising up black before him. Beyond it the road ran right to Killaloe, left to Ogonnelloe. And on that road the boreen branched off, to run past O'Sullivan's, and down to his own cottage and the lough. Almost home . . .

He misjudged the opening in the hedge, scratched himself on the brambles, reeled back, groped forward with one hand and charged out onto the roadway.

He had little warning – the impression of a giant shadow rushing towards him, and he lifted a hand to ward it off . . .

The blow struck his shoulder and chin and sent him down, rolling over and over in the dirt. Above him, confusion – a horse's scream, a man shouting, another swearing . . . and stillness. Afraid, he lay there and did not move, his face pressed into the damp earth, listening as the horses' hoofs ceased their confused tattooing and were still. A voice, quite close – 'Sweet Jesus . . . a child . . . ' and

15

hands, large and strong, were lifting him a little, turning him until he was gazing up into a face. In the darkness he could perceive that the features were even, could sense that the eyes held concern . . . but more frightening, the silk cravat, the well-tailored riding jacket . . . The boy's eyes widened in recognition.

'Dead dog here, sir . . .' A voice from the darkness near the hedge. The boy had squirmed, pulled back from the man's grasp before realizing what he was doing and had scrambled forward on his knees, hands feeling along the ground. 'Ruadh? Ruadh . . . ?'

But once more the hands had grasped him, turned him about. 'At least you're alive . . . Who are you? Do you belong to Tineranna?' The boy did not reply, but recoiled a little in the strong grip. He was afraid of this man and yet . . . there was something good about him . . . Something that reminded the boy of his own father, the clean smell of horses, the faint whiskeyness of the man's breath. Yet this solitary comfort vanished too, when he realized when it was he had last spoken to this man. He was there the day they put Da into the ground. He had been wearing black and had made a speech that made Ma cry . . .

'Come, boy – I want your name.'

The boy moaned in Irish, 'I want to go home . . . let me go home . . .'

The voice by the hedge growled, 'You answer Mister Kelly proper, boy, or it's trouble you'll be in. Now speak up – and in English.'

And the boy knew that voice, too. Rough, it was, with an upward lift when you least expected it. A small, dark man. On Tineranna he was referred to as The Northerner. The boy's father had not liked him. The man holding him said, 'Come, tell me your name. I won't hurt you.'

The boy looked up into the shadowed eyes for a moment. 'Denny-Joe. Denny-Joe O'Brien.'

The men exchanged glances. Kelly said, 'Aidan's boy . . . Your father was my groom.'

'Aye . . .'

'Aye, *sir*,' said the voice behind.

'Aye, sir.'

Kelly's hands were heavy on the boy's shoulders. 'You'd think the son of the finest horseman in County Clare would know better than to run in front of a horse's hoofs.' In the darkness the boy dropped his eyes in shame. 'How old are you, Denny-Joe?'

'Nearly six . . . sir.'

'You very nearly didn't reach six, young man. You ought to know

16

better than to run across a road without watching for horses.'

'Came close to killing Mister Kelly, y'young divil – y'know y' made his horse throw him?'

The boy's eyes widened in horror. But William Kelly smiled, and straightened. 'There's no harm done . . . '

'The boy ought to be . . . '

'That's enough, Nathan.' Kelly turned towards his horse.

Nathan sighed elaborately. The boy heard him move away a little. 'I'll throw this dog in the ditch and cover it, sir.'

'No!' The boy whirled, headed for the dark shape that was Nathan and launched himself at him. Groping, his outstretched hands came in contact with the stiff, cold fur that was Ruadh. Nathan felt the small arms wrench the dog from his grasp. A moment in shock, then irritated, he reached for the boy's collar, 'Y' fekkin' little . . . '

'Nathan!' The tone was sharp, and made the farm steward stop, surprised. Kelly turned to the boy, 'What happened to your dog, Denny-Joe?'

And the kindness in the voice was worse than his terror and the boy's throat closed on the sobs that threatened to rise from deep within him. He would not cry . . . He would not . . . 'In the brook . . . beyond Finlea . . . '

'He was drowned?'

'No! She's sick! Sick, that's all! Me Ma will fix her . . . ' He began backing away, 'Me Ma will make her better . . . ' Again the arm stretched out and held him firm.

'Your dog is dead, boy.'

'No!'

'You must let Nathan bury it . . . '

'No! Y'll not be putting Ruadh in the ground!'

Nathan said, 'Lemme box his ears for him, sir . . . '

'No . . . ' A sigh, 'Aidan . . . ' and this man, the owner of Tineranna and its big house, was down on one knee, drawing the child closer to him. 'You were named after your father and I shall call you Aidan, now. You'll be taking your father's place as head of your family. Did your mother not tell you that?'

'She . . . she said . . . I was . . . the man of the house, now.'

Nathan Cameron moved impatiently. 'For the love of . . . '

'Shut up,' Kelly said. 'A man, Aidan, does what has to be done. However painful it may be to him. Do you understand?'

The boy looked at him for a long moment. His voice only a whisper, he said, 'Is Ruadh really dead?'

'I'm afraid he is.'

'She. Ruadh is a she.'

'Let Nathan put her in the ditch, Aidan.'

A long pause, then, 'Aye.'

The little body was taken from his arms, and Nathan, wary of another outcry, laid the puppy in the ditch gently enough, and with his boot loosened dirt and stones until the body was covered.

When it was done, Kelly turned and mounted his horse. 'Nathan,' he said over his shoulder, 'put the boy up behind me.'

'Forgive me, sir, but . . . ' A lowering of the voice. 'The boy's probably crawling with lice, sir . . . '

A strong treble voice from below them in the darkness, 'I'm not!'

'You heard him, he's not. Now put him up behind me. I want to make certain he gets home safely.'

With another sigh that whistled through clenched teeth, Nathan grabbed the boy around his middle and swung him up upon the chestnut hunter. 'Hold on around my waist, Aidan, and keep your feet forward. Don't squeeze the horse in the flanks or we'll both end up on the road again.'

'I know,' the boy said calmly. 'Me Da showed me.'

Kelly smiled, and they set off at a walk. Past the big house of Ceelohg, the Osborne's property, past the high wall that divided it from Tineranna, past the line of cottiers' hovels, past the driveway that led down to their right, the tree-lined driveway that led to the big house of Tineranna . . . and the boy felt a kind of shame and a kind of pride that the master was going past his own home and its comforts to ride down a darkened boreen to bring him home.

His mother was standing at the half-door when they rode up. William Kelly swung him to the ground, and he ran to her. 'Denny-Joe!' She was out the door, had scooped him up into her arms. He clung to her, legs about her waist, hands about her neck. With the soft familiar smell of her, the nightmare of the evening pressed down upon him, his grief seemed all the greater in this haven of safety. 'Ruadh . . . Ruadh is dead. She drowned, Ma! She *drowned*!' And it was worse in the telling, and the tears would have surely come – but she sighed. It was a short, sharp sigh, not soft with the expected sympathy. His face was pressed into her neck, her slight arms were around him, and when she spoke he sensed, rather than heard, the edge to her voice. 'Never mind, Denny-Joe. Never mind.'

Slowly hiccuping, he pulled back in her arms to look at her. But her eyes were directed upwards towards the man on the horse. 'I want to thank y', sir, for bringing him home . . . '

Kelly smiled, negated his action with a shake of his head, then asked, 'How are you managing, Mary?'

18

'Well enough, sir. It's grateful I am for your help . . . '

'The boy's dog – he seemed very fond of it . . . '

'Only a stray, sir. It was the best thing to happen, as it . . . '

'One of my setter bitches has had a large litter. I'll bring one of the pups to you in the morning.' The boy heard this, and screwed his head around to gaze, blinking, at the landlord.

Mary said, 'Thank you, sir. It's the soul of goodness y'are to mind the boy's feelings – but he'll get over it . . . '

'The litter was a large one.' Kelly repeated, as if this solved the only possible problem. He stayed for a few minutes longer, asking her how she had managed to plant the acre behind the house. Terry O'Sullivan had helped put in the seed potatoes, she said, and Daniel McDonnagh had done as much as his time allowed. Kelly had smiled at this, and nodded, as if the thought of the young Killaloe lawyer dirtying his hands at farming was somehow amusing to him.

The boy, held close to his mother's chest, could feel the stiffness of her body. He wondered if his mother didn't like Mister Kelly – or was it that she didn't like what he was saying? For when he said, 'How long has it been now, Mary? Six months, since Aidan died? Don't mourn him too long. Either Terry or Daniel would make a fine husband', Mary's grip on the little boy almost crushed the breath from him.

When the two horsemen had turned up the boreen, and the sound of hoofs faded, Mary was still holding tightly to the child. 'Who does he think he is?' she was muttering above the boy's head. 'Believes he can choose my husband for me like I was a brood mare . . . '

'Ma – y'r squeezin' me too tight . . . '

'Arra, *you* . . . ' Her attention brought back to him suddenly, she let him go. The hardness of the ground sent a shock through his bare feet, but he had little time to cry out. His mother's hand had grabbed his wrist and he was dragged into the cottage, stumbling behind her. 'What was the meaning of *that*, tell me.' The half-door, then the full door were kicked shut behind them and she slammed the bolts into place. 'Tell me!' She was bent over him, shaking him by the shoulders, her face contorted with rage. Thomas, the younger child, looked up from the settle bed in the corner and watched the two, his dark eyes wide open. He had never seen his mother so angry. It frightened him, and his mouth puckered and he wondered if he should cry, but this new, wild Ma was so very strange that he could only stare, silent.

'What did you tell the master?'

'N . . . n . . . nothing!'

'Did you ask him for one of those pups? Did you? If you did,

Denny-Joe, so help me, I'll . . . '

'No, I didn't! I didn't!' He wriggled free somehow and backed off until he stood against the door. He gazed at his mother, angry himself, now. Angry, yet uncomprehending.

She was hissing, 'How did y' find it, anyway? You must have eyes like a hawk, sure!'

It took him an instant to realize what she meant. 'Ruadh?'

'Of course, Ruadh! How did you find her?'

'In . . . in the water – by the bridge . . . '

'Why couldn't you leave well-enough alone and come home like a decent lad! It's your own fault, Denny-Joe! I told you to lose that dog, I told you!' She was shouting, now. 'There's nothing in the house but half a bag of potatoes – half a bag, Denny-Joe! The cottiers are better off than us! I won't get paid for Mrs Curran's laundry until Tuesday – and that won't keep us long . . . ' She was crying, now, crying as she shouted, and the two little boys on either side of the narrow room cringed back against the walls. Thomas, on the bed, crammed his fist into his mouth as he always did when frightened. He wished his mother would stop, but still the sharp voice rang on. 'There's no room in our life for sentiment – do you understand? So you can blame yourself! The dog had to go! But now you, you little balbhan, you find Mister Kelly and get another little beast for us to feed. And a purebred setter! Sure, you heard him! He thinks we'll be grateful – and we have to pretend to be. Anything happens to *this* one and he'll want to know why!'

She stopped suddenly, the white anger leaving her face, and she flushed suddenly as she met her son's gaze. He was pressed back against the door and he did not appear to be breathing. His dark hair fell over his forehead, still wet with mist, and the wide-set brown eyes, so like his father's, regarded her with an opaque stare.

'Denny-Joe . . . ' she began.

His voice was a whisper. 'You killed Ruadh.'

Curse her tongue, she had given it away. He was too sharp. Or was he so like his father that he was equally able to perceive her deceptions? Her lips formed the 'No' he wanted her to say. But her honesty would not allow it. Instead, gently, she reached for him.

But he was having none of that. He shrank back even further. 'You killed her, didn't you?'

'Denny-Joe, listen to me . . . ' She pulled him to her. He struggled back, hating her; but she was strong, and tender too, now, and he could not fight her. She drew him to the hearth, sat down on a low, rope-webbed stool, holding him on her lap. He sat there, pulled back away from her.

20

'We're poor, Denny-Joe. Do y'know what that means?'

'I want Ruadh . . . '

'No. No, boy. Not any more. Mother of God, Denny-Joe, I didn't want to hurt you. You and your sharp little eyes – no one else would've seen . . . ' He was crying again, and she stopped, gazing at him, his body held stiffly from her, the tears running down his stained cheeks, his mouth held firm with wounded pride and resentment. It was too much for Mary. Her own soul had shrunk back from the deed she had performed at the brook, and she cried now with the memory of it. The two held each other, the boy finding his mother's tears double cause for his own.

Thomas, from his corner, could not see his mother crying. But the fact that she now held Aidan to her and had ceased her screeching at him made him feel comforted. Often, he woke in the late evenings and found Mary holding Aidan like this, or sitting beside him, talking to him as she sewed or mended. The atmosphere, to three-year-old Thomas, was something like normal.

'You'll understand when you're older, Denny-Joe,' his mother was saying, 'you can't have all that you want. Loving you means doing the best for you – and sometimes that means hurting you a little, too. You've got to learn to accept the hurting and carry on, anyway. That's what it means to be a man, Denny-Joe.'

The boy listened, his head against her breast. Someone else had spoken those words to him – Mister Kelly. Mister Kelly who said, 'I shall call you Aidan now.' He must tell Ma. Aidan, it is, now. But the fire was warm and he did not want to speak. Later. He would tell Ma later.

Thomas watched as Aidan's head drooped, watched as his mother stared into the fire a long time, the coals tinting her dark hair with strands of crimson. Then he lay down and turned his back on the two of them and fell asleep, his fist still held to his mouth.

Three times fourteen was . . . Well, three times four was twelve, put down the two and . . .

'I can't see why you're making such a fuss!'

'A dog, William! And a valuable one at that!'

Devlin Kelly raised his head from his work. Every time he came to a difficult sum his parents raised their voices. Three times four is twelve, put down the two carry the . . .

'They'll probably eat it!'

'Oh, don't be . . . !' William Kelly stopped, glanced over to the desk to find his son gazing up at him. He smiled a little, placed his hand on the thick fair hair. 'Carry on – I'll check them when you're finished.'

Devlin lowered his head once more. Three times one is three, plus one is four . . . Forty-two . . . He underlined it triumphantly.

His mother was saying, 'I simply can't see the purpose in giving a dog to a family that is already starving . . . '

'They . . . they shouldn't be. I've been too busy lately, with the meetings in Limerick – it's taking more trouble than we thought possible, gaining support for public education . . . I haven't had much time for the tenants . . . '

'Nor for your own family . . . '

'Caroline . . . '

'Very well. But why this sudden interest in Aidan's child? I've seen him. He has a blank face. No character at all.'

'You're wrong.' William walked to the hearth and dropped to his heels to stir the turf sods with the poker, 'I see his father in him, perhaps. A kind of tenacity . . . '

'Stubbornness . . . '

'Perhaps. But for his father's sake alone I should be doing more for the family.'

'Did the woman complain?'

'My dear, have you heard any of my tenants complain?'

'Pride. Self-centred pride. Back home in England . . . '

'You're not back home in England.' There was an edge to William's voice, and Caroline looked up from her embroidery. In a moment William would begin a monologue on the position of the degraded Irish peasant, quoting facts and figures in an attempt to prove that the British government was responsible for the millions of starving people on this inhospitable island. She could not bear it, and forestalled him. 'It wasn't your fault Aidan O'Brien died. It was his own carelessness . . . '

'He was a fine horseman – and he was never careless.'

'He knew the horse was temperamental. To go into a stall alone with it was foolhardy. You can't go on blaming yourself.'

'I'm not trying to take the blame. I'm not laying the blame anywhere – but the money I gave Mary has obviously run out. I must do something more for her.'

'You don't have to.' Caroline addressed her fast-flying needle. 'No one would expect you to . . . ' And she stopped, sensing without looking up that he was watching her . . . with his cold look. This was what she called it – the detached, appraising look that fell on her as if she were a stranger, and made her feel alienated, afraid. When would it stop, she wondered, this fear that he would cease loving her, would regret marrying her? And yet she was angry. She, a Retcliffe, who had given up so much to bury herself in this Georgian damp-trap, courted by the foolish wives of the Protestant landlords, despised by the Catholic population. Even William had lost a lot of popularity amongst his Catholic intelligentsia friends by marrying her. Bad enough that she had been born Protestant, but to be English, as well . . . Not all her piety, nor all her donations to the Church won her anything but lip-service gratitude from the town of Killaloe. She never asked herself why she was disliked, whether it was something in herself. She was a Retcliffe, that sufficed. But in this backwater, no one appreciated the fact.

And yet, she had no real regrets. When she had met William Kelly in London she had loved him from the start. Loved his intelligence, his humour, his strong, even features and the direct grey eyes. For him she had left her position in society, her family, her religion, exchanging the gaiety of the house in Grosvenor Square and the country estate in Wiltshire for the eternal *sameness* of Ireland. It was a prison of her own choosing – but no less a prison; lit only by the love she had for her son, the beautiful child so like her – and this tall Irishman, her husband, whose glance could still make her afraid.

'If I assist the family, it's because I wish to,' he said, now. 'And I'll be giving Mary O'Brien some work here at the house. Something in the kitchen or the garden, where she'll be able to have the children with her. She won't like charity, but she needs help.'

And she's pretty, too, Caroline thought, remembering the dark-haired young woman she had often seen when the carriage drove past on the way down to the lough. Mary O'Brien was pretty, and still young . . . Caroline remembered that the girl's mother had been housekeeper here, that Mary herself had worked at the big house until her marriage to the groom. She thought of a young William, with that girl close by each day . . . And even if this was unfair, the girl was desperate, now. She would not dare refuse should William . . . She bit her lip and lowered her head over her sewing.

But William had never considered Mary O'Brien as a potential conquest. Caroline's jealousies were groundless in that he never considered any woman any more than herself – and that was little enough. For he was totally involved in the social reforms of his time. Not pushing himself forward – his sense of duty bordered on a kind of zeal, and he was only too aware that the estate needed his constant care – but he worked tirelessly and unsung within the Repeal Movement, and had given money and support to O'Connell when County Clare elected him to Parliament – the first Irish Catholic in its history. In doing so, William gained disfavour from the Protestant landowners, who had begun to be friendly on his marriage to Caroline, yet the gesture did little to bring him closer to his own tenantry.

William Kelly was rich, after all. He may be Catholic, the people reasoned, and he may be kind-hearted in his way – but he owned titles across six thousand acres that had once been theirs. The British could argue that all this happened five generations ago, but the hunger for one's own land is something one does not forget. And the resentment passed down from father to son, and they resented the power of the Kelly family even as they were forced to accept the concessions that power afforded them.

So the old suspicion warred with her gratitude as Mary O'Brien stood outside her cottage the next morning and listened as William Kelly told her of the position for her at the big house.

Eightpence a day if she would tend to the vegetable garden and help the cook when needed. 'Yes, sir . . . God bless you, sir . . . ' gazing up at him attentively, and already thinking of the regular wages and what the money would buy. The potato crop would pay the rent, thanks to the work of Terry O'Sullivan and Daniel Mc-Donnagh – but this news meant a few chickens – a pig, perhaps. And later . . . Mother of Mercy, a cow of their own. It would be like it was when her husband was alive. No. It would never be like that again. But she would survive. She smiled up at William Kelly, drawing her two boys closer to her.

Thomas clung to his mother's skirt, fist in his mouth, and gazed upwards in fascination at the giant chestnut thoroughbred. If he reached up, he could, perhaps, touch the horse's underbelly. Soft, copper-coloured fur . . . Thomas debated whether to let go of his mother, but the horse snorted suddenly and he started, burying himself deeper into the folds of her skirt and not looking again at the horse except over a fold of the rough homespun. Better, he decided, to stay where he was.

The sack tied to the saddle was the only thing that interested young Aidan. Aidan, who stood by with his hands behind his back and his shoulders slightly hunched, watching the struggling, whimpering bundle. He had woken beside Thomas in the middle of the night, had remembered and sobbed silently, convulsively, into the blanket. He did not want the new dog – he would tell them he only wanted Ruadh . . . but this shape in the bag was the size of Ruadh – the whimpering sound like Ruadh . . . Was it possible – there was a mistake, Ruadh wasn't dead – had made her way to the big house – this was a surprise . . . she was back, she was . . .

The setter pup came out of the hessian all tongue and claws and

24

soft red fur. The boy lowered his head over it with the pain of his disappointment, already aware that he must play a part before the expectant adults. Not Ruadh . . . no more that thin and fearful tinker of a dog. This dog's coat was just as red, deeper russet, if anything, and soft . . . and how small and plump he was – how clean!

A little gentleman of a dog, to be sure – and confident! It crawled all over him, licking his face furiously, chewing his nose, his ears, then scrambled from his grasp to rush about them in circles, hurtling around the horse's feet with a velocity born of hysteria before tearing off down the road towards the lough, chasing a slow-lifting seagull. Aidan ran after him, scooped him up and brought him back. Not Ruadh . . . but walking back to the cottage, turning his head back and forth to avoid the pup's all-pervading tongue, he knew he was won. But his footsteps slowed as he saw the expression in his mother's dark eyes as she gazed at the dog.

'And one more thing . . . Aidan can help with the dogs – exercising them and feeding them – there'll be food to spare for the pup. Later I'll have the boy taught to ride.' Aidan stared up at him. To ride! To be a groom, and even a jockey, winning races all over Ireland, like his father . . . He smiled up at William. 'He looks a bright boy,' the man said.

Mary's hand went to her son's hair. She only smiled in answer, but her pride was tangible. The smile remained on her face as Kelly rode off, and the boy watched her carefully. 'Well, Denny-Joe . . . '

'Aidan, Ma.'

Her smile broadened as she looked down at him. Thomas was clamouring to hold the pup, and the elder boy reluctantly handed it over. Her hand on his shoulder, Mary turned back to the cottage. 'Well, Aidan . . . things will be all right, so.' She was not looking at him, and he dared not ask further questions, hoping only that this cryptic comment meant he could keep the dog.

2

The following morning dawned clear, the varied greens of the late summer lying in cool splendour beside the bright blue of Lough Derg. The world seemed to Aidan to be full of promise. On hearing the news of their luck, Mrs O'Sullivan had volunteered to mind Thomas and the pup for the day, and the two seemed content enough when Mary and Aidan left them at the cottage door and headed up the boreen.

To the big house, the boy thought excitedly, conscious that today brought something different, something of vital importance to their lives. Every spider's web within the ivy-covered stone walls, every lark that hovered, weightless, over O'Sullivan's field, seemed to the boy to be new and miraculous things, part of a day that pledged some wondrous happening somewhere ahead of them. He ran and skipped most of the way, kicking up dust with his bare feet.

And the big house – an adventure in itself. Double-storeyed, with tall gables and pointed dormer windows in the steeply-pitched roof.

Cook showed them through the kitchen and along a small, cold passage which led to the main hall. Here, at the centre of the house, was the office where William Kelly and Nathan Cameron worked.

Only Nathan was present this morning, and Mary stood at his desk while he outlined her duties, conscious of her dislike for the little Northerner, and conscious of his own dislike of her. He had loathed her husband, resented his popularity and his power on Tineranna, and his resentment was easily transferrable.

Aidan, uninterested in their talk, went to stand at the office door. From here he could catch a glimpse of the broad hall that ran towards the front of the house. On the floors were rich carpets of an intricate design that would surely take all day for one's eyes to trace. And the floor itself was of a highly polished stone that he had never seen before. The furniture that lined the walls was of dark, shining wood; carved dressers and chairs richly upholstered. On the walls were paintings in gold frames. From this distance he could not make out what they were of, and he longed to walk about the hall, to stand on tiptoe and study them.

'Aidan, are you listening?'

26

'Yes . . . sir!'

The adults had finished speaking. Nathan Cameron was behind him, pulling the door further open.

The boy and his mother were led outside into the kitchen garden, a half-acre of vegetables and fruit trees, surrounded by a high stone wall. The smell of the plants in their warm, rich soil came to Mary and Aidan like spices from some distant country. They raised their heads and inhaled. Here were potatoes and cabbages such as they had at home, but Cameron was pointing out squash and butter beans and marrows – strange names that made Aidan smile and glance at his mother. But she was nodding at Cameron, fingering the plants, memorizing his instructions on their watering and care. 'You probably don't know how to cook half of these, but . . . '

'My mother was housekeeper here at Tineranna until her death, Mister Cameron. And I worked as a housemaid there myself when I was a girl.'

'Your mother?'

'Mary Brogan.'

'Ah, yes. I've heard her name mentioned. She died soon after the old master.'

'Yes. It was before you came.'

Aidan became aware of a stillness between the two adults. A very slight tightening of the atmosphere. His mother was looking at Mister Cameron with her usual calm expression, yet her chin was a little raised. Aidan could see no meaning in his mother's setting a time upon Cameron's arrival, but the remark was not lost on Nathan. So the woman had pride, like her husband and her wee brat. This peasant woman was insulted when he questioned her culinary knowledge. So she reminded him of something that no one in Killaloe allowed him to forget for very long. He had been at Tineranna only six years. He was an Ulsterman, a Northerner, and a Presbyterian to boot. He submerged his anger, as he always did, and smiled grimly, looking more like a battered little devil than ever. 'Take them radishes, now . . . ' he continued, and walked on down the path, pointing out the vegetables as they went.

Aidan had begun to be bored with the sameness of the plants until a small tree, espaliered against the wall, caught his attention by its sweet smell. Food, he thought suddenly, hungrily. All this was food. Growing from . . . sure, nothing at all! Little seeds, according to Mister Cameron. Aidan saw two small red balls amongst the branches on the tree, reached up a hand and touched . . .

'Leave them apples alone!'

He pulled his hand back, quickly. Nathan Cameron scowled at

27

him, then turned back to the mother.

Apple . . . could he eat it? It was a beautiful colour, and had felt firm and warm beneath his hand. Would it be sweet? It had smelt fresh, and sharp. He wondered what the inside of it looked like, and followed his mother with a reluctant backwards glance at it.

They were shown to a gardening shed against the wall, where seeds were kept in labelled jars on the shelves. Hoes and spades leaned in the corner and cobwebs festooned the low ceiling.

'Mickey Ryan Dubh is getting too old and rheumaticky to handle the grounds and the garden,' Nathan was saying as he headed back towards the gate, 'but I still don't think it's any job for a woman.'

Mary was folding her shawl and placing it upon the path, but looked up. 'And why not, Mister Cameron? It's clean, and it's light – and sure it's no more than I'd be doing in my own garden, should it be as bountiful as this.'

Her smile held no warmth in it, Aidan noticed, and Nathan, meeting her look, merely scowled before opening the gate and heading off towards the stables. But in a second, he was back, his scowl even deeper. 'There's something else. Mister Kelly said that the boy is to wash his hands and face and report to the house at ten o'clock – Cook will call out for him,' he added, as Mary was about to deny possession of a watch. 'Ten o'clock every day for three hours of schooling with Master Devlin and his tutor.' The woman stared at him. Continued to stare after he had turned his back a final time and let the wooden gate swing shut behind him.

She turned to find her son gazing up at her. He knew she would not allow this. She would not permit him to be dragged alone and clean-faced into the big house. Alone in the big house! For it to swallow him up in its opulence. Alone! 'Tell him no, Ma. Tell Mister Kelly no!'

'*No*? What're y' talking about, "no"? Schooling, Aidan! Reading and writing! Adding up numbers! D'you not understand?'

'I don't want to! I don't want to!'

'Are you mad? Is it an eejit you are?' She knelt down beside him on the path, pushed the dark hair out of his eyes. 'Do you not know what this means? It's a way out, Aidan. You'll not have to be breaking your back as a farm labourer all your life . . . '

'I want to race horses like Da!'

'You'll not! Well, we'll see. But having the learning means you've got a choice, Aidan.' She stopped, realizing that the future meant nothing to the little boy. 'Maybe,' she added smoothly, 'they'll give you something to eat after your lessons.'

His eyes grew wide. 'Do you think so?'

28

'I don't know. You'll have to see. And if you work as hard as you can at your lessons . . . I promise you this. I'll take you into Killaloe and buy you some books of your own.'

'What kind of books?'

'Books about men who went adventuring – books about far-off places. The library of the big house is full of them – I used to look at the pictures in them, but I never knew what the words meant. Now you'll be able to tell me.'

'I will,' he said stoutly. Then, with a frown, 'Do we have the money to buy books?'

She smiled, though her heart ached a little that the penury of their lives had thus communicated itself to him. She realized with a pang that there was little of the child in Aidan. 'We'll have the money,' she said.

Her confidence was no longer feigned. In five short minutes she had found hope. A goal, something beyond the day-to-day realities of getting enough to eat for herself and the children. Aidan would have his books. She would work hard here at the house. And she would get up earlier and continue to do Mrs Curran's laundry as well. It would take her months of saving, but Aidan would have his books.

She instructed the little boy on how to pull the weeds from the garden, and place them in a neat pile. When the small figure was hunched with preoccupation over the task she turned and picked up the hoe. Another man's hoe, she thought, to till another man's soil. It was her lot, and she accepted it. But not Aidan. Not this for Aidan.

When Cook called him he was already standing by the pump, his feet and face and hands pink from the icy water. He followed the forbidding plump figure into the kitchen, but stopped at the door to the passage when her hand was suddenly clapped down hard on his shoulder.

'Sit down there – put those on.'

It took him a few seconds to understand her strange Northern English accent. This was another thing he would have to become accustomed to – nearly all the house staff at Tineranna came with the mistress from London. Aidan blinked at her, then followed her pointed finger.

A pair of boy's shoes lay on the floor beside the door. They were far too large for him, but made of beautifully soft patent, and there were two shining buckles on the toes. He stared down at them, then up into Cook's impatient face, then he sat down on a nearby stool and placed his feet into the shoes.

'Well, if you don't look a sight . . . ' She was almost smiling. At each hesitant step the boy took the shoes flopped awkwardly on his feet, threatening to make him stumble.

Cook pushed him down on to the stool once more. 'You'll have to wear 'em,' she said, fetching some rags and removing the shoes to stuff the toes before jamming them back on the boy's feet. 'You're to wear them when you come for your lessons – we can't have you tracking mud over the carpets.' She pushed him through the door into the passage, and along to the large, marble-floored hall. 'Don't trip on the rugs. Lift your feet. The next door's the one.' When Aidan turned around, her starched white figure was disappearing back around the corner.

As he walked along the corridor he could hear a young Anglicized voice intoning, 'Eo . . . die naves . . . portum int . . . intrantes videramus.'

'Very good. And the next?'

'Pompeius naves quas . . . quas in noc portu invenerat ad pugnum ex . . . expediebat.'

'Excellent, Devlin, excellent!'

Aidan tapped hesitantly, and the same voice called, 'Come in!'

It was a sunlit room, looking out over a wide stretch of lawn. A fire burned in the grate, for the ceiling was high, the house itself a cold one, and the room was sparsely furnished with only a dresser, a table with several books upon it, and two chairs.

He entered the room shyly, shutting the door behind him. At first he barely noticed the boy at the table, for his attention was rivetted on the teacher. He had somehow been expecting a forbidding figure, someone hard and grey like Father O'Callaghan, only worse. And yet this man in sombre black was young, with straight brown hair and an open, pleasant face. He was smiling at Aidan, and Aidan smiled back.

But the tutor's eyes were nevertheless taking the boy in, flicking over him, summing him up. Lord, this was a baby. A mere six-year-old, and small for his age, too. Still, his gaze was direct, the face showed intelligence. 'Come here, Aidan – I'm James Thomson. Have you boys met before?'

Devlin sent a sharp look at his tutor. Even at nine, he resented the easy camaraderie with which Thomson spoke.

'No,' he said.

Aidan's smile remained on his face as he turned to look at the boy seated at the table. A handsome boy, with thick fair hair and blue eyes. He wore fawn trousers and a short blue jacket; there was a black bow at the neck of his fine, white linen shirt. Aidan continued

to smile, he would have liked the handsome older boy to return it –
but the blue eyes held no warmth. They flickered over Aidan's
body, taking in the threadbare shirt and trousers, the bare feet in the
incongruously smart, ill-fitting shoes, and slid away back to his
book. 'Shall I read the next exercise? I know them all.'

'Just a moment. It would be fitting if you greeted the child.'
Devlin looked up at his tutor. 'Gentlemanly,' Thomson added
pointedly. 'Master Devlin, this is Aidan O'Brien.'

'How do you do.' Flatly.

Aidan repeated the phrase softly, then swung his eyes back up to
the teacher. A baby . . . Thomson sighed inwardly. William Kelly
and his philanthropic schemes. The children were too dissimilar,
and Devlin's resentment was palpable. Thomson could tell that this
was not going to work.

'Come here, Aidan. Sit down beside Master Devlin.' The young
tutor handed the boy a slate and chalk, conscious as he did so that
the boy would never have seen such objects before. He explained
them, held the child's hand within his own as he showed him how to
hold the chalk, then placed upon the table a piece of paper, upon
which he had written the first three letters of the alphabet. 'I'd like
you to practice writing them while I continue with Master Devlin's
Latin lesson.'

He turned away, picking up his book, and the strange, halting
words began again. Aidan took up the chalk and drew a very shaky
letter A on his slate. He had a fearful desire to get up and run out the
door. Beyond, in O'Sullivan's cottage, the puppy would be whining
for him. Samhradh, he called him, summer, since that season had
brought him the gift of the dog. When he returned home he would
take the pup running, along the lake's edge to O'Donoghue's farm.
Seamus and Thady would be impressed. Samhradh was not just a
sheep dog, he was a hunting dog, a real thoroughbred.

'Is that the best you can do?' Devlin Kelly looked amused. Aidan
flushed, and bent his head over the slate. This time the letter looked
straighter. Let Master Devlin laugh. He would learn.

He could think of no reason why the older boy should dislike him,
but as the week progressed, it became evident that Devlin wanted no
part of him. Aidan suffered sarcasm when Thomson was present,
ridicule when he was not. The boy found a small green frog awaiting
his bare foot within the black patent shoes. He found his carefully
written alphabet smeared across the slate if he was foolish enough to
look away for a moment. On Friday, his chair was pulled from
behind him as he was about to sit down, and he banged his head

31

heavily on the table. Thomson entered the room just after this and chastised them for their rough play. Devlin had smiled, and Aidan tried to. Through all that week he kept his unhappiness to himself, faced with his mother's pride in his new-found learning and Thomson's steady look of reproof when any incidents disrupted the lessons.

There were no lessons on Saturday, and Aidan spent the morning with Nathan Cameron, learning the names and the feeding routine of the twelve champion setters in the Tineranna kennels. He saw Samhradh's sire and dam, and in a separate pen some distance away, his eight gambolling brother and sisters. All were bigger than Samhradh. 'Yours was the runt of the litter,' Nathan said, holding up one solid, wriggling puppy for comparison. 'He'll never grow as big as this one will. Wouldn't even have lived if we'd left him with the mother.'

'Why?'

''Cause she's only got eight titties, hasn't she? I fed your little bastard with milk when I should have let 'im die. But the Master would have none of that. He's too soft-hearted.' And he stared at Aidan under his brows as he dropped the puppy down amongst his brothers and sisters. Aidan put his hands behind his back and stared back at Nathan.

Mary noticed a new quietness, a withdrawal about the boy. She told herself that it had to happen, his world had to expand into places that did not include her. But she ached for him when she heard him sob occasionally in his sleep. In the mornings, without asking him any questions, she would give him gentle lectures on the differences between themselves and a family like the Kellys, how wealth gave people certain rights, and stressed that there was no fighting this. It was only to Daniel McDonnagh and the Currans that she betrayed any fear of what Aidan might be suffering at the big house, mentioning the problem to them after Mass that Sunday.

'Sure a bit of teasing and a few bruises is a small price to pay for an education,' John Curran said, his narrow shoulders squared proudly in his new Sunday suit. He had worn it to Mass today for the first time, a kind of visible proof that his recent venture from farming to tavern-keeping was a success. Rocking on his heels a little, he glanced over to where the children were playing by the church wall. 'Now I come to think of it,' he added, thinking of the scuffles his own children were always having, 'bruises are a part of growing to manhood – would you be trying to protect the lad, Mary?'

But it was his wife who answered. Molly Curran had once been so like the small, dark man she had married that folk had taken them for brother and sister. Now, six children later, she had grown physically in ratio to their financial success, and was a little round, black-eyed woman, quick and determined – the real power behind the family's enterprises. 'And what kind of landlord will Master Devlin make, tell me, if he's allowed to enjoy the luxury of cruelty at his age? Why aren't there schools in Killaloe? Decent schools, where our children don't have to suffer indignities at the hands of the Kellys and others like them? Cromwellian Helpers . . . '

At the bitter phrase, the timeless insult levelled against any Irish family who had worked with Cromwell's invaders in the bloody 1640s, the group at the church gate stiffened. John Curran looked around him nervously. 'Hush, woman, that's past and gone . . . '

'Bad blood will tell,' Molly said stubbornly.

Daniel McDonnagh, standing by Mary, broke in placatingly, 'It won't be long before there'll be education available . . . '

'Arra, the English will never allow it,' John Curran muttered. 'They want us kept in ignorance. Where would they be if every Irishman knew how to read their legal papers, their contracts?' His wife was scowling at him and he grinned, realizing that he was about to begin a diatribe against the British legal system. Instead he turned to Mary. 'But for young Aidan, now. This is a grand opportunity for him. Different from when I was young – the hedge school up by Finlea . . . Father O'Callaghan drumming the learnin' into our heads . . . ' They all turned unconsciously to gaze at the tall, stooped figure of the old priest, now speaking to Caroline and William Kelly by the church door. 'Aye, it was worth it – don't I own a tavern, now? Sure where would I be when the Prods came round selling their whiskey if I couldn't add up the cost of the stuff?'

'When the new schools are built . . . ' McDonnagh began.

'Dreams. You're dreaming, boyo . . . '

'O'Connell will make sure they're built, Mister Curran! Now he's sitting in Parliament we'll see changes in this country. With Catholic emancipation . . . '

'*Emancipation*, is it? Is that what the text books will say? This year of our Lord, 1829 – the year of Catholic Emancipation!' He scowled up at Daniel furiously. 'Emancipation is a word men use instead of freedom – because it doesn't quite mean freedom! The British pay lip-service to Catholics holding public offices – and then they raise the franchise from forty shillings to ten pounds per man. Ten pounds before you can vote! How many cottiers can afford *that*! And you're optimistic enough to call that emancipated!'

'Well . . . '

Curran was away, now. Even his wife's frown had no effect on him. 'If you took your mind out of your lawyer's papers and looked at the realities of life, you'd know how far we have to go, young Daniel. Watch the cottiers leave their hovels to go begging each spring while their potatoes are growing . . . Talk to someone from the Dublin slums like Corrie O'Neill . . . And only last week the O'Donoghues had to part with one of their sows to pay the tithes for the bloody Protestant church. What right do the Protestants have to tax Catholics, anyway? And look at Mary O'Brien, here – how many more widows are there in her plight? Sure she's fortunate that William Kelly is the man he is – some Catholic landlords are worse than the Protestants! Get the English out, lad. Get them *out*, with their taxes and tithes and high rents – then I'll believe Ireland is emancipated.'

'But it's a beginning . . . ' Daniel persisted, and was cut short by a guffaw from John. Mary watched as the young lawyer flushed. Poor Daniel . . . Mary had to agree with John Curran – Daniel had been too protected by his lawyer father. Like William Kelly, he had money between him and the more galling outrages of British domination. Daniel saw hope everywhere he looked. He saw a new Ireland and was prepared to work for it without realizing how very far off that dream lay. While England's army spread out across Africa and Asia, bringing her own idea of civilization and education to her darker skinned brethren, eight million Irish lived in starvation and ignorance on her very doorstep. Mary felt a tenderness for Daniel, a concern for what would happen to him when the truth finally became clear. But then, she smiled to herself, Daniel would continue anyway. No amount of disillusionment could really dim his fervour. He would acknowledge the crushing reality, but never defeat. He was, she reflected, lit by some fire unknown to the rest of them. What a beautiful, yet terrible gift, Mary thought, was hope.

And he turned to her, then, suddenly, and smiled. She had the feeling that he had read her thoughts, such was his smile. But he merely said, 'William Kelly told me about the setter pup. It was kind of him, but I wondered how you'll manage . . . '

'He said I was to take some scraps from the big house to feed it, and Nathan Cameron is to give me some of the rabbits he traps to feed the kennel dogs – but still, the animal will be a trial.'

The brown eyes held hers. 'I'll come to the cottage every few days, should you like, and help Aidan train the dog. Bad enough having a pup without it being stupid and disobedient.'

She thanked him, and smiled up at him, and her thin dark face was suddenly pretty.

*

34

'Daniel McDonnagh's talking to your ma,' Maura O'Donoghue said.

Aidan looked up from where he sat on a headstone swinging his legs, drumming his heels against the inscription. 'So?'

'What'll you do if they start courting? What'll you do if he marries your ma?' The other children turned to look at her. Maura was small, red-haired like all the O'Donoghues, but her face lacked the openness of her brothers and sister. Maura's face was a pinched, pale oval, the slanted green eyes sharp, the little pointed chin obdurate. She stood now in front of Aidan, smiling her characteristic half-smile, looking like a rather malevolent *bean sidhe*. She was very clever with her tongue, too, and Aidan didn't like her. He scowled at her.

'I'd like it.'

Martin Curran, the eldest of John Curran's six children, gazed up at Aidan from where he was drawing patterns in the dirt with a stick. 'Would you, to be sure? He owns a horse . . . but he's so thin, and always dressed in his best . . . ' He surveyed Daniel's black frock coat disdainfully. His own father, even in his new suit, looked comfortable, approachable, more like a father should look. 'He looks like a priest,' Martin added.

Seamus and Thady O'Donoghue, their red heads bent over a furtive game of knucklebones, looked up at Aidan. They rather envied him his reputation for being the son of the famous Aidan O'Brien. Envied him, too, the fact that he had only one younger brother and was not caught as they were at the head of a family that seemed more like a string of paper dolls with every year.

'If Daniel wwwas your nnn-new da, Aidan,' Thady said, 'he'd let you rrrride on his horse, www-wouldn't he?' And Seamus, always impatient with Thady's stutter, added, 'Maybe he'd buy you one of your own. You could be a jockey, maybe, like your own da.'

Aidan turned consideringly back to Daniel McDonnagh. If he married Ma, it would mean not only a pony, but Ma would stay home all day, as she'd done when Da was alive . . . She wouldn't have to work at the big house, and surely Aidan wouldn't be made to continue lessons with . . .

'What're you doing?' The voice came sharply, and all the children started.

Devlin Kelly stood a little further down the path, his dark Sunday suit and shiny top hat contrasting with the pale gold of his hair. His eyes singled Aidan out. 'You shouldn't be sitting on that headstone, Aidan O'Brien,' he drawled 'it shows disrespect for the dead.' The children looked at Aidan and at each other. 'They might haunt you

35

for it.'

Aidan almost jumped down, but controlled his nervousness and met Devlin's gaze. A few other children, Minogues and Brogans and O'Byrnes, playing quietly by the gate, began to drift over, seeing Devlin and curious that the son of William Kelly was suddenly drawn into their midst.

Aidan saw this from the periphery of his gaze, saw them coming, yet did not let go of Devlin's glance, could feel that there was a challenge here, somewhere, and the children moved quietly, sensing a confrontation.

In their small world, Aidan had always held a special place, not only due to his father's reputation, but because he was a fearless little fighter with a black temper that disregarded odds and usually brought him victory. Now, here was their leader confronted by someone out of their class altogether, the heir to the farms most of their fathers tilled. The rules were suddenly changed, and they gathered in interested groups. The O'Donoghues, Seamus and Thady, stood up; the small and belligerent Curran brothers, Martin and Tom-Joe, so like their parents in their swarthiness, took two steps towards each other. The four Minogues clustered together on his right, the O'Byrne girls on his left . . .

'He's right, Aidan.' He turned, then. Maura O'Donoghue was gazing at him, her eyes laughing at him. She had someone more powerful than she standing near, and she felt safe. 'You should get down,' she said. 'Sure even now that person down there is no doubt planning a terrible revenge on you.'

'For what?' Defiantly.

'Sure for the insult, of course. Would you like someone to be sitting on your grave when you die?'

Aidan scowled at her, unable to think of a reply.

Devlin moved closer, 'What's his name?' He peered at the headstone. Aidan gripped it with his hands, moved his legs out of the way and gazed upside down at the inscription. 'You needn't stare at it, you can't read,' Devlin said. Aidan felt his face turning red. Devlin was scowling at the inscription, written in Irish. 'His name was Thomas Michael O'Reilly, and he lived from 1751 to 1816. An old man, and crotchety to be sure. He'll be after you, Aidan O'Brien.'

'He won't.'

'He will. He'll come creeping down the hill late tonight – at midnight – with clanking chains and moss between his toes . . . ' The children moved closer together in their cliques, but there was a smothered laugh from Maura. Devlin glanced over at her, apprecia-

36

tive, and seeing his pleasure, a few of the other children laughed also.

Seamus O'Donoghue, tall and freckled, slightly older than the other children, was one of the few seemingly unawed by the landlord's son. 'Why should he have moss between his toes?'

'Because he's rotting, of course. He's a skeleton, with strips of flesh hanging from him, and . . . '

'And only a few hairs on his white skull,' Maura put in gleefully, 'and black hollows where his eyes should be . . . '

Aidan remained where he was, his skin prickling uncomfortably, but conscious of Maura, hiding her spiteful laughter behind her hand, and of the mockery in Devlin's eyes. The latter he could face – had he not been suffering it all week? But now all his friends were watching. His friends and the precocious Maura O'Donoghue, and this, more than anything else, kept him clinging to his seat.

'He's getting angrier by the minute,' Devlin warned.

'I don't care.'

'You will. He'll come for you tonight.'

'For what? Sure and what would he want with me?'

And it was Maura who said, 'Why, to take your soul away, of course.'

And there was a dreadful hush at this. Only Devlin looked at Maura with something like admiration, turned back to Aidan and opened his mouth to continue this new attack.

'Stop it! Stop it, Maura!' All heads turned, and even Devlin Kelly's attention was momentarily distracted from the hapless Aidan.

The speaker was a tall girl of about eight, her thick, gold-brown hair so rich a colour that Devlin's blonde curls looked dull by comparison. The hazel eyes were large, expressive, in a face strangely mature for her age, the features clearly shaped and nearly perfect. Even at six years old, Aidan was not unaware of how pretty Anna O'Hagan was. Now, having the girl not only notice him but come to his defence, was rather overwhelming. He could only grip his headstone and stare.

But Anna's eyes were already unsure, seeing the startled faces turned towards her. Maura, who usually followed Anna's lead, now looked sulky and defiant; worse, the young master was looking at her crossly, obviously annoyed with her for having spoilt the game. She said, uncertainly, her gaze not upon Maura nor Devlin but somewhere in between, 'You shouldn't tease him. He's only small . . . '

'I'm not.' Aidan found his voice at this slight, 'I'm six. I'm big.

37

I'm not afraid, not of any one . . . '

Anna's eyes opened wide, and for one pleasurable moment, Aidan thought that she was impressed with his words, but then he realized that she was gazing over his shoulder, her eyes filled with terror . . .

All Devlin Kelly's threats came back to him with the rush of movement from the corner of his eye, the feel of the great hands around the waist—

'Arra, y' young divil!' a deep voice shouted, and Aidan was heaved up and off the headstone with tremendous force, hurtled, screaming, into Maura and Devlin, and losing his balance, stumbled and fell heavily on to the rough stones.

Father O'Callaghan looked taken aback by the boy's reaction, but scowled, turning his mouth down into a suitably severe expression. 'You keep a respect in you for the dead that lie in this churchyard, young Aidan. Y' hear me?' And he stormed off, the black cassock clinging to his legs in his long stride.

'You were white! White as a sheet!' Devlin Kelly roared with laughter. And Martin Curran's voice, 'He's tore his pants! Look, he's tore his pants!'

And he had indeed, the worn fabric having caught on a rough stone. He brought his hand around and felt the tear and the bare skin of his behind, and scarlet, began to sidle away. And all the while, the children reeled about with laughter, subsided weak with laughter, hung over the headstones, doubled up on the mounds and hummocks. Even Anna O'Hagan laughed, turning away to hide her smile from him. Aidan gazed at each of the children in turn, wildly, then whirled, headed for the low stone wall, scrambled over it, and ran.

Hundreds of years before, on this very hill, his ancestor, Brian Boru, had built his palace of Kincora; now it was a site of shame and degradation from which the child felt he would never recover. He ducked into the first lane, ran down the slope of the Aille Vaun to the canal bank, and turned left, up-river, towards home. But he did not go home. Past the huddle of cottages and hovels at the edge of the town he ran, then left the road at the first clear field and scrambled up towards Craglea. It seemed to tower over him, its huge slopes shadowed in green grass but bare of trees. He did not look back towards the village, as if by ignoring it, he could make it vanish, cease to exist.

He did not cry. He was beyond that, now. It was rage that filled him. Rage against Devlin Kelly, Father O'Callaghan, Maura O'Donoghue – and at the Currans and O'Donoghues who did not defend him. They were not his friends, he told himself, having come face to face for the first time in his life with the instability of human loyalties. Martin and Tom-Joe, Seamus and Thady – they were not his friends any more. He was going to climb Craglea. He would build a cabin at the top of it. And he would not come down. Never again.

Yet Craglea, too, was haunted. The huge hill, not really a mountain, part of the rounded range called Slieve Bernagh, was the haunt of the *sidhe*, the fairy, the pagan goddess Aoibheal. When Terry O'Sullivan visited Mary, he would sit with Aidan and Thomas and tell them of her – how Craglea, and particularly the large rock on its eastern shoulder, was her domain. How she controlled the winds on Lough Derg and kept the clan Dalcassian, of which the O'Briens were a member, under her special care. He told them of the battle of Clontarf, when Aoibheal had given a magic cloak of invisibility to her Dalcassian champion, how she had watched with pride as he had slain the Vikings with great ferocity from behind the cloak's safety. And the rumour of a miracle occurring had spread throughout the Dalcassian camp, and all the Irish had wondered who was responsible for the enemy who fell dead without visible cause. And the young champion could not conquer his vanity, and had flung off the cloak and cried, 'It is I! I who kill the Vikings with the ability of ten men!'

And from the midst of battle, a Viking archer saw the handsome young man in glittering armour suddenly appear – and aimed his bow and let fly an arrow that slew Aoibheal's beloved where he stood.

And she had gone weeping back to the mountain, Terry said. And Brian Boru, the High King, was slain, because Aoibheal was wild with her grief and had left the Dalcassians. The Irish won the war, but Aoibheal did not rejoice. She wept for days and Lough Derg was grey and the rain fell and the wind howled. And still, to this day, Aoibheal wails in the wind, cries in the wind that blows about the crest of Craglea. And she stands at her rock that faces the east, still hoping to see the favourite returning.

'Pishogue!' Mary would mutter, 'Superstition! Heresy, that's what you're speaking.'

Aidan liked the story. Even now, his senses made fearful by Devlin's talk, he did not find anything so very frightening here on the slopes of Craglea. This rock against which he leaned was not Aoibheal's rock – his legs were too short to carry him more than a quarter way up the slope – it was one of two boulders that protruded out of the hillside, facing towards the village. He had sat down here to rest for a while – and stayed. The rock was warm against his back.

39

The sun shone fully on his face and both these things gave him comfort. The ground itself was still damp – it had rained the night before – and the sun had not quite dried this little hollow, made by sheep, perhaps, long ago, and this dampness would be uncomfortable after a while. But for now he was content enough to sit, knees drawn up, eyes fixed sightlessly on the lough and the narrow bottleneck of water where it became once more the River Shannon.

Blue, the depths of Lough Derg this Sunday morning. Yet the sunshine only seemed to mock his unhappiness. The shame. Oh, he was so ashamed. Damn Devlin Kelly – now that was a sin. He remembered Da using that word and Ma saying 'Hush, that's a sin . . . ' But damn Devlin Kelly anyway.

He squirmed on the damp grass, put his hand behind him and felt the tear in his trousers. What would Ma say? She'd be angry – beat him, perhaps. He puckered his face – but no. He disdained to cry. Too angry, still. It was good, he realized, being angry. Not half as unpleasant as being ashamed. He had done nothing wrong, after all, he thought suddenly. And hungry. He was hungry, now. His mother had made bread the night before – bread such as they had not seen since Da died – crisp and brown on the outside, and soft and brown on the inside . . . He half came to his knees, preparing to stand, when the sound of feet through the thick summer grass made him pull back, further back within the shadows between the two rocks.

The footsteps came closer, then stopped. Someone was panting, short of breath after the climb, then – voices. Two voices, whispering. Aidan held his breath. He did not want to be discovered, not with the tear in his trousers . . .

'Aidan? Aidan O'Brien?' Light voice. Familiar but unplaced. 'It's me, Anna O'Hagan. Come out.'

Anna? He scowled. She'd come up here with Maura O'Donoghue and Devlin Kelly – all of them come to torment him again . . .

'Aidan, I'm sorry I laughed at you.' Silence. 'Aidan? Aidan, you'll not be sulking with me, will you?' He pulled back through the gap between the two rocks, and stood on the other side, his back against the rough surface.

He was flattered by the pleading in her voice. She sounded contrite enough. He put his hands behind him, the back of one hand pressed into the palm of the other, and both pressing together the tear in his trousers. He had a scowl already prepared, but it vanished at the sight of Anna's companion. There was no sign of Devlin Kelly, there was only the thin and carrot-headed Maura. He stared at her, and she ducked her head a little.

''Twas all in fun,' she murmured, 'I'm sorry y' tore y'r clothes.'
She looked up at Anna, then, and so did Aidan. Anna was nodding,
and the boy suddenly wondered if the apology had been entirely
Maura's idea. Everyone knew she was Anna O'Hagan's shadow;
unalike as they were, the two girls were always together.

'Aidan?' Anna said. 'I've brought you something.' She was holding out her hand to him, the fist closed. He reached out, curious, and
found she had placed a small holy medal in his hand. 'It's special.
The Bishop himself blessed it for my father.'

Aidan raised his eyes from the little silver talisman to Anna's face,
serious, earnest. 'I don't believe what that Devlin Kelly said. About
Mister O'Reilly coming for you. He'd be in heaven or hell by now,
I'm thinking. And if he's still in purgatory he'd have better things
than you to think about, sure. I don't think he'll come for you at all.
But in case he should,' she added, 'that'll protect you.'

He gazed at her silently, unable to comprehend this kindness.
She looked at the ground between them. Beside them, Maura
O'Donoghue watched them and stood first on one foot, then on the
other. She was clearly bored, but Anna was not to be hurried.

Finally, 'Is it true you're beyond at the big house every day?
Learning to read and write?'

'Yes.'

'Will you . . . tell me sometimes? Will you come by our house
and tell me? About the things you've learnt and what the big house is
like?'

'I will sure.' He was surprised. Could the girl be envious of the
nightmare lessons in the schoolroom? Yet he was about to tell her
that he could already write his name when—

'Will you promise?'

'I promise.'

She had backed away a little. 'I have to go, now. Me ma will want
me home. Come, Maura.' And the two girls ran off down the hill.
Aidan took two steps to follow, but remembered the state of his
trousers. Decorum triumphed, and he walked slowly after them,
soon losing sight of them when they scrambled through a hedge.

When he reached home, his mother beat him. Three strokes of
the stick for tearing his trousers, another three for disappearing after
Mass. It was expected. It was fair. He did not cry very much.

Late that night when the wind howled and the shutters rattled and
the scamperings began in the loft, he reached down behind the bed,
and in the corner where the two walls met, his hand found the little
silver holy medal. For three weeks this secret protected him from
the marauding Mister O'Reilly. When his mother found it clutched

in his hand one morning, she extracted the whole story from him. Not angry or scornful, she found a little cord of leather and hung the medal about his neck. Thereafter, even in the winter, he walked relatively unafraid through the dusk. And at night he slept snugly, waking, sometimes, to hear old Mister O'Reilly roaring his impotent rage around the cottage walls.

He was not to lose the medal until several years later, while swimming in the lough with Tom-Joe Curran. But he did not forget the incident, nor Anna O'Hagan's kindness. It was the beginning of a friendship between them. Anna would visit Aidan's cottage, or he would take himself to the large farm her parents leased from William Kelly. With her, he found a sensitive friendship that he could not find with any of the Currans or O'Donoghues. Anna was something apart.

Though he continued to visit Mary, Daniel McDonnagh's help was not needed in training the pup, for William Kelly himself took the little setter in hand, and the landlord, the boy and the dog spent much time together. Mary worried, at first, that the man's interest was a temporary thing, a manifestation of the master's power, a kind of game that would pall quickly and leave them poorer than ever, struggling to keep the dog fed, and with Aidan, who came to worship the man, embittered and hurt when Kelly's interest moved elsewhere.

But it came to be seen that the master was genuinely fond of the boy. Within eighteen months the dog was showing himself adept in the field, and yet William remained concerned with the boy's welfare. The lessons in the schoolroom continued, Nathan Cameron was instructed to teach Aidan to ride, and from then on he helped in the stables as well as the kennels.

As he grew older, he went about the property with Nathan, and was taught to set snares and, proving himself responsible, to shoot game for the master's table. William himself often took Aidan shooting, a bored and complaining Devlin tramping beside them when he could not avoid his father's invitation.

Caroline Kelly treated Aidan with aloof condescension, and Devlin, seeing this, continued to regard the boy with barely disguised hostility. But it was obvious that this scruffy little Irish child held some important place in William's thoughts; beneath his protection, Aidan came and went at the big house with, as Caroline complained once, an air of confidence and a gloss of manners that were far above his station in life.

And Mary, as time passed, found this, too, a cause for concern. It

42

was all very well to be a kennel boy, a gamekeeper, a groom – even a jockey, God forbid! But an educated one? Aidan talked of distant lands she had never heard of, was better at mathematics than Master Devlin himself, he told her proudly . . . But was all this knowledge safe? Would he be taught to see too much, and then realize, when grown to manhood, that he was just a poor farm worker after all, and be made to limit his sights to a one-acre patch of potatoes and a two-room cottage?

Yet she could not deny that Aidan was happy. To have the horses and his lessons and to take Samhradh out on the bog with William Kelly was all a boy could wish for. He did not envy his friends when the public school was finally opened in Killaloe in 1832. Sure, Master Devlin was thirteen, and would have James Thomson with him until he left for university in Dublin. And Aidan was to share those years. To be made, instead, to sit on hard benches all day, surrounded by other children – including girls! – that would be fierce boring. And with that thought in mind, even Devlin could be tolerated.

3

Devlin was lost. He realized this with a sense of shame that chilled him. Lost on a hunt. No reason would be adequate when he told his father. No words would mitigate the scorn on his father's face if Devlin returned home, was waiting for the field when it arrived back, exhausted, victorious. He had to find the riders now, had to catch them up . . .

He cantered his pony up a rise and stood on the top of the hill. The land spread out before him, stone fences dividing the faded green of the winter fields into neat squares . . . smooth hills . . . a beech wood . . . scattered, grazing cattle – but there were no riders.

His spirits sank. So he had lost them. Stupid, stupid Chloe – he yanked the reins in and struck the horse a stinging blow across the ear. She dodged sideways, snorting, rolling her eyes and twisting the neat gold head back towards him. Stupid Chloe – refusing the fence, making everyone impatient with him. His father's cross voice had shouted from half-way up the other slope when he had turned on his huge grey hunter to look back at his son. 'For God's sake, Devlin!

Take the gate! Go round and take the gate, you little fool!'

Everyone had heard. Celia Retcliffe, his pasty-faced English cousin had flushed in embarrassment for him, but even she, with her perilous seat and weak hands, had managed to get her cobby little bay over the fence. And her brother, Corbett, riding at the tail of the field after his horse balked at the brook – even Corbett had taken the fence easily, turning as he cantered up the slope and laughing at Devlin. Fat Corbett, who had pimples on his face, yet who could still get his hunter over a four-foot wall . . . Devlin had tried to follow, but still Chloe refused, turning at the last minute, her haunches tucked beneath her, her head struggling away from the bit.

So he had taken the gate, dawdling, now, in his rage and embarrassment, defiant and unhappy, wishing that he could have stayed home. Mama was driving to Limerick today. They would have shopped for a new cravat for him, perhaps, or a book. It was too bad to have to be thundering about on horseback. And why? To watch some wretched fox torn limb from limb by the hounds. Ugly sight. He hated it. And scowling, thinking these things, he had topped the rise to find the field of riders gone. They had ridden over the next hill and disappeared who knew which way. An hour of searching did not help. He passed two men working in the fields, repairing a stone wall, and a girl going out to milk a cow, for it was late afternoon now, but there was no information about the hunters.

He did not deign to ask directions back to Tineranna. He had recently turned sixteen, he was a man, now. His pride would not allow him to admit that he was lost, and so close to home. And the men did not recognize him – saw him only as a boy of good breeding and wealth. His thin face beneath the thick fair hair remained haughty and grew almost angry when one of the men offered to take him to the main road to Killaloe. He had thanked them with scant grace and wheeled Chloe, tearing across a corner of their potato field, crushing the new plants, and ignoring the shouts of protest behind him as he took the hedge in a beautifully collected leap. Why hadn't his father been there to see *that*?

The twilight was deepening, setting on fire the tops of the furthest hills, and he was cold, despite his well-tailored hunting jacket and his gloves. 'Where *are* they?' he muttered aloud. Home already, perhaps. If he could only get a glimpse of Lough Derg, he could get his bearings – but this eternal sameness of slopes . . . He urged the tired Chloe up yet another hill, thinking as he did so that this would be the last they would climb. If he could not see the field of riders from here he would go to the nearest cottage, pride kept in check, and ask to be shown the way home.

44

But there they were! Riders, forty of them, the exhausted horses trotting, or cantering slowly – mouthing the bits, throwing their heads restively, lathered white with sweat but still eager to be home.

Chloe, too, had seen and smelled the other horses, had whinnied a greeting to her stable-mate, William's big dapple grey hunter, and Devlin had difficulty reining in. Chloe fidgetted, lifting her forelegs up and down, up and down, eager to be away to the others. Still Devlin held her in. He could see his father riding beside the Master of Foxhounds, the strict protocol that demanded the latter's leadership now forgotten in the easy camaraderie of the homeward journey. He could hear the laughter and the voices as the men and women chatted and turned calling to each other. But most of all, he was watching the hedge.

Four men in dull-coloured clothes made bright by the sunset were working on his side of the barrier, digging and pulling at the blackberry bushes that grew faster and spread wider than the hawthorns themselves. The men waved and called greetings to the gentry as they rode past – but these things Devlin barely observed. The hedge itself was dry and brown and about four feet high, and his eyes were upon this while his thoughts were upon his father. Chloe was freshened, now, eager. She could take that hedge, tall though it was. His father would look up, would be angry with him, but he would see with what style Devlin rode, would be proud of his son for this one moment at least.

Devlin dug his heels hard into Chloe's flanks, and gave the mare her head in the steep downhill race. He was a good rider, he knew. He could almost feel the eyes of some members of the field as a call went up. The farmworkers shouted something, far to his right – he heard his father's voice call his name in that same instant that he rose in the stirrups, flinging his arms forward and leaning back as he had been taught, giving Chloe freedom from the bit with which to judge her own landing. Only in mid-air, the mare stretched her length and seemingly transfixed there in mid-flight did he see that the land dropped sharply on the other side, saw the wet black soil, the broad pool of water waiting. And *down* – thrown forward, the reins ripped from him, Chloe's scream going on and on, as the earth crashed into his side and darkness drowned him like the black water itself.

Someone was shaking him and screaming. Far-off, the sound of his father's voice called his name . . . But no. He opened his eyes to find his father's face contorted with grief or rage, his father's hands gripping his shoulders – yet the screaming . . .

It was Chloe. Standing in the pool, hock-deep, terrified, attempting to lunge out of the water but unable to move – her shattered

45

foreleg, that fine-boned leg where the hair turned sharply from gold to white, spilling red into the water. Water red from the sunset. From the sunset. Not Chloe . . .

'You did this, you young fool! Look at her! You little monster, I could kill you!' Deadened, deafened, the boy could only gaze into his father's face, his mouth open wordlessly, his eyes wild.

'William! *William!*' It was Robert Osborne, the Master of Fox-hounds, 'Leave the boy, for God's sake! Here's a pistol – it's loaded – use it, man! The animal's in agony!'

William let go of his son and Devlin stumbled back against the hedge. When he turned, his father was holding a light pistol, em-bossed with silver. It was one that Devlin had often admired, a gun that never left the person of Osborne, the owner of Ceelohg, an Englishman always nervous of marauding highwaymen and Terryalts – but now it lay in William Kelly's hand, the silver glinting crimson in the light, its muzzle levelled at the struggling mare. Devlin found air in his lungs, was on the point of shouting 'No!' when the pistol was lowered suddenly and William had turned to face the group.

'Ride on, all of you, if you wouldn't mind.' The riders looked at each other, then back at William. All the women in the party had already cantered off, over the next hill; toughened horsewomen, all, but unable to witness what they knew was inevitable. The remaining men looked uncertainly at William, but his eyes were on his son, and after only a second's hesitation, the horses were turned and the field rode off.

When they had gone, William turned the pistol about and Devlin found it thrust suddenly into his own hands. 'You do it!'

The gun almost dropped from paralysed fingers. 'No,' he breathed.

'You took that jump on an exhausted animal – a mere pony. A beast with less heart than she would never have done it for you – but she did, and now you can blame yourself for what happened. Shoot her.'

'No! I can't!'

'Do it, you little . . . !'

'No!'

'Look at her!'

'No!'

'By God, Devlin, I'll have you face up to your responsibilities. Look at her!' Brutally, he took the boy's face between his hands, twisting it until he faced the mare. Devlin sobbed, struggled to free himself, was let go only to find the gun in his hand, his father's iron

46

grip forcing the pistol towards the horse's head, the relentless voice in his ears. 'This is your responsibility. Be a man, Devlin, for God's sake . . . '

'No!'

'Shoot!'

'No! *No!*' It was almost a wail. For a long moment, William looked at his son, too angry to acknowledge the boy's misery. He let go of the gun, leaving it in Devlin's limp grasp, and stepped back. 'I shall leave you. I know you'll do what has to be done.'

Devlin stared at his father in horror, but William had already turned away and was mounting his own horse.

'Father, I can't! I . . . '

William's voice was cold. 'I do not want you in the house, Devlin, until this thing is done.'

Devlin turned away, trying to keep down the sobs of rage and terror that rose in him, and when he next dared to look up, his father was silhouetted upon the top of the hill, riding away, leaving him there. On the crest the figure paused, stood still like a gilded statue of a centaur, above and beyond Devlin, and he could not bear it. He turned his face away; when he next looked, his father had gone.

The seconds stretched into a minute . . . two. A thrush called, softly, further down the hedge. Still he did not move. He wanted to run, to catch up with his father, not to be left alone in this darkening field . . . and yet there was this . . . thing.

He looked down at the still form of the creature on the ground before him, and something broke inside him. He lashed out with his foot, 'Bitch!' he shouted. 'Bastard! You're to blame . . . !' His hate had found a release and once, twice, he kicked the animal, until to his horror it cried out, a soft-breathing whinny of agony . . .

And someone was beside him, had appeared from nowhere and the gun was wrenched from his numb fingers. 'Let me! Jaysus, Devlin, let me . . . !'

For an instant, Devlin thought it was his father, returned to help him face this, but the voice . . . O'Brien stood there, a scarecrow-like little figure in an out-sized coat, but holding the gun with confidence, pointing it down at the horse's head . . .

Until he died Devlin would hear that shot. Deafening, painful, exploding close to his ears. As a man he would wake up to stare across a blackened room, seeing the horse lying with its head on the edge of a pool of scarlet water. In time William would forget the incident. But Devlin would not. He would never know if his father knew the truth; would read, in his father's face, the cognizance of his own cowardice, his worthlessness. He would grow to resent his father for seeing these things in him, yet would never speak of them. So the wedge was driven between them, shallow, but firm. And by this boy.

'I would have done it myself.' And to his shame he was crying once more. He snatched the gun back, and stepped away. 'I would have. I would have done it myself.'

The boy was only about twelve, but tall, almost Devlin's height. Dark hair in his eyes, dark, solemn eyes that held no clue to what he was thinking. He said only, 'I couldn't bear it. I'll tell no one.'

Devlin wanted to hit him, make him cry out, smash the calm face; but he backed away. 'I'd have done it myself . . . ' His voice broke on a sob, and he turned and ran. Ran up the hill where the last scarlet light hung in the sky.

4

Aidan arrived home dazed, silent. He would not speak of what had occurred, did not wish the wide-eyed and curious Thomas to know how shaken he felt. Thomas worshipped him, and Aidan, who normally treated his brother with good-natured carelessness, was vain enough to wish to keep his image untarnished. Only late that night, in bed, when his mother came to kiss him goodnight and the impressionable ears of Thomas were closed in sleep, did he speak of what had happened.

' . . . And he kicked her – *kicked* her! – and I'd have liked to have killed him, Ma . . . '

'Be quiet with that kind of talk. I know how you feel, Aidan, but you're never to lift your hand against Master Devlin, do you hear?'

'But Chloe, Ma! Chloe! She was the cleverest horse on Tineranna – it was me who exercised her, me who taught her to jump – I know!' He lowered his voice. 'It's Devlin who should've been shot, doing a thing like that. If I was his father . . . ' He tried to rise, his eyes filling with the memory, and she pushed him gently back.

'But you're not his father. William Kelly is his father. William Kelly who owns this land, who owns us.'

'No!' He almost shouted the word, and Thomas stirred beside him, murmuring in his sleep. Aidan clenched his teeth. He could not bear the look of resignation in his mother's eyes. 'No, Ma,' his voice hoarse. 'No one owns us.'

'Maybe not. But sure he holds our lives at his whim. He can throw us out of this cottage – and we'd starve to death. Where would we be, Aidan, if it wasn't for the Kellys' charity? Now let me hear no more talk of striking back at Master Devlin.'

'He's cruel. And a coward. I think I hate him.'

'You do no such thing. Hate is a sin, Aidan. Don't you be jealous and bitter, now.'

'I'm not jealous.' Samhradh, who had been sleeping curled by the fire, unfolded himself and trotted over to Aidan. He put a hand on the dog's head, and the animal sighed with gratification. 'I just get tired of having to remember what's good manners when I'm with Devlin, when himself doesn't have any manners at all, for all his being well-brought-up. Why is it only poor people who have to be good?'

'Everyone should be good.'

'Devlin isn't.'

'Then the Lord will punish him.'

'I don't think I can wait that long.'

'Arra, stop.' She stood up. 'We must accept things the way they are. The Kellys are wealthy people and they're our landlords. Have been for more than two hundred years . . .'

'Who owned the land before them?'

'Aidan, lie still and rest, now.'

'Ma? Who owned the land before the Kellys?' He had rolled over on his side to gaze at her, pushed Samhradh's head aside the better to see his mother's face.

She hesitated. 'We did.'

'*We?*'

She came back and sat at the foot of the bed. 'When Cromwell gave land in Northern Ireland to his English soldiers, they dispossessed the real owners. These were killed or had to flee to the west. Some of the Irish helped Cromwell – traitors, they've been called, Cromwellian Helpers – but a lot of them had no choice and I can't blame them – the English were too powerful. These Irish were dispossessed too, but were given parcels of land in Connaught. And as a better means of defence, the land within a mile of the Shannon's western shore was given to families known to be completely loyal to the Crown. God knows,' she scowled, 'what the Kellys did to deserve it – some of the tales of those times . . . Most Kellys are good Irish families – these Kellys have been marrying and mixing with the English for two hundred years.' She paused, then said, 'Maybe that's what makes Master Devlin the way he is – he's Irish,

49

and yet he's not one of us. It's not even a matter of money. His mother is a stranger. Perhaps Devlin feels like a stranger, too.'

Yet his mother's forbearance left Aidan unmoved. 'They took O'Brien land? They took *our* land?'

'That's past and gone . . . '

'Daniel McDonnagh says that there were once woods on Craglea and the rest of Slieve Bernagh. That the English cut down the trees and sent the timber to England. When the mountains had trees on them – they were *our* mountains?'

'Aidan . . . '

'And the lough . . . *our* lough . . . Why did we give it all up, Ma? Why?'

'It was a matter of staying on as tenants, or being killed, Aidan. So many have fought, and died. Your own grandfather, and your uncles – your father's older brothers – weren't they killed in the Rebellion of 1798? And fine young men, all of them.'

Aidan murmured, 'Our land . . . '

'Stop, son. Those days are gone. Sure, go into Killaloe and you'll not find a stone of Brian Boru's castle. The O'Briens are scattered all over Ireland, all over the world, with so many other Irish.' She touched his hair, filled with pity and helplessness. She said gently, 'Things will be better for us, one day. But we must be patient, and work hard. The answer doesn't lie in fighting, Aidan. You have to learn to *wait*. When you're Irish, it's the greatest thing you can learn.'

'Sometimes,' he said, 'you don't have any choice.'

She had stood, but now turned back to gaze down at him. He was right, God help him. And he looked so like his father, scowling at her determinedly, pulling the succinct truth from her words, that she had to take the bucket as a pretext and go outside for water, to hide her desire to cry.

That November evening was a cause for local celebration: from her cottage, Mary could hear the sounds of music and laughter from the O'Sullivan's house, but was glad that she had made the excuse of Thomas having a chill to avoid attending. That afternoon Terry O'Sullivan had married Oona Ryan, a tall and attractive dark-haired girl from Tuomgraney, whom he had met at a *ceili* two years before. He had become tired of waiting for Mary. All the local people knew this, Mary herself knew it. Terry's mother had died only the year before, and it was hard for him to look after himself. He had waited for her long enough, he told Mary, the time was right, now.

And she had refused him. His broad, good-natured face could not credit it. He had stared at her, roared at her, accused her of playing him off against Daniel McDonnagh: had said vicious, wicked things, then had gone off to drown his disappointment in every public house in Killaloe and Ballina, telling the story of his broken heart to all who would listen. A month later he was engaged to Oona Ryan.

Two years before, Mary had moved the two boys into the room and the double bed that she had shared with her husband. She herself slept on the small bed in the kitchen; that way she could work late at night and not disturb them. She sat up late this night, listening to the music, thinking of her own wedding, her marriage – and perhaps because of this, when she fell asleep in front of the fire, it was to dream of Aidan, the boys' father.

He had come swinging down the hill past O'Sullivan's, as he had done every evening of their life together; his coat held over his shoulder, whistling; drunk, as like as not, but pleasantly so. She would run to meet him – had never grown out of that habit, even when the boys had been born – loved to watch him as she met him, the black eyes merry, smell the warm whiskeyness of his breath and the faint horse-smell that always clung to him. The finest jockey in Counties Clare, Limerick and Tipperary – and Mayo, too, had not Spartan gone down with him at the last jump and Fitzpatrick taken the trophy. Even Fitzpatrick had said it was luck, only luck – 'Bad for you, good for me,' he had said after the trophy had been handed to him, and he had shaken Aidan's hand. Mary had almost burst with pride in him. When Mister Fitzpatrick had called through Killaloe five years ago, Aidan had been dead only nine months. 'A fine horseman, and a fine man,' he had told Mary, and pressed a gold coin into her hand. 'For the boys,' he said, 'may they grow up just like him.'

God forbid. Mary turned to glance through the doorway to the bed where the children slept. She could do nothing to prevent young Aidan working with the horses. It was a job, and she was grateful for it. But it made her afraid, thinking of him working there, in the same stables, the same stall perhaps, where the crazed English stallion had killed his father. She would not mention her fears; she hoped that Aidan's love of horses would give way before other opportunities – else what was the point of all this education?

She brought her legs up beneath her and hugged her knees. He knew so much already; his arithmetic was excellent – and he had even taught her to write her name, a source of great satisfaction to her. Yes, this learning was a good thing, and besides, lately she had been considering the other avenues open to him; perhaps a job in one of the stores in Killaloe. Perhaps the Protestants would consider hiring a Catholic boy, if he could calculate well. Who knew? Even a store of his own one day – and Thomas . . . Thomas could help him run it.

Thomas. She frowned over the problem of her youngest son. He was nine, now. But already she saw him as a person, complete, what he would be when he was a man. Lazy, she thought. She glanced once more into the other room; the light of the candles fell on the sleeping Thomas. Aidan's dark hair, but finer features; he'd be a more handsome man than Aidan – but lazy, a dreamer. She sighed. Aidan would have to look after him, even as he did now. But an education would help. Thomas, too, must be taught to read and write. This new school recently opened in Killaloe – he must attend it; she would ask Daniel McDonnagh about it when he next came to call . . .

Daniel. Her arms tightened a little in their grip on her knees. Daniel . . . was he the reason for her dream of her husband? Was it a guilty conscience that bothered her?

He'd come past only three days ago and already she found herself wondering when she'd see him again. And scolding herself, too. Years, now, she had been waiting. Hoping that the warmth in his eyes as he gazed at her would become something more. Too long. Too long she had loved him. Was she a fool for doing so? Everyone spoke of how fond he was of her, and how it was only a matter of time before he asked for her. Did he not adore the boys? And they him? What was he waiting for, she thought impatiently, a sign from heaven? She frowned. This was not an altogether ridiculous statement. Daniel's faith measured so highly in his life. She had often been afraid that his academic leanings would finally find their place only in the tranquillity of a seminary. She could see him as a priest, and smiled at the thought. The priesthood should contain men like Daniel, with his kindness, his humour. Thank God his independent spirit baulked at the thought, or she was sure she would have lost him to the Church long ago. She frowned, considering. What, then? What had made him hesitate for so long? He was young, it was true, only twenty-eight . . .

The banging of a fist on the barred door. 'Mary?'

'Yes?' She had sprung to her feet.

'It's Daniel. May I speak with you?'

Her heart thumped hard. She felt guilty, awed, as if she had conjured him up. Opening the door, she stepped back, not looking up at him, afraid of the welcome written on her face.

'I know it's late, but I saw the light still burning and I had to tell

52

you.'

Surprised at the tightly constrained excitement in his voice, she forgot her own embarrassment. Shutting the door she leaned against it, staring at him as he marched over to the fireplace, turned and faced her, his eyes glowing.

'I've been accepted into Maynooth. Maynooth! I'm to leave straight away!'

Oh so glad of the solid door at her back. Feeling the blood drain downwards from her head, but her hands behind her gripped the bar of the door. She would not faint. She would not fall.

'Mary? Did you hear? The seminary at Maynooth . . . '

'Yes. Yes, Daniel. That's wonderful.'

'It is. Oh, it is.' He stood before her, took her arms in his hands, the warm pressure of his grip willing his pleasure, his excitement into her. 'Mary, I've prayed so hard – even . . . even you, you know me so well, don't know how hard, how long I've prayed. All these years I've known I wasn't worthy – I lacked the self-discipline, the humility. I went back to the president of Maynooth year after year, and he said to be patient, that I would know when I was ready and so would he . . . and he was right. This time, when we met, I could say to him that I was sure. He looked at me for a long moment – and then he embraced me. Mary, there were tears in his eyes. He said, "You will be a good priest, Daniel, I know it." '

She could only stare at him, feeling a hollow, a vacuity growing within her. She had known. Known all these years. The glow in his eyes that she could not understand, the courage, the quiet force of his will – all, all God-given.

'I'll . . . we'll miss you.'

'I'll miss you, too. You've given me so much – all I am, I think – I owe so much to you.'

'To . . . me?' She only breathed the words.

'Your courage, Mary. Your faith in the face of so much hardship. And your goodness.'

She shut her eyes, She could not bear it. The loved face aglow – but not for her. The love that radiated from him – but not for her. Any minute now he would say that she had been his inspiration, and she would strike him, or run out the door, or perhaps both.

'Mary, you are happy for me, aren't you?'

No! she wanted to scream. *No, I love you! I want you! I don't want to give you to God!* And suddenly she saw years of emptiness waiting for her with his leaving: the loneliness would creep from the corners to possess this room for ever once he walked from the cottage, never, perhaps, to return.

'Mary?' He was worried, now. Intelligent, beloved, ignorant man, stepping close to her, holding her hands. 'Mary, you are happy for me, aren't you?'

Her love was too great, even for her hurt. 'Yes,' she said, and smiled at him.

Aidan woke early after a night filled with dark dreams of hedges and screaming and scarlet pools. He shivered when he woke, sprang from his bed and dressed, knowing that he must leave the house quickly, quietly; action the only panacea against the memory of the day before. His mother was still asleep on the settle bed in the kitchen, dark shadows beneath her closed eyes. She was awake late last night, worrying about me, perhaps, of what Devlin would do now.

He let the dog out the door and followed it silently, making up his mind to bring something back from the big house kitchen for her. Some currants, perhaps, or a piece of left-over pie if he could talk Cook into parting with it.

The wedding celebrations were still in progress at the O'Sullivans'. Through the first light of dawn, Aidan took Samhradh past the lighted cottage with its sounds of lugubrious piping and voices, on up the boreen and across the Killaloe-Ogonelloe road, up into the hills.

He was glad his mother hadn't married Terry O'Sullivan. He liked him well-enough. He was great crack when he had a few jars in him – but he had a few jars in him nearly all the time, and Aidan knew his mother didn't like that. Besides, sometimes Terry became nasty drunk; Aidan had seen him beat a horse he was shoeing at the Tineranna forge – the horse would not stand still, and Terry had beaten it. Would have beaten Aidan, too, when he declaimed against it, had not Corrie O'Neill heard the shouting as he passed, and defended the boy. That was a proud moment for Aidan, Corrie O'Neill, the giant from the Dublin slums who had once been champion boxer of all Ireland, coming to his defence! The man was something of a legend already, travelling about the country, giving lessons to the gentry; a monolith of a man, standing six feet five in his bare feet, with shoulders like a plough horse and a face battered and scarred so much that it became a joke for the ladies to try to guess at the kind of features he had been born with.

Aidan scrambled up and down the hills towards Finlea, the dog ranging in broad circles around him, and he wondered at the life that Corrie O'Neill must lead. To have people's respect – surely that was the best thing about being a man. If he could only fight like Corrie

O'Neill . . . if he was only as big as Corrie O'Neill. But even at twelve years old, Aidan had no illusions about how tall he would walk through life. To be the son of a jockey put limitations on you, for sure. But maybe that wasn't so bad, he reasoned. His father had stood only five feet three inches, yet people had respected him almost as much as Corrie O'Neill. Perhaps the secret lay not so much in what you were, or what you did, but how well you succeeded . . .

Samhradh was barking, short, sharp barks, and had darted off ahead with a whine. Aidan considered calling him back, but let him go. It was not a rabbit; the dog's tail had waved in good humour, the whine had been one of recognition. He peered through the half-light, all that these winter mornings allowed at eight-thirty, and found a man standing by a clump of thorn bushes on the crest of the hill. Samhradh was fawning at the man's feet, rubbing his head against the man's hand, and Aidan recognized William Kelly.

He stood smiling as the boy approached. 'You're restless this morning, too, Aidan.'

'Yes, sir.'

They both stood silent a while, watching the pale reaches of Lough Derg become mottled bronze and silver as the sun rose, and the humped shapes of the Tipperary hills on the opposite shore separate themselves from the grey sky.

Aidan was thinking of the events of the day before, wondering what, if anything, the master knew about it . . .

'Chloe – Devlin's little hunter. She broke her leg yesterday. She had to be put down.'

Aidan was staring at him. But of course . . . he could not know that Aidan had been there. The boy was not tall enough to be seen over the hedge, and Devlin— 'Oh,' he managed, staring at the ground, trying to think of something to say.

Kelly glanced at the lowered head, took the silence for shock. 'You were very fond of her.'

'Yes . . . I . . . trained her . . .'

'I know. But these things happen.' There was an edge to the voice. Aidan looked up, but the man's gaze was fixed on the lake below. For a long time they did not speak, then, 'You've made remarkable progress with your horsemanship,' Kelly began, 'you are your father's son, no doubt – but . . . I have often thought that perhaps you should leave the work at the stables – for a few years, at least.' Aidan was gazing at him in horror. 'Don't look like that. What I was about to suggest was that you attend school in Killaloe . . .'

'Master Devlin doesn't want me in the schoolroom anymore.' He had blurted it out without thinking, and could have bitten his tongue immediately afterwards.

'Devlin? What has Devlin to do with it? It's something I've been meaning to speak with you about – you're mature for your age – you have had to be . . . but you're only twelve, Aidan. You should be at school, in the company of other boys and girls . . . '

'But I love the horses! Sir, you'll not send me from Tineranna?'

Kelly looked discomfited at this outburst. 'Aidan, I wish you to have a complete education. To keep you working at the stables when you could be at school is virtually child labour . . . '

'But all I want is . . . '

'Don't interrupt me. There are more things for a man to do in life than ride horses. When you're older, I could arrange for you to work as a clerk, to become a lawyer. You could be a great asset to Master Devlin if you became a lawyer. The commercial side of running a large estate becomes more complicated each year . . . '

Aidan's mind was still struggling over one phrase. 'How could I be an asset to Master Devlin? You run Tineranna, sir.'

The grey eyes turned upon him, the handsome face smiled a little, patiently. 'Aidan, I will not always be master of Tineranna. When I die, Devlin will own all this. He'll need help from men who are loyal and clever.'

Aidan was gazing at him in horror. Never had he considered this. Never. Devlin, spoilt, vicious Devlin, as master of Tineranna . . . It was impossible, inconceivable. His mind refused to accept the thought.

William Kelly was saying, 'There will be time for you to make up your mind what you want to do with your life – but these years of learning are important and the school could perhaps teach you more than James Thomson. And besides, you and Devlin are not friends, are you?'

It was Aidan's turn to feel uncomfortable. 'Sir . . . I tried . . . '

'I know. Your father and I were friends immediately, and remained so until he died. But I was not . . . protected so well as Devlin. Life was simpler, then. The barrier between landowners and farmers was not so great, it seemed.' His voice had faded slightly, as if he were speaking to himself. Then he looked across at Aidan. 'Thomson thinks you should stay. And I think Devlin has benefitted from having you share the lessons. But I feel you'd be happier as a schoolboy for a few years.'

'No, sir,' the boy said, meeting the man's eyes. 'I'll go if you want me to. But I don't want to.'

The man sighed. 'Very well. But if you wish, you can change your mind.'

'I won't, sir.'

5

Both Aidan and Thomas noticed a change in their mother. She worked just as hard, but silently, withdrawn from them. They did not connect it with Daniel McDonnagh leaving Killaloe for the seminary; they were simply puzzled, uncomfortable, they tried her patience with small acts of naughtiness and found a temper suddenly flaring in her, breaking the bounds of her usual fairness. She was sorry, afterwards, strangely so, and would hug them and weep over them, puzzling them further.

Yet as the months passed and the winter brought the year to a close, she gradually returned to something like normal. Summer came, and the summer after that, and Aidan realized that she was not quite as she had been – something had gone out of her, that winter of 1835. In the winters that followed, she would sit by the hearth, reading over letters, friendly, cheerful letters that arrived more infrequently and, finally, ceased altogether. The neighbours began to say that Mary O'Brien would never remarry, that she still secretly grieved for her husband. Oona O'Sullivan said nastily to Molly Curran and Kitty O'Hagan that Mary still had a secret *grá* for Terry. Whatever the reason, the widow O'Brien kept much to herself, was patient and gentle in her relationship with her growing sons, her dark eyes filled with some sorrowing that neither of them would ever guess at, could never name, let alone remove.

But they were growing quickly, their horizons broadening, their interests taking them further from her. Thomas was doing well at the school in the village, and Aidan was spending more and more time in the stables of Tineranna.

Despite his initial determination to stay on in the schoolroom, Devlin's attitude, though it no longer manifested itself in outright provocation, shed a pall over the enjoyable lessons. The atmosphere was heavy with resentment, and Aidan, after a further twelve months, voluntarily quit the schoolroom; he had made up his mind, and it was to the horses that he gravitated. He could not bear being indoors for long, knew, as the years passed, that he could never – even for William Kelly – give himself to the long years of close study involved in a legal career. So Samhradh now followed him on exercise gallops through the countryside as he trained the

57

hunters, and stayed put on command at the corner of the stables when Aidan led one of the thoroughbreds out on to the practice track. Aidan loaned the dog to William Kelly on several occasions, or went out with the landlord and his English visitors as the dog went through his paces. William overcame his disappointment that the boy wanted no further education, consoled himself once more that he was Aidan's son, and gave him more responsibility about the stables. He was proud of the boy's riding, which won him several races in Limerick and Scarriff, and he was proud, too, of Samhradh, glad that the dog had not been put down as a pup; that he made up now in talent and intelligence what he lacked in physical perfection as a prize setter.

'We should get him back,' Devlin said, once, watching the dog trot back to them, ignoring the black retriever who had flushed the mallard and now carrying the dead bird back to lay it at William's feet. William was blowing the smoke from his gun and reloading it, and turned to stare at Devlin. Almost eighteen, the boy stood as tall as his father, though with his blonde hair and deep blue eyes, his features favoured his mother. William sighed. Even the sentiments he expressed were words that shadowed his mother's mind. A gift was a gift, to William; he was proud that the O'Brien boy had done so well with the dog, pointed him out and showed off Samhradh as a triumph over the pup's inauspicious beginnings. Never had it occurred to him to envy the peasant child his possession. But how like Devlin. How like Caroline herself. The petty jealousy.

'He was a gift to the boy,' he said briefly, taking up the mallard and placing it in the sack, stroking the dog's head.

'We could buy him back . . . '

'Be quiet, Devlin. Do you have no sense of honour?'

The words were like a slap. Devlin felt his face flush, then pale just as suddenly. His father did not notice, was striding out once more. Devlin found he had stopped breathing. Even at eighteen, a man, now, his father's scorn burnt into him like a brand. He had been trying to help. He had seen the longing in his father's eyes as he watched the dog. Yet because Devlin voiced what his father was obviously thinking, he was punished by the backlash of his father's guilt. Of course he wanted the dog. But proud; too proud to ask for it. That won't happen to me, Devlin promised himself, following his father's footsteps through mud that sucked at his boots. Not pride nor honour will get in my way when I want something. Why should Father allow the O'Brien boy to triumph over him? Where was the pride in that?

They shot two more birds, then turned back towards Tineranna. His father said abruptly, 'How are your lessons with Corrie coming along? Has he made a fighter of you?'

Corrie. Devlin had forgotten him. The man would be waiting for him even now. He took his watch out and looked at it as he said, 'I'm improving, I think. Corrie gives me a lot of encouragement, but sometimes I think it's because he needs the employment. After six months I feel I should be able to trounce him by now.'

'Don't be so impatient. The pugilist's art takes years to master.'

Devlin had his doubts about it being an art, but refrained from saying so. He did not enjoy getting himself bruised by the heavy fists of Corrie O'Neill, seeing his warped nose and scarred eyebrows dancing before him tantalizingly, always just out of reach of his own fists. It was barbaric, and he loathed each approaching lesson with the ex-boxer. Just as he loathed the hunting, the shooting, all the bloody games that his father insisted he play, and play well. Was this the measure of a man? As if in answer, his father moved ahead of him a little, and Devlin found himself watching his father's easy walk, the gun at his shoulder, the cloth sack stained scarlet, swinging with each stride. This was a man. All that Devlin wanted to be. Why was the state made so difficult for him to attain? And must it be equated with the ability to hurt, to kill?

He found himself longing once more for London. His mother had taken him there only last spring – they had been to parties, and on shopping sprees. Had driven through the city in his grandmother's smart new carriage. Had gone riding in Hyde Park, and felt the admiring glances of his grandmother's friends. His mother was still very beautiful, and he – he was handsome, there was no sense in denying it. His skin was clear and his blonde head stood inches over Corbett Retcliffe and the other boys. At one of the entertainments organized for him he had heard them snickering to two young ladies that his father was an Irish Papist. He had walked over to them, bowed to one of the girls – the prettiest – and asked her to dance. And she had, without a glance at Corbett or his friends. It had been wonderful. London was wonderful. London was where he belonged, not tramping through boggy marshes in County Clare behind a man who would not notice should he, his own son, vanish behind him off the face of the earth.

'Keep your guard up! Keep it up! No, too high!'

'Ow . . . !'

'That'll teach you.'

William and Devlin walked into the stable yard, and stopped. On

59

the patch of grass in the centre, two figures were circling each other, eyes on each other's face. One, huge, beefy, his stomach straining at the tightly cinched trouser belt, the muscles of his massive shoulders working as his fists moved slowly, slowly, carefully, before him. The other figure tiny by comparison, slight, slim-hipped, wiry; yet the bony shoulders were broad, the neck short, promising strength. And quick – Lord, how quick those feet! Devlin stared at the figures, bitterness welling up.

'Aidan!' His father's voice, laughing. Devlin turned, but William had already moved forward. 'You two look like a bear and a terrier!'

The two turned, startled, then O'Neill had returned William's grin. 'Sir, I'll be tellin' you the truth – but this terrier's got it in him to win – bear or not. Maybe not for a few years yet, but begod, he's got it in him!'

William raised an eyebrow. 'Is that so? This brat?' Aidan knew the master's moods; kept silent, respectful, but his eyes danced and he moved on the balls of his feet, up and down, while they talked. 'How old are you now, Aidan?'

'Fourteen last week, sir.'

'You're tall for your age.' The boy stood almost at medium height, even for a man.

The boy grinned. 'No, sir. I haven't grown an inch since last year – this is as high as I'll get in the world, I'll be bound.'

William grinned. 'Get back to work, now. I'd like that bay hunter exercised fairly frequently this week – I'll be taking him out this Saturday.'

The boy touched his forelock, picked up his homespun shirt and walked away towards the stables, pulling it on as he went.

'I'm sorry to be seen sporting with the boy, sir,' Corrie was saying, 'but Master Devlin was late . . . '

'That's all right.' William was scowling after Aidan. 'I've always been interested in the boy – his father was more of a friend than a servant. We were raised together . . . I'd hoped young Aidan and Devlin might have the same relationship – but it seems not.'

'Your son's a loner, sir. If I'm not speaking too boldly,' Corrie hastened to add.

'No. No. I'd be glad of any help in understanding Devlin. Is he enjoying these lessons?'

'Well . . . he likes them better, now that he has more confidence. So much of this game is mind over matter, y'know. At first he hated it, and I knew it, so I took it real slow with him. But now it seems he's gettin' a certain knowledge, certain tricks, making the most of himself – I mean, he's tall, so he's got a good reach – a fine asset to

60

begin with . . . '

'Good.' William was apparently satisfied, and looked around. But Devlin was nowhere in sight.

Corrie, the battler, the scarred veteran of a career that began in the back streets of Dublin, from whose gutters he had emerged aided only by his fists and a steady, philosophic nature, gazed around also, then brought his gaze back to his employer. Poor bastard, he thought. You've got the wrong son, and that's the truth.

Devlin found his mother in her sitting room. It had once been the schoolroom, but it was unrecognizable now in the clutter of spidery tables, tassled drapes, the crowded grouping of china figures, all Caroline's little treasures, on every surface. She was sitting by the fire with her embroidery and looked up as he entered, her eyes sparkling somewhere in their blue depths with the welcome that made the boy suddenly calmer, confident.

'Mama.'

'Darling boy, sit down.'

'I shouldn't stay, I have a boxing lesson.'

'Corrie can wait. You've been shooting,' she said, taking in his muddied boots and breeches. He raised his eyes to her, and in the silence as they gazed at each other was perfect understanding.

'I brought down a water hen.'

Her mouth turned up a little. 'Congratulations.'

Suddenly he was grinning. She smiled openly, then, reaching out to place a hand upon his, said, 'You're being very patient, Devlin. I'm proud of you. It makes your papa so pleased that you like the things that he regards as important.'

'Hideous . . . ' he began.

'You're his only son. It's so important to him.' Her eyes glowed once more and she leaned forward, her voice dropping a little. He noticed, suddenly, the lines around her eyes and mouth. It made her look different . . . not quite as beautiful. But her words. She was saying, 'In a year or two, I'll take you back to London. Ostensibly for a visit, but I'll make some excuse – we've plenty of time to think of one. And we'll stay. A year – two years. We'll manage it,' she said, seeing him straighten, warming to the sudden joy in him. 'We'll think of something.'

'But . . . Father. You'd leave Father to go to London with me?'

Caroline kept the smile on her face. Only inside was there a tightening, a hardening. How could he know? He, for whom she did all things, including keeping a facade that she still adored his father. She looked at his face – strong, beautiful, trusting. He was every-

61

thing to her; could she not lean forward and speak? Hiss the truth, the burdening truth, that she was tired of the struggle to gain William's attention, tired of fighting his impatience with her, his boredom with her; tired of the little spears of his coldness when she would try to enter his world, his thoughts. A harmless comment on his political affairs, the troubles with the rebel groups, used to solicit a hard look, then a turning away, a scowl. Yet even this had changed. He would no longer look at her, would keep his eyes where they were. Would sigh, quickly. Would continue speaking as though she had not spoken. And she spoke only through love of him. Only to make him see that he was bleeding himself for nothing over these stupid, servile creatures – less than human except in their cunning. But he would not listen, *would no longer look at her*. And the love weakened, perished and dried up at its out-reaching edges.

To her son, she said calmly, 'Your father has his life here. You know that he is happiest here. Why, he probably won't even miss us.' She smiled. They both smiled, but their smiles were pinched with the years of their hurt.

William came to fetch his son. As he was striding down the hall to the sitting room the butler was answering a rapping at the front door. William stopped, hearing the low growl of voices below the high, clipped tones of his servant. 'If you'll come in, gentlemen, I'll see if . . . '

'It's all right, Barnes.'

The group looked up in relief as they saw him approach; Curran was there, and Father O'Callaghan, O'Flaherty and Flannigan, the two other Catholic landowners of the district, Cormac Regan, spokesman for the tenant farmers – but most surprising, Osborne, McDougal, Robinson, Clarke, educated, enlightened men, but Protestants, all four.

'We look at it this way,' Osborne began, once the others were seated in chairs about the library. Osborne himself stood, his bulky body rocking on his heels, his gaze full on William. 'We've been patient too long with this terrorism . . . ' A sound from Regan, and Osborne turned on him. 'That's enough, Regan. You're one of my tenants and a damn good farmer, but we all know you have your hand on the pulse of every gang of Terrys and Whiteboys! But we're not arguing that.' He turned back to William, 'I'll admit that we four have been pretty well left alone. The county knows that our rents are fairer, that we live on the land ourselves and aren't off whoring about London on money bled from the tenants. The county also knows how we stand on the subject of tithes – we've fought the issue just as

62

bitterly as you Catholics.'

'You telling us that you'd like it removed altogether? You think London is going to pay the wages of your ministers?' It was O'Flaherty, scowling up from the depths of his armchair.

'Let them come to us. To the landowners,' Osborne said.

'With respect, sir, the landlords would take it out by increasing the rents . . . '

'Regan . . . '

William interrupted. 'Osborne, I can see you're right – even Regan can see it – increased rents or not, this system is grossly unfair. Making Protestant farmers support their own church by force is bad enough, but to ask Catholics to pay the same tithe when their own churches lie in ruins and they haven't food to feed themselves is barbaric.'

'We've been fighting this issue for generations,' John Curran growled. 'Back in '98 the blood spilt like it was civil war – and it might yet come to that.'

'These agrarian outrages will solve nothing.' This from Robertson. 'The Terry raids are cowardly and for the most part unwarranted . . . ' The atmosphere in the room was tightened after his words, and he lapsed into silence. They may be agreed on the injustice of the tithe system but more than half the room was Catholic and who knew where their sympathies lay? A man would be wiser to watch his words.

From the corner came the quiet, dry voice of Father O'Callaghan. 'Enough discussion, gentlemen. We all feel the same way on this.' He turned to William. 'As Mister Osborne has said, neither he nor any of his Protestant friends have been attacked by the Terrys, and you being the man you are, William, have had no trouble either. But the situation is worsening – the English troops are everywhere. Mister Osborne had an idea; he and his friends came to see me, and I collected Mister Curran and Mister Regan and came to see you immediately. We need your help.'

William switched his eyes back to Osborne. 'What was this idea?'

'I've written to a friend of mine, Sir Charles Carlton, in Tipperary – as you know the trouble's as bad there, if not worse. If Protestant and Catholic landowners from both counties could get together, have petitions signed, went to Dublin, perhaps . . . *Together* something could be done.'

'That's admirable, Robert,' William scowled, 'but what support do you have for this scheme amongst your Protestant friends?'

Osborne flushed uncomfortably. 'Very little,' he admitted, 'we four only from Killaloe – but,' he added as O'Flaherty, Flannigan and Regan stirred, 'there'll be more in other parts of the country. For God's sake!' He turned to the room at large, 'We stood together to get O'Connell into Parliament, didn't we? Would you have a Catholic in the House of Commons now if some of us hadn't been behind you?'

Everyone stirred, assent, dissent – William cut across the rising voices. 'He's right,' he said loudly. 'We need each other.'

6

'But I've not been to Tipperary . . . '

'Devlin, you're needed here.'

'Father, there's nothing for me to do here – Nathan Cameron could run things very well in our absence . . . '

'No, Devlin. This is an important visit we're making, and it could be dangerous . . . '

'I'll be more help to you than Aidan O'Brien.'

William looked up from his papers. Sorting out which to take was hard enough, but Devlin's voice kept cutting across his concentration. 'Look, son. The boy comes as groom and manservant to both Mister Osborne and myself. He'll be useful. If you feel you could groom horses and polish our boots for us for ten days then it's pleased I'll be to take you and leave young Aidan behind!'

Devlin's face was pale and set. Yet he said, 'All right, Father,' calmly enough, and left the office without revealing his rage.

He left the house immediately, had Nathan saddle his thoroughbred and rode off across the fields and on down to the lough. It was Saturday, and he passed the O'Brien cottage without looking at it, in case the boy was there. All his thoughts focused on his resentment; his one chance to escape from Killaloe for a while, and it was denied him.

On the shores of the lough, a group of children were skipping stones across the water. They were laughing, placing wagers as to who could beat the others. Their laughter floated clearly up to Devlin, both mocking and inviting.

Aidan O'Brien was amongst them. Devlin frowned, and allowed the horse to pull the reins through his fingers as it lowered its head to graze. He held the reins slack, and watched the figure down on the

64

lough's edge, wondering at the hate within him. It was senseless, this bitterness, he knew it. The boy had nothing, was nothing. In a few years he would be a stooped little old man like Nathan Cameron, with a lined face like a dried potato, still cap-in-hand, saying 'Yes sir, no sir,' to further generations of Kellys. Why, my father owns you, Devlin thought. And when my father dies I shall own you. You are nothing. You signify nothing.

But did that matter? Down there on the shoreline, Aidan O'Brien was laughing, his stone having skimmed ten times across the water and beaten the red-headed Seamus O'Donoghue. Now Tom-Joe Curran took up a stone, but his projectile skipped only three times; the 'Arra!' of disappointment carried clearly back to Devlin. The others were still laughing, and Aidan placed a hand on Tom-Joe's narrow shoulder, gesturing with the stone in his other hand, how to flick it, the force in the turn of the wrist. The other children listened to him – Devlin watched each face – then Tom-Joe tried again. Five times the stone skipped, now, and there were murmurs of approval.

Devlin had not quite realized that he was riding down towards them. Only when the faces were gazing up at him, the group parting to stand about the horse's head did he suddenly find that he had no reason to be there.

'Master Devlin.' O'Brien touched his forelock. One or two of the older girls in the group curtsied. But the laughter had stopped. Each face gazed up at him expectantly.

Devlin was desperate. 'Skipping stones,' he said coolly.

'Yes sir.' The smile was still on O'Brien's face. Devlin, wondering if he was mocking him, stared at him hard. If he could only find some insolence in the boy he could complain to his father about him. But the smile was open, guileless. And for the first time Devlin wondered how Aidan saw *him*. Always, he had presumed the boy hated him. Devlin had everything, after all. And his mother always said that the poor hated and resented the rich. Aidan's smile held neither hatred nor resentment. Was he being clever, or was he too stupid to be resentful? He had been clever enough in the school-room, but these past few years they had barely spoken. They were no longer small boys; they could reason, and make decisions based on their own judgement . . .

'Would you like to try, sir?' Aidan was saying.

Devlin stared at him. Even some of the other children turned to the boy, wide-eyed at his presumption.

But Devlin dismounted. He threw the reins to Martin Curran and bent to run his eyes along the stones on the shoreline. The children looked at each other. No one dared say anything. They watched as

65

Devlin selected a suitable pebble and moved it around in his hand, feeling its shape, its weight. He had tried skimming stones before but had never been very good at it. It had passed the time, down at the pond behind the stables, when his father had been busy with accounts, when his mother had been ill with a headache, or when he had become tired of riding or sitting in the library with a book.

He took a stance, brought his arm back, then heaved forward, lobbing the stone across the lake's surface. Rings spread out in its wake, catching the light – once, twice, three times, four . . . and nothing. Devlin stared at the final ring, melting into the others, fading outwards. Only four. He was mad. He should never have tried. It was beneath him. Madness. And he was conscious of the silence around him. Silence that went on and on as he kept his eyes fixed on the water and felt the hot, prickling flush spread up from the tight collar at his neck. He was sensitive enough to know that there was no mockery in that quiet group. If he could feel the smiles he could have whirled, struck one of them. But this was a waiting silence. And still it went on.

'Try again.'

It was the boy's voice. Devlin turned to find him standing beside him, a flat, perfectly formed stone held out towards Devlin. He stared at it. Pinkish grey, it was, and smooth. He had not heard the boy stoop to pick it up. He must have had it all the time. In his pocket or in his hand. A perfect pebble, formed by nature as if its only purpose was to bounce across the surface of this lough. And held out, now, towards him. Not ingratiatingly, nor reluctantly, Devlin saw, looking into the wide-set brown eyes.

And he hesitated. To bounce one stone was a token gesture. To accept another was to enter the game, to be *involved*. And more than this; Devlin realized that never before in all these years had he and the boy faced each other as equals. Indeed he had never turned to gaze fully at the boy in his life, to ask himself what he was, how he felt. Now, in the outstretched hand and its offering, in the dark eyes and the open face there lay something of import, a new beginning. Devlin's gaze locked with Aidan's; he reached out. For an instant his fingers touched the firm brown hand and the pebble, warm, smooth, was placed in his palm. The beginnings of a smile began on Aidan's face – and Devlin's hand, unsure, failed to close quickly enough. The pebble rolled off his hand and fell between them. Both dropped their gaze to follow it.

Devlin's face had not changed expression. It had been cool, tight-mouthed as his hand went out. Cool, too, as the stone fell from his grasp. Martin Curran, behind him, whispered, 'He didn't have to do that.' And Devlin, whose first thought was to bend and pick up the stone, froze. Aidan's eyes came up to his, puzzled, the smile gone. The instant for retrieving the pebble passed. Still they gazed at each other.

'I must be going. My father wants to discuss the Tipperary visit with me.' He turned, pulling the reins from Martin's grasp with scant grace, and mounted the horse.

When he had gone, Martin picked up the stone, wiped the damp of it on his shirt and handed it regretfully back to Aidan. He muttered again, his eyes on the vanishing Devlin. 'He didn't have to do that.'

They all strolled up the hill towards the O'Brien cottage, straying in groups like meandering cows, the companionship sufficient to preclude anything but desultory conversation. It was only Thomas, walking beside Maura O'Donoghue and Anna, who could not forget the incident. 'Why did you bother to give him the stone anyway?' he scowled across at Aidan. 'What's he ever done for you?'

Aidan walked on, silent. He did not understand, himself, why he had made the gesture. He did not like it when he acted without forethought, it puzzled him.

It was Anna who said, 'He's lonely.'

They looked at her. She was nearly sixteen now, and could be expected to come out with these grown-up reflections.

'Of course Devlin's lonely,' Maura added, 'no one wants to be near him, do they? If he wanted friends he should be more pleasant to people. None of the other landlords' sons have anything to do with him – he thinks himself above everyone in Killaloe.'

Aidan's voice had begun to break some weeks before. The observation he now made surprised them as much for its adult sentiments as for the clear baritone that issued from him. 'Devlin can't bear to fail. That's why he won't try.'

'You can't judge him like that,' Anna said, 'just because he doesn't fit into life here. Perhaps he just isn't meant to be a farmer, perhaps he'd be different in Dublin . . . '

'Why are you defending him?' Aidan rounded on her, his voice breaking in mid-sentence, making him more cross. 'Have you got a bit of a *grá* for him or what?'

'Can I not discuss a man without . . . '

'A man, is it? Not eighteen yet – and does he act like one, I ask you?'

'It's jealous, you are, Aidan O'Brien, because he's tall and good-looking . . . '

'If you like pretty, girly looks in a man I suppose he is good-looking . . . '

'I don't. He isn't . . . !' She was becoming flustered under his attack.

'He wouldn't look at you, anyway.'

Maura and Thomas stared at them as they faced each other. Anna was flushing. 'Sure it's a matter of indifference to me that Devlin Kelly looks at me or not. And if you were a gentleman, Aidan O'Brien, you wouldn't be suggesting that I cared.'

He leaned forward. 'But I'm not a gentleman. I'm a stableboy, amn't I? I don't put on airs about my station in life.'

'And it's just as well, because a stableboy is all you'll ever be! It's all you're fit for!'

They stood unmoving, Anna close to tears, Aidan white with rage, then he turned and stormed across to the cottage. Thomas, with a puzzled look between his brother's back and Anna's scowling face, followed. Anna and Maura heard him say as he caught up with Aidan, 'Don't let her worry you – all girls are stupid, aren't they?' Aidan kept walking.

Maura saw that the curious children had stopped, were planning on waiting for Aidan to emerge; she turned to see what Anna would do and found her already continuing up the road. She ran to catch up. 'Why did you bother arguing with him?' she asked, falling into step. 'He's just a child, really, for all Mister Kelly trusting him so.' But Anna only scowled ahead, pulling her shawl closer against the rising chill of the wind. Maura continued. 'You couldn't expect to stay friends with him forever – he's a *boy*, rough and selfish, so.'

'He's changing,' Anna said grimly, 'I hardly see him anymore, it's horses, horses, horses, or it's Corrie O'Neill. All that fighting – he thinks more of his muscles than his brain, now.' She was quiet a moment, then said, 'We used to talk a lot – about lots of things, far-off countries, and things we'd do when we grew up . . . He's no fun at all, any more, he's too serious.'

'It's all those years with Master Devlin. Aidan must hate him something fierce . . . '

'Och, no . . . '

'He would, sure. I know I do. If it weren't for the Kellys our fathers would own their own land . . . '

'Oh, don't let's talk of that!' Anna grimaced a little and shook back her hair. She wore it loose, today, and Maura did not like it. Anna's hair was thick and honey brown and further pointed out the uneven physical differences between the two girls. Maura's hair never grew any longer than half-way down her back, and it was thin and straight and a harsh orange. 'My father's always talking of land

68

reform,' Anna was saying, 'of how things should be as they once were, making us all speak the Irish when we're at home – he's living in the past.'

Maura's eyes studied Anna carefully for a moment, then she said, quietly, 'Does Aidan not talk a great deal about land reform? I seem to remember . . .'

'Oh, yes, he does that. And I listen, and agree with him. But it's all a waste of time, is it not? You can't let the men know you think that, but it's so, and I'm almost bored with pretending.'

'Then don't.'

Anna turned to smile at Maura. 'You say that only because you can't pretend. You're too honest, Maura. I'm not sure if men will like that. Try to lie a little; sure it can't do any harm, and it makes people feel much more at ease with you if they don't think you're criticizing them all the time.'

She had spoken quite ingenuously, and walked on. Maura stood still, and the look in her eyes as she gazed at her friend's back held little that would have set her at ease. But by the time she had caught up with Anna, Maura's expression was veiled, her gaze on the ground. She asked, 'Who do you like best? Aidan or Master Devlin?'

'Oh, Maura . . .'

'Who?'

'Aidan, of course, although . . . Would it not be wonderful to be married into a family such as the Kellys? Would it not be wonderful to wear dresses such as the mistress wears?' She turned, expecting to find Maura as enthusiastic about the fantasy as she was herself, but found, instead, that Maura was scowling at her.

'I think the mistress is selfish and cold-hearted. She's hated by everyone. Would you like *that*?'

Anna sighed. 'Och, Maura, you're fierce boring, sometimes. Why do you always have to be so *realistic*?'

Maura stuck out her lower lip. ''Tis the way I am.'

'Aye, and I love you for it.' Anna gave her a hug.

Maura looked a little mollified. After a moment's walking in silence, she said, smiling, 'I think Aidan was jealous because you defended Master Devlin. I think he likes you.'

'Aidan? Of course he does.'

'*No*. As a *man* likes a girl. *You* know.'

'Oh. Well . . .'

'Why don't you lead him on, see if he'll become moonstruck like Seamus is over Sarah Minogue, writing her notes and walking her home from Mass – then you can laugh at him and show everyone his letters and he'll look a fierce fool, and . . . '

'Och, no – how cruel.'

'But he insulted you just now. You should pay him back, make him look like . . . '

Again the infuriating honey-coloured hair was swung back over Anna's shoulder; it came to Maura that the gesture was made whenever Anna was disturbed over something, and she stored the knowledge away. 'No, Maura,' Anna was saying. 'I like Aidan. He's my friend, do you not understand?'

'A better friend than I am?' Maura challenged.

Anna's fingers twisted in her hair. 'It's different.'

'Ah,' Maura said, and thought, *because he's a boy, he's more important*.

They had reached a point in the extensive grounds of Tineranna that was a great favourite with those children who dared Nathan Cameron's wrath by coming here. This corner had once been acres of formal garden, but had been the first casualty of William Kelly's drive for economy when he had inherited the estate. Much of what had been lawn and neat squares of shrubbery were ploughed under and planted with oats and rye, and all that was left untouched was the small wood, which William could not bring himself to decimate, even in the interests of agriculture. So the narrow track through beech and ash and oak, which led to a now-overgrown folly and a once geometrically neat maze that had become a solid mass of impenetrable privet branches, was rarely used. Its chief attraction, for the children, lay in the centre of the wood, where the road rose up in a shrug over the unnecessary presence of a man-made, crescent-shaped pond. Shut off from cow and sheep, it was used only by the fat and lazy gold carp that could sometimes be seen through the weeds and the lilypads.

On the little stone bridge, Anna and Maura paused, from habit, looked over into a clear space of still water, and studied their reflections.

Anna was thinking of Caroline Kelly, and, looking at her own even features, comparing them with the mistress's. Why, she thought, unconsciously lifting her hair up on to her head in its heavy masses of waves, I'm prettier than the mistress. Her face is longer – she looks more mysterious and aloof – but sure, she may only be cold, as Maura says. I have a nicer mouth . . .

Maura glared so hard into the water that it seemed to her that it should ripple, boil, where Anna was reflected, preening herself. She did not try to understand why she felt as she did, could only grip the stone parapet, and compare Anna's face with her own. *It isn't fair. It isn't fair.*

Anna was saying dreamily, 'Wouldn't it be wonderful to be admired, and sought after, and to have gentlemen calling on one, and hovering about three deep at balls and dances?'

Maura, who had never been admired by anyone in her life, merely sniffed. She turned away, and was about to make a suitably caustic reply to her friend's flight of whimsy, when she saw Aidan O'Brien approaching.

'He's come back.' She hissed to Anna. 'Look you, he's coming. See what he says, see if he'll apologize . . . '

Aidan sauntered on to the bridge. 'Anna?' She did not immediately look up, and under Maura's triumphant gaze he wandered to the other side of the bridge as if he were only pausing on his way. 'Anna, can I speak with you?'

She looked up, then. 'Of course.' She smiled at him.

Maura stared at her in horror. She whispered, 'Don't forgive him too soon. Make him say he's sorry. Make him . . . '

'Will you come walking with me?' the boy asked.

Anna hesitated, looked between Aidan, standing legs apart, confident, smiling; and Maura, pale beneath her freckles, her gaze pleading, as if she already knew the answer.

'Alone,' Aidan said meaningfully, and Maura's gaze swung from Anna's to lock with the boy's.

'All right.' And Anna was moving away from Maura, on across the bridge to stand beside the boy, and was falling into step beside him. Another minute and they would be out of sight around a bend . . .

Then, as if pulled by the force of Maura's will, Anna stopped, and turned. 'I . . . I won't be long, Maura. I'll call to see you in a little while.' Maura did not speak. Again a slight hesitation,'Do you know the white muslin blouse with the lace trim that you've admired? I want you to have it. Mam says you can, for . . . for I've outgrown it. I'll bring it with me.'

Still Maura did not speak, and Anna, wretched, turned away and moved off with Aidan along the boreen. Maura heard the boy say, 'Why do you bother with her? She's not important to you, sure. She can't be.' She did not try to distinguish the words in Anna's murmured reply.

Not important.

Maura stood as if made from the same stone as the bridge itself. She felt the rush of blood from her neck suffuse her face, but still she could not move, gazing after Aidan O'Brien as if she could kill him with her eyes. *Not important.* Who was he that he could say that of her? She would show him. She would.

She turned away, and once more her face appeared below in the dark water. Narrow, pale face, flanked by the dreadful, limp, brassy plaits. When she was grown . . . and beautiful . . . yes, more beautiful than Anna. And he would see her at Mass, or at a *ceili*, and wonder who she was. Her hair would be darker – Holy Mary, please let her hair grow darker – and she'd wear it . . . just so, about her head, and she'd wear earrings like Mam, and Aidan O'Brien would look at her. *Really* look at her. And she would be important.

'What're y' doing? Why're y' after wrapping y'r hair round y'r head?' Laughter in the voice. Thomas O' Brien stood there, smiling, kicking at a fallen branch with one bare foot, his hands in his pockets. 'Y' seen my brother?'

She opened her mouth to give him a setting down, stupid, ill-mannered, coarse little boy that he was, no better than his brother – and then she stopped. Like Anna, she smiled. Like Anna, she said in a pleasant, teasing voice, 'Sure, why are you always following Aidan about, Thomas? You could do anything, I'm thinking, and not have to run to Aidan for advice.'

'I could and all.' But Thomas looked puzzled.

'Then why don't you make your own friends, and go about your own affairs? Sure everyone . . . ' *Laughs*, she was about to say, but no. 'Everyone knows you're sharper than Aidan. Did you not write the best essay in the school this year?'

'Aye.' Thomas, discomfited, was looking about for Aidan, but the two had long since vanished.

'And you're taller than he, though you're three years younger. And you're better looking . . . ' She was delighted; the boy was blushing scarlet, moving the brown feet in the dust yet unable to drag himself away. 'Stand up for yourself,' she admonished him, trying hard not to laugh outright. 'You don't need Aidan. Why, you're worth two of him . . . ' But she burst into laughter, and laughed the harder as Thomas's face came up, smiling. He could not see, could not understand that she was ridiculing him. 'Oh, Thomas, you're such a . . . ' She stopped, and stepped away, before she said *fool*. For she did not want to ruin this few minutes' work. It was oddly satisfying to have the young idiot gaping loose-mouthed and smiling at her as he was. She turned and ran off, laughing.

She went walking, up on the hills, filled with restlessness that the sudden confrontations had awakened in her. She had enjoyed the way she had been able to play with Thomas, but it did not compensate for the humiliation she had felt at Aidan O'Brien's hands.

She saw them, once. She hid behind a hedge and watched Aidan

72

and Anna walk past, their heads together, talking earnestly, as friendly together as they had ever been. Maura stayed out walking for a long time.

She was not yet home when Anna called, but found the little white muslin blouse on her bed when she returned. She sat down, and studied it.

Like new, it was, with a fine lace collar and lace about the sleeves. She had coveted it for years; and now it was hers.

She could not prevent herself, so filled was she with a nameless anger. She went to her own sewing basket and took from it the fine little sewing scissors that her mother had given her for her thirteenth birthday. Carefully, methodically, she cut the blouse into small shreds, and later, when the family was asleep, stirred the embers of the kitchen fire, and flung the scraps upon it.

7

That ride to Ballingarry was fixed in Aidan's mind in the years to come. He would remember the small things: the snow on the broad crests of Slieve Bernagh behind them as they crossed the Shannon into Ballina; how, on the stone walls on each side of them, the melting snow made miniature falls and rivers down the moss-covered rocks and along the snow-edged ditches; the way a fern, jutting from a wall, glinted in the light, its fronds encased in ice, perfectly preserved, as if set in glass. The way William Kelly laughed and told funny stories when it began to snow once more, when Osborne had begun to grumble and Aidan's shoulders slumped with tiredness.

They were laughing, all three, when they rode into the tavern yard in Nenagh, and the evening became to the boy a warm blur of voices laughing, shouting, raised in discussion. From a small settle set back from the crowd, he fell into a fitful sleep while trying to understand the long English words being bantered about; repealists, anti-tithe campaigns, civil and religious liberty, municipal reform. He woke in the morning to a quiet room smelling of stale pipe tobacco and ale, to find himself covered with a rug, and the tavern-keeper's wife bent over the fire, heaping sods of turf on to the fading embers.

He felt he had had no sleep at all, and only the cold rain that fell as they rode on that day kept him from dozing in the saddle. The weather cleared, however, as they rode into Borrisoleigh, and it was before a cold, clean wind that they continued after a late midday meal.

Dusk fell, and the landscape took on a grey sameness; Aidan, with the spare horse, fell slowly behind, and never realized that he had been dozing until he awoke suddenly to the neighing of horses, the shouting of men, the flare of torches. He had no sense of where he was, the countryside was in darkness around them; against the gaudy glow from the lamps and flaring branches he could just make out William Kelly and Robert Osborne, their finely-bred horses rearing up in terror – and then Aidan, too, was plunged into the centre of the brightly-lit nightmare.

Thin, angry faces were raised to him, hostile hands grabbed at him, a stone struck his forehead. In his panic, the people meant nothing to him, a force, merely, to push against with his horse's chest. He did not understand them, hungry from the poor yields of a bad harvest, unable to buy food as well as pay their rents, angered further by tithes taken by force; their cows, their pigs, linen or lace handed down from mother to daughter for generations – taken to pay the wages of a minister not of their faith. The gentry had underestimated their anger; the meeting between the landlords and tithe owners and proctors was tragically ill-timed.

They were shouting, shouting, and Aidan knew he was somehow a target for their anger; but worse than his own fear was the sight before him of William Kelly's grey hunter, plunging and shying riderless amongst the crowd, and Robert Osborne's horse, the saddle empty and slewed sideways, the reins flying, charging terrified through the crowd, back the way they had come. Once, he thought he heard Osborne's distinctive voice, and looking to his left could see a building in the shadows of the hedge; then a shot was fired, somewhere before him, and another, and he could see scarlet uniforms through the flickering lights, above the heads of the crowd. Another shot, this time quite close, and his horse reared, catching him off-balance. When the pony's feet slipped beneath it on the muddy roadway it went back heavily on its side, Aidan going down with it, slammed hard into the ground, feeling an excruciating pain shoot through his leg. All shouts, legs, muddy bare feet. They were kicking him – Mother of God, they were going to kill him – he would die here on this unnamed country road in the darkness, miles from Tineranna, from Ma . . . die here without reaching Mister Kelly . . .

'Aidan! Aidan! Aidan O'Brien!'

Mister Kelly's voice! A volley of shots thudded against his ears, someone screamed in pain – and then he was grabbed beneath the arms, grabbed and hauled to his feet . . . his leg . . . ! The pain in it made him groan, fall – but the arms were strong, they held him up, dragged him along, the acrid smell of gunpowder closing his throat, choking him. More hands in a doorway, grasping him, drawing him inside, voices . . .

'Where did he . . . '

'Brave lad!'

'He was calling for his master . . . '

'Kelly . . . '

'Which is Kelly . . . ? One of them's dead . . . '

Aidan was trying to raise his head, separate the voices with their Anglicized tones, raise his eyes to the room in which several dark-suited men seemed to have taken shelter, search their ranks for Mister Kelly . . .

Robert Osborne lay on the floor; a thin man in a clerical collar was bending over him. The broad face of Ceelohg's owner seemed sunken, the wide cheekbones prominent, the skin pale almost to transparency beneath grey hair scarlet with blood. Aidan's heart, which had contracted with terror at the stranger's murmured words, now lurched into life at the sight of the big man lying there. And he was ashamed to acknowledge a seed of thankfulness that it had not been William Kelly . . .

Yet, as he watched, Osborne's face suddenly flinched at the curate's touch, a tentative dabbing at the scalp wound with a handkerchief, and the eyes opened. 'Take your hands off me, sir!' the voice said, only a little lower than his normal tones. The voice at Aidan's elbow said, 'Thank Christ!' and the boy turned, knowing by the words that he had been mistaken; this same voice that had called his name in the road was not William Kelly; the man who helped support him was a stranger, gazing at him with concern, and pity . . .

They had not closed William Kelly's eyes. As Aidan limped across the room to where he lay, it seemed that the man was looking at him. But on his knees by the body, holding the cold hand, the head remained turned a little, the grey eyes gazed beyond him. The boy touched the face, and gripped the hand tighter. 'Mister Kelly? Mister Kelly, sir?' He cradled the loved body in his arms, rocking it to and fro, but still the grey eyes gazed beyond him.

'Ma? Ma!' Thomas's voice through her sleep. 'Ma, there's a carriage outside!'

75

She raised her head from the mattress. It was still dark, but a rooster crowed somewhere, and beyond this accepted sound came the snorting of a horse, the movement of carriage wheels, and approaching footsteps.

She was out of bed, pulling on her skirt and blouse, when the hammering began on the door. 'A moment, I'm coming!' she called. Thomas stumbled out of the bedroom, tucking his shirt into his trousers, and went to the mantelpiece to light a candle. Mary opened the door.

A fine mist was falling, and the woman, half-asleep, thought with superstitious wonder that a visitation had come to her. A giant of a man; the light from the candle and the turf embers that Thomas was stirring bronzed the large sculptured features, the head of tight grey curls, the massive arms holding a boy to his chest. For an instant her heart contracted with an amazement close to terror, then all visions of Saint Joseph faded. It was Aidan held like a baby in the man's arms. Aidan – still, white, his temples bruised, jaw swollen.

With a moan her hands stretched out, but the man had already moved forward, ducking within the low doorway, pushing past her.

'He's all right, Mrs O'Brien, he's all right, I'm thinkin'.' He glanced around the cabin, and then walked swiftly to Mary's bed, beside the fire, and placed Aidan gently down upon it. When he straightened, Mary was already on her knees beside the bed.

'I'm Corrie O'Neill, ma'am. Perhaps the boy's spoken of me . . . '

'Yes . . . ' she barely glanced at him, her hand stroking the boy's forehead nervously. Thomas had gone to close the door, and now stood at the foot of the bed, gazing from his unconscious brother to the faces of the two adults.

Corrie was running his hands expertly over the boy's face, neck and body. 'As I thought, no bones broke. But he's been unconscious most of the way home. The blow on the head, for sure.'

'How did it happen?'

The boxer took a deep breath. 'They never reached Ballingarry. Half the countryside was up in arms, y'know. Feeney the tithe proctor took a sow from a widow named Coogan – worth three times the tithe they owed, I heard. The woman was ill anyway, but when she died that night, didn't her two boys, young Dan and Michael, blame Feeney for it? They borrowed a hunting piece, and went after him. Didn't kill him, I'm sad to say – the Lord will forgive me for wishing him dead, the Lord knowing Feeney for a black-hearted gombeen man worthy of hell . . . The night was misty and the shot

76

took him in the shoulder only. But they hanged Dan and Michael yesterday . . . '

'But Aidan . . . '

'A few of the gentry and the tithe proctors met at one of the big houses – when they were leaving, they were seen – a mob gathered, followed them – things got nasty . . . ' He looked up at her. 'That's when Mister Kelly and Mister Osborne and your boy met them, on the road, bad luck that it was. I heard about it in Thurles, from Mister Osborne. He was hiring the carriage that's out there, now. I decided to come back to Killaloe with him – the man needed as much help as he could get.' He stopped. Mary's face had been turned to him, and he was conscious of speaking for longer and in more detail than he need have done. He had known Aidan's mother was a widow – he had not known how pretty she was. He felt awkward and cursed inwardly that it had to be himself that brought such bad news to the house. Strain was already written in Mary's dark eyes. He put his hand in his pocket, and drew out a small packet. 'Look, it's a grain of tea I have here . . . ' He glanced at the white-faced Thomas. 'I know you want to hear everything, but I've ridden all night, and I'd be grateful to you . . . '

Embarrassed at her own thoughtlessness, Mary was already on her feet, her worry over Aidan momentarily finding outlet in activity. Thomas placed more sods on the fire, while Mary filled the kettle from the bucket of water, and hung it upon the hook above the flames.

In a moment of silence, when the three had sat down to wait for it to boil, Corrie looked from one anxious face to the other, hesitated, then said abruptly, 'Mister Kelly – William Kelly – was killed yesterday.' He hurried on, not wanting to look at their faces, his eyes on the hearth before him. ''Twas the mob – half-starved miners and farmers and farmers-that-was, evicted over the past month. They weren't aimin' at Mister Kelly, nor at your boy, 'twas the tithe proctors, the tithe owners, they were after. The police were called out. Ah, it was a foolish time to decide anything – not in Tipperary, anyway. A few of the gentry were struck with stones, that's how Mister Kelly died. The police fired into the mob, then; two men were shot, but they're still alive. The police are trying to find the one who was responsible for the stone that killed Mister Kelly. They won't find him, but they'll bring in the ringleaders – even those that never lifted a rock. They'll be transported, sure.'

Thomas drew his stool closer to his mother's. As their hands reached for each other, Corrie, his mouth grim, said, 'I waited in the kitchen at Tineranna while Mister Osborne was within with Mrs Kelly. He sent a message down that she was "too distraught" to have the added burden of your boy at the big house. I was to bring him home, and have one of the grooms send for the doctor.'

'He'll be coming?'

'Soon, I hope, ma'am.'

She had turned towards the boy on the bed; for a moment Corrie thought she would weep, and he wanted suddenly to reach out, take her hand, say something. She looked so helpless, yet at the same time he knew she was not helpless, that she had made herself very strong, and it moved him. He glanced around at the clean, impoverished room. How did she cope, alone?

She was crossing to the bed once more, was sitting on its edge, gazing at her son. He was so still, so white . . . What if he should die? Her Denny-Joe, her Aidan Og . . .

She was still watching him when the kettle began to splutter, so that it was Corrie who made the tea, handing a cup to her, and one to the still, pale-faced twelve-year-old, who barely managed a smile of gratitude, stiff with shock, before turning back to his brother.

Thomas thought, this could not happen to Aidan, not to Aidan who could do anything, Aidan who was infallible. Thomas's small world was shaken for the first time. He pulled his little stool closer to Aidan's bed and willed his brother to open his eyes.

Doctor Reed, when he came later from the village, could say little about Aidan's condition. He would wake in his own good time, he told Mary, and undoubtedly with a headache. He was to be kept warm, and must stay in bed for several days; Doctor Reed would call again the following day.

'And how will I be after paying for this . . . ?' Mary murmured to herself as she watched the doctor drive away in his carriage.

'The mistress – Mrs Kelly – she's taking care of it, ma'am.'

Mary was horrified to realize that Corrie O'Neill stood on the path close behind her, and had heard the words she had addressed to herself.

He looked a little abashed. 'She told me to tell you so,' he added. 'She's grateful for what Aidan tried to do – Mister Osborne said he went through the crowd like a wild thing, trying to reach Mister Kelly.'

There was a silence. Mary was not too sure whether she ought to invite the man inside once more, or to thank him here on the path, and give him the hint that it was time he should be leaving. He was very large, and he watched her too intently, and she wanted to be

78

alone with Aidan and Thomas . . .

A movement in the field caught her eyes before she could speak, however, and they both paused as Anna O'Hagan came racing across the pasture, her brown hair flying loose behind her. It was beautiful hair, thick and almost to her knees; she caught it on a bramble as she clambered over the low wall and paused, wincing, to disentangle it, before running up to Mary. 'God save you, Mrs O'Brien, could I go in and sit with Aidan, if you please?'

Mary nodded. 'Be very quiet, Anna.'

Anna was already off towards the door after bobbing a quick curtsey in Corrie's direction. 'Mister O'Neill . . . '

Corrie nodded, and watched her enter the cottage. The O'Hagan girl. Her father was a tenant of a goodly-sized farm, further towards Ogonnelloe. Grown into quite a beauty, he mused, and remembered drinking with her father the night she was born. Lord, was it sixteen years ago? How many miles since then had he put beneath his horse's feet? And how many more, a sobering voice asked him, did he have left?

'Anna's a grand girl,' Mary O'Brien was saying. 'She and Aidan have been friends since they were children.'

Corrie was thinking, the woman has fine eyes . . . and . . . and an agelessness about her. Two half-grown sons, and she looks like a girl . . . He cleared his throat. 'There's a match there perhaps, one day, ma'am.' She had been half-smiling, and now the smile disappeared. Corrie had made an effort at levity, anxious for something to say, but was sorry he had spoken. 'I did not mean to be bold,' he added, searching her eyes for a reproof.

But Mary smiled. There was gentleness in this man, as well as strength. In the dark hours of that morning she had fluttered around his bulk in the small kitchen, like a bird finding a bull too close to her nest in the grass. She knew nothing of him but what Mrs O'Hagan and Mrs Curran had told her. He had been born in the slums of Dublin, had earned a small fortune by the use of his fists, and now travelled to the big houses all over Ireland, earning money teaching fisticuffs to the sons of gentlemen. He had even taught Aidan some weeks back; had filled the boy's head with all sorts of nonsense until every fine day had the boy dancing before his shadow on the cottage wall, darting and dashing and sending Thomas into paroxysms of laughter. Mary had not liked it; she disapproved of the tales relayed to her of bloody fights in Belfast and Cork and Dublin, of men maimed, and fortunes wagered and lost. A dangerous man, this Corrie O'Neill, she had decided; dangerous and brutal. And then he had come into her life carrying her son like a child, had watched with her in the hours before the doctor came, had sat talking gently to Thomas while she watched Aidan, and had made them tea, moving quietly and capably about the room.

Of a sudden, she found that she would be sorry when he left. She glanced up at him, and realized that he was still studying her. 'You're not being bold,' she assured him. 'I think of Aidan as a child still. Of course, he's nearly a man – and a man should marry. Yes . . . ' she said carefully, thinking of the matter for the first time, 'I think I'd be pleased if he married Anna. A gentler, sweeter-tempered girl one couldn't find . . . '

'And you,' he found himself saying, 'you have not . . . There is no one who has made you consider marriage again?'

Now he *was* being bold. She threw her head back, to stare at him. Och, he was huge . . . on tiptoe she would not reach his shoulder. How did one quell such a man with a look? Standing there, gazing so fixedly down at her, features blunt and unmoving as if he were carved from one of the sandstone outcrops of Slieve Bernagh behind him. 'No one,' she said.

And only in saying the words, did a picture of Daniel McDonnagh come sharply, painfully to her mind. 'Good day to you, Mister O'Neill. God speed you.'

And she walked away from him, gathering her shawl around her, holding it close.

For the fifth time that day, Devlin entered the room where his father's coffin lay. He stood for a long time, unthinking, gazing down at the still features, the pale hands folded around ebony rosary beads.

Devlin had not cried; had felt he should, but could find no tears inside him. His mother's hysterical grief in those terrible hours before dawn had left him unmoved. Each of the five times he had entered the room he had come in disbelief, gazed down at the body and willed himself to believe that the spirit, the man himself, had gone for ever. It was not fair . . . there had been no time. How was he to have made the man understand him? He was cheated even of saying goodbye.

Robert Osborne, coming along the hall from a visit to the almost prostrate Caroline, paused in the doorway, and watched the boy for several seconds. At first it seemed to the Englishman that Devlin's face was working, moving in grief, perhaps; but as Osborne moved further into the room, he saw it was only the light from the many flickering candles playing along the planes of the boy's face. He stood immobile, oblivious to Osborne's presence.

80

Not gifted with words, Osborne cast around in his mind for something to say to the boy. He had no children himself, his wife had died thirty years ago. He knew little of the kind of words that were needed here. Yet he almost said, 'He loved you very much.' His mouth was open to say this, but he shrank, at the last moment, from the too foreign sentimentality of the words.

Devlin was thinking how young his father looked – much younger than his thirty-eight years. A gruff voice behind him said, 'He had great plans for you.' And the boy turned to find Robert Osborne standing there, frowning self-consciously. Devlin gazed at the older man for a long moment, then turned back to his father.

Great plans . . . Yes, undoubtedly. I am his heir, after all. Great plans . . . that only. And he knew, now, that he would not cry. He would not cry at all.

8

Aidan improved slowly, though he still had difficulty moving his left leg. Doctor Reed told Mary that it was a torn ligament and would mend itself in time, and she was to keep the boy rested. Aidan, uncharacteristically, did not argue. He lay, during those first few days, sleeping or drifting in a half-world of his own, eyes fixed somewhere beyond the cabin wall, at times not moving when his mother called his name, at times starting and staring at her as if she were a stranger to him.

Four days after the accident, the doctor and Mary helped the boy move back into the bedroom that he shared with Thomas, but being in his own room made little difference. He answered questions, but never spoke of his own accord. Samhradh, ignored, curled at the foot of the bed, miserable.

That afternoon Mary left Thomas looking after Aidan and went to William Kelly's funeral. Once again it was snowing, but softly, without a wind. It fell gently, hissing on to the drab, darkly clad crowd; the women in black; veils on the inner circle, shawls on the cottiers' wives at the outer circumference. The only colour in that crowd, Mary noticed, were the uncovered heads of the O'Donoghue men; faded bronze on old Liam's head, russet on Seamus's, deep copper on Thady's. Young Maura's bright orange hair was decently covered by a dark grey shawl, and she stood close by her mother, holding her little sister Bridie in her arms, their eyes on the ground as the voice of Father O'Callaghan rolled over them.

'Ashes to ashes . . . dust to dust . . . ' The beautiful, grim finality of those words.

Caroline Kelly, invisible beneath the heavy black veiling, leant weakly against her son. Around them, people were thinking what a comfort he must be to her. Standing at a level with even the tallest men in the crowd, the light gold of his hair paling further under the fall of snow, the boy gazed bravely into the deep wound in the soil, and when he went forward alone to sprinkle dirt on the coffin, it was only his demeanour that stopped the crowd whispering at this very Protestant gesture. They were shocked; but he did not notice. His hand did not tremble, his control did not waver. The pale, handsome face did not weaken at all.

Mary returned to find Aidan alone in the house, seated before the fire in the kitchen. 'They're having a dinner up at the big house,' he volunteered, before his mother could speak. 'Nathan rode down and asked if Thomas could help in the kitchen.'

'He shouldn't have gone off like that without asking me.' She shook the snow from her shawl at the door and came inside, looked at her eldest son and found herself glad that this had happened; Aidan was looking pale and tense, but he was showing some concern for the world around him. 'The dinner's for the guests,' he said quietly. 'The ones that came for the funeral.'

Mary looked over at him, then sighed, walked to the peg and hung up her shawl before coming to sit with him by the fire. She noticed, then, the pot hung over the flames, could smell the rich earthy smell of potatoes boiling in their jackets. 'You put the supper on the fire?'

'I've done it before . . . '

'The doctor said . . . '

'I had to do something. Why didn't you tell me the funeral was today? I should've . . . '

'I wouldn't have allowed you to go, Aidan. And besides . . . you have no need to feel badly. You said your farewells, Mister Osborne said.'

'I hardly remember!' Aidan burst out. 'It's like a bad dream I've had.'

'Then think of it in that way. Put it behind you. Remember the master as he was.'

It was inadequate, and she knew it. She bent to check the potatoes in the pot to cover the fact that she had no words that would help

82

him. 'We have to think of the future, now,' she said, in a more positive tone. 'Molly Curran told me that she and John think the Kellys will go back to England.'

'They're Ceelohg tenants,' Aidan said loftily. 'What would they know of Tineranna affairs?'

Mary replaced the lid of the pot, sat back on her heels and looked up at her son. 'They might go back,' she said, 'I can't see the mistress nor Master Devlin taking any joy in running the estate. They may hire an agent – John O'Casey, or Jim-Pat Flynn . . . '

'They wouldn't . . . !' His eyes searched hers, two red patches appeared on his cheeks, and she realized, suddenly, how much this thought distressed him.

'Perhaps not,' she said cheerfully. 'Sure, you're right, and it's probably only gossip.'

He did not answer her, and turned to gaze into the fire. The setter, Samhradh, who had been asleep at his feet, now stirred, as though it knew its master was disturbed, and thrust its head beneath the boy's hand. He stroked the deep russet head without taking his eyes from the flames.

Mary glanced at him, became afraid that he was slipping from her once again. She began to chatter about the local news; there was talk of another steamship to be brought to Killaloe to augment the passenger service to Portumna. 'With these new ships it's amazing to think it only takes twenty-four hours to get to Dublin.' She smiled over at him.

He looked over at her when he sensed her waiting for his response. 'That'll be grand,' he said. 'Would you like to go to Dublin?'

'Och, no! Why should I? Can you see me on those grand streets in this dress, without a pair of shoes to my name? Passing ladies in fine silks with parasols . . . ' Her voice trailed away a little. 'It would be nice,' she began again, 'to see the dresses and parasols.'

Aidan watched her face. He felt a rush of tenderness for her. She was so beautiful, and looked so wistful. He almost said, 'One day I'll buy you as many silk dresses and parasols as you'd like!' But he knew it would break her reverie, anger her; she would be ashamed of her dreaming, and round on him for reminding her of its futility. No, he would not speak of it. But he *would* do it.

His mother moved about the room, taking down the rough pottery plates and the three spoons from the odd set of cutlery given to her by the old mistress, William Kelly's mother. Aidan leaned back in the chair, listening to the comfortable, familiar sounds, attempting, as he had been all afternoon, to place his confused memories of the past five days into some order. 'Corrie O'Neill,' he

83

said, without preamble.

'What?' His mother looked over at him, a little sharply.

'Corrie O'Neill. I remember him talking to me in the carriage on the way home – you said he was here . . . did he say when he was coming back? Where did he go?'

'To visit with Mister Osborne, then on to Limerick, I believe.'

'When will he be back?' the boy persisted.

'I don't know, Aidan. How am I to know now?'

'I don't know. I thought he may have said. I thought you might have heard.'

He lapsed into silence, watched his mother setting the table with deliberation, a frown on her face, and he wondered at her abrupt change of mood.

But Mary had been merely startled at his perspicacity, for she had been thinking, at that moment, of Corrie O'Neill. He had looked at her with interest, as if he found her attractive, and he was a well-travelled man, one who had seen a great deal of silk dresses and parasols in his life, to be sure. And it had been pleasant having a man about the house again, even for such a short while. Once a person became accustomed to his great bulk he was a relaxing companion. Nowhere close to the intelligence that Daniel possessed, but then, she thought with a kind of irony, not as complicated, either. She could not see herself being forced to search Corrie O'Neill's eyes as she had Daniel's. Most of that nightmare morning Corrie had shared with her his gaze had been upon her. Wherever she had moved about the kitchen the harsh planes of his face had turned towards her, and the eyes – brown eyes, soft as a child's – had followed her movements. Not lasciviously. With curiosity, interest . . .

Arra, it's a fool I am. Too long alone, I think; too long without a man, and my thoughts becoming bold. Why, I'm . . . she calculated carefully, I'm thirty-one years old! – and thinking thoughts like some foolish girl about a man like Corrie O'Neill! She said aloud, 'Aidan, we'll eat by the fire, I think. I don't want you . . . '

The knocking at the door startled them. Mary, holding Aidan's plate, slowly, slowly, placed it back on the table. Aidan gazed at her, noticing the rigidity of her stance. Why did she not call to whoever-it-was to enter? He looked back at the door. Too heavy a knock for Anna, and Thomas would not bother to knock at all.

'It might be Mister Osborne, Ma,' he prompted. 'Didn't he call a day or so back?'

'He did, of course. He said he'd return . . . ' and she was moving to the door, straightening her hair back from her face as she went.

Anna O'Hagan stood there, smiling broadly, a bundle in her

84

arms, the long honey-coloured hair in two braids that fell past her hips. 'God save all here – may I come in and visit a while, Mrs O'Brien?'

Mary stood back with only a faint murmur of assent, and Anna came in, chattering that her mother had sent her with some pork from the pig they'd just butchered, and she'd brought some new books from the schoolmaster to read to Aidan. She stopped, then, seeing him, and Mary watched the smile between the two of them as their eyes met. She found herself thinking of Corrie's words. A match.

She looked at Anna. A beauty, to be sure. And clever, though her learning had not brought her above herself. She had patience, and a sense of humour; she was born to be a farmer's wife, and she would do it well. Mary watched them, sitting by the fire, Anna displaying the new books to her son, and, practical as ever, she wondered what dowry Paddy O'Hagan would provide for his daughter. Enough to rent the extra field back from the O'Sullivans . . . enough for a cow perhaps . . . 'Put the books away and eat with us, Anna. When Thomas comes home I'll have him walk back with you.'

Between mouthfuls of potatoes, Anna said calmly, 'Did y'hear about Maura O'Donoghue?'

Aidan and Mary looked up. Maura – red-haired, pale and so thin . . . Thoughts of illness, accident, crossed both their minds . . .

'She pushed Master Devlin into a bog this morning.'

Aidan roared with laughter so sudden that he upset his plate a little; then roared the louder when some of the boiling liquid fell on his leg.

'Stop spluttering potatoes all over the room! Arra, have y' no respect? The poor young master made a fool of and his blessed father not cold in his grave . . . ?'

But Anna was laughing too, now. She placed her bowl of food down upon the floor for fear of spilling it, and doubled over, laughing.

It was an infectious laugh: the kind that makes people nearby smile without realizing what the joke is all about, and Mary was forced to stop a smile herself as she scolded them. 'Will you put y'r head up, Anna O'Hagan – y'r hair is fallin' in the plate! And stop the noise, now. It's unseemly, that's what it is!'

Anna forced some control into her voice, 'It really isn't a laughing matter, Mrs O'Brien, and that's the truth. We were both sent to the kitchen with more eggs, knowing that the big house was filled with people, all over-eating with their grief . . .

'Y'know the big hedge that runs from the garden down towards the lough? I was on the one side, closest to the house, and Maura was on the other – we were looking for old birds' nests in the branches. And when we got to the marshy place just before the hill begins to rise, I heard a horse on the other side of the hedge. I was just about to call to Maura when I heard a voice, "You're the O'Donoghue girl." and a pause, and then Maura says, "Yes, sir" meek as y' please. The hedge was too thick for me to see through, but I ducked down and looked – I could see horse's hoofs and Maura's ankles and nothing more. But it was Master Devlin's voice all right. I saw Maura try to move past, but his horse stepped in front of her, snorting, and she pulled back. Next thing Master Devlin has got down from his horse – I could see his boots, shining black they were, as he walked towards her.

' "I've seen you at Mass . . ." '

' "Yes, sir," she says.

'And then he says, very slow-like, "I have often admired your hair . . ." ' '

This in Anna's creditable imitation of Devlin's anglicized baritone, and Aidan again roared with laughter.

'Whisht!' his mother said, furiously, and turned quickly back to Anna. Could this be true? Impossible! But she listened, mesmerized.

'And after a little, Maura says, "Thank y', sir," and it's unsure, she is, I can tell. And who wouldn't be?

'And I don't quite know what happened next, for I could only see their feet, but Master Devlin has stepped close to her and Maura gives out a kind of squeal, and looks as if she's about to over-balance backwards, but she didn't. Oh, but there was eggs fallin' all over the place – but neither of them noticed, Maura stepping back a bit, and Master Devlin goes to follow – and she must have pushed him! He over-balanced, reached for his horse – but it pulled back, frightened, and Master Devlin fell!

'*Then* I could see all of him – lying his length in the mud, mud over one side of his face and that fine hair of his . . . I could hear Maura running for her life up the hill to the house and the young master shouting, "I'll have you whipped, you . . ." ' A glance at Mary. 'I won't repeat it, but, "I'll have you whipped! I'll have you transported!" And he put his hand out to raise himself and placed it on one of those brown eggs Mrs O'Donoghue's so proud of. He screeched like a stuck pig he did, and raised his head and yelled after her again, "I'll have you transported, you . . . !" Oh, a filthy tongue he has, to be sure!'

'And what were you doing all this time?' Mary asked.

'Sure on my knees with my tail in the air watching through the hedge! I had to stay there, too, while he rubbed mud down his horse's shoulder, and on its knees. Then he mounted and rode after Maura. Very slowly.'

Aidan had stopped laughing, was smiling grimly at her. 'He'll tell them his horse went down with him.'

Anna nodded. 'To be sure he will. But I'm almost sorry he doesn't take Maura before a magistrate. How I'd love to stand up there before all Killaloe, and tell them what really happened!' Her usually mild hazel eyes were flashing fire as she said this, and even Mary had to smile. 'Do you think I wouldn't? Stop laughing, both of you! Why should Master Devlin be allowed to behave like that?'

Mary stood up, and moved to the table to refill the bowls, still smiling to herself. She had her back to the door when the knock sounded. It was Anna, laughing, who opened it to Thomas . . .

But it was not Thomas. It was Corrie O'Neill.

And Anna found herself almost forgotten in the following moments. Aidan, who obviously worshipped the big man, had eyes only for him, and Mrs O'Brien was fussing about at the dresser, fetching another plate, her face flushed, smiling, and Mister O'Neill kept turning his cap round and about in his great hands, and grinning like a schoolboy, telling them he'd accepted an offer made him by Mister Osborne, to work as a blacksmith on Ceelohg. ''Twas my first profession,' he said, 'and a steadier one than using my fists. Now we'll be neighbours, so.'

Anna had smiled her pleasure, but made no effort to join in the excited conversation. She turned to gaze into the fire. Something was bothering her, and she did not know quite . . .

She still hugged her adventure to her. She studied it once more, glad that she was warm and ignored by the others. The incident in the field had excited her somehow – and yet there was this dissatisfaction, a small resentment. Maura had handled the situation very clumsily. Maura had no tact; for all her cleverness, she did not know how to behave like a woman. It shouldn't have ended with hurt feelings and broken eggs and muddy, embarrassed faces. It should have been harmless, and amusing . . . and gentle, and . . . rather beautiful. It should have been romantic, it should have been . . . me.

9

For the remainder of 1837 there was little outward sign of change at Tineranna. Aidan had feared that many of the horses would be sold; Devlin had never shared his father's interest in either racing or hunting; but Aidan was given no new orders, and continued exercising and grooming the horses through the winter. Soon he began to relax a little, thinking that perhaps things would be allowed to continue as they had always done.

But Caroline was making plans. She had an adequate income of her own, and a small but fashionable town house in London that had been leased to a Professor of History at London University. He was duly given notice in November that she and her son would require the house permanently when the lease expired the following March.

Devlin, jubilant, walked about in a state of suppressed excitement for this time, attending to the business of the property with Nathan Cameron, but barely tolerant of the man's persistent suggestions and explanations on the running of the estate. Devlin was bored by the complicated breeding programme William had begun to improve Tineranna's large dairy herd, could sit through the necessary book-keeping only with the utmost self-discipline. As if I'll be here, he thought, as if I'd bury myself here. And Nathan would notice the boy's impatient scowl, and be afraid.

And Aidan, seeing Nathan worried, became afraid also. For as time went on, the air of excitement about the mistress and the young master became more pronounced; an excitement not in keeping with a family in mourning. It was the kind of energetic good humour they had betrayed whenever a trip to London had been planned, but this could not be a shopping trip. Neither was it a visit to the mistress's own family, for the Retcliffes had been wintering on their own Irish estate in County Carlow, and had arrived in time for William's funeral, only to depart again immediately after. It was all very puzzling, ominous . . .

Aidan found himself doing a variety of work that winter, as Nathan was forced to delegate more tasks to concentrate on the bookwork. Helping the farm labourers lay down fodder for the cattle and sheep,

88

Aidan would pause and gaze out over the neat fields, grey with frost, and he would feel frightened. For himself, for his mother and Thomas; all their lives had been given to this estate. And he trembled for Tineranna itself.

Despite Mister Kelly's taking care of his poorer tenants when bad times came, despite his expensive interests in racing and hunting, he had been forward thinking in his attitude to farming. Tineranna paid for itself, and some years even prospered a little; while to the north, near Scarriff, and to the south, in Tipperary, landlords lived like kings on crops and land already mortgaged, and their tenants huddled half-starved in cabins that would not house Tineranna pigs.

It was a grand place, Aidan thought, gazing down to where the hills lowered their shoulders into the grey waters of Lough Derg. But it took so little to swing the balance! He looked around at the many acres and the neat cottages of the tenants with the small potato gardens at the rear. How soon could the debts mount up, the productivity lapse, the rents be raised on the cottiers' farms? And a bad harvest, perhaps, and poor yields of potatoes . . . Then the rents would fall behind, there would be evictions, the cottages pulled down and the gardens ploughed under. Cattle and sheep would graze contentedly upon the slopes, and hundreds of people sent out upon the roads to die.

Aidan would shiver, and if he was working beside Nathan, would glance at the little man and wonder if he should ask him. All the fear-filled questions. 'Nathan, do y'think they'll sell the horses? Nathan, do y'think they'll dismiss some of us should they go away? Nathan, will there be evictions?'

But Nathan, gnarled, surly, hunched in his battered jacket, his mouth pulled down in perpetual concentration, was equally forbidding to the boy now as he had been nine years before, when they had battled on the roadside for possession of a dead puppy. Nathan was clever, Nathan was nearly always just, but one did not chat with Nathan. The most natural phrases somehow dried up half-spoken, when he would scowl more deeply, and raise his shoulder a little, warding off friendship as if it was a physical assault.

But all those on Tineranna were nervous, apprehensive, that winter. From the comfortably-off tenant farmers such as the O'Hagans and O'Donoghues, down to the poor cottiers on their single acres, their houses huddled together along the Killaloe-Ogonnelloe Road, all had the fear upon them. Would the land be sold? Would there be evictions?

It was not until the day after Little Christmas, the feast of Epiphany, that they knew. As many of the staff and tenants who could come were called to a meeting in the courtyard outside the kitchen. All came, nearly six hundred men, women and children. A light mist was falling, and some of the old ones and the children were beginning to cough badly, so the meeting was brief. By the gate leading to the kitchen garden, Mary, Aidan and Thomas saw young Master Devlin follow his mother out on to the step. In clear tones he thanked them for coming and announced that due to business problems connected with his father's estate he must go to London for some time. Most of the horses and the kennel of dogs were to be sold, but – and here an audible and apprehensive intake of breath was heard from the yard staff – there would be no dismissals, due to the problems of keeping the house and grounds in order.

The intake of breath was let out in one long cheer of relief; only Aidan and Nathan glanced at each other silently in a rare communion of thanksgiving.

No one was surprised when Nathan Cameron was made agent for Tineranna. The tenants who disliked him said he'd been hoping for this all along; only Aidan knew that Nathan did not relish the idea.

'You think Master Devlin's gonna be puttin' money back into this place?' he demanded of Aidan, once, when they were exercising two of the hunters. 'No! He'll want it all for living like a prince in London. And when the place isn't producin' what it should, *I'll* get the blame. And if we have a bad year – d'y' think he'll appreciate what we're goin' through from over there? He'll want those rents come what may – and there I'll be, stuck in the middle.' He stared ahead for a long time.

Aidan said, 'Mister Cameron? You could say no . . . '

Nathan's head came round sharply, 'Yes, I could. And some gombeen man like O'Casey or Flynn would be hired in my place, and they'd be collectin' rents and pocketin' what they could of the crop money, and robbin' tenants and Kellys alike. Godalmighty, boy! Did y' think I hadn't thought of that?' They rode in silence, then he said dolefully, 'I've never had any friends, but by God, I've never made enemies, either. This will bring them.'

The Kellys were to leave in early February, and were to stay with Caroline's brother, Lord Hallswood, at his country home in Wiltshire until the move to London in March. Since most of the Tineranna house staff were English, having shared what Caroline called her exile, they would be returning with her, going immediately to Grosvenor Square and setting up the house ready for their arrival.

Amidst all the final decision-making, the packing of trunks, the shifting of furniture and the bringing out of dust sheets, Devlin found his impatience mounting. Some relief was gained in the planning of the sale of the horses and dogs, and he enjoyed the company of the landlords, who rode sometimes from two or three counties away to stay in Killaloe and ride and shoot with him. Even these previously hated pastimes were somehow enjoyable, now, in the shower of praise that fell upon the training and breeding of the animals. If the credit truly belonged to his father and Nathan Cameron he failed to worry unduly about it, and found himself in his father's office at nights, looking through the animals' pedigrees, the better to acquit himself with the visitors.

It was during a discussion with four of the men in the library after a morning of shooting that one of them asked about Samhradh.

'Oh, he's getting on, you know,' Devlin smiled. 'We hardly work him at all.'

One of the visitors from Tipperary asked if the dog didn't belong to one of the tenants, 'a clever lad, dark as a gypsy . . . '

'O'Brien,' Devlin said shortly. 'The dog needed care when it was a pup. It was loaned to the boy to look after.'

'Would he be for sale, now?'

Devlin looked up. There was an infinitesimal air of waiting about the room, and he gazed at all the faces in turn before saying, 'No. No, we'll be taking Samhradh to England with us.'

'Ah.' The man was disappointed, but smiled with good grace. 'Can't say I blame you. The Wiltshire trials are in July, are they not? What a stir that dog will make there!' He turned to the others. 'I offered William Kelly any sum he wished for Samhradh, but he refused to discuss it. I still say that's the best setter in Ireland . . . '

The following midday, while the gentlemen were lunching at the Curran's inn in the village, Devlin rode down to the field where he knew Aidan O'Brien would be working.

Here the cows had broken down a section of the wall, and the boy was replacing the stones carefully, locking each into place by fitting each angle perfectly into its corresponding space.

Devlin disliked dismounting to talk to any of the farm labourers; he felt self-conscious, ill-at-ease with them, preferred as much distance between them as possible. This boy he knew well, but still he remained mounted, watching the boy work.

Aidan must have seen him, but he did not pause; he lifted a fallen stone to the wall, shifted it expertly amongst its fellows until it was firmly in place, and only then did he look up at Devlin and remove his hat. The length of time taken was just short of insolence. 'Good day t' y', sir.'

91

Devlin inclined his head a little. He had been right in thinking that this would not be easy. The boy had changed somehow. He did not look so . . . young. The eyes that held Devlin's were steadfast, the mouth firm. He looked older than his fifteen years. Had Ballingarry done this? Devlin asked himself, did it take death to make a boy into a man? And he felt a sudden, sweeping resentment, pushed to the back of his mind until now.

For why, of all people, did it have to be this boy? Osborne had told him that his father had died in the boy's arms . . . Not Devlin's, or Caroline's, as it should have been, but this stranger, this peasant – and it was to help other creatures like him that William Kelly had died.

Devlin swung down out of the saddle, but kept his distance. He began abruptly, 'I wish to buy the setter back from you. I can offer you a fair price, one that will undoubtedly help you and your family. Ten guineas.'

Aidan stared at him. Was Devlin mad? 'Sir, Samhradh has passed his ninth year – he's an old dog . . . '

'I wish to use him for breeding.'

'But . . . he's not fit for breeding. His jaw is overshot; he's far too small . . . ' He almost added, 'It's because of these faults that he was given to me in the first place.' But this seemed to reflect on Mister Kelly's kindness, and he was silent.

Devlin was saying, 'I know all this. I know as much of the dog's history as you – I have his pedigree and it's a faultless one. I will take charge of the breeding programme in Wiltshire and . . . '

'I don't want to sell him, Master Devlin.'

'Don't be absurd. Ten guineas . . . '

'Even so, sir. I don't want to sell him.'

The voice was low, quiet, but unmistakable in its firmness. Devlin gazed at him, speechless. He had been confident of an ultimate victory, had planned no strategy for a dignified withdrawal. For never in his life had he been denied any possession. To be refused now, by this cottier child, was unthinkable – and refused a dog that had never been paid for, that was rightly his in the first place. 'You are above yourself, boy. My father never meant you to keep that dog . . . '

Before Aidan could stop himself, he had cried, 'That's a lie! Mister Kelly gave him to me! Out of pity for me when my own dog died. Samhradh was a gift . . . !'

Devlin's hand gripped the riding crop, but he resisted the urge to bring it up and across the boy's face. 'I am offering you a fair price,' he continued with a forced calm. 'Very well, twelve guineas. You

92

cannot refuse that.'

Mother of God, but that was a lot of money! Aidan had never set eyes on so much in his life. He thought of the rent, of the presents he could buy for his mother and Thomas . . . and Anna. But to lose Samhradh! The dog had been with him almost as long as he could remember. He was more than just a dog, more even than a faithful companion. He was the generous gift of a man who had raised Aidan up and had him educated, given him visions of worlds out beyond Killaloe. Samhradh was the last link with a life that he was afraid was gone forever.

'The dog's not for sale, sir.'

For an instant Aidan thought Devlin was going to strike him. He had moved closer, and had half-raised the riding crop – but then he stopped. Aidan could have understood it, should the boy have hit him, he himself was amazed at his audacity in refusing the offer, but he was not prepared for the words that followed, clearly enunciated, more anglicized than Devlin's normal speech. A voice he'd never heard.

'So at last you think you've found a way to spite me. You think this means that we're even, somehow, don't you? You think to boast to your friends that I wanted and couldn't possess something that belonged to you. You're a fool, boy!' He was so angry, now, that he took another step forward, and Aidan, more in amazement than fear, took one back, bringing himself up against the wall.

'My father had you taught to read and write because he was fond of your father. Your father . . . ' this with tremendous scorn, 'was an ignorant peasant whose only ability was that he could ride a horse well. In intellect he was no better than the beasts he worked with, and neither are you! You owe your entire existence to my family. We keep you in meal and potatoes just as we keep our horses and cattle. Without us you couldn't survive! You are *nothing*. You contribute nothing. You are a parasite yourself, and you dare to presume that you own that dog – that you own anything!' And here followed a string of obscenities in Irish and English – stable language, kitchen language – that the younger boy was amazed that Devlin had heard, let alone understood.

Aidan was blind to everything but the boy's contorted face, deafened by the venom of his words and could not manage to rally his wits. The gentry did not speak like this to mere farm labourers. The gentry did not abandon their control and stoop to such behaviour. It was appalling, terrifying, it could not be happening . . .

He did not realize it then, but this was the first time the pattern of his existence was threatened, the first rent in the fabric that was the established social order in which he had been raised. Here was the unprecedented spectacle of Master Devlin lowering himself to coarseness and vulgarity. Aidan should be cringing, whining, begging pardon and mercy . . . But he did not.

Rage had overtaken him. Rage that this weak, self-indulgent boy was all that remained of the generous William. His words were born of this rage, fed by his unspoken grief, by the years of Devlin's ridicule. The demand for Samhradh suddenly represented a thousand demands locked in his racial memory.

'Your father would be ashamed!' he shouted. 'He would be ashamed to hear you speak so! He gave his word that the dog was mine – but that doesn't matter to you – what your father did, what your father was, doesn't matter to you! You have no honour! You're not like your father at all! *You have no honour!*'

The words struck to the well of Devlin's being. He did not know what he was doing: he felt each truth strike through him like needles through flesh, he did not feel his hands go out, the push that he gave the boy's chest that knocked the air from him, made him stumble back, half-fall against the wall.

Aidan himself almost welcomed the physical contact: he yearned to strike back, had clutched at the wall, placed one foot behind him to propel himself upwards. And the rock came towards him. He saw it, saw the hands, white-knuckled, clutching it; noticing all in fantastic detail in that split second fraught with death. A large rock, from the top of the wall, slammed down towards his eyes – and turning his head sharply, suddenly, it was only by seconds he avoided the boulder that would have crushed his face. It pounded into the wall beside his head with a heavy metallic sound that sent shocks through his spine. He lost his balance, fell, saving himself on one arm, propping himself up on the marshy ground and staring upwards at the older boy.

Devlin stood like a statue, all anger gone, ashen-faced and gazing at Aidan with eyes wide with shock. For long seconds they remained as they were, then Aidan was climbing to his feet; his voice was low, but his fists were clenched, and there was something in the contained power of him that made Devlin take a step back before he realized it.

'You try that again,' Aidan O'Brien was saying. 'You try that again, and landlord or no landlord, I'll punch your face in, Devlin. A fair fight it will be, though. If that's what you want.' And when Devlin did not speak, 'Is it a fair fight you want?'

And still Devlin did not speak. The seconds passed, then his gaze began to slide sideways, off and away from Aidan, at the same time

94

as his feet moved him back, back, away from the threat of the other boy, and towards his own horse. The eyes and the slowly moving feet seemed to work against the boy's will, but still he moved away, until groping backwards brought his hands in contact with the fallen reins, and turning he could throw them over the horse's neck, and mount. He rode away without another word, without looking back.

10

It was Caroline who came to fetch the dog.

Devlin had brooded about the house, white-faced, for more than a week. When pressed he had explained about wanting the dog, but never dreamed of telling her the whole truth; that his actions had terrified him, and that he feared reprisals. He did not leave the house, in case he met with Corrie O'Neill, now known to be a frequent visitor to the O'Brien home, or the red-headed O'Donaghues who had been brooding silently ever since the incident with their sister, or the Curran brothers, little, dark-haired, black-tempered devils who would undoubtedly join Aidan O'Brien on a Terry raid against the Kellys with very little hesitation. Telling his mother about Samhradh, he thought she would smile, tell him that he could have a new dog when they reached England. But she listened gravely, asked questions, watching Devlin's pallor and his faltering manner and believing that, odd as the desire was, he was making himself ill through not possessing the dog.

'You made the mistake, dear,' she told him, gently, 'of going to the boy with the offer. He is a child, after all, and still ingenuous. The person who will understand the practicalities and who will control the boy if necessary, is the mother.'

'I didn't think of that.'

'When you want something very badly, Devlin, it is well to meditate first on the best way of going about it. People will not always fall in with your plans, my dear, one must think well ahead. It is rather like a game of chess.'

They were in Caroline's sitting room, seated together on the chaise longue, the morning sunlight falling on their backs. Devlin felt warm and suddenly comfortable. As they smiled at each other, he noticed that his mother looked very well, even more beautiful in her black mourning. It came to him suddenly that she was happy. That she had not been so happy for as long as Devlin could remember. He wondered if his father's death – even though she had mourned him wildly in her grief – had not in some way been a release to her.

She put her hand to his head, stroked the thick gold of his hair, lingered against his cheek. They were so much alike! She said, 'I shall go to see this O'Brien woman, and you shall have the dog, I promise.'

Mary was alone in the cottage, some weeks later, when Caroline drove up to the door in the brougham. Conscious of an apron soiled with turf ashes, of her straggling hair, Mary stood petrified in the doorway and watched the footman open the door and lower the steps, and the strikingly beautiful figure in black step down and move towards her. From the corner of her eye she noticed a cart draw up behind the carriage, a lone man sitting in it. Behind her, in the cottage, Samhradh was barking, attempting to push past her and outside.

'Down!' Mary said sharply, 'Stay!' and Samhradh, desperate in his curiosity, stared wildly at her. 'Stay!' He sat, moaning, begging with his eyes, but she shut the half-door on him and walked outside.

She dropped a curtsey, offered a shy, 'God save you, ma'am,' and was about to invite her into the house, when Caroline lifted a hand.

'I have come about the dog, Mrs O'Brien.'

Mary's heart contracted. Had Samhradh been chasing sheep? Had he bitten one of her servants? 'My son wishes to buy him. Were you aware that Master Devlin offered your son Aidan twelve guineas for the dog?'

Mary felt the blood leave her face. Twelve guineas! Why, the rent for the cottage and its single acre came to only ten pounds a year. Twelve guineas! For a dog! 'No. No, ma'am, he did not tell me.'

'Perhaps he thought the figure unfair,' Caroline said smoothly, 'I have with me fifteen guineas . . . ' She gestured and the footman approached, bearing with him a cloth pouch from the front seat of the carriage. 'I trust you will agree with me that fifteen guineas is a more than fair price for a dog of his age. Your son could not possibly have any objection to that amount.'

'With . . . with respect, ma'am, Aidan is fond of Samhradh. That, more than the money, I'm thinkin', is what . . . '

'You are the boy's legal guardian. It is up to you to teach him values in life. You have two children to keep. This money will help a great deal. Is it not time your boy learnt that human life is more important than sentiment?'

It was over quickly. Too quickly. Later, she did not remember how. The gold was in her hands and Samhradh, led by a smart strap of leather attached to a studded collar, was being lifted unwillingly into the back of the cart. Mary was given a piece of paper, after Caroline had read the words to her in her clipped English tones, and she was asked to sign it. Had they thought of everything? The footman stood there with the ink, dipped the quill into it himself and handed it to her. Leaning the paper against the carriage, she signed a trembling *Mary O'Brien*, thankful at least that Aidan had shown her how to write her name, that they were not shamed in this, before Mrs Kelly and her liveried servants.

And they were gone. She was standing in the yard, holding a heavy bag of coins to her breast, listening to the howling, howling . . . fading by the second, from beyond the hill by O'Sullivans.

Gone! Samhradh gone! How would she tell the boy, *how*? The cottage was empty, the sack before the hearth where the dog slept was still mussed slightly where he had disturbed it in his hurry to bay at the visitors. She threw the money on to the table, stooped and took up the dog's rug, tossing it on to the fire. Let there be no trace . . .

She flung herself down on her bed in the corner, curling her fingers into the blanket, feeling the sobs rise towards her throat. Foolish, foolish, these tears! What right had they to have had the dog for so long? Were they gentry that they could indulge themselves so? The rabbits that Aidan was allowed to shoot, the scraps from the table at the big house – these could have fed a family of four! She had lost sight of this, all these years beneath William Kelly's protection. It had done them no good. The years that were to follow would be hard, and all the harder to accept when they had memories of comforts and full stomachs behind them. With Samhradh gone, a burden was lifted. But how would she tell Aidan? How?

There was a brief knock at the door and it opened immediately. She had no chance to rise, to wipe her eyes, before Corrie O'Neill was across the narrow room and seated on the edge of the bed. Its wood creaked dangerously beneath his weight.

'What's this?' A smile in the deep voice. 'God save you, I could hear the bellowin' before I reached the gate – like an orphaned calf, I thought . . .'

'Stop it! I wasn't!' She attempted to rise but found herself pulled, instead, to the massive chest.

'Hush, now. I know what's happened, I saw the carriages.'

She had stiffened to pull away, but at the knowledge that he

97

knew, and understood, she relaxed against him, felt herself begin to cry again with equal turbulence. 'I sold . . . the dog! She demanded it, and . . . I sold him! I had . . . no choice!'

'I know, I know . . . '

'I shouldn't be weeping. I did what I had to do. I'm not a weak woman . . . '

'I know that, too.'

'I did not . . . care for the dog. It has no soul, has it? It will be better looked after by the Kellys . . . '

'It will, that. He's a clever dog, they'll look after him like he was a prince, they will.'

'We couldn't have kept him! Not with bad times coming . . . '

'Why should bad times come?' His voice a little sharper.

'The Kellys . . . going. It'll mean bad times . . . They won't keep us all working for too long . . . '

'You'll not be depending entirely on the Kellys.'

His words did not make sense. She frowned into the serge of his jacket, began to push away to lift her face – and found herself imprisoned. She felt him sigh, yet still the iron grip of his arms did not shift. His breath was on her hair, and she realized suddenly that he did not want her to look at him. And immediately upon that thought was that she should not be here at all, half-lying on a bed in the arms of a man she hardly knew. But before she could move or offer a protest—

'With my fighting I earned a lot of money, but I spent it all.' His voice was low, tight. 'If I added it all up, sure there'd be enough to buy a farm. But it's gone.' The regret in his voice made her pity him, and she almost tried once more to lift her head to gaze at him, but did not; aware instinctively that the pressure of the arms would tighten again should she try. 'Mister Osborne is good to me. I'm putting a little money by, the past few months. I could still travel to Limerick to teach boxing there – though it'll mean I'll be away a good deal. You have the boys, though, you'd not be unprotected here.'

She felt her heart lurch suddenly, a panicky feeling spreading through her, the massive chest and arms no longer a refuge of safety but a threat, a cage. And she tried to push away from him then, tried to turn her head, to push at his arms in their grip upon her shoulders; but she remained held unmoving in his grasp, like a wren enclosed in a boy's strong hands.

'Hush, hush . . . ' The voice against her hair, gentle, disembodied; no part, it seemed, of the arms that held her. 'Hush . . .You knew it would come to this. Could I have walked away and left you for good and all, that night I brought your boy home? You so small

98

and alone? You haunted my steps all the way to Limerick, you walked ahead of me all the way back, until I ran the last miles.'

Again there was silence; she remained stiffened, wide-eyed but blinded, against him.

Softer, even now, 'I've had other women. Many of them. And not all . . . low women, bad ones. Some were ladies, they . . . It was who I was, you see. I didn't approach them. I didn't need to. I am a man, I don't apologize for all this, sin though they say it is. I have never hurt anybody. Not even with my fighting. You can sense a man letting go of life – can feel it, through your fists as you strike him. I would always stop. I don't have a temper. I don't want to hurt. Winning was enough. With women it was the same. Those that softened to me – who would have loved me, perhaps – I had to leave. I've never married. I always felt I would die in the ring . . . It made me afraid, to die leaving a woman and children. And besides this, the women I met . . . ' Again his breath, warm on her hair, and no words followed.

For a long time they remained motionless, then, slowly, she found herself able to rise, until she could gaze at him. Lord, how ugly he was, with his pock-marked cheeks and the flat, chiselled planes of his cheek bones. His mouth was large and scarred to a strange, crooked droop, and his nose was mishapen, almost entirely without a bridge. With his mouth closed he breathed loudly – she found herself thinking that he would undoubtedly snore.

But the eyes. The eyes were clear and brown and deep. And they gazed back at her with the candour and sincerity of a child. 'You know what I'm asking.'

She did not answer. She was wondering what it would be like, to allow this man to do to her the secret things that her husband had done . . .

He shook her, slowly, gently. 'Come. You know I can look after you. You need someone to look after you.'

'I . . . I don't know.'

'You've been alone too long, and that's the truth. Do you mourn your husband still?'

'No. I . . . '

'Are you afraid to lie with me?'

'No,' she lied, startled. His dark eyes studied her own. She felt herself colouring, but dared not look away; he would sense her embarrassment, realize the lie. She sensed he did not fully believe her now, but he nodded, slowly.

'Then there's nothing more to be said, is there? Where would you like to live? There are three rooms at Mister Osborne's . . . '

'No. I must stay here.'

'The estates adjoin, it wouldn't be far for Aidan . . . '

'You don't understand. This is O'Brien land . . . '

'*What?*'

'It is! It . . . it was. Before Cromwell, it was. Even if Tineranna can't belong to my sons, they belong to it. Do you understand?'

He stared at her. 'No. I grew up living in an attic one week, a hovel the next, beneath a bridge the next. I belong to the streets of Dublin. No piece of land owns me. But we'll stay here if you wish.'

'I haven't said I wished for anything.'

She said it sharply, gazing at his coat button. He did not move, and after a long pause she raised her eyes to his. He was looking at her with a faint smile to his crooked mouth. She waited for him to speak, expecting to be coaxed; but still he was silent. Finally, she said, 'I hardly know you. My boys hardly know you. I want more time.'

He said, 'I can wait.'

He was due back at Ceelohg and left soon after, promising to return early that evening. She was pleased that he did not embrace her again or try to kiss her before he left. But when he had gone, and she turned to find the Kellys' bag of money upon the table, the first acute pain of recollection was lessened somewhat. Corrie was returning. He would be here when the boys came home.

Aidan had been sent to Tuamgraney to deliver one of the hunters sold at the auction. It was the big grey that William had been riding the day of his death; a highly strung yet good-natured beast, and Aidan took leave of it with a good deal of regret. Handing the halter, with which he had led it from Tineranna, to its new groom, he felt again the painful wrench as if he were losing part of his past, even his identity. He tried to shrug it off without success and rode his little bay hard on the return trip, seeking to lose his thoughts in speed and the wind that rushed past him.

Riding past O'Donoghue's, he found the two ponies belonging to Martin and Tom-Joe Curran tied to a post outside, and feeling the sudden need of companionship, he rode down the boreen and into the yard.

He heard the voices immediately, above the barking of dogs and the wailing of the youngest O'Donoghue child, all issuing from the rear of the house. He rode around into the stable yard, still finding himself impressed by the neatness of the cobbled ground and the white-washed outbuildings. Liam O'Donoghue was prospering to be able to pave his yards and build extensions such as he had. All of five rooms their house was, each as clean as the big house itself. The three older O'Donoghue children did not work on the farm, but were sent to school in Killaloe; even the eldest, Seamus, who was almost sixteen. Mister O'Donoghue set great store by learning, was determined that one of his boys should study for a profession. For this reason Aidan, who had had some regrets after giving up his schooling at twelve, was slightly envious of the O'Donoghues, not under the same pressure to earn money as he himself was.

Really, the O'Donoghues seemed to believe in learning for learning's sake; even Maura was still at school; a girl, and fourteen at that. And everyone knew she was too sharp already for her own good. Aidan felt most of the family's strangeness could be traced to the father, Liam. He was one of the few men in Killaloe who insisted his family speak and read Irish, certain that within their lifetimes the Irish, and even the English, would come to realize the beauty of the language. He aggravated those people in the parish who tried to emulate the English by being as Irish as he possibly could. Only with a landlord like William Kelly could Liam O'Donoghue have prospered as he had, they said. He even refused to answer when people called him by the English equivalent of his name, William. English and Irish alike regarded him as more than a little eccentric. It was rumoured that his wife could speak French.

In the haggard, the field where the hay ricks stood, a horse and fodder wagon were standing abandoned, and beside it, watched closely by four children, Thady O'Donoghue was fighting Martin Curran.

It was a good-natured fight, judging by the laughter; but Thady's nose was bleeding, and the little girl, Bridie, was frightened, howling loudly and clutching at Maura's skirts. Maura was ignoring her, jumping up and down with as much excitement as her brother Seamus or Tom-Joe Curran. Aidan did not need to look around to know that Mr and Mrs O'Donoghue were not at home. They would never have tolerated the boys scuffling, let alone Maura excitedly urging on her champion, waving her thin arms in the air and stepping on her small sister's feet in her enthusiasm. Bridie howled all the more.

Thady was getting the worst of the fight though he was taller than Martin. Martin would never grow to be even middle-height, but both he and his brother Tom-Joe were perfectly in proportion and compact; and being a year older than Thady, Martin was not as gangling, had come to grips with the limitations of his size, was better able to co-ordinate himself.

And Martin did not know caution. Aidan looked at him and

doubted if he even knew fear. Once the Currans had detailed to him an incident with the headmaster of the village school. He had come upon the children teasing the Curran boys for their size and their swarthiness, and he had delivered them a lecture, then, on the Firbolgs, that ancient race, who inhabited this land long before the coming of the Celts. They had all been short, and dark, the Firbolgs, and were noted for their courage and their ferocity in battle. This had raised laughter of a not-displeasing kind, and from then on the Currans bore the occasional aspersions with better grace. Whether their ferocity was inherited, or all their own, Aidan thought now, it stood the slightly-built Currans in good stead.

Of the group in the haggard, it was Bridie who saw him first. Her excited cry of 'Horse, horse!' made Maura and the two watching boys turn, and the two antagonists, feeling themselves losing their audience, stopped for a moment, eyeing each other warily, before welcoming Aidan.

'Have y' got time t' fight me? Sure I've been itching to fight y' these three months gone!' Martin stood on wide-planted feet, flushed, but untired.

'I've got to get back to work,' Aidan grinned; but still, he dismounted.

'We won't take long. First one to call stop loses. How's that?'

'Sure y'll be here all day and all night if that's the rules.' Maura glanced wryly between them. She lifted the clamouring Bridie and placed her in the saddle of Aidan's horse, taking the reins from him. 'Go on, I'll hold the horse.'

He glanced at her, amused. She was a bloody-minded little thing, to be sure. Anna, now, though three years older than Maura, couldn't abide fighting, turned away cold-faced when they'd come upon one – which was often enough in Killaloe.

Thady had soaked his handkerchief in a nearby water trough and was squatting on the ground, holding it to his nose as Aidan approached. 'Hand me y'r coat,' he called through the cloth, and Aidan pulled off his jacket and tossed it to him. Martin was already dancing about him, his black eyes dancing over him, readying his entire energy, summing Aidan up, judging the best opening.

But it was over before Martin knew it. One minute he had rushed at Aidan who waited, balanced lightly on the balls of his feet, gazing calmly over his raised fists, and the next there was water running down his neck and into his ears and he was flat on his back gazing up at the ring of faces.

'He knocked you out!' the O'Donoghues crowed.

'He didn't, he didn't! Try it again! Come on, O'Brien!' Martin

102

struggled to his feet, 'You just try it again!' But the world was an unsteady place once he was on his feet, and his brother had to grasp his arm to stop him falling.

'Come, Martin, that's an end to it. I have to get back to work . . . ' Aidan peered into his face as he swayed a little, 'Are y' all right?'

The fist came up sharply, striking him on the lip, and he reeled back, tasting blood. Martin was on him at once, but although the blows rained down upon him furiously, there was no forethought, no judgement. It took Aidan an effort to push free of Martin's weight; then he was on his feet, feeling his own temper now, when the deep voice of Liam O'Donoghue cut across them, freezing them, fists up, like statues.

'I've got a blackthorn stick here that'll break the head of any boy I see in this field when I've counted to ten!' he roared. They glanced up. The tall, craggy-faced farmer was standing at the wall near the cow shed, indeed brandishing a heavy blackthorn walking stick. 'One!'

There was a hasty scatter. The Curran boys had scrambled over the fence and round the house as fast as they could go. Maura had lifted Bridie from the saddle of Aidan's horse and was dragging her off towards the gate leading to the house. Seamus and Thady had picked up abandoned pitchforks and were running across the field to the haystack and waiting wagon.

'Come here, boy!' The authoritative voice brought Aidan to a halt with one foot in the stirrup. 'Come here, I say!'

Aidan led his horse over to the wall, conscious that his lip was dripping blood down his chin. He half placed his muddy hand to it, but O'Donoghue had grasped his wrist. 'Arra, y'dirty young devil! Where's y' handkerchief!'

'I don't have one, sir.'

'What's the matter, Master Aidan – don't the O'Brien noses run like other folks'?'

The boy looked up, incensed, but found a clean white linen handkerchief held out to him.

'Get you on home and dont let me catch you fightin'. On my land or on anyone else's, d' y' hear?'

Aidan took the handkerchief with a cool 'Thank you', and holding it to his lip, mounted his horse.

He was late getting back to Tineranna. Nathan did not entirely trust his story of a fall from the horse and kept him longer than usual after the feedings, mucking out the stall made vacant by the sale of William's hunter. But once the new hay was down on the floor –

fresh, sweet-smelling – Nathan gave him threepence, growling that he had done a good job, and staring at him fixedly for a moment before turning abruptly away. Aidan pocketed the coin, pleased but puzzled.

He walked home tiredly, stumbling occasionally as the moon had hidden itself behind ragged grey cloud, and across the fields it was only the light of O'Sullivan's cottage that prevented him from losing his bearings. He climbed the fence near their door and kept on down the boreen, seeing now the lights of his own home twinkling between the boards of the shutters. Samhradh was quiet, tonight; he usually heard the boy's footsteps a long way off and bounded out the door in welcome. Asleep before the fire, Aidan thought, and his smile as entered the cottage was directed in front of the hearth . . .

Nothing. No rug. And a silence that was strange, pregnant, from the three people at the table. 'Where's Samhradh? Is he hurt?' Still silence. His mother's face anguished, Corrie O'Neill's awkwardly scowling, Thomas's pale. Thomas had been crying. 'Where's Samhradh?' Aidan shouted, 'Where is he?'

'Aidan . . . ' Corrie began, but Mary had laid a hand on his arm, and stood. 'No, I should tell him. Son, the dog's gone. The mistress came today and gave me fifteen guineas for him. I had no . . . '

The boy gave a cry of such agony that the words dried in her throat. The cut on his lip had opened, and she had the added terror of seeing the blood on his face as he whirled and flung himself awkwardly out the door.

He didn't hear the voices behind him, his whole being yearned to be up at the big house; he would find Devlin and kill him – yes, kill him for this!

Sobbing, unseeing in the blackness of the night, he crashed into the wall, tore his hands on the blackberry bushes growing over it, reeled back and had taken no more than three strides up the road when he was caught, yanked about, and shaken until his teeth chattered.

'Where do y' think you're goin'? What do you think you can do . . . !'

He struck out at Corrie, furious at the restraining grip, and felt his fists bruise themselves against the stubble of the heavy jaw. 'Let go! I'll kill him! The bastard, the lying, thievin' . . . Let go!'

'They've gone, Aidan! They left this afternoon on the steamer to Dublin! With the dog! They've gone to England, boy! Gone!'

The moon came out from the clouds in that second that Aidan stiffened, showing Corrie his white and bloody face, the dark hair falling into eyes huge with hurt and rage. Tightly from his con-

104

stricted throat, 'I'll . . . kill . . . him!' And a cry, with which he flung himself back in Corrie's grasp, 'I'll kill him!' He struck again and again at the man who refused to let him go; with the moon out, Corrie could see to block the blows aimed at his face, but he allowed them to rain upon his body, always keeping one hand holding tight to the boy's arm or shoulder. 'Let go o' me, Corrie! I c'n catch 'em! I'll take one of the horses! Let me go so I can catch them!'

'It's no use . . . '

'Let go o' me! I'll kill him, I tell you! He's a thievin' murderin' little bastard! He deserves it! I'll kick his brains out of his head! I'll cut his fekkin' throat, s' help me God! Let go!'

The blows he aimed at the huge and passive body connected, but seemed to have no effect at all. O'Neill simply tensed himself and took what came. But Aidan was tiring, slowly tiring; despite himself, he could feel the blows weakening.

'You don't know 'im – y' don't, Corrie . . . Corrie, f'r God's sake! I saw him . . . at a hunt . . . he killed his little mare, a beautiful little mare, and he killed her! Made her jump . . . and she fell – and him kicking her! He kicked her and kicked her, and swore at her – he's mad! He's a bastard! He'll kill Samhradh! He'll kill him, Corrie! Jaysus, you don't understand . . . Corrie . . . '

'They've gone.' The deep voice heavy as fate. 'They've gone, boyo. The dog's gone. You must face it.'

The boy stopped, suddenly. The finality of the words was at last seeping into his enraged mind, the futility of any action now obvious to him. It was over – these long years with the loping red dog at his side. And he cried, then, his head butted against the giant's chest, hating himself for his weakness.

Corrie placed his arms around him in an awkward embrace, searching his mind for some words, any words . . .

But it was Aidan's voice, low, savage, that broke the silence.

'I'll not cry again. Never again. I don't care what he does, I'll never give him that victory over me. I won't. Not ever again!'

11

The tithe question, responsible for so much tragedy and injustice in Ireland, underwent legislation in the following year of 1838. As Robert Osborne had foretold at the meeting of landlords at Tineranna, the amount was reduced and was now collected directly from the landlords. Aidan read the report in the *Limerick Chronicle* while on a visit to Anna one Sunday afternoon. Devlin Kelly read it in his own copy of *The Times* in the breakfast room of the house in Grosvenor Square. For the remainder of the day the thoughts of both were upon William Kelly.

Aidan's grief would never entirely leave him, nor would the private resentment against the fate that had ordained the senseless death of the landlord who had befriended him. But his initial fears for Tineranna and for his own future seemed, as time went on and no dreaded announcement came from London, to be unfounded.

The depression of the 1820s and early 1830s was over; now harvests were good, prices higher, and more and more cattle, pigs, sheep and grain were loaded into the many barges in Killaloe to be taken to markets on the east coast. Travellers going to Dublin and emigrants leaving their homes in the West and Midlands boarded ships on the canal after spending their last days giving their custom to the local inns and business houses.

Work was easier to come by, with the steamship companies and the Shannon Navigation System providing employment. In the two years 1841 and 1842, Molly and John Curran proudly married off their four daughters, all to young men working on the river trade.

At the party to celebrate the last of these weddings, Molly Curran had said to Mary, 'It's a grand year f'r weddin's, that's what it is!' Her eyes roamed pointedly towards Corrie O'Neill and back again.

'For those that wish them,' Mary had said, almost curtly.

On Tineranna, the threat of possible eviction was forgotten when the rents were paid and the potato crops at the rear of the cottiers' mud cabins blossomed and greened and grew, and the meal months, those months when the old supply of potatoes ran out and only the thin stir-about porridge kept families alive until the new crop came in, were shorter, it seemed, in the bounty of the harvests, and the waiting weeks of spring did not hold so much fear.

Nathan Cameron settled in as agent for Tineranna, and every Sunday at the Presbyterian chapel sent up his own dour prayers of thanksgiving that the crops were good and the rents came in on time. Even the dismissal of five of the farm workers, ordered by Caroline when London expenses required her to cut costs somewhere, was done with a minimum of ill-will, the men keeping their cottages and gaining work with the Navigation Company that enabled them to pay the rent. Nathan breathed a sigh of relief; another crisis averted. He wondered how long his good fortune would last.

Mary finished her work looking after the garden as soon as the Kellys had left, and it was Robert Osborne's servants who held the key to the padlocked vegetables and fruit trees. They came periodically and plucked whatever was ripe and in season for their own master's table, but did no gardening. The plants went to seed, and weeds grew in the neat rows that Mary had tended, the espaliered trees grew bushy and asymmetric, the raspberries and the blackcurrants marched forth unchecked across the paths.

The stables at Tineranna lay empty but for the four draught horses. Aidan was offered work by Richard Clarkson down river at O'Briensbridge, working with the stable of racehorses that he was building up; but though the work would have been easier than the virtual farm labouring he was now doing on Tineranna, he found he could not bring himself to leave the estate. The big house was beginning to need new paint on the window sills, and the lawns and flower beds were becoming too much for the skeleton staff to cope with; to leave the property to work somewhere else, even with his beloved horses, seemed to be the final act of betrayal to the place that had raised him.

Now, on gale days, when Nathan sat in the narrow office collecting the rents, Aidan went with his mother on an inspection of the house. For Caroline had left this instruction with Nathan, that it should be Mary O'Brien, daughter of the trusted housekeeper, who should take charge of the quarterly cleaning and airing of the house. In view of the Samhradh incident Mary would have liked to refuse Nathan, but the call of the big house was too much, and even Aidan felt its effect. He wandered alone through the halls while his mother, Anna O'Hagan and Maura O'Donoghue swept the carpets, removed the dust sheets and took them outside to be shaken, wiped down the mantelpieces and the ornate picture frames. His mother was unimpressed by the house, or made an appearance of being so before the other, younger women; for hadn't her mother been in charge here for thirty years? And hadn't Mary herself spent each day here as

107

a parlour maid, until her marriage? Mary was all business on gale days.

It was Aidan who went before them alone through the rooms, seeing the upstairs portions for the first time, feeling the presence of the Kellys everywhere; Devlin's bedroom with its deep blue drapes and ornate four-poster bed; Caroline's room in its shades of cream and rose; and William Kelly's room, where the tapestries of hunting scenes and outdoor fetes depicting men and women in strange and lavish costumes moved upon the walls almost as if alive in the faint draught from the door. Even empty for so long, there was a faint smell of leather, sandalwood and pipe tobacco that hung about the room and made the man's presence almost tangible.

He was filled with a strange restlessness after gale days, and would find himself walking to the O'Hagans' house in the evenings. He and Anna would sit before the fire and he would listen to her chatter of her impressions of Tineranna; she, too, was impressed by it, but by the luxury of it, the superficial trappings. Perhaps this helped put the place into perspective for him, there was always something sad, mysterious, almost portentious about the house that affected him deeply. To discuss the thickness of the rich carpets, the pattern in the Wedgewood dinner service, somehow enabled him to escape from his own uncharacteristically morbid thoughts.

Two days after gale day in summer, 1843, Anna walked with him halfway home through the lingering twilight. Climbing the hill across O'Sullivans' field, she broke a long silence to say, 'Ma and Da say y're not to visit alone anymore.'

He looked up, astounded. Her face was down, watching the grass at her feet. 'Why? What's wrong? I've done nothing. Sure they were grand with me just now . . . '

'You don't understand. This is the last time I'm allowed to walk with y' by myself, and that's only to tell you. Aidan, I'm turned twenty-two last February. My parents think it doesn't appear right that we're so often in each other's company. D' y' not understand?'

They had stopped walking, and he gazed at her in disbelief. Not to see her alone anymore? No clambering up the smaller hills of Slieve Bernagh, no walks beside the lough, no talks long into the dusks of summer, or beside the hearth in winter? Because she was now twenty-two?

'But we're friends!' he burst out. 'They know we're friends!'

'We can't be anymore! I have to have a husband, Aidan!'

The word hung in the air as if she had tried to conjure up the devil himself. A *husband*!

He was shouting. 'That's the most stupid thing I ever heard!

That's madness! What would you be wanting with a husband? Babies every washing day and plain hard work! Y'll get old before your time y' will! Old and scrawny and ugly! It's madness!'

He stormed on, up the hill, stopping after ten paces to find she was not following him. He stamped back to her, an idea born of desperation forming as he watched her face, merry with amusement.

'I'll marry you meself I will.'

'*What*?' Her eyes opened wide, 'Och, stop, Aidan! Y're a child!'

'I'm nearly twenty . . . !'

'You'll not be twenty 'til winter.'

'That's soon enough. I'm not a child . . . !'

'Aidan, stop.'

He stopped. They stared at each other, Aidan still angry, Anna with her usually tranquil features creased by a troubled frown. She loved him. They had never spoken of it, but both of them knew; they were too much a part of each other not to know. And Aidan's love for her shone out of his face with his despair. Anna thought her heart would break. The three years between their ages had never mattered, no more than the fact that his colouring was dark and hers fair. He was part of her, the most important person in her life. They thought, felt, dreamed alike . . .

Aidan's world was completely shaken. Having Anna with him was something that he had always taken for granted. They would always be together – they belonged together . . . How could her parents do this? The magnitude of the problem before him made him feel disarmed and helpless. He was losing her! Losing her to some spalpeen who'd . . . who'd lie with her, kiss her, place his hands upon her body . . . Hers! His Anna! His!

And they were rolling over and over in the grass, last year's thistles cracking and going down before them as their struggling bodies slid down the hill into them, nettles stinging their legs, all disregarded as they fought.

Anna could not speak, Aidan's lips pressed hard against hers, his tongue, bitten between her strong white teeth, still claiming, exploring her mouth, choking her cries. His emotions had found release in the cataclysmic awakening of his body, and he could no more have stopped than said, 'Go, marry whom you choose.' For she was his, his . . .

The force of his kiss pressed her head back upon the earth; he had both her hands pinned in his one above her head, and was groping surely up beneath her dress and petticoats . . . Drawers! Damn these O'Hagans and their pretensions at gentility! Drawers! And a strong drawstring held them tight around her waist. He tugged and fumbled at it while she writhed beneath him, took his mouth from hers to bellow, 'Where's the string t' these . . . !' But she began a scream, and he was forced hastily to close her mouth with his once more.

One of her hands came free – he had to use both his to imprison them again – and her knee, free of the emcumbrance of her skirt, came up between his legs with all the power of her young body behind it.

The explosion of agony blew him God-knew-where; he squirmed in some pain-filled purgatory between reality and unconsciousness, feeling his lower body crushed, mutilated, his stomach heaving, his lungs bursting. From somewhere far away he could hear Anna O'Hagan calling, 'Aidan! Aidan . . . !' Her voice would fade away then become clearer only to fade again . . .

He found he was breathing again; little gasps of cold air drawn into his lungs, he closed his mouth on the taste of bile, and something gritty – earth. His face was pressed into the ground, his body still dry-retching its protest. And from the blackness, 'Oh, Aidan – did I hurt you?'

'A-haugh!' A laugh, a choke, a shout; all he could manage through the pain. He willed his hand out, could not feel it moving, but willed it out towards her voice.

She was holding it, when he opened his eyes. Moreover she lay on the ground close beside him, her handkerchief in her other hand, dabbing at his face. He closed his eyes, smiling, and after a moment felt the weight of her head descend hesitatingly to his chest. He was breathing easier, now, though his lower body hurt like the devil and every nerve in him seemed ready to scream. Somehow Anna's hair so close to his face, smelling faintly of lemon soap, the feel of her breathing and the warmth of her coming slowly through his shirt was comforting. They lay there for a long time, then he said slowly, 'If this is love, then I'll join the priesthood so I will.'

'You'll make a poor priest if that's all the self-control you're possessing.'

'I dunno what came over me – God's truth. You believe me, don't you? I've always treated you with respect, have I not?'

'You have. 'Til today.'

'Jaysus . . . ' The enormity of what he had attempted suddenly dawned upon him, and he wiped a hand across his eyes as if the gesture could as easily take the memory from him. 'Jaysus – I was an animal, wasn't I? What would Father O'Callaghan say?'

'I shouldn't tell him if I were you.' Her body was trembling slightly, and he realized that she was laughing. He placed an arm

about her shoulders, smiling through his discomfort. '*Gra gal . . .* '
he murmured, 'My heart's love . . . '

'Oh, Aidan, y've a poet's soul, sure.'

'Stop coddin' me. I may be three years younger than you but I'm
stronger, begod.'

'That you are.'

'Today has taught us that, at least.'

'It has.'

'And I'll take no more nonsense about marryin', understand?'

'Aidan, Ma and Da . . . '

'You say no. Just that. Every slicked-up boyo who comes courtin'
y' – y' say no. And keep saying no. Until I'm old enough and wealthy
enough to bring you home. Mother of Mercy, Anna – could you be
happy with anyone else but me?'

She opened her eyes, amused by his arrogance, and propping
herself up on to one elbow, gazed into the depths of the wide-set
dark eyes, at the stubborn jawline and the mouth that promised both
strength and humour. 'No,' she said gently, 'no, I could not.'

The clouds were pink and gold and lilac in the east. They brushed
themselves off as best they could and started once more up
O'Sullivans field. Aidan walked with difficulty and his legs felt
weak, but it was only when they were nearing the crest of the hill that
Anna said, 'Aidan, will y' be able to climb the fence all right?'

He took a deep breath, 'Tonight,' he said, surveying the four foot
wall before him, ' I shall take the gate.'

They stood there a moment, hesitated, then, gently, he leaned
over and kissed her mouth, briefly. Even then the wakening
response of his body caused him to grimace in discomfort. 'Get you
on home, now, they'll be worrying about you.'

'And rightly.' She flashed a quick smile at him, then she turned
and ran off, back the way they had come.

Reaching home, her parents put the flushed cheeks and non-
communicative manner down to disappointment and chagrin over
Aidan. She had fought bitterly against the edict, and they, too, were
upset for her. But facts had to be faced; she was of a marriageable age
and comfortable background – her only brother being a sickly child
of three, Anna, as eldest daughter, might yet inherit the farm – it was
important that she find a capable husband, from comparable background, who would help her look after the place.

'It's for your own sake, Anna.' Her mother stood worriedly over
her in the meagre illumination of the candle.

Anna, lying in the large bed beside her two sleeping sisters, said,
'Yes, Ma.'

111

'For after all, once you're safely married and settled, you'll be able to bring Aidan to your house as your husband's friend. He's a fine boy, Aidan – I don't know any finer – but he belongs to your childhood, and that's over, now.'

Anna flushed, remembering the force of Aidan's mouth, the strange and terrifying pleasure of his hand on her thigh . . . 'Yes, Ma.'

When she fell asleep it was to dream innocent, comforting dreams of him. Once they were by a pool, gazing at their reflections; another time they were walking along the boreen leading to his house, and somewhere, someone was calling his name. 'Aidan O'Brien!' And again, louder, hostile, now, 'Aidan O'Brien!' It was her father's voice.

She sat up in the dark of the room, conscious that her two small sisters had stirred also. They were two years apart in age, Eileen and Deirdre, but of a size and so much alike in their fair looks that strangers often took them for twins. They sat bolt upright beside Anna now; she could see the pale blurs of their faces. Ma's voice could be heard murmuring something low, persistent – and then another voice, a woman's, unrecognizable.

The door opened, and Ma entered, again holding the candle. At the same time Da was shouting, 'I don't care! It's done! Even if no one knows! It's done!'

Ma was saying quietly, 'Get dressed, Anna, and come into the room.' She left the candle on a stool and went back to the kitchen. Anna pulled on her clothes, her heart beating hard with fear, listening to the low fluttering of the women's voices, the ominous dull deepness of her father's voice, like the beginnings of a storm wind across the lough.

Oona O'Sullivan it was who sat there by the hearth opposite Anna's mother. Oona O'Sullivan whose thin face and embittered expression was lit into almost prettiness by the flushed look of triumph she turned on the girl. Before Anna could understand its meaning, her father, standing ramrod straight before the fire barked, 'Is it true?'

'Da . . . ?'

'Is it true what Mrs O'Sullivan says to us? That you and Aidan O'Brien lay together in her field tonight?'

They had been seen! She turned startled eyes to Oona. The sallow face was serious, demure; the momentary beauty lent by malicious vantage had left her. She looked as she was, a dried up, still drying, young woman, burdened with a good-natured drunkard of a husband and too many children too soon. Her youth had been the first

112

thing to dry up, then the light in her eyes, the softness of her skin. Her womb would be the last thing to dry up. She dried from the outside in. Anna looked at her with ill-disguised animosity. What right did she have to spoil this new, this beautiful thing between herself and Aidan? What right did she have to use their love as a mouthpiece for her own bitterness? Anna glowered. 'We wrestled. That's all. We did nothing wrong.'

'Anna, it's shame you've brought on us! Shame!' Tears started in Kitty O'Hagan's eyes.

Oona clucked sympathetically, 'Pray don't upset yourself, Mrs O'Hagan. I only came t' tell you before it became the gossip of Killaloe.'

'You did rightly, Mrs O'Sullivan.' Paddy O'Hagan glanced at her, 'And we're obliged to y'.' To Anna he said, 'Well, are y' satisfied that y've brought this dishonour to us? I ought t' be flingin' y' out of the house! Stoned, y' should be, like they did in old times! You were there at Mass last Sunday! You heard Father O'Callaghan read from the Bible about daughters who played the harlot in their father's house . . . !'

'Da, I've never done such a thing . . . !'

'Stoned, y' should be!'

Her mother rocked back and forth on her stool in agony, 'Oh, the shame! How can we hold our heads up . . . '

'But we didn't . . . !'

'To play the whore after the decent upbringing we've given y'!'

'We rolled around a bit on the grass, Da!'

'Mother of Mercy, I'm so ashamed!'

'Whore! Harlot!'

The little boy, Michael, had awoken at last and ran into the room; clutching at the hunched shoulders of his hysterical mother and gaining no recognition, he added his own feeble wail to the clamouring. Eileen and Deirdre crept from their room and stood in their nightgowns in pale amazement against the wall.

'I ought t' shoot him. The little fox! The sly young creepin' devil! Both of y' shot!'

'Da, I tell you I never . . . !'

' . . . In an open field with 'im, y' little slut!'

'Holy Mary, Mother of God . . . ' her mother moaned.

'Y'll have to marry him, now, damn his eyes! Y'll have to marry him as soon as we can arrange it!'

All three women gazed at him in horror. Even Oona O'Sullivan thought this was going too far. She ventured, 'But Mister O'Hagan – he's only nineteen . . . and his prospects, as a stable hand . . . '

Paddy faltered a little. He'd forgotten that. The boy was tough, well-proportioned, mature, somehow. Paddy began to have doubts. There was a rumour that Master Devlin disliked Aidan – if he should lose his employment . . .

'Well . . . ' he growled, 'betrothed, then, until he has some security to offer her.' He whirled on Anna, 'To bed with y' now. I'm sick t' look on y', that I am! Get away!'

In the bedroom Anna chose to lie closest to the wall. When Eileen and Deirdre questioned her she was silent, her face turned from them. After a while they heard her crying; the bed moved with her sobs. They left her alone.

But Anna was laughing. Laughing at Oona O'Sullivan, at her parents, at the irony of a fate which had punished her by giving her what she had most wanted, yet dared not hope to possess.

12

The scene between Paddy O'Hagan and Mary O'Brien the next morning was a violent one. Mary was alone in the cottage, for Aidan was at Tineranna and Thomas had, since the previous autumn, been working as a dockman on the river trade, and she was horrified and frightened at O'Hagan's rage. She refused to believe that any indecency had taken place. Lord, was the man a fool not to know that his own daughter could be trusted? And Aidan – he was a boy. He did not look at Anna in that way, did not consider her as a woman – and desirable. Mary rounded on O'Hagan, once he had stopped his ravings of sin and shame, without, herself, clearly thinking the matter through. She refused to discuss it with him, she said, until she had spoken with her son. Yes, even then she refused to speak to him, evil-minded as he was. He was to send Anna and his wife that evening. She would not stand his recriminations a minute longer.

Paddy was not a strong man. His rage was born mostly of a fear for his own good name and a bitter resentment against this threat to his usually calm existence. He had always admired Mary O'Brien, her resilience as a woman alone, rearing sons. He grudgingly admired her even more, now, standing before him bristling like some wild, dark cat, protecting her own. His invective ran out like the last drops of foul water from a pump, and he replaced his hat grimly and left.

114

She had been sewing a new shirt for Thomas, but now, though she seated herself and took up the work, the needle stayed idle in her hand, and she stared blindly into the hearth. She would go and find Corrie.

She did not want to, sat there arguing with herself against the subtle dependency he had built within her, denying her need of him. After all, what could he say to her? Could he know more of the workings of Aidan's mind than she did herself? And then she reminded herself that her son was no longer her baby, her child. He was grown to manhood, was accused of actual intercourse. Lord God! How was she to broach this with Aidan? She wished suddenly, fervently, for daughters – one could speak of such things with daughters . . .

Her shawl was about her shoulders and she was out the door, closing it behind her and facing a light, clear day, Lough Derg throwing a bright blue reflection back at the sky. She passed the O'Sullivans', her eyes in front of her, not daring to look at the cottage, not daring to trust herself yet to speak to Oona. Children were playing in the boreen but Mary walked through them unseeingly, as if they were no more than a flock of geese. She could feel Oona gazing after her from the window. There would be time to speak her mind to that meddling witch when she had the whole truth.

It was nearly a mile along the road towards Killaloe to Ceelohg, past the two dozen or so cottiers' hovels, windowless, evil-smelling. The children were thin, unhealthy-looking in their pallor; it was the meal months again, the last of the potatoes were being eked out while the new crop greened and matured in the small plots at the rear of the cabins. These families would be living on one meal of potatoes a day. Sometimes not that. Mary shivered as she passed them. It did not seem so long ago that she had brushed close to their desperation.

When she reached Ceelohg's forge it was to find it empty. A stable boy told her that Corrie was checking rabbit snares that morning, and he pointed up into the hills on the far side of the road. It did not occur to Mary to turn back at this stage, though it was a steep climb up to where the trees darkened the hill's crest. Her chances of finding Corrie within the narrow paths through the forest were remote, but she kept walking because she could not face the return to the cottage, to the waiting.

But Corrie saw her approaching. She had her head down for most of the climb, out of breath, concentrating on each step, thinking of him; finally she looked up to see him standing there above her, the rust brown of his jacket and trousers against the branches of the larch and birch trees making him seem to have sprung from the wood itself. He held four dead rabbits, the soft bodies swinging slightly in his grasp.

He smiled at her, his eyes sliding over her figure, taking in the swing of her skirt from her hips, the way her laboured breathing pressed the thin material of her blouse against her breasts, full breasts, heavy for a woman of her size. A wisp of dark hair clung to her forehead with perspiration, her cheeks were pink . . . She had come looking for him. Unheard of in all these years of his patient waiting. His smile slowly broadened with this knowledge. But, 'What's wrong?' he asked.

'I . . . ' She faltered. How to begin? Without realizing, she had placed a hand on his sleeve.

Corrie held her to him, feeling the fire that always smouldered for her within him leap suddenly in his loins. And she had come looking for him! He became conscious of the covering of the forest behind him, had stepped back in order to draw her with him between the trees.

'It's Aidan. And . . . and Anna. There's . . . they say they've been . . . Oona O'Sullivan told Paddy O'Hagan – she saw them . . . 'she began to peter out as she saw his face harden. ' . . . In the grass . . . ' she finished lamely, wondering at this strangeness come over him, the twisted mouth more wry, the eyes narrowed. The hands that held her above the elbows were tightening, tightening . . . Was he so angry? She did not realize his morals were so strong . . . did he not wish to be involved? She wished she had not told him. She felt a flush of shame creep up from her neck and began to turn away. But the hands on her arms were like iron bands. 'Corrie – y'r hurtin' me . . . !'

'I ought to have known . . . ' Quietly.

'Known what?' She was afraid of him, now, somehow. In the five or six years of what she termed their friendship they had not been as close as this since the day Samhradh was taken. Corrie had not dared to come so close, but Mary, never fully awakened sexually, could not reason why, and after a while had accepted the relationship as it was. 'Corrie . . . ' She smiled at him, he liked her to tease him, 'Corrie, you must help me – I don't know where to turn . . . '

'Aidan,' he said heavily. 'And Anna. Have been lyin' together. Is that it?'

Her flush deepened. 'Well, that's what . . . '

'A girl of marriageable age and a boy who knows what's between his legs and what it's for . . . '

'Corrie!'

116

'And you're surprised at it.'

'It's a sin! A sin, and you know it!'

'They're in love! Always have been! You knew they'd marry! It's natural for them to find each other, want to know each others' bodies . . . '

'Corrie, let me go . . . '

'Why is it a sin? Because they're not married? There's no one else in their lives, only each other. They'll marry eventually.'

'I thought you could help me! I see now you won't! I was wrong . . . !'

'What would you have me do? Talk to Aidan? Tell him to behave himself? He's a man, now. Why should he not have what is his right? Why should he not lie with the woman he loves?'

And she stopped struggling in his grasp, and gazed up into the tortured eyes and heard beyond the words. She realized, suddenly, what these years had been for him. Not content, complete as they had been for her. Years of pain. Waiting, waiting . . .

'Oh, my dear . . . ' She was against his chest, her eyes closed. 'Must we speak of this now? You've waited so long, can't we . . . '

'I've waited long enough. I've waited for you to come to me, more fool that I am. It's done, now. Over.'

For a few seconds she gazed into his obdurate face with a feeling of terror that he meant not to see her again. But he had taken her arm and walked back into the forest. Mary had to follow, her skirt clinging to the deep grass, tripping her. Light branches parted for him and flew back, slapping her face and body. 'Corrie!'

In a space beneath a gnarled oak whose wide-reaching branches created a large and green-tinted dome above them, he turned to her once more. 'It's over,' he repeated. 'The waiting's over.'

She stood there a long time. Only one of the great hands held her arm, not tightly. She could have run. But all the frustrated passion of those years was upon his face, and she knew she had hurt him enough. It was more, too, than her comfortable love for him. Her eyes were level with the lower button on his shirt. The skin of his chest was brown and matted with grey hair. Often her eyes had sought that place, wondered at the difference of him, the foreign, maleness of him. She reached her hand up now and touched it, felt the hair spring slightly beneath the pressure of her palm. Some half-forgotten feeling stirred, deep in her. She took a little intake of breath. 'Yes,' she said.

He was knowledgeable, gentle, as patient and as controlled in this as in all things. He was as proud of his lovemaking as he was of his fighting, his ability as a blacksmith; as modest about it as a man can

117

be only when he is completely sure of himself. Women, well-educated, articulate women, who knew all the ways of loving and were not shy to speak their needs had taught him a great deal. He was looking forward to teaching these things to the frightened woman now trembling beneath him, her black hair, which he had loosened, spread out upon the grass around her. She would not look at his body, kept nervously trying to cover her own. He felt a pity for her, and suddenly remembered Lady – what was her name? – who had had him move every large mirror she could find into positions around the bed and then had stood on a stool and made him rub cream on to her naked body while she surveyed herself from every angle.

Mary drew herself back from a trough of the waves of pleasure that were beginning to come with his slow caresses, to gaze up at him worriedly.

'Why are you smiling?'

'Because I'm happy,' he said.

He picked her up like a child in his arms and carried her down the hill. She squealed and laughed and scolded that someone would see them. He replied grimly that he hoped they would. In case she thought to change her mind it would help if Father O'Callaghan added his persuasion, in the interests of morality.

He would not let her put up her hair, and it blew about them in the wind. She buried her head in his neck, holding tightly to the massive shoulders, smelling the soon-to-be-familiar odour of his skin. Her body felt sticky, evil and glowing, somehow. She had not climaxed, but never having known one, did not feel disappointed, was rather pleased to hold on to the pleasure.

Corrie knew this, but was content, for the moment. It was not much different, schooling horses or women. One didn't ask too much, too soon. He felt younger, powerful, secure that this woman would love him for ever. She had been worth all the bother. They had a lot of time to discover each other. He tossed her into the air a little, and caught her, laughing. They had a lot of time.

When Aidan finished feeding and watering the draught horses that evening, he found Corrie waiting for him outside the stables. 'Come,' he said, rising from his seat on the edge of the water trough, 'I'll walk home with you.'

They took the long way, round by the Killaloe road and up the boreen, not cutting through the fields and over O'Sullivans' wall.

118

And all the way they talked. Corrie was blunt and noncommittal in the retelling of Paddy O'Hagan's story, Aidan ashamed, vehement in his assertions that nothing more intimate than a wrestling match had taken place.

'I would have liked it otherwise,' he admitted, gazing up at the giant's profile challengingly, 'but she wouldn't – and I'm glad, now. I don't want her to be ashamed. I want it to be right between us. I want to marry her one day.'

'Well, it seems you'll get your wish,' Corrie said mildly. Aidan stared up at him. 'The O'Hagans will insist on a betrothal . . . '

'Will they?' His eyes were alight. Anna – Anna betrothed to him! Promised to be *his* wife! He had unconsciously quickened his step, felt the spring in his boots, wanted to gambol a little, to run all the way to the cottage . . .

Corrie's hand on his arm was as heavy as a boulder. 'Have you thought of your mother? You can't go dancing in there as if it's the best news you've heard this twelve month.'

Aidan stopped, stiffened. They gazed at each other. 'Lord, she'll be shamed. Shamed before all the neighbours . . . And mad – she'll be spittin' mad at me!' Suddenly getting home was not such a pleasant prospect at all. 'It must be faced, I suppose.' His shoulders came back a little. 'After all, I'm tryin' to do the right thing, aren't I?'

Corrie suppressed a smile. 'I think your mother will understand,' he said, as they fell into step once more.

'You don't know my mother as I do.'

'No,' carefully, 'but we had a talk this afternoon. I think she'll understand.'

'How do you *know*?' the boy insisted, but Corrie had put on a longer stride and was out in front of Aidan, signalling an end to the conversation.

When they entered the cottage, Anna was seated by the fire, her hands in her lap, demure beneath her mother's gaze. When she saw Aidan her face lit up; and Mary, watching him, saw the desire in his eyes as he looked at the girl. Dark, those eyes, and so like her husband's, his father's, that an irrational jealousy rose like bile in her chest and throat. Had she been blind? He did look at her in that way. He did. He had a man's knowledge, now. He was no longer a part of her, he was gone from her for ever.

A shifting of space, a sudden filling of the atmosphere around her, an intangible sensation of pressure . . . Corrie was standing behind her, not touching her, his head held, she knew without looking, at just such a casual angle that he could see her face. She felt her mind being scraped, felt at once violated and less alone. Corrie . . . Corrie . . .

The following day, the first thing Anna did was to call on Maura O'Donoghue, and to take her walking in Tineranna's overgrown gardens.

'And I'll wear Ma's wedding dress, of course. I showed it to you, once, do you remember it? Sure, there's not a grander bridal gown in all of Clare! Why, I'll bet Caroline Kelly didn't have a finer one . . .' Anna trailed off a little. She was puzzled, had brought Maura to the rather poetic setting of the little bridge over the pond on this, the first morning of her betrothal to Aidan, so as to have the right atmosphere for her announcement – and Maura merely stared at her, the thin little neck held stiffly, as if a sudden move would shatter her. Anna was a little piqued; she wanted squeals, hugs, delighted congratulations, and plans, wonderful plans that she could make and dream about with her friend . . .

Her friend turned and walked off the bridge, went slowly along beside the water's edge, and Anna stared after her. What was wrong, what had she said? She hurried after Maura. 'We'll make a new dress for you, also; something in a peach colour, that would suit your colouring so . . .' Anna had taken Maura's arm in hers, but Maura shook her off.

'I don't want a new dress for your wedding.' The voice was savage through pale, set lips. 'I'll not come to your wretched . . . ridiculous wedding!'

Anna stood, as pale as if Maura had slapped her face, hard. She murmured, 'Maura . . .'

There were tears in Maura's eyes, her eyes filled with them and looked emerald green, a deeper colouring than Anna had ever seen in their depths. The tears did not spill over, they stayed, while Maura worked her small mouth, half-speaking, changing her mind, and finally saying, her voice a little lower, but no less bitter for all that, 'You're very stupid, Anna. And you're vain. You can honestly think no further than walking down the aisle of a church in your mother's gown. As if that's all that marriage means. Lots of babies to Aidan O'Brien – is that what you want? Then don't expect me to be happy for you, for you're a fool!'

Anna smiled a little. 'But I *do* want lots of Aidan's babies – it's perfectly natural, Maura. What's the matter with you?'

Maura had turned away. This time Anna did not follow her as she walked off, slowly, along one of the paths. What was the matter with

120

the girl? She was being so silly – it was almost as if she were jealous . . . Anna ran along the path. 'It won't change anything, you know. We'll still be friends!' she called to the unforgiving, narrow little back, 'I'd miss you too much, if we didn't see each other, Maura. We've been friends for so long. Nothing will change!'

Maura stopped, turned. For a long moment she regarded Anna, who slowed, waiting. 'Yes,' Maura said, 'we'll still be friends.'

'It won't be happening for a long time, yet. The wedding, I mean. Two years at least . . . '

'Oh . . . ' Maura, it seemed to Anna, looked a little happier at this.

'Things will go on as they are, so. And we won't talk about it again, if you like.' Anna caught up with her friend.

'I don't mind talking about it.' Maura smiled, if a little shakily. 'I was just . . . surprised, that's all.'

'You thought, "Now everything's going to be changed . . . " '

'Aye, I did, sure.'

'Aren't you a little eejit . . . '

Maura found herself being hugged. She patted Anna's back, disentangled herself, and fell into step with the older girl, back towards the bridge, 'Aye . . . ' she murmured. Then, brighter, 'But . . . it's silly not to talk about it. I'm . . . I'm used to the idea, now. You must tell me what he said, how it happened. You must tell me everything.'

13

There were rumours in the village about Aidan O'Brien and Anna O'Hagan, but no one who knew them was particularly surprised about the betrothal. Aidan had always been fairly mature for his age, and the two had been friends for so very long. Besides, it was a good time for betrothals, for young marriages; with the bad times behind them and the future looking bright for crops and prices, more people were marrying young, having families. All over Ireland, the population was growing, at a surprising, almost alarming rate.

Yet all was not birth and beginnings. Robert Osborne, the genial and generous Englishman, died of a heart attack only weeks after Mary and Corrie were married, in August, 1843. His funeral was one of the largest in the history of the town, and for days a steady stream of visitors came to his grave beneath the shadow of St Flannan's square turret. His tenants particularly mourned him, and waited in apprehension for the arrival of Osborne's brother from England.

Thomas, to the wonderment of the village, left his work as a dock-man, and became a fisherman, late that same year. He had always loved the river, had hoped for this opportunity for years. But even then, the means of his success were not what he would have wished.

The community of men that fished the Shannon and Lough Derg were a close and jealous bunch. There were those who belonged to fishing families, and those who did not, and Thomas did not. All the fishermen had sons or brothers or nephews who went out with them, rowing on the still water of the lake, or poling the boat in the rapids near the bridge, holding it steady while the lines were set. Thomas had watched this every morning before he went to school; the men part of a canvas in tones of grey and pink and pearl, at one with the roar and hiss of the white water beneath them. It appealed to the romantic in Thomas, to the dreaming patience of him. There were seasons here on the water, the treachery was one of Nature's, not Man's. He could be happy, here. He went many times to Fish Row, spoke to small brown leather-skinned men bent-shouldered in their woollen jerseys. But all had sons, brothers, nephews.

So Thomas worked on the shore, carrying goods to and fro from the many boats and ships. And at Mass on Sundays, and whenever opportunity presented itself, he studied Maura O'Donoghue. Sharp, she was, so sharp; always a quip on her lips, the smart answer for everything. She liked Thomas, he knew, because he laughed a lot at her words. Thomas had a lot of laughter in him, a lot of good feelings to give, but no smart answers, no fast words. Maura on the other hand, had always had the answers – yet no laughter. It was strange.

Thomas began to feel responsible, he wanted to grow up quickly, be a man, earn money and respect. He continued to pester the fisherfolk in the village.

In December, 1843, a storm blew up suddenly, just before dawn. The fishermen, undaunted, went out. One boat did not return. The bell from St Flannan's rang dolorously at four p.m., and the villagers paused at their work, looked at each other, crossed themselves. The three sons of old Packy Brady were being carried into Killaloe for the last time.

Three days after the funeral, the old man, more stooped, grey-faced beneath his tan, came to the O'Brien cottage and asked for Thomas.

122

Now, like Aidan, he was independent; a man, at last. And the first person that he sought out, to share his hopes for the future, was Maura.

He found her walking with her younger sister, Bridie, down by the lough, and waited until the little girl had seen some of her friends and run off to play before he spoke seriously.

''Twas a tragedy, right enough, but with me there, Packy won't be alone working the nets, and I'll be where I've always wished to be.'

'On a boat?' Maura's eyes were following the younger children, chasing each other up the slope of *Beal Boru*, Brian Boru's fort, the high, circular wall of earth now the only sign that a fortress had once stood there. Maura laughed. 'It's mad you are, Thomas O'Brien. You could work in a store, or an office – you were clever with figures at school. Bobbing about on that white water, with those rocks waiting to tear the bottom out of your craft – that's a fierce foolish career.'

Thomas did not know whether to be flattered or hurt. He searched about for something positive to say. 'Your mother needn't bother buying fish each Friday, now. I shall bring some. For free.'

'Thank you. How wonderful. Sure you're the soul of thoughtfulness.' She had only glanced at him during this speech, and to her amazement Thomas did not seem to notice the sarcasm.

'Sure it's nothing. 'Twould be an excuse to see you.'

She turned to find him blushing, his thin, good-looking face lit by a foolish smile.

Well. So that was how it was. Maura felt a gratifying wave of pleasure sweep through her, and she studied Thomas in this new light. Not simply a friend she had known since childhood. Not simply an appendage to Aidan O'Brien, but a young man who found her attractive, who wanted to be with her.

He shuffled his feet, uneasy yet pleased to be the subject of her scrutiny. In lowering his head to gaze at the ground, she could see how dark his eyelashes were, how well-formed his features, how soft the dark, waving hair that the wind blew across his forehead. Much better-looking than his surly brother. Much better-tempered, a nicer boy altogether . . .

And she turned away in impatience, for she could not bear to look at the round-shouldered, smiling coyness of him, the bright openness of his face, the joy he had in being with her – all were an affront.

Why, she thought, I could lead you about as if with a collar and chain. You'd never stand your ground, never fight back. You'd look at me like a spaniel who's been whipped for no reason. A spaniel,

123

that's what you are, with your soft eyes and your eagerness to please.

'I'm going home, now,' she said, and turned away, her chest suddenly aching with a nameless sort of pain that needed thinking over, brooding over . . . She called Bridie, who ignored her.

'I'll walk with you . . . ' Thomas was saying.

'No!' As his long legs matched their stride to hers. They stopped. She turned to glare furiously at Bridie, then turned the same gaze to Thomas. 'I want to walk alone.' She did not care if she was being rude, for the more she looked at that face which was so like and so unlike Aidan O'Brien's, the angrier she became. 'I want to be alone, don't you see?'

'Well . . . yes.' He took a step backwards and stumbled on a loose stone, stood looking at her with his dark spaniel eyes, and his dog-like acceptance of her, and she turned and ran, not stopping when his voice came to her. 'I'll call to see you – if I may.'

'Yes!' she called over her shoulder, 'Yes, sometime . . . '

'And you call to see me – will ye?'

She stopped abruptly. Stood still, then turned slowly. He stood with his head bent forward, his gaze on her face, awaiting her reply.

She bit her lip, then found herself smiling a little; the weight in her chest had lifted slightly. 'Visit you . . . Your mother won't mind?'

'Och, no. You . . . you'll come, then?'

She took a deep breath. 'Yes,' she said, softly. 'Yes, I'll come.'

Mary O'Brien had hoped, on marrying Corrie O'Neill, that they might have children together. Yet the months passed, and no child came. Corrie, philosophical, did not seem to mind. It was hardest on Mary, and made harder by the laughter that floated down the hill from O'Sullivans. Twelve children, Oona O'Sullivan had borne. And all were living. Thin, fox-faced children, all alike. Puny and mewling when they were born, not fine, healthy babies as Mary's had been. And Oona was tired, screamed at the children, was exhausted further with each pregnancy, each giving of life. Mary longed for it, and hated Oona with a vengeance.

As time passed, Mary gave up hoping, instead turning to Corrie for consolation, planning with him improvements to the cottage and to the new half-acre he had rented behind the present potato field.

He was still working at Ceelohg, and chafed sometimes under the yoke of the new owners, Edward Osborne and his son, Hubert. They were quickly eradicating the goodwill attached to their name; had raised the rents to double that they had been under the old master. Now, in 1844, some tenants were threatened with eviction, but as the crops were good, the rents – high as they were – were paid promptly on most gale days. But the warmth that had existed between landlord and tenant, and had made Ceelohg exemplary in the parish, was gone. The estate was a business, crops and rent. Not people. The people were incidental, replaceable. If the tenants gave up the farms there would always be others to take them up. Land was the only means of livelihood; there were starving people even in these days of prosperity. People on Ceelohg and indeed every estate, hoarded and saved each penny towards the rents, the presence of the itinerant beggars a constant reminder of what happens when their potato fields are no longer their own.

The rents on Tineranna, too, were raised in 1845, but again, the tenants paid. There was no choice, no higher authority to whom they could go. Corrie found the rent on the cottage almost doubled because he, Aidan and Thomas had built an extra room on to the back; a separate kitchen for the moment, but it would be Aidan's and Anna's, eventually.

Corrie remonstrated with Nathan Cameron about the raised rent, calmly, but towering over the little man in such a tilted and threatening pose that Nathan's palms began to sweat.

'It's not my doing,' he said, 'I sent my report to Master Devlin – I mean, Mister Kelly – and had t' mention the addition. He drew up the rent prices, not me. I just got t' collect 'em.' And this was true.

Nathan was paler, thinner than ever, now. His hair was whitening quickly, and his skin was translucent, somehow, as if all his energy went into the running of Tineranna and there was little left over for himself. 'I do my job as best I can,' he told Aidan and Corrie. 'I didn't ask for it, but it's all I've got. If I'm dismissed, I'm finished.' And this, too, was true.

Property was everything. If one owned land, the law stood by one's shoulder. The melodramas of forty years later that would make clichés of people cast out into the snow, would raise no laughter in Ireland. It happened. Whole families would be thrust forcibly from their cottages, the children to die in ditches, the babies to freeze at their mothers' breasts. It was not murder. It was the landlord's right. And if the workhouses were full, and the benevolent groups were already struggling hopelessly to cope, then it was no one's concern. The money from these years of good harvests went to pay mortgages on most of the estates in Ireland, or to keep the owners, living for years in England.

On the plantations, large and small, in the South of the United States, the slaves were fed and housed; though regarded as little more than animals, still their lives were valued. The lives of the peasant population of Ireland in the early 1840s were valueless. More than half of the country's eight million people lived in a state of degradation and starvation unparalleled in the western world. Ireland was without equal, without equity, without hope.

In Killaloe the number of people whose poverty bordered on the starvation level was low, about an eighth of the population; fairly favourable compared to most parts of Ireland. Yet even these cottiers did not see themselves as part of an impoverished whole. The problems in their lives could not be political ones, when the decision of the day was how to make three potatoes feed four people, or six, or ten. And if there were potatoes enough there was the rent, the crops, the fear of cholera or typhoid, the whims of the landlord or his agent – always something immediate, personal.

So the rumours of a new potato disease in other countries raised discussions and apprehensions, but no real fear. The cottiers returned from their jobs of harvesting corn and oats on the estates, and gazed at their own single acre of potatoes in some pride and satisfaction. It would be a good year.

In February of 1844, Anna O'Hagan had taken the position of maid to two elderly ladies in the village. Molly Curran had found the position for her, and helped persuade her parents into letting her accept it. It had piqued their pride somewhat; they were comfortably off, they did not want the village saying that they had to put their daughter out to work. But Anna wanted to go. She had seen the two women, the Misses Fredericks, often. They were the maiden sisters of the curate of St Flannan's Cathedral, the thirteenth-century Gothic church, now Protestant, whose great square turret dominated the Killaloe skyline. The Misses Fredericks had been Belfast born and raised, and their manners and knowledgeable dress sense fascinated Anna. They went on regular shopping trips to Dublin, returning with much finery with which to dazzle the villagers. It was their one vanity. They were kind and good-natured, if a little self-centred, and after a while Anna began to feel very fortunate, being so close to a sophistication she had never known, and she watched, and learned, with a great deal of interest.

Aidan did not seem to share her feelings on the matter. They went walking one afternoon, on one of Anna's rare days off, and strolled through the tangle of spring growth in the now unkempt grounds of Tineranna. She had suggested the walk, but seemed preoccupied to Aidan, barely concentrating on his words.

'You'll be leaving the Misses Fredericks soon, though,' Aidan was prompting. 'You'll not want to keep working there after we're married, I hope.'

'I hardly think they'd allow you to sleep in the attic with me. But they might let me live out . . . '

'It's too far from Tineranna. Anyway, I'll want you at home.' He scowled at her. 'You do still want to marry me, don't y'?'

'Oh, you know I do!' She had placed an arm through his impulsively, then hesitated, as he was about to kiss her, and let him go. She faced him earnestly, 'I'm learning things, Aidan. How to set a dinner table, and what proper manners are, and all about clothes and being a lady . . . ' She stopped at the growing look of distrust on his face, then burst out, 'Oh, don't spoil it for me! I'll know that life for such a little time!'

He gazed into her face as if struck. He lived for the day he could take her home to the cottage on the lough. A bed in their own room . . . It was a thought that he kept before him constantly. It was a goal, the reason why he had worked so hard, putting shillings by in a piece of calico beneath his mattress. When the potatoes were harvested and sold, he would have twenty pounds. Enough, even, to take land of their own, a whole cottage to themselves! But to Anna this was not the focal point of her existence. She loved him, he knew it, but the new room at the cottage meant an end to a pleasurable way of life for her, the beginnings of household chores, motherhood, drudgery . . . And he felt a keen twist of pain that this was all he could offer her – and himself, his love for her. But she was strong, he told himself, as he himself was strong. Their love was not a dependence, a crutch, a grasping need for reassurance. If it had been they would have defied everyone and married long ago. It was a warm thing, dependable, sure.

But his desire for her body was no comfortable sensation. It was more and more difficult to keep his thoughts from her, his hands off her. The desire was a thing apart, it boiled in his blood. And she was asking him to wait.

'You're twenty-four,' he said fiercely, to cover the confusion of his feelings, to still his understanding of her. 'You'll be an old maid, soon.'

'That I won't.' Her smile was superior. 'There's plenty of men in Killaloe who'd have me at thirty-four, let alone twenty-four.'

'You think so?' He half-smiled, scowling at her.

'Yes. Because I'm pretty and I'm clever . . . '

'And humble as a nun.'

'No.' She showed her white teeth in a laughing smile. 'I'm not humble. But neither are you. We're well-matched in our arrogance at least. Come, Aidan – please don't scowl at me – promise we'll wait another year?' Her grey eyes were widened to him pleadingly. She looked beautiful, with her thick brown-gold hair up in braids on her head. To look so appealing at that critical moment did not help her cause at all.

'No,' he said. 'We'll be married after harvesting.'

'Aidan . . .'

'After harvesting. We've waited long enough.' His face was determined, his eyes burnt into hers; the very closeness of his body was suddenly a kind of threat. 'You don't know what it's been like! You . . . ' he faltered. 'You don't know.'

She was buoyed up by a kind of power. He was admitting that he wanted her! She had begun to forget the physical part of loving – beneath the watchful vigilance of her parents all these years, their relationship had reverted, much of the time, to the gentle friendship of their childhood. She remembered, suddenly, that grappling tumble in O'Sullivan's paddock. Aidan had not forgotten, she was sure. Why, he probably thinks of it quite often . . .

'After harvest,' he repeated. 'Or I'll know that y' don't love me at all.'

'But I do!'

'After harvest, then.'

'Aidan, y'r not fair.' But secretly she was glad that his need of her was so great, and she admired him for taking a stand. She wanted to marry him. She liked the feeling when they stood close together and his dark eyes looked searchingly through her. She turned to him, now, and without speaking, as if he knew her thoughts, he folded her in his arms, held her to him . . .

It began to rain, sparse, heavy drops, and they both looked up, then laughed into each other's face. 'Jaysus, Mary and . . . ' Aidan began to swear, but Anna took his hand, began to run. Together they raced across the overgrown lawn, pushed through the rioting scarlet rhododendrons that bordered the path. Suddenly she was gone from beside him.

'Over here!' Anna was running, her petticoats flying, through the now teeming rain, towards the kitchen door of the big house. Aidan had been headed for the gateway to the stables and barn, and swerved, vaulted over a low hedge, and met up with her again on the step. She was just turning the large, ancient key in the lock, and even as Aidan reached for her, the door opened and they both almost fell into the kitchen. The door shut behind them, and Anna was leaning against him, laughing, her hair saturated, fragrant against his cheek. 'Where did you . . . ' he began, but she had raised her face, and her cold, damp lips had found his, and they were warm, suddenly, despite the chill of the kitchen, the dampness of their clothes.

They groped their way down the dark passage to the main hall, holding hands. 'Do you suppose there's rats?' Anna asked.

'Devlin's gone to England,' Aidan said. 'Where did you get that key?'

'Molly Curran and your mother are to do the monthly cleaning on Monday, are they not? Molly's ill with a cold, and she asked me to give the key to your mother. Maura will probably go with her. You can take the key home with you when you go. Ooh . . . '

They had come to the main hall, and stood watching the light, turning scarlet and green and gold as it filtered through the stained glass fanlight above the door. It lit the large black and white squares of marble on the floor, the rich rugs, the gilt of the heavy picture frames along the walls.

'You've seen this before,' Aidan said. He did not like the awe in her tone. He knew this section of the house, his childhood had been spent here. It was redolent of memories of William Kelly, and a rich sadness threatened to overtake him. 'You've helped clean the house often . . . '

'Today I've come to visit,' she said archly. 'And besides, one never becomes accustomed to opulence, sure. Or, at least, I won't.' She looked at him expectantly, and he, after a moment of pretending ignorance, formally offered his arm, and they sailed rather damply down the length of the great hall.

She was enraptured with everything she saw, and Aidan felt torn between amusement at her childish delight and his own heaviness at the ghosts that seemed to hover invisibly in the great empty rooms that had once been filled with warmth and life. She ran all over the house, and he followed her, until, when they were downstairs once more in the formal sitting room, he realized that there was very little light coming from between the shutters on the windows. Anna was waltzing about the room, had lost none of her energy nor enthusiasm. She pulled all the dust cloths from the furniture, and threw herself down on a chaise longue covered in aqua and dove grey brocade.

'Arra, wouldn't it be grand to have a house such as this?'

He came to sit beside her, smiling down at her, for he suddenly realized that she knew as well as he how late it was. 'Well, yes. Yes, it would . . . '

She sat up, teasingly, just as he was about to bend to kiss her. 'You don't sound very sure.'

'I've never thought about it.' The faint light, a beam of it, fell

129

across her hair, turning the brown of it to a rich bronze. He touched it, placed his hand under it, stroked where it began to grow, silky-fine, on the back of her neck.

'Aidan,' she said softly, 'I see candles on the mantelpiece behind you.'

He looked at her. They smiled at each other. He rose, and lit the half-burnt, dusty candles in the holder. There were four of them, they smoked, and threw strange shadows on the wall. Behind him, Anna stretched. He heard her say wistfully, 'But don't you wish you could be certain that your life held . . . something grand . . . something far out of the ordinary? Don't you ever long to know that you'll one day possess . . . ' and her voice became very soft, so he at first did not catch her words, ' . . . something of real beauty, that will make everything worthwhile?'

He turned to her, and stood watching for a moment, as the light flickered upon the curves of her cheek and neck. 'I have everything I want,' he said, simply.

She came to him across the carpet, reached up and placed her hands on either side of his face. He was delighted when she kissed him, gently, of her own volition. 'I'd like to be like you;' she said, as his arms came around her and he held her to him.

'Like me? In what way?'

'You're happy . . . inside yourself.'

'Because I have you.'

She leaned back in his arms, 'It's more than that. You're sure of things, of yourself, of the world.'

'Och, no.'

'Yes, you are. You're the most obstinate man I've ever known, but you're fair – people know they can trust you.'

'Who? Everyone? Och, stop!' He threw back his head and laughed, and the candlelight danced in his dark eyes, and Anna nestled close to him. 'All these compliments,' he murmured, smiling at her, and she was glad that he was pleased, that his delight meant that he did not notice that her heart was beating faster, that a warmth was spreading through her, responding to his nearness.

He had an attraction that went beyond being merely handsome, she decided; she could have wished that he was taller, that his features were finer, more aristocratic . . . It came home to her in these surroundings that Aidan would never have the grace or the charm of, say, Devlin Kelly. But there was an intensity, a sense of almost overwhelming confidence and power that exuded from him, as if, no matter what happened in his life, his sheer will would carry all before it.

130

And it was odd, but putting these feelings into words for the first time, made her afraid. She realized why she had always loved him, for he possessed the certainty that she herself lacked, and realizing his strength she came to see the extent of her own weakness. She was not sure of anything, she thought with the first dawnings of self-knowledge; there was not one constant thing in her life, beyond this fierce young man she now held, whose warm hands were upon her body, whose warm lips were exploring her mouth, gently, insistently . . . There was no anchor for her frail soul that was swayed easily, too easily, on the slightest current. No anchor but Aidan . . . Aidan . . . and she clung tightly to him, gave all she possessed to him in her love and gratitude that here, here, was her only safety.

14

They walked home through a darkness that smelled of warm, clean, wet earth, hearing the drip, drip of water from branches overhead. Her head down, Anna admitted that she had volunteered to bring the key to Mary from Molly Curran.

Aidan walked with his arm about her. 'You knew what would happen,' he said.

'I knew,' she said, gently. 'We've waited too long, Aidan. I feel like your wife, I . . . I wanted to *be* your wife. We'll meet often, now, won't we? And if a baby comes – we'll be married as soon as we suspect.'

'Why wait for a baby?' he asked. 'I can tell you at least one good reason why I'd like to be married tomorrow . . . '

'We must save our money for as long as we can . . . '

'And if people find out that we're meeting in secret?'

'Sure and Aidan O'Brien, I think you care more for my reputation than I do!'

'I care a little for it, if you don't. We'll wait for a baby if that's what you want, but it's the strangest thing I ever heard in my life . . . '

Anna's parents were furious with her for being late, and for several months they were more strict about her meetings with Aidan. Yet he and Anna managed to meet occasionally, in the woods on Tineranna, in the over-grown folly, and twice more, since Aidan had found a board that was loose on one of the scullery windows, in the big house itself.

'When's this baby going to arrive?' he demanded one night, when they were lying, clothing adjusted and at peace, postponing the inevitable walk home through the winter darkness.

'Don't wish for it, Aidan. Sure we've been lucky so far.'

'If you call it lucky that I'm forced to share a bed with Thomas – who's smelling more and more like a fish market – instead of lying next to you, all legal-like in matrimony, then we have different ideas of good fortune.' He held her away from him, the better to study her face, 'It's the Misses Fredericks and their grand house – that's what's keeping you from marrying me, is it not?'

'I . . .'

'Come, no lies, now.'

'I've never lied to you! I'm happy there, that's true, and I'm happy knowing that I'm able to save a little of my wages and now I can contribute towards our future . . .'

'We have everything we need . . .'

She propped herself on one elbow and frowned down at him seriously. They had taken a chance, so cold was this January night, and had lit a fire in the hearth. The light burnished Anna's hair to copper, her eyes looked very dark; 'What do you want, Aidan? Your father's little cottage by the lake? Do you want nothing more?'

He thought hard. 'My own land. I'd like that.'

'Where?'

'Why, here, of course. On Tineranna. I'd like part of Tineranna, to hand down to our children.'

'Oh.'

'Where else should I choose? This is home. This is my people's land.'

'Yes,' she said, 'of course.'

And he did not know why she seemed dissatisfied, nor why he himself resented that she seemed so.

The firelight was warm, for the sods of turf from the cellar were long in drying and burnt well. He fell asleep wondering at Anna's moods of late, and woke slowly, as if drugged, to a half-dream of footsteps approaching. Then he was awake, and still the soft footsteps kept coming, slow, almost hesitant.

He opened his eyes and narrowed them to peer into the darkness beyond the glow from the fire. Anna was asleep upon his chest, her weight heavy on him, and he knew he would not be able to move quickly to defend them . . .

From the direction of the door, through the gloom, Maura O'Donoghue appeared like a pale ghost, a cream wool shawl over her

132

head and shoulders and the pale grey of her dress. She stopped when she saw him awake and watching her, and her mouth set itself a little as she took in the two bodies, lying on the couch.

For a long moment neither Aidan nor Maura spoke, then: 'I . . . I saw light between the shutters, and could smell smoke . . . I thought there might be a fire. I . . . I climbed through the scullery window . . . '

He studied her. Maura's voice was soft; Anna, on his chest, had not stirred at the sound.

'You're very brave, Maura,' Aidan said, coolly. 'Were you not afraid to come into a burning house? I think I would have been coward enough to run screaming to Nathan Cameron in the gate lodge, if it was me.'

She did not answer him, but pursed her lips and looked down at Anna. Aidan tried not to grin; he could feel that one of Anna's legs lay between his own, and Maura's distaste and condemnation were evident in her eyes. Anna stirred, looked up into his face, then followed his gaze, turning about to where Maura stood. 'Oh,' Anna said.

Maura was looking away. 'I'll go. And . . . ' she paused, 'I'll not say anything. I've seen nothing.'

They watched her leave, silently, and soon after, both feeling the same sense of violation of their world, they rose, and left the house themselves.

Aidan, though he did not mention it to Anna, was resentful of Maura's prying, for sure, it could be called nothing else. He waited, in the weeks to follow, to see if Anna came to him less frequently.

She did not come at all. They met under the watchful gaze of Mr or Mrs O'Hagan, and Anna was vague, Aidan thought, when he pressed her to try to get away alone. He suspected Maura O'Donoghue had told Anna's parents of the tryst in the big house, or at the least, had threatened to, but Anna denied this, saying her mother was simply naturally suspicious just now, and Aidan could not argue on the matter.

But he began to press her once more for a wedding date, for he had the feeling there was something wrong, that something was moving behind his relationship with Anna and beyond his understanding. Whether it was that Anna was changing, whether it was the effect of Maura or Mrs O'Hagan upon Anna's sensitivity and strong desire to please, he did not know. But seeing her on Sundays or an occasional Saturday afternoon was no way to find out. It was like pursuing a shadow.

'Just a little longer,' Anna pleaded, 'I know the waiting is making you unhappy, but . . . '

'It is that.' It was early autumn, and Aidan and Anna walked up and down the boreen outside the O'Hagan house, in full view of Mrs O'Hagan at the window. A light mist was falling, but they were pleased to be in each other's company and paid it no heed. It always seemed to be raining, lately. A dank mustiness was in the air, like the depths of a long, damp winter. 'It's been months since I've seen you alone, do you realize that? All summer and half the autumn we've been chaperoned like irresponsible children, and I don't like it at all.' He turned to face her, and the intensity of his gaze almost frightened her. 'After harvest, Anna. That's when it must be. You're my wife in all but name, and now it's time you belonged to me completely. The first week in November it will be . . . '

'That's only weeks away!'

'The first week in November.'

'I'll have to give notice to Miss Lilian and Miss Augusta . . . '

'Then do it. I'll see you next Sunday. You can tell me your decision then.' And he turned and walked away.

He had never walked away from her in anger; she felt bereft, incomplete. She hated it when anyone was cross with her. And now Aidan, Aidan was truly angry with her.

She had never told him how much she had prayed that each time they had loved each other that a child would grow within her. It never happened, and she had wept about it. The child would be the excuse for leaving the Misses Fredericks, the child would be the beginning of her real life. But in the meantime . . . in the meantime there was the house in Killaloe, and the fine furniture and her pretty uniform with its lace pinafore, and Miss Lilian had heard her strumming the piano, and was now teaching her to play . . . so kind they were! Why didn't the baby come, and make it easy for her to put that life behind her? Making decisions was never easy for her. She wished she could be like Maura, to whom everything was thus and so. Anna felt herself cursed with the ability to see awesome possibilities in any given direction.

Aidan disappeared over the hill. The narrow road, banked by the eternal grey stone walls, was empty. It reproached her. She had let him walk away, angry and alone, and it would be seven days before she would see him again. And she thought, suddenly, that her bed in the attic of the three-storey house in Killaloe was narrow and cold. She thought of running after him – had taken a few steps – and her mother called out to her. Anna paused. She could have pretended not to hear – but her mother was ill and tired lately, she did not want to worry her . . . She had paused too long. She faltered, then turned and walked slowly back to the farmhouse.

The next day there was more rain, cold and soaking, pushed before a bitter east wind that bit into the face and hands.

Aidan woke at dawn, hearing his mother and Corrie speaking in murmurs from the kitchen. Thomas had already gone down to the boats; his side of the bed was empty and cold. Aidan lay there for a long time, his hands behind his neck, gazing up at the beams above his head, hearing the soughing of rain into the thatch, thinking that in four weeks he would be sharing his bed with Anna. No more Thomas with his fish smell and his long toenails. Aidan gave thanks for his blessing of only one brother. Some of his friends slept five in a bed! No, Thomas was all right. It would have been wretchedly cold without him all these years, and at least he did not snore.

He dressed quickly and came into the new kitchen. The wind did not rattle the casements so loudly, here, for the window faced away from the lough, but Aidan paused in the doorway. He wrinkled his nose. The piece of bacon and thick porridgy stirabout was not the smell that first greeted him.

'What in the devil is *that*?'

From their seats at the table, Mary and Corrie looked at him blankly. He stepped gingerly around the kitchen, sniffing periodically.

'Can't you smell it, Ma? Is it a dead mouse in the roof?' He had tracked it down to the shutters. The draught blew the vile odour through the cracks between the boards.

Corrie had stood. 'I thought I smelt something bad during the night – a dead cow, perhaps, washed up from the lake.'

They were both heading back to the front room, taking down their coats. Corrie opened the door, and as they stepped out into the watery light of dawn, Mary called after them, 'Come back in directly. Your breakfast is ready now.'

They closed the door behind them and stood there, almost wincing. It was a sickening smell of decay, washed towards them on the wind. They looked down towards the lough, and had begun to step down the hill, when Corrie took the boy's arm. 'Check the field, first.' And indeed, the smell seemed to grow stronger as they rounded the cottage. Aidan could not understand it. Could something have died, begun to rot, in the time since he had last seen their fields? A cow? A pig . . . ?

They clambered over the low fence into the one-acre potato field, and stopped, transfixed.

At first it seemed as if the crop had vanished: the sea of bright green plants had gone, disappeared. They moved closer. The smell, that vile smell, was all around them. Decay was all around them. The plants lay, dark brown, jelly-like, flattened on to the earth like wet seaweed. The two men broke into a run, through the ruin of their crop, up the field to the fence which divided the original acre from the new paddock. Corrie was over the fence as if it did not exist. Aidan, his breath in dry sobs of fear in his throat, scrambled after him.

The cry his stepfather gave froze his blood. Corrie was glaring, wildly, pushing the air with his hands as if to block the sight from him. But it was not to be fought. Slowly, he relaxed, his breath the only sound above the soaking of the rain.

They stood there, silent spectres in an alien landscape, motionless, with the wind flapping their coats darkly, heavily around their legs, like black sails. Aidan went slowly down on his knees, stiffly, like an old man, heedless of the stinking mud, began burrowing around a blackened plant slowly, surely, almost with care, heaping the mud between his knees. His fingers after a while separated, seeking, sifting into the soil for the bulbous roots . . .

His hand went through the potatoes as if they had been sour cream. Through them! A skin, holding nothing but vile-smelling fluid. He shivered, felt panicked, contaminated. The thing was horrible, and he plunged his hand into the mud, and wiped his hand back and forth in the mud, trying to rid himself of the vile touch of the stuff. He was sobbing dryly, and dared not look up at his stepfather. He lowered his head and sobbed. And he thought of Anna, of the O'Sullivans, of the thousands in their hovels around the outskirts of the village. There they would be frantic, running from house to house, field to field, thinking perhaps it had only been their crop to suffer. Men who never saw a shilling in their lives, who paid their rent in labour, or potatoes. Who ate only potatoes. There would be people running everywhere, all over the parish, like ants when a boot crushes their nest, mindless, uncomprehending, their whole existence ripped from them.

And from the cottage, as if from another world, they heard Mary calling their names, telling them to come in out of the rain, that they'd catch a chill, that their breakfasts were getting cold.

15

Thus, for the moment, the decision whether to marry was taken from Anna's hands, taken from Aidan's, also. There was no crop for the O'Brien–O'Neill family of Tineranna, and Anna, seeing the worry written on her own father's face, knew how badly things stood and did not press Aidan on the matter. It was the opportunity she had half-desired, to continue working for the Misses Fredericks, and her parents were grateful, now, she could sense, that she had the position.

Yet for Anna it was not the same. It was one thing to postpone marriage and enjoy oneself; it was another to be forced to work because one's man could not afford a wife. And she felt guilty, too, these days, serving up the delicacies of ham and vegetables, salmon and roast chicken to the fastidious old ladies – and eating the leftovers herself – when outside the very windows a steady stream of itinerants, beggars and unemployed workers tramped back and forth all day, every day. Under orders from the ladies she was not to give alms; she had to stand at the door and gaze down into haunted, hunted faces and tell them no, there was not enough in the house, they were to go to the Relief Depot where they could purchase Indian meal, or be given a few ounces of the coarse stuff free if they had no money.

Yet at the Relief Depot there was never enough food. The land-owners, clergy, professional men and wealthier tenant farmers sub-scribed to the relief fund with generosity. The strong bond that existed between most landlords and their tenants kept the poor of Killaloe alive. In the years to come that would be called The Great Hunger, no one died of starvation in Killaloe. Elsewhere in Ireland they died in their hundreds of thousands.

Aidan stared at the ruin of their fields and asked himself for the thousandth time how it could happen. Some potato fields had been spared; Killaloe had lost only three-quarters of its crop, theirs was gone, and O'Sullivan's, and O'Hagan's – all the farms on the edge of the lough.

There were some reports in the papers. Some experts said the disease came from the atmosphere, was carried down on the rain.

Others said it was borne on the wind. Aidan could see in the dying leaves of the O'Hagan's plants, a minute whitish band growing around the destroyed area of leaf and stem. He did not understand it, could not know that the white matter was comprised of microscopic fungus tubes, the visible part only a hint of the extent of the whole, spreading itself through veins and tissue, devouring the plant's nutritional juices, changing the chemical consistency, leaving a putrefying mass of dead cells. Each fungus tube produced thousands of invisible spores, spread on the wind and beaten down through the soil by the rain. In dry conditions the fungus could not exist, but in the wet summer and autumn of 1845 the blight spread and multiplied, destroying the livelihood of millions.

Always there had been starving in Ireland. The relief funds that the British government sent were absorbed in 1845 without noticeable difference. As 1846 progressed, the situation worsened as what little food there was left was consumed, and profiteers raised the price of grain.

And Britain was loathe to commit herself further. Why weren't the landlords supporting their tenants? But in Ireland nearly three-quarters of the landlords' total revenue went into paying mortgages and other debts. Britain's relief plans were meagre, and came years too late to avert disaster.

The O'Sullivans were ruined. They fell behind in the rent in '45 and '46, and Nathan Cameron hinted darkly at eviction. Things were little better for the O'Hagans, who sold their cows and pigs one by one and lived on their own supply of grain.

The Currans could not manage the running costs of the tavern and their farm and the tavern had to go. They retired back to the cottage on Ceelohg, to plant more potatoes in the hope that 1846 would be a bumper year and they could recoup their losses. They had risen from farmers to businessmen once, Molly declared to her menfolk, and begod, they would do it again.

Even the O'Donoghues were not immune from the effects of the collapse of Ireland's fragile economy. They had had more acres under potatoes than most of the farms of that size, and now there was nothing for it but to part with some of the luxuries that they had come to take for granted. The horses were sold, the superfluous furnishings vanished from the house, and after that, the silverware of which Maura's mother was so proud.

Late in January, 1846, when unprecedented cold was gripping Ireland, adding much to the suffering, Caroline and Devlin Kelly returned to Tineranna.

A change had come over Caroline. To her dismay, she had found London society trivial and shallow after the first excitement of being there. There were men who would have courted her, for after all, it had been years since William's death, and Caroline was still an attractive woman. But the men, too, seemed shallow. They did not exude the same power, force, as her husband had. She looked at them, meticulously dressed and beautifully-mannered, and found them wanting. She found herself lying awake at nights, remembering William Kelly in the early years of their marriage, when he had stared at her as if she were a goddess whenever she walked into the room, as if he could not believe his good fortune in possessing her. How they had strolled in the garden for hours, hand in hand; how they had ridden to hounds together, coming back to Tineranna to bathe and fall into bed tired, but eager for each other's bodies. How she had loved him! And there was no one like him, no one! She forgot the later years, his impatience, his growling preoccupation with the estate and the problems of the parish. She forgot her own resentment of him, her withdrawal that had made the last four years of their marriage cold, loveless; he would kiss her hand in parting each night, each to their own room. If she had only known! Why did he have to die before she could realize his value to her?

And she would weep, then, thinking of the rest of her life, stretching forward, barren, purposeless. In London she took to going to Mass and saying prayers for William's soul, walking heavily-veiled to the Catholic church rather than be seen by any of her fashionable friends who had politely forgotten that she had changed her religion for William's sake. It was here, one morning, when the priest was offering up prayers for the starving in Ireland, that Caroline was suddenly inspired with the thought of returning to Tineranna. Later, it seemed to her that it was William's voice that spoke to her, as if he hovered nearby, telling her to go, that this was what he wished, that she should continue his work. It gave her a sudden and terrifying purpose to her life: she felt special, chosen, as if the Deity Himself had called her by name.

She went to Mass every day, stayed in the deserted church to say five decades of the rosary, wanting, she argued, to meditate on this being the correct path. In truth she was subconsciously worrying about Devlin's attitude to this plan.

At first he laughed, feeling that this new religious fervour on his mother's part would burn itself out, but the weeks passed and still she remained determined. She would go to Tineranna. He may stay in London if he wished, but go she would. And when he finally realized that she meant every word he exploded like a firecracker, shouting in a childish rage that was heard in the servants' quarters. She was selfish, foolish; she was living in the past, she could do the peasants no good at all. They would resent her as they had always done – had she not read in the papers that the White Boys and Terryalts were on the loose again, refusing to pay rents, threatening tenants who did pay, wanting a confrontation with the landlords? The owners and their families lived in terror – not a day went by without some attempted murder in County Clare. A landlord or an agent was a marked man. Did she understand? She could not possibly go back to that alone and unprotected, and if he accompanied her – why, he would be a dead man within the month!

'The people need me,' Caroline murmured. 'Your father would want me to go.'

'Father would want us to stay alive! Would you have us go back there and risk our lives for such people as that drunken Terry O'Sullivan, or that ungrateful brute O'Brien? Now *there's* a man who'd see me dead rather than look at me! And . . . and only just last week I was dining at Lady Bramley's and Trevelyan was saying that we weren't fighting a famine so much as the greed and slothfulness of the Irish themselves! And if the word of the head of the Treasury, who should know more of the situation than anyone else, isn't good enough . . . '

He was pink with rage. All his plans, the careful life he was building, despite the handicaps of an Irish upbringing and a Catholic father – all to be nullified by returning to that bog, that nightmare of a life! He walked from the room, confident that this show of displeasure would awe her into abandoning the scheme.

But the following morning she greeted him in the breakfast room by saying that she had made arrangements for an allowance to be made to him through their bank – his own income would be hard pressed to cover the upkeep of the Grosvenor Square house.

Devlin stared at her across the table, watching her place small bites of bacon and egg into her mouth, chewing calmly, while his own food became cold on his plate. 'You mean it, don't you?'

'Certainly I do.'

'I can't understand you, Mother. When we left Ireland, I presumed it would be for ever . . . '

'Oh, no, dear. Your father would be broken-hearted if we abandoned Tineranna altogether.'

'Father is dead!' His fist came down on the table. The silverware jumped. For a moment their eyes locked, the features of the faded woman and the young man so astonishingly alike.

'Yes,' Caroline said quietly, 'Your father is dead. And Tineranna

140

is your responsibility. But if you will not come, I cannot force you, Devlin. I will go alone.'

It was another fortnight before she left. Devlin kept a hostile silence between them except for necessary discussions about the town house and her business affairs. Only three days before Caroline was to leave did Devlin finally agree to accompany her, seeing at last that nothing he would do or say would prevent his mother returning to Ireland.

And yet, arriving there, Devlin was pleasantly surprised. It was not as bad as he had feared. The sons of many of the Protestant landowners of his own age had been educated in London, and he saw more of them now than he had done in the isolated years of his childhood. They were not rough, or uncouth, he felt; they had returned with some gloss of manners and taste. And they, too, were curious. Young men, who would never have dreamed of calling upon him had he remained at Tineranna, came now – for he was suddenly more Retcliffe than Kelly. The balance of his Anglo-Irish background had shifted. His mother was a Retcliffe, after all; and they were a highly attractive pair, socially capable, and known to have made quite a success in London despite the mistake of Caroline's marriage.

Yet it confused the landowners and their wives that Caroline still made such a show of going to Mass. 'Once a day – quite an excess!' one Miss Fredericks remarked to her sister. And after eight years, surely Caroline could come out of mourning? This summer's wide-skirted silks and taffetas, the low-necked muslin day dresses, came in delightful shades of sky blue and pastel green, quite suitable even for a woman of Caroline's age. But one had to admit she looked stunning in black. The finely-boned face and firm, sweet mouth, the perfect skin and the brilliant blue of her eyes beneath her gently swept-back blonde hair; she looked unusual, mysterious, at the dinners and balls; her charisma all the more attractive because she was totally unconscious of it.

For Caroline went to the entertainments for Devlin's sake alone. She would not always be here – she often had the feeling that God did not mean her to be long separated from her husband – and her efforts socially were to use her name and rank to solidify Devlin's acceptance into the upper echelons of Clare, Tipperary and Limerick society. She had always been a quick, nervous, impatient woman, who demanded to be amused constantly. Only just capable as a hostess her conversation had been stilted, self-conscious, trivial. Now she began to relax, and gained quite a reputation for her graciousness, her ability as a conversationalist – which among the

141

hearty and self-interested landlords, meant a woman who listened well and asked a minimum of clever questions. If the truth was known, Caroline was only half-listening. These people she spoke with did not matter; very little mattered any more, but fulfilling what she felt William expected of her.

Amongst his new friends, Devlin had a particular fondness for Hubert Osborne. From their large stable of horses, Hubert and his father, Edward, leased carriage horses and two hunters to Devlin and Caroline until they decided to build up Tineranna's stables once more.

It was while out riding with Hubert on Ceelohg, trying out the horses, that Devlin noted that three of the cottages on the Killaloe–Ogonnelloe Road had disappeared. 'Did you evict them?'

'Oh, Lord, no! I want to avoid that for a while! All three families agreed to emigrate – we packed them off to British Columbia.'

'Are many of the cottiers emigrating?'

'Hundreds. And a good thing, too. They're leaving the parish like fleas jumping from a dog – terrified of the fever, the fools. They take it with them, of course. They die in their hundreds on the ships – big hue and cry over the state of *them*, too. Coffin ships, they've begun calling them. Have you heard?'

Devlin had seen one ship being loaded in Liverpool, the half-starved, poorly-clad crowd being herded into creaking, decrepit hulls. The smell of disease and death was already upon them; it was not a pleasant memory. 'Yes.' Devlin scowled down at the piles of rubble that marked the cottages; down the road a little were several more, still standing, turf smoke issuing from the chimneys. Further along again, were the cottiers' hovels that belonged to Tineranna. 'Do you think you'll end up evicting?' Devlin asked. 'You've more tenants than we have, and Lord knows, we're finding it hard enough to collect the rents.'

'Oh, I'm sure it will come to that. Father and I are waiting until more troops are moved into Killaloe. These Terryalts are becoming more and more brazen – Father's already had a proscription posted against him – found it on the Cathedral door two Sundays ago.'

'What did it say?'

'Oh, demands that Father should forego collecting rent this year, like those philanthropists Clarkson and McDonald.'

'Could you?'

'Why the devil should we?' Hubert turned to frown challengingly at Devlin. He was a well-built young man of twenty-seven, two years older than Devlin, with sandy hair and a pale, handsome face marred by a weak lower lip that nearly always protruded, through

142

laziness or belligerency, or both. 'It's rather like war, you see. Both sides know that they're not going to get anywhere unless they unite. The Terrys are demanding that tenants shouldn't have to pay rent. They're even attacking their own people who do pay their rent because they see it as a weakness in the ranks. And there are those of us landlords who say that this wretched potato famine shouldn't be made an excuse to threaten the economic structure of the country. It's only one harvest, after all . . . '

'You don't feel anything for the people at all?'

'My dear boy, what can I do? If I went out and sold Ceelohg and everything else I possessed to give to the poor, it would be a drop in the ocean, the state this country's in, right now. The only thing that'd correct matters is to lose about half of this squalid, less-than-human population.'

'You're a stranger, Hubert, you don't understand Ireland's history . . . '

'Oh, don't get sensitive – I wasn't including your father's people in amongst that lot!' He waved a negligent hand towards the row of hovels before them.

Still Devlin felt nettled. 'But you don't understand these people . . . '

'Do you?' Hubert's glance was incisive. 'You haven't been to visit any of your tenants, have you? Old Clarkson goes down to hand out loaves of bread to his creatures outside their very doors. From what I've heard of my Uncle Robert, he'd have been doing the same thing. Did you know my uncle well, by the way?'

Devlin had a sudden memory of standing by his father's coffin, of hearing Robert Osborne's voice and looking up to see him there, awkward, embarrassed, *Your father had great plans for you.*

'No,' Devlin said, 'not very well. He . . . seemed a kind man.'

Hubert's lower lip was for once held firm, determined. 'Kind men make poor landlords.'

Devlin had indeed been avoiding his tenants. Nathan was kept busier than he would have been in Devlin's absence, planting himself between his master and the farmers who came to the big house to petition for reductions in this year's rents, and the cottiers who came begging for food at the kitchen door. His own cottiers! Devlin watched them approach, limping in rags up the drive, looking like moulting birds; and later, hurrying away, bright-eyed, watchful, clutching a small loaf of bread, a tiny parcel of meal.

Devlin felt ill looking at these creatures. He could remember them in his father's day; thin then, too, and dirty, but warmly clad

143

and a strangely happy people. After harvest frequent sounds of music had floated up from the huddle of cottages; fiddles, *uilleann* pipes, the flat, tambourine-shaped barawn drum beating out the gay rhythm. Now all was silent.

He watched the faces of these miserable people, half-expecting to see Aidan O'Brien amongst them. But he did not. And when he checked over the rent books with Nathan, he found that the O'Briens were one of the few families who were not behind in their rents.

'Why is this?' he asked Nathan. 'They had an acre and a half under potatoes. Nothing more.'

'Y'r father always paid Aidan and meself in cash, sir, like the house staff. And I didn't think to change it. A blessing it's been to both of us, sir.'

'So he's saved enough money to pay the rent.'

'Yes, sir.'

'What are they living on? The extra money his mother has earned caretaking this house couldn't have helped very much.'

'Well, perhaps I didn't mention it in my letters, sir, but Mrs O'Brien-that-was, is Mrs O'Neill, now. She married Corrie O'Neill.'

'Good Lord, that battered piece of granite? My boxing instructor?'

'The same, sir.'

'Good Lord,' Devlin repeated, laughing a little.

'Before the bad times, he'd go off to find work teaching in Limerick, sir. Still goes there every once in a while. And he's employed on a regular basis as a smithy over at Ceelohg. And then there's Thomas, sir.'

'Who's Thomas?'

'Aidan's younger brother, sir. Become one of the best fishermen on the river, old Packy Brady says . . .'

'I see.' Devlin tapped his cheek with his quill. He was illogically aggravated that things were going so well for the family. They seemed to be a jump ahead of misfortune every time. How did Thomas break that wall of insular kinship that existed amongst the fisherfolk? And what attraction could a dried-up little woman like Mary O'Brien have for a man like Corrie O'Neill?

'Where is O'Brien working now?'

'Over with the men clearing the ground on the slopes, sir.'

Nathan had sensed Aidan's mood at the news of Devlin's return, and had purposefully placed him as far as possible from the big house.

'Good,' Devlin said unconsciously. Then, 'O'Sullivan's. Two years without paying . . .'

'Well, yes, sir. But twelve children he's got, sir, and they're all in a bad way . . .'

'And O'Hagans – Paddy O'Hagan has thirty acres.'

'A lot of it was under potatoes, sir, and then the weather ruined his barley . . .'

'Damn it, man! That's not my concern! He owes me money from – what? Five gale days! How does he expect to pay me?'

'Sir . . .' Nathan shifted his weight from one foot to another, feeling the sweat break out between his shoulder-blades. 'O'Hagan's forced to work at the slate quarries out of Ballina, his daughter's taken a position in the village. They say they'll be able to make it up this year, sir.'

'When the new potato crop is in.'

'Yes, sir.'

'And how are they going to afford seed to plant this new potato crop? And I hope, Cameron, you're not going to say that they're asking me to pay for it.'

'No, sir. I think . . . I think Father O'Callaghan is buying seed, sir.'

'From his own money?'

'Yes, sir. For those farmers who have no way of replanting, sir.'

'I don't know, Cameron . . .' Devlin leaned back and stretched, not taking his eyes from the rent book before him. 'It seems to me that you could have managed this business a lot better. The cottiers are one thing – their houses and conacre plots take up valuable room, but their labour pays their rent, until they began begging at the kitchen door they were not a liability. But the farmers! Men like O'Hagan, and O'Donoghue with forty acres!'

'O'Donoghue's only three months behind, sir.'

'O'Sullivans are two years behind, and Ryans eighteen months, and Minogues six months . . . They'll have to go, Cameron, do you understand? If the rents aren't brought up to date by next gale day, they'll have to go.'

'Sir . . . I've thought of eviction meself, sir, long before this, but the people are desperate. They're organizing themselves into gangs and there's not a night goes by without some outrage being committed . . .'

'I know all this . . .'

'It's the oats and barley, sir. We've got the finest harvest of any estate in the parish this season. It's the oatcrop they'd strike at, first, sir. And the hay. The estate's so large – one couldn't have guards in all the hay paddocks. The fodder for next winter could go up in flames, sir. It's happened already, over in Ballina. Beggin' your pardon, sir, but I was thinkin' of these things . . . '

'Yes . . . ' Devlin stared at the pages in front of him, frowning. Damn the man, he was right. And so was Hubert. It *was* a kind of war.

'I'll not be intimidated by Whiteboys and Terryalts, Cameron. But I see what you mean – we must avoid a direct confrontation as long as possible. Talk to these people again. Tell them of my impatience. They saw bad times under my father's ownership, too, and yet rents have always been paid. I expect the same respect shown to me.'

He rose, and to Nathan's muttered 'Yessir,' was about to leave the room, when, 'Sir . . . ?'

Devlin turned. 'Yes?'

'There was something else, sir, that I was wondering. Nothing to do with the estate . . . The dog, the one that you took to England for the Wiltshire Trials . . . was he a success? I've often been curious, sir, as to whether he did well.'

Devlin studied him. Nathan had no interest in dogs, but he had even less interest in Aidan O'Brien. This was uncharacteristic . . . But the man was waiting for a reply.

'He did very well in Wiltshire – I retired him for breeding, after that. He died only six months ago.'

'Fifteen years old . . . ' Nathan said without hesitation. 'A long life for a dog, sir.'

'Yes.' And Devlin left then, not knowing why he bothered to lie. The time for the 1840 Wiltshire Trials had not come about when Devlin, at the house in Grosvenor Square, had received a letter from the steward of his uncle's Wiltshire estate. Mister Kelly knew, he wrote, that the Irish dog, Samhradh, had not been really fit since the voyage to England, and he felt it his duty, the dog being valuable and obviously prized, to notify Mister Kelly of the dog's death. The veterinary stated that death was caused by a wasting sickness. The steward finished with the assurance that all in his power had been done to save the animal, and any queries could be addressed to the veterinary surgeon . . .

But Devlin had all but forgotten the existence of the dog. He even felt a certain guilt over his actions in bringing the dog from Ireland. It wasn't really necessary to prove anything to O'Brien . . . And because the pettiness of the gesture embarrassed him, he threw the steward's letter away and pushed the thought of Samhradh to the back of his mind. It was one of those silly mistakes that every man

146

makes in his life. He would not think about it anymore.

But he thought about it on the way to the stables at Tineranna, angry with Nathan Cameron for stirring the memory, the futility of the gesture.

But Nathan was grimly pleased, and reminded himself to tell Aidan that Samhradh had lived to such an age. It was the one piece of good fortune that Devlin Kelly brought with him, and that was pitiful enough. He sat down at the desk and chewed the inside of his cheek, staring at the open page of the rent book.

Devlin rode into Killaloe to visit Hubert. The latter had recently purchased a three-storey house in the village, 'very cheaply' he claimed, and he had been wanting Devlin to see over it. Hubert could not bear living at Ceelohg, with the steady stream of beggars passing up the drive; anyway, he was used to the bustle of town life. His father, Edward, was against this idea of a town house, but Hubert felt it was his only escape route, his sanctuary, for he did not always agree with the now elderly Edward, and wanted somewhere to go when the old man's querulousness sent Hubert forth from Ceelohg in a rage.

Devlin called first at the Royal Inn, one of Hubert's favoured haunts, and finding him absent, had turned the corner in front of St Flannan's Cathedral, and had headed up the High Street, when he heard his name shouted.

Turning and reining in his horse, he saw the curate, John Fredericks, coming out of the wrought-iron gates leading to the church yard.

'Consulting the sexton,' he said, after greeting Devlin and shaking his hand. 'Two more deaths due to fever during the night.'

'Cholera?' Devlin felt afraid; he had shaken the man's hand. It was known that the priests and curates of both Catholic and Protestant churches worked tirelessly nursing the sick.

'No, typhoid. One of the Minogue children, and Sarah Brogan. I fear there'll be more, and quite soon. Doctor Reed wants a fever hospital set up in preparation – isolation is the only way to stop the spread of the disease. May we count on some support from you, Mister Kelly?'

The man was blunt, to be sure . . . 'Well, things are bad at Tineranna with all the cottiers . . . But yes, I can promise you I'll do what I can.'

'God bless you, sir. And here – are you busy now? I was going to the rectory, and then I was going to dine with my sisters. Would you care to join me?'

Lord, he could not imagine anything more deadly boring . . .
'I'm afraid I've promised to dine with friends, but perhaps another
time . . . ?'

'Surely, surely . . . Lilian and Augusta would love to meet you
and hear the latest news from London. They feel fearfully cut off
here, I'm afraid.'

'Of course. I shall visit soon.'

As Devlin rode on, he imagined what Lilian and Augusta looked
like. Feminine forms of their brother, he decided, small, with
narrow shoulders, a habit of nervous laughter and of standing too
close to one and speaking earnestly into one's face.

Hubert was upstairs, amid packing cases, sorting through his
porcelain collection and arranging it in a French cabinet of inlaid
walnut.

'Couldn't one of the servants do that?' Devlin waited until the
butler had gone and threw himself in a chair by the window.

'What, trust one of those rustics with objects of this value? Don't
be foolish!'

Devlin picked up a bisque shepherdess from a packing case beside
him. 'I went over the rent books today . . . '

'How's the situation?'

'I'd really like to evict – but I'm worried about the Terryalts.'

'With good reason . . . Ah, you've got my little shepherdess.
Charming, isn't she? More than a hundred years old . . . Have you
heard about the typhoid?'

'I met Fredericks, just now. He told me two villagers had
died . . . '

'That's nine this week. They're dropping like frozen birds, dear
boy – just look at this little dancer – sixteenth-century Venetian,
absolutely priceless. I do love to have my treasures around me . . . '
Hubert turned the piece this way and that within the cabinet, then,
satisfied, reached for the shepherdess. Develin watched him arranging it, almost amused by Hubert's fastidiousness in getting just the
right angle. The interest in the tiny and delicate objects was at
variance with the rest of Hubert's robust nature. It displeased
Devlin, somehow. Collecting porcelain was not . . . manly, he felt.
His father would never have considered it.

He turned to the window, listening to Hubert's prattle of the pure
simplicity of a parian statuette, and his eyes fell on the windows of
the house opposite. In a small room at the corner of the neat, grey
stone building, a woman was sitting at a mirror. She wore a dress of
some dark material, black or very dark brown, and her hands were
raised to her head. She was three quarters turned from Devlin, and

he could not see her face, but her waist was tiny, rising attractively to a line of white neck above the collar of her dress. The hair was a honey gold in the afternoon sunlight. Devlin listened to Hubert, but could not take his eyes from the figure opposite. She was removing pins from her hair, and suddenly it fell loose, down her back. Down, down. Devlin found that he had inhaled sharply. The woman was seated on a stool, and the hair touched the floor. When she stood up, it would be almost to her knees. And she sat there, brushing it. Languid strokes, as if she gloried in this possession. One hand held the hair away from her, the other brushed, once, twice, thrice . . . Devlin felt his right hand clench each time, as if he himself held the brush. He wished he did. There was something unconsciously sensuous about the woman's movements . . .

'I'd appreciate it – do you think you could?' Hubert was saying.

'What?' Devlin turned sharply.

'I said could you collect my latest piece for me when you go back to London? It's a T'ang pottery dog. I won't begin to tell you what it cost me, but I want it over here and I don't trust the dealers to . . . Devlin, are you listening to me?'

'I'm sorry, I was thinking about the estate . . . '

'Then don't. The wretched problems are always there, ready to swallow you up. Forget it, in the interest of your own sanity. By the way, will you have lunch with me? You arrived at precisely the right time to be invited to lunch . . . '

Devlin grinned. 'Thank you, yes.'

Hubert rang for the butler, and while he was engaged ordering the meal, Devlin, his gaze once more out the window, noticed John Fredericks walking up the street. In case he was seen watching, he pulled back a little, but the curate, his mind already intent upon his coming dinner, did not look up, but turned abruptly up the steps of the house opposite.

Devlin gazed with interest as the sound of the bell, inaudible to him, made the woman at the mirror start. She had bound her hair round and round at the base of her head in a tight chignon, and now hastily finished pinning it, stood and pulled on a starched white apron, and had disappeared from the room.

Devlin waited, more impatient than the hungry Fredericks below. When the servant, as she obviously was, opened the door, he had a clear view of her face as she smiled down at the curate.

'But she's beautiful . . . '

'Who?'

With a shock he realized he had spoken aloud. He turned to find the butler gone, and Hubert already at the window beside him. They both looked down; but the door of the house opposite was just then closing on the curate's back.

'Why . . . the maid. In the house across the street. That must be where old Fredericks's maiden sisters reside . . . '

'That's right. Yes, I've seen the girl. Quite pretty, though a little robust. I like petite brunettes, myself. Much more fun, I've found. Although . . . I did think of laying that little abigail. Damn' difficult, though. You'd think *she* was made of porcelain, the way those old women fuss over her. I swear, it's harder to find a good class whore in Ireland than it is to find a decent pair of boots! Shall we go down to the dining room and have a sherry?'

16

Devlin sought out John Fredericks two days later and gave a generous donation towards the building of the new fever hospital. When the grateful curate again suggested luncheon with his sisters he found the handsome and aloof Mister Kelly only too delighted to accept.

The Misses Fredericks had brought their own cook from Belfast, a woman experienced in traditional English meals as well as quite adequate imitations of French dishes, and Devlin was pleasantly surprised by the quality of the food. And with the fluttering old maids speaking volubly to the table at large, turning their heads this way and that, each one treading on the tail of the other's conversation, Devlin had plenty of opportunity to take short glances at the maidservant.

'Annie', they called her; and 'dear'; sometimes running them together with their heavy Northern brogues, 'Unnie dearr . . . ' Although the girl remained respectful, answering, 'Yes, ma'am', with eyes lowered, their familiarity was astonishing to Devlin. How it must have seemed to the Protestants of the town he could not guess, though perhaps the ladies' eccentricities covered even this breach of social etiquette.

Perhaps it was the frequent 'Unnie's' that confused him, but they were well into the meal before Devlin, catching sight of the girl in a quiet moment, standing at the sideboard with the sunlight from the window falling full on her cheek, recognized her. Anna O'Hagan!

The little laughing witch who had been part of all his early memories; one of the crowd of unruly children from whose ranks he had been forever barred.

It was then, knowing her background, fitting her into a history of which he was as equally knowledgeable as any, that the first real feeling of desire for her stirred within him. From his first sight of her through the windows, she had been an attractive curiosity, like one of Hubert's porcelain antiques. He had wanted only to view her from a closer vantage, from different angles. But much of her mystique had suddenly gone. She remained beautiful – at close quarters she was doubly attractive – but she was suddenly human, *available*. Her father was one of his tenants! And what's more, the man was fifteen months behind in his rent.

Devlin nodded in agreement with the chatter at the table, kept smiling down into his plate. The only mystery surrounding the girl now, was how she had grown into such a beauty from the gangling girl who had seemed all eyes and elbows and knees. She would be . . . Good Lord, almost his own age! She could not possibly be married, have borne children, she looked eighteen. Why was she *not* married?

After the meal, Miss Lilian asked Anna to play for them. Rather self-consciously she took herself to the piano and played a few haunting traditional airs, simply, but with expression. The Misses Fredericks were obviously proud of her accomplishment. 'She could play almost at once, by ear,' Lilian said. 'So I taught her a few notes. Now she's taught herself so many pieces, Mendelssohn, and Schubert . . . play one of the Schubert songs for Mister Kelly, Unnie dearr . . . '

He saw her alone for a few seconds at the door as he was leaving. She helped him into his coat, and he watched her, taking as long as he dared. Her eyes were dropped demurely, and he felt he must make her look up, acknowledge him.

'I didn't recognize you at first, Anna O'Hagan. I used to see you about Tineranna often as a child.'

The eyes came up to him, then, and he had the feeling they were studying him as appreciatively as he did her. He smiled a little, confident that she would not have seen any man as well-dressed, as polished as himself in this small town. The appreciation on her face, innocent as it was, was no more than he was accustomed to receiving in drawing rooms and ballrooms back in London. But there was a difference. Never had he been perused by a face as lovely as this one, and he inhaled slightly with the emotion of seeing those strange

151

brown-green eyes, eyes like the depths of shadows in a leafy forest, raised to his. Before he could stop himself, he had said, 'You've become beautiful. You're wasted here.'

He was filled with embarrassment, but later did not regret the words, for a glow appeared, surprise and wonder and perhaps gratitude, in the forest depths of those eyes. She murmured a goodnight to him, and the door was held for him. Devlin left quickly, but carried the memory of those eyes with him. For of course, it was not bland flattery to Anna O'Hagan. No one, he thought, would have thought to tell her she was wasted in the uniform of a maid. It was her place. He delighted, in the days that followed, that he had found this unspoilt girl. And to think that she had been here all the time . . .

Devlin lunched with the Fredericks every Thursday for three weeks, despite the confusion of the Dean, and his own parish priest, Father O'Callaghan, always worried whether Devlin's Protestant background would lure him away from the Church. But he went to Mass with his mother every Sunday morning, and from the carriage window, returning home, watched Anna O'Hagan leave and head off home on foot with her family and friends.

She would return to the village in the evening. Devlin knew this, and waited, each Sunday afternoon, in a field from which he had a view of the boreen leading to the O'Hagan farmhouse. For three Sundays he had no luck, and he had Nathan Cameron set up several low jumps in the field and set his good-natured hunter at them, worried that his tenants would think him mad if he spent too much time in the one field with no obvious reason. Several people stopped to watch him, Aidan O'Brien, and the Curran brothers, and Maura O'Donoghue. Devlin ignored them, set his horse at the beastly fences and told himself the ridiculous exercise was worthwhile – or would be, if he could only catch the girl alone . . .

And he almost missed her. He turned after taking a brushwood fence and ditch – in desperation he had asked Nathan to make the fences more difficult – and Anna O'Hagan was walking along the boreen, was almost out of sight behind a small copse of beeches.

'Miss O'Hagan!'

She had already turned at the sound of his horse's hoofs, thudding across the grass towards her. She came over to the wall as Devlin drew rein on the other side, his heart beating fast at the suddenness of the meeting. He dismounted as she was bobbing a curtsey to him. He smiled at her. 'I'm glad to have met you. To tell the truth, I chose to exercise my horse in this field so that I might see you.' Some instinct had told him that it would be best to tell the truth to this girl,

152

for even now her eyes were watchful, her smile not altogether certain. 'My mother and I are sorting through a great deal of the bric-a-brac in the house at the moment, and I've found several pieces of music – quite a pile, actually – that I'd like you to have. Are you busy now? Could you come back to the house with me?'

It did not take very much to persuade her to come. She was not ridiculously coy, and after confirming that the mistress would not mind – that she was, in fact, spending the afternoon with Lord and Lady Devlin, distant relatives of his father's, in Limerick – she assented. They walked along the paths together, and he told her of the concerts he had attended in London, of great singers he had met. She was intelligent, and not at all ignorant, and the longer they spoke, the more he felt bewitched.

And Anna entered the front door of Tineranna with the young master himself, and not all her nagging doubts nor niggling guilt could have persuaded her to forego the experience. She entered the big house like a lady, and nodded to the amazed English butler like a lady, and went to the large drawing room where she had spent so many evenings with Aidan, and was served tea and tiny sandwiches – like a lady . . .

Devlin's manners were wonderful, he spoke to her with a sensitive interest she had never known before, and there was no trace of condescension in his tone. Nor did he attempt any physical contact but sat in one of the grey velvet chairs and she sat in another. The green and silver brocade chaise longue was now pushed back against the wall, and Anna tried not to look at it. It spoilt the wonder of the moment with its memories of something more earthy, a union that seemed at this moment a tie with a life infinitely inferior.

The music he had for her was in a separate pile on top of the grand piano in the corner. Aidan had wanted her to play it for him, and she remembered this now, against her will, as she sat down and played through some of the pieces, Devlin standing close behind her. His left hand sometimes touched her shoulder as he reached forward to turn a page. It was an opera score.

Mozart's *The Magic Flute*. 'I imagine Pamina to look like you,' he said. She smiled as she played but made no reply. It had not been flattery, she felt like a princess . . .

They paused, once, and she realized he was staring down at her, and to cover her own feelings of pleasure in the knowledge, she asked, 'You don't play yourself, sir? I would like to hear you . . . '

'I don't play.' The voice suddenly firm, his eyes not looking at her, but beyond her. 'I wished to, as a child, but my father thought that the piano was a waste of time for a man. Particularly for the owner of an estate.' She understood his tone, now. There was a bitterness there. She felt a sudden pity for him. But the handsome face was turned down towards her and he was smiling at her. ' "For God's sake, Devlin!" he used to say. "If you really want to waste your time with music, hire a pianist to play to you while you're doing your accounts!" ' She laughed with him, and he held his hands to her to help her rise – and he had taken them harder than he should, and had pulled her to him.

All her pity for him, her growing understanding, vanished abruptly in the feel of his mouth upon hers – she was surprised at the feel of it, wet lips and slack, and a groping, yet hesitant tongue that pushed at her clenched teeth in a pleading sort of way that was matched by his voice when he pulled back to murmur between kisses, 'Please . . . please . . . like me . . . please like me . . . let me . . . ' a frightened whine in the voice that she wished she could stop her ears to, if her hands could only be free of fending off his fingers, mauling, pinching painfully at her breasts . . .

Someone knocked at the door. And she was free, so suddenly that she half-stumbled and her hand came down in a discord upon the keys. Devlin was upon the other side of the room, staring out the French doors into the shadows of the trees that encroached near the terrace. He called over his shoulder, the clear voice calm, 'Come in!'

Anna was watching Devlin, and did not look at the butler as he announced that Mister Hubert Osborne was waiting in the upstairs drawing room . . .

'Tell Mister Osborne to wait – I shall be up in a moment.'

'Yes, sir.'

When the man had gone, Devlin turned to look at Anna. She was shaken, he could see. One of her hands held the piano as if for support, the back of her other hand was held to her mouth. He wondered, with a shock, if he had hurt her – he had certainly frightened her – and he cursed his lack of control.

'My dear . . . ' He had to step around one of the chairs to reach the piano, but she was too fast for him. She had moved swiftly around the other side of the chair, and had found the latch on the French doors . . .

He caught up with her outside, only because he did not take the steps from the terrace but leapt down to the lawn and raced across to head her off as she was about to run down the path, through the overhanging trees, that would take her to the driveway.

'Miss O'Hagan – forgive me . . . !'

'Let go of my hand, Master Devlin . . . I shouldn't have come!' He was horrified to see that there were tears on her cheeks. 'I'm

154

wicked for doing so. I've only myself to blame . . . '

'Don't be a little idiot – we were alone, and I took advantage of you. You were too beautiful, sitting there . . . I lost control of myself. It was unforgivable of me. But I'll ask you to try to forgive me. Will you?'

She stopped struggling to free herself, seemed to hesitate. He added, 'And your music – you've forgotten it.'

'No, sir. It was wrong of me to accept it. You must forgive me . . . '

'For what, pray? There is a piece of music I didn't show you – I sent to Dublin for it, especially for you. It's the latest piece by Moscheles – it was all the rage when I left London . . . '

She raised her eyes to his; she was a little calmer, and her voice was firm. 'Sir, I cannot accept it. It's very kind of you, sir. Very kind. But I cannot.'

Lord, such pretty manners . . . And wasted here. Wasted! He imagined, suddenly, the stir she would make in London as his mistress – to take her to the concerts, the ballet . . . She would revel in it, she would be a queen . . .

'Please, sir, let go of my hand . . . I shouldn't accept the music at any time, but being betrothed . . . '

'What?'

His voice came too loud, she almost started. 'Yes, sir.' Her chin came up. She looked directly into his face. He was watching the line of her neck, the fine, pale cream of the skin at her throat; her words took seconds to register.

'I'm to be married to Aidan O'Brien.'

Devlin's eyes did not move from her neck, could not if he tried. A weight had suddenly appeared in his chest, stopping his breath.

Yet he was calm. Very calm. Slowly he brought his gaze to her face, and he smiled once more. 'And when is this marriage to take place?'

'Well . . . after this year's harvest, sir.'

'Presuming . . . there is a harvest this year?'

She stared at him. 'If there is a harvest, then, God willing, we will marry, sir. And . . . both Aidan and myself being tenants of Tineranna for so long, we hope for your blessing, sir.'

The green-gold eyes were looking challengingly, fearlessly, into his face. By God, she knew what he was up to! Intelligent, and courageous as well – it was too much to be borne . . .

He let go her hand, and stepped away. He said, 'I shall have the music sent to your house later today. It's yours, Anna. If young O'Brien would deprive you of it because it came from me, then I

155

would be very disappointed in him.' *And so will you*, his parting glance said.

Anna did not wait to see him walk away, she turned and walked quickly along the path. When she knew she was out of sight of the house, she broke into a run, the tears of her confusion and her shame running down her cheeks. She was bold, she had thought herself above her station. And what had possessed her to think for a moment that Devlin Kelly, with his pose of good manners, was a better man than Aidan? She longed, then, for Aidan's firm arms around her, the warm confidence of his lips on hers . . . making her forget the taste of Devlin Kelly . . .

There was a trough of water set nearby, under a tree and she went to it, bent over it, and rinsed out her mouth in the clean water, shutting her eyes to the mossy stone walls of the trough. She rinsed and spat, and scrubbed at her lips as if the master's mouth had left a stain upon her.

Devlin claimed a headache, and sent a piqued Hubert home to an unwelcome Sunday dinner at Ceelohg with very little good grace. He poured himself a large whiskey when his friend had gone and sat down by the fire in the downstairs drawing room, gazing at the now silent piano.

That girl and Aidan O'Brien . . . unbelievable. It will never happen, he decided, not knowing whether he was prophesying or promising himself. It will never happen.

A week later, exactly one month after her arrival in Ireland, Caroline Kelly was dead of typhoid fever.

Devlin had been too preoccupied with his feelings for Anna to notice how his mother spent her days. Some philanthropic work with the ladies of her acquaintance, he presumed; and Caroline had been helping with the food distribution in the village: but recently, seeing the tiredness of Doctor Reed and his handful of nursing staff, the exhausted features of the Catholic and Protestant clergy, she began to go with Father O'Callaghan to visit the fever patients.

There was little even the experienced nurses could do; give the patients drinks of water, place damp cloths on burning foreheads. Keep the patients as clean as possible in times when sanitation and hygiene were practically non-existent.

Caroline, in her long, sweeping skirts, moved among these victims, horrified and sickened by the sight of swollen, discoloured faces, the weeping sores, the delirium, the gangrenous hands and feet. She wore gloves, which she had burnt before entering her own

156

house; her dress was washed immediately she arrived. But on the eighth day of her work with the sick, she woke feeling ill. Her wrist had been bitten by lice the previous day, lice from those poor, filthy bodies, and the marks had itched all night. She had scratched them, and made them bleed . . .

She collapsed on stepping from the carrriage at one of the cottages and was driven home once more. Devlin, visiting Hubert in the village, was sent for immediately. He came hurtling through the doors of the big house and took the stairs three at a time, only to be met by Doctor Reed, who said he was not to approach her. Medicine was sent from Limerick, an opiate-based mixture that lessened Caroline's suffering but could do little to stop the advance of the disease.

Devlin defied Doctor Reed's orders and sat by the bed, watching helplessly as his mother, unconscious, slipped from him, occasionally stirring to whisper endearments to William, reliving some early memory. Devlin wanted to grip her, shake her, call her back . . . But within a week, she was dead. She died without regaining consciousness, without recognizing her son.

Hubert cancelled a particularly exciting cock fight in Limerick to stay with Devlin, the day of the funeral.

Caroline was buried beside William, and this time it was raining. Cold rain, that turned to sleet half-way through the ceremony, yet Devlin looked around at his shivering people, some without coats or shawls, hollow-cheeked, hollow-eyed, and cursed them.

She had died for *them*. With her beauty, her gentleness, her pathetic, misguided kindness – she was dead. And these scraps of humanity, these unwanted pieces of effluence, of whose scurrilous existence England had been trying to rid herself since the Statutes of Kilkenny in 1366 – these still lived. And it no longer occurred to Devlin that through his father he was one of them. He had spent too much of his life trying to forget the fact.

His uncle, Roger Retcliffe, Lord Hallswood, and his cousins, Celia and Corbett, arrived from Carlow in time for the funeral. Tired from the long journey, fearful of colds and any germs the wind might have blown towards them from the crowd of farmers and cottiers, they had retired early to bathe and lie in their beds, wondering, each of them, how best to convince Devlin to sell Tineranna and return to England permanently.

Oblivious to the plans being hatched upstairs, Devlin stayed up late, drinking. Hubert Osborne kept him company, whiskey for whiskey, toying with a piece of eighteenth-century Dresden while

Devlin stared out the windows. He could see only his own reflection, and a pale moon, warped slightly, with the varying thicknesses of the old panes.

'I don't understand it. Any of it. She was not happy with my father. She loved me more than she loved my father. Yet she came back here, knowing what it was like. Could she have wanted to die?'

'Nobody wants to die, Devlin.' Hubert turned the porcelain figure around and around, feeling the cool smoothness of the glaze. 'Not even these wretches in their hovels outside the village. They, of all people, should be seeking oblivion. It's almost frightening, you know, this Irish tenacity for life . . . '

Devlin appeared not to have heard. When, after a while, he spoke again, his voice was sad, bewildered. 'My mother was a vain, silly, weak woman. Yet these last few weeks . . . at the end of her life, she became very brave. What could cause that to happen?'

Hubert shrugged. His own mother had died in childbirth, and he had been brought up by the careless ministrations of a series of nurses chosen by his father more for their physical attractions than for their maternal instincts. He placed the figurine on the table beside him and squinted at it through his whiskey. 'I don't pretend to understand women. They're like an inhospitable island – other than the bay between their legs there's little about them that requires charting. Not wishing to sound disrespectful, dear boy . . . ' as Devlin turned to him abruptly. 'But I'm not the one to help you interpret your mamma's actions. Mothers aren't really women, anyway, are they? I grew up thinking of mine as somewhat above Queen Charlotte, and somewhat below the Virgin Mary.' When Devlin smiled a little, Hubert leaned forward towards him.

'Look here. Go and plough your pretty little maidservant – you can manage it, if you're clever. Or go back to London and throw yourself into an affair with an actress. Don't, for God's sake, sit around Tineranna, brooding over your empty rent books – you'll go mad.'

Devlin seated himself in an armchair, staring in front of him. Hubert was right. It was a woman he needed right now. He wanted to cry upon a woman's breasts. He wanted a body beneath him that he could hurt. He wanted Anna O'Hagan.

17

Of all the East Clare legends of how the Terryalts got their name, the most popular in Killaloe is this: There was a man by the name of Terry Alt, a most pious mild-tempered man, of excellent standing in the Protestant community, and of such gentle good manners that he did not have an enemy in the world.

Returning home from church, one Sunday morning, he found that his carriage could not pass down the street. A fight had taken place between some of the more unruly villagers, and a man lay unconscious on the side of the road, surrounded by a crowd of concerned friends. As his carriage slowed, Alt put his head from the window, gazing at the bloody form in concern, and called, 'What's happened here? Who did this?'

And it was one of the local wits who made history by saying gravely, 'T'was the work of a man of savage character to be sure, sir. A more fierce-tempered devil you wouldn't find this side of hell, sir. T'was the man they call Terry Alt, sir, and that's the truth!'

Stunned silence at his audacity, then chuckles, then laughter at the expressions that fled across the embarrassed Alt's face. He blushed scarlet, could think of no reply, and in the face of the crowd's huge enjoyment, tapped his cane upon the carriage roof and had his driver move on.

But the incident was not forgotten.

'Would you believe that Mister Alt knocked down a man outside the church, last Sunday?'

'No!'

'God save y', Mister Alt! Have you won any fights lately?'

'Move out of his way, boys! It's Terry Alt, himself!'

And the secret societies of the district, the groups of desperate men who met at night and waged a war of retribution on the more corrupt landlords, began to sign their warnings and proscriptions, not 'A friend' or 'Molly McGuire' but 'Terry Alt'. His name became as common a word as Whiteboy, one of those who wore a white armband on their raids, or Lady Clare Boy, who would dress in women's clothing, scuttling up to burn hayrick and barn in borrowed skirt, and shawl around the face. The Terryalts used no insignia, but their crimes were violent, destructive, and the ridicule and publicity almost destroyed the man whose name they had taken. He left the parish, went to live in County Wicklow, and was never heard of again, leaving his name to go down in infamy on the Tipperary and Clare shores of the Shannon.

The authorities found a way to deal with the societies in the late 1820s. Immediately after their trials, those men found guilty were chained in wagons, taken to Limerick, and loaded into ships that would take them to Cork, from thence to be sent to penal colonies on the other side of the world, *without seeing their families to say goodbye*. It was this, the horror of no farewells to their loved ones that broke the spirit of the family-loving Irish. The countryside quietened down until the Tithe Wars; and flared up again, worse than ever, when the famine began.

The Osbornes recalled several hundred acres from tenants, despite the protests, and left many farmers with little more than a few acres on which to plant next season's crop. The soil was left to lie fallow, for grass to grow, because cattle and sheep could be certain to bring in a good return at market in these times. Many of the landlords in the parish did this – though not all succeeded. There is a gentle field, rich and green in spring, behind lichened grey walls, on the road from Killaloe to Limerick. In early spring, at dark of night, fifty Terryalts came silently with hoes and spades, dug up the valuable new grass, and ploughed it under the rich black soil, in those quiet hours before the dawn. In the morning, the grazing land lay ruined, fit for nothing . . . Nothing but potatoes. The land was easily rented. To this day the people of Killaloe point it out to visitors, laughing, and call it the Terry's Field.

Aidan and Thomas helped Martin and Tom-Joe Curran plant the potatoes on their five acres – all that was left of the thirty-five they had farmed until the Osbornes resumed control.

Aidan worried that the hot-tempered Currans would find some way of lashing back at the landlords; but he had not reckoned with the legacy of the fever. All the Currans contracted typhoid in 1846; Tom-Joe and Martin survived – Molly and John did not.

For a long time after the deaths of their parents, the wild talk, the fight, went from the two brothers. Their olive-skinned faces were sallow, and except for their talk of politics, their belligerency seemed channelled into hard work and determination that this year the crop would be better than ever, that they would gain once more the security for which their parents had worked for so long.

It was Martin who talked the most of William Smith O'Brien, of the articles he had written in *The Nation* newspaper. Smith O'Brien

160

said that they should no longer follow O'Connell's peaceful policies, that having a free Ireland was worth any means they could muster, that they, in the country, should refuse to pay the exorbitant rents . . . When Martin was not quoting Smith O'Brien, he was citing John Mitchel, and Charles Gavan Duffy. They wrote brilliant prose, placed forceful arguments, quoted irrefutable facts. Aidan listened, and worked. Martin talked, and worked. It was Dublin, Thomas put in. All that was fine for Dubliners. What did insurrection have to do with this year's seed potato – or the lack of it?

The rain swept down the panes of glass, blurring the view of the faded lawns, the bare branches of the oak trees that lined the drive. Hubert, after the final hunt of the season, was staying to dinner at Tineranna, foregoing the ball in Killaloe because one of the young ladies with whom he had been flirting now had a decidedly proprietary look in her eye. 'Another waltz and she'd be arranging herself in the most flattering pose for a proposal – and not the kind I had in mind,' he grumbled to Devlin. 'Why must women be so confounded *serious*?'

Devlin merely smiled, and bent to the fire to stir the sods of turf. He heard Hubert say, 'And what about you and that little abigail? Have you made any progress?'

'Progress? No, I've been very busy with the estate . . . '

'Too busy to do anything about that little piece? That's *indecently* busy!'

'With Mother gone, there's a lot of legal matters to be sifted through,' Devlin insisted. He rose and went to the sherry decanter, filling Hubert's glass, then his own, before seating himself in his chair and gazing into the flames.

How could he explain to Hubert that he was afraid to seduce Anna O'Hagan? Gone were the days when an Irish chief could demand the right to a bride on her wedding night. If Aidan O'Brien found out that Devlin had had intercourse with Anna, he would kill him. Devlin knew this with a certainty born of more than knowledge of O'Brien's personality. Perhaps it was the years of schooling together, those years of proximity and constant resentment, binding them together like two brothers insomuch as they did not need to question what a particular reaction would be. They would know, instinctively.

If Devlin told Hubert that he was afraid of one of his own tenants, Hubert would laugh. He would suggest getting the man out of the way, a trumped-up charge of stealing a sheep, a bag of oats, that would earn him seven years in Van Diemen's Land. He could hardly

161

interfere with Devlin's plans from there.

Devlin had already considered this plan himself. There was some satisfaction in it, to be sure, but there had also been tales told of men who had managed to return from their banishment, after waiting years, to kill the landlord or agent who had had them imprisoned. And if any man with blood on his mind could come back across thousands of miles, it was O'Brien.

He remembered him at the funeral, a short, powerfully-built figure, standing between Corrie O'Neill and Anna O'Hagan. Their eyes had met for a moment, and O'Brien had nodded almost imperceptibly, the rain soaking his hair, plastering it to his forehead. His hair was black in the rain, and he looked almost demonic beside Anna's fair colouring and gentle expression. Yet they were standing together. They belonged together. Betrothed. Promised. They *would* lie together . . .

The thought more than depressed him. It filled him with an impotent kind of rage, had done so each time he thought about it, in the month since his mother's death. Hubert's bantering and coarse references to Anna throughout the dinner did nothing to improve his mood. He drank more and more, and Hubert, matching him, became more quiet and lugubrious as the evening progressed.

Back in the library after the meal, glasses of port and cigars in hand, Devlin and Hubert discussed the possibility of returning to England. For Hubert, it was a dream; his father controlled him with iron purse-strings, but for Devlin . . . why not? Sell Tineranna, Devlin thought. Forget the past.

'No more tenants and beggars, no more fog and bog and fever,' Hubert recited, 'no more Maidservant Whatzername to trouble your waking hours.' He looked up, brightly. 'I have the address of a certain lady in Bloomsbury, who . . . '

'What would you say . . . ' he was growing tired, his words slurring, 'What would you say to the idea of my marrying that Maidservant Whatzername?'

Hubert stared at him, and burst into laughter. 'Oh, really . . . '

'No, I'm serious . . . '

'You'd be the laughing stock of London!'

'What if nobody knew where she came from?'

'Don't be absurd! Of course they'd know – her accent . . . '

'She could be Irish gentry . . . '

'Well, yes, I suppose . . . '

'Her manners are superb. She plays the piano, she could be taught a little French . . . '

Hubert straightened slowly, a smile growing on his face. 'I say, this could be rather interesting when you think about it . . . Of course, you couldn't carry it off indefinitely. Word will get around . . . '

'But by then she'd have conquered everyone. You know what a stunner she is . . . '

'That's right. With her looks . . . your money . . . Lord, what a laugh – she could be the hit of the season!'

'I could buy her easily with a lease to her parents – fifty years, minimal rent . . . '

'Oh, they'd beg you to take her! But Devlin, you don't have to marry her, you know. Why not take her back to London and place her in a little house and then marry some heiress. Much more sensible idea.'

'But a gamble. What if I don't like the heiress? She'd undoubtedly be spoilt. I've known this Anna O'Hagan since we were children – she'd be grateful for anything I give her. And what's more, she's far more beautiful than any of the debutantes I've seen in London lately.'

'True . . . It'd stop your advancement, though.'

'I do not with to Advance. Let my children Advance. It takes too much energy.'

'Your mama would turn in her grave, Devlin.'

'My mama also married beneath her. She, too, fell for the romance of the Irish. The difference was, she didn't know how to handle Papa. I know how to handle Anna O'Hagan.'

Hubert had his head in his hands, laughing. 'Oh dear . . . We must sleep on it, we must! The absurdity of it! I'm drunk, Devlin, far too drunk to plot elopements tonight. Have I been invited to spend the night? Good. We'll discuss it again in the morning – when it will all seem thoroughly ridiculous.'

But Devlin awoke excited and determined. It was madness, perhaps, but he had not had enough madness in his life. He could not see that Anna would let him down socially; but if she did he could always retire her to an estate in the country with the children and live quite happily in London, more or less as he did even now.

In the morning Hubert seemed to have no remembrance of the conversation. He sat at the breakfast table, hung over, cross. Devlin ignored his grunting bad temper and turned his attention to a letter from his uncle, Lord Hallswood, who had now returned to London, entreating him to come to England as soon as possible. Devlin smiled at the expensive writing paper, the family crest. What would Uncle Roger say to this plan of his?

While Hubert grumbled at the under-cooked bacon, Devlin

wrote a quick letter, promising that he was soon returning to London, and would write to them from there. He stood at the window and watched the servant ride away with the letter, down the drive. The view from the window saddened him. All of Tineranna saddened him. He was empty, somehow. He felt a kind of guilt, that he did not miss his mother more, that he was not more grieved by her death. He could not admit to any feelings of resentment against her, yet he subconsciously knew that she had courted her own death, that she had, at the end, moved away from, and beyond him. She had chosen to die, had left him; after all those years of demanding that he be her own boy, her only love, the reason for her existence. He felt betrayed, hurt. He would never forgive her for dying as she did.

Only once, in the ensuing days of careful thought, did Devlin consider returning to his old way of life in London. He mentally reviewed every eligible young woman that he knew, both in London and in Wiltshire. There were gracious women, it was true, some of whom Caroline herself had approved as possible choices, but none offered him any excitement. Never had he felt anything but admiration for their wit, or their beauty, or their fortunes. There was no challenge to any of them. They came, each of them, from the same mould.

He became more excited, however, the more he thought of the problems of marrying Anna O'Hagan. Getting her away from Killaloe was a problem in itself – not to mention grooming her for life in London society. He resolved he would have to move quickly, not allow any second thoughts for either Anna or her parents.

Devlin would have been disconcerted to know that his attentions to Anna had not gone unnoticed by the Misses Fredericks. After each of his visits they would wait until Anna was in her room in the attic, and flit between each other's rooms in nightgowns and wrappers, to sit on each other's bed and talk about the possibility of a love match, an elopement.

It appealed strongly to the frustrated romantic which lay hidden within each little bird chest, that these two beautiful young people, so separate in education and background, yet so wonderfully suited in looks and temperament, should find each other – and in their house.

Of course, there was Aidan O'Brien, but Lilian discounted him immediately. A surly-looking brute, a real peasant. Augusta, who had once had a four-year-long unvoiced passion for the family blacksmith, declared that the boy had 'wonderful shoulders and quite fine eyes . . . ' to which Lilian replied that fine eyes did not

164

keep a wife, and that young O'Brien could offer their Unnie little except hardship and fifteen children. This mention of the unpleasant realities of life quelled Augusta immediately.

Devlin timed what he hoped would be his final visit to the two women at three o'clock the following Sunday afternoon. Anna, he presumed, was at home with her family.

Yet this was one of the few times that Anna and Aidan were allowed out alone.

Michael, the only O'Hagan son who had survived his infancy, was ill with the fever. He tossed and turned on his bed of straw – the mattresses had long been sold – in a corner of his parents' room. Anna, on arriving that morning, wondering why her parents had not met her at Mass, found her mother gaunt with lack of rest, her father asleep with exhaustion after his six days on the roadwork in the sleet, working beside neighbours and cottiers as weak as himself from cold and malnutrition. The younger girls stayed in their room, were forbidden near Michael for fear they, too, should catch the fever.

Anna, perhaps closest to nine-year-old Michael than any of her family, begged to stay and nurse him, but her mother was adamant. She must not enter the room. She could go to Mary O'Brien and visit with Aidan. Spend a day on the mountain, perhaps – somewhere away from the house and the threat of the sickness. With a final look at Michael's pink, distorted face, Anna went, stumbling along the roads to the cottage on the lough.

Aidan took a piece of bread and cramming it into his coat pocket, took her hand. 'Come – we'll climb Craglea.'

They managed to find a wagonload of fodder going to Finlea, and the farmer sat them up behind, their legs over the edge. It was cold, and overcast, but there was no scent of snow on the air, and the clouds were thin and moved too fast for much chance of rain. Beyond Finlea, they left the wagon and headed up the shoulder of Craglea, and at Aoibheal's Rock they stopped and seated themselves, eating the bread and gazing down at the hills of Clare, vanishing into the mist twelve miles distant.

Anna was quiet, her thoughts with the little boy back at her parents' cottage. Aidan's mind was on their own future, running on tracks of thought worn smooth over the past few weeks. He had been restless for some time, worried, again, what Devlin would do with Tineranna, for how long he could depend on the five shillings a week that his position afforded him. He had seen so little of Anna, too, in these past months; she had seemed, for a while, irritable and critical of him, most unlike herself. Could he not comb his hair more often? she would ask him, or, would he not be gracious enough to stay in his

Sunday shirt and jacket when he called on her? Odd little criticisms that he would laugh at, and comply with. But it bothered him. The strain of the long years of waiting was telling on both of them – it had been months since they had loved together . . . He looked sideways and studied her perfect profile, the tendrils of honey-gold hair that escaped from its knot at the nape of her neck and blew about her face. He realized he could not live without her much longer. Tom-Joe Curran had recently married, despite Martin saying that he could ill-afford a wife. Now there was a baby on the way, but sure Tom-Joe seemed to be managing, and he was happy, by God.

And Aidan's restlessness, in these weeks away from Anna, included the future. To live day to day, year to year, dependent on the whims of Devlin Kelly, away in London, filled him with resentment. The potato blight, in its far-reaching consequences had shown him how fragile the Irish economy was, how tenuous his own small place within it. To have so little choice in the matter – that was the galling thing. What good were all the books he had read, that had taught him of different places, of clever and ambitious men, when he himself was imprisoned in a narrow life of subsistence from which there was no escape? Though some had. Canada. America. It was possible to build a new life there, though Aidan had no illusions that it was any easier to make a living. Too many Irish had fled their country, desperate, carrying the various fevers with them. Both Canada and the United States had made it difficult for the destitute Irish to enter their countries. But if one had money . . .

'Next year . . . ' he said carefully, 'if we have a crop of potatoes that we can sell . . . I'd have enough money to take us to America.'

Anna turned to him, her eyes alight. One of her cheeks was distorted slightly with her mouthful of bread. He grinned at her. 'Would you like that?'

She swallowed abruptly. She had been sitting there quietly, wondering whether to tell Aidan of the frequent visits of Devlin Kelly to the house in Killaloe, of the terrible incident at the big house, but with his news all uncomfortable thoughts vanished. 'Yes! Oh, yes!'

'You wouldn't miss Killaloe?'

'Well, yes – there's my family. But my place is with you.' She was gazing at him with an intensity he had not seen on her face for some time. 'My place is with you,' she repeated, 'I'm sure of that now.'

'I've never doubted that for a moment.' And his arms were about her; she leaned her head against the comforting roughness of his jacket, and they sat there for a long time, content to feel the warmth of each other's bodies. Then,

'Anna? It's been so long . . . '

166

She looked up at him. 'It's been my fault – I've been foolish, and selfish . . . '

'Let's get married straight away. Well, in three days. On Wednesday.'

'What about the banns?'

'To hell with the banns! We have the room at the cottage ready. Could you put up with staying there for a year, until we leave for Boston? You wouldn't miss the life in the village?'

Anna considered only for an instant. Now that there was some future, some light of escape, no matter how distant, she felt she could give up the household in Killaloe. In America, she and Aidan would manage to build some security for themselves and their children.

'Yes,' she said. 'We'll have the wedding on Wednesday.' She glanced at him mischievously. 'And can you keep your thoughts pure until then, tell me?'

'I will not, sure . . . ' And he pulled her down on to the ground, and for a moment they rolled in the heather together, before Anna, breathless, managed to hold him back from her.

'Stop, will you!' She could barely speak for laughing. 'Only three days, Aidan! Let me have these three days as a maiden, and . . . '

'No . . . ' he growled, rolling over until he lay upon her.

'Please, Aidan, I'm serious now . . . '

'Arra, y'r not.' He looked hard at her face. 'You are.'

Slowly he sat up, leaned his elbows on his knees and gazed at her. She adjusted her dress, drew it down well over her drawn-up knees and gazed equally soberly at him. 'It means something to me. To wait. To prove we can do it, perhaps. When you love me next, I want it to be as your wife, Aidan.'

He pulled her to him, rocked her a little in his arms. 'We'll wait,' he said. 'Sure we've waited this long.'

She was silent a moment, then said consideringly, 'I wonder if we'll be bringing a baby to Boston with us? I hope so . . . in all this time we haven't made one.'

'How many times have we lain together? Seven? Eight? Sure and if we don't take a baby to Boston with us, after a year together, it won't be through lack of trying.'

He kissed her hair, and she was surprised to hear him say, after a pause, 'I'd like to have a daughter. A daughter that looked like you. We'd dress her in blue silk, with them white lace pantalettes . . . ' He took her hand and studied it. 'And she'd play all day with a hoop or a ball . . . And you'd teach her to play the piano . . . And she'd never do work any harder than embroidery – and neither will you.'

She gazed up into his face. The dark eyes burned fixedly down into hers. She did not laugh at his dreams. She alone, of all people, felt the rage that flickered sometimes within him, that would one day find an outlet and flame forth quite capable of carving his name upon whatever place in the world he stood. It was right that it would be America, a country just coming into maturity, like themselves.

They stood up, and he kissed her, while the rising wind moaned a little around Aoibheal's Rock, and the first drops of rain fell on Anna's upturned face.

She would not let him go into the house with her. Kissed him, instead, at the entrance to the boreen, and made him go on home. So Aidan did not see the carriage that stood at the door of the O'Hagan's cottage.

Afterwards she found it hard to piece together the happenings of that evening. Who had spoken first? Did someone tell her that Michael was dead, or did she know, instinctively?

Both her parents and the younger girls were in the kitchen, at one side of the room. Devlin Kelly stood at the other. She could not even remember if he greeted her. Did he nod, speak to her, did he look at her at all? And was he mad to come to a house of fever – to stay at such a time?

The door to the room where Michael lay was closed. She remembered stepping towards it, being led away . . .

And the room that she had shared with her sisters. She and her mother, sitting on the edge of the bed, her mother's face buried in her hands, the feeble light from the rush candle flickering on the grey in her hair, on the pointed shoulder blades that stuck through the thin cloth of her dress. Between sobs, her mourning for her son was combined with the terror of Master Devlin and his unheard-of demand.

'It's a lie!' Anna stared at her mother. 'He doesn't mean to marry me! He'll use me and then throw me out. Don't be foolish, Ma!'

'He says . . . he says Father Collins is comin' from Scarriff. Praise God, for he can give the last rites to Michael . . . '

'Ma, stop cryin' . . . Oh, don't, or I'll start, too! Ma, tell him to go! Tell him no, Ma! I don't believe him – how could you believe him?'

Her mother looked up at her. 'Didn't I tell you the priest was coming? At dusk, he says. He'll marry y' here, he says, and give us a copy of the marriage paper, to show anyone . . . '

'T' show Aidan, so he'll not come after me.'

The women gazed at each other.

168

Anna said softly, 'You want me to do it, don't you?'

Her mother lowered her eyes to the floor, unconsciously looking for the pattern in the small rug that had lain beside the bed. But the rug, too, had long gone. She reached for Anna's hand and held it tightly, only then raising her eyes to gaze at her. 'He's got a piece of paper with him – he says it's a lease – fifty years, at one pound a year. And no rent to be paid for the next five. 'Til we've recovered from the bad times, he says. And four bags of meal and oats to come each month . . . '

'I'll want to read that paper.'

'I told him that. Anna . . . ' the grip on her hand tightened, 'Aíne Asthore . . . Would you be unhappy as his wife? It'd be consolation, would it not, to know that your children would never starve . . . would never go in need of a doctor, like . . . if Michael had had a doctor . . . !'

'It didn't help Mrs Kelly.' Anna could not stem the brutality in her words. She felt a trap closing . . . closing . . .

'Anna, please . . . !'

Her children. Hers and Aidan's children . . . So real only two hours ago? And suddenly her children were Devlin Kelly's children, who would never starve or die in need of a doctor . . .

'I must talk to Aidan . . . '

'He says no. He says you must leave for Dublin tonight. He must be in England by next week . . . '

England! Anna found herself trembling, as if the cold room were even colder. She clamped her teeth together to stop them chattering. 'I can't do it! I can't do this to Aidan!'

'Don't be a fool!' Suddenly her mother's fear turned into anger. 'Aidan O'Brien is young, strong. Y' stupid slieveen – do y' think he'd be pining over you? He'd be married to another within the year! And you thinkin' he'd be broken-hearted!'

'This is the only chance for you, and for all of us, Anna. You let Master Devlin ride away tonight and we'll be evicted within the week – you know we're behind in the rent, and he's not the man to take a refusal from the likes of us!'

I led him on. The thought came sickly to her, I led him on with my dimpling smiles and demure looks and my vanity at his attentions . . . She put her hand to her eyes. 'I want time! I must have time to think!'

'You can't! You must go with him! Why, he's even got a letter from the Misses Fredericks . . . '

'*What?*'

'He's told them – he read it out to me and your Da – they're "pleased and proud" they say, that you've been so honoured. "Pleased and proud", Anna! They say y' could find no finer gentleman anywhere than Mister Kelly.'

No finer gentleman . . . blackmailing a starving, grieving family . . .

'Am I to leave before Michael's wake? Before he's buried?'

'Michael . . . will have no wake. No one will come to a house of fever, Anna, you know that. No one but the priest – and Devlin Kelly. That alone should prove his love for you. And this . . . this is more important than the funeral. It means a new life for you, and for all of us. Get up, now. We've kept him waiting long enough.'

Anna came out into the room and went straight to Devlin. White-faced, she lowered herself into a curtsey, and without looking at him, thanked him for his generous actions towards her family, and said that she would be honoured to marry him.

Father Collins was puzzled by the actions of Devlin Kelly, not only the unusual connection he was making, but the haste in which the marriage took place – the bride's brother lying dead in the next room, the bridgegroom's mother only three months in her grave. . . Yet strange things happened to people's emotions in these times. He questioned both parties about their sincerity in this contract, stressed that it was a sacrament, and bound each of them to the other for life.

Both Devlin and Anna answered calmly, determinedly. If the bride seemed a trifle nervous, this was only to be expected, and Father Collins, who had a private suspicion that there was probably a child on the way, was kindly towards Anna, and respectful of Devlin, for standing by the girl.

Aidan went for a walk with Thomas that evening. It was a long time since they had talked, and Aidan needed a sympathetic ear in which to pour all his plans for Boston.

'I'd wait a while before I told Ma,' Thomas suggested. 'And anyway, a lot depends on this harvest. If the crop fails again . . . '

'It won't. It can't. No two years in a row!'

'Whatever happens, you know I'll help all I can. I think goin' to America is a good decision – though what Ma will say, I don't know.'

They had come farther than they meant to, walking briskly because of the cold. When they came to the Killaloe–Ogonnelloe Road, Thomas turned about, ready to go back. Aidan hesitated.

'Ah, come now! You saw her not four hours ago. Anyway, she'll be back in the village by now.'

'Perhaps not, with Michael ill. She was always close to young

Michael. I might go see how he is, anyway. I could go into the village tomorrow morning and tell her.'

Thomas headed homewards, and Aidan turned up his coat collar and began walking towards Ogonnelloe. His mind was still on Boston. One of the Hogans had come back with a comfortable sum of money saved. He'd worked at a timber mill in the west – rough living, he said, but good money – enough to return home and lease a small farm.

A carriage was coming along the road towards him; he watched the lamps on either side, bouncing up and down as the vehicle hit ruts in the road. They were travelling fast – and heavy-laden, too, from the sound of the springs creaking in protest. He recognized it as the Kelly's brougham when it was still a hundred yards away, smiled grimly to himself, and stepped well to the side of the road.

He saw the woman before she saw him. In the dark, satin-lined cloak, his confused mind thought that it was Caroline Kelly . . . At the same time that he realized it could not possibly be, she had leaned forward, called his name . . .

'Anna!' he screamed. The thunder of the carriage passed him, he felt the wind shift his hair, his coat. 'Anna!' He was running, running after it . . .

Even as the driver shouted to the horses and they broke into a gallop, he had grasped the edge of the loaded luggage tray, clung to it as he felt his arms jerked, his legs fly out behind him . . . He tried to run a few steps but the horses were travelling too fast, too fast . . .He screamed her name over and over, could barely hear the sound above the pounding of the frantic hooves. His legs were dragging along the road, his bare feet dragging over the jagged rocks and stones, and the calling of her name became a cry of pain, over and over, 'Anna! Anna!' And he dare not let go. Would not let go. With every ounce of power in his shoulders he clung on, uncomprehending of anything but the knowledge that to let go was to lose her for ever.

At a turn of the road his frozen hands defied him, and he crashed to the roadway. He lay there, looking up as the two carriage lights jounced away, growing smaller in the blackness.

He crawled to the side of the road, planning to raise himself by grasping the wall, but remembered nothing more. He was still lying there when Corrie and Thomas found him, late that night.

171

18

Anna O'Hagan's elopement provided grist for the mill of gossip for many months.

The O'Hagans were, after the shock of Michael's death, proud and almost boastful of the match. Nathan Cameron was jubilant. Not at the marriage itself but that it had made Devlin so preoccupied in his last days that no definite orders for evictions were made, and as things stood, Nathan was to go on as agent as usual.

The O'Briens, as the family was still known collectively, despite Mary's marriage to Corrie O'Neill, kept silent, much to the O'Hagans' relief. They had expected an uproar, recriminations, perhaps violence – but they heard nothing. Aidan did not appear for two weeks. To the many enquirers Mary said that he was ill: in those days, when almost every house was visited by typhoid, cholera, relapsing fever, tuberculosis or pneumonia, it was not regarded with suspicion.

Mary was afraid for him, now. When the wounds on his feet and legs had healed, he went back to work on Tineranna, ploughing the fields behind the draught horses, going for long walks in the evening, barely speaking to anyone. He drank too much at the public houses in the village, and he looked for fights – and found them as often as not – coming home with eyes glinting and bloody knuckles.

Without Anna, he began to see more of his brother, and the Currans, Martin and Tom-Joe, and Seamus and Thady O'Donoghue. The latter two had helped one of their father's friends from Finlea, Dan Clooney, set up a barley still amongst the thick bushes on the shoulder of Craglea. For the promise that they would warn him when the revenue police set out from Killaloe to scour the district, Clooney bequeathed several bottles a month to the O'Donoghues, and on these special occasions they would meet in one of the glens in the folds of Slieve Bernagh and share the booty with the others. 'A sss-select group,' Thady had told Aidan the first time it was mentioned. 'Nnnn-now that you're nnn-not getting married, y've no reason to sss-stay sober, have you?'

Aidan had tended to stay close to home, these past few years; when he was not with Anna, he preferred the company of Corrie and his mother, their gentle banter, and Thomas's occasional astute remarks, made more surprising, coming as they did, with a deprecating grin or an air of absent-minded wonder.

Now he needed more than his family. The gap that Anna left in his life was a wound, a physical hollow that ached with nerve ends. The bottles of potcheen imbibed in the glen, the jokes and the laughter of the O'Donoghues, the dry bitterness of the Currans, all affected him in some positive way. He needed people, for away from them, faced with his own thoughts, he felt himself dying a little at a time. Not all his hard work during the day, nor the hesitant reactions of sympathy from Corrie and Mary could help him. Everything left him unmoved. He watched the starving thousands who moved through the village to the soup kitchen, and stared incuriously, as if he had joined the madness that possessed the world. He stood on the pier, flanked by Thady and Seamus O'Donoghue, and watched the boatloads of grain leave the district and its starving people; it no longer puzzled him that the newspapers reported fund-raising attempts in England while that country's government allowed the Irish grain to be exported. Thanks to his years in the schoolroom at Tineranna, he knew that *laissez faire* meant to leave alone; but he no longer burnt to know *why* England refused to interfere in Irish trade when she held the power to keep the grain within reach of the people. He no longer raved at reports in the London *Times* that criticized the backward Irish farming methods, when the country that governed Ireland made no attempt to introduce agricultural reform. Long ago he had wished that he did not understand the broader issues, did not know that this wholesale slaughter could have been avoided, longed for the ignorance of the cottiers who shut their doors and lay down when they felt the fever come upon them, who died believing this to be the will of God, not to be questioned, not to be fought. Now Aidan had reached that point of indifference.

But even that was not allowed him for long. For the fabric of his whole life was disintegrating around him, and in the most horrific way. It was not the destruction of the economic and social order of things, not even the families that packed their belongings and left on the steamers to emigrate, leaving cottage and farm to fall into ruin. It was the deaths.

A month after Anna left Killaloe with Devlin, Maura O'Donoghue's small sister, Bridie, died of cholera in the new fever hospital. Within two months, both her parents, too, were dead. Maura caught the fever but refused to go to the hospital. Thady, gentle, hesitant, stayed with her, nursed her until she recovered. He would not let the worried Thomas visit, but after she had recovered, it seemed that his concern had some thawing effect on her attitude towards him. She went often, then, to the cottage on the lough.

She did not single Thomas out, sometimes even arriving when she knew he was not at home. Even Mary was puzzled by these calls from a girl who normally shunned close contact with anyone but her immediate family; but Mary put the change down to loneliness, to Maura missing her own mother.

'Her parents and sister gone, all within three months, the poor girl. Aidan, you should be more kind to her, talk to her when she visits . . . '

'Me?' It was mealtime, and Aidan looked up from his plate of cabbage and turnips and hard bread to gaze scowling at his mother. 'But she comes to see Thomas . . . '

'Nonsense. They're friends only. She comes to visit all of us. You could find a lot to talk about if you tried. Make an effort to be polite, son, she's a good child.'

But good child or not, Maura O'Donoghue made Aidan uncomfortable. Her questions were too astute, her tone could be almost mocking; she drew him back from himself when he did not wish to leave his own thoughts. When she came to visit, he stayed only long enough for good manners to be satisfied before leaving to visit the Currans, or to head back to O'Donoghue's, or to sit brooding in a corner of a tavern in Killaloe, and wait for some excuse for a quarrel with one of the villagers.

She stayed late one night, after Thomas had left to set the eel lines. Corrie was pretending great interest in whittling a new pipe, and Mary, determined not to carry the entire conversation, lowered her head over her sewing, after giving Aidan a look as definite as a command that he should not make for the door. As he was casting about in his mind for something to say, Maura began, 'Thady and Seamus were saying tonight, that if the crop is safe this year, then we might emigrate.' All three looked up at her, startled. 'But I don't believe they really mean it. Seamus is sweet on Sarah Minogue.' Her disapproval was evident in her tone. 'You were plannin' on goin' to Boston,' she said to Aidan. 'Will you not be going, now?'

'That was a while ago.'

'Have things changed so much?'

He stared at her, wondering how anybody could ask such a question. As if reading his mind, she said, 'America meant a new life for you and Anna – but with Anna gone you have to think of yourself.'

Damn her impudence! He felt himself flushing, knew Corrie and Mary were listening – even from his mother he could feel the silent waves of agreement. 'I'll wait a few more seasons . . . There's no hurry. I still have my position at Tineranna . . . '

'I thought you didn't want to stay working there for ever.'

'Who told you that?'

'Anna.'

'See here, Maura, what is it to you?' The words were out before he could stop them; he could not bear the way she could talk about Anna in such a nonchalant manner, as if nothing had happened, as if she still saw her sometimes in the village, or walked home with her from Mass.

He was conscious that Corrie and Mary were looking at him. To reprove Maura like this when she was a guest in the house was unheard of. Yet when he looked at her, she showed no sign of embarrassment, was watching him in an almost amused manner.

She changed the subject then, began talking of the spring dance to be held at Minogues later that month, the first ceili since the blight had struck. 'Though it won't be the same without the Piper Brogan, and all the families have . . . have lost someone.'

It was the first time Aidan had seen her falter, and he looked at her for the first time, keenly, taking in the fact that her blouse was frayed around the cuffs, her skirt around the hem – and she wore no shoes. An O'Donoghue with no shoes!

And he remembered the winter of 1839, the fight he had had with Martin Curran in the O'Donoghues' field, with the haystacks piled high, and the barn full of oats and corn – and Maura's grim-humoured father, Liam, handing him a white linen handkerchief to wipe the blood from his face. And he pitied her, and he understood, suddenly, the flippancy that cloaked her brittle courage.

Maura was listing off the people coming to the party, families sadly depleted by fever and other illnesses, and the many young people gone on the ships to Boston and Quebec. Aidan watched her face, thin, sharp-featured, the slanted green eyes with their pale lashes, the freckles that covered her nose and cheeks. She had lost almost everything, now worked in the fields beside her brothers, without humour it was true, for as Seamus said, Maura had been born without it, but without complaining, without bitterness. Her mouth, Aidan noticed, was not unattractive. He was surprised to see that it was fairly full, and did not turn down at the corners . . .

She was looking at him. He looked away, abruptly. She rose, then, and thanked Mary for allowing her to visit, had placed her

175

shawl around her shoulders and stepped to the door before Aidan grudgingly read his step-father's look of reproof and offered to walk her home.

He walked quickly, silently, his hands in his coat pockets. A few times she had to take a little run to keep up with him.

'You're angry with me,' she said, after they had passed O'Sullivans'.

He glanced at her. 'No. Why should I be?'

'I talked about Anna. And your plans for America. You're not planning to go to America at all, are you?'

'No.'

She was silent, then. When he looked at her, she was walking with her head down. 'You still mourn for Anna, don't you?'

He stopped dead. 'Look you, Maura! Y'r a talkative slieveen, y' know that? What's it to you what I do or what I'm feeling?' He could see her shape, there on the road before him. He could not see her face. She was silent once more, looking very small. It made him more angry. 'Y'r too sharp, you know that? You want to get inside a man's head – and no man likes that in a woman. Just take care, Maura, or y'll end up like the Misses Fredericks – a dried-up little old maid . . . '

'Och, no . . . '

'No man wants a woman who makes his thoughts uncomfortable . . . '

'It's the truth that's uncomfortable, not me.'

'You too!'

'I could get a man if I wanted one.'

'Don't be so sure.'

'You don't know, do you? Just because you don't find me attractive . . . '

'I never said that . . . '

'Not all men have to have someone like Anna.'

'What's that supposed to mean?'

She had begun to walk away. He took her arm. 'It wasn't her beauty I loved – at least, not all. She was loving and gentle and . . . '

'You don't have to tell me that! She was my friend! Like a sister to me she was! Do you think I don't know her, worry about her? You! All you can think about is how miserable *you* are! How would you like to be her, locked up in some grand house, never to see your parents again, never to talk to anyone but Englishmen and Devlin Kelly!'

'What a little fury y'are to be sure!' he said in amazement. He still held her arm.

176

'Oh, let go of me! Go back to your hearth and your self-pity!'

Now he was holding both her arms, and the warmth of her and the scent of her and the frail femaleness of her arms within his hands made him want her suddenly. He had pulled her to his chest and kissed her, almost before her words were out.

He had never kissed any other woman but Anna, had never held another woman close – and with part of his mind he was amazed to find, in Maura O'Donoghue, a pliancy, a giving in the very way her body fitted against his. He had kissed her almost in play; suddenly it was serious, for Maura did not make the slightest objection, did not attempt to struggle. When finally they pulled away from each other, it was to realize that the kiss had lasted a long time, too long. Both were horrified; Aidan that his body could betray him into wanting another woman in the way that he had wanted Anna, and Maura in her shame that she had so given herself away.

She pushed back from him, took his stance of shocked stillness to be one of amazement at her audacity, then turned, and ran. Up the boreen and away from him, praying that he would not follow.

She had to stop before reaching the farmhouse door. Stood gazing back the way she had come, breathing heavily, waiting for her heart to stop pumping so she could face her brothers calmly.

When she entered the house they grumbled at her long absence – they had had to serve up their own meal from the pot – they were just about to come searching for her – she shouldn't wander about at night with so many desperate people on the roads.

She washed the dishes and they knelt to say the Rosary, Seamus leading and Maura and Thady joining with the response. The gentle monotony of the prayers calmed her somewhat; her mind extracted the most from the words, 'Pray for us sinners . . .', having consciously to take care that she did not say these words any louder than the rest.

Alone in bed that night, she could not sleep.

Aidan O'Brien had never looked at her. Never seemed to see her as anything more than an appendage to Seamus and Thady. For of course, he had Anna. Anna who was everything he had said, not only beautiful, but gentle and kind . . .

And foolish . . . and vain. She tried to stop her mind from acknowledging these thoughts, for she had pitied Anna her fate, and despite Maura's joy in knowing Aidan O'Brien was free, she missed Anna. Already, she had the feeling that she would never know such a friend again.

She writhed on the bed, disliking the conclusions when she compared herself to Anna, she who was not in the least beautiful, who could never be called gentle, and most of the time, though her faith meant a great deal to her, chafed against the ideals drummed into her by Church and parents. She had resented any scraps of their precious food her brothers insisted she give to the poor who came to the door; she went to visit houses of illness only when she knew her reputation amongst her neighbours would suffer if she did not. She wanted people to think well of her. She longed to be admired as Anna had been admired. Somehow it had been easier for Anna. And Maura was too honest with herself to believe that this was only because Anna was beautiful.

She did not know where the problem lay. She always consciously tried to say, to do the right thing, manners meant a great deal to her. Yet she knew she had few friends except for her brothers. Seamus and Thady liked her because, away from the censure of their friends, they could talk to her as they could to a man. She was clever, had political opinions of her own, and could do funny imitations of Father O'Callaghan and Nathan Cameron and even a creditable imitation of Devlin Kelly, in a sniffy sort of anglicized voice which made her whole family laugh. Now, with their parents and Bridie gone, the two boys leaned on her more than ever. She sensed this, and it comforted her. It made up a little for the loss of Anna, who had enjoyed Maura's occasional barbed wit and had a placid enough temperament to accept Maura's swift changes of mood.

'The world is upside down . . . upside down . . . ' she muttered into the lumpy straw mattress. Her mother, father, Bridie, Anna – all gone from her this year – and Aidan O'Brien, who had loved and been loved by her best friend, who had never noticed Maura as a woman, suddenly holding her to him in such an embrace! And she had enjoyed it!

She was bold! Och, she was bold! To visit the O'Briens so often . . . Mary was kind – but she was no fool. Did she suspect? And poor, foolish Thomas . . . No, she would not think of Thomas, sure he was not her responsibility. Aidan was all that mattered. He did not love her. Not yet. But the way he had held her, the force of his lips – he wanted her.

She felt disloyal. And yet, elated, too. She was not as beautiful, as womanly, as fine as Anna O'Hagan. But Anna O'Hagan had not had Aidan O'Brien in her arms tonight. Maura had. And she would again, she promised herself. She wanted him to surrender his feelings to her, to give her the gift of placing her at the centre of his world. All his love. All of it.

Beyond the need for this possession, she did not consider anything at all.

178

19

Thomas took his resentment to the river, worked on it, walked by it, let the sense of permanence that flowed with it flow over him. He lost his ready smile and the dry jokes dried within him, and he kept his secret, as he had always done, to himself.

Had Maura ever been more than fond of him? With Aidan, her wit had gained a sharper edge; sometimes Thomas had wondered if she was not seeking his attention somehow, but Aidan had always laughed good-naturedly, had never joined in her banter, and Thomas had relaxed. There was Anna, after all.

Holding the boat steady while Packy Brady set the lines, watching the dawn turn the sky to rose beneath the thirteen arches of the ancient bridge before him, he told himself that he should have spoken sooner . . . But no. He knew with the characteristic honesty that marked his relationship to life that Maura had loved Aidan all along. No timing would have been right. His only hope went with Anna O'Hagan.

It did not occur to him to fight what he saw happening between Maura and his older brother. He knew instinctively that Aidan was stronger than he was, that while he would not, perhaps, make Maura as happy as he himself could have done, Aidan was more capable; Aidan was a fighter, could grasp life with both hands and wring what he wished from it. He understood life, accepted it. Thomas watched life from a distance, did not understand it, was a little afraid of it.

Seamus and Thady were pleased with the frequency with which Aidan began to call upon their sister. They would have liked to tease him, but remained sensitive enough to Aidan's feelings for Anna not to wish to push him inadvertently in any direction. It was Aidan's own mother who betrayed misgivings.

One evening when Corrie was visiting Limerick, when Thomas had gone to bed and only Mary and Aidan remained by the fire, he said, 'You're very quiet, Ma. Would it be about Maura that you're thinking?'

She looked up at him from her sewing, catching his incisive glance, the smile that showed confidence in his guess. She lowered her eyes, stabbing the needle back and forth. 'You don't love the girl.'

'No.'

'Y're not planning on marrying her, then, are y'?'

'I . . . Yes, I think so.'

'Don't, Aidan.'

'Don't? I'm nearly twenty-three, Ma, old enough to make my own decisions. Anyway, you had no objection to me marrying Anna.'

'Anna is not Maura.'

He said tightly, 'We both know that.'

'They're very different women, Aidan. Maura comes from a fine family – but the pair of you are ill-suited, son.'

'I've known her all my life – we've never quarrelled . . . '

'You've never been together to quarrel – to get to know each other at all.'

'I know her brothers . . . '

'You'll not be marryin' her brothers.'

Aidan shifted restlessly on his stool. 'I know she's got a sharp tongue,' he admitted, 'but I can handle that . . . '

'Oh, y'can! I'll be tellin' you somethin', Mister O'Brien, accept a woman as she is before marriage, because that's what you'll be getting, only more so! If a woman suddenly becomes tender, loving, in a way she wasn't before, it's because she was always so . . . '

'Perhaps I see that in Maura . . . '

'You do not. Because it's not there in Maura. She's not *hiding* her feelings. She's twenty-two, now; I've never known her to smile kindly at a boy, let alone lovingly. She had a good man for a father, and a kind-hearted mother; she had every reason to grow up happy and good-natured like Anna – but she hasn't. She's too deep, Aidan . . . What it takes to make Maura happy, I don't know. But I know you can't give it to her. You'll both be miserable.'

'I need a wife, do I not?' he persisted, almost crossly. 'I'll not be single all my life, thinking . . . thinking of what might have been. I'll not look back. I know Maura, and she knows me. She's honest, and fair, and reasonable, she'll do her duty by me, and I'll do . . . '

'*Duty*? Yes, son. She'll do her duty by you as your wife – duty, I'm thinking, would mean a good deal to Maura. But what of warmth, Aidan, what of caring . . . '

'She'll do all that,' he said stubbornly. 'You'll see.'

Mary opened her mouth to speak further, but even as she did, she knew it was too late. The set of his jaw as he gazed into the fire was so like his father's, that wild, hard-drinking Aidan who had not lived to see his twenty-eighth year. How she had mourned him! Years and years. Yet had he lived, would she have been happy? She was happy with Corrie; she grew afraid, sometimes, realizing how much happiness he had given her; in the midst of this death and destruction that went on around them, no one had a right to be as happy, as well-loved as she was.

And she had wanted this same happiness for her sons, too. The right kind of wife. She could not help but see bitterness in Maura O'Donoghue – and God help her, there was bitterness enough in Aidan. She realized it suddenly, gazing at his fixed expression, the broad mouth with the mobile corners, now turned down slightly, his thoughts, she knew, on Anna. What hope could there be of happiness between him and Maura? For both of them, Anna would always be there.

And there was Thomas. Would it do any good to tell him what she suspected, that Thomas was in love with Maura? No, it would solve nothing. The glow in Maura's eyes had only ever been for Aidan; the girl was not astute enough to see that Thomas had qualities that were just as valuable as his brother's. Mary shrank from interfering; Thomas, after all, had never spoken to her of his feelings. If she mentioned her suspicions to Aidan, he would go to Thomas and demand to know what he felt, bullying him in a good-natured way to speak up – and Thomas would be made even more wretched than he was.

'Aidan . . . ?' she said softly. 'At least wait a while. Wait until you forget Anna a little. It's been less than a year, and if you marry Maura now, you'll always be comparing them, Aidan. And Maura will know.'

He did not take his eyes from the fire. 'I don't want to wait any longer. Maura understands about Anna. She was her friend, remember. There's nothing to be gained from waiting.'

And so he proposed to Maura O'Donoghue two days later, when they were climbing one of the hills on Tineranna, between the O'Donoghues' cottage and the big house. Lough Derg was blue in the warm sunshine of the summer, and their cheeks were pink with the bite of a crisp breeze and the haste of their climb.

On reaching the top of the hill, Maura, suddenly overcome by the scent of the grass, the beauty of the view before them, the joy of being alive and having Aidan with her, began to run along the crest of the hill. Aidan, laughing, followed her, watching her thin, boy's hips, her narrow shoulders. As she began to tire, slowing to a trot, he burst out suddenly, 'Will y' marry, me, Maura?'

Her heart missed a beat with shock. She stared in front of her for a long moment, slowing to a walk and finally standing still. Only then did she turn to him.

'Will I what?'

Aidan, too, came to a halt, embarrassed suddenly. He shoved his hands deep into his pockets, rocked a little on his heels. He wondered uncomfortably if she was going to laugh at him. 'I said, will y' marry me?'

Maura had not been expecting this. She realized suddenly that none of her dreams of him had ever led this far. She liked to be near him, found herself jealous of the time he spent away from her – but marriage was something in the future. And somehow, she still saw him as being part of Anna – and she did not want to do this. The jealousy of her friend bit into her more than it had ever done.

''Tis an amazing man y' are. Not six months ago you were in love with Anna O'Hagan – and here you are proposin' to me.'

He scowled at her. She realized she was waiting for him to speak. To hear him say . . . what?

But he was silent, and she turned from him. 'If I married you, all Killaloe would be laughing at me.'

His chin went up. 'And why is that?'

'They'll say . . . ' and she turned to him, to see his face, 'that you only married me because you couldn't have Anna.'

And still he was silent. They faced each other like two protagonists, neither moving but for their hair, whipped about their faces by the wind from the lough. So she was forced to say softly, 'It's true, isn't it?'

'What of it?' Uncomfortably, hating his inability to tell her some lie, any lie. But the look of hurt that appeared on her face was brief, and replaced by a slow smile.

'If Anna O'Hagan wouldn't have you why should I?' And seeing his reaction, 'Maybe I should find meself a wealthy husband, too . . . ' She turned away, but he had moved too quickly, had taken her arm and whirled her about to face him.

'Would you be thinking of that, now? Sellin' yourself t' some gombeen man, perhaps, who's made his money bleedin' others?'

'Y'r hurting my arm!' Then, glancing up at him, sharply, 'It's bothered y'are, still, Anna going off like that . . . '

'She did it for her family and you know it . . . '

'Does that make you feel better, Aidan? Maybe Anna just preferred Devlin t' *you*!' And she pulled away from him, angry, now. 'Why me, then? There are others y' could ask . . . '

'I know you.'

'Is that *all*?'

He shrugged, helplessly. Lord, the woman was difficult! He had thought it would be such a simple thing – almost a business agreement. She was alone in the world, they were both of marriageable age, what could be simpler? He struggled for words. 'You'd have no cause t' find fault with me . . . I'm a good provider . . . I've got my job at Tineranna . . . There's the room at the cottage, and enough land to provide for us and the children . . . '

'Children? Children, is it, now? T'be sure, y'are a practical man, Aidan O'Brien. I haven't said I'll consider y'r offer, and here y'are plannin' the family . . . All sons, I'll be bound.'

'Of course,' he said, unthinkingly, then seeing the look on her face, he had to grin.

And seeing this, her expression softened a little, and she took a step towards him, hesitantly. ''Tis a fine smile y' have, when y' bother . . . '

'Well, then . . . ' And he went to place his arms around her. She stepped back.

'I'll not be marryin' y' for y' smile. Y' don't smile often enough, Aidan. I could die in the waitin' . . . '

As she went to turn away again, he stepped quickly in front of her, realizing, now, that she was playing with him. 'Let's put an end to all the nonsense now. Will y' have me, or not?'

His hands were at the small of her back. Again he felt her suppleness, the potential giving in her . . . But she was frowning up at him.

'Is that all y've got to say?'

Exasperated, he almost laughed at her. 'Woman, what more do you want?'

She averted her face from him, turned to look down at the lough. Her voice lowered. 'A woman wants . . . more. Y' could start by saying y' loved me.'

There was no change in him. His arms still remained about her, warm, strong; yet his silence was tangible with feeling, and when she glanced at his face, he, too, was frowning down at the water.

'Ah . . . ' she breathed, and the very exhalation hurt her, some-how, 'I see . . . '

And she was gone from him, walking down the hill in the direction of her home.

'No!' he called, 'Wait! All right, I don't love you. Anyway, not yet.' She had slowed, halted, her shoulders straight. 'We know each other . . . we won't be having any romantic notions in our heads – but we won't be giving each other any nasty surprises, either . . . '

He watched in relief as her shoulders relaxed, and she turned to him, the old smile of amusement on her face.

'Well?' He walked down towards her, took her shoulders and

shook her gently. 'What d' y' say? Is it a bargain we have?'

And Maura knew she would accept. Saw the terrible chance that she took, the potential unhappiness that awaited her, but knew she had to accept. She wanted him for her own. For him to belong to her. Not to Anna. She would make him forget Anna . . . 'All right . . . It's a bargain.'

And they gazed at each other, almost shy. The kiss he gave her contained none of the passion of their first – the scene had drained him, her reminders of Anna were disquieting. Besides, he was late for work.

'I'll be over to tell Seamus and Thady tonight.'

'All right. We can have the banns read this Sunday . . . '

He nodded, remembering, suddenly, unwillingly, the day on Craglea with Anna. *To hell with the banns*! The madness, the joy just to be there beside her.

And he looked at Maura, small, pretty in a sharp, pinched way, and for an instant he hesitated. It was the only time he queried whether he was doing the right thing for her. But he said, 'Well . . .I'll be seeing you tonight . . . '

And he walked off at a tangent down the hill, towards the big house, leaving Maura gazing after him for a long time.

That night, Aidan, Seamus and Thady went walking, leaving Maura to clean up after the evening meal. Thady paused at the end of the boreen and looked into the blackness of the Killaloe Road.

'We m-might run into some Terryalts . . . '

'Which ones?' Seamus said jauntily. 'Regan's boys, or Connolly's or Duffy's mob? Come now, Thady, you know 'em as well as I do; they'll not be after the likes of us.'

'Perhaps the police will fff-find us. Perhaps they'll think www-we're Terrys . . . '

'If it's not one side, it's the other. Are you afraid of everything?'

'Nnnn-no. Just police and Terryalts. And I don't mmm-mean Regan and Connolly. There are others, y'know. Everyone's got a grievance, nnn-nowadays. Sss-some might not stop and ask wwww-what side www-we're on.'

Seamus sneered at his brother. But all three knew that the dark roads and boreens were natural hiding places for robbers; and starving men, with hungry children sheltering in ditches and hovels, roamed the countryside at night searching for unprotected crops and unguarded sheep and cattle. Aidan agreed that they should not go too far.

The moon appeared and disappeared behind cloud, but the night

184

was fairly mild. Aidan walked between the two brothers, feeling the companionship of their silence. He had always felt close to these two, closer even than to Thomas, whose introvertedness puzzled and sometimes aggravated Aidan. But Seamus contained Aidan's own restless energy, and Thady, for all his voiced trepidation, always entered into the roughest game, the riskiest gamble, with as much spirit as his brother.

'Now y'r marrying Maura, will y' come to live with us?' Seamus asked. 'We've four rooms in the house. And even when I marry Sara Minogue, there'll be room for us all.'

'I thought about it, and I thank you, but Corrie'll be needing help with the harvesting, and I'm closer to the big house where I am. Besides, as you say, you'll have Sara. I don't fancy the thought of Maura and Sara in the same house, d' you?' The O'Donoghues grinned, they did not.

'Hold there! Who would you be?'

All three stiffened, halted. Dark shapes arose beyond the wall to their left – rustlings in the grass – more shapes to their right.

'I said, who would you be?'

'Aidan O'Brien, Thady and Seamus O'Donoghue. Who would *you* be?'

There was a slight air of relaxation to the two groups. 'What're y' doin' out, O'Brien?'

'What's it to you?'

'You watch y'r step, boyo!'

'Aidan . . . ' Thady's hand lay cautioningly on his arm.

'Is it Cormac Regan? It is, isn't it . . . ?'

'Never you mind. Answer me – what're you doin' about at such an hour?'

'Walkin'.'

A pause. Regan's suspicion was tangible in the silence.

'Will y' take an Irishman's oath, you three?'

In the darkness, Thady and Seamus glanced at each other, then at Aidan. 'Www-well . . . '

'Speak up, now!'

Men were climbing the wall on the right to join them on the roadway. There were about half a dozen and they pressed the three slowly, inexorably, towards the voice on their left.

'Come,' Regan said, 'will you take the oath?'

Thady was pressed against Aidan's chest by a tall brute of a man who was treading heavily, threateningly, on his toes. 'I don't see www-why not . . . Seamus? Aidan? Can yyy-you?'

'Come into the field.'

It was not an invitation. Hands grabbed their arms, and they were half-hauled over into the pasture. It was Osborne land; Regan was one of Osborne's tenants. Aidan looked around at the men, and in the brief seconds of escaped moonlight, he thought he recognized several of them, and if he was right, they were all Osborne's tenants; all men with a grievance, and desperate.

'We got a Bible, here . . . ' Hands were still holding the boys' shoulders; before them they saw only the pale band that was Regan's shirt sleeve beneath his dark coat, they could not see the Bible.

It was Seamus who was pushed forward first, who found the leather-bound cover thrust into his hands.

'It goes like this, "I," ' – There y' give y' name – "believing in a free Ireland governed by Irishmen, pledge myself towards that goal, and promise to stand by my fellow countrymen in their efforts to keep the land that rightfully belongs to them." '

There was a silence. The hands on their shoulders tightened a little.

Seamus cleared his throat. 'That's it?'

'That's it. Will y' say it?'

Again they turned to look at each other. Aidan saw a sudden movement, heard Seamus give a sharp cry, 'Me arm!' But he had taken only half a step towards him when hands were holding his arms, his neck. His fear gone, he had something to fight against, almost managed to throw them off, but there were more of them, at least four of them; he felt smothered, his arms pinned to his sides . . .

Seamus was groaning, 'All right, all right! Let go me arm!'

The pressure must have been eased. After a pause, Regan began, ' "I, Seamus O'Donoghue . . . " '

'I, Seamus O'Donoghue . . . ' A tight, resentful voice. Seamus repeated it word for word. Regan and the Bible moved on to Aidan.

'Y'll get life imprisonment f'r giving oaths like that . . . ' Aidan's hand refused to take the Bible. The hands still held him tightly, and he was raging inwardly. Regan stepped close to him.

'This oath is all we've got, boy – standing together is all we got. We can't go t' the courts when we're turned out on the roads. What would you have us do? Lie down like dogs and let bastards like them two Osbornes kick us to death if they choose? If y'r not with us, O'Brien, perhaps y'r thinkin' of informin' the police . . . ?'

Someone brought a knee up into the small of Aidan's back. The pain through his kidneys brought him to his knees. He heard Regan's voice say mildly, 'Not too rough, there . . . '

And Thady's voice was saying, 'I'll swear it! Give me the Bible

186

here. Don't hit him! Give it here!' But someone had taken Aidan's further silence as stubbornness, and a blow hit him over the right ear, almost immediately followed by a strong bare foot slammed heavily into his ribs. His head went down, buzzing with lack of oxygen, and all he could hear above this noise was Thady repeating the oath after Regan, and a kind of misplaced wonder that Thady, in his efforts to draw the mob's attention from Aidan, had not stuttered once.

'Now you . . . ' Regan's voice was close. The man was standing over him. Aidan tried to put out a hand to help himself rise, the men holding his arms leaned down on him, pinning him there. Regan took his hair, pulled it back, forcing Aidan to look up into his face.

'What's the matter with you, boy? You've had Devlin Kelly raise y'r rents so high that there's not a family that c'd afford t' pay them . . . '

'His could,' a voice suggested.

'That's right.' Regan nodded, 'Y'r fortunate, boy, with y'r brother on the river and y'r ma married to Corrie O'Neill – but the rest of us aren't so lucky. We won't get anywhere with our demands unless we work together. If y' don't think of y'rself, think of y'r neighbours, think of the cottiers. And who would you be wanting to protect, anyway? Devlin Kelly? Why, everyone in Killaloe knows he took Anna O'Hagan . . . ' The blood pounded in Aidan's head, but the nightmare would not end, he could not move, and Regan's voice went on, remorseless. 'There's not a man here that doesn't feel for y', boyo. She was your woman . . . '

'Shut up, Regan!' he managed to shout, through the man's words, 'Shut up, shut up, just shut . . . ' Someone's hand was clamped over his mouth.

'Don't you realize . . . ! If we'd been organized then as we are now, we could have done something?'

'You couldn't have stopped him.'

It was Seamus who spoke. Regan straightened and turned to him. 'We could have made him wish he'd never been born.' And his voice was low with his rage. 'He's worse than any of the others! He's Catholic, and he's Irish – he's turned against his own kind.' He looked down at Aidan. 'What about it, boyo? Will you stand with us?'

Aidan felt the hand removed from his face. Still he was silent, could feel the rage making his tensed muscles tremble, could feel Regan's patience begin to wear, his fist was raised in exasperation.

'He won't give in to that kind of treatment.'

A new voice, but familiar. A figure appeared beside Regan,

having pushed forward from the back of the crowd. 'Aidan?' He knelt in front of him and Aidan recognized Martin Curran. Before he could speak, Martin was talking, softly but quickly, urgently. 'Aidan, we're desperate. I haven't talked much about it, but . . . most of us here haven't got more than a few weeks' food – the meal months have never been like this, Aidan – and Osborne won't help!

'Do you know where Tom-Joe is now? Do y' know why Tom-Joe isn't here? His wife's dying – Bridget is dying – of consumption they say, but they've had no more than three bowls of stirabout between them this past week, three bowls between her and Tom-Joe and the baby! No! Don't start askin' why we didn't come to you – it's too late for any of that! You've had no thought for anything but Anna, you haven't looked around at anything that's happening! It's not just here on Ceelohg, Aidan – it's all over Ireland. We have to *do* something! And Regan is right – we have to stand together!'

The two stared into each others' faces, then Martin said, more calmly, 'If they let you up, will you promise not to fight? Will y' take the oath, if y' stand alone and no one touches y'?'

After a silence, 'Yes.'

'Y're word y'll not fight 'em – they're like as not t' murder y', Aidan, I swear it . . . '

'I won't fight.'

Martin stood up, glanced at Regan. The older man said, 'Let him up. Leave him alone.'

Gingerly, they let Aidan loose, and he slowly got to his feet.

'Come then, repeat my words – "I, Aidan O'Brien . . ." '

'I, Aidan O'Brien . . . '

' "Believing in a free Ireland ruled by Irishmen, pledge myself to that goal." '

'Believing in a free Ireland ruled by Irishmen, pledge myself to that goal . . . '

And when he had finished the entire oath, Regan held out his hand. 'Come, boy, shake hands with me. Martin's been wanting to get the three of you with us for weeks, now . . . '

Aidan stared at Martin, who caught his glance and looked down, awkward, embarrassed about the incident. Regan was still waiting.

'Shake hands, O'Brien – show there's no bitterness between us.'

Aidan put his hand into Regan's, deaf to the few sounds of soft, relieved laughter from the men. No bitterness between them . . . Aidan looked at the others, crowding about, now, to shake hands with Seamus and Thady. Bitterness was all they had. Perhaps not for each other, but it bound them together. It was a brotherhood of bitterness.

The three walked homewards together, Aidan between the two O'Donoghues, sullen, scowling, his arms and shoulders bruised, his dignity equally as outraged.

'Come now, Aidan – if only Tom-Joe or Martin had come to us quietly and explained, we'd have joined the Terrys willingly enough . . . '

'Yes, 'twas their mmm-methods you're annoyed about, nn-not their objectives . . . '

'Their what?' Seamus leaned forward to stare at his brother.

'Ah, don't pretend t'be mmm-more ignorant than y' are.'

'Listen, Thady . . . !'

'Shut up, the pair of you, can't you?'

They glanced at him, sensing the rage still within him, and for the next hundred yards they walked in silence.

It was a silence that was to end in death. All three, looking back on that quiet walk, realized that a sound from any of them would have averted what happened. If Seamus had made a rejoinder to Thady, if Thady had looked up and noted that the moon was shining clearly, now, if Aidan had voiced his resentment of Regan's coercions . . .

They were at a corner of the road; to their right was one of Osborne's fields, dark olive green in the night, a sea of full-grown new potato plants. Aidan and the O'Donoghues were not Ceelohg tenants; they did not know of any reason why someone should be in Osborne's field weeks before harvesting . . . But a figure was there, scrabbling furiously with a spade, then dropping to his knees to burrow in the earth with his hands.

It happened too quickly for them to give warning. One minute the creature was alone, the next a large and powerfully built figure rose from the shadows, arms raised, and without a word brought the handle of a spade or pitchfork down upon the kneeling man. Once, twice, three times – the watching men heard the skull crack each time.

'No!' It was Thady. Aidan grabbed his arm – even in the moonlight he had recognized Hubert Osborne. But twice more the weapon came down; twice, before the cry seemed to penetrate Hubert's consciousness. He was filled with fury – three nights he had been waiting to catch this culprit – three nights while his enraged proprietary feelings mounted higher. He sought only to punish, to retaliate . . . He stared upwards at the three figures on the other side of the wall; two, tall, red-haired, and between them a shorter, dark, heavily-built man . . .

Aidan had grabbed both their arms. 'Run!'

They sped off down the road, each of them sickened, terrified, frightened with the fear bred into them, that the powers of the landlords were limitless, and they had witnessed one committing murder – and they had been seen!

Past the rows of cottiers' hovels, past the main gates to Tineranna, slowing only at the boreen leading down to O'Sullivans. All three were breathing heavily, leaning against the stone wall in exhaustion. Aidan glanced back along the road, turned to the two brothers. 'Get you home. Don't tell Maura anything . . . And if the police come, we saw *nothing*, d' y' understand? One of y' come to tell me if there's any news – and over the back way through O'Sullivans – we're not to be seen together, the three of us, for a few days, at least . . . '

'Aidan . . . '

'Go now! Osborne may be sayin' already that we did it!'

They separated, Aidan half-trotting along the boreen, the O'Donoghues walking quickly off along the road towards Ogonnelloe.

Only Mary was still awake when he came in. She had her head bent over her sewing, only glanced up at him before lowering her head once more. 'I suppose there's an end to it. It can't be undone – my blessing I give you only because you'll have need of it.'

He gazed at his mother as if she was bewitched, and then realized that she knew nothing other than that he had been to see Seamus and Thady, to discuss Maura and the marriage. Only a few hours ago . . . He debated telling her everything, but decided to wait until morning, and he crept off to bed to curl up beside the sleeping Thomas.

He slept fitfully, a sleep full of nightmare figures in darkened fields. He awoke when Thomas arose, yawning, to go down to the boats, and fell asleep again after dawn, a sleep of exhaustion that was abruptly shattered when he found Thady O'Donoghue shaking his shoulder, telling him in stuttering, barely intelligible phrases that the man murdered by Hubert Osborne last night was Tom-Joe Curran.

20

The potato crop had failed again. During the week after Tom-Joe's death; the light, warm rain fell, and in Minogues' fields, in O'Byrnes', O'Sullivans', all over Clare, all over Ireland, the potato plants wilted and died. And this time it was total failure.

Aidan, Thomas and Corrie stood amid the foul-smelling remains of their crop, and gazed silently at each other. All the money they had saved had gone to pay the rent, all Corrie had earned that spring and summer in Limerick had gone towards buying new seed. Seed that had sprouted, grown into fine and healthy plants, only to blacken to jelly one wet afternoon in September. Blacken almost as they gazed at them.

The only one of Aidan's friends who seemed not to recognize the peril of the situation was Martin, still driven almost to distraction in his grief. It took all Aidan's and Regan's persuasion to prevent him from murdering Hubert. 'Y'd be a fool!' Aidan told him at one of the Terrys' now frequent meetings. 'They're expecting you to try something. Y' never see Hubert Osborne out, without he's got four or five friends with 'im – all with two muskets apiece. And if y' did manage t' kill 'im – even if the others didn't recognize y' – y'd be the first man they'd come lookin' for, Martin.'

'Am I to do nothing, then? You know Neill Hogan overheard some talk at Osborne's tavern – some of Osborne's friends layin' bets that he'd be off to America before the coroner gives his decision. . . '

'He wouldn't try that,' Seamus said. 'No matter how much he'd like to – it'd be an admission of guilt . . . '

'Och, you!' Martin almost snarled. 'You three stood there and watched it happen . . . !'

Aidan said, 'Now just watch y'r tongue, Martin . . . '

'If it was Devlin Kelly did this t' Thomas, Aidan, y'd have his head on a spike by now . . . '

'And have me own in a rope tomorrow! Don't be a fool, Martin! We'll get Osborne, but not by any foolhardiness . . . '

'The British justice system wouldn't have favourites,' Seamus said drily. 'Let's just wait and see what the coroner says, and what our magistrates think of an Englishman in the dock for once.'

'I'm not waiting around playing games, Seamus . . . !'

There was a sound in the darkness, and one of the O'Byrne boys, on guard with the group's only musket, called, 'Who's there?'

'John McNamara!'

The group parted as the man almost fell into their midst.

'Where've y' been?' Regan demanded. 'Y' could get shot, arrivin' late like that!'

'Been in the village. Father Walsh . . . the new curate . . . '

'What about him?'

'He's dead – came down with the fever yesterday . . . Father

O'Callaghan, the poor man . . . he wept, Cormac, I saw Father O'Callaghan weep!'

The group was silent for a moment. 'Father Walsh was a good man, and a brave one. I think we all oughta go to the wake – I mean, to pay our respects.' Several men crossed themselves. 'God rest his soul gently,' Regan said.

He turned to Martin. 'I don't want to hear any more about Osborne, Martin. Or from any of the rest of you, y' hear? We'll make a move when it's safe, and not before. Now, let's go into the village – in twos and threes, not all in a group like a bloody regiment on the march.'

Aidan went with the others to pay brief respects to Father Walsh's body. The curate had been in Killaloe only six months, but had been well-liked and fearless in his determination to visit and nurse the sick. Father O'Callaghan, his thin, long body further stooped in his sadness, met them at the door. Why, Aidan thought, the man must be nearly eighty . . . yet the eyes were clear and sharp beneath the grey eyebrows, the handshake was firm. Father O'Callaghan still steered the ship that was his parish, and until he died, the hand would be firm on the tiller.

Father Collins of Scarriff was there. He knelt on the other side of the coffin, his head bent in prayer. Aidan reminded himself that this was the priest who had married Anna to Devlin. And yet he felt no resentment against the man; Devlin would have arranged things well; Father Collins would have had no more choice in the matter than Anna's parents, than Anna herself.

Father O'Callaghan was to have married Aidan and Maura, but within a week of Father Walsh's death, came even more startling news. Martin Curran came one wild night with the sleet lashing across the lake before a bitter east wind. He stood inside the closed door, the water dripping from his thick, blue-black head of curls, smiled a little for the first time since his brother's death, and announced that the new curate of Killaloe was Daniel McDonnagh.

Aidan was pleased. Though only ten when Daniel had left for Maynooth, the man had nevertheless been a constant visitor to the house, almost a father figure in Aidan's early years, and even Thomas had vague and comfortable recollections of a tall, thin man in black, who gave him rides on his horse.

But it was not the same Daniel McDonnagh who walked down the gangplank of the *Lady Landsdowne* that September of 1846. He had left Killaloe a young man, burning with love of God and mankind, excited at the prospect of studying with the greatest theologians, of

192

learning how to interpret God's words, how best to preach those words to the people.

For the years of his training, Maynooth was still under the influence of the elderly French expatriots, royalists forced to flee during the turbulent years of the new century, who brought to Maynooth and to the minds of their eager pupils all their conservatism; the respect for order, a belief in Divine Rule, a faith in whatever monarch the Lord chose to set over them. All teaching was coloured by this, all scriptures and history interpreted through these narrow sights.

The Bishop of Killaloe himself, as well as Father O'Callaghan, had received such training. Daniel, however, had questioned much in this rigid atmosphere, had been chastened, admonished, for querying his instructors' views on social justice and liberty – had been threatened with expulsion for reading and daring to quote the works of Voltaire. He was told to fast, to pray, to purge himself of rebellious thoughts – told this by some of the greatest ecclesiastics of the times. Told year after year, as his world narrowed around him, and the life of the village he had left became, it seemed, a meandering pattern of days, without meaning, without purpose. *Here* was the reality. And when he saw this, in his fifth year at Maynooth, he knew that the Order of Existence, God's ordained Order, was all.

He stayed on at Maynooth, and became an excellent teacher; he who knew all the rebel's questions because he had asked them all, now had the answers, concise, witty, sometimes barbed. He became feared, and a great favourite, at one and the same time.

He did not really understand why he requested his Bishop to be allowed to return to his own parish. It was a time of emergency, and the people, who were his own people, needed help. At the age of forty-two, after fourteen years in the seminary, Daniel McDonnagh came home to a Killaloe greatly changed.

His welcoming party was held at his parents' home, above their family drapery business in the village. Daniel moved through the groups of guests smiling, laughing, appearing to be enjoying himself greatly, but within himself he was appalled at the poverty that seemed to be everywhere, at the threadbare clothes even on such people as the O'Donoghues and Currans, comfortably-off farmers when he had left. And so many faces absent – three of the Brogans, Liam O'Donoghue and his wife and child, Packy Brady's three sons, Tom-Joe Curran . . . the names went on and on.

Aidan proudly introduced his stepfather to Daniel. Corrie shook his hand, liked the thin priest with the sensitive, scholar's face, but could not help the stab of displeasure when he saw the warmth with which Mary and the priest greeted each other. They had been friends since childhood, Father McDonnagh had explained to Corrie, but resting his hands on Mary's shoulders, gazing into her eyes. And the look she returned him!

The unfamiliar knot of suspicion stayed with him as they walked home. He kept remembering the fondness with which Mary had always spoken of Daniel, how he had been friends with her first husband, had helped her in the first days of her widowhood. They walked silently together along the road and down the boreen, the only sound from Thomas and Aidan, who had drunk too much at the party and were reeling and laughing at some distance behind them.

'You loved him, didn't you?' he asked abruptly. Mary did not answer, it was as if she had not heard. 'Didn't you?' he persisted.

'I wondered what you were brooding about,' she said softly.

'Well? Will you answer me, woman?'

She turned to look up at him, and he wished he could see the expression on her face, but it was too dark, her features were a blur. 'It's true that I loved Daniel,' she said, and it took all his will not to stop walking, yank her around to him, but her voice came softly, calmly. 'I loved the boy that he was, his gentleness, and his dreams. 'But . . . ' she turned to gaze ahead into the darkness, 'it wasn't the sort of love for *sharing*. Not the kind you can build a marriage on. Our love's big enough to include the boys, and soon, Maura, and *her* babies . . .

'I knew when I saw Daniel again that he was right to join the priesthood. I don't know how he'll cope with all he has to face here, but I know he couldn't have seen us through these bad times – he couldn't have guided the boys, nor loved me with such patience all these years. Mother of God, no man could have loved me the way you have! No man could have given me the happiness you have!'

Aidan and Thomas saw their parents pause, then saw Corrie bend, with a laugh, and scoop their tiny mother up into his arms. They stopped in surprise to see it, the giant walking jauntily along in the dark, Mary trying not to laugh, pretending to be cross with him.

'Y' great eejit!' she was saying. 'Put me down! What will the boys think? You'll not carry me all the way home – you'll not!'

'And why not?' Corrie's voice floated back to them, 'Sure y'r as light as a child in me arms . . . '

Corrie was walking quickly, and they were soon out of sight. For some reason the two brothers did not move off immediately; witnessing a scene of such warmth seemed to fill each of them with sombre thoughts.

194

Aidan said, almost grimly, 'It's possible to love twice in one's life, isn't it? *They've* done it. It must be possible. Don't you think?'

Thomas began to say something, stopped, then said, his voice like a sigh, 'I hope so.'

Aidan, heedless of his parents' advice, and even the well-meaning cautioning of Father McDonnagh, married Maura O'Donoghue in early November, 1846.

He was late for the wedding. All that evening before his friends had dogged his footsteps in a good-natured guard of honour, but he longed to escape, to be alone to think. The chance came when it was decided that the supply of potcheen was insufficient for the festivities, and eight of them headed up Craglea to visit Dan Clooney. It was early afternoon, and they did not have to begin fasting for the nine o'clock service until midnight; they had plenty of time, so they stayed. Aidan and Thomas, Terry O'Sullivan, Martin and the O'Donoghues, Roddy and Gerry Minogue, all seated themselves around the floor of the tiny cottage, drinking a great deal of the liquor. When midnight crept up upon them with a sleety rain that beat against the little house, they stared out into the bleak darkness, decided to a man to spend the night, and went back for one last jar. In the morning, when they awoke, Aidan had gone.

'What do you think of that, now?' Seamus, after they had searched the hut's environs in the weak morning light, stood and scratched his bright hair.

'Fine manners for a guest of honour, to leave without saying goodbye . . . ' Clooney scowled around, his dignity as host affronted.

Seamus turned to Thomas, 'You're his brother – where would he go?'

But Thomas only smiled his gentle smile, and shrugged. 'Home to get ready for the wedding, most probably.'

'What foolishness.' Gerry Minogue sat down on the ground, rubbed his burning eyes.

'Indeed.' Terry O'Sullivan half-collapsed beside him, he himself had decided to risk his soul and not fast at all, imbibing potcheen until sleep had claimed him half-way through a jar, 'What man with all his wits rushes off to be early for his wedding, tell me?'

They sat and pondered the disappearance for some while, then marched hopefully in a group around the hut three times, hulloing as they went. After this expedition, they returned to the hut to collect the potcheen, and wended a steady but meandering path down the mountain, Gerry Minogue leading his donkey with the valued provisions, and all seven calling Aidan's name all through the descent.

Aidan lay curled at the foot of Aoibheal's Rock. He had lain down there to rest, to clear his thoughts, to prepare himself for the wedding; but he fell asleep to dream of Anna O'Hagan.

They were seated here, the two of them, as they had been the last day he had seen her. Her hair was blowing loose about her, and her arms were about his neck. He was gazing into her eyes, black-lashed, haunting, the changing shadows of moss green and russet in their depths. He gazed at her unbelievingly, at the warm smile upon her lips, the few sprinkled freckles across an otherwise faultless skin. She was his again! He did not question the miracle, was talking to her only of the joy of having her here with him, how they would run away together – that day – that very minute!

'Yes,' she said, pressing her face into his chest. 'Oh, Aidan! I've missed you! I've missed you so!'

And suddenly, they were running together, along the crest of the hill, just as they had done as children, but she was faster, now, faster than he was . . .

'Come back, Anna! We must go, now! Anna, come back!' But she was running down the hill from him, towards the lake. 'Anna, come back!' And a rumble of thunder echoed over them as he reached her, took her arm . . .

Who was this, with her back to him, pulling herself from his grasp, walking away from him down the hill? Her hair was loose, it floated about her knees, but it was not the brown-gold of Anna's, but long and straight and silver as the moon's path on water. A black dress swirled about her like seaweed floating on the tide. Not Anna. Not Anna when she turned, the face beautiful, and smiling amongst the strands of silver that whipped around her like a veil of cloud, of mist . . . not Anna! But smiling at him, beckoning him, one white hand held out to him, then curled back towards her . . . And he tried to cry out, because he knew the woman in black was powerful beyond his comprehension, that she had taken Anna, and wanted him. And he screamed, seeing death in the touch of the white hand that reached for him; death was the promise of the lips that moved silently in invitation . . .

When he started up, it was to find Dan Clooney bent over him, grinning broadly with his yellowed teeth. 'Sure, I thought y' might have gone off by y'rself. Y' looked like a man whose thoughts lay heavy on his mind . . .'

'How . . . did y' find me?'

'How? An' you after givin' a bellow like a calvin' cow! C'mon, lad, or y'll be late f'r the weddin'.'

He helped Aidan to his feet, half-supported him as the storm broke above them, and through the rain Aidan, his mouth a line of grim acceptance, made his way down the mountainside.

Two hours late, he finally stood at the altar rail and promised his life-long loyalty and fidelity to Maura O'Donoghue.

Maura was furious, she seethed inside, yet, conscious that all the village was watching her, she kept her chin high, smiled a little. She knew, from studying herself in the mirror, that she looked better when she smiled. She wanted to look beautiful, today. She wanted people to remember her as beautiful.

Daniel McDonnagh, watching the patient waiting of the young bride, had undergone a change of feelings as to the outcome of this marriage. Now, gazing down at the demure pale face beneath the veil, and the owlishly blinking Aidan, he could not help smiling. Perhaps, he thought, the difference in their characters might work for the good.

In those bleak times, men and women grasped at any chance for gaiety and amusement. So Aidan's and Maura's wedding was a beacon in the dark month of November; for though the food was not as plentiful as it might have been, there was enough potcheen and good will to spread three times among the farmers, cottiers and villagers alike who gathered at the O'Donoghue house. Even with the Piper Brogan dead, he had four sons whom he had trained well, and who played manfully all through the evening, despite the frequent necessary stops to assuage their thirst: Jim-Joe, who had inherited his Da's pipes; Tom, who played the fiddle as well as any man in East Clare; Francis, who played the barawn, the flat goatshide drum; and Diarmuid, whose tin whistle could sound so haunting that one would swear that it was Aoibheal herself who sang around the eaves.

Long into the night the festivities went on; Aidan, for the most part separated from Maura by the crowd, kept glancing at her every now and then, asking himself even in his still drunken state, how all this had come about.

About two o'clock in the morning, the guests began drifting away. At half-past two, the Brogans left, and once the house was quiet of the bouncing rhythms, people began yawning and making their way to Aidan and Maura to say farewell. Corrie, Mary and Thomas were the last to leave, taking Thady and Seamus with them. For a week the couple would have the house to themselves, then the O'Donoghues would return, and Aidan and Maura go to the house on the lough, to the new room that Aidan had made ready so long ago.

And it was now that Aidan was to learn his first lesson of Maura's character. Alone together, finally, his head splitting, his eyes burning, he shut the door on their departing families, and smiled at her. A thoughtless smile, one of relief that she, too, must share, that this business was over, they could rest . . .

But her small, pinched face was even more cold, and she gave him such a look of fierce dislike that he stood amazed, had not fully gathered his wits before she had turned and walked off into the larger bedroom, shutting the door behind her.

'Maura?' He stepped to the door. 'Maura?' He entered after her, and found her standing by the window, her small frame stiffened with controlled rage. But Aidan could not know this, he saw only the paleness of her dress, silvered in the light of a full moon, and gilded where, behind her, the flames from the hearth reflected on the lace of the gown that had been her mother's. The hair that lay in heavy coils around her head was like flame itself; yet her face, looking out over the fields, was pale as the moon. She seemed made of conflicting elements. Warmth and cold seemed to meet in her, and Aidan, puzzled, fascinated, could only close the door and lean against it, gazing at her.

'You didn't want to marry me,' slowly from almost motionless lips. 'You never wanted to marry me.'

'That's not so.'

'Y' weren't going to come to the church at all. You'd changed y'r mind.'

'No . . . ' A few steps into the room. 'I arrived at last, didn't I?'

'An' a fool you looked. Everyone laughing at us. Father McDonnagh grinning so hard he could barely read the service.'

'Father McDonnagh has a sense of humour – somethin' my wife lacks.' He was close to her, now, reaching out his arms for her.

'Arra! Don't you touch me . . . !'

'On our wedding night?'

'There'll be no weddin' night, y' hear me?' She pulled back away from him against the wall. 'There's another bedroom – y' can have that one, or there's this one, but you'll be sharin' neither of them with me!'

'Look now . . . ' He stepped forward.

'Take another step and I'll scream, then what'll they say down at Minogues'?'

'I don't care a damn!' And as he rushed at her, taking her in his arms, she did scream, loudly and shrilly. 'Holy Mother of . . . !' He

198

clamped his hand over her mouth. 'What'll they be thinkin' over the way?'

'I don't care!' She pulled from his grasp and backed off against the dresser.

He shrugged helplessly. 'What're y' goin' on like this for? I got a little tipsy before the weddin' – many a man has done that . . . '

'You were two hours late – two hours!'

'I . . . I lost track of the time . . . '

She was clutching the back of the chair behind her for support, close to tears but her chin up determinedly. 'Y' weren't gonna come! Y' weren't gonna marry me after all!' Her voice was shrill.

'Maura, that's not so!'

'What were y'doin', then? Thomas says y' got lost on Craglea. Did y'?'

'Well . . . '

'Y' didn't. Where were y'?'

'I was on Craglea . . . '

'Y' know Craglea like the back of y'r hand! Ah! Ah, I know! Y' went by the big house!'

'I didn't!'

'Y' did! I can see it on y' face!'

'Why in God's name . . . !'

'Did y' think she'd be there – the new mistress of Tineranna? Could y' see her runnin' out to y'? Were y' hopin' she'd appear suddenly and say, don't do it, Aida, I still love . . . '

And this time it was he who stepped away, one hand raised warningly. 'Now, stop it . . . Stop!'

Maura stopped, then gave a cold, moon maiden smile and said with infinite care, 'Anna's probably with child by now.' She received the desired effect. He gazed at her as if she had placed a knife to his ribs. 'If she'd conceived straight away, she'd be . . . let's see . . . She'd be about four months gone, so her belly'd be swollen like . . . '

He roared 'No!' but she talked through him, the pale green of her eyes glittering. He cared! He still cared! She did not have time, yet, fully to digest this. Afterwards the hurt would claim her; but now, triumphantly, she drank in his pain, unwittingly making it her own.

There was a long silence. Aidan and Maura gazed at each other, like wounded animals. Then he turned away to the window.

It was only when Maura placed her hand on his arm and said, 'Aidan . . . ' that he realized she had been saying it for some time. He turned to her because he knew he must, looked at her and felt nothing.

She was saying, 'Aidan, I'm sorry. My tongue's horrid harsh when I'm angry . . . ' And it was she, now, who saw coldness in his face, moonlit and remote.

Why had she spoken like that? She had not meant to. Not like that. She wanted him to be relaxed, happy, his arms around her. Then he would talk to her, tell her all his feelings for Anna. What it had been like between them, what they had spoken of, and how it was over, now. But the look on his face! She had lost him.

'Are y' . . . sorry y' married me . . . ? Aidan . . . ?' He had turned back to the window. She tried to pull his stubborn torso around to face her. 'Aidan . . . ?' she pleaded, embracing him, 'Aidan . . . don't turn y'r back on me.'

Slowly he raised his hands, placed them on her shoulders, and gazed down at her, searching as if trying to find an answer, a possible guide in her face. 'I shouldn't have married you,' he said softly, 'for your sake.'

'I'm not sorry.'

She was staring up at him, and in her eyes he did read a message, a possible way to go. He ran his hands down her body from her shoulders, and she moved suddenly into his embrace, placing the length of her body against his. Again he felt the pliancy, the giving in her, and he held her to him fiercely, a protection against the cold of the night, against the desolation within him.

21

Never had there been a winter like this. As the cruel irony of Christmas passed over them and the New Year approached, the gales grew fiercer, the driving sleet and hail thudded like shot against the walls and roofs. Besides making life uncomfortable for those within doors, it shortened the miserable lives of those without, those crouched in ditches and doorways over the length and breadth of the country. The falls of snow, that turned fields and forests to white glory, buried the dead and the dying both, as if nature were covering her shame.

It was only the responsibility of looking after Tom-Joe's widow and little girl that prevented Martin from carrying out his threats against Hubert Osborne. He grew thinner, brooded more and more, when it became obvious that Hubert's name and influence kept him out of prison; the coroner accepted one hundred and fifty pounds bail and Hubert retired behind locked doors at Ceelohg to await the day of his trial. This did not worry him unduly, the magistrate was, after all, a good friend of his father's – but the threat of retribution at the hands of crazed Terryalts worried him a great deal. He read his books on fine china, two loaded pistols on the table beside him, and gnawed at the quicks of his fingernails, listening for every creak and shift the old house made, hearing Martin Curran in every sound.

Martin complained bitterly to Aidan and Thomas, made it quite clear he had little faith that anything could be done through legal channels, relieved some of his coiled energy in his talk of the political agitation in Dublin, paraphrased the writings of the young rebels who had seceded from O'Connell's Repeal Association. 'John Mitchel says that Tenant Right is the most important issue – that we're justified in using whatever means we have to keep our land for our own! And he's right! If the country could only organize itself we'd put an end to the kind of system that set Osborne free – the kind of system that upholds his claim to land that was never his in the first place!'

At the January Assizes, Hubert Osborne was found guilty of man-slaughter, but was released after a solemn and severe diatribe by the magistrate upon the excessive violence used in Hubert's defence of his property.

'Land ownership is a trust,' he said, 'and we must fulfil our responsibilities in protecting that land for our heirs to come. But greater than this is the responsibility of a fellow human's life, when we are in the position of ending it or preserving it. I find you guilty for the reason that the blows you inflicted upon the deceased were excessively harsh, and although I believe you had no wish to deprive the deceased of his life, that was nevertheless the outcome. I order you to pay thirty pounds compensation to the widow Curran, and be bound over to keep the peace . . . '

The roaring of the crowd drowned the end of this speech. Hubert, standing with his slack mouth trembling and the hair standing up at the back of his neck with fear, felt the noise and the hatred all around him. He did not need to turn around to know that only his own tenants were silent. The Regans, the Brogans, the Currans them-selves, would be staring at his back amidst their friends' calling out for his blood. He could feel Martin Curran's malevolence like ice water against his spine. These were the ones to be afraid of. These silent ones. The waiting ones.

The day after the trial, Hubert left Ceelohg under a heavy police escort, and boarded the steamer *Avonmore*. Within a week he was in London, and it was his father, Edward, who had Tom-Joe's widow presented with the money.

'Blood money,' Martin spat. He and the other sixteen men that now comprised the Terryalts, were crouched in the O'Donoghue barn. Ouside the wind screamed around the building and blew in gusts beneath the ill-fitting door, making Aidan, closest to it, shiver within his coat..

'It'll keep the woman and child alive,' Regan volunteered.

'It's too late for Bridget. When Osborne's man brought the money to the house, she couldn't rise off the bed. She just looked at him. I don't even know if she heard what he said. With the money, I sent for the doctor. He hardly looked at her. He said she'll be dead within the fortnight.'

All the men were silent. Martin stood and walked to the end of the building, then turned to them, a small, dark figure against the pale straw bales banked against the end wall; the pitiful store of fodder that was all that remained to the O'Donoghues. 'Tom-Joe's dying should have taught us something,' Martin said. 'That the law is for the likes of the Osbornes, not for us. There's no use us trying to fight all legal-like, as O'Connell wants. No more is there any hope in waiting, in keeping out of trouble, in prayer, like Father O'Callaghan and Father McDonnagh would have us believe. Y' stand still and let them take somethin' from y', they'll only be back to take something else.'

'If y'r gonna talk rebellion again, Martin, you'll be wasting y'r breath,' Aidan said. 'We're with y' the same as most people, but you can't fight on empty stomachs.' He jerked his thumb backwards at the door. 'There's y'r army out there, dying in the snow. They'll not be thinking of followin' any man except for food to stay alive. Could you offer them that?'

Martin glared at the shadowy Aidan, could feel in the quiet shifting of the men that the calm logic had struck home. 'It's easy for you. You have a job all year round, five shillings a week, come what may. The rest of us are living on charity or on what we have through sellin' off stock and furniture. You can afford t' sleep well at night, Aidan, probably wishing you were at home in bed right now, with y'r position to go to in the morning. But for most of us there'll be nothing to do but think on how hungry we are . . . '

'Or go to the mines and the Shannon Authority,' a cottier put in, 'and hope some poor devil's dropped dead at his post so we might take his place.'

There were mutterings of grim agreement. Regan's strong voice cut in. 'Sit down for a minute, Martin . . . '

'I want to know . . . !'

'Sit down!' Such was Regan's tone that Martin walked unwillingly back to his place.

'Now, listen, I've begun to agree with Martin . . . ' There were grunts of surprise and startled questions. 'Not altogether – let me finish! So far, we been waitin' f'r them t' make a move before we tried t' right matters. When Colford evicted the Ryans Ruadh, we hamstrung his horses. That didn't stop the Ryans from dyin' of pneumonia, nor keep their children from the workhouse. When Parish discharged four good men with families dependent on their wages, we burnt his haystack—'

'Didn't give us our jobs back.' A morose voice from the shadows.

'That's what I'm sayin'. We been workin' for revenge only, hopin' that what we do will make the landlords think twice before tryin' somethin' similar. And y' got to admit, if we're havin' any effect, it's none that we can notice. Things go on the same . . . '

'Then why don't we . . . '

'Shut up, Martin! I think it's time we reconsidered what we're about. Now the crops have failed a second time, there'll be bad times comin' . . . It'll be hard enough stayin' alive without worryin' about burnin' haystacks and cripplin' creatures that haven't done us any harm . . . '

'Are y' sayin' we should let them get away with raisin' rents and evictin' and . . . '

'I'm sayin' we should think more careful-like before we risk gettin' caught! Jaysus, Martin. Only last week Tommy Ryan was transported for burnin' down Thomson's barn. You think it's gonna console his Mary and the children all the ten years he's away, to know that Thomson'll have to buy fodder? Use y'r head, boy. We got no way of fightin' back, like Aidan says. I propose we look after ourselves and our families as best we can while these bad times are on us.' He took a deep breath. 'Raise y'r hand if y've ever done any poachin'.'

The men looked startled, glanced at each other. 'C'mon, c'mon, now,' Regan said impatiently. 'If y' tell me y' never took a rabbit or a snipe in y'r lives y'll be damning y'selves as liars. C'mon, up with y'r hands!' And he led the way by raising his own.

Slowly, hands were raised, until Regan, peering about, could note with satisfaction that there was not a man in the group with both his hands in his pockets. 'Y' do me proud,' he said. 'There's no telling me that God meant us t' starve while some Englishman claims ownership of every small creature in the fields. Now keep y'r hands up if y've ever . . . em . . . poached a sheep.'

The hands were lowered, raised, lowered again in guilty confusion. Giving a few seconds for their consciences to assert themselves Regan counted seven men with their hands raised, their expressions watchful, nervous or belligerent. Regan leaned forward. 'I propose,' he announced, 'that these men teach us all they know. That we take straws t' decide which men – one of these . . . experts, and two of us beginners – go after the sheep. We choose flocks from amongst those men who deserve to lose stock or who can afford it – and it's usually the same thing. We kill two sheep on every raid, butcher it on the spot, and take the meat away with us. It's divided amongst all the families and eaten *straight away*. The bones must be buried carefully – not beneath the hearth or the turf stack – that's the first place they'll look.'

There was a long silence as each man considered the plan. It was one of the cottiers who spoke first, saying 'Mutton . . . ' with such unconscious longing in his voice that all the men burst into laughter.

Maura wiped her mouth with her apron and turned back to the door of the cottage from which she had run so unceremoniously only seconds before. Mary looked up from the hearth as Maura, white-faced, sank down upon a stool. 'Better?'

'It's not fair.' Maura lowered her head into her hands. 'The first three months are supposed to be the worst, you said. Here it is four months, and me bein' ill all the time. There's little enough food as it is,' she added bitterly, 'without me bringin' it up again afterwards.'

'It's different for every woman,' Mary said calmly, arranging the coals over the lid of the pot oven. She stood up. The onions and trout fillets within the heavy iron vessel would cook slowly but well within the covering of turf.

What a blessing it was that Thomas insisted they eat the extra fish he brought home. They had even come to like it, to prefer the taste of salmon and trout and eel; but even pike and perch were not unpalatable with the skins removed and a coating of butter added.

Mary was conscious that the neighbours thought them peculiar, and pitied them this diet that was a tasteless, unappetising burden, inflicted upon them on Fridays and at Lent. To live perpetually upon a diet of these glassy-eyed, foul-smelling and slimy creatures was regarded with repugnance. And Thomas, bringing home extra fish for a few of the poorer cottages, found that the gaunt occupants either refused his offer outright or were completely ignorant of how to clean and dissect the fish.

Maura watched Mary cleaning up the table after the meal's preparation: at the sight of the fish head, she lowered her face again and moaned. 'Maybe it's the fish that's makin' me ill. Maybe if I had some potatoes . . . '

'Foolishness.' The older woman took up the onion skins and threw them on the fire where they crackled into flames and flavoured the harsh turf smoke. 'You're feelin' ill because your baby's announcing his coming. When he feels sure y' know, he'll rest quiet.'

'It might be a girl,' Maura pointed out. 'There's been mostly boys in the family, I know, but this might be a girl.'

'Do you want a girl?'

'No,' she said. 'I want a boy, one that looks like Aidan. I don't think I'd know what to do with a girl.'

'You'd love her just the same. Now come, if you're feelin' better, y' can take these down to the shore.' She picked up the cloth on which she had gathered the remains of the trout and handed it to Maura. 'Take it right down to the water's edge where the gulls will find it. And mind how you go.'

Maura went out into the dusk, treading carefully in bare feet between the patches of snow that still lay on the ground. She felt tired, heavy already, although as yet her pregnancy was not visible. Her ankles were swollen, however, and she did not seem to have any energy since the baby began to make demands upon her body.

She emptied the cloth on to the ground and already some late-flying gulls were wheeling closer to investigate. She left them rasping their delight over the find and turned back to the house, her eyes resting on the O'Sullivans' cottage as she walked. Oona O'Sullivan had gone through this nasty business of motherhood not once, but twelve times! And look at her, Maura told herself, old already, and her only thirty. And what was the purpose of all her suffering? No sooner did she get used to having a child, watching it grow up, then Phut! Dead. Four of the O'Sullivan children dead in two years. It was senseless. Maura kicked out with her swollen foot against a shallow bank of snow, watched the white fragments fly before her. It was all senseless.

The feeling of futility remained with her all that evening. She would not allow Aidan to touch her as they lay in bed that night. 'I just don't want to. And besides, hadn't we better . . . stop that kind of thing?'

'*What*?'

'Don't shout! I don't think such goin's on is right, Aidan. I mean, its purpose is the creation of children, isn't it? Well, I'm carryin' a child . . . '

'But it's fun, too . . . ' A heavily muscled arm snaked across her shoulders, the hand fastened on one of her small breasts: it was swollen and hard with the changes within her.

She did not shrink from him. But as he moved to cover her, he heard her sigh, softly. When it was over – and it was over soon enough – she went straight to sleep. He lay beside her, face down, with one arm flung across her belly, and wondered at his disappointment.

Was the failure within himself? Had he expected too much of her? She loved him. She showed it when they lay together. Endearments. The hands that fluttered at his face. But before they were married, when he would hold her to him, it seemed that her body had craved his as much as he had wanted her. He would embrace her and find no reticence, no holding back. Her body fitted to his as if it belonged to him, this promised gift of herself that had so warmed their friendship that he grew tender towards her. Yet this pliancy, this giving that had so flattered him and helped heal his bruised feelings, he now saw as a sacrifice, an offering. The yielding of herself was not wholehearted. Her pliancy was a deceptive willingness. 'Let me please *you*,' he had begged once, forgetting his own desire for a moment. The hands continued their fluttering at his neck and shoulders, 'But you are. You're near me,' she replied. He did not know why it was not enough.

The next morning they were terse in their disappointment of each other. Aidan went off in driving sleet and spent the day on the roof of one of Tineranna's barns, replacing slates that had blown away in the gale winds of a few days before.

Terry O'Sullivan worked with him, and Aidan was glad of the company as they fitted and wired the slates into place with hands that cracked and bled from the cold.

Terry kept singing to himself, often interrupting himself to cough, doubling over, his whip-thin body wracked with the convulsions of his chest, until Aidan told him to get down, that he would be falling off with the force of the wind and his lack of controlled balance. But Terry stayed, doggedly working and singing as the sleet soaked through their thin coats and the hail thudded into their backs.

'I'd like t' be in America, now,' Terry said at one stage, pausing to reach into his collar and remove two hailstones. 'In the southern states, like Mississippi or Georgia. Somewhere where it don't get cold. This work'll be the death of us . . . ' He was stopped by a coughing fit so sudden and violent that Aidan had to reach out a

206

hand quickly and take his arm to prevent him from toppling backwards off the roof.

'Tell me, now,' he continued, when he recovered, 'is it for this that I trained as a blacksmith? Is it for this that you became the finest horseman in East Clare?'

'We have no choice,' Aidan replied. He tried not to think of horses, these days, of the freedom he had enjoyed on practice gallops and in training the young hunters. He glanced up at Terry, found him wiping his mouth on his sleeve. There was blood on the damp homespun. Aidan stared, and barely heard the words.

'Sometimes I'd like to walk off Tineranna. If I knew that Oona and the children could stay in the cottage, I'd go travelling. Try to get work as a blacksmith somewhere else. Even America. If I had the fare, I could go to America and send for Oona and the children later.'

'You . . . you should, perhaps,' Aidan said. 'Go somewhere warm, I mean.'

Terry glanced down at his sleeve. 'Och, many a man's got consumption and got over it. It doesn't worry me unduly. It's a better life I'm after, see? F'r the children. If I thought I c'd get away with it, I'd join the Terrys, go robbin' coaches and get me some money.'

'The Terrys don't rob coaches.'

Terry turned and looked at him, a little too closely, a little too long, Aidan thought. Then, 'Anyway, I'd do somethin'. This work is as like to break a man's spirit as his body. Isn't that so?'

'Yes.'

'Anything would be better than this. A man's justified in wanting something better, is he not?'

Aidan looked at him again. Could he know something? Could he possibly know that Thady and Martin and one of the cottiers had taken a Tineranna sheep two days ago? Regan had refused to hear of Terry joining the group. He talked too much with the drink in him, he said. Oona had found two packages of meat on her doorstep on different occasions, but had not asked questions. It was wisest not to. Did Terry suspect why he was not accepted, and resent it? Aidan wondered at the different depths in the man. Terry was not all good-natured ribaldry. There was a bitterness here, too.

Aidan lowered his head to his work. 'We're wasting our breath. There's no better life for any of us. Tineranna is all we have. Without it neither we nor our families could survive.'

'But in America . . .'

'There is nothing better. Nothing changes.'

It was late afternoon when they finished the roof. Neither of them had thought any longer about their conversation, although they were both to remember it later. They climbed down the ladder and replaced it within the barn, then went across to the stables where a small fire was lit in the tack room, and the thin porridge-like stirabout that was the midday meal provided for them, bubbled sullenly over the flames.

Aidan was discomfited to find Nathan there. Though he knew Tineranna could well afford to lose a few sheep if it meant keeping families alive, he was nevertheless conscious of his connivance in telling the Terrys which flock to choose, when Nathan would be most likely to check them. It was food for the others, for their wives and children: yet to Aidan it was still theft, and never more so than when he looked into Nathan Cameron's face.

Nathan had been standing by the hearth, his shoulders slumped, gazing into the flames. He started as Terry flung the door wide on entering, letting it bang back against the wall. 'Stop y'r noise, y' great spalpeen! Any groom knows not t' go slammin' about in the stables.'

'Who's to frighten? Ginger and Brownie? It'd take more than a door openin' t' make them lift their hairy feet.'

But he shut the door quietly enough, and both men bent over the fire, Terry spooning the gruel into wooden platters. They sat down to eat, after Nathan had shaken his head at the offer of a plate. They ate their meal hurriedly and gratefully, not questioning themselves as to why Nathan was here. Even in weather such as this, he was out and about, checking the flocks and the barns and crops, three and four times a day. But now—

'There's half a bottle of potcheen on the shelf. The other men have had their share already.'

They looked up at him in amazement, Aidan with the last spoonful of stirabout half-way to his mouth. Like puppets moved by the one hand, they turned. There was indeed a bottle on the shelf, half-filled with clear liquid. Aidan finished his last mouthful of food as Terry rose to fetch the bottle.

'Just a minute. I've somethin' to tell y' first,' Nathan said. They turned to him, took in the grim lines around his mouth, the stubborn stance, the determined set to the narrow shoulders. Aidan felt sweat run down his back, despite the chill of the room. He and Terry glanced at each other. Nathan was saying, 'I've had a letter from Master Devlin . . . Mister Kelly. He's decided to put Tineranna on the market. It's to be advertised both in the Irish and London newspapers.' He paused for a moment, sensed rather than saw the white, shocked faces of the two men. He hardened his voice and made it toneless. 'And five of the men are to leave their employment. Mister Kelly mentioned the five by name. Roddy and Gerry Minogue, Kieran Corcoran, and you two. I'm to pay y' up to today, and give y' all an extra day's wages, but y'r to finish up this evenin'.'

He left them, then, standing there gazing after him. Aidan's feelings of guilt were forgotten. Their work. To finish this evening. This evening!

Terry sat down shakily, and gazed across the hearth at Aidan. 'What . . . What'll we do?'

Aidan dragged himself back from thoughts of Maura and the unborn child, to stare at Terry unseeingly. 'We do what he meant us to do. We sit here all afternoon with the potcheen – and we try t' think what the devil we'll do tomorrow.'

'Yes, but . . . ' Terry began to cough again.

Aidan looked at the bent head with pity, and felt one more reason for his growing anger, one more person for whom he was afraid. He gazed into the hearth, thinking of Devlin sitting in his study, writing in his small, cramped handwriting, the letter to Nathan Cameron.

'You first.'

He looked at Terry to find the bottle being held out to him.

Terry said, 'I marked the bottle half-way. You drink yours first.'

Aidan took a deep breath and downed his share of the potcheen while Terry looked on, hungrily. On a stomach half-empty, the liquor burnt into his mind immediately. Whatever it was made from, for in those days it could not be potatoes, it was a potent liquid indeed, and the edge of his vision and his wits blurred a little.

Terry emptied the bottle, and gazed at it with a regretful sigh. 'Did y' think it was the truth he was speakin'? Did the master really say it was us that was t' go? Or was it somethin' Cameron thought up out of his own little black mind?'

'It's Devlin. Damn his eyes . . . He doesn't deserve to own this land. His father'd . . . He doesn't deserve to live. If he comes back to Ireland, I'll kill him, Terry. I swear to God, I'll kill him.'

22

The weather began to improve after April, but thousands, ill-nourished, weakened, had succumbed to consumption, influenza, bronchitis, pneumonia, or exposure to the weather. Thousands more had died of the typhoid that reached epidemic proportions that spring. Killaloe's fever hospital, a wooden-walled structure erected in a field to the west of the village, was built to hold fifty patients. But it was soon overflowing when the wake of the famine brought not only typhoid but cholera, the swift-moving disease that flamed through whole families and could kill within twenty-four hours of the first sign of fever.

And the hungry, the homeless – no longer merely thin beggars. Some now devoid of nearly all human characteristics, skeletal puppets that limped through streets and along the roads between the towns. Parchment-skinned spectres, claw-like hands reaching, 'The hunger is on us . . . ' Small living mummies of babies held to flat, dry breasts, babies too weak to cry. Children with round pot bellies, stick arms and legs and heads too large for their shoulders, mothers pushing the children forward. 'Some bread for my little boy, your honour, the hunger is on us . . . ' 'Some milk for the baby, ma'am – a drop only. The hunger is on us.'

One of the ladies of Killaloe wrote a letter of protest to the *Limerick Chronicle*, declaiming against the numbers of beggars and itinerants allowed to crowd the streets. But such lack of sympathy belonged only to a minority. In Killaloe, as elsewhere, the Catholic and Protestant clergy and the Society of Friends – the mercy-giving Quakers – laboured to save as many of the people as they could. It was a never-ending task.

Aidan had walked through the lacerating raw winds and sleet of that spring to labour beside Corrie and Martin, Seamus and Thady, at the Government Relief Works, the new road from Killaloe to Clonlara. All over Ireland, groups of half-starving men had laboured all winter in freezing conditions, burrowing roads through the countryside. Most of the works were ill-planned, badly engineered, some to be abandoned, roads from nowhere, leading nowhere.

Like us, Aidan thought, watching the men swinging picks or

shovels while the late-falling snow collected on their hair and their bent backs, and at the women, gathering up the stones in emaciated arms, scuttling back and forth to the piles of earth, their pinched, haggard faces lowered beneath their shawls. They laboured from dawn until nightfall. The women for sixpence a day, the men for tenpence. They were all people he knew. Some were cottiers who spoke only Irish, who had lived solely on the potato, whose close-knit world had for generations revolved only around their families and their Church. Suddenly the potatoes were gone, their children were dead or dying, and no one explained how this had come about, what they had done wrong. Only the Church could speak to all of them, and she could tell them only that it was the will of God.

Even the small farmers with whom Aidan was on closer terms, found it hard to understand how their world had been turned so abruptly into a nightmare.

They, like the cottiers, should be spending winter and the chill days of spring indoors by a warm fire. The potato harvest would be in, there would be not much work to do until the spring planting: it did not matter that they owned little warm clothing, that few possessed a pair of boots. But now it mattered. Now, in the long hours spent shifting and carrying loads of earth and stones through the bitter winter that went on and on. They dropped in exhaustion by Aidan's side, they were taken home to their houses or to the fever hospital. People he had known since childhood, Minogues, Ryans, O'Byrnes, Reddans, Hogans . . . some he would never see again.

The threat of fever was everywhere. He lived in terror lest he unknowingly brought it home to Maura and the unborn child. Yet he must go off each day, mingle in that crowd before the supervisor, pray that he would be chosen to work that day, that he would be given a ticket to show to the overseer, that they would have the tenpence to buy meal for stirabout or, if Corrie, too, was working, to hide some of the money beneath the mattress towards the price of rent and this season's seed.

On the days when he was not chosen, he would often visit Nathan. It was as if he could not keep away from Tineranna, that every so often he had to visit the practice track where he had trained the thoroughbreds, the bog over which he had tramped with William Kelly and Samhradh, as if he had to set eyes on the big house, that in the solid bulk of the grey walls he received a reaffirmation that there was some goodness, some hope. He had been talking nonsense, that day on the barn roof with Terry. He had been feeling sorry for himself, saying that nothing changes, that there was nothing better.

211

There was something better. He had been befriended by a man like William Kelly, had been allowed to glimpse a world where men did not simply labour with their hands, but sought after knowledge, appreciated beauty and even created it, in words, on canvas. He had seen that world in those lost days in the schoolroom, so taken for granted. He had seen that world – and he had been loved by Anna O'Hagan. These two memories alone gave him hope.

Nathan himself seemed to welcome Aidan's visits. He would pause in the unloading of hay to the winter-starved cattle and stand talking of the weather, of the chances for a blight-free harvest, even opening up to the younger man about the state of Tineranna itself, as if Aidan, no longer an employee, could now be counted on as something of a friend. Aidan knew he had no family, no confidants. Perhaps the responsibility was becoming too great even for Nathan to manage, without the release of unburdening his thoughts.

On one of the first warm days early in June, after searching the stables and nearby fields for him, Aidan found Nathan in the big house. The kitchen door was open to the sunshine and the warm breeze. Aidan knocked and entered, gazing around him as he did so. The hearth was swept bare where once Cook had plied her culinary skills, bare too, was the space beside the door where Devlin's old shoes had waited for him each day.

Nathan met him in the hall, did not smile, but beckoned to him. In the office where the tenants came to pay their rents each gale day, Nathan sat down tiredly behind the desk. He waited only until Aidan was seated in a chair before saying without warning, 'Master Devlin's coming back.'

Aidan stared at him. 'With An . . . With Mrs Kelly?'

'No. Only himself.'

In his disappointment there was a kind of relief. He did not want to see her, it would hurt too much. And only then did he remember Maura, the pathetic white face above a body swollen with his child. He said quickly, 'Why is he coming back? I thought he hated the place.'

'He wants to collect some of the paintings and furniture.'

Aidan felt his hands clench, a sudden sick feeling claim him. 'Tineranna's sold then.'

'Not yet. With bad harvests and fever epidemics buyers in London are wee bit cautious. But it will be sold,' he said mercilessly, 'Englishman or gombeen man, someone will buy it.'

Aidan frowned at the floor, shrugged with an effort. 'It's nothing t' do with me anymore.'

'It is.' Something in his tone made Aidan look back to him. 'He wants me to evict. He wants the O'Sullivans out – they're three years behind in their rent. And he wants the cottiers out – they're behind, too – and he wants the land under pasture, he says. And he wants you out.'

He felt cold. The room was warm, but he was chilled to the bone. The unbelievable. The terrifying. The nightmare that dogged all of them. The finish.

He had risen to his feet without realizing it, was standing by the desk, and gazing down at the agent. 'But . . . Maura. The baby. Mother of God, Nathan, you wouldn't be after . . . '

The harsh voice sliced across his words. 'I haven't said that I'll be doin' anythin'! Stop standin' over me like some avengin' angel an' sit down! . . . That's better . . .

'This isn't any more to my likin' than it is to yours. You think I don't mind seein' this estate go to ruin before my eyes? The oat crop can't carry the whole upkeep of this place. I've been told to cut down on the land sown this year; I've been told t' sell off the cattle and sheep. And now he says evict. Evict people who were good tenants and loyal employees before these bad times. I tell you, it's not worth it to me, this position, seein' all this come about. I who remember William Kelly, may his soul rest gently.'

'But . . . what if he demands you evict? You can't fight him, Nathan . . . '

'I've written back warnin' him that he'd be doing this at grave risk. I've warned him about the Terrys before, and he seemed to be a bit nervous of them.' Aidan found the levity for a small smile. 'And wipe that smirk off y'r face! Hooligans with a grievance y' might be, but y'r hooligans all the same, and y'll be punished, the lot of y'!'

Aidan stared at him. 'What makes y' think . . . '

'Haven't I known you since you were five? Didn't I try to take your dead dog from y'r grasp, and didn't y' flay into me with y'r puny fists? I could've broken y'r head, but y' didn't think of y'r chances. You were wronged, and you fought without thinkin'. It's what y'r doin' now.' The hard little black eyes pinned Aidan to his chair.

'A man doesn't have many choices in these times.'

'I know that. We have no say in the way our lives are run. But when something like these evictions are placed before me, I . . . '

But Aidan was never to know what Nathan was about to say. His own name was shouted outside, loudly, urgently, growing closer.

'It's Thomas . . . My wife, Maura . . . the baby's due any . . . ' He had risen and tripped over the chair leg, flung himself out the door and down the hall.

213

Thomas was running across the yard, still shouting, waving his arms. 'Ma says to fetch y' quick, the baby's about here!' Aidan began running and Thomas fell into step as he came abreast. 'She's only been . . . in labour . . . four hours . . . ' he puffed as they ran, 'Ma says it's the quickest first babe . . . she's ever heard about . . . ' But Aidan was running faster, and Thomas, already tired, kept the remainder of his energy for keeping up with him.

Maura's son was born before the men arrived. Aidan held the wriggling, bellowing little bundle that was his firstborn and marvelled over him. The perfection of his hands, the thick black hair, the roar of rage and hunger that emitted from him.

It was not until later, sitting by Maura's bed, feeling a completeness and quietude he had never known in watching the baby at her breast, that the memory of his visit to Nathan intruded itself. He could not tell Maura, he knew, gazing at the thin, freckled face that in motherhood was beautiful. He could tell Corrie, and Thomas. . . . He shifted on the stool, resenting bitterly this encroaching threat that came now, of all times. He would not tell Thomas and Corrie yet, he decided. He would see Nathan again, would find out for certain before he threw his family into panic.

'Have you thought of a name?' Maura smiled at him.

'Hm? No. No, I hadn't. Have you?'

'Well you were very fond of the old master, weren't you? William. And my father's name was Liam – shall we call him William?'

Aidan scowled, consideringly. Then, 'I'd rather have the Irish version. Liam.'

Her eyes widened in surprise. 'Och, Aidan! Folk will think we're bog Irish, sure.'

'Why?' And she could not understand that he should look so fierce so suddenly. 'We should be proud of being Irish, not ape the English. Your father felt the same. And the master – he would, too. I'm tired of compromising with the Saxons. We'll call him Liam. They were fine men, both his namesakes. He couldn't do better than grow up like them.' Maura looked up at him, and he was surprised to see her eyes fill with tears. With an unaccustomed demonstrativeness she had reached out and taken his hand, was holding it tightly.

'Why . . . what's the matter?' he asked.

'Nothing . . . I don't know. You won't go away, will you?'

'No. A few of the lads'll be over, but I won't let 'em make too much fuss. Och, don't cry now . . . '

'It's not unhappy I am . . . I don't know . . . '

He moved his stool closer, and awkwardly stroked her hair.

214

Women were a mystery. If she was happy, what was there to cry about?

The tears splashed down on to the baby's thick hair, but Liam suckled on, oblivious, content.

23

When he brought Anna O'Hagan Kelly to the house in Grosvenor Square Devlin was still elated, tense, after the circumstances of his marriage. The magic had not faded, he could not believe his good fortune, could not take his eyes from her, hated leaving her. He aggravated his secretary, Percy Cole, by consistently avoiding all business matters except when absolutely necessary; the matters pertaining to the Wiltshire estate were neglected, and his friends, most of whom he shared with Hubert Osborne, found that the once fun-loving bachelor was no longer a bachelor, nor much fun.

He was constantly with his new wife. They visited shops; dressmakers, shoemakers, milliners, parfumeries; Devlin seemed to enjoy it all. Anna, intelligent and blessed with a good ear, spoke a carefully enunciated Mayfair almost at once, which delighted even the sceptical and rapier-tongued Hubert, who returned to London soon after the Kellys, and often visited them. Because of the recent death of Caroline Kelly, they did not entertain lavishly, but many people, due, a great deal, to Hubert's publicity, came to call. Many were censorious of the abruptness of Devlin's marriage, but they were curious, all of them, to see the Irish beauty that it seemed all society was speaking of. They made some friends among these people; surprisingly – and the patronage did a great deal to aid their position in society – they were taken up by one of Hubert's cousins, young Simon Beresford, Duke of Orwhitton, and his new bride, Serena. 'Well!' Hubert had muttered to Devlin when Simon had invited the Kellys to spend a few weeks the following autumn at his lodge in Inverness, 'and to think if you hadn't looked out my window in that beastly little town house in Killaloe, none of this would have happened!' Anna swept into people's lives with her beauty, her charm, her natural good manners and her new, impeccable etiquette; it seemed that Devlin's laughing prophesy would become reality, Anna would, that Season, come close to reaching the pinnacle of social acclaim.

She was like a child with everything she saw; indeed, despite her calm dignity, her almost eerie ability to mix with all the ranks of people, there was always something childlike about her, a fragility. At night, in the large, canopied bed she would cling to him more for solace and reassurance than passion, and cried, sometimes.

'I'm afraid – so afraid!'

'What's bothered you?' Devlin would ask. 'Was it the Ambassador drooling on your hand all night? It *was* a compliment, you know. . . '

'No . . . not the Ambassador . . . not just him. Everything.'

'You're happy, aren't you?'

'Oh, yes!' Her face came up to his. 'I never thought . . . It's wonderful – life is wonderful. You've given me so much.'

'And you love me?'

'Yes. Yes, I do.'

'Say it . . . '

'I love you.' But always, it was said quietly, seriously. And, he realized, never looking directly at him, never gazing into his eyes.

That spring and summer of 1846 was the happiest Devlin had ever known. They went walking in the cool of the parks, shopped for gifts for friends and for each other, occasionally visiting the theatre and the ballet, and Devlin, on these evenings, watched men watching Anna, in a gown of black silk studded with jet beads, and felt that his heart would burst with his pride in her.

Once or twice he wondered if her gentle smile might not mask some regrets at leaving her home and family. He had stressed to her on leaving Killaloe that there should be no further contact between their families, and, knowing the severe social structure of their times, Anna could see why Devlin made his request. She could bear it, she said. Her parents would understand. Their marriage was an irrevocable step that divided her for ever from her past.

Devlin believed her, he realized later, because he wanted to believe her. Something was indeed wrong in their relationship. He discovered it only in retrospect, and that infuriated him, for he should have found it out himself.

Serena Beresford called to see him one day in January, when Anna had gone to a luncheon held by Devlin's cousin, Celia Retcliffe.

'It's not my place to tell you,' Serena said, and proceeded as if it was, for she was a strong-minded, confident young woman, long indulged by her parents and now equally indulged by the easy-going Simon. 'Anna is very unhappy. She's been unhappy for months. I've told her to tell you, but she won't, so I've come to tell you myself. She's miserable, Devlin, and you've got to do something about it.'

His first reaction was one of strong annoyance. He leaned back in his chair and drawled, 'My dear Serena, is this a joke? My wife is perfectly happy.'

'Then why do I find her in tears so often when I visit – on days, by the way, when she feels sure that you won't be at home. All the poor child can think about is Ireland and her family.'

'No!'

'Yes. She's told me so.'

'She's said nothing to me! Never mentioned them . . . '

'Well, she wouldn't, would she? She worships you, she's pathetically eager to have your approval, the silly little thing. Really, Devlin, though I shall miss her terribly, I think you should take her back to Ireland.'

'No!' He had stood, crossed the room, in his agitation, without realizing it.

'Can't you say anything but "no"? You can't make the problem disappear by burying your head in the sand.'

'How can I take her back to Ireland – there's a famine in Ireland . . . the disease, the horror – my mother, remember—'

'Oh,' she said, immediately. 'I'm sorry, I'd forgotten the cause of your mother's death. But this famine can't be all that bad, can it? You'll be all right yourselves – just don't let people *breathe* on you . . . '

'Really, Serena, sometimes you're a fool!'

'Not often.' She stood up. 'At least I know when Simon's under a cloud. You don't seem to know the slightest thing about the workings of Anna's mind.'

Devlin had turned, was staring at her. He decided he loathed Serena Beresford; he hated bullying, outspoken women. But her words disturbed him more than he cared to admit. And when Serena had gone he sat in a chair by the window for a long time, watching the snow fall on the square.

Serena was right. He knew nothing about Anna. He had been too delirious in his possession of her, his pride in her, to look beneath her quiet smile, her acceptance of her new life. Take her back to Ireland . . . Oddly enough, he missed Tineranna himself, sometimes, it was as if the house held part of him and he needed to go back to reclaim himself – but that was nostalgia only, for he knew better than to take Anna back there . . .

His hands were shaking, for he knew, now, what made him afraid, what had been pushed to the back of his mind all along. How could he have been so blind as to believe she could have forgotten Aidan O'Brien? He was still studying his shaking hands, and now dropped his face down upon them, felt his cheeks wet with tears. He knew why he dare not take Anna back, why he could not.

But were they any safer here in London? 'He's here, too,' he murmured. 'Wherever we are, he'll be. Wherever we go, he'll follow.' The dream was shattered. Devlin wept for the loss of it. She had been perfect – and she had belonged to him. Now, he saw the flaw in her, the treachery, mourning a man she had loved, still loved. He did not question any other reason for Anna's unhappiness, he realized now, his fear had never left him. He had been a fool to believe that they could be happy. Now he had faced the truth, and he could never look her in the face again without the knowledge that she was not what he thought her to be.

He had a bag packed and left the house for his club. He stayed there for three days, alone in his room for a great deal of the time, and the demons of his suspicion kept him company. He began to wonder at her forwardness when they lay together. On at least two occasions, when he had been tired, sleepy, she had been the one to reach for him, had made it clear that she desired him. He had been flattered, then. Now, he thought, after only a few months of marriage, should a woman be so bold? She had not cried nor screamed nor protested at all on their wedding night at the inn on the way to Dublin. Given her rigid Catholic upbringing, there should have been some display of modesty, a little unwillingness. Instead, a quiet acceptance, though she had cried – yes, she had wept afterwards . . . His comfort lasted only a second. His nails curved into his palms; she wept because he was not Aidan O'Brien.

He took up pen and paper, and wrote to Nathan Cameron that he would soon be selling Tineranna. In the meantime, economies must be made . . . No – he paused – he shrank at evictions. Five men must be put off – and Aidan O'Brien was to be one of them.

At the end of three days he returned to the house in Grosvenor Square, knowing, within him, that their life together would never be the same.

Anna tried to speak with him, she cried, begged him to explain what had happened; he looked at her coolly, told her she was being ridiculous, and when she was driven almost into hysterics, he calmly left the room and locked himself in his study. He gained a fierce sense of pride for coping so well with the end of his illusions. He did not lash out at Anna with recriminations, that would solve nothing; but there was a secret sense of power that he had never before known in seeing her wretchedness. No one before in his life had been so dependent upon him.

When she told him, only four days after his return from his club, that she was carrying his child, he was delighted, kissed her cheek, and told her she had made him very happy. The hopefulness in her eyes was, he thought, almost pitiable. He told her, then, still holding her hands, that she would need her rest in the months to come, and he would, for that time, move back into his old room. He left her before she could speak or begin the tiresome weeping. He was glad of the excuse to move out of the room they shared; to lie all night beside someone almost bristling with unspoken resentment must, he thought, be one of the most unpleasant fates in the world.

He did not miss her body. He did not miss her at all. It was as if they had learnt all they could of each other, said all there was to say, in those first few months of their marriage, and, for Devlin at least, there was nothing more to be said. Separate bedrooms and a permanent partner to accompany one to the opera . . . he was filled with a kind of sadness that perhaps his own marriage was no different from anyone else's.

Hubert tried to console him, one evening at their club. 'I suppose marriage is something all men must go through at least once.'

'Like mumps?' Devlin suggested.

'Well, mumps can be permanently damaging.'

'So,' said Devlin drily, 'can marriage.'

Serena and Simon were silent on the matter; sometimes Devlin caught Serena watching him narrowly, but there was precious little to make her suspicious. In public Devlin and Anna presented a united face of domestic harmony. Serena spoke no more of Anna being unhappy. Devlin suspected that Anna knew who had begun all the mischief and spoke little, nowadays, to anyone of her problems.

On Devlin's suggestion they moved at the end of summer to Burnley Grange, the Wiltshire property he had inherited from his mother. Orwhitton, the Beresford's seat, was only a few miles distant, and Serena promised to go there in the autumn, to stay for the birth of Anna's child.

From the beginning, Anna hated Burnley. She hated its brooding silence, for it was miles from anywhere, and the farmworkers and servants were a withdrawn and sullen people, as if the atmosphere of the place had, over the generations, stifled their enthusiasm for life. She hated the building itself, made of grey stone that must have been dragged for miles across the countryside. The villages nearby, Biddestone and Castlecombe, and even the great houses such as

219

Orwhitton seemed, by comparison, warm, friendly places where normal people who preferred to smile when they could, went about their lives. Burnley Grange, with its thick, grey, damp walls, its surly staff, the semi-circle of ancient moat outside the windows, the still, green surface a breeding ground for annoying insects, created an aura of hopelessness that smothered one like an invisible fog.

Devlin loved it, before his marriage he had brought several friends for weeks at a time; the hunting was excellent, and there was much gambling, drinking and displaying of horses and marksmanship. Devlin, while he gained little pleasure himself from these pursuits, liked playing host. Yes, a pleasant time was to be had at Burnley – but that depended a great deal on one's company. By Christmas Devlin was so disturbed by the sight of Anna's swollen body, further exacerbated by what the doctor called 'fluid retention', that he made some excuse of pressing business in London and returned to the capital. There, he told Hubert, he would wait until it was all over. Serena Beresford wrote to him from Wiltshire soon after, telling him that she had taken Anna to Orwhitton for the birth of the child. Devlin was piqued that it was not to be born on his own estate; yet if he wrote that to Serena she might very well relinquish her care of Anna only to insist that Devlin take it upon himself. He wrote an effusive letter that thanked Serena for her concern.

He was troubled, at this time, by the dream that had so often haunted him; he relived the day of the hunt, the day the mare, Chloe, had died. And always his last memory was that of Aidan O'Brien's face, not a boy's face, white with shock as it had been on that day, but the face of the man O'Brien had become – and he was laughing, laughing . . .

It was after two weeks of suffering this dream, his waking hours still haunted by what must have passed between Anna and Aidan O'Brien, that he finally wrote the letter telling Nathan Cameron to evict the O'Brien family. He felt better after that, did not think to question that Cameron might hesitate to carry out his orders. Devlin was too busy to check with the agent that it had been done, for he had more pressing problems on his mind.

'What will I do with Anna once the child is born?' he wondered aloud to Hubert. They were having a sherry together before leaving for the opera. Devlin had been busy with a round of parties, lately, sleeping late and ignoring his mail; now Hubert sat with his feet on an inlaid mahogany and mother-of-pearl table and tore at the envelopes, handing the contents to Devlin, unless they were bills, whereupon he tossed them directly on to the fire. 'When's it due?'

'A few weeks – I have to think of something soon.'

220

'Leave the girl at Burnley. You can't keep living the life you do here if you bring her back.'

'I'm not sure I want to keep living the way I do. I've slept the past five nights with five different women, just to keep you company when you visit your . . . '

'Don't say a word against those ladies. They're the central purpose of my life.'

'Why?'

'What?'

'Why are they the central purpose of your life? What are you trying to prove?'

'What do you mean by that?' Hubert looked up suddenly, his tone deadly.

'Nothing. It's just that I don't see the point in sleeping with as many women as you do . . . '

'Because I'm a man, and I enjoy it. Real men do.'

Devlin felt stung, really hurt. He placed his sherry glass down on the table beside him, afraid that there was going to be a quarrel, sudden and ugly.

'Oh, damn you . . . ' Hubert picked up another envelope, ripping at it savagely, 'If you don't like it, then don't come with me – but don't whine about it, Devlin. I dislike you when you whine.'

'I don't. I . . . '

'Oh, Lord.' Hubert was staring at the letter.

'What? What is it?'

His friend looked up, and grinned. 'We'll forget about the opera. Let's go out to Monique's and get roaring drunk. This is from Simon at Orwhitton. You're a father, dear boy. You have a son.'

In the spring, Anna could forgive Burnley. She returned there with Devlin and her young son, and found the place almost charming. Daffodils bloomed in the dark moss against the walls, and the peach and cherry trees that lined the moat dropped pale pink blossoms into the water. Devlin seemed to wish to stay, so she did not mind the thought of a future at Burnley.

She was happy, terribly happy. It was as if, for all the heartache of the past years of her life, God had at last given her recompense. Her pride in the child, long-limbed and sturdy, with soft brown hair and dark blue eyes, was a tangible thing. It warmed even Burnley.

Devlin found nothing of particular interest in his son, other than his very presence. A man should have a son; it was, he knew, one of the unwritten tenets of masculinity, and he was quietly pleased to have produced one before Hubert Osborne. He was less pleased about the child's name. Anna, ill after the boy's birth, had requested that he be named Michael, after her small brother who had died the day of their marriage. Devlin thought the name too common, too Irish, but acquiesced for his wife's sake; so his son came to be baptized Michael William Simon Kelly.

Devlin was not unconscious of the change in Anna after the child's birth, and he felt oddly jealous, shut out. It was doubly strange in the face of what he knew to be his neglect of his wife for the past few months. Having the child there made Anna smile. She no longer needed Devlin's presence nor his approval. Serena had been arguing for weeks that Anna must not look after the child herself, but have a nurse, and had insisted that Peggy Lacey, her own childhood nurse, be 'loaned' to the Kellys. Anna resisted, but Devlin insisted that the nurse be employed.

He stayed at Burnley most of that year, surprising no one more than himself. He had his own room, and rarely visited Anna's apartment at all. She had asked him to her room, once, a month after the child was born; but he said she must think of her own health, and that, at least, was true. The doctors agreed that another child would be a risk. Anna accepted Devlin's reasons with her usual calmness, and Devlin relaxed a little.

She decided, that autumn, to learn to ride. Devlin's cousin, Celia Retcliffe, had come to stay at Burnley for a few weeks, and had brought three of her hunters with her. She offered to teach Anna, and a quiet, broad-backed gelding, well-used to the side-saddle, was procured for her to learn upon. Devlin did not know whether to approve or not. He spent most of his own days seeing to the estate, much neglected in the past several years, often having to ask the advice of Simon Beresford and his steward. He watched Anna and the smaller figure of Celia on their rides about the estate, told himself that it was a good thing that Anna was keeping busy; but something about her new-found contentment irritated him. He had hoped for a civilized relationship, a mutual respect. Now he possessed this – and it was not enough.

Once or twice, that winter, he hunted with her, riding by her, to check if she would manage the fences. But he need not have worried. Anna's seat on Celia's bay hunter was secure, her hands on the reins gentle but capable; and she laughed, in her confidence, in her delight, as they took the fences together, her husband and herself, their horses in unison. It would have amused Devlin, too, if he could have regarded riding to hounds with any feelings other than loathing.

For he hated hunting, never could forget the horror of the death of the mare, Chloe. The dream still haunted him on some nights. Celia, who seemed perfectly happy to stay on at Burnley through the winter, went in his place. Devlin preferred to remain at home, claiming the responsibility of the estate. It was on one of these hunt days, when he needed a new pen and came looking for one in Anna's writing desk, that he found the letter.

It was not an entire letter, but a fragment. A triangular piece from a page that had been torn carelessly, hurriedly, in quarters. Some of the words were scored through, different words written over the top. Ignoring the words crossed out, it read,

> *I do not understand*
> *to try to explain, though*
> *before me even as I write this*
> *a strength I pray will enable you*
> *A loving heart, my darling, I know*

It was a rough draft, it seemed, of a letter – in Anna's handwriting. Devlin stood there, with the tantalizing, unfinished phrases staring back at him. Slowly, he reached behind him for the desk chair and sat down, his gaze never leaving the fragment of paper. Then suddenly, with a sob, he was on his feet, running to the wastepaper basket. He rifled through it – but there was no more of the letter. He checked the fireplace for ashes of paper, but no, all evidence of the letter was gone.

Only for the briefest moment had he considered that this was a communication to her parents; he dismissed the idea immediately, for there was a tension even in the few words that he had that hinted at more than filial devotion.

He was withdrawn, preoccupied, Anna and Celia noted, that night at dinner. When they had retired to their own rooms, Anna made up her mind to speak to Devlin the following day. She had just dismissed her maid, for she liked to comb out her hair by herself, when the door opened and Devlin walked into the room.

He stopped, seeing her seated at her mirror, a wrap over her nightgown. The hand holding the brush stopped its action abruptly and she sat gazing at his reflection in the glass, not bothering to turn.

'I'm glad you've come,' she said. She placed her brush down upon the dressing table, moved it amongst the other articles on the surface until their placement seemed to suit her. Devlin, watching her, felt that she knew why he had come, was feeling her guilt, was perhaps afraid of him. 'I couldn't bear it.' And she turned to face him, and he saw no fear on her face, but a kind of anger. 'I couldn't bear it when I came back to the house this evening and found that look upon your face again. The cold look, that meant you were holding something unpleasant to yourself, and wouldn't share it with me – I knew I was bound to go through what I endured in London . . . '

'What *you* endured . . . !'

'Ah. Now we'll get angry, will we?' Her chin came up. 'At last. I'm glad you're angry, Devlin. We may be able to have some real communication between us at last, even if we're after shouting our heads off and waking Celia and Michael and every servant in the house. I'd welcome it, if I could find out why you've been behaving in the callous, foolish way you have . . . '

'Callous. I, callous. And foolish . . . Do I not have cause,' he shouted, 'to withdraw from you? That's what you complain of, is it not?'

'It's jealousy, isn't it? Serena told me that she'd . . . '

'Yes, jealousy! I've a right to be jealous!'

He was approaching her as she said, 'It's in your own mind, whatever it is that causes this rage of yours – your own imagination. . . '

'Call this my imagination!' He was holding the piece of torn paper before her face. She had to pull back a little to focus on it, but recognized it immediately, and snatched at it. But he was too quick for her.

'Where did you get that? Where did you find it?'

'Who is it addressed to? Did you send it? Did you?'

'It's none of your concern.' But her face had coloured a little, and she looked worried, now.

'You did send it, didn't you? This was only a draft . . . It's O'Brien, isn't it?'

'No!'

'Don't lie to me. You've been writing to him all along, writing love letters to him, and he's been writing to you. Where are his letters?'

'No, Devlin, there are no . . . '

'*Where are his letters*!' He had yanked her to her feet, and was shaking her hard. It was almost gratifying to have her within his grasp, feel himself stronger than she. His frustration, his hurt, boiled over, and he slapped her, hard, twice, across the face. 'You slut!' he sobbed. 'You bog Irish whore! You must have slept with him. Did you? Answer me. Did you sleep with him? Was O'Brien your lover? *Was he your lover* . . . !'

She pushed away from him, retreated from him. 'What do you want!' she screamed at him. 'What do you want me to say? Yes? Do you want me to say yes?'

He followed her, slapped her again. 'Tell me . . . !'

'Yes!' she shouted, sobbing. 'Yes . . . !'

His closed fist struck her temple and she fell hard, striking her head on the sharp corner of her writing desk. She lay still.

'Anna?' he breathed into the silence. 'Anna . . . ?'

'Oh, my God . . . ' The voice came from behind him. He started, whirled to find Celia standing there, just inside the door. She was still fully dressed, gazing in horror at Anna's crumpled body, then moved forward, ignoring Devlin entirely. She knelt on the floor, touched Anna's cheek, then felt her head carefully. There was no mark upon her face but the pink imprint of Devlin's palm. She could almost have been asleep.

Celia was looking up at Devlin. 'Help me carry her to the bed.'

Anna moaned, 'Devlin . . . ' as they lifted her, and again as they placed her on the bed. Celia tucked the covers about her, and turned to Devlin, white-faced, her little black eyes sparking with anger for the first time that Devlin had ever known. 'You fool. You absolute idiot. If you've killed this girl, Devlin, I'll see you . . . ' Anna moaned again, moved her head a little on the pillows. Celia bent to her, then raised her eyes to Devlin. 'Get a doctor, don't just . . . '

'No . . . ' Anna murmured, 'No . . . ' She opened her eyes, looked from one to the other. 'I . . . I'm all right. Did I fall?' She looked at her husband, and her eyes welled up with tears. 'Oh,' she said.

'Anna, I . . . you know I didn't mean it. Anna?' He moved closer to the bed, and Celia backed away a little, giving him space. 'Anna . . . Dear God, I didn't mean it! I goaded you . . . Forgive me . . . forgive me . . . ' Down on his knees by the bed, he lowerd his head upon her breast and wept.

She smoothed his hair. 'Och, stop . . . ' she said softly. 'It's all right, my dear . . . it's all right . . . ' After a long while, it seemed, she whispered, 'Lie beside me, Devlin. My love . . . ? I need someone to hold, tonight . . . don't you?'

He suddenly remembered Celia, turned to her, and found her gone; she had left the room, closing the door softly after her.

Devlin undressed and slid into the bed quietly beside his wife. He held her in his arms, and their union was brief and clouded by emotions that went deeper than physical passion, that lay unspoken between them, distancing them even in their intimacy.

Later, they drowsed together. Devlin said, sleepily, 'The letter – it was to your family, wasn't it?'

'Yes,' she said, 'it was to my family.'

'Did you send it? I'd rather you didn't. Have you sent it to your parents?'

'No . . . '

'You know how I feel about it. Ireland is behind us. You belong to me, now. Can't you forget about the past? For Michael's sake? He'll be raised an Englishman.'

She did not move or speak for several minutes, and he wondered if she were sleeping. Then she said, 'I'll not write to anyone at home. I'll forget Ireland. My place is with you.'

He drew her closer to him, buried his face in the fragrance of her hair, and fell asleep.

In the morning he slept late, and Anna was gone when he awoke. He remembered that she and Celia were to hunt today, and did not worry about her absence. He had things to think about.

There was a new beginning for them now, he felt sure of it; it had been born in the anger of the night before, a surety of her love for him. And he realized the depth – there were no depths – to his feelings for her. He had been a fool, a coward . . . He had so much, and he had nearly thrown it all away.

In his new feelings of being closer to her, part of a unit, he visited the nursery to see his son.

Michael, born in February, was now nine months old. 'A fine, bonnie boy . . . ' Peggy Lacey enthused, handing the wriggling, strong little infant to his father. Michael's face above the collar of the cream woollen dress was the soft pink-and-white of a well-cared-for baby, but the features of the man he would be could vaguely be seen in the small face. The nose was already promising to be high-bridged, the eyes were already a dark grey, the hair was thick and dark brown.

'He looks like my father,' Devlin mused to himself, and though the thought did nothing to endear the child to him, he had to laugh at the machinations of nature that brought the same features into a family, time and again, whether they were welcome or not.

The child Michael brought his brows together and scowled at Devlin, as if he sensed the laughter was not to include him, and the censure in those grey eyes made Devlin roar the louder. 'It's incredible! What a fate! It's simply not fair!'

Peggy Lacey was puzzled, and when Michael set his chin, opened his mouth and roared his own dislike of the man holding him, she clucked forward and brought her chick back to the warmth of her own breast. 'Tut, sir, you've frightened the little man . . . '

'God help me—' Devlin could barely speak. 'I'll grow old with that scowl levelled at me!'

He was still laughing as he came downstairs and found Simon

Beresford handing his hat and crop to the servant at the front door. Simon, white-faced, met Devlin at the foot of the stairs, and told him that Anna, on a clear run across a field, had had an attack of dizziness, had dropped her reins and fallen from the saddle. By the time Celia and Serena, riding closest to her, had reached her, Anna was dead.

24

Aidan found work with the Shannon Navigation Scheme soon after Liam was born. With some relief the following gale day, he was able to pay Nathan the past six months rent that was owing, though he wondered if it would make any difference to Devlin's threat. There were other farmers with more land than the O'Briens, who were two or three years behind in the rent. Why should Devlin be so anxious for them to be gone?

The idea of a vendetta occurred to him. Could Devlin resent him so much? But no. They were both mature men, now. Aidan was nearly twenty-four, Devlin would be twenty-eight. And he had everything, after all – land, money . . . Anna. Aidan told himself that he should be the jealous one.

And yet he found he was not. With his work on the river came a certain security; Corrie discontinued his soul-destroying haunting of the Relief Works and with Thomas's help, attacked the two fields behind the cottage with a hand plough and grim determination. They planted potatoes in the house field as usual, but the extra half-acre behind it was sown with oats. Thomas argued that the blight could not possibly strike three years in a row, that if they would only gamble a little and put in potatoes, they could make a good profit at market when so few farmers were willing to risk the cursed crop yet again. But Corrie asserted that they had gambled enough, and Aidan agreed with him. Should the potato fail them yet again, the oat harvest would at least pay the next year's rent, and give them enough grain for their own use through the months ahead.

And there was the baby. Liam's presence in the house changed everything. He was a kind of tangible future; thinking of him growing into a boy, and on to manhood, gave a different aspect to the lives of everyone in the house. Life was not only a round of work and sleep and thankfulness that they had survived that day, that week, that season. Here was someone for whom they were building a future.

Liam grew quickly. He was a contented, laughing child and Maura, who adored him, grew more contented also. Her questing soul and great need for love and its acknowledgement found its purpose in the child's demands. The waspishness with which she had begun to treat Aidan in the latter stages of her pregnancy vanished as she was kept busy fulfilling the baby's needs, and sharing with Aidan her pride in the child.

In their intimacy at night, however, there was no new spark of warmth. But here, too, Aidan began to accept things the way they were. Immature, he told himself, to expect a good wife to be all things. He began to forget what it was he had expected, his feelings of disappointment grew fewer; when he reached for her acquiescing and pliant body, it was to lose himself in the gift of her; and when he unconsciously realized that she was more content with as brief a union as possible, he took his vicarious pleasure without trying to prolong it. So their days were content, and their nights, too, became a habit; an unspoken and unquestioned function that neither distracted from, nor in any way added to their existence.

They watched their potato fields with dread, but the autumn was dry, and in October the potato stalks were healthily drying also, fading and browning as God meant they should, and when harvested the potatoes were fine, fat specimens. Thomas grumbled for months that they should have heeded his advice, that they'd have had twice as much money had the extra field not been planted with oats. But they had enough. They could pay the rent and buy more seed, and they would have bread and potatoes aplenty this twelvemonth.

Others were not so fortunate. With the blight, seed had been scarce and the land sown under potatoes was smaller in area than it had ever been. Some cottiers had walked off their useless plots early in the famine, in desperation had made themselves homeless in order to comply with the ruling that no free food was to be given to occupiers of a quarter-acre or more. When this harsh edict was abandoned in 1846 it was too late for thousands, and many of the ones who held grimly to their hovels and garden plots had no money to pay rent, without considering seed potato.

Many farmers who could have afforded to plant were as anxious as Aidan and Corrie, and the fields which in August would have been green with blossoming potato plants, now, in autumn, waved in pale gold undulations of wheat or barley or oats. And these crops, too, were sold for rent, and most of the rents paid off mortgages, and no one had enough money except the middlemen, the gombeen men, who bought the crops at the lowest possible prices and sold it to the unfortunate populace at prices unheard of in more settled times.

The O'Sullivans were three years behind in their rent. They had been able to afford only a quarter of the seed that they usually planted, and it was a meagre crop that was to pay rent and keep the family for twelve months.

Mary sent Thomas each Friday with a fish for them, and usually some bread as well, saying that she had made too much, that it would spoil. Oona still had her pride, Mary thought, as she wrapped the bread in a clean cloth, though God save her, that was near all she had. And she remembered with shame her resentment of Oona O'Sullivan, her shame that had grown greater over the years as her packages of food to the family had grown smaller. Only three children left. Three, while Timothy, Anne, Patrick, Conan, Michael, Margaret, Flannan, Mary and Kate became only names for vanished faces.

The cholera swept through nearly every family. When Maura remarked that they had, praise God, been lucky so far, Mary replied drily that she had never known an O'Brien man who had died of illness or old age. 'War kills them. Or horses,' she added. 'They go out like men would wish, anyway. It's violent, but quick.' Maura had looked at her with her slanted green eyes, and wondered whether to be comforted or not.

There was no sound except his own footsteps, a shuffling rhythm, back and forth through the frost-dry grass, and the faint notes of an owl, further up the hillside, hunting in the heather. 'At least one of us is happy to go hunting this night . . . ' Aidan muttered.

He yawned and stretched; he should not have volunteered to go forth tonight, twelve hours of swinging a pick on the muddy river bank had exhausted him. Thady and Seamus were probably equally as tired, that would explain their being late – probably asleep by the fire in their exhaustion – probably forgotten all about the raid on Tineranna's flock . . .

He had been waiting more than an hour, was impatiently deciding to return to his own cottage, when he heard the murmur of voices, the soft slur of bare feet through the dead grass, and he looked up.

They stopped on seeing him, stopped so suddenly that for a moment his mind played tricks upon him and he wondered if the shapes in the darkness were not Thady and Seamus after all.

The figures came towards him, slowly, but the familiar walk of each of them was unmistakable.

'What're y' doin', creepin' around like that?'

They stood before him, silent, hands in pockets, and in the moonlight, he could see the awkward smile on Thady's face, the frequent glances he cast his brother. 'Www-we been over with the Mmm-minogues . . . They sent one of the boys t' fetch us . . .Mmmmaster Devlin is back, Aidan.'

There was a silence. Was Anna with him? Could she have come with him after all? He would not ask them. Could not. His place was with Maura, and they knew it. He said, 'That shouldn't have made y' an hour late. What were y' doin'? Drinkin' his health?'

'Nnnn-no, Aidan . . . '

'We've wasted enough time. C'mon.' But as he turned up the glenside, Seamus had taken his arm. 'Wait, now. There's somethin' y' should know.'

'What?'

'Mrs Minogue was cleanin' the big house for the master . . . '

'That should have been my mother's doing . . . ' Aidan interrupted.

'But y'r nnn-not in favour at the mmm-moment, Aidan, y' oughta know that. Nn-nor y'r family, neither.'

'They've been there two days – the master and some English servants. No one knew, Aidan. Besides Nathan Cameron. It seems Master Devlin didn't want anyone t' know.'

'Is he mad? How can he hide in the big house without someone knowing?'

'Aidan, Mrs Minogue thinks that Devlin is . . . Well, he's lookin' terrible, and he's actin' worse. Drunk all the time, she says, and yesterday mornin' he had that fight with Nathan Cameron . . . '

'What's this? Why?'

'Mmm-Mrs Mmmm-Minogue was cleanin' the downstairs hall – and she couldn't help but hear, she sss-said. Mmmm-master Devlin was yellin' at Nathan, "Mmmm-onths ago! I told y' mmm-months ago!" But she couldn't hear what Cameron ss-said.'

Aidan knew. Staring in front of him, he lowered himself until he was sitting on his heels. The other two followed, squatting beside him.

'An' Mmm-master Devlin was shouting that Cameron was disloyal, an' a rogue, an' all sss-sorts of names she couldn't understand. An' then he's shoutin' for Cameron t' go. T' get out, off Tineranna. An' then it www-was quiet for a ww-while – and Cameron came through the door, holdin' sss-some mm-money in his

230

hand, and starin' at it, an' he looked up at Mmm-Mrs Mmm-Minogue as if he c'd see the very www-woodwork through her. And he walked out into the yard, she ss-said, an' Gerry Minogue said he sss-saw 'im with a bundle on his back, walkin' towards Sss-Scarriff. Ww-white like a ghost, he was.'

'No . . . '

Seamus said, 'Flynn has been appointed agent for Tineranna.'

'*No!*'

'Ww-what's the matter, Aidan? Flynn couldn't be worse than that little Orangeman as an agent, now could he? Aidan?'

He had turned away, his first thought to go looking for Nathan there and then. The man had no relatives, no friends, if he became ill on the roadway . . .

'Aidan?' Seamus spoke sharply. He turned. Again they were standing very still, gazing at him. 'There's more.'

'Anna . . . O'Hagan-that-was . . . ' Thady managed. 'She's dead, Aidan . . . '

'He could hardly bare to speak of it, Mrs Minogue said . . . '

'Know y'r mm-married to our sister, but we knew how you . . . '

' . . . Couldn't get any details, just yet, but it happened not long ago . . . '

'He loved her, Aidan . . . Mrs Minogue said he could barely speak he was that stricken with grief . . . '

'Spending all his time drinking with Hubert Osborne . . . '

They fell silent, abruptly. Aidan looked up at them. 'He's back, too, then?'

'Aye . . . ' almost unwillingly from Seamus.

'Aidan?' It was Thady at his elbow. 'We don't have to go after any sheep tonight. Y' can go home.'

Aidan tried hard to gather his thoughts; he was filled with the memory of his dream on Craglea, the day of his wedding. He had felt Anna leave him, had gone through with his own wedding only because he had known in that waking moment, that Anna was gone from him for ever. He dragged himself back to the present, 'Regan . . . ' he began.

'Regan met us as we were coming here.' Seamus took his other elbow. 'C'mon, we'll tell you on the way home.'

They walked Aidan to the boreen, explaining as they went that Regan had heard rumours of a police patrol later that evening, that he could not be certain if it were true or not, but they should not risk a raid that night. They would leave it, they said, for a week's time.

He did not answer them, and they walked in silence for most of the way, as if sensing the desolation within him. Seamus's few sentences and Thady's occasional halting comments were all to the effect that Flynn, with his reputation for ruthlessness, could be no worse than Nathan Cameron. Aidan thought, then, to tell them; but words were trapped within him, they rose to his mind but withered with his hopelessness before they reached his lips. He wanted to explain Nathan to them, but he knew he would become impassioned at their stupidity for not realizing the narrow tightrope the agent had walked over the years.

And Anna dead. He realized, on the walk through the darkness with Seamus and Thady, that he had expected either Anna or himself to die soon after this separation. But somehow he had thought it would be himself.

I have Liam and Maura. He said the words over and over as they walked up the road. I have Liam and Maura. But the cold sickness remained within him, and their names conjured up no image of hope.

25

Aidan insisted they leave him as they came to the entrance of the boreen. Even then he noticed through his own preoccupation that the two of them were worried, nervous, intent on getting him home. What are they afraid of? he asked himself. That I'll go kill Devlin because Anna died as his wife?

He watched Thady's restless shifting from one foot to the other, listened to Seamus telling him to go straight home, that Flynn had taken his new position seriously and had hired men to patrol Tineranna. 'Ww-with guns,' Thady added, giving Aidan a push towards the lane. 'Get you on home, now. Ww-we'll see you in the mm-morning.'

Aidan walked away from them slowly, puzzled that they waited until he vanished into the dark before their own footsteps faded away down the road. He stopped, then, and stood alone in the darkness of the boreen, heard the wind roar up on the hillsides, and keen around him through the chinks in the stone walls, the dry tangles of blackberry bushes.

He could not go home. He did not want the warmth, the watchful looks from Maura and his mother. He did not want the questions, nor to break down and tell them what he knew Flynn's appointment would mean.

He would have to tell them, he thought, retracing his steps back towards the road, but he needed to think of the manner of it. It needed careful thought. There would be hysteria from the two women. He knew that. Corrie would be staunch as always. Thomas would pale, and sit tight-lipped, and wait for someone else to make a decision. But his mother and his wife would be terrified. He could not face the look in their eyes. Not yet. Not tonight.

He crossed the road and headed up into the hills, pausing, once, when he heard a noise behind him. Could someone be following him? He stood there, near the wall he had just climbed, turned and looked back the way he had come. An empty road; empty, too, the entrance to the boreen. Yet for a while, in his tiredness and his nervous susceptibility, he could hear rustlings and scrapings behind him, at a distance, back there in the shadows. But who would be after him on such a night?

He chose the most difficult face of Craglea, and scrambled up the slope, feeling the need to pit himself against something, to spend some of his anger in physical action. He paused for breath half-way, and turned to gaze back at the moon-shot lough, and the narrow neck of water that fled past Killaloe. Almost at the crest he paused once more, and knew he could go no further. It was bitterly cold, and here the wind tore through him and wailed around him as if Aoibheal herself resented the intrusion of a man upon her domain at this hour of the night. He crouched down in the lee of a rock, as he had used to do when as a boy he felt the world had turned against him. Like a wild creature, he felt better for his isolation; it was only in those darkened cottages below that the dignity of aloneness in death or grief was denied one. Yet he was a result of that warm and over-close huddle of humanity. All through his youth his thoughts had been trained to allow him to take his place within that community. But there was no solace for him there now.

The moon hung low in the sky when he heard the shots. He had shifted, stretched, and decided to uncurl himself and prepare for the slithering descent to the lough, when one, two and three, the explosions cracked in the clear air and reverberated crazily between the hills around him. Where? From where did they come? His eyes scanned the still darkness of the slopes below him. Nothing had changed. Was it Tineranna? Flynn's men? Seamus and Thady – *had* they gone straight home? He was standing, had started off at a tangent down the treacherous slope.

There were men abroad. Too many men. Coming down through the fields towards the road, he saw a group of horsemen riding fast from the direction of Killaloe. He crouched in silence and waited, and as the hoofbeats faded and he began thinking it safe to stand and continue walking, three figures, low in the shadows of the stone wall to his left, suddenly sprang up, oblivious to him, leapt the fence and ran, quietly, quickly, along the road after the horses. He began to follow, heading in the direction of the O'Donoghue farm, and passed yet another figure, running, this time, back towards the village. It was madness . . . Aidan crouched low beside the wall; in the dark he could hear the man's heavy breathing, could not recognize him in the darkness, but something in the loping run . . .

'Thady?' Aidan hissed, 'Thady O'Donoghue!'

But fatigue forgotten, the man, Thady or not, had bolted off once more like a rabbit, leaving Aidan to stand gazing after him, watching the exhausted figure lurching off into the blackness. Was it Thady? If it was, he would have recognized Aidan's voice, surely now. Aidan hesitated. The more he thought about it, the more certain he was that the figure had been Thady O'Donoghue. He scowled after the man, and of a sudden impulse, turned and headed after him, towards the village.

Even there, it was pandemonium. Lights in windows that should have been shuttered and in darkness. The heavy tread of the booted police and the military, horses' hoofs sounding sharp and threatening on the cobble stones, echoing back and forth across the narrow street.

Aidan crouched in yards, in doorways, and watched the mobilization of the town's forces with a kind of fearful excitement. All this for sheep thieves? Surely not. The thought occurred to him that any number of the groups of Terryalts or Whiteboys may have staged a robbery, burnt a hay field. That was it. And there had been violence. An agent shot, perhaps . . . And with a feeling of horror he remembered Thady and Seamus. Their efforts to put him at ease, their denials that anything would change under Flynn's administration, their determination to get Aidan inside his own cottage with his wife and child. Thady. It *had* been Thady on the Killaloe road!

He stood gazing around him wildly, trying to gather his thoughts, to put himself in Thady's place. He had run away from the direction of his home. So they knew who he was, had recognized him. Where in the village would he go? And why the village at all? Why not up into the hills?

And he remembered, then, something that Regan had told them. 'Think twice. Don't do what they'll be expecting you to do.' He remembered Reddan's barn, behind the public house, where once Regan had hidden for four days when he thought he had been seen and recognized while on a raid. The barn was safe. The barn it would be.

He made his way along the narrow side streets, keeping away from the High Street with its lights and activity. Still he could not say that he was not followed, that he was not seen, for the poor crouched in every doorway; as he moved past hands were held up to him, fingers clutched at his coat, weak voices murmured to him. He hurried along, not pausing, knowing even as he did so that he might be exciting suspicion. The homeless moved slowly, without apparent direction or purpose. No honest man with a clear conscience, no matter how starving, would move this quickly down streets soon to be searched by army and police alike. He felt the eyes follow him, but could not slow his steps. At the corner of the barn, he collided with a figure turning into the narrow street. It reeled back, a fist raised – and only as Aidan went to block the blow did they stop and stare at each other. It was Martin Curran.

'Jaysus!' Aidan breathed. 'What in God's name are y' doin'?'

'What're *you* doin' here? How did y' know t' come here?'

'Where else would Thady come?'

'Sh! Get you within and don't be rousing the whole street.' Martin was pushing him around the corner and into the doorway of the barn. The low and rotting door swung back after them with a protest of its rusty hinges. In the silence and the dark, Aidan and Martin gazed at each other's shadows, listened to their breathing.

Martin said, 'They told y' about Anna, didn't they?'

'That's . . . over with.'

'Aye. And you should be home, so.'

Aidan ignored him, went to walk further into the barn, when Martin's hand was tight on his arm. 'You put the fear into me when you're so quiet. Why are you here, Aidan? What would you be thinking?'

'Nothing.' But his voice was shaking with supressed rage. 'It's not a night when I'd wish for any thoughts of my own.'

'It wasn't Devlin's fault, Aidan . . . '

'He married her . . . '

'She could have died as your wife just as likely . . . '

'Their marriage was unlawful in the eyes of God . . . !'

'Keep y'r voice low . . . !'

'He forced her to marry him. Nothing but evil could come from it. But it should have been Devlin that died . . . '

'Whisht! There's been . . .'

'It should have been Devlin, not Anna!'

'There's been enough of that tonight.' Martin's voice was low and strained, 'Enough of revenge and bloodshed, d'you hear me?'

Aidan stared at him, drew him over to a place on the floor where moonlight shone down through a hole in the slate roof. It was his turn to grip Martin. 'What were y' doin' tonight, you and Seamus and Thady? Where were y'?'

From the rear of the barn a slight sound made them both whirl. A shifting in the darkness . . . 'It's all right, it's us.' It was Regan's voice, but Seamus and Thady were close behind him as he moved out into the faint light.

Martin said, 'He should be out of here. He's got a wife and child. If they come and find him here . . . '

'He's right. Aidan, this is no place for you. Get you gone, now.'

'No. I want to know what happened tonight! If you were at Tineranna I had a right to be there! Why wasn't I told? Did y' not trust me?'

'Aidan, y've got yyy-young Liam an' Mmm-Maura t' think of . . . '

'Y' couldn't wait t' get rid of me tonight, could y'?'

'No, we couldn't,' Seamus interrupted him, 'We couldn't trust you anywhere near Devlin Kelly. We had more important things to . . . '

'Jaysus.' He stared from one face to another. 'Is it a madman y' think I am?'

'Aidan,' Regan said, 'Get you on home. The less you know, the safer you'll be.'

'I'll not stir until I'm told what's happened. Is . . . is Devlin dead, then?'

'No. But better for you if he was . . . ' Regan said, and stopped suddenly, listening. They all stiffened.

Bare feet, running along the street outside, laboured breath and running feet that kept going, past the door to the barn, away from the village. There were more stirrings, now. They could feel the street astir. The bundles of rags gathering themselves into human shape. Moving past like ghosts. All five in the barn stood still as if spirits were passing in their midst. Aidan was left with a feeling of tension, a nameless fear that he had not known before.

It was Seamus who broke the mood, he stepped forward and the light from above fell on the red hair, threw the high freckled cheek bones into prominence, but masked the eyes. 'Tell him,' he said to Martin. 'He won't go until he hears it.'

Martin had been standing with his hands behind his back. As he

236

glanced at Seamus, he let them fall to his side, watched the look on Aidan's face as he saw the sleeves stained darkly, even held them up a little, surveying them blankly.

'We weren't at Tineranna. We were at Ceelohg. Devlin Kelly was there, too. His horse was outside. He was visiting Hubert Osborne. The fool came back with Devlin, y' see. Came back to Ceelohg . . .

'We didn't know it at the time. We went to get ammunition, about twelve of us. We all had guns, but none of them were loaded. We surrounded the house and demanded what food and ammunition they had. In answer, they shot at us. We . . . we rushed the house, then, dragged them outside. They'd put out the lights, until we got 'em outside we didn't know who we had . . . Old man Osborne, Devlin Kelly . . . '

'He was out of his mind with fear,' Regan interrupted. 'Kept screamin', "It's Aidan O'Brien! Aidan O'Brien, I tell you! He's sworn to kill me!" And cryin' out for Hubert Osborne to help.'

Regan stopped and turned to Martin. Aidan stared at him, his mind filled with the thought of Devlin being dragged across the broad sweep of Ceelohg's lawn, feeling his, Aidan's, hate in every heavy hand that gripped him.

Martin was saying, 'I found meself holding Hubert Osborne. Me and Roddy Minogue and one or two others. When I saw it was him . . . I hit him. I had a musket, and I struck him with it. I don't know how many times. They dragged me off him, and we ran, then. I don't know how many times I hit him. But he's dead. I saw his brains in the moonlight. He's dead.'

Aidan stared at Martin for a long time. The words made no sense. Bravado, that was all. Young Martin had always had a great temper, and a mind for exaggeration. They had grown up together. Knew each other like brothers . . . Not murder. No. Not Martin.

But his memory of the night slotted into place like a macabre game. The shots, Thady fleeing along the road . . .

'You didn't stop when I called your name . . . '

'Mm-Mother of God, was that you? How ww-was I to know?'

'I saw three other men – runnin' scared they were . . . '

'We got away as best we could,' Regan said. 'It went wrong, all wrong. I'll not be blamin' Martin for what he did. It was no more than the law should have done, if we had justice in Ireland. But we panicked and ran away. We didn't get what we came for.'

'Ammunition . . . '

'Yes. It's like a war, Aidan,' Seamus said. 'Now Nathan Cameron's gone from Tineranna and we've got that gombeen man, Flynn – waddling around on his little short legs, with his silk

237

waistcoats, like a goose through a paint pot. He'll be the end of us. And not just Tineranna tenants. He's not only evictin', he's patrolling with armed men. Soon every landlord'll be after copyin' him. We can't stay home and starve, and we can't go lookin' for food as we did. We had to get ammunition and more arms – we got to fight them on their own terms!'

He had heard the words before. But it had always been the Currans who had urged social awareness. The meetings by the fireside, going back to '45, and the dark heads of Tom-Joe and Martin, bent over copies of *The Nation*, reading aloud articles by Davis, Mitchel, Duffy, Dillon, that grew from the urgings for a solid political unity to demands for a national uprising, violence, rebellion. He stood there gazing at the four of them, Regan's plain, honest face, Thady's earnest, kindly one, Seamus the fine-featured intellectual, Martin with his swarthy skin and dark soul. All of them, farmers, once, sheep thieves, now, in these bad times – and tonight made violent men, murderers.

'Aidan,' Regan was saying. 'Get you home, now.'

And his own voice was answering, calmly, as though it no longer belonged to him, 'No. I'll stay. We're in this together – our oath, remember? – and you may have need of another man.'

'Aidan, y'r mm-mad!' Thady gripped his arm, 'What of Maura and . . . '

But it was already too late for persuasion, too late for escape. The sound of booted feet – running towards the door there was a dull thud, and the sounds of splintering wood . . .

'Run!' Regan yelled. There was only a second lost in shock and they were after him, heading back into the dark of the barn, towards the rear door, someone – Thady? Seamus? – grabbing Aidan's arm.

'No! Up here!'

They were climbing the broken ladder to the loft. Aidan's heart was lurching with fright, his breath already laboured. From below they heard the shout to halt, saw the faint light glint on a raised musket . . . The explosion was deafening, but Aidan had no time to realize where the bullet had gone, who was screaming. The figure above him had wriggled up through a hole in the roof, was reaching down, taking his shoulders, and hauling him after. Only on the roof, crouching there for a second, did he recognize Regan's face.

They were off, scrambling over the slates, on to the next building. He heard Regan say, 'Here! Behind the chimney . . . !' But Aidan was now in front – when he turned, his foot skidded on a loose tile and he lost his balance. Checking a cry, he rolled with it, over and over three times, clutched at the eaves vainly – but it was a low-roofed building, this, and only eight feet from the ground at its end. He landed on the mudddy alleyway and was up on his feet before his terror had allowed the recognition of the fall.

And noises behind him! He was running, running down the narrow deserted street, no bundles of rags in doorways, now. It was then he knew that a trap had been set. Someone had seen . . . someone had told . . . any one of the starving hundreds of beggars whose eyes would have followed them.

He reached a corner, and had no time to turn before he heard a shout of 'Halt! Stop there, you!' in stentorian tones, a harsh English voice, there behind him. In a year of taking mutton from forbidden fields he had feared tó hear that voice. It was more of a nightmare now, here in this confined alley, this narrow street of his own village.

Wood from a doorway exploded in splinters as the shot tore the air apart. He ran wide-eyed, mad with fear like a rabbit, no plan, no understanding, just to escape . . .

He had doubled back without realizing it. Here was the High Street and Reddans, here were men, more soldiers . . . and horses! For the first time, some reasoning penetrated. The horses were tied fifty feet from him. He had time to rake his eyes along them, chose the tallest, a bay thoroughbred whose head was already raised, gazing towards the sound of his running feet . . .

A man rushed out from a doorway, a scarlet coat that tried to grapple with him. Rage and fear drove his arm, he felt the nose break under the blow of his fist, kept moving, had his hands on the reins, jerking them free, was into the saddle and carried off in four huge strides that even then seemed to take him back, back . . . He was at Tineranna, schooling a bay steeplechaser . . . Cara, Mister Kelly had called her . . .

He was at the top of the village, before him the Catholic St Flannan's, and a dozen mounted men were coming from the direction of Ogonnelloe. He pulled the horse in, wheeled her even as they saw him, even as he looked back the way he had come and saw the four men coming after him, whipping their horses up the street.

He did not realize until afterwards that it was the barracks yard into which he was headed. A pistol shot had exploded, his horse had bounded off to the left in fright – and suddenly the opening in the stone wall was there. It never seemed to be a dead end for him. Cara, for it was Cara, was mad with fright, as mad with fright as the man on her back, in whom she had utter confidence as a rider. It was over before either of them thought about it. One minute they were careering across the cobbled yard with the shouting crowd of soldiers behind them, and suddenly the wall was in front of them. And they did what it was in their nature to do. They jumped it.

It was six feet high, and two feet thick, and the soldiers told no one about it afterwards. Short of saying the man was bewitched, or the horse, or both, they could find no explanation. The Catholics amongst them stared and crossed themselves. The Protestants merely stared. And both lost fifteen seconds in controlling their horses and their wits before charging out of the yard, finding the streets empty, dividing their numbers in two to follow the road to Ogonnelloe and the road to Finlea.

The regiment had already been searching the countryside that evening; their horses were tired and were gradually falling behind Aidan's fresher mount. The seven men who followed him to Finlea were more than a mile behind him when he passed the darkened farmhouses and was out again on the open road.

He had had no conscious thoughts since stealing the horse, but now, after several glances behind him and finding no mounted men within sight, his thinking began to clear, the fear began to recede a little.

He had been seen, that was certain. Even if he managed to prove he was not one of the men present when Osborne was murdered, he was guilty of horse stealing. He cursed his own panic, thought with swift, sudden clarity that he would have been better off giving himself up. But he had run. No matter what came from this night's work, he was a wanted man. The penalty for stealing a horse was seven years transportation to Van Diemen's Land.

To hide. This was his only chance, now. To remain in hiding until Corrie and Thomas could get money for his passage to Boston. It was nothing new. It had happened often enough to the Terryalts. Boston or Van Diemen's Land. Boston or death.

He found the fear had returned, but a cold, sick fear, now. To leave Maura and the baby. To leave everyone, everything. For one thoughtless escapade.

Looking around to his right, he could see where the shoulder of Craglea rose up into the hill's crest, humped against the sky . . . And he remembered, then, the old man, Clooney, with his cottage and still, high on that slope, far from the eyes of the revenue police. Aidan was drawing rein, sliding from the horse's back, and with a slap to the mare's rump, sent her off down the road. He wondered if she would forget her new owners in her fright, and smiled, as he climbed over the stone wall, at the thought of Cara leading their pursuers to the gates of Tineranna, where she had been born and bred.

There were white ruins ahead of him in the dark. He stared at the pale shapes of free-standing walls, trying to place them . . . There had been cottages here. Four or five cottiers' huts. As he approached the ruins, skirting around them in case someone had returned to build a hovel amongst them, he remembered a rumour, that one of the landlords from Finlea had managed to persuade some of his tenants to emigrate. This, then, was all that was left; a few chimneys standing, a few walls supporting nothing at all. One window hole stared sightlessly across at him.

And even as he walked, glancing at that aperture and away again, there was a shifting of the darkness within it, and a scuffling on the stones. Aidan turned to it sharply, the hair rising on the back of his neck.

'Sir?' A woman's voice. 'God be with you, sir. Will you help us? I beg you, sir!' Quicker, as Aidan turned away, took two hurried steps. 'I beg you, sir, I know you have no food . . . some water, sir, *please*.'

'I . . . I have no water.' He was scowling helplessly towards the invisible voice, edging backwards up the slope.

'My child is dying, sir . . . !' A wail, the wail of true grief in the voice. 'I've carried her from Scariff – the workhouse is full . . .She's dyin', sir! I can't leave her to go to the brook . . . Please, sir!'

Aidan stopped, glaring back at the window with resentment, wanting to turn, to leave . . . Something heavy landed in the grass near his feet. He started in terror, only the woman's voice calmed him. 'There's the bowl, sir. Please, sir . . . the brook's down beyond the trees behind you.'

Hoofbeats on the road! He half-turned, the terror taking control of his body, and the woman's voice, relentless. 'There's another in here, too. A man near death too, sir. For both their sakes, if you're a Christian, sir . . . !'

The hoofbeats were deafening, soon the heads of the riders would appear above the stone wall . . . He reached down and grabbed the wooden bowl, running fast and bent low to the ground, tripping on the uneven soil, down to the shelter of trees, the bubbling of water. He fell on his face among the twisted tree roots, listened as the riders charged over the stone bridge close by his head. They were coming for him, coming, coming, roaring down upon him with drawn sabres, Anna was dead, his friends were dead, and now they were coming for him. He had bitten his lip and it was bleeding into his mouth. His twittering, gibbering thoughts had him lying on the ground, paralysed, and it was only slowly and with all his concentration that he realized that the hoofbeats had long faded, that he had been lying there for some minutes, unable to rise.

He clambered to his knees, groped his way to the muddy edge of the brook, and filled the bowl with water. Slowly, with infinite care, he carried it back towards the ruins. Laughed, in his state of shock and despair at his ability to walk so carefully, conscious of every drop of the liquid. It was madness, madness . . . Death in this ruined field, death waiting on the road. So carry your bowl with care, do what you have to do. It did not matter. Death in the fields, death on the roadway . . .

'Are you there? I've brought . . . ' the hands came through the window opening and groped along his arm, snatching the bowl from his grasp. The 'God bless you, sir,' was almost lost under the childish wail that issued from somewhere in the shadows. Aidan heard the death in the weak protest, stumbled back and half-turned. 'God go with you,' he said.

'Aidan O'Brien?'

The voice stopped him. Man's voice. Familiar. 'Is that Aidan O'Brien?'

Jaysus-Mary-and-Joseph. It wasn't Nathan Cameron . . .

'Come back if you're Aidan O'Brien. Come back, man.'

They would be coming back, soon. Turning their horses, milling about at some crossroads in the dark where the moonlight showed empty boreens dipping down between the hawthorn shadows. He had begun to walk away.

'Aidan . . . ?' Like a blow between his shoulders. There was no doubt. There could be no running.

He lay crumpled in a corner by a fallen wall. Aidan took a flint from his pocket and struck a match. The face was almost unrecognizable. The fever had taken hold, the pustules on the bloated face were bleeding, the dry cracked lips opened to gasp for air. 'It's Aidan?'

'Aye . . . '

'Why have they left me alone out here? Why isn't Cook here to nurse me? Cook was always sent down with some gruel . . . ' An emaciated hand snaked out and grasped him, took his wrist in an irresistible hold. 'Have y' been makin' trouble for me in the kitchen? Have y'?'

'No . . . No, Nathan . . . You know I wouldn't do that . . . '

The match went out. The grip on Aidan's wrist slackened as if the man's energy failed with the light.

'Fetch me . . . some water, Aidan . . . from the barrel.'

He looked up and around before realizing that the older man thought he was still in his room above the stables at Tineranna. He

242

stood and groped among the ruined masonry. 'Woman? The bowl, if y' please. Woman . . . ?' Groping blindly, he found her, took the empty bowl from her, made his way down to the brook once again.

Terror in returning, terror in holding the bowl against those feverish lips, the malignant sores. Yet he conquered the fear. He had seen mothers abandon their children when the typhoid came upon them, had seen husbands leave their wives in cottages to die alone, so great was the terror of the disease. Yet he stayed – for already, nothing seemed to matter very greatly.

Nathan muttered to the boy about William Kelly – had he arrived home? Where was he for so long? Why hadn't he seen to it that Nathan was looked after? Aidan squatted by him and listened, gave answers as best he could, found himself almost mesmerized by the misplacing of Nathan's thoughts. Could he believe it? How easy it would be! Those distant good days, the stables . . . Yes, Fleur had given birth to a colt – yes, the master had seen him. There were thirty-three horses in the fields, eleven in the stables – Master Devlin and the mistress were riding to hounds next week – Cider Glass would be sure to win the next race in Limerick – the master was in Killaloe. Yes, he would be back. Soon, quite soon . . .

He had been sitting there in silence for some time, when the woman's voice spoke quietly from beside him. 'He's gone, sir.'

'What?'

'Sir, cross y'self for the sake of his soul, sir, God rest his soul gently. Could you not tell, sir? He's been gone these three minutes.'

A touch on the older man's wrist. Silent the pulse within that narrow frame. Gone the force that had bullied him, constricted him, taught him, helped bring him to manhood.

'Get you gone, sir. In the morning I'll bury him with the stones. Get you gone, sir, before the soldiers are after returning.'

He was pushed a little, stood up and stumbled backwards. The moon was behind a cloud. He had no final sight of Nathan, no sight at all of the woman or her now silent child. 'God go with you,' he managed to say.

'And with you.'

He groped for an opening in the wall and was off, heading up the slope, away from the road, into the hills.

He had climbed these hills all his life, loved to climb, even when exhausted, placing one foot before the other, eyes on the rocky soil, the heather and hardy grasses, feeling at one with them, stubbornly clinging to these hills where he belonged.

He gained some of his old sense of comfort now, as he climbed, and he left behind him the horror of Nathan's death, all the horrors that were part of this night, and concentrated on walking up, up. His goal lay somewhere in the darkness above him. He would not think of what was behind him. If he tried he could do this . . . If he were strong, he could do this . . . put it behind him, don't look back. For there lay the horror and the madness. Never, never look back.

26

Jim-Pat Flynn climbed down from his horse with difficulty. He was short, and fat – fat, his tenants thought, as no man had a right to be in these times – and his movements were hampered by arthritis that attacked him particularly in his knees. He strove to hide it, never complaining – except to his wife, who paid more fully for his agony than even he did – for it would not do for his clients nor his tenants to think him unfit in any way.

He would have to get a pony and chaise, he thought, approaching the broad steps of Tineranna. He climbed them one at a time, secure in the knowledge that there were few servants in the house to see him, and all of those doubtlessly clustered about Devlin Kelly, after his fright that evening.

He was proved right in the five minutes that it took Masters, Devlin's valet, to come downstairs to answer the bell. Half of that time, Flynn was sure, the frightened Englishman had been peering at him through the window, trying to decide if it really was the new agent, or one of the Terryalts on a stolen horse.

'Is the master in?' Flynn stepped through the door.

'Yes, sir.'

'Show me to him at once.'

Masters closed the door and led the way up the stairs to the first floor drawing room, bristling with indignation. Flynn sensed it, sniffing the man's discomfort with delight. To be an Englishman, yet forced to take orders from an Irishman such as he – oh, it was amusing, all right! Kelly must be paying the man a fortune, to make it worth his while to suffer these indignities in silence.

Devlin was seated by the fire, a large brandy on the table beside him. His normally pale face was ashen, unhealthy. 'Come in, Flynn. Masters, you may retire. We'll be leaving early, remember.'

'Yes, sir.'

With the closing of the door, Flynn moved closer, arranging his face into a combination of concern and righteous anger. 'I trust y've recovered, sir. It was a bad thing, sir, so it was, and I thank God you're safe.'

'They would have killed me, too.' Devlin's eyes, bloodshot and dark-circled, burnt upwards into Flynn's. 'Would have killed me without a thought, if they hadn't been frightened off.'

'Cowards, sir, each and every one of them.'

'The blood frightened them.' Devlin's voice was low, his gaze now fixed on the fire. 'They'd never seen so much blood. They knew Hubert was . . . dead. Poor Hubert. He was my best friend, Flynn.'

'I know, sir, and a finer gentleman you'd never meet. Those that did this thing will be caught, sir, the police have a list of their names.'

'O'Brien was there. I know O'Brien was one of them . . . '

'Yes, sir. Mr Osborne has sworn that he saw Aidan O'Brien amongst them . . . ' He stopped as Devlin lifted his head to gaze at him keenly.

'Yes,' Devlin said finally, 'He was there. He'd have killed me.'

'They always were a trouble-making lot, sir. My father has tales of the O'Briens – nine of them killed in the troubles of '98 – rebels they were, the lot of them. Aidan's got their bad blood, sir. Mad for revenge, sir, that's . . . '

'He has no reason to seek vengeance against me. Haven't I allowed him to remain as a tenant, even after he was no longer employed on Tineranna? His whole family would be starving on the roads if it wasn't for me!'

'Yes, sir, that's right, sir. He's after bein' one of the most ungrateful of spalpeens, sir. But he'll be caught, sir. They'll all be caught. Clare isn't big enough to hide them.' He watched worriedly, as Devlin turned once more to gaze into the flames. Flynn was not at all sure that O'Brien was amongst the men at Ceelohg. True, he was rumoured to be a Terryalt, so he might just as well hang for murder as be transported. Something about the man seemed to bother Devlin Kelly, so the sooner he was out of the way, the better.

'Flynn, pour me another brandy, would you? Pour yourself one, also.'

' . . . The decanter is empty, sir.'

'Damn. Ring for Masters, will you? Or . . . you'll find some in the dining room if you care to go down.'

Flynn did not; but Devlin seemed to expect him to, so he left the room, and shutting the door after himself, leaned on the banister

245

and hopped painfully down the stairs. They were carpeted stairs, and his uneven progress was masked by the thickness of the pile. The hall was black and white marble, brought at God knows what cost from somewhere in Europe. By the light of the lamps – Kelly had given orders that the lamps were to be left burning – Flynn easily found the dining room, had reached for the decanter of brandy and taken a long swig straight from the bottle, when the sound of breaking glass shattered the silence, had him choking, coughing, as the burning liquid found its way into his lungs.

He was not a cowardly man – what could the broken window mean but more Terryalts? His eyes still smarting, he reached the door, blowing out the lamp, and taking from his belt the revolver that never left his side. He could hear Devlin Kelly's voice calling out his name, demanding to know what the noise meant. He did not answer, strained his ears past the sounds of his master's shouts, heard no further noise in the hallway.

He opened the door, checked quickly around the doorway, towards the front of the house where the window had shattered – he sensed his mistake even as he heard the quick inhalation of breath beside him, knew in that split second before unconsciousness claimed him, that someone had been waiting for him.

Devlin came out of the room carrying one of the French duelling pistols he had never fired. It was loaded, now, had been loaded since he had returned to the house from Ceelohg. But even this was inadequate, and he knew it. He had been mad to return alone. Pride, that was it, a kind of shame in remembering his screaming for mercy. He had returned in a desire to show that he was master of Tineranna, was not afraid. He had refused a police guard, and they had not insisted, feeling that the mob was scattered, too frightened to make another attempt that night.

The lamps had been blown out, there below him in the hall. He had not thought of that. He realized that he was a sure target, silhouetted against the lamp on the hall table behind him. He froze with fear, torn with the desire to throw himself back into the drawing room and lock the door, yet terrified to turn his back on what waited in the shadows below him.

'Mister Kelly.'

He lifted the pistol. 'Stay where you are.'

'I want to talk with you.' Distinctive voice, gravelled, rough . . .

A shadow moved in the dark, and Devlin tightened his grip on the gun, felt the smooth trigger give, the explosion that pushed him back into the table, rocking the ornaments and the lamp upon its surface.

In the silence as the shot faded, the objects rocked absurdly, clocks in syncopated time, winding down. The shadows cast by the lamp, banister rails, Devlin himself, swayed about on the dark wallpaper, flickering maniacally. Devlin remained frozen, watching his own shadow in its macabre dance and pressing the trigger again and again in his terror – the pistol aimed now at the shadow, the hammer clicking home harmlessly.

'Mister Kelly.'

He threw the gun, heard the shape below him grunt with pain as the pistol struck, had half-turned –

'Stay where you are! I swear I'll break down every door you hide behind! I swear it!'

And Devlin stayed. He could place the voice, now, knew who it was even before the heavy feet climbed up from the darkness into the pool of flickering light.

Corrie O'Neill's great blunt head was raised to him as he climbed. Slowly, Devlin found himself losing some of his terror. Corrie O'Neill. Here was an adversary he knew, had controlled from his boyhood. An extension of Tineranna. A tenant.

'Lay a hand on me, O'Neill, and you'll hang. You know you will.'

'Maybe, and maybe not.'

'For God's sake, man. There's been one murder already, tonight! What is it you want? I have no money here, no ammunition! Tell your murdering friends to go – there's nothing for you here!'

'I came alone. I'm no Terryalt.'

'Then what . . . '

'I want the truth from you. You'll not be saying that Aidan O'Brien was at Ceelohg tonight. It's you that's made old man Osborne say he was. The old man's mad with fear and grief . . . '

'If he saw him there . . . '

'He did not, and neither did you! When Mrs Minogue came and told us of your wife's death, I went looking for Aidan. I saw him coming home with the O'Donoghues. When they left him, he headed up towards Craglea, alone. I followed him most of the way.

'You said there'd been one murder already tonight. There was, and it's sorry I am for Hubert Osborne, may his soul rest easy. But you're after having two murders committed. And one resting squarely on your hands.'

'O'Brien was there,' Devlin said stubbornly. 'Edward Osborne knows what he's saying . . . '

'You're lying!' It was a shout, a bellow, that made the crystal prisms on the hall chandelier jangle musically in the shadows.

Still Devlin felt unafraid. He had known the gentle fighter for too long; but the big man was stepping towards him, up the stairs, and Devlin, despite himself, was backing away down the hall, step for step.

'Tell the truth. For God's sake, you'll not be using your own hatred to punish a man like this. Aidan wasn't there . . . '

'He was!'

'Mister Kelly, God forgive me, but . . . '

'Keep back!'

'Tell the truth! Admit it . . . !'

'He was there! He deserves what comes to him! He deserves to be punished! He . . . !'

'Y' lyin' little coward!' And the hands were around his throat. Devlin stumbled backwards against the table, only now realizing that something had snapped within the old boxer. He had lost control, and Devlin knew in the instant that the fingers closed on his windpipe that the man would kill him.

'Tell the truth! The truth, damn y'!'

Devlin's hand groped behind him as he lost his balance. It found the heavy bronze statuette that his father had bought in Florence. His hand closed around the smooth metal neck of a shepherd boy. He brought it up and around with all the weight of his trapped body. His neck screamed in the iron grip, but the statue landed heavily behind the giant's ear.

Corrie's eyes remained fixed on Devlin's face, but he felt no pain when the metal base of the statue drove through the thin bone of his skull. He died instantly.

It was Devlin who felt the full horror of that moment. The statue's edge remained fixed in the skull, the dead hands remained gripped around his throat, the dead face gazing at him in hatred. For two seconds they stood there, before Devlin's terror freed his body, and he screamed, screamed as he pushed the body away from him, watched as it toppled backwards, bouncing off the banister one moment, off the wall the next, watched the splashes of scarlet mark its progress down into the darkness. Still the sounds of the fall went on and on. Devlin put his hands to his face, screamed again in horror at the blood that covered his right hand and sleeve.

He was crouched on the stairs, his arms over his head, his own panic the only reality, when he became conscious of a voice, a soothing voice – but from there, below him . . .

The downstairs hall was filled with light, the shadows gone.

Devlin did not immediately see the sprawled body because Jim-Pat Flynn was standing before it, just shaking out the match with which he had lit the lamps. He gazed up at Devlin with concern.

'It's all right, sir,' he was saying, 'It's all right. I saw the whole thing. We'll think of something, sir. It'll be all right, you'll see.'

There was a pause, while Devlin stared at him, blankly. Flynn was suddenly afraid for the man's sanity. He must remove him from the house, take him to stay at Ceelohg, perhaps, old Osborne would appreciate his presence . . .

Flynn walked up the stairs to where the landlord was crouched, the fair head down on the knees in a posture of despair. As if to a child, Flynn spoke gently, took the man's arm and helped him to his feet, guiding him back into the drawing room, keeping him turned away from the sight of the stairs.

27

The Sidhe of Craglea was dancing once more through his dreams. He awoke in terror, remembering nothing except the vague feeling of her presence, the woman in black, with her long pale hair.

He gazed around him at the shadows of Clooney's cottage, seeing strange figures everywhere until his vision cleared. Clooney's cottage. He had scrambled up here, had knocked and called out, had finally entered to find the single room empty. The still had disappeared. Had the revenue police found him at last?

There was no food at all. But the bedding was dry, and there was turf left by the fireplace. He lit a blaze, and leaned back on the thin mattress, resting only, he would not stay . . .

He was almost thankful for his nightmare. Birds were calling sleepily in the furze, and the dawn would soon break over the crest of the hill. He had not meant to sleep. He could not afford to.

The memory of the previous night was upon him before he had propped himself up on one elbow, checking the still-dark sky outside the window. The panic began to rise in him once more. Losing Anna, losing Nathan – and God knew what had happened to Thady and Seamus, to Martin and Regan. All he wanted was a place to run to, a safe place, somewhere he could sit quietly and face his grief. But he must run, and keep running. There was no going home for him, now, no going back. Even to have been seen with the Terrys last night would carry a heavy prison sentence. To have helped them was to be one of them.

He stayed there on the bed, for the first time allowing the full impact of what had happened to settle upon him. Maura, Liam, his mother, Corrie, Thomas . . . He could never go home to them again. Too many Terrys had been trapped that way. Wives moving through their chores with set, white faces, and the waiting gleam of red coats and brass buttons silent in the half-shadows of the room. Waiting . . .

He did not know exactly when the sounds became footsteps. Here on the mountain, Clooney's cottage had long become part of the heather country. Nature moved all around it, the birds, the deer, the small wild things of the hills – but the rustling that his ears had become accustomed to, suddenly had a pattern, a slow and cautious rhythm.

He was on his feet, groping towards the door. On the wall there – hadn't he seen a walking stick, a broom? Any weapon, anything. . .

The knocking at the door had him reeling back against the fireplace, blindly looking about for some way of escape. The only windows were two tiny apertures, placed on either side of the door. Why hadn't he realized this? He had been a fool to come here – he was trapped . . .

'Aidan? Aidan O'Brien, are you there? It's Father McDonnagh. Aidan . . . '

The sense of relief brought him half-way across the room – but here he stopped, as cautious as an animal. The priest must have heard the faint movements within the cottage. 'I'm alone, Aidan. I came alone. Open the door.'

He lifted the latch, stepped back and let the priest, a darker shadow in the night, move silently into the room. There was a slight and awkward pause as Aidan shut and bolted the door; then the priest broke the silence, moving to the fireplace, muttering of the cold. He threw more sods of turf on the fading embers, and still kneeling, addressed the acrid smoke.

'Clooney was arrested last week. He'll get six months imprisonment, poor old devil. I saw him yesterday. I doubt if he'll survive. The fever is rife in the prisons.'

Aidan's thoughts were suddenly on Nathan Cameron. 'I found . . . '

'And what about you?' The priest talked through him, turning and gazing at Aidan, squinting in the gloom. 'How will you survive prison, I wonder?'

250

'Me? I'll be damned if I . . . I mean . . . '

'Let it stand. You are damned, and you know it.'

Aidan felt himself pale. 'Father, I wasn't there at Ceelohg! I swear to God! I met Martin and the O'Donoghues in Killaloe! I . . . '

'They say you were there.'

'What? Who said that?'

'Devlin Kelly and Edward Osborne.'

'They're mad! I was . . . !' he stopped.

'Yes?'

'Father, they're lying . . . '

'If you weren't there, Aidan, where were you?'

'I was . . . – was walking. On the slopes below. I wanted to think.'

'You knew what they were going to do . . . '

'No! They didn't tell me. They didn't trust me to keep my temper. As if I'd want to soil my hands on Devlin Kelly! They'd . . . told me about Anna. I wanted to be alone.'

'Is that the truth, Aidan? You wouldn't lie to me?'

'No, Father.'

For a long moment they gazed at each other. The priest stood, and in the flames from the fire, he watched the open, intense face of the boy before him, and nodded, slowly. 'But you were a Terry, weren't you?'

Silence.

'Weren't you?'

'Yes.'

'You were on a raid tonight?'

'No. Thady and Seamus . . . they called it off.'

'You have no witnesses, so. If Osborne and Kelly say that you were at Ceelohg, you have no way to prove them wrong.'

'Am I guilty, then, just on their word?'

'They have power and influence, Aidan. They're well-respected citizens. Their word will be believed.'

Aidan backed away, his eyes narrowed. 'And you – do you believe them?'

'No. I can understand Thady and Seamus leaving you behind.'

'They'd no right . . . !'

'Don't be a fool! Things are bad for the cottiers – even for the O'Donoghues, God save them – their education doesn't help them in these times. But *you* – your family has enough food to live on, a house over your heads . . . '

'They're my friends! You've said yourself how much they stood in need! In times like these, men have to stand together . . . '

'What kind of talk is this? Sedition, is it? Have you been reading the rubbish that Mitchel and Duffy have been publishing?'

'Aye! We all have! And they're right! All I've seen these past five years convinces me they're right!'

'They're doomed men if they keep up that talk!'

'You don't understand! Here in Clare . . . '

'Have I not been burying hundreds of bodies each week?' The priest was trembling. 'Don't dare to talk to me of starvation and disease, telling me that I don't know how things stand in Clare, Aidan! I could write the history of this county in my own blood and it wouldn't tell the horror of it!'

'Then you can't be blamin' us! Damn it all, Father, I haven't done anything that any sane man wouldn't do! We have a right to live, to control our own lives! The land was ours! Not England's, but ours! We have a right to it!'

'Would you be having more scenes like the one at Ceelohg? Would you have your land by murdering the landlords one by one?'

'It's our land! *Our land*! They've bled it dry, and us with it! We're bein' blown away like dry seed on the wind, and you want me to stand by and watch it happen!'

'The changes will come slowly. Perhaps not in our lifetime, but certainly not now, boy! You tell me to look at the people – *you* look! And then tell me if these folks are capable of fighting for anything more than their next mouthful of stirabout! They're broken, Aidan, totally demoralized. Your revolutionaries have to have visions, to be able to see tomorrow as a reality and fight for it.'

'Some of us are prepared to fight for it . . . '

The priest stepped to him, took his arms in a tight grip. 'Some of you? How many are left, Aidan? Thady is in prison – he'll be transported for life, if he's not hanged. Martin will certainly hang.'

'They caught them? After we fled the barn . . . they caught them?'

'They caught Thady and Martin.'

'And Seamus. Did Seamus escape?'

'Seamus is dead, Aidan.'

The silence. The silence went on and on, while he waited for the priest to retract his words. But Daniel McDonnagh only looked at him, his face a pale shape in the flickering darkness.

'No,' Aidan said, finally.

'Seamus is dead.'

'Y'r lying!' He had whirled away to the window, stood there gripping the ledge. He wanted to take hold of the priest, shake him, strike him, make him admit he was lying. He did not dare let go of the ledge. The voice followed him relentlessly.

'Seamus ran from the police. They called for him to stop, but he didn't listen. He was shot three times in the back.'

'*No!*'

The priest walked up behind him. 'Why are you so shocked? They were all prepared to die. That's what Mitchel and Duffy are teaching, aren't they? You wanted to go with them – it could have been you.'

'But Seamus . . .'

'Seamus knew the risks he took. He was a rebel born out of time – a scholar who saw too far into the future for his own good. He should have been here in '98 – his dreams and his death were wasted. But he risked only his *own* neck . . .'

Aidan turned slowly. 'What d'you mean?'

'You've got a wife and an infant son. What right did you have to go off playing games of catch-me-if-you-can with the police?'

'It wasn't like . . .'

'What good would it do Maura for the English to shoot you? What would you have proved if you were led off in chains to Van Diemen's Land for administering your pathetic rebel oaths? All your glory wouldn't feed her and the babe – not all your petty heroics . . .'

'That oath was sacred! What we believed in, what we tried to do . . . It was for the good of everyone! It was for Ireland that we wanted to . . .'

'It was for yourself!'

Aidan stared at him. The priest's voice softened. 'You'd never let me talk about Devlin Kelly. All these raids on the Anglo-Irish estates – it was your own little war you were fighting, wasn't it? Revenge. Pure and simple, Aidan.'

'No. Things . . . happen. Gradually. So slow that you don't realize how you change. But you *have* to change; it's either that or die, or go mad. It happened to all of us.'

'The famine.'

'Yes.'

'I know. In some ways, I understand. I've seen things . . . terrible things . . .' Aidan had a feeling that the priest was looking through him, beyond him, as he spoke. 'They don't prepare us for this. To be able to stand suffering of this magnitude . . . so much of it. Hundreds, thousands of people . . . and the children . . .'

'Then you understand . . .'

'No!' The focus of Daniel McDonnagh's eyes came back to Aidan sharply. 'I know I mustn't doubt. In the worst moments, I remember the prayer, "Lord, I believe. Help thou my unbelief." ' He took Aidan's hands in his, 'You must think on this, too. I came

253

looking for you – all the places you'd visited as a child – I wanted to find you before the police . . . '

'The police . . . ?' Aidan's voice a hiss.

'I wanted to ask you not to wait for them to find you. To have faith, Aidan . . . '

But he had pulled back from the priest. 'You're after asking me to give myself up! You expect me to walk into the garrison and give myself up!'

'Aidan . . . '

'No!'

'It'll go better for you . . . '

'*No!*'

'It'll prove you're confident of justice. It'll help prove your innocence.'

'It'd prove I was out of my mind! You just finished tellin' me that all Killaloe will believe Devlin Kelly and Edward Osborne . . . '

'Someone may have seen you on your ramblings – someone who'll speak up for you . . . '

'What poor eejit is goin' t' stand up to Devlin Kelly?'

'Aidan, you have no choice in this matter! You can trust me to do the best I can for you – you know that, don't you?'

'Yes, but . . . '

'What chance would you have of escaping? No one has any money to help you get to America – and the fever on the coffin ships would endanger your life much more surely than staying here and facing trial. Either way you're lost to Maura.'

'I could go to Dublin . . . '

'Man, every soldier and policeman in Clare and Tipperary is out looking for you! And worse than that, there's hundreds of starving men and women who'll turn you in for the reward. Money to buy food for their families – do you think they'll hesitate to betray you? Be sensible, Aidan. You have no hope, only to tell the truth . . . '

Aidan had walked away a little, sank down on the bed and stared before him. Again, he felt the breathless, panicked feeling that had claimed him by the bridge. It pressed down upon him. The strident twittering began in his ears, and he leaned his elbows on his knees, placing his hands to his head.

Daniel McDonnagh, taking the gesture for one of despair, stayed where he was, by the window, and watched the younger man for some seconds.

Finally, Aidan said, 'Leave me for a while, Father. Bless me, if you would – then leave me. I'll follow you into the village.'

'I . . . . Yes. I suppose it would look better if you came alone.'

254

Aidan got to his knees, received the priest's blessing, then rose. They gazed at each other.

'Your word that you'll come after me.'

'I swear it.'

'God be with you.'

'And with you, Father.'

The priest turned and left the cottage, shutting the door after him. Aidan sat back on the edge of the bed once more. He made no effort to set his thoughts in order. There seemed to be black walls at the edges of his consciousness, he could only go so far, then found himself frightened, trapped, unable to see any way of escape. The moment ended here. There was no future, no sense of tomorrow. The despair was total. His whole life had been building to this – the walk into Killaloe. He signified nothing more. It was then he thought of suicide, briefly, the shame filling him almost immediately as he thought of the priest and his promise to him.

He stood up and left the cottage, walking up over the crest of Craglea, through the grey shapes of heather, barely visible in the first faint light.

He came down the hill on its steepest slope. Though it was still too dark to see far, he wanted to know that he had a distant view of Tineranna and his own cottage.

He was half-way down the hill when he heard the voices. He had been picking his way carefully amongst the half-buried rocks in his path, not looking up, and the eerie sound of keening, when he knew himself to be quite alone, had all his memories of the woman in black rushing down upon him. The hairs stood up on the back of his neck, and he stumbled in his fright, losing his balance and rolling over and over for ten yards down the slope before he could clutch at a tuft of grass and save himself. He lay there, bruised all over his body, conscious that his trouser leg had been torn, and his leg gashed. But worse than this was that the keening was closer . . .

He scrambled to his feet, fear claiming him completely, and sprang off down the slope. Home! Mother of God, he was going home, and if he ever set foot on Craglea again . . . He dived down into the glen, came up to the top of the hill that overlooked the road.

The lights of the procession stopped him, had him standing there, gaping in amazement and breathless exhaustion. A crowd of thirty people or more were passing, all carrying torches. At the centre was Minogue's ass-cart, the donkey picking its way almost daintily along the road, as if conscious of the solemnity of the pageant. Dark-coated men, slope-shouldered, the light of the flames on set faces, walked on either side, or marched in a group behind. Then there were the women, an unrecognizable huddle of dark shawls, arms supporting children, or each other, faces lowered. And the wailing, wailing rising from them into the paling sky like some macabre anthem.

Who was dead?

He bent low, running down the road, waiting there, crouched behind a hedge, until the group had passed him. When he raised himself to look over the top, there was the procession, trailing away from him.

There was a slight figure, walking at the tail end, limping badly and unable to keep up with the others. Roddy Minogue, who had injured his leg when working at the silvermines some weeks before. Aidan had him by the throat, whirling him away to the side of the road, half-supporting him.

'It's all right. It's me. Aidan O'Brien. I couldn't let you cry out.'

'Aidan . . . ? Holy Mother of God . . . '

'I can't stay – who was that in the ass's cart?'

'Aidan . . . '

'Who was it? Was it one of the Terrys? Was it Regan?'

'It . . . Och, Aidan! It's Corrie – it's y'r Da, Aidan!'

In the latter years of his life, when time and distance enabled him to look back over those years, he still could not remember much of the remainder of that night. When the pain of the memory had gone, he wanted to know. To place himself somewhere within that night-mare; for his own self-knowledge to account for his feelings, his actions. But it was missing from him, and always would be. Although he knew the circumstances of Corrie's death, he had no recollection of hearing them from Roddy Minogue. He passed what he later realized to be three days without any memory.

Though twice he had dreams. He could not feel them to be anything more.

He was standing in the main hall at Tineranna, and later, in the tapestry-hung room that had belonged to William Kelly, speaking as if to the man himself, making hurried apologies, begging his pardon for something . . . for what?

There was another dream, of his waiting. And pain. Pain in his hands. Of gazing down at them and finding them covered with burns. Of hearing someone say 'His hands!' and looking up to find a group of Tineranna cottiers gathered around him in a semi-circle – at a safe distance. They were outside, it was sunset – or was it dawn? The men and women looked at him with fear, and he found himself trying to explain to them, too. An apology. How necessary all his actions were. They stared at him as if he were a spectre, and he began to feel as if he were. They crossed themselves, and moved away from him, and he did not really care. They were incidental, they did not touch his purpose, his waiting. He knew instinctively that they would not try to stop him, as he stood in the shadows at the head of the drive.

And he was right. For as they heard the sound of the horse's hoofs, it was as if they knew, and they drifted off, melting into the shadows. They did not disapprove of what he would do, neither did they wish to witness it.

Devlin's horse reared back at the sight of the flames, but its rider had already flung himself from the beast's back with a cry. He began running across the lawn – and it was then that Aidan O'Brien stepped in front of him, the short, powerful figure silhouetted against the flames, instantly recognizable. And this time there was no escape.

This was all Aidan knew. The limp body falling finally from his hands, watching the face and feeling nothing. He straightened, looking up just as the roof collapsed in a mountain of flame, and the windows of the west wing began to flicker as if the house was possessed. He did not notice the ten mounted and exhausted policemen ride up. He was still standing there, gazing at the blazing destruction of Tineranna when they placed the irons upon his wrists.

28

Devlin was running through a burning forest, calling for his father. 'Father!' he screamed, 'Father!' The smoke caught in his lungs, he could not speak, knew that if he did not find his father soon, something dreadful would happen, he would be lost, lost . . .

Aidan O'Brien stood some distance away, looking coolly at Devlin before walking calmly away through the woods, almost disappearing in the shadows. Devlin tried to follow, dodging all the time the flaming twigs and branches, the crackling, hissing limbs of trees tortured, consumed in scarlet horror, falling across his path.

A hedge, and O'Brien was disappearing through a narrow gap in the foliage; desperate, now, Devlin ran after him, pushed through blindly in an effort to escape – stopped and screamed. There was a

drop of several feet on the other side; he held to the thorny branches
of the hedge to prevent himself from falling down, down, into the
scarlet pool that waited below. The dead horse lay on the other side,
and standing over it was O'Brien, as he had been as a boy. All was the
same, suddenly, as it had been that day of the hunt, the gaze that
O'Brien gave him was the same look of pity and disgust.

'I didn't mean it!' Devlin screamed at him. 'I didn't mean it!'

He looked about him, but there was no longer anywhere to run,
the flames had followed him through the forest and now were
burning all around him. The very grass, the hedge caught fire, and
he must walk into that scarlet pool to escape . . . The smoke was
choking him, killing him, there was no escape . . . no escape . .

'Yes, Master Devlin, yes, there is, sir . . . you're all right . . . '

'No escape . . . no . . . ' He was speaking aloud. He opened his
eyes, turned his head to look about him – winced with the pain – and
the whole horror of the past night came back to him. He studied his
surroundings warily; a bedroom, expensively, comfortably
furnished.

'You're at Ceelohg, Master Devlin.'

'Smoke . . . ' he croaked, half-sitting up.

'Aye, it's that fireplace, it's not been used for many a year – 'tis
settling down, now, drawing nicely.'

Devlin had stiffened, for focusing on the speaker at last, he found
himself gazing into the face of Kitty O'Hagan, Anna's mother, and
his heart contracted with fear. 'What are you doing here?'

'I . . . I asked Mister Osborne if I could tend you, sir. You were
brought here from Tineranna – Mister Osborne's staff have their
hands full, sir, tending himself – he's taken it all very hard, sir, and
him not a young man, neither.'

'Hubert . . . he's dead, isn't he?'

'Yes, sir. Many died this night.'

He looked up at her sharply, but she was smoothing the counter-
pane he had disturbed in the terror of his dream. Her eyes were
lowered, but he could sense no hidden animosity within her, only a
kind of pain. He knew what she wanted to hear, but . . .

'What happened? You must tell me. Was Aidan O'Brien caught?
Did they arrest him . . . ?'

'Aye, sir. Aidan is in chains, along with Martin Curran and Thady
O'Donoghue. And it's a blessing that John and Molly Curran and
Liam O'Donoghue and his Maire aren't alive this day to see the
shame that's been brought on their names . . . Would you like a sip
of water, sir?'

There was a decanter and glass beside the bed. 'Yes . . . ' Devlin

258

croaked, while his mind was stumbling to absorb all the happenings of the night. 'O'Brien was a fool . . . coming back to Tineranna after what he did at Ceelohg . . . ' He drank thirstily from the glass that Kitty O'Hagan held to his lips.

She was saying, almost to herself, 'Revenge, sir, for Corrie O'Neill . . . ' and still there was no censure in her voice, the voice was calm, accepting of all horror – or did it only seem that way? 'They say that young Curran and O'Donoghue are denying that Aidan O'Brien was at Ceelohg this night . . . '

'He was there! I saw him . . . !'

'Pray don't distress yourself, sir. Lie back . . . ' Devlin had finished drinking and she pushed him gently back against the pillow.

Devlin did as he was bidden. 'And the others . . . ' he continued. 'There were at least fifteen or twenty men at Ceelohg tonight – were any more arrested?'

Again the eyes, eyes so like Anna's, but faded with grief and hardship, were masked. 'No, sir. They've sent Aidan and Martin and Thady to Ennis Gaol – those three only. Roddy Minogue told me he saw them being taken away in a carriage with a great many armed policemen. The Constabulary are not after takin' any further chances this night. Seamus O'Donoghue's body is at the hospital – along with Corrie O'Neill's . . . Maura O'Brien and Mary O'Neill would like the bodies of their menfolk at home, I've heard . . . '

'I'll not have wakes held on Tineranna for such men as they – O'Donoghue murdered my best friend – O'Neill would have killed me in cold blood tonight . . . I'll not have such men made into heroes, and you can tell that to my tenantry!'

She stood silent, passive. 'Yes, sir.'

He wondered how she could come here, tend him, knowing that most of her friends would despise her for it. But he had married Anna, had been her daughter's husband, and this mattered, this was almost a blood tie.

'I meant to come to you,' he said, now, knowing he had to tell this lie, felt it was necessary to justify himself. 'I was coming myself, that's why I didn't write to you from England . . . '

'I heard from Mrs Minogue.'

'She must have overheard something she shouldn't – I've spoken to no one. I . . . I was too distraught.'

'I know, sir.'

It was probably no secret that he had been drinking heavily with Hubert Osborne, all the way from Dublin and ever since they arrived. There were no secrets, here. The woman's gaze when she

259

did look directly at Devlin was pleading. She had lost her daughter, and she wanted to know how . . . how . . .

'I . . . I must tell you – Anna was . . . '

Her eyes filled with unwilling tears, 'Sir – I want to know, believe me, sir, I do – but you're ill, sir, you came very close to dying, and the doctor says you must rest, and not talk.'

'It was a hunting accident,' he said, for though he was tired and his throat ached, he felt he must tell her that much. 'She fell from her horse . . . '

He did not know what else to say, vacillated between wishing the woman would leave, and wanting her to stay, needing some other presence in the room to keep back the shadows beyond the lamplight.

'Did . . . did she suffer, sir?'

'What? No. No. She was unconscious. She fell, and . . . she died, instantly.'

She opened her mouth as if to speak, but, perhaps distrusting her own emotion not to overcome her, she broke off and turned to the door. 'I'll leave you, now. I'll be in the next room. God bless you, sir. Rest quietly.'

The door shut behind her. Rest quietly . . .

There was a small clock on the mantelpiece. The hands stood at three a.m. Would it never be morning . . . ? Rest quietly . . . Soon the woman would come back, and he would have to tell her more. She would ask, was Anna happy? Why had she never written? Were there no children of the marriage?

Devlin winced with pain as he unconsciously set his jaw. Michael was his, Michael was more Retcliffe than Kelly, despite his looks. Michael would be raised as a Retcliffe should be raised. Devlin would not share him with these people who were little more than peasants. Michael would not be torn apart by two different cultures, religions. Michael must have what Devlin never had, a sense of *belonging*. With ambitious schemes of changing his religion to Anglican, his name to something more suitably British, Devlin fell into a deep sleep.

The next morning he told Kitty O'Hagan only of the accident, of Anna's happiness until that moment. He did not mention the existence of Michael. He left the woman with a warm memory of her daughter's last months, content, accepted into London society – a lady.

She left to return home, and Devlin sighed with relief. Masters, his valet, helped him dress, and he went downstairs to sit with

Edward Osborne, slumped in his chair in the drawing room; and in the silences, for the grief-stricken man barely spoke, and then only about Hubert, Devlin silently made his plans to return to England immediately after the trial.

'Sir,' he said gently, into a long pause. 'I know how difficult this is for you, but I feel we must discuss what happened here last night.'

'No point . . . Hubert's dead . . . '

'Yes, sir,' patiently, 'but we want to capture his killers, do we not? All of them. Now, as far as I know, there were five men that I recognized, Cormac Regan – who seems to have disappeared from the face of the earth, though I don't doubt they'll find him – Martin Curran, Aidan O'Brien, Seamus and Thady O'Donoghue . . . Can you think of any more?'

'I . . . no . . . I . . . ' There was a pause. The skin on the old man's face looked like grey parchment. When he next spoke his voice was a little stronger. 'You're sure O'Brien was there?'

'Of course. He struck Hubert as they left the house – you were behind me, perhaps you didn't see him then. But you must have seen him in the garden – he laughed when they struck Hubert down. You must have seen him . . . '

'Yes . . . In the shadows . . . ' the old man murmured.

'He had a torch . . . '

'Yes . . . I'm almost sure . . . '

Kitty O'Hagan did not go directly home to Paddy and her two remaining daughters. She went, instead, to the cottage on the lough, to Mary O'Neill, Thomas and Maura O'Brien.

Kitty told them the details of Anna's death. Other than that, they spoke little. The day was grey, a mist was falling, but still the smell of damp ashes came to them on the faint wind from the ruins up the hill.

'Did he tell you . . . about Corrie?'

'No, Mary. And sure, I couldn't be asking him. I wanted to know about Anna.'

Mary was silent then, and the only sound came from the fire and Liam, lying in his cradle, crooning to himself, oblivious to the atmosphere in the room.

'They say . . . the police sergeant said, that Corrie tried to kill Master Devlin, and he had to strike Corrie down in self-defence.' Kitty repeated news that she knew they must have heard already.

'Lies . . . it'll be all lies – and they'll be believed.' The taut, bitter words came from Maura.

And Mary raised her head slowly, looked at the girl. 'No,' she said softly, 'I followed Corrie outside, tried to talk to him, make him stay at home . . . I saw his rage. He'd followed Aidan, he knew he hadn't gone to Ceelohg. No one will believe that, sure. But Corrie . . . Aidan was his son in everything but name. He'd have killed to protect Aidan. God forgive me, but there may be a grain of truth in what Master Devlin and that gombeen Flynn are saying.' She turned her dark eyes to each of them in turn. 'And I hope so. Corrie's dead and nought will bring him back to me. But I pray he had his hands about Devlin Kelly's throat once before he died.'

Thomas was staring at her, horrified. She looked apologetically at Kitty. 'I'm sorry, he's your son-in-law . . . '

'No longer. My girl's dead, and there's an end to my loyalty to the Kellys.' She hesitated, then continued. 'We have a bit of money saved. Paddy's talking of going to Boston. He has a brother who works in a shipyard, he might find a position for Paddy. The girls will go into service. We'll find our way. But I'll not stay on Tineranna much longer. No, I'll not be at the mercy of such landlords any more. America is the only hope for us.'

Maura looked at Mary and Thomas. There is no hope in sight for us, she thought, as she rose to see Kitty to the door. They would be forced to stay here, to die here, with the shame of what had occurred always with them. And Aidan would be sent to prison for years, she was certain of that.

She felt a wave of nausea sweep over her, and was drawn out into the open air, chill though it was. She swallowed hard as the smell of burning wood came to her nostrils. Up the boreen, beyond O'Sullivans' field and the bare trees of the gardens, drifts of blue smoke still rose into the leaden sky.

I'll never forgive you for this, she promised Aidan in her mind, never . . . never.

Clemency. It was a word that stayed in Aidan's mind during the time of his trial. Those who believed in him, in his innocence, kept asking for it. The court, it seemed, was intent on refusing it. Aidan remembered his trial only vaguely. Someone spoke at length, pleading his case. Father McDonnagh, aye. 'Devlin Kelly had killed Aidan's stepfather, a man he had loved as if he were his natural father . . . ' His mother told of Nathan Cameron's death, of the news of Anna's death, pleaded that the shock had unhinged her son. Both had sworn, others had sworn, that Aidan had not been at Ceelohg. But that, after all, was the main matter. That was why his mother had had to be led from the courtroom, losing control, held close in Thomas's arms. 'There can be no clemency in cases such as this . . . ' the judge was saying, sternly.

Because of Terry O'Sullivan. Terry clean-shaven, who had been given a new coat, Terry who had stood up stone-cold sober and said that he had seen the men go off towards Ceelohg, had recognized Aidan O'Brien amongst them – yes, he was positive, Y'r Honour, and what's more he remembered Aidan O'Brien threatening the life of Devlin Kelly, oh, months ago, Y'r Honour . . . the day news came that they were to be dismissed, it was, Y'r Honour . . .

'I'll kill him if he comes back to Ireland.' *In the harness room at Tineranna, yes I said that. The poor bastard wasn't lying now, at least.* 'I swear to God, Terry, I'll kill him.'

Transportation for life . . . The words meant nothing to him, no more than the pontificating diatribe against what the judge called 'Agrarian Outrages'. Well, he thought to himself, were we being Agrarianly outrageous? He wanted to share the joke with Thady and Martin but thought better of it. Thady was weeping. Aidan looked back at the judge who was placing the strangest little black cap upon his wig . . .

'Martin Curran, you have been found guilty of murdering Hubert James Osborne at Ceelohg on the 19th of December, 1847 . . . ' No . . . ' . . . sentence you to be taken to a place of execution . . . ' *No* . . . ' . . . there to be hung by the neck until you are dead.'

'No!' Aidan roared, and Martin, face set into a mask, had gripped his arm.

'Leave it, Aidan. 'Twas what I expected. Leave it, man . . . '

' . . . may God have mercy on your soul . . . ' the judge intoned.

In the prison, the Ennis Gaol, they were separated from each other. Aidan shared his cell with five other men, all younger than himself; one had burnt an evicting landlord's haystack, another had stolen bread from a street stall, two more were pickpockets, and the fifth had stolen a calf and killed it for food. It was the bread thief who, a few days later, broke through Aidan's grim self-isolation to tell him that the following morning was the scheduled hanging of Martin Curran.

Aidan's brain began to come alive, unwillingly, from that moment. If the worst was to come, he realized in the long wait until morning, it would come, and no blotting it out could avoid it.

He was waiting at the grill in the cell door when first the guards, then the chaplain and Martin, walked along the corridor.

'Martin!' he called, and his voice broke on the word.

Martin stopped, looked up, said to the men, 'One word with him?' and when the guards nodded, Martin approached the door.

'I'm glad to see you.' The white teeth in the thin, brown face were visible for a moment in a wry smile. The voice, always quick, sharp, was gentle, as if he had a great deal of time, when all his short life he had lived as if there was never enough. 'They let me see Thady, too. I'd hoped you'd forgotten. It's something I'd rather my friends slept through.'

'Martin . . . ' Suddenly there were no words.

Martin said, 'Don't fret about being sent to Van Diemen's Land. They say it's not as bad, sure, as it used to be. Take Maura out after you as soon as you can. Raise your son away from Ireland and her troubles, Aidan. Don't have him end up here like us.'

'I . . . I'll not.' The guards were approaching. 'God go with you, Martin!'

'And with you.' The too-thin brown face smiled once more, then he was walking away, was out of sight.

Aidan waited at the grill, his head pressed against it. Soon, from the cell window behind him, he heard the roar of the crowd gathered at the scaffold outside the gates. A bell tolled. It was over.

29

Two weeks later, a guard appeared at Aidan's cell door at eleven in the morning. 'Y've got a visitor, O'Brien. A lady.' He had been told he would not be permitted to see any relatives in the time before he left for Spike Island, the high security prison where he would await transportation to the colonies. Now, not questioning in his excitement, he followed the guard out of his cell; another guard fell into step behind him, told him to slow down as he almost ran along the corridor.

Maura was standing when he entered the sparsely-furnished visitors' room, and she would not seat herself at the table. Her face looked strained, her lips pale. 'I can't stay long . . . '

Aidan glanced at the guard who had positioned himself just inside the door. The man was used to such scenes, kept his gaze on the narrow barred window and his face impassive. For all anyone could tell, he was lost in his own serious thoughts, and was oblivious to the two people in the room.

'Maura . . . why did you not come sooner?'

She did not answer him. She looked at the floor between them.
'Maura?'
'I couldn't.'
'That's it? That's all?'
'I couldn't. I'm here now because Father McDonnagh said I should see you . . . '

Aidan gave a snort of laughter, 'And it takes Father McDonnagh's influence before you wish to see me?'

She raised his eyes to his slowly. There was no warmth in her gaze. Nothing there. To avoid acknowledging this, he said, 'Is Ma well?'

'Well as she can be, with Corrie gone from her.'

He almost winced. 'And Thomas, and the baby?'

'Sure we're managing.' She hesitated, then she said, colouring slightly, glancing at the impassive face of the guard, 'There's another child coming, Aidan.' He stepped towards her. 'No, keep back from me – I'll not touch you.' All in the dull, cold voice.

'Maura, about Van Diemen's Land, I'm told life can be good there . . . I'll be free sooner than if I'd stayed here, and . . . '

'It doesn't matter.' Something in her tone made him stop, 'Here or there, it doesn't matter.'

'I'll have a shorter sentence if I keep out of trouble – you and the children can join me . . . I've heard there are opportunities there, and on the Australian mainland . . . '

'I'll not live with you again . . . '

'We can have a new life, there. I'll make it up to you . . . '

'You received a life sentence, and even . . . '

'Twelve years, and I'll have my ticket-of-leave . . . '

'Will you not listen to me?' she said fiercely. 'Even if you did return to Ireland – and I've heard that on a life sentence you'll not be allowed to do that – *I won't live with you again*. The child coming doesn't change anything. Our marriage is over. I'll try to keep the truth about you from the children as they grow older . . . '

'You'll tell them I've died, will you?' And her gaze slid away from him. He stared at her. 'Mother of God, you'll not,' he breathed.

'They shouldn't have to live with the shame . . . ' she began.

'You can talk about the shame I've brought on you, and still contemplate telling my sons such a lie? You're after being ashamed of me! What kind of dishonesty is that you're talking!'

She said tightly, 'I'll not have my children pay for your sins.'

They stared at each other. He leaned across the table that lay between them, his brows black, his eyes dangerous in his rage. 'So you'll punish them by taking them from me – taking even the knowledge that they'll be told of me – and not for their sakes,

Maura. For your own. For your own need to revenge y'rself on me. And you can't even be honest about it. You're a hypocrite, Maura, a cold-blooded, small-minded little shrew – y'r not a woman at all. I don't think you ever were.'

She had pulled back, white-faced, as if he had struck her. The guard muttered, 'Go easy, O'Brien . . . ' But neither husband nor wife heard him. She backed away, trembling, and he immediately regretted his outburst, could not think of the words that would now call her back, cancel out all he had said.

At the door she turned; he thought she had had a change of heart, and began to step around the table, to hold her, but she was speaking through stiff lips, 'Shall I call the child after you?'

His anger exploded, 'Call it the devil,' he burst out, 'and to hell with both of you!'

She left the room. He heard her footsteps, quick, firm, leaving his life.

He threw himself out the doorway. The guard grabbed for him and held him, thinking he was attempting to escape, but Aidan stopped in the corridor, 'Maura!' She paused with her back to him, slight shoulders squared. 'Maura,' he could barely speak her name for the rage that consumed him, 'if by some chance it's a girl . . . call her Clemency.' He wrung the word out, almost choked on it.

Maura was silent. He screamed after her, 'Did you hear me!'

Her voice floated back to him as she continued to walk away. She did not turn. 'I hear you,' she said.

That day was market day in Ennis and the streets were crowded. Carts rumbled past filled with screeching, protesting pigs, russet-coloured cows strolled up the centre of the road, square hips swaying, occasionally pausing to lift their tails and soil streets already turgid with deep mud and refuse. Dodging unseeing through a flock of sheep, unmindful of the shepherd's complaints when she scattered them before her, Maura crossed the high street, ignored the beggars lined against the walls, hands held out pleadingly towards her.

Why could it not have been Thady she was permitted to see? No, she was deemed by law to be closest to her husband, had been allowed to see him on compassionate grounds – clemency, indeed! – in order to tell him of the coming child. Why could she not have seen Thady? Her heart ached that he should be undergoing the same dreadful sentence as Aidan. Thady must have been coerced into the crimes they said he committed. Aidan would have revelled in them.

She wondered where the pig selling was taking place – Paddy

O'Hagan had taken five young pigs to market today, and she was able to ride beside him on the cart. He had warned her he might be all day, she was to meet him when she finished at the prison . . . She shivered, feeling somehow contaminated, sullied, by that great grey building in whose shadow she had left her husband. She wanted to speak to someone, put it from her.

She had several hours before they would be leaving for home; she paused, and felt a little giddy, her head ached . . . of course, she had not eaten since five that morning. If she could find a cheap stall, she could perhaps purchase a small bread roll . . .

Everywhere there were animals – the smell, the noise of animals. She turned down a side street, and into a quieter row of buildings. A carriage rolled past her, but its presence did not intrude on her consciousness until she heard voices and the vehicle had drawn to a halt at the side of the road.

Devlin Kelly was standing before her, one hand still upon the door of the carriage. He lifted his hat to her, and held it in his other hand. She stopped short, not believing for an instant that he could be waiting for her. But he spoke quietly, respectfully, 'Mrs O'Brien? Forgive me for intruding upon you. I've been in Ennis on business; can I presume you've been to see your husband?'

'Yes, sir.'

'He's well, I trust. And your brother?' he added.

'They're both well enough, sir. They leave next week for Spike Island, so the Assistant Superintendent told me.' She wished he would leave. Standing still made her feel dizzy, and she did not wish to speak further about Aidan, nor this place called Spike Island . . .

'Are you feeling well?' To her horror, his hand was upon her arm, and worse, she was *not* feeling well.

'I'll be on my way . . . ' she murmured, and went to move past him.

'Nonsense. How are you returning to Tineranna?'

'By cart. Paddy O'Hagan's after selling his pigs . . . '

'He'll not be returning for some time, isn't that so?'

'Yes, sir, but he's expecting me soon . . . '

He was calling a street urchin over to him, giving him a penny and telling him to deliver a message to Mister O'Hagan at the pig market. Then he turned back to her, as the boy ran off. 'Climb into the carriage, Mrs O'Brien. Please.' And his voice was kindly. 'I'm driving to Ceelohg, and your cottage is little out of my way.'

'But, sir . . . ' He was drawing her insistently towards the carriage, pulling down the little steps for her. 'No false pride, please. This is a strange situation brought about by the strange times . . . '

267

They were both in the carriage, Devlin shut the door, seated himself opposite her and gave the signal to drive on.

'This is kind of you, sir.' She spoke stiffly. Strange, indeed. What would Mary say when the carriage drew up? And Thomas? And still she felt ill. What would Master Devlin say, should she be sick over his blue leather upholstery? 'I . . . I was sorry to hear about your wife, sir.' She made herself think of something other than the gentle movement of the coach. 'She was my closest friend for many years.'

'I know.' His smile held a little sadness. She noticed the grooves in his cheeks; he looked older than his twenty-eight years; the past few weeks had taken their toll on Master Devlin, also. 'I'm sorry about your brother Seamus. I'm sorry about Thady, and your husband. We've lost a great deal, you and I.' The voice was little above a murmur, his gaze fixed upon the view of the streets outside.

Maura thought, there's something not quite natural about Master Devlin. His words sounded queer in the extreme; Aidan's ravings seemed almost endearingly human by comparison.

Devlin was saying, softly, 'I don't know why I came back here. I was mad to do so – I've solved nothing. Yet it's hard to drag myself away. It has a hold upon me, I can't tell what it is, and I can't break the spell . . . '

Arra, he's sensitive, she thought. He senses things other people don't – or won't. Perhaps that's been his trouble all along. She realized she was staring at him, and looked away at the view herself.

There was a pause, while the coach began to sway, once off the cobblestoned streets and out onto the roads, then Devlin said, 'Forgive me for asking this very personal question, but I care about your welfare. Are you with child, Mrs O'Brien?'

Maura thought she would faint with embarrassment. Her figure was not distorted, how could the man tell? How . . .

'Please don't be distressed, I can tell the answer from your reaction. I was able to guess only because of your faintness back there. I'm no expert on these matters, but you must take care of yourself. It's not fair upon the child.' And again his gaze was fixed outside. 'It's the innocent that suffer most, do they not?'

Had Anna's death, followed by his friend Osborne's unhinged him? She had the feeling he was moving in his own mind, and only occasionally acknowledging the outside world. She found she pitied him, and had to forcibly remind herself that this was the man who had claimed that Aidan was with the Terryalts at Ceelohg when Thady had claimed he was not; that this was the man who had killed Corrie O'Neill; that this was the man who had tried to make improper advances to her near a hedge on the day his father was buried. It was hard to reconcile this picture with the man before her.

They spoke little on the drive home, even when it began to snow and the window frosted up, and he insisted she place both carriage rugs around her knees. He asked her if her family had enough money, and she told him of Thomas's fishing and that they had enough to eat. He asked if she had other children, and she told him with quiet pride of Liam. He asked her if she would one day join her husband in Van Diemen's Land, and she said, 'No, sir.'

And the silence within the carriage matched the silence outside, and they drove the rest of the way to the cottage door without speaking.

Mary and Thomas were amazed when she stepped down from the carriage, turning to thank a shadowy figure within.

'Master Devlin?' Thomas echoed, when she told them. Mary simply looked tight-lipped.

'I couldn't say no, Ma,' Maura defended.

'I know, child. Sure I'm glad he came along. And Aidan . . . he's well? And Thady?'

'They let me see Aidan only to tell him of the child. I couldn't see Thady, but they say he's in good health.'

'Will they survive, do you think?' Mary's face was clouded with her terror at the thought of their journey.

'Aidan will.' Maura spoke without thinking, then added, 'Both will.' But Mary had already caught the note of bitterness in Maura's voice. She knew, then, that there had been no tenderness in that farewell.

Devlin, they heard, left Killaloe in the *Lady Landsdowne* two days later. They never knew exactly which day Aidan and Thady left Ennis, to be taken by cart to Limerick and thence by ship to Spike Island in Cork Harbour. The prison officials had found it best to secrete their prisoners away, avoiding the possible reactions of distressed and resentful relatives and friends. So Mary, Thomas and Maura did not know that it was August of that year, 1848, before Aidan and Thady and one hundred and seventy other prisoners left Ireland for Hobart Town, Van Diemen's Land.

Thomas found their destination on a map. It was a wedge shaped island, off the south-east tip of Australia. Not as large as Ireland, and set, it seemed, far into the southern-most ocean, as if the continent of Australia, like a huge ship, trailed the island behind it like a dinghy. They wondered if it would be cold, the island seemed to be set so close to the ice caps at the bottom end of the world.

It was as if the two men had died. Thomas wished he had not seen how far away they were to go. 'Any further,' Mary said bitterly, 'and they'd be coming back again the other way.' They tried to forget that most men and women who were transported were never seen again.

Maura thought of this as she lay in her bed in late August, 1848, and watched tiredly as Mary and Kitty O'Hagan washed her new-born daughter. Clemency, Aidan had wanted to call the child. Sure he never meant it. Did he? He never would have expected to have a daughter, anyway; Maura had not believed it herself. 'Och, stop . . . ' she had muttered at Mary's delighted cries that it was a girl. And, Maura noted, a small and thin and ugly one at that.

They were placing the creature, cleanly wrapped in soft linen, into Maura's arms. Maura gazed down at it. This was Aidan's legacy; shame and poverty and despair – and this wizened, hairless thing with no redeemable features except a wilful tenacity to keep breathing.

'She's hungry, Maura,' Mary prompted, and Maura glared up at her mother-in-law. Oh, if Mary's breasts were not dried up, if she only had the milk to keep the creature alive, Maura would have flung it at the woman. Mary would have been ecstatic – only look at the softness and regret on her face now, as Maura opened the neck of her nightgown and pushed the greedy, snuffling little head at her breast.

'I've not much milk,' she said, flatly. 'If I don't get more, we'll have to find someone to wet nurse it.'

Kitty O'Hagan nodded. 'Cormac Regan's wife is still suckling her youngest – she's a fine big girl, Sissy Regan, and she's milk a'plenty . . . '

'I'll not have the wife of that man suckle this child,' Mary's eyes flashed.

'Mother of God, Ma!' Maura suddenly burst into tears, 'I've more reason than you to hate Cormac Regan – him and his murderin' schemes – all my family he's cost me! But I'll be having his wife here if she'll feed the child!'

'Of course . . . of course.' Mary was sitting on the edge of the bed, comforting her. 'We'll tell her to call this afternoon. Don't fret yourself, Maura.'

Maura still sobbed, in her relief. Mary was such a sweet, kind fool. It almost irritated Maura that the woman was so very insistent on seeing the best in her.

Later, the still-hungry child cried itself to sleep in its cradle by the bed. It was the same cradle that had rocked Seamus, Thady, Maura herself and little Bridie. Maura's thoughts were grim as she swung it slightly, to and fro. Perhaps the cradle was bad luck . . . Thomas came in from the river and gazed down at the sleeping baby. She looks like you.'

'Och, she doesn't,' Maura snapped. 'She's ugly.'

Thomas looked stricken. He stared hard at the baby, then looked back to Maura. 'She's like you, only not as pretty,' he amended.

She had to smile. Dear Thomas, he'd die rather than believe he had caused pain to anyone.

'What will you call her?' he asked, now.

'Mary Clemency Kathleen.'

'Clemency? Are we Quakers, now?'

She grimaced. ''Twas Aidan's wish.'

Thomas repeated the name several times, went to gaze at the child and repeated it. The child stirred and opened its eyes. Its hair was fine gingery down, the eyes a strange, pale grey-blue. It seemed to look directly at Thomas as the small mouth opened and it yawned. Maura smothered a giggle; sweet, tedious Thomas – even the baby had summed him up.

'Will we call her Mary, or Maura or Maire?' Thomas asked, 'Sure, we'll have every form of "Mary" in the house . . . '

'We'll call her Clemency,' Maura said, bitterly. 'Let Aidan live with it in the future. Not that we'll ever see him again.'

The baby had begun to cry. It was Thomas who bent and lifted her up, surprising Maura by his capable tenderness. 'We'll see him again,' he said, definitely. 'I know Aidan. He'll come home to us somehow.'

Thomas sat down at the table that night and wrote a letter to Aidan, telling him the news of the village, his joy at being an uncle once more, and stressing that he would look after the family until Aidan came home again. He asked his mother, who was preparing the fourteen-months-old Liam for bed, to dictate her own message to her son, and she smiled, and did so unselfconsciously, exhorting him to have faith, to keep his pride in his name and his race, and to believe that they would all be together again.

Thomas kept his face turned away and had difficulty writing on the damp patches his tears made on the paper. The ink would spread, and he did not like to think that Aidan would know that they were unhappy. He went into the next room, then, and placed a sheet of paper and the pen before Maura, and asked her to write her own message.

It was one of their few quarrels, and it was one in which Thomas walked away the victor. She did not want to write to Aidan – there was no point . . . She could not tell Thomas that she never wished to see Aidan again. Thomas insisted. The news of the child's birth,

Aidan must know that he was the father of a baby girl . . .

Maura, sensing his obstinacy, finally scrawled a letter.

'You must address it yourself – it must come from you, Maura . . . '

She scrawled the vague address he suggested – how it would find its way to the other side of the world she could not know – she handed it back to Thomas almost savagely, lay down, and turned her face to the wall.

Cormac Regan had relatives in America. It became well-known, after only a few weeks, that the reason the police could not find him was because he was headed for New York. Soon it was known that Sissy Regan was receiving money from America, and it was accepted that her man had escaped. She was a good-natured, naturally maternal young woman, who had no objection at all to feeding Maura's daughter; she had far too much milk and Maura too little – it suited them both, she said.

In time, Mary and Maura forgot their resentment of Regan. They liked his wife, struggling to raise the children Regan had left behind, a boy of four and another boy of only two weeks old, when the raid on Ceelohg occurred. Mary and Thomas were glad for her when, in April of 1849, she received enough money to join her husband in New York.

Maura's own milk, to her chagrin, showed no sign of disappearing, and forcing herself to do the best for a child who was always reluctant to take cow's milk or stirabout, Maura supplemented Clemency's diet with her own milk for fully a year.

There was no bonding of mother and child by the act, however. Maura could find no good reason for the child's existence, it was so unfair that she had to be burdened with this, what people knew to be a criminal's child, when the future looked so bleak. As she grew older, Clemency clung to Maura only for her own comfort; when she was fed, or dry, or feeling brave enough, she would wriggle out of Maura's arms and toddle away. Liam had not been like that. Liam had been a warm, laughing, affectionate baby. But she had wanted Liam.

It was Mary who was closest to the child, who came to look after her more and more. And it was just as well. Maura felt guilty for that, forced herself, often, to tend to the child, cuddle it, sing to it; and the child watched her, from quiet eyes that had turned as green as Maura's own; watched her until she was strong enough to push her mother's arms away, and move off on her own. It was as if the child blamed Maura for everything. And she had done her best.

*

272

The potato blight had struck again in 1849; the family survived due to Thomas's work on the river, and the hard times, the changes that had come to their world, drew the five closer together.

Packy Brady succumbed to the cholera in 1852, and it claimed Doctor Reed and Father O'Callaghan in that same year. Twelve months later, when a new outbreak of the disease struck the parish, the two Misses Fredericks, despite walling themselves away within their townhouse for much of those years, caught the infection, and died within a day of each other.

The O'Hagans and the O'Sullivans migrated to America, though the families who left in what came to be called the coffin ships, often took the fevers with them. Kitty O'Hagan had promised faithfully to write to Mary O'Neill when her family arrived safely; Mary never received the news.

Yet Roddy Minogue arrived one clear morning in March 1853, with a letter in his hand. 'It's for Mrs O'Brien!' he called, seeing Thomas first, up on the cottage roof, mending the thatch.

'For Maura? Who's it from? Who's it from!'

Roddy ran up, and held the letter upwards towards him. 'Sure how am I supposed to know, Thomas O'Brien, when I never had the learning like y'rself?'

Thomas reached down and took the envelope. It was barely legible, crossed and re-crossed as it was with directions and strange names; but he could make out the original address, and Maura's name. It was Aidan's handwriting – the letter was from Aidan!

He longed to open it, wished fervently that Mary would return from walking with the children to Beal Boru, Brian Boru's fort, and even more that Maura would return from the village where she had gone to buy their few meagre supplies. Thomas stood up, searching the boreen for her, and he was rewarded by the sight of her. Roddy had returned the way he had come, was waving to her as she approached, and Thomas shouted, and waved too, waving the letter in his hand. Mary and the children appeared also, they must have met at the top of the boreen. Now they were stopped by Roddy Minogue, who was speaking to them, pointing back towards the cottage. Thomas shouted again, 'Maura . . . ! Ma . . . ! It's from Aidan . . . ! Aidan . . . !' He found he was weeping in his joy, 'It's come!' he shouted. 'He's alive . . . ! He's alive!' It was then, waving the letter furiously above his head that they might see it, that his foot slipped and he went down, missing his grab at the wooden ladder, falling the short distance and landing in a heap on the grass near the water barrel.

There was no specific pain, he was pain all over, but he did feel like a fierce eejit – they were all running up to him, gathering around him. 'Sure, I'd bounce . . . !' he was laughing, and still crying. 'Ma, stop howling like that – I'd bounce, I'm tellin' y', I'm that glad! Look, Maura! Look!'

His laughing face was pale; he was holding the letter towards her; but Maura was looking beyond it, at the strange angle of Thomas's left leg, bent beneath him. Maura took the letter with stiff fingers as Thomas's hand fell back, limply, and he fainted, his face white against the green of the spring grass.

30

To Devlin's consternation, when he had returned to Burnley Grange, it was to find Celia Retcliffe still in residence.

'I stayed to make sure Michael was well cared for.'

'Peggy Lacey . . . '

'Is only a servant. Michael is my kinsman, Devlin.' She turned from the drawing room window where she had been gazing out at the rain-stippled moat, the rain-swept drive. She smiled at him. 'I shall leave tomorrow for Retcliffe Hall – no one need know I did not return the day before your arrival. My virtue will not be compromised.'

Devlin tried not to look startled at the thought of anyone suspecting anything remotely immoral occurring between himself and Celia.

His cousin was tiny, small-boned and plump. She had inherited none of the vivacity of her petite French mother, and her features, though her complection was faultless, were too ill-assorted to be beautiful; the small black eyes, that in her mother had added appeal to a heart-shaped face, in Celia looked like currants in a suet pudding. Worst of all, she had inherited the jutting, rounded Retcliffe chin. Caroline, thank God, had avoided it. In the Retcliffe men it gave character and distinction; in a woman, it was a disaster.

'Nonsense,' Devlin murmured gallantly, 'I'm very grateful to you for staying – it was kind of you.'

He had wandered to the bookcase, about to search for some reading matter to pass the evening away; they had dined together and he knew already that he had no further topic of conversation

274

with Celia that could interest either of them. But he was wrong.

'What will you do now, Devlin?' she asked.

He looked up at her. 'Do?' he queried. 'This evening, you mean?'

'The rest of your life, my dear. You had a month in London with poor Hubert, and another six weeks, hideous though they must have been, in Ireland. Somewhere in that time you must have come to some decision about your future without Anna. There is Michael to be considered.'

'Peggy Lacey is remaining here at Burnley. And when Michael is about five or six, I shall send him away to school, I expect. By the way, what do you think of calling him William, instead? It's his second name, after all, and much more suitable to an Englishman, don't you think?'

The firm chin was set. 'I think you should call him Michael. It was his dear mother's wish.'

Devlin, chastened, turned away to the bookcase. The pause went on and on. He perused the books and searched in his mind for something to say. He did not like having Celia speak of Anna. There were too many unspoken questions about Anna's death; he had, to keep his sanity, to force himself to forget. He had hoped Celia had also forgotten . . .

'You'll be shocked by my forwardness. But I must speak out. I've come to care deeply for little Michael – I care even more deeply for you, and the attachment goes back years and years.'

Devlin, stunned, turned slowly to face her.

Cheeks pink, the little currant eyes were lit by an inner fire. Except for that chin, which was raised and trembling ever so slightly, she was almost pretty. 'Do you remember the visit we made to you at Tineranna in 1835? Your horse fell at one of the jumps and you had to shoot it. I was only thirteen, but I think I loved you in that moment, seeing your father so angry with you, and you so white-faced and frightened – you'd been punished enough.

'You were left alone out there to use the gun yourself; I watched from my bedroom window for you to come home. It was raining when you arrived, walking up the drive in your sodden clothes, clutching the gun – I thought my heart would break. I sat next to you at dinner, and tried to be kind to you. You didn't notice. You never noticed me. Not then, nor in any of the visits we've made to each other's homes.'

Devlin was appalled, it was the last thing he needed. 'Celia,' he said coolly, in order to put an end to the embarrassing scene, 'please don't be foolish.'

'Just listen to me, that's all I ask. I wish us to be friends, companions. A marriage of convenience only . . . '

'A marriage!' he roared.

'Don't shout. Don't lose your temper. You have a very bad temper, Devlin, a childish temper. Everyone knows it. Think of that.' He did not know what she meant, but she was continuing. 'And think carefully, very carefully, about marrying me. I shall be a good wife; I've been trained to be a social asset to my husband; I'm very rich, and I love your little boy. You both need me.' He tried to speak. 'And I can offer you this – my father is no fool, he'd like to see us married. He'd settle a great deal upon any children we may have, for I needn't tell you that Corbett's gambling and dissipated lifestyle has been a severe disappointment to our father. He would be very pleased, Devlin, if you would change your name to Retcliffe on our marriage.' There was a pause, here, she knew she had Devlin's attention. 'There would, you see, be a great many advantages.'

'I don't love you, Celia.'

She smiled, amused. 'I know that. I shall settle,' she said, with what he suspected was irony, 'for your kindness and regard.'

There was a long silence. Devlin studied her deeply for the first time in his life. He considered her background, her personality and character. Then he said, 'What if I say no?'

She took a deep and shaky breath, 'Then I shall tell the authorities that Anna died as the result of the beating you gave her. Percy Cole heard the struggle, Devlin, so did Masters, and the maid, and Peggy Lacey – their loyalty to you would not, I'm afraid, stand up under cross-examination in a court.'

He felt ill. He growled. 'Why would you wait so long . . .'

'You intimidated me. I was afraid for the child.'

The silence went on for a long time. 'I shall leave you, now,' she said, and swept off towards the door. 'We shall speak of it tomorrow morning. I realize you must have time to consider. Good night, Devlin.'

He was staring at the floor, feeling as if a trap were closing over his head. She had paused, and he looked up at her. He realized that he had never acknowledged that wistfulness in her face; yes, it had always been there when she had looked at him, even as a child. He had never considered her at all; she barely existed for him. 'Remember,' she said gently, 'that I do this only from my great regard for you.' And she left, closing the door softly behind her.

Of course, it would be impossible to murder Celia, though during that long, sleepless night, Devlin considered every means of doing so. There were simply too many witnesses; he couldn't kill Celia and

Peggy Lacey, Cole and Masters and the upstairs maid, short of burning the house down.

The answer he sought, the means of escape, did not come. The next morning he spoke civilly to Celia, she returned home to Retcliffe Hall, near Salisbury, and a suitable twelve months later, an announcement of engagement was printed in *The Times*.

Devlin converted himself and Michael to the Church of England, and in June, 1849, in Salisbury Cathedral, he married Celia Retcliffe. Soon after, he changed his surname to that of his mother and his new wife. He burnt the Kelly family bible, attempted to remove all trace of the name.

Celia had been right; she was an excellent helpmate, and they kept, for the most part, a cheerful distance from each other in the house. There were other compensations. Doors opened to him now that he had hitherto not known existed; his uncle, now his father-in-law, Lord Hallswood, pressed him to consider going into politics, and Celia's dowry, he found, made him richer by several hundred thousand pounds.

Yet resentment built on resentment. All through that year of their unofficial engagement, Devlin had brooded. He kept Anna's apartment exactly as it had been, had it cleaned and dusted, but moved nothing within it.

Sometimes, even after his re-marriage, he would go into the rooms, take out her clothes, touch them, weep over them, beg her forgiveness for his weakness, his infidelity. He regarded his present marriage almost as a kind of penance that he must suffer, so great were his feelings of culpability in her death.

Michael gave him no solace. It was as well that Celia loved him, for Devlin could not, despite everything, warm to the boy. It was not only his uncanny resemblance to William Kelly; it was the fact that Anna had died, and the child had remained, and it had been Anna who had been of paramount importance to him.

The years seemed to tumble in on Devlin; from the time of his mother's death he had been swept along uncontrollably by a flood of circumstances that had given him little sense of achievement or happiness. He was born under malign stars, he told himself, and settled into a morose hopelessness; nothing seemed worthwhile.

He took little joy in his marriage, gave Celia children in the hope that it would keep her busy, deflect her feelings for him. In his mind there was only Anna, and he thought back to their nineteen months together with increasing longing.

Two children were born to Devlin and Celia, both daughters. The eldest, Caroline, died of meningitis at a year old. With the birth of the second child, a year later, came the greatest shock. Celia, in perfect health, had a sudden haemorrhage after the child was born, went into a coma, and died the same day. When the infant did not much outlive the mother, Devlin was almost relieved. Celia's death, so close on his mother's and Anna's, filled him with horror. More frightening still was his lack of grief, that when the coffin containing mother and child was lowered into the ground, he could feel only that a weight had been lifted from him. It was as if the penance was over.

Lord Hallswood and Corbett's grief was real enough. They stayed on at Burnley Grange after the funeral and talked endlessly of Celia in terms of potential and promise, and dragged out reminiscences that went on hour after hour, over port and cigars, until Devlin was dizzy with the alcohol and the blue fumes that poisoned his drawing room. The two men, in their clumsy, hearty way, were very fond of the grey-eyed and silent Michael, now six years old; Devlin realized their own lives at Retcliffe Hall were empty, purposeless, and that they could stay on, thinking of Burnley as some kind of jolly club, for years.

Finally, in an effort to rid himself of his guests, he told them he was taking his grief to Ireland, would stay with Edward Osborne and arrange, finally, the sale of Tineranna.

Lord Hallswood and his heir finally left. Devlin had had no intention of returning to Ireland, but on the very night they had driven off, he changed his mind.

Celia, feeling, perhaps, that she had already pushed Devlin enough, had never insisted that he clear Anna's belongings from the house. Now, as before when puzzled or depressed, he spent an hour sitting on the edge of her bed, lost in thought.

He went to her desk, and, for the first time, looked with care through her papers, needing to find something to stir the memory of her more closely.

In a pile of receipts and long-paid bills, he found the letter. It was face down, and at first, his heart sickeningly loud in his chest, he thought that it was the final draft of the letter fragment he had found. He did not want to be confronted with the fact that she had lied, that she had written to Aidan O'Brien . . .

The letter was addressed to him, Devlin. It was dated the 17th of November 1847. It was the day she had died.

My Dearest Love,
   I want to write this, though I should tell you. You are before me

now, asleep, and I do not wish to wake you.

Some quarrels can be good things, many true words can be spoken in anger that, could one overlook the manner in which they are spoken, can lead to a greater understanding.

I learnt last night, during our terrible quarrel, exactly how much you needed me, my love and my reassurance.

My dear, they are yours, though I have been too self-conscious to be too open about my feelings, not knowing how they would be accepted.

Please do not allow jealousy to ruin all we have, I want the following years to be a time when we are drawing closer to each other, not further apart. You are all that matters to me, the only man I ever loved. What occurred between Aidan O'Brien and myself was an innocent, childish affection that left me when you appeared in my life. I have been happier with you than I ever thought possible.

I should tell you this, I long to tell you this

There was no period at the end of the letter, and it was not sealed. She had not bothered to place it where he would see it – was undoubtedly planning on giving it to him herself, or, more likely, had decided to tell him, later that evening, when she had returned home . . .

He read the letter again, and he wept in his longing for her. But even then, he did not know if he believed her or not. He placed the letter in his pocket, and after checking that there was nothing else in the desk of any personal interest, he left the room. He read the letter again, downstairs. He was to read it so often that the folds of the paper would, over the years, soften, and tear. He wanted to believe she meant all she wrote, so, as time passed, he came to believe it. The thought occurred to him, sitting alone the following morning after a solitary breakfast, that the letter was, in a small way, similar to the fragment that he had found . . .

He put his face in his hands. He needed time to think . . .

Percy Cole knocked on the door and entered the room, to ask what papers he would be needing to take to Ireland.

He did not stay long with Edward Osborne at Ceelohg, for he found the man introverted, querulous, inclined to exist in the past and resent any mention of the present. The future he dismissed bitterly, lived only, as he told Devlin openly, for his own death. Without Hubert, there was no purpose. He mentioned Aidan O'Brien, too, went over and over that night at Ceelohg . . .

Devlin, who felt his own fragile nervous system could take no more morbid thoughts, left Ceelohg and took a short lease on Willow House, an attractive grey stone building on a slight promontory of land across the Shannon in Ballina. The view of Killaloe from the Tipperary shore was not one he often saw, and he liked it; he felt safer, at a distance from Tineranna, though he could see the hills of the estate from the gardens that ran down to the river and a view of the salmon weir.

He put off visiting Tineranna for several days in the rounds of visits to friends on surrounding estates. He visited Limerick, the shops and the establishments of several discreet ladies to whom his friends introduced him, bought and read several books and generally enjoyed a quiet time, healing himself slowly, putting his life, he told himself, in order. Decisions would have to be made, during this trip, about his future. Should he return to Ireland, where he half-felt he belonged, despite everything, or stay in England? Go into politics or begin to take a serious interest in his several estates?

He was not pleased to hear from Jim-Pat Flynn that three years before the empty stables at Tineranna had been fired. Flynn insisted that he had written to Devlin, telling him of this. Devlin could say nothing, as he knew he barely looked at the regular letters from Flynn, only at the financial returns.

And these were depressing enough. There was much hardship everywhere. Devlin could see this, the ragged crowds in the streets were more numerous than they had been years before. Elsewhere in Ireland, he had heard, whole villages had boarded up their houses, died quietly of starvation.

For Devlin, his horizons, his view of Ireland, ended with Tineranna's borders. And on a cold, overcast day in April 1853, he rode his hired horse along the Killaloe–Ogonelloe Road, through the heavy iron gates, rusted open for years, and on down the main drive of Tineranna.

The driveway twisted and curved, the beech trees almost meeting their still-bare branches overhead. Last summer's leaves lay blackened on the ground, and softened the tread of his horse's hoofs.

He had not come back this way since that night, more than five years before. He remembered the sight of the house in flames, knew that little of it would have survived, yet as he rounded the curve in the drive his heart contracted at the unwanted, uninterrupted view of wild shrubs and lawn grown into pasture, of reeds and lough, where the eye had once been accustomed to the solid, comfortable symmetry of the big house.

It left a space within the landscape, a space, Devlin realized, drawing his horse to a halt, within himself.

He tied his horse's reins to a low branch, and walked on alone, across the long and frost-faded grass to where the broad, mossy front steps led upwards – to nothing at all.

Ivy and other creepers had taken possession of all that remained, the foundations, the fallen masonry, and shattered, blackened slates. Many years had settled the ruins into solidity, and he could walk over them, with care. It began to rain, softly. Devlin did not notice.

Here was the entrance hall, broad and imposing . . . There had been the fireplace where his father's setters and retrievers had lain on the expensive rugs . . . Here was where the staircase . . .

He turned away. Here had been his mother's sitting room, and before that, it had been his schoolroom . . . He smiled at the memory of Aidan O'Brien, little and ragged, falling like a clown when Devlin had pulled his chair from behind him. How ridiculous he had looked, and the hurt and reproachful glance he had given Devlin as he pulled himself to his feet . . .

Across the hall was the drawing room . . . The way the French doors had let the sunlight stream through . . . Anna at the piano . . . Mozart's *The Magic Flute* . . .

He realized, now, that it was raining, and quite heavily. He shrugged to himself; there was nowhere to go for shelter, the stables and the barn had gone . . . He glanced over towards them, and paused, because he thought he saw a movement between the shell of the barn and the crumbling walls of the stables . . . But no. He waited, and all was still.

The rain continued to fall steadily, and Devlin found it impossible to think himself back within those warm, safe days; he no longer saw Tineranna as it was, but looked around and acknowledged the broken wreck of what had been his home. It was gone, and with it all those people he had loved and so taken for granted.

He had been foolish to come, and he shouldn't have come alone. Not only was it depressing, but it could have been dangerous. Why, he could have been followed by some maniac who bore a grudge against landlords in general – and Tineranna's, perhaps, in particular. Flynn had made him enemies enough, it was clear . . .

He looked around, worried, now. They may be hiding at this moment, behind that hedge – that wall – five or ten of them, ready with their heavy, blunt weapons, as they had been that night at Ceelohg . . .

He turned his head sharply, remembering the faint movement he had seen near the stables. His foot rolled on a piece of loose masonry and his right ankle turned, causing him to go down hard on one knee, scraping skin badly from his right hand and sending a shooting pain through his wrist. He did not move, despite the agony, and remained still . . .

In the shadows beneath the low branches of an early-leafing oak tree, before a broken gate that leaned drunkenly on one hinge by the charred stable wall, two figures in black stood staring at him.

Black hoods over white faces, dark holes for eyes, their whole demeanour was a waiting malevolence that was more terrifying than any earthly creature could be. He opened his mouth, in his terror, to scream, 'Go away . . . !' but one of the spectres was moving forward towards him.

The legs and feet were bare, and Devlin saw this with relief; the figures were immediately made more human. Two women. One took the arm of the other who had stepped forward, and they spoke together, low, urgently. Then the first was moving forwards again, and the other had turned and had passed through the broken gate, was disappearing into the grey mist that clung about the trees.

Devlin was conscious that his ankle throbbed, it hurt to place his weight on it. His right wrist hurt, if possible, even more, and was clearly swelling, the heel of his hand bleeding profusely.

'Sir . . . You've hurt y'rself.'

It had been the shadows of his own fears that had lent horror to the figures: the face was thin, pale, but no ghost, nor one of the walking skeletal figures that lurched pathetically along the highroads. At her feet was a basket containing young nettles.

'It's nothing,' he said, feeling foolish, wondering, now, how long the women had watched him, whether they had laughed at him. 'I know you, I believe . . . ' For the woman before him was familiar, his memory of her was a disturbing one, yet comfortable in that she was part of his past . . .

'I'm Maura O'Brien, sir. Maura O'Donoghue-that-was.'

'Oh. Of course.' He tried his ankle again, and it almost failed him, he came close to falling once more, had to put out his left hand to steady himself.

'If I'm not being too bold, Master Devlin – may I help you?'

He was furious with himself, wondered if the woman carried any germs with her, the fevers were still rife everywhere. But he had little choice, his ankle was sprained, his wrist also, if it was not actually broken. 'Yes, please – if you could help me to my horse.'

She was small, but strong for all that. His arm about her made the dark grey shawl slide back, and her hair was exposed, a bright, light

282

red without a touch of grey, the eyes that glanced up at him occasionally were a clear green, but the lids were dark-shadowed. Of course, she could not be as old as she had first appeared; she was, if he recalled, younger than himself. The lines in her face were fatigue, he decided, and hardship. He thought of the basket of young nettles, he knew the peasantry cooked them like a vegetable. Not only hardship, but hunger.

She helped him mount his horse, and stood looking up at him, her old-young face, instead of hatred, held a look almost like concern. He had found her attractive, once, remembered with some embarrassment attempting to kiss her in a field . . .

'Will you be all right, sir?' she was asking.

'I will, of course.' He paused. She was backing away. O'Donoghues, once among his wealthier tenants. He remembered speaking to this woman in his carriage on the way back from Ennis, well-spoken, articulate . . .

'You have some education, I believe, Mrs O'Brien?'

She stood still, her chin came up, 'Yes, sir. I was at school for eight years.'

He sat thinking, his gaze on the mottled, swollen skin of his wrist. He would be doing no writing for weeks, even if it were not broken. 'Can you come to Willow House, over in Ballina, tomorrow? I have correspondence pertaining to my estates in England that must be attended to. You write a good hand?'

She almost smiled, she was sure of her own achievements. 'Yes, sir.' And added calmly, 'I'm an excellent speller, too.'

'Good. Oh . . . ' he paused, 'Call into Crotty's Emporium this afternoon – I shall leave an order there for you to have a uniform fitted. You don't object? A simple black dress. And shoes.' He did not add 'stockings' but he would see to that, also.

She was looking startled at the turn of events, but through her embarrassment that her clothes were ragged and not fit to grace a gentleman's house, her sense of propriety and her pride asserted themselves. This was Devlin Kelly. 'Sir, I don't know if I would be the best person to . . . '

'I will be staying in Killaloe only a month or six weeks. Would eight shillings a week be sufficient?'

It was a man's wage, and more than generous. 'Yes, sir, but . . . '

'There are few people left whom I remember.' His words, his tone, surprised both of them. He looked down at her rather startled expression. 'I would like to see a familiar face about. You, I believe, could use the employment. Between the hours of nine and four I think would suffice. Will you come?'

She hesitated for only a moment, 'I will, sir,' she said, and dropped a curtsey to him.

He rode off, smiling at her manners. It was good, he thought, to hear an Irish voice again. The accent . . . of course. The accent was Anna's.

The news of her position in Master Devlin's house met with silence back at the cottage. Then Thomas was telling her no, no she must not accept. Devlin was a man on his own, with financial power over her and there was, he reminded her, no love lost between Devlin and Aidan's family. 'What would Aidan say, tell me?' he demanded, his face uncharacteristically grim.

'Aidan's gone,' she almost snapped. 'And of what use was his letter telling us to emigrate when we've not enough money to buy food—'

She stopped, could have bitten her tongue for her thoughtlessness. All their savings had gone towards paying the doctor's bills – the new physician in Killaloe had known something of setting bones correctly, and he felt that Thomas would be able to walk again almost normally – but for at least four months he could do nothing but lurch about the cottage with his leg in a splint.

Their diet was one of unrelenting fish, brought by sympathetic friends from Fish Row. The meagre supply of vegetables from their own garden had all but disappeared, the Meal Months were almost as threatening to them as to the poorest cottiers. The best of the food went to Liam and Clemency, and the adults tried not to think of the last months of spring and early summer, waiting for the potatoes and cabbages to grow, grow . . .

Usually the thought of eventual emigration to Australia kept their spirits up – though secretly, Maura had no intention of leaving. Aidan's letter from prison had spoken well of the new colony; but it had also told her that somewhere in the Pacific Ocean, her brother Thady had died of a lung infection, contracted in the damp of the cells on Spike Island. He had been buried in a Christian ceremony at sea, Aidan wrote, attempting to comfort her with this thought. As if anything could console her for the fact that all her family were now dead. She no longer had any reason to leave Ireland. Aidan was not enough.

Aidan wouldn't want her to join him when Devlin was paying the fare, Thomas was now telling her, stubbornly. And Maura had to walk outside, so irritated was she with Thomas's lack of vision. He could not see that now they were saved. Sure even Aidan, she knew, would understand. Methods meant little to Aidan, it was results only that counted. Suddenly she understood a little of her husband, and was grateful for his teachings. Thomas would have the family starve for their good name – she would not.

'Thomas doesn't understand.'

She turned to see that Mary had followed her outside.

'Yet you hate Devlin even more than Thomas does, Ma.'

'I do. I couldn't stay this afternoon to speak to the man. He killed my Corrie, and I'll not forgive him ever. But sure I pity him. Wasn't he walking over the ruins, wearing his fine clothes and all unmindful of the rain, talking to himself. It's glad I am that I could see it. The man's haunted. And in my heart I'm satisfied, for he'll not forget Corrie and Aidan any sooner than I will – and my memories are more comfortable than his, sure.'

'Then you think I should go?'

Mary looked at her fully, 'We've little choice,' she said.

Devlin's wrist was broken, he wore it heavily bandaged in a splint and resting in a sling about his neck. Oddly enough, against his dark jacket, it made him appear even more handsome. He was irritable with the pain for many days, for he had to rest his sprained ankle, too. Maura read his correspondence to him, copied out replies as he dictated them, checked figures for him in ledger after ledger, sorted his untidy file of bills and receipts, stoked the fire, even read to him from his books.

For some reason he liked this. She did not think she was a very good reader, her voice, she felt, lacked expression, but he liked to hear her, and she read John Carlton's grim *Black Prophet*, and Dicken's latest works, Devlin leaning back in his chair and closing his eyes.

Sometimes she worried that he slept, for he never told her to desist until she had to break off to place a turf sod on the fire, or they were interrupted by the cook-cum-housekeeper, Mrs Ryan, with afternoon tea.

They grew closer to each other without Maura knowing that it was happening. Perhaps Mary's own admission to pitying the man was what began it. She enjoyed the knowledge that he found her of interest. When she arrived in the mornings his blue eyes, on seeing her, were alight with some emotion that intrigued her even as it made her recoil. Men were all the same. She felt superior in the safety of her position; she was self-contained, the inner core of her could never be touched. When Devlin first told her he wished her to become his mistress, she did not, to her own surprise, panic, run

285

away, nor was she angry with him. Her reaction was totally against her own character, and she knew it; but there was a harmlessness to him, the sheer depth of the loneliness behind his request robbed her of false modesty and self-pride.

'No one will disturb us,' he was stroking her cheek with his hand. 'Masters and Mrs Ryan have the night off. There's no one in the house.'

She did not pull away, but she began to cry, quietly. Told herself, as he led her insistently along the corridor to his bedroom, that he could not touch the *real* part of her that mattered; if Aidan, whom she had loved, had not taken her soul to him in those heated moments of union, then this man could not. And she liked this man, he needed her . . . he was kind, and he needed her . . .

He lit the lamp, and she stood there, as her own reflection came slowly to life in the large mirror over the dressing table. 'Sir, this is wrong . . . ' *You have no choice, no choice* . . .

He was undoing her dress fastenings. It was odd, but there was little of Aidan's passion about him. She had liked kissing Aidan, it was the groping, the loss of her autonomy, the sense of violation that she hated about the act . . . Devlin was almost clinical, he did not seem annoyed at the tears that would insist on rolling silently down her cheeks. Tears with Aidan meant tenderness, loving words – she had liked that – but his tenderness made him take forever with the act, prolonging her embarrassment with his insistence that she, *she* could enjoy this beastly coupling . . .

She shivered in her thin cotton shift. 'Sir, you may regret this later, and . . . '

'I won't.' Coolly. 'And my name is Devlin, Maura. We're about to become intimates, it would be fitting if you ceased calling me "sir".'

'I . . . I'll try . . . ' He was kissing her, strange, strong, hurried kisses, curious, passionless, as if he were driven as much as she into this embrace. Held hard against his chest, she said, 'Sir, the lamps are very bright. Might we not have the darkness? Will we turn the light down, sir?'

His voice was a sigh, his hands pulling her shift down over her shoulders, 'No, madam, we will not.'

She lived in a strange dimension during that time, one that she could never, in years to come, acknowledge in terms that she could understand, as a Catholic, as a wife, as a moral woman trying to raise Christian children. She respected Devlin for sparing her feelings and making their times of union as brief as possible; if it was painful, it was over quickly, and his manners were more considerate, if

286

possible, afterwards. Devlin demanded little of her, she felt he understood her more than Aidan did. They were . . . they were friends. How odd that sounded! But often, when he had spent himself upon her, he would talk to her, tell her of his life with Anna, of his son Michael – trusting her alone with his existence. The O'Hagans had long gone, but she felt privileged, and kept his secret; she could understand the changing of his name, his desire that the child be secure in his surroundings. Children, in the end, were the most important things, the only permanence in life.

He stayed longer in the village than he meant to, and Maura felt special, important in his need for her. She listened to him in a way, she was certain, no other woman had; both his wives, she decided, had been vain women who thought more of themselves than of him. Sometimes he wept within her arms, was incoherent. That he clung to her, made her glow within herself. How could this be wrong, when she was helping him?

Yet she would be denounced by the whole village, she knew, if their relationship became public. But soon he would return to England; then she would go to confession and receive absolution and be given a penance, and all would be well again.

She had been terrified she would conceive his child – and when it happened, she was almost relieved that the worst she had feared had occurred. She did not tell him, avoided the problem, for surely, surely, he would leave soon, and this natural penance would be hers to bear alone. His value was greater than hers, she told herself, he must be saved. She would think of saving herself later.

Thomas and Mary knew what was happening. They said nothing. It was a terrible conspiracy between all of them – in a way, they were all guilty, Maura told herself.

She was ill for a week with what she at first feared was fever, but it turned into a mild influenza, and she recovered with no ill-effects. It was raining the first morning that she felt well enough to go to Willow House, and Mary tried to persuade her to remain at home. But no, she had made up her mind she would tell him of the coming child. He would know how to cope with the problem, could advise her. He was a man of the world and had experience of these things. Adoption, perhaps, or – and she liked this thought – perhaps he would take the child back to England and have him educated there, perhaps raised in his own grand house in London with Anna's boy.

The pains began when she was level with *Beal Boru*, the misty rain sweeping in and almost obscuring the circle of dark trees on the lough's edge. By the time she reached Killaloe itself she was able to walk only a few hundred feet before stopping to rest. The road by the canal was deserted, it was an unusually harsh summer storm, and even the beggars were crowded into doorways, talking in huddles; no one noticed her in the driving rain as she walked along the canal path. She took off her shoes and walked barefoot, and when she began bleeding she was glad of the lashing rain. The blood washed away from her heels, she left bloody little footprints along the path and over the stone bridge into Ballina.

Devlin's valet, Masters, had contracted the same influenza virus that had attacked Maura and a quarter of the parish. A thin young man, prone to asthmatic attacks and further weakened by years in London fog, he had little chance against the virus, and though Mrs Ryan tended him he died two days afterwards. Today had been the day of the funeral, and Devlin had returned to Willow House completely unnerved. He had been mad to stay merely to carry on a dalliance with that rather dull little woman – he spent the rest of the morning packing his own belongings, and told Mrs Ryan that he would see no one . . .

'You'll have to see her yourself, sir,' Mrs Ryan stood at his study door, looking agitated. 'Mrs O'Brien is standing there on the doorstep and says she won't go away 'til you see her . . .'

'Did you give her the envelope I left with you?'

'I tried to,' she held it out to him, 'but she said she'd take it from your hands only.'

'Damn.' He snatched the envelope from his housekeeper, and stood undecided.

Mrs Ryan said, 'She looked very ill, sir. I asked her to come in for a moment, just to wait in the hall, but she would not. Half-fainting she is, poor creature . . .'

Devlin went to his desk. There was more than a hundred pounds there; he took fifty and placed it with the fifty already in the envelope. Mrs Ryan found the weightier package handed back to her. 'Explain to her. I've lost Masters, and I'm very upset. I can't see her, nor anybody. I'm returning to London this evening. Explain. I can't bear to see her if she's ill – I can't bear it.'

'Yes, sir.' She threw a last, speculative glance at her employer and went downstairs.

Maura was leaning against the wall of the house, and Mrs Ryan was frightened by the sight of her. She had become weaker even in these few minutes. 'Child, he can't see you. He said to give you this . . .'

'Tell him I'm ill, that I . . . .'

'He especially can't see you if you're ill! He's just lost Masters,

288

missus, and he's fierce upset,' she lowered her voice. 'No stomach at all. You know, *squeamish*. He's given you plenty of money to make up for losing the position – take it, girl, and . . . Och, come inside with you, y'r ready to faint . . . !'

'No! No . . . I'll be on my way.' She took the envelope from the housekeeper.

'You're sure you'll not come in and rest – you can sit in the kitchen. He'll never know you're there.'

So she must hide from him . . . 'No. I'll be going.'

Still she did not move. Reluctantly, Mrs Ryan stepped back. She said, 'I must go, then, and help him pack – he leaves for Dublin and then on to England this very afternoon, he's after tellin' me now.' Maura stared at her. 'Well . . . if there's nothing more I can do for you, girl . . . Get you on home, now, out of this weather, 'tis horrid harsh. God bless you, missus.' And she closed the door.

Father McDonnagh found Maura wandering in the streets and brought her home. She wakened from her delirium long enough to see him minister the last rites to her. It was over. She would be forgiven . . . She whispered her sins to Father McDonnagh and there was no recrimination on his face. He absolved her, blessed her, and Maura was free of pain at last.

Devlin stood at his bedroom window and watched the wind on the river whip the water, always wild, to grey caps of foam that had no sense of current but boiled among themselves. The view of the sturdy bridge and St Flannan's turret, the thatched-roofed cottages that clung to the slope of the Aille Vaun, gave him no feeling of permanence. He knew he would not return to Ireland again. Oddly enough it had been Aidan O'Brien's wife who had given him the only sense of direction he had been able to find in all these past years. *Children*, she'd said, *give the only permanence in life*.

He had been chasing a shadow all this time, running without any real goal but to see himself as a man, strong, self-sufficient. And doing this only by hoping for the reflection of his image in someone else's eyes, his mother's, father's, Anna's . . .

He felt immeasurably sad, and yet relieved, that he would now return to England, and be – only himself. There was no real adventure waiting out beyond the years for him.

Tomorrow . . . Tomorrow belonged to Michael.

Devlin knew better than to believe that he himself could do more than caretake the fortune he had inherited – nearly three quarters of a million pounds – from his parents and Celia. He did not understand business and finance, and loathed the sort of men who did. He could not face the idea of politics, the civilized savagery. But Michael . . .

He felt a vague stirring of hope within him. Nothing like the sense of excitement he had once known in his dreams for his own future, but perhaps all the more secure, now, because this did not depend upon his own resilience. Michael had been born with wealth, position, and a pleasing appearance that might yet make him a handsome man. The only stumbling block to a great career would be a character flaw within that man himself. How old was the boy? Five? Six? He could be taught . . .

Devlin stood and paced slowly about the room. *Children are the only permanence* . . .

Maura did not know until much later how close she came to death. She drifted in and out of consciousness for days, for after the miscarriage an infection set in and her delirious dreams made it hard to realize what was real and what was not.

Gradually, she was able to take broth; Mary or Thomas fed her from a spoon, and she felt useless and weak and a burden to them. Often Father McDonnagh came, sat by the bed and spoke to her, and this cheered her.

She awoke one day from a half-sleep to realize that Clemency was being scolded by her grandmother. Maura could hear the voice, controlled, angry. Why was she late home, why were there scratches on her face and arms . . . ?

'I hit Flan Minogue in the eye. He scratched me like a little cat, he did – so I hit him in the other eye. He doesn't know how to fight at-all at-all.'

Maura turned her head, focusing on the family group. Liam was looking up at his sister from the alphabet book Maura had been using to teach him to read. 'Why?' he asked, for both Mary, at the fire, and Thomas at the table with a newspaper spread before him were too surprised to speak, 'Why did you hit Flan?'

'He called Mam a hoor.'

'What's a hoor?'

'I didn't know, but I knew it wasn't good – I hit him, so.'

Liam nodded. 'I would have too, I'm thinking. He's a right rogue, that Flannan.' He returned to his book.

Thomas had blanched, Mary had flopped on to a stool, turned startled eyes towards Maura, then Thomas – all three adults looked at each other.

Clemency was fetching from a drawer the wooden farm animals

290

that Thomas had carved for the children. Liam left his book and joined her; they looked like twins, Liam brown-eyed, Clemency green-eyed, their hair darkened to auburn, curling around their faces. And to the children's astonishment, after Clemency being scolded, they were told to take the toys outside. Mary stood at the door, and watched them run to a favourite patch of grass beneath an elm tree some distance from the house.

'I heard,' Maura said.

They were silent a moment. The word 'hoor' still hung in the air between them. The Irish pronunciation softened the word, but the meaning remained the same, *whore*.

Maura's cheeks burnt. Hot tears spilled from her eyes; and suddenly Thomas, free of his splint, now, but still unsteady on his feet, lurched across the room to sit on the stool by her bed, hold her hand in his. 'It's all right . . . Och, don't cry . . . I'll be back on the river this week, we'll be all right, so.'

'I'm ruined . . . ' she murmured, 'Sure I've brought ruin on your name . . . '

Mary's voice was strong, bitter. 'You've not, y' little eejit. Devlin Kelly has. And that's nothing new. The saints preserve me from women who blame themselves for a man's failings. Hold on to your pride, girl – no one else will hold it for you.'

Maura was not listening. She had thought, with Father McDonnagh's compassion and blessing, that the stain would be wiped out, could be forgotten. But she was wrong. For all her life the whispers would follow her, she would see the knowledge of her sin in the eyes of every neighbour, every villager. 'What will we do? What will we do?'

'We?' Mary came to sit on the bed, faced Maura fully. '*We* will do nothing. But you and the children – arra, that's a different matter.' She gazed fixedly at her daughter-in-law. 'You three should be going where you belong.'

'What? Where?' she muttered, then, seeing the stricken look on Thomas's face, she knew. 'No!' she said. 'Van Diemen's Land – Australia – no! Twelve thousand miles, Mary! Thomas, she's not serious! Twelve thousand miles from home!'

Mary went to the mantelpiece; in an empty canister she found the grubby, worn page that had been read and re-read so often that Mary could quote from it as if she could read it herself. 'Aidan's letter says he'll be free in twelve years – nearly six have passed already . . . '

'That letter was years getting to us – and we've heard no more of him . . . '

'We'll come to join you eventually. Father McDonnagh knows a priest in Dublin who knows the Bishop of Hobart Town, he says His Lordship is kindness itself and takes a special interest in the families of convicts.'

Maura winced at the word. Mary's voice went on, quiet, insistent. 'You have enough money to see you settled there, Maura. Maybe what happened was God's will, for your place is with Aidan, girl.'

'Thomas, tell her she's wrong! Thomas, tell her it's a mad scheme. Twelve thousand miles, Thomas . . . !'

Thomas's head was lowered over her hand, held tight within his own. His voice sounded strange, and so soft that she could barely hear him.

'Your place is with Aidan,' he said.

Part 2
VAN DIEMAN'S LAND

Who built and laboured here?
The wind and the sea say
– Their cold nest is broken
and they are blown away.

They did not breed nor love.
Each in his cell alone
cried as the wind now cries
through this flute of stone.

JUDITH WRIGHT

31

The first sound was the key turning in the lock. He had been dozing, and his first thought was that the priest had returned. But no – that had been last evening, hours ago, surely. He waited, watching the blackness where the door should be, tensing his back against the damp wall. The light would appear before him, slightly to his left. A long sliver of light it would be; grey, if it was morning, brighter if broad daylight, gold-tinged lamplight if it was still evening.

The door did not open. He stared hard at the darkness, feeling his heart begin to pump with excitement. Morning, noon, or night? Which, which? Or . . . morning. It had to be morning. What a trawneen he was to be sure. It would be breakfast time.

And still the door did not open.

He launched himself at it before he realized what he was doing, bashed his fists against the cold iron of it, screamed for them to open it. 'I won't be played with, y' fekkin' gurriers! Open the fekkin' door or close it but don't . . . !'

It swung open and he almost fell through. The light from the small, barred window blinded him, the rush of clean air made him gasp. He fell to his knees on the stone floor, his only impression that of the dark blue uniform that had stepped smartly back to avoid the assault.

'The Sergeant spoke to us, O'Brien, we had to answer. Get up, man. And keep your temper if you don't want another three weeks in there.'

He held on to the door jamb and rose to his feet.

'Keep your eyes half-shut. It's always like this to begin with.' The clank of metal as the man's musket was changed from one shoulder to another, a hand on Aidan's arm, then they were walking, along the narrow passageway, up a flight of stairs, a hallway before him, dark blue jackets on either side of him . . . another door opening, more light, a breeze on his face . . . the yard. Grey-clad figures moving towards him. He stopped, almost recoiling.

'I'll help him . . . ' Hands reaching.

'No,' he said. The two guards were gone. Bastards – they allow a man an hour's exercise at night, then release him into this blinding inferno . . . Hands, helpful, took his elbow. He swore, whirled away violently, and almost fell; through streaming eyes he saw the wall in front of him. He lurched at it, found it, placed his back against it and wiped his eyes with his sleeve.

'Leave him be.' Treloar's voice, the unmistakable rise and fall of it. 'Leave him alone for a while.' Half-blinded by the glare as Aidan was, he knew the group would have been comprised of the new men, O'Farrell, Walsh, O'Dowd, Costelloe and some of the younger English prisoners who had seen him fight Crawford, seen this last fight with Grant, and wanted to befriend him for some weak-minded reason of their own, as well as finding out what solitary was like, how he had borne it . . .

He moved off, along the wall, and when he was at a distance from the men, he lowered himself to the ground. He did not lower his face into his hands, though he would have liked to. Grant or Crawford or one of the other bastards might pass some comment and he did not want to fight again, did not want solitary again, not so soon. He shaded his eyes from the sun, and blinked cautiously at the paving stones that covered the ground before him. He could hear, in the distance, the rumble of cartwheels over a cobbled roadway, and the strange warbling call of the Australian magpies in the trees beyond the wall. The sun burnt into his skin; this hot, impossible January sun that warmed the ground until it hurt the hand to touch it, and brought from the surrounding hills a resinous smell of eucalypt trees, unknown and exotic to Aidan's senses.

The heat was not yet unpleasant. He shut his eyes and luxuriated in the warmth, his mind preoccupied only with the sensation – like an animal, he thought. He was hungry, too. They had obviously forgotten his breakfast. Feeding time. How like an animal. Yes, that was it. An animal in the sun.

He opened his eyes every few minutes, and after half an hour he could see fairly well. He leaned his head back against the wall and watched the men moving about the yard. He saw Grant, narrowed his eyes . . . the thick-featured Grant held his gaze with equal animosity, but Aidan did not move. Grant felt the madness in O'Brien's droop-lidded stare, a brute, total singleness of purpose. He'll start again, Grant thought, if I smile or move. And the thought thinned his blood, robbed his gaze of life, until his point of focus blurred and slithered down to O'Brien's boots and away to a group of men among whom he could blend himself.

Aidan shut his eyes, and gave himself up once more to the sun. Killaloe in summer, the coolness of the bright grass, the blue of Lough Derg . . .

296

Footsteps beside him, and he looked up, squinting into the glare, muscles already tense. Will Treloar sat down beside him with a sigh, leaning his heavy arms on his knees. Aidan relaxed a little, letting his gaze wander to the wall of the cell block opposite him. There was shade, there, and several groups lounged or squatted in the coolness, talking in a desultory fashion as if the heat had already robbed them of energy. Aidan watched them, and made no effort to greet the man beside him or even acknowledge his presence.

Each day since Treloar had joined the *Hyderabad* in Cape Town, and until the fight with Grant, he had come to sit beside Aidan. He was no fool, the man's talk could not be called chatter. Treloar was not lonely, he had made friends amongst the other prisoners, so he was not desperate for companionship. Yet regularly he had sought Aidan out, told him any rumours he may have heard of what awaited them in the colony, what the land was like and where they may be sent, never minding that Aidan did not welcome him, rarely spoke and never responded with any interest.

Treloar was born in Cornwall, had left his hometown of Lost-withiel under a sentence of seven years. Aidan's ship, the *Hyderabad*, had picked up Treloar along with forty other prisoners reassigned from the leaking *Calcutta*, when it was made unseaworthy after a storm.

At twenty-eight, Will was three years older than Aidan, and often spoke of how much he missed his young wife, Sarah, how short a time they had had together before his arrest. Then Aidan would turn, wanting to walk away, punch the man, silence him at all costs. For the longing in Will Treloar's voice touched something deep inside Aidan that he kept rigid and controlled. When he thought about Ireland at all, he thought about the past, he did not want to imagine the present, what his family were suffering. And Treloar always seemed to sense the discomfitting silence, and changed the subject smoothly. Often he said nothing for hours on end, and then Aidan forgot him altogether. His mind roamed back to a Killaloe of his own choosing, a past more real than the reeking prisons of Ennis, Spike Island, the *Hyderabad*'s hold, the black cell beneath this, the Hobart Town Gaol, and amongst people more real, more dear, than these grey-clad, stubble-haired figures who now shared his existence.

Will Treloar broke his silence to say, 'Look here – you've been in that pit three weeks, Aidan. T'would break the spirit in a man to keep returning to it. And you'll be doing that if you can't keep out of trouble.'

Aidan said nothing, kept his eyes before him.

'I tell you this because I can't see how you'll survive. And . . . and for Thady's sake, God damn it! You weren't there when he died, Aidan, you were in solitary even then, not two days out of Cape Town, t'was. I was there.'

At least he had the boy's attention. Aidan was looking at him, at last. Will had been regretting his promise to young O'Donoghue. 'Talk to Aidan . . . ' Thady had begged him. 'Try to befriend him . . . ' But all through the voyage south Will's attempts had met with failure; the one-way conversations with O'Brien had begun to make Will doubt either Aidan's sanity or his own. On the boy's release from solitary, Will would make one more attempt, he vowed, and it would be his last. One could talk to a stone wall for just so long.

'I know you don't welcome my company,' he went on, 'but Thady knew you were taking this bad, leaving your home, your family – and he did say you were driven to what you did. We have landlords in England, too, but nothing the like of what 'ee have in Ireland. Thady told me all about it.'

Why had Thady befriended the Cornishman, Aidan wondered. I do not need anyone, he scowled, why should Thady worry for me? Why should Thady tell all my affairs to a stranger, and an Englishman, at that? Will had always been an interloper, now he was doubly so. Aidan wanted to continue grieving for Thady alone, somehow to come to grips with his guilt that he had not been there . . . Thady had been fading before Aidan's eyes ever since they left Spike Island, yet when the end had come, Aidan had been three days in a creaking hold four feet by four feet; when he rejoined the other prisoners it was to find Thady gone, his spirit released, his body consigned to the merciless blue of the sea.

He wished, now, that Treloar would go away, but the man seemed to be waiting, perhaps for Aidan to speak. The Irishman glanced across at Will, took in the broad face, the mild blue eyes, the light brown hair that even close-cut as prison regulations demanded, managed to form tight waves upon his head. He was not looking at Aidan, was watching Stimson saunter across the yard, yet still there was this waiting quality about him.

Stimson came to a halt by a group of young men opposite. Two of them stood at a look from the older convict and moved off. Stimson sat down beside the remaining boy, a nineteen-year-old Dubliner called O'Dowd, and smiled at him, speaking in a low voice. It was a common enough sight. Both Aidan and Will remained unmoved at Stimson's expression, at the fear on the boy's face, the tremulous smile, the unsure gaze. Stimson had been seeking the boy even on the voyage out.

Aidan dragged his gaze from them, lifting his eyes to the barred windows, the offices above the cells. A blue-coated figure moved in one of the apertures, disappearing back into the shadows as if he had been gazing down upon the men and become bored by their ugliness, their hopelessness. And why not?

'You'll do what you've the wish to do,' Will was saying, 'and finish with your neck in a noose like . . . '

'Stop it, Treloar, or I swear I'll . . . '

'Hit me and you'll get not only solitary but a flogging besides.'

They gazed at each other. Treloar was right; even now, from the corner of his eyes, Aidan could see the sentries on the gate move closer together, their faces turned towards him . . . He leaned back against the wall, making an effort to unclench his fists. Treloar said, 'You can't go on feeling responsible for what happened to your friend Martin – he knew the risk he took when he did what he did. Thady said he died with courage . . . '

'Aye.'

'Then might it not be possible for you to live the same?'

Och, but he was clever with words, this one. Aidan looked at him, and as their eyes met he could see, suddenly, what had made Thady warm to him. He was a good man, this Will Treloar.

As if encouraged, Will was saying, 'You don't see what Thady knew almost straight away, that transportation to this colony doesn't mean the end of everything. Hark 'ee to the other Irishmen – you d'have better food and bedding and more clothes here than back home. The Famine hasn't touched this island. They d'say there's jobs and land for all if we work for it . . . '

He stopped. He had not become so impassioned in expressing his hopes before. O'Brien was at least listening to him now. But what good would it do? He cast a glance at the younger man's stony features, facing dead ahead, scowling, and his own good-humoured face buckled into a wry grimace. He could not get through to the man. He could talk till the cows came home. He had done his best; the man was waiting for his death, would let no one divert him. 'No one can help you but yourself,' Will said desperately.

The young Irishman growled, 'I need no help.' And they were silent once more.

They were each thinking of Thady, a mixture of sorrow and a kind of resentment. They each wished the other would go away, but each stayed because of the dead boy, because Thady even now had a hold upon them.

And while they were preoccupied with their own thoughts, they were unconsciously watching the pantomime of Stimson's interest in the Irish boy, O'Dowd. Stimson's voice low, earnest, O'Dowd's answers monosyllabic, his discomfort obvious. Several men in the yard were glancing at the two, someone laughed . . .

Will was wondering what to say next, if anything at all. Then Aidan took him completely by surprise. He said, 'I'm sorry. I realize you're trying to help me. I'm glad that you tried so to fulfil Thady's wishes. I had no idea he'd asked it of you – though sure, it's like him. 'Twas a great responsibility for you – he must have thought highly of you to ask such a thing.' Aidan was gazing full into Will's face. Will stared, taking in this speech, surely the longest O'Brien had made in the four-month voyage from Ireland.

Will's knowledge of human nature was broad, but his categories were few. A man was straight, worthwhile, or he was not. He had been a farm labourer and sometime poacher in the hills to the north of Lostwithiel. In his attempt to escape from a determined game-keeper he had pushed the man, making him fall awkwardly. Will was recognized and captured later, the keeper's broken arm result-ing in a conviction of felonious assault.

Will had his own ideas on justice, not always complying with Her Majesty's courts. Thady, now, had been convicted of being an accomplice to murder. But Will had liked the soft-spoken, well-educated young Clareman, had understood what had driven this stuttering, sensitive boy into joining the Terryalts. He understood Aidan, too, though with his silences, Will considered, he seemed a trifle thick between the ears . . .

Now, gazing into the broad, stubborn face, the clear, slightly slanted dark eyes that held his own, their scowling intensity gone, Will changed his mind. There was intelligence here, and a depth of understanding. Lord, boy, he felt like saying, where have you been all this time? Instead, 'You'll see,' he told Aidan. 'T'won't be so bad, here. We're tough and we're clever, 'twill be all right for us.'

It was then that Stimson stood up and sauntered off towards the latrines. A few minutes later O'Dowd followed. There were coarse remarks bantered about when they had gone.

We become animals, Aidan thought, watching the men's heads go together to discuss the two. These years take our pride from us. There's no escape. What will we have left to us when they set us free?

He got up without a word and moved off, away from Will. For the rest of the morning he sat by himself, shoulders hunched, staring in front of him, as he had always done.

The convict system in which Aidan and Will found themselves seemed simple enough to their eyes; the rules, regulations, the discipline, fast and brutal, that accompanied breaches of those rules.

300

Yet by that year of 1849, when Aidan and Will arrived in the colony of Van Diemen's Land, the convict system was in the throes of an upheaval that had begun years before.

England was fast tiring of the complaints and pressures of the wealthy free settlers in Van Diemen's Land. Some had come, pouring all their capital into farming or businesses, others had arrived virtually penniless and through their own endeavours had made their fortunes. They wanted their say in the governing of their adopted land; they had children who had been born here, who regarded themselves as Australians in general and Tasmanians in particular. There were petitions, constant agitation – open up the land, stop transportation, give us self-government, remove the name of Van Diemen's Land and its stain on the memory of the world. Give us Tasmania.

The home government, however, had already lost the United States as a depository for Britain's criminals with the War of Independence in 1776. In 1840, due to persistent pressure from the Australian colonists on the mainland, transportation to New South Wales had ceased. Britain could not afford to lose Van Diemen's Land. The many changes of policy and administration in the 1840s, therefore, were a conscious effort on the part of a giant empirical system, largely ignorant of the enormous difficulties, posing new schemes for a country twelve thousand miles distant. It made few compromises to placate the free settlers, the main aim was to continue a prison system that relieved Britain of the sight and a great deal of the upkeep of her criminal classes. Van Diemen's Land had been founded as an island prison, and as such, the government insisted, it would remain. Those free men who chose to settle there must abide by the laws and accommodate themselves to the real purpose of the colony, and not raise their voices in complaint against a situation they had known existed from the start. There were attempts, early in the 'forties, to stop immigration altogether, and the number of convicts sent to the colony was, for a period, doubled. The island was a fortress, its walls were being strengthened, the colony turned back in upon itself.

But despite the many efforts by the home government, the economic situation in Van Diemen's Land was only further aggravated, the labour market of the colony was flooded with ex-convict and ticket-of-leave men; unemployment soared, wages fell, and the free-born workers, unable to compete, left the island in their thousands for the mainland. All over the colony, men were idle, embittered.

If Will had known all this, his optimism may have been daunted,

301

for when the *Hyderabad* sailed into the Derwent Estuary in December, 1848, it was to find the convict system in the throes of confused adjustment to what was the eighth major change to the system in ten years. The free settlers were reaching a point of exasperation. Would there be no end to it, 'this extravagance of upstart theory', wrote the free settler and writer, the Reverend John West, '(this) fitful experiment without end . . . '?

Aidan, on a life sentence for the attempted murder of Devlin Kelly, and for being an accessory, with Thady, to the murder of Hubert Osborne during the raid on Ceelohg, only narrowly missed being sent to Norfolk Island.

This was the very worst of colonial prisons. The small island in the South Pacific was the depository for those convicted of serious crimes in Britain, and those incorrigibles who had committed second and third offences in Van Diemen's Land.

But Aidan, arriving with the only life sentence among two hundred Irish Whiteboys, sheep stealers and petty thieves, had his case examined in a favourable light. The Irish convicts were known to be better behaved, to adjust more readily to their surroundings than their English counterparts. While Aidan's crimes, recorded in the far right-hand corner of the convict register, looked serious, he was young, yet, and perhaps, just perhaps, he was redeemable.

32

On the thirtieth of January, 1849, three hundred of the prisoners confined at the Hobart Town Gaol were mustered in the main yard. Each was dressed in a new suit of clothes; grey, for the short-sentence men, black and yellow for those, like Aidan, serving a life sentence. A feeling of anticipation ran through the entire group, for they were on the move at last. One by one their names were called, the ticket-of-leave men in their cheap civilian clothes, to go to hiring depots throughout the island; the short-sentence prisoners handed over to their new masters or their overseers. And while they waited, the hot sun burnt down upon their heads. A few men fainted, and were tended to by their companions. Still Aidan waited.

Men were marched off, out the huge gates and past the gallows, into the noisome bustle of Murray Street, until, at the end of three hours, only thirty men remained. The officer who had read the assignment lists surveyed them, folding up his papers. 'You remaining men have been assigned to one of two probation stations south of Hobart Town; either Brown's River, where you'll be working on the roads, or Southport, where you'll be clearing the channel for navigation.

'Most of you are serving life or fourteen years; many of you have already been through some years at Norfolk Island, Macquarie Habour or Port Arthur, and quite a few of you have only a few years to serve before becoming eligible for tickets-of-leave. After a certain time at the probation stations, your characters and behaviour will be assessed, and many of you, those that deserve such treatment, will be assigned as farmhands, servants or clerks for the remainder of your sentences.'

He unfolded another list, read the names of those of the Southport contingent, then that of Brown's River, Aidan and Will Treloar among the latter. And as he finished, the officer looked up, adding, with a touch of ascerbity, 'I will take this opportunity of reminding those of you who have been long . . . *resident* in the colony – Garson, Oldfield and the rest of you – that you've come very far; don't slip back or it will be Port Arthur for you – or worse. O'Dowd, O'Brien, you new men – and you, Treloar, your barbarous conduct on the *Calcutta* landed you here amongst this lot . . . ' Aidan glanced behind him. Will had been scowling at the ground, now looked up at the officer. 'All you new men will be carefully watched – by good behaviour and hard work you'll earn the marks that will result in easier labour and a shorter sentence.'

An Irish voice behind Aidan murmured, 'God bless British justice.' The officer had not heard. He gave the order to the sergeant and the men formed a file of twos. The gates were flung wide and they were marched out, sentries at each side, before, and behind them.

It had been late afternoon when Aidan had first arrived in Van Diemen's Land. By the time he and the other prisoners had been marched from the moored *Hyderabad* up Murray Street to the gaol, dusk was falling. That brief, violent Australian dusk that threatens, waits poised, then descends into night without warning. He had time only to note the beautiful, broad harbour, the ships' lights already breaking up the patterns of mast and spar on the gold-surfaced water; Murray Street's frowning Government office buildings, and Mount Wellington, grey in its shadows, amber-pink where the dying sun claimed it. It dominated everything. He had kept staring at it as he marched, found its shape and depth of colour threatening, its eastern face striated with deep grooves, like the partially exposed bones of some monstrous prehistoric animal. In Killaloe, the mountains lay low, kept their distance. This monolith loomed over the township, pushed it with its shoulder towards the sea, as if the land wanted no part of it.

This was all he had seen that first day; the darkness had fallen before the gates on the gaol swung open to receive them, and too soon had come the skirmish with Grant and the deeper darkness of solitary. Only in his night-time walk about the yard did the sleepy carolling of a magpie and the scent of the gum trees remind him that Mount Wellington and the lesser mountains and hills waited darkly, quietly, just beyond the boundaries of the town.

A pretty town, he thought, now, walking the broad streets, largely ignored by a populace too accustomed to columns of grey-clad, close-cropped men shuffling along, to more than glance at them. Aidan noticed that the houses were well-spaced, and nearly every one had a broad veranda before it, to shield it from the harsh Australian sun. And flowers in the gardens! Riotous colours lining the pathways, and against the walls roses, flowering jasmine, honey-suckle, growing up to frame neatly-painted doorways.

So different from Ireland. There, only the owners of the big houses would bother with such frivolities as flowers, only they could afford to waste valuable land so. All the cottages Aidan knew were devoid of ornamentation, only the potato plants opened fragile white or purple blossoms each spring . . . Or they had done so, once. The memory came to him, swiftly, unbidden, of fields of wet, dark travesties of plants, everywhere the smell of decay . . . and the people, those creatures huddled against walls and hedges beneath the snow . . .

As they turned their backs on the town, marching down Hampden Road towards the Sandy Bay Road, they approached a row of neat, timber workmen's cottages. A woman came out one of the doorways, and stood shaking a tablecloth from the step. She paused, holding the cloth to her as the men passed, watching them with a kind of pity. None of the men spoke, though they all looked at her; most of them touched their caps. Before they had passed, a small boy ran out of the house after the woman, and tugged at her skirts, 'Mama! Can I have a cake? I saw them on the dresser – Mama? Can I have a cake?' Then his ears caught the sounds of the awkward march, the squeaking, scuffling, dragging of boots in the dust. His hands still held tight to his mother's skirt, but his eyes opened wide and he watched in silence as the line of men went by.

'Cake! Did 'ee hear 'im?' Will's voice from behind. 'The house was small, they weren't rich folk – but they had cake! I tell 'ee, this country . . . '

One of the overseers from the Brown's River Probation Station, a sandy-haired, slab-cheeked man, roared, 'Shut up, Treloar!' Will shut up.

They walked in silence then, down towards the beaches, where the road curved round, following the shoreline. For more than two miles they had the view of large, splendid homes amidst landscaped gardens to their right, and the broad and magnificent harbour to their left. Aidan was amazed. There was natural beauty on this island – he had been led to believe that it was a windswept and desolate place – and more than this, there was obviously money to be made here, for these houses were veritable mansions, they belonged to wealthy men, who must have just reason for remaining in the colony.

Gradually the houses became less frequent, the bush claimed the roadside once more, and they marched between heavily wooded mountains and the broad estuary, coming closer all the time to where the curved arms of land released the Derwent into the sea.

The road was climbing, now, up over a hill, down to cross a steep ravine easily, over hundreds of tons of stone laid down as a causeway. By convicts, Aidan thought, marvelling at this, and the giant cuttings through the hills.

About seven miles from Hobart Town, the road ran around a mountain thrust close to the shoreline, and then doubled back, into the shadows of the mountain's southern slope, clinging to its side, round and down in a curve, to rise slowly and traverse the top of a level-backed headland. As they walked into the blueish shadows of the mountain, turning their backs, for the moment, on the sea, Aidan could make out the Brown's River Probation Station, the single and double-storied buildings within the high walls. It lay about a mile distant, at the foot of the next headland, where the road down to it left Brown's Road and wound down through cleared pasture to the sea.

They passed the Superintendent's stone house on their left, single-storeyed here at the road, dropping down to three storeys at the rear, where it sat at the edge of the slope running half a mile down to the water. They turned off the Brown's Road on the southern side of the small valley, down the steep track to the probation station. Once again, heavy iron gates swung shut behind them.

They were gathered in a group before the brick storehouse, and from the steps the Assistant Superintendent announced that they would now be given a meal, and the afternoon would be spent in each being issued their bedtick, rug and blanket. After making up their bunks, they were to have the evening free until evening muster.

They filed into one of the two mess rooms, were given bowls of a reasonable vegetable soup and a piece of the heavy, stoneground bread; they ate at the benches with the few probationers who were not out on the road that day. They were allowed to speak at meal-times, here, but kept their voices low, grouping around the Brown's River men, who were all too eager to talk to the new prisoners. Only Aidan ate his meal in silence, but he listened to the talk about him. Will Treloar, in particular, on the opposite side of the table, was asking questions of a middle-aged man who had been in the colony twenty years; Aidan could hear the rise and fall of Will's voice become even more pronounced in his supressed excitement at the talk of this new country. He's like Seamus O'Donoghue, Aidan thought grimly, fekking optimist . . .

That night they did not settle down immediately. Aidan on an upper bunk at the far end of the dormitory had the end wall window close to his head, and lay listening to the crickets in the scrub, the faint and constant hiss of the water on the rocky shingle of the bay, and the whispering of the men within the walls. Finally, a thought that had been bothering him since the muster in Hobart that morning, made him lean over the edge of his bunk to gaze down at Will.

'What was this barbarous deed you committed on board the *Calcutta*?' Somehow barbarity and Will Treloar seemed mutually exclusive.

The faint moonlight through the barred window gave little illumination. Aidan saw Will's white teeth flash in a grin. He had his arms folded behind his head. 'I fell on a guard.'

'Jumped him? That was a foolhardy . . . '

'*Fell* on him. I was climbing down the ladder after our exercise and I missed my footing. One of the guards always stood at the foot of the ladder t'see we came down in orderly fashion; this man, he wasn't looking, an' I had no time to warn him – I fell and tried to catch the ladder and missed – we went down like stones, the two of us. Only he was knocked unconscious, out for three days. They put me in the solitary confinement hold for a week.

'I'd already had words with the man, y'see. He beat one of the younger lads. When I found out, I asked the guard aside. Watch it, I said, for I killed a man in Millbank, I said, and I could do the same

306

for you. He didn't like that, 'tis always the way with bullies, but he never forgot it. When I fell on him he swore I did it on purpose. By that time he didn't care what I thought of him, as long as someone kept me away from him.'

Aidan lay back on his bunk, staring at the ceiling, wondering at Treloar's ability to take such matters with acceptance.

From outside in the tree tops, a bobook owl called softly, and before Aidan could speak to Will once more, O'Dowd, on the bunk level with Aidan on the opposite wall said, 'It could almost be a cuckoo, couldn't it?' There was a pause, for no one knew to whom the boy spoke. 'Back in Raheny we had a cuckoo in the woods behind our house. It . . . '

Aidan had stiffened. This was the kind of talk he could not bear, and he broke in harshly, 'There's no point in thinking of the way things are at home . . . '

'I have to,' the boy rejoined, half-sitting up, turning a pale blur of a face towards Aidan. 'I have to think of it, even if it drives me mad, for sure the thought of this place will drive me mad sooner.

'My little brother was ill, he could be dead, by now. If I was only in gaol in Dublin . . . I could bear fourteen years in a Dublin gaol – they could send me messages . . . But, *here* . . . Mother of God, we're twelve thousand miles from home!'

A little Manchester man, nicknamed The Bantam for his cockiness, his gameness, now asked O'Dowd why he was transported.

'Robbing a tavern,' O'Dowd murmured. 'It was left untended, y'see. The owner caught me going out the door with ten pounds or more, and some bottles of wine. At the trial he did me a kindness and didn't mention the money. He knew more about this business of transportation than I did – like as not I'd have hung, but for him doing that.'

Nat Garson, a small, slope-shouldered little Cockney whose string of convictions had taken him to penal stations all over the colony, put in, 'An' I s'pose that was the first time you ever stole a farvin', isn't that right?'

'It was! I'd no job, no money, and my family . . . '

There was laughter from the other bunks, and as O'Dowd raised his voice above the noise, still protesting innocence at least until that moment of weakness, a heavy Lancashire voice from the darkness interrupted, 'Now, *me* . . . ' Oldfield, Aidan realized, like Nat Garson, a multiply convicted prisoner. 'I break into houses for the sheer love of it. Half the amusement is to see the insides of places they'd never let me close to should I approach 'em in broad daylight. Once I robbed a pantry of ham and cheese and the best cherry pie I

ever ate, topped off by a bottle of French wine. All imbibed, my
fellow sufferers, in the centre of a four-poster bed. My only regret
was that I didn't think to bring a lady friend along . . . .'

Laughter, then different voices began speaking up, anecdotes
competing against each other. The voices rose higher until a clang-
ing sound from the end of the room had all the men lying flat, silent.
A bright light appeared at the opening in the cell door, then was
partially blotted out by the sentry's face being pressed to the opening. 'Keep that noise down!' he bellowed into the silence. 'Just shut
up or you'll all be in chains tomorrow!'

No movement. Nothing. The face, then the square of light,
vanished.

For a long moment the only sounds came from outside, the
crickets in the scrubby undergrowth, and then, hesitantly, the
bobook called, twice.

Softly, a man three bunks along from Aidan said, 'There was this
house *I* broke into where the owners were still at home . . . ' He had
a smaller audience, the talk became localized, no man daring to raise
his voice to address too many. Aidan lay listening for a moment, then
bent once more over the edge of his bunk.

'Treloar? *Did* y' kill a man in Millbank?'

'No,' the Cornishman snorted. 'Can't stand violence. I d'push
gamekeepers, an' fall on soldiers, but I've never been in a fight, a *real*
fight, in my life.'

'Arra, get away. Not one?'

'No. I'm big, y'see. When trouble threatened all I did was to draw
myself up and say, "Is that so?" Mebbe I've been lucky enough to
meet only cowardly bullies, or perhaps I'm a better actor than I give
myself credit for, but every man to date has backed down. I think,
on the whole, life is easier when you *look* like a fighter. You probably
needn't fight, either, Aidan – but you're such a pugnacious one that
I d'think you enjoy it.'

'Look you, Treloar, it's not that . . . .!'

'You see?' The voice was laconic. 'You're the easiest man in the
world to get roused. Perhaps, in a way, you're more fortunate.
There are times in a man's life when he'd be well-served by a temper.
But I don't possess one, and that's that. My Sarah, now. A small
woman with a violent temper, curses me often-times for not arguing
with her. She says I'm a dull man t'live with, not quarrelling a
tuppenceworth.'

He fell silent, perhaps waiting for Aidan to contribute to the
conversation. But Aidan remained quiet, gazing into the dark above
him. He had been right in what he had said to young O'Dowd.

308

There was no use in looking backwards. Here was what mattered, surviving, finding some means to get away . . . It was an unusual feeling for him, but he found himself wanting to speak to Will about it; had anyone escaped? And where did one go? But he did not speak, knew instinctively that while Treloar would not betray him, the man would do all in his power to talk Aidan out of escape. Will was patient, in ways Aidan was not. Brave, too, but not a man to take risks. Aidan thought suddenly, something in him reminds me of Corrie O'Neill.

Already he was accustomed to the other men, no longer heard them breathing heavily, snoring, occasionally coughing, muttering, whimpering in their sleep. His last thought was that he must think of something, some means of escape. For he would not spend the remainder of his life here. He would not.

The old lags were saying that this was no different to any probation station of the past eight years. It irked them that so many of the newly-arrived men had gained tickets-of-leave, they complained bitterly that all the good jobs would be taken by the time they were released. Each had a good reason why he should have been given his liberty long before. Only the younger men, the first offenders, found the Brown's River Station to be a kind of release in itself, a comparative freedom, after the cramped prisons and ships' hulls of the past twelve months.

The next morning, Frederick Lawrence, the Superintendent, a sunburned, straight-backed figure, stood before the men after morning muster.

'Brown's Road, now frequently called the Channel Highway, was entirely built by convict labour. Most of the men assigned here are working in gangs to keep the road in order, some others are working on a road under construction from Fawcett's Rivulet towards the area above Hobart Town called Ferntree.

'Some of you men will be working on Brown's Road, some on the new section to Fawcett's Rivulet, but all of you are expected to fulfil your tasks well, and without undue pressure from your overseers. Do your work well, remember the rules of this station, and things will go well for you while you are here.

'This barracks are hampered, at the moment, in that we have at present no resident chaplain or medical officer. Any illness should be reported to your overseer or the officer on duty, and he will approach me to authorize the fetching of the medical officer, Dr Reynolds, from Hobart Town. Usually the chaplains are in charge of the reading and writing classes, but until some gentleman is assigned to us, you must have your lessons when possible. The Reverend Wills from Hobart Town visits this barracks each Sunday for Divine Service, and whenever his duties allow at other times, he will hold reading and writing classes.

'Your timetable will be consistent with most probation stations in the colony. Being the summer months, you will work from half-past five in the morning until six o'clock in the evening, with three-quarters of an hour for breakfast, and a midday meal of one hour. On Sunday, the previously mentioned Church of England service will take place in number one mess room, and afterwards an inspection of all convicts will be made by myself and Doctor Reynolds, in the main exercise yard.

'Bibles are provided in each dormitory, to be kept, when not in use, on the shelf provided for them. Various other books of a religious or improving kind, are available for loan at any time; for these you will approach the Assistant Superintendent, Mister Clyde. Now, are there any questions?'

A shuffling amongst the lines of prisoners as each looked at his fellows, but no one raised his hand. Lawrence stepped aside, and Clyde read the lists of those assigned to the maintenance gangs, and to the new work on the river road to Ferntree.

Aidan was glad to find himself working on the latter. He did not mind the six-mile walk each morning, and was always pleased by the sight of the broad, cleared fields dotted with small farmhouses, as they came down the road towards Brown's River each day.

It was timber country, stringybark, which, dressed, was sold as Tasmanian Oak, and the huge blue gums, up to two hundred and fifty feet, grew right down to the river's edge. There were other trees, swamp gums and peppermints, but none as valuable as the blue gums; Aidan liked to see them where the river's edges were untouched, the young trees throwing pale blue-grey reflections amongst the trunks of the dark-green leafed, mature parent trees. There were timber mills nearby, tracks snaked through the bush, and the mill owners bought some of the more valuable logs from the station, providing horses to pull the naked, limbless trunks along the tracks to the mills. Aidan worked on a saw with Will Treloar much of the time. However, because he had experience with horses, he was sometimes allowed to accompany a particularly unwieldry tree trunk, with the workman from the mill, along the bush tracks, helping to unsnare the log on corners, or encouraging the team of heavy draught horses. He supposed himself lucky to have even this amount of variety in his work. A man who was good with an axe used only an axe, sometimes for the entire ten hours a day. The old lags,

310

who had known an easier life under the old probation system, muttered more bitterly than ever. And none louder or more frequently than Nat Garson.

The little Londoner was a braggart, and violent, but he knew the colony like no one else, and Aidan, in the evenings and on Sundays, listened to the tales of bushranging and escape attempts with interest. It whiled away the time, and the Lord knew he had plenty of that.

But despite the hard work and the friendships he was beginning to make among these men so different from his own experience, by the end of his sixth week at Brown's River the monotony of their life had begun to grate on Aidan's nerves. The food was better here than at any other time in his imprisonment, and with his body returning to its old strength, he was somehow thinking more clearly, noticing more, beginning to question.

'For what will it be used?' he asked the overseer, once, as the man stood watching Will and Aidan sawing.

'What's that?'

Aidan paused. 'The timber. We take it into the mills. They bring it out again – for what will it be used?'

The man's name was Camley, he had been in charge of the men on the trek from Hobart. He had a flat, incurious face and a seemingly unconnected bellow that could be heard at enormous distances. He stared at Aidan from pale eyes.

'The timber,' he prompted, '*This* timber.'

'Yes.'

'You're the first man who's asked that. You got ambitions, O'Brien?'

'No. Just curious.'

'Curious. A curious proby. You are ambitious. Planning on heading for bigger things when you leave here?'

'I was only asking. Forget it.' Aidan turned back to the saw and the waiting Will Treloar.

As the teeth bit into the wood, rasped their length, Camley said, 'Building. Some of it's sold to settlers hereabouts, the rest is taken into Hobart Town. It's sold there. This stuff here, blue gum, it's used for boat-building a lot, too, sold to the shipwrights round Battery Point. Though them that can afford it, of course, buy Huon pine.'

'Why Huon pine?'

Camley stared at him, shook his head. 'Ignorant micks . . . ' he murmured, and turned away.

Aidan had taken half a step towards him in sudden rage, when

311

Will Treloar's hand was on his arm, a warning grip. But Camley, too, had stopped, was scowling up the slope to where their newly-made road followed the top of a low ridge before swinging down in a curve to where they now stood.

All three stared up at the hooded single-seated buggy, brand-new and painted a dark blue, and its pair of matched bays. It was an incongruous sight on that broad bush track, the horses stepping delicately past one of the logs being harnessed to a draught horse team, and the probation station's cart, being loaded with firewood by O'Dowd and Oldfield. The driver of the buggy was almost invisible in a dark coat and a wide-brimmed hat. The face was turned towards the men in the gully, then glanced back to realize that the road very soon petered out into scrub. The buggy continued for a few yards, then the horses were turned expertly and headed back the way they had come, the driver's eyes now intent on the road before him.

Camley left them, walking over to a group whose axes swung like pistons as they lopped limbs from one of the fallen trees. Nat Garson put down his axe and went to speak with Camley.

'C'mon,' Will said, and he and Aidan picked up their saw. But they had barely begun before Camley called out.

'O'Brien! Come here!' Aidan began to walk over, as the overseer turned and bellowed for Oldfield to take Aidan's place on the saw with Will. Then he turned back to Aidan. 'Show me if you can be trusted. I'm sending you back to the barracks with the firewood – you and Garson. You've seen the stables before, make sure the horse is rubbed down and fed before you unload the wood.' He took a piece of paper from his pocket, wrote out a hurried pass for them, and handed it to Aidan. 'Try to bolt and I'll have your gizzards for breakfast, I warn you.'

As they set off, the old half-Clydesdale, Rameses, stepping out with more energy than he had seemed to show at any other time, knowing that they were headed home, Aidan glanced across the seat at Nat. The man's gaze was fixed on the road ahead, and there was a kind of tension in his body, as if he were as eager to be back at the barracks as Rameses, and would race him at that.

'What's the matter?' Aidan asked.

'You'll see, you'll see . . . '

Aidan shot him another look, but still Nat remained oblivious, and they did not speak again until they climbed a hill, could see down to where the newly-turned yellow soil of the roadway dipped down into a gully, heavily shaded by the surrounding hills and the

312

arching trees. And there, at a distance of a hundred yards, was the blue buggy.

Rameses had already smelt and seen the other horses, had whinnied a greeting and broken into a loose-limbed trot, swinging his large-as-dinner-plate hoofs out to the side as he went. Aidan grinned, half at the unheard-of interest in the old gelding, and half at Nat Garson, squirming on the seat, grasping Aidan's arm, hissing, 'You see? You see? Now there's a girl, mate, *there's* a girl . . . Thought I was forgot for a while there, but nah, not 'er Nat, couldn't get by wivvout 'er Nat. Just look at 'er!'

The driver of the buggy had stepped down from the vehicle to stand waiting for them. Tall and heavily built as the figure was, the dark coat did not cover trousers, but a long skirt. In the heat of the afternoon the woman must have been sweltering; even as they looked, she peeled off the coat, leaving the hat upon her head, rakish, incongruous.

Nat leapt down from the wagon and raced forward into the woman's embrace. Aidan, puzzled, slightly embarrassed, drew Rameses in behind the carriage, pulled on the brake, and glanced behind him, up the hill to where the road disappeared over the crest.

'Don't be nervous, boy.' The woman's voice was deeper than Nat's. 'I paid Camley two guineas for these five minutes. Come down here.'

'When?' Nat was saying, his arm still around her, one hand moving up and down her back, up and down as if to implant the shape of each well-covered vertebrae in his memory. 'When did you see Camley, Ettie?'

'He came into the pub a week ago. Don't worry, he'll look after you all right from now on.' She smiled into Nat's eyes. Aidan, standing before them, felt unnecessary, an interloper. He should walk away a little, he thought, but the woman was controlling Nat's flagrantly wandering hands and was smiling at Aidan.

He found her at once attractive and repelling. There was a faint dark down on her upper lip, and she exuded both the smell of an expensive perfume and that of an unwashed woman's body. She was massive, taller than he, with a broad, square jaw that spoilt a face that could have been magnificent, if not beautiful. The lips were generous, the nose large but fine, and the eyes so dark that they appeared all pupil. The hair was bright gold, unreal, but pulled back demurely enough beneath the mannish hat. The cloth and the lace of her dress were expensive, and there were pearls hung from her earlobes. Aidan held himself rigid, staring at her. This was as close

313

as he had been to a woman in fourteen months.

'You're Edward O'Brien,' she said.

'Aidan, Ma'm. There's no English equivalent of the name.'

'Aidan . . . ' she drawled, and her eyes narrowed as she smiled and studied his face. 'Clinging to your Irishness. They'll bash that pride and stubbornness out of you pretty quick here, my lad.' She broke off to slap Nat sharply with one jewelled hand, 'Listen to me, stop your groping! There's tobacco for you, in my reticule on the seat.'

'You get it, mate,' Nat mumbled.

Aidan stepped to the buggy, found a large reticule purse, glanced at the indulgent Ettie, and found two packets of tobacco in the jumbled contents of the bag. 'There's papers there, too, and pipes.'

'God, Ettie, where would I be, without you?' Nat hugged her.

'In the shit, as per usual. Now listen, anything you – wait, O'Brien! There's a letter in there as well. Right at the bottom, prob'ly.'

Aidan pulled out a soiled and creased letter, the seal half-missing. He barely heard the woman's voice, 'The captain of the *Tory* brought it into my inn – someone had told him I knew a lot of lags, wanted someone who'd get it to you safe. When I found they'd turned you into a proby with Nat, I brought it myself.'

He could not take his eyes from the crumpled envelope, the smudged but precise handwriting . . . Maura.

'Your sweetheart?' Nat had looked up, curiosity getting the better of him. One hand remained behind Ettie, once more playing on her backbone, up and down, playing her like a keyboard, trying to draw forth some chord of response.

'My . . . wife.' He could barely speak; nothing, nothing in these past fourteen months had affected him as did the sight of that light, schoolgirl-like hand.

Boots sliding on gravel. He looked up to find Nat and Ettie already at the edge of the trees. He half-opened his mouth, but Nat screwed his head around to say, 'Keep watch, there's a lad! I'd do the same for you!'

Aidan stood paralysed, his face scarlet, the letter held forgotten in his hand. They could not mean to . . . They had disappeared, the branches falling back behind them, the whispers and laughter becoming fainter. Still he stood there.

What a place. And what people. With convicts and screws coming along the road any minute . . . He gazed back once more at the scar in the forest along which the men would come.

Nothing yet. Glancing towards the now silent scrub, he walked to

314

the heads of Ettie's horses, pushing Maura's letter into his shirt as he did so. He did not dare read it now . . . What to say should Camley and the others come? He scowled into the bushes. When would they finish? Begod, they could be there for an hour . . . And it must be six, or close to it . . .

The flush began to creep up his neck once more. He tried not to think of what they were doing. He had Maura's letter, he would read it later that night, when he was calm, when there was nothing else to think about . . .

He shifted his trousers a little, stroked the head of one of the bays, muttered to himself, 'Standing here like a great trawneen, holding the fekking horses,' he growled, 'it's the story of me fekking life.'

Later, he regretted not reading Maura's letter then, for though Nat and Ettie were fifteen minutes in their private reunion, Camley kept the others back. Aidan had Rameses already rubbed down and eating his chaff in the stables by the time the rest of the men returned.

Camley said nothing, and the men had their dinner on the long table in the mess just as usual, except that Nat was unusually quiet, and greeted every comment and look from his companions with a smile of secret satisfaction tinged with looks bordering almost on the compassionate.

Aidan, his strict Catholic upbringing confronted by obvious pro-fligacy for the first time, swung about in an atmosphere of savage and conscious hypocrisy. He shovelled potato and beans into his mouth and gnawed his small elastic piece of meat, refusing to talk to anyone.

After dinner, the Anglican minister arrived unannounced, and one of the interminable lessons took place. Aidan found himself reading aloud to the men from a battered copy of Bunyan's *Pilgrim's Progress*, while the illiterate amongst them struggled with writing out the alphabet. It was towards the end of the lesson that Aidan asked for permission to go to the latrine, leaving the room while O'Dowd was stumbling through *The Slough of Despond* and all the stubbled heads were bent unwillingly over their slates.

Discipline at Brown's River was not strict, the locked doors and the armed sentries outside meant that, while within the walls the men were regimented, they were not watched individually, isolated and guarded each moment. In the corridor outside the mess room, Aidan was not surprised to find there was no guard on duty at the door; he knew there would be two, wandering about the lower floor of the building, and their measured tread in their heavy boots would give him ample warning of their approach along the stone corridor.

315

There was a heavy door leading into the latrine, it had no lock, and was used less for privacy than to help keep the smells localized. Aidan shut the door behind him, went to the one flickering lamp and pulled the letter from his shirt.

The writing seemed oddly hurried, for Maura;

Killaloe,
29th August 1848.

My Dearest Husband,

I trust this letter finds you in good health and spirits. We are all well, here.

Our daughter was born this morning. She has red hair and is rather small but seems very healthy. I have decided to have her baptized Mary Clemency Kathleen, and she will be called Clemency, as this was your wish.

Your son is well and growing daily. He has your features but his hair has changed to that dark red of our beloved Seamus.

Our prayers are always with you,

Your devoted wife,

Maura O'Brien

And on the following page, in a stronger hand, the letters neatly formed;

Dear Aidan,

This is truly a cause for celebration, is it not? Your daughter is a grand girl, the image of her mother. That's better than looking like you, don't you think? Your boy Liam looks more like you except for his hair which is a real O'Donoghue mop, and his voice is even louder than yours.

Aidan, we all believe we shall see you again before much time has passed. You have courage and sense and I know you'll try to stay out of trouble and come home again. Things have not been bad here sure. We've weathered worse, have we not?

Terry O'Sullivan was given money from the magistrate for giving evidence against you. While the English have this practice of paying witnesses how can they say there is any justice in Ireland? Terry and and Oona will be leaving soon for America with their two remaining children. They live in the village, afraid of Terryalts seeking revenge, perhaps. Cormac Regan they say is gone to New York.

Do not be bitter with Terry O'Sullivan, now, Aidan. He was a weak man and will n ever forget what he did God help him.

Your affectionate brother,
Thomas O'Brien.

316

Aidan was smiling at the schoolroom English; he had not known that Maura and Thomas could write so well. And then he read, still in Thomas's hand,

Your brother pens this for me. I wish only to say I miss you and pray for you my darling son.

He leaned his head against the wall and closed his eyes, so strong was the picture of his mother before him.

It was then that the door opened behind him. 'What've you got there?' The guard stood, smiling, a dark, lean and loose-jointed man, like many of the guards, an ex-convict himself. He had always looked more incongruous in his uniform than did most, because it did not fit him, too long in the waist, too short in the sleeves; the trouser cuffs flapped about his ankles when he walked, but no one laughed. He had a vicious temper, even the other screws kept their distance.

And it had to be him, smiling, now, his hand held outstretched for the letter . . .

He moved quickly, aiming for Aidan's wrist and the papers; Aidan pushed himself off the wall, took a step along its length, holding the letter behind him – but the screw, enraged, was on him, the papers torn from his grasp, he heard them rip, realized he held only a piece of the margin in one hand even as the other was reaching out, had the guard by the neck, squeezed his thumb there while grasping the man's wrist, pushing it down and out.

He saw the sheets of paper fall, clutched futilely at their erratic flight down. The guard had grasped his neck and was bellowing for aid – but all Aidan could see in his horror were the pages face down in the urinal, the water always in the bottom of the receptacle even now blurring the ink, soaking into the paper . . .

The idiot would not let him reach them, would not let him go. Aidan squirmed around, holding tight to the man's arm, let go only to bring his fist up towards the other's chin. The blow sent the man hurtling back against the opposite wall, where he slid down, unmoving.

Aidan picked up the saturated sheets, there had been at least half a page he had not read . . . The writing was gone, leaving indecipherable grey blurs on the paper. It was useless . . .

Hands were grabbing him. 'Here, look what 'e's . . . ' 'McCutchen, McCutchen . . . !' 'Y' rotten . . . !' 'Y' bastard. . . !' His head was flung hard back against the wall, knuckles smashed into his mouth – he was blind, could not get his arms free – a blow to his stomach and a buzzing that grew louder, threatening to drown out even Camley, bellowing above them all. 'Don't kill 'im, y' stupid gits! Don't bloody kill 'im . . . !'

33

The voices had been speaking for some time.

'I never thought O'Brien was bad as all that. There are lots worse. Nat Garson once knifed a man at Macquarie Harbour. No one could prove it was him, though.'

'What, killed a man?' Irish voice.

'O' course. But to hit McCutchen, a *screw*, and one of the worst of 'em . . . '

Aidan could not reconcile the talk to the shouting that had preceded it. Had he been unconscious? Had he . . .

A voice said, 'He's coming 'round.'

'Aidan?'

He opened his eyes to Will Treloar's blurred features; he blinked, turning his head away.

'Aidan?'

'I'm all right,' he murmured. He was not. His head hurt like the devil and his shoulder ached as though his arm had been wrenched from its socket. He turned back to gaze up at Will, taking in, now his vision had cleared, the fact that he was lying on his bunk, and more faces were grouped around Treloar's in a worried tableau.

'It's morning, Aidan,' Will said. 'One of those scaley bastards knocked you cold . . . '

'It's a bad morning for you.' Oldfield, the fifty-year-old house-breaker, the sunburnt face lined like a walnut beneath the grey stubble of his hair. 'They'll send for the magistrate from Hobart Town, no doubt. You'll be sent back to Hobart – maybe put on a ship to Port Arthur. Second offenders who . . . ' Will jabbed Old-field in the ribs.

But Aidan had already closed his eyes. Port Arthur . . . the high security prison on the Tasman Peninsula, sixty-five miles or more from Hobart, accessible only by boat, or by a narrow neck of land. To escape on foot one faced the savage guard dogs chained almost nose to nose across the isthmus, or one swam – and faced sharks. Few had escaped from Port Arthur and lived.

318

'Why did y' have to hit McCutchen, Aidan?' It was young O'Dowd. ''Twas worse than Will leppin' on that guard on the *Calcutta* – they'll not let it go by without punishing you, that's certain . . . '

'Och, stop.' Everyone was so interested in his inevitable punishment. He'd tell them to go to hell, but it was difficult to speak. He placed a hand on his face and felt his swollen upper lip, could taste blood in his mouth where his cheek had been torn on his teeth.

The bell rang outside in the corridor. There were stirrings all around as the men in their bunks rolled over, grumbling, sat up and began climbing to the floor. The wooden platforms squeaked in protest, and creaked in release.

Bolts slammed back, a draught of air. 'Come on, you lot!'

More grumblings and mutterings. A cheerful voice called, 'O'Brien still alive?'

Will turned his head, 'He'll live longer'n you, Bantam.'

'Haw!' from The Bantam.

Then Nat Garson's voice, 'Chin up, O'Brien! Nearly all of us've been in Port Arfur – ain't 'alf bad, food's better if anythink!'

'Fall in, all of you! All except O'Brien! You get to sleep in, O'Brien!' Because it was a screw who made the joke, nobody laughed.

The three by Aidan's bunk already had their boots on. As they lined up to tramp outside, Will placed a hand on Aidan's shoulder, and gave it a squeeze. Aidan winced. Will said, 'Mebbe t'won't be so bad – they didn't throw you into solitary straight away. Garson says try not to move around much until . . . '

'What? Why?'

'They'll rub. The chains.'

He stared into Will's face. Will almost smiled, awkwardly, then thought better of it. Nothing could comfort here. 'You're in irons, Aidan.'

'Fall in, Treloar!' roared from the opposite end of the dormitory.

With a final worried glance, Will was gone, stepping into line behind O'Dowd, and the door shut behind them.

Aidan raised his head, hearing at the same time the faint clank of chains about his legs. He sat up, staring, moaning a little under his breath with the horror of being trapped, confined, that was a thousand times worse than being in the blackness of solitary. Chained . . . chained! Not the irons in which all the Irish prisoners had been marched to their ships, chains somehow made tolerable when all his fellow exiles shared the degradation. Why, they had sneered, laughed about it, muttered insults at their guards in Irish, and knew all the time that the fetters were temporary. These chains that bound his ankles each to the other were two feet in length and weighed twenty pounds. The bands were held by pins, firmly hammered into interlocking sockets. 'While I was still unconscious, while I couldn't fight . . . Damn their eyes, damn their souls t'hell . . . ' He was tearing at the iron bands, ripping his nails, making the metal bite into the flesh of his ankles. Useless . . . it was useless . . . Sobbing with rage he drew his feet back to kick futilely at the wall, but the sound of the bolt on the door being drawn back once more, made him pause. He lay propped up on his elbows, trying to control his laboured breathing, watched as the door opened and the guard approached, boot soles squeaking, the too-short trouser cuffs flapping about the ankles.

'Put your boots on, O'Brien,' McCutchen said, 'The Superintendent wants to see you.'

Aidan gazed at him, taking in the dark bruise on the side of the man's chin. He stood there, dark eyes glowing with malevolence, holding, incongruously, a broad-based broom in one hand. The convicts themselves cleaned the barracks, two men mustered each week to clean the dormitory. Aidan eyed the broom with suspicion as he lowered heavy-laden legs to the floor. He sat down on Will's bunk and pulled on the heavy convict issue boots over his bare feet.

McCutchen said, 'You think you're lucky, I daresay.' Aidan kept his eyes on his laces as he tied them. The man went on. 'If this happened in the Tench you'd be bleeding from seventy lashes this morning. And all for what? Because I dropped a letter from your Irish whore into the piss.'

He was laughing. He snorted and roared with genuine laughter, and Aidan's self-control was gone. He was on his feet, had taken one and a half steps forward – too fast, the broom came sliding forward, turned on its side. It hit the chain and pushed it backwards violently, pulling Aidan's foot back with it. Off-balance, he fell heavily on to his side. He half-rose – and found the point of the broom handle pressed into the base of his throat.

No humour now in the face above him. 'You're an animal, O'Brien, that's what you are. And I don't care about shoving your teeth through your head like I ought, because what's waiting for you in this colony is worse than anything I could do to you.' His voice was soft with anticipation, 'I've seen 'em just like you, full of grit to start with, won't take no pushing around . . . and I seen 'em come back from the coal mines and Norfolk Island, skinny and sick with scars like ropes from their necks to their knees. An' the fight gone, O'Brien. Like rag dolls with the stuffing removed. If they got their balls is a matter of no difference, they ain't got the heart to screw even a tart, the old lags. And that's where you're headed, old son . . . ' The broom handle stroked Aidan's face, forehead to chin, almost gently. 'That's where you're goin'.'

He allowed Aidan to get to his feet; outside the cell door they found two sentries waiting; McCutchen did not follow as the two guards fell into step beside Aidan, matching their paces with his, along the corridor, out the door and across the yard. Until they entered the Superintendent's office, Aidan could feel McCutchen's eyes upon his back.

The guards remained with him while the Superintendent spoke. An ex-naval officer, Frederick Lawrence had the bearing and the clipped, confident manner of a man used to command; there was little about the man, except his very presence here, that hinted that his career had been disappointing, his ambitions frustrated. His men, the motley collection of soldiers of fortune and ex-convicts who served as guards and overseers, certainly never guessed it. These were fairly peaceful times, many relatively capable men in the military forces had found a shortage of opportunities for advancement, had reached their middle years and realized that they would go no further in their chosen careers. But Lawrence, at least, was not one to take out his not inconsiderable bitterness on those around him.

He was almost bald, his blonde hair having receded to a point where it clung to an area not above his ears, but the hard face was handsome, the grey eyes calm as they ran over Aidan's body from face to toes and back again. He took his time speaking.

'How old are you, O'Brien?'

Aidan gazed at him, knowing the man had his record close to hand, knowing that he knew very well how old he was. 'Twenty-five . . . sir.'

'You're a trouble-maker, aren't you?'

'I . . . ' he stopped. He would not banter words with this man. He chose a point on the wall above Lawrence's head and kept his eyes there.

'I'm not going to ask you how you managed to get that letter, I know you won't tell me. But you were aware that all mail must be forwarded to the officer in charge of the probation station, and it would have been handed on to you after inspection. In the circumstances Officer McCutchen was justified in presuming that the letter was suspect, and your behaviour at the time only seemed to confirm that. Do you have anything to say for yourself?'

Silence. Lawrence played the game too, and was quiet for a long

321

moment, though Aidan felt his face was being scrutinized.

After a long time, Lawrence leaned forward a little and continued, 'You cannot keep lashing back at those in authority, O'Brien. I have the feeling that it hasn't come home to you, yet, that however strong you feel yourself to be, this system is stronger. Keep pitting yourself against it, and you'll be the one that's broken.'

Still Aidan said nothing, and Lawrence leaned back in his chair. 'I'm not sending for the magistrate from Hobart. He'll take weeks to arrive, and when he does, he'll undoubtedly order a flogging. That, no matter how well you deserve it, is something I will try to avoid. You're intelligent, and well-educated, you have every reason to make a success of life in this colony once your time is served. From what I've seen of floggings, in the navy and in the convict system, it seems only to harden a man, to make him even more defiant, and reckless. You're too young for the lash – yet keep going the way you are . . . ' He opened a book whose place was marked, and tapped the paper. Aidan looked down and saw his own name at the top of the page. ' . . . And this record that follows you won't record merely solitary confinement. Use your head, O'Brien. In this colony nothing is forgotten, it's all here, black on white – you can make your own future here, or destroy it, it's up to you.

'You're to wear those irons for three months. I take this decision upon myself, because in solitary you're little good to yourself or anyone else. It's been tried on you twice, and had no effect. For such a man as you seem to be, chains just might teach you something.

'You're to spend the rest of the day chopping firewood and cleaning the stables. You'll be back on the roadworks tomorrow – and expected to fulfil all your taskwork as usual. You're dismissed.'

Aidan touched his forehead dutifully, one of the guards opened the door, and all three left the room.

34

And back to the forest, 'the bush', the old lags called it, as if the scrubby vegetation that went on for miles was one entity.

The bush; the giant eucalypts, their meagre, drab, grey-olive uniformity of leaves, the harsh, prickling bushes that grabbed at one's clothes with dry, invisible claws, the alien birdsongs from the

322

fluttering groups of currawongs, parrots, magpies and native finches that whistled and squabbled fearlessly in the branches above their heads, even as the men hacked and sawed the timber. And lizards and snakes, *snakes* . . . it was a monstrous country, Aidan thought, the day he almost trod upon a tiger snake and stopped, frozen in sweaty terror.

It rippled with silent fluidity across his path, over a rock that made it hump its body, as if flaunting the perfect brown and ochre pattern on its back, then with a final flick of its tail, it was gone. Aidan stepped on, cautious, watchful, and for the rest of that day every bent twig upon the ground seemed to start and slither at the corner of his vision, every fallen and blackened branch was watching him from lidless eyes. A monstrous country.

Nat Garson, for some unintelligible reason of his own, had taken a liking to Aidan and had Ettie procure a pair of leather leggings, 'up-and-downers' as Nat called them, to protect Aidan's already blistering ankles from the irons. Nat handed them to him one evening in the dormitory before lights out. There was a piece of light rope, too. He tied one end around Aidan's waist and looped the other end around the middle of the chain, pulling it up off the ground before tying the ropes end. 'Now you'll move freer.'

Aidan walked up and down the room, and found it to be so. He stopped by his own bunk, feeling awkwardly indebted to Garson. He fumbled beneath his mattress and brought out the remains of his carefully hoarded tobacco and went to hand it to the man.

'Nah! What're you on about?'

'Take it. You've gone to a lot of bother sure.'

'Not me. Ettie, maybe.'

'You asked her . . . '

'Ettie'd do anythink for me,' he said simply. 'Gawd knows what a woman like her sees in me, but she sees somethink worthwhile. It's no trouble to 'er to help me, and no trouble for an old lag like me to help you. You got guts, though you don't make no big noise about it. We all admire you for it. As for Camley,' his thin face broke into a grin, 'it's him that's been doin' all the go-betweenin' – ol' Ettie'll have been greasin' his palm proper, don't you worry. So keep your tobacco – Gawd knows when you'll get more.'

Will did not like Garson, could tell that the little Londoner was clever enough to surround himself with men stronger than himself, and Will did not like to see Aidan dragged within that sphere of influence.

'I don't trust them,' Will said once during the midday meal break.

Aidan sighed, knowing that Will had been building up to this

323

lecture for some time. He himself felt that he saw Ettie and Nat clearly enough, but while they saw fit to be kind to him, he could see no harm in the friendship. The sun was warm, only that morning the chains had at last been removed from his legs, and he did not want a quarrel with his friend.

'Garson is a killer,' Will was saying, 'and the men tell me that Ettie Harding runs a brothel – and she owns the building. Where'd a woman like that, an ex-convict herself, you can be sure, get the money to buy a tavern, set it up as she did?'

'Hmm. Em . . .'

'Hmm, em . . .' Is that all you've got to say?'

Aidan grinned at him. 'It explains the orange hair and the ear-bobs. I've never met a woman of ill-repute, would you believe that? We didn't have any in Killaloe. We may have had once, mind y', but knowing Father O'Callaghan he drove them out like St Patrick did the snakes . . .'

'Are you going to be serious?'

'No. These are bad times, and this is a country on the edge of hell – I'll not be throwing stones at a woman who's been kind to me, make her living how she might. And God knows what forced her into it. Sure, *we're* not exactly where *we'd* wish t'be, are we?'

Will glared at him. Aidan scowled back.

'I don't want you to land in more trouble than you are already.'

'What're y' like?' Aidan burst out, 'I'm hauling logs on this fekking island with my legs in irons, til this morning! What more could happen!'

'Solitary and floggings. Port Arthur – more solitary and flog-gings . . .'

'Och, stop.'

'Forget about Ettie Harding, Aidan . . .'

'What, the only woman I've seen in a twelvemonth . . . ?'

'Forget about her and put your mind to coping with all this, keep y'r temper, and do nothing to single yourself out so they d'make an example of you. You're not really here for life – you've heard the old lags talking – most lifers d'have their tickets-of-leave in twelve years! 'Tis not that long, is it? Aidan?'

But Aidan had stood, seeing Camley glancing at his watch, and had already moved off towards his work before the overseer began to bellow at them to return to their tasks.

Aidan lay awake in his bunk for some time, that night, thinking, as he often did, of his family, particularly of his daughter, wondering if

324

he would ever see her . . .

He did not realize he was dozing until a cold hand gripped his arm.

He rolled over quickly, half-sat up, fist raised, before the voice hissed, 'Shh. Quiet – lissen, O'Brien!' Aidan was gazing into Nat Garson's shadowed face. He lowered his fist, and the little cockney whispered, 'Thought you was about to kill me.'

'You'd deserve it sure, creepin' up on a man like that . . . '

'Be quiet a minute . . . ' Nat paused, listening to the breathing of the men around them, then ducked his head to the lower bunk to check that Will's snoring was not feigned. Aidan, puzzled, was leaning over the bunk after him when Nat's face reappeared within an inch of his own. Aidan was not prepared for the blast of Garson's foul breath full in his face. He threw himself back against the wall.

Nat took his arm. 'Did you hear me?'

'Sorry . . . ?'

Hands took his shoulders, shook him, 'An escape! D'you hear me? It's our only chance . . . ' He loosed his hold, pulled back. 'You're not yeller, are you, mate? You're not scared?'

'No . . . No . . . '

Nat leaned forward over the bunk. 'I bin driving the firewood back to the barracks this past month – Camley got Ettie t' meet me on the road yesterday. She'll handle everything, clothes, a passage to America . . . Are you listening, O'Brien?'

'Yes, but . . . '

'No buts. Are you with me or not? This is my sixteenth year here, O'Brien. I can't stand it any more – *I can't!* Are you listening? Why are you cringing away like that?'

'We . . . we can't talk here, someone will hear. Can we talk tomorrow? Outside?'

'I can't. We're safer here – even Camley can't know. Lean forward so I don't have to talk so loud . . . '

'Listen, Nat . . . '

'*You* listen!' Aidan thought he would faint. The gale of rotting air from that black-toothed cavern swept over him, the words were meaningless. 'Ettie . . . Mountain . . . A hut close . . . Ettie . . . food and horses . . . Ettie says . . . '

He thought of turning his face to the wall – but there were rumours of someone who had offended Nat Garson, who later had had the intrepidity to trust his back to the man, and had finished with a knife between his shoulder blades. His own options were few, and yet the risk of being stabbed seemed almost preferable to . . .

Nat was saying, 'So I'll see you then.' And he was gone. Aidan almost fell out of his bunk with panic. When, when? he wanted to shout.

He found he had stopped breathing. He lay and listened to the different sleeping sounds of the men around him, drawing in fresh air and trying to cope with this new thought. Escape.

He was filled with a wild, sudden excitement that it *could* work. Nat was an old lag, he'd know the right tricks, and he knew the bush; and Ettie had the money, the contacts . . . It had to work!

But when was he to speak to Nat again? Not tomorrow, he'd said it was too dangerous . . . Aidan wanted details, he had been half asleep, he would say, tell me again. But the thought of finding Nat once more, while still in the confines of the already stale room . . . He could not bear it. He rolled in his blanket restlessly all night.

And in the morning there was no opportunity to speak to the man. Nat would glance at him meaningfully and move away, obviously wanting no talk of a conspiracy to arise.

For a whole week Nat avoided him, then, in the afternoon, as Aidan, Will and Oldfield were loading pieces of dry timber on to the cart for the barrack's wood supply, Nat, within the cart, asked the nearby Camley, 'C'n I take O'Brien with me? The Bantam's on yard duty, can't ask him to unload all this.'

'All right.' The overseer had turned away. Aidan had been concentrating on loading the lengths of stovewood, now looked across at Garson at the same time as Garson glanced at him. And Camley had turned, had seen.

Perhaps the man knew that something was afoot, and that he had no part in it. It seemed to Aidan, later, that Camley was endeavouring to protect himself; he was a man who thought of every possibility. For he said, now, 'Bailey will go back with you.'

Neither Aidan nor Nat faltered; Aidan lifted the logs on to the cart, merely nodding at Camley's words, and Nat kept neatly stacking the wood. But Camley had not moved off, instead his flat-featured face was gazing from one to the other for fully half a minute before turning and bellowing for Bailey.

It would have been the perfect opportunity to talk, Aidan was thinking, watching Bailey, a guard who had joined the Convict Department after serving as a sailor for years, come rolling across the clearing. He climbed agilely into the front of the cart, his musket between his knees, held securely by broad, heavily-tattooed arms. Damn y' t' hell, Aidan thought.

'You drive,' Garson told him. 'You know 'orses better'n me.'

Camley was still standing by, but made no objection to Aidan taking the reins. Nat, in the back, found a relatively secure seat on the pile of stacked logs and gave Camley a royal wave as they set off. Camley stared after them, unsmiling.

Wending their way back along the new road, Aidan wondered if he and Nat would be left alone to unload the wood; Bailey had little imagination, he did not seem to question the decision for a guard for two men who had, until now, been trusted. He sat stolidly beside Aidan and looked at the road. Perhaps he would take Camley's order literally, accompany them back to the barracks then leave them to go off to the guards' quarters for a cup of tea . . .

Bailey was falling. He pitched straight forward from his seat, struck Rameses upon the rump, making the horse start forward violently, and disappeared between the shafts of the wagon.

'Jaysus-Mary-and-Joseph!' Aidan was pulling on the brake, hauling at the startled horse, only glanced backwards – and stopped.

Nat Garson stood poised on the pile of wood, one eighteen inch log held in one hand. Even now he was throwing it down, jumping out of the wagon. Aidan vaulted from his seat to the ground, and bent to see the unconscious Bailey lying in the dust. On the other side of the vehicle Garson was on hands and knees, dragging the musket from beneath the body.

'You've killed 'im!'

'Leave 'im! Leave 'im and come on!'

Aidan was dragging at Bailey's boots, pulling the man free. Nat was wild, panic-stricken, his feet dancing on the road. 'Leave 'im, I tell you!'

'I'll not leave him t'be trampled!' He took the man's shoulders, pulled him well out of the way of the wheels and the horse's hoofs. He bent over the man, and felt his chest. 'He's still breathing . . . Jaysus, the blood . . . '

'Had to knock 'im out, di'n' I? C'mon!' Nat was already across the road.

So this had been it? Aidan hesitated. He had not been prepared at all. He stood and glanced around them. They had not yet left the new road to turn north to Brown's Road, were only about three miles from Camley and the other convicts. There was no one in sight; before and behind a turn in the new road swallowed the yellow-dust surface between the tall gums.

Nat had paused a little distance into the scrub; at the base of a twisted stringybark, long ago struck by some disaster and recovered into a weird and somehow threatening shape, Nat was scrabbling furiously. Aidan crossed the road to him slowly, watched as the older man pulled up a large package, dusted the earth from what became obvious as two blankets and two oilskin bags containing what must be food. 'Run on ahead!' Nat was urging, 'That way!' he gestured. He was taking a compass from one of the oilskin bags, holding it in his hand as if it meant more to him than anything else in his existence. Aidan was still standing there. Nat threw him one of the bags, and one of the blankets, then he was off. 'Run, y' great git! We have to lose them by nightfall!' He was disappearing through the trees, heading south, and Aidan, his brain clearing, headed after him.

He had difficulty keeping Nat in sight despite being taller, younger and fitter. Nat ran like a maniac, heedlessly, sightlessly, ignoring Aidan's calls. Aidan himself set a dogged pace, judging his footing with as much care as he could, looking up occasionally to see Nat's small frame leaping ahead of him between the trees like some scruffy and demented forest spirit. He wanted to laugh, he was filled with an exultation that brought him close to tears. He was free.

35

By nightfall they had reached an area above Margate, skirting the roads and the small farming community. As they paused on the slope of a hill, Nat pointed off into the distance. 'See it? Cathedral Rock. That's where we're headed.'

Aidan could see it, through a break in the trees; of the same mountain range as Mount Wellington, but its slopes were steeper. In the fading light it looked very far away, and forbidding. 'You'll not be tellin' me, I trust, that we have to climb it?'

'Nah, don't be daft! That's our landmark, that's all. Tomorrow we head for it.'

It took them four days to reach the lower slopes of Cathedral Rock. They had little food left, only a small piece of salt pork and two biscuits each, and both were close to exhaustion.

Two days later, having scrambled over the shoulder of the mountain, the food was all gone. Still they walked, half-running, sometimes, when a sound in the scrub behind them filled their minds with fears of tracking dogs, tired police and guards with accounts to settle . . . The bush, a terrifying enough place at any time, was now haunted with imagined warnings of boots and muffled barks and whines, drawing closer, closer . . .

They found a stream, running noisily between banks of tree ferns, and took off their boots and walked in the shallows for a mile or so, despite the numbing cold of the water. Would it confuse the dogs? The two men replaced their boots and followed the creek down-stream, through a chill rain, and prayed the diversion would at least delay their pursuers.

It was Nat who tired first. Aidan saw him stumble, fall, and by the time the Irishman had reached him, Nat was on his knees but making no attempt to rise. 'F'r God's sake, Nat, we can't keep this up – where are we supposed . . . '

'I told 'er she should've been waiting for us! I told 'er it's too risky . . . That's it! That's finished it!' And he was weeping, his face in his hands, loud sobs that shook his body.

Aidan stared at him, appalled; to imagine that this wilderness had the more experienced man defeated shook him terribly. 'Och, stop – it's not that bad. We'll find our way. You're just tired.' His own knees were shaking with fatigue. 'We'll rest a while and then start again.'

'You don't understand! I followed all Ettie's directions! I used the bleedin' compass! But we're lost! We're lost!'

'We can't be! Just stay calm, Nat . . . '

'Round the base of Cathedral Rock, she said; we done that. An' head directly west comin' down, and we come on this clearin' – only there *ain't* no bloody clearin'!'

Aidan sat down in front of the sobbing man, 'Well . . . what's in the clearing?'

'What d'you mean, what's in the clearin'?' He aimed a furious blow at Aidan's face and missed. 'Nothink's in the clearin'! What d'you expect to find in a clearin', *trees*?'

'Mother of God, Nat . . . '

'We're finished, O'Brien!'

'We're not! Now listen to me. Listen!' Shouting at Nat dissipated some of his own fear. How blind he had been to trust Nat's self-sufficiency; he had been in the bush for years, but never under his own volition, never having to make his own decisions. Aidan took his shoulders and shook him. 'If it's important that we find this clearing, then we will. Perhaps we came too far north; we'll go back to the top again, and move more south-west, this time . . . '

'There's no point,' Nat sniffed, wiping his nose on his sleeve. He was beginning to be ashamed of his outburst. 'We'll be flounderin' around all night. Let's just sit 'ere an' Ettie'll send someone t' look for us.'

'That could take days!'

'What else can we do?'

'Climb a tree,' Aidan cried in desperation, 'Look for this clearing of yours . . . '

Nat reared his head back to stare at the giant eucalypts above them. 'Climb one of *them*?'

'If you stand on my shoulders you could reach the lower branches . . . '

'Gahn! I'm not climbin' no tree! *You* climb it!'

'I can't, man! I'm too heavy for you to lift . . . '

'Well, that's that, ain't it? You can't climb the tree an' I *won't*.'

Aidan picked the man up by his shirt front, struggling against the desire to punch the blackened teeth. 'Nat, if you don't climb that tree . . . '

Nat kicked out at him, catching Aidan on the shin; the next moment the little man had bent, groping at his ankle . . .

The knife glittered in the fading light, short but lethal, held blade upwards, expertly. Nat's face was white, his control gone. Once Aidan looked into Nat's eyes he did not dare to look away, knowing instinctively that to display either hostility or fear would push the other man too far. Instead he said quietly, 'Kill me and you're alone. Night's coming on, and you'll be alone.'

He paused, watched as Nat's eyes flickered, his mouth working a little. He looked sullen, then suspicious; the colour was returning suddenly to his face; he swallowed, glanced down at the knife, and lowered it. Aidan had a hold on Nat's arm, now he let go and took a step back, calmly, still watching Nat's face.

'Gahn, didn't think I'd really do you in, didja? We're mates, you an' me. I just don't like bein' pushed an' pulled about, that's all. You wouldn't know what it's like – you strong blokes don't 'ave no worries. We little-uns get sensitive-like you know? C'mon, shake 'ands.'

They shook hands, Aidan guardedly. Nat grinned self-consciously, and replaced the knife in its leather sheath strapped to his calf. 'Ettie gave it to me when I last met 'er. She thinks of everything, Ettie does. What'll we do, O'Brien?'

The suddenness of the question was surprising in itself, the tone of frightened appeal had Aidan at a temporary loss for words; Nat Garson, leader of his own little clique of vicious and desperate men, now turning for help and advice from *him* . . .

'Mountain River,' Nat said. He had evidently decided to be helpful. 'That's where Ettie's waiting – a hut on Mountain River.

330

This might be it.' He said hopefully, looking at the stream. It was no more than twenty feet across.

Aidan sighed. 'We'll follow it, so.'

They walked until there was no further light in the sky. Nat propped. 'Let's rest, shall we? Eh? I'm fair done in, O'Brien.' Aidan sighed, and agreed. Clearing the ground of stones, they lay down upon the rather damp leaf litter, and each drifted off immediately into a light and fitful sleep.

She was there again. Even in his dream he was amazed that she could follow him so far. She walked towards him from downstream, moving easily up the slope between the blackened trees. *No!* he cried out in his mind, but still she came calmly towards him, the Sidhe of his dreams on Craglea, the white hair blowing about her like a cloud, the same smile on her face, the pale hand in its black sleeve held out towards him, beckoning, the inaudible voice calling . . .

He awoke shivering, turned his head, gazing in the direction from which she had come. Nothing there. The moonlit trees and that was all.

He was cold, even in his blanket. His shirt and coat were thin, and gave little protection from the damp ground. He wished for another blanket, a roof, a bed . . . There would be a frost in the morning, already he felt the stiffness on the blanket about him. Perhaps they'd be warmer if they kept moving, sure they could see before them . . . He raised his head to look at Nat. But the older man was asleep, curled in a ball, snoring softly.

Aidan slept no more. He woke Nat at dawn, and all that next morning they stumbled on, following the water's edge. The trees were thinning out, the ground became less rock-bound. They found native grasses again, and, once, horse-dung on a path that led from the creek away through the trees. The stream was much wider, now, but whether this was the river Nat was looking for, he had no idea. The area abounded in waterways, and the surveyors of the colony seemed optimistic when naming them.

But across the stream from them, coming into sight as they walked, was a grey hut of split timbers and a bark-shingled roof. It lay in a five acre clearing; a slanted, slab-built barn stood drunkenly a little distance away, and horses grazed before it, their legs hobbled.

'Ettie-e-e!' Nat screamed, so close to Aidan that he flinched. The little man ran along the bank, hurled himself into the water, and half-waded, half-swam across the river, yelling whenever his head appeared above water, 'Ettie-e-e-e!'

Aidan waded into the stream; the water reached only to his chest, and he was able to see clearly as a man and a slim, fair-haired girl appeared at the door of the hut, staring down towards the two men. Aidan thought for one sick moment that Nat had made a mistake, this might be a settler who would turn them in for the reward.

But even as he watched, the two at the door were pushed aside, and Ettie Harding, still fastening the hooks on her bodice, came charging out of the hut, her bright orange hair loose down her back, and flew into the damp and desperate arms of Nat Garson.

Ettie found dry clothes for them while the girl, who was introduced as Ettie's step-daughter, Matty, prepared a meal. The man, Jimmy West, an old crony of Nat's, fired questions at the two men, and Nat, between mouthfuls of cold mutton, bread and butter, and strong, sweet tea, told of their escape, leaving Aidan to eat in silence. When they had finished, Matty poured more tea in their mugs, and then the fire was doused. The five of them sat about the rough-hewn table, the bush flies buzzing about them, and talked of what course of action they should follow.

'It'd be madness to go back to England, Nat. You've realized that?' Ettie prompted.

'In a few more years,' Nat whined, for the thought of life without London was unthinkable, 'they'll forget, and with a new name I won't be recognized.'

'You'll be drawn back to the old haunts. Someone will dob you in, have no fear of that.'

'She's right.' It was West who spoke. He was a heavily-built man of about Aidan's height, whose good looks had long ago been diffused by drink and long exposure to the sun of this country. His eyes were heavy-lidded, dark-circled, with puffy bags of skin beneath them, the line of the mouth altered by the sagging leathered skin of his cheeks. 'There'll be no more London for you, Nat. Too many men have been caught in that way.'

Ettie said, 'I've got you a berth on a ship to San Francisco, love – you and O'Brien both. You'll have to work as sailors, you won't mind that, will you?'

Nat did. In bitter terms he complained to Ettie, while Aidan could only stare at the woman, whose matter-of-fact words had brought his dream of the future suddenly close.

The others had forgotten him in their efforts to help Nat see reason. Aidan turned to gaze into the steaming ashes of the hearth, his mind racing ahead to the letter that he could write to Maura from America. He could work there, earn enough money to send for his family. He found his nails biting into the palms of his hands with suppressed excitement.

West, too, seemed to feel a sense of victory, a sense of release. He stood up suddenly and headed for a corner cupboard. 'Rum! This calls for rum! We'll drink a toast, we will!'

The liquor was poured into pottery mugs and the four made a toast to their intrepid venture, and drank deeply of the raw, burning liquid. Aidan's eyes were watering; Matty, who had refused a drink, was smiling at his discomfort from her seat by the wall. She had a mass of curling, almost white-blonde hair pinned up upon her head, and an alert, mature expression that somehow did not fit with her softness of features.

The other three were laughing, drinking without economy from a small keg, the excitement of the escape still upon them. Aidan sipped from his mug more cautiously, wondered, briefly, at the good sense of them all indulging themselves so heedlessly when 'the traps', as Nat called the police, were most assuredly searching for them. But the three were obviously certain that the worst was over, and gradually their confidence and the strong liquor conquered Aidan's unease and reticence. When West asked Aidan where he came from in Ireland and why he had been transported, Aidan told them, not holding back any of the details. He found quick sympathy in them, for hunger had stalked each of them as children, wherever in Britain these three were born. The details of the Famine were not too unusual for them not to understand, neither the gnawing hunger and desperation, nor the decision to steal. He began to lose their attention only when he found himself justifying his actions, giving the reasons behind the Terryalts' formation, trying to explain what made honest farm labourers plan thefts, robberies, murder . . .

Nat had taken over the conversation; Aidan's recounting of wrong-doings and retribution had sparked some memory within Garson, and he began to recount a tale of vengeance, long ago, in the grey streets of his youth . . . West took it up, told the story of his own transportation for robbing a shopkeeper who had once beaten him when West worked for him as a child. Vengeance and the memory of vengeance ruled the table. Their eyes shone, they threw the liquor down their throats and barely waited for each other to finish his or her story. It happened to me, to my father, to my cousin, to a friend, to a friend of a friend and it's true, so-help-me-God . . .

'He beat me every day . . . ' It was Ettie speaking. Aidan raised his head from where it lay on his arm, and pulled his mug towards his mouth. 'He beat me with his belt, the buckle end, and when I didn't scream loud enough, he beat me with his fists. I was young, only seventeen, and thin – I wasn't the woman I am now . . . He kept me half-starved – the only child I ever carried was born dead because that man beat me. I never had another child.' Aidan drank deep of the rum, then became conscious of something within the cup, bumping against his lip. He pulled back and squinted down into the vessel's depths. It was dark – how had the room darkened? It was almost night. He could only just see the fly, stuck there in his mug of liquor. He stared at it in some resentment.

'It wasn't as if he was poor, either. Every penny that the tavern made was put in a box with a lock on it, and kept beneath loose floorboards in the bedroom. He didn't show me where it was. I stood in the dark of the hall one night and watched him place the week's takings in with the rest. I'd never seen so much money. That decided me. He'd eat scraps from the table himself, and give me the same, only less of it, all the time moaning how bad things were for him. I had enough, then.'

The fly was swimming valiantly round and round in the rum, rowing furiously with its wings, round and round . . . Aidan made three attempts before he managed to scoop it out of the cup with his finger. He flicked it out on to the table; it hit with a note of protest, then recovered and buzzed damply away towards the open door and the grey light of the evening sky.

'I did it all in one night. Put all the arsenic in his dinner, in the stew. He was drinking heavily, he always did on a Sunday. Everyone knew how heavily he drank. I watched him crawling around, dying. Couldn't tear myself away. It didn't take long. Thin as I was, I dragged him to the stairs, and dropped him down. He was so heavy I could barely lift him to do it, thin and ill and half-fainting as I was, but I did it.'

Aidan, careless, had gone to take a swig from the cup at the beginning of this. He still had his face buried in it. Did not move for a long moment, blinking sightlessly, feeling the blood leave his head, his shoulders, turn his hands to ice as her words registered. He lowered the mug. Ettie was not crying. Why did he feel she would be crying? She had a knife in her hand, still greasy with mutton fat, and was scoring the table in jagged lines, her mouth pursed, eyes narrowed with the memory.

'You done right, love. No one c'd blame you.' Nat placed his little paw over her large white one, and gave it a comforting squeeze. West agreed, nodding his head on his thick, short neck. Aidan could not move. And to his horror Ettie, sitting opposite him at the table, raised her eyes to his, and stared at him with those large and

334

luminous eyes, waiting for him to speak. He could say nothing. She smiled, slowly; kept her eyes on him as her lips curled gently, waiting, knowing his horror, his terror. 'Yes,' he could say, or 'Uh huh,' or 'Em . . . ' or . . . But his throat was closed permanently. He would never speak again, never move again.

The dreadful parody of a woman leaned over the table to him. 'The first time for anything is always the hardest. Like you and this Devlin Kelly you tried to kill. You thought you had. That's the most important thing. Next time it'll be easier for you.'

'An' you should know, love.' Nat was hugging her. 'My poor Et's had a hard life, O'Brien. The rogues who've taken advantage of her! A woman has to fight back best she can.'

'The second time didn't go so smooth-like. I did it slow, this time, so he was real sick before he croaked. But his relations got nasty greedy because I got all the money. There was talk of an inquest. So I got out of England, came here. I've heard since that things settled down. The police weren't really suspicious, it was me that was nervous. I could go back there tomorrow if I liked.' She smiled at Nat. 'There's so much I'd like to show you. Where I grew up, and all. So many things to share with you, I'm looking forward to that. But not for a long time, pet. I'll have to join you in San Francisco first.'

Nat, Aidan found, was looking at him, and smiling. He glanced back at Ettie, ''Ey, Et – look at O'Brien. Are you 'orrified, boy? Ettie's only killed three men; less than I have. And there was good reason, don't you believe otherwise. If they'd treated Ettie proper, she wouldn't have done what she did, would you, girl?'

Ettie looked around them carefully. Aidan was puzzled until he remembered the girl, Matty. He realized with some thankfulness that she had been gone from the hut for sometime.

'I married the girl's father in 'forty-six. A widower he was, with four kids. I wanted a fresh start by then, and he had a good farm he'd worked up from nothing. I'd have done good by him, boy, I would have, so help me God. But he was a nagger; carp, carp, carp, all the time. Nothing I could do was right, though I tried to be everything for that man. The kids hated me, and that hurt, too. I did my best for 'em, their own mother couldn't've fed and clothed the little bastards better'n me. But nothing I did was good enough.

'We had a fight one day when we was alone in the shack he called a house. It was easy, and quick, this time, I was a lot stronger by then. There'd been bushrangers about, it wasn't hard to pretend I'd come back from the cows to find him there, the axe left by him, and all the valuables gone.

'What with the money I'd brought with me from England, and the sale of Harding's farm, I had enough money to buy my tavern in Hobart Town. I took good care of the kids – got the three boys jobs in the city at an age when most would say they were too young to learn, but they were strong and bright boys, they're doing all right, I've heard.'

'And . . . Matty?' Aidan could barely speak. The girl was no more than nineteen; he could not bear to think of all she had witnessed in her short life.

'Matty works with me at the tavern. She's a good girl. She does as she's told. She doesn't take after her father at all.'

Aidan was saved from further comment. His mind had been rejecting his situation for some time, now his stomach, too, rebelled. 'I . . . I . . . Excuse me!' He bolted for the door, his hand to his mouth. Behind him their laughter exploded, the force of it pressed him out into the night, plucked at his nerves still, as he headed away, down the hill, running awkwardly, almost buoyantly, in the new-found release from the weight of his chains.

He was ill by the bank, then stooped gingerly to the water and washed his face. He was trembling violently, and his mind could not function, his body failed him. He stumbled up the bank and fell, lay on the grass where he had fallen and did not move.

'Are you all right? . . . Are you all right?' A shifting of grey shadows before his eyes. Matty was on the grass beside him. Her closeness; a different smell, a woman smell. Maura swept close to him from the recesses of his memory. 'Are you awake?' Matty asked.

'Yes.'

There was a long silence. He could sense her searching about for words. He wanted her to go away, yet his pity for her kept him silent. He raised his head, stared at her face, wondered at the nightmare that the girl had lived through, and how much of the truth she suspected. Was Ettie Harding usually so loose-tongued with a few jars in her? Could she be so careless? Or was her loquacity due to her joy in finding Nat Garson once more?

And how long would Nat Garson last? A sudden picture appeared before Aidan of Ettie Harding in five or six years time, bored with Nat, aware, now, of his whining cowardice. Was Nat so self-interested, so self-confident, that he could not see that he, too, may become a victim to Ettie's disillusionment? Aidan owed no real loyalty to Nat, but could not prevent himself from half-retching at the thought of Nat's probable death. They were mad! All mad!

Matty's hand was on his neck. He said, 'I'm all right.' And he was. He would not think about it. He lifted his hand to his neck and

336

removed her hand, giving it a small squeeze of gratitude to lessen the rejection of her touch before he let it go, and raised himself to his feet. She fell in beside him as he moved slowly and with great care towards the now-lighted hut. But when they were closer, she took his arm.

'No, not yet. Over here.' She tugged at him. He stumbled, and felt ashamed before her. A fine figure he must look. Cannot hold his liquor, cannot walk straight . . . She was leading him into the barn. One of the horses whinnied to them, softly. Suddenly she disappeared from beside him. He peered around, and found her sitting on a stool, or barrel, by the door. He looked about him, felt about him in the darkness, but there was no other object on which to sit. His feet rustled in straw. He paused, suddenly aware that he did not belong in this darkened room with a girl who was not his wife, who disturbed him strangely. But then, he did not, at the moment, belong anywhere. His mind dwelt for only a second on that grisly company within the hut before it reeled back once more. Better where he was. He sat down on the straw.

'Matty? Do you know your way out of here?'

'Out? How do you mean? Back to Hobart?'

'To a road, at least. Do you?'

'No. I don't think so. Ettie says I've got no head for details, and she's right. I haven't got any sense of direction, either.'

'Can you remember which way you rode in here? Was it over the creek?'

'We came up from Huonville, following the river. But we had to cross a lot of creeks – without Jimmy West, we'd have got lost.'

He placed his elbows on his drawn-up knees, his face in his hands.

'Aidan?'

'Aye?'

'Aidan . . . That's a funny name. Aidan . . . I like it – it suits you.' They were silent a moment. 'Aidan, do you want to leave? Without Ettie and Nat and Jimmy? You'll get lost. Men die in the bush, starve to death.'

He knew. He had gazed at that possibility only hours before, but . . . 'I've got to get away,' he said.

'Why? Why can't you wait and we'll all go together?'

He could not answer her, knew only that he must get away, and soon. And then the chilling realization came to him that he would be leaving her behind.

She rose, before he could speak again, and came to sit beside him. He was suddenly uncomfortable, nervous, the nearness of her frightened him.

'Please, Aidan . . . Don't leave. Ettie has it all worked out, really – she can make sure you get clear away. You don't want to get caught like so many of the lags, do you? They stumble back into the prison barracks after weeks of starvation. Is that what you want to happen? And you'll be flogged, then, for sure.' She reached out a hand and placed it on his own. 'Please, Aidan – trust Ettie, she's . . . '

'Ettie . . . ' It was a moan that escaped from Aidan's lips; even the name sickened him. He turned to gaze at the girl beside him. He opened his mouth to speak, but she had bent forwards, and he found her lips pressed tight against his, her hands in his hair. He over-balanced, and she was pushing him back on the straw, murmuring, 'Don't push me away, please. Only hold me . . . You're good, you're a good man, I can tell. You're not like the others . . . '

He held her by her shoulders, felt the well-rounded flesh of them. She tried to press herself against him but managed to do so for only a short moment before he held her away from him again. 'What others! What're y' talkin' about?' He spoke savagely, almost with-out control, for her full breasts had for a second been pressed close to his chest and such a wave of desire had passed through him that he felt almost faint. He wanted to possess this girl, wanted it desper-ately . . .

'The men at the tavern. Oh, I've had men before. But so few I like. I've . . . It's been a rotten life – you wouldn't believe it. You Irish are different. You've had poverty, but . . . Oh, please. You don't understand. Just stay with me, now? Hold me. We won't go no further if you like. But I'm lonely, and I'm frightened out here . . .

She was kissing his cheek, his eyes, his forehead all this while, her soft little hands were inside his shirt, moving over his skin. She kept up her stream of words, pleading, flattering, and Aidan listened to them and was reprieved from further thought, from doubts and the threatening atmosphere around him, and he gave himself up to the feelings, to the ease of it.

It was quick, almost anti-climactic in the brevity of the act. They found each other, spent themselves; and he found himself lying on top of a girl he did not know, whose face he could not remember. A stranger to him. He did not know how to act. Nothing in his experience had prepared him for this. He moved away from her carefully. Heard her sigh and adjust herself, her clothing. For a long moment he lay there, until the arm upon which he was supporting himself began to ache, and he lay back slowly in the straw. He fumbled at his new trousers, covering himself, fastening buttons. And still he lay there, gazing up at the roof where missing wooden slates allowed the geometric shapes of sky to appear, deep indigo and scattered with stars, above his head.

She had moved, risen, but soon came back to him. He felt blankets being laid over him, then she was beneath them with him, and despite the turmoil of his emotions, and his recent climax, he felt his body stirred by her once more. Softly, unaware of this, she said, 'I knew you was a good man.'

He turned to gaze at her; her hair and face were as pale as the straw upon which she lay, he could barely see her. 'What?'

'I said, I knew you was a good man.'

'I . . . You . . . But you don't know . . . Sure how can you tell from that?'

She sighed, almost impatiently. 'It's not what you did. It's what you're *doing*.'

'What am I doing?'

'You're still here. Here beside me. That shows some feeling on your part.'

He had been thinking of standing, and this remark froze him entirely.

'Matty, I must leave . . . '

'You don't belong with Ettie and Nat and Jimmy, I know that. You're a decent sort, one can tell. But, see, sometimes you got to make the best of things.'

He did not like her preaching to him. 'I know that, but . . . '

'Take me. Life on a farm looking after the younger boys. And Father. What a bastard he was. You wouldn't believe all I had to put up with. But that's what people are, and you can't change them. The same with Ettie. She don't care for me at all, and that's all right with me. It's good to be left alone. I'll meet a good man one day, at the tavern, and I'll marry him, and get away from it all. I'll have my own house, and maybe kids. And then I'll do what *I* want.'

Her voice had risen in pitch with suppressed excitement. She had sat up, was looking at Aidan, but it seemed to him she was not seeing him. 'See, if it wasn't for Ettie there'd have been no hope for me. I can put up with her; she's not all that hard on me. Dad was the one. If Ettie hadn't done what she did, I'd have done it myself, if he'd touched me just once more . . . ' She trailed off in her anger. Then, 'I never told Ettie I knew. I'm not that stupid.' She sighed, and cuddled next to him, she did not seem to notice the rigidity of him, that he was barely breathing. 'Ettie buys me pretty clothes and at least there's always plenty to eat. We have jellies on Sundays. Could you see my old man letting us have jellies?'

'Matty . . . ' Aidan's voice came out with difficulty, 'Matty, how old are you?'

'Fifteen,' she said, defiantly, 'What's that got to do with it?'

36

He left her at dawn, lying on her side asleep, one fist to her face, like the child she had never been. He had taken one of the blankets, moving carefully so that he should not disturb her, and walked from the shed into a mist-hung morning, heading downstream. The dog discovered him, but instead of setting up an alarm, it fell in beside Aidan and appeared to wish to join in on the excursion. Aidan threw stones at it, and it finally slunk back towards the hut, gazing at him over its shoulder with reproach.

About a mile downstream, where the water ran swiftly but shallowly over almost exposed rocks, he stripped off his clothes and held them in his arms as he waded across, half-laughing aloud with the shock of the icy water. On the opposite bank he dressed, then headed off into the hills. He had no idea where he was going, if he wanted, indeed, to be anywhere at all. He was angry with himself for not having the stomach to tolerate Ettie and Nat, to use them for his own ends. The anger remained wordless, he did not carry on a debate within himself. The knowledge was there that he could *not* tolerate them, that even the freedom they could procure for him would not compensate for the periods of restrained disgust and, yes, terror, that he would have to undergo in their company. He had always been a loner, he would rather take his chances alone. Even now, directionless, afraid, there was a certain sense of release, even of mounting excitement, that he had no longer to bear the company nor the responsibility of another human being.

He did not think of Matty. Lying awake beside her while she slept, he realized he could do nothing for her, he had neither the money to give her, nor the necessary time to enlighten her as to her danger. He had no way of helping her to escape from Ettie, to begin a new life. And would she want to go? Throughout the night he had wondered, decided, hardened himself against the idea of caring about her. When he left her it was with one look of pity; by the time he was five miles into the scrub-covered hills, she no longer existed for him.

He was changing, and he did not know that he was changing. The buoyancy of his steps through the small bushes and shrubs and fallen branch litter was as much due to his lost sensibilities as to the chains that had fallen from him. It was as if nothing in this country claimed him, nothing touched him. The past was dead, there was no future, all that existed was now – and he himself. He no longer even indulged in thoughts of death. He had *become* his instinct for survival, there was room for nothing else within him. Nat, Ettie, West and Matty had made sure of that. He would leave nothing of himself for others to claim, nothing for them to recognize, to covet.

He thought once, briefly, of Will Treloar; found he missed the man, the only friend he had ever made away from the tight little community of Killaloe and the boys with whom he had travelled into manhood and, almost, into death. He had a feeling he would see Will again. Realized that he wanted to see the man again, to apologize, to explain his running off . . .

But sure, that was madness. Will would be glad for him, but would expect nothing. He would not see Will again. How could he? For he was *not going back*.

He had been travelling downhill, and stopped on seeing a narrow creek, running between boulders at the foot of the slope. He did not recognize the terrain at all, but had not expected to. He stooped at the water's edge and drank of the cold stream, noticing, as he did so, the strange paw marks in the mud. Unrecognizable. Wallabies? The short, rotund wombats? The savage little creature that looked and sounded like a cross between a dog and a pig, that they called the Tasmanian Devil? He could not remember all the names of the animals here, they were all weird, the most innocuous of them threatening in their very strangeness. None were likely to attack him unless he cornered them, and he planned to keep his distance from anything that lived and moved in this wilderness – but he would have to spend his nights amongst them.

He stood up, looked about him, and went to sit on a flat-topped rock where he could gaze down at the water, and think. He was not going back to Brown's River. So where was he going?

The mainland. The vast continent to his north, separated from this small sister colony by Bass Strait, two hundred miles of water. Aidan knew that much. He must find food, and then he must find the coast, and then a boat – pass himself off as a free man – could one do that, or would one need papers, proof of one's identity? And he realized, suddenly, how impossible it was, why the other convicts had laughed at the various escape plans suggested by some of the more reckless prisoners. He remembered tales of men brought back, as Matty had warned, starving, out of their minds. Or dead. Those who had tried to escape and failed. For the country itself was the

341

killer; the brooding, hostile country that now lay grey-leafed and silent but for the occasional call of a bird, invisible amongst the foliage. The very silence seemed menacing, the hesitant bird calls a warning. Go. You do not belong here. Go away.

He shook his head, refusing to allow his imagination to work upon his mind. He had decisions to make, and they must be made clearly, and without delay.

Hobart lay to the east, he knew this; most of the settled areas of the island were to the east, and north-east. He had only to follow the rising sun, to rest at noon and turn his back on the setting sun, and he would come to civilization, then . . . Then he must take his chances, face the possibility of being recognized, recaptured . . . and what then? Port Arthur, almost certainly; the high security prison on the Tasman Peninsular, a longer period in chains, perhaps a flogging . . . But they would not catch him, they would not! Better death than to live like this for the rest of his life.

He stood up. The sun was only half-way up the sky, and the creek, for a while, at least, ran towards it – east. Aidan started off once more, trying not to think of the hollow rumbling of his stomach. He would think of food later. Now, he must travel as far east as he could, while his strength lasted. Freedom before food. Freedom before anything.

He found he need never stray too far from the creek, for though the waterway meandered a little, it invariably came back to an easterly direction, growing larger as it was joined by other, smaller streams, until it was almost twenty feet across, running brown and sullen between sloping banks. That first night, Aidan slept on a high, flat rock above the creek, lulled to sleep by its music, too exhausted to notice or care about the scufflings and snufflings that continued all night, and the evidence of more paw marks by the water's edge when he awoke the next morning.

As he stooped to splash his face and drink, a wombat on the other bank, upwind of him, and almost blind in the sunlight, waddled its way down to the water for a last drink before retiring for the day into its burrow. It paused and sniffed the surface with its broad, blunt snout, blinked its tiny, myopic eyes, and, as if satisfied, plopped both its fat front paws into the water, and lowered its head to drink. Aidan smiled at the sight of it, sat on his haunches and watched until the animal had had enough, had shaken the water from its face, spraying its dark brown fur with droplets, and padded away up the slope, its sizeable rear end shaking waggishly as it went.

All the morning and into the afternoon, Aidan walked, stooping to drink frequently at the creek's edge. He watched the surrounding

342

scrub for any sign of plants or trees whose berries would provide food, but the small, hard specimens he did find smelt resinous and foreign, and he trusted to his instincts and threw them away from him.

In the afternoon, when he had been walking so long that the whole journey had begun to have a dreamlike quality about it, he saw the clearing. It was across the creek from him; about twelve acres that ran up the slope from the water, and finished in a small brick dwelling with a slab-built kitchen attached, and two timber sheds, all sitting comfortably on top of the rise. Beyond that, he thought, there would be a road, sure. And, one way or the other, a town. But the real objects of his attention were much closer; six large apple trees, well into their twentieth year of growth, spreading their branches picturesquely not far from the water's edge. The house itself was framed by branches dotted with dark red fruit, and the ground around the trunks was littered with windfalls. Aidan pulled back amongst the untamed scrub on his own side of the stream, feeling the warmth of the fading sunlight on his back, watched the trees hungrily, watched the house for signs of life. Nothing stirred. But he could not fool himself, it was too neat, too well-tended, to be abandoned altogether. He pulled further back into the bushes, sat down where he could still have a clear view of the house over a stunted shrub, and waited.

At sundown there was still no sign of life, the kitchen chimney did not smoke, and no lamps appeared within the windows. Aidan considered waiting until complete darkness had fallen, but he was curious, too, to find what road may lie before the cottage, and he would need to see, to decide which way to go.

The setting sun threw a pinkish glow upon the bricks of the house, the grey of the vertical slabs of the kitchen, upon the brown and twisted trunks of the apple trees. He rolled his blanket into a tight cylinder, and held it above his head as he waded into the water. Deeper than he had thought, much deeper, and fast-flowing in the centre. The blanket was saturated, heavy as a stone, but he some-how held it beneath his left arm and swam awkwardly across the short distance of deep water. He arrived dripping, and cold, and walked back upstream to the apple trees already shivering, glancing at the dark and silent house, wringing out his blanket as he walked, cursing his foolhardiness; why did he not wrap it around a rock, throw it across the stream? He was a brainless one, to be sure . . .

Among the windfall apples, now, the sweet smell of the fruit was all around him. He dropped the sodden blanket, bent and picked up a deep cherry-coloured, slightly wrinkled apple, bit into it after only

343

a cursory glance. He ate five of them, three or four bites apiece, and in between, bent to pick up more of the fruit, piling them into his shirt that he held away from his body.

'I've got a gun pointed at you. Don't move, mister.'

The voice came from behind him, from the scrub at the edge of the clearing. He paused, his chest full of fear, his mouth full of apple, the core still held in his right hand, his left supporting the knobbly burden against his stomach. He turned around, slowly.

At first he could see nothing, then the figure separated itself from the trees. He had thought it was a woman's voice, and he was right. A small woman, holding a gigantic and ancient musket to her shoulder with incongruous but chilling confidence. She walked with a pronounced limp, dragging her right foot after her, but such was the lightness of her movements that even then she made almost no sound through the dry grass. 'Been watching you all afternoon, from the kitchen window. Thought you were planning on robbing the house. Were you?' The question was underlined by a threatening movement with the gun.

Aidan swallowed an enormous piece of unmasticated apple, painfully. 'No, ma'am!'

'Too busy stealing my apples. Didn't notice me sneaking round on you. Shovelling 'em into you like a pig you were.'

She fell silent. Aidan waited. Dare he run for it? She would shoot him. Dare he tackle her for possession of the musket? He was at a distance of about twelve feet. She could still shoot him . . .

'There's worms in those apples.'

He blinked, stared at her.

'I got all the best of the fruit up at the house.' Still he stared at her. He did not know how young he looked, how wet, and cold and frightened. He had called her ma'am. 'In a pie,' she added.

But she was no fool. All the way to the house, she kept the gun at an easy angle, and, once inside, she sat him down at the far side of the table, in the corner, where he would be at a disadvantage if he tried to rush her. She placed the gun by the chimneypiece, and lit a lamp.

The bronze light showed a face that had seen too much sun, too much hardship. She could have been forty, or forty-five, but he knew instinctively that she was little over thirty.

'The colony's in a disgusting state, I'm telling you.' She took down plates from a rough dresser against the wall, and opened the meat safe, a wooden frame over which pieces of hessian had been fixed, and from within it brought forth the remains of a leg of mutton. From the cupboard appeared a few cold baked potatoes and the promised apple pie. 'You're the third man this month, stragglers, down-and-outs . . . the government brings you out here and gives you those tickets-of-leave, or calls you a probationer – or have they given up that idea? I can't keep track of what's going on in the Convict Department. And they set you loose to find your own work, make your own way – and the crops bad and there's not enough jobs for the free men who want them. There's my John gone logging up the Huon – it was that or trying his luck shearing on the mainland. Don't sit there, boy, there's your knife and fork, eat, why don't you? The Lord knows when he'll be back – don't bolt your food, you'll throw up and it'll go to waste – if they make a man a convict, let him be a convict, I say. Make some decent roads in this colony, or even better, open up some more land for free settlers. And when a man's no longer a convict – well, let him go. Set him free so he can go back to . . . Where do you come from?'

'County Clare, Ireland.' Through a mouthful of meat.

She gazed at him, nodded. 'An Irishman. No wonder you look such a baby.' He stared at her, but his hunger got the better of him, he continued gnawing as she spoke. 'All the young ones coming here, lately – I've read about it in the Hobart papers, most of them here for stealing food – in the middle of a famine. Suppose you were one of them. You've the eyes of a child. Why were you transported?' He gulped, swallowed, choked. 'Suppose you were stealing a sheep, were you? Or a calf?'

'Sheep, ma'am.' Truthfully enough.

'How old are you?'

'Twenty-five.'

'How long before you get your pardon?'

'I . . . I don't know.'

'There! What a mess! What an ill-run, inconsistent, lop-sided disaster this colony is turning out to be! How typical! You don't know when you'll get your pardon! And do you know why?' She leaned across the table to him, the eyes in the sharp little face glittered, the broad and thin-lipped, rather quizzical mouth turned up a little, 'Because the colony's run by money-grubbing opportunists who are here to make a tidy fortune, then retire to their farms in Surrey and to the devil with the rest of us, who came here to make a living, to stay here. Now isn't that so?'

'I . . . haven't thought much about it . . . '

'Of course it's so! You wait until you're ready to buy land of your own, and see if I'm right.'

He lost three or four of her following sentences because of her words. Land of his own? A farm like this – land of his own . . . He was in an atmosphere of normality here, that's what it was. The thought made sense here in a way it never had when Will Treloar dreamed about freedom and a farm and tried to interest Aidan in the future. But it was before him, now, in this kitchen, in this little woman who was limping about her domain, lighting a fire in the hearth, setting the kettle above it for her strange, yet seemingly accepted visitor. He felt as if he were beginning, somehow; awakening, becoming real. She talked to him like a man, like a person. He realized of a sudden that her life must be desperately lonely.

She had been quiet for some seconds, studying him, now caught the change of expression on his face. 'I've been talking too much.' Her tone was almost apologetic. He denied this, but she smiled. 'Oh, yes, John tells me often that I chatter . . . It's the difficulty of storing up all your thoughts, until you meet another soul. This country can be a lonely place.' She looked at him kindly, 'But no doubt you've discovered that for yourself.'

His thoughts were on his home, and they both understood this. 'Yes, ma'am.'

He was amused by her, but her loquacity and her trusting nature did not make her seem foolish. He realized something in him had appealed to her, down there by the bank. If it had not, she would have sent him on his way. She liked him. The thought warmed him, that she did not see him as an animal to be caged and watched, nor was she wishing to use him, for his strength, as Nat and Ettie had, nor for the brief comfort of his body, as Matty had demanded.

He was shivering in his wet suit, yet she made no offer of a change of clothes, and somehow he did not wish to ask. They drank their tea sitting by the fire, and his clothes steamed.

'I wouldn't come here again,' she was saying. 'If I had my life to live over, I'd still choose my John, but I'd make him stay in England, I would, none of this traipsing around the world just so we can say we *own* the land we're on. Things were settled, back home. You knew who you were, you knew your place in the scheme of things – you always had your family about you. Here . . . Well, John has a sister and brother-in-law in Launceston, at the north of the island, doing very well they are, too, and they need to, with sixteen children. John and I never had children. That's why I'd like to go home. Your family get to be important to you as you grow older, and there are no kids to worry over, to fuss about and fill your time with their comings-and-goings. With your own family you can share things even a husband can't know about. Memories, I mean. What it was like . . . You must have found that, being out here, no one close by that you grew up with . . . '

Thady. Aidan's tired mind was wandering. The last of them. Thady, y' red-haired young balbhan, why did you have to die then? Why couldn't you have fought on?

'Did you have dances, where you came from?'

He dragged his gaze back from the flames to look at her, startled. 'Excuse me, ma'am?'

'Did you have dances? The waltz, the mazurka, the polka – dances like that.'

'No. No, in my town it was the Irish dancing. We'd hold ceilis, and it'd be reels and the *gabhairin bui* and the . . . '

'No *proper* dances? No balls?'

They were not for the likes of us, he thought wryly, remembering the summer dances on the terrace at Tineranna, watching from the shadowed garden with Seamus or Thady, as William Kelly and, later, Devlin, had whirled Anglo-Irish girls in pastel silks round and about . . . 'No, ma'am,' he said.

'I used to dance. We weren't poor, my family. Even when we first arrived here, John and I were doing well. Maybe things were bad everywhere in the world, I don't know. But when we lost our convicts to this probation system in 'forty two, and the harvest was bad two years in a row – it near finished us. Now they say they've finished with the probation system, but who has the money these days to take on ten, twenty convicts the way we did back in the thirties?

'We've sold a lot of the land, the three hundred acres we cleared. Didn't get much for it. We own sixty acres along the creek, here. We'll clear it when we can afford to take on more help.' She stared into the fire for a long moment.

Aidan was exhausted, and was controlling his yawning with difficulty. Yet he was alert enough to contrast this family's hardship with Will Treloar's visions of a fortune to be made in this colony. It was the same wherever one went, Aidan thought dully, to have vision wasn't enough. Hard work wasn't enough. One must see the bad times coming. Some men could do that. Some men made fortunes, while others were ruined. But the good, never the good, the patient.

'I have a gown – it cost as much as a farmworker's wages for half a year. My father bought it for me, for a ball at the manor house. I still have that gown, brought it half-way round the world with me. That's how foolish we women can be sometimes . . . '

She was gazing into the fire, and Aidan was filled with pity for her, and a kind of fear. Would Maura look like this in another fifteen

347

years? The mouth set in permanent lines of grim acceptance, the hands that lay in her lap were rough, and marked with scaly sun spots.

'You may yet be wearing the gown again, ma'am. When your husband comes home, and times improve, there'll be . . . '

She was shaking her head, laughing, 'God bless you, everything they say about the Irish tongue is true!' He was blushing, annoyed with her, now. 'Ah, boy, I'll never fit into that gown again, tiny, frothy, godless little thing that it is – and just as well. Even if I could fit into it, and the pale green of it didn't make my skin look like a newly-tanned piece of pigskin, I won't be limping into a ballroom in this colony or any other, with one leg shortened and stiff as it is. But you've a kind heart, boy, for saying otherwise, knowing that was what I wanted to believe.'

He was puzzled, slightly horrified at her honesty. Why say what she was really thinking? Why mention the bad things, the sad things that always lurked behind their words? They were real enough, the horrible realities of life – who could forget them? Why bring them out, in all their hopelessness, their possible terror? Far better to cloak them in words, beautiful and kind words; it made life more pleasant.

She was leaning forward to him. 'When you live in this country of Australia, boy, you're better off facing up to the truth straight away. Face up to it, and carry on anyway. Don't lie to yourself, and don't lie to others, and save the flattery for the wealthy squatters if you need them for anything, and then use it sparingly, they're no fools. Acknowledge the truth, and know who your friends are, that's what I'd tell you.'

She gazed at him kindly, then leaned back in her chair, easing her leg forward. 'The dray rolled over, coming down Brown's Road. I was trapped under it for two hours until John could get to a farm and get help to lift it off me. The knee never healed. But still, no use crying over things like that, is there?'

She was standing up. 'I'll get you some blankets. You can leave your things by the fire to dry and sleep here until the morning. Just don't tell all your friends about the place. I don't want a whole stream of half-starved Irish landing on the doorstep.'

'No, ma'am.'

He could not believe his good fortune. A bed beneath a roof! A fire! And, undoubtedly, when he awoke, breakfast!

Later, when she had given him the two blankets, he heard her bolt herself into the front section of the house. But he was not bothered by that; to be allowed to sleep within the house at all had been

348

beyond his hopes. He stripped off his clothes and lay in front of the fire, wrapped in the warm, rough blankets.

He woke three times in the night and added more wood to the fire, turning his clothes on a stool before it, and in the morning, when he awoke from his last, exhausted sleep, the clothes were dry.

He dressed quickly, in case she should return and find him half-naked, or worse; and he filled the kettle and placed it over the flames before tidying the room as best he could.

She was pleased to find the kettle singing cheerfully when she entered the room, and she chattered to him as she made an oatmeal porridge, flavoured with cream and sugar. When they had finished, and he knew how many brothers and sisters she had, and the names of all John's sixteen nieces and nephews in Launceston, he dried the dishes as she washed them in a bowl before the fire. He took up his blanket, dry now, and then hesitated. 'Ma'am, if there's any work I can do to help you before I leave – cutting some firewood, perhaps, or . . .'

'No, you'd best be going on to some place that can offer you a permanent job. I'd like to do that, but not the way things are at present. Call back here someday. Maybe in a few months things will be better.'

She walked outside with him, into a crisp, clear day, the winter sun lighting up the green of the grass, the brown of the frost-bitten patches. They walked up the paddock to the top of the driveway, and Aidan saw at last where the house lay.

The crest of the hill continued for about two hundred yards ahead of them, it was transected by a narrow brown road, and beyond this, more meadows, rolling down the slope. Before him, for miles, was a deep, broad valley, green and rich, and dotted with orchards and farmlands, the hills on the far side hung with mist that was even now rising into the heat of the sky. 'What is this place?'

She glanced at him with amusement, 'Don't they tell you anything about this country? This is the Huon Valley – see the river down there?'

Between thick trees that grew down to the water's edge he caught sight of the broad, brown stream, the surface caught the light, and threw it back at him. 'That's the Huon. Some of the richest farming land in the colony, perhaps in the whole of Australia.' She turned to him. 'Come back again. Meet my John. He's a good man, he'll give you good advice on how to make your way.'

His heart ached, suddenly, realizing that this strange English-woman was offering him friendship. 'Thank you kindly, ma'am, I'll be doing that, to be sure.'

'Where are you heading, now?'

He thought quickly, 'Back to Hobart Town, I'm thinking.'

She pointed to the left. 'Hobart's that way – this is the bridle track from the city to Victoria, or Huonville as they're starting to call it – there's a lot of confusion with Victoria the colony – not that it takes much for the mails to go astray in this country. Well . . . Goodbye.'

'Thank you, ma'am. God be with you.'

She looked slightly abashed at this very Irish, very Papist farewell. But she smiled, 'And with you.' And as he turned to walk away, she called, 'What's your name?'

He hesitated, 'O'Brien, ma'am.'

It was only slight, the faltering in her, the faint hurt that he did not trust her with his full name. 'Good luck, O'Brien,' she said.

He travelled in the bush more and more as the houses grew more frequent. He climbed the hills and skirted well around the groups of farm houses at the lower point of Brown's Road. It was slow progress, and he was beginning to be afraid. The lame woman had trusted him, had not asked for his pass, or his ticket of leave. No one else would be so naive, should he be found in like circumstances again.

Once, on a hill overlooking the dirt road upon which he had laboured with the road gang, a dog appeared from nowhere, snarling at him, snapping at his heels. Aidan bent and picked up rocks, pelting them at the animal, but still it came after him. He was swinging at it with a fallen branch, when someone shouted, from down in the gully, 'Beau!' or 'Blue!' the voice called, it was too far away for Aidan to make out the word. But the dog heard, hesitated, stood still; its eyes still on Aidan, yellow, malevolent eyes in a mottled ginger and slate-coloured head.

The voice called again. The dog turned, whined its displeasure at the interruption, and trotted quickly down the hill in the direction of its master.

Aidan went on, hurrying as much as he could over the rough ground, between the thick, snarled bushes. He slept that night in the meagre shelter of a half-burnt-out tree, his back propped up against its charred black inner wall, exposed, now, and affording him a view down the slope and along a section of Brown's Road.

His one blanket was not enough, now. The cold kept him awake, shivering, most of the night. And it was this that allowed him to hear them approach in the morning.

Police. He awoke from a half-doze with the knowledge already in his mind. He could hear the slight sounds of disturbed branches, small stones. Not animals. Too heavy, too many of them; with his body to the ground, he could feel the vibrations. Boots. Heavy boots. He waited only a few seconds, his heart lurching, stomach tightening with terror.

He whirled, over and up to his knee and one foot, had time to see three of them, all of whom he recognized from the station. One of them, smiling, was McCutchen. Behind them, at a distance, was a man in a grey cap, holding, at the end of a rope, the roan-coloured dog, snarling towards Aidan as the guards moved in. Sounds behind him, beside him, strange men in police uniform, guns to their shoulders, confident, impassive.

He would have gone with them quietly if it had not been for McCutchen. Even the police and the other guards were taken aback by the suddenness of the blow. They had turned down the hill, the manacles once more on Aidan's wrists, and McCutchen was suddenly there, at the prisoner's shoulder, and an exhortation to move faster was accompanied by a rough clawing of Aidan's shoulder, and a sharp, heavy blow to his kidneys.

Both hands came around, in his rage, catching the guard full in the middle of his chest – and back, one more blow, though he knew he should stop, even as his fists swung back, and McCutchen's nose cracked under the weight of the Irishman's chains and his hate.

Someone's hands were about his throat, pulling him backwards, blows were striking the backs of his knees until he went down, and only then the pressure on his throat was eased. Someone was shouting, 'Get 'is arms! Get 'is arms!' and above it all, McCutchen or the dog was howling, howling – a heavy weight was on his legs, they were grabbing for his arms, pinning them down, and someone was kicking his ribs, his back, his head . . .

37

He was beaten twice after that. Once on returning to Brown's River Station, just before being flung into the solitary cell, and once by three of McCutchen's friends, guards at the Hobart Gaol. By then he had learnt the difficult lesson of not defending himself, to block the blows only, as best he could, and wait for their hate to expend itself. Not even the most tolerant of the guards would allow one of their number to be bested in a scuffle with a prisoner; it frightened them, threatened their idea of their own status, and they would close ranks to force the miscreant into submission.

He had had no opportunity to say goodbye to Will. In solitary only until nightfall, Aidan was dragged out and thrust into the back of a cart, the chains on his wrists fastened to a ring on the vehicle's side.

A mist had been falling; as the cart climbed the hill to Brown's Road, and turned right, around the bend in the mountain, Aidan could look back at the lights of the station; the bakehouse, the store, the prisoners' barracks, clustered below him in the gloom of the valley. Beyond it, the harbour shone gold-flecked with the light of the half-moon. He was suddenly homesick for Will, Oldfield, O'Dowd . . . He did not want to leave Brown's River Station. And he knew he would not see many of those men again.

Three days after he arrived at the Hobart Gaol, the Medical Officer, Reynolds, examined him in his cell. Aidan's face was still bruised, his kidney area was tender, one rib was cracked. Reynolds, a slow-speaking, laconic man with a broad, droll mouth and thick crop of yellow hair, lost all of his dry banter as the examination progressed.

'Who did this, O'Brien?' Silence. The dark, stocky Irishman with savage, silent eyes, and a mouth set against the pain, refused to speak about the injuries at all. Reynolds persisted, 'You're protecting them, O'Brien, can't you see that? Think of the other prisoners that you'll help save from treatment like this.' Silence. 'Think of your own satisfaction when the bastards are dismissed.' A faint smile to the Irishman's mouth, a grateful glance, for Aidan liked Reynolds, but still he said nothing. The word of a prisoner counted little against that of a guard, who would say, in this case, that all the injuries were inflicted in attempts to prevent the prisoner from escaping . . . And besides, the guards, like McCutchen, had long memories, and he was already marked out from among the other prisoners – the man who had smashed McCutchen's nose. They watched him, hopefully, for further signs of defiance. Aidan, for the first time in his life, began to learn the technique of passivity, the art of patience.

The Superintendent of the gaol visited him, and he was questioned closely about Nat Garson; why they had chosen to escape the way they had, what, or who, was waiting for them in Huonville. But again he kept silent.

The Catholic chaplain visited him, exhorted him to help the authorities as much as possible, stressed that things would go better for him. But he knew he could say nothing of Nat and Ettie. If he

352

did, in order to gain some minor indulgence from the court, there would still be the future to contend with, Nat and Ettie's vengeance frightening him less than the thought of living with the memory of his betrayal of them, for all his life. Better to bear what lay ahead of him.

Again the knowledge that he was alone worked on his courage. Things could get no worse than this, sure. He would keep to himself, see it through, somehow. *They* were out to break him, to make him conform. They were more powerful than he, because they understood the system, and he did not. He must conserve himself, not lash out blindly. He had made mistakes, too many, by trying to fight without thinking of the repercussions. And he had made a mistake, too, in trusting Nat Garson – even, yes, in trusting Will Treloar, because friendship was one more dispersion of energy that should go towards watching, learning, making moves that could be advantageous.

He stood immobile in court, while a tired-looking magistrate studied his case, his crimes. The room was cold, even Aidan's new suit of canary-coloured wool did little to keep out the chill of the room, the dampness that came with the misty rain outside.

Everyone in the court seemed tired. Or perhaps they were ill. The magistrate and the clerk of the court had colds. They sniffed often into handkerchiefs, and the court recorder had a rattley cough that regularly interrupted the proceedings. The energy in the dark-panelled room was at a low ebb. Aidan thought grimly, standing with his manacled hands resting on the railing of the stand, that none of them, not one of them, really wanted to be here. Yet here they were.

' . . . . You are a violent, unthinking brute,' the magistrate said, in a measured, almost bored voice somewhat affected by the congestion in his nose, 'and you will learn that society does not countenance your actions, will not tolerate them.'

Did he have anything to say for himself? 'Five years hard labour at Port Arthur,' the magistrate pronounced into the silence.

And Aidan could bear no more, was leaning forward, shouting.

'Y' miserable old yeller-faced gombeen! Y' shrunken old disappointment! Y' fekkin' old *cuvair* . . . ! *Geochach* . . . ! What d' y' know of hunger and poverty, y' great *leicin*! Y' bourgeois old fart!'

After a shocked silence, the court had erupted – the judge had fallen back with his mouth open, was then hammering for silence, his usually sallow face suffused with rage and embarrassment. 'And two weeks' solitary confinement for contempt of court!'

Guards were trying to hold Aidan, to drag him off. He was waving his powerful chained arms and knocking them back as they grappled with him, roaring, swearing, blaspheming in a rage of furious Irish.

Ettie Harding, at the back of the court, had her white lace handkerchief crammed into her mouth, tears in her eyes, and was rocking back and forth, convulsed with laughter.

The *Lady Franklin* was a newer, more comfortable ship than the *Hyderabad*, and despite the chains, the men were well-treated on the short voyage around the Tasman Peninsula.

The prisoners talked amongst themselves, many knew each other – even Aidan felt he had seen some of the faces from his last detention in Hobart, but he made no sign of recognizing anyone.

'You're O'Brien, aren't you?' a voice from beside him said suddenly.

He did not know the man's face, features small and sharp above a jaw that was broad and heavy. 'Yes. Do I know you?'

'No. But we all know you. You're the dog that ran out on Nat Garson.'

Aidan decided he did not like the man's face. 'That I did not . . .'

'Y' did. He's on the run, now, because of you.'

'What're y' like? He was on the run from the day we escaped . . .'

'Well, you don't know everything, do you? Running off to save your own skin. I got the news through one of the guards. Nat nearly made it, was headed for Huonville, new clothes, food, everything, could have made it – but because you was nabbed round about there they was on the lookout for Nat. Couple of troopers challenged 'im, and 'e ran for it. Made the bush and got away, but they've gone in there with dogs, now. It won't take long before they bring 'im in.'

Others were listening to the conversation, silent disapprobation on every face. He had run out on a mate. Aidan felt his anger rising, looked away and made an effort to control his rage. No more trouble, no more . . .

'My name's Harper, I bin with Nat at Macquarie Harbour and Norfolk Island – we bin through more hell than you can think about. If he dies out there you're for it, O'Brien.' The voice had been thickening with emotion, but when the man struck Aidan across the back of the neck, the pain shooting up into his head, his first reaction was one of shock. He'd said nothing to the man, done nothing! But they were grappling, now, the chains on their wrists doing more damage than the blows of their fists. All around them the men were shouting, cheering, and one or two voices came through clearer than most, 'The guards are coming, y'fools! Stop it! Stop 'em!'

Boots, now, striking their shoulders, blurs of scarlet coats above them, and Aidan, who had been steadily losing the scuffle due to the injuries from his former beatings, was almost glad that the guards had arrived. More shouting, soldiers bellowing for quiet, but the excitement was contagious and it took some time to calm the men.

Aidan turned to look at Harper. The man glowered, but said nothing further.

One more enemy, Aidan thought, then hardened himself against the realization. He had been lucky in that most of the prisoners had been shouting, scuffling, and he had not been singled out by the guards. Harper would bear watching, to be sure, especially if bad news came through about Nat. But he would not allow the man himself to matter. He would not care about the complex and variable gradations of friendships and enmities within Port Arthur. He would put all his energies to surviving the next five years, and gaining his freedom.

Coming ashore at Port Arthur, Aidan gazed around him in wonder. Low, wooded hills surrounded the cove on three sides, and within the circle they and the sea provided the settlement was set out attractively; here the Commandant's house, its broad verandahs overlooking a landscaped garden and small jetty, here the huge three storey brick convict barracks, two hundred feet long by one hundred feet wide. There was a stone church, its steeple rising above well-spaced eighteen-year-old oak trees now losing their dry brown leaves. And there were cottages, stores, a hospital, a turretted watch tower, the stonework and masonry of a superb standard, and numerous timber buildings, each linked by paths and roads through broad stretches of lawn, dotted with ponds and fountains, past shrubs and flower gardens still providing an occasional flash of colour with some late-blooming flowers.

Into the large brick prisoners' barracks, a cell of his own, six feet by seven feet. From the window he could see the harbour, and the low grey promontory of Point Puer, where the boy prisoners, aged from nine to about seventeen, were given a rudimentary education and taught a trade with which they could earn a living when released in Hobart Town. Beyond Point Puer lay the little, wooded island called, one of the returning prisoners had informed Aidan, the Isle of the Dead. It was the burial ground for the settlement. For a few moments Aidan stood at his cell window and contemplated the lonely two acre burial ground. How many convicts had come here – and stayed, their bones interred on the small island and their ambitions, no less real than Aidan's own, buried with them?

But he turned his back on the island, and thereafter, when he looked at the view, he did not allow himself to consider it. It would not claim him. It would not.

'One, two, three, *heave!*' the overseer would roar, and the dozen or so men would lift the giant log to their shoulders, some would step out from beneath, now the log was in place, and those men left holding its weight would set off, down towards the timber yards. From a certain angle only the log and the men's legs were visible, and the log-hauling parties had long ago gained the name of 'centipedes'.

The work was hard, but somehow he found the life here easier to bear. Port Arthur was far better planned than the Brown's River Probation Station; the people who had established this settlement nineteen years before had known what they wanted, and the rigidity of the system, the strict attention to every detail, the monitoring of each moment spent outside his small cell, meant that all Aidan's basic physical requirements were met and there was no real need for him to think at all. There was an established time to rise, to wash himself, to begin eating breakfast, to cease eating breakfast, to begin the march to the timber grounds, and at night, to march back again. He noted, not for the first time, how time passed so much more quickly when one was exhausted. In the timber carrying gangs many men would collapse and need a stay in the large, well-equipped stone hospital. There was a high incidence of heart disease at the settlement, but no sooner was a man designated as no longer fit for the work, than another took his place. Labour was the one resource that Port Arthur had in abundance.

He had hesitated to write to his family, not knowing how to explain that he had had his hopes reversed, and did not feel sure, now, when he would have his ticket-of-leave. Finally, he decided to write anyway, asking them to come as soon as they could, and mentioning the twelve-year period in determined optimism.

For time was passing, and there were even odd, fierce ways of measuring his own progress. He had learnt something from observing Nat Garson – one needed allies. He gave up smoking, and his ration of tobacco became a valued commodity. He talked to the strong, surly loners, the men like he himself had been. He listened hard to their stories, and he remembered details that meant a great deal to them. He won the confidence of a number of these men, slowly, over several months, and Harper, who had been waiting his moment, suddenly found that it was too late; O'Brien seemed always

356

to be surrounded by men as grimly aggressive as himself. He had gained what passed for friendships in the settlement, yet no man was really sure of O'Brien. He was respected, he could be amusing, yet despite his interest in others, he himself gave little or nothing away.

His thoughts were disturbed in October of 1850 by the arrival in Port Arthur of William Smith O'Brien, one of the leaders of the Young Ireland movement whose words had so fired the Currans' and O'Donoghues' political fervour. Aidan had heard of the pathetic attempt to raise the Irish nation to rebellion while he was in Spike Island Prison, awaiting transportation. The call to arms was ill-timed, the leaders ill-prepared, there was no food, no arms to distribute to any volunteers. The rebellion which was not a rebellion finished with one hundred and twenty people, only thirty of whom were armed, finally capitulating and dispersing after a bloodless confrontation with troops on a farm near Ballingarry. That same Ballingarry, in Tipperary, that had witnessed the death of William Kelly. To Aidan it was almost ironic. The Cabbage Patch Rebellion, as it would later be known, was as pointless as William Kelly's death. The failure had come as no surprise to anyone with any knowledge of the horror and despair that stalked the Irish countryside. Aidan had often wondered if the young intellectuals who had tried to raise the country, had any knowledge of what faced the starving cottiers and small farmers; most of the people who had followed them to Ballingarry had done so, Aidan believed, more in the hope of gaining food for themselves and their families. Filled with heroic dreams, blinded by political and military naiveté, the Young Ireland leaders seemed not to have considered these facts.

But their motives had been grand, sure. None could argue with that. And he pitied Smith O'Brien.

He saw him one day. Aidan had cut his arm rather badly on a splintered log that had rolled from the men's grasp, and was being escorted by his overseer to the hospital. As they climbed the road to the large brick building with its classical facade of columns, the overseer pointed out three men coming down the steps. 'Smith O'Brien,' he said. For one, tall, well-built, stood out in civilian clothing. Behind him, fairly close to him, walked two guards. Aidan could hear the prisoner's voice, the Anglicized Dublin accent as he turned to one of the men behind him, 'Do you have to walk up my back, Hamerton? To where should I escape?'

This irritability did not seem to anger Hamerton at all. The three men turned up beside the hospital and headed for the cottage that stood alone behind its high wall, for the political prisoner did not associate with the rest of the felons at Port Arthur. It was a strange punishment meted out by the Crown.

Smith O'Brien walked back to his private gaol leisurely, his hands held behind his back, and would have appeared to be out for a stroll for the pleasures of the spring morning were it not for the two guards following doggedly in his footsteps.

'There!' the overseer said. 'And we think we have troubles. If I have to be a prisoner I'd rather be neglected than be taken so well cared of as that man. Watched night and day, t'would drive a body mad.'

Aidan was consumed with envy when William Smith O'Brien was released from Port Arthur and his cottage prison, persuaded by his influential friends in the colony to accept a parole, a ticket-of-leave, upon his promise not to escape from the colony. He went to live at New Norfolk, where he was joined by his family. Aidan watched from his cell window as the ship carried his fellow countryman out of the penal settlement towards his new life. Aidan himself could eat no dinner that evening. And that night, for the first time in years, he cried, lying on the hard pallet in the dark of his cell, muffling the sounds with his blanket so no one would hear.

In August of 1852, when Aidan had been more than three years at the settlement, there was a change in the position of medical officer, and Milton Reynolds, who had been stationed at the Hobart Town Prisoners Barracks, was appointed to the post. He spoke briefly to Aidan during his first examination of the men, a brief parade before the lines of convicts during muster.

'O'Brien, isn't it?' The mild blue eyes studied him.

'Yes, sir.' Aidan had liked Reynolds, was pleased to be remembered.

'You look fit enough. What work are you doing?'

'Carrying timber, sir.'

Reynolds frowned. 'And how long have you been exercising your intelligence doing that?'

'Three years, sir.'

'I see. But you can read and write, can't you? I seem to remember you reading to the men at Brown's River, during one of the lessons.'

'Yes, sir.'

Reynolds nodded and moved on. For a few weeks after, Aidan thought he might have a change in his duty. Of course he was sentenced to hard labour, but educated men were so rare in settlements such as this, where most of the guards were ex-convicts and very few, even among the free-born, could write or calculate with any real ability. Aidan went over and over the doctor's words, his expression, it had seemed to displease him that Aidan's education was wasted. But perhaps the frown meant only that the medical officer disapproved of a man with education stooping to violence and absconding, as Aidan had done. Perhaps the man despised him for throwing away his opportunities when he had the learning and should know better. A lot of officers had lectured him on this when they had seen his record.

Another three months passed, until October and the sun returned to warm the settlement, turning the grey harbour to blue, and the lawns of the settlement to brilliant green. The flowers, roses, carnations, daisies, anemones, began to show themselves in the neatly-tended borders, and the gardens of the cottages. Aidan, who had laboured through the winter days when the cold skies poured down rain and icy sleet, welcomed the change, the return of the warm weather.

But his work went on the same, his life went on the same. Meal times were the summital moments of his day, the meat and vegetables which he regarded with almost religious solemnity being the only real pleasure between stone cell and deep forest. At the tables there was a rule of silence, and Aidan did not mind. His life became almost like the period of his transportation, when he was locked within himself. But this was different, this was a conscious choice. He was not driven within his own mind. It was a place he chose to be. There was no energy to think, or worry or plan when he was at work, and at night he slept, exhausted, immediately he lay upon his bunk. For him the time was passing quickly.

One morning late in October, no one came for him. All along the line of cells, even as the bell that announced the moment was still ringing, bolts were being drawn back – but the noise drew closer, passed his door, went on. Feet scraped, shuffled, and chains clanked, out into the corridor, marched in time, shuffle shuffle, clank clank, past his door, down the stairs, until there was silence. He waited. This was Port Arthur. There was a purpose. Nothing here was left to chance.

He remembered, suddenly, that today was his birthday. The thought amused him – had they given him a holiday?

Half an hour later, a guard arrived with a bowl of gruel and a piece of bread, the normal breakfast. 'You'll be called for at nine,' the man said. 'The Assistant Superintendent wants to see you.'

The news threw him into a sudden panic, the situation lost any humour it possessed. It couldn't be something to do with Reynolds, that was three months ago, now. Then what? Sure he had kept out of trouble in all this time, even the few threatened skirmishes begun by

359

some of the men working with him had failed to involve him. He had stared at them with the knowledge that he could undoubtedly have broken their heads should he choose, and yet his anger was not flaring as it had done once. Even with Harper on board the *Lady Franklin*, it had been Harper who struck the first blow, it had not been his decision to fight. No, he realized, he did not want to be intruded upon, to have his feelings baited forth from him. He protected them. And so he had kept out of trouble.

Bad news from home. Mother of God, could that be it? The fever had been rife when he had left, and someone had told him only a few weeks ago how bad things were, the fever killing thousands . . . A death in the family . . . Ma. Maura. Thomas – the baby? Liam? Oh, Jaysus, not Liam . . .

He was sick with fear by the time they came for him. 'What is it? Is it news from my family?' But the guards did not know. He had been praying all morning, prayed hard, now, all the way to the Assistant Superintendent's office.

The guards left him at the door, stood outside waiting, and Aidan entered alone, suddenly embarrassed to find himself again within the civilized surroundings of carpets and desk and heavy, comfortable chairs. He removed his cap and touched his forelock to the two men in the room, Davidson, the Assistant Superintendent, and another man seated by the window, a burly character with dark hair and red side-whiskers. Davidson introduced him as McDowell, master builder for the several settlements on the peninsula.

'You can read and write, lad, can ye?' A heavy Scots burr.

Aidan could feel only relief. No disaster! 'Yes, sir,' he breathed.

'Can ye draw?'

Aidan looked perplexed. 'Draw, sir?'

'Not pictures. Plans. C'd ye draw plans?'

'I . . . don't know, sir. I've never done it before.'

'How many years schooling did you have?'

'Six, sir.'

It was Davidson who interjected, 'Six! What cause does a man with six years education have for breaking the law and getting himself sent here?'

'The learning did little good in the Famine, sir.'

Davidson's eyes went down to his desk. The familiar sheet of paper lay there. 'On your record you were designated as a farm labourer, O'Brien. Why a mere labourer? Did you hold a more responsible position before that, and abuse it?'

'No, sir.' His chin came up. 'It was working on the land that pleased me, sir. I was a horse trainer before the Famine, sir.'

McDowell spoke up. 'And your six years' education, did you not learn anything about degrees, angles . . .'

'Geometry?' Aidan smiled, understood. 'Sure, I was very good at that, sir.'

McDowell took a piece of paper from the desk, drew three diagrams with figures upon it. 'Give me the cubic feet in those, find the surface area in that.' He handed the paper to Aidan, tapping the diagrams with the pencil.

The Irishman was suddenly cold with embarrassed fear. It had been so long . . .

'Sit down there.' McDowell gestured to a chair in the corner. 'Take your time.'

What if he couldn't do it? What if he had forgotten? The two men began talking between themselves; the weather, the new shipment of supplies from Hobart Town . . . Aidan's mind was a blank, he felt that the figures and shapes meant nothing . . . But there, that was familiar; an idea formed, a memory surfaced . . . it was coming back to him. Begod, it was simple, sure! He began to feel pleased with himself. He finished the sums, checked them again, cleared his throat, handed the paper to McDowell.

'Ye took long enough,' he growled.

'It's been years, sir.'

The builder ran his eyes over the figures, looked over at Davidson. 'He's right.'

'I don't know.' Davidson was scowling at Aidan. 'You have a history of violence, O'Brien. You might as well know that Doctor Reynolds has recommended you to Mister McDowell for a position, though I have my doubts about your suitability.'

Aidan's heart was lifting, lifting; he could sense McDowell's restlessness, impatience. He had impressed McDowell, he knew. The man had need of him.

'Your record since you came to Port Arthur, however,' Davidson went on, 'is exemplary. The overseers are pleased with you. Not only have you remained calm in the face of several attempts to draw you into arguments,' (did nothing go past the notice of the overseers?) 'but on one occasion you actually prevented a fight from breaking out . . .'

The midday break, two high-pitched English voices being raised unintelligibly close by. He had looked up, roared, 'Shut up, can't you!' his voice too loud, disproportionately so. The two men, the argument caused by strained nerves and exhaustion, lapsed into silence. The overseer had been standing by, watching, had said nothing.

361

'. . . In view of your record over the past three years, if Mister McDowell wishes to take a chance with you . . . ' Davidson continued, while McDowell hurumphed, looked severe but agreeable, 'then you will be reassigned to his office, to work as a draftsman, and whatever other duties Mister McDowell sees fit you train in.

'This makes no difference to your sentence – you will be here for five years, and one violation of the trust we have placed in you will involve your immediate return to the gangs.

'You may go with Mister McDowell now, and he will show you your duties.'

Outside the door, McDowell dismissed the guard, and the two of them walked, almost *strolled*, down towards the harbour. Aidan was confused with the sudden freedom, the day had abruptly taken on an unknown quality – he did not know how he would be spending his time. The mystery of it, the sudden change, had his mind reeling with delight. He tried to concentrate to answer McDowell's questions, on his home, his family, his work at Brown's River, but it was with an automatic courtesy. He looked about at the water, the wheeling gulls, and felt like singing.

'Most of the plans are drawn up in Hobart,' McDowell was saying, 'but there are always changes to be made – and if it's one thing that the Convict Department hates, it's last minute changes. It was all very well when they were designing places like Hobart Town and Port Arthur itself – but I've got to erect buildings and re-furbish buildings and move buildings from one side of this cursed peninsula to another, and they won't always send out some artistic-type architect from Hobart Town. They send plans drawn up in some office in Murray Street and neglect to think that I might have to contend with a rock the size of Malta in the way.'

Aidan was shown the office where he would be working, and shown also over the carpentry shop and the now nearly empty shipyards opposite the Commandant's house, for the great days of ship-building at Port Arthur were over. Once or twice a ship called in for repairs, but the slips were rusting, the stone piers no longer crowded.

Yet on a bench in the shipyard workshop, they were sanding a newly carved spar; the wood was a strange colour, a pale cream-gold. The place was scented with it, a clean, almost aseptic smell that was more than the usual smell of a carpenter's shop. And suddenly he knew. This was Huon pine, brought from the upper reaches of the Huon Valley, one of the last pieces to be carved and fitted to a ship in Port Arthur where once nearly every ship had been made of the

362

prized wood. Aidan put his hand out to the spar, touched the wood; stroked it; it was so fine-grained it felt like silk.

'Ye touch that timber like it was a woman,' McDowell said.

Startled, Aidan's hand came back. McDowell was smiling at him. 'Ye've a feel for timber.'

'No,' Aidan said, 'I've not had much to do with it. Except haul the logs about.'

'That wouldna give you a love for it. No, but ye've a feel for it. I ken you'll learn. I ken you'll be all right.'

38

He sat at a desk most of the day, seated on a stool, copying plans, making up requisition lists, writing letters based on McDowell's scrawled notes, adding up figures, filing bills and receipts. When there was no paperwork to be done, he went down to the carpentry shops, or went with the master builder himself to one of the building sites on the Peninsula, where McDowell would show him how the plans he copied so carefully became reality, and he even worked, at times, with the boat builders themselves. Over the months he learnt to work the steam press; to replace damaged planks; he worked the caulker's mawl, learnt the intricacies of turning mast and spar, the fitting of them upon the floating hulls. He scrambled over the decks and into the rigging of seven vessels in the years following, felt a part of each one, an elation that was overwhelming, and a sense of loss that was almost as overwhelming when a ship that he had helped to repair set her sails once again and glided between the Isle of the Dead and Point Puer, to vanish from sight.

He now slept in one of the large dormitories and moved down to his work with the trades workers after breakfast. It was summer, so work began at five-thirty.

Yet it was more than work to him. It had been so long since he had laboured at anything that taught him new things. Not since the early days of training and racing the Tineranna horses, each animal a challenge, each race or fair something new, exhilarating. He had laboured on at Tineranna long after William Kelly had gone, after the horses had gone, for the love of the land itself. But there had been no challenge there. In the plans that he began to draw under

McDowell's guidance, in the trying of his judgement on the working of the wood beneath his hands, he felt his mind come once again alive, as if part of him had been asleep for years and years. The lessons learnt in the schoolroom with James Thomson came back to him, but clearer now, for he could see how these things could be applied, and he rejoiced when some almost forgotten piece of knowledge turned like a key in his mind as he gazed at McDowell's plans and designs.

The Scotsman told an incredulous Davidson that O'Brien's understanding had staggered him. 'He'd have made a fine engineer or architect – I can't understand where he gained the kind of knowledge he possesses, but the lad comprehends everything I tell him.'

Aidan understood why. He remembered his resentment of James Thomson seldom allowing him more than a brief study of history, Latin, geography. Anything he learnt in depth was by taking the books home to the cottage after school hours. In the schoolroom itself, while Devlin conjugated verbs and learnt the names of the Kings of England by rote, Aidan was given one mathematical problem after another, until he was even outstripping Devlin in his knowledge of arithmetic, geometry, algebra. Devlin did not mind; he learnt his own mathematics under sufferance. Aidan had felt that Thomson had regarded him as inferior, not clever enough to learn more than a little of the other subjects. Now he understood Thomson, and sent up a grateful prayer for the tutor, wherever in the British Isles he might be. For Thomson understood what Aidan, then, could not have comprehended. That a man born in poverty could never make his way upwards by chance, only by calculation. To understand further and deeper than those around him. Thomson had known, had hoped, that Aidan would take up a trade, if he did not follow William Kelly's plan and be articled to a lawyer. And with both these possibilities in mind, Aidan had had, from the beginning, the most practical education possible. His most formative years were spent having the basis for a technical career drummed into his head to what was, for the time, an exceptional standard. Thomson had told nobody. That it was done would be enough. Aidan would learn himself, one day. Let him go to his beloved horses. Thomson had given the boy knowledge. Only life would teach him wisdom.

Now, Aidan began, for the first time, to consider what he would do when he gained his freedom. McDowell was right, he enjoyed working with timber. He could work for a boat builder in Hobart, perhaps; he had heard that they built many fine vessels at Battery Point, and with the knowledge gained from several years here, he

364

might be able to find someone who would employ him. Or there were the timber mills themselves – hadn't the lame woman of the Huon Valley said that her husband was logging Huon pine thereabout? He was glad, when he thought about her, that it had not been her who had turned him in. She would undoubtedly remain in ignorance of him being an escaped convict, and he was glad, too, of that.

He thought it was strange, sometimes, that if he had not been recaptured he would not now be doing what he was doing. While he was not happy, he was almost, for the first time in years, content. It wanted only his freedom, his family, to be complete.

And the certainty came to him as the years passed, that he would not return to Ireland, that he would stay in Australia. Will had been right. This was the New World for both of them.

'They've caught Nat Garson at last. Have you heard that?'

Aidan had seen little of Harper since their arrival in Port Arthur. Occasionally he would whisper jibes at mealtimes, but for the rest, he would keep his distance, waiting, Aidan suspected, for an unguarded moment, and for news of the missing Nat. Now it had come.

Harper kept his eyes on the plate in front of him, and was pushing food on to his fork. He held it close to his mouth, to disguise the fact that he was speaking; there were guards watching the men constantly. 'He's been in the prison hospital in Hobart for months. No wonder – on the run in the bush – through all them winters. He's got lung fever – he's better now, though. He'll be comin' here on the next ship.'

A long silence. Aidan kept chewing the same piece of meat, doggedly. He was angry with Harper for telling him this. Sure it was nothing to him. Nat, with Ettie helping him, had had a better chance of escaping than he had. His patience was beginning to wear thin, he had had enough of Harper and his insinuations . . .

Harper kept chewing, shovelled more meat and potato on to his fork and held this too, close to his mouth. 'If you'd stuck by him, 'e'd have got away. He'll be out to get you, O'Brien, just wait. And I'll help him. Nat's got a lot of friends at Port Arthur.' There was a faint murmur from men opposite Aidan and to the other side of him.

Still he did not speak, though he realized, now, that he was seated amongst enemies. Time and his safe removal from the logging centipedes had dulled his senses, he was no longer as fearful as he had been, all those years ago – was it really five years? – since he had arrived at Port Arthur. His rise in position had caused him to lose touch with most of the men. Many he had known, he realized, had been transferred to Hobart long since.

'Nat'll kill you, O'Brien.'

'Nat can try, Harper.' He finished his meal, and rose to return his plate.

He wondered, that night, if there was anything to be done – but there was not. He would not, now, be transferred from Port Arthur, he felt sure, for transportation from Britain had ceased in 1852, and most long-term prisoners, even from Norfolk Island, were now being transferred to Port Arthur until it came time for their tickets-of-leave. Aidan, too, would undoubtedly complete his sentence here before returning to Hobart Town. It would be strange – he had barely seen the city, but felt there would be many changes. It was no longer the centre of a far-flung penal settlement; the year before, in 1853, Van Diemen's Land ceased, officially, to exist, and the new, free colony of Tasmania came into being. Aidan wondered, wryly, if he would live to see any more of it than Tasman Peninsula, and the Isle of the Dead.

As the weeks passed, the mutterings around him grew stronger, more frequent, and spurred on by Harper, more men, bored with their routine, were becoming interested in the story. Harper told it well. An old lag had escaped, offering to take an inexperienced man with him. And the young dog had bolted, leaving his friend to his fate.

And what a fate. Worse than being captured and flogged. He had been discovered, almost starving, in a squalid and half-derelict shepherd's hut in deep bush. The police had found him when they had been called into the area to investigate growing complaints of sheep stealing and various petty thefts from remote farmhouses. When he had finally been apprehended, he had wounded a policeman by attacking him with a scythe. Already weakened by the severity of his life on the run, he had developed pneumonia when incarcerated once more in Hobart Town Gaol.

This news came through one of the guards at the Port Arthur hospital. Nat had indeed arrived on the next ship, but was too ill to begin work. The Superintendent complained to Hobart that the prisoner should not have been sent. But Hobart declared he had been fit when he left the Hobart Gaol, and thereafter he was the responsibility of Port Arthur.

So weeks went on, and Nat did not appear.

In the meal line one night there was a shuffling in the group of men behind Aidan. As he turned around, he was struck, hard, in the small of the back, and he went down with a cry, the pain exploding into his legs, up his spine, and into his brain. He could only just hear the shouting and the scuffling of feet going on around him.

Three men were questioned and given two days solitary. The guards knew that something was afoot, that it was a matter of retribution, but did not have any proof of who the ringleaders were. This type of vendetta was common at Port Arthur, and many mysterious deaths occurred as a result. In the guards' quarters they began to place bets that O'Brien would not last more than a fortnight after Nat Garson's release from the hospital.

The threats became more frequent. The animosity came at him from every side. It ceased, as the weeks went on, to be a challenge to him, a game. Aidan's nerves were strained by the waiting, the constant pressure of the ill-will, and he did not even understand it. Were they mad? Or was he mad, for not knowing what he had done?

Christmas Day was spent much as any Sunday, with church services in the morning, and an address by the Commandant in the afternoon. But there were extra rations at dinner; and some ladies' club in Hobart Town had sent cakes. Each convict had a thick slice and a glass of rum with which to toast the Queen's health.

Aidan looked around the mess room during the meal, expecting, somehow, to see Nat Garson; and Harper, too, he could see, was beginning to become impatient. Why wasn't Nat released? Was he more ill than they suspected? Aidan did not know whether to hope that Garson was alive or dead. The only difference it seemed to make was whether Nat killed him himself or if his grief-stricken cronies did it for him.

It was towards the end of the evening that there was sudden silence from the end of the room. A hush, broken only by excited whisperings that spread along the tables, replacing the laughter and shouting like the sudden drop in wind before a storm.

From the main doors, Doctor Reynolds was approaching, down the long space between the tables. And beside him walked Nat Garson.

Most of the men in the mess room had either known Nat Garson or known of him. But here there was nothing to remind them of the tales they had been told, or the man they had known. The first feeling that ran about the room was one of disbelief.

Nat's hair was white, receded from a forehead discoloured with sunspots and scabs; the flesh had fallen away from him, leaving the rather long face creased heavily about the mouth and nose, and shadows beneath the flat cheek bones. His shoulders were two points through his shirt, the arms held loosely, slackly by his sides.

367

He walked with a slight limp, his entire left side seemed to be awkward, his left arm swung unnaturally. He moved with his head down and stopped, looked up, only when Harper, as Nat passed, said, hesitantly, 'Nat?'

For a long moment, Garson did not speak, but studied the man, and only slowly did a smile come to his mouth. 'Why, hello, Jack. Are you here?'

'We're . . . all here, Nat. Alf, Jocko Morton . . . we're all here.'

'Ah.' Smiling, nodding, Nat looked up slowly, cast his gaze around the table, found out the men he had known, and greeted them, gently, fondly. But unlike Harper, there was no real concern on the faces of these other men; rather their gazes slid away from Nat as his eyes caught theirs, and they mumbled their greetings and turned a little, looked about, embarrassed, unnerved.

The whole room was put in fear. Not physical fear. It was more subtle, more terrible than that. Garson had walked into their midst not as a legend come to life, but as an embodiment of their own unconscious dread. For the most part these men had long ago given up any real interest in the outside world and its broader issues, politics, social events, the cultivation of any further knowledge than that which they possessed. It was not even a conscious letting go, it was a long spiral down into hopelessness. All they were left with, particularly those on life sentences, was their strength and their cunning. Nat Garson, now, embodied their greatest fear, which was not even death, but almost as certain as death for those who knew in their hearts they were not capable of adapting to the outside world. It was the end result of a life in the prisons, a fate that awaited each of them. They would grow *old*, and perhaps, probably, their spirit would fade also. One lost the will to battle for the petty rewards of prison life, the best bunk, an extra plug of forbidden tobacco. Without one's strength and one's cunning it was a living death. And from the vicious anticipation with which they had waited for Nat's arrival, they were faced with the appalling spectacle of their own future in the defeated grey figure who limped among them, recalling faces from his past.

Aidan was so jolted by the change in Nat that he had no room for apprehension, as the little man moved along the benches to where he sat.

Nat's gaze found Aidan several feet before he reached the Irishman. His eyes lit up and he moved forward quickly, Reynolds at his side, hovering watchfully. Aidan felt the hairs on his neck rise, and wondered if Reynolds was going to allow Garson to attack him there and then. The eyes were wild, Aidan was recognized, a target. The room held its breath.

'O'Brien?'

Aidan stood, climbed over the bench.

'O'Brien?'

''Tis I, Nat.'

'How are you, O'Brien? You all right, boy?'

'Yes, I . . . grand, Nat. And you?'

The eyes burned back into his, unnaturally intense. 'Have you seen Ettie? I bin away a long time, O'Brien. Ettie's all right, is she? I waited, but she never came for me . . . '

'I don't know, Nat . . . '

'Someone in Hobart Gaol told me she'd gone to Melbourne with Jimmy West. Long time ago. She wouldn't do that, would she?'

'I . . . don't know.'

The light went out of Garson's eyes slowly, very slowly. There was something almost uncanny about it, as if his energy was being drained from within. As if Nat had no control over his loss of attention, of focus. His gaze wandered, he looked bewildered, turned to Reynolds. 'I'm tired. C'n we go back, now?'

'Certainly.' And they left, Garson to return to the hospital, and the men in the mess room turned to each other. And the buzz of their shared amazement, their voiced conjectures, grew to a dark, low rumbling.

Aidan's gaze sought Harper's. The man only stared, there was no real expression in his face. Morton, across the table, was talking at him, questioning him, and he dragged his gaze back from Aidan to turn and answer.

Aidan was one of the first to return to his rum and his piece of fruit cake. He felt suddenly light, almost cheerful. Whoever killed him, it would not be Nat Garson. And if the supposed victim could forget his grievances, then perhaps his friends could, also.

The shipyards had long lain abandoned; there was little growth at the settlement and no new buildings were undertaken. Repairs could be done by convict labour, and many free tradesmen, including McDowell himself, decided to leave the settlement. McDowell could not hide his delight. Six years at the settlement had been enough for the Scotsman, he was looking forward to a return to civilization.

Aidan lay awake at night and pondered his own future, wondered if he would be able to provide for Maura and Liam and Clemency.

This had been his eighth Christmas away from home. He had no idea if they were well, did not know if Maura had received his letter, written at Brown's River nearly six years ago. He prayed that she had, that she had written back immediately, that there was a letter from her, somewhere between Killaloe and this far-flung settlement that seemed, to him, to exist at the very edge of the world. He wanted to write to Maura again, to tell her of all that he had learnt here, but first he would wait to see what her reply would be to his suggestion that the family should emigrate. But he was becoming impatient, and even persuaded Milton Reynolds, when he was to go on leave with his family to Hobart, to check that a letter had not gone astray in the circuitous machinery of the Convict Department. But the months went by and no letter came.

When Nat Garson's health improved, he was set to work in the gardens about the settlement. Under the eye of the overseer in charge of the grounds, he and the other invalid and elderly prisoners clipped hedges and pruned bushes, raked the leaves from the lawns, cleared the fountains and ponds; not forced to work hard, but kept busy. Nat rarely spoke, but seemed content. When Aidan passed him on the way to or from the workshop, Nat would look up from his work and call a greeting.

Harper was nonplussed. For Nat to lose his mind was one thing, for him to become friendly with the dog who, in Harper's opinion, had caused his insanity, was the height of unreasonableness. He pondered the problem long and hard, considered the sharpened piece of steel he kept hidden in the hollow of a tree near his work in the large vegetable gardens. He went over his plan to waylay O'Brien in the latrine, the only place where any privacy was available for basic deeds such as murder and the passing of bodily wastes. He would fondle the piece of steel with growing regret. It was hardly worth it; Nat was not burning for revenge, had become increasingly interested in horticulture, much to his friends' disgust. And those who had been righteously outraged on his behalf were left feeling a little foolish. So they did nothing.

With about a hundred of the more well-behaved prisoners, one Sunday afternoon, Aidan was allowed to seat himself on the lawn outside the church and listen as the children of the officers and soldiers gave a concert. Inside, the church was filled with proud parents, men and women who lived in small brick or timber cottages dotted about the settlement, who lived almost normal lives, raising their children in the midst of a thousand violent, desperate men.

The convicts on the lawn, however, were doing a reasonable imitation of piety that day, as the childish voices rose and fell. Once,

370

the minister introduced Emily Reynolds, Doctor Reynolds's daughter, Aidan thought; and a clear young soprano rang out in a hymn, Protestant and foreign, yet the beauty of it touched him.

He began to think of Maura, of Liam and Clemency, of the other children who might be born should Maura join him here. He wondered if she would, remembering that their relationship had never been a warm one. Could they forget their own disappointment with each other by planning their children's futures?

He had been the one to fail her, he admitted to himself. His precipitous marriage, his refusal to leave Tineranna for more profitable employment, the Terryalts' raids, that last black night in Reddan's barn and at the big house – each step he had taken had hurt Maura. Each decision had been made by drawing on the feelings within himself, without considering her at all. And with this realization his perspective shifted. He went over all these events once more, seeing them from Maura's point of view. A series of constant abandonments, betrayals. Things will be different, he promised her in his mind. Trust me and come, things will be different.

The prisoners were half-way back to the barracks before the congregation spilled out the church doors; Aidan heard the children's voices and turned. Saw the officers in their dress uniforms, the women in their best summer prints, small boys in dark suits, and little girls in white muslin dresses with blue or pink sashes. The children ran down the lawns, calling to each other, laughing. He marched on, holding the sight within him, calling it forth, as time went on, whenever his spirits were low.

His spirits plummetted whenever he came in contact with Nat Garson. Not that the little man did anything himself to affect Aidan. It was the sight of his pathetic, shrunken figure and the memories he conjured up. The Englishman had become progressively out of touch with reality. Nat would talk, now, to no one except his flowers, would even rage at them sometimes, as if they were defying him in their refusal to grow the way he wished. There was talk among the officers of having Nat placed among those prisoners classed as lunatics, and separated from the rest of the settlement. But it was a simpleness that marked the change in Nat. His world was bordered by the hundred yards from his cell to the stretch of garden and lawn that was under his particular care. He ate, washed, slept and went to church on Sundays because the obedience to the bells, commands, timetables, had been indelibly impressed upon his mind over the years of his imprisonment. While he could still cope with life in the prisoners' barracks his eccentricities were overlooked. Men left him alone for the most part, even Harper, who of all men found the change in Nat most unnerving; but Nat, muttering to himself, did not notice that he was alone.

The Tuesday after the concert, Aidan passed Nat on the way back from the workshop. The avenue was lined with young oak trees now in their full summer foliage, and between the trunks rose bushes had been planted. Nat was on his knees, his tools around him, digging up the soil around the roots, weeding, and shaking the earth from the weeds with oaths and curses. He looked up at Aidan briefly, and even nodded in recognition, but kept working at the infringing grass seedlings and thistles as if they were a personal danger to him.

Aidan walked on after returning Nat's greeting, but paused a little further on to turn back and watch for a moment. He remembered the night in his bunk at Brown's River when Nat had scurried up to him in the dark to tell him of the plan to escape. The desperation in the voice. *'This is my sixteenth year here, O'Brien! I can't stand it anymore! I can't!'* And he had been right. Aidan could not connect this broken wreck of a man with the strong, malicious little villain who had charged off before him through the scrub, prepared to face possible death from exposure or starvation, willing to gamble his life for his freedom.

Don't let it happen to me. Aidan prayed, God, don't let them break me. Holy Virgin, don't let this happen to me. Give me strength. Let me survive . . .

There were other people on the lawn. Aidan did not become aware of them until Nat did. Afterwards all that happened passed in a blur of images, clear, like a dream can be clear, but unreal, as a dream is unreal.

Nat straightened, stared off along the flower bed, away from Aidan. Reynolds was walking with his two youngest children, a boy, only a toddler, in a white frock, who was crowing to himself, running off away from his father on small, unsure feet. Reynolds called him, took chase, laughing. The girl, thirteen or fourteen years old, her brown hair in long braids, had reached out her hand, was picking a rose.

Aidan knew from the way Nat stood, knew from the set of his shoulders; he had no need to see the man's face to know that it was white, contorted until it was no longer Nat's face. Aidan began to run even as the man bent quickly, had taken up the pitchfork . . .

'No, Nat! No! No, no!' Aidan screamed with his heart, with his mind, with every ounce of his energy that was not involved in running, running, arms out groping at the space – stop him, stop him – crying out to the human in Nat, the man in him, the feeling, thinking being of him.

372

The hurled pitchfork javelined through the air, the child was stumbling backwards, screaming. She fell, the heavy pitchfork landing short of its target, pinning her ankle to the ground. Nat had the sharp-edged trowel, was already running, quarry before him, just before Aidan's groping hands – so close, so close . . .

He caught him and they fell heavily together, the breath knocked out of both of them – but Nat was a fiend, a mad thing, with a strength that took Aidan by surprise. He was fighting for his life before he could fully realize what was happening. They were rolling over and over, crashed against the trunk of an oak tree, half-rose and fell again, Nat's mouth open all the time in a scream, an unending unearthly scream – they were falling, rose bushes tearing at Aidan's face – his eyes were blinded, the pain . . .

The pain was in his side, he choked and could not breathe against it. It was robbing him of breath, of life – but he must not let go, he must not . . . Thorns tearing – can't see, can't . . .

But the newly-turned earth, he could feel it, the warm earth was against his cheek and all was silent, and that was better somehow.

39

He held tight to Maura's hand. He felt if he let go, he would drown, dissolve away. He gazed up at her and tried to tell her what he was feeling, how he had tried to do his best for her. Yet he had been wrong. He knew this now. He would try harder. He would.

But she would go away, leave him. And he was never surprised, only disappointed. 'You're cold! Cold!' he shouted once, and the face that swam before his was not Maura's face at all, but a stranger's, a woman with dark hair, dark eyes, who gazed at him in concern. She had cool hands, her cool hands were on his forehead . . . He asked her who she was, and she told him, but the words meant nothing and he felt her slipping from him. 'Tell my wife I'm here,' he asked her as she blurred and faded. 'Tell my wife I'm here . . .'

They all moved through his dreams, Maura, Anna, his mother, Thomas, Corrie. Sometimes he knew he was dreaming, Doctor Reynolds would be there, real, feeding him some bitter fluid from a small glass, and Aidan knew that all he had just seen had been illusion. He would try, then, to hold on to reality, knew he must be ill, groped for the reason but could not find the will-power or the stamina to keep his thoughts clear, controlled.

The Woman in Black was there, also. But by this time he almost expected to find her. Yet her power was somehow diminished, his visions of her were brief, he was not really frightened, felt almost detached; she was crowded out by the scenes of his childhood. The dead that were not dead to him, the lost who were not lost to him.

He woke in the evening, and the dark-haired woman was sitting on the edge of his bed. There was something different in her smile; she looked quite happy. 'Welcome back, Mister O'Brien . . . '

'Ma'am?'

'I'm Mrs Reynolds. You've been very ill.'

'I . . . feel it.' He tried to smile.

'It's been five days.' At the lack of expression on his face, she added, 'Since it happened. You do remember?'

He tried. A wave of sick fear. 'Nat. Nat Garson. He . . . he went mad. Your daughter . . . ?'

'Emily's foot was protected by her boot, her ankle was bruised only. We have you to thank for her safety. I pity Mister Garson, truly I do – but I cannot see how they can justify his being allowed such freedom when all the time he carried such violence within him. My husband says it's impossible to tell in most circumstances, but . . . '

She appeared too distressed to go on. Aidan noticed the dark circles beneath her eyes, realized all the time he lay ill she and her husband had been nursing him. Five days! He looked about him, and realized with a shock that he was not in the prison hospital. This pretty room must be in Reynolds' own house. He put his hand to his left side, but his movement was jerky with his lack of co-ordination, and he grimaced with the pain that shot through him. The damn garden trowel . . .

And he saw Nat's face, once more, as he had seen it the last time, eyes distended, mouth working, the very essence of madness, the personality of the man gone, submerged by his overpowering rage. The child had nearly died – he himself had nearly died . . .

His mind had only begun to grapple with the reasons that caused the incident. But he was tired, too tired . . .

In the following weeks he had to scold himself in case he became complacent; he was enjoying himself too much, the fuss that the Reynolds family made of him was comforting indeed. The child Emily would read to him, as Margaret Reynolds sat sewing, and the small boy played on the rug by the bed. The Commandant visited

374

him, his cool praise had Aidan feeling disconcerted, embarrassed. It had been over so quickly, had he done anything more than any other man would have done?

Reynolds sat with him of an evening, and they smoked their pipes and talked. From Reynolds, Aidan found that Nat Garson was in the asylum. The little cockney's moods now fluctuated from deep depression to wild rages, and Reynolds could not see that he would ever be cured.

Aidan could not help thinking often of Nat, trying to trace the man he had known at Brown's River, to their final meeting on the deceptively gentle lawn of Port Arthur. Now Nat lay apathetically in his cell in the insane asylum, mumbling to himself and recognizing his gaoler's existence only when an order would break his regimented routine – then the violence within him would erupt and he would attack, not caring for the odds against him. All this Reynolds told Aidan, and he realized the bitter lesson that Nat had taught him.

I'll not lose my reason again, he promised himself. I'll not panic and lose sight of my main objective. I'll not fall into a pattern of days to the extent where I cannot see where the channel of my life is carrying me. I'll not be complacent, ever, because a man's destiny is not all in his own hands – no matter what his reasons, that man beside you may wish to destroy you. And it may come as suddenly as that attack upon the lawn.

And later I must be so much more careful – for until now I've had only my life to lose. Some day I will have so much more. Some day, with money carefully saved, I shall be almost wealthy – begod, I *shall* be wealthy – and I shall have so much more to lose. That must not happen. I must take care of Maura, I have Liam and Clemency to think of. I'll not have them live in poverty – I must leave a legacy for them. Nothing must prevent that, nothing and no one.

The next morning, Emily came to read to him. Margaret Reynolds was busy in the kitchen close by, and Aidan could hear her humming, smell the warm, sweet yeastiness of bread baking, as the childish voice followed the misfortunes of the hero and heroine of Dickens's *Old Curiosity Shop*.

But after reading only a few pages, Emily stopped and looked up from the book upon her knees. She was wearing a blue smock over her dress, and her feet, in black patent boots over black stockings, were crossed on the rung of the chair. In a hushed voice she said, 'Mr O'Brien? Are you a desperado?'

His first reaction was to laugh at the earnestness at which the question was asked. But he controlled himself, and answered with equal gravity, 'No, Emily, I don't think so. Why do you ask?'

She looked disappointed. Ignoring his question she asked, 'Were you a bushranger?'

'No.'

'Oh. What did you do then? You must have done something extremely wicked to be sent here.'

He thought carefully. 'I burnt down a house. It belonged to someone I didn't like.'

'Was *he* a wicked person?'

'Well – I believed so.'

'But still, you shouldn't have burnt his house.'

'No. I realize that now.'

'Do you think you've been punished enough?'

'Oh, I'm sure I have.'

'I want to know, you see, because I want to include you in a letter to Berrima, she's my older sister, she's sixteen, and a great chore to me. She wasn't allowed to come here because she's *impressionable*. I'm not, you see. Well, not as much as Berrima. And it becomes very boring for her, living with Aunt Charlie . . .'

'Who?'

'Uncle Charles and Aunt Charlotte. We don't call either of them Charlie in front of them. Don't tell Mama I call them that.'

'I promise I won't.'

'Uncle and Aunt Charlie are very rich and very strict and have no imaginations. That's what Berrima says. So she said for me to write to her whenever anything exciting happens. She's writing a book, you see. And nearly being killed by a pitchfork is exceptionally exciting, is it not? So I'm writing to tell Berrima all about you. That's why I was hoping you were a bushranger. But we'll have to make do. It's not your fault,' she added kindly.

'Thank you.' He was beginning to enjoy himself. 'Tell me about Berrima – that's a strange name.'

'It's a town near Uncle and Aunt Charlie's property in New South Wales. It means "black swan" in Aboriginal. Papa and Mama were living there when Berrima was born. There's also a prison there,' she added wryly, 'but Papa didn't think we'd be staying long enough in Australia for it to matter. Now we've been here years and years and everyone's heard of Berrima Gaol, and they all think Papa is a trifle eccentric. I was born in Sydney, and Richard – that's the baby – in Hobart. Just think if he'd called us all by the places in which we were born, we'd be Berrima, Sydney and Hobart Reynolds! I'm glad to say, though, it was only a phase on Papa's part.'

376

'And is this Berrima's first novel?'

'Oh, no. Berrima is very literary. That's what you call people who are always scribbling. She draws and paints, too. But she becomes thoroughly ill when she sees prisoners in chains. She ran away from Mama when we first arrived in Hobart Town, and followed a crowd thinking it was a parade, but it was a hanging, and she saw it. She's not feeble in any other way, but she still becomes upset whenever she sees men in chains. And while Uncle and Aunt Charlie are living here in Hobart Town – they travel about to their different houses, you see, they have three, one in Hobart, one in Berrima and one in Melbourne – then *our* Berrima stays with them. I wish Papa was rich, also – I think he deserves to be – but Uncle Charlie is the eldest brother, you see, so he has all the money. It's scarcely fair, is it?'

'No.' Aidan, bewildered, tried to follow this family history.

'Being rather sagacious myself – Papa is always telling me I'm sagacious – I have to take pity on Berrima, even if she is terribly spoilt. So I'm writing to her about my lucky escape, and suggesting she calls it *A Brush With Death*. But I doubt if she'll follow my advice.'

'Sure, why must you send all the exciting details to Berrima? Why don't you keep them and write *A Brush With Death* by yourself?'

She stared at him, and her eyes came alight. 'Oh, but . . . ' she faltered, 'Berrima is the literary one.'

'I've not heard of any rules that says one can't be literary and sagacious, too.'

'Oh . . . ' She squirmed on her seat. 'I could, too, you know. I can tell it much better than Berrima because I was *there*.'

'You were, sure.'

She glanced at the door. 'I can't leave now, Mama said I must read to you.'

'Read to me a little longer, and then tell Mama I'm tired and I'm having a nap.'

'All right. Thank you!' And she returned to *The Old Curiosity Shop*, and for the next ten minutes Kit Nubbles and Little Nell moved through their harrowing adventures at an alarming pace.

He heard progress of Emily's novel regularly as the days went on. He was also privileged to read the young author's letter to Berrima, saying that, 'something very exciting has happened and I very nearly Lost My Life, but I will not tell you now as I am writing my own book about my experience. I will send you a copy when it is Published.'

It brought a rather churlish reply from the more experienced scribe, who claimed that Emily was a selfish little pig and had no pity for her and did she have *any idea* what it was like living with Aunt Charlie? If anything at all exciting had happened, Emily was to write back immediately and explain *everything*, or she would regret it.

Apparently Milton and Margaret had not told their eldest daughter of what had happened, and for the following weeks Aidan enjoyed the politics, strained diplomacy and downright blackmail that went into the sisters' correspondence. He was young again, saw the world, for a while, with Emily and Berrima's naiveity and fearlessness. They knew what they wanted, and they reached out, eagerly, joyfully. They awakened something in him that he had forgotten existed. A sense of optimistic anticipation, of joy in life.

He was almost well, could stand and move about the room, he wondered when he would be ordered to return to the prisoners' barracks and his work at the carpentry shop, and feeling restless, a burden to the household, made up his mind to speak to Milton Reynolds about it.

There was neither the need nor the opportunity. That evening, Reynolds entered Aidan's room, sat down in a chair, and told him he had been with the Commandant. After some delay, the awaited papers had finally arrived on the *Lady Franklin*.

'You're to return to Hobart Town, to work at Everard's boat sheds at Battery Point. McDowell arranged it for you – he said you'd like to work with ships, is that right? I've met Everard – a hard exterior, but he's fair, and his men think highly of him – you'll like the old man.

'By the way, I'll be taking my family back to Hobart in a few weeks – I have enough money saved to go into private practice. We have a house in South Hobart – you're to visit us, O'Brien, I mean that.'

Aidan was staring at him, not daring to hope . . . 'You mean, I've been transferred, an assigned convict . . . '

'No, dear chap – my God, didn't I explain? You've been granted your ticket-of-leave, man! Your ticket-of-leave!'

378

Part 3
MAURA

I gave and I gave and I gave without stinting
On Candlemas Day in the church my heart's minting,
For your eyes' smiling, brighter than corn-ears dew pearlings,
And your mouth's singing, gayer than the dawn talk of starlings.

With wile I'd have won you, with kiss and with wooing,
With wile I'd have won you, with silence and suing.
With wile I'd have won you, when the barley was turning,
But the blade was but sprung when you left me love mourning.

. . . You have made me the jest at the reaping,
The tale of the market, the show for the peeping,
The corn for the flailing of tongues at the threshing,
The hound that the switch of their laughter is lashing.

SEÁN O'CIOLEAN
Translated from the Irish by Sean O'Ciolean by
Fiabard O'Farachain

40

He followed Terrier Adams along South Street, Battery Point. 'Here it is.' The little man stopped at the second house in a terrace of four. Clean red brick outer walls, convict made; white painted window sills – and Mother of God, flowers in the narrow stretch of ground beside the short path from the gate to the front door.

'This is my house?'

'Well, not all to yourself – four of us here. Wonder what we'll call you?'

'Pardon?'

'We've all got nicknames – everyone at Everards. You have a nickname? Guess they call you Paddy, eh?'

'No.' His voice heavy. Once or twice men in prison had attempted to call him Paddy. He did not like it, and often had to fight to persuade them of the strength of his opinion. No one had insisted.

In the end, the men at the shipyard called him The Mick. And strangely enough he did not object. It was easier to bear, given the fact that no man at Everards had the name he was born with. And he would prefer, he thought, to answer to 'Mick' rather than one of the strange names such as were chosen for the other men. In his house, alone, were Terrier Adams, so named because on the few occasions when he could be aroused to anger he went for a man's throat and clung there grimly; The Dragoon, a huge, heavy man who had never undergone military service – he had jumped from a window to avoid capture by police while engaged in forgery, had broken his legs and now walked with a peculiar march-like tread, and Ah Poo, whom Aidan had expected to be Chinese. Instead he found a little Welsh-man with chronic bronchitis, who hawked his phlegm and spat it out, his name a euphemism for the sound that betold his presence everywhere.

At first Aidan found his independence strange, as a ticket-of-leave man he found himself responsible, once more, for his own be-haviour; the regimentation had gone from his life, the bells, the heavy tread of the guards, the bars at the windows – all gone. Instead he rose six days a week at the sound of Terrier's alarm clock, stumbled out of the bedroom that the four shared, into the kitchen-cum-parlour, in the tiny house. They brewed tea and prepared their midday meal before heading off, their tin billys packed with bread and meat or cheese. Up South Street to Hampden Road, down to the bay and the shipyard, while the dawn was just touching the sea between the two arms of land that embraced the Derwent estuary.

The men at Everards were rough, mostly ticket-of-leave men or assigned convicts, but not hardened types such as he had known in the prisons. Many of them had been quite happy to have been transported here, regarding Van Diemen's Land as the beginning of a new life; once off the stinking ships, they had never known any life but that of a probationer on public works, or an assigned servant. For those who, until then, had known only a life of semi-starvation in city slums, and then the teeming hulks and prisons of Britain, the small wages and the good food and gentle climate of Hobart Town represented the best time of their lives. '*Home?*' echoed Terrier once, by the fire in the kitchen, when Aidan had professed home-sickness, 'Home? for God's sake – *why?*'

And Aidan thought hard, and the periods of homesickness changed to the more definite longing for his family. He wrote again to Maura, telling her of the Reynolds family and his transfer to Hobart; and he wrote a separate letter to his brother, knowing that if he could persuade Thomas to emigrate then his mother would come also.

'Such ships as we are building here,' he wrote to his brother. 'Cutters, ketches and schooners, two and three masted – to see them in the harbour here would swell your fisherman's heart to bursting. All along the Point, each week sees a new boat or ship launched.

'Never would I have believed that I could love the water; sure I thought often times you were mad to bucket about in your little boat on the river. But here it is different. To *make* something, Thomas. To see it grow beneath your hands, to turn the wood to a thing that is almost alive on the sea.'

He'll think I'm turning poet, sure, Aidan thought, embarrassed when he read the paragraph back. He took the precious sheet of paper, and almost crumpled it, but stopped, shrugged, and wrote on with a grim smile;

'You must bring Ma and Maura and the children. You *must* come, and you will see, and know for yourself.'

He knew it would take months before a letter came back and probably many more months before there was enough money to bring his entire family to the colony. He curbed his impatience by throwing himself into his work, into learning as much as possible, and the weeks passed quickly. He lived with a hope, a confidence, that he had never felt before, and it reflected on his attitude towards his work and his fellow workers. Milton Reynolds checked with Everard, the master boat builder, a dry salty little herring of a man, who was as impressed with Aidan as McDowell had been.

A month after Aidan left Port Arthur, Milton Reynolds wrote to him at the cottage, inviting him to dinner on the following Sunday.

Aidan had contemplated the letter for an hour. Since arriving in Hobart, he had mixed with free settlers, shopkeepers, neighbours, clients of Everard's, and he had become aware of the suspicion and contempt with which most immigrants treated ex-convicts. Even those who were doing well for themselves, who preferred to be called emancipists to differentiate between themselves and those who remained in the lower dregs of the community, close to the threat of imprisonment once more.

So Aidan's eagerness to continue his friendship with the Reynolds family was fading a little now he knew something of society's attitude towards men such as himself. Reynolds would definitely be risking the disapprobation of his peers by having Aidan in his house. 'Give the man a few guineas,' he could almost hear the Hobart Town lawyers and doctors saying. 'That should recompense him sufficiently. He'd prefer to drink a few guineas' worth at the tavern, old boy, than sit stiff-necked at your dinner table.'

Not that Reynolds would take that kind of advice. The man was kindness itself. But the invitation was issued primarily from gratitude. Why, Aidan did not even possess a suit of clothes other than the one he went to work in. How could he, dressed as he was, face an evening in the Reynolds' home, with perhaps some of their other friends, free, middle-class friends, present as well?

He wrote a letter to the Medical Officer, and told him that he would be working on Everard's accounts that Sunday. He hoped it was not too obvious a lie. It was the only excuse he could think of; to say that he was ill would bring Reynolds post-haste.

There were some misgivings as he dropped the letter in the post box. But sure there was no choice left to him. One day, perhaps, when he was free, when he had a better suit of clothes, he would visit the Reynolds. But he would not be beholden to them now. He would not have them ashamed of him.

Terrier Adams brought a woman home with him that Saturday night. Both Terrier and The Dragoon had had their tickets-of-leave for some three years, and possessed more contacts and consequently a more interesting social life than either Aidan or Ah Poo.

'Even so,' muttered Ah Poo to Aidan and The Dragoon as Terrier and the lady, a faded and over-blown flash of brown teeth and crumpled yellow taffeta, vanished into the bedroom, 'I dunno where he found her.'

Aidan was tired, would have liked to go to bed, but with only one bedroom in the house, all three remaining residents grudgingly respected Terrier's right to his infrequent recreation, and they sat in uneasy idleness by the fire until well past midnight.

'Shall we try the taverns?' Ah Poo suggested. 'They say the Barley Sheaf is a fine place for drinking these days.'

'Nah. Reveille at nine tomorrer. Remember that widow I met at the Bonaparte's Arms? She's asked me to drop by sometime, got a little farm at Glenorchy. So I'm going on manoeuvres meself in the morning.' The Dragoon had long ago found that the only way to cope with his unasked-for nickname was to take the joke further, and he peppered his conversation with as many military terms as he knew. It had reached the stage when Terrier would remark that, 'To 'ear 'im talk you'd swear 'e was Wellington's adjootant.'

Ah Poo laughed, now, at The Dragoon, then spat into the fire, 'Lucky devil,' he said, and turned hopefully to Aidan.

'No, we'd best stay home,' he said. 'It's late.'

None of the men in the cottage seemed to know of Aidan's association with Nat Garson and Ettie Harding. Those men at Everard's who might have read the report of the Brown's River escape in the newspaper and linked Aidan to the event, were wary enough of him not to mention it. In the circle they moved in, a man's past was his own concern. So Aidan was able casually to probe about Ettie Harding and Jimmy West. They had gone to Victoria, Ah Poo asserted, and it was not known when they would come back. Here The Dragoon interrupted. 'You should see the lass that's running the Barley Sheaf now.' His large bony face came alive with the thought. 'Ettie's daughter, or niece or somethink. A fine girl. Wot a bosom!'

'Used to be such a little mouse, she did . . .' Ah Poo said.

'But she's come inter her own, now Ettie's not about. Half of Hobart's in the bar of the Barley Sheaf these days, and it's not just for the rum or the ale, I can tell you – though she don't water it down like Ettie did. A lot of 'em come to look at Matty. And some do more than look.' The Dragoon winked, 'But only the few. She's choosy, is Matty.'

Matty. He did not mention that he knew her. He could not understand why her name should affect him, but it did. They had lain together in a tumbled-down barn, out of loneliness and pity for each other. Yet the memory of her body remained with him. In his sleep, he dreamed more of Matty than of Maura, his wife. And he

384

would wake in the night and bring his body silently to a point of release, and afterwards almost cry with his loneliness.

Should he go to the Barley Sheaf? Should he? He knew that he wanted her body only, and that was wrong, was unfair. He was married, could offer her nothing. And there had been that hardness to her, a hardness even he himself did not possess, that would always prevent him trusting her or opening his heart to her. No. Matty belonged in his past. Soon Maura would be with him, and he would no longer dream of women with fair hair and brown arms and full breasts. No. With Maura he would forget that.

He worked late one evening at the beginning of August, so he was alone when he left the shipyard and walked up the narrow, mist-hung streets of Battery Point, the gas light throwing yellow patches of light upon the black and glossy cobblestones, slippery underfoot.

There were sounds of laughter and loud talk coming from the cottage; sounds that ceased abruptly with his hand upon the latch and the protesting squeak as the door opened. He stood there, conscious that there had been a sudden burst of activity just before he entered. The Dragoon had just straightened, turned a poker face towards him, a face that had only now been laughing, Aidan had heard him. He surveyed them all, Ah Poo, making a great show of bending to stoke the fire, and Terrier, rocking on the back legs of his chair. 'Good evenin',' Terrier said.

''Evening. What's happening here?'

'What's happening? Nothing. Dinner, you mean?' Ah Poo grinned, turned and spat into the fire, and smiled brightly back at Aidan. The Welshman's front teeth were missing, an accident that greatly aided his aim, he claimed. 'There's no dinner tonight. We're going out to dine. We've been invited.'

Aidan sensed rather than heard the presence behind the door; he glared at Ah Poo, then stepped aside quickly, shutting the door after him, facing the hiding figure.

Will Treloar stood there, mouth fixed in a comic expression of suppressed laughter. But on seeing Aidan's shocked expression the laughter burst from him, he stepped forward, lifted the Irishman off his feet, and swung him around the room.

'Leggo, y' great eejit!' Aidan gasped as his ribs bent within the Cornishman's exuberant grasp, 'Leggo, damn' y'!'

They talked over the top of one another while the other men took up their coats and Ah Poo placed the screen before the fire. Then out into the night, towards a small tavern in Cromwell Street that Terrier recommended.

They sauntered along Hampden Road, Aidan and Will slightly behind the others, talking of the changes the past seven years had brought them.

'I've had my ticket-of-leave four years, now. I'm working down on the docks – hate it, too – hate living in the town. But the money's fair, and I'm that glad to be out of prison grey.

'Oh, but I've better news than that. A letter has come from my Sarah. She says she's sailing on the *Tasman*. She'd have left afore now. I been to see the shipping office. She'll be here in another two months, Aidan!'

The Irishman's heart was gladdened for his friend. He placed a hand on Will's shoulder and said, ''Tis glad I am for you, boyo – fierce glad.'

'And you?' Will, sensitive, turned his own fortunate story aside for the moment. 'Will you press for an unconditional pardon, and return to Ireland?'

'No. I've written to my family and asked them to join me here.' And still it hurt, to admit it openly: a defection, a betrayal of Killaloe, a way of life, his heritage. 'No, I want more of life than Ireland can give me.'

They ate and drank and laughed together until two in the morning, at the tavern in Cromwell Street. It made a great hole in their wages, but none of them begrudged it, least of all Will. Having made few friends amongst the hard-drinking wharf labourers, he was pleased to find himself at home with the ill-assorted foursome from South Street. There was a seriousness, a quiet ambition, that marked each of them, and that night became the first of many that the five would share. The nights in taverns were few, for all were saving their money. Most nights Will would call at the cottage, and the five would share a dinner of mutton and potatoes, and smoke, and argue and talk of their plans for the future.

The subject of the gold discoveries on the mainland occupied a lot of their conversation; yet they were cautious, each of them, none had any plans, just yet, to pack up and try their luck 'across the Strait'.

'Look what happened in California,' The Dragoon said soberly, during a dinner at the Bonaparte Arms a month after Will had entered their lives. 'Fortunes were made over there, all right, but more spirits were broken and good men ruined.'

'Only if they were careless.' Terrier was the one most optimistic about the rushes. 'If you went with enough money to keep you – if you made sure you didn't go into debt . . . I dunno – I think it'd be worth goin' just to try your luck. It's the fools who go ill-prepared, with little or no equipment, expecting to pick up nuggets from the streets – they're the ones who'll fail.'

It was during this speech that Aidan looked up, idly, towards the door that led to the main hall of the inn. There the stairs wound up towards the first floor and the rooms available for rent. Aidan stared. A man and woman were receiving a key from the innkeeper, and a servant was carrying a small trunk up the stairs. They were a respectable couple, neat in dark, conservative clothing. The woman's face beneath the dark straw bonnet had looked familiar when for a second she had glanced towards the dining room; the walk, as she headed towards the stairs, was halting, awkward. It was the lame woman of the Huon Valley.

Aidan rose from the table, and had crossed the room into the hall and was standing in front of her before he had quite realized that he had moved. 'Ma'am? Excuse me, ma'am – I'm Aidan O'Brien – you wouldn't remember me . . .'

She stared at him, then, 'A-ah.' The eyes crinkled at the corners, 'Yes, I do. The man who was stealing my apples. A few years ago, now, isn't it?' She turned to the narrow-shouldered, craggy-faced man beside her, 'John, you remember me telling you about this young man, don't you?'

John glared at Aidan, studied him for a moment, and grunted. He had the thin, pale face of a man whose health was not good.

'Forgive me for addressing y'r wife, sir, but she was very kind to me when I needed help.' He turned back to the woman, 'I wanted to say thank you, ma'am.'

He would have turned away, but the man said, 'You wouldn't be looking for work, would you, young fellow? With half the working population going to the mainland to chase gold, I'm short of a rousabout for the farm.'

And only in the face of this offer to return to the land, did Aidan realize that he was happy at Everard's. 'Well, sir, I'm working at one of the shipyards here at Battery Point, but . . .' He suddenly thought of Will. 'But I have a friend, a fine worker, a country man from Cornwall, I could introduce him to you, Mister . . .?'

'Frazer.' said John Frazer, and turned to his wife. 'I'll take you upstairs, my dear, then return to meet this man O'Brien suggests.'

Aidan could barely contain his excitement when he returned to the four men, and explained hurriedly to Will about the Frazer's offer.

'A house,' Frazer said, after he had been seated, and had questioned Will about his history,'small enough, two rooms, plus the kitchen.' He turned to Aidan. 'It's the old house that you'd remember. We've built a bigger place since, have some more land, now, too.' He turned back to Will. 'It means you'll have some place to bring your wife. Perhaps she would like to earn some extra money, too, by helping Mrs Frazer in the house occasionally.'

For Will it sounded perfect. The description of the country filled him with delight; the idea of a house for his Sarah was the final touch.

In their excitement at Will's good fortune, they did not go directly home, but went on to two more taverns; Aidan and Will, less accustomed to the harsh liquor of the colony than the more experienced trio from South Street, followed their lead about Hobart Town in a happy blur. There were uncomfortable moments when troopers entered the taverns, but the constables were bored, or cold, or looking idly for some man in particular, for they simply eyed each man in the crowd balefully and drifted out again.

Once, in the third tavern, Aidan thought he saw someone he knew. Someone he knew and didn't like. It bothered him. When he looked again, peering through the smoky haze, the figure had gone. Jimmy West. Jaysus-Mary-and-Joseph, that's who it had been. He stood and looked about – but no, the man had gone.

'Whatsa matter?' Will asked, tugging at Aidan's coat.

'Thought I saw a man I knew.' He sat and leaned across to The Dragoon. 'What tavern's this? Not the Barley Sheaf, is it?'

'Nah!'

Ah Poo intercepted, 'You wanta go t' the Barley Sheaf? You wanna go there?'

'No, no . . . sure I just wondered.'

They were careless that night, buoyed up with good will and several bottles of rum, much more than they were used to drinking. When they turned into Hampden Road and heard the footsteps behind them, they were not unduly concerned. The Dragoon turned, and noticed the six or seven men moving casually along at some distance behind them. Will was talking of his new position, asking Aidan for details of the farm, the countryside, of Mrs Frazer's personality. 'Would she be a good mistress? Would my Sarah be happy working for her do 'ee think?'

Aidan answered as best he could, but even he, at this stage, was becoming conscious that the footsteps behind them were not as casual as they had at first seemed. Indeed, the pace appeared to have quickened ever so slightly.

'Boys?' The Dragoon spoke. 'I fear we're about to be called upon for active service.'

'What're you talking about?' Ah Poo, who was a little hard of hearing, was the last to notice that they were being followed.

388

'I think,' The Dragoon explained, 'we've fallen in with some footpads.'

Each of them stiffened, the hairs on the backs of their necks standing up. All glanced behind them. The seven men were walking purposefully, now, their eyes intent on the five companions; they had dropped any pretence at casualness.

'Any weapons?' The Dragoon asked nonchalantly. All answered in the negative. They walked on more quickly, avoiding the desire to run. The Dragoon could not, and none of them considered leaving him to dash for it. They turned into South Street. There The Dragoon propped, took hold of the picket fence that protected one of the small gardens, and yanked. The three foot long piece of wood came loose in his grasp. He handed it to Terrier, and pulled out another for himself. The others were quick to follow him, and picket after picket came loose with a squeak of reluctant nails. Within the house a curtain moved, twitched, Aidan saw it. But no sound came from within. No one in Hobart Town would rush out on to the doorstep at such a time, beatings and robberies were too frequent, the men who prowled the streets after dark too well armed and sinister of purpose to confront openly.

The five waited, tensely, their weapons held ready.

Their pursuers swung about the corner, almost running now, slid to a halt on seeing they were expected – but attacked nevertheless.

Aidan missed with his first blow – the man's hand came up and something hard struck Aidan's arm – he yelped and dodged back. His assailant held a short piece of metal pipe in one hand. Even as Aidan watched, while his friends were roaring, punching, bashing, falling, attacking, all around him, the man before him had pulled a knife, lunged forward with a growl.

It was a lucky hit. Terrier, who had once watched a cricket match in London, said that Aidan's swing would have won him a place on a top British team. He brought the picket down and across to the left with all his weight behind it, feeling the wood crack even as the man's forearm splintered. The cry of pain and rage came later, seconds later, filling the street and the silent village – lights sprang up all over South Street and across in Hampden Road; Battery Point awoke, opened its windows, murmured questions to the night.

The two camps stepped back to survey each other, then the seven glanced about the street now coming to life, and backed off. They cast looks at each other, then turned and ran off, the sound of their boots on the cobblestones sending staccato, hammering echoes up between the houses.

The five limped home, comparing injuries as they went. Terrier had had to spit out one of his lower front teeth, his lip was bleeding and already beginning to swell; Will had caught a blow to his ribs and had difficulty breathing; both The Dragoon and Ah Poo were bleeding slightly from their foreheads, and Aidan nursed his bruised arm, unable to move it, feeling it beginning to swell in his grasp.

Yet there were no broken bones, nothing seriously wrong with any of them. 'Lucky, eh? We showed them,' Ah Poo muttered, holding a bloodied handkerchief to his face and hawking into the gutter with satisfaction.

Will stayed the night at the cottage in South Street; in the morning he helped the men explain to the irate neighbour, and lent a hand to replace the pickets upon the fence before heading off to his own work.

Aidan had his suspicions about the reasons behind the attack; and it was that evening that he found out for certain, for when he finished work and headed out the shipyard gates with his three friends, Matty was waiting for him.

The light blue eyes appraised him as he hesitated, and walked towards her. She was the same, yet not the same. Her face had lost some of its plumpness and was a woman's face, the bones strong but well-moulded. Although her skin was pale, it was perfect, she had no need of the faint touch of rouge that she had applied to her cheeks. She wore a dark blue cloak over a striped mauve and blue silk gown that was almost too fine for day wear. The bonnet, however, the same dark blue of the cloak, made her appear conservative enough. But there was a suppressed excitement about her, an eagerness in her face that he had not seen before. Her eyes ran over him, and she smiled – a confident smile.

Some of the men had been whistling or calling to her, as they came off-duty – some recognized her and addressed her by name. Even Terrier began dancing a little, showing off, and called, 'G'day, Matty darlin'! Goin' my way, love?' Until Aidan had begun to move towards her. 'You know 'er?' he hissed. 'Hey, Mick – you know 'er?'

Aidan said merely, 'I'll see you at home,' and walked across the road to stand beside the girl. Terrier, Ah Poo and The Dragoon gazed at each other, then sauntered off up the hill, each man determining to question Aidan later. Other men, acquainted with Aidan's temper, ceased their teasing and strolled away with feigned carelessness.

A thin wind was blowing off the harbour, the glossy blonde side-ringlets beneath her bonnet danced. Aidan stared at her, feeling awkward and embarrassed. It was as if her knowing smile told him that she knew of all his dreams of her over the past seven years.

'I had to come.' She spoke first, and he was thankful; thankful, too, that there was no time for formalities, the silences in which their shared past and its discomfiting memories would surely drown them. 'I had to come to tell you. It was Jimmy West's doing. He saw you at the tavern and sent some of his friends after you. Oh, he hates you like poison, Aidan, him and Ettie both! You've got to be careful.'

He gazed at her, only barely comprehending. 'I thought they'd gone to Melbourne . . .'

'They did. They came back a week ago. They . . .'

More men were coming from Everard's and along the street from the wharves and warehouses and other shipyards. They stared at Matty as they passed. 'Look,' she said, 'walk with me – if it gets back to them that I've been seen talking to you Ettie'll kill me.'

They began walking, and because there were people upon the street with them, Matty kept to safe subjects. She asked how he had returned from Port Arthur so soon and listened as he recounted his story. But only half his concentration was involved; the innermost part of him was reeling with the thought that West and Ettie Harding hated him so much that they would have him attacked amongst four of his friends – and with the fact that Matty was beside him.

Her hands were demurely beneath her cape, the faint perfume of her floated up to him every now and then. Before, she had been pretty, now she was beautiful. She kept glancing up at him, and even if he could forget what it had been like, their brief and desperate union, the look in her eyes was willing him to remember.

Things had been well for her, she said, as they passed South Street. (A while further, he thought, not willing to admit he did not want to lose sight of her.) The manager of Ettie's tavern had proved incompetent and Matty had virtually taken over the running of the place. 'So when Ettie came back, only last week it was, she saw I had my uses after all – I'm much better at figure work than she is for a start, I do all the accounts now. She's as poisonous an old bitch as she ever was, but she pays me well. She can't afford not to, particularly now, with everyone headed for the goldfields.'

'Matty?' He brought her, and himself, reluctantly back to the main problem. 'I don't understand about Ettie and West. It angered them that I left the hut as I did – I can understand that. But the hut was never discovered. Sure that'd convince them that I never told the police. I wanted to go on alone, did you tell them that? Didn't they understand?'

'Oh, they did – or, Ettie did. Jimmy just went along with Ettie's opinions, as always. It was after that, when Nat panicked and ran from the traps at Huonville. The police couldn't find him, but neither could Ettie. She started thinking then, that if you hadn't left Nat, he'd have been able to bluff the police – with you there, he wouldn't have lost his nerve the way he did. She had months and months to get to hate you, Aidan. She'd lost Nat and she had to blame someone.'

'She hates me enough to kill me? Was that what they were trying to do last night?'

'I don't know. I heard Jimmy saying yesterday that you're never alone, always with those other three.'

Her eyes were on the ground, she was silent a moment, then looked up suddenly. 'Aidan, can't you leave? If I get you some money, will you try to escape? I can get you on a ship to the mainland – I ain't got much money, but it'll get you that far.'

'I'll not run away from the likes of them, Matty. Besides, I've sent for my wife and children – I have to stay here and build a future for them.'

'It won't be much of a future if you're dead.'

Her mouth was a tight line. He did not understand the expression on her face, could not know the jealousy that consumed her. For he had forgotten her, this was obvious. He was not to know that she had not forgotten him, indeed no. She had been thinking of him so very often in the time since the escape. The narrowness of her life, the strictures of it, the sameness of her days, gave her immature imagination ample scope with her dreams; she embroidered a character for him, to the end of her days she would believe that he was the one man who understood her totally. And without her being aware of it, the very fact that Ettie Harding hated Aidan, made him that much more attractive to her.

'But why?' he was saying. 'She has to be mad! Nat Garson – didn't he take the same chances that I did? There were no guarantees that either of us would come out of there alive . . .'

'It doesn't matter now!' she said in exasperation, 'Why do you have to try to *understand*? There ain't nothing to understand. Ettie is Ettie. When she hates someone, she wants to destroy them. Haven't I known her nearly all my life? And she's no different to a lot of people. Spend all your time questioning, Aidan, and they'll be able to trick you, the people like Ettie and Nat Garson. They live their whole lives waiting to gain an edge over somebody else. They don't ask "why", they simply want, and they take.'

Her voice and face were suddenly hard. She was not looking at him, but before her, lost in nightmare memories that did not have to

392

be told in order to chill him. There was something about this girl that almost frightened him. The callousness, the bitterness within her.

'Well . . . I'm grateful to you for warning me . . .'

'I worry about you.' She was gazing fully at him now, had stopped walking, so he was forced to stop also. 'I've been worried about you all this time. I care about you. See?'

He was taken by surprise, both by the vehemence of her tone, and by the nearness of her, for she had stepped very close to him, their bodies were almost touching. He realized she wanted him to speak, and floundered about in his mind for something to say . . .

But Matty was studying his face, whispering, 'You'll come home with me, won't you? I've wanted to come to you all this time, but I was too angry with you. You knew where the inn was, but you never came looking for me. I've waited all this time, ever since they let you out of Port Arthur, and you never came once. I hated you, then.'

There was hatred on her face even now. And desire. They were mingled. Aidan stood before the nakedness of her feelings and felt something like dismay, even as his body was responding to her. He wanted her, he knew he would have her. But, dear God, what did she want with him?

He was a bedraggled-looking ex-convict, in a threadbare suit that did not really fit him, with no money with which to amuse her. There were men in this town, he knew, coarse, handsome, laughing young men who were free, and rich, and who would take a woman like Matty and give her whatever she desired. They would laugh at the same things, skim along the surface of life, with fine wine and fine clothes as long as the money lasted. Aidan was haunted by his past, he did not laugh often, and to spend time in sheer enjoyment had been so remote from him in the years of the Famine and his imprisonment that even his occasional longing for an idle existence filled him with a kind of guilt.

Yet that shallow, laughter-filled life was what Matty desired, was all she had been accustomed to. It was obvious in the expensive, over-trimmed dress, in the precision of her curls, the subtle rouge upon her cheeks and lips, and, most of all, in the boldness of the blue eyes.

Even while Aidan wondered about her motives, Matty knew she had made the right choice. She had forgotten how good-looking he was, the pride of his walk, the strength of his shoulders. It did not matter to her that he had a wife and children. So many of the convicts left families behind in Britain. But why should he send for them? Why not ask a friend to fabricate a story that his wife was dead, as so many of the lags did, so they could marry again here in the colony? What sense was there in dragging some shrivelled little Irishwoman, old before her time, no doubt, all the way to Tasmania? She'd die within a few years if she didn't die on the voyage. Matty smiled grimly. Irishwomen didn't adapt well to the colony. She'd seen them in the streets, with a dozen children in tow, drained, made ill with child-bearing – had heard the Irishmen in the tavern complaining that their women were homesick, couldn't take the dry heat of the summers, the coarseness, the 'godlessness' of this raw new country. Let her stay where she is, Matty thought bitterly. He's changed, anyway. He'll never be the same man as he was when he was in Ireland.

But he was the right kind of man for her. A good man, she had decided, that night in the barn on Mountain River, and a tough man, resilient. The kind of man who would eventually win some respectability, who would take care of her when she was older. For she had seen Ettie attempting to flirt with some man who took her fancy, had seen the older woman's humiliation when the man had turned to one of the younger women in the tavern. Surely, Matty had decided at a very early age, there was nothing worse than growing old. Unless one was respectable. And rich. For that she needed a man who was capable of carving out a fortune from this colony, and holding on to it. A man who was self-centred, a little vain, and yet possessed of scruples. Such a man was easily manipulated by a clever woman.

She did not think about the fact that he did not love her. She did not like to admit that. She survived on her dreams of the future with him. And each moment spent with him, each small victory, would grow into a time when his life was so entangled with hers that he could not escape. It was ideal. He was ideal.

And it would take so much time, this game of ensnaring, and he would be so busy, for much of it, in his struggle for security, that she would be free to enjoy herself as she wished. He was the kind of man who would never suspect his woman of being unfaithful, he was too full of himself, too sure of his ability to make things into what he wanted them to be.

So Matty saw Aidan. And as they turned up into Cromwell Street, and she led him silently into a white-washed cottage set close to the road, she was very sure of him, very sure of herself.

Aidan was consciously not thinking of Maura. He wanted Matty, needed her caring, her touch, desperately. He would not think of Maura, he would not . . .

This was Matty's only mistake. She thought she saw him very clearly; her conscious decision to love him came from fitting him

394

into the scheme of her life as she wanted it to be. But the loyalty which she desired to awaken in him was strong already – but not for her. His stubborness, which she hoped would be her bulwark against the unknown future, was already firmly in place, inextricably attached to the sense of responsibility that Mary and Corrie had instilled in him, with his Irishness, his Catholicism, with Maura.

41

Aidan had never thought much about such intangibles as love and understanding. One possessed them, or one did not. Matty's need of him made him consider; he thought of Maura, and his memories of her were fresher, clearer. Regretfully, the romantic veil of distance and time was also falling away; he saw her with fondness, but without sentimentality, he could see, again, that Maura was not an affectionate woman, he saw the emptiness awaiting him when he would try to share his thoughts, his desire for touching and comfort that seemed to repel her.

Matty gave him affection, he loved her body and he craved it, he hated being away from her, wanted to know that she was always close, so that he could reach out, touch her. But there was no real communion of minds with Matty; she talked of the scandals of Hobart, and painted pictures of others people's shames and misfortunes, and then laughed her deep soft laugh, expecting him to join in her amusement. Matty longed for the day, she said, when they could go out to dine together, to the theatre together, quite openly, and she would describe their fine clothes and the horses that would pull their carriage. 'And everyone will be sorry that they'd sneered at us. We'll show 'em. Don't you worry. I've never forgotten them that hurt me. You're like that, too. We'll get even, won't we? One day.'

'I don't think I care,' he would say. 'You can kill y'rself with bitterness. I'd rather put it behind me . . .' But her hands would be in his hair, her lips on his, and he would forget that they could not agree on anything, forget that their souls were strangers.

For when the time came to cease touching, to begin talking, there was nothing to say. But Matty talked. 'You liked that, didn't you? I never felt like that with no one else, really and truly. Was it as good for you? Is it like that with your wife? I bet it isn't. I bet she don't understand you like I do. I bet she don't know what you want at all. Did you like the way I . . . ?'

And the act would be reviewed, in all its detail, unless Aidan stopped her lips with a kiss, and she would laugh, that deep, confident laugh, and stretch like a cat; and he would feel alone again, regret his presence there, would want to be gone. Until the memory of her stirred, a day or two later, and he would be back, in the little house in Cromwell Street, and the dance of their shallow passion would begin once more.

'Do you have other men?' he asked her, one evening.

'No. I don't want nobody but you.'

'But you won't have me forever . . .'

'Why do you have to keep reminding me, Aidan?'

'Because I'm afraid you may forget it.'

She rose from the bed and walked to the dresser, surveying herself in the mirror above it. 'I could find a man if I want one, don't you worry.' She turned to him, and he tried to concentrate on her face, hating her power to make him desire her. It was her hold over him, it was his weakness, and she knew it. Stood there, knowing it. 'Would you care?' she asked, now, softly. 'Would you care, Aidan, if I had another man here, after you?'

'No,' he said.

And she laughed, and punished him for his lie by pulling on her petticoat and going downstairs to make a pot of tea, humming, knowing that he wanted her again.

It was Sunday, and as he made his way back to South Street, he could hear the bells of the various churches ringing their summons over the town. He closed his mind to it; plenty of time for Mass and confession when Maura arrived. If he went to confession now he would be told he must not see Matty again, and he knew, no matter how much he would have liked to obey the priest, that he could not give her up; not now, not yet.

He turned into Colville Street, and was passing a row of workmen's cottages not unlike the group in South Street, when two men stepped out of the doorway of one of the houses. He should have been warned, for they had not come from within the cottage, had obviously been standing in the doorway. They both wore dark suits, fashionable but of cheap quality; their hair was neatly brushed, their faces clean-shaven, but there was something indefinable in their manner, that despite the attention to detail, from their hats to their shiny shoes, they were not gentlemen.

They came to a halt close to him, one either side of him, the perfect position to take his arms – but no. They stood quietly, smiling fiercely, making no move to lay hands upon him.

'Good mornin', Mister O'Brien. A lovely day for a stroll, ain't it?'

Aidan had stepped back to swinging distance. He had already marked out which one would be likely to attack him first, and growled, 'I'll enjoy shovin' your heads up your arses, lads, so come on, if y'dare . . .'

'We ain't come to fight.' The bigger of the two spoke up with something like offence in his tone, adding, 'Not today, we ain't.'

'You do us an injustice, Mister O'Brien. We have no grudge against you whatsoever. You are overly suspicious, my dear sir.' He was dark-skinned with little black eyes, this one. Though smaller than his companion, his eyes glittered with more zest at this meeting; this was the one to watch, Aidan thought, small, like Nat; probably, like Nat, a knife man, quick, agile . . .

'We got news for you, that's all.' The taller man had sandy hair and very pink cheeks and nose. His ears stood out, crumpled a little around the edges as though they had been crimped with curling tongs.

There was a silence while they waited for Aidan to ask what news this was, and Aidan watched both of them, saying nothing.

'My friend and I,' said the little dark one, when no curiosity was obvious, 'are in the employ of Mrs 'Arding. Ettie 'Arding, whom I may safely say, I think, is not wot you'd call a friend of yours.'

Aidan sighed, and stepped around them, but they were in front of him again, with an alacrity that caused all three of them to collide for a moment. Again the shifting backwards for space, the watchfulness . . . 'Please 'ear us out, Mister O'Brien, for this concerns you greatly. We ain't in the 'abit of molesting law-abiding gentlemen upon the streets unless there is good cause.'

'Get to the point and then off with y'. I've no time for the likes of Ettie Harding, nor for you.'

'But you can spare a great deal of your time, can't you, for Mrs 'Arding's stepdaughter . . . '

Oh, Jaysus – so Ettie knew. And Matty would be in danger, was undoubtedly in danger at this very moment . . .

'Now,' the little dark man continued, 'Mrs 'Arding ain't got no objection to Miss Matty enjoyin' 'erself as she sees fit. She's a broad-minded lady, is Mrs 'Arding, and powerful fond of Miss Matty. But the fact is, Mister O'Brien, that our mutual friend Nat Garson has died in Port Arthur. And that news 'as upset our employer considerable. She cannot even go to poor Nat's fun'ral, for as you know, 'e'll be buried in an unmarked grave on the *Île de Morte*. It's very sad, Mister O'Brien, very sad indeed. And it becomes even

397

more unfortunate, for I'm afraid that I must tell you that our employer has quite made up her mind that you are considerably to blame for poor Nat's demise. And with that thought in mind, she's decided to kill you.

'Now, we do not wish to cause you undue distress, but we all felt you should know. With a bit of advance notice, you can tidy up your affairs, like. Make provision for your widow and children, see.'

Aidan was circling them, and this time they did not attempt to stop him, but the voice went on helpfully, 'We don't know at this stage 'ow we're goin' to do it – I think Mrs 'Arding is goin' to try to persuade Miss Matty to 'elp out a little – bein' family. She may poison you – Ettie's prob'ly taught 'er lots about that. But you keep right on visitin' Miss Matty, and no doubt you'll find out for yourself in good time . . .' Aidan did not run. He walked as slowly, as casually as he could, on down the street, while Crimp-Ear's laughter and the unrelenting voice followed him, 'We'll all be at your fun'ral, Mister O'Brien. All Nat's friends and yours! It'll be a lovely occasion, Mrs 'Arding is looking forward to it . . .!'

He walked in a kind of shock, unable to comprehend the evil that had just confronted him. They were looking forward to killing him – were even stringing it out, playing with him, expecting him to panic, to try to run. Ettie would send spies out, would perhaps be watching him even now, drinking in his fear.

He went directly to the South Street cottage, and was relieved to find, on opening the door, that not only was the house devoid of assassins, but empty also of his friends. He needed to be alone, to concentrate and to plan.

They were devils, to be sure. No, no, wait – there was no 'they'. It was Ettie Harding, she it was who was behind this. He was restless, prowled up and down the small parlour. He noticed the empty grate, and lit a fire because he was cold, a cold that had little to do with the mild spring day outside. It gave him something to do, setting the twigs upon the paper, lighting matches – his hand kept shaking, the match would go out in the draught from beneath the ill-fitting back door – placing the larger pieces of wood upon the flames, carefully, in order of their size . . . *Matty. They'll ask you to kill me, Matty. And if you refuse, what will Ettie do to you? What hope is there for either of us?*

When the hammering on the door began, Aidan was so startled that he overbalanced as he whirled, still crouched down by the hearth, and fell backwards, forced to place his hand out against the soot-encrusted wall of the chimney. 'Fek!' he breathed, throwing himself forward, on to the rug, slapping at the sparks that still clung to his singed sleeve. 'Who is it!' he roared.

398

And from outside came the calm, educated voice that Aidan would have known even should the name not have been mentioned. 'Doctor Milton Reynolds.'

He was across the room, opening the door, could almost have wept with a mad kind of relief. 'Come in! Well! Grand it is t' see you. Sit down . . . Can I make you tea?'

Reynolds was sniffing, 'Not if that smell is indicative of your culinary skills – what is that odour?'

'Oh – me sleeve.' He turned his arm over to show the scorch mark. 'I fell into the fire – but I'm all right sure.'

Reynolds was looking at him quizzically, but said only, 'I've come to take you back to South Hobart with me, Aidan. Margaret and I want you to come to dinner.' Aidan hesitated, and Reynolds spoke more firmly. 'No, you'll not give me any of your excuses. I don't know what your reason was, last time, but I know for a fact that Leonard Everard has never worked on a Sunday in his life, and neither would he allow his employees to do so. So come along, my dear fellow, Margaret is expecting us.'

Aidan stumbled for something to say, some way of refusing politely, but the moment was postponed by the appearance in the doorway of his three room-mates. 'Phew! What's burnin'? O'Brien, what've you been doin'?' They were laughing, Terrier was carrying a bucket filled with crayfish, one of the large crustaceans held in his hand, prepared, Aidan knew, to shake the creature in his face – but they stopped on seeing Reynolds, and sobered immediately. 'After-noon, Guv'nor.' Terrier nodded, and the others chorused the greet-ing after him. 'That your carriage outside, then?'

'Yes,' Reynolds smiled. Aidan came to himself, introduced the men to each other, then began to explain that he could not come to dinner, much as he would like to . . .

'Why not? Do you good. Go on, mate, go why don't you?' Ah Poo urged.

'Scorched 'is jacket, didn't he?' The Dragoon turned Aidan's sleeve about to show the burn. 'Thought I could smell it as I came in. Can't make a fire without doing yourself a mischief. I'll loan you my coat, your shoulders are broad enough.'

'It's not the coat . . .' he began to protest.

'An' 'is shirt's frayed like it was fringed round the cuffs an' collar. Can't go like that. Scruffy-lookin' piece you are . . .' Ah Poo was heading for the bedroom, came back with the best of his two shirts. 'Change into this, just don't spill champagne down the front of it.'

Terrier, too, began to laugh, 'How wide's your backside, O'Brien? Small as mine? Loan you me new trousers if you don't go an' split the seams on me.'

Reynolds stood by amused as the friends pulled and bullied Aidan into a corporate wardrobe of clean clothes. 'There,' the Medical Officer laughed, as Aidan stood before him, complete with tie and linen handkerchief. 'You look the picture of conservative good taste. You have no appointments elsewhere *this* time, I take it? Then shall we go?'

Of all times for a dinner invitation, Aidan thought, climbing into the double-seated buggy, for never had he felt less like being polite, well-mannered, playing with children, attempting to believe that life was clean, gentle, safe.

Along Hampden Road they drove, towards Hobart itself, past other carriages on Sunday outings, families in their best day clothes, on their way to or from church or to pay calls in the suburbs. At the top of the hill they turned left into Davey Street, and climbed still higher, along the crest of the hill, towards South Hobart.

The Reynolds' house lay behind a tall hedge of alternately-planted hawthorn and privet. Within the garden early blooming roses were set amongst beds of daffodils and jonquils, the scent of the latter was blown towards them on the breeze. The house itself was double-storeyed, built of the attractive red brick of so many of the Hobart houses, and made to appear larger than it was by the broad verandas that surrounded it on three sides.

'A grand house, sir,' Aidan volunteered, impressed. Compared to his own cottage in South Street and the one in Killaloe, this was a veritable mansion. Not as large or as impressive as Tineranna, of course, but what did that matter? This was a home where he was a guest. He had been invited. As the horses trotted down the gentle slope of the driveway, around to the rear of the house and the stables, Aidan realized that this day marked his entrance into middle-class life. Convict and peasant, his education and manners had counted for little until now. But there, at the foot of the garden, where a broad stream ran, was Margaret Reynolds, Emily and the baby, Richard, even now waving and walking towards him. In this country, in this family, he was accepted. It was a beginning, a glimpse of where he could be, what he could hope for.

The smell of the roses and the honeysuckle that grew over the nearby wall floated heavily around him. Emily was running up the slope towards him, in a blue plaid silk dress, white-stockinged legs pumping. She collided into him and he hugged her, and the child's arms around him, her excited chatter, the animated face that was raised to his made him glad he had come, and he pushed his fear behind him.

'I'm so glad you came! Why haven't you come sooner? Now you can meet Berrima. Berrima!' But there was no sign of the eldest Reynolds child. 'Oh.' Emily's face fell, and she surveyed the large garden crossly, 'I told her not to go away . . .'

Why was this not his family? He walked about the lawns and down to the edge of the stream, with Reynolds and his wife and the toddler between them, and he envied his friend his house, his wife and children, the closeness that they seemed to share. It was wrong, this envy, and he felt ashamed of it, but acknowledging it did not make it go away. He found consolation in telling himself that he would have all this one day. He would work hard, and he would build a house such as this; if he kept his courage all things were possible . . . Then he would remember Ettie and her threats, and his heart would sink, and he wondered what on earth he would do.

It was not an open fight, this, it was not an obvious struggle with an adversary who stood before him. He hated the fact that it was a woman who was his enemy, and he was afraid of her, too, for, from the little he knew of her, Ettie's rules were her own. But I'll stay alive, he thought. I'll not let her kill me. I might have to kill her, if it comes to it. But she'll not rob me of all this. I shall have all this, and to the devil with her.

Milton Reynolds had been calling Berrima periodically during their walk about the garden. Emily had been running in and out of the house and all about the grounds, hunting for her.

'She's not usually shy,' Margaret Reynolds explained.

'Rather the opposite. Berrima!' Reynolds called crossly, glaring about the grounds.

Aidan was the first to see the pale shape amongst the willows, the flat-bottom boat moving slowly downstream towards them. 'My God . . .' It was Reynolds, beside him. The adults moved to the water's edge, Reynolds lifting the little boy, Richard, into his arms.

'I found it in the willows near Colonel Atkins' house. Isn't it wonderful?' The face was lowered in concentration, punting the barge-like boat along, keeping it out of the shallows. The thin little form in white muslin with a red tartan sash looked incongruous atop the vessel, the large sun hat giving her the look of a mushroom afloat in a paper boat.

'Berrima, that is not our punt. Now take it back.'

'No, Milton, she can't swim.' Her eyes on her daughter, Margaret clutched her husband's arm. 'Berrima, don't panic, bring it here.'

'Berrima, take it back!'

'Just let me give the children a ride, Papa, no one will know . . .'

'No, you must . . . !' And more tightly, 'We have a visitor, Berrima . . .'

During this exchange the boat came closer and closer to the bank, through the willows, now, and Berrima's hat caught on one trailing branch and was pulled back on to her neck.

Aidan gasped, feeling almost ill with the shock of seeing the face before him. Mother of God, it was Anna. Anna at fifteen or sixteen, smaller, the hair a little darker, the face a more pointed oval, perhaps, but the features – that smile, those eyes . . .

She was Anna in miniature, like a doll made of china, Aidan thought with sudden, savage bitterness that tore at the heart of him. A doll without the character of the original. Even at sixteen there had been a grace, a calmness about Anna. This bold little toy was dancing on the spot, unmindful of the rocking punt, laughing and teasing her father; she tossed her head, gestured with her hands, and generally gave the impression of possessing too much energy for her small frame. It exhausted Aidan even to look at her.

Yet he could not stop looking at her.

'Take it back!' Milton, embarrassed to red-faced and un-accustomed fury, roared at the girl.

'Oh, all right . . . !'

She dug the pole deep into the water and pushed hard, as angry, now, as her father. The pole stuck in the mud, her grip was slack as she went to pull the pole free – she was over-balancing, falling, Margaret screamed . . .

Aidan had learnt to swim in the shallows of the Shannon with Thomas and the Currans; now he did not hesitate, even to glance at Milton Reynolds. He flung himself into the water, and plunged after the girl, searching in the reedy, muddy water with his hands. He grabbed at her hat, but it was floating free – he could hear Milton behind him, 'For God's sake, find her . . . !' the voice breaking. 'For God's sake . . .' He pushed aside the punt, which had moved slightly with the current, and dived again, groping along the creek bed – his hand touched cloth – he pulled hard – found her waist and rose to the surface, dragging her with him.

Part of his brain was detached; he had seen too much violence and his mind was cool, looking at the small face so close to his own, the heavy hair falling back wetly, the eyes only now opening to gaze at his own features. Brown eyes, not hazel, dark eyes like his own, and widening with shock.

'Thanks be to God . . .' Margaret's voice, and Aidan came to himself, pulling the girl towards the bank. He stumbled up into the shallows. His burden was small, light in his arms, and he handed her over to her father with something like regret. Her hair had come loose and was cascading down her back, past her hips, hair as long as Anna's – he wanted her to turn around, now that they were out of the shadows of the willows, wanted to see that face that drew him while it embittered him.

The daughter was being reefed up the bank, petticoats clinging, and received a sharp push towards the house, 'Go to your room, miss!'

One last glance to her father, 'Really, Papa . . .' Then she had turned and was walking with what remained of her dignity, up the slope towards the house. Emily ran after her. Margaret, with an apologetic look at Aidan, murmured, 'Thank you . . .' and followed.

At the top of the slope treble voices were raised, 'You stole it! You stole that boat and embarrassed Papa.'

'I didn't steal it . . .'

'And in front of guests – you were showing off!'

'I wasn't – shut up, you little prig.'

'I'm not a prig – and anyway, I'd rather be a prig than *childish* . . .'

'Shut up, shut up, shut up!'

And the conversation finished with the slamming of a wire-screened door. Emily came down towards them, smiling, satisfied, innocent.

'My dear chap, I can't thank you enough,' Milton said, as they headed up the slope. 'The sooner McHale, below us, removes that wretched dam he's built across the creek and it returns to its humble little trickle, the safer I'll feel . . .'

Aidan changed into the fresh clothes provided for him, and handed his saturated finery to the Reynolds' housekeeper with a pang of guilt – how would he explain this to the three at the cottage?

Before dinner, he and Reynolds returned the punt to its mooring upstream, creeping away after the deed was accomplished, like fugitives, back to their own camp along the bank.

'Dear Lord,' Reynolds breathed, as they stumbled over the roots of willow and she-oak as quietly as they could, 'I feel like one of the lads at Port Arthur. I can't think how they could enjoy this type of adventure. The idea of Colonel Atkins catching us is terrifying – and I'm only returning the dashed goods.'

Aidan had to laugh, and then laughed at his ability to laugh. He was no more a part of Port Arthur than Reynolds himself.

They ate supper by candlelight in the formal dining room. A

servant, plump and coarse-voiced, obviously a convict herself, once, though well-trained and unobtrusive, served them soup and ham and leg of lamb and five different vegetables, and Aidan could not believe that the evening was a reality. Only Emily ate with them at the table, and he could see by the lack of surprise upon her face that this was average fare for Sunday dinner. To follow, there was trifle with thick whipped cream, or apple pie with chocolate ice cream, and Aidan, who had never in his thirty-two years tasted any of these, tried them all.

After dinner Margaret and Emily left them, and the two men took their glasses of port and their cigars out into the garden and the cool of the night. Seating themselves on a bench near the water, they were both silent for a while, listening to the bell-like sound of a frog, and the rushing of the creek over rocks, further down the stream. Aidan leaned back and gazed up at the night sky and thought that he could quite happily die at this moment.

'Are they going to try to kill you?' A calm, clinical voice from beside him.

'Jaysus . . .' Aidan breathed, after a silence. 'You'll be after making me bring up that entire meal . . .'

Reynolds laughed softly. 'I'm sorry. I suppose I wanted to catch you by surprise. I wanted to make sure you wouldn't lie to me.'

'Sure I've never done that.'

'Sure but you'd have tried just now. "No, sir, I'm all right, sir. I can handle it, sir." '

'I don't like it when you ape me,' Aidan growled.

'You don't like it when I'm one step ahead of you, as I am on this matter. Will Treloar wrote to me from Huonville, he's heard from another ex-convict that you were a marked man. Because of Nat Garson's death.'

Aidan waited for him to continue, but Reynolds was quiet, busying himself with sipping from his glass of port. When he lowered the glass his gaze was questioning, even in the meagre light, the last of the swift, Southern dusk. Aidan could see that he was waiting.

'There was a woman,' he said with difficulty. 'A . . . a friend of Nat's . . .'

'What was her name?'

Aidan went on quickly, and told him, without mentioning names, of the escape from Brown's River, finishing with the threats made that afternoon.

'Who is she, Aidan?' Reynolds, undaunted, repeated.

'I can't tell you that.'

'You could have her arrested. Don't you see? Damn it, Aidan,

404

none of this would have happened if you'd told the truth when they brought you back after the escape. What possible loyalty do you owe them? Nat's dead, the woman is nothing to you, is she?'

'Mother of God, no!'

'Then why are you even hesitating?'

Aidan smiled wryly. 'Honour among thieves, Doctor.'

'I shall punch you in a moment . . .'

'But . . . it would be an idea, wouldn't it?' His mind was suddenly racing. 'If she *thought* I was going to the police.'

Reynolds said gruffly, 'The woman's stupid, it's the first place any right thinking man would go . . .'

'Och, no, I wouldn't say that. Any one *she'd* come in contact with would have something to hide, to be sure. She'd be feeling quite safe.'

'Tell her that you have proof of her complicity in the escape . . . ? Something that would undoubtedly send her to gaol for seven years . . .' Milton murmured thoughtfully.

'And I gave it to my lawyer!' Aidan was almost crowing, 'I gave it to my lawyer, to be opened should anything happen to me! Arra, she'll be following me about Hobart with bandages and salve, in case I fall and hurt meself!'

'I wouldn't go so far as to say that. But it may prevent her wreaking vengeance upon you. Of course, she may decide that the pleasure of killing you is worth the risk.'

But Aidan was buoyed up, now, convinced that Ettie would be bluffed.

'I'd rather you sent the woman to gaol,' Reynolds muttered, still not completely convinced.

'She'll get out eventually, and then she'll stop at nothing. By then I'll have Maura and the children with me. No. I'd rather challenge her now, when there's only my life that'll be in danger.'

'She'll not harm your wife and children, surely.'

Aidan's next words sounded incongruous with the lights of the house behind them, and, before them, the moon rising over the tops of the dark willows, silvering their upper-most branches. He spoke matter-of-factly, and had no idea how the words chilled Reynolds. 'She's killed before,' he said softly. 'It doesn't seem to bother her. I don't think she'd hesitate to kill my family if she thought they stood in her path, if she'd profit in some way.'

Reynolds sighed. 'I'll take your word on this, though the woman sounds more demon than human. I'd go straight to the police, you know, despite your protests, if I wasn't afraid it might force their hand. Don't try to face these things alone, Aidan. This is what friends are for.'

Aidan was moved, turned to the man. 'You're very good, sir. It's grateful I am for all you've done for me.'

'You can thank me by staying alive,' Reynolds said drily. Aidan laughed and looked away, and Reynolds studied the younger man. Saw the dark eyes burning in the face that prison had robbed of its youth, the lines etched around his mouth, premature lines that marked the years of hardship, of confusion, beyond reason or hope.

'Once in a lifetime, perhaps,' they had told him, on joining the Convict Department, 'you'll find a good man in there. But you'll be fooled time and again if you're not careful. Even the best of them will let you down. They're doomed to failure, most of them, can't help themselves. The job'll break you if you allow it to.' Reynolds had been careful, but had always resented the words.

He had helped several men, men from slum backgrounds mostly, but also a few country boys who had found themselves here very early in their criminal careers. They had gone out from the probation stations and had made new lives for themselves. Reynolds had kept track of them, none had backslided, and these were men of no education who drank and gambled and lied as a matter of course. Products of their backgrounds, they played at life according to the rules of their street, their village – only now they moved more cautiously, having found the world wider than they thought, having accepted their own responsibility for their destinies.

This one was different again, Reynolds thought, he did not bother to flatter or lie to gain an advantage. Aidan's honesty counted for him, in Reynolds' view; but his violence, which Reynolds did not for an instant believe was gone forever, must be repressed and channelled.

He said consideringly, 'I don't really understand how you came to be here at all. If you could only control that dratted temper of yours I'm sure you'd still be a free man, back in Killaloe. You've never really belonged with men like Nat Garson . . . '

Aidan's voice came softly in the gloom, the words measured. 'No. I share something in common with all of them, all the men in Port Arthur or the other prisons. We took what we wanted. Whether money or revenge. We took it. That's why we're here. Sure maybe it was meant to be. In a way, I'm after thinking it was the best that could have happened. I don't know. I think that sometimes.'

Into the silence there was the sound of a door opening in the house behind them, and Margaret called them inside to say goodnight to the children.

★

406

He had been irritated that Will Treloar had written to Milton Reynolds without writing first to him. But the following morning a letter arrived at the cottage, from Will in Huonville, telling him that he was worried, to take care, to contact Milton Reynolds and the authorities, not to try to take on Ettie alone. At the end of this advice, in a change of tone, he told Aidan that Sarah had been taken ill, had not made the sailing of the *Tasman*, and might not arrive for several weeks.

Aidan had planned, that evening, to go directly to Ettie Harding, but postponed the inevitable confrontation when a second delivery was found to have arrived at the cottage during the day. It was a large parcel of clothing, including the cleaned and pressed wardrobe of his friends, as well as a lightweight summer suit, two shirts and a pair of boots. The accompanying letter said he was to keep the suit he had worn home from the Reynolds' home the night before. All the clothing fitted, and Aidan glared with suspicion at his room-mates, all affecting excitement for him, and airs of innocence.

'We never helped him, we never told him nuthin',' The Dragoon asserted.

'He's a doctor, gotta make quick decisions all the time, ain't he? Probably c'd look at you an' say, "Ah, a size fifteen and an 'alf collar, I'll stake me life on't",' Terrier put in, breathing on the shine of the boots and polishing them with a swift brush of his sleeve. 'Don't look gift shoes in the toes, me boy. Wear 'em, an' shuddup.'

He spent the rest of that evening writing to Will and to Milton Reynolds, thanking them both for their concern and their help. When he finally went to bed, stepping between the bunks of the snoring companions, it was with the thought that tomorrow would do just as well for visiting Ettie . . .

He was annoyed, the following morning, to find that this plan, too, had to be discarded. A new ketch was to be launched, the *Virginia*; her owners were prevented from coming to Hobart Town to collect her, and Everard, taking a crew from the shipyard, decided to deliver the ship himself. 'My wife will be coming also,' he told Aidan, 'down to Dover, south of Huonville. We'll return on the packet tomorrow. I've a crew of four chosen, but I feel you should come along.'

'Sir . . . there's some business that I have to . . .'

'Put it off, put it off. That's an order. It's about time you saw something of a ship besides its innards.'

It was a warm autumn morning such as Tasmania sometimes bequeaths on its weather-wary inhabitants. There was a holiday atmosphere as the little ship sailed out into the Derwent Estuary,

Everard at the wheel, rejoicing in his return to the sea. Mrs Everard stood in the bows like a plump little figurehead, and Aidan scrambled aloft and hauled on sheets with the rest of the crew, managing, for the first few hours, to be in everybody's way.

When they had set their course and the activity had calmed a little, Everard pointed out the various landmarks to those of the crew who had not sailed from Hobart before. 'That's Opossum Bay to port, and Brown's River to starboard. You were there, weren't you, O'Brien? Township's coming along, now . . . Hullo, who's this coming?'

The latter remark was addressed almost to himself, but almost as if she had heard, his wife had turned aft to shout, 'It's the *Tasman*, Mr Everard!'

Everard was short-sighted, but would never admit to this. 'How the devil can you tell at this distance, woman?'

'By her size, Mr Everard, and the shape of her bows!'

'She's probably right,' Everard muttered. 'Eyes like a gull has for whitebait, that woman.' He turned to Aidan. 'Built just up from us on Secheron Point, the *Tasman* was, only a few years ago. Passenger ship on the London to Melbourne run. Full of gold-hungry opportunists, no doubt, but with any luck there may be some settlers for this colony aboard her.'

'She's early, is she not?' Aidan asked, remembering that Will Treloar's wife, Sarah, was to have been aboard the *Tasman*.

'No such thing as a timetable on the ocean, boy. They've made it – the sea's littered with too many who don't. Mrs Everard!' he bellowed suddenly.

She turned. 'I think Captain Prescott is in command, Mr Everard, I seem to recollect that he is.'

Everard merely hurumphed, by which sign Aidan took it that the capable little figure in the bows had once again anticipated her husband. Aidan was interrupted in a quiet smile by the old seaman telling him to go below and fetch the conical loud hailer. 'We'll ask Prescott what sort of a voyage he had . . .'

When Aidan returned from his errand the low line of the Tinderbox Hills was off to starboard, and to port was the deep semi-circle of Half Moon Bay. Ahead of them, from the direction that benefitted greatest from the south-easterly breeze, the *Tasman* bore down upon them, nearly all her canvas out, as if she knew she was almost at her journey's end.

Everard turned the *Virginia* and the crew leapt to take in the slack; it appeared as though the ketch would pass directly beneath the tall ship's bows – but no, they skimmed along beside each other, 'Ahoy!'

from the poop of the *Tasman*, and 'Ahoy!' from Everard, who called one of his sailors over to take the helm.

The *Virginia* was downwind and the crew could clearly smell the stench of fouled bilges and cattle and sheep pens that bore the effects of nearly five months at sea. The passengers clustered at the railing to gaze down at the trim new vessel as the two captains traded greetings and information. Aidan was conscious of how the *Virginia* must look, blue paint shining, brasswork flashing, her snowy canvas arched out to catch the wind. He was proud to be part of her, proud to be with Everard, glad to be who and where he was. He wanted to shout to the tired and travel-sick emigrants that yes, this land was good, that even a prisoner could be free, that visions could be real, here, such as they never could be at home, that he, Aidan O'Brien was proof of it all.

They were close, so close to the side of the larger ship, and the faces of cheering and waving passengers went past in a blur . . . But one did not. There. Aidan had glanced away for a moment, but his eyes came back . . . There. A woman, running along the length of the deck, pushing people out of her way . . . Over the shouting of the two captains, the calls from the other passengers, her voice was faint, almost inaudible, he could see her mouth working, her arms waving . . . A little woman in dark clothing . . . His heart ached suddenly, for it could almost be . . .

'Leonard, be quiet! That woman is trying to hail us!' Mrs Everard put a firm hand on her husband's arm.

The two vessels were pulling away from each other. The small figure in black dress and brown cloak was growing smaller by the second . . . she was tearing at the drab bonnet, and it came away in her hands – her hair was bright flame, as bright as the sunlight on the railing she gripped so hard as her final words came floating down to them, 'Aidan! Aidan!'

He almost screamed, but was turned to stone, could not move – there, the child, the boy, pulling at his mother's arm – there the little girl in dark coat and bonnet – and there the ship's officer walking to them, the woman pointing, clutching at the man . . .

Aidan had thrown himself across the deck. 'Turn about! Turn about!' he shrieked. 'For the love of God, turn the ship about!'

'*What?*'

'*Turn about!* Sir, please, sir!' He could not know how demented he looked, mouth working, the tears streaming down his face, he actually shook his employer. 'For God's sake, sir! Turn about! It's my wife! It's my wife and my children!'

42

It was only Everard's reputation, in the end, that released Maura and her children from the *Tasman* in a manner so irregular, mid-estuary, so close to the official landing place and the Tasmanian authorities.

'We'll see them first thing on our return!' Everard bellowed across the water, as the long boat reached the side of the *Virginia* and Aidan scooped Maura up on to the deck, into his arms. The passengers on the deck of the *Tasman* roared and cheered, but Aidan and Maura were oblivious to them.

Clemency was lifted up to them, and the three embraced, the auburn-haired, solemn-faced eight-year-old not deigning to cry, though her face puckered in alarm as this strange dark man crushed her and Ma to his chest. Could this be him? Could it? 'Are you my father? Are you? Are you my father?'

The man was holding her in his arms, staring into solemn green eyes that appraised him critically. 'Aye,' Aidan tried to calm himself, realizing the child's apprehension at such an emotional scene. 'Aye, that I am, Clemency, I'm your da.'

Liam, more cautious, held out a hand to Aidan. Aidan took it, then grinned. The boy was suddenly grinning too, then they were in each other's arms. The boy's eyes were alight, strange eyes, brown eyes, but with that russet tinge to the pupils so often found in brown-eyed redheads. The features of the face were Aidan's own, but the eyes gave Liam an intensity that he owed no one. 'I knew we'd find you,' he said almost fiercely. 'I told Ma, didn't I, Ma? We did find him!'

'That we did, Liam, we found him.' Her face was thinner than it had been, there were lines around her eyes and mouth that had not been there before. Only now, looking down at her in her worn cloak and faded bonnet did he realize how much she must have suffered. But she was smiling, linking her arm into his, and the three turned to wave to the *Tasman*, now once more heading away from them, up the estuary towards Hobart Town.

'Aidan,' Maura said earnestly, 'I must tell you – Mister Clarkson, the magistrate, opened your case again, and he's decided to show clemency . . .' She was laughing. 'That's truly the word he used, and you're to have your ticket-of-leave, Aidan!'

'I have it, woman!' he was delighted to tell her.

'You do?' And already her quick mind was working ahead, 'This might mean your pardon then – would it? If they granted you an unconditional pardon, we could return to Ireland, could we not?'

'Aye, perhaps . . .' He was watching his children, running along the deck. Eight and nine years old they were, thin as whips, but healthy . . .

There was no time to assimilate the news of his possible pardon. He wanted to look at Maura and his children, gaze and gaze at them, and the rest of the little crew of the *Virginia* were not about to ignore the new passengers.

'My dear, I'm so delighted that this adventure has given me some female company on board.' Mrs Everard was positively glowing with the reflected romance of the incident. 'Aidan, you must detach yourself from your wife long enough for her to come below with me – the galley, my dear, has clean hot water and a mirror, and if your trip was anything like ours was, twenty years ago, you'd like to avail yourself of both. Time enough for introductions later.' And as she swept a smiling and grateful Maura towards the hatch, 'Mr Everard, I'd suggest Mr O'Brien be relieved of this watch so he can show our new cabin boys over the ship.'

'Exactly as I would have suggested, Mrs Everard, if you'd given me time.' Everard thrust out his chin belligerently.

'I'm sure you would, my dear.' She patted his cheek as she passed him.

There was an air of unreality about the day, from that moment on. They walked for'ard, Aidan and the excited children who seemed already to accept matters, taking Aidan's hand, skipping at his side, asking him where they were going. Would they see a kangaroo? Why had Aidan been away for so very long? When would they see Gran and Uncle Thomas again?

The sun shone on blue water and green hills, only the drabness of the trees belied the dream that they could be somewhere off the Irish coast. No going home, Aidan thought, and tears were still so close to him that he wept into the wind, with no one to see him but his son and daughter, their russet heads turned away, to face the new land. No going home, no going back.

Maura joined him on deck bearing a large hamper, while Mrs Everard followed with mugs of tea. Introductions, then, and questions asked and answered, and Aidan could not take his eyes from his wife, glowing under the kindness and attention. The children sat

411

between them, speaking over the top of one another and dropping sandwich filling down their clothes. Maura would scold them, but even this, to Aidan, was part of the miracle. These messy, talkative, good-natured children were his. This demure woman, speaking intelligently of the economic situation in Ireland in answer to Everard's queries, was his woman. He could not understand that this could happen, all he had longed for through the silence and loneliness of years was here before him, without warning or announcement, after a morning that had begun like any other.

All was changed, he thought. All his planning, his painstaking decisions, his feelings of ambivalence. Tomorrow would be different from anything he had expected, his life was taking a shape that he had not foreseen, and as yet the details did not occur to him. He rubbed his cheek against his daughter's red-brown curls, knew he could face whatever would come. He had Maura and the children with him, whatever happened now could only be for the good.

He had no real details from Maura regarding her voyage, how she had managed to find the money for their passage, who had arranged it for her. The Everards were so interested in the latest news, when they realized that Maura read *The Times* – Father McDonnagh's copy, Aidan suspected – and had mingled with the English passengers on board the *Tasman*, that they tended to monopolize her attention. It was not until that evening, when they berthed in Dover and were led to a little waterside inn in which they would spend the night, that Maura and Aidan were alone. The door was shut, the children were asleep in their beds against the wall, and husband and wife stepped toward each other.

'I had to come, I had to,' she breathed against his shoulder. 'With Thomas's help, I saved enough for our tickets. Your mother and Thomas will come also, Aidan, when the money is available. We shall work hard and send for them, will we not? They are my family, too, now, all that I have – and I miss them, Aidan, I miss them both so much . . .'

She was sobbing again, and he held her to him, felt such a wave of tenderness for her that he could almost have wept once more himself. Instead he raised her face to his and kissed her, gently, upon the lips.

He became aware that the bed was so very close to them, a large, English bed that would fit two of them comfortably. 'Look you,' he pointed it out to her, 'even the beds are bigger than those at home.'

She insisted on sleeping in her petticoat, and was nervous about the children waking and seeing them. Aidan, in his joy at finding her again, was gentle, tolerant of her fears, told himself that this was not

412

Matty, and he could expect no sudden passion in Maura, perhaps he could never have that. But sure, she loved him, she had moved her own world aside to follow him. In her quiet devotion she gave him an anchor, from that very first day, with which to face whatever would come. It was the one thing that he never doubted; through all the grim adversities and sudden upheavals that they were to know, he never again doubted that she loved him.

It was the Everards who found them accommodation when they returned to Hobart. At the lower end of Bath Street, Battery Point, close to the narrow little beach, Everard had a boat house. Half-straddling a pier that ran out into the water, the weatherboard building had a small attic above its single large room, it was roughly-made and draughty, but Aidan's as long as he wished.

For Maura, who swept and cleaned and painted the walls with whitewash while Aidan made tables and chairs from barrels and off-cuts from the timber yard, it was perfect, more than she had ever hoped for. She had come prepared to face a broad and untamed, lonely land; instead she was mistress of a house nearly three times the size of the cottage on Tineranna, with a view across a stretch of water as equally broad and majestic as Lough Derg. Here she did not have the Tipperary hills, far across the lake's surface, but she had the sunrise each morning, could stand on the pier and watch the pale pink fingers of light move up the estuary from the far edge of the sea.

Aidan, because he was happy, put the thought of Ettie Harding from his mind. Sure the woman was all threats, for hadn't he been free and walking the streets of Hobart Town this month or more since Ettie and Jimmy's return from Melbourne? He was careful, watchful, but came to think more and more that his panic had been born of his emotional isolation and loneliness.

Now it was all he could do to leave the house every morning to go to the shipyards, he wanted to be with his family, and working six days a week, twelve hours a day, gave him so little time to grow close to them. Liam was all right, Liam was grand, sure, an uncomplicated, sturdy little boy. Clemency was another matter, she did not appear to be close to her mother, but seemed, all the same, to resent Aidan's relationship with Maura. Should he place an arm about his wife's shoulders on returning from his work, the thin little face would be there, below him, sidling between them, glaring with ill-concealed animosity. He remembered his own slight jealousy of Corrie O'Neill had faded very quickly, once he had become accustomed to the changes in the household, but in this he seemed to have little help from Maura.

413

'Don't, Aidan, the children are watching . . .' when he tried to kiss her.

'The children must see that I'm powerful fond of you . . .'

'I'm busy cooking, Aidan, I can't move with y'r great arm around me.'

Perhaps he could have accustomed himself to this, for maybe he was asking too much that she should feel at ease after so long a separation. But at night her reticence was even more pronounced. The glad eagerness for his arms that she had shown in the inn at Dover calmed, to his disappointment, to their usual tussle of wills. 'I want to hold you – close, close . . . is that wrong?'

'Too much is wrong. Too much is Lust.'

'Not if we're married. If we're married it's not wrong.'

'Too much of *anything* is wrong.'

Oh, Maura, little housekeeper of the emotions, meting and doling affection like treacle from a jar, waste not, want not . . . Thin white arms pushing him away, 'No, Aidan, we did it last night.'

She had taken to going to Mass every day, and that, too, bothered him. He went with her on Sundays of course, had been to confession and done penance for his affair with Matty. But Mass every day? 'Even piety can be carried to extremes,' he grumbled to her once.

So Maura went to Mass alone each day, while the children were at school, and Aidan would wonder about it, this new religious austerity about her. Had it been the Famine, had she seen too much?

She did not like to speak about the Famine, nor what it had been like in Killaloe these past nine years. But something in her was changed, some spark of life had gone from the sharp green eyes. She used to walk along the little pier of an evening, when the dishes were washed and the children in bed, and Aidan read the *Hobart Leader*. 'I'll just step out for some air,' she would say, and she would leave the boathouse, never asking Aidan if he would like to come too.

He sensed she wanted to be alone, but it disquieted him. He could never settle to his reading, knowing that she was wandering about out there under the stars, wrestling with some unknown problem she could not, or would not share with him. Occasionally he would follow her, after a while, finding her on the narrow wooden pier, looking at the lights of Sandy Bay to their right or the scattered lights of the few farmhouses on the eastern shore.

Aidan had built a fence of strong four-foot pickets about their front door, complete with a little gate, and this gave the children a kind of terrace on which to play, while keeping them safe from the water below. But out here there was no hand railing, just the

414

ill-fitting planks and a sheer drop ten feet to the water.

'I worry about you here. Can't you walk beyond on the sand?'

She would shake her head, say she was very careful and sure-footed. Once she answered, 'This has become my home,' turning to smile at him in the moonlight. 'I know each of these boats, their comings and goings. I know their owners and crews like you were used to knowing each potato plant in our field.'

He searched for the right word. 'Is that sarcasm in your voice?'

'*Sarcasm*? Och, no. Don't be thinking I'm unhappy, Aidan, for I'm not. I'm very content. More than I have been in my life.'

'Is that right?'

'Aye, to be sure. Don't I seem content?'

'I want you to be happy.'

'Happy . . . ' Only faintly the word came to him, the voice had the same lost sound as the water lapping about the wooden piles that supported the jetty.

He expected her to continue, but she did not. Finally, he said, 'Maura, what is it? Why can't you tell me?'

'There's nothing to tell.' Her face, white in the moonlight, came around towards him.

'You're keeping something back from me.'

Again the heavy silence. Then, 'Did you have other women, Aidan? No, no, don't answer! Don't tell me. I know how you are, how much . . . that sort of thing . . . how much it means to you. You're not the kind of man who could say no to temptation.'

He did not want to lie to her. But neither did he wish to begin the sad and troubling story of his relationship with Matty. This was Maura, whom he had known all his life, Maura who could not forget, let alone forgive.

The little pale oval of her face was turned up towards him. 'I understand. If it happened, it's over. We belong together, in the sight of God. If . . . if these times, bad times, have forced us to sin, then we have asked forgiveness and can put it behind us. Can we not? Aidan?'

'Aye. Yes! Of course!' And his arms were around her, and for once her arms were about him, and she was holding him tightly, her face buried in his jacket. How tiny she was, how frail! He kissed her hair, her face – and found it wet with tears.

'What's this?' He held her while she sobbed, harsh sobs that racked her body. 'Maura, Maura . . .' he crooned to her as if she was a child.

'Evil, evil . . .' she was muttering through the paroxysms that shook her.

'What? Who?'

'I . . . *I am* . . .'

He remained silent, then, held her and waited, knowing she had something vital to say.

'It was hard – oh, you don't know how hard! Watching the streams of starving people going back and forth on the road to Scarriff. All over Clare, into Tipperary, 'twas just as bad . . . arra, Aidan, people were dying on the roads, they were eating *grass*, Aidan!'

'I wanted to leave, I knew we had to come to you. I didn't want our children growing up amongst scenes like that! Or . . . perhaps the fever would take them like it did my little sister Bridie, and so many of the children.

'In spring of last year, April it was, but wet and cold, the master came back to Tineranna . . .'

'What "master" are y' talking about? Devlin?'

'Yes. He came back. It was raining that day, a grey bleak day it was, and your mother and I were picking young nettles in the old garden of the big house . . .'

'Why should you and Ma be picking nettles like beggars? Was not Thomas on the river? Was he not looking after you?'

She hesitated. 'Angry he'll be when he finds I've told you.'

'Told me what?'

'He didn't want you to know, he's better now . . .'

He had gripped her shoulders, 'Thomas? Thomas is ill? Tell me!'

'He fell, Aidan. Mending the thatch he was, when he fell, and broke his leg.'

'He'll walk now, he'll be all right?'

'Aye, he's back on the river, now. But for all that winter of last year, it was bad times for us. That's why Mary and me were picking nettles at the big house, and how we came to see the master . . .'

'Stop calling him that.'

'Mr Kelly, then. Wasn't he walking over what's left of the house, slipping on the stones, tripping over the ivy that's begun climbing over the ruins. He had no coat on, as if he'd ridden from the village and had been caught in the rain. Sure he nearly fainted when he saw us.'

Maura hesitated, and when she spoke again, it was as if with an effort. 'He . . . the master fell, and broke his wrist. He asked me if I'd take a position at his house – a secretary, write his letters for him. He knew who I was, Aidan.' Her face swung up to confront him again. 'He knew who I was, and yet he asked *me*. Out of pity, 'tis the only reason sure, that I can see, for he'd remember your ma in your da's time, and me an O'Donoghue, in bare feet like a tinker now!

'And could I say no?' She was standing stiffly away from him, almost shrieked the words at him in the release of her pent-up feelings. 'Could I say no to eight shillings a week – no matter what – for I wrote his letters and kept his accounts – all that spring and summer and autumn, Aidan! And . . . and . . . . whatever he asked of me, to keep the family alive, I'd have . . .'

He had reached for her, held her close in his arms as she cried again, tears of relief, now, for her secret had been shared. He laughed softly, kissed her hair time and again, 'Och, Maura, is that all? Sure and I had visions that you had killed a man at the least!'

'You don't understand . . .!'

'I do, I do.' He rocked her in his arms. 'Did I not share his schooling for half my childhood? I know the man, have no fear of that. He took my dog, he took Anna; he's an envious eejit so he is. I've no doubt he tried to take you also, grá gal.'

She had stiffened in his arms, 'Aidan . . .'

'But I know you. He'd not succeed with you. Trying to lead you into sin . . . Och, don't struggle, you don't let me hold you often enough – I don't want you worrying about it any longer, Maura. If it's to Devlin I owe your being here . . .'

'And I paid for a doctor to visit Thomas, Aidan. And I bought food . . . Without Master – Mister Kelly, I couldn't! I had to . . . '

'Then it's all the more reason I have to be grateful to Devlin, and I shall tell him so, when we meet again.'

He was highly amused, thoroughly delighted. He tried to imagine Devlin's efforts to seduce Maura, Maura who refused to be seduced by even her own husband, but he had to leave off the pictures in his mind because he began to laugh, and that would hurt Maura. To her it would be no laughing matter.

'You're feeling guilty for taking money from a man who was my enemy. Yet it's past now, all of it.'

'No, Aidan! It's . . .'

'Past! Past, Maura. I have no bitterness for the man. He's a superstitious fool with not a drop of his father's courage in him – he'll live with Corrie's death upon his conscience for the rest of his life. Let him go. Let him have his fine house in England – he's haunted by the past you can be sure, or he wouldn't be walking about Tineranna in the rain. He's lost what's most important to him in the world, can't you see that? But I have it all.'

He paused. She grew aware that he was gazing down at her consideringly, that light in his eyes. She was worn out with grief, with remorse. The excess of feeling left her drained, sleepy. Aidan, however, was the reverse, she could sense his excitement, feel his body warming to the thought that she was *his*, and when they entered the house once more he would want proof of that. She almost said, *I am not your belonging, rescued from Devlin Kelly. I am not like your dog, like Anna. I belong to myself*. It would sound prim, petty. He would not understand.

43

Everard handed the letter to him the following day.

> *Dear Aidan,*
> *Ettie is playing games only just now, she wants you off your gard. Plees com to see me 30 Napolean Street it is very important and erjent.*
> *Matty.*

To visit Matty would place in danger all the happiness he had known these past few weeks; even as he was lying to Maura, telling her he wished to visit Ah Poo, Terrier and The Dragoon, even as he was shutting the door against Maura's tight-faced disapprobation, for she did not like his three friends, thought them coarse, boorish; even as he walked up Napoleon Street, he knew that he was risking all that he had built so carefully since Reynolds had had him released from the timber gang.

The house was neat, its facade flush with the footpath like so many of the Battery Point houses, the windowboxes filled with geraniums, the front door painted deep green; even here, as he stood in indecision on the doorstep, he could hear Matty singing inside.

He hesitated at the sound, wanting to turn and walk away. It was over – yet did Matty realize this? 'I'm a great trawneen,' he murmured to himself. 'Should never have begun.' Yet he stepped to the door and knocked.

Och, but she was lovely, still he could see this and appreciate it. She wore a dress of ivory lace which would have cost a working man's yearly wage. The pale, curling hair, drawn back into a heavy chignon, the dress, and her creamy skin gave her a look of fragility

418

that Aidan knew to be deceptive. She flew into his arms as soon as the door was shut behind him, kissing him hard and hungrily.

'Where've you bin? Aidan, I bin going mad here by myself. I thought Ettie'd scared you off.'

'No, it wasn't that.' He turned his face away from her kisses. 'Don't, Matty, we have to talk.'

'Yes, I know that.' She had withdrawn from him, crossed the room and when she turned again to him, she was suddenly cool and in control of herself. She smiled. 'You've changed, you know. Once you couldn't wait to hold me. Why, I remember one night, on that very rug in front of the fire . . .' She stopped, sensing something from the look on his face. 'Well,' she breathed softly, 'all things do change, don't they? Ain't nothing that stays the same.' She sat down on the couch, and after a pause, he seated himself in a chair. He noticed as he did so, that all the furniture was different, of better quality; only the guilty rug was the same, and a few good ornaments. He wondered why she had moved from Cromwell Street.

'Has Ettie been threatening you?' he asked, finally. 'That's the main reason I haven't been to see you. I know that you're dependent upon her. I'd not like to see you in any trouble because of me.'

Could she tell he was lying? The smile on her face deepened until she laughed, softly. 'You don't have to worry about me. Nah, Ettie wouldn't hurt me, I'm too useful to her. It was you I was worried about. Now Nat's dead she's as set as ever on doing you in.' She paused, waiting. He did not speak, and she frowned a little, studied his face. He was thinking, *She's playing with me. She wants me to be afraid.* And he smiled a little himself, and told himself that it was all he deserved, for not loving her, and he liked her a little less, felt a little less sorry for her, because she was the sort of woman who enjoyed another's distress.

Matty said, 'It's you she wants dead, not me. What are you goin' to do?'

'Nothing.'

'Nothing? An' your wife and kids here . . . ?'

'If Ettie was going to have me killed she'd have done so.'

Matty was really puzzled, now. She covered this by snapping at him. 'Confident, ain't you? Don't you underestimate Ettie, Aidan. Other fellows have. Don't forget my father, he was thick enough to turn his back on her one day, and look where it got him.'

'I haven't forgotten anything about Ettie.' *Nor that she raised you, girl, taught you to hate, taught you greed and robbed you of gentleness.* He was tired suddenly, weary of all of them. He stood up, but Matty was quick, and she, too, was on her feet, across to

419

him, her arms around him, her face against his neck. Despite himself, the scent of her stirred him.

She was moving her hands over his body. He reached for her shoulders, and pressed them hard until she was still. When she looked up at him he steeled himself not to gaze at her lips, full, half-parted, waiting lips. He gazed instead into her eyes, beautiful and too knowledgeable. They were the real Matty. He saw that she was not really afraid, was not really distraught at losing him. Her eyes were confident, as he had known Matty always to be confident. Her hands were wandering his body and she was sure of her hands and sure of his body's response.

'I don't want you to go.'

'I must, Matty. We must stop this now . . .'

'I know you don't love me. It's got nothin' to do with love . . .'

'But it should, don't you see that? I don't love you, Matty, sure I've been using you. Find someone who will love you . . .'

'I don't need that. I don't expect you to understand. You only know women like your wife. I'm not like that. I've seen too much. I don't need love and all that sort of talk. I just need you, I need you touching me . . . that's all. And not forever – I never asked for forever. I was goin' to ask you to take me away.' Quickly, as she felt him start to pull back, 'But that was just to protect you. I don't want Ettie to kill you, Aidan. I don't love you, I don't love no one. I seen too much. But I want you alive, and with me for as long as you can be.'

'Matty . . .'

'I don't love you, I don't need you . . .' Her hands were on his body, her mouth on his. When she pulled back, and drew him by the hand towards the narrow stairs, he could do nothing but follow her.

Aidan had written to Milton Reynolds to tell him of Maura's arrival, and two days later Reynolds called in at the boathouse. He impressed Maura with his good manners and gentle humour, and told them of a picnic he had arranged. He would like the O'Briens to join his family, the following Sunday, on a jaunt to Kingston Beach. Maura looked first at Aidan, her eyes alight, and he could tell she was happy that they should accept.

Aidan had been working long and difficult hours at the shipyards; Maura had had much to occupy herself making the old boathouse comfortable, so the Sunday excursion, two weeks before Christmas, 1856, was a matter of excitement and a relief from labour for both of them. Only the children accepted the treat as if it were their due, waiting impatiently on the terraced section of the pier for the sound of horse and wagon to come down the hill. They travelled in a large

420

dray that Reynolds had hired for the journey, the two men taking turns to drive, and Maura, Margaret Reynolds, Emily, Berrima, Richard, Clemency and Liam, all bouncing about in the back with rugs and cushions and picnic baskets.

Already the little settlement at the mouth of Brown's River had begun to be known as Kingston. It was a pleasant beach, a curve of yellow sand with a rocky headland at each end and a view, across the water, of Opossum Bay.

Aidan could tell that Maura was enjoying herself, though even now, after four weeks in the Australian summer, she could not become accustomed to the flies that buzzed and clustered about them. She had sewn red buttons on to her sun hat on loose threads of cotton, and they danced in a fringe when she laughed. And she laughed often that day.

After the meal, the adults walked along the beach and watched the children playing at the water's edge, their shoes and stockings removed, paddling in the surf. Berrima was carrying Richard piggyback, and Clemency walked beside the girl. At seventeen, with her hair up, Berrima seemed the picture of sophistication to Clemency, and worthy of emulation. Aidan had already noticed that his daughter had spent so much time with the English emigrants' children on board the *Tasman* that she had lost some of her Irishness. She called him 'Papa', not 'Da'. He saw her, now, copying Berrima's walk, her gestures; oddly enough it irritated him. Emily was less flamboyant, but eminently more suitable, he felt, as a model for his daughter.

Without preamble, Maura said, 'Anna. That's who it is. Young Berrima – she looks like Anna, Aidan, does she not?'

Margaret Reynolds had heard. 'Anna? And who is Anna, Mrs O'Brien?'

Maura had spoken without thinking of the nearness of the other couple. She nearly glanced at Aidan, but did not. Only he noticed the slight colouring to the freckled cheeks, 'She was my friend. Our friend. Back home.' She raised her head; Margaret Reynolds was gazing at her. 'She was a beautiful girl, she grew into a fine woman. She married well, and went to live in England.'

Reynolds said, 'Well, I should like Berrima to grow into a fine woman, but I don't think I'd like her to go home to live in England. I hope all our family remains here.'

They went on to speak of the possible benefits of sending their children back to Britain to be educated, and the subject of Anna did not come up again.

So even Maura had noticed the resemblance . . . Aidan scowled down towards the shore where the children walked. Emily was now walking beside her sister, her thin plaits an unfortunate mousy brown beside the rich dark chestnut of Berrima's, Clemency's auburn curls, and the thick fair hair of young Richard. Aidan liked the droll Emily; she would grow into an interesting and astute woman. Maura's likening Berrima to Anna only contrasted the two further in Aidan's mind. Berrima was vain and shallow – she did not have the depth nor the constancy of Anna's character. He wondered if Milton and Margaret protecting Berrima was the best thing for her; Emily seemed to cope with Port Arthur and any other unpleasantness life brought her. He felt that the parents were indulging the talkative, precocious Berrima at the expense of Emily. But still Berrima fascinated him, even while she irritated him. To see Berrima was to see Anna come to life once more.

He was thinking of this when he found that Maura had paused, allowing the Reynoldses to move further off from them. She faced back down the beach towards the children for a moment, hesitated, then, 'I thought we might have . . . I hoped I was with child. But I'm not. I'm sorry.'

'With child? Already?'

'I've been here a month.'

'Aye, but there's plenty of time, Maura . . .'

'I'm thirty-three, Aidan, same as you. I want as many children for you as I can. Fine sons like Liam to help you with the land.'

'We'll keep trying,' he said close to her ear, and nuzzled it.

'Och, *you.*' She blushed and laughed and pushed him away a little.

Oh, that was a grand day. The best day, perhaps, of all their days together. Though when he tried to analyse it afterwards there was nothing special about it. It was simply a time of relaxation and laughter, when the future seemed as close and yet as limitless as the blue of the bay or the blue of the sky. A simple day, unclouded by pain or fear. Perhaps that was it: the gift lay in the simplicity itself.

Back home through the dusk, the bay always on their right, deepening to cobalt and indigo in the fading light, past the narrow road, overgrown now with weeds, that twisted down to the abandoned Brown's River Probation Station; the lights of carriages before and behind them, the children singing carols about cold Northern Christmases all through the journey of that warm Australian summer's evening.

It was the next day that Maura wrote to Mary and Thomas, and described their new life; Aidan was pleased with the letter, pleased with the tone of it, for Maura's pleasure in this life was apparent in

422

her writing in a way that was not always obvious in their day-to-day life. Often her fatigue and the strain of her situation as an ex-convict's wife wore on her nerves and she would be sullen and shrewish, and Aidan would wonder if her coming here was the best thing for her after all, whether she would ever adapt, come to see this strange city at the end of the world as home.

But in the letter she exhorted them to come, wrote unconsciously effective and, for Maura, prosey descriptions of the harbour and its lively shipping in order to stir Thomas; described the food and the shops and a growing Liam and Clemency who missed their grandmother, in order to instil the same restlessness in Mary.

They attended midnight Mass on Christmas Eve, walking back through the brightly-lit streets busy with revellers and devout alike. Liam had been sleepy, Aidan had chided Maura for not allowing him to sleep during Mass, but she had insisted that he should be awake, would pinch and shake him a little when he looked to be dozing off. Yet outside in the night air, both children recovered their energy and spirits and half-danced along beside their parents, chattering excitedly about Father Christmas and the possibilities of what he might bring.

Aidan smiled. In his own childhood there had been no such thing as Father Christmas. But Liam and Clemency would be visited by that mythical figure, bearing a set of toy soldiers in green uniform that Aidan had made in his spare time, and a wax-faced doll that had an expression on its face, Aidan told Maura, as if it had its toes stepped on while its mouth was full of toffees.

Aidan felt a warmth of gratitude for the Almighty, and a certain pride in himself that the children would have these gifts. As he unlocked the door and they stepped inside, he was thinking how long it would take for the children to fall asleep, and hoped they would not wake their parents too early in the morning.

It was a dead thing. Long-dead putrifying flesh, their noses told them, and they pulled back from the doorway. 'Oh!' Maura cried out, but Aidan was pushing her back, grabbing Liam by his shoulders, reefing him out the door, almost bowling Clemency over. 'Go downstairs,' he told Maura, his heart thumping with the shock, the knowledge that someone had been here, could be waiting within with that thing. 'Get you down the stairs on to the sand.'

'Aidan . . .'

'Do as I say. Take the children and go.'

'What was that . . . what was that?' Liam was demanding, 'Something smells, what is it? Ma, what is it?'

She hurried them through the little gate and down the stairs. Aidan

waited for a moment to make sure she was safely out of the way, but
had only just opened the door, bracing himself against the desire to
gag at the sickening smell, when from below on the sand came the
rumble of a man's voice, a squeal from Clemency, Maura's voice high-
pitched in hysteria, 'Aidan! Aidan!'

He took two bounds downstairs, vaulted the handrail and
dropped the last six feet to the ground, seeing the dark shadow of a
man before him, he struck out –

'Nay! Aidan! Leave off! 'Tis Will!' Aidan's blow was blocked by
two heavy forearms as Will ducked and covered himself, and the
shock of the contact sent an agonizing pain from Aidan's fist clear
up to his shoulder. Will was holding his forearm, 'You've broke me
arm, damn ye!'

'You, y' great trawneen! What are y' like creepin' about like that!'

They clutched their arms and glared at each other in the darkness.

'Would it be Mr Treloar?' Maura's voice.

'Aye. Mrs O'Brien?'

'I'm sorry. I thought . . . I was afraid.'

''Tis all right now,' Aidan reached for her. He looked about. 'Are
you alone, Will?'

'Aye. I've been with the lads at South Street. Thought 'ee
mightn't be awake and I nearly went back, but I heard your voices.'

'He tried to introduce himself,' said the shadow that was Maura.
'But it was terrified I was . . .'

'What *smells*?'

They had forgotten the children.

Clemency demanded, 'Make it go away, Ma, or Father Christmas
won't come. I don't want him to think our house smells.'

'What's the matter with 'em?'

'Come upstairs, Will. Maura, will you be all right here now?'

'Yes. I'm sorry. A great eejit I feel . . .'

'Don't. None would blame you, sure.'

Aidan started up the stairs again, drawing a puzzled Will with
him. At the top near the gate, the dreadful smell came to them
through the half open door. Will sniffed, 'Phoo, is it you or me?'

'Quiet.' Aidan opened the door slowly. 'Light a match,' he told
Will, standing before him protectively.

'Don't know as t'would be wise, mebbe the air will explode . . .'
But there was a scratching sound and the sudden flaring of light;
Aidan reached for the lamp beside the door.

In the glimmering light as Will put the match to the wick, they
could see the dog, hung from a beam in the centre of the large room.
Will took up the lamp and they walked slowly forward towards the

424

macabre sight. The creature was long dead, its exact breed was impossible to determine, it hung on a thick piece of rope by its neck, the body stiff, unnatural, swinging slightly in the breeze from the doorway.

Will, being the taller, climbed upon the table and cut the animal down; while he was doing so, Aidan went to the loft and came back with a shovel. Will handed the rope and its burden gingerly to Aidan. 'A rare good Christmas gift. Who did this? Ye d'know, don't 'ee?'

'I'll go bury it . . .'

'I'll come with you . . .' Will jumped down from the table top.

'No. No, you look after Maura and the children.' He walked quickly outside and down the steps. Maura, on the sand, shrank back, Liam attempted to step forward.

'What is it, Father?'

'A dead dog.'

'In *our* house?'

'Come away, Liam.' Maura drew the child back from inspecting the grisly remains. 'You're after burying it?' she asked Aidan.

'Aye. Get you upstairs to Will, he'll look after you. It'll be all right now.'

Clemency's voice followed him along the beach. 'Poor dog . . .' she said sadly. 'Who put him there? Who . . .?'

He buried it near the road, deep in the loose, sandy soil, and the harder he worked the more the rage was boiling and thickening within him. When he finished the task and returned to the boat-house he paused at the foot of the stairs . . .

No. No! Damn it, he'd not let them get away with it, he'd not allow them to do this to his family! He leaned the spade against one of the wooden piles, turned on his heel and walked quickly up the sand to the road. He half ran up Bath Street, for he knew the Cornishman would call him back, try to prevent him from his course of action. But he wanted a confrontation, wanted it to be on his terms. And if he died, he would take one or two of them with him, begod.

He had kept his own counsel, relied on himself; for all the years of his imprisonment he had not been part of the dark dealings, the malignant struggles for vantage and dubious, small scale power within the groups of other prisoners. But certain information was overheard, names, deeds, useful contacts, and heard often enough, much of it, until, now the need had arisen, he knew exactly where to go.

First, a return to the cottage in South Street where an amazed

Terrier, Ah Poo and The Dragoon listened to a calm and controlled plea to loan him ten pounds. 'Until the holiday is over and the banks open – I . . . I can't wait until then, y'see.'

They knew Aidan, knew this request was out of character. Ah Poo scratched his head. 'You don't want it for that doxy that you've been sleeping with, do you?'

'Shut up.' Terrier studied Aidan. 'Why do you want it, boy?'

He took a deep breath. 'To buy a gun. For self-protection only.'

They stared at him, the enormity of it striking each of them. They turned and gazed at each other, but remained silent, sensing that Aidan wished that whatever quarrels he had remained *his* quarrels, that by the customs of the world in which they moved, each man's past was his own secret, unless he wished to tell.

They weighed the matter up within their minds, then Terrier stood, The Dragoon climbed awkwardly to his stiff legs, and they were fumbling for their money belts at their waists.

The room where Mullins lived was, if anything, smaller than any of the rooms in the South Street cottage. And it was dirty. Aidan stood trying to close up his nostrils with the force of his will, against the fetid odour from the dirty cooking pots, the filthy nest of blankets in the corner, even the dirt-encrusted rug upon the floor seemed to have absorbed the odour of the unwashed little man before him.

Mullins had a bladder problem; whether through illness or laziness it was very noticeable. Yet Mullins was a paradox. Aidan's reeling senses told him that Mullins had not washed for years, yet the man was dressed in a suit of the latest style, already showing wear in the cuffs and elbows and knees, as well as the droppings from numerous meals down the front of the vest and the once white shirt.

Mullins was nicknamed The Toff. When out and about on his shady dealings, he carried a cane and wore a top hat. It was common knowledge in the town of Hobart that Mullins always dressed in the height of fashion. Always. For until the new season's clothes arrived from England, The Toff would never be out of his latest suit, even to sleep.

'A fine weapon, this.' In the flickering light from the fire and the coarse candle on the mantelpiece, Mullins gazed down at the pistol on the table. 'It's worth every penny.'

'How many times must I be tellin' you, I don't have twelve pounds.'

'It's not easy for a man such as myself. This is a dangerous trade for a gentleman to be in. The authorities have narrow ways of looking at things, like. They can't understand the necessity of the

426

service I provide, that gentlemen such as yourself can't always go to a gunsmith in Macquarie Street . . .'

'I know all . . .'

'You've got to see my . . .'

'I'll give you nine. I told you . . .'

'Nine for a pistol such as this? Brand new! Bought off a Yankee sailor, never used it, he said . . .'

'Nine is what I think it's worth . . .'

'Ten, sir. I'll let you have it for ten because it's late, and I'm tired, and you're a hard man, I can see. I can't win with you, that's obvious, you're determined and me that has to count the pounds and live in humble squalor will just have to . . .'

'Nine. *Nine pounds.*'

'Ten, and I'll throw in this – see? A beauty, isn't it?' The knife appeared from nowhere in Mullins' hand – Aidan started, but the blade was held away from him, the weapon lying flat on Mullins' discoloured palm.

Aidan took the knife gingerly. It was a dagger, its handle white bone, the steel of its blade honed to a sharp point. He did not know how to use a knife in combat. But, he thought grimly, I'll learn fast enough, I'm thinking.

Aidan scowled at the man, but knew that he had to agree, the night was passing and he could waste no more time. Mullins was watching him greedily as he pulled ten pounds, in notes and coins, from his pocket. He counted it into Mullins' hand with a heavy heart.

Mullins was already placing the money carefully in his vest, taking a dozen shells from a drawer, and handing them to Aidan. It was done. He placed the knife in his belt, the pistol in his right hand coat pocket, the extra bullets in his left. He thanked The Toff briefly and headed gratefully for the door, and fresh air.

The clearness of the night was a blissful relief, he paused to breathe it, to breathe the cool air into his lungs, before setting off towards Elizabeth Street, and the Barley Sheaf tavern.

He stood for a moment inside the building, surveying the crowded bar, but recognized no one there. There was a closed door at the back of the room. He crossed over to it, opened it and stepped quickly through.

No one noticed his arrival. The red light from the lamp-shade fell on the various tables, the men standing or sitting about, intent on the games of chance being played out. Men's fortunes were being won or lost, and few bothered to glance up. Aidan, standing with his back against the closed door, his hand on the gun, ready to spring, to

427

shoot, to dodge, found himself feeling rather foolish. He was standing there awkwardly, changing his weight from one foot to another, when a voice rang out from behind, 'What're you lookin' for?'

He turned, expecting to find Jimmy West, or at least one of the two men who had told him of Nat's death, but this man was unfamiliar, and there was no recognition, simply annoyance, in his face.

'I'm looking for Ettie Harding. Or Jimmy West,' he added. 'It's important.'

The man surveyed him narrowly. Then, 'They're upstairs – first door on the right.'

Aidan nodded shortly, and headed off towards the stairs, feeling the man watching him all the way.

This time the manner of his entrance was justified. Ettie Harding, thinner, more haggard-looking, glanced up from her desk; Jimmy West, gazing over her shoulder at the ledger, went pale at the sight of Aidan – then both of them were fumbling for the top drawer of the desk.

'Stop. Don't try it.' The gun was in Aidan's hand. He held it steady, pointing it at Ettie. She and Jimmy were still.

'You're mad, O'Brien,' West whispered.

'Maybe I am, and maybe I amn't. Just don't move!'

Ettie leaned back in her chair. West straightened, and moved back a little from the desk. They stared at Aidan. 'Y're animals,' he breathed. 'Y're worse than animals – y're as filthy as that creature y' hung in my house tonight. Y' terrified my wife and my children – those who have done you no harm. I ought to shoot you where you are. Y' deserve it, sure!'

'What're y' talkin' about, O'Brien?' Ettie's eyes narrowed, 'We never done nothing to your house . . .'

'Then one of your men . . .'

'It's Christmas, O'Brien, what d'you take me for?'

He could only stare at her, the ludicrous but genuinely affronted dignity of her. And Aidan noticed then, the loose skin of her large frame, the cheeks slack and the features so changed that if it were not for the bright gold of her elaborate hair and the still bright luminosity of the dark eyes, he would not have recognized her.

She's ill, he thought. And yet that knowledge did nothing to stir pity within him, he had the memory of his family's terror, the thought of Jimmy West in his house, *his house* . . . In Ettie's illness he felt only a sense of ultimate resolution, saw only his one way of breaking through to her.

His words came slowly, deliberately, with a cruelty born of his

428

rage. 'I'm here because I want one thing and one thing only – leave me alone, damn y', or y'll regret the day you tried to appease your own guilt by blamin' me for Nat's death.' Ettie began to speak. 'Shut up! Nat was a coward and a weakling and he couldn't have made it alone in the world anyway. You tried to help him to a freedom he knew he couldn't cope with – if anyone killed him, you did. I've left a letter explaining everything with my lawyer – it'll be opened if I die violently – the police will be banging on your door a few hours after. And you'll not want to spend your last days in the horror of the Female Factory, will you, Ettie? One coarse cotton dress and no one to arrange y'r hair? No men, no liquor . . . Just women as evil as y'rself and younger, Ettie, younger and stronger . . .'

'You don't scare me, O'Brien . . .' But her eyes belied her.

'An' when you die, Ettie,' his imagination took control of him, 'when you die and all y'r friends have disappeared who've been involved in killing me, then my friends 'll come forward – and they'll dig your body up, Ettie, from whichever hallowed ground y've bought y'r way into, and they'll hang y'r body on a tree in the scrub beyond Ferntree – an' the crows'll pick y'r eyes out and you'll rot and no one will find you! An' it's all you deserve, y' great harpy, for what y're doing to my wife and children!'

'You're mad, O'Brien!' she shrieked, 'You're a ghoul, y' know that? You're sick in the head!'

'No more 'n you! We're all mad! So leave me be! Leave me and my family be, Ettie, or I'll follow you to hell so I will, to see you suffer!' He stopped. He had blurted out more than he had meant to – he was angrier than he had thought possible.

When they had not touched his life, kept out of his way, he had forgotten about these two, shutting his mind to the memory of their mindless violence, their malevolence and unremitting resentment. He had seen it all at the hut on Mountain River, but now, through reasons that he could not fully fathom, their venom was directed at him, and his contempt for them, in his defence of his family, flared into open hatred.

They sensed it, did not move. He opened the door, pocketed the gun, and closed the door after himself quickly.

He took the wrong turning at the foot of the stairs, and found himself, to his chagrin, once more in the room of crimson-tinted gamblers, a world he had never seen before and could not look at now, could not stop to study. He expected any minute to hear footsteps behind him, to feel the bullets in his back at the same time as he heard the explosions from the gun. The forced calm of his walk from the room filled with the intent figures seemed interminable.

429

Even afterwards, in years to come when he would visit, briefly, the expensive gilt and red plush gambling houses of Sydney and Melbourne, they would bring back the same sick feeling, the same sense of danger, of potential death.

Down the corridor, past the crowded bar that reeked of ale and cheap alcohol. Out into the damp street, to walk quickly away, towards the harbour, and home.

A cool rain began to fall as he crossed Morrison Street, around Parliament Square and into Salamanca Place, near the docks. His heart was still beating fast, his nerves taut, his very step still truculent and aggressive, so that the various groups of men who haunted the wharf area, the lazing scavengers of the night, leaning in doorways, waiting in alleyways, watched him walk past with his hands jammed into his pockets – and allowed him to walk on.

He turned up Kelly's Steps, the narrow stone stairway that bridged the steep rise from Salamanca Place to Kelly Street above, still wondering if anyone was following him, perhaps waiting for him, or would he now be left in peace?

The figure stepped out of the shadows at the head of the stairs. Aidan had no time to fumble the gun from his pocket – he brought his hand up, loose, swept it up and across, dodged even as he felt it connect with the man's face, dashed up the last few steps, had his weight braced to push the man down the steps when something in the shadowy figure made him pause.

'Will!'

'This is the second time tonight y've set upon me . . . !'

'Will, f' God's sake, how was I to know . . . ?'

'I can't conceive how you'll survive, Aidan, behaving as you do. What mischief have you been up to? Where have 'ee been?'

'Will . . .' he began, then said, 'Come home. We risk our lives standing here talking.'

They turned along McGregor Street. 'Terrier told me what had happened, why 'ee needed money . . .' He talked louder over Aidan's growl, 'I knew it was something to do with Ettie Harding . . .

'Aidan – you don't know how lucky you are, to have Maura and the children . . .' There was a look of pain about Will. Aidan slowed his pace, tried to study the man in the dim light. 'I mean it,' Will was saying, and he took Aidan's arm suddenly, and pulled him about to face him—

The bullet ripped through Aidan's side, he knew he'd been hit by a bullet, the explosion was still ricocheting about between the buildings . . . the two men, standing close to each other, gazed into

430

each other's eyes with the same bewildered look. All Aidan could think of was that Will must have shot him, Will had shot him . . .

But Will was crumbling, falling, his weight crushing Aidan to the ground, the man's grip on his arm like a vice, and blood – blood everywhere, wet and warm, now cold as Will rolled away from him, the face lifeless.

The bullet meant for Aidan had passed first through Will.

44

Quick footsteps, muffled, running footsteps, there to his left – and Aidan was on his feet and running in pursuit, stumbling, slipping on the uneven soil of a vacant piece of land. He ignored the pain in his side, and held a hand to his chest as he ran, not caring, now, whether he died or not. But he would catch this figure before him. Catch him and kill him.

The man had scrambled over a fence. Aidan could hear the sound of booted feet fading across a cobbled yard, as he himself vaulted the wooden barrier, half-falling to the ground in his haste. He felt the gun fall from his pocket, but did not pause to pick it up, and tore down the side of the cottage to the street.

The little circular road called Arthur's Circus, small drab cottages all around, was still in darkness. Very little light but there he was, speeding down Runnymede Street, back towards the wharves, towards the warren of yards and alleyways around the warehouses; once there he was lost for ever.

This knowledge and his hatred gave Aidan added speed. He caught the man at a corner. His grasping hands reached for the man's coat, tearing at him, dragging him back into the vortex of Aidan's unleashed violence.

There was blood all over West . . . so it was West, Aidan could see him now, the blood pouring out of his head; Aidan let him go as hands started to pull him off the man. 'Y're killin' 'im, y' brute!'

'Look wot 'e's . . .'

'See wot 'e done . . .'

'Against the lamppost! Look wot 'e . . .'

He would do it again, his hands itched to get at the man, to finish

431

him . . . but he backed away, still looking down at the bloodied, motionless Jimmy West, the gun that had killed Will lying near his hand, the blood upon it, also.

Aidan glanced at the faces around him, even as the men in nightshirts and coats were elbowing each other.

'Don't let 'im go . . .'

'Catch 'im, come on . . .'

'Alf . . . grab 'im, Alf . . . !'

He had turned and fled, back up Runnymede Street, across the grass at the centre of Arthur's Circus, ran with the terror now pumping through his veins where only a few seconds before the numbing rage had possessed him. His wits clear, details fixed themsevles within his mind, his wits racing . . . Left into Hampden Road, dodging through the streets, down the slope towards the Derwent's broad estuary, flowing like a black shadow beyond the shore lights.

He was possessed of a dreadful fear, above and beyond the threat to his life and freedom that followed him. It was the thought that *it was happening again*. Death in the narrow streets of a town, the death of a friend, a blinding desire for revenge, the knowledge that escape was his only hope, the running, running . . .

The years passed away as if in a dream and he was once more in Killaloe, panicked, helpless, bewildered, handicapped with the knowledge that this race for his life was in earnest, a reality, yet the reasons for the escalating horror of the night, the paths that led to this destruction were lost to him. *Why?* his mind screamed again as he had screamed to the flat and merciless faces of the grey housefronts of Killaloe.

He glanced behind him on turning into Napoleon Street, and seeing no sign of his pursuers, leaned back against the stone wall of a building, breathing deeply, gathering his wits. Where to go? Home? That would involve Maura. Dear God, Maura . . . Doctor Reynolds? The man would insist Aidan give himself up. Lord, there was no hope for him. Assault it would be, this time, and back to Port Arthur, once more in chains. Will. *Will*. The man's face on the ground, as he had last seen him. *He died instead of me*. The thought ripped through his confused mind, had him leaning back with his eyes closed against the pain. *It should have been me . . .*

His mind processed three thoughts, quickly, wordlessly within his head without realizing it. This was total despair, the blackest pit of his life; he must go somewhere, get off the streets before they found him; he would go to Matty, take the risk of trusting her, while he sat down to think.

He started walking. He must not panic, must quell the rising taste of bile within his throat, must think coolly.

Here was the change from Killaloe, although he did not realize it. Somewhere in the forced discipline of the past years he had learned control, he was not running blind. In the silences of solitary and the work gangs of Brown's River and Port Arthur, he had confronted himself and studied himself and the past, and his actions within his experiences. Nothing could have prevented him beating Jimmy West, any more than anything could have prevented him from attempting to kill Devlin Kelly. Their actions had called up all the violence of his nature – but now he walked down the street above this harbour at the world's end, and no voices twittered and gibbered and called him down in a spiral to his own destruction. It did not occur to him to end his life. He had known the worst before, had thought that nothing could threaten his sanity to that extent again, but the depths were there, confronting him again, it threatened to swallow him into a maw of terror and hopelessness; and only he was different, and he did not know it.

He was aided in finding Matty's house by a faint light behind the heavy window drapes; Aidan hesitated, for it occurred to him that Matty might not be alone. He stood at the door and listened, but there was no sound from within. The night had turned chill, and he shivered in his coat that was damp from the rain. He knocked softly on the door. Silence. Behind him, a cat leapt up on to the fence of a nearby yard and he started, fear turning his stomach to ice until he saw the animal there, staring at him with incurious round eyes.

He knocked again. Still no answer. The flickering of the light told him that she had a fire lit, for despite the season it was a cold night.

Behind the houses a lane could be found, surely. He loped off, around the corner, and managed, by counting fences, to find the tiny yard at the rear of Matty's house. Climbing the fence, he went to the back door, giving a murmured prayer of gratitude to find it open.

The house was empty. He placed more wood on the fire, for he was trembling badly, and chilled with dry sweat. He checked the wound in his side; it was not bad, he had seen much worse caused by accidents and fights at Port Arthur. He should clean it, he supposed – but he was tired, so tired . . .

Matty had dreamed, the night before, that Aidan was dead. Ettie had come to her, and announced that Aidan had been shot dead by Jimmy West. The dream was so real that Matty carried her grief about with her all day. There were no Christmas celebrations for her; as the day progressed, her forebodings grew, and with these unwelcome feelings, her long-buried hatred of Ettie grew too.

It was a damp night, and she lit a fire in the hearth as much to warm her thoughts as to warm her body. She fell asleep on the couch, to dream the same dream, but this time she saw Aidan's body on the ground, lying on black cobblestones, his chest covered with blood. She awoke from a picture of Ettie's gloating face and ran for her cloak, a few belongings she had taken from the Barley Sheaf recently, and ran out into the fine misty rain.

She passed Jimmy as he was coming out of the tavern, took his arm and demanded what Ettie had done with Aidan O'Brien. He had been looking nervously up and down the street as she approached, and now opened his eyes wide, and pushed her hard, back against the door before running off, down the street towards the harbour.

Her reticule purse was heavy in her hand, but Matty felt quite calm as she climbed the stairs.

Ettie looked up, furious, as Matty opened the door. 'I said get after that . . .' She stopped, and in a lower tone, 'Get out of here. You don't work for me no more, you can just get your arse out of . . .'

'I passed Jimmy outside . . .'

'So?'

Something was wrong. Ettie was leaning back in her chair suddenly, and smiling.

'You done it, haven't you? You finally done it. Sent that poor dumb bastard out to do your dirty killing for you.'

'I'm too old to do it meself any more.' The dark eyes were dangerous slits. 'Get out, Matty, don't come mewling to me 'cause you lost a good bit of cock.'

'You wouldn't know about that, would you? Aidan never looked at you, let alone . . .'

'I had him! I had him at Brown's River!' She was rising from her chair. 'I had him in the bush at Brown's River and he was nothing! Nothing!'

Matty laughed. To Ettie it was sick-making, the beauty of her, the pale, calculating eyes, the confident depth to her laughter. Matty was drawling, 'Nothing . . . Well that just goes to prove you the lying old bag of farts I always thought you was – because I can tell you Aidan is *something*, Ettie. A woman couldn't forget the feel of 'im – why do you think I can't give him up? He's one in a million – but you wouldn't know that. That's why it poisons you that he's walking around, making love to other women . . . You wanted him

434

at Brown's River, oh, yeah – I'll believe that. You wanted him at Mountain River for sure – you were drooling over him the whole time . . . Are you looking for this?'

She pulled a neat little silver inlaid revolver from her half-open reticule. Ettie gasped, looked down at the desk drawer she had been fumbling through for the past several seconds.

'Gawd, Ettie – I ran this place for years while you were in Melbourne. Did you think I'd hand it back to you without having copies made of all the keys?'

Ettie's face was grey. She was sidling around the desk, looking at Matty and half-whimpering in fear. Her jowls wobbled, and Matty, who wanted the moment to be serious, was hard put not to laugh. Ettie was backing across the room, and Matty followed her, slowly, a graceful, pale cat stalking, stalking . . .

At the door Ettie turned and ran – Matty caught her at the head of the stairs. Her own heart was beating hard, but not in fear, no way, for she had waited, waited so long for this . . . the heavy piece of piping, lethal but slim enough to fit in Matty's capable hand, came out of the reticule. Matty was tall, fit, the blow was easily delivered, and thank God, no blood . . .

And in the end the precaution was unnecessary. Ettie lay at the foot of the stairs, two men bending over her, as Matty ran down, her purse closed, consternation on her face. Ettie's eyes were fixed on her, and she stopped in mid-step and almost stumbled. But no, the neck was at such a funny angle, surely it was all right. Matty came down the stairs, knelt in a graceful swish of silk skirts by the body of her stepmother.

'She's dead . . .' one of the men said, his face pale. Ettie Harding had seemed as indestructable as Mount Wellington itself.

'Bloody hell . . .' Matty murmured. 'And at Christmas, too.'

Aidan awoke with a start, dreaming that the Sidhe of Craglea was reaching out to touch his face – he shrank at her touch, cried out – and Matty was there, on her knees beside his chair.

'Well . . .' a nervous laugh from her. 'You're alive, at least.'

He managed a grin. 'Are you pleased?'

'Yes,' she breathed. 'You're like a miracle, you are. I really thought . . .' She stopped.

'What – that Ettie had done for me?' He stopped, remembered, and sat up abruptly, wincing with the sudden pain.

Matty fetched a bottle of whiskey and glasses from a cupboard. 'I'll pour us one, then I got to get you fixed up and home.' As the golden liquid glinted into the small glasses, she said, 'Jimmy did this

435

to you, right?'

'He . . . killed Will . . . aiming at me . . .'

'Treloar? Your mate? What happened? You get Jimmy?' All the attention of those light blue eyes were focused on him. 'Did you?' she insisted.

'I beat the bejaysers out of him – I hope to God I've not killed him.'

'I hope to God you have,' she said in an undertone. He heard her.

'I'm going to the police tomorrow.'

'Like hell you are. There's no need,' she added quickly. 'Not if you mean because of Ettie. I wouldn't even worry about Jimmy. No, now I think about it, he'd be pretty useless, poor Jimmy, without Ettie to tell him what to do.' He was looking up at her, the black brows creased. She patted his face, handed him his glass of whiskey, and said gently, 'There was an accident at the Barley Sheaf tonight, love. Ettie got roarin' drunk – not unusual – and she fell down the stairs. There wasn't nothing to be done for her – snuffed it real quick, she did.'

'Ettie is dead? But I was with her not an hour ago, or . . .' He caught sight of the clock on the mantelpiece, and rubbed his forehead, 'No . . . four hours ago . . .'

'Anyone recognize you?' Again the careful scrutiny.

'I don't think so.' She had turned away, was placing her own drink down upon a table. 'Matty . . . ' as she was about to leave the room. He stood, 'I'll go now – I have to find out if Will . . .'

'You have to stay here 'til I fix you up, you got to look neat in case they stop you on the street, don't you see?'

What Aidan could see was turning around before him, slowly, the fire, the coal scuttle, the mantel and its clock. He sat down again.

Matty fetched hot water, bandages, and dressed and bound the deep wound the bullet had scored along his side. He kept telling her sleepily that he was all right, he was grand, sure . . . He must find Will . . . He must find Will . . .

He lay on the couch and dozed fitfully. Soon she would move him to the bedroom. He could not make love to her, but she could hold him. Perhaps this was the best thing to have happened, she thought, watching his face, pale among the cushions, the dark hair falling across his forehead. He had come to her, not to his wife.

She turned to scowl into the fire. What a bore that Stephen owned this house – and how bloody lucky that he had gone to Melbourne for two months! She looked back at the strong face on the settee. What would he say if he knew whose house this was, that she had not one lover but three? Griffith Rodgers knew about Stephen, Stephen suspected, sullenly, the existence of Griffith and Aidan. But Aidan – it'd be more than her life was worth to tell him of the others. Or, she frowned, she hoped so. She liked the idea of him being wild with jealousy, unhappily could not see it occurring. She looked at him with some resentment.

'The woman hasn't been born yet that'll really stir you, you bastard.'

And the brown eyes opened, fixed on her, the mouth turned up a little on one corner. 'I heard that,' he said.

Nothing she could do that night would arouse Aidan. He lay on the bed beside her, and stared at the ceiling. She had changed into an expensive linen nightdress that she had never worn before. She wanted him only to kiss her, tell her that he loved her, but he was so silent. She was disappointed, bitter. This night was something she had planned for a long time. Stephen, the fool, was so besotted with her that he would have let her bring six men home and clear himself out of the way. She paused in her thoughts of how to arouse the man to think with displeasure of Stephen, small, pale, pathetic, a regular client at Ettie's brothel until he met her, because he could not, for all his neat lawyer's mind and well-ordered comfortable existence, bring himself to show affection. He had to trade for it. Would trade anything for it. Especially from Matty. Her own passion, lying beside Aidan, was fast fading with the thought of Stephen's quid pro quo if he learned that a man had spent the night in his house, in his bed. And she could take little more of it. If Aidan left without her she would have to stay here.

She had to think of something. She could not continue suffering Stephen's bony arms and damp, tentative kisses, not even for financial security. 'Aidan, just look at me.'

'No. Don't, Matty.'

'Aidan . . .'

'I'm trying to think, Matty . . .'

'Don't worry, love. I told you – tomorrow I'll find a place for you to hide. I'll get a boat passage, too, and maybe forge some papers. If you got money it can be done. We'll go to the mainland – you'll be safe, you'll see.'

She had told him this downstairs, and he had been too tired to argue. It was unbelievable that she could consider throwing her lot in with him, adapting to a life on the run, considering the way he had treated her. Yet it was something she wanted. He had watched her eyes dancing as she talked of the plan, to use her money to go to the anonymity and potential wealth of the goldfields.

He wondered where she would get the money. He had the suspicion that she would steal it, somehow, from Ettie. But he did not ask her.

For he was not tempted. Whatever held him to Maura, and he was no longer so blind nor optimistic to call it love, he could not do this to her. She had given him loyalty and support, and despite his failing her, she still showed a love for him, a pride in him, and gave him as much affection as she possessed. Maura deserved his loyalty. It was her upright character and unrelenting integrity that held him to her, across the thousands of miles, that would continue to hold him to her all the days of their lives together.

He slept, finally, for a few hours, and woke to find Matty wound about him; she was drowsing in that period of half-sleep. The dawn was a grey light at the casements. He gazed out, realizing he would be on those streets, somewhere, if it had not been for the girl beside him. He was filled with a sense of responsibility for her, a kind of gratitude that warmed him to her. She awoke and reached for him, and he made love to her with a tenderness that surprised both of them. The wound on his side opened again. 'Was it worth it?' she asked mischievously.

'Yes . . .' he said, reluctantly, still puzzled at the joy he could find in their lovemaking.

For Matty it was a wondrous thing, it filled her with a sense of victory, she saw it as the beginning of his love for her. For Aidan it had a sweet bitterness; despite Matty's pleadings, he rose, afterwards, and dressed, and with her curses and entreaties still ringing in his ears, he walked home to the boathouse.

She was building up the fire for tea-making, as she did every morning. He walked in and stood there, watching her. Slowly she straightened, and for a long moment they gazed at each other.

'He's been taken to the hospital,' Maura said, finally.

His heart lifted. 'Will, you mean?'

'Of course, Will!' she snapped. Then her face changed, and she came towards him, stood beneath him studying, he knew, the changes in his face. He walked past her, and sat down in his chair by the small grate where they did their cooking. 'What happened to you?' her voice followed him.

'Nothing,' tiredly. 'Leave off, Maura.'

And oddly enough, she did. She said only, 'Will came last night to tell us about his wife. He didn't know how to, before, kept it to himself – that's why you've not seen much of him. She died, Aidan. She never left Lostwithiel. Will came to tell us, and to give us Christmas presents. Yours is on the shelf, there.'

438

He could not even look where she pointed, and sat gazing into the hearth for a long time. There were no words of reproach from Maura, but the chill of her disgust with him fell all around him like a sleety shower.

When the police called, later that day, she lied for him. The children were awake by then, and Clemency asserted even louder than Maura that her father wouldn't leave them on Christmas Day.

An enquiry was made, but no real evidence was forthcoming. Jimmy and even Ettie had too many enemies amongst the criminal element of Hobart Town. The police had their own theory that it was a well-planned take-over of some of Jimmy's and Ettie's more unsavoury business concerns. Will Treloar, who could tell them nothing, must have been shot by mistake. And in this, at least, they were right.

Cora Frazer came to Hobart Town several times to visit Will, who was a long time mending, and often stayed at the boathouse. Aidan, who spent his time going between the boathouse, the shipyard and the hospital, shut his mind from a great deal of thought in that time. He knew Cora Frazer wished him to come to work with Will at the Huonville property, but his mind was considering broader avenues of escape.

He read, without really setting out to do so, everything he could on the many ambitious emancipists who had risen to positions of power and eminence in Australia. And these, he mused, were the ones who were not ashamed of their pasts, Greenway, Dry, Redfern, the wonderful Mary Reibey. Who was to know how many successful men and women, once they possessed their pardons, had changed their names, moved on to a different colony, or back to their own countries, and worked their way to a better future with a clean, though fabricated past? Terrier Adams had recently left for the goldfields – might he not do the same? It was worth considering.

With Milton Reynolds's help, he had applied for an unconditional pardon – this would mean he would be allowed to return to Ireland if he wished. He did not plan to, but he chafed, all the same, knowing he could not. He came home from checking with unhelpful, supercilious clerks in the Convict Department, one afternoon in early February, and found his brooding disappointment forgotten as soon as he opened the door.

The boathouse was empty.

The furniture was the same, except for Maura's little rocking chair that he had made for her. There was tea and bread and cold meat; the hearth was swept clean and a fire set ready for lighting. The tiny, hand-made cushions were gone from the bed, Maura's pillow was gone. He fled up the stairs to the broad loft. No sandy boots on the floor, no toys lining the narrow windowsill. The mattresses were gone from the two small beds.

The note was downstairs, propped against the pipestand that Will had carved for him as a Christmas present.

> *Aidan,*
>
> *She came to see me two days ago, your friend Matty Harding. She told me that you it was who killed the man we read about in the newspaper. She said, You see, now, the kind of man you married. Sure I saw the kind of man he had become.*
>
> *And you went to her. You went to* her *instead of me. You were betraying me with her since you came to this colony. You had better stay with her in Hobart Town. You and she are two of a kind, as she said.*
>
> *As you know, Mrs Frazer wants us to take up employment on her property – I am glad now that you did not consider it, though Will says it would have been the job of overseer. He says you could have been grand, you have the experience. But you never would consider it, and of course you never asked how Liam and I felt about it.*
>
> *Mrs Frazer had said I could help her in the house – I have taken the risk that she will take me alone, and have left with the children on the morning packet to Huonville.*
>
> *I called to see Will before we left and told him. He is anxious to see you of course, and he wants us to be together again. He is a good and kind man.*
>
> *Should you decide to come to the Huonville property, I must tell you that we will not be living together again as husband and wife. I have told no one the real reasons, of course, but you will understand. You have failed God, me, and your children, not once but over and over again. I can never forgive you.*
>
> *Maura.*

His rage was all directed inwardly. He sat down slowly into a chair, propped the letter against the sugar bowl in the centre of the table, and watched it from a distance, as if it were a painting. 'Well, well,' he whispered.

So he was free, was he? Off to the goldfields, would it be? Off to Matty to wring that pretty little neck? Off to the hospital to place Will's mind at rest? Bitch that Maura was, to upset him.

He rose, left the boathouse, and paused on the jetty, where he stood looking out at the soft grey of the estuary, at the lights beginning to flicker into life in the houses of Sandy Bay and Taroona. A ship's horn sounded mournfully from beyond Secheron

Point. He would go to Will. To Matty? No. She had ceased to exist for him. To the goldfields of Victoria? Maybe, not just yet. He would wait in Hobart Town for the damn Lieutenant-Governor to decide whether or not he was to be pardoned, and then he would go to the Huon Valley. He would write that evening to Maura, and to Cora Frazer. He would make a good wage as a farm overseer. He would go to Victoria with money enough to keep himself should he take a little time to succeed. He had no doubt but that he would succeed. And the children would be with him. He would succeed for the children.

A picture came to him, unbidden, of Berrima Reynolds. She danced along the deserted little beach to his right in the same way she had danced along the strand at Kingston; confident, careless, innocent of her power. If he left for Victoria, he would never see Berrima again. Half his age. Daughter of one of his closest friends. Sure it was a good reason to be going to Victoria.

In the final hours of that night, Matty woke screaming from a nightmare.

'It's all right . . . It's all right, Matty . . .' A man's voice beside her. The picture of Ettie Harding and the axe, the squalid bush hut, the blood – all vanished. She flung herself sobbing into the man's arms. It was very dark, and she could not, for the first few seconds, remember who it was she was holding.

'Poor child . . .' Cultured voice, slurred with drink and sleep. Of course, she was in Griffith Rodgers' rooms in Davey Street. So beautiful, Grif. She curled up into his arms, asking herself for the hundredth time why he was such a drunk. His family was one of the finest in Tasmania and the younger colony of Victoria. Grif had everything – and he chose to drown it all in whiskey. And he was so *nice*, most of the time.

He was used to her nightmares, and had fallen asleep once more, his mouth open. His breath was bad and she turned away a little.

Three nights before she'd gone to see *Macbeth* at the Theatre Royal. The bloke was good, but his queen wasn't up to much. Matty could have done better . . . then the queen had started walking around at night, having nightmares about doing the old king in, and Matty had forgotten to be critical. When that awful wailing started offstage, and the skinny messenger in blue tights came in and told Macbeth that the queen had gone and killed herself, Matty had made Stephen take her home. He was reluctant to go, saying that the best part was the sword fight at the end, but she insisted.

She had spent the next few days with Grif. He was more solid, a selfish bastard, but his arms were strong, and he made her feel safe.

Yet it should be Aidan who was holding her. There would be no nightmares if it wasn't for Aidan. She had thought Ettie alive was pretty hideous; Ettie dead was terrifying. Matty had gone to Aidan's wife, hoping he would come to her in anger. He had not. She should have told him what she had done, killed Ettie to avenge – as she'd thought – his death. Maybe he would have stayed then, out of . . .

Out of what? her honesty demanded. Out of pity? Guilt? She had been right not to tell him, neither of these things would hold Aidan O'Brien.

She stretched, and smiled at the ceiling. He would come back to her, though. Tomorrow, or next year. He was a passionate man, and that wife of his couldn't last to the first furlong post, let alone stay Aidan's distance. He'd be back. She cuddled into Grif, began stirring him with her capable little hands. In the meantime, she could amuse herself, Mister O'Brien, thank you very much.

45

It was nine months later, in September, 1857, that Aidan returned to the Huon Valley.

He could recognize no familiar face in the small crowd that had gathered to welcome the little steam packet. Still, he was not disturbed, asked directions to the Frazers' farm, and set out on foot to find it. One of Maura's few replies to his letters had told him that she and the children were living in the original farmhouse; Will had a room in the new homestead. It was a stone building of two storeys, he was told, about four miles further along the road. It was the only place like it, it would not be hard to find.

He enjoyed the walk, the sense of freedom after the narrow streets of Battery Point. And within his breast pocket, after months of waiting, he carried his Unconditional Pardon. This was the real freedom; he could go anywhere, his own master once again, and need no longer inwardly shrink at the sight of a blue uniform.

The knowledge added a buoyancy to his step; he looked around him with a satisfaction bordering on delight, noting that the gently sloping fields were as green as Ireland, and shadowed, on the hills, with virgin forest. Many of the farms were planted with orchards that were white with apple blossom, acre on acre, and their perfume came to him on the breeze.

At the top of a rise in the road he paused, for the skyline of hills and the surrounding fields were familiar to him. Only then did he see the house, two-storey stone, as it had been described to him, a few hundred yards further on. But here, here was where he was meant to be . . .

He gazed down the slope to his left.

It was half-hidden by shrubs, now, for someone had planted a garden before it. But it was the same. Two rooms of red brick, and smoke coming from the chimney of the kitchen at the rear. Behind the house, further down the slope, he could see the old apple trees, eight years older, eight years taller, than when he had rummaged amongst them for windfalls, desperate, starving, in the autumn of 1849. Now they were starred with blossoms, white petals fell from the branches as the breeze stirred them, and brought their fragrance to him where he stood.

There was a dream-like quality to the scene. He had to tell himself, 'They are there, my wife, my son, my daughter. They are there, in that house . . .' For it did not seem as if it could be real. He found the slip rails, and climbed through, walking slowly down the path towards the front verandah.

He knocked at the door. Silence, no footfall from within the building. He knocked again. Again silence. But a voice murmuring, somewhere . . .

He followed the sound, around the side of the building, past the wall and broad brick chimney that backed the kitchen fireplace. He stopped at the corner of the house, his gaze upon the scene of clear creek water behind the gnarled trunks and overgrown blossom-covered branches. From one of these – he began walking stiff-legged and disbelievingly down the slope – a swing was hung, and a girl of eight or nine was seated upon it, the thin legs in black boots and stockings stretched back and forth; the long plaits swinging behind or falling over the shoulders of a grubby white pinafore. One hair ribbon was loose; when she leaned back, it trailed along the ground. She was singing a song in Irish, about a daughter begging her mother to allow her to go to the fair.

Aidan joined in the chorus, and the light little voice stopped at the sound. She turned to face him, then smiled, slowly, and continued. Begod, but she was like Maura, the jaw a little more square, the hair darker, but gold-threaded as the sun through the branches touched it. She made no move, even when the song ended. Maura's eyes, green as the new leaves above her, watched him approach. 'Hello, Clemency,' he said, gently, and hesitated, did not know if he should reach for her or not – arra, he'd die, so he would, if she should push him away . . . He wanted to touch the copper of her hair, hold her in his arms and dance about the field with her, throw her into the air and hear her laugh, hear her call him Papa.

But they remained gazing at each other, each feeling awkward, shy, wary of the other.

He sensed someone behind him, turned, somehow expecting to find Maura . . .

Liam stood there, a school satchel over the shoulder of a blue shirt, his trousers short, above the knees and patched in several places, grey socks down about his ankles and short boots laced at the instep.

The boy stood like a statue, pale, staring, then, 'You came. You came back.' And he was into Aidan's arms, the two holding each other, rocking each other and weeping, and all the time the boy kept repeating, 'You came! You came back!'

'Of course . . . of course I did. Nothing would keep me away from you all!'

'Ma said you might not be home for a long time, that you might go to the goldfields first, or stay in Hobart and not come here – we were waiting for a letter from you . . .! Here comes Ma, now . . .'

Aidan stood still, looking up in the direction Liam indicated. Across the paddock from the large stone homestead, Maura walked briskly, her cotton dress clinging to her stride. She bent and climbed through the wire fence to approach them.

'There you are – wasn't I after telling you to come straight to the big house? Just look at you!' And it was not clear whether she addressed son, daughter or husband, her glance encompassed them all, but slid away. She reached, suddenly, for Clemency, and for a second the girl shrank back against her brother, feeling for Liam's hand. Maura was impatient, 'Stand still, Clemency – y'r ribbon is untied.' She refastened it, ignoring her husband.

Aidan stood confused, gazing at her, not knowing what to say. So often he had rehearsed this meeting, felt it to be important, for it affected the rest of their lives, but Maura, when she turned to him, was tight-lipped; studying him, but with no real animosity in her gaze, it was as if he was no more to be blamed for his absence than Clemency was for hers. They were tiresome, both of them a chore. But they were hers.

444

'Have you eaten?'

'Not since early this morning . . .'

'Oh. Well, you'll want tea, then, after your walk. Come within.'

And she turned and led the way up the slope to the slab-built kitchen that Aidan remembered. He felt like a guest, unexpected, tolerated, not altogether trusted. Only Liam's and Clemency's hands, slipped quietly within his own as they walked, gave him any confidence. Why, I was more welcome when I was stealing the apples, he thought.

The kitchen appeared much the same, though the walls looked as if they had been recently whitewashed, and there were flowers in small vases on the mantelpiece and the table. He realized Maura must have been caring for the garden. Back home in Killaloe there had been no desire, no need for gardens. It pleased him to find that she had this interest, but he wondered at what other changes the months had brought. They had had so little time together, less than two months, before West's attack and the events that had taken her away from him. He hoped that in some way the separation might work for good, that they both might have matured, their expectations of each other become more realistic, that there would have grown up within each of them a desire to please, to cherish the other. It would take time to find out. They were, at the moment, merely acquaintances, only the children holding them together.

He sat at the table in the same chair that Cora Frazer had shown him to, his back to the corner, this time in order to see all the room, his wife and daughter preparing the meal, the boy fetching more firewood from outside.

With their cups of tea, Maura placed an apricot pie before them. All four members of the family had a slice, but it was eaten in a strained atmosphere. It was not hostile, but there was too much unsaid.

'So, the Frazers have taken care of you? You've been happy here?' he asked Maura.

'Happy enough. They're kind people.'

'Uncle John and Will are going to Port Davey, aren't they, Ma?' Liam said.

'Don't speak until y'r spoken to, Liam.' And to Aidan she said, 'We've managed well enough. The children's school is just along the road – they've no need of that pony, but the Frazers spoil them as though they were their own.' She added, 'I teach needlework and French at the school on Wednesdays.'

He gazed at her in amazement. But of course. She was clever, and better educated than many women in the colony, it was a natural vocation for her. 'Do you enjoy it?' he asked.

'It means more money sure. Cora – Mrs Frazer doesn't mind.'

There was a pause. Aidan watched his daughter, pushing her pie about her plate with a fork.

'Clemency looks a great deal like you.'

Maura gazed at her daughter, but did not answer. Aidan, even in Hobart, had often noticed that there was never any real warmth in Maura's gaze whenever she looked at Clemency. He felt with a sudden cold certainty that Maura resented the child. His wife's gaze was still fixed on her, but he felt there was no fondness there, merely a clinical scrutiny. The memory came to him that down by the fence, when Maura had taken hold of the girl, Clemency had clung for an instant to her brother. Aidan lowered his head to gaze into the contents of his mug, and hoped he was wrong.

'Liam,' Maura was saying, 'you've finished y'r pie – you have chores to do.'

'But Father's only just arrived . . .!'

'The garden must be watered and the horses fed, Liam. They'll not be accepting any of your excuses.'

Liam excused himself and headed for the door, reluctantly, brown eyes turned back to Aidan as he did so.

'I won't be far away, Liam. You'll have to show me the horses, later.' And the boy smiled with a relief that was painful for his father to witness. How many years would it take before the boy could be sure that Aidan would not vanish without warning yet again? He realized that he was going to have to work to build trust in each of his children.

Maura turned to her daughter, 'Go and do your homework, Clemency.'

'I've done it, Ma.'

'Then go and study some more, your father wants to speak with me alone.'

It was neither true, nor fair. Aidan did not speak soon enough, in his surprise, and Clemency had flounced out of the room, glaring at her father as she went. He looked back at Maura, waited for her to speak, but she had begun to wash the dishes and he found himself gazing at her back.

'Do you want any firewood cut?' *Oh, Lord, I asked that eight years ago, too.*

'No, Will's cut plenty of wood.'

'Is there anything I can be doing, any . . .?'

'No. Just sit there. When I'm finished we'll go beyond to the big house.'

446

He did not like that term, felt it had no place in this new country, but he did not think it appropriate to mention his thoughts on the subject at this time. He sat down.

'You'll expect to stay here, no doubt,' she said.

He looked up at her. She rubbed the soapy cloth round and round the half-submerged plate, scowling at it with concentration.

'I didn't have any expectations.'

She threw a quick glance at him from the corner of her eye, eloquent even in its brevity. She said, 'You can sleep here in the kitchen, for I don't want people talking. And we'll see, Aidan. I'm heartsore, and that's the truth, I can't forget so easily all that's happened. I've tried, but I cannot.'

'I understand.'

'Do you?' She leaned the plate among the others, resting on an upturned cup. He noticed how red her hands were, how rough and spotted. They looked older than her thirty-three years. 'We've been together one year and three months, altogether – one year and three months, Aidan, out of the eleven years we've been married. I no longer know you. And what frightens me even more than this, is that I'm not sure I want to know you.'

'Are you after blaming me for all that's happened . . .?'

'No, not at all. Not for everything. You're a violent man, and I knew this when I married you.' She smiled a little. 'Perhaps it was partly this that attracted me to you. I mistook your violence for strength, Aidan, I wouldn't be the first woman to make that mistake. So I'm partly to blame.'

'Partly to blame . . . for our marriage, now? Are you saying that our marriage was a mistake?' He had told himself this often, but it hurt inexplicably that she might regret it.

'No,' she said, and he felt a kind of relief which had no time to settle before she said, 'I'd do the same again, for I love my children, and to wish you had not existed, is to wish them, too, out of existence. That would be a sin indeed. No, I'll not regret our marriage.'

'We've seen bad times, sure,' he said quickly. He did not like the calm, flat voice she used, this cold and hopeless voice. 'It's been hard on us both, in different ways. But I'm a free man, now, Maura. In a few years I can even afford to take us back to Ireland – we can return home, to Killaloe, if that's what you wish.'

'No,' she said slowly, drying her hands on a cloth and gazing out the window as she did so, as if she saw Killaloe out there, its grey walls and thatched roofs, and turf smoke hung about St Flannan's turret. 'No, 'tis sad but it's the truth, that we'd not be eating mutton

447

twice a day in Killaloe.' She added dryly, 'Not mutton of our own, anyway.'

He flushed, gazed at the floral centrepiece on the table. 'I've done my best for you,' he said, and it sounded surly, and totally inadequate, even to his own ears.

She was drying the dishes, polishing each surface, until it squeaked beneath the cloth. She replaced everything in cupboards and drawers until the kitchen was neat and empty as the silence between them, and then she turned to him. 'Come,' she said, closing the conversation like a cupboard door, 'We'll go beyond and visit the Frazers.'

He liked the Frazers' house; it was still very much a country house, not as grand as the Reynolds's town house had been, not as cluttered with pretty things; all was functional, here.

The furniture was heavy, and dark, but it was not crowded together. There were few potted plants, and the curtains were of cotton, not heavy plush. The only real colour came from the gay rag rugs on the floor.

Cora Frazer was in the kitchen when Aidan and Maura arrived – as did most friends to country houses – at the back door. She came forward to meet them as they walked into a room warmed by the heat of the dominating black iron stove against the wall.

Her hand was held out. Aidan took it, gazing down into a face that the years had marked, but had not robbed of any of its humour. 'Well, the prodigal returns! Mr O'Brien, it's good to see you. You've been sadly missed.'

'Thank you, ma'am.'

'We'll be glad to have you, now, especially. Has Maura told you?'

He glanced at his wife for a moment; Maura was saying, 'I thought it best to come from you, ma'am . . .'

Cora nodded slowly, 'My husband is gravely ill, Mr O'Brien. He's had consumption for many years, but this time,' she glanced upwards, unconsciously lowering her voice, 'the doctor is very worried. We all are. You see, he has this plan to go logging once more, a remote settlement on the other side of the island, south of Macquarie Harbour. From all I've heard it's a barren, cold spot, and even if he did go there, the climate would kill him. But he insists that he and Will are going, and in only a few months. Go along with this, if you please. I want John kept cheerful, hopeful, even to the end, if it should come. Will doesn't know, either. They both expect John to get well, think and plan nothing but going off to Port Davey together.'

448

'It may still happen, ma'am. Men have recovered from consumption before . . .'

She smiled. 'Bless you, you haven't changed. I begin to suspect that you are an optimist, Mister O'Brien. Is he, Maura? Is that what sees him through his trials?'

'Yes, ma'am. Aidan always believed that things will turn out the way he wishes.'

He looked at her, silently, aware of the unfairness of her words, aware, too, of the faint touch of spitefulness to her smile. She had an ally, she felt, they were two women together, she could shift the loyalty that had been enforced upon her, just for this moment. But Cora, too, had not changed.

'Well,' she said, 'in these bad times that can sometimes be the only thing we have to rely on, our faith in ourselves.' She gazed at him fondly. 'Port Arthur has taken its toll of you. You're no longer that boy that I found down by the creek . . . But it's just as well. The gold in Ballarat has spelled doom for many farmers here in Tasmania. If you want to make your way, you're going to need every ounce of toughness you've learnt, my boy.'

Maura had turned to the cooking pot on the stove, had lifted the lid and was stirring the contents. Cora glanced at her back, then headed out of the room. 'Come, I'll show you upstairs.'

It was apparent to Aidan on first entering the sick man's room, that Frazer was dying. It was also apparent after speaking to him for only a few moments, that his wife had been right, he had no knowledge of the fact.

'Good that you're here, O'Brien.' He smiled weakly. His cheeks were yellow, they folded like damp paper with his smile. 'We'll have to see that you stay out of trouble, now. You're too strong, boy. Have to find something worthwhile to pit your strength against. Burn yourself out, going back and forth to prison like that. Have to find something worthwhile . . .

'Take charge of the farm while I'm away at Port Davey – won't be long, a year or so – then I'll come back here and you can join Will as a piner. Lease the ground off me, buy it if you want – you'll make the money soon enough down there – make a fortune, all of us, in Huon pine. Seen it happen here in the valley, but all the good stands have gone, now. What do you say? You know timber, Will told me. Do you fancy the idea?'

'Yes, sir.' Aidan glanced at Cora, who was sitting quietly on the window seat nearby. His heart had begun beating faster with excitement, for it seemed to be just what he needed, some task that would utilize all that he had learnt. He had spent so much time wondering how he would gain enough money for the future, and here was the scheme, laid out before him, simple, and perfect. He knew how hard it was to lease the stands of Huon pine; competition among loggers was fierce, and one needed money and contacts. Frazer had both, and due to Will's recommendation, Frazer obviously felt Aidan to be reliable as a business partner. *Despite everything*, Aidan thought with wonder. *Despite everything, he trusts me, not only to pay for the lease, but to take care of his farm in his absence.*

He almost faltered then, for he knew that Frazer would not be going to Port Davey. Aidan had seen too many dying men not to know when a man's body had all but given up the struggle, when only the will kept the feeble heart beating, the lungs labouring. Frazer would not leave his sickbed, Aidan thought, and suddenly, selfishly, his own hopes were as limited, his own horizons narrowed to the dimensions of this room. He felt cheated, disappointed in the fall from his expectations – but caught Frazer's eyes.

'I've . . . I've little experience of farming in this country, sir. I only hope . . .'

'Oh, I won't be leaving for a while – have to rest a bit, get my strength back. This lung fever – had it before, never keeps me down for long. Plenty of time for you to find your way. You'll learn, O'Brien, don't worry. Wish I could leave Will with you, but he's burning to follow me to Port Davey – built for logging, that man. And pining is a sure thing, surer than gold . . .'

He looked up at Aidan. 'You two have been through a lot together. No need to ask this, I suppose, but you'll stand by Will, won't you? Things aren't looking too good for this colony – a man needs to know he can count on his mates – particularly someplace like the South-West. You'll stand by Will, won't you?'

It was the first hint that Frazer might have doubts about the future, might know he would not be there, with Will, in the South-West.

Aidan said, only, 'He's like my own brother, sir.'

'Good. I trust you. What Cora said about you, and what Will says.'

Will only ever saw the best in me. But he did not say this. He said, instead, 'Thank you. I'll do my best, sir. Would there be anything I can be doing this afternoon?'

'No, no, boy – spend this time with your family. Will has a room downstairs, and he usually eats with us, but I'll send him over to your house as soon as he comes in from his work.'

Aidan saw that Frazer looked tired. He stood up. 'Sir, I'd like to thank you for all you've done for myself and my family – my children are very fond of you, you've done more to help them than anyone would expect of an employer . . .'

'No children of my own . . . that boy of yours – real little man, that. And the girl – half ours, we think, sometimes . . .' He made an effort to smile at his wife, who stood by the window. She moved forward and took his hand.

'Your Maura's been company for Cora,' Frazer went on, 'and a great help to her when I've been ill. I'm only glad that you and your family will be here with my wife while Will and I are in the South-West.' His eyes kindled. 'You wait till you see that country, boy. God's Country. I swear, if He ever walked any hills besides the Holy Land, it's the South-West of this colony. It's the silence of God, O'Brien. That's what calls me back. Cora doesn't understand . . .' He smiled, patting his wife's hand. 'You will. It calls you. You'll see . . .'

He had drifted off to sleep. Aidan glanced at Cora Frazer; they left the room quietly.

When they reached the parlour downstairs, she paused and turned to him. 'Thank you.'

'For what, ma'am?' he asked, puzzled.

'For appearing to believe him. For helping him keep the dream alive. I don't know what it is about the South-West, what he thinks he sees there – mountains and forests, he says, but there are mountains and forests everywhere in the world. Why is this so different?' She was at the window, her arms folded, scowling out down the slope towards the creek.

Aidan had no answers for her, he was filled with pity for her. She seemed to sense this, turned and smiled grimly, 'Go talk to Maura – tell her she needn't stay after the meal is cooked. She'll need time to prepare her own meal with your appetite and Will's to consider.'

But it was hard to talk to Maura. Aidan wished that the Frazers had given him work to do, better that than standing by while a silent Maura cooked the meal in the large homestead, then walking with her back to the cottage where she prepared their evening meal in just the same mood of unapproachability. She expects me to make demands upon her, he brooded, considering her starched and inviolate white pinafore as she moved about the kitchen.

Aidan finally walked outside, and spent the afternoon strolling about the farm's boundaries; he saw Will from a distance, at least he thought it was Will, walking behind a pair of draught horses, while other figures moved across the field in his wake, sowing seed. He did not want to disturb them and turned back towards the cottage.

But, 'Coo-*ee*! Aidan . . . !' and Aidan turned to see the Cornishman running towards him, stumbling on the furrows, and Aidan was running to meet him.

He was caught up in the familiar bear hug, whirled about, they fell together. The men were introduced to him, a series of brown faces whose names he could not yet remember, but they welcomed him, and while he and Will chatted to each other, Aidan worked with them.

It was a grand finish to the day. Plough handles within his grasp, the talk of the men, of crops and weather, the sunset behind them turning the fields rose and vermillion before them. He took deep breaths of the smell of freshly-turned earth, the distant, spring-rich meadows. Like the soil that rolled and folded after the plough, this was the beginning, good and clean and straight the path . . .

It was only that night that he was able to talk to Will about Frazer, after the meal, when the children had been put to bed, and all three adults sat on the narrow rear verandah of the cottage, watching the last of the light fade from the sky, swatting idly at the mosquitoes that rose from the creek to whine about them.

Maura sat quietly, not joining in the talk, her head bent over some knitting, but Aidan could feel her listening, could tell that she had her own thoughts on the plans that Frazer had made. All day she had been waiting for Aidan to bring the subject to a decision – if the offer was made, would he go? She waited, contained in her resentment. He had discussed it with her, but she would not commit herself, she wanted to see how he would react, how much he thought of their happiness, their welfare. She did not think of it in terms of testing him, it was her duty as a wife to leave the decisions to him. But consciously or not, she was waiting on his choice – and if it was made against her own . . . she would think of it later. She would have to fight him. Wife or not, their lives had not touched in so long, that his existence here, now, must not be allowed to ruin all she, Maura, alone, had built up.

Aidan could not bear the silent disapproval that emanated from her; if she would only listen to him – all afternoon, when they had been alone, he had tried to explain that he aimed only for security for herself and the children, that initially it would take sacrifices on both their parts, but she would not answer this type of argument; even her silence said, *I have made enough sacrifices*.

'Come for a walk by the creek,' he said now to Will, and stood, feeling, rather than seeing, Maura's head come up. It was not fair to exclude her, but dammit, he decided, she excludes herself, her very bitterness is a wall between us.

When they reached the creek bank, Will said, quietly, 'Maura doesn't approve of the pining venture, you d'know that, don't you?'

'Aye. It means long absences from home. But sure, I wouldn't be going for some time . . .'

'Aidan, Aidan . . .' Will faced him, 'I keep my thoughts from Mrs Frazer and John, but I know as well as you that the man is dying. I don't know what Mrs Frazer will wish to do with the timber ground if John dies. I think it's best if you tell Maura you won't be going. To tell the truth, I don't know if I want to go, anyway – 'tis a cold, windswept place, I hear. I've kept up the pretence for John's sake – you barely know him – but there are few men like him, Aidan, in this colony or any other. Cora's a good woman, too. If John goes, I'd want to stay and help her run this place. You couldn't do better than to stay, also.'

Aidan scowled and was silent. For the thought of working another man's soil, for years and years to come, did not appeal to him. He did not come half-way around the world to do here all he had done in Killaloe.

Will's calm voice interrupted his thoughts. 'You're too quiet, Aidan. You are going to stay, aren't you? You won't be doing anything foolish like running off to the goldfields like Terrier did, are you?'

Aidan's chin came up, and seeing the movement, Will groaned. 'I might have known . . .'

'There has to be something more, boyo. I want land of my own . . .'

''Ee must work for it . . .'

'Sure and I will. But on seventeen pounds a year, it'll take for ever . . .'

'Aidan – just try it, will you?' Will's heavy paw was on his shoulder. 'Promise me you'll not go running off to the goldfields yet a while.'

'Och, no. Not with Mister Frazer ill – and I like this country, but . . .'

'That's all I need to know – you worried me. Go back to Maura, now, Aidan, and tell her you'll be staying. She's a nervous little thing, your wife. All this talk of going pining and gold-digging will frighten the life out of her. Don't talk about it for a while, yet.'

Aidan growled, 'All right,' somehow resenting Will telling him what to do. But Will was slapping him on the back, grinning. They shook hands, and Will loped off up the hill to the homestead.

Aidan walked along the creek alone, swearing softly at the mosquitoes, but unwilling, yet, to return to his own house. He glanced back towards the lights of the cottage – Maura had gone back inside, now, he could see her shadow moving on the curtains. He did not want to face her yet. The night air was cool and he needed more time to think.

Maura must have left the cottage then, for it was only a few moments later that he heard her footsteps through the grass, heard her speak his name.

'Aidan? Will you come inside, Aidan?'

He found himself feeling churlishly obstinate. Why was she asking him inside? It was not as if she *wanted* him with her.

'The night air is damp,' she said. 'You'll catch a chill.'

'Woman, I've known worse conditions.'

She was silent. He was annoyed with her, the calm coolness of her, her lack of feelings. His homecoming was an anticlimax. He thought self-pityingly that Liam was the only one who truly welcomed him.

Maura remained silent. She shifted her weight from one foot to another, and he saw her once again, suddenly, as she had been in childhood, Anna's shadow, small, freckled, silent, overpowered by Anna's grace and good humour. Maura herself was never truly honest with her feelings, she distrusted everyone, it was not just Aidan. She hoarded her feelings to her, hoarded others' feelings to her. Was that why she had been Anna's friend? Because Anna was a creature of feeling, of open giving, and Maura caught some of this in reflection.

'I've made your bed in the kitchen.' Maura almost mumbled the words, it was clear that she did not feel quite right about this action, but she was determined in it nevertheless. Aidan scowled at her in the dark, his mouth a grim smile. He wondered what she would do if he suddenly tumbled her on to the green grass, took her here on the bank of the creek . . .

And it was a terrible thing, but the realization came to him that he did not want her. Neither here on the grass, nor on a bed within the cottage. On the surface he was angry. But more frightening, where his hope and desire for her comfort had been, all these past years, there grew from this moment, a kind of desolation, a bleak emptiness. He could only stare at her, waiting for this feeling of aversion to pass. But it did not. It only grew as he tried to tell himself he *did* want her. His anger, his repugnance grew. And within him there was nothing. This rage and disappointment would pass, but within him the void remained. This was an ending.

'Yes,' he said, the word a sigh. 'Yes, I'll come inside now.'

She had raised her head. When he went to move past her she said, 'Aidan. Forgive me. I know it's hard for you to understand . . .'

It was perverse of her. Almost as if she knew that he was tired of

454

her, tired of fighting for recognition in her sterile world, she had stepped towards him, placed one thin hand against his cheek.

Still he did not want her, but her touch filled him with a kind of rage – and he kissed her, hard, more because he knew she would not like it, to shock, to disgust her. He felt savage and cruel and he kissed her even as he hated her.

She was struggling in his arms, pulled back a little from him, trying to wipe her mouth with the back of her hand even as he still held her elbows, was drawing her towards him once more . . .

'Leave her alone! Leave her alone!'

He had no time to turn around. The blow struck him in the small of his back. He had been standing on the uneven slope, facing downstream, and the force, sharp, unexpected, made him lose his balance. He turned, reaching out – and found nothing there to hold, took two steps to regain his balance – and was falling, the icy shock of the creek water closing over him, filling his lungs . . .

He rose struggling to the surface, half-laughing, knew as he turned, confused, looking for his bearings in the dark, that the attack had come from Clemency. She must have woken, missed her mother, and come searching for her . . . he stood in water up to his waist, gazed up laughing at the two – and stopped.

For Maura was striking Clemency, and both were screaming. Maura hit her and hit her, across the face, the body, wherever her enraged hands could connect with the child and Clemency crouched, her arms over her head, and screamed.

Aidan scrambled up the bank and threw himself across to them. He separated them with difficulty, Maura was now shaking the child, Clemency's head rolling on her neck like a rag doll.

'Stop it, Maura! Stop it. What're y' like!'

She stood back, still crouched, her gaze on her daughter. 'It's typical of her, the sly little beast!'

'She couldn't know, Maura. She thought I was hurting you . . .'

'It's a viciousness in her. She has a temper like nothing in my family.'

'She's a child!'

'And she'll have to grow out of such behaviour, or I'll make sure she does.'

The child was still screaming, crouched on the ground. Maura reached for her but Clemency pulled back, squealed and pushed Maura's hands away. 'Oh, all right, walk by yourself in the dark and I hope the banshee gets you!' Maura walked away quickly. Aidan could tell that she was crying.

He would have run after her, but Clemency had thrown herself down upon the grass and was sobbing violently.

He got to his knees, squelching and dripping. The coolness of the night air was now icy to him. Clemency raised her head. He could not see her face, and wondered how to approach her. 'Poor dear. Poor little rebel. You're not after receiving much gratitude f'r y'r pains, are you?'

More sobs, but from the set of her head she was watching him carefully.

He reached out his hands slowly, and touched her hair. 'Come, she'll not be angry with you long, sure. She'll get over it.'

How could he make her trust him? What did one say? He kept on repeating endearments to her. 'Poor little dear. Clemency? Clemency *asthore* . . . don't mind, little one, don't cry, little rebel, sure crying won't do any good.' He stood up, wondering if he should pick her up and let her scream, pick her up like a struggling, protesting foal, and carry her into the house.

But Clemency, too, was struggling to her feet. She tripped on the hem of her dress, but finally she stood. Her breath still came in shaking sobs, but she was reaching up to him.

He stared at her in amazement, then bent and picked her up. He tried to hold her away from him as he walked, but she leaned into his shoulder, placing one arm around his neck.

'You're wet,' she said.

'Aye, y' little divil, wet indeed.' And he was laughing softly, could not stop laughing.

She pulled back from him to peer into his face as they came to the cottage and a light from the kitchen fell on them.

'We're a fine pair are we not?' He hugged her a little. She kept looking at his face, studying him.

Her bed stood in the parlour of the cottage, not in the bedroom that Maura shared with Liam. It was because Clemency had nightmares, sometimes, and kept the boy awake, Maura had said. Now Aidan found Maura to be within the bedroom, the door shut. It was just as well, he was too angry to speak with her.

He found Clemency a nightdress from a cupboard, and it was when he was helping her with the hooks on her dress that the meagre light from the candle fell on the bruises on her skin.

Some were darker than others, some were yellowing and fading. Already tonight's assault had raised pink marks on her arms and on one of her cheeks. He held the child near the light and studied the marks, feeling a rage he had never yet known possess him. He sang to Clemency all this time, *The Old Woman From Wexford*, changing his voice for the different characters, and making her smile, but all he could think about was the bruises, made, he knew, with some heavy stick, the imprint was clear upon the pathetic little back and shoulders. He dressed her, continuing the song, but in his rage his voice shook, his hands shook. He placed the child in her bed and stood talking to her until the green eyes, wide, suspicious, closed gradually in sleep. Even then, an occasionally shaky inhalation of breath would make her body tremble.

He backed away from her, turning to the bedroom door. He moved slowly but with a deadly deliberation; pulled at the handle as he went to step inside – but the door was locked.

'Maura?'

He turned the handle and pushed with all his weight behind it. He could feel a pulse beating in his cheek.

'Maura?'

Silence. He pushed against the door again – and then stopped, remembering the children.

His voice shaking, he spoke clearly. 'Maura, I'll tell you this once and will not speak on't again. Don't raise your hand to that child again, Maura. D'y'hear me? For if you do I'll be after raising my hand to you with all the force of a shebeen-haunting, potcheen-drunk cottier, Maura. You understand? *Don't strike that child again.*'

Then he went to his room, pausing by the bed for an instant, to gaze at the sleeping child before he blew out the candle.

He was tired and slept soundly, dreaming, at one stage, that he was back in the carpenter's shop at Port Arthur, the smell of the fresh timber, the sounds of the many hammers were ringing in his head . . . Someone was knocking at the back door, he realized the sound had been repeated several times, growing louder each time. Aidan, disoriented, sprang up, stubbing his toe on the leg of the table, forgetting he was no longer in the boathouse. He half-fell across the table surface, cursing, and the hammering was repeated.

'Aidan! Mrs O'Brien! Are you within?'

Maura entered the room from the parlour as Aidan opened the door. Will stumbled in, wearing his trousers, the top buttons unfastened, his nightshirt hastily tucked into the waistband, his feet bare. 'Mrs O'Brien, he's gone. John's gone. He died just now, he . . . he choked . . . Aidan?' He turned to face his friend, the blue eyes wide with shock. 'He's gone, Aidan.'

Aidan had half-stepped forward, but Will sat down on one of the chairs, still gazing before him. Unseeingly, the man stared in front of him, then his eyes filled with tears that ran, silently, down the brown cheeks. Aidan, feeling helpless, placed a hand on his friend's

457

shoulder. From behind him, in the main part of the cottage, he could hear Clemency begin to wail, softly, and, closer, Maura striking a match to light a lamp.

Aidan noticed, that night, how tense Maura became, that after helping Cora lay out the body, she had come home and vomited, several times. The following day she was ill with a headache.

By the time of the funeral, however, she had recovered.

It was Cora who worried Aidan. Unlike Will and Maura, her grief was not obvious. Throughout the visits from sympathetic neighbours and the ordeal of the funeral, she remained calm, almost detached. All who knew her realized she carried her grief within her, refusing to face and recognize it.

'What are we going to do?' Maura asked Aidan. More and more she and Will were turning to him for advice. He had had no time to settle into his new life before being plunged into the responsibility of the farm and both households. Aidan found it hard. If Frazer had only lived a little longer . . . But, 'What are we going to do?' Maura asked.

'Wait,' he replied. 'She's a woman of common sense. A realist. She'll come to terms with this. It must be in her own time.'

So for the most part, Cora stayed on the first floor of the homestead, came downstairs dutifully to smile palely at her well-meaning neighbours, then retreated back to her room, or the room she had once shared with her husband.

Somehow news had reached the community that Aidan had been in gaol, and there was some suspicion of him. People said that something must be done about that ex-convict who had taken advantage of Cora Frazer's grief, who now seemed to make all the decisions on the farm, and rode about giving orders like an overseer.

Had they known it, Aidan had hesitated about this, believing Will to be the one to take charge. But Will claimed he worked better under someone else, that he did not want the responsibility, for he was not accustomed to it. So Aidan, following his nature, took control.

He knew people talked about him, criticized him. When he drove the wagon into Huonville to pick up the supplies ordered from Hobart, he could hear the little town murmuring behind its hand. In the stores, on the jetty where the packet was moored, 'That ex-convict . . .' 'The ex-convict overseer . . .' 'The fellow who's taken over the Frazer place . . .' Occasionally he heard the word Emancipist, knew that only his position of trust on the property earned him the name. And it pleased him. Maura could not understand this, hated to see the curious looks that people gave her, especially the women. 'Of course, her husband was a convict . . . A convict. . .' she imagined them saying. And when a few artful women, whose own background, had Maura only known it, would not have borne close scrutiny, commented, 'Your husband is a handsome man, Mrs O'Brien,' she thought only that they were mocking her with their sarcasms. The hard featured, powerful figure of her husband was not the soft-eyed boy she had married. To her, his face bore all the malign influence of those years in prison. It was the face of a man who had seen too much death, who knew how to cause it while managing to evade it himself. A remorseless tactician. He was a man who, had she just met him, she would not have liked at all. She would distrust him. The dark eyes and the quiet force of his will would make her afraid. And he was her husband. And still she did not like him, still she was afraid.

Aidan gradually became used to the whisperings about him. They were minor irritations, they did not affect his purpose in life. For Maura, whose horizons were narrower, who cared most for her family and their position within their peer group, the gossip was torture. From the time Aidan was arrested in Killaloe – where the murmurings were, if anything, sympathetic – she had had to contend with the fact that she was made different, pointed at, talked about. It was the single thing that most embittered her: that Aidan's actions had brought his family into disrepute. All their misfortunes had stemmed from this.

The men who worked on the farm, local labourers, many of them uneducated Irish, were resentful of Aidan for only a brief time. It became obvious to them that he was fair, could deliver an order or admit a mistake with equal honesty, that he was a man of some education who yet seemed to understand what their lives were like. From the jealousy that he had been a convict as they had been, had risen far above them while they remained in a life of hardship, they came to take some good will from the fact that though Mr O'Brien was 'gintry' he had known the horror and dishonour of chained servitude as they had. He would often share a joke in the Irish with them, would arrange some extra supplies if one of their children or their wives were sick. They could only compare him with other landowners, who could have them imprisoned if they broke their contract of employment and left for a better job, or other farm overseers who were cheating both owners and workers alike, lining their own pockets. O'Brien was all right, the working man confessed over his beer in the Huon Valley pubs. He was straight, and decent. He understood.

Aidan liked his work, was pleased to see, in the months that followed, that Cora was slowly, slowly, beginning to take an interest in people, to spend more time downstairs with Maura. The children helped. She was very fond of Liam and Clemency, was especially fond of the little girl. Maura began to feel happier. 'I don't so much mind the gossip, now,' she admitted to Cora as they had morning tea one day in the big homestead kitchen.

'Gossip? What gossip?' Cora looked up sharply.

'Och, you wouldn't know. Aidan being an ex-convict. When he first arrived here it was all folk could talk about.'

'Well, Huonville isn't exactly Paris, y'know. There isn't much happening to occupy people's minds.'

'But it shames me. You don't know how it shames me.'

Cora sighed. 'My dear, if they were throwing stones I'd think you had something to worry about. But this is Tasmania, Maura. Everyone here has some contacts with convicts or ex-convicts. Don't brood about it, girl, or I'll lose patience with you. You have your husband and your children . . .' Cora's eyes were wide, not fixed on Maura, and the Irishwoman could have bitten her tongue for complaining. 'Thank God for your blessings, Maura. Aidan is a fine man. It doesn't matter what the world thinks of you both. It is what you think of yourself that counts.'

Whether it was Cora's words or the grudging acceptance of those around her, Maura began to realize that basically she was quite happy with her day-to-day life. It dawned on her that the Irish who worked on the farm treated her husband with respect, and when they nodded to her as she drove to or from school to teach, it was more than the respect for a schoolmistress that she had come to know – there was a certain warmth in their greetings now. Their respect for Aidan brought her closer to them, she seemed less formidable, this Irishwoman who taught French. They smiled when they called good day to her. This appealed to Maura. She told herself that they were ignorant men and women, possessing no education and probably more deserving of their prison background than Aidan, but she enjoyed their good will, the deference they showed her. She wished some of her friends in Killaloe could know that Aidan was now a farm steward, earning twenty guineas a year, and even having his meals in the big house, all of them, Aidan, Cora, Maura, Will, Liam and Clemency, seated about the table in the dining room – like a family. It was like her own life had been, before the great hunger.

Aidan took the packet into Hobart a week before Christmas and remained two days, ordering supplies. While there he bought his Christmas gifts; a pocket knife for Will, a sewing box for Cora, a new bonnet for Maura – dark blue with a bright blue lining – a copy of *Every Boy's Annual* for Liam, and a prettily-dressed rag doll for Clemency. Even with his Christmas shopping, and the supplies he had to order at the grocers and produce merchants, he had a whole afternoon free before him.

Back at the Shipwright's Arms, in Battery Point, where he was staying, he had the gift he had made for the Reynolds family, a pair of bookends carved from Huon pine. He had not seen the family since the picnic to Kingston the year before. He and Milton exchanged letters, and Will, too, corresponded with the man who had befriended both of them; but Milton had had much to do, setting up his private medical practice, and Aidan was grateful not to be called upon for polite visits to the Reynolds home – and Berrima.

Throughout the journey to Hobart Town he told himself he would send the parcel by messenger to the house. But when he had filled his supply list, done all he had to do, he found himself returning to the Shipwright's Arms, shaving and dressing with care, taking up the parcel, and, cursing himself, calling a cab to take him to South Hobart.

46

It was useless to struggle. Twist and turn as she might, the strong brown hands held their grip on her shoulders. Miranda closed her eyes as she fought, for she knew that if she looked up into those jet-coloured eyes . . .

Was jet any real colour? She crossed it out and wrote *dark*.

. . . she would be lost. But she was tiring, quickly, her breath came in deep sobs, and finally, her large, limpid . . .

She was furious, her eyes wouldn't be limpid. Another line through the word.

. . . her large, frightened eyes were raised to his.

'We are alone,' he said, and his voice was so low that she could barely hear it above the howling of the wind outside the cave. 'My brave crew, gone. Even the gallant sailors of your English Queen's Navy – all lost in this storm. It is Fate,' he whispered, and he pulled her into his arms for a

kiss that robbed her of all her power. The great brown arms about her were crushing her, she could feel his heart beating within his broad chest.

When finally he pulled back a little, it was to gaze at her with all the possessive interest of a man who now held a valued and long-coveted treasure within his grasp. The saturated gown of pale pink tarletan shot with mauve and the matching mauve sash that now trailed limply behind her on the white sand of the floor of the cave . . .

'Miss Berrima, are you listening? There's a Mister O'Brien here to see you. Or, really, to see you papa, but when I told him . . .'

She growled, over the flying pen, 'Send him away, Nellie.'

. . . might not have been covering her, such was the boldness in his black eyes.

Miranda lifted her hand and struck him, full across that broad and mocking mouth, and as he cried out, she managed to twist free of his embrace.

But she was hampered by the clinging wet gown, and he had moved faster than she. He stood, now, blocking the mouth of the cave, and her only route of escape.

Nellie coughed a little. Berrima ignored her.

His legs in the black thigh boots, were planted wide on the sand, the heavy white trousers and white silk shirt were damp and clung to the heavily muscled body.

Thankfully, the door shut behind Nellie. Berrima sighed, placed one hand to her hot face. The sun poured through on her, curled, as she was, on the window seat, and her stays were uncomfortably tight.

The broad shoulders in the black velvet jacket were squared, she knew, with the determination that she should not escape. His head was turned on one side, slightly, the gaze in the wide-set eyes, black as coals, studied her with a confident anticipation. The cynical mouth, twisted slightly . . .

Nellie coughed again. Berrima, irritated, ignored her, and then she remembered that she had heard the door shut several minutes before.

He stood with his back against the door. His legs, in the brown knee boots, were planted wide on the carpet, and the bleached moleskin trousers fitted well over strong thighs and narrow hips. The shoulders in the brown corduroy jacket were broad, the neck short and powerful. The features of the face, too, were broad, too much so to be called handsome. The hands, square, powerful, held a brown paper parcel, and a broad-brimmed felt hat. The head was turned on one side, slightly, the gaze in the wide-set eyes, black as coals, studied her with a confident anticipation, the cynical mouth twisted slightly.

Berrima scrambled to her feet, staring at him. She began to gasp, 'Who are you . . .?'

When his hands were holding her elbows, she told herself she knew exactly what it was. She should not have had Nellie lace her so tightly. That was it. And she should not have been sitting in the sun for so long. And she should have eaten lunch, and she shouldn't have risen so quickly.

'Lie you down there . . .' Great heavens, he was pushing her back to lie prone on the window seat. 'I shall fetch your servant . . .'

'No!' almost a yelp. She scrambled to a sitting position, saw that she had stopped him almost in midstride. He turned back to her, his gaze solicitous.

'You're ill,' he said. 'It would be best if . . .'

'I'm not ill at all. I'm as healthy as a horse.' To prove it, she stood up and moved carefully to a chair out of the sunlight. She sat down, and with the remains of her composure she gestured for him to take a seat, also.

He remained standing. 'I think that you should call your maid, Miss Reynolds. If you'd like to retire for a while, I can wait here until you return.'

'I don't need to retire. Why should I retire?'

He looked uncomfortable. Because she had felt embarrassed, she did not come to his rescue now, but continued to look at him inquiringly. It was her very first mistake.

'Because I believe your stays are too tight, Miss Reynolds. You have a charming figure, but my hands should not meet around your waist.'

A paralysing flush was creeping up her throat. 'They don't,' she hissed.

'They do. I caught you as you were about to fall, and I assure you, I could enclose your waist with an inch or two to spare. I don't think that's very sensible, do you?'

Only to think that not half an hour ago she had been wondering why nothing ever happened to her. Half an hour ago she had been thinking that except for kissing Mark Ellis twice on his visit last Sunday, she had not had one decent adventure in her life. She had begun to write a poem entitled *Bourgeois Womanhood*. But somehow it was impossible to put down, in rhyme, the sense of emptiness that filled her days, that filled, she felt, the days of every woman she knew. She had been for a walk that morning and seen fishermen's wives down on the docks, screaming out the value of the fish and the crustaceans on the tables before them. She had seen them talking and flirting with strangers who stopped to buy, and Nellie, who had accompanied her, had been forced to pull her away with an admonition that her papa would not approve at all of his daughter staring at those shameless creatures.

Yet to Berrima it seemed that those badly-dressed, careless women were enjoying a freedom that she would never know. Only fancy being able to speak to anyone one chose! Why even Nellie, who was one of seventeen children and had been placed in the orphanage when she was three, now earned money that was her own, and on two afternoons a week – for Milton Reynolds was a generous employer – Nellie could sally forth and do precisely as she pleased.

Berrima's parents were kind, wonderful people, and she loved them dearly – but she felt, often, and today more than any other, that her goal in life was to be ornamental. Until the day when she married, and then she would have to work like the very Dickens – and still be ornamental.

The poem she had attempted had run no further than,

> How to aim for graciousness,
> a womanly gentility,
> When all the world beyond
> Throbs with sights and sounds and goals
> Whose brightness ever overshadows
> This good, grey life
> They tell me suits me best?

She had always been too partial to Browning. The Browningesque mode was not large enough to encompass her yearnings, the terrible sense of futility, knowing too much, wanting too much, and no outlet for her energies. Only her piano, her needlework, her watercolours. And one must, of course, be careful that one did not appear too proud, too forward, in speaking of those.

So she retreated with Miranda: *The Twenty Second Miranda Adventure – A Pirate's Revenge*. Miranda who was an expert horsewoman and swordswoman and crack shot – and who only occasionally managed to place herself in perilous situations from which a romantic adventure with the darkly handsome and dangerous Don Rodrigo would ensure. That afternoon she would escape from the cave and find the pale, blue-eyed Jack Mainwaring-Smythe unconscious on the shoreline, and she would nurse him back to health.

The notebook was on the floor, face upwards, her round schoolgirl's hand almost legible from where the man stood. Berrima, partly to cover her embarrassment, walked to it and picked it up, before he could anticipate her.

'I assure you,' she said precisely, and she placed the notebook beneath a copy of *Vanity Fair* on the table, and tried to look as if this was a natural thing to do, 'I am quite comfortable – Mister O'Brien. That is your name?'

'Aye.'

'I was very busy at midday and didn't have a chance to eat luncheon – and I was seated in the sun . . .'

'Does your father know you wear stays?'

'Mister O'Brien, I don't really think it's proper for you to talk about my undergarments!'

'I seem to remember your father giving me his opinion on women's corsetry, once. That it was most unhealthy . . .'

'He does know! At least, he knows I have them. Really, I don't find this conversation very congenial, Mister O'Brien.'

'You look as if you're becoming heated once more, Miss Reynolds. Don't you think you should retire and have your maid loosen them – I'd hate to see you have another attack of the vapours.'

'I'm becoming heated because I'm cross! I won't be talked to in this manner! If you continue, I shall tell my Papa . . .'

But she couldn't, of course, for Papa, who had been inveigled into allowing her to buy stays to wear for the various balls and dinners this season, had no idea that she was taking advantage of his absence to wear them today. She had had Nellie lace her into them, in the period of boredom between finding the poem unsuccessful and retreating within the powerful world of *Miranda*.

Really, it was very odd, how he had suddenly appeared, as if he had simply stepped from the pages of *A Pirate's Revenge*. Don Rodrigo. She studied his face. Yes, feature for feature, he looked quite villainous enough to ravish a woman in a cave on a Caribbean Island – or anywhere else, for that matter. She realized, suddenly, from the amused look on his face, that she must have been scowling at him. She said, trying to remember her manners, 'Have you known Papa very long, Mister O'Brien?'

'Yes. About seven years.'

'That long? I don't remember meeting you before.'

And he was aggrieved, really annoyed. *She did not remember him.*

'I've been away a great deal.' Then quicker, 'I'm overseer on a property in the Huon Valley.'

'That's a very pleasant place, I've heard. Papa means to take us there, when they've built a better road to the area. And do you only come to Hobart Town once a year at Christmas?'

'No, I . . . Yes, I have been. But I'll be coming more often, now.' He said this because he was gazing into her face, and could not have said anything else.

For it was Anna before him, Anna as she had been, only the setting, her clothes, were different. Anna in a blue-sprigged, white muslin gown, the bodice bloused just a little for the sash was tied around the new, tiny waistline. Aidan, with his eye trained by years of carpentry, knew it would measure barely sixteen inches. He wanted to slap the girl. What a vain, silly little creature she was, to be sure. As feather-headed as Caroline Kelly.

She was watching his expression change. The broad mouth twisted a little as he looked at her, and she thought he looked particularly unpleasant. Where had Father met this man? He looked more and more dangerous by the minute. It was rather wonderful.

He was standing, had gone to the cabinet where he had dropped his hat and the package, now held the latter out to her. 'I've brought a present,' he said abruptly. 'For your family. For the library. You have a library, I remember. It's for the library.' *Oh, God . . .*

She took the proffered gift. 'Thank you so much. I shall place it under the tree – there . . .' She bent and balanced the parcel amongst a pile of others beneath the decorated pine tree that stood in the corner, and her petticoats rustled and her hair – she wore it in a long plait that finished with a blue bow – fell over her shoulder and brushed the floor.

The back of her neck and shoulders were exposed, the skin was very white, but there were a few moles there, and they contrasted with the white of her skin. He wanted to touch them. His body ached with the desire to touch them . . . He was responding to her presence with an alarming intensity, and was furious with himself. She's an empty little doll, he told himself. She has no depth, no character. A self-centred child who'll grow into a self-centred woman. She was not even as pretty as Anna – her chin, on closer scrutiny, was more pointed, the mouth slightly broader than Anna's had been. And the whole, so much tinier. She lacked Anna's stature, in whatever way one wished to use the word.

Berrima straightened, turned to face him, and felt once again the veiled intimidation that she had sensed before. It was not actually harmful, not in any physical sense. Rather it was a kind of crowding, as if the man's presence was powerful enough in itself to make the room seem too small, her own position untenable. He was too confident, she decided, as if it were his house, not hers.

They were saved from further assessment of each other by the return of Nellie.

'It's Mister Ellis, Miss Berrima. I've shown him into the library.'

And Aidan was never to forget the look of anticipation that claimed Berrima's eyes for a brief second. Sensitive as he was to

466

every movement she made, he was oversensitive in his interpretations, for he had to make every moment with her count, every nuance therefore signified something more.

The look of pleasure that momentarily lit her face, now, was to convince him that she was in love with Mark Ellis.

He watched her with a scowl as she made a pretty apology to him, and excused herself, saying that she would return very shortly.

He was left alone, waiting with his own sense of pleasure in the outcome of this afternoon, for twenty minutes, then with impatience for another ten. It was as he rose to leave that his gaze caught the notebook that Berrima had been scribbling in as he had come upon her, and, savage with piqued masculine pride that she could so easily forget him in the presence of someone he immediately assumed to be young and callow, he removed the exercise book from beneath *Vanity Fair*, and leafed through it.

Thirty minutes passed before he realized that he had been seated on the window seat, totally engrossed in Miranda's hair-raising exploits, all that time. And still Berrima had not reappeared. He rose to his feet, almost regretfully replaced the book. How on earth could he ask her what happened next, without betraying himself?

He went out the door into the hall, smiling broadly. The notebook only served to strengthen his opinion of Berrima. She was pretty, and she had a thousand stories in her head, but it was painfully obvious she was completely out of touch with reality. He thought of *Vanity Fair*, for he had read that novel at – of all places – Port Arthur.

It did not seem at all odd, to him, that the twenty-second *Miranda* adventure should be placed beneath Thackeray's study of a fascinating, vain and shallow woman.

He found Nellie bent over with her ear pressed to the keyhole of the closed library door. Even from where he stood, Aidan could hear the tense voices from within the room.

He walked about Nellie and stood in front of her, silently. She stiffened, her gaze on the toes of his boots, and her frightened young eyes followed his body all the way up to the swarthy face with its hard mouth and even harder eyes. She swallowed, audibly, and made a little choking attempt at speech, but he was saying, quietly, 'I think you'd best interrupt, Nellie. Could you inform Miss Reynolds that I must be leaving?'

He did not think her eyes could open any wider than they were, but terror added to their roundness until she looked like a ringtailed 'possum caught in the glare of a hunter's lamp.

'M-me? Oh, no, sir. No, sir, I couldn't. Reely.'

'Nellie, I must be leaving . . .'

'But reely and truly, sir, I couldn't go in there, now. It wouldn't be right, sir, I couldn't . . .'

'Nellie, you're supposed to go in there . . .'

'Such a dreadful scene, sir – Doctor Reynolds should be here, sir. It's up to him, sir . . .'

'How long have you been working here, Nellie?'

'F-five weeks, sir. You won't tell Miss Berrima I was listening, will you, sir? You know they'd send me back, and I think the world of the Reynoldses, reely and truly – I felt I had to listen, Mister Mark's awful cross, an' I didn't know what to do . . . If the master was here, it'd . . .'

He moved her aside, and stood at the door. He could hear the voices quite plainly.

'It was only last week!' Ellis was saying, in something like exasperation. 'I can't believe that anyone's feelings could change inside seven days! Are you so heartless . . .?'

'How was I to know you were serious? John Hempinstall proposed to me on the evening of Emily's birthday party – and he never meant a word of it. Nobody does. I'm only eighteen, Mark, and really quite silly for my age, anyone will tell you that. It was . . . a game. That's all, a game.'

'I trusted you. I believed you.' The tone was heavy with accusation and despair. Aidan tried to feel for the young man in his blighted hopes, but the words struck him as being so much like one of Jack Mainwaring-Smythe's utterances that he started to laugh.

'Oh, sir.' Nellie's little voice, heavy with reproach.

'I haven't told you this, Mark, but there's an old friend of my father's visiting us at the moment, and I really have to return to . . .'

'You let me kiss you. You let me kiss you twice. That, to me, sealed our promise to each other. But it meant nothing to you. You undoubtedly give your kisses away to anyone who asks you!'

'You horrible, spiteful creature! How dare you, Mark?'

'Who else have you been kissing, Berri? What other man have you been promising your love to? John Hempenstall, obviously. And Edwin Trask, and Peter Bartlett? I supposed you've kissed them, too!'

'Nellie will hear you, Mark! The whole house can hear you!'

'But I want to know. I merely want to know.' Cruelty now in the voice. 'And if you don't care much about giving your affections away, then I deserve more than you give to me!'

The sound of a piece of furniture being bumped, a startled cry from Berrima – and Aidan had hammered on the door, and entered.

468

'Milton!' he roared, heartily, then, 'Oh, I'm terribly sorry.' He paused, attempted to look confused, and was pleased to note the young man was now at a safe, albeit reluctant, distance from Berrima. 'I heard the voices, and I naturally thought Milton had returned.'

Berrima leapt gratefully into the breach. 'Mister O'Brien, this is Mark Ellis. Mark, this is Father's friend I told you about . . .'

'Mister O'Brien . . .' Beneath the curling black hair, the handsome face was pale, the blue eyes guarded. Mother of God, this was the handsomest young man Aidan had ever set eyes on – what was the matter with this girl? Mark Ellis's eyes kept coming back to Berrima, burning with intensity.

Berrima was saying, 'My parents haven't returned yet, Mister O'Brien, they're visiting friends on the Eastern Shore . . .'

Aidan smiled at her and gave a yank to the tapestry bell-pull by the fireplace. Almost immediately, the door opened, and the young maidservant stood there, pink in the face.

'Nellie,' Aidan said, 'we'd like tea. Mister Ellis, you will be staying for tea?'

'No.' Stonily. 'No, thank you. I must be going.'

'Nellie,' Berrima said, and her voice grated with Mark's like two pebbles, 'will you fetch Mister Ellis's hat?'

'Yes, miss.'

'I can see myself out.' With a final glance at Berrima, the young man left, and Nellie followed him out, shutting the door.

In the terrible pause that ensued, Berrima turned to look at Aidan. Now Mark was gone, the bluff humour had fallen away. He was standing by the fireplace, studying her, and his gaze was rather critical. She was glad that he had arrived when he did, and yet – and yet he must have heard everything, to burst into the room like that.

Still he gazed at her, and it was rather like the look her father would have given her if he had been a witness to the scene. She felt herself blushing, and she did not blush often, was furious with herself.

She said, making herself crosser by the subdued tone of her voice, feeling more and more like an errant schoolgirl every second, 'Nellie usually serves tea in the parlour – shall we go back, now?'

'By all means.' The black eyes seemed to sense her confusion, and were amused by it. He opened the door for her, smiled down at her, impudently, she thought, as she swept through.

She seemed to gain courage once back in the more informal atmosphere of the little parlour, met his steady gaze, and thought of at least three ways of explaining matters. The trouble was, each

469

sounded worse than the one before it.

'I suppose . . .' She moved about the room, touching the furniture aimlessly. 'I suppose you'll tell Papa.'

'You must think I'm a great *ceolan*.'

'What's a *ceolan*?'

'A blatherer.'

'You mean you won't tell him?'

'I didn't say that. To tell the truth I am a bit of a *ceolan*. If you were my daughter I'd want to know. I'd turn you over my knee for being so damn silly.'

'Silly?' Her chin came up.

'Young Ellis doesn't appear to be a man to be trifled with. He's no callow youth. If you want to practice breaking men's hearts, do it on someone closer to your own age. You deserved that scene just now. Perhaps I should have left him to it.'

'I don't want to break men's hearts! And you've no right to lecture me, Mister O'Brien, bounding through doors at people and ordering tea without as much as a by-your-leave.'

'Would you rather I hadn't interrupted?' he asked quietly.

She gazed at him for a second, then, 'No,' she said softly, resentfully.

A tap at the door, and Nellie arrived with the tea things. Berrima felt decidedly ill at ease at the thought of having to play hostess to this man. While Nellie was setting the table, Berrima took the opportunity to study him, for he was walking about the room, now, scrutinizing the various paintings on the walls, standing before each of them, with his hands behind his back, his chin thrust out.

She did not find him particularly handsome. She liked men of Mark's build, tall and slim, with fine, sensitive features. Yet she had to admit there was something attractive about the sheer power of this man. It was not simply the physical strength, the hard face and the steady, perceptive eyes, so dark that they appeared black most times. There was something in the personality of the man that dominated the room, even when he had his back to it. He did not turn until Nellie had left them.

Aidan had begun to relax back into his sense of enjoyment. He moved to the chair opposite her, and seated himself. He watched her for a moment, then, his curiosity and the rekindled jealousy of Mark Ellis gaining the better of him, he said, 'And could you be telling me why you've decided to refuse Mister Ellis's suit?'

'Mister O'Brien!' It would not do to antagonize the man and she would not give him any more information than he already knew, 'That was rather an unpleasant scene, I'd rather not discuss it.'

470

'Of course.' Apologetically. 'I suppose I merely feel sorry for the young man. It can't be easy to have one's hopes blighted in such a manner. Although,' he shook his head, 'I rather doubt the wisdom of his choice for a wife. You are, it appears, rather fickle.'

She handed him his tea cup in silence, refusing to be baited. Who was this man? He looked vaguely familiar. She would ask Emily. Emily was the one with the retentive memory. Emily remembered everything.

He saw Berrima frowning at him slightly, saw her genuine puzzlement. Obviously she did not remember anything about him at all. He did not want to remind her. Did not want to be the ex-convict who had saved her sister's life. He did not want any past, only now; he did not want to speak, to move; he wanted the moment to go on, that would be enough, that would be more than enough.

He could not remember when he had felt so intensely happy. To be with this girl, and in these surroundings; he had always loved this house. The furniture was delicate, the colours of walls and drapes warm but muted; he had forgotten the beauty of these rooms. The softness of the carpet made him want to take off his boots and curl his toes into the pile, as he had once curled his toes into the summer grass on Tineranna.

That was the problem, he thought soberly – he brought the country with him. To this girl he must seem like a 'bushie', or at the most like a poor farmer, a cockatoo, or 'cocky', farmer, whose land was successful only in terms of these avaricious native birds. Such was the joke. And Aidan did not even deserve that title, for the land he worked was not his own. And he felt suddenly awkward, his skin too brown, his feet too large. Amongst the fringed velvets, the crystal vases and china ornaments of this room he was aware that he did not belong . . . But wasn't that up to himself? Who, after all, had the right to tell him where he belonged, what he could do, if his ambitions were too great, beyond his reach? No one, he thought, fiercely. And his sense of well-being began to reassert itself. I have the power to be *anything*.

Berrima had read his expressions correctly, the critical gaze around the room, his sudden dissatisfaction, his final look of confidence, of arrogance. But she connected these emotions with herself, with the scene he had just witnessed. His scowl had been one of censure. Only the final look of well-being puzzled her. Then she thought with a sinking heart that he might, like the Reynolds family, be Quaker – if he was, and a very strict one, he might feel it his duty to report this whole episode to her father. He might even denounce her at Meeting! Was that the reason behind his grim smile? Was he one of these terrible, fire-and-brimstone members of the Society of Friends who denounced dancing and gay clothing, and . . . she felt ill, wished she had taken his advice and escaped upstairs to loosen her stays. O'Brien, O'Brien . . . *Was* there anyone at Meeting called O'Brien? Where had she heard that name?

His gaze was back studying her face, looking for . . . what? It puzzled her, and unnerved her a little. She looked about for something to talk about, something that would take his mind from herself, and her gaze fell on the copy of *Vanity Fair*. 'Have you read *Vanity Fair*, Mister O'Brien?'

Aidan's gaze followed hers to the book, 'Yes, I enjoyed it very much.'

Berrima relaxed visibly with relief. 'I'm only half-way through it. I'm not really sure I can bear to finish it, I'm so worried about Becky Sharp. She's so delightfully evil that I'm sure the author has some dreadful fate in store for her.'

Aidan smiled. 'Shall I tell you what happens?'

'Oh, no, don't! My apprehension lends a great deal of excitement to my quiet life. Of course,' she went on, 'one can tell that Becky is going to be a villain when one reads that she had dark hair and slanted green eyes. To have slanted green eyes gives one no choice but to be sly and malicious. An analogy to cats. Physical clichés always annoy me, Mister O'Brien, don't they annoy you? Being dark and rather villainous-looking yourself? In *Ivanhoe*, it was the same, the hero had blond hair and blue eyes and the wicked Sir Brian was dark . . .' She was chattering. She knew she was chattering. Anything to keep those dark eyes from scanning her mind.

As she paused for breath, he said, leaning back in his chair, 'So I look like a villain.'

Ah, he was vain, too. She smiled wickedly, with her head on one side. 'Only to young girls who read too many romantic novels. But, yes,' she studied him, 'you do look rather like a desperado. You'd make a good pirate.'

For some reason this amused him greatly. 'Really?' He raised one eyebrow, and succeeded in looking even more brigand-like.

'Really. But a gentlemanly pirate. The kind of pirate who'd offer one a glass of red wine before he made one walk the plank.'

He laughed aloud, then, and now that his laughter was not directed at her, she thought how different he looked when he laughed. Why, she thought, he is handsome, when he smiles. It was bad temper, she decided, that put those lines on his face.

Aidan was delighted by her. He had not been so amused since. . . He could not remember. How young she was, now naive,

472

yet how clever, seductive in her very playfulness. He could not take his eyes from her, dreaded the time when her parents would come home, when she would be relegated to the background as a well-brought-up girl would be.

Who had taught her to be so confident? The Reynoldses? Surely not Uncle and Aunt Charlie . . . And he felt saddened, suddenly. For it came to him that soon, perhaps quite soon, she would be changed. She was beautiful, and some man would marry her, and children would come, and responsibilities, perhaps hardship. The free spirit in her would be harnessed, tamed. Her unusual honesty and originality would bend before the need to act as respectable wife and model of behaviour for her children.

He had little idea of women, remembering only the changes time had brought to Maura. He had no real knowledge of women's resilience, could not fathom that the middle and upper class women in pastel silks that he had seen, could possibly have any courage or tenacity of their own. They were a race apart, and Berrima belonged to their group.

He had long ago written the story of what had undoubtedly happened to Anna in Wiltshire, how she would have been bowed down by the strangeness, the hostility, of the English surroundings. And if Anna's spirit had been broken, Anna who was good-natured and pliant, how much more suffering was in store for this little creature? Berrima was talking of the Christmas presents she had for her family; he watched her as she spoke. This was a girl of finer metal than Anna. More brittle, less likely to take strain and stress. She would never adapt, he decided, to a life of hardship, could not even cope with what Anna had coped with in Killaloe, seeing the lines of dying beggars, seeing her friends and family die about her. Within an unhappy marriage, Berrima would languish like a caged skylark. He could not bear the thought of Berrima embittered, her life desolate. It won't happen, he decided to himself. Not to this one.

A tapping at the door brought Nellie. 'Pardon, Miss Berrima. A boy has just come from your parents to say they'll be dining with the Hempinstalls this evening.'

Damn. Aidan had finished his tea. Without Milton Reynolds and an invitation he could not possibly stay alone with the girl during dinner. Reluctantly he stood, as Nellie left the room, and bowed slightly to Berrima. 'Thank you very much, Miss Reynolds. I must be leaving.'

'Oh.' To Aidan, she looked surprised. Indeed, Berrima *was* surprised, and puzzled at her feeling of disappointment that he was not staying. He was not really as ill-mannered as she had thought; in

473

fact, she found him rather interesting. But she, too, rose from the table.

She saw him to the front door, and there they paused. She said to him rather earnestly, 'You will come back tomorrow, won't you? About four, I think.'

'I was going to leave on the packet tomorrow morning . . .'

'I see. Of course.'

He gazed down at her. She had lowered her eyes. He watched the dark chestnut of her hair, pulled back from a central parting to the plait at the nape of her neck. The hair shone gold where the light struck it. Did she *want* him to come back? 'I do have some business to attend to. I was saving it for the next trip . . .' he lied suddenly.

'I'll tell Mama and Papa to expect you.' She was smiling up at him. It made his heart contract; looking at her gave him a kind of tender pain that he thought he would never feel again. It possessed him, this pain. He felt the nakedness of his feelings, his attempts to deal with it must be written on his face. 'I'll come back tomorrow, at four.'

She held her hand out to him, and he took it. Not Anna's long and graceful hand. This was short-fingered, broad-palmed, a capable little hand. He wanted to hold it even while he wished the fingers were longer, ached with the knowledge that this was not Anna, not Anna . . .

He bent over her hand like a gentleman would, and in doing so, felt like a gentleman for the first time in his life. Then he let her go, but the touch of her had unnerved him; a silence followed, then he murmured a good evening, and left the house.

When he had gone, Berrima stood for a few minutes in the hall, watching him, through the lace curtains at the window, as he walked up the drive. When Nellie spoke, behind her, she almost started.

'Miss Berrima, I couldn't help overhearing. Don't you remember, your mama and papa are spending the day with Doctor and Mrs Trask in Sandy Bay – you was supposed to go with them . . .'

'Oh, dear . . .' Berrima looked stricken.

'Will I run after him, miss?'

But Berrima had stepped between Nellie and the door. 'It's a little late. His carriage was waiting outside.'

'Ah.' Nellie's round eyes remained on her mistress's face. 'I see, miss.'

'Yes,' said Berrima, and walked back to the parlour.

She took up her notebook and pen, but was overcome by a feeling of restlessness that would, she knew, prevent her from writing further. Preoccupied, she went upstairs to the room she shared with

474

Emily, and without really knowing why she did so, she bent and pulled out the small tin trunk from beneath her bed. She placed the notebook amongst its twenty-one predecessors. She was to write a great deal in her life, but this was the last of Miranda's adventures.

47

He was turning into Trumpeter Street and was about to cross to the Shipwright's Arms, when a voice hailed him. A tall, very thin man, standing beside a carriage. 'Hey! O'Brien!'

Another of the men who had known him in prison? Aidan waved, went to go on, but 'Hey, O'Brien! Come 'ere!' He stopped. The man was beckoning to him. He might as well go, there might be some news of Terrier, Ah Poo or The Dragoon – though crossing towards the man, he did not look familiar . . .

'Aidan?'

Matty's face appeared at the carriage window as he reached the vehicle.

What was their relationship that the first shock of seeing her, the first remembrance of Nat, Ettie, their coarse, corrupt way of life, could be swept away in only a few seconds, and he was glad, glad to see her; the bright, artfully-painted face, the same pale, dangerous eyes. He was reminded suddenly of Berrima's words. Despite the curling tendrils of fair hair, the blue of the eyes, Berrima would insist that Matty was a villain. And Berrima would be right.

'You look well,' she said, smiling at him. 'The years should've left some mark on you, Aidan, but they haven't. Most old lags – I dunno – they got a kind of look about 'em, y'know? But you – hell, y' look like a gentleman.' She said this not in flattery, but as if she was speaking aloud; almost reluctantly, resentfully. So the result was that he *was* flattered, for he knew she was speaking the truth. Her compliments had always been rather heavy-handed, yet clumsy, she was not actress enough to hide the fact that her motive was usually concerned with herself.

He smiled, said nothing. He did not tell her she was beautiful, for she was, and she was waiting for him to say so. He did not understand why, but he enjoyed this small act of spitefulness, watched her growing more annoyed.

'You're cruel, Aidan. You're not polite, you're not. But still . . .'
She sighed, lowered her eyes – Matty attempting to appear demure
made him grin even more. She reached out and touched his
shoulder. 'Climb into the carriage, Aidan. We'll drive for a while.
No harm in that, is there? Two old friends like us?'

He was laughing, softly. Matty felt a resurgence of all her feelings
for him. She had come from curiosity, for her new lover was rich,
weak and demanding, and her emotions and her material needs were
so entangled with him that she could not begin an affair with Aidan
once more – would certainly never allow him to possess her as he
once had. She was older, now, she had learnt the practicalities of life.
But she looked at the brown skin, the bold, dark eyes, and for all her
rationalizations she wanted him. The bastard never loved me, she
thought. He never cared for me. Cares more for that skinny shrew of
a wife of his . . . But, 'Come on, Aidan. Life's short, my dear, isn't
it? A brief drive about the city, along Sandy Bay Road, perhaps, or
up to the Queen's Domain, to look at the view.'

He climbed into the carriage. The afternoon had exhilarated him,
he was too wild with the reckless energy that Berrima had inspired in
him to worry about caution, the future, or Matty's motives. He
wanted to laugh, to forget everything but the present; to see as much
of life in this moment as he could, for he knew his senses were
heightened as they had never been before.

'One of the lads from the Barley Sheaf recognized you yesterday,
saw you leaving the Shipwright's Arms, and came an' told me.
That's how I knew where to find you,' she explained.

'Ah,' he said.

She watched him, scowling, and grew more petulant, he could
tell, as the drive progressed. He had not once complimented her on
her looks, let alone on the smart carriage and stony-faced driver.
Aidan had not forgiven her for paying that visit to Maura, for losing
him his children, all those long months.

And yet for all this, he was glad to see her. He despised her, and
yet he wanted her. When she leaned forward and placed her hand on
his knee, her sharp eyes filled for once with a gentle seriousness, he
covered her hand with his own. 'Can you forgive me? For causing
you all that trouble? Can you forget, Aidan?'

'Och, no. I'm not going to forgive you. And I certainly won't
forget.' His eyes were narrowed, they looked at her boldly, and she
felt a little thrill, a kind of challenge, the more delightful because she
suddenly knew that he was not to be fooled, perhaps never had been
fooled. That he was as clever as she, as strong as she. Stronger,
perhaps. Yes.

She leaned back and looked at him critically. That was it. This boy whom she had attempted to use all those years ago, the boy whom Ettie and Nat and Jimmy had laughed about, ridiculed behind his back – this boy had become a man, and had beaten them all. They all three lay in unmarked graves, Nat because he had died a convict, and West and Ettie Harding because it was Matty's final revenge.

And Aidan O'Brien sat there smiling; virile, confident. Stronger, in the end, than all four of them had been together. Ettie had been a fool, Matty told herself, and until that moment she had never thought of her stepmother as a fool. Ettie knew men. Yet she did not know this one. She tried to destroy this one – when she should have made a friend of him. A friend – and more. There had been a time when he would have, perhaps, been desperate enough to accept her favours. But she had threatened him, alienated him, when he had the strength that Ettie needed in her men.

Matty would not make that mistake.

At the Domain they alighted from the carriage and walked about a little under the cool stars, looking at the lights of the city below, the moving glow-worms of ships' lights on the harbour.

They spoke little, then. It was as if what lay between them was too fragile a thing – both felt it. They were happy to be there, happy to be with each other, but a word, a sigh, a movement at the wrong time could bring back the bad things, the bitterness or the boredom of their love affair, and both needed the good, the frail glow of its memory tonight.

They walked away from the carriage, into the dark, and he kissed her. Strange and disturbing, that he kept thinking of Berrima. Wanted to hold Matty, to recapture the passion of being with Matty, but when he opened his eyes, he wanted to find Berrima there in his arms. 'I want to make love to you,' he said to the dark shadow that was Matty/Berrima, and she laughed. 'Come back to my hotel with me.'

She said nothing, but her mouth came up to meet his, softly, her sharp little teeth worrying his lip, gently, but threateningly.

He took her arm and moved her firmly towards the carriage, before he decided to remain in the darkness of the gardens, take her there in the sweet gum-tree-fragrant leaf litter. He gave the address to the driver, and when they climbed into the carriage, this time he sat by her side.

The horses were moving at a smart pace towards the city. However, when they reached Elizabeth Street, the driver did not turn the carriage left towards the harbour, but turned right instead – and headed up the busy street, away from the direction of Aidan's hotel.

'You're being kidnapped,' Matty smiled at Aidan's suddenly scowling face. 'Aren't you pleased? Aren't you flattered? Not many men get kidnapped by women. An' if you want to know if my intentions are honourable, they're bloody not, so there.'

He gazed at her, trying not to grin. What a little witch she was! Always, always, her own way. Was this her legacy from Ettie? 'I told the driver the Shipwright's Arms . . .'

'Before you got into the carriage I told him to ignore whatever directions you gave. He was to take us home.'

'Home?'

'The Barley Sheaf.' When his silence betrayed his amazement, 'I managed to keep the lease. It was hard, but I did it.'

'I'm glad. I did wonder how you fared.'

'Did you really.'

'Aye . . .'

'Liar.' She said it calmly. 'You never think about me when I'm not about, Aidan. I got to wind myself around your neck before you so much as look at me. Like a kid, you are. No concentration.'

He laughed. 'Matty, let's go to the Shipwright's Arms. The Barley Sheaf . . . has bad memories.'

'Nah. It's home. I've changed everything. You won't recognize it.'

'Stop the carriage, Matty. Now.'

'If you're going to take to a life of crime, do it right. I've begun a kidnapping, and I'm gonna see it through.'

'Do I have to jump out the door?'

She glanced outside. 'The traffic's moving pretty fast. Some baker's cart'll knock you down and you'll be trampled into the horse dung. I wouldn't advise it.'

He, too, glanced outside. They were in the middle of the street and carriages passed on either side of them, moving at a good pace. He turned back to her, his eyes narrowed. She smiled, liking the idea that he could not move without her permission. Briefly, at least, due to the congestion of Elizabeth Street, he was all hers.

'I can't go there with you, Matty. I won't.'

She stared at him. He stared back. The moment of their intimacy was trickling away like sand between their fingers. She was stubborn, was used to her own way. But he meant what he said.

She put her head out the carriage window, and said, 'I changed my mind, Ned – it's the Shipwright's Arms – turn at the next street.'

She leaned back into her corner of the carriage as the driver turned the horses, and gazed at Aidan. 'You needn't think you've got everything your own way.'

'No?'

'No. You might not have noticed – I dare say you haven't – but I've changed, too. Like you, I've taken to gentility. It don't suit me just now – I mean, I'm genteel enough on the outside, but it takes time to work its way through the system, like; but I don't want to spoil it by doing something low class, like sleeping with a strange man.'

He studied her, wondering where this game was leading. Almost to play for time, he said, 'And I'm a strange man?'

'Oh, yes. Goodness me, yes. You're about the strangest man I've ever met.'

'And you're telling me that because you're now a lady, you won't continue to be my mistress?'

She raised her eyebrows. 'Continue? Was I ever?'

His arms were about her, fingers in the thick coils of her hair, pulling them back until she was forced to gaze up at him. 'Yes, and a devil of a time you led me. The most unhappy period of my life, so it was, and why I'm sitting here with my arms about you I don't know, except that I'm mad, perhaps. You will sleep in my bed tonight, Matty, or I'll take you here and now and wave your drawers out the window for all Hobart Town to see.'

'You wouldn't – Aidan!'

'Your word? Your word as a traitorous, lying, thieving little . . .' he stopped.

She lay half-beneath him, laughing. 'Whore?' she suggested.

'Sure, that's the word.'

'I'd kill any man who called me that.'

'You'll not be killing me.'

'No, but – Aidan, don't! I . . . you can't . . .' She could barely speak for laughing. 'People can see through the windows, Aidan!'

'Your word, madam? Before I outrage all your sensibilities . . .'

'All right! Yes! Let me go!' She sat up, arranged her clothing, straightened her bonnet. Eyed him, after a moment, dangerously. 'Just to set the matter straight,' she said, 'my word isn't worth a damn.'

'Matty,' he leaned over, speaking gently, tracing the line of her jaw with one broad, capable hand, 'nothing about you is worth a damn.'

Her claws came up to his face sharply. He caught her wrist, twisted it downwards, savagely, until she gasped. They stayed like that for some seconds. Then, still without moving, she said coldly, 'What does your wife think of you now? Climbs into bed with a stranger these days, don't she? You know it, too.' His eyes narrowed, 'Yeh. You know it. Something dead inside you, lad, hey?'

Suddenly he wanted to let her go, to thrust her from him. She always used to say that they were alike. Hinted even a few minutes ago that they shared even their facade of gentility. Aidan did not like it. Until that moment, he had thought his gentility real enough. He thought of Berrima, and realized it had to be real. Matty made him doubt himself. She dragged him down and made him face his dark side. He brooded over her only slightly less malevolent form, and realized from her smile that she knew this, even prided herself on it.

'I don't need you,' he said.

'You been sayin' that a long time.'

'I don't.' He did not care at this moment what she did, where she went. He should not be here. It was to go backwards, and he was not going backwards, he was not even standing still. He was moving outwards and upwards, and he was not looking back.

'Ah, yes,' she murmured, as if she spoke to herself, 'you understand, now. You understand, and you don't like it. But there ain't no going back, Aidan. You can try all you like, but there ain't no going back.'

'What are y' talking about?'

'Remember what I used to say? I seen too much. I didn't have no expectations of you, because I'd seen too much.' She smiled, lied smoothly. 'It never really mattered to me if you left me or not. You were useful to me, that's all. There's no room in my life for all that sentimentality, really. Sometimes the pretence of it will work, though.'

'That's all it was?'

'Yes. Does it hurt your pride to know that? I wanted you, all right. But not to the point where I was banging my head against the wall because I couldn't have you. I ask you, was it in character for me?'

'No.'

'There. See, I'm as ruthless as you.' This time it was she who locked her hands in his hair, pulling his head back a little. They studied each other for a long moment.

'You've never been sure,' she said, slowly, 'what part I had in trying to have you shot, have you?' He was silent, his face unreadable. 'An' you're not a liar, don't understand lying, so all them things I told your wife, they stick in your craw too, don't they?' Silence. Her voice was low, 'An' I'm your whore, am I?'

'Yes,' he drawled, waiting for the nails to find his neck, careless, now. She was breathing faster. When she leaned forward and her mouth found his, hungrily, demandingly, he was completely taken by surprise.

She stayed that night with him, and never again, from the moment of that kiss, did he ever confuse her with Berrima, or anyone else. Matty's reasonings, he was forced to admit, were her own.

In the morning, she lay in bed beside him and told him about her new life; told him of Griffith Rogers, young scape-grace son of a high-born Hobart family, who had made such a difference to her life.

Aidan was not displeased that there was someone else, with prior demands. Rogers' high living was described to him, the trips he and Matty took to Melbourne and Sydney, the gambling, the music-halls, the jewellery that went in and out of hock should a bad period arise and luck failed them. It was, Aidan knew, the life that Matty had always craved. To live high and dangerously, skimming wildly along the knife's edge between unlimited pleasure and ruin.

'And there's Stephen, of course. I still see him sometimes. He's useful, in his way, but nothing like the excitement of being with Griffith. Ain't that the nicest name – Griffith?'

'Who's Stephen?'

'It was Stephen's house I moved into in Napoleon Street.'

'My God. Does he know about me?'

'No, though I suppose he had his suspicions.' She went on to speak of Griffith Rogers, how he had often proposed to her, but she preferred her freedom. Yet she loved him. She could tell that Aidan did not really like hearing these details. Not that he cared, but he liked to believe that when he was with a woman, all her attention was upon him.

Yet the pull of Aidan's indifference was enormous. He could not *really* be careless of her. And if he was, he must be made to care.

They ate luncheon together at a small restaurant in Elizabeth Street, and afterwards, sensing his restlessness, a preoccupation, Matty left him. He helped her into her carriage, wondering briefly what the driver thought of all this – nothing could be read on his set, grey-whiskered features.

'Send a message to the Barley Sheaf next time you're in Hobart.'

'I will.'

'Take care. I need to know you're all right, Aidan.'

'I'll see you soon, I hope.'

She held his hand until the carriage, moving forward, pulled it from his grasp. He was not sorry to see her go.

He bought a shawl for Maura that afternoon, spending a great deal of time over his choice, going from store to store. He even thought of buying her another bonnet. He stared in the window of quite a few milliners – but each time he thought of a choice he realized he was imagining it on Berrima. So he settled for the shawl, an embroidered one of blue silk with a heavy fringe. It was a little more than he could afford, and he smiled as he realized it was undoubtedly bought from a sense of guilt. Would Maura be pleased with it? If she knew why he felt driven to appease his conscience by buying it for her – would she care?

48

He returned to the Shipwright's Arms, bathed and changed his shirt, arranged for his bags to be sent to the packet, and paid his bill. At twenty minutes to four he took a cab to the house in South Hobart; if anything, even more nervous than he had been the day before.

She was in the garden as he drove up. He saw her as he walked through the front gates, had begun to head for the house, but now changed his mind and walked down the drive towards her, calling 'Miss Reynolds!'

Her head came up, and she stood still, smiling, watching him approach. Her hair was pulled back from a central parting in wide coils at the nape of her neck, the rather severe style softened by the ruffles of lace at the throat of her dress, palest soft green muslin, the ecru of its trimmings highlighting her fair complexion. He drew closer, slowly, so that he could study her. She held a tiny parasol of the same beige lace above her head, though here the trees shadowed her quite adequately. He wondered if she had forgiven him for the scene of their meeting yesterday, and was relieved to see that her smile was warm – she actually looked pleased to see him.

'Mister O'Brien . . .' Again the hand was held out to him; he took it, wanting to pull her forward into his arms, to kiss her, taste her lips, feel that perfect-looking skin against his cheek – to see if she was real, if she would respond to him like . . .

Of course he had let her hand go, after a brief, faint pressure and

482

the correct stiff bow over it. Of course they were standing with the correct three feet between them and their language was as cordial and informal as if they were surrounded by a hundred guests at a garden party.

'I have an apology to make to you, Mister O'Brien. Last evening I was rather ill with a headache . . . it was undoubtedly the . . . scene you witnessed between myself and Mister Ellis. A scene,' her eyes came up to his with a faint challenge to them, 'that you would be quite correct in saying I brought about myself.'

'I might think it, Miss Reynolds, but I would not be ill-mannered enough to say it.'

A smile pulled at her mouth. It was a generous mouth, like Anna's, even the small white teeth were like Anna's. He had been staring too long at her mouth, could tell by the look in her eyes as their gaze met that his feelings had betrayed him a little, she was watching him quietly, had moved back a little and turned, strolling slowly along the path towards the creek, and he walked with her. 'You see, I'd retired to my room by the time Mama and Papa and Emily and Richard returned – and this morning I woke to be told by Nellie that they have, all four, gone off once more, for their Christmas visit to Doctor Trask and his family.'

She had not been looking at him, but now threw a glance sideways to him – a sharp, considering glance, almost nervous in its brevity, and he had the absurd feeling – or was it an absurd hope? – that she was not telling the truth. 'So you see . . .' A nervous little laugh. 'I have not had the opportunity to tell them that you would be calling. I've sent a message to the Trask's house, to tell my parents you'd be visiting, but as yet they haven't returned.'

Was there a faint flush to her cheeks? They were walking in the sunlight just here, perhaps he was imagining it, or it was the heat. Sure, that was it, he scolded himself, there was no way a young girl, with a handsome fool like Ellis dangling after her, would be arranging time alone with the likes of *him*.

'I am . . . glad, a little, to be able to see you alone for a few moments,' she was saying.

'Eh?' His head came up, sharply.

'I wanted to tell you again that I'm not in the habit of having scenes such as that you heard Mister Ellis speak of.'

He smiled. 'I think you can rest easy that I didn't think you were. I was teasing you yesterday, and it was ill-mannered of me.'

'Then you won't say to yourself, each time you meet me, "Ah, there's that Miss Reynolds that led young Ellis on and tried to break his heart." I don't like to think that you thought that.'

'What would you like to think I thought?'

She caught his glance, was amused, suddenly. 'I don't know . . .' She walked ahead a little, and he watched the sway of her skirt, was pleased to see her naturally small waist was no longer confined by the ridiculous stays. They came to one of the willows that were planted along the creek's edge. She walked beneath the branches, leaning back against the trunk so that Aidan, coming behind, could see only a little of her skirt, and her parasol. 'I suppose I should like you to think I was ladylike – rather like my Mama. Gracious, you know.'

'Well,' he drawled, considering for a moment, 'Yes, I believe you're ladylike and gracious enough.'

'And gentle and kind, and sunny-natured and very clever . . .'

'You're asking a great deal of my perspicacity. Besides, if you're so much of a paragon, it's a fierce boring young lady you must be, and that's the truth.'

'I'm not boring, but I'm not wicked, either.'

He walked about the trunk, stood smiling at her. 'Yesterday you wanted to be wicked.'

'Don't keep talking about yesterday.'

'All right. And to set your mind at rest, I don't think you wicked. Foolish, perhaps, but I hope you've learnt your lesson and will treat Mark Ellis and any other man who comes courting you with a little more wariness. Physical appearances, as I think we've agreed, can be deceptive. When it comes to the opportunity to hold a woman such as yourself, all men can be villains.'

She laughed, delighted with his speech, and he realized that he had somehow moved too close to her, and that though her back was pressed against the trunk of the willow, she betrayed no sign of feeling threatened, nervous. She smiled up at him with the same amount of warmth, as if she trusted him. And it was this realization, more than anything else, that prevented him from grabbing her by her shoulders and pulling her into his embrace, to kiss her hard and lingeringly. She was eighteen. *Eighteen*. And more than that, she was Milton Reynolds' daughter.

He had walked away a little. Here a tree branch hung quite low; he reached his hands up to it, gripped it, leaned there, feeling his chest ache with a heaviness and confusion that he had not known in years. He did not understand it, knew only that he wanted these moments with the girl to go on – and yet more than that – he wanted to wrench from it all the delight that it promised. And the hopeless-ness of it all made him grit his teeth, grip the willow branch hard with his hands against the desire to cry aloud. He wanted to weep.

Yes, like a great *maicín*, a spoilt baby crying for a star, seeing it only as a toy just out of reach.

Berrima had sensed something of his despair, it was there in the massive back and hunched shoulders, the grip of the scarred hands on the branch. She ran about him, came up almost too close to him, gazed up into his face.

He dragged his eyes from the wooded hills opposite to look down at her. He looked at her the way he would look at a stranger.

'Mister O'Brien, are you . . . are you in trouble? Is that why you've come to see my father?'

'What type of trouble? No.' He half-smiled. That odd lift to a broad mouth that was made for smiling, but which seldom did. 'No. It's no trouble I'm in.'

'But you are unhappy.' She half-lifted her hand, made a helpless gesture – but she had come close, so close, to touching him. His heart lifted at the realization. She had almost touched him; against all propriety, her pity had stirred her to it. That, and his arms leaning on the overhead branch. She had felt safe enough. If it had not been for the years of excellent training she had received, training as to what-was-done and what-was-not-done, training never to over-step the boundaries of good manners, especially when alone with a strange man, sure she would have touched him. She's a touching person, he thought with a kind of joy. That's why she ended up in Mark Ellis's arms. She is easily stirred, affectionate. Like Anna . . .

'You . . . you come from Ireland?' she was saying, speaking with care, her tone hesitant, 'You've experienced the hardships of the Famine there, then.'

'I have.'

'Some experiences . . . can leave scars, I should think. It must be hard to forget.'

She was very close to him. He saw the changing shades of brown within the pupils of her eyes, eyes that never lost their focus on his own, and he felt pulled down into their depths; his sense of reality was fading, and the strangeness of their conversation was not, at that moment, strange at all, but natural, intuitive, right.

'You find something good,' he said into the darkness of those eyes that claimed him, 'and you're lucky even to recognize it.'

'Because of what has happened in the past?'

'Aye. And the terror that it may happen again. Loss. Pain.'

'A repetition . . .?'

'Life may be a repetition, God forbid. The same mistakes, over and over . . .'

'But when something is found, as you said, something good, of value . . . one should hold on to it . . .'

'One should, but circumstances . . .'

'It may mean breaking the chain of repetition.'

'I'd like to believe that.'

Their breath touched each other's faces, so close were they. He had forgotten who she was, where they were, forgotten everything but the gaze that joined with his, the mind that joined with his. He did not know if their bodies touched, felt afterwards that he had known her, the feel of her against him, every part of her matched and fitted to him. It was a possessing, and a being possessed, and he would never be free again.

Yet it could not be, for his hands still gripped the branch above their heads, and she was not touching him, but he felt her pulse matching his, so near . . .

It was she who kissed him, rising up on tiptoe and pressing her lips to his. Soft, yielding, her lips were, yet there was a chasteness to the kiss, it reminded him that her body and his body were separate. The physical touch of their mouths upon each other threw into contrast the union they had known a few seconds before. He felt puzzled, and not a little unnerved. When she pulled back from him, the same emotions were mirrored in her face.

They stood there, their bodies not each other's, nor their own, and he slowly lowered his hands – almost, not quite, touching her shoulders, her arms, as he did so.

They could not speak, and now could not meet each other's eyes. There was embarrassment between them, a feeling, Aidan was sure, that they had both betrayed themselves. He did not know what to say. Cursed himself, thought of Milton Reynolds's trust, and cursed himself again.

'Shall we go into the house?'

He had not meant his voice to sound so harsh. Her gaze came up to him sharply on hearing the edge, the coldness of his tone, but he had not seen her clearly, had already turned away, needing action, movement. His body still throbbed with the memory of whatever had passed between them.

He did not understand it, did not want to understand it. The enormity of it did not bear thinking about. He had survived all these years by closing a door upon his more sensitive emotions. He felt threatened, now. He needed to know he was in control, and he put the emotions, the whole incident behind him, and regained that control.

They were almost at the house when a carriage came around the

486

side of the building. Margaret and Milton were the first to see him and call a greeting, Emily and young Richard – how they had grown! – turning down the slope, then exclaiming with recognition, scrambling out of the carriage, running towards him.

They clambered about him like young puppies, each demanding attention, and as he had feared, Berrima stepped back and allowed them their way.

'Mister O'Brien . . .' It was Margaret Reynolds coming towards him, and he took her hand, then Milton was approaching, and while they were exchanging greetings, he could not help but hear Emily say to Berrima:

'Your new dress is very pretty. Is Mark here?'

'No.'

'Oh.'

'I don't need Mark's presence to persuade me to wear a new dress, Emily.'

Aidan was glad he had other excuses to smile. She liked him, she must like him . . . He walked inside with the parents and the two girls, while Richard was sent to lead the horse and carriage to the stables and search for the groom.

The evening was ruined in a perfectly innocent way.

Aidan had blinded himself to the inevitability, had, he told himself later, wanted to believe that it should not matter; but when, over the main course of cold turkey and roast pork, Milton said, 'And how is your wife, O'Brien? And the children?'

Aidan swallowed his food in one lump, kept his eyes on Milton, and did not dare glance at Berrima. 'They're all well, thank you.'

Margaret Reynolds began to speak in her quiet voice, but at the same time Berrima was saying, 'How old are your children now, Mr O'Brien?'

He was forced to look at her. Her gaze was interested, her mouth smiled, but there was something veiled in her eyes that became more pronounced as she gazed at him; as if there were something within her that needed concealment, something vulnerable.

'Liam's ten and Clemency's nine, Miss Reynolds.'

'Clemency,' she murmured, her gaze falling away from him, for now she must remember. 'Such a pretty name.'

He did not know how he would get through the remainder of the meal. His face felt cold, the muscles tight; for the next few moments he kept cutting his food, placing it in his mouth and swallowing it without remembering to chew it. Around him the clatter and the chatter went on, and Berrima's white face was a blur only as he swung his gaze up and down the table between Margaret and

Milton, answering their questions.

'It seems so long since we've seen the children,' Margaret was saying. 'We'll hardly recognize either of them. You must bring them to visit us on your next trip to Hobart. When will that be?'

'I've no idea – but, certainly, they shall come with me on my next trip. They would be delighted to see you again.'

The conversation went on, they were asking him about the farm and Will Treloar. Aidan dared not look at Berrima for fear his feelings would be obvious. He did not really acknowledge what they were speaking of, and answered automatically. Only during a discourse by Milton on the appalling state of the track from Brown's River to Huonville did Aidan dare glance over at her. She had her head lowered, and was moving her food about her plate with stiff little gestures. Once she raised her eyes to his and she did not smile, did not attempt to smile; the gaze slid away again, down to her plate. She looked very young, very hurt.

It was obvious to him now that she had known nothing of his past. It would all come out tonight, when he had gone, the whole sordid tale, and how they liked him despite everything. Better that she had seen her parents last night, better that she had known before he saw her again. She would look back on their last scene in the garden and regret it; she would see his behaviour as cheap, so wide is the gap between what is acceptable from a single man and what is acceptable from a married man with a family.

Suddenly he wanted to explain to her, wondered if it were possible to be alone with her before he left. To explain – what? But he must try, he could not bear that he should leave, not to return for God knows how long, and have her think badly of him.

But he had no chance to speak to her at all. For as dessert was being served, Berrima addressed her mother, 'I'm afraid that I may have spent too much time in the sun this afternoon, Mama. My headache is returning. Would you and Papa and Mister O'Brien excuse me if I retire?'

No! Aidan wanted to bellow. 'Certainly, Miss Reynolds,' he murmured, standing, as Milton did, as she rose and swept out of the room.

Aidan left at nine, and Milton drove him to the wharf. He turned about, as they headed up the steep little drive, and looked back at the house, lit with a warm glow from within, and wondered which room was Berrima's, when he would be able to see her again. And what she would say when he did.

In the room she shared with Emily, Berrima undressed into her

488

nightdress and sat for a long time before the mirror, ostensibly brushing her hair, but for the most part merely gazing at her reflection. It was strange. She had looked so pretty this morning. Tonight she looked tired, and *old* — she looked at least twenty-three. Her lids looked puffy as though she had been crying, and she had not. And there was no colour left in her cheeks. She looked sallow.

She was not consciously thinking anything about Aidan. It was more a kind of shock, a kind of waiting for the acceptance of the news. She had no idea of time passing, until Emily opened the door and tiptoed into the room, stopping on seeing Berrima. 'Oh. You're still awake.'

'My headache is better. Has he gone?'

'Mr O'Brien?' Emily smiled. Berrima noticed her expression softened. It was a strange thing, the evening must be bewitched, for the normally rather plain Emily was very pretty, with her cheeks flushed and grey eyes alight. 'Isn't he the kindest man? I'm so cross that you couldn't leave a note for us last night – I never would have left the house today if I'd known he was coming. Undo my fastenings, will you?' Berrima helped her with the thirty or so hooks and eyes at the back of her skirt and bodice.

'Why?' Berrima asked almost petulantly, 'What's so special about Aidan O'Brien?' *She had kissed him — and still she was not sorry* . . .

'Oh, *come*, Berri, you can't pass him off like that. He's important to me, at least.'

'Why you?'

The last fastenings were unhooked, and Emily turned to gaze at Berrima in amazement. 'I thought you were behaving in a peculiar manner when we went in to dinner. You dropped behind with Papa and I heard you ask Papa where he met Mr O'Brien. I thought I'd die with embarrassment – it's fortunate he didn't hear you.'

'Papa gave me such a black look. Why?'

'Don't you remember? When I was at Port Arthur – a crazy old convict went mad and attacked me with a pitchfork, and Mister O'Brien – who was a convict himself – threw himself at the madman and saved my life. It was all too dramatic . . . ' Emily undid the fastenings on her three petticoats and they fell to the floor. She was picking them up to hang them in the cupboard alongside her dress when she saw Berrima, and stopped. 'What are you looking like that for? You've gone white. Berri? You can't mean to say you'd forgotten *everything*?'

Berrima was seated stiffly before the mirror, the brush held forgotten in her lap. 'A convict?'

'Like Mister Treloar. Though I think Mister Treloar is nicer looking. He has such a kind face, and I like the way his hair curls, don't you?' She sighed, 'It was such a tragedy, his wife dying. One can tell just by looking at Mister Treloar that he's known and lost a great love.'

She half-expected Berrima to tell her, as she did often, lately, not to be a sentimental little idiot – but when she glanced up, Berrima was still, silent.

'I fell out of the Atkins's punt.' Her voice was dead. 'And he . . .'

'Of course! I'd forgotten that – gracious.' Emily plopped down upon the bed. 'To think of it – he's saved both our lives. Berri – you must write a book about it. Why, someone may even publish this one! Of course, it would be better if he married one of us, in the end. I've begun to like romantic endings. What a pity he's already married to someone else . . . '

It was strange to see the usually ebullient Berrima so subdued. Emily spoke with the faint maliciousness of a younger sister, 'You did know he was married, when he came yesterday?'

'Of course.' Primly.

She was curious, however. 'If he wasn't married,' she persisted, 'would you like him?'

'I like him now.' Berrima smiled at her sister in the mirror.

'You're trying to shock me, and I won't be shocked.'

She was pulling off her garters and stockings, but stopped and looked up at Berrima. 'You were upset, though, weren't you, when Papa asked about Mrs O'Brien?'

'Not at all. I tell you I knew. Mister O'Brien must be quite old, at least thirty. He'd have to have a wife somewhere.'

'I suppose,' with a little smile, 'that you were hoping she was back in Ireland, or dead or something.'

Berrima leaned her cheek on her hand. 'Yes,' she said wistfully.

'He is attractive. I've never forgotten him, but then, I knew him a great deal better than you.' She was folding her clothes neatly. 'You didn't have much chance for conversation when he hauled you out of the water, like a wet cat.'

Berrima glared at her in the mirror, hating her smugness. 'You're getting a little tubby, Emily. Shouldn't you speak to Mama about stays?'

Emily paused, unconsciously pulling in her stomach. She reached for her nightdress. 'I happen to agree with Papa that stays are bad for one's health, they restrict one's vital organs. Anyway, I'm not tubby, you're only jealous because I found Mister O'Brien first.'

She looked over at Berrima with new suspicion. 'What did you talk about all yesterday afternoon? It's not enough that Mark Ellis is making a fool of himself over you, but I'll bet you were flirting with

490

Aidan O'Brien, too.' Then she stopped, seeing that Berrima had frozen, was gazing into space, 'What's the matter?'

'Oh, Emily. The things I said last night. I was nervous, because I liked him. Oh, Emily.'

'What, what? What did you talk about?'

'Books . . .'

'So?' Emily's voice came muffled through the folds of her nightdress.

'How could I?' Berrima walked up and down the room, 'I told him — we were talking about appearances — I told him he looked like a villain.'

Emily's head popped out of her nightdress. She thrust her arms into the sleeves, 'Of all the . . . when he's been in *prison!*'

She said crossly, 'How was I to know he *was* a villain? People who are villainous have no right to go about being sensitive about it.'

'But he's *good*. He's a very kind man, and he saved our lives, and I think *you're* villainous!'

'It was a game, that's all. He was playing too.' She smiled suddenly. 'Really, he has a good sense of humour. I like him immensely. *Well*.' She sat down on the edge of her bed. 'Who'd have thought it. He really is a desperado.'

'I heard things from Papa . . .' Emily sat down at the dressing table and began to take the ribbons from her hair.

'What things?'

'Why Mr O'Brien was transported, things like that.'

'Tell me.' Berrima pulled her feet up under her nightdress. 'I won't allow you to go to sleep — I shall jump up and down on you unless you tell me everything you know! And all about the way he saved you from the mad convict, too. *Everything*, Emily.' But before Emily could speak, Berrima added impatiently, 'Really, I can't understand why these things should happen to you, you don't have the kind of spirit to appreciate these adventures. It should have happened to me.'

'I seem to remember,' Emily said primly, 'that you said something of the sort at the time.'

Will met him when he stepped off the ship the following morning, waiting with the wagon to load the supplies. Even his friend's wild call of welcome and excited handshake could not dispel Aidan's reticence and gloom. It lifted only when Will, almost dancing with excitement, told him that Cora had reconsidered. She would sell the lease of the timber grounds at Port Davey to them. They were to leave for the South-West immediately after Christmas.

49

It was a letter from her sister-in-law in Launceston that had decided Cora. She wrote that her daughter and two of her sons were 'brooding and quarrelsome and in need of change and some hard work. Could you find them something to do on the farm? They are all strong and healthy, especially Bella, who can chop firewood faster than either Billy or Tom, but they are good boys nevertheless and will eat anything .'

So just before Christmas, Billy, Tom and Bella arrived at the farm, and a week after Christmas Will and Aidan, Maura and the two children, sailed for the distant south-western settlement of Port Davey.

It amazed Aidan that Maura insisted on coming. 'Cora doesn't need me here,' she said, as they walked home from the large homestead one evening. 'You saw Bella in that kitchen – the girl was made for farm life. She left me nothing at all to do. The two boys are as strong as oxen and so glad to get themselves free of their parents and all the other children that they'll do right by Cora. No, Aidan . . .' and she did a very uncharacteristic thing and took his arm, 'you've been trying to talk me out of going for three weeks now, and I'll not be letting you succeed. I want to go with you, can't you see?'

'I *want* you with me.' He tightened his hold on her arm, in case she should decide to pull back. Physical communication between them was so rare that he wished to make the most of the moment – it bespoke a warmth between them, a friendliness that he could not pretend to himself always existed.

But since his return from the visit to Hobart Town there was a cordiality between them that came gently at odd moments and surprised him.

He was more patient with Maura's moods, better able to understand the frustrations under which she laboured. He was kinder, and it puzzled her, but secretly pleased her. Often he caught her gazing at him appraisingly, and his guilty conscience told him that she suspected – or worse, knew, in her heart – that he had seen Matty. But except for these odd moments, when she would tell him some anecdote of Liam's behaviour with a smile, or be more than usually patient with Clemency, or ask Aidan a question mildly when she would once have snapped at him, their life went on as before. It was enough, however, this new friendship, to make him believe that they might start again. Ridiculous that this friendship should only really be beginning now. He considered rather bitterly that it was his due – and hers, he should not be forgetting that – from the very beginning. It should not take adultery on his part before they decided that they liked each other, could live amicably. He wondered how long it would last, thought of the hardships awaiting them in the bleak, wind-raked wilderness of the South-West, and thought that it could mean hell for both of them should this uneasy truce fail and their habitual animosity return to undermine their confidence.

As for Maura, she had had her suspicions that something – some mysterious something – had occurred while he was away in Hobart. He had returned too content, he smiled easily. And the blue silk shawl – it was totally out of character for him to buy a gift of such extravagance.

Yet it was not suspicion that made her decide to accompany him. For there was far less danger of him taking another mistress at Port Davey than if they stayed here in Huonville. It was the realization that with the good money that everyone agreed that they would make there, they would not be short of food, or other supplies. She did not care so much for Aidan's talk of riches, not even for land of their own. For a good life and the respect of her friends was all Maura craved. The year here with Cora had given her a confidence in herself. From the moment that she realized that it was a definite thing, this pining venture, she sat down and worked it out clearly, stopped bracing herself against Aidan's will out of habit. Her new-found confidence made her realize that however primitive the conditions would be at Port Davey, they would be mild compared to the deprivations of the Famine. She had fed her family exclusively on fish before, she could do it again, should the worst come to the worst. And Aidan had promised, in his early pleadings, that they should take furniture and other comforts with them, that he would build her a proper cottage, with three rooms.

And with the knowledge that she could, if need be, cope with the worst, she began to see benefits in the project. She would have Aidan all to herself. They and the children would form a unit, and the years ahead, as they became more accustomed to the isolation, would bind them together and make up for all the years apart. She would find out what it was Aidan was searching for, would be able to probe more easily in the aloneness of that small settlement, and might yet come to understand this man. She had loved and married him, yet he still remained an enigma to her. They would be able to forget their past differences, perhaps, and people in Hobart, too, would forget about his convict background. They could, once they had enough money, return not only to respectability, but independence.

And once she had made up her mind, she quite looked forward to the adventure, and chose the household things they would take with them with some excitement.

The only misgiving she had was caused by her interview with the local schoolmistress, Miss Hinchy, who tried, in a determined manner, to keep Liam in school. 'Even if it's boarding school in Hobart, Mrs O'Brien.' In the past year Maura had become quite friendly with the woman, but resented this. 'He's a gifted child, you ought to know that. He not only craves learning, he needs it. Port Davey will pall on him within six months and he'll regret leaving.'

But Maura, who had packed so many of her books, felt confident that she could take charge of both the children's education. 'And besides,' she told Miss Hinchy, 'Liam is a working class boy, he'll be a working class man. There's not much point, I'm thinking, in the learning, when he'll only follow after his father.'

Miss Hinchy wondered if she mistook the faint bitterness in Maura's voice. 'And if Liam wants to be a teacher, or lawyer?'

'Och, get away! How could we afford the learning for that?'

'There are scholarships . . .'

'Not for the likes of Liam. Not for emancipists' sons.'

'That's not so . . .'

'No. Besides, Liam is too young. If we go to Port Davey for five years or so, and at the end of it he's still keen on the learning, then Aidan will have the money to indulge him.'

She said almost the same thing to Aidan when he queried the wisdom of disrupting Liam's education. But her answer did not satisfy the father any more than it had the teacher.

And Aidan was close enough to see an added aspect. The fact that Liam was decidedly, visibly, Maura's favourite child.

The boy still slept in the same room as Maura; Clemency slept in her bed in the little parlour, and Aidan remained on the settle bed in the kitchen. The matter had preyed on Aidan's mind for months, now. It had to change. He had given Maura plenty of time to adjust – the arrangement had been something that had been temporary, while they decided if they had a future together or not. Now she had made up her mind that she would accompany him to Port Davey, Aidan determined that the present sleeping arrangements would not follow them.

Maura returned from a visit to the homestead one evening to find Liam curled up in the settle bed in the kitchen.

'We've changed places,' he told his mother, happily.

'What?'

'Father and me. He's sleeping in your room, now.'

'Oh, he is . . .'

'You don't mind, do you, Ma? All the boys at schools sleep with their brothers, and the mothers and fathers sleep together . . .'

'Liam!'

The boy paused, puzzled. 'What's the matter? Don't you like sleeping with Father? Does he snore? Is that why you make him sleep out here?'

'No. You don't understand.' She headed for the parlour.

'He's sleeping in your bed, too.' She stopped to gaze at him. 'Mine was too short for him. His feet stuck out – he looked fierce funny when he tried it out,' Liam giggled. 'He said he'd best sleep with you – for his feet get cold.'

Wordlessly, Maura turned and went through the parlour, past the sleeping Clemency, and into the bedroom.

Aidan lay propped up in the double bed, his pipe in his mouth, reading his newspaper. She brought her eyes quickly away from his bare chest to gaze at Liam's bed in the corner. It was stripped of bedclothes, the mattress bare.

She turned back to Aidan, trembling so with rage and affronted pride that she could barely speak. 'That was a low, cheap trick.'

'Ah. Yes. Perhaps.'

'Get out, Aidan! I'll not let you get away with it! Get out of this room!'

'There's not a bed in the house that's vacant, Maura. That'll fit me,' he added.

'I despise you, do y' realize that? I'll not go along with it! I'll not be sleeping with you, Aidan! I'll not let you touch me!'

After a short pause, he said mildly, 'You're presuming, my dear, that I wish to touch you. The argument we're after having is connected with sleeping arrangements, not conjugal rights.'

'I don't believe you.'

He shrugged, looked back at his newspaper. 'Suit yourself.'

There was a long and tense silence. Tense, that is, for Maura. Aidan looked very comfortable. He turned a page, puffed at his pipe, continued reading.

'Are you naked under those bedclothes?' she asked, finally, when she could bear the silence no longer.

'Very,' he said.

'And you try to tell me you merely wish to sleep with me,' she scoffed.

'I merely wish to sleep naked with you. 'Tis fierce hot, Maura.'

'It'll be cold in this bed, Aidan.'

'I'll not be minding that. Come, don't let's be arguing. The children will wake. We must at least give an appearance of having a natural, normal marriage, Maura. You wouldn't want them to grow up thinking our marriage was not a success, would you?'

Her eyes flickered. She did not like to think that he might be right. How had this appeared to Liam? Did he question his parents' relationship in his mind? She was confused; had begun taking their estranged relationship for granted. It was not fair of him to do this so unexpectedly, and she with no chance to gather her wits, to fight him.

'Maura, are you going to stand there all night?'

'No.' She marched to the bureau against the wall, and pulled open the lower drawer, 'I shall sleep in Liam's bed.'

'I shouldn't advise that.'

She was kneeling by the bureau. Something in his voice made her pause. 'And why not?' without turning.

'Because I shall be forced to get up, and pick you up and bring you to this bed. In all my manly glory, Maura. This way, at least, you can pretend that I finish at the waist.'

She stood, glaring at him, feeling close to tears. 'It's not fair of you!'

'It's what I want.'

'And what of what I want?'

'Would you like to have a little cottage in Huonville, Maura? Or would you like to stay here with Cora? She won't mind. The children can stay with you, until Liam's old enough to come pining with me.' He saw her stiffen, and added, softly, 'And he will, Maura, you know he will. I'll send money to you and the children, but we'll not live together again.'

She stood gazing at him, silently. 'Or,' he continued, 'you can come to Port Davey with me. Mr and Mrs O'Brien, whom God hath joined together; helping each other, planning together, raising their children and romping beneath the blankets each night. I shall teach you to romp beneath the blankets, Maura, if it kills you. But not tonight. Sure, gazing at your pretty, bad-tempered face has put me off my lusting, and that's the truth. I shall read the newspaper, instead. But soon, very soon, I shall begin arguing about conjugal rights – and I will win. And you know I shall win. Now put on that pretty nightdress with the pink ribbons threaded through the lace –

I've often seen it hanging on the clothes line. I'll read the paper – I won't look.'

He disappeared behind the *Derwent Chronicle*.

She stood for a long moment in indecision. She did not like the tone of his voice, had long ago realized that the degree of his anger and the expression of it were in adverse proportion. She would have felt more confident if he had bellowed at her.

Eyeing him resentfully, or, rather, eyeing the newspaper resentfully, and the puffs of smoke that issued from behind it – for he was as good as his word and did not look – she undressed and put on the nightdress. She crept to her side of the bed and gingerly climbed between the covers.

He yawned, turned another page, kept reading.

Three-quarters of an hour passed. He re-filled his pipe twice, then let it go out, kept it in his mouth, chewing the stem as he read, carefully, studying every sentence in a way she knew he did not always do. It aggravated her. He was playing with her. He would wait until the lamp was out and then throw himself upon her. He had learnt to be cruel in these years in prison, she had noted that.

Finally he sighed, yawned once more, elaborately, placed his pipe on the table by the bed, dropped the newspaper on the floor, and reaching up, turned the wick of the lamp down until the room was plunged into darkness.

'Goodnight, Maura,' he said, gently.

'Goodnight,' tightly.

Silence. It went on and on.

She did not remember falling asleep, but she woke, several times, to his gentle breathing. Twice, he touched her accidently, harmless gestures of a man used to sleeping alone. She began to relax. He had some honour left, after all.

When she woke in the morning, with the first light struggling between the drawn curtains, it was to find herself asleep in his arms. And worse, as she stiffened, was the realization that she had been there for some time. She felt him stir, sigh. 'Maura?' he murmured into her hair, 'Do you remember that argument I said we'd have over conjugal rights?'

A dreadful silence.

'No, Aidan.'

'Yes, Maura.'

'No, Aidan!'

'*Yes, Maura . . .*'

50

When, years later, Clemency was asked about her childhood memories, she did not think of Ireland. For her, her real life began in the South-West.

Clearest of all her memories, perhaps because it was repeated over the years, was the cry, 'Father! Father's coming! The boat's coming!' And running, running through the bush, down the slope, along a narrow track where the wet, green grass dampened her skirt and her thick black stockings; to stand with other children and adults and gaze upstream, listening for the 'Coo-*ee*! Coo-*ee*!' with which the bushmen called to each other, wait and watch the softened, mist-bound river's mouth.

In winter, the Davey River ran between clouded, dripping banks, the river itself appeared to roll from under a cloud, and through the mist would come the dark boat and the two men. And she would be lifted to her father as he stepped ashore, held in the great damp arms, and there was laughter, as they all returned home together.

Her world, like the world of everyone around her at the settlement, revolved around the great logs that floated, bound together as rafts, down the river. The men talked about the size, the quality of the logs, the price that they would fetch in Hobart Town; the women talked of the weather, and how easy or difficult it was for their men to be working, they talked of the trips to Hobart Town when enough logs came down the river, and they talked of leaving, and the time when they would not have to gaze from their front doors to the lonely stretch of beach that was Settlement Point. To the days when the air would not be filled with the whine of the saws, and the chug of the engines from the saw pits, as the pine was trimmed and barked, smell the woodsmoke and the mutton bird oil that greased the machinery.

For Clemency, it was a magic place, a huge canopy of life where exciting things were always happening, yet where she knew almost everyone, and she felt safe, secure. Except for the compulsory schoolwork in the mornings, Clemency kept herself out of her mother's way as much as possible, for when she was not following Liam about, there were the Malone girls.

At first they were a blur of faces, pinafores, black legs and dark, curling, unruly hair. But gradually she came to separate them; the tallest was Franeen, then there was Bridget, Geraldine and Mary-Kate, who was only a little older than Clemency. There were male Malones, also, happy, heavy-booted, loud creatures, who worked their own mill. They did not really matter. The girls washed their brothers' clothes and waited on them at table, then scuttled out to the bush again. Franeen was Responsible, which meant she could be trusted not to let the others fall into the water, but, if truth were known, they often did. All the Malones could swim like mermaids, and in their rambles by the edges of river and creek, in the building of rafts to float on streams, of bridges across them, or tree houses in the King Billy pines over them, there were many catastrophes.

Clemency learnt to swim early, playing naked in the water with the Malone girls. When she fell into the creek fully clothed, it was only a matter of being smuggled into the Malone's cottage, where Mrs Malone would tut-tut, and find her some clothes of Mary-Kate's, and dry her own before the fire, and feed them all barm-brack, cake spiced with dried fruits and nuts.

When Clemency was back in her own clothes, the children were off again to play, always with the dark little good-natured gypsy of a woman cautioning her, 'We'll not be after worrying y'r Mam about this, will we?' Oh, it was a grand life!

Maura could feel the estrangement growing between her daughter and herself. The child seemed, when she had to spend her time indoors, to be always sidling about her. As Clemency grew older, it began to bother Maura. She saw Clemency not as a clinging burden, but as an independent creature who would one day be a woman, and it came to Maura that they were not friends.

It was hardly surprising. There was this secrecy, a slyness to the child, that Maura never could tolerate. She liked people to be open with their feelings and emotions, perhaps because she herself found it difficult to be completely free in betraying her feelings; she liked others about her to be more confident.

Clemency . . . crept. She walked softly, spoke little, and seemed to see everything. Sometimes when she did speak, it was to say something so adult, so astute, that it was obvious that she saw everything. Yet she shared nothing. She had always been like this.

Yet now Maura wished she could break through somehow, and explain to the critical mind behind those eyes all that had happened, why it had happened. Sometimes she would like to see some emotion upon that bland little face, even if she had to strike her, as she used to when she could not bear the sullen, resentful gaze any longer. Tears were better, tears made the child seem human. She could feel warmer towards her, then. But now, now the child had grown too far away from her. She walked into the house each evening and it was like a strange child wearing a familiar mask. Clemency made Maura think often of the legends of the changeling. What if the faeries had come, and out of mischief, had taken away the laughing daughter she could have loved, and left instead this prickly, introverted child? How they would laugh. And somewhere, she would muse bitterly, there would be a dark-haired little girl, who looked like Aidan, who smiled like Thomas, who would be puzzling the bejaysers out of an obstinate, soured, wasp of a woman who deserved Clemency for a daughter.

Now, Liam – Liam was a joy to her. His mischief was caused by pure high spirits. He was thoughtful, and kind-hearted, in a gruff, manly way. The only shadow on her life was that Miss Hinchy's words were proving correct. The fact was, the boy was too bright. Even Maura, now, began to see more of a future for him than working with his father. She wanted the best for him.

He had devoured all the books in the settlement, hounded the skippers of the whaling and sealing ships that sometimes moored off Whalers' Point, to be allowed to borrow their books, even read disused volumes on navigation. Most of her day was spent supervising his lessons, helping him, and it gave her a pleasure that she did not know in anything else.

But lately, Maura was watching him, and her heart would he heavy, because she knew she would soon be faced with a decision she did not want to make.

At first Aidan had longed for more frequent trips to Hobart Town – and Berrima. But there seemed to be so much more to be done at the settlement, things that led to more money – and that thought was beginning to take precedence with Aidan over any other. He thought of Berrima often, dreamed about her at night, made love to the clenched-fisted Maura, and thought of her. Sometimes, but less and less frequently as the years went on, he thought of Matty. But he wanted to be rich, more than he wanted to look upon Berrima, to make love to Matty. Matty he could live without, Berrima – all he could do was to look upon Berrima. Better to do it from a position of sufficient wealth and prominence that she might be tempted to look back.

Yet he visited the Reynolds family at least once each year, on his annual trip to Hobart. Berrima was always there, looking more like Anna with each year that passed. And there, too, nearly every visit, was Mark Ellis. Aidan teased Berrima about him, but she would

500

never be drawn into a quarrel, simply lowered her head and smiled to herself, and would not make any retort.

Maura, on one of the visits when both families dined together, was horrified to hear that both Berrima and Emily were helping their father in his surgery and at the city hospital. She was concerned that they were exposed to disease – not to mention sights that well-brought-up young ladies should not have to witness – but Milton claimed that his daughters were of inestimable help to him. Emily, particularly, he said, knew a great deal about medicine already, more than a great many of the men who passed in Hobart Town as medical practitioners. Maura admitted to Aidan afterwards that it was hardly the sort of thing she would wish to boast about, had it been Clemency.

'All that dreadful knowledge – what man is going to want to marry a girl who knows everything about him from his brains to the workings of his bowels, tell me? She'd inhibit him, make him suspicious. Sure, Milton Reynolds is raising himself a pair of fine intelligent old maids, you mark my words.'

They were in their hotel room in Hobart Town, and Maura was regarding Aidan from her chair, the book she had been reading held forgotten on her lap in her concern for the Reynolds girls' prospects. Maura had been fitted with glasses this trip, for her eyes had for a long time, now, been failing her. They were gold-rimmed spectacles, small, in order to fit her small, narrow face. He never said so, but he did not like them; she had a way of looking at one through them that made the green eyes glitter, like hard emeralds.

He did not argue with Maura over the matter of Milton's peculiar ideas on education – Maura was even more horrified the following year, to find that Richard, now seven years old, was dissecting rats and frogs in order to study anatomy. The fact that the child had a scientific bent and a leaning towards following his father into medicine, was not excuse enough for Maura. She began, privately, to regard the Reynolds family as little short of a group of necromancers. 'Unnatural,' she muttered.

Yet the family exerted some hold over her, as it did over Aidan. Maura liked Margaret Reynolds, and in truth owed the family so much that she tolerated Milton's strange ideas, and ceased, on the annual visits, to ask what the children were doing these days?

Aidan, each visit, waited for the announcement of Berrima's engagement to Mark Ellis. He dreaded it, hated the emotions that beset him; surely, at his age they were ridiculous? He found the young man outgoing, friendly. He had no reason to dislike Mark Ellis, yet could not help resenting him. He was, Aidan thought, too much at home in the Reynolds house.

Over and over, he told himself grimly that Berrima would be wise to marry Mark, that she was a fool not to see that he obviously loved her. Yet Aidan's jealousy sat in his chest like some bitter pill that would not be digested. In 1860 he decided not to go to Hobart Town, but allowed Will to take the timber, sell it, and buy their supplies for the next twelve months.

Maura, too, surprised him by deciding to stay, that year. She had, she claimed, everything she needed, here. Aidan did not understand it, but had noted that she seemed, in these years, to be very content.

Aidan spent the time that Will was away – a month that somehow lengthened to two – building a lean-to laundry-cum-bathroom at the rear of the cottage, and working with the Malones in laying the keel of the little ketch that he had planned on building for so long.

Will, too, had been busy these past years making additions to his modest one room cabin. It had prompted Maura to comment, 'That boy's planning on marrying again . . .'

And indeed, it seemed as if Will had that in mind. He came back from his two-month visit in late 1860 with several new shirts and trousers and a pair of boots that he wore only when one of the families had a child, a wedding or a funeral. Aidan questioned him, teased him about the identity of the girl, but Will became coy, embarrassed, claimed there was no girl; at least, no girl that would look at him with interest, who would be mad enough to follow him to this lonely settlement.

Their life was hard, their work exhausting. But the logs piled up in the pens near the river's mouth, and the money piled up in the bank in Hobart Town.

They spent weeks at a time upriver, where their timber ground lay, living in what the piners called a badger-box, badger being the title many used for the native wombat. The 'box' was a ten-by-fifteen-foot hut built on an A-shaped frame, its roof-walls of bark and the ridge covered with grasses.

All through the autumn months from February till May, Aidan and Will cut the timber, rolling it on log 'skids' down the steep slopes to the creeks. From every hillside, it seemed, in these upper tributaries of the Davey River, axes rang and saws rasped like asthmatic giants among the timber, but each man knew his boundary, and no one trespassed on another's ground. Aidan and Will, Malone and his boys, Lane and Raymond, Bradley and Taylor and others nearby, saw their families back at Settlement Point only when they returned every few weeks for supplies, then it was back to the cutting and rolling, the clearing of the little creeks and streams, in preparation for the winter rains.

The South-West of Tasmania possesses the highest rainfall in Australia; with the winter storms the many creeks begin to swell with swift, brown water, and the logs, each marked with the piners' own brand – for Aidan and Will it was a shamrock carved into the wood with the small axe – would go down the creeks and channels to the Davey River, helped by the men in their little, stubby-ended boats that bobbed, keel-less and easily manoeuvrable, amongst the logs.

Will and Aidan's boat had been bought from the Malones, and they had spent the warm Sundays of their first autumn learning how to handle it, first on the calm lower reaches of the Davey, then, as the true test, through the narrow bottle-neck of Hell's Gates. There the bare cliffs towered high above them on either side, and the river turned in a sharp curve, so that approaching in a winter's flood, when the sky was hung with low cloud, they could see nothing before them but sheer rock, and yet were thrown forwards through it – 'Like being swallowed by a whale,' Will had murmured shakily, the first time they brought their logs down and came to a relatively slow drift in the broad river once more.

At the pens, the brushwood and log-fenced floating yards, the men would claim their own timber.

They had both been confident, when they came to Port Davey, of their ability to cope with the life; confident, being strong men, that they would succeed at whatever they had to do. But the boat was a challenge to them, taking turns, one with the oars, one with the iron-tipped prodder, and a few dunkings had them realizing that what they needed to cultivate was balance and agility, and quick, accurate judgement. They earned the amusement and eventually the respect of the Malones and the other more experienced piners. They were determined, and they worked well together. Eventually, they could fly through Hell's Gates nose-to-nose with Malone and his sons, with the logs thundering together about them like the Clashing Rocks of Greek mythology, and laugh. 'But me heart's in me throat,' Aidan admitted, 'every time, so it is.'

If they worked hard, they played hard also – nearly all the men were drinkers – but an occasional spree was never allowed to affect their work or their judgement. The one thing that all at Port Davey shared, and this applied to the women, too, was a fierce ambition. They stayed, and they worked hard and they tolerated the cold, the rain, the presence of the strange, dense, temperate rainforest around them, the loneliness and the primitive conditions, because the market in Huon pine was excellent, and here they could earn the money quickly, for the farm, or the business that each of them craved. It was not a gamble, as the goldfields would have been, neither was there the brash, lively, ever-changing panorama that would have compensated much for the hard work and rough conditions. All life at Port Davey was tuned to the land, and the land was tuned to the seasons.

For those who could see miracles in a snow-hung tea-tree, reflected in a pool, who could find a miniature world amongst mosses and sedges and the brilliantly-coloured fungi that clung about the tree roots, who could find something majestic and splendid in the changing cloud patterns across the faces of the rock-bound mountains, or the raw sweep of the button-grass moors to the north-east; for those who could see these things, the South-West gave back a thousand-fold. Those who came and made their money and left could never forget it. Many returned, time and again, never free of the pull of the place. Whalers, sealers, piners and prospectors, came to take, and left part of themselves behind, never to be free, completely, ever again.

There were dangers here, too, inherent in the work and in the very land they trod upon. Though the piners were tough and took few risks, the felling of the logs, the rolling to the water, the clearing of the channels and the freeing of the snarled logs in the race to the mouth of the Davey, caused accidents at times. And the icy winds from the Antarctic, that froze mast and spar and broke ships and men meant that for every piner buried in the little cemetery, a sailor, or sealing or whaling man, lay nearby.

Some men simply became lost. Shipwrecked sailors, on the rugged, barren coast, lone prospectors, even surveyors, had been known to disappear in the thick rainforest, most dying of exposure in the cold. And there was another danger for the unwary, that of the horizontal scrub.

Its botanical name is *Anadopetalum biglandulosum*, and it deserves the complexity of the title, but those who know it call it simply, horizontal. It grows in low lands and gullies, parent trees reaching upwards until the mainstem bends with age, and the branches from this fallen trunk rise skywards, becoming mainstems themselves, interlacing together, falling, sending up more subsidiary branches. Eventually it becomes a woven mass of vegetation, almost impossible to walk through, and strong enough for a man to walk upon should he step down upon it over the gully it has choked, sometimes to a height of more than thirty feet. It requires care, this walking on horizontal scrub. Some new growth can lack support from beneath, and one may fall, down between the tangle of branches, sometimes to the forest floor, and the branch that has let one fall springs back into place. One can disappear without trace.

Yet the little group of pioneers – never, until the idea was pointed out by their grandchildren and great-grandchildren did they regard themselves as anything as romantic as pioneers – lived and worked and suffered in the snow and storms of winter, and some came to regard the place as home. One of these, surprising no one more than herself, was Maura.

Somehow, she had made a home in that wilderness. Aidan would have thought it impossible; she herself would have shared that view, but there was something in that wild and untamed country that touched something within Maura. She found herself responding to it in a way that she had not to any of their homes in Tasmania. There was a sense of unity to the little settlement that was missing in the far-flung group of farms in the Huon Valley.

When the Malones ran short of supplies, and the O'Briens joined with several of the other families to loan them flour, salt meat, sugar and tea; when Lane hurt his foot, each of the men spent a few hours with Raymond to help out; and Maura did not resent this, had been warned that it sometimes happened in the settlement, and she received a sense of well-being through being able to help her neigh-bours. She made a friend of Lane's wife, Maggie, who shared Maura's love of books; they exchanged whatever reading matter they possessed, and discussed authors; it was as close as Maura had come to having an intimate woman friend since Anna O'Hagan.

And she had been right; here, there was no one with whom she had to share Aidan; he had come to love the South-West as she had, but his work was arduous, and she was at the centre of his home, the warmth, the comfort he returned to after the weeks upriver. Aidan came home to her eagerly, stepped off the boat to her eagerly, and she could tolerate his fondling her at night, since it meant that he watched her with gladness in his eyes, and he talked to her, often.

In 1861, as the winter drew on towards its close, and Aidan and Will brought the last of their logs down the swollen river, Aidan somehow thought Maura would be looking forward to visiting Hobart Town.

'But there's so much to do here,' Maura murmured, looking around the small garden where she had planted potatoes, cabbages and onions, for it was now September and spring. 'I'm not sure I want to go to Hobart Town this year, either.'

The wind was rising. Aidan had been making another water barrel for the house, had come out to fetch Maura, could not help but admire her, the tenacity and her desire to keep working – the garden meant a great deal to her. 'It's only for a month, Maura. We've not been back to Hobart for two years. I know how you feel – Will and I want to be finishing the ketch, and starting our own mill – but even for these things we need to go to Hobart Town. And I'll be wanting to see my bank, also. We've enough money to invest in a little something, now – we should consider it.'

'All those newspapers you study,' she said, looking at him, unsure. 'And the books on business – do you really think investing is the best answer? Would we not be happier if we bought our small farm?'

'We've been through this before. A small farm will take us nowhere at all. We need money first, Maura. Lots of it. So we can make sure we keep that farm.'

'Yes,' she sighed. 'But don't take risks, will you, Aidan? Don't gamble our savings on anything with any risk . . .'

'You know me better than that,' he growled.

And she smiled. Yes. Much of his reckless nature was now controlled. Or perhaps it was just where money was concerned. He would have to be careful, Maura thought, with this new greed he had acquired. In some ways it made her feel secure. She knew in her heart that they would never be poor again. But it was a preoccupation, this study of stock markets and business affairs. Sometimes she would have preferred it if he had come home and sat down with four of his mates and a few bottles of whiskey, like other women's husbands. Even her own father had not been so preoccupied with making money.

She said, now, 'You go to Hobart Town, and . . .' Her mind leapt ahead, she made a decision suddenly, irrevocably. Aidan had looked over at her. She had been toying with the handle of the spade, now pulled it from the ground to push it firmly back into the soil; a decisive sort of gesture. 'And I want you to take Liam with you.'

'But you and Clemency . . .'

'You don't understand. Liam . . . Liam should not come back here. I want you to take him to a good school in Hobart. The best, Aidan. Liam must have more learning.'

Aidan gazed at his wife in amazement. She did not meet his look but scowled over her garden to the encroaching tangle of bauera, the native dog-rose, at the edge of the scrub. The thick vine was starred with delicate pink blossoms, but it would take over her garden if she allowed it, and lay it waste.

'Jaysus, this is sudden, is it not?' He almost said, you mean you'd let him go away from you, for a year at a time – but he did not.

She turned to him. 'Miss Hinchy back in Huonville tried to warn

506

me – but I thought I knew best. You've been helping him with his mathematics – you know he can work with figures as well as a twenty-year-old, and he's only fourteen. And he's read so much history that he can tell you dates and descriptions as though he were there, sure.'

Aidan was hurt a little. He had had plans himself for Liam, could see them working together on the new ship he was building; in only a few more years they'd be equals, working together, like Malone and his boys. Maura's words were a threat, they took away that dream figure of his grown-up son, who worked shoulder to shoulder with him. Put in his place a dark-coated, sophisticated figure – for some reason he thought of Mark Ellis – and it was as if Maura had robbed him of a friend.

'You'd be proud of Liam, would you not? Should he go to university and become a lawyer, or doctor?'

'I would, sure. But have you asked Liam? What does he want?'

She turned away again, and he realized how dreadfully this scheme was hurting her, and his own possessiveness of his son was forgotten in his knowledge of what this was costing Maura.

'Come,' he said, and took her hand. 'Let's find him.'

They walked down to the water's edge, where the sound of children's voices floated up to them through the dusk. By the river's edge there was a tree house built long ago by the Malone boys, and now inherited by their sisters. There were Bradley and Raymond children, as well as Malones – the tree seemed full of Malones, the black-stockinged legs swinging. Maura took her hand from Aidan's, long before any of the children could notice. 'Look at those Malones – and there's another on the way, they tell me. They're like the O'Sullivans all over again . . .'

'Don't,' Aidan said, that depleted family rising before him, the little coffins that had been carried out the door . . . the wailing.

She looked at him, sharply. He smiled, wryly, in apology, but she understood, crossed herself, and murmured, 'Aye, 'tis not right to compare them.' And she turned to gaze at the Malones, playing as they were, they tumbled everywhere. 'It's a soft country, Aidan,' she said. 'It's kind to us, is it not?'

'It is,' he said, and he was glad that she could see this. He was always half-expecting Maura to be homesick, to wish to return to Ireland. Each good thing she expressed about this country made him relax a little more.

'Liam!'

His son dropped out of a tree, and ran up the slope towards them, barefooted, hair mussed and scattered with leaves.

507

'What would you feel about going to school in Hobart?' Aidan said grimly, without preamble.

At first the freckled face was unreadable, then it broke into a grin, and the wiry little arms were flung around his father. 'Do you mean it? Do you mean it, Father? A proper school? Ma? Is it true? Can I?'

Maura's hand was gripping Aidan's arm as if drawing support from him, 'Yes,' she said, and her other hand touched Liam's head as he embraced her.

The mother and son walked up to the cottage together, their arms linked. Aidan called Clemency and followed behind them, watching the two in front and thinking, without jealousy, that a great deal of the affection Maura contained was given to Liam. Liam who, with his natural self-confidence and ebullience, did not really need the concentrated devotion. As Aidan watched, the boy wriggled free of his mother's arm, and strode along beside her, chattering, waving his hands about.

'Papa?'

He glanced down at Clemency, and smiled. Her face was very grubby, and her thick auburn hair was spikey with twigs and dry leaves, 'Papa, you won't make me go to school, will you?'

'Ma helps you with your lessons, does she not?'

'Aye. But later. You won't make me go to school later, will you? I don't want to leave here ever.'

'Education for women is a fine idea, Rebel. But rest easy, I'll not be sending you anywhere you don't want to go.'

'Promise?'

'Promise.'

One small hand patted his face. 'Good,' she said, firmly.

His heart felt lighter. Clemency was still here. She would not be leaving him for a long time. He could cherish her in a way he could not cherish the laughing, capable boy.

Aidan thought that the way the family was grouped as it walked up the hill, was rather typical; Maura with Liam, Maura who had not checked to see what had become of Clemency. Aidan loved both his children equally, could not understand Maura having a preference. But perhaps he worried more about Clemency, understanding the relationship between mother and daughter in the early years, when Maura had been under the strain of poverty, and not knowing if he, Aidan, was to be released or not.

He saw shadows, sometimes, in Clemency's eyes, and he did not know if these were due to a highly-strung, moody personality, or a direct result of her early estrangement from her mother. He did not discuss this with Maura, who said often enough even now that he spoiled Clemency. But he felt driven, in some way, to compensate her. He spent a great deal of his free time with her, liked to hear her questions, to answer her, to know that she responded to his interest, was less reserved with him, laughed with him, tried out already her little store of flirtatiousness and persuasive charm.

Perhaps he did indulge her; he thought her plottings extremely amusing. Maura said he was encouraging her in deviousness and avariciousness. Aidan replied that she was learning that diplomacy was the key to successful social exchange. But that was teasing Maura. He had the feeling Clemency knew he was aware of being cajoled. They understood each other, he felt. But Maura would scowl, and repeat her prophesy that Clemency's character was being ruined.

It was that night, the night that they decided that Liam should go to school, that they heard the screaming.

It was unearthly, terrifying, rose and fell above the wail of the wind, and both Aidan and Maura sat up in their bed, first with the thought that one of the children had come to harm; then, as the two little night-shirted figures fled through the door and on to their beds, both wide-eyed with fright, they wondered briefly, superstitiously, about banshees, so eerie was the sound.

Aidan lit the candle. They sat there for some seconds – then the sound was cut short abruptly. They knew, now, that it was human, that only unconsciousness or death could bring such a cry of agony to such a halt.

Aidan was out of bed, pulling on his trousers over his nightshirt, and everyone was speaking at once; the children clamouring to go with him, Maura begging him to be careful.

But he had barely pulled on his boots before they heard voices; men's voices, murmurs and curses, and boots on the muddy path, then a heavy banging on the door.

Now Maura was up, but the two children were quicker even than Aidan, had fled through the door to the kitchen, and were fumbling with the latch on the front door. Aidan reached them as they began to open it, had only enough time to scoop up Clemency, stood holding her beneath one arm as the force of the wind blew the door back. The crowd of men, beards grizzled with snow, capped heads hunched into their coats, came in, with God-save-you's, and thank-ye's and smiles of gratitude pinched with the cold and their fear.

They bore a stretcher between them. It dripped wetly, darkly, on to the scrubbed slab floor. 'Come in – there's a bed, there—' Aidan indicated Liam's settle bed, and backed off, into the bedroom,

509

dragging Liam by one arm. 'What is it? Who is it? What's he . . .?' He pushed them both into the middle of the bed, grated, 'Stay there,' in such black tones that they shrank back. He followed Maura, now wearing her dress, a shawl thrown over her shoulders to hide her unfastened bodice, out into the kitchen.

'We're from the *Maid of Erin* . . . This lad – 'tis Heath, that's his name . . . It's his head . . . '

'Came down off the spar just as we was making it safe into Bond Bay . . .'

'He's been screaming all the way from the ship . . .'

The man's face did not bear looking at. Maura turned away. She went to the fire and began to light it, to hang the kettle in place. Water, yes. They would need lots of water . . . She thought she would be ill, but keeping busy, keeping her back to that bloodied thing on the settle, kept her mind from the horror that threatened to engulf her.

'Only twenty-five, Heath is. Done for, now, I expect.'

'An' there's no doctor here?'

'No,' Aidan said, glancing at Maura; somehow he expected she would know a little about these things, but a glance at her averted, white face, told him that he could discount aid from that direction. 'I . . . ' he went to the curtained shelves, took down some cotton pillow slips, 'Here, keep these pressed against the wound. I suppose . . . ' He wracked his brain. 'Hugh Raymond is the most experienced piner, here. He's had to attend to a lot of accidents. He lives up the track about a quarter of a mile . . .'

'Mister, we can't carry Heath all that way through this weather . . .'

''Twas hard enough getting him to shore . . .'

'Yes, I understand. Of course he can stay here. I'll go beyond and fetch Hugh.'

'I'll go.' Maura had stood, and before Aidan could stop her she had looped up his own oilskin jacket from the door, taken up one of the sailors' lanterns, and was outside in the storm.

'Maura!' He ran after her, catching up with her at the corner of the house. 'Maura, what's the matter with you?'

'I can't stand it – do you not understand? I won't have that . . . that thing in my house. The blood! Did you see it?' Her voice was rising, 'He's dying! I'll not have him die in my house!'

'Maura, Stop it! Do y' have no pity in you at all!'

'No! Take him to Malones', or Bradleys' or the Raymonds' house – but don't leave him in my house!' Her voice was almost a shriek. Aidan shook her.

510

'What're y' like? Give me that coat. Get you inside and try to be useful.'

'I can't bear to look on him, Aidan!'

'Then don't! Help the men as much as you can, find them fresh bandages, make them tea – I'll go to fetch Raymond.' He gave her a push, back towards the lighted doorway, furious with her, and went off up the slope through the screaming sleet, pulling on his jacket as he ran.

Both Raymond and his wife came back with Aidan; bluff, sandy-coloured, capable people, they knew only as much of injuries as a lifetime spent in logging camps had taught them, but this was often of as much value as any of the doctors of the time knew.

For the unfortunate Heath, Mrs Raymond claimed, there was little that even the best Hobart doctors could do. They bandaged the lacerated face, but it was the wounds to the head that were the main cause of concern. There were no cuts above the hairline; only on the man's forehead, but the skull was obviously fractured in at least two places.

'What do we do?' one of the sailors asked.

'Keep the wounds clean, and wait,' Mrs Raymond said stiffly, 'and either he'll live, or he'll die.'

'We're sailing tomorrow, if the weather clears . . .'

'You'll go without him, then. He'll not be moving for some time.' It was her husband who spoke. He was rinsing bloodied hands in the basin of water, and turned to Maura, seated white-faced by the hearth. Neither he nor his wife were very astonished at her inability to deal with what had happened. She was such a frail little thing, and very bookish. If she had taken control of the situation calmly and competently, they would have been amazed. 'The weather will improve tomorrow, Missus. We'll move him up to our cottage,' he said, now.

'Thank you.' Maura could barely meet the man's gaze. She was consumed by her sense of guilt. She felt pity for the injured sailor – she did, sure – but her fear was greater than her pity. Her fear crushed her, she huddled there by the fire beneath the memory of her mother's death, her father's death, and – oh, the worst – Bridie's! Bridie who had been ten years old, who had held her rag doll and cried for her mother . . .

Aidan knew nothing of this, Aidan who had told her she had no pity, who had pushed her! Let Aidan watch a ten-year-old child die of typhoid fever, and then let him talk of pity!

Hugh Raymond took the five sailors back to his cottage, and his wife stayed the rest of that night with the O'Briens. She was patient with Maura, felt secretly that the woman appeared to be in some kind of shock. The two children had long ago fallen asleep in the large bed. Martha Raymond tucked Maura in beside Clemency, and bade her get some rest. She and Aidan stayed up for the remainder of the night, drinking tea and discussing the young man who lay so still upon the bed in the corner.

It was strange, Maura thought, afterwards, that the incident should mean the beginning of a coolness between herself and Aidan, the loss of their tentative sense of companionship built up quietly over the past five years. She should have told him, she thought later, of why she had behaved as she did. But all that night and the next day until the weather cleared, and the sailor, Heath, was taken up the hill to Raymonds' cottage, she had felt trapped within the prison of her own memories. She took the children to Will's hut and went through their lessons there, and Will did not mind, came to view the man on the bed and the appalling injuries to his head, and did not appear to resent Maura for her lack of sympathy, did not regard her as callous. No one did, she thought. Except Aidan. Oh, he said nothing, not even when the little cavalcade wended its way up the slope towards Raymonds' cottage. He made no comment at all. But she could feel his accusations there, all the same, in the way he turned to look at her, before taking up his axe and walking down to the woodheap to cut more firewood.

That, Maura often thought later, had been the time to speak. But speaking of such things had always been hard for her, sometimes the words came out awkwardly, and if they did so now, he would think, perhaps, that she was making up excuses. He could say, quite correctly, 'You nursed Liam when he fell and cut his leg badly, you've nursed him when he's had a cold.' And she would say, 'Yes, because I love him, because he is my son and depends on me.' And he would say, 'You nursed Clemency when she had the whooping cough.' 'Yes, because she, too, is my child, and there was no one else to help – I am all they have . . .'

But he did not speak, and she did not have to justify herself. She said nothing at mealtimes nor after he had come back from visiting the unconscious Heath, nor when they lay in bed together that night. Once, Aidan would have questioned her, she thought. Back in Killaloe he would have questioned her, for he could not bear, in those days, to think that there was a mystery close by; that there existed something that he did not understand. But after the years in prison, he had learnt to live, it seemed, with mysteries, with things he did not understand. Then Maura became stubborn, and not a little hurt. He did not even *try* to see her point of view, he did not

512

even ask why. It was easier for him to accuse her, he preferred to blame her. If he really cared for her, he would bring up the subject first. But he did not care, believed the worst of her, as he had always done.

Two weeks later, in early October, with the man Heath still very ill, Liam, Aidan and Will sailed for Hobart Town. The two men would return in four weeks, but Liam would go directly to his new school, to remain there until the school holidays in December, which he would spend, that year, with Cora Frazer in the Huon Valley.

He went quite happily, feeling himself on the brink of a new world, glad to be free of a life he had found stultifying – due mostly, though he could admit it to no one, to his mother's loving pre-occupation. At their parting on the beach, he tried to look sad, but he could not join in her tears, felt sad only for her sake. 'You go along and be happy – I'll be all right,' she kept saying, and he felt heavy-hearted at her unhappiness while at the same time resenting her for trying to hold him back with remorse, even now.

He felt more moved when he looked down at Clemency, whom he had always protected from rougher children – and from Ma. Who would look after her now? As the boat pulled further and further out into the bay, he knew Clemency would not be crying, would say nothing at all. Her eyes would be huge in the small face beneath the mop of auburn hair so like his own. Yet all through the voyage, and in the nights of his homesickness in the dormitory that first year, it was more often Clemency's face he saw when he thought of that farewell on the beach.

51

The first four days in Hobart Town were spent at Risby's mill overseeing the unloading and measuring of the timber. For these first few days, Liam still followed Aidan like a shadow, as if the time for parting was too close for either of them to feel entirely comfortable.

There were new clothes to be purchased for himself and Liam, and the embarrassment and confusion of ordering clothes for Maura and Clemency, and with only measurements to guide him. He sent these latter parcels directly on the first ship back to Port Davey.

Liam's application to enter St Andrew's School was at first regarded with misgivings, but after a day of tests it was more than clear to Father Glynn and the other teachers that Liam was well ahead of any of his age in the school. Though he was fourteen, he was small for his age. They decided to place him amongst the fifteen-year-olds, confident that he would cope with their standard.

As they left the school grounds, Liam gazing around him at the tall stone buildings, Aidan said, 'They'll be older than you, these lads, and bigger. Are you sure you wouldn't rather be among boys your own age?'

'No. I want to prove I'm smarter. And anyway, I'm strong. If they begin bullying me, I'll thrash 'em.'

Aidan had taught Liam to fight, but now worried at the tone of confidence in his son's voice; he glanced down at him sceptically, but the look was lost on Liam.

Aidan and Will spent three days with Cora Frazer on the farm, helping Billy and Tom with the spring ploughing, then boarded the packet together, to return to Hobart.

Will was silent for much of the trip; Aidan had begun to wonder if Cora's niece, Bella, was the reason for Will's new clothes and his silence then—

'I went to visit Doctor Reynolds on Tuesday, while you were at the school with Liam,' Will said.

Aidan looked at him in surprise. 'You said nothing about that.'

'No. I . . . it didn't turn out to be a pleasant visit. I needed time to think back on it.' He was standing gazing out at the coast of Bruny Island, and suddenly Aidan thought he understood.

'I had to ask Doctor Reynold's permission, you see. Oh, Lord, 'twas embarrassing. He called her into the room and asked her if she wanted to marry me and she said 'twas all a dreadful mistake and burst into tears. Aidan, 'twas like being caught up in one of those music hall dramas. I've never been so humiliated in my life.' The great hands gripped the railing, the great shoulders were hunched. Aidan could think of nothing to say, was so taken aback by the Cornishman, whose usual optimism and reserve carried him through any grief or distress he might suffer. But now Will was openly miserable. Aidan himself felt as if he had been punched in the stomach, and found difficulty breathing.

'But, boyo . . . when did all this happen? When did you propose to Berrima?'

'Last year. All this year I've been working, living for the day when I could bring her home to Port Davey . . .'

'Home to . . . ! All year! Why didn't you tell me?'

514

'I . . . I don't know. She wanted it kept a secret, and I suppose I thought you'd try and talk me out of it. She's not exactly the resilient type, is she? I thought you'd tell me it'd be wrong to bring her to the settlement.'

'And so I would. Mother of God, Will! Can you see her there? What kind of a life would it be for her?'

'Maura manages.'

'Maura was brought up in Ireland, she's seen the Famine. She wasn't cosseted in such a house as the Reynolds'.'

'But she's such a sensible girl . . .'

'Sensible?' He was filled with unreasoning rage. 'That little eejit! She deserves a good whipping with a riding crop – first Mark Ellis, now you.'

There was a pause. Then Will said, 'We d' talk about Emily, do we not?'

Aidan stared at him. '*Emily*? You proposed to *Emily*? But when I said Berrima . . .'

'Did you say Berrima? I'm sorry. I'm that grieved I don't know what's going on about me . . .'

'You were jilted by *Emily*?'

''Tis hard to believe, isn't it?'

'Well, she's still very young . . .'

'Nineteen. A grown woman who knows her mind. I hope.' The blue eyes scanned his friend's face, 'Unless you're telling me that I'm too old for her. 'Tis good for a man to be older than his wife. Twenty years is not too big a gap if a man is fit, young in his mind.'

Aidan's heart was heavy, for this could be himself, breaking his heart over Berrima. There was no hope, Aidan knew, could not understand that Will did not know. Love made men fools. He saw himself in Will's place, and felt ridiculous. Both of them infatuated at almost middle-age, with girls young enough to be their daughters. Aidan writhed.

'Twenty years is not unreasonable,' Will was murmuring wistfully. The wind whipped the light brown curls around his face, a face more alight with emotion than Aidan had ever seen it. 'I haven't forgotten Sarah, but – Emily is special. She's made me feel alive again. Oh, I know I be only an ignorant bushie, but Emily loved me, Aidan! I d'believe she still does! But for some reason she's become frightened. Perhaps her parents talked her out of it.'

'If she loved you, Will, nothing they said would make any difference.'

'I don't believe that. A young girl, who's been as closely brought up as you say – she'd hold her parents' wishes in some standing.

Doctor Reynolds wasn't unkind about the matter – rather the opposite – but I just think that something is wrong.'

When he did not continue, Aidan said, 'She'll write to you, Will, she'll be in touch should she change her mind . . . ' But he could see that this was little comfort to Will.

'I'd like you to talk to Doctor Reynolds.'

'What?'

'You'll be seeing the family when we return to Hobart, will you not? You could talk to Doctor Reynolds, find out if there's some reason why he doesn't find me a fit husband for Emily. And . . . and you might be able to speak to Emily, also; she might have a message for me.'

Aidan felt out of his depth. The complications of his own life were enough; Maura brooding back in Port Davey, his desire, foolish though it might be, to see Berrima again – and now he was drawn into the triangle of Will, Emily and Milton Reynolds. He had never been much of a conciliator, he thought, having done most of his settling of matters with his fists. This task of diplomacy Will had given him made him feel awkward.

He approached the Reynold's house the following day wondering how to broach the subject.

His welcome was as warm as it ever was. Young Richard dragged him off to the large attic room that had once been the nursery, to see the elaborate train set his father had had sent out from England for his last birthday. Margaret then accompanied him down to the parlour for luncheon – but mother and son were the only members of the family in whom Aidan did not sense some kind of shadow.

Emily he could understand, and Milton, for they had had the responsibility of blighting poor Will's hopes. But there was a reserve, too, in Berrima, something at once grown-up, which was natural, at twenty-two, yet not, he believed, natural to her. All through luncheon, she did not address any comment directly to him, though she smiled readily enough. Sometimes he found her regarding him quietly, but her eyes would be lowered, or move away to one of the others, if he met her gaze directly.

It was during the meal that Milton Reynolds said, 'You'll stay with us for a few days, won't you? Would Will mind? You said in your last letter that you were interested in the property next door – I hear it's going on the market in the near future, we could see over the grounds.'

Margaret joined in, 'Indeed, yes, you must stay.' As did Richard, Emily and Berrima – although the latter was much more controlled in her pleadings than the other two. Polite, only, Aidan thought –

but he knew he would accept. To stay in the same house as Berrima! He coloured a little, said thank you, he would be delighted, and put the thought of Will, who would have to stay alone at the hotel, from him in his sense of pleasure.

In the afternoon he returned to the Shipwright's Arms, and explained to Will, who smiled, and said he understood, that he did not mind at all – but Aidan would, would he not, talk to Reynolds that very night, come to see him the following day? Will was agitated and restless. He helped carry Aidan's bags down to the cab, wrung his hand, and said, 'I'm depending on you, Aidan. Talk to them as soon as you can.'

Aidan drove back to the house in South Hobart, wondering at love's power to overwhelm one. Was Will going through all he had suffered for Anna's sake? If so then he must be miserable indeed, and Aidan knew that he would do all he could to help. All the way up Macquarie Street in the carriage he rehearsed ways of bringing up the conversation with Milton.

But that night, after the men had been left alone with their port and had once again, as on that evening so long ago, taken their glasses and cigars down to the garden, it was Milton who brought the subject up.

'I'm glad you could spend these few days with us. I'd like to have you for your entire visit if I didn't think Will would feel . . .'

'Aye. Under the circumstances.'

'He's told you then? I'm glad – I needed to speak with you about it, Aidan. Tell me, is he taking it very badly?'

'I truly believe he loves Emily. He's taking it badly, so.'

'I was afraid of that. I want you to know, Aidan – and I said the same thing to Will on Tuesday – that if Emily loved him, I'd be pleased to have him for a son-in-law. I meant it. I don't think Will believed me. I think you will, for you see the same qualities in him I do.'

'It's a fine man he is.'

'Yes. But last year, when these little trysts were taking place at various gatherings here – and I had no idea they were as serious as Will now informs me they were – Emily was going through a rather trying time.' He glanced over at Aidan. 'I think she was rather jealous of Berri – you know how Berri's had Mark Ellis dangling after her all these years. And more than that – I've a feeling that there's always been some small amount of jealousy between Emily and Berrima. Emily is so exceptionally clever, and Berrima is the more striking in looks and temperament – they each had cause to feel a little envious as they were growing up. They're good friends, now, for Emily is more confident. I think we can thank Will Treloar for that. Probably because he is older than the majority of young men Emily meets, he was the first to see past her reserve, her shyness. When he left to return to Port Davey last year, he left behind a young woman who saw herself, for the first time, as being very attractive. I've no doubt that last year she truly believed herself to be in love with Will – but he was the first, you see. She's matured beyond that relationship – it's been supplanted by something else . . .' Milton hesitated.

'There's someone else?' Aidan's hopes for Will plummetted.

'Aidan, my family are members of the Society of Friends – does that mean anything to you?'

'You're Quakers, then. I've the greatest respect for Quakers – they did a grand job in the Famine – or tried to. They gave of their own food to us, and died of the fevers, nursing us. The Quakers have a fine name in Ireland.'

'For three hundred years we've always believed that men and women were created equally in God's sight. Our daughters have always been educated equally as well as our sons, and at Meeting, our women can preach, and lead prayers.'

'But, Milton, Will is Protestant – Methodist, I think . . .'

'Aidan, Aidan! It's not a matter of religion. What I'm attempting to explain is that Margaret and I have brought up both our girls to use their intelligence, not to shrink from learning. And lately, with the women's suffrage movements in the United States and England becoming more voluble, we've thought that perhaps there might be more for our girls than simply becoming decorative . . . appendages to their husbands.'

Milton looked embarrassed. Aidan was thunderstruck. He had never, in his life, heard talk like this. He was never to know it, but this last shocking description was one of Berrima's, and Milton was equally surprised to hear his daughter's propaganda come from his own mouth. He took a deep breath. 'I'm sending Emily to New York, Aidan. She wishes to be enrolled in medical school. She wishes to become a doctor.'

Aidan could only stare at his friend. 'Emily? A doctor?' He tried to imagine Emily examining him for abdominal pain and almost laughed. But then he remembered the wives of the over-worked doctors at the old penal stations, who, he had heard, often nursed the convict patients. And he remembered Margaret Reynolds at Port Arthur, when he was recovering after Nat had stabbed him. Yes. If women could nurse – indeed, though the fashion was to treat them as frail, delicate creatures, they were yet

518

expected to nurse, to lance boils, bandage ugly wounds, to lay out bodies – if women could do all these things, why could they not be doctors?

Milton said, 'I suppose you find the idea preposterous.'

'Och, no! It's just surprised I am!' He thought of Emily, as lovely, now, in her own way, as Berrima, soft brown hair and quiet, intelligent grey eyes. Yes, these past few years, Emily had gained in confidence – it was this that made her beautiful. He placed Emily in Maura's place when Heath had been carried through the cottage door. And he said, quietly, confidently, 'Emily will make a fine doctor.'

Reynolds seemed to relax a little, placed a hand briefly on Aidan's shoulder, as if – and this pleased Aidan – his opinion had mattered. Aidan was not to know of the ridicule, the expressions of horror, even the insults that Reynolds had suffered in the past few months, when he had attempted to discuss the matter with fellow doctors and academics.

'Papa?' A light voice behind them. Aidan's heart lifted, but it was not Berrima.

Emily said, 'Richard is ready for bed, Papa. He'd like you to say goodnight.'

Milton went off towards the house. 'I'll be back directly,' he said to Aidan, 'I'll bring us some more port.'

Emily stood smiling in the dim light from the house. She did not follow her father back inside, but moved down the slope to stroll beside Aidan.

There was a silence for a while, then, 'Your father told me you're after leaving for New York.'

'Yes. Did he . . . did he mention when?'

'No, but I take it it'll be quite soon.'

'Tomorrow, Mister O'Brien.'

'*What?*'

'It was decided some weeks ago, but after . . . after speaking to Will, I asked Mama if we could leave earlier. She's coming with me, you see – just for a few months. I'll be staying with her uncle in New York – he's a surgeon.'

'Emily, forgive me – but this isn't an effort to avoid Will, is it? He'd be the last person to make himself foolish by forcing his attentions on you . . .'

'Oh, I know that! I do know that! But – I had to avoid seeing Will before I leave, Mr O'Brien, I couldn't bear it. For he wouldn't understand. Papa said you would – but I know Will. I care for him deeply, Mr O'Brien, I want you to know that. But I'm not the right

519

woman for him. And . . . and I must leave for the United States soon, for there are very few universities there that will allow a woman to study medicine – but certainly my chances are better there than in England. I won't even be able to begin immediately, I'll have to study privately with my great uncle – perhaps for years – before I can be admitted to a course. You see, they'll expect a great deal more promise from me than from the average male student.' She smiled a little sadly.

'I see.'

Again the silence. Aidan thought of Will, back in the Shipwright's Arms. Will with his new-found pleasure in his appearance and the additions to his cottage. *Aidan, she's made me feel alive again.*

And suddenly he was angry with Emily. It must have communicated itself somehow, for she said, 'I meant to tell him, Mr O'Brien, when he wrote to me and told me of his new cottage and his plans for us. But it seemed such a cowardly thing, for me to crush the hope out of him like that. And he wasn't simply the man I was in love with. He was my friend, as well.

'But then he arrived last week, and I was called into the parlour to give him my answer. How could I tell him the truth? That I wish to spend my life treating disease and illness – facing sneering fellow students and narrow-minded lecturers and ignorant people . . . How could I tell him I'd chosen this over him?'

'You should have tried,' Aidan growled.

'Perhaps. But I can't risk him trying to prevent me. I've broken with him, now. It wouldn't be kind to see him again.'

'Are you sure you'll be happy doing this?'

She looked directly into his face. 'My father has brought us up, Mr O'Brien, to have faith in our own strength and intelligence. Neither Berri nor I were ever taught that because we were female we were somehow inferior in intellect or wisdom. I don't think that I should be studying medicine because I am any cleverer than a dozen girls I know. It's just that I have confidence in myself, you see. And we, the first, will have to have confidence above all else. Yes. This is what I want.'

He gazed at her, sensing and admiring the strength of her. He said gently, 'This may break your heart. Do you see that? The opposition, I mean.'

'Yes, I know.' Emily smiled a little. 'Perhaps Will will be pleased to know that I, too, will be suffering.'

'Arra, no. Don't say that, you do him an injustice.'

'Yes,' she admitted, 'I suppose I do. Will you tell him, Mr O'Brien, will you try to explain to him?'

520

'Miss Emily, you don't know . . .'

'But he'll listen to you! You're his best friend.'

Aidan ran his fingers through his hair, felt himself to be a piece of timber in a press. He was to talk Emily into joining Will; now he was to talk Will into letting Emily go. He wished he were back in Port Davey. Hell's Gates was a more pleasant position than this . . .

'There you are!'

Berrima stood on the flagged path that led to the house. He had only to raise his eyes and she was there. Her dress was all pale pink flounces, in a flimsy sort of fabric that the breeze played with.

'I'll go inside now.' Emily stretched out her hand and Aidan took it. 'I know you'll do your best to explain. I want to know he's forgiven me. It's presumptuous of me perhaps, in the circumstances, but I would like to know that. If he thought I was doing the right thing, it would give me such courage.' And she was gone, walking, half-running, up the path and into the house.

And Aidan was left alone with Berrima.

He held the glass of port at an odd angle, forgotten. The other hand held a cigar that had long gone out. They both realized the silence had gone on for too long. She tried to smile, 'Well. Have you solved all the problems?'

'You know about all this?'

'Oh, yes. Not only am I Emily's confidante, but I saw Will for a few moments before he left the house on Tuesday. I felt very sorry for him. Everyone seems to have the greatest confidence that you'll see *their* side and will be able to do something.'

'There'll be only one victim.'

She hesitated. 'Yes,' she said softly. 'Poor Will.'

He turned and began to walk along the lawn a little, keeping within the range of the lights of the house. He hoped she would fall in beside him, and he was right. It was a mild night, only a faint breeze blew. He could smell a fresh floral scent from Berrima, and then remembered she wore a nosegay of rosebuds at the sash of her gown.

'How is your wife?' she asked politely.

'She is well, thank you.' His gaze was on the ground before them, he did not look up. She was able to study his face for some minutes.

'She did not come with you this trip . . .?'

'No. She actually prefers to remain at Port Davey. She has many friends there. She is not used to city ways.'

A drab, Berrima decided smugly. Even her own mother had described Maura O'Brien as a colourless little thing. Berrima cast a quick glance sideways at Aidan, the broad shoulders in the dark suit;

If he were my husband he should not go off to the city alone.

She almost resented her feelings for this man. While she was fascinated with his humour, his toughness, his obvious resilience, she could not but help think that it was unfair that none of the men she had met in the past years had made her forget him. His was the face she used in all her fantasies of a dark stranger, somehow threatening yet fascinating, that fed her imagination in all those years when she was maturing into adulthood. They were innocent dreams. They had little to do with this man, who was, after all, beyond her reach. But she could not quite forget the feelings that had stirred within her when she met Aidan. It made her wonder about love. On the one hand there were the feelings of excitement engendered by Aidan O'Brien, on the other – and this was where love, real love led – there was the rather dull routine of motherhood and housekeeping, the companionable friendship that her parents shared. Mark wanted her to experience both feelings, but she knew, somehow, that they were mutually exclusive. Some common sense within her had stopped her, telling her that she was too young, that if she had once met a man who had filled her with warmth, respect, or pity, excitement, if she had found it once with the mystical, mythical Aidan O'Brien, then she would find it yet again. What she had not expected was to find all those feelings returning with the very man who had first stirred them within her.

Aidan was watching her, wondering hopefully, briefly, if she, too, might take it into her head to study medicine. But no. This was the author of the twenty-two *Miranda* novels. Beneath that very attractive bosom beat the heart of a true Romantic. She would marry for love. And it had to be Mark Ellis. Aidan's jealousy, unreasonable as it was, possessed him totally. He looked at her, saw how lovely she was, and wanted to preserve her somehow. To keep the moment as it was, now, to have her always look like this, like Anna. Not to be his, Aidan's, perhaps. But not to belong to anyone else, either. It was senseless, it was selfish. But he wanted her smile, her touch, her physical presence as much as he ever had. The mind behind the eyes, Anna's eyes, held little interest for him. He knew her. Knew her type. Many of the landowners' wives and daughters in Killaloe had been of such a type as Berrima was. Caroline Kelly was one of them. Her soul was like a familiar-looking stretch of landscape. Foreign, perhaps, but nothing really different. It did not stir him at all, he did not desire to explore it, let alone to claim it. But someone else would. Soon, perhaps quite soon. He asked, 'Will you marry Mark Ellis?'

She stopped walking, and he sensed a withdrawal, an emotional withdrawal. She stared at him from a long way off, as if he were some form of lower life. 'You have no right to ask me a question like that.'

He smiled, but it was not a pleasant smile. 'I care about you. I ask merely from my interest as an old and trusted friend of the family. Well? Do you think you'll marry him?'

She was blushing; he could see her heightened colour as she glanced away, first towards the house, then down towards the creek and the darkness, as if realizing that the shadows hid her face. After a quick glance at him, taking in his calm stance, the shadowed watchful eyes, she said softly, 'I don't love Mark. I don't want to fall in love with anyone. It means only one thing, doesn't it? Getting married, and having ten or twelve children. I . . . I'm a little like Emily in that. I want something more. Not wealth or position,' she added hastily, 'for a woman gains that, too, from a clever marriage with the right, socially-ambitious husband. No, it's something more than that.'

He waited for her to go on. She was gazing up at him rather earnestly, and he found himself moved by her obvious trust in him, to speak so to him, even when he deplored her sneering at values to which he had always ascribed. Wealth and position were all that mattered, really. One was not safe unless one possessed them, and by now Aidan did not really care about the methods used to gain them. And marriage being distasteful to her . . . He stood studying her and told her silently that if he was married to her it would not be such a chore, even if twelve children did come along. The begetting of them would be worth it, begod.

He said, instead, gently, 'Berri, what is it that you want?'

She turned almost frightened eyes to him. He could not know it, but it was surprise and gratitude that was on her face. He did not treat her like a child, as her father did, but through his fondness – he must be fond of her, she thought, or he would not be bothered speaking with her like this – he did not dismiss her words. She felt that though he did not understand, he accepted her opinions, her ideals, unformed, clumsy though they were.

'I envy Emily dreadfully,' she said, 'because she has this goal of studying medicine. I envy my mother because she's so totally satisfied in being an excellent wife and mother and hostess. All I am is just a mass of . . . of *wanting*, without any direction. It's like yearning for something that has no name.'

'You're dissastisfied,' Aidan said. 'You're young and dissatisfied with the life that has been forced upon you.'

'But it's going to continue to be forced upon me.' And when he frowned a little, 'You don't understand, do you? What are the choices? Marriage – or spinsterhood. Dependent on my husband, or dependent on my parents.'

'Everyone's dependent on someone,' he growled. 'Even the husband to whom you claim you will be nothing but an appendage,' he borrowed Milton's words, did not notice her look of surprise, walked on, scowling. '*He'll* depend upon his employer – even if he's a high-ranking politician, he'll sweat over each election ballot. We're all imprisoned in some kind of dependence. Unless . . .'

'Unless what . . . ?' she asked when he did not finish.

'Unless one is very rich. Unless one has land. Lots of land.' His features looked very hard, his mouth tight, he was not looking at her, was scowling up at the stars.

She thought of a dozen things to say, all clever, all rather helpful, patronizing things, for he was wrong. He was ambitious for money, she realized, and always having sensed his doggedness, his determination, she realized he would succeed at his goal. But he would change. He would be trading only one dependence – whatever his might be – for another. He would not own the land that he longed for so very much. It would come to own him.

She half-opened her mouth. He turned to her, rather expectantly. She realized, quite suddenly, that she nearly always had his attention. It was pleasant. But puzzling. There was so much she did not know, did not understand. Her feelings of comfort, almost completeness, when she was with this man, must be illusory. What could she, Berrima Reynolds, twenty-two years old, not overly intelligent or perspicacious, hope to understand about a man of the complexity of Aidan O'Brien? Let alone to scold him on the shallowness of his ambitions. It was unlike her, even to wish to attempt to change anyone. They were worlds away from each other in years and experience. They would grow further apart as time went on. And she felt sad at that thought; a kind of heaviness settled upon her.

She was not looking at Aidan. When she gave a little sigh, short, sharp, he was disturbed. He studied her face in the half-dark, and wondered if he had done something to annoy her. But she smiled, and said, 'Papa is a long time, isn't he? Shall we go inside?'

And he walked up the steps beside her, sensing her mood had changed. He thought of something clever, trivial, to say to her but there was something in the angle of her head, a slight droop to her shoulders that prevented him.

How changeable she is, he thought. He could not understand, even now, how she could look so much like Anna, and be so completely different in character. One always knew what Anna was feeling, and why. And there were never any storms within her breast anyway, to be sure, for she was a capable, placid girl. She was reasonable, Aidan told himself, and glanced sideways almost crossly, to the pretty child who walked beside him. He hoped Mark Ellis was a patient man. Begod, he would need to be patient to cope with this one's whims.

Berrima glanced up and caught his scowl, and wondered if what she had said made him disapprove of her. That bothered her. She did not understand why, but this man's approbation mattered. Was it because their first meeting had been so inauspicious? That she was trying to convince him that she was after all, a lady?

He should not matter. He was ill-mannered, and sometimes interfering. Her life, whether she married, whom she married, was not his concern.

He drank too much that night, and was glad that Reynolds matched him drink for drink, and did not appear to mind. For Aidan's brain, unfortunately, remained clear, and there was little blurring of his feelings. He had a suspicion that Reynolds was wondering, after all, if he was doing the best thing for his daughter. 'Always believed in equal rights for women,' he murmured at one stage. 'But somehow it's easier to hope that some other woman, somewhere, does something frightfully clever and paves the way. When it's one's own daughter up there, being pointed at, ridiculed by idiots who are afraid of change – well, I don't know, somehow I wish I could say, "Stay at home, Emily, stay at home, dear, where it's warm and safe. Let someone else be the first." But if everybody thought that, nothing would ever get done, would it?'

Aye, Aidan thought blackly, and tried to concentrate on Emily and not think of her sister.

And in the night, in his bedroom that faced over the rear garden and the creek, flecked with moonlight, he fell into a drugged sleep and dreamed of the Sidhe of Craglea. She walked towards him up the hill, and now there were willows growing all around. And his heart ached, because it was Anna, and he moaned in fear because it was not Anna, and she came so close to him, grasped for his arm with her long fingers, and he only just escaped.

He lay awake for a long time, and wondered, not for the first time, what the dream meant. It seemed to occur, he thought, whenever he was contemplating something wicked. Was it a warning?

He could not deny he wanted to make love to Berrima – God forgive him, if he thought he could seduce her, he would. He could afford to keep a mistress, now . . .

But that was foolishness itself. Milton and Margaret were his friends, he could not be thinking these things. Besides, she was too quick, was Berrima, she'd be after seeing that there was little to compensate her for the loss of her reputation.

It was hopeless. Like Will, also, undoubtedly, passing a restless night, he was torturing himself for nothing. He shouldn't have agreed to stay in this house. Of what use was it, to be so close to Berrima? It was not as if he truly cared for her. She who looked so much like Anna – yet who was not Anna. He could never forgive her for not being Anna. But even then, he found himself looking forward to morning, to seeing her, freshly-scrubbed and neat in one of her pastel summer dresses, perhaps a little sleepy, still, sitting there at the breakfast table with him.

He felt his body responding to the thought, and rolled over, violently, with an oath. Arra, he was mad for staying in this house. Mad.

He was caught up in the plans and packing and removal of trunks, the next morning, and it was not until they were at the wharf, and Emily and Margaret were taking his hand in farewell that he realized that this was actually happening, that Will, now, would have no chance to say goodbye to Emily at all.

But he looked down into the girl's face, and read there that she did not wish this; there was a gratitude, there, that Aidan had followed her wishes.

Then it was over, it was too late; the *Tamar Maid* was moving easily, beneath her cloud of canvas, down the broad Derwent estuary, bound for Melbourne.

Preoccupied, he saw the subdued Reynolds family into their carriage, made excuses that he had to visit his bank, and left them, feeling that they would wish to be alone with their own sense of loss. And he, Aidan, had to be alone, also; how to tell Will? How in God's name to tell Will?

He did go to his bank, playing for time, hoping some ideas would come to him, but then, in his single-mindedness, and his pleasure in the meeting with the manager, Austin, Aidan momentarily forgot Will and his problems.

'There are many pieces of real estate on the market at the moment,' Mr Austin said. 'Have you considered investing in land, Mr O'Brien?'

Aidan had, in truth, been thinking of a timber mill. But the idea of city real estate intrigued him. With Austin's recommendation, he visited several land agents in the city, and spent the rest of the day looking at vacant blocks close to the business centre, choosing one, finally, in Davey Street. It was expensive, but from the situation, and the drainage, he could see that it would be worth it.

He went back to the bank, settled the matter of deposits and surveyor's fees, and explained his idea to Austin.

'A whole building of doctors' room?' Austin repeated after him, but as Aidan went on, he could see the advantages. That was why the man had been at such pains to find a block with excellent drainage, for the sewage question, in Hobart, like any other city, was always a problem. Milton had spoken to him time and again of the difficulty in finding clean, sanitary surroundings in which to set up a medical practice. This would be the first time, to Austin's knowledge, that anyone in Hobart had begun to construct a building that was designed specifically for that use. Austin himself was intrigued with the idea. According to O'Brien, he had a friend in the medical field who could work with the architect and give him a definite idea of what was required of the rooms.

When Aidan finally left the bank, Austin, who had walked him to the door, stood lost in thought for a few seconds. He had begun the interview that morning with the assumption that O'Brien was a cautious man, of little imagination. Now, Austin drifted back to his desk under a completely different impression.

Aidan was still considering all the details of the deal when he arrived back at the house, and realized, only on walking down the drive, that he had completely forgotten to go to Will at the Shipwright's Arms, should have told him what had happened . . .

He had begun to turn, but stopped, seeing Berrima kneeling by one of the flower beds. His hesitation was gone. 'Good afternoon,' he called.

She looked up, and rose to her feet. It was a pity, he thought, to disturb her; in her gardening gloves, lemon dress sprigged with tiny flowers, the ribbon on her broad straw hat a matching lemon, and a full, pale green pinafore, she looked a picture, bent over her work.

'Good afternoon,' she smiled. He was learning the complexities of these things, had come upon her and called heartily, would have passed with a comment on the pleasant sunshine. But she had waited until he was closer, had greeted him almost gently, looking directly into his eyes, and his brashness left him and he stood before her with the air between them weighted, waiting.

'I'm afraid I'm the only one home at the moment. Papa is at a meeting at Richard's school. Shall we go inside and have tea?'

'No. No, the sunshine is more pleasant, don't you think? It's only a few moments I have, I must see Will . . . Would you walk with me? Or,' he added hastily, 'would I be disturbing your work?'

527

'Not at all.' She bent to her basket on the ground, exchanged her gardening gloves for a pair of white lace gloves, and began to walk, a few feet between them, about the grounds.

It was a chore, Berrima thought, this social chatter, as she described the spring blooms and the plants her mother had for the garden. She liked Aidan immensely, wanted to ask him about his life in Ireland, longed to ask him about his experiences in prison. Yet the rules of propriety must be observed. Not for the first time Berrima chafed under them. When he told her of the vegetable garden he had planted at Port Davey she was happier. It was not difficult, by means of a few clever questions, to have him talking about his children, and Will, describing the forest and its creatures, his plans for the cabin and eventually buying his own farm.

Yet as they headed down the slope towards the water, he seemed to feel that he been talking too much, began to lapse into silence, smiled rather awkwardly and spent a great deal of time scowling about the willows and the encroaching hills opposite as if preoccupied.

'Are you hot?' she asked now. 'Would you like to return to the house?'

He looked up in surprise, 'No, not at all. Though I suppose I should be going . . . fairly shortly . . .' He petered out.

There seemed, almost, to be so much unsaid, Berrima thought, as they walked down to the creek, slowly, and then along under the willows.

She felt excited, and somehow guilty, and yet she had walked like this with Mark often enough and had never felt anything of the sort.

Aidan was silent, now, and even when they reached the boundary of the Reynolds' property and the overgrown garden of the much larger estate next door, they kept walking in silence. They halted only when a hedge of overgrown blackberry blocked their path.

'It's almost a jungle, this property,' Berrima said, finally. 'Colonel Atkins died about eighteen months ago intestate. Until someone sorts out the will, the house is falling into disrepair, and the gardens . . .' She swept her hand over the view of overgrown shrubs, from which Aidan could just pick out the glass of several greenhouses, and one or two fountains and ponds. 'This was one of the first large houses here. The name of the property is Glenleigh. It's a pretty name, isn't it? No doubt the land will be divided up to build more cottages. Though it's a pity, isn't it?'

'Yes,' he said. But he was studying her, not looking at the garden.

They were almost beneath the shadow of a huge willow, and he

528

took her arm, drew her gently within its shade. 'Miss Reynolds,' he began, and then stopped.

The memory of that day, four years before, when they had stood quite near this spot, came clearly back to them, now.

Her voice came firmly, surprising him by the maturity of it. 'How long will it be, do you think, before I forget you? I'd like to be able to, you know. It's not just a matter of will-power.'

He had reached for her without realizing it, held her by the narrow shoulders and gazed at her, too stunned to speak.

'You try to shut me out – don't, Aidan. Don't. I've loved you for four years . . .'

'Arra, stop, Berri . . .'

'I will. That's all I wanted to say.'

He still held her by her shoulders, hard, as if he were drowning; and he was, could not speak, still, for the emotion within him stopped his lungs, his mind. She said, 'Say something, Aidan. Say something.'

His hands still gripped her shoulders. 'I don't believe you.'

Long seconds passed, it seemed. He said, 'You believe this now, I know. But it will pass, sure. And you'll . . .'

She was in his arms, her tears were wet against his cheek, and she was holding him, cradling him almost, her lips were against his cheek, his neck, his ear, with more tenderness than he thought he could bear. *Anna . . . Anna . . .*

'Oh, my dear . . .' she was saying, 'You do believe me. Aidan . . . Aidan, in your heart you know. You do . . .'

He was holding her tightly, kissing her, and he was lost, lost in feelings so long forgotten, so strong and overwhelming, that he did not know where he was; he existed in a timelessness that was here yet was Killaloe, that was all his experience and yet nothing he had known before.

Only slowly, slowly, did he come back to himself, his arm about her waist, the other behind her head . . . it was the feel of her that was wrong somehow, the smallness of her that was Berrima, Berrima.

He pulled back from her, gazed down at her, willing himself out of the maelstrom of his own feelings, with the terrifying realization that the girl *understood*. The child, this ignorant, cruel child understood. Saw his past and his desires such as no one else had, possessed the power to see within him and *understand*. His hands on her shoulders were trembling. What a power she would have over him if he let her. He had betrayed himself and because she wanted him –

now – now, on one of her whims, with her astuteness and her intelligence she had seen through him. She could possess him in a way that no one else could, but Anna. Little Berri, with her bright mocking eyes, who was so far removed from him in background and education that, for all her naive talk of love, should he say 'Live with me', she would laugh in his face. Walk away laughing.

They did not know what made them turn. It was not a conscious sound, perhaps it was the shifting of light as the new-green fronds were pushed aside.

Will stood there. Like a great brown bear that had received a stunning blow, and had not yet gathered his wits to shake himself, he stared.

Slowly Aidan's and Berrima's arms dropped to their sides. They did not look at each other, both waited for Will.

'I . . . I asked at the house. They said Miss Reynolds was in the garden . . .' His face, above the fair beard, was beginning to turn scarlet. Perspiration popped out on his brow, and he stuttered a little over some of his words. 'I . . . brought you your cheque. Your half of Risby's payment.' Will's hand came out, giving Aidan the slip of paper. Another pause, then he was backing away slowly, 'Thought you'd be back at midday. Thought you might need it . . . that's all.' He turned, and began walking away.

Aidan glanced at Berrima, pressed her arm, and walked quickly after his friend. 'Will!'

The man stopped. 'Will, there's . . .' An explanation? Was there? 'Will, you mustn't think . . .'

'It's your business, what you do, Aidan. Yours and Maura's.' He stared out before him, as Aidan groped for some words to alleviate the situation. Will hesitated, then, 'Did . . . did 'ee see Emily? What did she say?'

Oh, Jaysus!

Will was gazing at him. 'Well?' Eagerly, then with a trace of resentment, ''Ee did remember to speak to Emily, did 'ee? And Doctor Reynolds?'

'I . . . I did, Will.'

'You didn't come to see me.'

'No. I was going along directly.' Aidan felt himself flushing now. 'Will, the decision was made already. And . . . it was Emily's decision . . .'

'She said that?'

'Yes.'

'There's someone else.'

Aidan could hardly bear to look at the man, the sheer misery of

530

him. 'No. No one else. But she's gone away, Will.'

'*What?*'

'She's sailed for America. She's going to attend the university . . .'

'But – that's mad! How can she be gone! She was here yesterday . . .' His gaze caught Berrima's, who was approaching them. 'She was here yesterday,' he repeated, and he looked lost and dazed. 'Are you lying to me, Aidan? Miss Reynolds, is it the truth he's speaking?'

Berrima swallowed. 'Yes. She left on the ship this morning, Will, with Mama. There's a letter for you, up at the house.'

She led the way. In the hall the house was cool, and not one of the three spoke as they entered the darkened parlour, the curtains partly drawn against the glare of the sun. Berrima drew off her sun hat, and threw it on to the settee. The clock ticked, and that was the only sound as Berrima took the letter from the escritoire and handed it to Will.

He stood holding it for a long time. He looked up at Berrima, and then around at the room, carefully, whether hoping that Emily would somehow appear, or bidding it farewell, it was hard to say. Finally, his eyes caught Aidan's, and remained there, with a steady – yes, almost venomous – look that frightened Berrima.

Then he turned and was gone out the door to the hall.

'Will!' Aidan caught his arm at the front door. Berrima was behind them, saying, 'Will, please don't leave like this . . . You're *our* friend, Will, not only Emily's . . .'

Will's eyes were only for Aidan, whose hand was still on his arm. His voice when he spoke to the Irishman was very calm, very quiet. 'Let go of me,' he said simply. 'Just let go of me.'

Aidan took his hand away, slowly. 'Will, let me . . .' But he was gone, the door slammed after him.

For a long moment Aidan and Berrima stood there, not looking at each other, Aidan's hand still on the door-knob, but knowing it was useless, now, to go after the man. They stood there until the door at the end of the hall opened, and quick little heels tapped their way along the parquetry of the floor, 'Miss Reynolds? Pardon me – but would you and Mister O'Brien like tea?'

Berrima looked up at Nellie, wondered what the servants had heard, but Nellie's round face was suitably expressionless of anything other than helpful concern.

'Yes,' Berrima said tiredly, 'thank you, Nellie.'

The servant left, and Berrima and Aidan went back to the parlour. Berrima shut the door after them, and went straight to Aidan, into his arms. She was crying. 'It's dreadful,' she murmured. 'I'm so ashamed. Poor Will. It's dreadful . . .'

He had no time to savour the moment, knew that she had come to him only for comfort, as she would have come to her father, or her brother had he been old enough to understand. He stroked her hair, feeling only tenderness for her in her confusion.

Carriage wheels were approaching down the drive. Aidan placed his hand upon her shoulder, knowing in his heart that this was the last time he could see her alone. 'Dry your eyes, Berrima,' he said gently, firmly. 'Then go to meet your father. For us to be caught in a compromising situation twice in one afternoon would be too much to bear.'

52

Berrima spent several minutes alone with her father, explaining (How much? Aidan wondered) about Will's visit and abrupt departure. When they drank tea together, it was only young Richard who had any appetite, for the three adults all felt some culpability in the gentle Cornishman's unhappiness.

Aidan excused himself immediately afterwards and went off in search of Will.

But Will had gone, the clerk at the Shipwright's Arms told Aidan. The *Union* brig had just sailed for Port Davey and Will had only just missed it. He had hired a cab and had raced to meet it at Sandy Bay, would get one of the yachts to take him out to the ship.

Aidan waited at the inn until nine at night, in case Will had been unsuccessful and returned, but then headed reluctantly back to the Reynolds' house. He thought hard all the way through the streets in the dark, and decided to explain to them that his visit would be cut short. He tried not to let them see that the reason was predominantly Will, but he knew that they guessed.

For the remainder of his stay, he did not see Berrima alone again. He was left with the impression of a brightly coloured, flustered bird, who was not capable of staying still; she danced all over the house, spoke to him, it seemed, only on the way to somewhere else. The scene in the garden had shaken her, obviously, Aidan thought, there was no longer any feeling of intimacy between them. It was as if the scene at Glenleigh had never taken place.

He bought the equipment needed for setting up a saw-mill, and arranged for the machinery to be sent on the ship with him – it took days, and he was angry with Will, who should have been here to help. As it was, the choices and decisions were Aidan's – not to mention the expense. He vacillated between wanting to talk to the man or box his ears the minute he set eyes on him. Perhaps talk to him and then box his ears . . . He was kept busy, also, discussing the new building with Milton, who, to celebrate, organized a dinner party on the evening before he was to leave for Port Davey. There were two other couples invited; Austin, from the bank, and the chosen architect, and their wives. They were both attractive women, gracious and good-humoured. Aidan watched the guests. They were all the same age as the Reynoldses – about ten years older than Aidan, and he could not help but see himself and Maura hosting such a party. Maura, if he could only talk her into facing a dinner party, would look very pretty in a jade-coloured gown such as the woman beside him was wearing.

Mark Ellis was also invited and Aidan was impressed once more by the man's looks and bearing, noticed how even the married women in the party took whatever opportunities they could to study the tall figure with the black curling hair and dark blue eyes. His manners were gracious, and his wit sharp. He looked at Berrima with such gentle warmth that Aidan almost missed a question being asked of him by one of the men, so puzzled was he over the matter of the two young people. Berrima smiled at Mark, laughed with him, but there was none of the warmth that glowed in Mark's eyes. What's the matter with her? Aidan asked himself. What on earth is she waiting for? Does she think she'll find a finer young man than Mark Ellis? And he wished, in this new detachment, that he could see her alone, just once more, to tell her not to be such a little *maicin*, to take pity on poor Mark who had loved her these four years, at least, not to play with him like a little temptress. He'll go one day, Aidan prophesied, and then she'll be crying like a child that's lost a precious, familiar toy. And she'll tell herself that she should have responded sooner, should not have waited and dreamed away the important years, like himself, and Anna . . . Berrima made his heart ache.

He pulled himself back from the past and turned to the woman and man beside him, who were talking with longing of a visit home to London they were to make in two years. Aidan questioned them about the city, and the woman, homesick as she was, responded with delight. He was not really bored. London was an important place.

533

He would go there one day. Perhaps send Liam to be educated there. He had realized long ago, due to his reading and during his prison term, that no information, however bizarre or seemingly useless at the time, was ever wasted.

But at the back of his mind, and only a matter of five feet away from him, Berrima sat smiling, and he could feel an ache that was prescient of a longing that he knew would haunt him over the next twelve months, that he was so close to her, for days at a time, and was yet so far away.

He sailed to Port Davey on the *Maid of Erin,* and as if sensing his mood, the weather responded with lowering clouds and an ominous sea that threatened and threatened and finally broke in rage, as they neared the north of Recherche Bay. They crept in here for safety and were forced to remain for two days, Aidan preoccupied with his thoughts of the saw-mill, of Will, and Berrima, while the other men played poker and stared at the sky.

By the time he reached Port Davey he was tense from apprehension.

But only Malone was there to greet him when he was rowed ashore. The machinery was to follow, but Malone suggested it might wait for a few hours. 'There's been an accident,' the little Irishman said, taking off his cap to run his hand through his bush of wiry black hair. 'Jock Lane – went off with the surveyors to find that track to Huonville they keep talking of. Drowned, he did.'

'Lane? How?'

'His swag was too heavy – y'know what he was like, even on the way to his ground – he liked his food, Lane did . . . And always carrying extra things just in case – axe and knives, heavy stuff. They were crossing a stream leading into the Spring River, swollen by the storm, an' the log rolled, an' didn't he fall, God rest his soul! Hugh Raymond was following behind him – tried to grab at him, but missed, and didn't both of them go in. Raymond grabbed hold of the log and wasn't washed away – Lane was swept down into deeper water. They dived for him, but by the time they found him he was dead. The pack was too heavy, kept him under.'

'They've brought him home then?'

'Sure they're after buryin' him beyond, now. An' Maggie'll be givin' him a wake – *after* the buryin', like the English do. A dull affair it'll be without the corpse, I tell her, an' hardly fair – but she's English an' you have to respect their strange ways. Will y' be comin' beyond now? They saw the ship comin' in and said they'd wait the service for you.'

534

So Aidan walked with Malone up the slope to the little burial ground, to attend Jock Lane's funeral.

There was no minister, but the Captain of the *Union* read the funeral survice, and all the two hundred or so residents of Port Davey, their ranks swelled by a few sailors, sealers and whaling men whose ships lay in Bramble Cove, stood about respectfully.

Maggie Lane was weeping violently, leaning against Maura's narrow shoulders, Maura's thin arm about her. Clemency stood beside her mother in one of Maura's capes, because it was black. It fell to the child's heels, and with her cap of short red curls, she looked like some Gainsborough figure of a young prince.

Hugh Raymond stood with his rather square, sandy head bare and gave a eulogy for Lane, praising his fairness, his skill as a piner, his good nature and his kindness when others were in trouble or ran short of supplies. There were mutterings and murmurings of assent as each loved characteristic was voiced. 'In short, he was a good mate and a fair man to deal with, and a good husband . . . wasn't he, missus? And we can't go wrong if someone says that about us when we turn up our toes, can we? That's about all I got to say, I reckon.'

There were a few murmurs of 'Good job . . . well said, Hugh,' and then the captain was completing the service, and they began to fill in the grave.

Malone put a hand on Maggie's shoulder. 'And hasn't he got a Huon pine coffin, missus, that won't be after rotting – and won't his remains – God rest his soul gently – be all the one piece, come the Judgement Day.'

Maggie wailed the louder. Malone looked abashed, then patted her arm.

'She needs a tonic, missus,' he said to Maura. 'Why don't we take her home and give her a drop of something to settle her down a little?'

Maura looked rather coldly at Malone, but urged the almost-fainting Maggie out the little cemetery gate and up the hill.

Clemency had seen Aidan, let go of her mother and rushed to him, laughing. He swept her up into his arms and hugged her. 'Five new dresses!' she told him, oblivious to the solemnity of the occasion. 'You sent five new dresses – and a bonnet – thank you, Papa! The dresses are too long,' she added soberly, 'but Ma said I'll grow.'

'You will, sure.' He looked up at that moment, and saw Will Treloar filing out the gate with the crowd of men.

Aidan called his name, but he could not have heard. He did not turn around. Aidan was about to call again when someone came up to stand beside him. Aidan turned, and looked into the battered face of the sailor, Heath. He knew the man only by the injuries, although the swelling had gone down. The wind whipped the thick, straight brown hair about his scarred, handsome face. His eyes stared fixedly at Aidan, who was taken aback, confused by the intensity of the gaze.

Hugh Raymond also paused, stopped. 'You remember Heath, don't you?'

'Yes, of course. Good day to you – I'm glad you're better.'

The gaze remained fixed on Aidan's face for a few seconds, then dropped to his feet. He did not move.

Clemency said, 'Mr Heath's been sick. Haven't you, Mr Heath? You hurt your head.' With a child's aptitude for description, she tapped her forehead with her hand.

Heath's face broke into a grin, showing surprisingly white, even teeth. 'Head!' he said, touching his now-healed wound. 'Sick!' he scowled. 'Hurts!' Clemency scowled also, nodding sympathetically.

My God, oh my God . . .

Heath's two shipmates from the *Maid of Erin* were gazing at him with questioning horror. He smiled at them without recognition, then turned and began following the crowd out the gate and up the hill.

It was Hugh Raymond who said, 'O'Brien? Welcome back.' The two shook hands, and Raymond nodded after the figure of Heath, with a worried shipmate on either side of him, walking slowly, rather clumsily up the slope.

'He was lucky to survive at all, y'know. I don't know what's to become of the man. He'll never sail again. Since Lane died he's been helping Maggie with chores – simple things like fetching firewood, can't trust him not to cut off his toes with the axe just yet – he's still clumsy. A few of us here thought of giving him odd jobs to do, letting him stay here at the settlement. He's not crazy, see. But he's so slow. Set him loose in Hobart Town and he'd starve to death. Crying shame it is, he's a good-looking boy. No family that anyone knows of – no other name.'

Aidan nodded. 'Let him stay. We'll find something for him to do, and with God's help he might improve.'

They fell into step behind the trail of mourners. 'You're back early,' Raymond noted. His broad, rather full cheeks with their ruddy tan dimpled a little with a sly grin. 'You and Will had a quarrel, did you? He's been walking about under a cloud ever since he arrived back.'

There was no point in lying, the settlement was too small for Will's coolness to go unnoticed. 'Yes,' Aidan said briefly.

536

Raymond nodded. He was not the man to pry. 'He'll get over it,' he said, 'once you two start work again. Hard to dodge falling trees and bob about in a boat with a man and keep a grudge going.'

'Aye.' Aidan hesitated. 'I'm sorry about Lane, Hugh. You'll be after missing him.'

Raymond walked on for a few paces in silence, almost as if he had not heard. Then, 'It's more than that, that's not the hardest part. The worst is thinking what I could've done that might have saved him. If I'd have grabbed for him a bit faster, if I'd dived for him a bit deeper . . .'

There was a silence, and Aidan said, 'Aye.' His mind was suddenly, unwillingly, peopled with a great many ghosts, and he wondered how many he, Aidan O'Brien, could have saved. William Kelly, Anna, Corrie, Tom-Joe, Martin, Seamus and Thady . . . 'I understand,' he said.

Aidan thought he would be able to speak to Will at the wake, but the obdurate Cornishman fenced himself within a group comprised of Malone and several of his sons, and though he spoke to Aidan in an ostensibly normal way, the Irishman could tell that he was not to be forgiven so easily.

Maura took Clemency home about an hour later, and an hour after that, Aidan, too, left. The supplies and the machinery for the mill were unloaded from the ship by Aidan, Will and the Malones, who swung the heavier pieces out on a winch to their little ketch, and stored it at their own mill until Aidan and Will began building. The operation was typical of the friendship and cooperation between the men at the settlement.

Maura and Mrs Malone, foreseeing how tired and excited the men were, prepared a supper at the O'Brien house, and Maggie Lane, shocked and damp with tears, was fetched from her now-empty house to dine with them.

Maura sat her between Taylor and the eldest of the Malone boys, and Aidan, across the long trestle table, realized it was the best thing for the little widow. Both men directed most of their attention to her, partly out of pity for her situation and partly, Aidan suspected, from genuine interest.

There had always been something appealingly childlike about Maggie Lane, despite the fact that she was at least thirty. Her eyes were blue and large beneath hair very dark with not a touch of grey. She spoke with a hushed voice, rather breathless, as if everything was of great wonder to her. Her taste in books, Maura had told Aidan with a touch of disapproval, was 'towards the light novels'. She was not a practical woman. Both Maura and Aidan had wondered how she would cope with her widowhood. But watching her now, with the assiduous attention of the two men, Aidan and Maura both felt that somehow Maggie would manage quite well.

It was the beginning of the end of the close friendship between Maggie and Maura. They never became enemies – indeed, never spoke a rude word to each other, but Maura's disapproval was obvious when, a few weeks later, Taylor moved from his tent into the spare room in Maggie's cottage.

'It could be innocent,' Aidan suggested, when Maura, tight-lipped, recounted the news. 'I mean, she's a woman on her own, now.'

'Arra, who'd harm her here? She could look after herself. She'd be better off giving a home to poor Heath – isn't he after living in that abandoned shack of Hungerfords? I visited him yesterday during the rain, and the roof leaked near the chimney. Why doesn't Maggie take pity on him, now? No,' they were in the parlour, and Maura was sorting the washing into piles of those that could be boiled, and those that could not, 'no, she's after looking for another husband, and if she can't have a husband she'll have the next best thing. It disgusts me, so it does.'

He thought, she cannot understand anyone wanting anything so very badly. She cannot imagine that Maggie may lie awake at night in that great bed, and miss the touch of someone else, miss the breathing, the feel of a man's body.

Maura stood up, took one basket of washing. 'Och, I've remembered, I've loaned my soap to Will – could you go beyond and fetch it for me, Aidan?'

He glanced at her, but went willingly enough. It was obvious that she was giving him yet another excuse to patch up the mysterious quarrel between himself and Will. He could have told her it was useless, that Will, obstinate and angry in his hurt, and with a new, brooding intensity that Aidan had never seen in the man, wanted nothing to do with him. There were excuses enough. They were kept busy at this time of year, repairing their houses, tending their gardens, and for Aidan and Will there would soon be the new mill to build. But so far, Will had put off beginning the work. To Aidan the postponement was ominous, and he decided to extract an explanation from the man, along with the lye soap.

It was a clear morning, with already the promise of heat, and Will was at the trough behind his hut, doing his own washing. The shirt-sleeves were rolled up over the hairy brown arms, and he whistled tunelessly between his teeth as he scrubbed a pair of overalls in the sudsy, none-too-clean water.

'Will?'

Will merely looked up. No smile, no 'Good morning', just the black resentment of the gaze. *You great brat, you maicin, I'd like to dunk you in that water and clear the nonsense out of your head . . .*

Aidan had noticed that most of Will's wardrobe was already on the line. 'Maura was wondering if you had finished with the soap.'

Will still did not speak. He glared at Aidan for several seconds, then picked up the soap and hurled it at him.

It would have been funny in other circumstances, trying to catch the slippery wet cake that refused to stay in his grasp. When he finally held it firm, he turned furiously on Will. 'And what was that for, tell me?'

'I wish it was a rock! I'd like to knock your head clear off your shoulders! 'Tis no more than you deserve after what you've done, y' scaly bastard!'

'What *I've* done? What the hell have *I* done?'

'You let them send her away! You let them talk her out of marrying me, you probably told her yourself that it'd be a mistake . . . !'

'That's not true, Will. An' if you stopped to think for a moment you'd know the truth.'

'She's gone! That's all I know, and you knew, and you never warned me so I could stop her! And when I came looking for you, there you be, with your arms around—'

'Now stop it!'

'Too busy, perhaps, was that it? Involved in a little seduction yourself and too busy to think of my happiness and Emily's . . .'

'What you saw wasn't what it seemed . . . !'

'I saw! I heard her! "Oh, my dear," she'd say, and kissing your face she was, and half-crying! You've probably broken her heart, too! They should have kept you in prison, Aidan, they should've thrown away the key! Maura would be better off without a man like you!'

'Will . . .' Aidan felt the blood leave his face, took a step forward, used every ounce of his will not to rush at the man, to strike that contorted face, a stranger's face.

'I remember that Matty woman in Hobart, overheard people gossiping about you and her. And now this! And that'd be bad enough! But to ruin my chances of happiness – you're a bitter, twisted, spiteful man. An' I'll be leaving Port Davey, Aidan. I don't want to work with you. I never want to see you again.' And he turned back and headed towards the corner of the house – but stopped dead. Aidan had moved after him, had reached a hand for his shoulder. 'Will . . . !' He saw Maura standing there by the corner of the house, standing as if made of stone, white-faced, gazing at Will. Only slowly, slowly, did her eyes leave Will's face and move to Aidan's.

It was Will who finally spoke, Will who stood scarlet, wishing the ground would swallow him entirely, Will who, for the first time, saw in that narrow, little pale-faced figure, something of the remorselessness that she rarely showed to the outside world. It frightened Will, who had only ever seen Maura's quiet capability, who never in his knowledge of women, of his Sarah, Cora Frazer, the Reynolds women, and the Maura he thought he knew, had seen such icy malevolence, such strength of purpose. It emanated from Maura in waves, and it was all Will could do not to step back in the face of it.

'Maura?' Will said, but she wouldn't look at him, or acknowledge him at all. He turned to Aidan, who was watching his wife with expressionless eyes, waiting.

'Leave us, Will,' she said, eyes still on Aidan.

'Maura, please, I was . . . I never meant . . .'

'Leave us, Will.'

Will could bear it no longer. He walked quickly past Maura, half-ran down to the water and the boat shed and the whine of the pit-saws. Away from the virulent maelstrom of emotions between the two at the cabin. Yet he was not untouched. He could never be free of the memory of that scene, could never forget Maura's face. He would watch the marriage in years to come as if he were partly involved – and he was.

Maura, when Will had gone, walked forward to Aidan, and held out her hand. He stared at her, not understanding, until he remembered the cake of lye still held tight within his fist. He stared down at the soap. His grasp had made corrugations in it, for it was rather melted. He gave it to Maura. Their hands did not touch. Then she had turned and walked away, back towards their own house.

Aidan did not follow. It was not that he did not want to face her, it was better to get that scene – and it would be a scene – over and done with, but he knew better than to think that the matter would stop there. He needed time to consider what she would do, how he would react to it. He knew with a sense of certainty that nothing would be the same, after this moment. He walked down to the water, where narrow, clear waves rolled upon the white sand with barely a flicker of foam, and he breathed deeply, and thought, *All has changed*. The very air seemed changed, the colour of the water and the quality of sunlight on the hills and mountains seemed changed.

He doubted if Maura would leave him. She could, easily, he

knew, for Cora's letters to them repeated the fact that they were missed, that they must return to the Huon as soon as they could. Cora, he knew, would give Maura a home with her, no matter how many nieces and nephews filled the red brick homestead.

No, Maura loved it here, loved the wild magnificence of the place, loved the people and their kindness and their self-reliance. She had sent Liam from her, and stayed. She could assimilate what she would see as Aidan's adultery, and still stay.

It came to him suddenly that, except for one thing, he would not mind if Maura did leave. It was better to face loneliness than the strain, and over the years it had become more and more of a strain, of her watchful disapprobation. The silent criticisms, and worse, the subtle struggles in the bedroom, the excuses and the impatience, the feeling that he was less of a man and more of a beast to force himself upon her: these were tiring him. No, he thought, with something like wonder, he would not miss Maura. He would feel alone, but free in his aloneness, to be what he was; there would be no green and accusing eyes reminding him how he had failed her.

But Clemency. He would not have her taken from him; moreover, he knew the child would not wish to go. It could not be any real surprise to Maura, though oddly, it remained an annoying thing that Clemency preferred to be with her father than with her mother. When Aidan thought of the early years it was to be expected. But he had not been there then – there was so much of her childhood he had missed. She was growing up so quickly, she was changing each time he came down river for supplies. It was always Clemency who reached him first. To be honest, it was Clemency he first looked for. He fancied that he saw something of himself in the child, but her features favoured Maura. Clemency adored him, and accepted him as he was. It more than compensated for Maura's brooding silences, her inability to reach for him, her lack of tenderness. He did not think any further than this, that Maura may leave, but Clemency must stay. The details meant nothing to him. And anyway, Maura would not leave. She would move her belongings and her stiff little unyielding body into Clemency's room, and continue, to the outside world, to be a loving wife.

And this time, when she left his bed, he would not bring her back to it. The years of forcing his attentions upon her had tired him. Her reluctance no longer amused him, he knew now it was not feigned from false modesty or the desire to use some emotional hold over him. She simply did not like sexual intercourse, had no desire, despite his patience, the discussions he attempted – which horrified her more – to learn to like it. She did not fear it. It simply was not

541

important, did not interest her. He could have tried further, but not when it was a matter of indifference to her.

He turned and walked up the hill to the cottage. He did not look for Maura at the wash trough at the back of the house, felt that she would be within, waiting for him. And he was right.

She sat at the table that he had made himself from celery top pine, its surface scrubbed almost white with the daily sand-soap cleaning. Her hands rested on the table's surface. She did not look up immediately he entered. He closed the door behind him and pulled up a chair opposite her. Only then did Maura look at him.

She had surprised herself in her calmness, there was no rage of grief and shame and bitterness in her, as there had been when she had been initially told by Matty of the affair, all those years ago. There was only a dullness within her. She had not yet had time to study it – it was curious. Did it mean she no longer loved him? She studied his face. No, it hurt her to gaze at those features, into those dark eyes. They possessed her, he possessed her, in a way he would never allow her to possess him. She hated him, and when she knew she hated him she knew she was not free of her love for him. Not for the first time, she wished she *was* free of her love for him.

'To make certain,' she said, and it came as a surprise to her that her voice sounded so calm, almost mellifluous in her new calm, 'that I am not wrong in my assumption, and my decisions, you must tell me, Aidan, as a Christian and an Irishman – you have made love to that woman, haven't you? You've visited her since I have been with you, and you've lain with her. Haven't you?'

He gazed at her, did not dare speak, because he had almost asked 'Who?' and that would have compounded everything.

'I knew she wouldn't let go.' Maura's voice was a little lower. She stared at the table, at a spot between them, and spoke almost as if to herself. 'She told me she wouldn't let go, that she'd wait for you, no matter how long it took . . . She told me how she . . . how she liked you lying with her. That she was a fitter wife for you than me, because you were alike . . . She was a beautiful woman – so much younger than me. When she spoke like that I was afraid, for I could see that she was right. She was more suited to you than I was. Of course, she was little more than a whore . . .' The green eyes, dark now, almost all pupil, raised themselves to him, 'but that didn't matter. You were her kind of man, by then, and she was your kind of woman. Killaloe was a long time ago, Aidan. You're not the same. You'll never be the same again.'

They were quiet for a long time. When Maura sighed, it was as though she was tired. Aidan, who had braced himself for her cold

542

fury, her white-lipped spite, could only stare at her. She placed the bunched fingertips of her right hand to her right eye, rubbed it a little, waved a droning fly away from her face with the other hand. She did not even look angry. Only tired.

'Matty Harding. You see, I haven't forgotten her name. Almost as if I was after knowing we'd hear from her again. Have you slept with her since you came back to me in Huonville?'

'Yes,' his voice was a whisper. Only briefly did he debate telling her of the innocent embrace he had shared with Berrima. Maura would not believe him – and should she? How innocent had that embrace been, after all? 'I didn't sleep with her this trip, Maura, I swear it. Once only, before we came here. Once in four years.'

'But I can't believe you.'

He stopped. And he thought, watching her, you don't want to believe me. You're bored with the whole business. You can't be bothered believing me. And it did not matter to him.

She said, 'Clemency and I will be returning to Hobart Town.'

This mattered. 'No, you won't, Maura.'

'I'll not stay with you, Aidan.'

'You've been saying that for years, sure. You might not be happy with me, girl, but you're happier than you'd be without me.' Her eyes narrowed a fraction of an inch, but she made no comment. 'We need each other, Maura. The children need both of us. What sort of an effect would it have on Liam, how would the parents of the other children at St Andrew's react, if it were known that his parents lived apart? Society doesn't countenance such things, Maura, not even in these parts of the world. And the Church would not approve.'

She was staring at him, then she said in a deadly calm voice, 'You great, bullying, sanctimonious hypocrite. How dare you mouth threats to me of what the Church approves or doesn't approve. Does the Church countenance adultery, Aidan? Does the Church countenance your lying naked with that painted blonde whore?'

'Does the Church countenance a woman refusing to sleep with her husband, refusing him affection and tenderness when he works and sweats his life away to provide her with a home of her own and security for the rest of her life? Don't talk about breaking vows, Maura, for you broke your vows long before I did!'

She was white, leaned back as if he had slapped her. 'What do you mean?' she whispered.

'You're as guilty as I am, sure!'

'What do you mean?'

'You never—' he stopped. What was he doing, after all? In his guilt, more for the sudden and overpowering desire for Berrima, which was by far a greater betrayal than his brief and meaningless unions with Matty, he was forcing the blame upon her. Was she to blame? For Berrima? For Matty? He could think of no answers, it was all too complex, had begun so many years ago. It no longer mattered, he realized, whose fault it was. Things were as they were.

Maura looked as if she was still waiting for him to speak. But the silence went on. He was tired, now, too; could see why she had appeared the way she had when he came in. Really, there was nothing more to be said.

'I don't want to lose Clemency,' he said, and it was because he was tired, and tired of pretending, and because he knew she was tired, that he spoke honestly.

Clemency. There was no marked change on Maura's face. She lowered her gaze to the table once more because she was afraid to meet his eyes, afraid that her own eyes would give her away. *Clemency*. It was the child he did not want to lose. Of course. With his wilful self-centredness, the child was a possession of his. She said, 'You don't love Clemency. No more than you love me, nor your boat, nor the new saw for the timber mill, but all must be taken care of, for it would not do for Aidan O'Brien to be known as a man who did not take care of his possessions. But you care less for me. For I resist you, will not allow you to use me in the way you use all your other possessions. I resist you, so you can afford to lose me. You're quite well off now. You could buy a new possession like me. Better equipped to deal with the strangeness of this colony and your city-bred friends; coarser and shameless, a woman who'd meet your animal wants. A younger woman, not bowed down with child-bearing and poverty and shame. Yes, I'm not important to you anymore.

'But you'll not be keeping Clemency. You can't. Not even a court of law would allow you to have the child with you if you were cohabiting with a harlot like Matty Harding . . . '

He interrupted with a dull voice. 'You're a fool, sometimes, Maura, for all your learning. I want things to go on as they are. I'll try to do without other women. When you've been able to make some pretence of tolerating me – even if you don't want me in return – I haven't gone to anyone else.'

'I'll not be blackmailed!' Her voice was harsh, the small hands on the table made into fists.

He paused with his mouth open. 'Is that how you see it?' He gazed at her. They had never in their sniping, snapping, growling arguments, ever reached beyond the stage of pointing out one another's shortcomings. This was the closest they had ever come to any kind of

544

discussion about their separateness, the gulf of understanding between them.

He leaned forward, amazed at this business-like entente between them, amazed at the dispassionate interest in his own voice. 'What does marriage mean to you, anyway? What was it you wanted for your life, when you married me?'

She considered his aloof eyes as she considered the question. She thought, he could only be talking like this, in this tone of voice, if he does not care. These are questions a man in love never asks, for fear he will hear an answer that will hurt him. But beyond the gall, the wounded pride, she was honest, and she answered honestly, innocently. 'I loved you. You were the man I chose to share my life with. The man I wanted to work beside in the fields, to raise our children together. I thought we would plan together and read by the fire of an evening, and talk about books. You never read books anymore – only those that concern business. You used to be interested in far distant places, in travelling . . .'

This time he interrupted more sharply, 'Perhaps I found it was different to talk about travelling than to do it, to live life instead of reading about it. I don't want another man's dreams, I want my own.'

'Killaloe was good enough for all our people before us . . .'

A hot rejoinder rose to his lips but he pressed them closed against it. Smiled a little grimly, and leaned back. 'Och, no, my darling. You can defend the old ways all you like, call forth the past Aidan O'Brien as being a far superior young man to this thirty-eight-year-old relic. But don't be after telling me that we were happier in Killaloe, that *you* were happier in Killaloe. No. God forgive me, but the Famine was the only thing strong enough to shift me out of my dream world, prison was the only thing to make me hardened to the idea of settling for mere comfort. I want it all. I want it *all*, Maura. If you can't live content with my greed – and you must consider that it makes me equally as uncomfortable as it does you – then I'll help you leave and see that you want for nothing – but I'll be giving you and the children security, *real* security if it kills me. And since you and the children are the reason I risk my neck and my fingers with axes and saws all day, I want you around to see the effect of my labours.' His words were arrogant and he knew it, she loathed him to speak so and he knew it. 'Face it, Maura. You'd be unhappy away from me. You're unhappy with me. Why not stay where I can watch over you and alleviate some of the bitterness.'

'Do you think I care about that? Fancy clothes such as you brought back for me? French bonnets and later a fine house and carriage? Do you think they matter to me?'

'You can treat them with scorn. I'll be buying them for you whether you live with me or not – fo you're my wife and I'll take care of you if I have to lace you into those velvet gowns myself. And think how miserable you can make me by telling me that it's all meaningless. What would be the point of hating me from the other side of Tasmania? I might forget you, Maura, if you're not about to plague me.'

Only on this last sentence did her eyes narrow. 'I don't want to plague you. I only want what other wives have the right to possess – their husband's love and loyalty. To have someone to share life with, not to be shut out. You've always shut me out. You give me material possessions, but you don't give me yourself.'

'You demand more than I have to give, Maura. It was the problem long before Matty, even before I left Ireland. You always wanted me to be something I'm not.'

She said sceptically, 'That implies I don't know you, never did, and I understand you better than anyone else on this earth, Aidan. If I did want to change you, to what would it be?'

Someone kinder, slower, someone who did not care for riches. Someone who would, as she said, work in the fields with her. Someone who found joy in books for their own sake. Someone who took joy in the passing seasons and watched them with interest and appreciation for beauty, not trying to hold time back, as he did, not someone who sees in the years of his life only what he should have achieved, a man who will spend the rest of his days attempting to catch up. And I will never know when I have caught up. I will never know what my potential was. I will keep stretching myself to find out, until I die.

The words came into his mind, but he did not say them. Wondered, suddenly, briefly, if this very reticence that claimed him occasionally was what Maura meant when she said he did not give of himself.

He was possessed of an enormous weariness, and he saw that there was no more point in trying to pretend. Each time he tended the ragged thinness of his marriage, the fabric tore elsewhere, simply with the pressure of his attempts to mend it. It was as useless as a rotting piece of silk, could be kept only as a reminder of the past, a world, a way of life, that was gone.

He realized that all through this conversation his arrogant flippant pressure for her to stay had been externalized. Keep the status quo. Future benefits. Not once had he said, 'I love you, I need you with me.' And he could not say it.

'You haven't answered me.' And her mouth was a line of bitterness, for she had seen that he had forgotten her. Already his mind had moved beyond her. 'What is it you think I want you to be?'

He sighed, and raised his head slowly, and in that sound, that gesture, she knew it was the end between them. Her heart failed within her.

'It doesn't matter, does it?' he said heavily.

53

Will was not seen again for some time after his quarrel with Aidan. After a few days even Malone and Hugh Raymond and a few others began to worry. But Aidan was too angry with Will to care, and too busy with his family problems.

He and Maura argued long and bitterly over Clemency during that time. Aidan insisted that the child could stay with the Malones – one more child wouldn't matter, and Clemency practically lived in that house even now. Aidan would attend to her lessons when he came back from the timber grounds for supplies – and he would come back more often.

Maura had all the correct arguments on her side, that the little girl belonged with her mother, that in Hobart she would have Liam at home with her, and she, too, could attend a proper school. But she listened to Aidan's arguments grimly, not allowing the slightest hint to appear that, except for her sense of duty, and her fear of what the settlement and her friends back in Hobart and Huonville would say, she would dearly love to let the father have his way, and keep the child.

Aidan began raging at her, sensing that his case was hopeless, that though he could, due to the legal situation of the times, not only keep Clemency but compel Maura to remain with him, he knew he would not enforce this. Though the law saw the wife as being a possession of the husband, to take her property, to choose her friends, and forbid her access to her children, give her as much or as little money – even if it had been hers on marriage – as he chose, Aidan's rage would not allow him to stoop to it. He had read of the scandal of Charles Dickens' marriage and felt it was no credit to the man. Yet he could not bear the thought of leaving the prattling,

547

vulnerable child to Maura's bitterness and resentment. It was true that Maura had not lifted a hand to Clemency in years but neither had she reached for her in affection. Aiden spent most of these days with the child, wondering what to do. He knew in his heart that Malone's house was not what he wanted for Clemency, either. None of the family could read or write, Malone's mathematics were all done mentally.

He considered, briefly, returning to Hobart, leasing a ground of timber closer to the capital, but the money was in Huon pine, and that was here. The money was here. He tried to explain to Clemency, but the child kept repeating that she wished to stay with him. This was his one weapon against Maura, but he could not use it. He wanted the best for the child, and that was to be found in Hobart, not in this wilderness.

So when Maura left on the *Balmoral*, she took Clemency with her, struggling, scratching like a little animal, howling, screaming, reaching back with her arms to the man on shore as the boat pulled away, bobbing on the swell, towards the waiting timber-loaded ship.

For Aidan it was a new kind of grief, it tore the heart from him. He told himself that she would have all the material things that Port Davey could not provide, she would attend a good school, would learn, and would grow up to be a lady. He repeated all these things, over and over, as the little voice called 'Papa! Papa!' Clear as a bell across the water the voice rang, and it echoed in his sleep for years afterwards, the third estrangement, the third betrayal.

He stood on the shore for a long time, watched as the two figures were helped aboard, watched as the *Balmoral* raised her anchor and set her sails, turned her prow away from him, in the direction of the open sea. Watched until it vanished in the heat haze on the water around Whalers' Point.

He was very conscious that his grief was for Clemency alone. It was Clemency that he longed to have back here; where his longing for Maura should have been there was only emptiness, like a shallow depression over a long-healed wound. Beyond his yearning for the child who loved him, was a kind of surprise that his marriage had ended. Oh, they would undoubtedly share a house in Hobart, when he came to visit once a year, but he would be like a boarder in his own home, the way they had lived in the cottage on Frazer's property when he had returned to Maura. But this time there would be no dissatisfaction, no fear on her part, no twisted, controlled desire on his. Perhaps, he mused, they might, now, be friends at last.

He turned back up the slope from the beach, to the houses that appeared strangely quiet, deserted, for all knew that Maura was leaving and no one wanted to appear as if they were curious, prying.

They had been watching, however, and though they left him alone that day, when evening fell one of the Malone boys came to invite Aidan for dinner, and the next day Hugh Raymond arrived with a cask of rum, helped Aidan to mend the fence around the little vegetable garden, and later sat drinking with him on the verandah that faced the water.

They did not talk about Maura or Clemency. It was if the two were within the house, or, perhaps, had never been here at all. The cause of Hugh Raymond's concern was Will.

'He must be upriver. There's little he could do by himself . . .'

'Nonsense, he's probably felling trees to right and left with that axe. He doesn't need me.'

There was a slight bitterness in the voice. Hugh narrowed his rather sandy lashes and followed Aidan's gaze, fixed on nothing, the distant view, Whalers' Point, around which the *Balmoral* had disappeared this time yesterday. O'Brien looked tired, as if he had slept little. Almost, Hugh was glad of the disappearance of Will. It was something, no matter how aggravating, that might take O'Brien's mind from the loss of his family.

'The boat might have overturned,' he said now, and Aidan turned to glare at him. Raymond shrugged. 'It's been known to happen. Might have over-balanced, leaning out to free a snarl of logs – fallen in, hit his head . . .'

'Arra, get away . . .'

'I think we should go look for him.'

'He's sulking, as you said. My going after him won't do any good. He's probably ashamed to face me.'

Raymond glanced at him. Ashamed? 'But, O'Brien . . . it's not just me who's worried. Several of us are.'

After a pause, Aidan said, 'I think he wants to be left alone.'

'Because of this girl? Was it that serious then? He didn't break his heart, did he?'

'Yes.'

'What's he blaming you for?' Even as the question came out Raymond regretted it. He had been good mates with O'Brien for four years now, but it sounded like prying. It was a personal question, and Raymond felt embarrassed.

'She went away. He thinks I could have stopped her.'

Raymond felt relieved. 'Ha!' He expelled his breath on a hoot of laughter, 'As if anyone can stop a woman once her mind is made up.'

'Two days,' Aidan said suddenly.

'What?'

'We'll give Will another two days. Then we'll go look for him.' Aidan turned to Raymond, almost scowling. 'And when we find him, I don't want any interference.'

'Interference . . .?'

'Aye. Because I'm goin' to belt the bejaysus out of him, and I don't want any man to try to stop me.'

The following day the *Maid of Erin*, loaded with Malone timber, was due to sail at dawn. Usually there was a group down at the beach to hand last minute letters and packages to the captain to be delivered in Hobart Town. When the *Balmoral* had left, Aidan had been allowed to be alone with his thoughts. Now he stayed away from the farewell group on the sand, though he had considered sending a letter to Clemency on the ship. No, he would wait, for to stand there and see the ship pull out would leave him with a restlessness and longing for his family.

He was involved in moving the furniture about; somehow it made it easier to gaze at the familiar objects, harder to imagine Maura, Liam, Clemency there if the objects were in a different place.

And then, behind Clemency's bed as he moved it from the wall, he found her favourite doll. Arra; that will make the separation harder for her. He held the thin and rather grubby rag doll, face faded from much kissing and hugging and motherly scrubbings with a flannel, and sat down on the bed, slowly, as if all his joints ached. He did not know how long he sat there, did not realize that he held the soft toy to his face, until a heavy knocking on the door made him start violently. He put down the doll. The din was repeated before he could cross the room to the door. Heath stood there, breathing heavily, as if he had been running. 'Mr Raymond said . . . I should . . .' His brow furrowed. 'I should . . .'

'Hugh Raymond wants me?'

'Yeah. Mr Raymond said to come. Will.' His scowl was a little relieved, 'It's Will.'

'*What?*' He had grasped the man's shoulders, 'What about Will?'

'Yes.'

'What about him? Is he ill? Has he . . . has he drowned? Was it the boat?'

'Yes,' Heath said happily. 'Will. Boat.'

Aidan rushed out of the house and looked about, but there was no solemn procession coming down the slope. The only people to be seen were down at the beach, loading up the small boat in which the sailors already sat, waiting for the fourth man to step aboard.

The fourth man was Will.

He was busy. He was loading small trunks and bags into the boat,

550

and did not notice Aidan approaching. The group of people did, and moved aside as he strode into the shallows, grasped Will by the shoulder, whirled him about and struck him full on the jaw.

'That's it, is it?' he roared, not hearing Raymond's pleas from the sand to go easy, to cool down. Aidan's gaze was on the other man, scrambling to his feet in the water. He had not reached his feet before Aidan kicked out with his foot, struck Will on the shoulder with one heavy, waterlogged boot and sent the man backwards into the surf, to disappear from sight for a moment, while Aidan, beside himself, continued to roar.

'Packing y'r bags, are y'? In the night, it was! Sneaking off, y' gutless trawneen, sneaking off without a word!' Will's head appeared, his shoulders, he backed away as he found his feet. 'Well?' Aidan roared.

Will stood silent, dripping, in water up to his knees. Aidan waded to him, thumped the man's chest with one fist, to the side of his head with the other, and a jab to his nose before Will's knees buckled. 'Talk, damn' y'! D'y' know what you've done? You and your petty tempers! D'y' know she's gone and Clemency with her? Clemency's gone from me, you great oaf, you great prattling fool, and it's all your fault!' He was crying, glad of the water that splashed over him, for no one knew, and he let his grief flow from him.

He slapped at Will's face, once, twice, hoping to sting him into some sort of response, but Will bent his head with the blows. Only as Aidan waited, fists ready, did the Cornishman murmur, 'I couldn't face you. I d'know what I did. You've the right to hate me.'

The dull words drove Aidan mad, he struck at Will again, catching him on the cheek bone and opening a small cut. Only then from behind him he heard the sailors' voices, 'We got to go! She's about to weigh anchor! Is 'e coming?'

'And you'd leave me to build the bloody mill by meself! With the loggin' season about to start and no partner! Y' selfish great *maicin* running away to hide your pathetic broken heart! Emily never loved you! She never loved you! So what do you know of loss! You've lost nothing! I've lost my daughter!' The memory of the doll in the cottage came to him, and he struck the impassive face before him, once, twice. 'I've lost my little girl, y' fecking bastard!'

'Is 'e coming or not?'

'Have you got nothing to say? Nothing at all? What the hell did y' expect me to do here, y' cowardly good f'r nothing?'

The horn from the ship wailed across the water. 'We're goin' mate! Y'r luggage is on shore!'

Will had lumbered to his feet, and when Aidan lunged for him he turned slightly, the blow grazing his forehead, but he had Aidan now, one great wet arm around his neck, pressing backwards, the other twisting the Irishman's arm up behind his back. They struggled and floundered. Aidan could not breathe, the arm across his neck was like a vice.

'My father taught me wrestling.' The gentle voice, through the scarlet wash that was blotting out the sea and hills and sky. 'He said my greatest advantage was my strength, to wait for the other man to tire. You're quick, Aidan, you're fast with your fists. You should have kept your distance, you let your temper get the better of . . .'

They lost their balance, fell, and for a moment Aidan was almost able to wriggle free, but Will had found his feet, and stood up once more, pulling tighter at Aidan's neck; with Will's extra few inches of height Aidan was pulled off his feet. He kicked and churned at the water impotently, his own weight, held as he was by the neck, choking him.

The red hills were darkening, darkening . . . Jaysus, he's killing me . . .

The world moved slowly, back and forth, water flecked into his face, he was on a ship . . . no, someone held him, the blood drummed in his ears, a sickening view of shallow water churned by boots . . . clear voices. That was the frustration, the voices were so clear and he could not answer them . . .

'No, he's not heavy. But could you and the lads take my luggage back to my cabin, Hugh? I'd appreciate that.'

He was lying on the settle bed in the kitchen-cum-parlour of his own cottage. Will Treloar was seated at the table, one of Aidan's week-old Hobart newspapers spread out on its surface. He looked up, gazed at Aidan quietly.

'Get out,' the Irishman growled, but it was all growl and no words at all. His throat was on fire, his neck felt as if it had been broken. He rasped air into his lungs and tried again, 'Get out!' That was clearer, but either Will's hearing was poor, or he was being wilfully unco-operative, for he remained where he was.

'I'm not going to leave the settlement,' he said finally. 'You were right, I was running away. I'll stay and help you build the mill, but we won't be partners, if you like. Perhaps Hugh Raymond will join you in't – I d'understand if you don't want to work with me any more.'

Aidan was disadvantaged; all the bitter recriminations he wanted to hurl at the Cornishman used breath and throat muscles that he felt

552

he would rather protect. Will seemed to sense this, and smiled. 'You won't be arguing with me today, Aidan. I should get out all my say now and leave you, while I have things all my own way.' He sobered a little. 'You d' want me to stay, don't you? I'd have left but you were standing between me and the boat. I did think, if you really wanted me gone, you'd have stopped thumping me and let me climb aboard. But you didn't.'

'I hadn't . . . finished . . . with you.'

'No.' Will grinned. 'I'm sorry, Aidan, I took all I could. I lost my temper, too. And everyone staring at us, I thought I'd best end the fight.' He fell silent, perhaps waiting for Aidan to speak, but the Irishman rose slowly, swallowing painfully against the dizziness, the rising wave of nausea.

'Are you all right?' Will asked.

'Oh, I'm fine. Me neck's broke and me throat feels like it's been cut, but don't let it bother you. Couldn't you have punched me on the jaw? Did you have to half-garotte me?'

'I don't know anything about fisticuffs. I didn't want to hurt you. Just stop you.'

'Aye, you did that.'

There was a silence. Will shifted his feet, awkward, embarrassed. Aidan, too, wondered what to say. He had thought his temper was behind him for ever. How puerile of him to attack the man like that. He glanced up. Clemency's doll was propped up on the mantelpiece. He pulled his eyes away from it, rubbed them, ran his hand through his hair.

Will was saying, 'Aidan, we've both had a lot of hurt – but we're mates, are we not? Partners? You have more to blame me for, than I do you. In this week away up river I had plenty of time to think. And you were right. Emily couldn't have loved me. She wasn't the meek little creature who would let her parents make her decisions for her. She's an intelligent girl, and strong, and honest. That's why I loved her, Aidan, for one needs a woman like that.

'I reread her letter over and over, and I saw I was wrong to blame you. And when I thought of all I said, the grief I'd caused Maura . . .'

'Och, stop, get away. You caused no grief to Maura. That's something I've been doing very well, by myself, for years.' His voice was rusty, painful, but even through this, Will could hear the bitterness. Aidan moved to the fireplace, and searched for matches on the mantelpiece – he must move that damn doll soon . . .

'Will you have tea?' Grudgingly.

'Yes. Thanks.'

553

The match caught the dry grass, then the twigs, then the logs, and the fragrance of burning eucalypt, like no other woodsmoke in the world, slowly began to fill the cabin.

'Aidan?' Will asked, as the Irishman swung the kettle over the flames. 'Aidan, Maura's not gone for good, has she? She'll come back.'

'Aye, she'll be back, she'll be back, sure. She's not a city person, is Maura. She was born to the lakes and rivers and mountains, y'see. She'll miss them, she'll be back.' He looked at Will confidently, and was relieved to see his friend's relief.

'We'll work hard, this season,' Will said, with something like his old optimism. 'And we'll have the mill built in no time at all. And we'll work on the ketch, too, shall we? She could be in the water, come spring. And we'll leave here in a few more years – another three years? We'll have enough for our farms, then.' His voice changed, 'I'm sorry, Aidan. About Berrima. She's a lady, same as her sister, and I know she wouldn't do anything wrong. Neither would you. I should have believed you.'

'Let's forget it, Will, it's behind us.'

'So much depends on these next few years. I don't want any bitterness between us, we need each other's help to provide for our families, to give them a better life than the one we knew. We have to work together without tearing each other's throats out – at least, not often – that's what being mates means. So tell me you don't resent me, Aidan? Can you forgive me for losing Maura to you?'

'Don't be an eejit. I do, I do, sure. What time is it?'

'Midday.'

'There's some damper in the meat-safe, with some ham I brought back from Hobart – let's make this our meal. We'd best get used to the single life, I suppose,' he said, rather morosely.

54

Down on the slips, the little ketch, Huon pine throughout, took shape. Aidan and Will worked on her in the winter months while they waited for the rains to come that would bring the logs downstream. They worked on the boat carefully, without hurry, and in spring she was launched. They called her *Lostwithiel* after Will's birthplace, and sailed her round the bays and inlets of the large harbour, learning how she handled, preparatory to sailing her to Hobart, come summer. The Huon pine itself, was becoming more and more scarce; they were forced to move further and further up the creeks after timber, always leaving the young trees – 'Young!' said Will who never ceased to wonder at the time it took for a Huon pine to mature, 'They're only babies and they're 400 years old!' – and taking only the mature trees, growing between seventy and one hundred feet in height, being a relatively small species, but maturing at about five hundred years old.

'Even then,' Aidan said once as they walked further up the slope, exploring for better stands, 'these hills will be worked out soon. It'll be a pity, will it not? If we take all the Huon pine there is.'

'It'll grow again, we only take the big ones – though I don't know as how I d'approve of that scheme of yours. Many of the other piners are bringing out near twice as much timber as we are – 'tis not as if we be fishing for trout, having to throw back the tiddlers, Aidan.'

'Arra, is your brain in your gog, boyo? Even if we all left the young ones, a tree takes five hundred years to mature, and there'll be five generations or more who won't know what a real forest of Huon pine looks like, so.'

They had reached a gully that swept at an angle down the hill. Far below the horizontal scrub lay, covered with mosses to the extent that it looked like a false forest floor, and they could hear the gurgling of a small stream. Will paused, wrinkling his nose in distaste: despite years on the docks, scrambling up and down ladders, he had a horror of heights, and horizontal scrub made him nervous at any time. He scowled over at the Huon pines that lifted their heads amongst the taller timber on the other side of the gully. 'What's to look at?' he asked. 'What would these people be missing? Huon pine is just another tree. Just damned hard to get to. Do we have to cross this?'

'You can scramble down and try to go through, but you're just as likely to get stuck.' And Aidan trod out on to the springy branches with caution, walking about ten paces before looking over his shoulder. Will still hung back. 'Come on, can't you?'

''Tis all right for you. I'm heavier than you. I could disappear and that'd be the last you'd see of me.' But he stepped out gingerly, bent over and moving on all fours, searching this way and that for the firmest foothold. ''Tis a blessing this cursed stuff is rare,' he muttered.

Aidan was by now at the other side, and had scrambled up a short slope between the ferns.

'Nay, Aidan, wait, will 'ee?' Will made it to the other side with some relief, clambered up the bank, stood in an area where several young Huon pines grew, two and three bunched together on a 'fall-down', an older tree that had collapsed with age. The younger plants had sprouted in crevices in the bark, and it was difficult to imagine that these were three to four hundred years old, that the parent tree that now lay prostrate on the forest floor had been young, perhaps, when Nero was throwing Christians to the lions.

Aidan was somewhere ahead; for a moment Will was alone. He stood still, watching the moss-covered logs and the young trees, their offspring, reaching their straight branches up towards the light. It was soft, here, green and quiet and timeless; beyond, another bank rose, covered in ferns, and brightly coloured toad-stools gleamed amongst the emerald lace of the fronds and the velvet mosses.

For over five years, now, he had worked in the wilderness of the South-West. He had been on trips to the high moorlands, the buttongrass plains, and he had followed a little of Robertson's track. That well-meaning minister had scoured the South-West in his efforts to find all the aboriginals to convince them they should move to a reserve instead of being killed one by one by the settlers. The mission that had led to the last of the tribespeople living in exile at Oyster Cove, where they died all the same, of the white man's diseases and their own broken hearts. Will had been along that track, which wound south-east along the coast; he had seen long stretches of headlands and beaches, wild and magnificent, lashed by the cold seas of the Southern Ocean, forgotten by the rest of the world, loved, perhaps, only by that black and majestic race that was gone forever. Yet only now, in this glade that opened before him, did Will feel anything like an emotional response to the land.

Aidan had talked of it, often, but he was Irish, hills and streams seem to mean more to the Irish character. For Will . . . he was here to make money. The misty cliffs and pearled lakes, the snow-hung pines and eucalypts were a backdrop to a money-making venture. Only here, now, did he pause, feel something human and yet not human, in the very stillness, the greenness of the place. He moved forward slowly. He realized minutes had passed. He had forgotten Aidan. The strange and faery world possessed him, had him search-ing each tree, each fern, for he knew not what. Childhood stories of elves and nymphs and goblins came back to him, and he wondered, suddenly, if the black people had had stories like these, if they peopled their forests with small and magical spirits such as those back home did. He was understanding, now, how this could happen, could almost say aloud, there are some mystical beings here. I felt them, I know them. It would only be one further step to a lone man's mind to say *I saw them*. The further into that green shade he moved, the stronger the feeling became. He seemed surrounded by invisible forms and silent voices, and it was old, their calling, old, and sang in his genes, in the blood of his ancestors and he knew there was a message here, that this place wanted to tell him some secret, but he did not know, could not know what it was. He saw only green and quiet-growing things, felt their timelessness and almost wept with the pressing of their voices; he thought, wildly, inconsequentially, *Once I knew*. But that was not so. The call was to something Will Treloar had long ago lost, before his life, his father's life, before the Treloars had a name, yet Will felt the guilt of the loss as if it were his own. This shaded place sang to him a song that was not of his understanding, called to him to belong to it and he could not reach out. He had never in his life felt so much at one with the earth, yet at the same time so shut out from its secret. It hummed in the air about him, quivered behind each leaf, a millimetre and a million years beyond his understanding.

He pushed through the ferns, fighting to leave the feelings behind him, remembered Aidan once more and hoped he would have a joke, a caustic comment on Will's slowness, some means of disrupting the possession of the place. Aidan was nowhere to be seen. Only the still and silent forest, and the friendly, puzzled, questioning voices from around him. They did not threaten, they offered, and only in his frustration did he feel uncomfortable. He did not want to call for Aidan. One did not shout in such a place. He stood calmly and looked about, wondered, for the first time, if Aidan had sensed something of the same atmosphere. Will moved a little to his left, not knowing why he chose to take that direction. The sunlight slanted through the green canopy of leaves and threw golden shafts here and there. Moths danced in the lines of light, fluttering up to be caught, silvered for an instant in a beam.

He saw Aidan, then, not far in front of him, standing still, his head raised.

He had been there for some time, studying the tree before him. He had walked around and around it, and now gazed up into the branches. He sensed rather than heard the other's approach, and it was with a kind of resentment, as if Will were an interloper into a private world; knew even as this thought came to him that it was curious, that there was no rationalizing it. He hoped Will would not rush upon him, shout 'Where were you!' or 'What's this then?' He was braced for some comment about the tree, did not want to hear it,

557

wished, strangely, fervently, that he was alone, that he did not have to share this with anyone else.

But Will's approach was silent, and finally, when he stood beside Aidan, his head thrown back to gaze up at the tree, still he was silent.

After a moment he moved, around the trunk in the green-gold shadows, and came a halt at Aidan's opposite shoulder.

''Tis the oldest, Aidan. It must be. One of the oldest in the world . . .'

And there was room in Aidan's mind to wonder, he said it was the oldest. He didn't say it was the biggest.

They were silent once more, both walked about the tree, reaching out their hands and touched the grey-brown bark. There were older trees, there were larger trees, but they were not Huon pine, that pale gold, fragrant wood. Aidan thought of it, there beneath this rough bark, the sap that flowed, living cells that moved, divided, beneath that gnarled exterior. Two and a half thousand years, three? It was bigger by far than any Huon pine he had ever seen. Malone had once brought one down the stream, and a visiting naturalist had claimed excitedly that it had been two and a half thousand years old. He said it with excitement that faded even as he spoke, to realize that the tree was dead, that two and a half thousand years of growth would plank a ship or parquet a floor and no one would know that it was special, unique.

Will must have been thinking along the same lines, for he said softly, ''Tis older than Malone's.'

'Aye,' Aidan whispered back. Neither of them noticed that they were whispering. 'It'd be the tree that bred all those fall-downs.'

They stepped back a little. 'Old, old,' Aidan said. 'When the Pharoahs were building the pyramids, this tree was standing.' He turned slowly to gaze at Will and Will at him. They did not like to look at each other, each felt the other did not belong. The other brought man and civilization within this place. Alone, each of them had forgotten himself, had become, for a short time, part of the forest, part of the plan, almost kin to the earth and privy to her secrets. To look at each other made them feel heavy, awkward, self-conscious, corrupt.

They stayed for a little longer, then, when they left, it was together, slowly with one accord. From beyond the gully with its horizontal scrub the outside world called them. But the call from the glade where the giant pine stood sentinel at the centre came, puzzling, unquiet in its offer of comfort and solution. They stepped out on to the horizontal scrub, knowing that they would come back. It did not occur to either of them to take timber from this place, it did not occur to either of them that the other would. It was something they *knew*. The tree must stand, its offspring around it must stand, the glade must be kept safe. They wanted to return to it.

They walked the mile or so down the slope to their camp, and neither spoke. Now, in the familiar surroundings of bush they knew and understood, the feelings engendered back in the glade seemed slightly ridiculous. Both regarded themselves as realists, as men who wasted little time in fatuous self-indulgence or whimsy. Yet though they were each puzzled by this new emotion, it had struck hard enough, deep enough, for them not to wish to dissect it with words, to pull it apart in the name of logic. It was as if what they knew as words, what they knew of as logic had no place within that world they had just left.

And yet, they would never quite leave it. For Will, more than Aidan, who had always been conscious of trees as being something beyond a mere raw resource, the lesson learnt in the glade made him more aware of details that he had never before considered. Now, for the first time, the bush seemed alive for him. The flight of a green parrot from tree to tree overhead, the scent of the native shrubs that blended with the heavier eucalypt smell of the forest, once aware of these, he was never again to forget.

Locked as they were in their own thoughts, it was with something like resentment that they saw, as they came down the slope, Hugh Raymond and Heath rowing upriver towards them.

After Lane's death, Raymond had thought long and hard about finding a suitable new partner. Then, as Heath's coordination improved and it became clear that though his mental processes would never be the same as they were, he was a willing worker and eager to please his new friend Raymond began taking him out in the boat and trying him with an axe and saw. All this season they had been working together, and now as the cold weather was setting in and the rain had begun, they were upstream, like Aidan and Will, to await the first floodwater.

Hugh Raymond waved to them, 'Got some letters for you! Arrived two days ago with the *Constant*!'

Their hearts lifted. Letters! Only infrequently was there news from Hobart Town and as the winter wore on, fewer ships would be making the tortuous, dangerous trip around the south coast from the capital.

Raymond, sensibly, was the one to make the tea, while Aidan and Will sat down with their backs against the steep pitch of the badger-box roof, and devoured the contents of the letters. One for Will, a very fat one from Huonville, and three for Aidan, one from his bank,

559

one from Maura, one from Milton Reynolds.

He opened the bank's first. Yes, Austin wrote, the building of the new medical chambers in Davey Street was progressing satisfactorily, and they had had several queries from friends of Dr Reynolds regarding leasing rooms as medical surgeries. The plumbing and sewerage systems were of such a standard that all members of the medical profession who had seen the building were very impressed. Mr Austin felt Aidan would have no trouble in finding tenants for the building.

Austin was also pleased to announce that Aidan's bid for the late Colonel Atkins' estate, Glenleigh, the ten acres adjoining the Cascade Creek in South Hobart, had been successful.

This was the property adjoining Milton Reynold's house. Aidan was delighted. He had the designs already in mind for the several homes he would build, for future sale, keeping the main house and three acres of ground for his own.

He turned now to Maura's letter.

Hobart Town
13 March 1862

My Beloved Husband,

(How her endearing introductions amused him.)

> *Please forgive me for not writing earlier, it is some five weeks since I last wrote, I know, but there have been so many demands upon my time lately. It has taken me a great deal of time to become accustomed to the housemaid you insisted I have. I must say, Aidan, that you were wrong to claim that I would accustom myself to being waited upon. I have not, and there is a constant war between Jane and myself as to who should do the cooking and cleaning. Most people of my acquaintance seem to spend their time complaining of the laziness of their servants, but I wish someone would explain to this over-industrious girl that I wish to prepare my own food occasionally, and that she should not follow behind me and take dusters out of my hands.*
>
> *No doubt this must sound amusing to you, but it is not to me, sure. Margaret Reynolds visited me yesterday, and she had a discussion with Jane to the effect that if the mistress wishes to clean the floors she must be allowed to, and Jane retired to her room and wept and threatened to leave, saying that I left her nothing to do and was robbing her of her function in life.*
>
> *I would dismiss the girl if it were not for the fact that Mr Austin of the Bank visited me yesterday, to inform me that you have successfully*

560

bought the estate, Glenleigh, next to Margaret and Milton's.

I did not believe you would go through with this scheme, cannot see how it will benefit us in the slightest. Everyone knows that the colony is in an exceptionally bad state, and who knows if it will improve? Sydney and Melbourne seem to be growing more and more prosperous, due no doubt to their proximity to the goldfields, and Hobart Town is being forgotten. If we had a farm, Aidan, a very large country estate, I would rest easier, for land, a great deal of it, is the only security. You of all people should know that. To do as you are doing, buying city properties, and in such depressed times, is such a gamble. How can you bear to risk all you have worked so hard to gain on the chance of selling again at a profit?

I asked Milton Reynold's advice on this, but he says only that he trusts your judgement in these matters. Please, please, think carefully, Aidan. I would rather that we did not raise our heads so high at the risk of falling so low, should we be forced into bankruptcy. I will say no more about it, now.

Mr Austin gave me the key, and I drove myself and Liam and Clemency over to see Glenleigh. I must say I approve of the little gig, it is a convenient size and I am quite an expert, now, as a reinswoman. I am glad to hear that you do not mind my driving alone occasionally. To have a coachman would be the final straw.

Aidan, the house is far too large! If we had seventeen children it would be too large. Clemency asked if it was the bank where Mister Austin worked and sure it gives just that impression. And did you know that that mad Englishman who owned it (he died drunk in the parlour, Margaret told me) has animal heads on every wall? There is a lion and tiger in the drawing room and many other creatures poking their heads from above fireplaces all over the ground floor; Liam was in transports of delight, and Clemency wept with pity all through the inspection.

Afterwards I took her to the Reynolds' house, and she recovered only when we were served tea, including some of Berrima's wedding cake.

Milton and Margaret were most sorry that you could not be here for the wedding, though I gave your apologies and bought a pair of Wedgwood vases as a wedding gift. I wish you could have written yourself to thank Milton for the invitation, you could not be so busy that . . .

Aidan had stopped breathing, his heart thumping painfully. He crumpled Maura's letter into his pocket, picked up Milton's letter and began tearing at the seal.

It was dated six months before. What had happened to it at the shipping office? Why had it not been delivered to him?

His eyes ran down the page.

> *. . . So glad to announce that Berrima has finally consented to become Mrs Mark Ellis. If it is possible, could you come to Hobart Town for the wedding . . .*

He had stood, slowly, without realizing it, came to himself and his surroundings, only when Will, still seated, said, 'Aidan? I have some news. I . . . I've a letter here from Huonville. I didn't want to tell you all I was planning until I was sure . . . I'm to be married, Aidan, I've written to Cora Frazer, and asked her if she'll marry me, and she says yes.'

It took several seconds for Will's words to penetrate Aidan's mind, through his own pain and confusion. He dragged his gaze away from Milton Reynolds' barely decipherable, damning letter, and stared at his friend.

'Cora? You proposed to Cora? But . . .' He forced his mind to think. Will was gazing at him expectantly, waiting, Aidan knew, for a reaction, and a favourable one, at that. 'She's a fine woman, Cora.'

'Yes, that's it, y'see. I've learnt a great deal these past years, Aidan. 'Tis a woman I want, not a girl. Cora has lost her John, she d'know how it is, to be married, as I was, and to lose someone you love, as I did.'

'She's older that you are, Will . . .'

'Five years only. That doesn't matter. We were always good friends, Aidan. We d'understand each other. I don't . . .' he hung his head almost sheepishly, 'I don't want another love such as I had for Emily, Aidan. 'Tis destructive, such a love. I d'wonder, now, if what I was feeling had any reality in Emily at all. I wanted to be young again. Loving her made me feel young again.' Aidan was quiet, his gaze was locked into Will's, and each word went through him with the sharp edge of its truth. ''Twas foolishness, I see it, now. It couldn't have led to happiness. Cora understands me, she has a sense of humour, and she's brave, and strong in her mind. We'll deal well together, I think . . . Are you pleased, Aidan? Will you wish us well?'

Will had stood, and Aidan now grasped his hand. 'Aye, that I do . . .' He found it hard to speak, felt an absurd burning at the back of his throat and eyes.

Will was scowling at him, 'Your hand's frozen, Aidan, an' you be as white as a sheet – what's wrong?'

'Och, I'm grand, sure. But . . . It's Maura. She's not happy in

Hobart, and . . .'

Heath, behind them at the fire, was laughing at something Hugh Raymond had said; they were both laughing; in a moment, Will would tell them about his coming marriage, and there would be a celebration. Raymond always carried a bottle of rum in his boat. Without realizing it, Aidan was escaping, walking away, up the slope.

'Where do you go?' Will called.

'I need to think. I'll return soon.'

Will watched him go, worried, now. Then, too full of his own good news, he turned to the two men at the fire. 'I'm to be married. In a few months I'll be bringing my Cora to the settlement.'

They were delighted, they pumped Will's hand and laughed with him, even Heath, who did not quite understand but was glad to join in his friends' happiness. It was Raymond who looked about and caught sight of Aidan, disappearing into the scrub up the slope. 'Hey, where's O'Brien going?'

'I don't know.' Will paused wondering what had shaken Aidan so badly; Maura could be hurtful, he knew. Perhaps it was something to do with the children. Will was glad that he and Aidan had found the glade beyond the horizontal scrub; whatever Aidan's trouble, it would be a good place to heal oneself.

55

Now everything was changed. He could not bear the thought of living in the house that lay next door to Milton Reynolds and his family. Och, Berrima and Mark might be living with them! Aidan would see them every day and he could not bear that.

He decided not to visit them when next he went to Hobart Town, would write a letter to them, shortly, conveying his congratulations and his very best wishes – but he would not, could not, go to visit them.

Yet only five months later, when he was preparing to leave for six weeks in the capital, and most of the ships had loaded his timber of that season, barked and trimmed in the new mill, the *Maid of Erin* steamed into Port Davey, and on board were Berrima and Mark Ellis.

Aidan was coming out the doors of the mill with Will when the first long boat reached the beach. He saw one of the sailors lifting a woman out, saw the sun catch the chestnut hair beneath the demure bonnet, and even at this distance he recognized her, and his heart stood still. And there, the tall figure that leapt from the boat onto the dry sand; Aidan knew the supple, straight-shouldered figure to be that of Mark Ellis. He watched the young man take her arm, stood frozen to the spot in jealousy, and Will, hesitating a step, gazed from his face down to the group on the beach.

'Who is it?' he murmured. 'Is it someone you know?' But he stopped, then, his eyes narrowed, and in a moment, he too had recognized the couple. They were walking up the slope towards Mrs Malone, who stood, hands on her hips amidst a group of her children, watching, and ready to welcome the newcomers; interested, alive with curiosity to hear the latest news of Hobart Town.

The sailors were unloading valises out of the boat and carrying them up after the couple. There was much gesturing, and Aidan saw that Mrs Malone was telling the couple where his house lay, where the mill stood – but they had seen him, now! Were walking towards him! Oh, God . . . Aidan told himself he should move, should walk down towards them, should force a smile on to his face, a laugh, perhaps, a cry of welcome. Already Will had moved forward, was doing just that. But Aidan wanted to back away, stumble back into the mill, slam the great doors, to be alone.

More like Anna than ever before in her womanly maturity, and coming towards him, smiling, across the sand; the wind catching at fine wisps of her hair, pulling them free from the chignon below her bonnet, her face laughing, the brown eyes laughing. 'Mister O'Brien! Will!' she called, both hands out now. She reached Will first, and the man actually hugged her, then turned to grasp Mark Ellis's hand in both his, pumped hard – they were laughing, the three of them, all the bitterness of Will's last meeting with Berrima forgotten.

Aidan still stood, unmoving, feeling as old, as worn, as an ancient stone statue, part of the earth, not part of their warmth, their laughter, their loving friendship. I want no part of it, no part of it . . .

She had run on towards him – there! – she was running towards him, her hand outstretched – and he could do nothing but take it, press it warmly. 'Mrs Ellis.' And he smiled, he actually smiled, and wondered at the calmness in his voice, its friendly tone. It was not as difficult as he had thought it would be. For she was so lovely, and he cared so deeply for her. And her happiness, now that she stood before him, was so tangible, it came through the feel of her hand in his; there was a new vibrancy about her, Aidan thought, she loves Ellis. She is not near him, her back is to him, yet she feels at one with the man. She loves him.

All four turned up towards Aidan's house. Berrima had brought some fresh supplies for them, including seed cake and a plum pudding that she had made in preparation for Christmas. Aidan made tea, and there was a veritable feast at the scrubbed table in his cottage. Berrima brought letters from Maura, her father, and Liam, but Aidan put them aside and talked with his visitors.

It was Will who asked, after the news and gossip and messages from Hobart Town had been duly relayed, what brought the Ellises to Port Davey. 'For I'll tell 'ee, when Cora and myself go on our honeymoon, t'will not be to such a place as this.'

'Several writers have described the "rugged beauty" of the South-West,' Mark answered, with a grin, 'particularly in the past year or so. Don't be surprised if you don't receive more visitors as time goes on. When the weather's mild, the trip around the coast can be very pleasant. And I must say, the settlement is a surprise – all you need is a public house and a general store and you'd have quite a little village.'

Why was it that Aidan, watching Ellis, found that he did not like the young man nearly as much as he had on those occasions when they'd met at the Reynolds' house? It went beyond his jealousy, he thought, though that could be reason enough.

No, there was something new in Mark's attitude, a careless propriety towards Berrima; a cynical drawl to the voice, a smile that came at some of Will's or Aidan's comments where one wouldn't normally smile, being well-mannered – in short, a kind of patronization that had never been present before. She's given him confidence, Aidan thought bitterly, he has what he wants, and no longer needs to exercise his charm to its full potential. The blue eyes continued to look lazily out from beneath thick dark lashes, occasionally he would brush the heavy curls back from his forehead impatiently; the man was as handsome as ever, Aidan thought with sick envy, but now, it almost seemed, Mark knew the fact.

He was being uncharitable. There was nothing, really, to prove this change of personality – a man could not change so quickly, sure. It's all within myself, these feelings of jealousy that take vent in criticizing Mark. For it's he who sits beside her, not myself. It's he who'll hold her in his arms tonight, not myself. It wouldn't matter if the man was a saint. He has Berrima, and I hate him.

Later, Aidan and Will took the couple on a tour of Settlement

Point, rowed them up the Davey a mile or so, and when they returned, boarded the *Lostwithiel* and sailed around the harbour and into Bramble Cove where the whaling station lay.

For Aidan, the entire day was a nightmare. He had been able to cope with the fact of Berrima's marriage by putting it out of his thoughts entirely, putting his friendship with her away from him forever, had planned to be an acquaintance only, should they be forced to meet at Milton's house in South Hobart. And here she was, without warning, in this isolated world he had made for himself – had chosen for himself, for he had gone to Port Davey more than willingly – having seen Berrima that day he had interrupted Mark's love-making. He had almost run away, he realized now, because to see her too often would be too painful.

He hated her for coming here, for implanting her face against these hills, these mountains, for walking along this beach, for standing in the prow of this vessel with her face raised to the sun. Soon she would be gone. But she would never be gone. Wherever he looked, from this day on, he would see her. There was no escape for him.

Knowing she was Mark's wife made not a bit of difference to his feelings. He had hoped it would, but it did not. They stayed in his cottage that night, sleeping in the room that he had shared with Maura, the bed he had shared with Maura. And all night, each small sound the house made meant that they were making love. He lay there in the narrow bed in what had been Clemency's room, and thought of the two. Punched his pillow in rage and bitterness that they should come here, flaunting their happiness under his very nose, filling his house and his mind with the thought of their lovemaking.

It was not quite dawn when he realized that he could stand it no longer. His bed was damp with sweat, the sheets twisted into rolls beneath him. He got to his feet, groped for his trousers and pulled them on. Shirtless and barefooted, he left the house, closing the door carefully behind him, and walked down towards the beach in the darkness.

He removed his trousers, threw them down upon the sand with a harshly suppressed oath, and turned and flung himself into the sea.

He did not consciously have the idea before him that he would kill himself. He swam as hard and as fast as he could only to escape, to leave Berrima behind him, to leave far, far behind the thought of her body – white-skinned it would be, pale like Anna's – coiled about the brown body of Mark Ellis. And they had the right! Man and wife, man and wife . . .

He knew he must turn back, felt himself tiring, and could see the little islands off Fitzroy Point to his left. He had swum almost two miles! He must turn back, or head for shore, soon he would be too tired . . .

He stopped, and trod water for a short while, and it was then that the first cramp took his ankle. He flicked his foot about, trying to flex the muscle, but it tightened further, like a rope that pulled his foot down, imprisoning it in a tearing grip like ice-cold wires, tightening, tightening . . .

And it was out of his hands, he thought, and merely smiled, and lay on his back and tried to cope with the pain. It is out of my hands, now, if I live or die. He headed back to shore, not to the land closest to him, three-quarters of a mile from him to either side, but back to Settlement Point, moving slowly, mostly on his back, gazing up at the paling stars, and waiting for his body to fail him. Hours passed, it seemed to him, and the pain in his foot had spread to his knee. Still he waited to die, careless, now, his rage gone, his energy gone, the only reality to keep swimming slowly, calmly, driven by his almost unconscious will, a token fight for life.

Yet it was enough. His arms struck sand first, then his legs, and he could stand. He was some distance down the beach from his house, but he was back. He had made it . . . He rose to his feet and stumbled, limped up from the water. The breeze was cold on his skin. He stood in the shallows, threw his head back, brushed his hair back from his eyes, placed his aching leg experimentally upon the ground . . . The water still lapped about his knees, but he did not notice, forgot even the pain in his leg, remained with his head half-flung back, and gazed up the beach to where Berrima stood, watching him.

He lowered his arm very slowly to his side. He knew that even in the faint light of the false dawn she could see his nakedness, but he stood there, breathing heavily with exhaustion, and did not cover himself, did not apologize, did not speak at all.

Her hair was loose, falling half-way down her thighs; he could see her thighs, her hips, her waist, her breasts, the outline of them through the white lawn nightdress that the breeze pressed back from her body. She did not seem to notice, looked at him from amid the hair that blew about her, half-shook her head as if someone had spoken; and her eyes traced his body, unwillingly though it happened, he could feel her eyes over his body though her face was in shadow . . . only her hair, blown back from her, hair black in the moonlight, made her seem real. Other than this, she might have been a statue, so white she looked, so still.

She moved forward a little. The waves that rolled about his knees fled towards her, reached her bare feet, pulled at her, covered her, tugged her towards him. But she stopped, and only the water moved between them, only the water tugged and beckoned back and forth between them with its insistent rhythm. He could see her eyes, now, could see the fear in them. He told himself that he had only to reach out, to take her, hold her – but it was impossible. He did not understand the reality of this, for it could not be reality. This was little more than a child, half his age, who had been married less than six months . . .

It had turned cold. Berrima shuddered. She looked down, then looked away towards the house. She murmured something. Only after she had turned away, did it sound within his brain, 'Forgive me', soft as a prayer, and she was walking away, back up the slope. She did not look back once. He saw the door close behind her.

Only then did he allow himself to fall to his knees in the swell, fell forward on to his face and let the waves claim him. He did not understand, he did not. These things did not happen, it was not real . . . He crawled up on to the sand and lay there for a long time, the sea still tugging gently at his body, as if it, too, was questioning, was puzzled.

56

Somehow, he slept, on returning to his cottage and his bed. He awoke with the sun half-way up the sky, slanted in across his bed, lay thinking that the night could have been a dream, but every muscle in his body ached; and, further, he had been careless, his bed was gritty with sand, his skin smelt of the salt sea, his hair was stiff, and still damp.

There was a murmur of voices behind the door. He pulled on his clothes and went into the kitchen, to find Berrima, Mark and Will seated about the table, drinking tea. He had eyes only for the woman, at first, and gazed at her, hoping to see something written on her face of what they had shared the night before. For it seemed to him that they had shared something. They had been trapped in some dreadful moment that had not been of their choosing, a moment that for him – being a man, he told himself – had held a distinctly sensual pleasure. He pitied Berrima in what must have been, for her, an alarming experience, yet he could not but hope that she had felt *something*. Forgive me, she had murmured. She had been embarrassed . . .

Her eyes met his only for her brief smile, her quiet 'Good morning', and then they slid away, to the cupboard where she now headed, to fetch a cup for him . . . and she was busying herself with pouring his tea, with cutting more slices of damper. The men took charge of the conversation, teasing him for sleeping late, for allowing the liquor to go to his head.

That afternoon they packed a lunch of cheese and damper and plum pudding and rowed upriver even further, stopping to eat only after coming close to the mouth of Hell's Gates, calm, now, in the early spring, a swift current only, but too much of a chore to row upstream even at this slow, kind season.

After the meal, on the river bank, Will and Berrima went for a walk to search for tree orchids. Aidan watched them go, knowing that Will would ask Berrima about Emily. He's like me with Anna's memory, he thought, he'll never forget her.

'You know . . .' Mark said, leaning back against a rock and puffing at his pipe, causing Aidan's attention to return from the two figures along the bank, 'you know, it was more than simply the desire for a short vacation that brought us here.' Aidan looked at him suddenly. 'Oh, it was for Berrima, but I must admit that I had an ulterior motive, one which . . .' he glanced after his wife, 'I doubt she would approve.' He seemed to hesitate. Aidan, at this point, was intrigued. Mark scowled over the water to the opposite bank, lush and green, a tangle of myrtle, vines and ferns, 'You see, O'Brien, I never had it in my mind to remain a surveyor all my life. Particularly working for the government. The wages are fairly low, and now . . . Well, I expect I'll soon have a family to provide for.' He took his pipe from his mouth, and chewed a little loose skin on his lip for a moment.

Aidan, watching him, felt his palm itching with the desire to punch that handsome face. And for no other reason than his jealousy, and it was an unreasoning jealousy. He was a fool, sure, he must stop feeling so involved. The man was speaking of himself and his wife. His wife. Aidan felt sick with his envy, could barely disguise it. 'Yes,' he managed to say, 'a man must think of his responsibilities.'

Mark turned to him, eagerly, 'Yes, that's it, you see. That's why I've come to you, for I felt sure you'd understand. You're very fortunate in knowing timber – you've been able to put that know-ledge to work for you, here.' He waved his pipe about at the river and hills. 'But those of us without your specified knowledge must choose very carefully if we wish to branch out into business for ourselves.'

'Is that what you have in mind? Your own surveying company?'

'No! No, I expect that's the most obvious thing that one would think, but I was planning to move right away from surveying altogether.' He hesitated, then plunged on, 'I know the owner and editor of the *Derwent Chronicle*, O'Brien. He's a man who's suffered from ill-health for some time, now, and his doctor has told him to move north. He plans to go to the new colony of Queensland as soon as he sells the newspaper.

'I would like to buy the newspaper, but I need a partner. I wondered if you would be interested in the venture.'

Aidan inhaled too sharply on his pipe smoke and it went down his throat. He coughed, almost thankful for the incident, which gave him time to compose his thoughts.

He had planned never to see Berrima again, unless it was abso-lutely unavoidable, at some social function in Hobart Town. He had planned to put her from his mind for ever – or at least to attempt to do so. And now this. Partners with Ellis! Partners with Berrima's . . . he hated the word, hated to place it upon Ellis's handsome, confident features – Berrima's husband.

Partners. Dinner parties, family outings. Sunday dinners together, being godfather to their children. Growing old and pros-perous together, cheek by jowl. He started to laugh.

'Sir?' Mark queried, puzzled, perhaps a little chagrined, not knowing if he was being mocked. It was the first time that the younger man had called Aidan 'Sir'. How manners change, Aidan thought drily, when one wants something.

'How much is your friend asking for the business?'

'A thousand pounds. I expect we'd be paying about one thousand two hundred with legal costs. There's the lease on the building in Campbell Street as well.' His attention was now entirely upon Aidan.

'Yes,' Aidan said. 'I'll have to have my lawyer and my bank

570

manager look into the matter. If they believe it's a good idea then I think we could come to some arrangement.' He smiled, and Mark smiled too.

Jaysus, Mary and Joseph. Where would it lead? He rose and stretched, feeling delighted with himself. He did not care what happened. Berrima would be there, close to him, for the rest of their lives. He would cope with what pain that may cost him, later.

That night Berrima and Mark retired early, and Aidan remained before the kitchen fire with the letters Berrima had brought him, answering them now, so that she could take them with her when she and Mark returned to Hobart Town in three days' time.

He tried to concentrate on his descriptions of the visit and the progress of the season's work, and to shut his ears to the soft murmur of voices from the other room.

After a while this became difficult, and he was forced to put down his pen, for it was obvious that Berrima and Mark were no longer conversing, they were quarrelling.

He was tempted to go to the door and listen. Could not control his fierce feeling of enjoyment. But no, he could not stoop *that* low . . .

Neither could he sleep. The voices went on and on, until Berrima's was tearful, Mark's petulant. Aidan kept waiting for them to tire, but there was no sign of it. Finally he rose and dressed, and went to Will's cabin, calling his name through the window until he awoke and rose to let Aidan in.

He felt happier to be away from the couple in his own cottage, though he slept equally as fitfully – for his mind remained pre-occupied with Mark and Berrima.

It almost seemed as though Mark had visited Port Davey especially to ask Aidan about the newspaper. He struggled to cope with the fact that Berrima, far from existing on the periphery of his life, was going to be very much at the forefront of it; that it was not even through his own choosing, let alone hers, but because of Mark.

In the morning, he and Will breakfasted together, then walked over to Aidan's house, Will talking excitedly all the way of his plans for his marriage to Cora. Aidan was noncommittal about it, having doubts whether Will really loved the woman, and afraid, as he so often drew parallels between his own life and that of his friends', that the man was marrying the comfortable, placid Cora because he knew he could not have Emily Reynolds. He could not say this, smiled, instead, on cue, asked the appropriate questions in order to encourage Will in his plans, and tried to push his own doubts into the background. Cora was not like Maura. She was flexible, adaptable.

Will would not, in any case, be made unhappy by the union.

They could see Mark as they crossed to Aidan's cottage, a tall, dark-clothed figure striding along the beach, his face turned to gaze out over the harbour. Will, whom Aidan had told of the mysterious quarrel, now hesitated a few steps, stopped and gazed down the slope to the morose figure.

'Looks like they haven't made it up,' he murmured.

'It's their own concern,' Aidan growled, but Will had stepped away, down towards Mark.

'You talk to Berrima,' he said, 'she'll listen to you. I'll go talk to Mark.'

'Don't interfere, Will.' Aidan was aggravated, had totally taken the peace of his life for granted before the Ellises had come. He was forced to do too much thinking, too much feeling, these past few days.

'I'm not interfering. I'll talk about the tides. Unless he wants to talk to me.' Will grinned, and walked on.

Berrima was seated at the table when Aidan knocked and entered the cottage. There was a full cup of tea before her; it was cold, no steam rose from it. The girl looked up without surprise.

'Please, sit down, Aidan.' She smiled rather bleakly, 'You stand there as if you doubt your own welcome – and it's your house.'

He pulled up a chair, sat backwards upon it, leaning his arms on the back of it, and gazed at her worriedly. 'Berri, what's the matter?'

She watched him for a few moments in silence. 'Things . . . never happen quite correctly between us, do they?' she said softly, gazing into the tea cup, turning it slightly this way and that on the scrubbed surface of the table. 'You've been an unwilling witness to so many of my mistakes.'

He could only stare at her, so strange was it to hear her speaking like this. The ebullient child he had known was not evident in the controlled young woman in the dark grey dress and lace collar who sat before him. She raised her eyes to his. 'You must say no to Mark and this venture into newspaper ownership. Please, Aidan. Don't allow him to talk you into it.'

He sat very still, his mind racing. He said, very quietly, 'He told you about it last night, did he not? It was the first you knew about it.'

She lowered her head. For several seconds she did not speak. 'I wouldn't have come, if I'd known that that was what he planned to do. He wants it so much; yet it's beyond our means, we'd be forced to go heavily into debt to purchase our part of the business. And though Mark is very bright, and is so keen on the idea and would learn quickly, really he knows nothing about the press. Aidan, it's a foolhardy gamble. Don't indulge him. It would be at your own expense.'

Her eyes were pleading with him. He had the feeling that she would not – or perhaps could not – tell him the entire story. He leaned back in his chair, studying her coolly. He did not like schemes that threatened to lose him money; his money mattered a great deal to him. But neither did he like allowing a scheme that would keep Berrima close to him to fade from him, before it had even begun. He said, 'All great military campaigns began as fool-hardy gambles. Most great fortunes have been based on what appeared to be foolhardy gambles.'

'The people concerned knew what they were doing. And besides, a lot depends on if one can afford to fail. If Mark fails, he won't be unduly disturbed. His pride will be hurt, but he has wealthy, indul-gent parents, he'll have more money and another project very shortly. For you . . .' She looked uncomfortable. Aidan scowled and she saw it, and looked even more uncomfortable.

'I have less capital and few such sources of revenue,' he finished for her.

'I didn't meant to infer that . . . I was considering your wel-fare . . .'

'Commendable.'

The brown eyes were cool as agates. She wished she had not spoken. He went on, 'Shouldn't you be more concerned with your husband's welfare? If the venture succeeded, he would be accepted in a field that obviously means a great deal to him . . .'

'I must think of which is the wisest choice . . .'

'Madam . . .' he said, and could not keep the insolent irony out of his voice, wished to, tried to, but could not. The fingers that toyed with her cup glinted with a diamond ring and a plain gold band, and the sight infuriated him. He had not noticed them before, had always been too busy studying her face. Now he could not drag his gaze away from them. 'Madam, your husband may know little about business management, but I suggest your knowledge would be even less. And if, as you say, he could bear the temporary loss of money and dignity should the venture fail, then, sure, you should allow him to go ahead.'

'But you . . .'

'I can take care of myself.'

The silence went on. Berrima looked more and more distressed, until Aidan realized that she was close to tears. He felt as if he looked at her from behind an iron mask – he could not allow his face to betray the feelings that went on within him. It was prison that had done this to him, one set one's face, and after a while it was easy. It was the best defence against those who watched him greedily for a sign of weakness. Berrima, from very different motives, was looking for such weakness at this very moment. Her brown eyes were large, they studied his face, as if searching for some clue, some trace of feeling – but he betrayed none.

She lowered her gaze to the table. Aidan was thinking, oddly, that Maura had sat there, in just such a silence. A helpless silence, where words could do nothing but hinder understanding.

Mark and Will entered the cottage, then, Mark looking tight-faced, his gaze going quickly, consideringly, between Berrima and Aidan. He's afraid she's talked me out of it, Aidan thought, and wondered how to tell the man that it was otherwise. He did not understand Berrima's fear of the venture, she could not possibly know of some flaw in the scheme that Mark was not aware of. What possible reason could she have of not wishing the idea to succeed?

Aidan realized he would have to go to Hobart. Sure, this had occurred at a good time. He had been missing Liam and Clemency, and the deal had just been finalized for the land at South Hobart, and he had to decide on whether to build on the land he was subdividing on the Glenleigh estate, or whether to sell the blocks as they were. There were many things to do.

More and more he realized that he would eventually have to leave Port Davey. He had, in his land in Hobart, and investments made through the bank, in Melbourne and Sydney companies, the basis for a small, comfortable income. And he was considering consolidating these, buying land in the boom city of Melbourne, centre of the gold-rich colony of Victoria. He had become accustomed to making money. Now he felt more confident, even more ambitious. It was not enough to make money. He wanted to make it quickly.

Will made them tea, trying all the while to keep a conversation going, speaking about the weather, and how it would affect the men in terms of bringing the logs down the Davey. Berrima allowed him to take charge of the kettle, was watching Mark with concerned, almost frightened eyes. Her husband avoided her gaze.

Aidan wanted to slap them both, hurl them out of his cottage. Their brooding silences, their wealth of accusatory words, unsaid, hung in the air and disturbed him.

'I'll come back to Hobart in a few weeks, and we'll talk more about the paper,' he said now to Mark. He saw Berrima's head come up to gaze at him, then she had risen and walked over to the window. Mark looked delighted, laughed a little – but the laugh was lost under a roll of thunder.

574

Will rose from where he knelt coaxing the fire, and moved to the window to stand beside Berrima. 'We'll get a good storm.' He glanced back at Aidan with a grin. 'Don't you think it'll settle in?'

'How can you tell?' Mark asked.

Aidan said, 'Will likes to believe he can predict these things.'

'Is he often wrong?' It was Berrima who spoke, without turning, from the window.

'I'm getting better at it,' Will retorted cheerfully. 'Everyone should rely on their feelings. They'll not let you down half as much as trying to be logical and sensible about things.'

He had no idea why his words should depress and strain the atmosphere in the room, but the fact was, they did. He looked around at three people each silently, grimly, looking at nothing in particular.

The storm broke suddenly and fiercely. Will had little time to pull back, drawing Berrima with him, before the rain came rushing in on the wind. He pulled the wooden shutters closed, as Aidan struggled with the others. Berrima helped them go through the cottage, fastening the shutters against the storm. When they returned to the kitchen, Mark had lit a lamp.

'Shall we play cards?' he asked them, the thin, handsome face alight with a smile that included all of them. For whatever reason, his mood had gone. He fetched the chair for Berrima, a rug for her shoulders, for it was cold, and the four sat down, cheerfully enough, to play cards by the light of the lamp, while the wind howled around them and the thunder fell like an avalanche from the furious sky.

Later, the thunder faded, but for all that day the rain poured down, and evening came, and night, and it showed no sign of abating. Will decided not to go back to his own house, and slept on the settle bed in the kitchen, near the fire.

The next day the storm continued; Aidan and Will were secretly jubilant, for they could see, in their minds' eye, the creeks below their stand of timber, swelling their banks and pushing at the last of their logs, perhaps ready, at any time, to free them sufficiently to carry them down to the Davey and on down to the pen. They glanced covertly at Berrima and Mark, expecting them to be feeling confined, bored, resentful of the weather that kept them indoors. But Mark was pleased to have the opportunity to talk to Aidan about his plans for the newspaper, and even Berrima, who surprised Aidan by being philosophical about the drenching rain, curled up on the settle with one of Aidan's new novels, Dickens' *A Tale of Two Cities*, and seemed content.

Mark's back was to her, and sometimes Aidan would look up and

575

find her studying himself and her husband. He thought it simply that she was worried, still, about the soundness of the plan; but there was a considering quality about her at these times, strangely at variance with what he knew of the girl.

But all the happenings of the last few days had begun to shake his opinions – for what, after all, did he know of her? She was as wilful as ever, but it did seem that she was growing into a woman of forethought, whether her reasons for opposing the buying of the *Derwent Chronicle* were right or wrong. As on that day when they had embraced beneath the willows at Glenleigh, he found his idea of her beginning to change – so he fought it, now, as he had then.

She looked up every once in a while across *A Tale of Two Cities*, and the girl's eyes were now a woman's eyes, watchful, patient, apprehensive, as this man whom she had married, whose possession she had become, plotted and planned a life that would not only concern Mark himself, but which concerned her, whether she would have it that way, or not.

Yet his surprise at Berrima was not at an end. Towards evening they were visited by Hugh Raymond and Heath, who took off their oilskins and dried themselves by the fire and talked of going upriver the next day.

Will agreed, then, remembering their guests, looked sheepish, for it would mean leaving them alone in the settlement.

But Mark was saying, 'I'd like to come too; would it be possible?'

And before anyone could answer, Berrima said, 'And me, Mark. I made myself a suit based on Mrs Bloomer's design of several years ago – I still think they were very practical, and since the outfit is heavy serge, it should be ideal for this climate.' She grinned. 'I made it especially in the hope that I might see some of the wilderness – Aidan?' He turned stricken eyes to her, and found her watching him steadily, her face alight. 'Aidan, Mark doesn't mind if I come – will you take us?'

He turned to face the other piners. Heath stood with his good-natured grin, waiting for Hugh Raymond to explain matters; Hugh looked vastly amused; Will looked very much as Aidan felt, completely taken aback.

Mark had his arm about Berrima's narrow shoulders. 'Really, Aidan. She looks small, but she's a perfectly plucky little thing. The Governor's wife, Lady Franklin – back in the thirties – why, she used to trek all about the colony. Surely history can cope with two adventuresses.'

'In a boat,' Aidan breathed, 'through Hell's Gates in a boat with a woman . . .'

He caught her gaze. Her chin had come up. The woman was gone and in her place was the child he had known, the confident, indulged child who could not believe that anyone would prevent her having her way.

There was laughter in the room; already Raymond and Will were saying that it had never been done, but dammit, why shouldn't it be done? Only Aidan was silent. He and Berrima gazed at each other as if there were no one else in the room. He knew that to argue with all of them would be useless. Berrima knew it, too. Her brown eyes were sparkling with mischief and triumph. This time, at least, her gaze seemed to say, I believe I've won.

57

The decision was made in that mood of light-heartedness that claimed all of the piners at some stage, when bottled up indoors for days at a time by the steady soaking rains of the South-West. Yet the scheme was not altogether foolhardy. There had been rain for only two days: like as not the river had not risen all that much, and they had already brought most of their logs down. The men were even prepared to take fewer of their remaining logs, to come downstream earlier than they would have done, had the visitors not been there.

For Mark's charm, his good looks, his reckless spirit, and Berrima's obvious pluck had impressed Will and Hugh Raymond. They were flattered, too, that two city people would brave the violent and fickle Southern Ocean in order to see the pining settlement. They wanted the young people to enjoy themselves. They could both swim, they would not be coming back down in too much of a flood. And the piners were confident in their ability. Even Aidan and Will did not believe that actual harm could come to anyone. Aidan, Will, Raymond and Heath knew their boats, knew the river.

They set out just after dawn the following day. It had stopped raining, but the clouds still threatened.

Berrima appeared wearing the peculiar Bloomer suit: loose, baggy trousers, nipped in at the ankles, and a straight tunic over them that fell to her knees, the sides slit to her waist.

'I admit a woman can move better in them,' Will whispered to Aidan as they walked behind the Ellis's, carrying their boat on their shoulders. 'But they d'look *strange*.'

There was something eastern and exotic about the outfit – Aidan, in his reading over the past few years, had read reports of the fashion, but doubted, as the critics had, that the fad would last. It looked ungainly, and these were times when a woman would not risk looking ungainly. Better, they thought, the long skirts, however cumbersome, which made one appear to drift along the ground.

It was a pity. He enjoyed seeing Berrima striding out, for it appeared to him more natural than the fantasy that women did not possess legs. He liked to see the slim ankles in their laced leather boots. He wondered what Maura would say to the Bloomer outfit. Then smiled. It did not take much imagination to work out what Maura would have thought.

Hugh Raymond and Heath headed the procession for the first mile or so, but then the groups split up and re-formed. Mark would help one or the other of the men with their boat, and Berrima walked beside each of the men in turn, questioning them about the country through which they walked.

They carried a tent with them, but finding the Malones gone from their usual base at Three Hut Creek, they camped there for the night, Aidan wondering, not only at Berrima's good humour and obvious enjoyment in the venture, but at Mark's attitude; he seemed to think that his young wife was capable of tolerating any condition, facing any danger. It would have angered Aidan, this careless over-confidence, except that with each day that passed Berrima seemed to deserve that confidence.

Aidan kept himself busy, otherwise he could not have borne this. It seemed that Berrima would superimpose her presence upon his world until there would be no place left for him to go where he would not be reminded of her. And it was a new Berrima, this good-humoured, adaptable Berrima, who laughed when she fell over on a muddy bank, who hummed as she walked through cloudbursts, a Berrima he tried hard not to see, for she filled his heart even more in this setting – he was forced to respect her, to realize unwillingly that she had always held these qualities within her.

When they reached their own badger box and Heath and Raymond left them to continue upstream, Mark insisted on helping with the creek clearing: like Berrima, he did not seem to mind the cold rain, the heavy, oppressive presence of the rainforest all around them.

It was Berrima who was left with little to do but watch the men from the bank as they worked that first day. They had brought food with them, there was little need to do much cooking, and Will was worried that Berrima was bored. It was that evening before the fire in the badger-box that he suggested that Aidan take Mark and Berrima to see the giant Huon pine.

Aidan looked up, glaring at Will from eyes that appeared like coals in the light. Berrima, seeing them, felt tense, almost frightened.

Aidan was arguing with Will. Or rather Will was arguing against Aidan's low, flat refusals. 'No, I said. They'd have to cross horizontal. It'll be too dangerous!'

Will was staring at him in surprise. 'But . . . !'

The dark eyes bored into Will. He stopped, stared hard at his friend, not understanding, but feeling the tension in him, his displeasure.

'Yes,' Will mumbled. 'I'd forgotten.'

'I've heard about horizontal scrub, I'd like to see it.' She would not let him out of it that easily, wanted to stir him further.

'Och, you'd see it all right. It'll look grand, when you fall through it, and y'r swinging by y'r petticoats, thirty feet above the ground.'

Mark was laughing, and did not appear to notice Berrima's face, pink with anger, her compressed lips betraying her effort at self-control. The badger-box was very small, there was little room even for four people with perfect equanimity between them. The vibrations of resentment now made the atmosphere almost intolerable. 'Mark, let's go to the tent, now.'

'Why?' Mark looked surprised.

Aidan said, 'I didn't mean . . .'

'I quite understand, Aidan . . . Please, Mark, let's go to our tent.'

She rose and went out into the light, drizzling rain to where the men had pitched the tent further up the slope, in case, as so often happened, the water rose to the badger-box.

Mark looked after Berrima, scowling. He turned to the other two, and said tightly, 'She's tired. She doesn't mean to be ill-mannered.'

'Oh, we know . . .' Will looked at Aidan for corroboration, but he found none in the hard face that gazed into the flames. Will had a sudden desire to bash Aidan's head against the low roof. The great fool . . .

'I'll go to her,' Mark sighed, and rose. 'We'll see you in the morning.' He flashed his smile on each of them and was gone out of the little hut, into the dark.

He felt it in the morning, the subtle pressure from the other three to relent and take Mark and Berrima to the giant pine. But he was determined that there would be one refuge left to him, one place

579

where Berrima had not been, where he could go to escape from her presence.

While Aidan and Will went upstream to free the channels and their snarled logs, Berrima and Mark remained at the badger box. Aidan wondered if Mark's new inactivity and carefully not-quite-disguised boredom was a hint that seeing the glade with its tree would be a welcome diversion; yet if Aidan could not bear Berrima there, he could bear Mark there even less. Will should have kept his mouth shut.

It rained again just before midday, and the creek rose sufficiently to take fourteen of the logs down into the Davey. When Aidan and Will returned to the badger-box it was to find several logs banked up near the camp, and Raymond's boat pulled up on the slope, well above the creeping water. The brown flood water lapped half-way up the height of the badger-box. Raymond, Heath, Berrima and Mark were crouched in the tent. The rain hissed into a fire nearby, partly covered by a canopy of green manfern leaves.

'Good enough time to go,' Raymond reflected as the two arrivals were handed mugs of tea and buttered damper. 'Not going to get much higher, reckon we oughta go down soon as we finish this. What do you reckon?' He turned to the other three piners.

All reckoned he was correct; it only needed, now to decide who went with whom. Raymond obviously had it in mind that he would like to ferry Berrima. He had placed a grid of new timber on the floor of his boat, and insisted that his was the more stable craft. In the middle of the argument launched by this statement, it was only Berrima's voice that quelled the noise by stating she would be delighted to go with Raymond and Heath. She was flattered at their gallantry, and was by now so cross with Aidan's churlishness that she did not care to travel with him.

Aidan had time, occasionally, to glance at Berrima as they un-snarled the logs from the bank, and pushed them out into mid-stream; she sat bent forward slightly in the centre of the boat, holding on to both sides, watching with interest not only Raymond as he pushed at the logs with the iron-tipped prodder, but Aidan's boat also, where Will handled the oars, Mark sat opposite him and Aidan worked with the prodder.

They could not tell how many of the logs were Raymond's and Heath's, and how many were Aidan's and Will's, it would all be settled at the pen downstream, where the floating boom logs, tied to stakes into the riverbed, held the logs in place until they were ready for floating to the pits at Settlement Point, or to the ships that waited to load them for Hobart Town.

Occasionally Berrima's eyes caught Aidan's, and they exchanged a smile, for they were both tense, oddly at one, at the beginning of this venture, sharing the danger.

It bothered Aidan, now, in a way that it had not before, that they were doing this. How many times had he and Will brought their logs down? Several trips during each winter, for five years. There had been times when they had taken a third man down in the boat – but always it had been because of illness or accident; the day Heath had cut his foot, the day Taylor, one of the other piners, working further up the Davey, had dropped unconscious with a bout of pneumonia. Both times Aidan and Will had taken the ill man down the river, and it had been during no less severe floods than this.

But he was worried nevertheless, and kept glancing at Raymond and Heath, telling himself that they were capable boatmen; in an emergency they would save Berrima at the cost of themselves.

The first section was the trickiest, they went back and forth like saturated sheepdogs, poking and prodding the logs from where they liked to cluster quietly on the banks. They would urge them out into the centre, have the satisfaction of seeing them caught by the fast flowing river, turned length on and pulled, fast, away from them. Some would snarl again, further down, but as the river wound towards Hell's Gates it moved deeper, swifter, and soon there was no need to shepherd the logs, they fled before them of their own accord, down, down, towards the opening in the shining dark rocks.

Aidan sat down in the prow, and turned to Mark. 'Hold on!' he shouted. The younger man's face was pale, but alight with tense excitement; his grin was strained, he clung to the sides of the boat, but managed to shout over the roar of water, 'I'm all right! I can't see Berrima, though! Afraid if I turn around I'll fall in!' He was laughing, and Aidan grinned, looking back to where Raymond's boat was shooting down river, surrounded by logs, in their wake. 'They're coming!' he shouted. 'They're just behind us!'

It happened just as they entered Hell's Gates. Raymond's boat was close behind him, then, despite the roar of water, they heard Berrima scream. To Aidan it seemed to go on and on, the rocks caught it and threw the sound back and forth. When he looked back, Berrima was crouched on the floor of the boat, which had struck a log, slewed sideways, and was taking in water even as Heath struggled valiantly with the oars. Raymond used the iron prodder to push out at the logs, turning the boat to face downstream . . .

Aidan and Will were too well-trained to panic – but Mark was not.

He had seen, was on his knees with a cry, lost his balance, fell across the rocking boat. Will cried 'Watch what y' . . . !' They were slewing sideways . . .

'Aidan!' Will's cry – Aidan was falling – a pain in his legs as the boat tipped, overturned, fell upon him – the bulk of its blackness in the water above him, he reached for it, but it fled away from him. Then water, rocks, water, speeding past in a nightmare blur – reaching out, opening his mouth to cry 'Will!' only to find it filled with water. Water closed over his head, rasped him against sharp obstacles, butted him against concealed weapons beneath its surface, toyed with him, played with him; after five years upon it, the Davey had him in its power.

He must not lose consciousness, told himself to stop struggling, but it was hard not to fight against the inexorable pull – he was raised in the air, thrown down again, whirled about until he did not know which way he faced. Once he saw the boat, and thought he saw a man clinging to it, but it was gone in a swirl of white water and he was alone, the icy water freezing him . . . tiring him . . . he was vomiting water, choking on water, the water the only reality . . .

Will was ahead of him – he suddenly realized it was Will – there was the boat and the figure clinging to it was Will. The water was swift, but calmer now. He was propelled forward to Will and the boat, and swam as fast as he could with muscles that were exhausted with the struggle to keep afloat, towards the man.

'Will . . . ?'

Will turned, blood flowing into his eyes. 'Can't see,' he murmured. 'Daren't let go. I'm all right, you all right?'

Aidan clung to the boat. He put a hand on Will's shoulder, 'Yes. Stay there . . .' He looked around. They were out of Hell's Gates, in the broader stream of the Davey. If they clung here to the boat, they would be able to swim to shore somewhere near the pen, or perhaps Raymond and Heath were still safe in their boat and were coming . . .

He saw Mark, then, downstream at some distance, a dark hump in the water by a drifting log.

Aidan was tired, so tired. He looked back towards Hell's Gates. There was mist here, and he could not see a boat coming.

He looked back at the still form of Ellis. If he dies, it would not be Aidan's fault. He was probably dead . . .

'Stay here,' he repeated to Will, and pushed off from the boat.

'Where're you going?' The fear in the voice. 'Aidan?'

'I can see Mark . . .'

The current helped him. He kept the dark shape in sight as he swam towards it. Berrima loved him, must love him, to have married him. He bore Mark Ellis no real ill will except that he was Berrima's husband. Sure he could not be blamed for that.

Aidan reached him, pulled at the dark hair. The white face came free of the water, the eyes closed . . . He was too late. He tried to feel for a pulse in the neck – but his hands were like ice, they could feel nothing. His own strength was leaving him. With the last of it he heaved Mark's body up, over the log of Huon pine, and adjusted it so that the face was clear of the water.

There was a shout behind them, and voices. Again, Berrima's scream, his name, 'Aidan!' The rest was unintelligible. He turned, saw the boat coming down, the three seated in it, began to smile.

'Look out! Look out!' they were shouting. He saw the two logs coming fast towards him – his own log, over which Mark lay, was still slewed sideways to the current. Aidan dodged, and the first log struck the end of his own, furthest away from Mark. Aidan turned to the man's body, the blow had jolted Mark, he was sliding back into the water, Aidan caught, pushed him back . . .

He had no time, did not even see the log that had struck turned sideways in the current, collect its companion, close in a scissor movement – he could hear only Berrima's scream, felt only the pain explode in his body, as the logs crushed his lower spine between them– and the black water was dragging him down.

58

Pain. A nightmare, whirling storm of pain in which he was trapped, tossed about, helpless. His pelvis was fractured, and he was sentenced to month after month – 'perhaps a year', Milton Reynolds warned him when he finally regained consciousness – of lying on a hard bed and waiting for his body to mend, slowly, in its own time.

He was furious. Angry that they took him back to Hobart Town without waiting for him to regain consciousness; angry that he woke from his delirium to find himself, not in the cottage in Moonah, but in Glenleigh, the great house beside Milton Reynolds' home, angry to find that it was not Maura nursing him, but Berrima.

Maura had come, briefly, while he was unconscious. Her reaction was such that Milton had not suggested that she nurse Aidan, had suggested instead that the more experienced Berrima, with Mark – who had suffered only mild concussion and a sprained shoulder – stay in the new house. Milton left it to Maura to decide when she and the children would move from the cottage in Moonah to Glenleigh. But Maura murmured that the children must be close to their schools, and though she would visit the house she did not wish to reside there. Berrima and Milton made as good a story as they could to explain Maura's behaviour, but Aidan saw through their kind effort. He did not ask after her, did not ask, either, for the children. For as the months passed, Maura did not come. When Berrima suggested she drive to Moonah and bring the children to him Aidan was short with her, snapped that he did not wish to see the children at the moment.

You don't wish them to see you as you are, Berrima thought privately, you don't wish them to see you helpless. But despite her knowledge that his pride lay behind the decision, she did not press him. Berrima herself drove to Moonah many times to see the children, and to try to persuade Maura to change her mind. Berrima did not understand Maura, did not understand how the relationship between husband and wife could deteriorate to this extent; but she trusted that it was merely Maura's fear and horror of illness that kept her from Glenleigh. Berrima had known many people who suffered in this way. So while she was annoyed with Maura, she knew that the woman was not entirely at fault.

Aidan was angry at the pain and his enforced immobility; he could read, study his business affairs, but for such a man as himself that was not enough.

He was angry at Mark, with his gratitude. 'You saved my life, old man – I'll never be able to repay you.' But Aidan swore at him, told him he was not Mark's old man, that he did not want his gratitude and not to be a damned fool.

Three weeks after the accident, Will, Heath and Hugh Raymond arrived in Hobart Town, visited Aidan, sat in an awkward row and enraged him with their collective guilt.

When the visit was over, and they trooped downstairs to have tea with Mark and Berrima, they all proclaimed that they were relieved. They had thought to find him pale, thin, lethargic. Instead, he was surrounded by books and newspapers and notebooks, and his wits were sharpened. He had regaled them with a description of the timber business on the mainland, knew how much they would get for their timber before they had been to the mills, described the latest steam engines and sawing equipment to them.

'If he didn't do it so . . . so . . . furious-like, I'd be happy,' Will

584

said, rather miserably, holding the teacup awkwardly in one big fist, a muffin in the other. It was a large dining-room, but even so, Berrima smiled, the three piners seemed to fill it.

'He's keeping himself busy,' Berrima told them, 'I don't think he really wants to face the thought of how many months it'll be before he's well again.'

'He'll . . . come back, won't he?' Heath voiced the question that was in each of their minds.

Berrima looked at each of the open, simple, good faces before her. 'Yes,' she said gently. 'It was a clean fracture. Until now he's been very fit, his good health may mean that he'll heal quickly. We hope so.'

After a pause Will said, 'It must be hard on you. Him bellowing like that all the time.'

She laughed. 'I can understand it. He's never been really ill, has never cultivated the patience he'd need to deal with this. And I've been nursing for my father for several years, I'm accustomed to difficult patients.'

They promised, as they left, to come back the day after next. Berrima closed the door after them, and stood for a moment gazing around at the hall. She sighed as she crossed towards the stairs. It was a dark hall; Aidan had admitted to her that he had left the buying of the house in the hands of the bank and had never actually seen over the interior. Yet it was a comfortable house, she thought, as she climbed the stairs. Perhaps she could talk Aidan into having the hall repapered in a lighter colour than the brown and ivey-leafed pattern that so depressed her. Perhaps he would even have workmen enlarge the windows, let more light in . . .

Maura. She thought suddenly that it should be Maura who did these things.

Each time she visited Maura she found the woman nervous, apologetic, but adamant. She had been to visit Aidan once, she said, she could not bear to see him like that again. No, she could not go again. She would send the children if Aidan wished it, but she could not bear it, she could not.

Berrima discussed the matter with her father, but both agreed that there was little they could do. Milton suggested hiring a full-time nurse, but Berrima refuted the need for that. Aidan had saved Mark's life, Mark would insist that they nursed Aidan back to health. If Maura and the children would not move into the South Hobart house, then Mark and Berrima would stay as long as necessary.

She shut and locked the door of her own house in Battery Point with no real sense of despair. Even as a child she had loved the great house that had belonged to Colonel Atkins, the foreign smell of sandalwood that permeated all the rooms, for he had brought back many artifacts from his campaigns in the East; the large gardens with the follies and conservatories.

She paused, now, climbing the stairs, to look down over the now-overgrown garden. She was glad that Aidan had bought the property – even though he planned on subdividing and building cottages on the land, he had pledged himself to keep much of the gardens. She could understand that he liked the place, and felt a fierce pity for him in Maura's refusal to come here.

The more Berrima saw of Maura O'Brien, the more aggravated the younger woman became. Her father cautioned her to show understanding, the woman was of a highly-strung nature, and had been through God-only-knew what hardship in the Famine. The fact that she insisted on blotting her husband's illness from her mind, blotting her husband himself out of her mind, must surely show how disturbed she was.

Her father's forbearance, his ability to gaze at an emotionally-charged situation and be clinically detached enough to be compassionate, was all very well, Berrima thought. Privately, admitting this opinion to no one, she believed Maura to be a stony-hearted, selfish little scold who had no understanding of her husband, nor any desire to understand him.

Her hand tightened on the banister. How had he come to marry her, she asked herself, not for the first time; how could a man like Aidan marry such a woman?

She knocked briefly on his door and entered the room. Aidan had been reading; the newspaper from Melbourne was open at the Stock Exchange report, but he had let it fall back on his chest, and was gazing upwards at the ceiling. He looked over at her as she came in. 'Did I upset them?'

She slowed her pace, looking at him with concern. 'No. Why should you?'

'I talked at them, not with them.' He waited until she had sat down in the armchair close by his bed, her usual seat. She was wearing a mauve dress of light wool, a white bertha at the shoulders. With the petticoats and the broad crinoline that were the rage at the moment, the skirt of the frock was enormous. Berrima and Margaret Reynolds were the only women to visit him – he was unconscious when Maura had come, and sure these skirts would not appeal to Maura at all. But Aidan liked them. He was yet to see the wide-hooped skirts on anyone not possessing a tiny waist, and he

586

thought the fashion a pretty, if impractical, one. He thought Berrima looked like an overturned flower, blown along by the wind. It did not appear as if she had feet at all. Now, seated, the soft wool fell in folds about her. She was looking at him with the now-familiar compassion on her face.

'I suppose,' he said, 'the men's eyes nearly fell out of their heads when they saw this place, did they? They must think I'm a fierce fool, a real trawneen for buying it. It must be hard for you, after having your own home, to live in this mausoleum.'

'This house isn't a mausoleum. You love it, that's why you bought it.'

'It looks better looking at it than from it.' He was half-smiling.

'It needs only paint and wallpaper – perhaps to get rid of some of the heavy, dark furniture. And the drawing room is still full of stuffed animal's heads.'

'Mother of God, no! Is it? Why didn't you get rid of them?'

'I . . . I thought perhaps you might like them. A lot of men would.'

'Keeping decapitated heads of poor dead animals? Och, no, get away! Get rid of them, Berrima, please.'

'I shall,' she smiled.

He was studying her face. Perhaps it was his regret over his impatience with Will, Raymond and Heath, but he seemed more thoughtful. The frown, that perpetual frown of the past weeks since the accident, was gone from his face. With some relief she saw that the dark eyes were for once quiet.

Aidan was thinking, how has she stood the strain all this time? My own wife won't come near me – I'm only half a man, now. And this little one who I thought was so shallow, so selfish, has been tending me like a mother does a baby. He began to blush as he thought of the bathing, the bedpan duties that Berrima performed capably, dispassionately, without embarrassment. The first week after he had regained consciousness, each bathtime, each need to urinate was the cause of battles. 'I can do it meself!!' And he did not know what was worse, her quiet stubbornness going ahead with what she had to do despite his protests, or the knowledge – for he knew, as well as she – that he could not manage himself.

Aidan would have preferred to have Margaret Reynolds nurse him, even wished, sometimes, for Emily, now studying in New York. He would have felt happiest of all with a hired nurse – but Berrima would not hear of that. In her treatment of him she was proving herself capable, reliable, compassionate, patient. None of these qualities would he ever have ascribed to her. He had snarlingly told himself that she could not keep up the pretence, would dissolve into petulance at any time – he had even goaded her at times, hoping to see the spectacle. It would have vindicated his ill-opinion of her, justified him in his resentment of her. And his reasoning, as he lay there and gazed at her, was simple; Berrima as an unreliable, shallow woman could be dismissed easily from his thoughts; Berrima who betrayed Anna's characteristics and was truly as he had seen her these past few weeks, was a woman he could never forget.

But something was happening, through the anger that consumed him in finding himself trapped here, an invalid for the Lord knew how long; he could not help but see Berrima differently. He saw her each day; each day she was with him for hours at a time, and he could no longer brush away his knowledge that she was a special kind of person. It was odd, but he began to feel friendly towards her for the first time. He ceased to tease her, to treat her patronizingly; it was hard to be patronizing towards the woman who fed him, washed him, helped him on and off the bed-pan. Yet she never retaliated for all his patronizations, his sometime sarcasm. She helped him willingly, fondly. To have Berrima fond of him was almost more than he could bear.

'I've been a fierce burden to you, sure,' he said, now. Her eyes opened wide at this unheard-of humility. 'Half the time I growl because I'm unhappy over that. You're young, just married, you should be in your own home, taking care of your husband. Poor Mark must rarely see you, you seem to be always here tending to me, talking to me or reading to me.'

She looked taken aback, and avoided his eyes; her fluster was pretty to see. What a turn of events! He had longed to be in a situation where he might see her constantly – and here he was. From this position, prone on a bed as hard as the bunks at Brown's River, Berrima was very nearly all he did see.

'Mark doesn't mind. He's very grateful to you . . .' At one of his gestures of impatience, she said hastily, 'And it's no chore to nurse you, or to talk to you. You know that. You ought to know . . . in circumstances like that, it's no chore.'

'It should have been Maura. Your care of me is doubly gratifying in the circumstances . . .'

She said rather stiffly, 'I don't blame you for Maura not wishing to come.'

'Many would. I've not treated Maura well . . .'

'You're feeling sorry for yourself.'

He stared at her, surprised by the abruptness of her response, and began to scowl, 'I don't think I . . .'

588

'Yes, you were. Poor Aidan, abandoned by his wife in his hour of need, and it's his own fault for he drove her away. I don't believe that.' The hands folded in the lap of her dress gripped each other. 'You're a fine man, and any woman should be proud to be your wife. You're reliable . . . You don't . . . change, and play games with people. You don't mock others.'

'I mocked you. Many a time.'

She studied him, realizing there was something different in his tone. 'I never minded,' she said, softly. 'I'm grown up, now, Aidan, and I'm beginning to know how little I know. But when I was younger I was dreadfully sure of myself, sure that I could handle any situation.'

He smiled at her, 'I'm beginning to think that you can.'

'No.' Her voice was low, hard. She gazed at him with such a strange look on her face, a look he could not understand at all. He had not seen it before. 'I've learnt so much. Not that it's done much good.' Then she smiled. 'I'll have to see to dinner.' She rose, touched his hand briefly. He took it, and held it a moment while they gazed at each other, smiling. Then he let her go, and she left the room.

He was pleased with the gesture. It's because she trusts me, he thought happily. It's a sign of this new understanding between us. He did not really care for the reasons; to hold her was enough.

From that moment on it was easy for them to reach for each other. They often held hands while she read to him, letting go, calmly, only when someone entered the room.

Berrima thought, he is my friend. He saved my husband's life. It is innocent, it hurts no one. Somehow it gives him comfort. He is ill, he needs comfort. And I . . . I need comfort also.

Aidan was no longer so self-interested, so self-absorbed with his manic efforts at forgetting his illness. The initial shock had been absorbed into his mind, and he was beginning to cope with the thought of his slow recovery.

He was still troubled by pain, particularly at night; for in his sleep he could not help occasional, unconscious movements, small enough in themselves, but they wrenched his body, and made him cry out in agony. Milton had prescribed laudanum at night during the first weeks, but had cautioned Aidan against the use of it. 'Excellent painkiller,' he said, 'but addictive, it's been found. Opium in it, you know. That's what does it. So go easy with it, old chap, don't drink it like a hot toddy.'

Aidan disliked the word addictive, disliked the thought of being dependent on anything. Gradually he had cut down on the laudanum he took, and lately he was sleeping without it.

It took quite a few nights to realize that the muffled, raised voices and slammed doors, the lone horse that walked, late at night, up to the stables – Aidan's room overlooked the rear of the house – were not, as he had at first thought, a new circumstance, but had been going on for some time. He had simply not been awake to hear them. Berrima remained the same, cheerful, patient, but now Aidan studied the eyes that were faintly shadowed, the pale skin. This, too, was not new. He had thought it had been due to the strain of her nursing him, had urged her to hire more help than Nellie, who had come with her to her own house on her marriage, and now to Aidan's. Berrima had claimed that she needed no further help in the house, but now Aidan saw another reason behind this decision. There would be fewer servants to talk.

He decided not to waste time questioning Mark or Berrima, it would undoubtedly be useless. He decided to get to the bottom of the matter immediately, with the person who really understood what was going on. He decided to bribe Nellie.

'Oh, I don't know as I feel right about this, Mister O'Brien,' Nellie stood twisting the five pound note round and about in her hand, stepping from one foot to another and glancing at the door all the while. Mark was at the newspaper office, Berrima was shopping in Hobart Town, there was no chance of them being disturbed.

'It's grand that you're loyal to your mistress, Nellie.' Aidan spoke gently, wishing the girl would stop bobbing about like that, from his prone position it made his head swim. 'But it's Mrs Ellis I wish to help – and Mr Ellis, too, of course.'

'I can't say as I rightly think either is to blame, Mr O'Brien, not really. I don't want no trouble. I don't want neither of them hurt at all.'

'No, of course not. Nellie, could you stand still while you speak? Good girl . . . Nellie, is Mr Ellis in any sort of trouble?'

'Trouble? No, sir. Not that I know of. I think it's just the marriage problems between them, like. It happens with lots of folk. They get married, and then they find they don't like each other. It's that simple.'

She was right, dammit. But Mark and Berrima . . . 'What do they quarrel about, Nellie?'

'Oh, it's the same thing over and over. Mr Ellis – he will go out 'til all hours, and Miss Berrima – Mrs Ellis – will scold him for it, and most times she scolds him *before* he goes out, and it's got so I can't remember who started it, whether he goes to get away from her

590

scolding, or whether she's cross 'cause he goes.'

'What do they say to each other?'

' "You use me as a convenience! You don't love me!" That's what Mr Ellis says. "You want to change me! I am what I am!" an' that's not true, neither, 'cause before they was married you couldn't find a more serious nor sober young man than Mister Mark. An' Miss Berrima, she cries and says, "You've changed already, you got no heart! You didn't treat me like this afore we was married! You go off with your . . ." ' Nellie stopped, lowered her voice, 'She accuses him of goin' off with other women, Mr O'Brien.'

'And does he, do you think?'

Her eyes opened wide. 'Mr O'Brien, how am I supposed to know?' He continued to look at her. She relented. 'My brother's a bit of a wag. Not bad you understand, but a bit of a flash cove. He says he's seen Mister Mark at some gambling places.'

'So he's losing money . . .'

'Oh, no! He's not a card sharp or a gambler.' Her face softened, 'He's unhappy-like. Can't you tell? It's that sad. I don't reckon it's Miss Berrima's fault. But they can't talk to each other no more. If they ever did. She shouldn't have married him, Mr O'Brien, and that's the truth. He's good-looking and so persuasive, he could talk a woman into anything, that man. Fair breaks your heart when he smiles at you. He got real sick, y' see, noomonia, it was, just when he'd given up all hope of her marryin' him. But Miss Berrima visited him, and he begged so hard for her to take pity on him . . . That's how it was, y' see, Mr O'Brien. I can't tell you much more'n that. They'll settle down. All young couples go through times like this, don't they? It's a matter of getting used to each other, like.'

That evening, when Mark called in to Aidan's room before dinner, Aidan asked him if they could drink a whiskey together. 'I've not touched the stuff for six months or more – it's about time.'

'I don't think Milton would . . .' Mark scowled, but saw Aidan's face, and grinned. 'I'll fetch the bottle from downstairs.'

Aidan did not know what Mark told Berrima, but for more than an hour they were not disturbed. Aidan had two whiskeys, though he longed for more. He was not wrong, however, in his assumption that Mark would drink more than he.

They began talking about the newspaper. Mark was full of enthusiasm. Though they had hired an editor, it was not a permanent position. Mark was determined to take over that role in the near future. Aidan was pleased to see that it was not problems at the newspaper that were causing any stress in Mark. He allowed the younger man to talk on at length, then interrupted, 'I thought perhaps,' very carefully, 'that you had some worries about the business.'

'I? No, not at all. It's running splendidly. It's those free first copies that did it, and announcing that it was under new management.'

'I think Berrima thought that you were under some strain, that you felt you couldn't talk about it.'

Mark's face, instead of the open boyish enthusiasm, was suddenly set, cold. 'She told you that?'

'No. Berrima would not discuss you even if I asked her outright. You know that her first loyalty is to you.' Mark looked a little mollified. 'But I've noticed something in the air. You know, lying here day after day, tracing the plaster cupids in the ceiling, one's after sensing things.'

'You can hear us screaming at each other.'

'Yes. Things like that.'

Aidan half-smiled. Mark stood, and walked over to the window. It had been raining, and the garden was washed clean in the evening light. Aidan could see him, but only with difficulty, as Mark was half behind the head of the bed. He did not want to ask him to return, however. If Mark thought more clearly by the window, let him stay. Aidan gazed at the ornate ceiling above his head and waited.

'It'd be good to talk. My own parents wouldn't like to hear these things, and I can't go to Milton and Margaret . . . I have my own reasons to believe why Berrima married me.' He turned back to Aidan, saw that it was difficult for the man to see him, and moved closer to the bed. Aidan assumed Mark would speak, but he did not. He simply stood there, head turned on one side, the better to see Aidan's face, a calm look in his eyes, as though he studied a painting that half-pleased, half-displeased him. Yet gradually, imperceptibly, Mark's mouth was hardening. The eyes had not lost their calm, appraising look, but the mouth was hard.

Something was not quite right. Aidan's sixth sense that guarded his self-preservation, dormant since he had been released from prison, awoke with jangling nerve-ends, wordless messages. The part of his mind that helped him sense a warning in the false calm of groups of men who hated him, the shaped steel, the hidden razors . . . This silent alarm was now telling him to beware.

He could not ignore the warnings, lay looking up at Mark with his impenetrable look while his mind told him *he means me harm. He wishes to harm me*. And he tried to cope with the suddenness, the illogicality of these feelings. He did not understand. If he died

592

now . . . Mark's eyes had flickered to Aidan's pillow, and back to his face – Jaysus! – if he died now, he would not know why.

If he puts the pillow over my face, Aidan was thinking, could I fight him off? In these weeks I've grown weaker, and the pain would weaken me further. He's taller than me, but his arms and shoulders aren't as strong as mine. It'd be a fifty-fifty chance . . .

But the danger had passed. Mark had moved back to the window abruptly, and his shoulders were slumped. He placed his forehead against the glass.

It was over. Aidan began to breathe again, deeply. Could he have been wrong? No. No, look at him, the shoulders drooped in a kind of defeat. For a while, for a little while there, he had been ready for something. And Aidan smiled a little, realizing he was safe for all time. Now, Aidan drinking whiskey – which in his weakened state could have brought on a stroke – now was the right time to kill him. But Mark had not. Mark would not.

Only then the words came back, the last words Mark had said, *I have my own reasons to believe why Berrima married me* . . .

Myself? It was something to do with myself? He felt disproportionately elated for several seconds. But no, it could not be. Nothing had happened, nothing at all. Whatever reason Mark had for jealousy lay in his own mind.

'I'd loved Berrima for so long,' Mark was saying, his voice calm, thin, detached. He kept his gaze on the wet garden below. It was darkening by the minute. 'When she married me, I felt sure she loved me. I was ill, you see, and it wasn't, perhaps, a bad thing. The thought of losing me for ever was what decided her on marrying me, once I was well, but . . .' There was a long pause. 'There were things she wished to escape from, weren't there?'

Aidan waited. Then, 'Were there?' he queried.

Mark turned to him. Aidan thought, I shouldn't goad him. For he was realizing, at last, that for all Mark's good-humour and control, the man was unstable.

Mark smiled. 'Now, right now, I feel as if I've been a fool. A fool for allowing Berrima to marry me, a fool for believing that it would work out any better than it has.'

'She loves you, Mark.'

'No. She . . .' Again the silence, and Aidan waited, frowning, not knowing what to expect. Mark murmured, finally, almost sulkily, 'She's disappointed in me.'

'Not at all! You must stop – if you're looking for faults in your marriage, you'll find them, boyo. Try looking for what's good and strong in your marriage . . .'

'Does that help you in yours?' They stared at each other. Then Mark was saying quickly, 'No, I'm sorry, I shouldn't have said that. To have your own marriage fail, you'd see more clearly the reason why. I'm grateful for your understanding, Aidan.' He stood looking awkward for a moment, then said, simply, and Aidan thought genuinely, 'I appreciate what you're trying to do . . . I understand it's not easy for you. I *understand*.' His look was somehow intense. But then he smiled, quickly, almost too abruptly, waving his hands in a gesture that was strangely awkward for him, 'I've been drinking too much, I know that. It's the work, I suppose, and the worry over what's happening with Berrima. You've been trying to say that the fears are inside my own head.' Aidan said nothing, merely watched him. 'Yes, perhaps you're right. I think . . .' he gazed out the window once more, began tapping his fingers in a tattoo on the window sill, 'that I have been a fool.'

Still Aidan refrained from comment. Berrima came into the room, then, and the whiskey bottle was taken from them. She did not make as much fuss as the guilty pair had supposed, but commandeered the little that was left – Mark had been drinking seriously all this time – and hustled her husband from the room.

After that, the atmosphere in the house improved. Aidan would have liked to have spoken to Berrima, but kept postponing it. He told himself, as he had told Mark, that she would not wish to speak to him. But it was not that. He did not want, at this time, to look too deeply into Berrima's soul. He realized with an odd feeling that of all the women had ever known, he was a little afraid of her. Or, not of her, exactly, but of the feelings she awoke within him. They were of giant proportions – it was ridiculous, but he was afraid they were capable of devouring his reasoning. Berrima was like a Pandora's Box that he did not wish to look too closely into.

He waited to see if the talk with Mark had any effect. When it appeared that Mark was settling down, his fears – Aidan somehow sensed that they were concerned with himself – were put to rest, and Aidan did not see any reason to talk to Berrima about her marriage. Mark came home earlier, the bitter words in the night were no longer heard, and though Mark still drank – he took to sharing a bottle with Aidan every few nights – it was nothing that was uncontrollable. Aidan watched Berrima relax, regain some of her colour, saw that even Nellie was less tense, heard the servant singing occasionally around the house. It occurred to Aidan to wonder, sometimes, what the reasons were that Mark spoke of, that had resulted in that moment of danger when the two of them were alone. Had the man been foolish enough to believe that there had been something between himself and Berrima? He could have believed that, given Mark's possessive nature, his volatile, imaginative character.

What would he have done, Aidan smiled to himself sometimes, if he had known that my intentions towards Berrima were never anything but of the most dishonourable kind? He congratulated himself that Mark was over these suspicions, congratulated himself that he had placed the man's mind at rest. He went back to his Stock Exchange reports and bank statements and his study of real estate, telling himself smugly that even flat on one's back, one could manipulate people and situations if one was clever enough.

Aidan awoke from a doze and for a moment believed himself to be dreaming. Liam stood before him, at the foot of the bed, a chunky, well-formed boy of fifteen, now. His mouth was a tight line. Beside him, Clemency, almost the same height, the same dark auburn hair pulled back in tight pigtails that fell to her waist, stood gripping the foot board.

Liam said, 'It's true, isn't it? You've been ill all this time, and haven't wanted us with you. Hell's outhouse, Father! Why didn't you tell us? *Why?*'

Aidan came awake completely. 'How did you get here?' He stared at them, standing there like vengeful wraiths, the two freckled faces, the eyes, one pair brown, the other green, gazing at him accusingly.

'We took a cab,' Clemency said, 'We used our pocket money and our savings.'

'Why didn't you tell us?' Liam repeated.

'I . . . I didn't want to worry you, son. I'll be better soon.'

'You told all the grown-ups.' Clemency again.

'Aye,' her brother put in, 'You told everyone else. You told Ma. You'd have been better off telling us instead of Ma.'

'Why?' Although he knew, he did not want to find that they knew.

'You know what she's like.' Simply, stolidly.

Clemency came from behind the foot of the bed to gaze down at her father. 'I heard her talking to Mrs Ellis today. Ma was crying . . .'

'What a to-do that was! Hell's outhouse, Father, how could you let . . .'

'What's this "hell's outhouse", tell me? Where did you find that?'

'One of the boys at school made it up,' Liam said, with just a hint of sheepishness, before hurrying on. 'Why should Ma go on like that? I don't think she likes Mrs Ellis – and she was only trying to talk Ma into coming here . . .'

'Where's Mrs Ellis, now?'

'She's still there. Or she was when we left. I told Liam, and we both listened for a while, and then we came here. Does it hurt very much, Papa?'

'Yes, Rebel. If I try to move. If I lie still, I'm all right.'

'Will you . . . walk again, Father?' Liam's face was pale behind the freckles.

'Yes. There's no permanent damage done. The bone has to set, that's all. When the accident happened Doctor Reynolds stuck pins in my toes to see if I had any feeling in them. I very nearly bit his head off. He doesn't do it anymore.'

Only Clemency smiled, and it was a half-hearted smile. He realized, suddenly, that he had underestimated them greatly, both their maturity and their understanding. Clemency sighed, a little breathy sigh. 'To think you've been here all this time.'

'Well, we're not going back, and that's that.' Liam's brown eyes below the thick dark brows glared at Aidan over the foot of the bed. 'You can't chase us to hit us, Father, and we're not going. Please,' he added, a little to mitigate his defiance.

Aidan tried to scowl, but the two faces were determined – though Clemency took a step back, out of his reach.

He smiled, then, held his hand out to Clemency. As she took it, hesitantly, he addressed both of them. 'I want you here. Don't be believing for a moment that I don't. But your mother and I have had a difference of opinion . . .'

'You *always* had different opinions . . .' Liam began.

'Listen now. It would be grand, so it would, if we all could live together here. But your mother isn't strong, and she's not accustomed to nursing. Mrs Ellis is; and living here, I'm directly next door to my doctor. Do you see?' Oh, this was grand – liar that I am . . . But what else to tell them? What?

The auburn heads nodded. 'But Ma cries a lot,' Clemency said.

'Yes. And she talks of home all the time. Ireland, I mean. "Oh, if only we hadn't left home, oh, if only we'd stayed in Killaloe." '

Clemency said, 'She doesn't really mean it – she just wants to be poor again so she won't have to have servants.'

Aidan laughed. He pulled her to him and hugged her, despite the pain the gesture caused him. 'Do you think your Ma would like to live here? What do you think?'

They turned to gaze at each other. 'Well,' Liam stated gloomily, 'she's not happy where she is, sure.'

Aidan was silent, thinking hard. He had it in his power to order Maura to hand over the children to him. Legally he was head of the house, and possessed powers not only over the children, but over Maura herself. He could force her, by law, to return to his house, his bed. His mouth curved wryly. A grand victory, sure.

He looked up at the children, both watching him expectantly. Clemency said, 'Can we stay with you, Papa?'

It tore the heart in him. For if Maura had not been a good mother, he was no better as a father. Yet they wished to be with him.

'Liam, go to the dresser, there. Take a pound from the money you'll find in a wallet in the top drawer.'

'You're sending us away . . .' Clemency's soft little voice, almost a wail.

'Arra, Rebel, you know you have to go home tonight for sure. Take a cab again, and explain to your ma.' They both began to speak. 'I know you'll be in trouble, but you shouldn't have crept away like that. Tell her I want to see her, that we have to talk.'

'Will you ask her to come here to live? Will you, Papa?'

'I'll . . . I'll talk with her about it, Rebel. I can't do more than that.'

The children begged to be able to return the following Saturday, to spend the entire day, and Aidan agreed. But first they must check with their mother.

They left, then, a trifle apprehensive, but determined to have the business over with. When the front door shut behind them Aidan heard it echoing through the silent house, a final sort of sound. He wondered where Nellie had been during all this, then forgot her, turning to gaze at the oh-so-familiar ceiling and wonder what to do in the matter of his family.

Nellie appeared an hour later, apologized for being away, but she had to buy some flour for tonight's pudding . . . Was there anything she could fetch for him, now?

Only Berrima, Aidan thought grimly. He was about to say, 'No, thank you, Nellie', when the sound of the front door opening was heard, followed by Berrima's quick steps on the parquet floor. 'Yes, tell Mrs Ellis I'd like to speak to her, would you?'

Nellie left, and after a short pause, Berrima swept into the room. Her cheeks were pink, her nose was pink, for the day was cold and a keen wind was blowing down from the direction of the snow on Mount Wellington and the hills beyond.

'Oh, dear, I'm exhausted. So much shopping to do. I've told Nellie to bring us tea. Would you like that? Come, I'll put a few pillows behind your head.' She had walked over to him, taken the pillows from the lower shelf of the bureau, placed them behind his head. She smiled at him, and went to step away – but found her wrist suddenly held in a grip that made her wince. 'Aidan . . . ?'

'Sit down.'

'I was about to.' Her eyes went to her chair.

'Not there, here.' He pulled, and she sat down abruptly on the edge of the bed.

'Aidan, what's the matter? Let go . . .'

'So much shopping to do. So many little things you need for the house . . .'

'Yes. You told me you wanted new curtains in the drawing room, and I told you the couch needed recovering . . .'

'And my wife? Did you feel she would look attractive between the grandfather clock and the potted palm? Did you think the decor screamed out for a little red-haired woman with a perpetual scowl on her face . . . !'

'Aidan! Stop it!'

Still he did not let go her wrist. He was tensing himself, the pain was beginning to spread, down his legs, up to his shoulders; he tried to relax, but still did not let go his grip on her wrist. He had not realized how furious he was until he saw her. 'Damn your interference!' he breathed. 'Damn your insidious, helpful, officious little mind! You're a meddling little *maicin*, aren't you? If I want to see my wife, *I'll* send for her, do you understand?' The fingers of her other hand were tugging at the grip he had upon her. He imprisoned that wrist, too. 'I don't want Maura here. Do you not understand that?'

'I was trying to help!' She was close to tears.

'Help! And how would it help me, having her here, when I know what seeing illness does to her, tell me. She can't bear it! She'd only be after forcing herself to look on me, and her fear and disgust would be written on her face. Do you think I want that?' He shook her. 'Do you?'

'No! I didn't think! Aidan, don't be cruel . . . ! Have you no understanding? Let me be! Let go! You're cruel, Aidan!'

He stopped shaking her. Still held on to her, for it was good to hold her, the anger between them was good, the tenseness, the outpouring of rage. It was good, even Berrima's tears were stilled, she glared at him now, angry herself.

'I was trying to help you! It wasn't the first time I visited Maura! I've gone every few days, to tell her how you are, to ask her to visit you. She . . . she doesn't like me, I think she resents me for being able to care for you – but I understand her a little. We talked of the Famine, and all that had happened. There are reasons why she feels the way she does, Aidan, I understand perhaps better than you, for you've never taken the trouble to talk to her!'

598

'How dare you go sneaking off to her behind my back . . .!'

'How dare you say you don't want her in your house! She's your wife, and she loves you! And you have a duty towards her!' Still she struggled to pull herself from his grasp, but he would not let her go. 'I was trying to do the right thing! The best thing for everybody! It can't go on the way it is! It can't! You must bring Maura back! I can't bear it! You must! . . .'

He let her go, slowly, she was weeping again quietly, with the strength of her emotions, though she turned her face away, furious with herself. He reached beneath his pillow for his handkerchief. She glared at him, was about to deny the need of it, then finally snatched it out of his hand.

Aidan watched her. 'Ah,' he breathed, and there were words and words in the exhalation. So she had broken under the strain after all. Sure, he could not blame her. She had been grand – but in his selfishness, he had not noticed her tiring. He had preferred to grasp at the excuse of her troubles with Mark, when it was actually he himself that was the burden on her.

She had blown her nose, wiped her tears, now sat glaring at him. 'Surely I don't have to explain . . .'

'Och, there's no need to explain. I just . . . I'd rather hire a nurse, Berrima. I don't think Maura would come.'

'Aidan, you must understand . . .'

'I know Maura . . .'

'Aidan . . . Aidan! How can a man be so obtuse!'

He scowled at her, and decided to wait until she explained herself. She took his hand. 'Aidan, we are friends, aren't we?'

'Of course.'

'Sometimes, with friends . . .' He was looking at her suspiciously. He did not like the manner in which she was addressing him, as if he were a child, a simple child.

She began again, 'I owe it to Mark. I married Mark. I loved him, then, and it wasn't difficult – I loved his faithfulness, his patience, his gentleness – and he was so ill. He *needed* me. Yet I shouldn't have married him. To marry someone because you feel . . .' She lowered her head, and looked away. 'Cheated,' she said, her voice tight, constrained, 'thwarted by . . . by fate, I suppose – to marry Mark for the love that he could give me – oh, it was wrong. It was a childish gesture, and I'm so ashamed of it!

'And Mark knows – he knows! I think that's what's driving him mad. I must love him, I must make it up to him. I must give him all that I promised him the day we were married. I can't do it here, now. I'm right, aren't I? Aidan, it's best, isn't it?'

He said, through numb lips, forcing his numb brain to function, 'Aye, if Mark's jealous of me, he should take you back to your own house. Sure, I never meant to monopolize your attentions. I'll . . . I'll miss you. But what you say – it's perfectly good sense. Go back to your house with Mark, so.'

She still held his hand. He noticed she had stopped breathing, stared at him. He did not understand her intensity. Why should she feel guilty about wishing to spend more time with her husband? It only hurt him to hear her talk about it like this. She could not know it, he must not blame her, but it hurt that she wished so to be a good wife for Mark, that she wished to devote her love, her life, *to Mark*. Arra, he knew all that. Did she have to turn it into a drama for him?

She took a deep breath and rose from the bed. Like her husband a few days before, she walked to the window, and leaned her head against the glass. Aidan was filled with a feeling of *deja vu*. In a moment, Berrima would say, 'I've loved Mark for so long . . .' He could not bear it. His body began to prickle with pain that he knew was caused by tension. This ill-starred love affair was aggravating. To hear them moan about each other was aggravating. What malign fate had brought these two into his life, anyway? The cottiers in Killaloe – even Maura and himself – managed to simplify matters. Either one was rutting with one's wife, or one was not. He tightened his lips in savage humour; this was obviously one of the prices one paid for becoming middle-class. One had so much more time to wonder if one was happy or miserable. And even the misery must be graded and studied.

Watch her. Oh, God, Anna's profile against the pale light of the dusk! She will say, 'You must understand about Mark . . .' or, 'Mark and I . . .'

Without moving, she said, 'You are a selfish, complacent, boring, thick-skinned, ignorant swine of an Irishman.'

A few seconds had passed. He realized she was looking at him, that his mouth had fallen open.

'I can understand why your wife lives three miles across a city from you. I can understand how your constant self-interest and . . . blindness to her needs drove her from you. You couldn't even understand, didn't try to understand, what I've been doing in visiting her, in attempting to bring her here. You can't see any point of view but your own . . .'

'My point of view, as you put it, is fairly limited . . .' he began icily.

'Oh, no! Don't attempt that! Don't attempt to blame things on the accident! You'd be your old impervious, sullen self standing on

600

your feet or on your head, Aidan O'Brien.'

'What did I say?' he asked the ceiling with wild exasperation. 'Jaysus, Mary and Joseph, has the girl gone mad?'

'Yes! Oh, yes! That has to be it!' She was furious. 'It's my fault, all my fault!'

'What are we arguing about?'

'Nothing! Everything! You! Listen, Aidan, just listen for a moment.' She walked towards the bed. 'Today Maura agreed to consider returning. And she has every right to, and you have the responsibility to help her all you can.'

'Don't try to lecture me on . . .'

'You'll be well, soon. Next year you could be back cutting pine at Port Davey, who knows? But Aidan, what if you don't get well? What if this isn't as simple a fracture as Father believed?'

'Stop it,' he breathed. 'Stop it, Berrima.' His fingers itched. If he could reach her he would shake the life out of her . . .

'You must consider it! Hiring servants to look after you may be all very well – but Aidan, your capital may not last for ever. You don't need a servant, Aidan, you need someone who *cares*. And it cannot be me. Oh, my dear, it cannot be me.'

Her tone had changed, there was something in her voice that made him study her. The words went through him like steel – she was telling him that she did not care, could not care for him, though she pitied him.

In his own prison of his emotions, a captive of his past, he could see no further than this. Berrima, warm, loving, independent, trapped by duty and her upbringing, spoke the only words that she could speak. Aidan in his ignorance, heard only the words. Berrima reached to him from beyond the years of her training; obedience, graciousness, honour, integrity – these words, in kind and loving terms, had formed the path of her childhood. She could not break from that, for beyond lay chaos. This man meant chaos. She said, with forced calm, 'Maura is trying to do her best. She says she will come to see you, to discuss it. You'll listen to her, won't you? You *must*. Promise me you won't allow your pride and the bitterness of the past to intrude. Promise me!'

'Yes,' he said sullenly, hating her. He was losing her. She wanted to be free of him. He struggled to consider her point of view, that her place was with her husband, as Maura's place was with him, but the thought kept intruding, relentlessly, that he was losing her.

There was a slight noise from the doorway. The door was ajar. Someone coughed in the hall, then the door was pushed completely open.

601

Maura stood there. She came into the room, in her cape and bonnet; the quick green eyes, unsure, flitted from Berrima to Aidan. They both stared at her, almost superstitiously, as if their conversation had conjured her up.

'My cab passed the children's. We all came back together. When I couldn't find them, I realized where they'd gone, you see. I came after them . . .'

'We're so glad you did.' The warmth, the welcome in Berrima's voice as she smiled at Maura.

There was an awkward pause, for the warmth in Berrima's face was not reflected in Maura's. The green eyes behind the gold-rimmed spectacles were steady, unreadable. Berrima said, 'I don't know what's happened to Nellie. I'll have her send up the tea for you.' And she was gone.

Aidan wanted to call her back, to say, Don't go! You belong here, *you!* This is wrong, wrong! But his gaze caught Maura's.

He was taken aback to see compassion there in the green depths. Compassion with the fear, the questioning. It was strange, but he realized, suddenly, how frail she was. It was not only her build, for she and Berrima were both light-boned, fair-skinned. It was an emotional frailty that Maura possessed.

He wondered why she should look apprehensive, then thought of quite a few reasons why she would be. Why, he thought, for all her hardness, her unrelenting malevolence when enraged, she is really a weak woman. Berrima, little, young, silly Berri, is stronger than Maura. And he somehow sensed it was not the Famine that had done this to his wife. Maura would have been Maura even without the Famine.

She removed her bonnet, crossed the room to sit in the chair, Berrima's chair, and gazed at him. He thanked God that she did not begin her gambit with the inanities of asking after his health. Then he scowled, for she was thinner, paler . . . She began to speak, but had to stop to cough. It rattled in her chest. Aidan scowled in concern, but before he could speak, she said, 'I'll come and live here with the children, Aidan, if it's what you want.'

'Yes,' he said. 'It would be best.'

'I . . . I'd feel better, though, if Berrima and Mark would stay. Sure it'd be for a short time only, while I settled in. I've not been well lately. Only a chill, but my cough won't get better. I'd find it difficult to nurse you alone. I like Berrima and Mark very much, and . . . it's such a big house, is it not? Bigger than the one at Moonah. It'd be like home, having a lot of people about; sure I'd like that.'

'I would, too, sure.'

She smiled, as if it were settled; Aidan had no illusions, this was no reunion of souls, let alone bodies. Maura would be a presence in the house, but not the dominant centre of it. He realized that despite her guilt, she was undoubtedly happier living alone in Moonah. Thin as she was, the bonnet that now lay on her lap was quite fashionable, and she had looked well in it. She had made a separate life for herself; it would be no less separate for living under the same roof with him. Each time they returned to each other, it was with more aloofness than before.

Nellie brought the tea things, only two cups. Aidan asked after Mrs Ellis, and was told that she had a headache and was lying down in her room. She would not be down for dinner.

'Do you know,' Maura said, almost mischievously, after Nellie had gone, 'from the way Berrima speaks, I'd almost be thinking she had a bit of a *grá* for you.'

Aidan spoke, and only after he spoke did he hear the moroseness in his own voice. 'Why should she be after being in love with me when she's married Mark Ellis?'

'Och, I was codding you. She's simply fond of you, and respects you, the same as her father, I'm thinking.' Maura smiled as she poured the tea, with all the confidence of the mistress of the house. She smiled, yet the treacherous eyes had narrowed. When she spoke again it was about the children, but in her mind she was hearing, as she had heard as she approached the door, Berrima's words, and the desperate emotion behind them, 'You need someone who *cares*. And it cannot be me. Oh, my dear, it cannot be me.'

59

Australia was moving forward; the recession of the 1840s was behind her; the new machines, the new technologies, were being put to use in factories founded by men who had come from Britain and other countries as struggling emigrants. The squatters, those who had staked out their vast tracts of land, made their fortunes and now sat in their Antipodean castles in nervous splendour, listened to the terms Liberalism, Classless Society, Land for the People, then looked over their vast, untenable kingdoms, and worried.

The enormous effects of the Australian gold rushes were felt everywhere. Though so few made fortunes, the very fact that some had, and had moved upwards in this society that was based, not on titles or breeding, but increasingly more on wealth and its attendant power, made the people confident. Things could change. Life was not static as it had been back home. A man whose family had been peasants for generations, could become wealthy, begin his own colonial dynasty. Newspapers gleefully reported the cases of good fortune; the tales of misfortunes, hardship, failure and illness on the gold fields, did not interest people half so well.

Democracy was a popular theme; though the majority of the wealth in the country was still held by the squatters, who claimed that Australia's development was best served by a pastoral-based economy, few, as the 1860s advanced, could accept this.

In the more established cities of the huge colonies, chimney stacks rose and belched smoke, machines steamed and heaved and whirred; railways began to reach out from the major cities. The myth of the Real Australia was kept alive by the knowledge of the broad, seemingly endless plains of the interior of the country, where only the handful of squatters clung tenaciously to fight the land for their living. The Australian settlers had always clung to the rich coastal plains, where the land and the weather were more generous to them; now, in the cities that had grown up around the shorelines, the machines moved and made money. Together with the rest of the world in the latter part of the nineteenth century, men gathered to the machines. The true Australia, that nation of coast-dwellers, began to cohere, to question, to demand.

In Tasmania, ten thousand men left the colony to join the gold rushes of the 1850s, and this hampered the movement for the colony's political and social reforms. Those men who would have agitated for greater political freedom, for the lessening of the stranglehold on the land by a few landowners, had gone to the mainland in search of a better life.

Aidan lay on his back in the high-ceilinged room in Glenleigh, and read newspapers from each of the Australian colonies, and realized that he might be stultified by staying in Tasmania.

It occurred to him, briefly, to take his family and move to Melbourne. There he could change his name, invest his capital quietly, and begin afresh. Maura would like that. To remain in Tasmania would mean a greater struggle to achieve what he desired; land, a property of his own, and the increasing profits from other sources – timber, businesses, real estate – that would enable him to live confidently should crops and stock prices fail him. It was yet another lesson learnt from the potato blight, he thought bitterly. Never rely on one crop, one staple, no matter how certain it appeared.

Yes, Victoria, and its capital city of Melbourne – it had many possibilities. It had been at Ballarat, on the Victorian goldfields in 1854 that the Eureka Stockade had taken place; miners, driven to desperation by the severe licencing laws, and the corrupt police force that enforced them, had rebelled and declared an Australian Republic. Thirty-four miners had died in the ensuing skirmish. Though five policemen were killed, not a jury could be found who would convict the thirteen miners accused of high treason, and the miners' leader, Peter Lalor, Irish like most of the other miners at Eureka, had subsequently entered politics. Aye, Victoria was the place to be, now, Aidan thought. It was a rich and still expanding colony, and there was a growing middle class with a democratic and liberal outlook.

Or perhaps he should go even further north, across the border to New South Wales. Sydney was said to be a beautiful city. It had an excellent deep-water harbour – he liked that thought, for ships and the building of ships still interested him. And he had maps of Port Jackson, had studied the waterways around Sydney – so many rivers ran into the harbour – and where there was water, there would be industry.

Both colonies attracted him. The thought of making more money, of leaving his convict past behind, attracted him.

But then Berrima would walk into his room, and his thoughts of a new life would be thrown into confusion. A sensible man did not stay in a colony in which the economy was uncertain, simply because of a woman – and that woman another man's wife.

Maura and the children and the housemaid, Jane, moved from the Moonah cottage to Glenleigh. And Mark and Berrima, when Maura approached them, agreed to remain.

Many days the two families did not meet except at evening meal times. Maura, in the freedom that Jane and Nellie's presence forced on her, had begun taking up charity works; visiting poorer families in the city, and serving on committees, helping to decorate St Francis's church with flowers from Glenleigh's gardens.

And Maura appeared to be content, though her cough did not disappear, and she spent many rainy days in her room, afraid of a further chill. She had two rooms to herself in the furthest corner of the house – when Berrima suggested she and Mark give up their bedroom so Maura could be closer to Aidan, she gently refused, saying it would disturb matters, and that she was quite happy with

605

her rooms, overlooking the front garden and the new cottages being built on the property.

Early in 1863, Will married Cora in Hobart Town, and they called to see Aidan, Cora in a cream lace and muslin gown that had belonged to her mother. The reception was to be held at the homestead in Huonville, and Aidan had a suspicion that the ceremony had been performed in Hobart in order that he would feel included on the day.

Cora, her thin, rather plain face alight with happiness, clung to Will's arm, and they, both of them, brought such an atmosphere of pleasure and optimism to the great house, and to Aidan's sickroom, that he hated to see them leave.

Maura watched them as they chatted to Aidan, reliving the ceremony and telling him their plans for their honeymoon in Launceston before returning to Port Davey. And she felt a bitter envy. Envy and sadness, for what she saw as the inevitable disillusionment that awaited these two.

Aidan watched her face, and wondered what she was thinking, whether she was remembering the fiasco of their own wedding; if she had any regrets. Yes. She must, she must . . .

But sure, it would be different for Cora and Will. One could not find a woman further removed from Emily, Aidan thought, than Cora. Mature in her outlook, droll in her humour, one whom life had already marked but had not broken. Kind, but not over-imaginative, her needs were simple. No, she was not Emily. But in the end, Aidan wondered if Cora might not be a more suitable wife. The looks she gave Will were full of fondness, and when she rose from her chair, she reached out to touch her new husband's shoulder with a charmingly tender, possessive gesture. Yes, Aidan thought, an affectionate woman. It may all work out for the best, so. They were friends, their entire relationship had developed from their friendship. And he, too, felt a touch of envy.

He was able to walk out on to the landing to bid the couple goodbye. And over the next few weeks, he spent more and more time learning to walk again. Slowly, painfully, using first two sticks, then one, worrying about his slow recuperation, trying to brush away the fear that he would not be able to return to Port Davey.

And at the same time, he knew that as his health improved, so the time drew closer when Berrima and Mark would leave. He told himself that he should not ask for too much, Berrima could not remain within his house for ever, but the thought came back that he would like her to.

Berrima said to him, once, coming into the room to collect the washbasin and towels, for he now washed himself, 'You're happy, now, aren't you, Aidan?'

It was more statement than question. He looked up at her; he was dressed in a suit and tie, and was seated in the chair pushed over to the window. In the nearly seven weeks since Maura and the children had come to Glenleigh, it was the nearest she had come to mentioning anything personal since the night of their quarrel.

'Happy? Sure, that's a strange word to use. I don't aim for happiness. And while I'm using . . .' He began to gesture towards his walking sticks.

'No, I meant, you're happier, aren't you, now that you have your family about you? It's good to have the children here, isn't it?'

He smiled at her. 'And I think Maura's content, is she not?'

Berrima almost seemed to hesitate, but she returned his smile. 'Yes, yes, I think so.'

She had picked up the washbasin, but he was reluctant to let this new mood of intimacy pass, and said quickly, 'And you? Are you happy?'

Her back was half-turned to him. He saw the slight stiffening of her shoulders, the sudden, fleeting and unreadable change of expression on her face. She turned to him with her usual gentle smile, 'I don't aim for happiness, either. Rather, a kind of contentment.'

She placed the basin down again, and sat on the edge of the bed, frowning slightly. He felt a small thrill of delight that she wished to stay and talk.

'Mark's trying very hard to make a success of the newspaper. I don't see him as often as I'd like. He's pleased with the work that I do periodically to help him, has even asked me to the office sometimes, to learn a little more about the business. I'm very flattered.' Her smile flashed, her eyes alight. 'It's not every man who would wish his wife to be included in his business life, is it? He must trust me, and feel that I can be of some value to him.'

Aidan was gazing at her for too long. He could think of nothing to say, because what she was telling him did not please him. Berrima herself looked suddenly unsure. Went on, like plunging into a pool, the depth of which was uncertain. 'That's important to me, you see. To know that he trusts me, and includes me in his world, doesn't shut me out. The trouble we had recently, it's over – thanks, a great deal, to you. I'm . . . yes, I am happy, now. I have all I need. Mark is the same as he was when I began to love him; considerate and kind. A woman couldn't wish for a better husband.'

The towels were still held in her hands. Aidan glanced down to see that she was rolling the cloth's edge back and forth between her fingers, rather quickly, nervously; it was at odds with her calm speech.

'He's . . . We've thought of moving to Melbourne. Not now.' She saw him stiffen. 'In a few years, when the *Chronicle* might fetch a good price. Things are difficult in this colony, as you know . . .'

'I've often thought of Melbourne myself. I'll be going there briefly as soon as I'm well enough, to look about at investment possibilities there.'

'Oh.' Her face was calm. 'So you'll be coming back and forth quite often.'

'Yes,' he said. *I'll not let you go so easily. Melbourne or Sydney or Brisbane or back to England, I'll not let you leave my life.* 'To and from Sydney, also,' he said. 'I've occasionally seen partnerships in businesses there that interest me.'

'Oh,' she repeated, nodding in a preoccupied manner.

'When were you planning on going to Melbourne?' he asked.

'It's rather vague – a few years away, at least.'

The stitching at the edge of the towel was coming away with her picking at it. When he looked up, their gazes locked; both felt awkward suddenly, somehow embarrassed. When Nellie knocked on the door and entered they both started.

'Dinner's served below, Miss Berrima, an' Jane's comin' up with your tray bye'n'bye, Mr O'Brien.'

But Aidan, possessed of an impulse, rose to his feet, grasping the arm of his chair, 'I'll come down to the dining room, Nellie.' He ignored Berrima's protests. He was filled with a restlessness, an impatience with his weak legs and painful hip that bothered him more now than at any other time. Mark and Berrima were considering leaving; the whole world was on the move, it seemed to him. All things were happening on the mainland, and he must get well, he must, and he could be part of it.

It was now February, late summer. After dinner, a high spirited affair, in which the children were delighted to have their father join them at last, Aidan suggested that Milton, Margaret and Richard join them. Nellie was sent to fetch them from next door, and adults and children spilt out on to Glenleigh's terrace, lit by lamps that Liam had suspended from the branches of the trees. The young people played a short-sided game of cricket in the half-gloom, and the adults drank port or tea, and talked amongst themselves.

Aidan was reminded of the first time he had been asked to dinner at the Reynolds' house. In the days when Ettie Harding and Jimmy

608

West had turned his life into a nightmare. Even in the midst of their threats, he remembered looking at Milton's garden, almost the same view as he had before him now; looking at Milton with Margaret and their children and feeling isolated, envious; how he had wanted to possess all he had seen before him.

And in Glenleigh, he did possess it. There sat his wife, chatting to Berrima, there on the lawn was his son, stocky, strong, the man he would be already evident in his broad shoulders, the stubborn face beneath the auburn hair. And his daughter, running back and forth like a vibrant moth in the ridiculously wide, hooped skirt that showed the ruffles and pin-tucks of the ornate pantaloons beneath. They were fine children. He had a wife whom he could respect, with whom he shared many memories. It should be enough, he told himself.

Maura was not chatting to Berrima, she was talking quite seriously of the house, the difficulty of keeping it clean, the noise of the traffic from the road. It was not the first time she had brought this up, each series of complaints finishing with the hope that Aidan would soon agree to move to a farm in the country.

Berrima listened politely, was struck, again, by a kind of pity for this woman, who, really, wanted so little in life. To return to the land, was that so great a thing to ask? Maura had married a farmer, had she not?

Berrima thought, there must be times when you wonder what has become of the man you married. Is it this man, who, until tonight, has been surrounded by his books and his plans, who will take you and drag you into a better, more prosperous future, despite yourself? Do you know this man, I wonder?

Maura felt herself to be complaining, but could not stop herself. She had had a horrid day, one of the children at the orphanage she had visited had died during the night, and when she thought about it, she could not stop herself from shaking. She did not wish to speak of it, so she spoke of Glenleigh, instead. And all the while, she was thinking. In the country I'd be able to have a decent garden, and a cow, and I'd not allow Aidan to have more than one servant, and I'll not have to fill my idle time with charity work to justify my existence.

Tonight she hated Aidan, gazing about at the grounds through his pipe smoke in such a satisfied manner. Master of the big house, she thought with an inner sneer. She hated him for taking her life out of her hands, for giving her the idleness for which she had no desire.

She felt spiteful, *full of spleen,* wasn't that what the novels called it? What an ugly phrase. But she felt ugly. And this girl beside her, pretending empathy, this little miniature of Anna O'Hagan, was so very lovely. Even in the lamplight that flickered as the breeze moved the lanterns, her skin was like cream, her hair thick and lustrous, her energy seemed like a coiled spring within her. It made Maura restless, nervous, as if, if it chose to release itself, Maura doubted her ability to move out of harm's way quickly enough.

Berrima had been watching Liam, Richard and Clemency on the lawn, turned back to find Maura leaning forward a little, her eyes alight with malice. No. Not malice, it could not be that . . .

'You remind my husband of someone,' Maura said. 'Did you know that? You must have noticed how he watches you, makes much of you . . .'

'He's Mark's friend . . .'

'Of course. But he indulges you, does he not?' Maura said this with a laugh. 'It's because of Anna. You resemble Anna so closely.'

Berrima had been feeling uncomfortable, had been beginning to think that Maura's mood was malicious after all; she did not like what the other woman was saying, did not like to see the pale face and pointed chin thrust in so eager a manner, like a bird waiting for a chance to peck.

Yet, 'Anna?' she asked before she could prevent herself. It was not important, surely, yet it seemed important to Maura that she explain.

'She was a girl my husband knew in our village. She was very beautiful. She died. He hasn't forgotten her, not ever. When he first saw you, we agreed that you looked so much like her.'

Was this it? The only reason for the glow in his eyes when he looked at her? That she was a shadow of this other, dead girl? Berrima shivered, she did not want to believe this. Looked at Maura and knew that Maura wanted her to believe it. Maura had not liked the child Anna. How silly of the woman to resent the memory of a little girl who had died years ago, probably in the Famine. How possessive she was of her husband – as if Berrima was to be warned. Anna's tale was a cautionary one.

Maura had begun to cough, the fit became worse, and Berrima rose and moved to her, concerned.

'Are you all right? I'll fetch you some water . . .'

'No . . .' She was recovering slowly from the paroxysms, 'No . . . I'm all right, now.' She wiped her mouth with her handkerchief. The eyes were calmer, more tired, as if the coughing fit had released more than one kind of poison. What a strange woman she is, Berrima thought. She had nothing in common with Aidan but her Irishness. Had she ever been attractive, smiling, affectionate?

610

'Why are you studying me, girl?'

'I . . . I'm sorry, I wasn't aware that I was. Your cough is very bad, I was thinking that you must have my father see to it. It might be something serious.'

'It probably is.' Yet Maura was smiling. Berrima wondered if it was a grim kind of joke. She had a feeling that all Maura's jokes would be grim. 'I've had a hard life, child, that's what it is sure. For you, who've known only comfort, it would be hard to understand what those years were like in Ireland. Now, of course, we have a grand life – but one doesn't forget. Like Aidan. He can't forget. He has his mill and this grand house, but most of the time it's the memories of what's gone by that drives him. Oh, yes. Events of years past.' Her attention was fixed once more on Berrima, directly on Berrima so that the girl felt an instinct almost to recoil. But it was illness, it must be illness that lent such an unnatural look to those green eyes.

Maura said, 'He's never told you his story, has he?'

'No.'

'And he won't. He'll no longer speak of it, even to me. And I was part of it. And that's it, you see. Past events make you what you are. And we've been moulded by the same griefs, the same fears. Even the same loves . . . Yes.' The eyes lost a little of their focus, 'Even the same loves. We can never escape from these things – even here at the end of the earth, all that happened goes with us, is a part of us . . .

'And it can hold us together, too. That's why he can go off for months at a time to Port Davey or to Melbourne, and he'll still come back. Because his grief is part of him, and I understand that grief. Of all people in the world, I understand it. With me, there is no need to speak of it. I *know*. And that's what makes him return to me. Time and again. That's why he will always return to me.'

Aidan, across the terrace, looked at Maura's face, at Berrima's; he looked at Mark's animated form, addressing his parents-in-law; at Margaret Reynolds's pretty, gentle face, her shining, dark hair pulled back into a beaded net, at Milton's strong, humorous face. Aidan's family, his friends, his home. It should be enough, he thought once again, fiercely. But in his heart, he knew it was not.

In July of 1863, almost a year after the accident, only a few weeks after Berrima and Mark returned to their house in Battery Point, Aidan left on the steamer for his visit to Melbourne.

He liked the city, the well-planned, broad streets, marred only by the deep gutters which flooded with each fall of rain – gutters so deep

611

that every so often, a street urchin would drown in one. Small bridges linked the edge of the road with the footpaths before the prosperous shops. Melbourne was a gold-rich city, and it was growing at a mighty pace. Aidan, using only a light cane now, walked over most of the city, and never tired of the sense of movement, of growth.

His own banker, Austin, in Hobart Town, had suggested Aidan see his friend Carlisle at the Bank of Commerce. Aidan had no preconceived notions of what the man would suggest; he had, however, determined to be cautious at first, not to commit himself too readily.

Carlisle discussed several options with him, the very long, ruddy face, made longer by a rather mournful dark moustache (He looks like a Mexican bandit, Aidan thought, amused), frowning in concentration over steepled fingers. All the projects required more capital than Aidan would have felt comfortable putting forward. Yet it was obvious that this was a time, and a city, in which money was to be made.

'And will you eventually be settling here, Mr O'Brien?'

'I . . . Well, I'm not sure about that, now. It's my first visit to your city . . .'

'It's a fine city, Mr O'Brien, financial centre of Australia. And this will continue, I'm certain. When Federation comes to these colonies, we in Melbourne are very sure that our city will become the capital of Australia.'

Aidan smiled his most charming smile, 'And rightly so, I'm thinking.'

Carlisle took him out to lunch at a smart outdoor cafe; his partners, when he was leaving, tried not to register their surprise, as by Melbourne standards, Aidan was a relatively small investor.

But there was something about O'Brien, the sombre, thoughtful Carlisle told himself. Look at the clever way the man had managed to gain capital at a time when the Tasmanian economy was lumbering along and making very little progress. Part-owner in a successful newspaper, real estate developer, timber mill owner – albeit the latter was at the world's end at this place called Port Davey. One had to respect the man, he was an inordinately clever gambler . . .

It was then that Carlisle remembered Tweedie. He hesitated, for of all his clients, O'Brien was among those who could ill-afford to lose their investment. But then . . . 'Mr O'Brien, there is one possibility that I haven't mentioned . . .'

'Oh?' The Irishman, who was vastly enjoying a dinner of excellent roast beef, looked up, eyebrows raised.

612

'There's a chap called Andrew Tweedie, a very clever young man who made a considerable fortune on the goldfields – not as a digger, but as a storekeeper. He's one of those men who are blessed with good timing, and he managed to buy, years ago, land in what are fast becoming the suburbs of Melbourne. In some cases these blocks have been completely surrounded by a town, where until recently, no town existed. All this in a matter of ten years. The problem is, Mr O'Brien, that he refuses to sell any one of these blocks, he wishes to build stores upon them. But his capital now is rather low. The goldfields are not what they were, and competition amongst storekeepers is fierce for what business there is. We would take out a mortgage on any one of Mister Tweedie's properties, but . . . He is rather an odd character. I think he had rather a hard life before coming to this colony. Or perhaps, despite his cleverness and good fortune, he still has not grasped the ideas behind banking and finance. For whatever reason, he does not wish to go into debt.'

Aidan liked the sound of the man immediately. He listened with interest as Carlisle pointed out that Tweedie's splendid ambitions, though viable in theory, worried several potential investors. It appeared the man was determined to hold on to every block of land, to have all his kingdom of Tweedie Emporiums or none at at all; he wanted total control of the business side of the stores, and Melbourne-based businessmen were cautious of a man who had no experience of the more sophisticated consumers of the city. Nor of the intricacies of wholesale buying and retailing of these more luxurious goods.

Aidan was interested, and that afternoon they drove to Tweedie's house in Fitzroy.

It was no longer a house. In the two months since Carlisle had seen Tweedie, the thin, intense young Scot – whose long legs seemed even longer because their first view of him was up a ladder, painting – he had decided to go ahead with his first Melbourne store. He had sold his three stores in the gold towns of Chiltern, Dunolly and Ararat, and had begun transforming the large weatherboard house here in Fitzroy into a store.

'There's a general store on the corner, there,' he pointed out to the two visitors after he had cleaned his hands and strolled to the new glass windows that now constituted the front of the house. 'And there's a blacksmith's in the small street behind. In this shop here I plan to sell the kind of things those two won't provide. Household things that everyone needs but may not feel like tramping into the heart of Melbourne for. Ladders, hammers, saws, rope, calico, paint and wallpaper. Lots of people renovating their houses lately,

613

have you noticed?'

'Are all your shops going to be along the hardware line?' Aidan asked.

'No, though there's a need for it at the moment. You see, you have to think of the area you're servicing. I've got a block of land near one of the big theatres in the city – part of it I plan to turn into a restaurant, to open late for after-theatre suppers – you just have to think of what people want, and give it to them.

'As far as supplying the stores – all my stores – I know a London-based wholesaler. He's dissatisfied with the big Melbourne stores taking so long to settle accounts. I'm not like that, and he knows it, so he's willing, once I'm ready, to work with me. Come into the office – it's a bit of a mess – but I've got plans there of all the shops. You haven't seen them before, Mr Carlisle, I've had them drawn up only recently, but you'll see there what I mean.'

They stayed until eleven that night, and even Carlisle was impressed. The few times he had met Andrew Tweedie, it had been in the bank, the man had been neatly, fashionably-dressed and well-spoken, but nervous, Carlisle realized now, at his surroundings. Here, he was on his own ground, literally, and had, despite the bank's caution, gone ahead on his own initiative. His very enthusiasm tonight pleaded his case more eloquently than at any other time. Carlisle was no longer worried about Aidan's investment, and mentioned again to Tweedie that the bank would be pleased to negotiate a loan. In the cab on the return to the city, Aidan said, 'And what would you be thinking about it?'

'I think he will succeed, Mr O'Brien. Though he needs the bank's advice and a steady partner, like yourself perhaps, to curb any excesses. It should work out ideally – Mr Tweedie obviously wishes to manage the business, and you wish to invest while not wishing to have a great deal to do with the running of the company. Perhaps you'll change your mind if you decide to move to Melbourne, but if you wish to remain in Tasmania – you plan to go on the land eventually, I believe you said – the partnership may suit both yourself and Mr Tweedie as ideal.'

Aidan returned to Hobart as tense and excited as a man could be who is about to sink his entire assets in one make-or-break venture. The building in Davey Street would have to be sold – but he was fairly certain that a cooperative would be formed amongst the medical tenants to buy the building. The houses in South Hobart those completed, must be sold, and the vacant blocks of land sold as they were. Andrew Tweedie and Co. would open three stores in the next twelve months, in Fitzroy, South Yarra and Hawthorn, and

614

later, when they saw the returns, Tweedie said he would consider a bank loan to float the luxury central city store.

If it worked, Aidan thought, if it worked he could live anywhere he damn well chose, and still he would be secure.

He would keep his share in the *Derwent Chronicle,* at least until Mark decided – if he did decide – to sell.

The pining . . . He felt even more restless when he thought of Port Davey; with all that was happening in his life he could not really understand its appeal for him – but he wanted to go back, to begin working with Will once more. True, the market in Huon pine had slumped over the past year or so – with the economic situation in Tasmania there was little building, and the timber was not selling; the prices were not the mad, exorbitant figures that the wood had once demanded.

Yet he wanted to return. He did not need the walking stick any longer. When he reached home he would discard it. He would begin exercising, go up to Ferntree and cut firewood, put his body into condition for the final test, a season logging up the Davey. He had to do it. He realized, suddenly, that this was what bothered him, what had been nagging at the back of his mind all this past twelve months. Would he be the same? Would he lose his nerve at the thought of Hell's Gates? Would his body contain its old strength, would he find himself weakened, unable to cope with the arduous work? He had to go, to find out, to test himself.

All through the drive from the ship, up Macquarie Street to Glenleigh, he considered all that had happened, how he would explain to Maura. What would she think of a possible move to Melbourne?

It was a Thursday morning, early, and the Hobart residents were just coming awake. Curtains were just being parted, doors and windows opened, the milk cart went slowly up the street, and sleepy housewives, shawls wrapped about their shoulders and over their heads to protect them from the lightly falling mist, came out with their empty jugs and buckets to collect the white frothy liquid.

The carriage had already passed the corner where now a bank and offices stood in place of the old gaol where Aidan and Will Treloar had been first imprisoned. There was little in this attractive city to remind him of the horrors of his past. When one viewed things materially, Hobart Town had been very good to him.

Maura shared this opinion, was adamant that they stay in Tasmania, and surprised him, further, by pressing for a return to the South-West.

The children were delighted with this idea, both were eager to leave school and their happiest memories had always been of the Davey and Settlement Point.

It was a further challenge to Aidan, this return to the hard but satisfying life of a piner. His professional life was in order, sure he could do what he wanted to do with his time.

He had even found three ladies in Hobart, of generous natures and indifferent morals, and fell a little in love with each of them. He called on one or the other of them several times a week, and these three intrigues left him with little time or energy to brood over the fragile *entente* with Maura, nor the fact that he rarely saw Berrima these days. He felt rather smug that he could so compartmentalize his life, and was thus quite chagrined to find how easily Berrima could shake his resolve when he visited her in Battery Point to tell her of his decision to go pining once more.

'I think it's the most foolish decision you've ever made.'

Mark was at the newspaper office. Aidan was seated on the sofa, the remains of their afternoon tea lay between him and Berrima's chair. He reached over and took the last scone, spread jam on it deliberately and tried not to be aggravated. He must stop dismissing Berrima's opinions. It annoyed her. He had been very close to saying, 'My dear, you know nothing of these things . . .' The last time he had said that, a few weeks before, she had asked him to leave, and not come back if he was going to patronize her. She was now twenty-four years old, she had reminded him, and had a right to her opinions. She was right, of course. It was he himself who was to blame, he who wanted her to remain a child. Selfish of him – and stupid. He chewed the scone with studied casualness, swallowed and asked politely, 'Is that so, now? And what's made you think that?'

'Huon pine isn't worth the risk to your health and Maura's – not to mention your children's futures. What's Liam supposed to do at Port Davey?'

'He'll be helping me – because he wishes to!' As he felt she was about to interrupt him he added, 'I know that Liam must go to university – but he's only sixteen, there's plenty of time for that.'

'And Clemency?'

This was indeed an awkward problem, but he did not wish her to know that he was confused, and he began to raise his voice. 'I can look after my own daughter! She wants to come . . . !'

'Of course she wants to come – she's devoted to you and she'd follow you to the end of the earth. But, Aidan – you must see that Clemency is detached, a solitary child. She needs girls of her own

616

age, and in a year or so she'll be going to parties and entertainments, and meeting young men . . .'

'Young men?' He fairly roared, 'She's only fifteen . . . !'

'She's as tall as I am already, and she has all the outward characteristics of a woman, Aidan.' Berrima spoke softly, but Aidan listened, for she was putting into words things he had noticed; Clemency's sudden and premature blossoming had startled Aidan, was discomforting Maura, who found it hard, these days, to chastise or discipline a girl who stood three inches taller than she did herself.

He said, frowning, "Tis true, I've thought about that, and worried about taking her away from her school, and bringing her to a place where there are few women and hundreds of men . . . But the Malone girls are still at Settlement Point . . .'

'But as time goes on? She should be making friends here in Hobart, Aidan. It's here where her future will be. My dear, you will not always be here to take care of her.'

The line of his mouth, the set of his shoulders betrayed a forbearance that was ominous. The voice was very quiet, 'I can take care of my own children.'

'You can't give her a mother's guidance.'

The shock of her words left him momentarily lost for words. Yet such was the look in her eyes that he did not say, on recovering, 'She has Maura.' Ridiculous and hollow words they would be. Clemency had Maura's example, Maura's care, Maura's discipline. Guidance? Maura would say yes, she guided Clemency. But to Aidan the word meant something else. For himself, as a man, he thought immediately of Corrie O'Neill. I wanted to grow up like Corrie, he thought. Then, immediately, I don't want Clemency to grow up like Maura.

Berrima was saying, 'Maura is very prone to coughs and chills. It's become worse over the past year. Haven't you noticed? She's lost too much weight – I doubt if she'd have the resistance to fight if she contracted pneumonia or influenza at Port Davey.'

'I've worried about that myself, so I have. But she's fierce determined on returning with me. She has so many friends there, and we were . . .'

'You shouldn't be going back either.'

This was too much. He looked up at her from under his brows; she stood by the windows, and the fine, pale blue woollen gown, yards and yards of it over the broad hoops and petticoats, the full sleeves and lace collar made her look like a painting, the painting of a child. Such a slip of a girl. And standing there lecturing him . . .

Blue, he thought suddenly, unwillingly, had been Anna's colour. He hated it and was moved by it whenever Berrima wore blue. Now,

617

with the light from the garden behind her blurring her features, and from where he sat, lower than she so that she appeared taller . . .

'You fractured your pelvis. It mended extremely well, but in a damp climate you're almost certain to be affected by rheumatic pain.' Anna/Berrima became decidedly Berrima with this abrupt and, he felt, rather unseemly prognosis.

'Berrima, my pelvis is my own affair.' His tone was deadly, he was trying to force the issue, to make her withdraw in embarrassment, but she stood her ground.

'I've seen men in the hospital so crippled with rheumatic pain and arthritis that they can't walk. Many your age, Aidan, or younger.'

'I've had no pain for a long time.'

'The weather is warmer in Hobart than Port Davey, and it's not as damp.'

'I shall wear flannel drawers.'

'They won't help.'

'Two pairs. And I'll soak naked in hot baths each night.' The black eyes were bold, narrowed slightly.

Her cheeks were pink, she was trying not to smile. 'You're attempting to shock me. I'm not frightened at the thought of you naked, in a bathtub or not. If you remember I've seen you . . .'

'All right, all right. So you've no shame in you at all, y' needn't boast about it.'

She laughed, for he was beginning to blush himself, now. He glared at her. It was not easy to gain the upper hand with Berrima, lately. The physical power over him that she had had during the long months of his convalescence had left her with a trace of impertinence in her manner. He could shake this only by gaining physical power over her – to reach out, hold her, let her struggle until she found that he was stronger, admit defeat.

'Why are you looking at me like that?'

If you broke your pelvis, could I nurse you as you did me? It was on the tip of his tongue to say this, but she would slap him, and order him out of the house. So he stood, grinning, and picked up his hat. 'Propriety forbids,' he murmured, and bowed slightly.

'Aidan,' as he turned towards the door, 'Father will tell you – in fact, I know he means to – that all I am saying is correct. Neither yourself nor Maura should be going to Port Davey. For heaven's sake . . . !' Beneath the heavy blue folds he was certain she had stamped her little satin shoe upon the carpet. 'It's not as if you need the money from the timber – you have responsibilities here, and in Melbourne now.' She lowered her voice a little. 'You've moved beyond the pioneer's life, Aidan. Don't go back. Often the more

618

successful a man is, the more his life-style changes – the simple things must be put aside . . .'

'My life is complicated, sure,' he growled, glancing away for he felt that he might give his feelings away in the very look he gave her.

'We'll miss you if you go, Aidan.' The voice soft. It stirred him, and he did not look back at her for a moment, for he could not bear the fondness, only fondness that would be on her face. 'Think seriously about remaining here, will you? Please?'

He gazed at her, finally, their eyes locked; one of those long glances they often shared, when each wondered what the other was thinking. Aidan wanted to say, I have to go. It's best if my life moves fast, if I travel and keep on the move. There are things about myself that do not bear thinking about, memories that make me afraid. And my wanting you. That, too, does not bear thinking about. I must keep other thoughts in my mind. And it's easier, far easier, far away from you.

She was smiling gently, holding out her hand to him. 'Will you come to see us again, soon?'

'Yes.' He said the word on a sigh, took her hand briefly, and left.

Clemency met him in the hall at Glenleigh, came running down the stairs as he was turning the key, pushing open the heavy door. Her hair was ruffled, her face pale and set. 'Oh, Papa . . . Where were you all last night? Liam's looked everywhere . . . '

'What's wrong? What's happened?' He was not about to tell Clemency that he had gone directly from Berrima to a certain little brunette in Barrack Street.

She realized she was standing in the doorway, stood back to let him in, and shut the door behind him. Aidan dropped his bag in the hall, and removed his hat. 'What's happened?'

'It's Ma. That cold she's had all week – Doctor Reynolds says it's developed into a severe case of pneumonia.'

'Serious? It's not serious?'

'Papa . . .' she gazed at him helplessly, 'we don't know. Doctor and Mrs Reynolds have been coming over to check on her periodically. I've been sleeping in Ma's room. We're doing all we can, but . . .'

Later he wondered at the feelings inside him at that moment. It was not panic, it seemed inconceivable that anything should happen to Maura. It could not happen that way. Even separated from each other, he had always seen himself dying first. Maura was too much a part of his past, she was his last connection, in this far-flung colony, with Killaloe and the people of Killaloe. Later, he would feel the guilt that came with the knowledge that no feeling of tenderness, of real love for Maura herself, as a woman, as his wife, was awakened with this news.

He had started for the stairs.

'Papa?'

When he turned, Clemency was picking up a letter from the hall table. She handed it to him. 'This came yesterday – from Ireland. Read it before you see her, Papa. It may have good news you can tell her.'

He took the letter from her and glanced at it. 'I'll read it first, sure,' he said. 'It's from your Uncle Thomas.' And he had turned and was climbing the stairs.

In the sunlight from one of the long, narrow windows that lit the upper hall, he sat down on a heavy, carved chest, and read:

Killaloe,
30th March, 1863.

Dear Aidan,

By the time you read this, we will be on our way. We sail on the 14th June from Liverpool.

It feels strange, sure, and we are a little apprehensive about the trip, but have talked of it so much that we are determined now.

Father McDonnagh is glad for our sakes that we are going to a better life, but sad too I feel. So many people are leaving Killaloe. The river trade is quiet now. It is the railways, they are being built all over Ireland, and the river trade is dying so. The town is quieter, now. Father McDonnagh says we will never see it again as busy as it was before the great hunger.

Your news of being a landowner – and in a city! – was grand to hear. Ma has been boasting of you all over the parish.

We trust you are all in good health, we are so excited at seeing you once more, and Ma longs to see her grandchildren. This will be the last letter you receive from us. We will be in Hobart Town sometime near the 15th October.

Ma sends you all her love and best wishes,

Fondest regards,

Your brother,
Thomas O'Brien.

His hands were shaking, his mind in a turmoil. He stood up, moved down the hall to Maura's door. He opened it quietly, and entered.

Aidan had never been in this room. It was part of the new,

620

scrupulously polite peace treaty between himself and Maura. He had not wished to go to her rooms unless he was invited, and he had not been invited.

The walls were painted white and the furniture was of a light make, and, contrary to popular fashion, there was little of it. Indian rugs, the same type that had been right through Glenleigh when he had first purchased it, lay upon the floors, along with some bright rag rugs that he knew Maura must have made herself. It was a neat room, bare almost to asceticism. The only sense of life came from the three prints about the walls, interspersed with a crucifix and the votary light that Aidan had refused to have in the main hall downstairs. Without examining the prints, Aidan knew them to be Irish scenes.

Maura was asleep. He walked softly to the bed, sat down in the straight-backed chair by the pillow, and glanced over at the narrow, white-counterpaned cot on which Clemency had obviously spent last night.

When he looked back to the bed, Maura's eyes had opened. Before he could speak, he saw them fill with tears. She half-raised her head, but was too weak; the tears spilled down her cheeks, and one ran into her hair. 'Thank God you've come, Aidan . . . I've been praying that you'd come back before it's too late . . .'

'Maura . . .'

'I must tell you. About Master Devlin . . . And Anna . . . Anna . . . It was because of Anna—' He could barely understand her, she was sobbing hard. 'Aidan . . . I did only what I had to do! You know that! You know!'

'Maura! Och, stop, Maura.' He took her hand, held it fast.

'We can't be blamed, none of us . . .'

He stared at her. She had momentarily turned away from him. She knows it was a mistake, he thought, she knows, too. 'There's no blame, Maura. I have no regrets.'

She turned to look up at him, her eyes wide, intense, her tears stilled for a moment. 'No regrets . . .' It was barely a murmur. 'After all I've done to you. No regrets . . .?'

'Aye. Please, Maura, listen to me . . .'

'But I must tell you.' Her grip was so tight that her fingernails were digging into his hand. He knew she did not notice this, did not dare extricate himself.

'Maura, see what I have . . .' He made his voice calm, lowered it almost to a whisper. 'Lie back, Maura, look what I have . . .' He showed the letter as he would to a child who could not read.

She looked disoriented, panicked, bewildered by this piece of paper, uncomprehending how it could be important. 'What . . .'

'Maura, it's a letter from Thomas. He and Ma have agreed to come to Australia. Both of them.'

'Thomas? Mary and Thomas?' The eyes gazed past him, through him.

'Aye, both of them. So you must get well, so you can be with me when I meet them.'

'Soon? They'll be here soon?'

'They've already sailed, they'll be here in a few months, so.'

She lay very still, gazing before her. 'They're coming . . .' she repeated. 'They're on their way . . .'

'Aye, Maura.'

There was a long pause. He wondered if he should have spoken as he had, giving her news of such importance when she was already partly delirious. Strange that she should be as haunted by the past as I am, he thought. He wondered if all the Irish who left Ireland after 1845 had minds as preoccupied with the past and its memories. The Famine killed, and it maimed. More than any other effect, it maimed the survivors emotionally. Any stress seemed to draw himself and Maura back into its horror, its despair.

But Maura was calming, her breathing was shallow, but more regular. She murmured, so softly that he could barely hear, 'I must get well, so. I must get well.'

More than anything else these faint words stirred him, as if she were addressing some adversary. 'Aye, that you must.' Then, almost desperately, 'Maura, what can I do? Only tell me what it is you want, and I'll get it for you. But you must get well.'

Her face, the pale face marred by lines of suffering and illness, the narrow, green, intense eyes, moved around to him, studied him for a moment. A long, long moment.

'You'll not . . . you'll not be wanting us to go to Melbourne, will you, Aidan?'

'Melbourne? Why, no – we agreed we would not.'

'I thought you'd reconsider. I was . . . afraid, Aidan.' Her voice broke a little. 'I've never said it before, for I'm your wife, bad wife though I am . . . and it's no calling of mine to question your judgement . . . But oh, Aidan, don't make me go to Melbourne . . . ! This is my home, now – this colony! It's a little like Ireland, is it not? When Ireland was forest, before the people came. This is my home, now. I don't want to leave.'

'We don't have to, sure.' He became more certain as he spoke. 'I've found a business in Melbourne and I'll be investing in it.' He felt her tense, and hurried on. 'But I want a property. We always wanted a farm . . .'

'Promise me.' Her head was half-raised from the pillow, both her hands now held his.

'I promise you, Maura. We'll not leave Tasmania.'

'Milton Reynolds told me this morning that I can't return to the South-West.' Her eyes scanned his, 'Would you mind?'

'Och, no. We'll buy a farm instead . . .'

'Not a grand house, Aidan. A farmhouse, just a farmhouse. Amongst the hills, the mountains like Port Davey . . .'

'A farmhouse it'll be. White-washed and slate-roofed, on the banks of a lake. We'll find it, Maura. Just wait. Just wait . . .'

60

Mary O'Brien at first did not recognize her son. In the crowd of people pressed close around them, it was only Thomas's arm that prevented her from falling in the crush. She stepped aside automatically as a burly, dark-whiskered gentleman in a top hat stepped towards her. Her bonnet had been pushed askew – as she reached up her hand to straighten it, the stranger had assisted her, adjusted her bonnet for her, had taken her hand. 'Arra, no . . .'

'Aye, Ma. It's me, Ma.'

She gave a cry and was swept up into his arms. How strong he was, this hard-featured man in his fine clothes. How broad his shoulders – her son, her son . . .

And the three of them were hugging each other – who could ever tell that these two were brothers, Aidan and the narrow-shouldered and aesthetic-looking Thomas, his brown eyes soft, the features – had these two ever looked alike? – showing only his good-nature and intelligence. They clung together and they cried, all three, but Mary's tears were for the changes of which she dared not speak. *What have they done to you, my Denny-Joe, my Aidan og?*

She wondered further, in the next few months, as her son, this landowner, this businessman, went back and forth to Melbourne to sign contracts and have conferences with a man called Andrew Tweedie, who was not, as Mary told Thomas worriedly, even Irish. Not even English, but a *Scot*.

They lived, during these months, in the forbidding, sprawling red-brick house called Glenleigh, where Mary nursed the now-convalescing Maura, muttering all the time to Aidan that it was shamed he should be, to bring such a frail creature away from the good soil and clean air to live in damp rooms the size of a barn.

The building in Davey Street was sold to three of the medical specialists for a handsome profit, and the houses and land in the subdivision of Glenleigh were sold also. All the profits were sent to Melbourne and reinvested in Andrew Tweedie and Company. Carlisle at the bank was happy with the progress and, though it would perhaps be sometime before any large returns were realized, he had no doubts but that the venture would succeed.

Thomas was disturbed. He feared change more than he cared to admit, and this new, sharp, hard-faced brother of his intimidated him more than a little. His English clothes, his English way of doing business and – he would never dare speak of this – even his Irish brogue fading from the constant abrasions of dealing quickly, cleverly, with Englishmen of better education and equal greed.

Thomas, though his temperament remained as mild, his interest in the new colony quite genuine, began to be more than apprehensive. Aidan's schemes were frightening in their scope, more frightening still in the face of evidence that made it seem very likely that he would succeed. He wanted land, a great deal of land, but more than this, he wanted to be involved in some other businesses or industries that would further secure his hold upon that land. This, Thomas, who had seen the full effect of the years after the potato blight, could understand. But Thomas had thought that the rather odd partnership with the eccentric Andrew Tweedie would fulfill that need.

But no. Timber it had to be, and even a brick kiln, Aidan had mused, once. Building was going to be the trade for this new colony – land and building. Those were the places where money would be made. 'One day,' he promised Thomas, 'I'll build you a fishing boat – something like the *Lostwithiel*, only better still . . .'

Thomas had turned from the drawing room window abruptly. 'If I have a boat, Aidan, I'll pay for it myself. You'll not be supporting me long, I'm thinking. I want independence – not even for my own boat, sure – for I was born to be a farmer, I know that. I must do it my own way.' Two pink spots had appeared on his cheeks as he spoke.

'Of course, of course . . .' Aidan said placatingly, and had gone on to speak of the immediate plans for a timber mill and how he would need Thomas's help for a while yet.

624

Thomas began to feel foolish – and ungrateful. It was all very well to say that he wanted none of Aidan's charity, but he had been living well on it for years. They could not have afforded the little luxuries of bacon and vegetables and milk without Aidan's regular money sent over the past years. And Thomas did not fool himself that he would be able to buy land of his own without his brother's help. Aidan was an emancipist, Thomas a free settler, yet more and more in Australia as time went on it was money that counted. Aidan had money, and ambition, and a definite charm when he chose to exert it. Aidan would succeed where Thomas, unhampered by an unsavoury past, would surely fail. Aidan would succeed and push, pull, coerce and bully Thomas into being successful, too. Thomas stood and mentally cringed at the thought. Arra, he should have stayed in Killaloe. Was it a sin to desire a simple life? Yet how could he say that to Aidan, who did all these things not only because Thomas was his brother, but because he loved Thomas, and liked him, and wished to take care of him?

He had bought Thomas a horse, had taught him to ride, and his brother was not the most willing pupil. He suggested, now, that they combine their daily ride with a practical goal, and dine at an inn in Hobart itself. Thomas, who could see the sense in being a capable horseman, even while he regretted the necessity, agreed.

The streets were crowded, but Thomas handled his chestnut mare quite competently. Aidan, from the back of his own bay thoroughbred, was about to compliment his brother, steering his horse grimly through the drays and carriages and pedestrians when he happened to glance in a shop window, and saw Matty.

He kept riding, in shock at seeing her and at the feelings that woke in him. It may not have been her, it may not . . . but the woman had pulled back from the window into the shadows of the store – almost too abruptly – as their eyes had met. Pale eyes, the face thinner beneath a small hat set amongst pale curls . . . it had to have been Matty.

He reined in, sat chewing his dry lower lip, considering. But no logical thought came to him, no clear thoughts of consequences, repercussions. He must see her.

'I just saw a friend of mine . . .'

Thomas had ridden on, unknowing. He turned, halted his mount. 'Where?' he looked around.

'Back there. Listen, Thomas – you go on, there's an inn just there on the corner. Order a beer for me, and I'll be along directly.'

Thomas looked puzzled. 'Where is this friend?' he persisted.

'Back there in one of the stores. You go on, Thomas.' And Aidan turned his horse and rode back quickly, before Thomas could question him further.

He glanced back up the road as he tied his reins to the railing. Thomas was riding obediently on up the street. Despite his unease in the saddle, he looked well on a horse, Aidan thought, being tall and slim – a pity his confidence didn't match his capability. But then, Aidan smiled, realizing he had made a rather profound statement, that was always Thomas's trouble.

It was a general store, and large. Towards the front were the bolts of cloth and haberdashery and ladies' apparel. It had been a small blue lace parasol in the window that Matty had been admiring, her hand had been fingering it meditatively just as her gaze had caught Aidan's. She was nowhere to be seen as he stood at the front of the store and gazed around. Of an impulse, he bought the blue parasol, and when it was wrapped, he went through the store, slowly, looking for her. He became more and more certain that it was Matty. More and more determined to find her.

She was at the rear of the store; he saw at once that he had been correct, that she had recognized him, and moreover, knew that he was following her. She had her back to him, examining some gardening implements, hoes and spades, and these objects being so foreign from the Matty he knew, and the rather stiff set to her shoulders as she stood with her back to him made him even more certain that part of her wished to avoid him.

'Matty?'

She was still lovely, but there was some strain, now, about the mouth, some uncertainty about the eyes that had always been so confident. He studied her face, and liked the changes he saw. She affected him deeply. Her love for him was still written there, on her features, in the depths of the blue eyes. 'Hello, Aidan.'

They stood there, an awkward silence developing. Neither could think of anything to say. It had been so long, and, Aidan thought, she had the right not to speak to him at all. I put her in her carriage that day six years ago, and almost forgot her.

The silence was broken by one of the store clerks, who walked up to them, smiling, addressing Matty. 'Good afternoon, Mrs Rodgers, may I help you?'

She did not take her eyes from Aidan's. 'No, thank you, Mr Holmes, I was just looking for the moment.'

It was unwise. Holmes's 'Of course . . .' contained enough speculation to stir the gossips of Hobart Town, and Aidan dragged his gaze from Matty to stare after the figure of the store clerk as he

626

moved towards the front of the shop.

As if sensing his thoughts, Matty said, 'Are you worried about my reputation? You are, aren't you? And you can, now, for I have one. Yes, I'm married. Have been for three years.'

'Ah.' He smiled, nodded, and Matty, who was quick, as she always was, could sense that he was not pleased.

She said, 'Would you like to talk, Aidan? Or are you in a hurry?'

'I . . . Och, no, there's no hurry. My brother has gone ahead to the inn where we'll be dining.'

'Not the one on the corner – The White Cockatoo?'

'Aye . . .'

'I own it. Or rather, my husband and I own it. Let's go back there, now. Your brother won't mind if you're delayed a little.'

She led him out the back way, past the bins of grain and saddlery, the fresh, dry smell of oats and chaff, into the cold air of a rank back alley that smelt of stables and refuse.

They walked along the narrow lane, to the corner building, through a small gate into the yard, into the large, clean kitchen and along a passageway. Matty opened the door to her office. It was rather a masculine room, though she said that her husband had no real interest in the running of the inn itself and she was the one who handled the business. There was nothing about the furniture or the furnishings that reflected Matty; it was a neat and impersonal room.

She had shut the door behind them, he turned, gazed at her – and they were moving towards each other. It seemed perfectly natural, yet sometimes they pulled back from each other, from their hungry, demanding kisses, and their eyes mirrored the same perplexity. It had been so long . . . yet they wanted each other still. More strongly, perhaps, than ever.

'Enough!' she laughed, breathing heavily, pulling away from his embrace, backing to lean against the door. 'I can't compromise myself with you here.'

'Somewhere else?' he moved after her.

'No, Aidan. Sit down here, with me, and keep your hands to yourself . . .' They sat together on the leather covered settee that lined one wall, and stared at each other once more, greedily, questioningly. She laughed, softly, the old laugh, deep, quiet, the laugh that masked God-only-knew what thoughts.

He realized that he had never understood her, that that had been part of her attraction for him, from the beginning.

'You're lucky,' she said, 'that I'm such a simple soul.'

'Simple? You?'

'Yes. I either love, or I hate. Sometimes both at the same time, but never anything in between.'

'It must make day-to-day intercourse very difficult.' He was toying with one of her ringlets that fell behind her ear. Then he was touching her ear, playing with her earring, stroking the lobe of her ear. She did not understand what he meant, but had the feeling that it had nothing to do with the look in the black eyes that claimed her own. When? the dark eyes were demanding, When? She smiled. *Wait, you bastard. I waited for you long enough.* But she wanted him, wanted his touch, wanted more of it. She was surprised that she had not forgotten his touch. There was something familiar about it, and yet none the less thrilling for that. It was like a homecoming. And she did not like that, clenched her jaw against that thought. She realized she wanted him very much. He would not have to wait long; she turned to him silently as she realized this. It was not fair, not fair . . .

'I'm married, now,' she repeated, to distance herself from him, from the thoughts his touch rekindled.

His hand paused for a moment. 'Yes, you were saying. Are you happy?' No clue in the calm features, the cool voice.

'As happy as anyone is, I s'pose.' There was a fringed cushion behind her, and she played with the tassles of this as she said, 'I had a choice, see. There was two of them. Stephen. You remember Stephen, whose house I lived in in Napoleon Street? Dull and safe, that's Stephen. I knew I'd end up rich if I married him. I'd make him use his money cleverly – and he wouldn't let me spend it, he's that stingy. Tighter than a fish's arse, and that's water tight.

'But then there was Griffith. I told you about him. Comes from a good Hobart family. Thorough wastrel, but charming. Totally unreliable. That was my choice, you see.'

He took in the demure cut of her clothes, the dark blue pork-pie hat, delightful, but not outrageous; the outfit made Matty appear more conservative than he had ever seen her. She wore no rouge on her face. He smiled, the picture of her pleased him somehow. 'So you settled for middle-class stability and married Stephen . . .'

'Shit, no! I married Grif!' And they were laughing, suddenly. 'My God, Aidan, do I look middle-class? Do I? I'll shoot myself!'

They fell laughing on each other's shoulders – and he was kissing her once more. She was too near, and too alluring. He knew, whoever Grif was, that Matty still played life by her own rules. As if she had had heard his thoughts, she said, 'I don't feel awful doing this. Grif, he's led me a merry dance on more than one occasion, I can tell you. But that's why I love him and why I married him. I'll never be sure of him. He's as selfish as I am, and a lot meaner. I like that. I have to put up with the hard times – but it's living, isn't it?'

They were close, sat gazing at each other with some real understanding. Aidan was thinking, oddly enough, of Berrima. The personalities, situations, were different, but Matty's rationale covered his relationship with Berrima, too. He understood. Berrima made him feel more alive. He could never really possess her, but the pain of this knowledge was something with which he could cope. But the heightened sense of awareness that being with her inspired, Berrima's own particular magic, made it worthwhile. He could tolerate Mark's presence, his bouts of drinking, the facile duplicity and the occasional supercilious remark, knowing that Berrima was always close.

He nodded, his mouth held a trifle wryly, and looked up to see Matty studying him, smiling a little. 'And you?' she said. 'You still with your wife?'

'Yes. I mean . . . we share a house, if that's what you mean.'

'That wasn't what I meant. You're not sleeping with her at all, then?'

'No. It doesn't upset me.' And it was the truth, he found, wonderingly, 'We have a good friendship, Maura and myself, we have a great deal in common, and our shared past – we've known each other for so long . . .'

'Who are you sleeping with, Aidan?'

For some reason this embarrassed him a little. 'There are a few ladies of my acquaintance,' he murmured, 'with whom I spend an evening occasionally . . . They're diverting, charming, discreet . . .'

'They're whores?'

'Basically, yes.'

They gazed at each other a long moment. Matty thought, You son-of-a-bitch. Six years. Your life's been emptier than mine – yet in six years you haven't come looking for me.

She could not understand. Everything was so right between them; Aidan was a more demanding lover than even Grif was, especially lately, when the alcohol had begun to affect Grif's desire. Really, Aidan was a better man than Grif was. But for all that Grif possessed her in a way that Aidan could not. She began to understand what he meant by a shared past – there had been good times with Grif, there always would be, for he was wild and unpredictable, and she liked that. Their loving and their quarrelling were equally memorable. Perhaps it was that very basic weakness in Griffith that held her to him, a tie that was never there with Aidan. For Aidan never needed her, her alone. Grif did.

Aidan had risen, walked to the desk where he had dropped the parcel on entering the room. 'This is for you,' he handed it to her.

She had not seen him buy it, had noticed him within the shop only as he had come towards her, already carrying it. She took the brown paper parcel, and the shape of it told her what it was.

She bowed her head over it as she unwrapped it. It had cost ten pounds, it was made in Paris. She did not open the parasol itself but held it out, twirled it. 'Oh, Aidan.'

She had begun to think it would almost be worth the loss of him for the ego-soothing satisfaction of hitting him with it, telling him to go away. Instead, she told him, gently enough, 'Aidan, I can't have an affair with you.' She looked up, saw the dark eyes regarding her quietly, waiting. Damn you, she thought. She had forgotten this, he was the same the last time they had met. The impassive watching eyes with their secret light.

'Really, Aidan, try to understand. He's no gentleman, my Griffith, for all his posh Hobart relatives. He's beaten me more than once. He's a drinker, see.' She saw him scowl, and hesitated. She wanted Aidan, dear me, yes. But it'd send Grif off on a six-week bender if he found out, and like as not she'd get a beating or two. It was not the beatings that she minded, it was the risk that one of these days Grif would leave, as he frequently did, but this time never to come back. She knew that her husband loved her – but she could not push him too far.

Aidan sat gazing at her, his eyes faintly narrowed, the same cool, inscrutable look within them.

Here's another one, Aidan was thinking. Matty, for all her fire, her ambition, her downright greed, tied herself to a man who drank heavily, who treated her with little respect and sometimes with violence. Aidan had no proof that Mark had ever struck Berrima, but there were similarities here. Who would have thought that Matty and Berrima could share something in common? But there they were, each married to self-indulgent alcohol-addicted men; neither of them need stay and put up with it, but stay they did. They loved these men.

Aidan was angry out of all proportion. He had used his family's arrival and his business affairs as an excuse to put Berrima and her problems with Mark out of his thoughts. He was close against those problems now, unexpectedly; it seemed suddenly that these women were both as weak as their men – or weaker, for they had married them, knowing them as they were.

'It's a wonder you brought me here,' he said stiffly. 'What if he walked in now?' His hands were behind her back, unfastening her bodice before she could protest. He was practised in this, Maura

630

never used to like it to be easy for him . . .

'Aidan, stop . . .'

'Let's see what he'll do, shall we?' His face was pale, set, the dark eyes burnt into hers. 'Will he fight for your honour, Mrs Rodgers?'

'No bloody fear. Will you stop – how did you learn to do that? God, you're quick . . . Stop it!'

'What will he do, Matty?' He pulled her bodice forward, effectively hampering the arms that tried dutifully to push him away; kissed her lips, her throat, her shoulders . . .

'Oh, stop . . .' But it was a groan, 'You're a swine, Aidan, stop . . .'

'What will he do, Matty, your man of excellent connections? Horsewhip me? Horsewhip you? Begod, you're lovely . . .'

The conservative clothes, as it happened, fell away as readily as the conservative manners. Afterwards, he helped her with her bodice fastenings, helped her adjust her hat. They had not spoken, had glared at each other throughout their mating, glared while they were dressing, each still with his or her own bitterness, and both wondered at what emotion they shared; how, while their passion never seemed to die, neither did it grow into any real affection. They had made love almost savagely, yet both were satisfied, as they always were. It was as if this was their only gift to each other, and neither was content with it, for different reasons.

'I want to see you again.' He had noticed a decanter of whiskey on a bureau in the corner, went to it and poured himself a glass.

'Why?' she gazed at him balefully. 'You can get that from your whores, can't you?'

He glanced over at her, the face hard, the eyes cool once more. 'That doesn't deserve an answer.'

'Only because you don't have one. Pour me one of those, too, you selfish pig. A big one.' Her hand was held out, like a demanding child. Aidan laughed, poured her a whiskey, and brought it over to her. He had no idea where her husband was, but suddenly, it did not seem to matter greatly.

Thomas had become tired of waiting, and had almost finished his meal when Aidan approached the table, from the rear of the room. 'Did you come through the kitchens?'

'Yes. I've ordered myself a cheese and meat sandwich, I won't make you wait while I have a full meal. I'm not really hungry, sure.'

'Did you see your friend?'

'Aye.' Aidan's eyes scanned the two glasses on the table, one empty, one half-empty. 'Did you order a drink for me?'

'I did. You didn't come. I drank it meself, so.'

Thomas wondered why Aidan was being so very secretive. Who was this mysterious friend? Someone new to meet and talk to over dinner would have been interesting, sure. But Aidan ate in silence, quickly, as if he were very hungry, and drank two glasses of ale. He seemed tense, to Thomas, looking about the room, smiling slightly, and raising his eyes to the kitchen each time the door opened or shut as the waiters went back and forth. And he hummed to himself a little. It was very strange.

He was content that year – or so it seemed in retrospect. He looked back on those first few months after his mother and brother arrived in the colony, before the planned return to Port Davey, and he told himself that yes, that was one of the best times. He had Matty, whose husband seemed almost obligingly disposed to leave her alone at the inn for days and sometimes weeks at a time while he went on mysterious business trips. He only occasionally visited his more professional lovers; the dangerous affair with Matty fulfilled once more the need for affection, physical pleasure, and even a kind of companionship, for they were both mellowing a little in their attitudes to life, and to each other.

The firm of Andrew Tweedie and Company was thriving, and Aidan, with a mortgage on Glenleigh, was able to begin the building of a mill on land in the Derwent Valley, near New Norfolk.

Thomas was Aidan's shadow; he watched, and he learnt. By the time the mill was completed and producing, Thomas was conversant enough in the management of the business to feel nothing more than nervous agitation at the idea of losing Aidan to the South-West; to the thought that, together with a competent foreman brought from Melbourne at a salary that made the thrifty Thomas wince, he would be running a timber mill the size of nothing he had known in Ireland.

'I don't think Thomas is entirely happy about it,' Maura said, once.

'The only way Thomas will learn to be confident is if he does what terrifies him and finds out that the sky won't fall on his head. I know my brother, Maura. He has to learn – I can't hold his hand for the rest of his life.'

'I don't think that he expects that . . .'

'Then trust me. He'll do very well with the mill.'

She left the room, then, with a final glance at him that told him that she was unconvinced.

Aidan continued with his correspondence, seated at the dining room table, the sun warm on his back through the high, narrow windows. He enjoyed working here; it was a lighter, airier room than his office at the rear of the house. He was closer to the heart of the household; it was noisier, but he liked to feel he was at the centre of whatever was going on.

Maura had joined Clemency in the next room; he could hear his daughter playing the piano, and every now and then, Maura would pass a comment on the girl's interpretation. Her voice came like a light hum through the heavy door. The music was clearer, a slow, rather morose piece. It depressed him. The letters before him depressed him.

He sighed, lit his pipe and leaned back in his chair, scowling at the pages before him on the glossy surface of the dining table. Five letters, including one from Andrew Tweedie, and all pertaining to his mainland interests. He should be in Melbourne at this time – or somewhere on the mainland . . .

He could hear Maura's voice, now, raised suddenly. 'Don't thump like that! It's not a march!' The music stopped abruptly. An exchange of voices, low, tense, then the music began again.

Aidan smiled, grimly. Clemency did not thump, but there was a tenseness to the music, now. His daughter would never be a true musician; her emotions showed through her playing; try as she might to devote the required expression to each piece, it was a matter of chance if her mood matched that of the composer.

He tapped his fingers on the table; listening to Maura's voice was annoying him, even though he could not hear the words. Why couldn't the girl be allowed to play as she wished? Why must Maura criticize every phrase, as it seemed the high, droning voice did? He felt like going to the door and opening it, shouting at her to let the girl be . . .

He calmed himself with an effort, and wondered at his impatience. True, it was easy, lately, for Maura to annoy him. They had had several scenes together over the past few days – again over Aidan's persistent postponements of the return to Port Davey. Despite himself, he could not forget Berrima's reasoning, it was a step back. Yet any mention of Melbourne as an alternative and Maura would close up, refuse to discuss the matter. Last night he had shouted at her, called her obstinate, and this morning she had refused to speak to him.

He decided, of an impulse, to visit the newspaper, to visit Mark. With the mill and the correspondence that went back and forth to Melbourne, he had not often been to the offices of the *Derwent Chronicle* since his return. The last time he had spoken to Mark he, too, had been talking of leaving Tasmania. Berrima's Aunt and

Uncle Charlie had decided to move to Camden, closer to Sydney, and had offered their property near the town of Berrima to their niece and her husband at a very reasonable price.

Aidan, faced with the thought of losing Berrima, conjured up as many reasons as he could to convince Mark to remain in Tasmania. He knew, even as he left the house, leaving a message with his mother should Maura ask where he had gone, that Mark would undoubtedly bring the subject up once more. Mark, too, was restless.

Maura heard his horse on the gravel drive and left her station by the piano to watch him ride up the slope, disappearing behind the fuschia bushes by the front gates. Her mouth pressed itself into a line of disappointment. She had wanted him to apologize before he left – now he would go off to his bank in the city, or to Mark at the *Derwent Chronicle* office, and he would forget her grievance. He would come home and treat her as if nothing had happened, while she must spend all day with her gall, the tight, encapsulated memory of their quarrel, a bitter pill left to dissolve in her mouth, that would not fade, disappear.

'You haven't learnt that piece correctly – you've been playing it by ear, I can tell. Study the music – I shall want to hear it this afternoon.'

Clemency grimaced. Maura placed her hand on her daughter's shoulder, the stiff, awkward gesture, the only touch Maura could ever bring herself to make. 'You're improving,' she added, before she left the room.

Aidan's correspondence was in an untidy pile on the dining table. She stopped, annoyed, and gathered them up, impatiently crushing some of the letters and crossed the hall with them, into Aidan's office. Why couldn't he work here, instead of littering the house? The Lord knew, it was hard enough to keep tidy. He had an office in which to study these incomprehensible letters of business. Of course, it was a dark room, as he said, and the dining room was more pleasant and sunny, but everything had its place, Maura thought grimly, making a pile of the letters, neatly, in the middle of the blotter on the desk. It was a small thing, but typical of Aidan's lack of consideration.

She sat down in his chair, and swung from side to side a little. She liked this chair, it swivelled. This had been the first of its kind that she had seen. Sometimes she would pause in the midst of her sweeping and dusting and sit in this room, dark though it was, and smell the familiar smell of Aidan that seemed to cling with his pipe smoke in the air, and let her thoughts, for a short time, flow freely. It was pleasant . . .

She scowled. Lately there was so little time, and her thoughts could not be of her own dreams, her son's success at university, Clemency's excellent marriage match, the comfortable farm they would have, eventually . . .

For anger, lately, kept her fenced away from her few brief dreams, and she resented this. Lately anger consumed what little energy she had left, after the duties of the day.

Melbourne. The businesses in Melbourne. The prospects in Sydney. The Stock Market and the expansion of Andrew Tweedie and Company.

Maura stood abruptly and walked from the room, took up her bonnet from the hall stand, and walked on down the hall towards the rear of the house, directionless, knowing only that she could not remain still; her restlessness, this ever-present rage, would not let her rest.

Why should she be placed in a position where she should defend the life she had? And defend it, strangely enough, from the man who had given her all this. Aidan, who was meant to be closer to her than anyone, whom the Church told her was second only to God in her life, was the one who had brought her so far, and, now she was happy, threatened to take that happiness from her.

And she was not well. He had no right to do this to her when she was not well. The fever had returned, these past few days, the fever and the sense of weakness returned at strange times to make her stand still, reach for a chair, sit quietly for a moment until the faintness passed. She had told no one, resenting the fact that no one seemed to notice the strain that must show on her face. It was typical of the O'Brien selfishness, she thought, that no one asked after her health or well-being.

Down the back stairs, holding her hooped skirts close to her, for Glenleigh had been designed with no thought for the fashion of crinolines, and the back stairs leading down to the terrace were narrow.

Thomas was in the garden, spare frame, brown hands, working with a hoe at neat rows in the dark soil. The drab brown of his tweeds and his unfashionable trousers looked incongruous against the backdrop of an elegant greenhouse. He had not seen her, and she sat down on a bench beneath one of the trees, feeling slightly breathless from her haste and the exertion of the stairs, and watched him.

She had used to help him in the field of the cottage in Killaloe, in

635

those far-off days when he had been the man of the house and had looked after them. There was a calmness to Thomas. It had helped them through those black and terrifying days, had helped her through her fear and her shame. When Aidan was about, she almost forgot Thomas. The light of his spirit was a soft, steady light. It paled before Aidan like a candle in daylight. But it was no less strong, comforting, because of this uneven comparison.

She wondered if Thomas would every marry, ever till his own fields – and then decided, no, he would not. And perhaps, she thought bitterly, he was better off as he was. Sure what had marriage brought her? She and Aidan were not happy. Aidan was as much of a stranger to her as he ever was. And she had long ago given up attempting to understand him. It no longer interested her. He was like a clever, often peculiar, boarder in her house. Muddy boots, and papers littered on the table tops.

She realized with a dreadful sort of shock that she did not like Aidan. They played at war, they battled for supremacy; but it had been years since she had worried about him, wanted him near her, needed his touch . . . Why, she thought, and it was as if a heavy burden had been raised from her spirits, I don't love Aidan at all. If he left me today for some vulgar woman I would not mind. In fact . . . and her face flushed, she was appalled at her own thoughts, I would be relieved. It's not just this matter of him wishing to go to the mainland. It's not that. It's that we've become strangers. And yet we're tied together. Didn't God take this into consideration? She looked up at the white puffs of cloud that drifted over from the face of Mount Wellington. Two strangers tied together until they died. She shivered suddenly.

Thomas had seen her and was calling as he approached her, smiling broadly. 'God bless you! I'm glad you've come out into the sunshine.' She felt the warmth, the simplicity of his regard for her. After Aidan's detached personality, the force of his driving ambition, to be near Thomas was to feel welcomed, cherished.

'I'm tilling new soil, here, y'see. Himself won't be pleased that I'm taking up some of his lawn, but sure and isn't it a waste to see so many acres under grass and not a cow to be seen?

'I was going to come inside to fetch you in a little while, I wanted your advice. Do you think I should put in three rows of cabbages, or only two? And these tomato things that Aidan's so fond of – they're good to have with cold meat in the hot weather – should I plant them here, do you think? How much shade do they need? What think you?'

She had looked up half-way through his speech, ready to answer

636

him, but had to stop. She had wanted to tell him about Aidan's pressure to go to Melbourne, his blithe unconcern about their own wishes. At first she was amused at Thomas's excitement, the rather petty reasoning behind it . . .

Petty? What was petty? She had important news – Aidan's news. From Aidan's world. Business pressures. Prospects, Aidan said. She looked into the soft, humorous brown eyes, the face that was Aidan's, and not Aidan's, for there were no grim lines here, his face was as unlined as a boy's.

Two rows of cabbages, or three? Tomatoes or no tomatoes. These plants and seeds mattered to Thomas, he would live off them, if he had to. He gave to the earth and the earth gave back to him – it was not stealing, or plotting or cheating to gain another man's wealth. Petty. Who was petty?

He was still waiting for her to speak. The patient gaze, the handsome, gentle face bent forward slightly, for he was a lot taller than she. Always, always, that gentle face had been turned to her. Thomas in his field, Thomas whose reality was what he could see, touch, feel. Thomas who wanted so little, but all the right things, the good things.

I should have married you. Oh, Thomas, I should have married you! We would have been content, Thomas. *We want the same things.*

'Maura? Dear God, Maura?' his voice from a distance, he was stepping towards her through a haze.

'I'm all right. It's the sun. These silly new spoon bonnets give one's face no shade at all. I . . .' Holy Mother, was she crying? Weakness, tears of weakness, they simply spilled from her eyes unbidden, and she spoke as if nothing were happening, 'I think three rows of cabbages, Thomas. And . . . and . . .'

'Maura, come inside . . .'

He had taken her arms at the elbows, and the touch of him made her feel weaker still; the goodness, the safe, warm pleasure of his hands on her arms. This was not her. This was not Maura O'Donoghue O'Brien. No, this was some other woman, standing in the plot of fragrant, freshly-turned soil, her forehead against this man's chest, the tears of years of frustration, fear, humiliation, defeat and the acknowledgement of the truth at last.

'I'm sorry . . .' An excuse, any excuse. 'I've not been well lately . . . and this business of leaving – we can't leave, Thomas. We must be after putting down roots, Thomas, must we not . . .?'

But it was not Thomas who answered. 'Och, what's this, then?' Mary at the foot of the stairs, her thin little face screwed up with concern. Maura tried to speak, but it was Thomas who said, flatly,

'Aidan's upset her.'

'Arra, come within, child. Come and have tea, and tell us what that greedy little spalpeen has done now.'

So she was able to tell her story. They did not wish to leave, either, she could tell that. They talked of it over tea in the dining room, and she could tell that they were in accord, each of them. When Clemency came into the room, sat down near the window with a biscuit and listened to the talk, Maura could tell that even the child agreed with them.

If they could only persuade Aidan to buy the farm he had always spoken of – somewhere in the Derwent valley, or, even better, in the Huon valley.

Maura began to feel better amongst their companionship. She needed to have her feelings and beliefs ratified by others in order to feel completely secure. Anomalous thoughts frightened her.

She avoided looking at Thomas, for it was odd, so odd, but she was seeing things in his face that she had never seen before, and it awoke in her just such strange, unheard-of feelings that were capable of frightening her badly. There was no one to tell of this, no one who could inform her that her feelings for Thomas were normal, were right. This was something that could not be shared. Not ever.

She felt very alone. Thomas, once her refuge and calm strength, was now a threat. She hoped he would leave soon, to return to the mill at New Norfolk. Then, perhaps, these strange new feelings would go away.

At the newspaper office, Aidan was accorded the sort of welcome a major partner deserved, was told that Mr Ellis was not in today, but Mrs Ellis was in the printing room. One of the junior clerks was summoned to show him the way.

She was standing in the centre of a group of five or six men, one or two in business suits, but the remainder in shirt sleeves, with aprons covering them from their necks to below the knees of their trousers. The noise from the giant machine was deafening. Someone came running up with a sheet of newspaper, Aidan heard Berrima say, 'Thank God!' There was laughter and relief from all of them. 'Yes . . . yes, fine, Toby. We're away, now. I'll take this upstairs with me . . .' Only in turning did she see Aidan.

She smiled, but it was a smile in which exhaustion left little room for much enthusiasm. 'Aidan . . .' She came forward and took his hand. 'See this, Aidan . . . We had some trouble with the machine.'

'What? Already?'

'Only something minor. But with a daily newspaper like this we

638

were naturally beginning to panic. Heavens, I don't know where we'd be without Walter.' She glanced back at the huge, roaring machine, its reels of white newsprint whirring about, feeding up between the rollers. She smiled at Aidan. He had been the one to suggest they update the printing press. The Walter machine was the best in the world, both the Ellises and Aidan were extremely proud of it. 'Come up to my office,' she said, 'I need a cup of coffee after this, we all do.'

The sub-editors went their own way when they reached the first floor. Berrima led the way into one of the offices next to Mark's. *My office*, she had said.

She gave an order for coffee to be brought to them, and they entered the office, Berrima seating herself tiredly in the chair behind the desk.

'Berrima?'

'Mmm?' She was rubbing her eyes, with her wrists, for her fingers were black.

'Where's Mark?'

She paused, looked up at him with pink eyes. 'He's in Launceston – there was a fire in one of the stores last night – and he's writing the story.'

She continued to meet his gaze, despite the slight narrowing of his eyes that was meant to tell her that he did not quite believe her. Then he said, 'You're tired. I think I'll take you home.'

'Home?' She blinked at him, as if she had not heard the word before.

'Home. Your residence.' He was walking towards her, studying her face, 'Where you keep your tooth powder and your curling tongs – and your rouge.'

'Rouge?'

'You just smudged it.'

She fled to the cabinet in the corner, pulled out a mirror and stared at herself. He was right. Her eyes had watered and she had rubbed them with too little care. She flushed with embarrassment.

The reflection of his face appeared behind her in the mirror. She turned, and he had taken her firmly by the arms. 'What is the matter with you? Sure I'll wager you're as pale as death beneath that paint.'

The dark eyes searched her face, the concern they held, the strong hands that held her, the heavy shoulders in the perfectly-tailored jacket, so close to her, Aidan . . . Aidan . . . Always there.

'Take me home, Aidan. If you don't I think I shall cry here and now. Take me home.'

At the house in Battery Point, more coffee was ordered. This time they drank it, sitting quietly in the parlour whose bay windows looked out over the harbour. For a long time Aidan did not speak, for he wanted her to recover, to relax away from the tense atmosphere of the newspaper office.

Finally, he said, 'Where is Mark?'

She looked up at him, replaced her cup in its saucer. It rattled a little. 'I told you the truth. He has gone to investigate the fire in Launceston.'

'And when was this fire?'

She looked down into her almost empty cup. Softly, 'Three days ago.'

She thought his cup and saucer would break, such was the force with which he returned them to the tray on the table. She began, 'Aidan . . .'

'It's hopeless, you know that? Every time I visit the *Chronicle*, something else is wrong – Mark is drunk, or Mark is ill – and half the time I'm beginning to suspect it's the same thing.' He glared at her. She looked away. 'That's when Mark is here at all.' He tried to lower his voice, shouting at her wouldn't help. 'Dammit, Berri, it's not good enough. What's the matter with him?'

'I don't know. He does his best, Aidan.' Aidan made an impatient gesture. 'He does, truly. He's unhappy. Please, my dear. The paper is running well, you can't find fault with the sales figures. Mark isn't careless with his career. His drinking problem isn't any more serious than that of a great many respected men in this colony. You don't . . . We don't see you all that often – this is your first visit in two months . . .'

He was gazing at her, strangely, intently. She went on, hurriedly. 'It is coincidence, truly, that you find us in a state of disruption. Look at the sales figures, Aidan. See our accountant any time you wish . . .'

He had stood, was strolling over to the windows with his hands behind his back. His voice cut across hers. 'Quite a few times during these past few years, I've found you at the paper. "Visiting Mark at the office", that's how you explained it, I think. The times that you were at home, you'd been in the study – you never told me what you were writing at . . .'

He turned to her. She sat gazing at him. Her face was very white. Normally the emerald green of the dress she wore, with its ruffled bell sleeves and white lawn under-sleeves would have suited her beautifully. Tonight, however, it reflected in the translucence of her skin, and she looked a most unhealthy colour, almost green herself, her eyes dark-shadowed.

640

He asked gently, 'How long have you been running that newspaper?'

'No! That's not true!'

'Come, Berrima, no lies.'

'It's not true. I help Mark, that's all. And then only occasionally. You ought to know me, Aidan. I have no head for business at all. I'm not in the least logical . . .'

'Girl, I have long ago ceased to place any limitations on your capabilities – that is a compliment, by the way. And it annoys me when you denigrate your ability by denying it. I'm not concerned, if you want the truth, if you're running it or not, for it's running well. But I don't believe that it's Mark who's doing it. Stop giving him the credit – I won't.'

She slowly relaxed back into her chair. 'We . . . we have an excellent editor. He does a great deal of the work. The idea was for Mark to take over when he felt himself capable . . .'

'And when will Mark feel convinced of that?'

Her scowl deepened, sharply. 'Don't mock him, Aidan, he is my husband.'

'I'm not mocking him at all. I simply wonder when his flagging self-confidence will assert itself. Or is the truth that he's simply lost interest in the world of the press generally, and the *Derwent Chronicle* in particular?'

'You . . . you must talk to Mark. He may feel . . .'

He could not stop himself. 'I don't give a damn what Mark feels. I care what you feel. I can see what this is doing to you. What did you feel when you looked in the mirror this morning, Berrima? For I can tell you right now, you look like someone who's been underwater for a week.'

She stood, moved restlessly, 'It's the dress, green doesn't suit me . . .'

'Anything suits you. But not half-dead with exhaustion the way you are. I can't bear to see what he's doing to you, Berrima.'

To his horror, she burst into tears. 'Stop it! Stop it, Aidan! Don't you see that working at the Chronicle is all I have? There are no children – no children! And there won't be, now! And I must thank God for it! If I'm sane at all, Aidan, it's because of that newspaper, and I won't give it up to stay here and embroider table napkins, Aidan, I won't!'

'I can't fire y' if I wanted to, woman!' he shouted from the turmoil of his emotions and the desire to move to her, hold her against him, comfort her. 'You're not on the pay-roll! And don't be after screamin' like a harpy at me, it's not my fault that you don't have children! I'd – you'd – that's not . . . I can understand,' he burbled, flushing, as her face had come about and she was gazing at him, amazed. 'I can understand that you find some joy in what you're doing – your work can fill your life – yes, I understand the need for that. But if you've got courage enough to do that, then have a little more courage, and don't let Mark drain away your life. Leave him. Leave him, and come away with me.' And he almost gasped at his own words, his audacity.

She had begun to turn away but turned back to him, very slowly, as the words penetrated. 'What?'

'Come away with me. To Melbourne, or Sydney. It doesn't matter where.' He tried to control his voice, to keep the desperation from it.

She could only stare at him. 'Just . . . like that? Leave?'

'Yes. Get packed now, and we'll leave on tonight's steamer. I can arrange everything else from Melbourne. But you needn't come back here. Mark won't find you.' His heart was thundering in his chest. It was all he could do not to rush across the room and hold her, shake her, beg her.

She still stared at him. He swallowed, could not understand why he had spoken like this, now, only that he could not bear to see what was before him. Mark was killing her, killing her slowly . . .

'Why?' The word was barely audible.

'Because . . . you shouldn't have to live like this. Because you deserve some loyalty and respect and . . .' His face felt heated, he was embarrassed; her face looked so cold, so cold. He suddenly realized what he was doing, attempting to seduce the wife of his business partner, his friend . . .

'And you . . . you feel these things for me?'

'I . . . Yes. I always have. I've always . . . been fond of you. I knew your marriage was a mistake. I would have told you, too. But I doubt you'd have listened to me. You loved Mark, didn't you?'

'Yes.'

'Yes. So nothing I said would have mattered. Nothing I felt for you would have mattered.'

'Aidan . . . You haven't considered— You can't leave your wife, your family. You'd miss them. I couldn't . . . I have nothing to give you.' She had half-spoken to herself; when she looked up at him he was gazing at her intently, the eyes unreadable. He walked towards her.

The look in his eyes was a kind of threat that she did not quite credit, could not believe. 'You . . . you don't love me,' she said.

He stopped. 'I don't know what love is. I wasn't speaking of love. I want to take care of you. To see you laughing again, to be young

642

again before Mark drains you of all your joy and leaves you old and haggard. Mark won't age, he'll age you. You're the one who'll pay the price for his immaturity. He'll never grow up. You'll never be able to depend on him.'

She had half-raised her hand, almost as if to ward off a blow. 'I can't listen to these things . . .'

He took her hand quickly. It was not a friendly grasp. It was too tight, he was pinching her fingers. 'Leave with me, Berrima. Don't stop to think about it. If we think about it we'll both stay, and be miserable the rest of our lives. Take this chance. Gamble with me. I'm an excellent gambler.'

'You pity me. And you're unhappy – I know how unhappy you are. But you don't love me. You've never said anything before, you can't mean any of this . . .'

'I want you. I do mean that. I want you and I'll have you, Berrima. I'll not allow Mark or anyone else to destroy you. I swear before God, I want what's best for you.'

She paused, biting her lip. He moved forward, quickly, and had taken her in his arms before she could move away.

'Don't, don't . . .' Yet she was holding him, and even her voice betrayed her, lacked conviction.

'What will we do, Berrima, Berrima . . . ?' He breathed it like a song against her flesh. 'What will make you stop this senselessness, put Mark out of your mind? What, Berrima? Berrima.'

How could his voice be saying such things, crooning his thoughts, wicked thoughts, out aloud. Planning, plotting, like music his voice fell on her, but the words jarred. She did not wish to think of Mark, to think of anything. She wanted to forget, hear and feel only the music of his mouth against hers.

He had picked her up, carried her to the couch, and now . . . 'No!' The hands were rough, were upon her petticoats, 'No! Aidan, No!'

He kissed her – oh, his kiss was hard, now, and not pleasant, and his hands were hard and hot on her shoulder, on her thigh, 'No!' She tried to rise, turned her face away, but his weight was upon her, both hands were at the bodice of her dress. He pulled at it – she felt the jerk of the weight of his impatience, the fabric hurt her arms, cut into them as he pulled at it . . .

It did not tear. With an oath he yanked her into a sitting position, and pulled at it. Her breasts were all but exposed, but the bodice, the expensive emerald velvet, well-made as it was, did not give even under his grip.

Berrima watched as his face flushed, the dark eyes, almost all pupil, black eyes dark with desire and rage, calmed, fired a little. The mouth twitched, turned up a little . . . he was smiling. He looked into her eyes and he was smiling. He held her to him . . . she was trembling with shock and fear . . . and he was laughing. Laughing!

She did not understand, would never understand. He was talking to her, small nothings. 'Poor child, poor dear . . .' And he was adjusting her clothing, seating her on the edge of the settee, with gentleness and care, as if he were about to paint her portrait. He wandered, away, slowly, to the window, turned, and leaned against the frame, still laughing softly to himself. She could only gaze up at him, wondering if he had gone mad. Too frightened, still, by the violence of him, by the betrayal of her own body in wanting him, she could not understand what he was doing, what he was thinking.

He appeared quite relaxed, almost negligent. He was smiling, still, she could see that he was smiling at some thought that appeared before him. 'Berrima, Berrima. It's not really worth it, is it?'

He studied her, his eyes running over her, so that her hands went unconsciously to her bodice.

He said, 'I'll not be after taking you by force, Berrima. There's no point in thanking God for the strength of your bodice, for I'd have taken you anyway, with your breasts before me, or not.

'But it's not worth it, girl. It's not one quick mating I'd want of you. Is it gratified you are to hear that? I'd want more of you, Berrima. And I'd want to know for certain that you wanted me. I don't know that. I doubt if you'd ever tell me. You'd have let me take you just now.' And slightly louder, as she began to protest, 'The decision would have been out of your hands. You'd have had no choice. And later you could have reviled me with all the rage and wild epithets you wished, tell yourself what a cad I was – and I'd never know if you wanted me. Never know what you felt. You'd have had the experience without the responsibility of caring.'

'How dare you! How dare you insinuate that I'd want you!' She was consumed with shame, her mind raced, she flung the words at him. 'How dare you touch me, how dare you lay your hands on me, you behave like a criminal! You behave like a dirty ex-convict!'

'Yes.' He nodded mildly, his smile did not change. It infuriated her. 'There, you're beginning already. The experience hasn't made you prostrate with shock, at least.

'I can't promise this won't happen again. But I can promise I'll not take you by force. Not once, only once. For I couldn't bear it, girl. Do you understand?' Once more their eyes locked, and his were black and fathomless, and they frightened her. 'I couldn't bear it.'

'Why did you . . .' She did not know what she was about to say.

644

The shock was passing, and her tears were very close. She found she wanted him back, wanted him here – to hold her, only to hold her. But he was there, across the room, negligent, unfeeling.

'Why did I what?' An eagerness in his voice that did not reach his eyes. But a waiting, a tenseness about him.

Why did you say those things, why did you hold me? Why begin, then draw away from me? 'Nothing.' Sullenly.

He gazed at her. She did not like it, liked it less when he said, as if he had read her mind, 'I wanted to hear you say you wanted me. Wanted me even if you don't love me. I took matters in my own hands when I shouldn't have, but I'll not be continuing on with it, falling into the romance of it. Pluto and Proserpine – or something out of *Ivanhoe*.' He grinned, and oh, she hated him! 'It *is* a fantasy, is it not? To be taken by some man you really want?'

'No! I don't know! Not . . . not me!'

'Nor any woman, I suppose,' he said dryly. 'But you wanted me, and you would not say you wanted me. Oh, it's a fantasy all right, Berri. A fantasy for those who don't want to make decisions, to leave go of their pride and reach out. I'm not allowing you to do that.'

The thing to do, of course, was to throw him out. Rush out into the street and scream that she had been attacked. Or just leave the room with dignity. Or . . . But she stayed, because his calm voice made an unpleasant kind of common sense. And the truth kept her pinned there.

'Would you come away with me?'

'What?' She raised her eyes to his, disbelieving what she heard.

'I'm a stubborn wretch, aren't I? You see, you still haven't given me an answer. Would you come away with me? There could be no divorce, Maura would never agree to divorce me. But we could go somewhere where no one would know.' Still in that calm, detached voice.

She did not really believe what she was hearing. It went against all she had known of him. She could more easily believe that his violent passion could result in him raping her, than that he would consider this. 'Leave Maura, and the children?'

'Yes. I'd leave them.' And he would, knew it as he spoke, that though it would tear the heart from him, he would go with this girl. Would move heaven and earth to be with her.

'No. No, I couldn't. I won't even consider it. It's impossible, and you know it.'

They stared at each other for a long moment, then, heavily, 'Yes,' her sharp little voice summed it up. That was how she would see their union, it held no beauty, no attraction for her. 'Yes,' he said.

He wondered what would happen now, became aware that she was dangerously close to tears and wished him gone. Yet he was afraid. Never again, after today, would their relationship be the same.

He went, of course, to Matty. Booked into the White Cockatoo, and ordered a late supper to be brought up to his room. He could barely contain his impatience and rage when a manservant arrived with the food – he had expected Matty.

She arrived at two that night, after he had fallen asleep, letting herself in to the room and sliding into the bed beside him.

'I had to wait for Griffith to go to sleep. A whole bottle of French brandy I had to give him. You're an expensive hobby, my lad.'

'He's here? He's home?'

'He can't be out every time you call. He lives here, you know. And he does have first refusal.' She giggled, and wound herself about him. The darkness was thick, blinding; for a few hours, for a few brief hours, he was allowed to forget Berrima.

The hammering on the door awoke them. Matty, in terror, clung to him – for both of them expected her husband to break down the door at any moment.

But gradually the words seeped into Aidan's drugged mind. 'Father? Is that Aidan O'Brien in there? Father, wake up! It's me, Liam! Father, unlock the door! It's Liam, Father, unlock the door!'

He pulled on his trousers, whispered, 'Wait there, be quiet,' to Matty, and went to the door.

Liam would have thrown himself into the room, but Aidan took him by the shoulder. 'What's the matter? What's happened?'

'It's Ma, Father. She's had some kind of collapse. She's real bad, Doctor Reynolds says – he wants you to come home at once . . .'

61

'I arrived back at Glenleigh this afternoon,' Liam told him as they headed down the stairs and out into the inn yard. A sleepy young groom held their horses, already saddled. 'Doctor Reynolds was with Ma, he'd sent to the newspaper, but Mrs Ellis arrived to help, and she said you'd left. When they told me that I thought you'd have headed for the mill, perhaps, so I changed horses and came right back. It's only luck, sure, that I found you. Uncle Thomas said you often spend the night here.' Liam reached into his pocket and flipped the groom a coin. Aidan had a last view of the narrow, sly face, grinning, before they rode out of the yard and along the narrow lane towards the main road.

Milton Reynolds opened the door for them. He stopped Aidan with a hand on his shoulder as he was about to mount the stairs. 'Liam,' the doctor glanced at the boy over the father's shoulder, 'you've ridden hard – have a few hours' rest, will you?'

'But . . .'

'Your mother's sleeping. There's nothing that can be done until morning. We'll wake you if she calls for you.'

Liam went unwillingly up the stairs, glancing back, unsure, at his father. When the boy had gone, Milton drew Aidan across the hall, into the parlour.

'Aidan . . .'

'It's bad, isn't it? I can tell from your face . . .' He felt ill with concern, with guilt. He gripped his friend's arm. 'Tell me, dammit! What's happened?'

The room was in darkness, the shadows fell on Milton's face, the light from the hall made strange shadows on his cheek, 'Aidan, there's no easy way to say this . . . You must face it – I've done all I can do. She's dying, Aidan. Tomorrow, the next day – it could happen any minute. Double pneumonia, and a heart attack this evening . . .'

'Jaysus . . .!'

'She's too weak, Aidan. She's had the pneumonia for a week or more, and told no one how ill she was. And from what she tells me, she's had heart trouble previously, too.'

'What are y' like? Maura's never had a heart attack!'

'What? She never told you? She said she'd been having spells since the last trip to Port Davey – I was going to take you to task for not having her see me before this . . .' Aidan had turned away, into the darkness of the room. Reynolds's voice had faded on seeing the effect on the man. He groped along the wall for the light, found his matches and lit the gas. It hissed into life, sputtering a little.

'She never told me.' The broad back, shoulders hunched, the voice pain-filled. 'How can it be? She never told me . . .'

'She's a very strong woman, Aidan. Strong in herself, I mean. You know yourself of all she's been through – she's had a hard life – she's accustomed to coping. Perhaps she really believed she was invincible. I wouldn't put it past her. She has great spirit. It's that, I

647

think, that's kept her alive all this time.

'Go to her, now. But remain calm. She mustn't be excited.'

Upstairs he was terrified to see that the priest had been called, had administered the Last Sacrament, and was now kneeling in prayer with Thomas and Mary at the foot of the bed.

Aidan had forgotten to remove his hat, now pulled it from his head and dropped it into a chair. He bent his head until the prayers were completed, then, on the priest's suggestion, Aidan was left alone with Maura.

She looked infinitely small, withdrawn. Looking at her, the pale translucence of her skin, the stillness of her, he knew that Milton was speaking the truth. He stared, and stared, and willed his mind to accept the truth. That this frail little creature was Maura, that she was fading, had almost faded already, out of existence, and this barely functioning little shell was all that was left. He knew it was the truth. Yet he shook his head slightly. Perhaps there was a mistake, there must be something that could be done. He would call in a specialist in the morning, get a second opinion. There must be some other way, this could not happen, he would not allow it to happen.

The memory of the morning came back to him. Her silence, her wounded feelings – she had not spoken to him, he had hurt her so badly with his words the night before. Now she may die, he thought with horror, and she would die hating him, she would die not having forgiven him . . .

She had opened her eyes, was gazing at him. He opened his mouth to speak, but no words would come. What could he say? What?

He walked closer, and sat down on the chair that was pulled close to the bed.

The green eyes were huge, they dominated the tiny head, they glittered like green stones in the white face. And yet, she looked young – so very young, the bright orange hair in braids upon the pillow.

'Maura . . .'

'I'm glad.' She half-smiled. 'Is Father Glynn still here?'

'Aye, he's in the room beyond.'

'Good, it's kind of him to wait with me. So . . . much to do. I've left so much for . . . later. Later never comes, does it?'

'Maura, don't talk so . . .'

'Strange, isn't it? I'm not afraid at all. This is what's so . . . strange . . . today. I really feel as if I see clearly. It's God's . . . gift, perhaps.'

He was filled with horror at her words, her attitude. Fight! he felt like shouting at her, don't let go so easily, not now! Don't let yourself be beaten now! But he could not say this, did not wish to acknowledge what was happening, hated it that she could do so.

'Aidan, we'll have little time alone. Your poor mother, when I go it will take a little of the life from her. Help her all you can.'

'I will sure. But Maura . . .'

'No, don't take on so. Don't waste time telling me I'm not dying. There are other things – important things . . .' She paused, then said, suddenly, 'This is the first time . . . I'll get my way . . . and I want everything understood. The children . . . They're to go back to . . . to Ireland.'

'What?'

'You heard. They're . . . to be educated . . . in Ireland. Dublin. Trinity . . . for Liam. And a fine . . . convent – the best – for Clemency. You have money enough, now. You can afford it.'

'Maura, I can't have them go half-way round the world . . . !'

'They're Irish children! I want them . . . brought up . . . Irish. They mustn't forget.'

Aidan was becoming angry, despite his shock, his guilt, his fear – or perhaps because of it. 'Forget *what?* Being hungry and out of work? Forget the landlords selling the crops to England while we went without?'

'Aidan.' She held out her hands to him. 'Aidan, I'm asking you. I want to know that when I die the children are being educated properly – not running about like . . . tinkers' children.'

'They're happy here . . .'

'This country gives them no choice. I've thought . . . all day, Aidan . . . Lying here, I've thought about it. This country gives them no choice. Let them see what else there is. Other . . . opportunities.'

'I could send them to Melbourne . . .'

'Aidan, I'm . . . begging you, now. Let it . . . be Dublin. I'll not rest until you've promised.'

'The children are all I have . . .' he breathed. Their eyes met, then she had closed her own eyes, locked him out once more. *She knows that. She knows that . . . !*

Her breath came in little, shallow gasps. Her face was gaunt, and dangerously pale.

He said, 'I promise.'

'Say it. Say . . . all of it . . .'

'I . . . promise to y' – I'll send the children back to Ireland.'

And she relaxed a little, then, and smiled. 'Good . . . good. And you must tell them first thing tomorrow.'

'Tomorrow?'

649

'Aye. And they're to leave . . . soon, Aidan. As soon . . . as possible.'

She reached out and took his hand. She tried to smile, knowing that she had hurt him. But, 'You'll see . . .' she said, gently. 'It will be for the best, I know it.'

Maura died two days later. Clemency and Aidan had driven into Hobart, to the apothecary to have a prescription made up, and Liam, oppressed by the atmosphere in the house, had walked over to visit with Richard Reynolds not five minutes before it happened. Thomas, for want of something to keep his shaken nerves and helplessly restless body occupied, was digging in the vegetable garden at the rear of the house.

Mary had been sitting by the bed, working at her tatting in a patch of afternoon sunlight. Mary had no time to call for aid; it was Maura who said, suddenly, loudly, as she half-sat up with the pain, 'It was Thomas! Thomas, was it not? Why did you not tell me? We were all so foolish!'

Mary had moved forward, seated herself on the edge of the bed, holding the younger woman. 'Oh, Mother of God . . .' For she had known, of course she had known.

'I told the priest. Oh, Thomas . . . !'

When Thomas flung himself through the door, she had already gone. Mary was laying her back on the bed, adjusting the poor, distorted face, closing the eyes.

'Stay away, Thomas, leave us a while.'

'No! She's not . . . I was coming up to the house. I heard her voice. She called my name . . . !'

Mary's hands, gnarled, tender, had done their work, Maura lay peacefully.

Thomas said, 'She's not gone!' The control of years, the love of years, warring within him, his grief shattering his perpetual calm. 'No, Ma! She's not gone! She called my name!'

His mother's back was to him. It was stiff, her mouth held grimly. She said, 'She called for Aidan.'

A terrible pause, then, 'No, Ma. No. I heard her. She called for me.'

The black eyes came around to him, filling with tears and her love for him. No. No, it had gone on long enough, long enough. She would not have his life haunted by the thought that Maura had been his. 'She called Aidan, my dear. Why should she call you, *asthore*? She called for her husband.'

Thomas stared at her, 'Aye, but . . .'

Mary had stood, led him gently out of the room. He walked like a man whose spirit had left him.

650

62

The children left for Dublin two months after Maura died. It was as long as Aidan felt that he could justifiably wait, keep them with him. Liam was no problem at all, was delighted to go to Ireland, to study privately until such time as Trinity accepted him into a Bachelor of Law course. He was philosophical about missing the 1864 term, boarding in Dublin with independent means was not to be regarded as a disappointment. Clemency, however, was another matter.

'I don't want to go. And to a *convent*. Papa, it's cruel! You'll not be after doing it! I don't believe you!'

'Rebel, it's not what I want. It was your ma's last wish . . .'

'Then Ma wasn't thinking straight! She couldn't have been . . . !'

'Now you stop it! That's an evil thing to say!'

'She couldn't want me to leave Tasmania, to separate me from you! She couldn't!'

'She wanted you to have the best education, Clemency. You'll see London, as well as Dublin. And Paris in your school holidays – Liam has promised to take you . . .'

'I don't want to see stupid London or Paris! I want to stay here!'

'Clemency . . .' Her shrill little voice was beginning to grate on his nerves, for she was right in her wishes, and he had thought and thought and could see no way out of this. 'Clemency, I understand how you feel. But I have to do this thing for your mother's sake. It all comes down, Rebel, to doing what your mother would wish, or what you would wish. Your mother is gone—'

'And you're trying to make up to her.'

He stared at her. Through her tears the green eyes, Maura's eyes, glared at him. 'What?'

'You're trying to assuage your guilt. By fulfilling a last wish, and it wasn't a fair wish, a right one. Ma wanted to separate me from you . . . !'

'You stop talking like that!'

'If she'd asked you to kill me, would you have done that? I think you would have. For you'll be killing me, Papa, by sending me to that city on the other side of the world. I belong in this country, Papa! I was raised in the bush at Port Davey! I'm not Irish, I'm Australian!'

'Stop the performance,' he said grimly. His face was closed. 'I'm not after asking you anything, Clemency – I'm telling you, as your father. You're going to St Theresa's in Dublin, and there's an end to it.'

She had run out of the house, and despite Mary's pleas, he had not gone after her until two hours had passed, and even he was worried. He was placing his hat on his head, ready to leave to search for her, when she arrived home, with Berrima. She, too, tried to speak to him on the matter, but he remained obdurate.

'I have to do it, for Maura's sake.'

'Aidan, if you're a Christian you must see that Maura would no longer care about these things. It's Clemency's life – you must think of her happiness . . .'

'I gave my word.'

'Is your honour more important than Clemency's future?'

'I don't need you to tell me what to do, Berrima! I don't need your cold officiousness to run my life, nor my daughter's!'

He said these words because she was sitting before him, embodying his grief, his guilt, and still the driving force of his life. He wanted her, and he hated her, and he could not forget that this was the first time that she had come willingly to see him since Maura's death. He took a savage delight in compounding her view of him as heartless, an incorrigible fiend.

Berrima's eyes had widened with hurt, and she had left him to go to Clemency. After that, she did not come to Glenleigh again.

Clemency barely spoke to him in the weeks until she left on the clipper *Windward* for London.

Aidan, when the children had gone, spent more and more time in Melbourne, organizing the buying and re-selling of land in the new suburbs that were beginning to spread along the coast about Port Phillip Bay.

His letters from Liam, in the following years, were brief, the style staccato with excitement and optimism. His letters from Clemency were also brief, forced and polite. He knew that a nun must supervise the fortnightly letter-writing hours. He felt certain that otherwise the child who signed herself 'Your Dutiful Daughter', would not write at all.

Matty could not help him, although she tried. When he finally went to visit her, eight months after Maura's death, she welcomed him with all the passion of her nature. But their lovemaking, to him, was a failure. He did not climax, lay with the rest of his body tense, felt his desire falling from him. It had never happened before, and he felt embarrassed, waited for her to laugh at him, question him.

'That was lovely for me, mate,' she held him tenderly, but he could still sense her surprised amusement. 'But it wasn't much fun for you.' He still lay half upon her, and she held his head with her hands, the large, long-fingered, capable hands, and gazed into his face. She brushed the dark hair from his eyes.

'I'm sorry,' he said.

The deep, throaty laugh. 'Don't be. It's all right, love. You been through a bad time. I know what it's like. Bit of guilt there, too, I s'pose.'

He scowled a little, and went to roll away. 'Hey.' Her hand went to his shoulder. 'You have to face up to that. Lots of people go through it when their husband or wife dies. It's almost natural. I'd probably go off sex, too, if something was to happen to Grif. Aidan, love. Stop scowling. Let's just lie here, eh?'

But he was filled with restlessness, and dressed, and had his horse saddled, and rode on to the mill. Matty did not like him leaving her – Grif was away, and it was a real waste of time, a proper shame, that Aidan should come over all penitent and guilt-ridden and spoil what could have been two or three enjoyable evenings. It wasn't as if he and that Maura were *really* man and wife anyway. He couldn't *miss* her . . .

It was not missing Maura exactly. It seemed that he had taken her presence so much for granted, and his house was lonelier, colder, his world made more vulnerable by her passing from him. For years he had refused to consider the thought of his own death – Maura's brought the possibility closer to him. He would gaze at his reflection in his mirror before setting off to the mill, or to the bank, or the *Chronicle*, for this latter was the only neutral ground where he now met Berrima, and somehow, even resenting her, he needed to see her. He looked, in the full-length glass, fit, tough, well-dressed. The soft, flat-crowned hats with the five inch brims that he now wore suited him. He looked what he was, a wealthy man who had made his money on the land. He did not look old . . .

But he was old. The fact that he did not look more than thirty-five did not alter the fact that he was now forty-one. What if these unsuccessful matings with Matty – and lately he had taken to visiting Beatrice and Antonia, with the same results – what if these failed attempts were just the beginning? His sexual ability was on the decline . . .

There developed something panicky about his love-making, and nothing that Matty could do would convince him that tension was the very cause of the problem. And for her own reasons, Matty became worried. Perhaps she saw, unwillingly, that her hold over

Aidan had always been a primarily sexual one. And if this was so, she was going to lose him.

When, two months later, Mark Ellis announced that he wished to leave Tasmania and settle in New South Wales, Aidan was not driven, as he once would have been, to despair. By then he felt hardened to any further disappointment, hardened to any excessive feeling at all. The *Derwent Chronicle* was sold, and both Mark and Aidan made a good profit on their three-year investment.

Berrima and Mark left for the New South Wales town of Berrima, for which she had been named, in March, 1865. Aidan had not attempted to dissuade either Mark or Berrima from the move. Berri was polite, a little withdrawn when they met; Aidan, preoccupied with his own emotions to the exclusion of almost all else, did not know, after the scene they had shared the day before Maura's death, how to approach her.

In later years he wondered at the emotions that possessed him, that prevented him from taking Berrima and shaking an explanation from her, that drove him to work hard, drink hard, in order to avoid facing up to the situation. It would seem such weakness; a time spent in a kind of limbo – all movement, action, and yet superficial. He made money, but his life went nowhere at all. He watched his bank balance rise with a feeling of terror. He had killed Maura, he did not deserve to have so much. And he worked harder, to forget his achievements, achieved more in doing so, and tried not to think that there was no longer any real goal behind his efforts. The Celt in him took a perverse view of the matter in that he felt he had deserved to lose Berrima, deserved, too, the recurring impotence that began to claim him whenever he tried to make love to a woman. It was the wrath of God. He had killed Maura with coldness and impatience – he had taken years to do it. Now he was left with everything – and nothing. He had always been treated with suspicion in business circles. Now – unapproachable, over-sensitive, savage-tempered – men began to dislike him, and to fear him.

At home, Aidan brooded and grumbled and snarled. Mary ignored him much of the time, because he was, as she told him, too unpleasant to bother with. She did not really worry about Aidan, realized that this was something he would need to see through for himself.

She worried more about Thomas. She knew he had never slept with a woman in his life – his sexual urges, like his other emotions, were kept hidden deep within him. Mary knew that Aidan had found solace somewhere, he'd discovered it years before she and Thomas had arrived, for he and Maura had had separate rooms even

654

then. Whoever it was that Aidan was seeing would be the person to help him through this time. But Thomas . . . She could think of no way to help Thomas, watched him become more withdrawn, thinner, driven, like his older brother, to work long hours and for days and weeks at a time without a break in routine. But Thomas's nature did not allow him the outlet of bad temper and aggression. And his grief, she knew, was greater than Aidan's. Aidan had lost his wife, and now felt lost himself. And he felt guilty. It was obvious in the set of his shoulders as he stood leaning against one of the trees at Glenleigh, scowling over the garden, or in the grim lines in his face when he looked up from his newspapers or documents to glare into the fire for minutes at a time. Thomas had lost the only love he had ever known, and Mary moved about Glenleigh in those months after Maura's death with a prayer on her lips, most of the time, that her own action, at the end, had been the right one. Time would tell. The obsession with Maura *must* be over. Thomas – was she gambling too heavily on this assumption of her son's deep-seated common sense? – would not make a shrine within himself to the dead, in the same way that he had unselfishly served the living.

It was the only truly obvious sin that she had ever committed in her life, withholding the knowledge that Maura had called Thomas, at the end. It did not matter to Maura, did it now? And sure it could make a great deal of difference to Thomas. Time will tell. Holy Mother, understand and intercede for me. It was a white lie, Holy Mother, or a fierce pale one, at the very most.

After Berrima and Mark left Tasmania, letters began coming for Aidan, Mark excitedly praising the countryside, his prophesies that this area, called the Southern Highlands, would soon be amongst the wealthiest in Australia.

> *The land is, for the most part, volcanic – one can grow anything in the rich black soil. I must admit I was loath to follow Berrima's urgings to leave Hobart, but we are very happy here.*
>
> *We both miss you, dear chap. Don't you think that your business interests would be better served by being closer to Sydney? When the railway links Melbourne with Sydney, you would be in an excellent situation, here, since we are about ninety miles from Sydney, and the train to Melbourne will stop practically at our door.*
>
> *Berrima joins her wishes to mine, that we may see you here . . .*

One letter expressing sentiments like this disturbed him; when it was multiplied over and over in the months after the Ellises had left, Aidan reached the stage where he could hardly bear to open the

655

envelope. When he did, he found himself searching down the page for the words . . . 'Berrima misses your company – she claims she has no one to quarrel with . . .' 'Berrima sends her fondest regards to yourself and Mary and Thomas and begs you to consider removing yourselves to where we will be neighbours once more . . .', 'Berrima said yesterday that the region around Mittagong reminds her of pictures she had seen of Ireland. She said she wishes Mary could see it . . .', 'Berrima says you should all come . . .', 'Berrima says . . .', 'Come . . .', 'Come . . .'

One evening he walked by the creek at the bottom of the garden in Glenleigh, found himself drawn to the tree, the willow's branches bare of leaves, now, where he had once held Berrima.

Will had discovered them. Will whose heart had been broken by Emily. Will was now making preparations to sail the little *Lostwithiel* to Brisbane, Queensland, where he and Cora meant to settle. He had written to Aidan to tell him of the sale of the lease; Aidan had received the letter that morning and pulled it, now, from his pocket, and reread it; two new piners, Winters and Preston, had bought their stand, for a good price.

You'll not like this, Aidan –I didn't myself when they told me – but they've begun logging on the other side of the gully. I've been busy at the mill, and looking after Cora, who's still having sickness in the mornings, despite Mrs Malone saying it should pass by the third month. I didn't know that Winters would have started bringing the pine down so soon – not but that he has the right, Aidan, for he owns the lease, now. Anyhow, he came down river especially with the big pine, to show everyone. Malone says he should cut a section and take it to Hobart and put it on show. It saddened me, though, to see what was left of the tree, floating in the water off Malone's pit. It was rather like leaving an old trout go, was it not? A big old trout that had deserved the right to live.

Aidan thought of that green glade beyond the gully and the fall-down pines, and the ferns – and the giant tree, separate, apart, amongst the ring of its progeny. Gone, now. The peace and calm of the place shattered, the quiet beauty changed to a raw ugliness of low, truncated stumps, fallen branches, dead limbs. An ugly clearing, nothing special, nothing wondrous about it. A place where piners had passed through.

He thought of Port Davey, the broad, fjord-like harbour, the grey beauty of the place. He thought of Settlement Point, the cluster of huts and cottages, the smoke drifting from the chimneys into the cold air, to rise, misting the view of the mountains and to blend with the low-hanging cloud. He thought of the people in these houses, the Malones, the Raymonds, poor simple Heath, foolish Maggie Lane and her new paramour – these people had been his friends when he had been The Ex-convict; they had shared their companionship, their food, their tools, their labour, when he had been simply a struggling piner such as they were.

Aidan glanced over at the red brick house next door. There, in the warmth of those lamplit rooms, Milton and Margaret Reynolds, in their early fifties now, would live out the rest of their lives. They, too, had accepted him, along with his past; accepted him as he was.

Now his ambition had brought him close to being wealthy, he must move away, and he would find other friends. But he would be The Emancipist, the owner of this, and that, and the other. A useful man to know. For the rest of his life, despite being a reliable judge of character, he would never know, completely, if he were accepted for what he intrinsically was, or for what he had become. Here, among these people, he knew.

But within his pocket, crammed there unthinkingly before he had left his office to walk outside, was the latest letter from Mark. It was filled with bitterness; against the weather, the soil of his farm, the temperaments of his workers, even against the Government of New South Wales, for choosing to lay the precious railway not through Berrima township, but further to the east. 'The upstart towns of Mittagong, Bowral and Moss Vale,' he wrote, 'have the benefit not only of the nearby iron mine, but of the railway that is strangling this village to extinction. It was a mistake to come here . . .'

The rest of the letter was equally as gloomy – and worse, as of late, there was an unmistakable ingratiating note creeping into his prose. Aidan, knew, suddenly, that Berri had undoubtedly said very little about Aidan joining herself and Mark. Mark needed Aidan; the last few letters had contained the phrase, 'I am not managing half so well here, without your excellent advice . . .' and though Aidan no longer believed that Berrima truly was urging him to come to them, he knew that Mark spoke the truth; he could not cope. And if Mark was in distress, then so, tied to him as she was, was Berrima.

Aidan looked up at Mount Wellington, the last light touching its broad shoulder with dove-pink light. I can't stay, he told this island that had given him so much. I must go. I must.

Part 4
MITTAGONG

. . . There the little homesteads nestle in their green,
Opal where the mists rise, amber where the paddocks shine,
My own things around me and none to come between.

VANCE PALMER

63

It was late 1865 before all the business ties with Hobart were satisfactorily settled, and in January, 1866, after a last Christmas with Margaret and Milton Reynolds, Aidan, Thomas and Mary left Tasmania for the Australian mainland.

The journey seemed interminable; by steamer to Melbourne, then by train and coach, northwards, across the Murray River that divided Victoria from New South Wales. And more days spent in lurching coaches, more nights in hot, uncomfortable roadside taverns. And the scrub, endless scrub. Finally, after more than two weeks of travelling, the coach rattled over the boards of the bridge across the Wingecarribee River, and turned up the gentle slope to the township of Berrima.

They were there to meet the coach, Mark in a dark business suit, looking more handsome than ever in his maturity. Aidan could never rid himself of the slight envy when Mark stood before him, and he was conscious that beside the younger man he appeared not only of middle height and stocky but downright *short*. He tried to put the feeling from him, noticing with relief that there was no sign of dissipation in Mark's face such as there had been during the past years in Hobart Town. Despite the mood of foreboding in his letters, it seemed that he was not seeking some artificial release from his problems. He chattered as he walked them to the carriage.

'We've moved, you know. I found farming didn't really suit me, so I hired a manager for the farm and Berri and I bought a charming house in Mittagong. Far more exciting place.' He grinned at Aidan. 'A man could make his mark there, if he was clever, couldn't he, my dear?' Berrima merely smiled.

She was now, Aidan calculated, twenty-six, but even in the subdued lilac-grey of her costume, she looked nineteen. Bubbling with excitement at seeing them, she had rushed forward to embrace Mary, Thomas and Aidan without favouritism; and her smile, her laugh, the ring of her voice were still, even now, hauntingly, hurtfully, reflections of Anna.

Mark was helping Mary into the carriage, demanding why it had taken her so long to decide to come, that he missed her cooking and her sharp tongue. Mary, who enjoyed Mark's humour, told him to blame Aidan and his business affairs. 'Sure any place where there's a sunny climate and I'll be happy,' she said.

Berrima climbed in beside her. 'Actually the climate here is similar to Tasmania – the winters can be cold.'

Mary turned a baleful eye upon her eldest. 'If he'd told me that,' she said, 'I'd have stayed in Hobart.'

Thomas was helping Aidan load the luggage in the dray that was to follow behind them. He glanced up at the laughter in the carriage, and murmured to his brother, 'Berrima still looks like Anna, does she not?' His brown eyes were sombre. Aidan caught their expression with a kind of shock, and his brother smiled faintly, as if in a kind of apology. 'Aye, I've always been after noticing. Ma, too.' Mark was helping unload the cases from the top of the coach, and as they stepped forward to take them; 'But different within, Aidan . . .'

'I know that.' His tone was flat.

He had somehow expected that she would have changed. If he was honest with himself, at the back of his mind had been the hope that there was tension between herself and Mark, that she had finally seen Mark as he was, and wished to leave him.

Their house in Mittagong was a two-storey sandstone building, fronted by a wide, cool veranda, and surrounded by garden. It was an established and attractive avenue, Queen Street, with its view of the low mountains, and the neat brick and stone and weatherboard houses had a feeling of security and complacent well-being to them. Berrima's house, complete with the faithful Nellie, was a picture of warm stability, and Berrima, showing her guests over it, gave no sign that the atmosphere within the house was any different to that of its comfortable exterior.

The Ellises welcomed the three O'Briens, insisted that they stay as long as they wished, not to hurry and buy the first property they saw. Aidan, however, was eager to see as much of the countryside as possible. He invested in good horses and a carriage almost on arriving, and spent a great deal of time exploring.

As Mark had predicted on the first day, Aidan liked Mittagong. Nestled amongst wooded slopes, the few fine brick and stone shops and houses found themselves surrounded by slab-timber, mud brick or weatherboard buildings which had been raised hurriedly to cope with the growth of the place. This had been years before, in the 'forties, when the mine had first been established. Now the growth of the town had been slowing considerably, for the hope that Mittagong – with the first iron mine and steel works in the country –

662

would expand to a city, was receiving many setbacks. Several tradesmen brought out from Sheffield in England had even named the township New Sheffield amongst themselves. But the name had had little chance to catch the imagination of others. Not for the first time, the lack of nearby coal deposits, the cost of transporting the ore to the market in Sydney, the expense of the steel-making machinery, and most of all, the competition from the cheaper steel arriving from Europe, put the mine and the mill out of business.

Yet already, the railway had made a difference to the town, and at the time Aidan, Thomas and Mary arrived, there were plans of re-opening the iron works; more money was being poured into the purchase of up-to-date machinery, and there was hope that a petition for tariff protection might bring some aid from the government.

'The mine' was all anyone talked about, lately, in the pubs, in the street, at the dinner parties held in the large houses of the country estates – 'the mine', 'the plant' was on every man's tongue. It concerned the town, concerned them all.

Roger Pirie-Moxham, one of the most prominent members of the new Board of Southern Highlands Iron and Steel, gave a party only a few weeks after the O'Briens arrived. They were invited, Aidan suspected, less because they were newcomers to the district, as because they were houseguests of Berrima and Mark Ellis. The party was for Mark's younger brother, only just returned from England, to celebrate the success of his book of poetry, *Songs of Nattai.*

'Where's Nattai?' Thomas asked Aidan, in the carriage on the way to the party.

'Hereabouts, somewhere,' his brother replied, wrestling a little with the tight collar of his new dinner suit. 'This area seems to have more names than I can cope with. 'Tis a river, I think, west of Mittagong. In fact, Mittagong *was* Nattai until recently.'

''Twas also New Sheffield, and Fitzroy,' Thomas grumbled, 'I wish they'd be after making up their minds.'

'The railway station's to be called Mittagong. That'll settle matters.'

The whole district was new, in a state of flux, and Aidan felt happy in the confusion. At the Pirie-Moxhams' party he drifted about from group to group, and listened to the gossip, noting names, and memorizing details, characters, faces, that would help him in the future.

And yet, behind all this scheming, he had hoped that somehow, this evening, he would find an opportunity to talk to Berrima alone, if only while they were dancing together.

But though he managed to dance once or twice with her, and though she led him about from group to group, introducing him to people, the wealthy merchant families or the landed gentry with their private incomes, even one or two with minor titles who frequented the Highlands for the salubrious climate, there was no time for any serious talk between himself and the girl.

Aidan found himself, at one stage, left in a group comprised of Mark and a married couple, Helena and Hedley Warwick, both of families long-resident in the district. Mark was remarking that 'the trilogy' as he called the three towns of Mittagong, Bowral and Moss Vale, had, because of the Highlands' reputation for a healthy climate, more inns, between them, catering for invalids, than Bath in England. 'And since Mittagong has such a small natural spring, people are mostly forced to drink the ale, you see,' he said, seriously. 'But no doubt, they adjust, after a while, and probably have a better time of their stay.'

Mrs Warwick, who was trying not to smile, said disapprovingly, 'I fear you are very cynical, Mr Ellis. There, you and your brother greatly differ from each other.'

'Yes, thank goodness.' Mark looked across the gardens to where his brother stood, deep in conversation with a very pretty dark-haired girl. 'All the romantic tendencies in the family belong to Garth.'

'And his horsemanship – he won the steeplechase in Sydney only last month – one of the finest riders in the colony.' Hedley turned to Aidan. 'I'm glad we didn't lose him to England. Very fortunate for Australia that he has brought his talents home.'

'Yes, indeed,' Mark murmured, and sipped from his glass of punch.

Aidan was interested in this. It seemed that there was not a little jealousy between the two brothers. Mark, of course, was undeniably good looking; by comparison, the younger Garth was rather long-faced, his hair an indeterminate brown, and he was taller, moved with less grace than Mark did. Garth moved quickly, jerkily, and seemed ill at ease even in this group gathered to praise him. The only time Aidan saw him looking confident, at ease, was when the young, dark-haired beauty was talking with him.

And then, as he moved away from Mark and the Warwicks, he saw the girl's face full-on, and almost faltered at the sight of it. A birthmark, deep red and very noticeable, stained the left side of the girl's nose and upper lip. Aidan had thought, on first seeing it, that her nose had been bleeding, and he walked on, hoping he had not made any unintended show of shock at the sight of the disfigurement.

He found Berrima, and questioned her, seeing her expression soften as she turned towards the girl. 'Victoria Amberley,' she said. 'Garth has been in love with her for years. Did you not read the descriptions of the heroine in *Songs of Nattai?* That's why that book was such a success, Aidan. Garth put his soul into those poems.'

Aidan asked, 'Why didn't he just throw the girl over his shoulder and elope with her?'

'That's what I like about you, Aidan.' Berrima was unmoved. 'Your elemental attitude to life. My dear, it wasn't that easy. Garth has enough money of his own, certainly, but Francis Amberley – that's him over there, the big man with the grizzled beard – he's a self-made man, and he didn't have much patience with Garth's rather esoteric ideas on life. Victoria is still under age – Garth is hoping that Mr Amberley might reconsider his suit, now that he's a success in English literary circles.'

'So Garth came home to fetch Victoria?' Aidan looked between the two young lovers with interest. The story appealed to the long-buried streak of romanticism in his soul.

'He'd have come home at any rate. He loves Australia – it comes through in his poetry, don't you think?'

'I only . . . em . . . skimmed through it.'

'I see.' She looked at him with reproach. 'Well you won't escape the edifying experience of Garth's prose, for he's to read selections of the work this evening before supper.' She grinned, and Aidan groaned quietly.

He amused himself, after she had been swept off for the polka by Francis Amberley's son, Fitzroy, in having a discussion with the Warwicks. He had decided already that he liked Hedley and did not like his wife, for Helena was a woman possessed with great curiosity and a gift of seeming to censor whatever information she heard. 'Van Diemen's Land?' she repeated, when Aidan answered her query as to where he had been resident before coming to the Southern Highlands. 'How wise you were to leave. I can't understand how any free settler,' and she looked at him narrowly for a split second, 'can abide to live in a colony where the population is three quarters felons or ex-felons.'

Aidan debated, for a moment, telling her that he was an emancipist – but no. Let Southern Highlands society find out for itself. 'Och, ma'am,' he said with a smile, 'the figures are nowhere as bad as that.'

'No? Well, perhaps I exaggerate, but there are certainly many of them. One wouldn't feel safe.'

'I've not looked into it in any detail, ma'am, but I do assure you that there are few ex-convicts left in Tasmania. Most of them headed for New South Wales with the first goldrushes.'

Helena Warwick's face closed in on itself like a prune drying in the sun. To make matters worse, her husband, Hedley, giggled softly. He did not laugh; he was a man in whom all outward show of emotion was muted. Helena glared at him, and Hedley sobered, pushing his glasses up his nose, a gesture that Aidan was to see him repeat often when he was at all distressed.

Aidan had just opened his mouth to note that living in a district with its own infamous gaol, at Berrima, must provide Mrs Warwick with infinite opportunities to study human nature, and wouldn't her father have been after hiring convicts for farm work in the recent past, when Berrima swept up to their group. Aidan wondered how she had known, not realizing that the affronted look on Helena and his own expression of dangerous humour, was enough to bring her from across the lawn. She was complimenting Helena on her gown, then turned to Aidan to mention that Thomas and Mary were looking for him, and managed to guide him lightly but inexorably away.

'What a spoilsport you are, to be sure. Just when I meet someone interesting . . .'

'You mean when you meet someone foolish enough to quarrel with you – and Helena would. You'd be capping her exaggerations until she realized you thought her a fool and then she'd never forgive you. No – don't bother turning that innocent gaze on me, Aidan, I could see what was going to happen. In a way, I don't blame you; Helena is an overbearing, meddling, unbending, remorseless snob, I admit it; but because people are afraid of her, she has a coterie of sycophants. A powerful woman in this district, Aidan. And you – you set out to annoy her on purpose.'

Aidan was delighted. They had stopped, half-way along the path, by a small pool with a fountain playing. They were relatively alone, no one standing very near.

'I'm not used to polite society. I've not been moving amongst people lately,' he sighed. 'There are few people I can talk to, y'see. It's best to involve myself with my work. So I'm often tactless, I suppose, when I do try to move in polite circles.'

'Aidan, you were hoping she'd say something objectionable.'

'Och, no. I've been too long alone, I'm thinking, that's why I'm so gauche. It's not been the same in Hobart without yourself and Mark.

I'd come to depend on you both a great deal. When you left I missed you.'

How did it happen that he could stand there, simply stand there, not too close, and fill her mind as if the entire garden party did not exist? Without touching her, he moved her, without looking at her, he claimed her. She was afraid. Without realizing it, her eyes were searching the crowd for Mark. The spell was broken when Mark was about. When Mark was near, the threat disappeared.

His voice was low. She knew he was watching her. 'You're looking for an escape route.'

She could not meet his eyes. 'No,' she said, 'I was looking for Mark.'

The silence was very heavy, and so compelling was his gaze that she was forced to raise her eyes to meet it. 'It's the same thing, is it not?' he said, quietly.

She forced her mind back to the subject of his social adjustment, 'This isn't Port Davey, Aidan. It's not even Hobart. At the moment, you have no reputation at all. You'll be building one on the basis of the opinion these people will be making of you during these first weeks. They're hasty and inflexible, many of them, and it wouldn't hurt you, with that in mind, to set out to show the best side of your nature.'

'Och, Berrima, why so serious about it? People are the same everywhere – and they can take me or leave me. I'll not be after licking any man's boots, girl, you should know that by now.'

His very mildness of manner irritated her, his aloof satisfaction with himself. 'I don't know why I bother with you. I'd like to push you backwards into that fountain over there . . .'

'I'd be taking you with me. And you lecture me about guarding my new reputation . . .'

'You're arrogant, Aidan. You think you're an island, as Donne wrote, and you're not. You're part of the main, my friend. And this,' she made a slight sweeping gesture about the gardens, 'is it.'

He was looking at her with amusement. 'Truly? And what is it that these people can offer me, should I decide to betray the best side of my nature?'

'Aidan . . .' she was almost lost for words, 'I can't believe you mean that. Are you telling me that this has been your attitude all along? That people are there to be used?'

He frowned about them at the gathering for a long moment, knowing she had asked the question seriously. The moment went on and on, and she realized that he did not know how best to answer her.

667

She said, quietly, 'These are your people, Aidan. The men and women you'll be moving among for the rest of your life. Your children will be buried amongst these people. You are part of the Southern Highlands, whether you like it or not. If you object to that, you can leave, but sooner or later you must put down roots. You must integrate, become part of a community. That means giving, too, Aidan. Not just taking.'

'It'll be here, so.'

His eyes came back to her, and he smiled a little, but the expression on his face was unreadable. She was not sure that he agreed with her, had not quite realized, until now, the extent of his self-sufficiency. But before she could speak again, she had caught sight of Edward Lawler moving towards them.

Lawler, handsome, comfortably padded, smiling man, was the finest doctor in the district. He had no real need to practice medicine, indeed, to have any career at all; as a young man in his native Liverpool, he had been fortunate to meet and gain the affections of the daughter of a wealthy baronet. It appeared to be a love match still, for the two indulged each other and their brood of attractive, ebullient children. His medical practice was the only point of dissension between Lawler and his wife. She, having elevated him, would have preferred it if he had thereafter relaxed and enjoyed the view from their social position. But Edward was no snob, could see no reason why he should not be accepted anywhere – and he was invariably right. His wife brought with her from England a definite idea of Place. She only wished this new, raw country would find a sense of Place for itself. The upwards and downwards mobility of each of its citizens, enjoyed or suffered with the same grim humour, was unsettling in the extreme. And now she found Edward dragging her across the lawn to meet a dark, hard-faced individual, possessing shoulders such as no gentleman would consider respectable, and who, her husband informed her as they walked, was *Irish*.

Berrima, when she found that Edward was to be his usual genial self, and that his wife was bemusedly well-mannered, excused herself and went off in search of Mark.

She found him with his brother, looking on amused at the group of women who clustered about Garth. It was as she approached her husband that she heard Mrs Pirie-Moxham, in her nasal, piping tones, calling Garth up to the specially-erected rostrum.

Berrima and Mark stood at the back of the crowd, and in the half-darkness, as the applause died away, and Garth began to recite, Mark reached one hand behind Berrima's waist and held her. 'I love you dearly, you know,' he said.

She looked up at him, and the confusion she had felt, talking to Aidan, melted away. Here was safety. Here, surely, was real love. Mark, who knew all her failings, understood all her yearnings, who stood firm in the face of her restlessness and apprehension and loved her, loved her through everything.

'I love you, too,' she said. Garth's voice suddenly did not mean as much as discovering the reason behind Mark's words. 'Why do you say that now?' she whispered, 'Is it my new dress, or has something profound struck you, listening to Garth talking to his devotees?'

'You're flippant, tonight.' His hand tightened on her waist. 'You always come back from speaking to Aidan with that curious, brittle tone. He puts you on the defensive, doesn't he?'

'I . . . I hadn't thought about it. I suppose he does.'

Mark nodded. They had driven Garth to the party tonight and had looked forward to hearing him read, but later, for both of them, the memory of the recitation would be blurred. What would remain with them would be this strange conversation, one that neither of them had meant to take place. Even with the O'Briens staying in the house, and now Garth, there were many times when they were alone together, could have talked. It was odd that the words should come, now, here, in someone else's darkened garden.

'He threatens a great many people,' Mark said, 'one way or the other. He threatens me because he's so bloody-minded, and so successful at whatever he turns his attention to. I think I lack the concentrated drive that he possesses. And he threatens me in his attitude to you.'

She searched his face. The eyes were still warm, he smiled a little. 'I don't know if he's in love with you,' Mark continued, 'but he's fascinated with you. That's why he torments you, my darling.'

'Mark . . .'

'There's no need to explain anything. I don't believe, you see, that we go through life and have only one real love affair each. I worked it out, once, that in the average person's life there should be at least five people who were alike enough to make one happy. Sometimes, one meets two of these people at the same time . . . and then there can be problems.'

'Mark, I'm not in love with Aidan. I'm not!'

'I know, my dear. He doesn't have the sensitivity that you need in a man. But you admire his strength, and his odd sort of integrity, and his fierce loyalty . . . all the things I admire in him. And you're a woman, Berri. You find him physically attractive.'

His hand was warm on her back. It moved a little, in a gesture of comfort, for he saw her sudden distress. 'He is a very attractive man,

Berri. And he's dangerous, because he doesn't have time for other people's feelings. I've spoken to a man in Hobart whose wife used to know Aidan. His attitude to women is cavalier in the extreme. Many women find a combination of charm and money and hardness to be absolutely irresistible. If you hadn't noticed, Berrima, I'd have been worried.'

Still, she stared at him. 'Oh, Mark. Have you been brooding about this all the time? Why didn't you say something before . . . ?'

'No, no . . . there was no need. One has only to see the two of you together to know that there's no tenderness between you at all. And you're a woman that needs tenderness, Berri.' His hand was beneath her arm, his fingertips brushed her breast lightly, and she felt herself stir with a desire for him. But the calm voice was saying, 'Women are fools to love men like Aidan O'Brien. Emotionally such men are children. They've spent all their adult lives striving for success, developing their brains, their business skills, and they have no time to allow their emotions to mature – certainly they don't exercise them. The army is the same – among the officers, anyway. Perhaps women look at Aidan and think they'll be the one to awaken him. From what I've heard, a few have tried . . .

'But you, my dear, wouldn't allow yourself to start. That's why I had to say I loved you, just now. I watched him taunting you, over there, and you came close to stamping your foot with rage – but you don't regard him with the soft, foolish looks some of the widows and old maids have been casting at him ever since he arrived. I love you because you're not a fool, Berrima. And I pity Aidan – I pity him mightily, for he's intelligent enough to know you'll never love him.'

She was silent for a long moment. Her feelings were disturbed once more, for she had not been unaware, these past weeks, that Mark was drinking more heavily, and it had begun at the time Aidan had arrived. To know Mark was envious had not been difficult to surmise. As in Hobart, she had shouldered more of the burden of running the household and the property, and they carried on despite the problem. But she had not realized the extent of her growing bitterness towards her husband until this mood of unexpected empathy swept it away.

It was for such things as this that she had always loved him, the perspicacity, the ability to judge matters clearly, dispassionately, with gentle humour, and, yes, his tenderness. The other Mark, the one that alcohol brought forth, was like a nightmare figure. At this moment, she could put it from her, could believe it did not exist. The fact that Mark tried to understand her peculiar relationship with Aidan warmed her. That he could offer her an explanation for it

670

was doubly gratifying. And yet, his words took the problem further than she had ever dared. She, after all, had spent years trying to cope with her feelings for Aidan, from schoolgirl fascination, through the dispassionate business relationship built on mutual interest and respect, through to where they now stood. Wherever they now stood.

Mark, in acknowledging the reality of all this, made it impossible for Berrima, from that moment on, to pretend otherwise.

Aidan, on the other side of the crowd, was listening to the recitation with something like envy. How wonderful it would be to be able to think up such imagery, to be admired for one's intellect and artistic ability. Occasionally, in the crowd around him, he would hear a woman sigh at some particular passage. One, a rather gaunt figure whom he soon recognized as Helena Warwick, leaned over to her female companion with a creak of stays, and whispered, 'They call him the new Byron.'

Her companion, a round little woman in a great deal of maroon lace and pearls, nodded, and there were tears of sentiment in her eyes.

Later, the two women were part of a group by the supper table that crowded around Garth,

'I just love the way you . . .'

'How did you begin writing, Mr Ellis . . . ?'

'The only thing I don't understand is . . .'

'You know, I have a half-finished poem at home . . .'

'Where did you get the idea from?'

The same statements, questions, Aidan was sure, that Garth must have heard across England, Europe and America. Yet he answered them all with good-manners and recieved the praises with grateful modesty.

Later, Aidan began a discussion with Hedley Warwick, who was on the board of Southern Highlands Iron and Steel, about the chances for an early re-opening of the project, and so he missed what later became one of the most talked about incidents in the district.

He was aware, fairly late in the evening, of Garth, very pale, leaving the party – he seemed to be quarrelling with young Fitzroy Amberley, but then it became apparent that his friend was attempting to persuade Garth to stay. He broke away, however, and not long afterwards, he was seen, on a borrowed horse, heading off down the drive, very fast.

'Oh, dear . . .' Hedley Warwick murmured, 'he must have had another scene with Francis Amberley. I really thought he'd give

671

Garth his blessing, at this stage. After all, he's proved himself respectable with *Songs of Nattai*. He's not just a young wastrel with artistic pretensions. Tsk.' When Aidan did not reply, he turned back to him with a smile. 'He's rather formidable, our Francis. He's the Chairman of the Board of Southern Highlands Iron and Steel, you know. And the most thorough man you could imagine. You were asking about taking up shares – do you know that Francis insists on character references and holds extensive investigations into the backgrounds of *everyone* who's ever desired to put money into the project? Never knocked anyone back who's had the cash, mind you, but he must know one's background to an extremely detailed degree. And he rules those meetings like a damnable school-master. Rather a strange character . . .'

Aidan followed Hedley's gaze, and saw the big man, in his sixties, looking uncomfortable in his dinner jacket, come down the front steps of the house. He looked angry, and Aidan was not really pleased when Hedley Warwick chose that moment to call Amberley over to introduce them.

But he found the man keen, intelligent, and obviously obsessed with the success of the Mittagong mine. 'I was born here,' he told Aidan, 'My father was one of the first settlers in this district, and it's taken all his lifetime and half mine to build our property up to where it is today. I feel I can do the same thing with the mine – if the government give us half a chance. Are you interested in investing, O'Brien? I was talking to young Ellis about you earlier, and he said you were going to settle in this area, go into business in some form.'

'I was in timber in Tasmania.'

'Ah, yes, very safe. But mining is where Australia's future lies, O'Brien. And Mittagong was at the heart of it. Could be again. Think about it.' His rather pale, but intent, blue eyes, were very observant, and Aidan wondered if they caught his slight hesitation as he said, 'I'll certainly consider the matter of investing in the mine, Mr Amberley.'

And he was thinking, it's not fekking likely, if you're going to be scraping up my past for the whole of the Southern Highlands to talk about.

Amberley and his family, a pretty, dark-haired wife, young Fitzroy, who gave the impression, at age twenty, that he would be one day as positive and impressive as his father, and a rather subdued Victoria, left soon after that.

Aidan was feeling disturbed, wondering just how long it would be before news filtered up into New South Wales of his prison back-ground. And to blot out this worry, for he would not, could not

672

bring himself to expound on the matter to the world at large, he finished off a great many more whiskeys than he would have done, noticing Thomas regarding him disapprovingly and recklessly asked Berrima to dance with him, for the third time that evening.

She agreed only, he found, to scold him for not taking care of his mother at the supper table, and it was while he was listening to her diatribe, in a rather happy fog, that Fitzroy Amberley came running up the drive, across the lawn, to half-collapse in Mark Ellis's arms. His head was bleeding heavily, and his shoulder was dropped at a strange and awkward angle. Before he fainted, he managed to gasp out that the family's carriage had overturned. His father and Victoria were badly hurt and unconscious.

64

Francis Amberley died of head injuries five days later. Victoria, who suffered only slight concussion, and Fitzroy, with the cut on his head and a dislocated shoulder, recovered, in time, and were kept busy helping their mother in the difficult time of adjustment after Amberley's death.

The man's funeral was the largest the town of Mittagong had ever known, and a day of mourning was declared when all the stores and hotels closed in memory of a man who had done more, perhaps, than any other, to raise the town into a position of prominence in the colony of New South Wales.

Yet despite the widespread grief, there were two matters, Berrima noticed, in the months that followed, that meant something positive had come from the man's death. Aidan, she had always been certain, would clash in personality with the equally determined and aggressive Amberley, but was now, in his absence, seriously considering investing in Southern Highlands Iron and Steel; and Garth, now that paternal opposition was so tragically removed, was able to gain a quiet agreement from his friend Fitzroy and Victoria's fond Mama, to allow a marriage with Victoria when the year of mourning was over.

'It's almost supernatural,' Mark had noted, 'how Aidan can gain what he wants. Do you think he has a pact with the Devil?' Berrima was horrified at the way he could speak, sometimes, but was already beginning to recognize two Marks, the man she had married, and the bitter, malicious man, glass in hand, who seemed to dislike the whole world, and himself most of all.

Berrima found that Garth had an unsettling effect on Mark though the two brothers were close. She was not sorry when Garth announced that he would be leaving to spend several months with his parents at their home in Melbourne. Garth had an intensity, a cynicism, that was surprising in one of his age, and she often wondered if the very young and infatuated Victoria had seen this, through her joy and her pride in him.

Aidan would have liked to have left soon after Garth, but had not yet found a property that suited him. Still, it was becoming harder, after riding about checking properties all day, to cope with the old, bitter-sweet feelings once more, returning to a house where Berrima would greet him – yet knowing that the house was not his, that this woman that he wanted above anything else in the world, was not his.

It was Mary who first voiced what Aidan and Thomas had begun to notice, that Mark was beginning to seem agitated, restless. 'The boy's under strain, sure,' she told her sons, when they drove together one morning.

'Och, this is the normal Mark y'r seeing, Ma.' Thomas spoke without emotion. 'Are you not after remembering what he was like in Hobart Town?'

'I thought it was the pressure of running the newspaper.'

'It's the pressure of living,' Thomas replied drily. 'Mark's ambition and Mark's tenacity don't come in equal portions. He's an unhappy man, so.'

'Arra, you're a wise man, boyo.' Aidan felt a kind of delight in his brother's perspicacity.

'Don't be smug, Aidan, f'r you're possessing the ambition and tenacity of five men.' Thomas grinned at him. 'If Mark is weak,' and here his smile faded, 'he'll make up for it by manipulating. That's the way of things. He wants what he wants . . .'

'We're guests in his house, Thomas, I'll not have you speaking so of the man . . .'

'Arra, Ma, let me finish. Aidan, you'll not be doing Mark any good by taking care of his problems for him. Perhaps he'll be happier as a small farmer who can tell himself that he could have been successful. If you place all the power in his hands, and he hasn't the moral courage to deal with it, then you'll ruin him, boyo, can't you see that?'

'And when did all this occur to you?'

'I've been watching Mark watching you. His envy that you can

674

sum up a situation and take advantage of it. Yesterday he mentioned to me that he's had the idea of beginning a new newspaper in Mittagong. Has he spoken to you about it? I had the impression that he wanted me to broach the subject with you. That's what I mean about Mark – I'd feel better if he came straight out with these things.'

'He's hinted at it,' Aidan admitted. 'But he knows I've enough problems finding us our own house and land – and later seeing to Andrew's and my business affairs in Sydney.'

Mary said, almost unwillingly, 'Thomas is right in much that he says, Aidan. Help Mark and Berrima all you can, for they're good people, and they've been kindness itself to us. But don't go placing too much responsibility on Mark. His boyishness, his fecklessness is part of his charm. He could help you deal with your business associates, for he has more charm than you do, and more tact, often, *asthore*. But don't crush his spirit under paperwork and such.' Reflectively, 'Berrima could manage. Sure isn't it strange? Berrima would manage very well.'

Aidan had gained an added confidence in his observations of Southern Highlands society, and it was with a pleasurable anticipation that he approached the meeting with the new Chairman of the Board of Directors of Southern Highlands Iron and Steel.

Beecham Donaldson's house was a double-storeyed Georgian edifice, largest of any of the big houses Aidan had seen since coming to Mittagong. It lay in the centre of several acres of garden, was expensively and ostentatiously furnished, and possessed, Aidan was amused to notice, at least three liveried servants. Pretentious old bastard, Aidan thought, his eyes finding that of Donaldson's portrait as he walked past it and followed the butler into the library.

He was left waiting for half an hour, growing more and more furious as the minutes ticked away. Goddamn Donaldson, this was his way of showing Aidan his place. The board wanted his money all right, but they were not about to let him know exactly how eagerly they wanted it.

He prowled about amongst the books, all leather-bound, gilt-titled – and never read, he felt sure – and thought with chagrin of how much time he wasted dealing with people like Donaldson. The aggravating waste of time spent in small talk and petty politicking in order to get what he wanted.

It might be different, he thought, if he had to do business with people he liked. Where were the Reynoldses, the Will Treloars, of this world? Then he told himself bitterly that they worked for themselves, they didn't begin industries that needed to survive at

675

someone else's cost. Aidan's very ambition separated him from the men like Reynolds and Treloar, dragged him unwillingly into an arena peopled by men as ruthless as himself. The only difference was that these men wore disguises, their fine houses, the genteel gloss of their existence was an attempt to prove to the world that they had not left good manners behind.

Aidan had never possessed manners in any great depth, but he did not need a fancy show to prove that he possessed more than his share. Or so he told himself, as he scowled up at the chandelier high above the library, every candle burning in an extravagance of light. The truth of the matter was that he was too busy at this stage of his life to worry about superficial trappings. He wanted the basis for an empire, not a facade. He wanted foundations, solid, immovable, inviolable.

Donaldson sailed into the room on a wave of port fumes, assailing Aidan almost immediately with the twin guns of his officiousness and his bonhomie. 'O'Brien, dear fellow, so sorry for the delay – visitors, relatives of my wife's, you know. Awkward time for them to arrive, but one should be polite to family.'

'One should be polite.'

'Come, O'Brien, don't be stiff and formal, sit down.' He did not offer Aidan either port or a cigar. 'To business, now,' he said, as he settled his bulk in the chair behind the large mahogany desk. 'You wish to purchase some shares in Southern Highlands Iron . . .'

'I'm here to offer to invest ten thousand pounds. The board can take it or leave it.'

Donaldson had a hard time covering his shock, but he was an experienced actor in matters such as this, and his faltering was obvious only to one who looked for it. Aidan did, and was rewarded.

'Yes . . . Well, a very generous investment. May I ask how soon you would expect the agreement to be drawn up? Should the board be agreeable, of course.'

In other words, how soon can you get the money? Aidan thought. Donaldson obviously doubted that he possessed it. 'My bank manager could arrange the cheque immediately – should the board be agreeable.'

Donaldson had lost a lot of his geniality; he was himself, and gazed through Aidan as if trying to see the motives behind him. All business – afraid, suddenly, that he was dealing with someone who was not to be taken for granted. Ten thousand pounds – who would have thought it? And the coolness of the man – if that amount was all that O'Brien possessed, he hid the matter very well. The man was altogether too casual about it. Could this story of ten thousand

676

pounds be real? Or was it a hoax, an Irishman's mad joke? Donaldson grew pink in the face, gazing into O'Brien's cool eyes, at the thought that the man might be laughing at him. Donaldson did not like to be laughed at. But neither could he afford to take chances. If O'Brien was genuine, the company needed that ten thousand. It might just be enough to turn the tide in its favour. But how to know for certain?

'May I discuss this matter with your bank manager, Mr O'Brien?' There, that would call his bluff . . .

'Certainly – it's Mr Sutherland of the Bank of Commerce in Mittagong.'

Donaldson nodded, leaned back in his chair. Despite the fact that he had heard news that could spell success for the mine, he looked at Aidan with very little warmth. Sorry times . . . he thought to himself, when a gentleman had to deal with men such as this. Ignorant, unscrupulous . . . he had met them in Sydney and Melbourne – from a little gold squeezed from the mud of Lambing Flats and Ballarat they went from strength to strength on their cunning and their greed. While those such as Donaldson and his father – his eyes sought his sire's portrait above the mantelpiece – struggled merely to hold on to the wealth they possessed. Wait until the others heard this. Ten thousand pounds!

'I will approach the shareholders at our meeting tomorrow, Mr O'Brien. Of course it is up to them to make the decision, but I can see no reason why your offer would not be accepted.'

Donaldson made an effort to smile, to regain his superior, patronizing manner. For such a man as Donaldson it was hard to patronize a man – even an Irishman from Tasmania – who possessed ten thousand pounds in cash. Later he would tell himself how coarse O'Brien was, how rough and uneducated, and totally lacking in style and finesse. He would think of what O'Brien's children must be like – a blank-faced boy and a rabbity-looking girl – and imagine his line dying out within a generation with dissoluteness. And he would think with pleasure of his own wife, Imelda, who spoke four languages, his two strapping sons, and his five daughters, who always wore white and who were so wise and good that they rarely spoke, but played the piano beautifully. When he had had time to consider all these things, he would pity O'Brien. Until then, he sat in his chair and thought with bitterness that wealth was rarely distributed to the deserving, the discerning men such as himself. Life was unfair.

'Tell me, O'Brien, what is it about the iron industry that interests you particularly? Your background is . . . agricultural . . . I believe.' He spoke as if some soil still clung to the root of the word. 'I ask merely from curiosity.'

You ask only because you know the mine is a bad risk, and you wonder what it is I'm after. He smiled. 'I'm a bit of a gambler, Mr Donaldson, I feel there's a great future for iron in this country – I'm sure we'll eventually produce all the steel we'll need. I'm willing to take the risks involved in helping to see the industry on it's feet.'

'Risks? What risks do you mean?'

'Mittagong was the site of the first iron mine in Australia, Mr Donaldson – yet since 1848 it's been plagued by problems . . .'

'Management problems, my dear sir . . .'

'Perhaps. The administration has certainly changed enough times to stand a good chance of gaining *some* competent men . . .'

'I cannot be responsible for the mine during times when it was owned by other companies . . .'

'They were brave men, all of them. I think you're brave, also, Mr Donaldson. The transport problems that beset the mine all those years ago haven't exactly disappeared. What Mittagong needs, is a deep water harbour . . .'

'We're forty miles from the sea, sir . . . !'

'Unfortunate, is it not? A major disadvantage that won't hamper, for example, Beaconsfield's deposits, in Tasmania . . .'

'The quality of our steel was judged to be comparable to the finest Sweden steel at the Intercolonial Exhibition . . .'

'Of course,' Aidan said gently, 'I mention these things only to point out that we'll have our problems, will we not? The lack of government incentives, also . . .'

Donaldson's back had straightened, 'I think I am aware of the problems facing us, O'Brien.'

'The cost of producing the iron prices it out of the market – English steel can be imported cheaper than mining it here in Mittagong and shipping it to the cities.'

'That won't always be so, and you know it. Once the new equipment arrives from England and Dai Williams, the new engineer, is here . . .'

'It will take years, before we see a return.'

'It will be Australian steel, sir.' Donaldson's voice was deadly.

'And none shall wave the flag more spiritedly than I – should we have a flag of our own by then – but until that day when my country pays me back for my investment and my sacrifices, I remain a gambler, sir. We are all gamblers. Each selfless patriot amongst us.'

Donaldson's mouth almost twitched in spite of himself. Damn the man, but he was brighter than I gave him credit for! I'll recount this exchange to Warwick and Pirie-Moxham tomorrow – they'll hardly believe it.

Aidan put Donaldson's silence down to an inability to think of a reply. He himself knew he had gone too far. He was bandying words, for no other reason than to let Donaldson know that he was not ignorant of the situation. And that did not matter. Better for Donaldson to believe him ignorant. It had been a bad evening from the outset, he was feeling aggressive, knew himself of old that that was when he made his greatest mistakes.

I'm making enemies when I have enough without trying, he scolded himself. With a smile, he stood and held out a hand to Donaldson. The man got to his feet, as unwilling to take O'Brien's hand as O'Brien was to offer it. But they shook hands. Neither of them were fools.

He left Donaldson's house with a sense of satisfaction, yet possessed, also, by that now almost familiar sense of isolation. It seemed to press down on him in various degrees of aloneness ever since he had moved from Hobart Town. Often, as on this evening, riding back along dark country roads into Mittagong, he wondered if he should have left Tasmania at all. The very uneventfulness of his existence at Glenleigh now seemed a warm and secure thing.

But, he thought, is it Glenleigh itself I'm missing, or Glenleigh as it had been?

Thomas accompanied his brother, three days later, up into the hills to the west of Mittagong, armed with yet another map provided by yet another land agent. Thomas was remembering the day two years before when Aidan had taken him to see the miles of what, to Thomas, looked like wilderness, that was to be his mill near New Norfolk. Once more they were ambling on horseback up and down mountain tracks that were fit for hardy horses alone, and Thomas became more and more oppressed by the close-growing scrub, his feelings of having been here before.

'Aidan, for the love of God, this is a farm we're going to see, is it not?'

'Och, yes. What's bothering you, Tomás?'

Thomas scowled. 'Every time you give me my name in the Irish I know you're up to something . . . ' Aidan was laughing. 'I remember the last time you led me into country like this – I finished by spending years as the manager of a timber mill. I want to be a farmer, Aidan – do I have to hit you with a blunt object before you realize that?'

'What a sorehead you are to be sure. Haven't I promised you a farm?'

'Aye, for the three years that Ma and me have been in this country.'

'Patience, Thomas. 'Tis a farm we're going to, now.'

'How big? And if you say six thousand acres, Aidan, I'll knock you out of the saddle, so help me!'

Aidan was laughing too much to speak for several seconds, but made an effort to calm himself, and said, 'The farm's about two hundred acres.'

Thomas looked surprised. 'So small?'

'Arra, is there no pleasing you . . .?'

'But . . . so far from Mittagong? And along these tiny tracks . . .?'

'We shall broaden the roads.'

'Och, Aidan, it'll be a lot of expense . . .'

Aidan merely smiled to himself.

'And a house, Aidan? Is there a house?'

'Aye. Patience, boyo.'

There was a house. It had five rooms, each with a fireplace. It had the remains of a garden, with fruit trees, and, once, it had had a roof. Thomas stood on the stone doorstep and looked inside.

There were no longer any floor boards. A giant lizard flicked its blue tongue at them, before darting over the earth floor and disappearing through a crack between the bricks through which daylight showed.

'Arra, *fek*.' Thomas breathed. It was the first time Aidan had heard his brother swear. 'You're after tellin' me you'll settle happily into this place after Glenleigh?'

'Aye, and why not? What's the matter, Thomas?' Aidan mocked, 'Is it soft you're getting in your old age?'

'Sure it's you that's soft – in the head. I hadn't expected much of the house, Aidan. I can adapt as well as you, I'm thinking. But I had expected one or two little luxuries – like a roof.'

'Turn around, Thomas, study the view. Then imagine this house with a roof, and a veranda, and a fine kitchen.'

Thomas turned. He had been too horrified by the ruin before him to really look at the view.

The ground sloped down to a broad, swift-flowing creek, the track snaked down the green slope and over a wooden bridge, back towards the main road. It was a pleasant valley, small, secluded, grassland running by the creek as far as they could see, until the stream turned about a hillside and disappeared from sight. All around them hunched the hills, covered with tall eucalypts. It was a

680

beautiful place. The soil on the valley floor looked fertile, but there was so little of it.

'Aidan? The farm is two hundred acres, so. What's in the rest of the property, Aidan? How much timber do you have?'

Aidan stood on the front path, below Thomas, his legs apart, hands held behind his back as he had stood as a boy, his eyes on the low ridge of the hills behind the house. He was grinning to himself. 'Twelve thousand acres.'

'Jaysus, Mary and Joseph . . .!'

'In the hills behind this house, I'll build my mills. Not just one. Two – or three. And in Mittagong, I'll build a brick kiln, and have a timber yard, to sell my timber. For building is the thing in this country now, Thomas. Men are hungry for land, now, not gold. The gold is disappearing, but the land will be the thing to build an empire on. You wait and see. And they'll need houses, these would-be land barons.'

'And Mr Tweedie?'

'I'll not let him turn me into a shopkeeper. Andrew is a millionaire by now – on paper, at least. He can afford to hire a managing director for the Sydney business. I want to stay here. I want to build something, too. Something to leave to Liam when I go. The best land in this district. And my timber will buy it for me.'

'Och, Aidan, you have everything planned.' Thomas was dumbfounded. He could not believe what he was hearing. Knew it was logical, yet could not conceive that all this would happen. It was too much for him. He felt nervous, threatened; changed his weight from one foot to another. His hand was resting on the frame of the doorway. This was real. The house before him – he preferred to think of it. One thing at a time. Roofing, repairing, these things he understood. 'There's a lot to be done,' he murmured, looking around him. 'You've made up your mind, then?'

'Yes. The house is in the centre of the property, the timber we've passed through – that alone would make the logging worthwhile.'

Thomas shivered, he could not help himself. This property was *twice* the size of Tineranna . . .

When they had crossed the small, rustic bridge over the creek, Aidan reined in his horse and looked back. The shell of the house, its doorway and four black windows stared back at them blindly.

'What will we call it, Thomas?' Aidan said gaily, 'The stream runs through the centre of it . . .'

'Shannon . . . something,' Thomas said. 'Though sure this little creek's too small to name after the Shannon anyway. 'Twould be a mockery.'

681

'Shannon Creek . . .' Aidan considered.

'Hasn't it got a name? The creek, I mean?'

'Some Saxon name – we'll ignore that. Shannon Stream . . . Shannon Brook . . . Shannonbrook.'

'Shannonbrook. Aye, that's grand.'

'That's what it is, so. Shannonbrook.' He laughed softly. 'Shannonbrook One.'

'What?'

'There'll be others. I'll want to own *good* soil, someday, Thomas. The best in this district . . .'

'Aidan, the English own it.'

'We're all Australians here.'

'The Australians with English money own it.'

'Then, ' his brother said calmly, 'they must be persuaded into giving it up.'

He urged his horse forward a little too enthusiastically and the animal shot forward at a gallop, relieved to be turning homewards. Thomas, never a secure horseman, followed, struggling with his mount to keep it collected. At the top of the rise the horses had tired and they slowed them to a jog. Thomas turned briefly in the saddle and looked back down on the house, the bricks warmed to a bright rose by the sun. Shannonbrook number one. Hell's outhouse, as Liam would say – where will it end?

It was late that night, when the rest of the house had retired, and Aidan sat in the little downstairs parlour with his correspondence, that Berrima entered the room.

He had been humming to himself over the letters, making notes in the margin before settling down to answer the mail. He looked up, almost startled to see her there.

She smiled at him, and said after a moment, 'You're very pleased, aren't you? To find the property that you wanted.'

'It's a bargain, Berrima. No one can see the potential in it that I can,' he enthused, more to cover the emotion he was feeling at the knowledge that this was the first time he had seen her alone in all these weeks. 'It's poor country, y'see, and the eejits don't see its potential. I'll run a few hundred sheep, and with the stands of timber that I have . . .' He had already talked too much of his plans over dinner, he must not allow his nervousness to make him chatter, now. He stopped, went forward to the fire and placed more logs on it, then pulled forward her own little chair.

'I . . . I won't stay long, I know you're busy . . .'

'Not at all.' He left his work at the desk and sat down in Mark's chair, smiling at her.

She knew that he knew what this was all about. His eyes were kind, he was extremely satisfied with the land he had seen this afternoon. He was more . . . approachable tonight. Yet she wished she did not have to approach him, of all men.

'I didn't . . . In a way, I didn't want you here, you know.' Oh, that was marvellous! A wonderful way to begin! 'I mean,' she hurried on, 'I thought, in view of all that had happened . . . In Hobart . . . It was embarrassing – I didn't think you'd care to find yourself living so close to me – us.' She swallowed. The dark eyes merely watched her quietly. The humour had left the face, but neither could she read anything helpful.

'This isn't easy for me.'

After a pause, 'I know that.'

She had to stop herself from snapping 'then say something!' at him, for he must know, he must . . .

Instead, she said, 'I thought coming here was the best thing for Mark. His family were eager to see if the land here could be developed – but it's only now that we see how very long it will be before the township of Berrima will begin to recover.'

'It's not entirely the railroad's fault, Berri. Mark is no farmer.'

She said miserably, 'He had the background, his own people were squatters, he has an agricultural background.'

'That doesn't make him a farmer.'

'No. And that's it, you see. I hoped we'd . . . we'd be independent. Aidan,' her face turned directly to him, 'Mark was depending on you too much, towards the end of our stay. We . . . we all were. That's why we had to go.'

When she was silent, he said in puzzled tones, 'But you and Mark wanted me here . . .'

'Mark did. And . . . and now I see that perhaps he was right. Would you be willing to form another partnership – a newspaper in Mittagong? I think he has the capability and the knowledge, now, after the years with the *Chronicle*, to make a success of the editorship. Our . . . our financial situation isn't good, Aidan. I can't see how we'll manage another year farming here. And I don't want to go to Mark's parents in Melbourne.'

He was silent, gazing into the flames for a long moment, and she began to feel agitated, angry, felt that he was toying with her. Bad enough that he had the financial power that he had, to help them or break them, but he should not play with her.

He had stood up, was moving about the room slowly, and she realized he was considering. When he looked up, he said, 'Why didn't Mark approach me about this?'

683

'He would have. In time. But . . .'

'You didn't want to wait.'

'No, I . . .'

'Worry more about lack of money than Mark does.'

'Yes. No! It's not that he doesn't worry . . .'

'Mark comes from a Pure Merino family. They can live on their reputations. Being temporarily insolvent doesn't bother him as it does you and I, who were brought up to pay our bills.'

She was gazing into her lap. He saw that he was distressing her. Why are you so loyal to him, he wanted to scream at her. Why do I know even without asking you that you would never be unfaithful to him? What did he do to deserve this?

Berrima had swung back on to the safer tack. 'Mittagong is growing steadily, and with the railway linking us to Sydney and Melbourne . . .'

'Aye, there's a good market there for a district newspaper I'm thinking.'

'Then you'll consider it?' She had stood to face him. He hated to see the tenseness of her, hated to see how much this meant to her. He knew that she was troubled, knew that she would not tell him the true extent of it. But her desperation was there, on her face.

'No,' he said, 'I'll not consider it. I'll tell you now. I'll set up a newspaper in Mittagong, and I'll advance Mark the money needed for his fifty per cent of it. I'll even pay the editor's salary entirely from my own money. On one condition. That Mark is not the editor of the newspaper, you are.'

Shock, disbelief, pleasure, affronted pride, anger. He watched all these emotions move across her face. Then she had turned and walked to the other side of the room. She prowled about near her desk in the corner, as if she herself were cornered. He watched as she clenched her fists, turned to him, began to speak, then turned away – only to whirl on him at last. 'You're a devil, you know that? You like to play games, see what power you have over people! "Take the editorship." It's unheard of! What would people think! What would my parents say when I wrote to them? How could you suggest such a thing?'

'You haven't told me what Mark would think of it.'

'It would destroy Mark! I don't need to tell you that, you know it! It would be the last stab that would bring his self-confidence down in ruins around him. I shouldn't need to say it – you know what it would do to him!'

He sat down in the chair, half reached for his pipe, looked up inquiringly, 'Would you mind if I smoked?'

684

'Go up in flames, for all I care. One day you will, Aidan O'Brien – you'll disappear into a burning hole in the ground like the final scene in *Don Giovanni* . . .'

'I never had a classical education, though it's sorry I am to admit it to y' . . .'

'I despise you when you put on that fake ignorance . . .'

'It's a disguise. To hide how you wound me with your allusions that I'm bound for hell and damnation. And for what?' He puffed his pipe, looking at her gently through the smoke. 'For offering you only what you most want.'

'What . . . what *I* most want?'

'Something special, something of your own. Success at something in life besides being Mark's wife. A career.'

'A career?'

'You never used to be so hard of hearing. I think you understand me, Berrima. If I went into this venture, it's with the desire to see the venture a success, and to make a profit.' He turned his head on one side, watching her. 'I had an idea that such a venture might be suggested, but I had no idea, sure, that I'd ask this of you until right this minute. It came to me, as they say, like a bolt from the blue. You're more capable of handling the newspaper than Mark is. You know it, my dear.' The last added quietly, as she was about to speak.

He was free to observe her for several seconds as she continued prowling about the room. She felt his eyes on her, his quiescence, and it enraged her further. He was right, this was what she most desired, something new. Something . . . a goal. Something that would set her apart, if only in her own mind. A sense of importance. And he was offering it to her, knowing it would bring the safety of her world down about her.

He had picked up a china figure of a dancer and was fingering it, studying it, addressing it. 'We shall have to begin quite soon, go to Sydney, have the press ordered from England . . .'

'I can't do it!' Almost a scream from her. 'And you shouldn't have mentioned it! You shouldn't, Aidan . . . !'

'Only because it's what you want, what you've always wanted and have been afraid to do. Step out on your own, risk being regarded as unfeminine – what was it you once called Emily in one of your letters to her? A bluestocking. Yet you envied her, you later admitted.'

'That was years ago. I was a child . . .'

'Children have more vision, and often more moral courage, than adults, haven't you noticed? They don't have very strong consciences, perhaps that's it. I think I liked you better when you were a child. You hadn't allowed the world to tell you who and what

Berrima Reynolds was.'

'Berrima Ellis.' Her voice low.

'You don't owe everything you are to Mark's influence. But I can well understand what's happened. You've found it's easier to hide behind Mark, to make a martyr of yourself – and you are such a charming martyr. I'm sure I'm the only person alive who wants to slap you for it instead of praising you – but that doesn't prevent me from admiring how well you play the role . . .'

'You're trying to use this to drive a wedge between myself and Mark . . .'

'I'm stipulating my terms of business . . .'

'You're trying to make me more independent so that I have less need of Mark . . .'

'You have no need of Mark.' The face was dangerous, hard and dangerous – all the dark side of his nature showed through in the way he looked at her. 'Mark does the needing. That's been your excuse, your purpose in life for the past five years. I'm offering you something more. You'll be able to feel you're contributing something – using the brain God gave you and not hiding behind anyone – gaining the credit for your own work . . .'

'Not at the cost of my marriage!'

She had turned away, he had spoken in a low, tense voice, but the words reached her ears, 'What marriage.' Statement, not question.

She turned on him, feeling the blood drain from her face, and walked to him.

'You know nothing of my marriage. You know nothing about people at all – especially those closest to you. How dare you try to question the validity of my relationship with Mark. You can't hope to understand our need of each other – *of each other*, Aidan – because you've never needed anyone in your life. Certainly not Maura – don't interrupt me! – I've been in a far better position to study your marriage than you have mine, Aidan. I know that for the last five years of your married life you and Maura lived separate existences. Her pathetic little white room at Glenleigh – you were never allowed in it. She didn't want you near her! And why was that, pray, when you seem to see yourself as such an expert on human relationships? What marriage, indeed.

'How do you know what needs Mark and I fulfil in each other? We don't sleep in separate rooms, let alone separate houses, Aidan. Don't be shocked, someone who makes a study of other people's marriages shouldn't be shocked at the mention of such things. Marriage is for the procreation of children, is it not? Did you think that because there are no children in my marriage that Mark and I

686

have been as chaste as yourself and Maura? Oh, no – I tell you this only to add to your information, to help you with your studies – ' She hissed the words out, her face white and strained, she reminded him of a cat, flat-eared, dangerous, snarling. 'We have our compensations for each other's little failings of character. We have our lighter moments, our . . . secrets, our times of intimate communion. But you wouldn't know—'

One of his hands was in her hair, pulling her head back. The other gripped her throat, and she thought, I have pushed him too hard, too hard, and he'll kill me, now he'll kill me—

For a long moment they gazed at each other, with all that was between them written on their faces. And the rage left Aidan slowly, very slowly, with the knowledge of where he was, the knowledge of Mark, Thomas, his mother, sleeping upstairs.

He allowed her to straighten, and took his hands from her without haste. 'You lie with him.' Quietly, now, a deceptive calm to the voice, 'You lie with him, I know this. It comes as no surprise. Mark owns your body, for he is your husband. He may . . . do what he wishes with you. But the laws of Britain make no provision for a woman's mind – it lodges where it wishes. And I know you – and where your mind lies, little one. Sure the more grown up you become the more I see how alike we are. We were both born wanting more than we have. Our goals are different – but goals they are. I'll have your mind, so. Sure,' the honeyed voice, she had always loved his voice, fell over her like a cloak and beneath it his eyes had their will of her. 'Sure I have your mind already. Have your "marriage", your moments of intimate communion and to the devil with you. But that newspaper will be fifty-one per cent mine, and forty-nine per cent Mark's – and you will be behind that desk. I shall call in often, and expect you to be behind that desk.' And the voice was hard, suddenly. 'That's an end to it, Berrima. Those are my terms. You may take them, or leave them.'

He stood back from her, murmured, 'Goodnight, Berri,' and left the room.

Berrima stood for a long time, then, shaking, forced herself to go through the motions of dousing the fire, to extinguish the lights, trembling all the while. She climbed the stairs. No sound from the bedroom which contained Mary, nor the room that Aidan shared with Thomas.

She undressed and climbed into bed beside Mark, drew close to him, shivering, attempting to control her sobs. He woke, and placed an arm about her. Even the smell of whiskey on his breath, for he kept a bottle in the room, did not disturb her. She held him tightly.

'I thought I heard you arguing with Aidan,' he said drowsily, through sleep and the whiskey. 'Did you ask him about the newspaper? I was afraid that was why you were arguing. I meant to stay awake, but I was so tired . . .'

'It's all right. Just hold me, Mark . . . Mark, don't go to sleep . . . ! Hold me! Tell me it'll be all right. Mark?'

'Of course it will . . . What did he say? No, I expect.'

'He . . . he said yes . . . But . . .'

'Really? Good man . . .'

'I'll tell you in the morning . . . Mark? Hold me – hold me very tight. Hold me, Mark!'

65

When Berrima placed Aidan's terms before Mark the following morning, he amazed her. The reaction was not one of jealous anger, but of intense amusement.

'I might have known the old devil would think of something like this! It's why he's as wealthy as he is, you know. Really, Berrima, Aidan O'Brien is worth studying. I'm glad he's come – I feel I shall learn a great deal by observing the twisted paths of that mind of his . . .'

'Mark, we'll say no. He's playing a game. He's not serious . . .'

'Aidan doesn't play games, my dear. At least,' he added with a smile, 'not where money is concerned.'

Aidan, in the end, had his way. The little, bustling railway town of Mittagong was soon graced with a weekly newspaper, and to the amazement and horror of the local families, a woman sat behind the editor's desk. Mark, it was agreed with Aidan, would take charge of sales, and the arrangement, as far as the *Mittagong Argus* was concerned, worked exceedingly well. Mark had the variety that he needed in his work, and took a perverse delight in the stir that Berrima's position caused.

For the first few months people purchased the newspaper in the hope of finding mistakes. Some people, particularly Mrs Helena Warwick, who for weeks had written furious letters to the editor and defied her to print them, did more for the circulation of the *Argus* than if she had totally ignored the publication. Berrima printed every scurrilous attack in the Letters to the Editor section, and smiled determinedly in the face of the opposition.

Aidan, true to his word, came to the office frequently, and sat quietly, smiling, as she worked. So busy was she, that she did not pause to spend a great deal of time chatting to him; and since he did not expect this of her, his presence, sometimes reading copy or with a Melbourne or Sydney paper held before him, became almost companionable.

He did not betray it, but he was surprised at the courage she showed. Her patience when a reporter from a large Sydney paper arrived and demanded to interview her, asking impertinent, almost insulting questions, amazed him. Mark, too, was in the room at the time and heard the reporter's innuendoes that questioned Berrima's intelligence her ability, and that slid smarmily along the possibilities of her being masculine, 'unnatural', a dummy figure only to boost publicity, or even a socialist with the idea of 'propagating Marx's theories of anarchic total equality' in Australia. It was only Berrima who prevented Mark and Aidan from tossing the man out on his ear into the main street of Mittagong.

And the quiet dignity that she displayed when Mrs Warwick, righteously militant, led a deputation of wealthy, indignant ladies to the *Argus* office, telling Berrima that she was lowering the status of her womanhood by descending into the realms of trade . . .

But Aidan was no less surprised than Berrima herself. She paused in her work, sometimes, and wondered at the strength she had found within her. Why, I'm not going to pretend to be silly and giddy ever again, she thought. I . . . I honestly don't care if people dislike me for being capable and successful. I can't regret what's happened. I'm stronger, I've found something to fight for. And I'm not going to let anyone take that away from me!

Gradually, as Mittagong society found it could not deter That Adventuress, Mrs Ellis, it did the only thing it could do, and pretended that the situation did not exist. After the first damning battery of social disapproval, the threatened army skirted about the lost piece of ground, and pretended that it was not worth the bother of paying attention to it. But by then the majority of people in the district had already noted that the newspaper was interesting, factual, as up to date as a parochial newspaper can be, and the *Argus* was a success. When it became known even through the now defecting ranks of Mrs Warwick's army that the fashion pages of the *Argus* were more readable than that of many of the city papers – 'But Helena – she doesn't talk down to one . . .' little Mrs Corbett offered – then the scandal fluttered down into an uneasy rest.

*

Land to the east of the township was being opened up during these years, land so rich that the natural vegetation was as thick and lush as a jungle, woven with creepers, giant eucalypts courted by feathered cabbage palms and tree ferns, jewelled with mosses and multi-coloured fungi.

Up to forty feet in circumference, the trees grew, and Aidan, only weeks after the purchase of Shannonbrook One, was able to buy eight hundred acres of this land and build a mill concurrently on each property.

The wilderness that was Shannonbrook Two reminded Aidan of the South-West of Tasmania. When he had received Will's letter, in Hobart, telling of the felling of the giant Huon pine, he had tried to tell himself that the desecration of it, and the whole place, should not matter – that it may have been special, unique, to himself and Will, but to the rest of the world those trees meant nothing. Money, a piner would say. Even he and Will would once, perhaps, have said that. It was, he realized, that he had seen enough of the South-West to realize that it was not limitless, the resources not endless. Already there were voices in government circles who admitted the scarcity of Huon Pine, predictions that the species, already disappearing from the banks of the more accessible Huon and Davey and Franklin Rivers, would one day vanish from the interior streams and channels as well, that the species was doomed.

Aidan had made up his mind then, over Will's letter. He must institute some kind of replanting scheme on his properties, he must not rely on always having more timber available. His stands of timber must serve Liam's mills when he, Aidan, was gone. And Liam's son's, and his son after that. He must think of the future.

He began re-planting schemes on both properties as soon as the mills opened, and he had decided on something more. He had several acres fenced securely, and hung *No Trespassing* signs about it. Already Shannonbrook Two was ringed with newly-cleared farms, many of them bought by Irish immigrants, drawn to the area by the cheap prices and the soft, familiar climate. The nearest hamlet to the east, Robertson, named after the politician who had engineered the opening-up of the land, was soon renowned as the centre of the finest potato farms in the country. But behind its fences, Aidan's rainforest dreamed on, undisturbed. It was the only eccentricity found in a man who was becoming known to be land-hungry in the extreme. 'Call it reparation,' he would mutter, when questioned, and only Berrima came close to understanding what he meant.

*

The coming of the railroad brought a new prosperity to the Southern Highlands, and Aidan, with his diverse business interests, prospered along with his new home. He became more and more insistent during these years that his children should return to Australia; he wanted them to see the changes in his fortunes, the world he had painstakingly built for them.

But Liam, having graduated from his Law course with honours, went on to his Master's degree, and from there to accepting a teaching post at the university. It was only a tutorship, he wrote to his father, but for a Catholic, that was a good step, and Liam would like to remain for a year or two. Aidan, enormously proud of his son, wrote that he understood, and did not press Liam to return.

Clemency, who had insisted that she had no desire to see the cities of Europe, now spent a great deal of her time travelling between them. She was living with the family of one of her schoolfriends, the father of whom was Nicholas Brereton Mitchell, one of the foremost pianists and composers in Europe at that time. Even Aidan was impressed, for Clemency's letters were filled with the names of famous writers, musicians and poets. Although Christabel, Mitchell's wife, was Catholic, Mitchell himself came from wealthy Anglo-Irish stock, and most of Clemency's letters were addressed from the Mitchell's second home in Knightsbridge. She was happy, busy, and living a life of such obvious gaiety and excitement that he could not bring himself to issue a direct order for her to return to Australia any more than he could bring himself to bully Liam. He sent his children generous allowances, instead, and wondered, sometimes, what Maura would say, if she knew the consequences of her actions in insisting on a 'traditional education' for their children.

Thomas, with his savings and Aidan's help, had been able to purchase four hundred acres adjoining Aidan's. But Thomas had little time, in those first years, to settle to the business of building up his property. Aidan was over-worked as it was, with two mills to run and his business interests in Sydney and Melbourne. Despite himself, mostly from his sense of gratitude, Thomas found himself continuing to fill his usual role as Aidan's assistant. He chafed under this, at times, but could not bring himself to stand up before Aidan's careless, good-natured dictatorship. Mary and Berrima often told him to rebel, but he could never quite find the . . . the ill-manners to do so. Sure it wasn't as if Aidan *knew* what a bully he was. He simply took Thomas's loyalty for granted. And what could a man say in the face of that?

One matter on which Thomas found himself increasingly drawn

to confront Aidan was the amount of time he spent with Berrima. It would not matter if his visits, every few days, were made to check the entire business. But that was not so. Aidan arrived and ensconced himself in Berrima's office, if Mark was there or no, and there he would stay for an hour or more at a time. Often he left without doing more than nod to whatever staff he met. People were beginning to talk, and Thomas, seeing more than most, finally made up his mind to speak to Aidan.

'It's not that there's anything unseemly going on, sure. I know that,' he said, late one night in the homestead at Shannonbrook One, when their mother had retired for the night. 'But the townsfolk aren't to know that. And Berrima has a hard enough time as it is, with that Mrs Warwick, the old witch, cutting her in the street when they meet. People in this town have their attention fastened on Berrima, y' see – just waiting for her to make a mistake. If they could fabricate an illicit relationship between you . . .'

'Arra, get away.' Aidan had stood, moved away across the room. Thomas looked up, a little surprised at the vehemence of his brother's tone and movements, then set his mouth grimly. He was so transparent – and he was not the one to be hurt by all this, but Berrima . . .

'And isn't it always the way,' Thomas persisted, 'that people tend to blame the woman in these cases . . .'

'There is no case! And you're a fierce trawneen for even speaking as you are . . . !'

'I tell you this only because you should know what the town is saying. I care about your reputation – you have one here, you see, as far as I know, no one knows of your being in prison. It'd be grand, would it not, if you can truly begin afresh, here?'

'They'll find out sooner or later. Someone will recognize me one of these days . . .'

'Perhaps you should have changed your name . . .' Thomas immediately regretted the suggestion when he looked up to see the black look Aidan threw him.

'T' hell with what Mittagong thinks,' he growled.

'That's all very well for you to say. What about Berrima?'

'When Berrima asks me to leave her office because that old bitch Helena Warwick is spreading gossip, then I'll go willingly. But Berrima has said nothing of the sort.'

There was a silence, and Aidan turned to see Thomas gazing down at the floor unhappily. Jaysus, Aidan thought. He knows, so. He said quickly, 'Small towns always talk. You know what it was like in Killaloe. Berrima has taken the risk of people talking about her. She

692

knew what it would entail, same as Emily when she took up medicine. All the Reynolds children were raised to have faith in their own convictions. I hope I've raised Clemency and Liam the same way.'

'You still have to carry out those convictions – and it's easier, sure, if you don't have to do it surrounded by hostility on all sides.'

Aidan almost said, 'I'm used to it.' Could almost add, 'I thrive on it.' But Thomas would not understand. Since he had left school he had had the day-to-day security of life on the river. That was what mattered to Thomas – day-to-day security; his horizons were small. Aidan was glad of Thomas's presence, his aid, his droll humour that helped Aidan gain perspective. And on evenings like this, when he was drained in body and spirit from the constant details of his work, he almost envied Thomas.

He thought he would sidetrack his brother from his rather disapproving offensive. 'I've been thinking of buying some town lots in Mittagong. What think you?'

Stiffly, 'T'would be a good investment, you know that without my saying so.'

'Aye. Donaldson is selling the land he owns between Johnson's forge and the hardware store. Two blocks – sixty pounds for the two.'

'Reasonable.'

'Aye. And he mentioned something else, most unwillingly, I thought. The iron mine is in difficulties, he asked if I'd consider investing more money. And Pirie-Moxham wants to retire from the board – there's a good chance I may be voted into his place.'

This time Thomas looked up with real horror. 'Arra, what're y' like? Is it mad you are? Stark mad? That mine has bankrupted more men than . . . than . . .' He could think of no metaphor frightening enough. 'Och, you'll not be considering it, Aidan! And . . . And what about the other members of the board? Will they be after having you amongst their number? Pure Merinos, the lot of 'em, and they'd be failing with dignity, most of them, I'm thinking, rather than allow an Irishman to sit at the board table.'

Aidan was aggravated. 'Not all of them. There are some good men. Lawler, and Hedley Warwick . . .'

'Lawler is accepted because of that mad Honourable Sophia that he married. Basically he's a medical man of no more social pull than Milton has in Hobart. And Hedley Warwick won't defend you if his wife says you're not acceptable. You know she hates you only a little less than Berrima. If Warwick and Lawler did support you, they'd be lone voices . . .'

'We'll just see, shall we?' His voice was tight. Thomas was limited in his thinking – it was annoying, sometimes, one could not make him understand . . . 'That mine is the main bastion of wealth and position in this town, is it not?'

'One could have wealth and position without being a board member of Southern Highlands Iron and Steel.'

'Not so publicly.'

'What? Are you saying that it's important that others see that you're successful? Isn't being happy enough?'

'Lord, Thomas, I'm not happy!' Thomas stared at him. Aidan met his gaze with something like amusement. 'Dear God, man, do I seem happy to you?'

'Why . . . yes.'

'Then I'm a better actor than I thought.'

Thomas looked perturbed. 'But I can't see how becoming a shareholder in the mine will change matters – everyone knows they've had nothing but trouble since the day they began. How will losing money prove anything to the world? You'd be better off building a fancy house, and hiring an army of servants.' Aidan was scowling at him, but now it was Thomas's turn to feel annoyed. He shook his head, 'What is it you want, Aidan? What in the world do you *want?*'

His brother scowled into the fire. Finally, 'Everything.'

'You'll not get it.'

'I can try.'

'You could end up losing everything – you've already lost what's—'

He stopped. Aidan had looked up, was watching him. Thomas flushed. 'You've already lost what's most important.' He grew even more angry, felt ill with the unaccustomed anger when Aidan looked genuinely puzzled. Thomas said quietly, 'Maura, Aidan.'

He looked even more puzzled, then his face cleared only to stiffen with that dangerously cool expression.

'Are you saying that I gambled with Maura's life? Is that what you're saying?'

'I . . no. You . . . you loved her, I know that. You misunderstand me, that's all.'

Aidan continued to watch Thomas, then stood and walked to the cabinet in the corner and took out a bottle of whiskey and two glasses. 'You'll join me? I need this.'

'All right, a small one.'

Aidan poured, a goodly amount in both glasses, and handed one to Thomas.

'I said a small one.' Thomas gazed into the brimming glass.

'Drink it down. Do you good.' Aidan was seating himself back in

694

his chair. Thomas glanced up at him with sudden rage, but his brother was gazing into the fire. So typical of you, Thomas thought with resentment, we all take what you think we need, whether we like it or not. You have no knowledge of any of your family, and care little to find out. That's what killed Maura.

But Thomas sipped his drink. 'I thought when we came here that this country reminded me of Ireland. But that's not so, I see it now. I mean, it's as full of English as England must be. I can't help but notice that the farmers even of our own class – and those who don't possess as much land as we do – except the Irish out at Robertson – look down on us.'

'They suspect that because we're Van Demonians we're all ex-convicts, so.'

'It's because we're Irish Catholics, Aidan. We're surrounded, here, with people who think that God is an Anglican, and they show as much tolerance as Hubert and Edward Osborne, back in Killaloe.'

'Not all of them.'

'The real money in this district is held by people who came here in the early part of the century, Aidan – and newcomers who are poor cousins of the British aristocracy. It's impossible for you to wrest that power from them – and even if you did, you'd not be accepted by them.'

'You're saying I can't win?'

'Not if what you're aiming at is, as you said, everything. You can't have everything, Aidan. You know it yourself.'

'Yes.'

'Then for the love of God, count your blessings. Bring the children home from Dublin. With the political situation the way it is, it's not safe, anyway.'

'The Fenians are scattered, or dead,' Aidan said bitterly, referring to the failed rebellion in Ireland in '67, two years before. 'By the time we heard about the Rebellion, it was over.'

'You're not still giving money to the Fenians in Sydney, are you?'

Aidan stirred a little. 'I contribute still, yes. But they want organization, now, not guns. And the British aren't going to allow them that.'

'Aidan, bring the children home. And . ... and get married again. Don't sacrifice everything to your ambition . . .'

'I've not done that. I've not. I wanted security for Maura and the children, for *them*, you understand?'

Without considering, 'Perhaps they'd have traded the position of being wife and children to a wealthy landowner and businessman, for being the wife and children of Aidan O'Brien.'

'I don't like it when you set yourself to lecture me, Thomas.' The dark eyes gazed at Thomas from beneath black brows.

Thomas lowered his eyes to his glass. 'I mean only to help. I've loved you all. I hated to . . . I hate to see any of you unhappy.'

'It's a time of struggle, Thomas, the children accept that. Maura accepted that.'

The gentle eyes were raised to him, steadily. 'Aidan, it's been a time of struggle for you ever since you could walk, ever since you realized that there were those who lived in idleness in the big house, and those who planted potatoes to stay alive.'

'Are you after criticizing my ambition? Where in God's name would we be without it? I'd be working on Cora Frazer's farm in Huonville for twenty pounds a year, and you'd still be bobbin' about on the Shannon catchin' fish!'

'I'm not after criticizing your ambition . . .'

'It seems to me you are, and very strange it is, coming from you, who don't know the meaning of the word . . .'

'Are you saying I'm jealous of you?' Thomas's face had paled.

'I'm saying you've no right to criticize me for having the guts to pull myself up from where I was born to where I am now – despite Devlin Kelly and eight years in prison – and I brought Maura and the children and Ma and you, too, Thomas, with me!'

'Are you saying that I'm that small of heart and narrow of mind that I resent all you've done? Why, if anything, I pity you, Aidan – I pity you rather than envy you – for you had the best wife in the world – who – who – sacrificed everything for you and . . . and us . . . And you'll never know 'til you die, Aidan, just how it was! And you let her fade away from you without seeming to notice – you never knew her, Aidan! You were too self-absorbed to notice what your ambition was doing to Maura, to Liam and Clemency! If I'd . . .'

'Don't tell me what I should have done, what I should be doing, Thomas! Don't tell me what I should be thinking or feeling or how *you* feel I should treat my family! For I won't stand for it! Learn to solve y'r own problems before you try to lecture me!'

Thomas got to his feet, and placed his half-finished whiskey down upon the mantelpiece with such violence that most of the liquid spilt. 'I'll not be staying in the same room a minute longer with a bastard who has such a low opinion of me! I never asked for your help, Aidan O'Brien, and I'll not be made to feel like a parasite that's been living off you!' He stamped off into his bedroom, and came back dragging blankets and pillow.

'Jaysus, Thomas, where d' y' think y'r going?'

'To the barn, where the dumb beasts have more sensitivity than my own brother! And I'll be sleeping there every night until my own house is built on Killaloe . . . !'

'On what?'

'That's what I'll be calling my place! I'll not be working for you on that great tract of land – Shannonbrook Two indeed! I'll take my four hundred acres and I'll plant potatoes on it! And I'll call it Killaloe! I'll not be turning my back on my past like some people I could name!' Loaded with his bundle of bedding he struggled to the door, trailing blankets behind him. 'I'll have me own place, and I'll not set foot inside this door after that!' And he let fly with a stream of Irish, half of which Aidan could not understand, learnt, he was certain, from Packy Brady of Fish Row. Aidan was sure that none of it was complimentary.

The door slammed behind Thomas, and Aidan could hear him stamping across the yard, swearing, the two mongrel dogs they had acquired beginning to bark as they caught Thomas's rage and excitement.

Aidan sat scowling into the fire and did not move, even when one of the doors opened behind him and Mary came into the room. She wore her shawl over her nightdress, her grey hair in two braids over her shoulders. She moved to the fire and swung the kettle over the flames.

'So he's gone at last.'

Aidan raised his eyebrows, such was the calm tone in her voice. 'Och, Ma, he'll be back.'

'No, he won't. He's cut the tie at last, Aidan. And about time, too.'

'Should I call him in?' He was worried, now.

'Och, no. Let the eejit stay out there in the cold. He has his pride to keep him warm. Don't rob him of this moment, Aidan, it's been a long time coming.'

66

When Aidan awoke the next morning it was to find not only Thomas, but one of the horses and a wagon gone from the barn. Several tools, a hoe, shovel and saw, among others, were also gone.

Aidan, who had been rehearsing an apology through a sleepless night, strode back to the house, all remorse and sibling affection removed from him by what he described to Mary as Thomas's sneaking defection.

Mary hoped he would not stay about the homestead, brooding about this. She liked having the house to herself, liked working in the large kitchen that Aidan had had built at the rear of the homestead. She had more time for cooking and baking, now, for the heavy work was done by a woman from Mittagong who came four times a week. Aidan had insisted on her presence, and Mary to this day complained about the lack of need for her, but secretly it was a relief. She did not like Aidan or Thomas to know how tired she sometimes was.

'Charity has entered our lives,' Thomas had murmured drily when he had first met her. Charity Peebles was narrow, thin-haired, spare of words and warmth, but a tireless worker. 'She's as misnamed as Clemency,' Aidan complained one day, when a request for a cup of tea brought the response, 'I'm helpin' Miz Mary with the soap-makin' – you'd best get it yerself.' She was devoted to Mary, so despite her manners, or lack of them, she stayed on at Shannonbrook.

Today she and Mary clucked and fussed about the parlour and kept moving Aidan's papers from one side of the room to another while they swept and dusted. He had felt like a calm morning at home, answering correspondence and planning what attitude to take towards Thomas, but the dust and agitation the two women raised finally drove him to put the papers away and head for Mittagong.

He had managed to finish one letter, one of several he had exchanged with Matty over the past years; it was odd, but they did not seem to be able, quite, to forget each other. His sexual relations with the women he knew in Sydney were mechanical, lacking in any warmth; he went to them in the same way he would take a hot bath to soothe tired muscles. He found he missed Matty's affection. It was odd that it took so many years and so many miles before he realized that he had affection to offer in return. She was living in Melbourne now. One of Griffith's cousin's had an exporting business, and had given him a job. 'I'm still respectible . . .' Matty wrote, 'an't it awfull.'

He dropped the letter into the pillar box at the Mittagong Post Office and rode on towards the new properties. Only as he was passing the edge of the boundary to Thomas's land did he change his mind and ride into the scrub, instead of on to his own property, and the mill.

He found his brother in a clearing on the side of a hill, until now the only improvement that Thomas had carried out on the land. Aidan was guided through the scrub by the sound of the axe on wood, and stopped for a moment to watch.

A square had been pegged out on the ground, the soil cleared within it, and Thomas was off to one side a little, hacking at a stubborn sapling.

'Thomas?'

Thomas paused, but did not look up. This section of his land had been lightly cleared, once, but the forest was quickly regaining its control. Thomas looked as if it would happen in a matter of hours, not years, had already felled one small tree, stood with tense muscles as if even the time wasted in saying hello could result in some encroachment from the waiting scrub.

Aidan dismounted from his horse, tied it to a sapling and approached his brother. 'Thomas?'

'Get you on to your mill, Aidan.'

'Arra, Thomas, don't be childish.'

'Who's being childish? I'm building my home, Aidan, can you not see the line for the foundations? How is that childish?'

'It's childish to creep off in the night without telling me. I didn't know you wanted a house of your own so badly, Thomas. I'd have helped you with it . . .'

'You never knew what it was I wanted. You never asked.' Thomas leaned his axe against the trunk and turned to Aidan. 'I lived in your house all these years because I thought I was of service to you – that you needed my help at the mills, and about the farm while you were busy with your money-making ventures in the city . . .'

'And you were a help to me, Thomas – you are.'

'No. There's an end to it. Now I'm setting out on my own.' He gazed about the clearing, lowered his voice, unconsciously echoing Mary's words, 'And about time, too, I'm thinking.' He looked back to Aidan, and there was no anger now, in the voice, 'Perhaps you were right, I was thinking a great deal, last night, couldn't sleep for thinking – and the fleas in the hay . . . I was thinking it's easy to be pushed by you, Aidan. You're like a flash flood that sweeps all before it, and it's easier to go along with the tide than to struggle against it. Especially so when one's not used to struggling and prefers drifting on calm waters as I've always done. But now? No. I believe I have sheltered under your protection long enough. I don't understand your ambition, Aidan. I never will. But there's room in this country for men without ambition, sure the world is full of men without ambition, who simply want calm waters.'

'You'll be swamped by every wave that comes along – all the powerful, greedy men that you're always telling me run this country – if you don't fight them, they'll swamp you, and they'll sink you . . .'

'No. I'm too small for them to worry about, Aidan. I'm no threat. Men such as myself will float long after the storm's passed. For we've got nothing to lose. You're the sort of man that the wealthy ones, the greedy ones, will want to crush. You threaten the order of things, you make them afraid. To keep your empire, Aidan, you'll have to destroy some men along the way . . .' Aidan began to interrupt. 'That how's *they'll* see it, Aidan. And they'll think they'll be next, if you're not stopped.'

'Thomas,' Aidan coaxed, totally unaffected, 'Thomas, we went through all this last night. We do no good at all arguing. We're brothers, are we not? If we're surrounded by enemies, we should stand together, so.'

'Aye,' Thomas smiled, 'we're brothers. And I'm with you, Aidan, though you batter your head against the world, I'm with you. All I ask is that you grant me the freedom to make my own way.'

'Sure I've always done that.'

'You haven't. But do it now.'

'All right, then. Go. Stay. Do what you wish. As long as we're friends, Thomas. I can't abide that we're at each other's throats. And it worries Ma.'

'Ah.' Thomas leaned against the tree, scowling at the ground. 'I don't want Ma worried.'

'Nor do I. So will you come home, Thomas?'

'I'll . . . I'll stay until my house is built. I have to be on my own, now, Aidan.'

'Damn your pride . . . All right!' Aidan picked up the hoe from nearby, and headed off towards the square of string that marked the ground plan of the cottage.

'Where are you going?

'I'm going to help you build this house of yours. Not because I want to get rid of you . . .'

'No!'

Aidan stopped, turned. Thomas, pink in the face, stepped towards him. 'That's what I mean, Aidan. I haven't asked you – you just step in, pick up the hoe . . .'

'It's my hoe—'

'Shut up! And stop digging at my house. I want to do it myself, Aidan, can't you get it through that thick head of yours? This is all mine, and I want to do it myself!'

'Of all the pig-headed trawneens . . .'

'Look you Aidan—!'

'*Hello there!*'

They had moved close to each other, Thomas, for the first time in his life, angry enough to strike out to hurt. The voice cut across his anger. They both turned, saw the horse and buggy coming between the trees from the direction of the road. They gazed back at each other. Aidan looked amused; there was laughter on his face, and it made Thomas even angrier. At such a moment, not to be taken seriously was the last insult.

'Y'r a fekkin' gurrier . . .' Thomas hissed beneath his breath as the buggy, containing two strangers, moved closer to them, 'And you'll get where y' want to go because . . .'

'Ssh, Thomas . . .'

'Because you've got all the instincts of an outhouse rat, Aidan!'

Aidan reeled away, laughing to himself, and went to greet the arrivals, a man and a woman in a heavy, old-fashioned vehicle.

They were well-dressed, and plump like the pair of matched bays that pulled the carriage, but there was something genial about them. Aidan was overjoyed at Thomas's first signs of mutiny, and the friendly faces before him served only to put him in an even better mood.

He held out his hand, 'Good morning! Aidan O'Brien, sir, ma'am. And this is my brother, Thomas.'

'Ah, you are building here, yes? We heard the axe chopping and we come to visit – Heinrich Henke, and my daughter, Ottilia. We are your neighbours along the road, near the marsh. You know our house?'

'Yes.' It was Thomas who spoke. He came forward and Aidan politically stepped back and let Thomas explain that he was the builder, that Aidan had a property adjoining.

'Ah, the O'Brien mill, yes. But we know the overseer, Mister Dent . . . He lives on the property – you do not?'

'No, I'm living near the first mill, in the hills to the west.'

'You will be by yourself?' Henke asked of Thomas. 'All by yourself, here?'

'Well, yes.'

'No wife, no family?'

'Only Aidan's family – his children are overseas at the moment. We'll . . .' he caught Aidan's gaze, 'we'll be visiting each other frequently. And . . . and I hope you, too, will visit, Mister Henke. I've heard a great deal about you. You're something of a naturalist, I believe.'

Where does he find out these things? Aidan wondered.

'Ah, yes. The birds, the wildfowl. This is a good area for studying such a thing, the marsh attracts so many species . . . But not serious study, now. Not like Austria. My English is not good. So I am an amateur here.' He shrugged. 'The birds, they do not mind. They come back, I feed, I watch them.'

'I'd like to talk to you about them one day.'

'Yes,' with enthusiasm. 'You come and visit. We will show you. Yes, Ottilia?' And, turning back to Thomas again, 'We bought food, it is time for a meal. You working hard, here, we thought. And Mrs Henke says to take you some Austrian food – the best food when one is working hard. You will eat with us?'

Aidan and Thomas exchanged glances. 'Here, you mean?'

'Yes. We have brought. Sausage, yes? You like sausage? Wine, and cheese – and my beer I make myself. And very excellent bread . . .'

Ottilia was reaching into the back of the buggy and lifting out an immense basket full of food.

So the day that had begun so grimly for Thomas, took an unexpected and delightful turn. He sat on a rug upon the ground and ate strange, spiced continental food for the first time in his life, and laughed with Henke and Aidan and Ottilia, and all the time, beyond them, lay the square of ground that would soon become his house.

He noticed little about Ottilia Henke, other than that she was plump and pleasant and very pretty, with her bright blue eyes and honey-brown hair. She was silent much of the time, but when she spoke her voice held no trace of any accent.

The Henkes would be good neighbours, Thomas thought with some relief, for this morning it had been his anger that had driven him to measure and plot and chop at the timber; as the morning had worn on the silence had begun to descend upon him. He was not by nature a solitary creature, he liked to have people about him. The friendly presence of the Henke family only half a mile down the road, would do much to mitigate the loneliness of his first days living alone in the bush.

He heard a little of Henke's history as they sat there eating and drinking. The very strong beer made Thomas slightly drowsy, and more talkative than he normally would have been. Henke had not been poor in Austria, had come to this country with a small private income, as well as money saved from his position as Professor of Natural Science in Vienna. Farming had always interested him, and here he was revelling in the life. He and his wife made German sausages and cheeses that had an excellent reputation amongst their fellow German immigrants in Sydney and Melbourne.

But it mattered little, Henke said, whether he succeeded or failed, for while he could always have enough to eat, he was satisfied to be living the life that pleased him. That was the most important thing, yes?

Thomas nodded and agreed wholeheartedly, turning to gaze tellingly at Aidan, for this was precisely what he had always thought.

For his part, Aidan was watching Ottilia Henke watching Thomas. Never too openly, polite glances only as she served the food, or when Thomas addressed her. But when she was certain that he was vitally interested in something Heinrich Henke was saying, or when he was speaking with excited single-mindedness, she studied Thomas from her bright blue eyes, and it was obvious that she liked what she saw.

Aidan was delighted. He hoped the girl would gain courage and begin to flirt with Thomas as time went on. For all her demureness and good manners, she had a quiet confidence about her, and she was, Aidan judged, in her late twenties, with a woman's astuteness. If she decided to set her cap at a man she would stand an excellent chance of having her way – not that she would succeed with Thomas, more was the pity. Thomas was too set in his bachelordom to marry at this stage of his life. But even a good flirtation, to accompany Ottilia at a few dances, to dine at the Henkes' home and be treated to the full effect of her cooking and her bright blue eyes – sure, who knew what might happen?

He left them, still talking and drinking, to return to Shannonbrook Two, feeling quite content with the way the morning had developed. Thomas was right, he did need to more independent. Aidan should have seen this at the very beginning and arranged for Thomas to have his own house. But he had been too pleased to see his brother again, liked the idea of the family being together.

But it was not the same as life in Killaloe, he reminded himself, there's no necessity for us to huddle close together in one cottage – this country has given us the opportunity to expand. Yet it saddened him, too. He liked having Thomas close by. To have so many miles between them meant that he had no immediate friend with whom to share his plans. For while Thomas did not always approve, he always listened.

This country is dividing us, he thought, as he rode up the long drive of Shannonbrook Two, to the mill, dividing us as its vast expanses divide so many families.

Yet only two days later, his thoughts of this being a huge and lonely continent were wiped away with the realization of how small a world he actually inhabited.

He had attended the sheep sales at Camden, the pretty, established town almost half-way betweeen Mittagong and Sydney, alone that month, leaving Thomas in charge of the mills. It was while sauntering between the pens, gazing critically at the animals for sale, that he chanced to look up.

The man was elderly, distinguished, with an air about him that bespoke of years in the army, or perhaps the navy. Aidan would have noted only this, had the man not hesitated, stopped in front of Aidan. He began to speak even as some warning began to ring within Aidan's memory that he knew this man, that the memory was not pleasant . . . 'Mr O'Brien? Aidan O'Brien?'

Aidan scowled at him, 'I don't believe I know you, sir.'

'We have met,' the man said. He smiled a little, quite an open smile, it was as if he, too, were a little embarrassed by this meeting. 'It was a long time ago. My name is Frederick Lawrence. I'm the District Magistrate here in Camden. But in 1849 I was at Brown's River, Van Diemen's Land.'

Aidan felt himself pale. He attempted to cover his shock by smiling a little, and holding out his hand to Lawrence. The man's grip was firm, friendly.

'I've been meaning to call on you, O'Brien, to pay my respects and give my congratulations on your success.' He looked round them a little; the crowd was thin, here, and in a slightly lower voice, Lawrence said, 'I saw you and recognized you in the office of the *Mittagong Argus*, several weeks ago. I thought then, you see, that it would be best if I approached you rather than have you recognize me and think perhaps . . .' he paused.

'Yes, Mr Lawrence?' Aidan prompted.

'Well, the past is past, is it not? I simply wished to assure you that from this moment I have no memory of meeting you, O'Brien. You've picked up a few Merinos that I had my eye on,' he smiled, 'but further back than this sale, I can't remember meeting you before.'

They gazed at each other for quite a long moment, then Aidan took a deep breath, exhaled, and smiled. 'Mr Lawrence, though we've only just met, it seems we have sheep breeding in common. Would you care to come to the refreshment stand and drink an ale with me?'

'Thank you. I will.' And for the next hour they talked about their flocks, and the weather, and the soil and the price of winter fodder,

704

and Aidan was almost able to forget the fear that had momentarily claimed him.

It was in the train the following day, returning to Mittagong, that he asked the green hills that flew past the window, Did he mean it? Will he really keep his word and say nothing? Was I wrong to take the chance that no one would recognize me? Sure it's not too late, now, to make a clean breast of things, admit that I was in gaol, once.

But he knew he could not. The questions, the explaining, that would, of necessity, follow such an admission, chilled him. He did not want the future marred by this. He did not want people around him remembering things he himself refused to remember.

67

Gradually, Mark's old behaviour patterns were returning. Mittagong began to gossip about the Ellises once more, and some of the more vicious tongues hinted that it was having such an independent, emasculating wife that drove the handsome young Mister Ellis to be seen drinking too much at social gatherings, and even to be recognized going into hotels and houses of dubious character, where no man of his standing should be. Kinder souls began to wonder if it were not Mark's drinking that had forced the pretty little Mrs Ellis into taking up a career. After all, as Hedley Warwick, who had always rather admired Berrima, said to a stiff-lipped Helena, if the husband was not capable of running the family business, what was a wife to do?

Helena preferred to believe that it was Berrima's fault. The woman obviously took a masculine delight in working – there were no children, were there not? Berrima Ellis was not the type of woman who would have children. Poor Mr Ellis – no wonder he was driven to seek the comforts of liquor and coarse women. What did he have waiting for him at home? Not that Berrima Ellis was ever to be found at home.

Berrima left the day-to-day running of the house to Nellie, who, faithful as ever, had accompanied Berrima to the mainland. The house ran smoothly, and Berrima often entertained, but there were still tongues who said that her house was ill-managed – and what could one expect when the mistress is out until all hours of the day and night, puddling in printer's ink and putting on airs?

Gradually Berrima stopped entertaining; although she had made friends amongst some of the families in the town, Mark's behaviour was becoming more and more difficult to excuse – and hiding it was now out of the question.

Aidan, in March of 1869, was spending much of his time overseeing the clearing and fencing of Shannonbrook Two, and going to stock sales in Sydney and Goulburn. Still, the matter of Mark and Berrima preyed on his mind. On the three-hour train journey north to Sydney, or at his own desk, late at night, he would consider the problem – yet could think of no way to deal with it.

How many times had he talked to Mark on this matter? Jaysus, he thought, I lecture him more than I ever had to lecture Liam. At fifteen, Liam had had a greater sense of responsibility and pride in himself than Mark has now, at thirty-eight. There was, Aidan realized with a sick feeling, something really wrong with Mark. He did not drink merely to enjoy himself. He drank seriously, all his excesses were serious. It was as if, short of putting a gun to his own head, Mark wanted to kill himself. For he must know what he was doing.

He forgot them, briefly, a few days later, when he received a letter from Matty, saying that she had talked Griffith into allowing her to come to New South Wales on a brief holiday – *'and to look at Moss Vale. One of Grif's relatives is on the staff of the N.S.W. Guvnor, who as you know has his summer residets there. He don't speak to Grif, naturally. But things have not gon so well for us, here, and Grif thinks that Uncle Willoughby Rodgers might change his mind when confrunted with his godson. We can only hope.*

'I wont you to know I wont corse no trubble. Reelly this is the truth Aidan – Grif has so manny posh relatives you wouldn't beleive. We have to make the most of these opportunitys, dont we? There is more reasons, but I'll tell you when I com.'

He did wonder at the accuracy of her tale. He made inquiries and found that there was indeed a Mister Willoughby Rodgers who was a minor secretary of the Governor's. So in that, at least, Matty was telling the truth.

He did not know how much further to trust her. Obviously she was still with Grif, still committed to him, though he seemed to make a botch of whatever he turned his hand to. Again Aidan was reminded of Mark. He even thought, with mounting horror, that should Matty like the looks of the little hamlet of Moss Vale, he may very well be saddled with taking care of Griffith as well as Mark – all for the sake of their wives. But the idea was enough to tickle his sense of the ridiculous. There was no point in crossing one's bridges – he did want to see Matty again. So he wrote to her, and told her he would meet her train in Goulburn, that they would talk there, initially, and plot some way of seeing each other without compromising her yet-to-be established reputation in the reputation-conscious Highlands.

He lay in bed, that night, thinking of Matty, and fell asleep to dream of Matty and Berrima, Berrima and Matty, both moving through his mind, first one, then the other, until they became absolutely confused, and the dreams were somehow no longer pleasant, but unschematic, disconcerting and ominous.

When he found himself on the slopes of Craglea, near Aoibheal's Rock, confronted with the Woman in Black, his terror was boundless. For it was Berrima, for a moment, then Anna, then the stranger's face once more – and all the time the long silver hair blew about her face, and the long white fingers beckoned him. He tried to turn and run, knowing as he did so that it was of no avail. He found he could not move with any speed, his actions were slowed, hampered, and he almost screamed aloud in his terror. All through his adult life he had dreamed of this woman, and he knew what she represented, knew even in his dreams that the day he finally died, she would be waiting for him.

He awoke to find his nightshirt wound tightly around his legs, his body bathed in sweat. He lay still and listened to the first magpies and blackbirds calling sleepily from the trees in the garden, watched the dim light of dawn at the windows and slowly relaxed with the knowledge of where he was, that he was safe.

Aidan was still thinking of the dream as he rode, that afternoon, down the valley road to the mill at Shannonbrook One. There was a horse tied to the railing outside his office – a customer for lumber, he presumed, but Thomas, coming to the door before Aidan reached it, took his arm and drew him away a little from the building.

Over the sound of the engines and the saws' whine, Aidan shouted, 'What's the matter? Who's within?'

'Mark Ellis. He's been in Bowral all day, drinking. He's insisting on seeing you, Aidan, been swigging from a hip-flask this past hour while he waited for you. I didn't know whether to send him on his way home, or not.'

'You did right.'

As he stepped towards the door, 'Might you need any help?' Thomas asked.

He stopped. 'Should I?'

'Well . . . it's belligerent he is. I don't know if he's angry or if he's normally a nasty kind of drunk.'

Aidan grinned. 'The latter, I should think.'

'Poor Berrima . . .' His brother's words floated to him as his hand was on the doorknob. He did not pause, but his hand tightened its grip, and he entered the little office more abruptly than he would normally have, shutting the door behind him too sharply.

Mark was in a chair against the wall, beneath a print of Hobart Town viewed from the Eastern Shore; he was leaning back on the rear legs of the chair, and was just pulling the mouth of the hip-flask from his lips. He grinned. 'There you are. All hail, Brian Boru, High King of Ireland . . . !'

'Jaysus, Mark. What're y' like, coming here like this? Have you no sense at all?'

'I needed to see you, O powerful one.'

'You should be at the newspaper . . .'

'And so I shall. Soon. I shall return immediately. If not earlier.' He blinked lazily.

Aidan walked to his desk and sat down on his own chair, watched Mark, and waited.

The handsome face had become thinner, the dark blue eyes more shadowed. But the drinking of the past months had not detracted from his good looks, rather accentuated them. The finely-chiselled features were sharpened, not blurred. His effect on women would be heightened, Aidan thought, by the new pallor; he looked ascetic, like one imagined St Sebastian to have been. Women would want to protect him. One in particular did. *Yes, I'd miss him . . . Yes, I love him. I care for him . . .* He was filled with resentment. Mark Ellis had been given every opportunity in life, had been born with position, wealth, intelligence, good looks. He had Berrima. Every night of his life he could make love to Berrima, hold her to him. And he had betrayed everything, thrown it all away. Sat there, before Aidan, locked behind the blurred veil of alcohol, for he felt safe within its cocoon. *You will die in your cocoon,* Aidan thought, *it will kill you. And it will take years, curse you. You will have years in which to poison Berrima's life, too.*

'You are not pleased with me, coming here like this.'

The words drew no reaction. The hard features of the man behind the desk remained impassive. Mark licked his lips, glanced down at the silver flask in his hand as if he suddenly did not recognize it, and replaced it in his pocket. He tried to smile. 'I am not always drunk, you know. It seems as if each time we have a confrontation I am

708

inebriated, but I am not often drunk. You may ask Berrima.'

Aidan could have spoken. A tart reply came to his lips, but he remained silent.

'You're a formidable man, O'Brien. For us lesser mortals some fortification is needed before confronting you in possibly unpleasant circumstances.'

'You keep talking about confrontations.'

'Do I? Perhaps so. The fact is, I need your advice. I used to like to believe that I could cope totally upon my own. There is Berrima to consider, I can't go on taking risks that may affect her.' Did he imagine it, or was there a flicker in the jet-coloured eyes that gazed so coolly at him?

'I may as well tell you,' he went on, praying he had not been mistaken, 'that I have been gambling again. I'm quite heavily in debt, because I thought to make up the amount I borrowed from the *Argus*. No doubt you'll see what I mean when you look at the books.' His face was very pale. He glanced into Aidan's face and away again. Aidan had never seen him so tense.

'I checked the *Argus* accounts last month.'

A rather sick smile. 'Much can happen in a month. Kingdoms rise and empires can fall in a month.'

'Have you told Berrima?'

'No. How could I? She's not well, Aidan. She's been working so hard lately. I fear she's on the verge of a nervous collapse, and to find what I've done . . .' He did not go on.

Aidan was screaming to himself that he should have made sure Mark did not have access to the *Argus*'s funds – but how else could he have carried on his work? It would have been the final insult to the man.

'I was in Mittagong today, Mark. It's a wonder I missed you. I called in to visit you both.' He stopped, waiting to see Mark's reaction.

'Oh?' A flush began to creep up Ellis's throat. He wondered how Berrima had appeared to Aidan, prayed she had looked suitably peaky. 'Well, you'd see what I mean, then. Though she puts a brave front on things, one would think she was quite well some days, but then she'll break down completely when she's alone. I don't know how much more she can stand.'

Aidan wondered what it would be like to throw Ellis through the office window. It was now lunchtime, it would be a bad example for the men. But Mother of God, what a temptation . . .

'I've been thinking of returning to Melbourne, Aidan. As you know, my father owns quite a large surveying company in Melbourne. I've never particularly liked the idea of working with him before, because I've always wished to be independent . . .' His confident facade was giving way a little. '. . . But, to tell the truth, my health has not been what it was . . .' He caught Aidan's glance. 'It's not the drinking, Aidan. At least, not all of it. If I went home – to Melbourne – there may be some help there. You're a family man – you know that one's family can be of support to one in times of stress . . .'

'And Berrima isn't?'

He flushed darkly. 'Yes. Of course she is.' He looked down. His hand felt for the flask again, held it, trembling, as if he wanted more than anything else to drink, but controlled the urge. 'Something . . .' the voice came out tightly, the tension was growing in the man, the muscles stood out in his neck with his effort at self-control. 'Something is happening within me that Berrima can't . . . help. My hell is my own. I . . .' Aidan watched the trembling fingers, the knuckles white with the force of the grip. The next moment the flask was flung with all Mark's pent-up rage behind it, into a corner of the room. It crashed among the iron legs of a heavy old table, and bounced back beneath Aidan's desk.

The echoes died away into the air almost immediately, but it seemed to the two men that the repercussions went on and on. They stared at each other.

'It's so easy for you,' Mark hissed, and the open hatred on his face would have made a man less well-trained than Aidan pull back, scowl, show that he was shaken. 'It's so easy for you. You have the ability to take, and take, and never tire of it, or stop to think of the consequences. Berrima. All this time, it's been Berrima, hasn't it? Do you think I haven't known? Why, right from the beginning – from the first day I met you – you couldn't take your eyes off her. We've played the game, all of us, pretending we don't know what's going on – and all this time she's been committing adultery in her mind, if not with her body. I won't ask you if you've slept with her, I can honestly say that I no longer care.' Aidan had made a slight move, his face was white and dangerous, but Mark only smiled, began to laugh, softly. 'Are you about to go for my throat, Aidan? Please don't. You have men milling about in the yard outside, it will be all over the Southern Highlands by this evening. For people are waiting for you to disgrace yourself, for the veneer of respectability to rub off. To attack your business partner – and it could only be over one reason – would delight your enemies.

'And you have many enemies, Aidan. I am accepted in circles where you cannot move, and I tell you now, you have more enemies

710

than you would believe. You'd do well to be careful.'

He was frightened, Aidan realized. He was drawing on all his viciousness as a kind of defence. Was it only jealousy? Aidan was not disturbed. He had faced men many times more dangerous than Mark Ellis. All Mark had to fight with were words. He used them well, but Aidan could shrug them off.

But he was puzzled. Mark needed him. Why was he turning on him?

The silence went on and on. Mark glared, but slowly seemed to realize what he had been saying. He made no apology, but stood, and lurched for the door. Aidan had no idea if the man's awkwardness was caused merely by the alcohol, but now the anger had left his face Mark looked truly ill.

Aidan knew he would not return. He wanted to leave. Even Aidan could understand that need Mark had to run away, to return to the safety of his family. But he would take Berrima with him. He would be taking her from Mittagong . . .

'Mark!'

Mark paused, the door held open; he leaned in the doorway, his back to Aidan. From outside the whine of the saw was louder.

'Mark. Close the door.'

He wondered if the man had heard. Then he had closed the door, leaned against it. Before Aidan could speak, he said, 'That was unforgivable. Yet it's . . . the strain, perhaps. Forgive me for what I said.'

'I can't talk to you here, Mark. Will you go to the homestead? When did you last eat something?'

'This morning. I think. No, no . . . I didn't eat this morning.'

'Ask my mother to give you a meal, there'll be something there. Then go to bed in the spare room and sleep off the effects of that brandy. Are you hearing me?'

'Yes.' Almost sullenly.

'I'll be home about six this evening, and we'll talk. Only if you're in a fit state, boyo. Do you understand?'

'Yes. I . . . Thank you.'

He left, shutting the door behind him.

Aidan sighed and went on with his work, but at the back of his mind was Mark, his face as he had flung the brandy flask. He wanted it to go at my head. He hates me. The thought did not worry him unduly. He did not care about Mark. The memory came to him, suddenly, of the accident in the Davey, seven years ago. Should have let him drown, Aidan thought without vindictiveness. Berrima would have been free. I've been free these past five years. I could

711

have married her. She wouldn't want me, but I could think of some way of talking her into it. She respects me, she depends upon me to a certain extent. I could have fostered that dependence, made her believe she loved me. Five years! If Mark were dead. If Mark were dead . . .

His pen, signing his name to a letter, went through the paper with his vehemence.

Mark looked quite different that evening. Mary had always rather liked Mark; with her strong woman's liking for a rogue, she enjoyed his company and his wit. He flirted with her in a very gallant manner, and the dinner that the three of them shared went smoothly, with no shadow thrown over them by the scene at the mill. It was as if it had not occurred.

Mark drank only tea during his dinner, and coffee afterwards by the fire with Aidan, while Mary washed the dishes. They were quiet, for the most part, smoking, speaking only of generalizations until Mary bade them goodnight and went to her own room.

Aidan wondered, ever afterwards, what he would have said, that night. He wanted to keep Berrima. If that meant helping Mark, then he would help Mark – but they must stay in Mittagong. But with Mark's words, all Aidan's plans went out of his head, and never, afterwards, could he remember what he had been about to say.

Mark said, 'I realize what your feelings for Berrima are, you know. And I believe that she loves you. All those terrible, bitter things I said this afternoon – they have their roots in the truth. I suppose – all these years – I've been trying to compete with you. But it's no use. She should never have married me. If she hadn't, she'd be married to you, by now.'

He had not taken his gaze from the fire once. Aidan could only stare at him, and his first thought was that Mark might be mad. The crazy man who had sat in his office today, on the edge of violence, and this man who sat calmly, telling Aidan that Berrima loved him, seemed like two different people.

Yet . . . there must be some truth in it, he found himself thinking, there must be some truth is what he is saying, surely, or he would not be driven to such extremes of behaviour.

He studied Mark, and Mark glanced up and caught the look. 'How many years have we known each other now?' he asked, still in that calm, rather detached voice. 'Late in '57, wasn't it? That's twelve years. And we've been business partners for the greater part of that time. Yet I don't know you, really. I've tried. You remain an enigma – to a lot of people, I should think.'

712

'I could say the same thing of you.'

'Please don't. For you'll begin to say that you can't understand how I can waste my time and my money on my gambling and my drinking. You'll say you don't understand how I can waste my mind and my talents, and how can I bear to bring heartache to Berrima.' He looked at Aidan mildly, inquiringly, and at the back of his eyes there was a kind of pain.

Aidan said, quietly, 'You don't know yourself, do you?'

The barrier went up. Mark withdrew his gaze to the fire once more.

He said, 'Would you take care of Berrima, should anything happen to me?'

'Jaysus, Mark . . . !' Aidan felt a sudden, superstitious dread, remembering his thoughts that afternoon. 'Stop, will you?'

'That's all I want to know. Would you?'

'Yes. Yes, of course. But don't be after talking of dying, it depresses me.'

Mark smiled, and it was the old Mark. The chin came up, the firelight caught the fine planes of his face, lit the black curls and, for an instant, only, the blue eyes held no shadows. 'I had to find out. If anything happens in Melbourne . . .'

'Mark,' Aidan broke in, 'I don't know if Melbourne is the right decision.'

'I feel I'll manage better in Melbourne . . .'

'If you can't handle your finances here, Mark, what makes you think you'll be any better in Melbourne?'

'I'll have my family there.'

'But you're a big boy, now. You shouldn't need your family . . .'

'I need some stability!'

They gazed at each other. Mark dropped his head, rubbed his temple a little. 'I'd like a drink . . .'

'No.'

'I have a headache, Aidan.'

'You have a hangover, Mark. You're undoubtedly sober for the first time in weeks. Am I right?'

Mark shook his head slowly and grinned. 'Aidan . . .' he said, and when he raised his head his gaze was serious. 'Perhaps it's the best thing for Berrima, too, to come to Melbourne with me.'

Aidan tried to relax, leaned back in his chair, though he felt his body tensing. He did not like this. 'I think you should ask Berrima.'

'I have very little to do with Berrima lately. I think she'd come to Melbourne with me if I asked her – she came here to Mittagong willingly enough. I think she's done her best to be loyal, to place our marriage first. Will you try to stop us from going?'

Aidan looked at him in surprise. 'Stop you? How could I? I didn't try to stop you leaving Hobart for Mittagong, did I?'

'No.' There was a silence; when Mark spoke it was quietly, his voice burred, his hands rubbing his eyes. 'The right thing. Every one wants to do the right thing . . .'

Aidan waited, not understanding. The silence went on and on, Mark seemingly took courage from it, for he looked up at last and his voice was firm. 'I'm considering allowing Berrima to divorce me.'

Aidan had stopped breathing, was staring at Mark. Oh, God, let him mean it. Oh, God, don't let him be playing with me. He said, through tight lips, 'That would mean a scandal. I don't think Berrima would wish that.'

Mark smiled, and it was not a pleasant smile. 'She has coped with the gossip-mongers very capably, to date, has she not? I think she would settle down happily enough. She has her work, Nellie would remain with her. She'd have her father to help her should anything go wrong. And you. You said you'd help her.'

'Mark, I think you're talking a lot of rubbish. You don't want to divorce Berrima . . .'

'But I do need seven thousand pounds.'

They were staring at each other. Then slowly, slowly, as the ramifications behind the words became clear, written there in the fixed challenge of the blue eyes, Aidan rose and moved to the window. The curtains were closed. He walked further down the room. There were good rugs on the floor, and framed pictures on the walls. And here was Clemency's piano, brought with him from Glenleigh. It was a comfortable, attractive room. Aidan saw nothing of it.

'I need a drink, Aidan. Perhaps we both do.' The calm voice behind him.

'In the cabinet to y'r left.'

As Mark rose and was pouring two whiskeys, Aidan had dropped down into his mother's rocker. Mark turned around, glasses in his hand, to see him, the powerful legs in the fitted breeches stretched out, one booted foot crossed over the other. Aidan gazed into space, one great fist supporting his chin.

You look thirty-five, Mark thought bitterly. You've sold your soul to the devil, I believe. For wealth and eternal youth. Or perhaps you are so hard you've managed to defeat time. It has no effect on you. You won't soften enough to decay – you'll outlive us all.

He handed Aidan his drink. He took it without speaking, did not look up.

714

Mark's voice came to Aidan from a long way away. When he finally glanced up, the younger man was leaning his forearm against the mantelpiece, gazing down into the flames. 'I can see no way out, no way out at all.'

'How, in God's name, do you come to owe seven thousand pounds?'

No reaction. Then an infinitesimal shrug. 'It adds up.'

Aidan took a large gulp of whiskey. This was madness. If this had been any other man, Aidan would be laughing in his face.

Carefully, carefully . . . 'The sale of your land in Berrima wouldn't come near that figure . . .'

'I know. My parents would loan me the rest.'

'But you wouldn't want them to know.'

'No.'

Again the silence. Aidan could not gather his thoughts. He did not know whether to agree with Mark, or to bash the man's brains out. He was on sliding ground, he did not trust Mark . . .

'If . . . if I had the money, that would be an end to it. I haven't gambled for three months – that's why the accounts at the *Argus* are . . . the way they are. I had to use it to keep my creditors content.'

Aidan's anger was growing. He must not show it, but he felt it growing. How had Berrima come to marry this man? How had Milton Reynolds allowed it?

'And how do I enter into this?' he asked.

'If you . . . If you pay my creditors, I'll go to Melbourne alone. I'll provide Berrima with the evidence she needs to divorce me. I'll let her have whatever I own of the newspaper, to keep or sell as she wishes.'

'And I'd have Berrima.'

'Yes.' Only a breath.

Aidan was silent a long moment, then, 'Christ, you disgust me. I don't think I've ever met anyone in my life that I despise more than I do you.'

Mark was white. 'We are what we are,' he said tightly.

'Yes. I daresay it makes you just as ill to do business with me.'

Mark was silent.

'This will need arranging. I'll come back to Mittagong with you tomorrow and you can tell me who you owe money to and how much.'

'Aidan, I . . .'

'Don't you dare say thank you. Don't you dare tell me you're grateful. I don't know what, in your dirty little way, you see as my

715

relationship to Berrima, but I'll not be after buying her. Do you understand? I may help you. But it'll be for her sake. For I know something that has seemingly slipped your attention. Berrima wouldn't go with me, she wouldn't marry me even if she were free. She loves you. She knows you for what you are – a weak, feckless, spoilt little boy – and she loves you. She'd follow you into debtor's prison, you fool, that's the kind of woman she is. And I could kill you for your blindness, I could kill you for what you've done to her.'

Mark's glass fell from his hand. He did not move as it crashed on to the hearth, sending splinters of light everywhere as the glass exploded. He stared down at it for a terrible moment, then he had whirled, was across the room and out the door onto the verandah.

'Mark!'

Aidan could see him in the dark, running towards the barn, the excited dogs barking at his heels. Aidan followed.

When he reached the doors, partly open, Mark was lighting the lamp. 'What're y' doing?' For it was past eleven at night, and the road from the valley was difficult enough in daylight. 'Mark, for God's sake, you can't go running off at this hour.' He went to take the man's arm, but he had pulled away.

Aidan stood and watched him as he saddled his horse. Mark led the animal outside and still he said nothing; only when Mark was in the saddle did Aidan take hold of the reins near the bit. 'Are you listening? I'll come to Mittagong tomorrow and we'll discuss this.'

'No! Just leave me alone! Leave us alone! Berrima and I don't need you – we never did! It's all your fault! Everything! I ought to kill you! And you talk about helping! All this time she's thought of you as some kind of omnipotent god – you stretch out your hand and everything falls into place. She's never seen you as you really are, if she did she'd despise you as much as everyone else despises you! Leave her alone! She'd have loved me if you'd only have left her alone!'

His horse sprang forward and Aidan let go of the reins, was forced to step back quickly. Mark was swallowed by the darkness, and Aidan could hear only the sound of the horse's hoofs on the roadway, the clatter as they crossed the bridge. He stood for a long time after the hoofs had faded up the mountain road, gazing after the man.

716

68

The next morning, a message came for him to see Thomas urgently, but Aidan, accustomed to Thomas's tendency to panic when things did not go well at the mills, sent a message that he would be at Shannonbrook Two mill at midday, and rode into Mittagong.

It was Berrima who, after an interval, opened the door of the Queen Street house to him. Aidan walked directly into the parlour, trying to appear unconcerned that she was wearing a heavy velvet robe over what was obviously a lace-trimmed nightdress. He had the feeling that she would have stopped him at the door, but he walked too quickly, too determinedly.

Mark was not in the parlour, a breakfast tray set with one cup was laid out on a small table near the fire. He looked up at her as she came into the room, was about to ask Mark's whereabouts, but stopped.

She looked dreadful, as if she had spent the night in tears. 'It's Nellie's day off. Why are you here, Aidan? It's not seven-thirty, yet . . .'

'I'm sorry. I didn't realize it was so early. May I have a cup of tea?' He lifted the teapot, it was full.

'Yes . . . I'll get dressed.' She moved to the door.

'I didn't ask you to get dressed, I asked for a tea cup. This will do.' He had moved to a china cabinet and taken down one of the fine porcelain pieces that he remembered from the house in South Hobart; they had obviously gone to Berrima on her marriage. Without asking her permission, he poured tea into the two cups, handed hers to her. 'We seem to spend so much of our time together drinking tea. Do you realize that?'

She placed the tea cup and saucer down upon the table, avoiding his eyes. She moved restlessly about the room for a moment, finally saying, without turning, 'Mark told me.'

'Oh, Jaysus.' He replaced his own cup on the table and dropped into a chair, beginning to feel that the past thirty-six hours were a nightmare. 'Mark told you what?'

'About . . . about the seven thousand pounds.'

'Ah.'

'I . . . I want to thank you, Aidan, for what you tried to do.'

717

He was rubbing the bridge of his nose tiredly between forefinger and thumb, now raised his head slowly to stare at her. 'What?'

'Offering to loan Mark the money. We don't deserve your friendship, Aidan, we've abused it too often . . .'

'Shut up, Berrima.' He had dropped his head into his hands once more. Oh, God, he was tired. He had hardly slept last night, seemed to spend all his life, lately, on a horse going betweeen quarrels with one or the other of the Ellises . . . 'Is that what he said?' he asked now of her amazed face. 'Is that what he said, that I offered to loan him seven thousand pounds?'

'Why . . . Yes . . .'

'*Rawmaish*, girl.' He threw his head back to gaze at the ceiling. 'Mary, Mother of God . . .' he murmured, and stood up. 'Where is this husband of yours? Is he upstairs?' He was half-way to the door.

'He's gone out, Aidan.'

'I don't believe you. Is he in the main bedroom? I take it that this last "character failing" has not robbed you both of your intimate compensations. Or is he sleeping off his hangover in one of the other rooms?'

'He sleeps in *our* room.' Her face was white with anger. She took his arm to pull him back from the hall. 'He left *our* room early this morning to go to explain to his creditors.'

Aidan stopped. Studied her face and realized she was speaking the truth. He came back into the parlour and closed the door. 'And what,' he said, standing too close to her, 'is he explaining to his creditors?'

'That he'll be selling his share of the newspaper and the land at Berrima, and . . . and . . .'

'Come, Berrima, stop stuttering.'

'Really, Aidan, I needn't tell you any of this. It doesn't concern you – let Mark alone to solve this as best he can . . .' He was holding her arms and his grip was tight, and it was hurting her.

'It is my business – that newspaper is half mine, I think you may remember. Who is going to make up the difference in the money, Berrima?'

'Our parents. Mark's father in Melbourne, and my father.'

'*Milton* . . . ?'

'I wrote to him this morning . . .'

'Jaysus, Mary and Joseph, you little *maicin!* You'd be after worrying your father with Mark's nonsense . . .'

'Stop it! Do you think I liked doing it?' She was close to tears, 'We have no choice . . .'

He had not let go of her arms, and now he shook her, hard. 'When will it stop?' he said through gritted teeth. 'When will you wake up, Berri? He's ruined himself, can't you see that? And he'll ruin your father, too. He's got no right to ask your father to jeopardize all he's worked so carefully to build up. I'll not have it!'

'It's a family problem, Aidan! Don't make me more ashamed than I am, for God's sake . . . !'

'*You* ashamed? Mother of God, why should you be ashamed?'

'Mark going to see you – almost . . . begging like that. He didn't say that's how it was, but I can guess . . . I've never been so . . . I was so humiliated. Don't make it worse than it is!'

'It's worse than you think it is. He's a confirmed gambler, Berrima. A gambler and a drunkard, and he won't change.'

'He will. We must go away. He explained it.' He could feel her trembling through his hands. 'We talked about it. You don't understand . . . away from here . . . in Melbourne . . . it will be different.'

She was trying to pull away from him, but he held her firm. He now said, gripping her arms so tightly that she stopped struggling for a moment, 'Away from Mittagong? Or away from me?'

They stared at each other, in a kind of horror of recognition. For they realized that all the years had been leading to this.

She looked away, and he did drop his hands, then, needing to distance himself. He moved away from her, trying to choose words that would not frighten her, push her even further from him.

'You're not happy with Mark,' he said. 'There are no children involved. I'm free, now, Berri. Can't you . . . A divorce isn't the worst thing in the world, is it? For God's sake – we can't go on running about this country trying to avoid each other. You'll divorce Mark and marry me. That's what I think you ought to do, anyway.'

She was smiling a little. 'Why, Aidan?'

He stared at her. Did she want some impassioned declaration? 'I don't know. Why not? You love me, don't you?'

It was a grave chance he took, but 'Yes,' she breathed.

'Then the only thing that's between us is Mark.'

Something happened in her face, a shifting of expression that told of some anguish. Aidan knew, then, in the small pause, that Mark was reason enough. His voice low, 'You'll not stay with him out of duty. Out of pity. I won't let you.'

Her eyes, normally a light brown, seemed to darken as she raised her face to his. 'How dare you tell me what you will allow and what you won't allow!' She had whirled across to the other side of the room. 'You discuss my life, my future, with the patronizing tone that you'd use to a child! I'm not a child, Aidan, though you've always insisted on treating me like one. You have no respect for me – no real respect at all.'

'That's not true . . .'

'You don't treat me as an equal. Married to you I'd be as unhappy as Maura was – more unhappy, for I love you, Aidan, and I'd want to please you, and I'd adapt to your moods, good and bad – I'm more tractable than Maura—' He laughed at this, could not help himself, and she grew angrier. 'Maura managed to find some life for herself away from you. She ceased caring. And I . . . I couldn't. And you wouldn't let me,' she finished sullenly.

'So I'm an ogre, am I?' He walked towards her. 'Let me tell you something, Mrs Ellis – 'tis not I who have the strong character here, but you. If I have my foot on your neck half the time, it's because a man'd be a fool to let you gain power over him. You'd have him in a box and tied up with blue ribbon before he knew what was happening.'

'Aidan, you're insane! That's your own fears speaking . . .'

'You've done it to Mark . . . !' he lied in his rage, in his desire to hurt, and knew he had gone too far even before her hand came up and once, twice, she slapped his face, hard, with her right hand. For a second he did not move, then he turned to leave.

'I am stronger than you,' she said. 'I'm as much afraid of my love for you as you are of your love for me. But I don't blame you for it. I don't punish you for it. You're the child, Aidan, not me.'

He kicked the parlour door shut, savagely, and the key flew out of the door, landing near his foot.

And he had bent, picked it up, hands shaking with a rage he had not known in years, locking the door – and he turned on her.

She did not scream, nor, as far as he could remember, did she say anything at all. There was a moment when he thought he saw something like a kind of tenderness in her face, but it was at the moment of his own climax and was gone in the confused blur of his senses. Later, when he undressed at home, he found the scratches on his body, some had bled heavily; noted the bruises on his face and collar bone made with her vehement little fists. But when he took her in a struggle that began on the sofa and finished amid the debris of the over-turned table and shattered tea things, on the carpet, there were no words, nothing but raw emotion that went beyond love, lust, hate, longing.

Afterwards there was no tenderness. His body still beat hard with the pulse of his rage and desire as he stood at the window, tucking his shirt into his trousers, staring unseeingly through the lace curtains to a world that looked the same, but was not. He had possessed

Berrima, but in the cataclysm of the physical release there was no release from the emotional hold she had upon him. He stood at the window and watched the calm, leafy street, and waited for that carelessness that came when he had taken every other woman in his life, but Anna.

It did not come. He steeled himself not to turn around, knowing she still lay on the floor, her hair dishevelled, her body bruised. If he turned he would go to her, take her in his arms, cradle her like a child, and tell her it was all right now, he would take care of everything.

Any other woman would wish him to. But this one – no.

He heard her moving; his instincts were proved correct when he heard her say, 'You'd best leave.' The voice low, calm. When he turned she was standing, pushing her hair, which had tumbled loose from its combs, over her shoulders.

He stood for a moment, gazing at her. 'This isn't the end of it, Berri,' he said. 'That wasn't done in any sense of vengeance.'

'I know that.'

He said, his heart heavy, 'I didn't want to take you until you wanted me.'

There was a change in her expression. She came across the room to him, and placed her hand on his face. She was almost tender. 'We seem to take turns making dreadful mistakes,' she said. 'And each one pushes us further apart.'

'This . . .'

'No.' She smiled a little. 'I could have said, "Don't." ' Her tears came with her laughter, and he held her to him, then, forcing her head to remain upon his shoulder so she could not see the treacherous moisture in his own eyes. He kissed her hair, said, 'Get packed. We're leaving now.'

She was still in his arms, then, 'No, Aidan.' She spoke into the lapel of his jacket. 'No, my love. All I said was true. You're too strong for me. Until I know my own strengths, until I know how capable I am, I can't be with you. You'd destroy me.'

This was why he feared her, this ability she had that no one else possessed, to stir him to his very depths, up, down, back and forth, like a crazy, dangerous tide that moved, it seemed, on her whims. He yanked her back from him now, all gentleness gone from him, shook her, glared at her. 'Pity for Mark – that's what's keeping you here. You're worried that he'll destroy himself without you. He will, too. He longs to. Let him get on with it, Berri. Let him go, or he'll take you with him.'

'I need time, Aidan!' Tears close, her hands in fists against his chest. 'A separation from Mark – I'll go home to my parents in Hobart . . .'

'No. I'll not have you leave me again. I'll drag you back by the hair. Don't waste pity on Mark . . .'

'To walk out of this house into yours would mean the destruction of what little self-esteem he still possesses! I owe him this – some dignity in losing me. I'm all he has, Aidan, and he loves me . . .'

'And last night he offered to divorce you. For seven thousand pounds he offered to allow you to divorce him. Presumably so that I could marry you.'

He thought she would faint, she seemed suddenly so powerless in his grasp, staring up at him white-faced as if he contained the only recognizable form in a world of sudden chaos.

'It's not true . . . I don't believe you . . .'

'It is. I didn't want to tell you . . .'

'You're lying, Mark wouldn't do this to me, Mark wouldn't do this to me . . .'

'He would, y' little eejit! For God's sake, Berri, I . . . I don't know the words – I'm rough, and insensitive . . . I'm not young anymore . . . But I want to save you from this . . . Let me give him his money, and you'll be free . . .'

'Let go of me.' Her voice hard, through pale lips. 'Take your hands off me.'

'What?'

'Take your hands off me, Aidan, and leave me be.'

'Do you not understand? For that money he was happy to let you go. He was willing to go back to Melbourne alone!'

'Stop it!' She almost screamed at him, trying to place her hands over her ears to shut out his voice, 'Stop it!'

'I want to help you! Don't you understand that I . . .'

'I don't need your pity! I don't need anything from you!'

'Pity! That's the last . . . !'

There were white lines about her mouth. 'I wish I'd never set eyes on you. So you'd marry me, would you? Not because you loved me – you'd choke before you said that. You want me only to show how omnipotent you are. You know nothing of love, Aidan. Power means everything to you. You have no heart in you. Now take your hands off me and leave my house. Leave me some pride, Aidan, for God's sake. Leave me some pride, and go.'

He let her go, slowly, appalled. He could not gather his wits. 'Berrima, I've never meant to hurt you . . . Berri, listen to me. All these years . . .'

She was laughing. She sat down in a nearby chair, and she was laughing, and crying at the same time. 'Aidan, you hurt without meaning to. You have a great capacity to hurt. How dare you come here and tell me what you've just told me!' Her jaw tightened against her tears. 'Mark was right – we must get away from you – we must be independent . . .'

'Independent? You and that spoilt, drunken baby?' he shouted, stung by her words. 'Woman, I don't give a damn what the two of you do! Sure, you deserve each other! It was your husband who came to me! Your husband who made that foul offer to me . . . !'

She almost screamed, 'Aidan, leave me alone! I want to be alone . . . !'

'He doesn't care about you at all! Can't you see that? He offered to sell you, Berrima! He offered to sell you as if you were nothing more than a possession he'd tired of – because he knows I want you, that I've always . . .'

She had stood, had struck him. The blow of her open hand hit him smartly across the cheek and shocked him into silence. For a long moment he stood there, gazing at her in a kind of bewilderment. This blow he felt. It struck at the centre of his being.

'I'm no man's possession,' she hissed.

'That's not how I see you . . .'

'That's all you see in me,' her tone was bitter.

'Then I've helped you away from me. All I've tried to do for you made you happy, did it not?'

'You helped make me strong, Aidan. All that I've become, I owe, I believe, to you. But what was your purpose? Was it for me, Aidan? Or was it for yourself? To feel that sense of power in bringing me so far, only to destroy me utterly, at your whim? I will not be bought. Not by you, not by anybody.'

He took a step back from her. More than the physical blow to his face, the words stunned him, had his senses shocked, confused.

He did not, afterwards, remember leaving her. He had no last sight of her in his mind's eye, all was confusion. He rode back to Shannonbrook Two like a man who had received some great physical blow, too numb, yet, to sense the pain or where it would come from, knowing only that he had been hurt, hurt, and afraid to look for the cause, the injury.

Coming down Range Road, he could see the smoke. It worried him for it was in the direction of Shannonbrook Two and Thomas's Killaloe. One fire and the timber, and the newly planted plantations of eucalypts, would be gone.

But they told him at Henke's place that it was not a forest fire. It was Ottilia who ran out to the sliprails on seeing him pass, Ottilia who leaned, white-faced and pitying, over the rails and told him that his mill had been burnt almost to the ground.

69

Thomas thought Aidan's mind had become unhinged, as he walked about the smoking, charred ruins, muttering to himself. Thomas followed slowly, worriedly, at a little distance, seeing Aidan through the drifting smoke, brow lowered, jaw moving tightly, talking, talking beneath his breath.

The men were still working, carrying water from the tanks to throw upon what remained of the front wall of the building. Aidan seemed to come to himself as Thomas was approaching him, and called for the men to stop. The roof had gone, the rear of the building had disappeared altogether. 'Leave it, lads . . .'

'Mr O'Brien . . . ?'

'Leave it, now. You've done a grand job, sure. Take the day off and go home and rest. Call out here tomorrow morning and we'll discuss what work you'll be doing 'til we rebuild.'

'Sir?' One of the youngest men, a thin, dark-eyed boy called Maurie Templeton, 'We won't get the sack, then?' A few of the other men scowled at him, but all turned to Aidan expectantly, it was what had bothered each of them.

'No, damn it, I'll need all of you . . .' Cold mist of Tineranna, standing in the stableyard, dark-coated, shawl-wrapped figures waiting for the announcement from the back step, the relief on their faces, mirrored now, in these brown, bright faces before him. He felt a pain that was his past claiming him, the isolation of standing alone, as they drifted off, still calling their thanks and their goodbyes. He knew the thoughts in each man's mind, will he blame me, will I be the one to go? Aidan stood in his ill-ease. He was known as a hard, but just, employer. He had a tendency, these days, to bark orders. Part of this was because Tineranna still lived within him, the more powerful he became, the more analogies he found. The joy in his power would always be affected by his unwilling memory of being the worker, the hireling. He avoided large meetings of his workers for that reason; he could not forget, at those times, that he was no longer one of them, accepted. He did not like to see the

724

multiplied suspicion and awe on that sea of faces.

His office still stood, and the overseer's cottage. It was in the scrub behind Aidan's office that Thomas and the overseer, Frederick Dent, had found the two cans of paraffin.

'That's what's so maddening,' Thomas almost snarled, when the two brothers were alone in the office, pouring over the insurance papers. 'It was broad daylight – why didn't you come this morning!' He whirled on Aidan suddenly. 'Do you think I'd send for you if it wasn't important?'

'You have before, sure.' His brother looked up from his desk mildly. 'Don't go losing your temper now, Thomas. What could you have told me this morning? That Fred Dent saw something or someone skulking about the mill last night – right? It's happened before. We can only take more care, that's all, you'd have done what we usually do in these circumstances, mount an extra watchman at night. But in this case, what could we have done? Someone as bold as brass, came up the lower section of the valley, set fire to the building while the men were at morning smoke-o, and then headed off the way he'd come . . . '

'I sent two of the men to check the valley further down . . .'

'They'll find horse's hoofprints circling back towards the main road, and they'll have lost him.'

There was a silence. Thomas, still bearing a smudge on his left cheek, the shoulder of his jacket burnt badly, fell tiredly into a chair, leaned his elbows on the arms, and gazed at his brother over locked hands. 'So who did it?'

'I didn't . . . I don't know. I didn't think I had enemies of that kind . . .' He gave a bitter half-smile. 'Although Mark told me I did.'

'Mark? When?'

'Yesterday. Arra, in the middle of an argument, it was. It meant nothing.'

'Many words said in anger have some basis in truth, Aidan.'

Aidan looked up at him. 'Who could he have meant, for I'm telling you now that he's not in the mood to help me by naming names?'

'That fat Englishman over Glenquarry way – Pirie-Moxham. He has a little mill, did quite good business selling inferior wood, until you came along.'

'He wouldn't have the imagination to think of something like this. And he'd have to send one of his sons to do the deed for him; Pirie-Moxham couldn't get his bulk into the saddle, let alone do the kind of riding that'd take him out of that valley in a hurry.'

725

'He's one of the shareholders in the iron mine, is he not?'

'Aye,' Aidan agreed, 'and he resented my joining that little elite, you can be sure.' He took a piece of paper and wrote *Pirie-Moxham* in his round, firm handwriting.

'And Donaldson . . .' Thomas suggested.

'Only because he thinks I'm an Irish upstart? Oh, well, wars have begun for less reasons, sure.' He added Donaldson's name to the list.

'Helena Warwick?'

Aidan roared with laughter, and it was at this moment that a knock was heard at the door, and being open, it was pushed slightly.

Young, boyish features, straight brown hair suddenly visible as the trooper's cap was removed. Yet the eyes, for all their youth, were keen, they had passed quickly over Thomas, to Aidan.

'I thought to find you wild with anger, Mr O'Brien, or at the very least, severely aggrieved.'

'Put my mood down to hysteria, Constable.' Aidan rose as the policeman entered the office, and held out his hand to the young man. 'Peterson, is it not? This is my brother, Thomas.'

'Henry Peterson, sir.' He now shook Thomas's hand, and looking into the direct eyes, seeing the genuine smile, Thomas's first feelings of suspicion faded a little.

'Sergeant O'Hare asked me to handle the investigation, sir. I asked for it, for I've been meaning to make your acquaintance since I arrived in Mittagong, three weeks ago. My father's business partner – they have a mill and a firm of contractors in Ballarat – he knew you in Tasmania. Bartholomew Adams, his name is. He spoke highly of you, and asked me to send you his regards.'

No veiled threat, no hidden meanings within the green eyes that gazed at Aidan, yet the Irishman felt all his intestines tighten with the words. So this was it. At last it had happened. Soon it would be all over the town exactly what kind of man Aidan O'Brien was . . .

'I don't know any Bartholomew Adams.'

Peterson was no fool. He gauged from the closed face, the tight voice, all that the man was feeling. He went on hurriedly, 'They call him Terrier, sir. Terrier Adams. Small fellow, full of energy . . . He said that you and he shared a great deal of good and bad times . . . '

'*Terrier!* Hell's outhouse! Terrier Adams!'

'He met my father on the goldfields, Mister O'Brien. My father . . . he had spent ten years here at Berrima.' There, that would make the man understand.

Aidan looked at Peterson, for a while not comprehending. His father was in the police force . . . ? But the younger man's jaw had

726

tightened; he was gazing at Aidan with something like dignity, but there was a slight flush to his neck, above the high police uniform collar. 'Your father? Was in Berrima Gaol?'

'From 1841 to 1845. His original sentence was fourteen years. For stealing a horse,' the boy added, the voice was emotionless policeman's voice, reciting only. But Aidan saw the bitterness, the shame, and wondered, Do my children speak so of me? What have my actions cost them in pride and self-respect? They'd suffer as much as myself.

Aloud, he said, 'Thomas, how about finding us the whiskey bottle in the cabinet there? And three glasses, boyo.'

Peterson would not drink, but he stayed talking with them for two hours, managing, during tales of Terrier's business success in Ballarat, to gain whatever information Thomas and Aidan could give him concerning the fire.

'You should have reported it yourself, you know, not waited for me to come visiting,' he stated, finally, and despite the smile, there was a reprimand there. 'I know that you mustn't have a very high opinion of the police – my father came close to disowning me when he heard that I wanted to join – but truly, Mr O'Brien, we can help. Don't try to solve these matters on your own.'

There was a knock at the door as Aidan answered Peterson, and Fred Dent handed a note to Thomas.

'Peterson, I'm glad I've met you, and it's more likely, now, that I'll come to the police with such matters – but until now I've had no use for them. This is the first time since I've come to New South Wales that any attack has been made on myself or my property. But I have to tell you, if I find who did it, you'd better be close behind me, for I'm accustomed to handling these things myself . . .'

Peterson stood, smiled a little. 'Then I'll have to warn you not to, sir.' He held out his hand, and Aidan shook it. 'I'll be making inquiries – thanks for the list of employees, I'll be calling on them in the next few days.' He shook hands with Thomas, and left them.

Fred had already gone back to his brooding over the black ruin. Thomas stood at the door and watched the young trooper ride away. Then he turned to Aidan.

'Who's Mrs Griffith Rodgers?'

'What?' Aidan, who had only just reseated himself in his chair, looked up, Thomas thought, rather startled.

'Mrs Griffith Rodgers. There's a note here from her.' He handed the piece of paper, folded once only, to Aidan.

Regarding the slip-rail poles I ordered from you recently, could you

727

come to see me, regarding the length,

Your Obedient Servant, Sir,

Mrs Griffith Rodgers.

'Oh. She's . . . a new arrival. Planning on building at Moss Vale.'

'And she only wants slip-rails?'

'Just now, yes.'

'I'm going back into town – shall I call to see her?'

'No. No, I've got to call at the newspaper anyway. Come, we'll ride in together.'

He shoved the paper into his pocket, thanking God for Thomas's obtuseness, and they left the office.

'It happens to all of us,' said Matty, when they were alone in the corner table of the town's one decent restaurant.

Aidan's mind was still preoccupied with the memory of his mill. The sight that had met him, the charred wreckage of the building, the naked, blackened machinery. Now he was staring out the restaurant window; despite his surprise and pleasure at seeing Matty again, he could not get the thought out of his mind that someone wished to destroy him. 'It happens to all of us,' Matty had said, and Aidan looked up sharply, scowling. He did not understand, then realized they had been talking about the passing of time.

'What happens to all of us? Maturity, you mean?'

'Children.'

He stared at her.

She smiled a little, and it was a wry smile. 'You wasn't listening to a word I've said. Not that I blame you. That's why I came to Mittagong this morning – heard about the mill and all. Have they any idea who done it?'

'Nothing, yet. I doubt if they'll catch anyone. I'm going to call on Peterson at the police station this afternoon.' He looked at her inquiringly. There was little change in her, she was still lovely, her dress still the demure dark colours of the middle-class matron that she had been affecting for the past few years. At first he had been a little irritated that she had taken matters into her own hands and come directly to Mittagong instead of waiting in Goulburn as they had agreed – but looking at her, he was glad she had come early, and had come to him directly. It was over between them, but the warmth of their friendship remained for him. Matty knew him so well; there was no need to pretend, with Matty.

He asked, now, 'What made you say that? About children?'

She looked down at her food, toyed with it a little. 'That's my

728

news, you see. Just as exciting as yours, to me, anyway.' Again, the mouth was wry. 'You never came to see me for years, you swine, so you don't know. I had a baby, Aidan. A daughter. Emmy, I call her. It's really Emily, but I like Emmy better. She's five years old, now.'

'My God.'

'You've gone all white!' she laughed, her old laugh, low and throaty. An attractive laugh. Two farmers, seated behind her at a table, turned and glanced at her appreciatively.

'Do you mean – when I last visited you, you knew?'

'Yes, but you were so damned busy and preoccupied – you'd race in, fling your hat in a corner, drink a few whiskeys with me, grab your hat and be gone. That's all you did those last few months – you never stayed.' Her voice had slowed, the tone was lower.

'It was . . .' Suddenly he could think of no reason to give her. What could he say? He could give no explanation of these past years.

'It doesn't matter.' Matty reached her hand across the table, and touched his fingers briefly. 'It's just as well. Emmy could have been yours – and that would have caused problems all round.'

They smiled at each other. She said, 'Will you come to see me again, Aidan? And as I told you once before, I think, my intentions are dishonourable.'

'Matty, I've . . .'

'I know what you bin doing. You bin burying yourself in your work, and turned yourself into some kind of machine. Have you had any . . . diversions at all since your wife died? You can tell me.'

He thought, I must move quickly regarding Berrima, I must find Mark. Best get things settled with him before attempting to see Berrima again. Give Berri a chance to calm down, see the reasonable side of matters . . .

Matty took his silence and preoccupied frown to mean that there had been little or no diversion in his life. 'My God, Aidan. You got to do something about it, lad. It's like anything else athletic, you got to keep in practice.' She went on, on this theme, the low voice, part of memories of wild nights that began to come back to him from the past, continuing the conversation in a way that only Matty could. And he tried not to smile at her, tried not to laugh, and despite himself he was becoming aroused – and Matty knew it.

'Motherhood hasn't changed you, sure,' he said at last. 'Y'r as evil as you ever were.'

'I hope so.'

'And what does Griffith Rodgers think of the unexpected addition to the household?'

'He's been on one long bender ever since. Still, hoping for a son and heir next time.'

'Next time?'

'Well, there's a good chance . . . You know . . . I might already be . . . You *know*.'

It amused him to find her actually embarrassed about pregnancy, when a few minutes before she had been crude as she could be about the mechanics of reaching that condition.

'Does that bother you?' she asked, now, scowling a little.

'No. Why should it?'

'Will you come? Not now, when I'm staying at the hotel – but when I have my own place, will you visit me, like you done before?'

'You must be fierce sure that man of yours won't be home often.'

'I am.' Without bitterness. 'Being a father isn't making any difference to Grif, so why should motherhood make a difference to me? I do what I like.'

Aidan grinned. Suddenly, his gaze was caught by something beyond her, and she turned a little. A very well-dressed gentleman was just disappearing past the restaurant window.

'Who was that?'

Aidan's face was grim, his eyes still gazing at the place where, for a moment, the figure of Donaldson had been framed as he passed. 'A man by the name of Donaldson. One of the men who resent my presence in this town. To what extent . . . I don't know.'

'Donaldson? Are there many families about here called Donaldson?'

He looked back at her. There was something in her face, the faint frown on her forehead that she tried to smooth away with a smile when she saw him look watchful, intent. 'Why?' he queried.

'I just wondered. He's wealthy, isn't he?'

'He appears to be. The mine is eating away at everyone's assets – it's hard to tell how badly Donaldson is affected. Why, Matty?'

'A family joined my train carriage in Goulburn. When I arrived here in Mittagong last night, we all booked into the same hotel. I overheard them talking. A good-looking family – not rich, not poor – decent folk. Sam, the father's called. And two sons about seventeen and eighteen, Neil and Bram. The two boys sat in the seat behind me on the train. They was talking all the time about Mittagong, what it was going to be like – and they wondered what Donaldson was going to be like – like he was their employer or something.' She looked, for Matty, rather awkward, hesitant. 'I might have got the wrong idea, Aidan. But they talked about a mill. Donaldson's mill.'

'He doesn't have one.'

'That's what I mean – it's a new mill. Sam, the father, I gathered he was going to be foreman, or superintendent, or something, 'cause the boys were a bit crabby that they had to leave Goulburn for this job of their father's, and they were hoping that the mill was going to be worth it, see? That's the impression I got.'

What was Donaldson trying to do? It was impossible! Yet . . . why the secrecy? He had heard nothing about another mill being built.

His heart was hammering hard. He looked down at the food on his fork and replaced the utensil on his plate.

'Oh, God,' she breathed. 'Now I've begun something.'

'Don't be regretting telling me this, Matty. For the love of God, come and tell me any time you hear something like this.'

'But Donaldson wouldn't burn down your mill just 'cause he wants one of his own – would he?' She read the answer in the dangerous glow in his eyes. 'Oh. Well. I wasn't to know these things, not hardly seeing you these past five years . . . '

He was gazing out the window once more. She sighed, for she knew she would get no sense out of him now. When he turned to her it was only to ask Sam's surname. 'Russell,' she answered confidently. 'That's what the conductor called them. Sam Russell. And his wife's name is Tess, now I think of it. Pretty little woman, but tired. Like having all them great hulking men around her exhausted her.' But there was very little else she could tell him, there was no hint of where the mill was situated, or at what stage of completion it had reached. 'When the mill opens, is all they said. Hell, I didn't pay much attention. How was I to know how important it was?'

He saw her back to her hotel when they had finished their meal, and promised to visit her the following day, to drive her in his buggy to the little township of Moss Vale. 'There's nothing there, you know – the railway station and a pub or two.'

'Good, the land might be cheap. We'll make out, don't worry. We always do, me and my Grif. We land on our feet, like cats.' She grinned back at him as she left him, the smile that was the old Matty.

He headed back towards the new sandstone police station, so preoccupied with his thoughts of what Matty had told him, that when he collided with Donaldson as the man came out of Hutchins' general store, he nearly apologized and moved on. Instead, he planted his feet firmly in Donaldson's path.

'Ah, O'Brien.'

Aidan said nothing.

'I . . . heard of course. I've sent a few of my men to Shannonbrook Two, to . . .'

'Exactly when was that, Mister Donaldson? Not at about ten o'clock this morning, by any chance?'

'This afternoon, O'Brien – to see if they could be of any assistance . . .'

'To myself? Or to the owner of the new mill?'

Donaldson's features froze. After a tense pause, he said, 'Are you insinuating, O'Brien, that I would have anything to do with sabotaging your mill?'

'The timing is suspicious enough in itself, Mister Donaldson. I'd best look to my first mill, or the one you're building will have the market all to itself . . .'

'There's Pirie-Moxham . . .'

'He doesn't do business on the scale that we do. I'd be right in calling Pirie-Moxham an amateur, I think. You and I, however, are serious, are we not?'

'You're presuming that others have the same low tactics and high degree of greed as yourself, O'Brien.'

'I haven't burnt down someone's livelihood these past twelve months, Mr Donaldson.'

'But you could. You would. Your type stops at nothing. That's why you can dare stand there and accuse me of stooping so low . . .'

'You're building your own mill . . .'

'And what of it, sir? I have the right, if I so desire, to build ten mills . . . !'

'Not on the ashes of mine, damn you!' He stepped closer to the man, and Donaldson, for the first time, realized the rage within him. 'And I'll tell you this, boyo. I'll be after shooting the first man I see creeping about on my property. And I'll come to you, my old friend, should anything like this happen again – and I shall have your fat and greasy Saxon hide strung out on a barbed wire fence like a wallaby skin.'

'How dare you! None of my men have been near your mill except to help . . .!'

'Your help I can do without – and I will do without it. Start up your mill, damn you, your damn secret project! Y' love plotting in the dark, don't you? Like a fekking centipede under a rock.'

'Mr O'Brien?'

The two antagonists glanced up, scowling. The young police constable, Peterson, stood there looking solemn and official. He had a strong, large-boned face that would look better as he matured. Now, at twenty-five, he looked merely young, and raw. But again, the eyes held both the men. 'Gentlemen, I could hear your words

732

half-way down the block. If you're going to cause a disturbance, I suggest you come into the station.'

'I'll not go anywhere with this scoundrel. I'll not be seen talking to him. You go to the police station, O'Brien – it's where you belong.' And Donaldson stormed off, along the wooden footpath, his tread heavy in his fury.

'Mr O'Brien . . .'

'You found anything yet?' Aidan said quickly, trying to forestall him.

'No. Mr O'Brien, I can't have you making threats to people like that. If any allegations are to be made, the police will do it. Kindly leave this work to us.'

Aidan glanced at the young constable, who met his look stubbornly. Strange it is, Aidan thought, but this is one policeman I almost like. Perhaps that was why he now smiled grimly, where once he would have turned his back and walked off. Hal Peterson believed in what he was doing. Believed in the future of legal justice – perhaps he had been drawn into the police force in an effort to make sure that justice was done. To Aidan, that word was at best amusing, at worst a tragic misnomer.

'I . . . I want you to know, also, that I'll not be mentioning to anyone else what Terrier told me,' the young man added in a less formal tone.

'That I'm an ex-convict? Arra, you heard Donaldson just now – when they find out the truth, the people of this town won't change their minds about me – it'll vindicate their opinion.'

'A lot of people think highly of you, sir. The workers at the mine, for example, for helping to keep it running. They're afraid that when the mine closes, the town will die.'

'Och, no. The land's too rich.' He looked down the street at a patchwork town of impressive stone buildings side-by-side with tiny weatherboard and slab-built cottages. The main street, part of the Hume Highway that linked Sydney with Melbourne, was churned into dust or mud, depending on the weather, by the numerous horses and vehicles that passed to and fro, and even from here they could hear the sound of building in the streets behind the facade of shops and hotels. 'Mittagong won't die,' Aidan said confidently. 'It'll be here when you and I are dust, lad.' And he added softly, almost to himself, 'And my mills will be here.'

He did not call at the house in Queen Street again that day, but he spent an impatient hour at the office of the *Argus*, waiting for Mark to show himself. When he did not, Aidan left, leaving messages there, and at the various places in Mittagong where Mark was known to go drinking, that Aidan wished to see him urgently.

It was now nearly six, and he rode back to Shannonbrook One almost dozing in the saddle. What he needed most, he thought, was sleep. Then, in the morning he would take out the old plans of the Shannonbrook Two Mill, and he would order the timber from Number One mill to build it. Donaldson and his imported overseer, Sam Russell and sons, would not beat him, yet.

Tomorrow, too, he would arrange to see a representative of the insurance company – and he would go to see Mark Ellis.

For all his talk of refusing to buy Berrima, he thought with sardonic humour, that that was what would happen. It was a matter of supply and demand. Mark wanted money, and had only Berrima; Aidan wanted Berrima, and had the money to make Mark give her up.

Mark Ellis was mad, a man with 'roos in his top paddock, to be sure. Aidan felt exhausted just at the thought of the games he would have to play in the following weeks, months. But he would play them. He would buy out Mark Ellis. He would purchase that divorce, and he would have nothing further to do with Mark. He should have thought of it years ago. He had over-estimated the man, that's what it was. His moral courage and his love for Berrima.

His mother had a chicken roasting. The smell of it reached his nostrils as he came through the back door from the stableyard. But the kitchen itself was empty – no Mary, no Charity.

He found his mother in the parlour, seated rather stiffly before the fire. She rose when he entered the room.

'Ma?' It was the way she stood, something in her that radiated the fact that she had been waiting, tensely, for him to arrive home.

'Berrima rode out to give me a letter for you. She wouldn't stay – it was this afternoon, about two. I'm worried for her, Aidan. Read it – I'll leave you alone' – she handed him the white envelope – 'but when you finish, for the love of God, son – tell me what's going on.'

Dear Aidan,

I wish I did not have to write this letter, but I must. My dear, you need look no further for the person who burnt down the mill. It was Mark.

I cannot hope for you to understand – for I do not understand myself. He returned to the house at about twelve, white-faced, laughing, and told me what he had done. He seemed to think it was an enormous joke. I could not break through to him. It terrified me.

734

Aidan, I have done the only thing I could do, and have taken him to his family in Melbourne. There is no further use in my pretending that Mark is in his right mind. As I write this, he is sleeping. He broke down in tears about half an hour ago, and cried until he collapsed. I hope that when he wakes he will be more tractable. I must take him home to Melbourne. *I can no longer cope alone.*

It seems that once again, I must leave you to solve our problems for us. I wish there was some other way. But I cannot stay and see Mark placed in an asylum. I have seen the insides of these places with my father, and I would rather Mark be dead than to be admitted as a patient.

There is something else. Equally as difficult to write.

You are so much a part of me, Aidan. Yet I was never truly myself with you – looking back, I played the game of being half-woman, half-child because it seemed that was what you wanted of me. I'm not really a butterfly, never was – but I must have liked you a great deal and wanted your approval to suppress my own personality like that. Even as the editor of the Argus *I felt that you did not truly believe me capable, that I required watching. I married Mark as his child-wife – I can't go through life in that same relationship to you.*

We have been hurt so much by our unsuccessful marriages – yes, from this distance, I can admit to you that I was never really happy with Mark – you and I can't be together when all we would do would to carry our problems within this new relationship, destroying each other with memories of Maura and Mark at their worst.

Perhaps I always expected too much from you – though exactly what it was, now, I don't know. You were the first truly romantic thing to ever happen to me – and that, for an ignorant, over-protected young girl, can be seductive enough in itself. But, my dear, we never really knew each other – we could not allow ourselves to betray our real feelings, could we? We talked of plans, of ambitions. But who is Aidan when he is not building empires? Who is Berrima when she is not waiting for the magic?

My dear, for as much as I know of love, I love you. I have from the first – but there was Maura, and not just your pity for her, but my own. Neither of us could have hurt her.

I married Mark – Oh, Aidan, what are you thinking when you read this?! – because I knew I could never have you. I hated Maura at times, that she could share your house, your life, that she bore your children – that it could not have been myself.

I knew it would hurt you when I married Mark – foolish gesture that it was. It was my idea to come to Port Davey – it was that night on the beach, that terrifying night when I followed you from the cottage because I needed you – that I realized that I had made a dreadful, irrevocable mistake.

I must go. I've spent too much time on this letter already, and I must help Nellie with the packing. I would appreciate it, Aidan, if you could send our personal belongings to my parents in Hobart Town.

My love, there is so much more to say, there are twelve years of words that should be said, but cannot. We are part of all that has happened, Mark and Maura would always be between us, alive or dead. I could not face the future with the knowledge that I had failed to take care of Mark. He needs me, Aidan. You, my dear, are strong, and you'll survive. If I left Mark, even for you – my love, my love – I could not live with the guilt.

If there is any way of paying you back for all the expense, please rest assured, I will.

Oh, Aidan – don't come searching for us! This is Mark's last hope.

Goodbye, my love, Berrima.

He rode his horse into Mittagong as he once rode in the races of Limerick and Galway cities, with no thought but the goal at the end of the ride.

He left his horse in a white lather of sweat on the front lawn of the house in Queen Street, flung himself up the front steps, through the unlocked door, and into the darkened house.

Nothing. No one. Silence.

The bedroom littered with two suitcases, empty. Mark's clothes, Berrima's clothes, flung on the bed, the wardrobes agape.

He did not need to search the house. It had that empty, deserted feel to it. He knew that Nellie, too, was gone. That there would be discarded belongings, half-packed, then abandoned packing cases in several rooms of the house. But Berrima was gone. And she could not, would not come back. He lay across the bed, the large bed she had shared with Mark, his face against one of her robes, and he remained there, dry-eyed, fully conscious but unmoving, all night.

70

There was an enormous scandal. Mittagong was too small, and Mark
Ellis's debts too great for it not to be discussed in every circle.
Aidan's enemies delighted to think that he had been left to try to run
the *Mittagong Argus* as best he could, that, and the loss of his mill,
they said, with heavy tones and secret smiles, may just spell ruin for
Aidan O'Brien. Of course, he had investments in Sydney and
Melbourne – but who knew how much in debt he was? He could
have been struggling, all this time, to keep up appearances. And he
lived like a cockatoo farmer, anyway, out there in the hills. Ellis's
defection, and the loss of his precious editor might just break him.

Aidan shuffled his investments, sold some of his valuable shares in
Tweedie and Company, and managed to survive, to pay off the
receivers for the other half of the *Argus,* and to buy the house in
Queen Street with much of the furniture. He could not bear that
strangers would live in Berrima's house, use Berrima's things. He
had to have them, to keep them . . . None of his family dared to ask
the purpose. Deep inside they felt he hoped she would, one day,
return.

Aidan, however, was not prepared to wait. He went first to
Hobart Town, leaving Thomas to take charge of the building of the
new Shannonbrook Two mill. He was not prepared for the Reynolds
family to be as puzzled and hurt over the matter as he himself. They
had received a letter, Milton told him, telling them that Berrima was
going away with Mark for several months but did not say where.

Aidan stared at Milton and Margaret, took in their strained faces,
and knew they were not lying. Mark was not the only one who was
mad, he thought, the first seeds of anger beginning to grow amongst
his hurt and bewilderment; Berrima, too, was mad.

Milton accompanied him to Melbourne, and on the boat, they
talked.

'I knew she loved you. I knew it. That's my burden, you see, that I
allowed her to marry Mark, hoping that his love for her would wean
her affections from you. For it was hopeless, my friend, was it not?'
The blue eyes looked tired. Perhaps it was the dark sea of the Strait,
but it seemed to Aidan that his friend had aged considerably in the

past four years, the eyes had lost much of their life.

'I was married,' Aidan admitted. 'There was no hope for us. I didn't – I did nothing improper.' He traced his friend's face, it was important to him that Milton believed this.

'I know that. To tell the truth Margaret and I didn't know, until you came chasing down here three days ago, that you returned Berri's affections. I don't know quite what we could have done, even if we had known. As you said, there was no hope – but . . . I don't know . . . divorce should not be such a terrible shame, such a disgrace. Why, I know several marriages in Hobart Town that are shameful, in terms of the hell the couples put each other through. If . . . If I knew then, what I now now – I'd have told you to divorce Maura – or, rather, to allow her to divorce you. I'm sure she would have been happy enough – you two, God rest her soul – were more mismated than Berrima and Mark.'

'You'd . . . you'd have allowed me to marry Berrima? An emancipist such as myself? My crimes were worse than Will's . . .'

The blue eyes flashed suddenly, the voice grew cold. 'Have I been your friend for these past twenty years only to have to tell you now that your prison record doesn't matter to me? Are you so much of a fool that you would believe it did? Then it's no wonder my daughter makes mistakes in regard to you, Aidan, for it's a confoundedly blind and perverse character you are.'

'And now?' Aidan barely heard the words of that speech, only the meaning went to his mind, warmed him. 'And now? If I find her again? If she'll consent to divorce Mark? Would you have me for a son-in-law, Milton? Would you?'

'First find her, dammit!'

'Would you!?'

They gazed at each other, and Milton Reynolds smiled. 'I'd be proud. You should know that, man. I'd be proud.'

And they were embracing. The sea spray, cold and fine, stung Aidan's face, but he clung to his friend, felt the tears equally biting, sting his eyes.

'Aidan? There are two gentlemen over there who are looking at us very strangely . . .'

Aidan turned. The two gentlemen turned away and walked quickly off along the deck, shaking their heads. Aidan and Milton clung to each other, laughing.

If the Ellis family of Toorak, Melbourne, knew the whereabouts of their son and daughter-in-law, they refused to divulge it. Milton came back to Aidan with this news, for Aidan had remained politically removed from the family, waiting for news at the hotel where he and Milton stayed.

They were decent, snobbish, heartbroken people, Milton reported, and he pitied them. But they would divulge nothing, claimed they had not heard from their son, and felt that Mark and Berrima would reappear only when they wished to. 'I don't believe them, of course. I feel certain that Mark is in a private sanatorium somewhere, and Berrima is close by him.'

'I'll hire a private investigator.'

'Do you think that will serve any purpose?'

'We can only try.'

Milton returned to Hobart Town, waiting only to visit Richard at the university. He, too, had heard nothing from Berrima, but Milton did not tell the boy all the details of the matter, fearing that it would disrupt his mind from his studies. Aidan waited in Melbourne for three weeks, hoping for some report from the investigator. But there did not seem to be a trace.

He went home to Mittagong, visited the cold, silent house in Queen Street, the furniture covered in dust sheets. He wandered through the rooms, thought of Berrima's clothes, sent, with Mark's things, to Milton, lying in unopened packing chests in the attic of the red brick house in South Hobart.

He reread the letter, so often that it began to tear along its folds, but beyond the words that spelt 'goodbye', he could find no further message that would help him discover what she would do, where she would go.

He thought he had known emptiness, despair, before. He had thought, self-pityingly, that Maura's death, the death of his childhood companion, his fear of getting older, and the loss of his children to Ireland, were reasons for the despondency of the past years. But it was nothing to the feeling of helpless raging that possessed him when he realized that he had known, *had known*, in his heart, that Berrima had always loved him. Her words in the letter came as no revelation, they made obvious to him only the fact of his own blindness.

What had he expected of her? The blatant voicing of sexuality that Matty possessed? Or did he expect, because Berrima denied, on so many occasions, her feelings for him, that she meant the words, the cold, icy-cold words with which she tried to keep him distant – as Maura had meant her words of frigid denial? She was not Maura, any more than she was Matty. But somehow, in his own fear, in his own terror that this thing between them was too wonderful, too grand, that it would vanish like his relationship with Anna – in his insecurity over these memories of his past, he had created a Berrima of his own choosing. She combined all that was worst in all his women. He found similarities and rationalizations at every phrase she uttered. And out of these he built a wall that would keep the real Berrima from him. She was right in what she had said in the letter, that was what hurt him the most. *My dear, we never really knew each other.*

Gradually, almost unwillingly, now, he began to work once more, and found that if he kept long, impossibly long and very busy hours, he had little time to think, to lie awake and wonder where in this great continent she was, how she was coping.

Still, he refused to rent the house in Queen Street. He kept the key to the door on the ring that held the keys to his mills, and he called there, sometimes, and sat in the parlour, or in the upstairs bedroom that looked out over the rear garden and the crouched bulk of Mount Gibraltar, watching the sun turn its slopes to pink and rose and gold in the way he had watched Mount Wellington from Glenleigh.

He sold *The Argus* very cheaply, to a fussy, middle-aged, confirmed bachelor who had worked for years as a sub-editor of a Sydney newspaper, and now had saved enough money to purchase a country paper of his own. He was a narrow, unimaginative man, Enoch Wilkes, and Aidan received more complaints than he thought possible from Mittagong readers who regarded the sale as some kind of defection. Edward Lawler, the town's leading physician and one of Aidan's few friends on the board of directors at Southern Highlands Iron and Steel, complained that the *Argus* should be renamed *The Parochial Whimper,* and even Helena Warwick was overheard by Ottilia, in Hutchins' General Store, saying to Mrs Albertson, that 'whatever rubbish O'Brien and Ellis used to publish, it was at least *interesting* rubbish'.

He had some diversion, too, later that year, in the matter of Thomas and Ottilia.

He had returned very late from the new Shannonbrook Two mill one night, to find Heinrich Henke in the parlour, talking to Mary. She looked up, her black eyes sparkling, at her son, as Henke stepped forward, hand outstretched, with his usual good-humoured greeting.

Aidan was tired, was not pleased when Mary excused herself to go to bed. It would mean that Aidan would be left to entertain the man, possibly until the small hours. Yet, as Aidan went to the cabinet, and was pouring them a whiskey each, Henke said, 'It is a bad time – but you are so busy – very often I come to see you, but always you are

740

working. It is a simple matter, but important.' Here he stopped. Aidan, turning with the glasses, found Henke to be looking rather nervous.

Aidan was genuinely puzzled. 'Sit down, Mr Henke . . .'

And when he was seated, glass in hand, Henke began without preamble, 'You are the eldest male in your family, so I come to you with this matter. I would come to your father, if he were here. I would like to arrange a marriage between your younger brother, Thomas, and my daughter, Ottilia.'

Aidan, who had been looking mildly enough at the man, was now gazing at him in complete amazement. 'My brother?' he said, when he realized the silence had gone on too long.

Henke's eyes twinkled, 'You haf only one, I believe.'

'Yes. Yes, and he's . . . forty-three, Mr Henke. Sure, he's old enough to be arranging his own marriages. Marriage.' Aidan took a gulp of his whiskey.

'*Ja*, that is so. But I am, perhaps, old-fashioned. It is the way things are done in my country, and I think, in yours? Mrs Henke, she says that things must be done the right way. Though I know that this is a new country, and this talk we haf is . . .' He grinned, a little self-consciously, '*Formlichkeit* . . . What is the English . . .?'

'A formality?'

'*Ja*! The young people – they haf made up their minds, yes?'

'Have they?'

Henke blinked. 'Thomas has not spoken to you?'

'Em . . . no . . . He spoke to you, did he?'

'Ach, no – not yet. But he is a quiet one, yes? He will be pleased to have it arranged. Mrs Henke is a quiet one, she was pleased that her mother and father arranged our marriage – she feels Thomas would like it arranged by us.'

'But . . . Mr Henke . . . If Thomas hasn't mentioned anything – how do you know he wants to marry Ottilia?'

'He does.' Henke nodded calmly, 'Always he is at the house. Chops the wood for Mrs Henke, helps Ottilia milk the cows. Sings the Irish songs . . .'

'*Thomas?*'

'Yesterday, 'Tillia went to help Thomas hang the curtains at Killaloe – she did not come home until after dark.' He grimaced a little. 'So many windows there cannot be in a cottage. No. It is time, Mr O'Brien. They luff each other.

'In the marriage settlement, I give them one hundred acres and fifteen of my dairy cows – excellent Friesians and Jerseys – and there is family silver that . . .'

741

'Mr Henke . . .'

'. . . has been in the family for six generations. Ottilia is only child, so all comes to her and her sons with Thomas . . .'

'Mr Henke . . . ! I . . . I think we'd better find out for certain that Ottilia and Thomas wish to marry before we start talking about the dairy – dowry!' Oh, God . . .

For the first time, Henke looked unsure. 'You think that . . .that Thomas is . . . *playing games only?*'

'Thomas? Och, no. He wouldn't know how. But . . .' His head was beginning to ache with fatigue and the ramifications of what the man was saying. Could Thomas be toying with the girl's affections? He tried to imagine Thomas lounging about the dairy, singing *Eileen Aroon* to Ottilia . . .

But the more he thought about it . . . Arra, it would be great crack to see the boyo married off. And Henke was right – if ever a man needed to be pushed into matrimony, it was Thomas.

He arranged it all, as head of the house. Thomas was asked to come to Shannonbrook One for dinner that Saturday night, and Mary told to disappear after dinner. Aidan knew that she would be waiting up, listening for every sound, but she agreed this was the only way it must be arranged.

Aidan sat Thomas down in a chair in the parlour once the meal was completed, and questioned him ruthlessly about his feelings for Ottilia, plying Thomas with whiskey all this time, until by the end of two hours, he was mellow enough to admit that he had a fierce *grá* for her, sure, but as for declaring himself – not just yet. And as for marriage, well! That required a great deal of thought . . .

Poor Thomas wished he had not come. Aidan's belligerent solicitude was wearying him. And how could he tell Aidan the truth? With any other man he could say, 'I loved a girl, once. I loved her faithfully and steadily for nearly all our lives. And she died – and still I love her. There can be no one else for me.' He could say this to anyone else – but not to Aidan. So he parried, and dodged, and grew more and more ill-at-ease.

Finally. 'Mr Henke came to me, recently, with the plan that I should help arrange a marriage between yourself and Ottilia.'

'What?' Thomas was on his feet, his face white.

Aidan glanced at the clock on the mantelpiece. 'As a matter of fact, they'll be here in about five minutes, to discuss the matter.'

'Mother of God, no!'

'Thomas, it can't go on as it has, boyo. The girl's wild for you. Have you no pity?'

742

'Wild for me? 'Tillia?'

'Of course – begod, you're after breaking her heart – why else would Henke come to see me?'

'Ottilia? Loves me?'

'Arra, she's a lady, Thomas – you don't expect that she'd come right out and say it, do you? She's been waiting all this time for you to say something.'

'But . . . I couldn't – I mean . . . I don't . . . Oh, God!' He headed for the door. 'I'm going home – I'll not let you get me into that kind of situation . . .!'

'Thomas, if you walk out that door, I'll be after you, and if you'll remember the last time we wrestled – you were thirteen, I believe – I won, without difficulty.'

'Don't threaten me, Aidan!'

'Then come back inside, like a sensible man, so I won't have to embarrass Ottilia by having her find me sitting on your chest to keep you here.'

'I'm not going to marry Ottilia Henke! I'm never going to marry! *Do you understand?'*

'Of course, Thomas, of course,' his brother soothed. 'But I'm afraid your behaviour over the past months means that you'll have to clear the matter once and for all with the Henkes.'

They both heard it at the same time, the heavy creak of the old buggy, the clatter and roll of it over the bridge. Aidan went up to the white-faced, statue-like Thomas, gripped his shoulder. 'We'll send her in straight away, leave you to break it to her yourself. Be gentle, lad.'

Thomas Patrick O'Brien married Ottilia Anna Maria Henke in the little sandstone church of St Francis Xavier at Berrima, in February, 1870.

With a great deal of heirloom silver, seven Friesians and eight Jersey cows, they began their married life on the property called Killaloe.

His mother cried at the wedding, less at the sight of her son taking the pretty Ottilia as his wife, as in relief that she need not die with what she had begun to call 'that sin' on her conscience.

She had had only one reason for feeling real guilt in her life, only one time when she had deliberately set out to hurt another human being – and that person her son. Maura, at the end of her life, had called for him at last. And Mary had lied about it. It had been a dreadful lie, a dreadful gamble. Yet with what soon became apparent as Thomas's happiness in this strange state of affairs, her guilt had faded. She knew, in her heart, that had he known Maura loved him, nothing would have convinced him to be unfaithful to her memory.

You're a fierce fool, she would mutter to him silently, even now, when she would visit Killaloe, and see the puzzlement that sometimes claimed Thomas's face, for it was obvious that he still did not understand how he could be so happy. He felt in his way, his mother was sure, that it was not right, not *decent*, to be so happy. Even when his son was born, when he walked from the bedroom to show Aidan the ten-pound boy that he called Corrie O'Brien, with the tears of his happiness coursing down his cheeks, he still did not quite believe it. How could so much good happen so quickly – and to *me*? his bemused expression seemed to say, and Mary would feel like slapping him. He would never change. He would spend all his life asking Why Is This So, instead of acting on his impulses.

But 'Tillia was clever. She had made him, at forty-four years old, a husband and a father. Who knew what other miracles she might not perform?

The little family at Killaloe grew; Henry was born in 1872, Joseph in 1873. Aidan took great delight in his nephews. He wrote letters to Liam and Clemency and described their small victories on their path to boyhood, asked them, constantly, to come home and see their cousins for themselves . . .

But the letters from Dublin remained, in content, rather the same. Liam was now a junior lecturer – albeit a non-Fellow – in Legal History at Trinity. He was having a very pleasant time, keeping very busy, and did not see how he could come home this year.

Clemency was now twenty-five, and had been virtually adopted into the family of her friend, Catherine Mitchell. Even on Catherine's marriage, Clemency, who had become close friends with Catherine's mother, Christabel, showed no desire to leave her new life and return to Australia. Aidan was so taken aback at the turn his daughter's life had taken, that he did not share Mary's worry that Clemency should be 'lookin' for a daycent man and settling down'. He read his daughter's letters aloud to the family, and took a great interest in her life; he was secretly glad that she wrote as often as she did, and her fond memories of her family and of Australia convinced Aidan that she would eventually return. 'But not just yet, Papa – a little while longer . . . '

He did not wish to force either of his children to come back to him. But in watching young Corrie and Henry and Joe he missed Liam and Clemency, felt the need of their presence.

Early one morning in April of 1873, Thomas rode up to Shannonbrook One, just as Aidan was about to leave for the mill.

'Come walk with me,' Thomas said, 'I have something to show you.'

They strolled amongst the bare fruit trees in the garden. Though the autumn sun was warm, a thin wind was blowing from the south-west. Aidan was about to ask the frowning Thomas what business had brought him here at this hour, when Thomas pulled a newspaper cutting from the pocket of his jacket and handed it to Aidan.

It could barely be termed journalistic reporting. It was one of the scurrilous, venomously-worded pieces of copy that newspapers were permitted to print; four columns of it, dreadful innuendos and pitiless, vicious descriptions of the parties in a divorce scandal.

Mark Shaw Ellis, was sueing his wife, Berrima Anne Ellis (née Reynolds) for divorce on the grounds of adultery, and naming the younger son of an English Marquis, Sir Grantly William Balbrook, as co-respondent.

'It's a Melbourne paper,' Thomas pointed out. 'But it's all in the Sydney papers, too. Berrima's really in trouble, now, is she not?'

71

'I still find it hard to believe,' Thomas said, after Mass three weeks later, when they went for a walk along the edge of the creek, at Killaloe, while Mary and Ottilia prepared Sunday dinner within the homestead. 'Berrima – and the town still hasn't stopped talking about it. They stop in front of the Queen Street house, have you seen them? And they point it out to visitors – "That's where That Ellis Woman lived." They make me sick.'

He glanced over at Aidan's obdurate face. 'Aidan, you don't believe it, do you?'

'Mark gained his divorce, did he not?'

'Arra, Mark isn't in his right mind – even the newspaper hinted that he was under the influence of alcohol when he was being questioned. The man's mad – he'd have to be mad to put his wife through that horror, even if she *was* guilty.'

'He had witnesses, remember, he and his father caught the two of them in Balbrook's house – *in flagrante delicto* in the four-poster.'

'Still, it's so out of character for Berrima – there must be some reason . . .'

'What else would she be doing at the time? Showing him her birthmark?'

'Does she have one?'

'How do I know?'

A silence, then, 'Sure would that be what's bothering you?' Aidan looked over at him, blackly, 'That she never . . . showed you her birthmark?'

'Thomas,' Aidan said in a deceptively calm voice, 'I've been after noticing that your speech is taking a turning towards the lewd since you married . . .'

'Och, yes. That it has, I'm pleased to say. Sure I'm making up for the years when I didn't know about lewdness, Aidan. There's so little time, and so much to know.'

'Well, keep your smutty little mind off Berrima.'

'I can do that, sure.' Thomas's eyes were suddenly serious, 'Can you?'

He could not. He read and reread every description of the scandal in every newspaper he could find; he built up an idea of what had happened, from searching for the facts within the overlaying of coloured, cheap journalists' tricks.

Mark and Berrima had spent three years in England and Europe. Obviously, his parents had paid for this, in the hope that some cure for Mark's condition would be found. In London, Berrima had met Balbrook, charming, urbane, perhaps a kind man, for all that had happened, for it was obvious that he was standing by Berrima throughout the scandal.

When Berrima and Mark came home to Melbourne, Balbrook had followed them. Aidan believed, and he had no proof but his own feelings, his own knowledge of Berrima, that it was only then, realizing the extent of Balbrook's love for her, that Berrima had succumbed to him.

And Mark, being Mark, had known. Mark, being Mark, would have been waiting.

Aidan wrote three letters to her, asking only that she write back – offering any aid that she might need, his money, his presence – he would come to Melbourne immediately, if she would only ask him; but to none of these letters, despite the weeks in between them, waiting, waiting, did he receive a reply.

And he could not forgive her for this. Once more, as on those long nights in the months that had followed her precipitous flight from Mittagong, the duality of his feelings kept him awake, writing dialogue in which he insulted her, hurt her, comforted her, seduced her, depending on the violently oscillating pendulum of his emotions.

Yet there was much to do, with his business interests, that gave him ample scope, in those years, to vent a great deal of his resentment, against Berrima herself, and against those in the Berrima district whom he had always seen as standing in his way, who would not accept him. He had invested in Southern Highlands Iron and Steel, but the mine continued to lose money. Aidan found he was in a position to make loans, and take out mortgages on the properties of several of the investors. It was what he had hoped would happen when he had first invested himself in Southern Highlands Iron and Steel, and he vent a great deal of his spleen, or his gratitude, depending upon how he felt about the men concerned, as time went on, and payments were not forthcoming.

He ruined Pirie-Moxham, he made things very uncomfortable for Donaldson. He was able to offer sound advice to Edward Lawler, who as a businessman was an excellent physician, and he acted with surprising gentleness towards the Warwicks – for he came to like Hedley, and could see no way of sending the wife to the poorhouse unless her husband accompanied her.

Thomas was appalled by these machinations – even Matty, who was now living in Moss Vale in a rather run-down farmhouse she shared with 'Me kids and Grif, my boarder,' surprised Aidan by taking little delight in his victories.

'You're sneaky, that's what. You're like a spider in a web, you are.'

'Arra, what're you like? You've used men all your life . . .'

'Yeah, but I don't plan it like a bloody war, mate – I pick up what I can along the way. I'm a scavenger, I am. Not a bloody general. You scare me, the way you go on.'

He did not like it when she became moral. 'We're two of a kind,' he stated stubbornly. 'Your cheating on Grif didn't just happen. You have to plot hard enough to see me.'

They met at intervals every week or so, at a shepherd's hut Aidan had had built on Shannonbrook Two – at a great distance from the flock and any of the stockmen. The single room contained only a cupboard and a bed – all they'd need, Matty noted drily on first seeing it. Brandy in the cupboard and the bed covered with sheepskins. There was a fireplace, and this particular night they had lit a fire, and the flames threw strange, warm patterns on Matty's skin.

'That's self-defence, that is. He ain't staying home with me, most nights, I can tell you. You seen that new whore in town? Awful lot like old Ettie, she is – but fatter, and not as good looking, though I hate to say it. Well, Grif's been hanging around her establishment, I bin told. I haven't slept with him since – and he hasn't asked me. We got a chaste marriage, we have. You're my only bit of devilry, see? I got to have a hobby. With some ladies it's tatting, or embroidery – with me it's rolling around in the buff on a sheepskin rug with you.'

He was fortunate, he told himself, going between his games with Matty and his games with the board of directors, that he had such pleasant means of spending his time.

Matty had her third child that year. A boy at last, Aidan was even mildly hoping that it was his. Matty wasn't sure, but claimed as the months went on that the child – called, naturally, Griffith junior – was, in fact, progeny of Griffith senior. 'He's got a brown birthmark coming up on his bum – just like his dad's.' Matty said rather morosely, 'And he's gonna have a cleft in his chin, like Grif. Just as well, I suppose. You both got a boy each, now. Next time it's anybody's game.'

Yet in these four years he was kept motivated mostly from habit, he knew; habit and bitterness. Matty made him laugh, often, but she could not fill the empty space inside him.

Thomas said, once, when the two brothers were seated on the front steps of the Killaloe homestead, a low, meandering building with an enormously long front verandah, 'Are you certain that all these rather unfair business tricks you're after playing lately, aren't a kind of vengeance on Mark?'

'What?' Aidan was tapping the contents of his pipe out against the verandah railing, turned to gaze at his brother, amused.

'You never used to be so vindictive before Mark and Berrima left, Aidan.'

'Thomas, I'm more wealthy, now. I can afford to be a bit of a bastard, these days.'

'You avoided the possibility of being called that name, once. Now, it seems, you take delight in it.'

'It was necessary. I have properties, now, that I wouldn't otherwise possess . . .'

'You knew that the mine would fail, didn't you? It was what you were hoping for. You've lost about five thousand pounds of your investment, but to you it's been worth it. Those men – even the ones who didn't like you – they respected you. They went into your debt – and you foreclosed at the first opportunity . . .'

'That's business, Thomas.'

'It stinks, Aidan. They could have been your friends.'

'Never. Not that chinless Pirie-Moxham, nor Albertson nor

Donaldson. Anyway – Donaldson and Albertson will survive, they have other business interests . . .'

'Albertson is ill – did you know? He had a heart attack the day before yesterday.'

Aidan turned to him.

'Yes. And there are people in this town who are after saying that it was you who drove him to it.'

'Arra, get away, they wouldn't be saying that if the bank-it-was that foreclosed on him. He still has his house – great mansion that it is – I've two shops in Mittagong, and the three new ones in Bowral – how's that to affect Albertson's monopolies? He should have kept up the payments . . .'

Thomas's voice, soft in the darkness, 'The shame, Aidan.'

'He took his chances like everyone else. That mine has ruined finer men than Albertson and Pirie-Moxham – it's the price one pays for becoming involved in such a venture. If the government had given tariff protection, to see the industry on its feet, then Mittagong might well have become New Sheffield, who knows? But we've no harbour – it costs as much to get the ore to Sydney by train as it does to get the same amount from England to Sydney. The ships are practically fighting for it, to carry it as ballast on the return trip for more wool. How can Mittagong compete in those conditions? No, Thomas, I've talked to Dai Williams, the mining engineer – the heart's gone out of him. He sees we'll have to close the mine in a few months' time, at the latest.'

They were quiet for a long moment, for they both knew that this move would be bad for the town, despite the growing emphasis on dairying and market gardens and beef cattle that the land to the east was providing. An agricultural economy would not grow as quickly as an industrial one, Aidan thought. But sure, he was a farmer, before he was a businessman, no matter what his bank manager and Andrew Tweedie tried to tell him.

Thomas broke into his thoughts. 'Speaking of shareholders in Southern Highlands Iron and Steel, Hedley Warwick rode to Shannonbrook Two, today, looking for you. I should have told you earlier, but with young Joe's croup and all, it went out of my head.'

'That's all right, I'll call to see him tomorrow. Can I spend the night with you, here?'

'I'd not be turning you out to ride the distance to Shannonbrook One at this hour – even if you are seemingly becoming a bit of a gombeen.'

'Arra, Tomás – and how could I be after doing that, with a brother such as yourself to watch over my soul for me?'

749

Thomas aimed a good-natured swat at his head.

Aidan met Hedley Warwick in the office of the *Argus* the following day, as he was placing an advertisement for a tenant for the shops he had recently had built in the growing village of Bowral.

'Ah, O'Brien – I saw you as I was passing the window . . .'

'I was going to call at your office later – I believe you wished to see me . . .'

'I do. Will you be long here? I have something to show you.'

Aidan finished placing the advertisement with the clerk, tied his horse to the rear of the phaeton, and rode beside Hedley Warwick, eastwards out of town, past Killaloe and Shannonbrook Two. Warwick explained as he drove.

'You've been very patient, O'Brien, in the matter of the money I owe you. It has finally come home to me, however, that I'm not going to be able to repay you as soon as I'd hoped.'

'I've not pressed you . . .'

'I know. Frankly, considering the suspicion with which you were treated by many of us when you first arrived here, I think you've behaved with forbearance, Aidan.'

It was the first time Warwick had used his first name, and Aidan was oddly pleased.

'But I have my own conscience to consider – and I have a plan that may please us both equally. I'm taking you to see some land – it's not my own, it belongs to my wife, but she thinks it's high time it was sold. She's quite happy with the house on the Bowral road, and she's never been pleased with my idea of someday giving up my Sydney businesses and turning farmer.

'Helena's father, John Stewart, built his house on this property in 1828 – fine style of place it was. He had the gardens landscaped, trees planted . . . it was one of the earliest mansions in the Southern Highlands, and the real show place of the parish. Then the bushfire of '43 swept through – everyone escaped, but the house was destroyed. My father-in-law never rebuilt, didn't have the heart for it – and even Helena is saddened by the place. I don't think I could convince her to live on the property again.'

Aidan knew the place. His heart was hammering with excitement. It was further out of town, away from his centres of interest and he did not often pass the sandstone walls and giant, rusted iron gates. But when he did, he admired the place. It reminded him, somehow, of Tineranna, the overgrown drive of old oak trees, perhaps. He knew the ruined house – one could see a black chimney or two from the road – lay at the centre of the original two thousand acre grant

750

that had been made to Helena Warwick's father. *Stewartville*, the property was called. In spring the blackened chimney rose from a fairy garden of pink and crimson and white blossoms, and in autumn the hillside was a landscape painter's dream of gold and russet and scarlet and flame. No crops grew on that vast expanse of farmland, some of the richest in the district. There were cattle, allowed to graze freely over paddocks where the fences were mere visual boundaries. The cattle stepped over them and wandered at will. There was a manager, and two roustabouts living in small cottages on the property, Warwick said, but they could do little but tend to the exterior boundaries of the fences, and muster the cattle for market each spring.

'Am I right in believing you and your wife wish to sell me part of the Stewartville estate?'

Warwick sighed. He had a thin, aesthetic face, and wore glasses on the high bridge of his nose. Yet something about the man reminded Aidan a little of Father Daniel McDonnagh, and a little of his own brother, Thomas. Hedley Warwick, despite being Pure Merino, did not cling to his money, or desire more than he had. His position in the colony, related as he was to at least three members of Parliament and a high-ranking magistrate, seemed sometimes almost to embarrass him. He had been one of the first men in the district to accept Aidan, and Aidan did not forget it. He loathed Warwick's wife, however, sharp-nosed, tight-mouthed, petty-minded. He could not forgive the woman her campaign against Berrima.

Warwick now said, 'We would like to sell you the entire Stewart-ville estate, Aidan.'

And there it was. Standing here, at the top of the rise, where once a circular drive had seen chaises, landaus, broughams and britskas discharge some of the most famous names in early Australian history, Aidan knew that he had found what he had been wanting without acknowledging it. He looked around at the gardens, the ornamental fruit trees just beginning to show their buds, the azaleas and rhododendrons beginning to show their flashes of colour from amongst the tangles of blackberry bushes, the ground, where once there had been lawn, a mat of native grasses starred here and there with a hardy daffodil or jonquil. The scent of these latter came to him, headily, became part of his excitement.

He had lost sight of the dream of his own big house when Maura had died. Always, he had seen her as mistress of it, standing at the head of the stairs and welcoming guests in her quiet, capable way.

751

With Maura gone, the dream faded. It took all these years and the offer of these prize acres to awaken that ambition once more.

For Liam and Clemency would be home, soon. In a year or two. He'd need a bigger house to entertain their friends, so. Parties, picnics in the acres of gardens, balls and musical evenings . . .

He became restless, and prowled about the charred stones of Stewartville with the patient Warwick, imagining Liam and Clemency and a crowd of young people moving in and out of the French doors that would lead out onto the broad verandahs, strolling amongst the lawns and gardens . . .

He turned his attention to the once-landscaped gardens. It would take a great deal of work, but he would have the house ready by the time the children arrived home. The trees were magnificent: pines, beeches, poplars and oaks. Here and there amongst their roots the hardier patches of imported English grasses showed up a brighter emerald in the shadows. Down there, in the tangles of shrubbery, Hedley Warwick had said, were paths, and two or three pools and fountains.

Why hadn't Aidan thought of it before? His children would come home as adults, and they would soon, very soon, marry and have children of their own. Why – he looked behind him, and superimposed over the black ruins was the immense stone mansion of his imagination – this place will hold all of us. I will have grandchildren. Liam will eventually run the businesses, and I will grow old here. And the thought made him feel, oddly enough, more alive and young and capable, than he had for months, years.

He had lost sight of what he was building for – not only to take care of his children, but to leave something worthwhile in the hands of those children, and for *their* children, and their children's children. He would build something that was all his own, his final project, the centre of his empire. Shannonbrook Three.

Mary, Ottilia and Thomas were secretly delighted to see the change in him. It seemed he could hardly wait for the papers of sale to be drawn up, and then he was to be found at the new property every day, with several of the men from Shannonbrooks One and Two who were interested in working on the new place. Young Maurie Templeton came, and Jim Chaffer and several other young men who were interested in seeing what The Old Man would do with this brand new toy.

Builders came, and under the direction of an architect from Sydney, plans for a two storey, gabled, modern house of mansion proportions, began to rise on the ashes of Stewartville.

The house drove all thoughts of bitterness from his mind. It was odd, but he no longer lay awake at nights and dreamt of the dreadful revenges he would wreak on Berrima. He could never make up his mind, despite the passing of the years, whether his predominant feelings towards her were ones of love or hate. He could not even accept the ambivalence of his emotions and realize that he both loved, and hated. His thoughts swung about, savagely, and he called on her in his love for her, his fear for her; and he hurled curses at the night that covered her, brought down imprecations upon her head, wherever she was hiding from him. When he made love to Matty, it was Berrima he possessed, and sometimes it was all he could do not to call out her name. He felt guilty for this, for Matty was his friend, and he used her, shamelessly.

But now, with his joy in Shannonbrook Three, he found his feelings for Berrima, too, mellowing. It had been five years since he had seen her, and he began to see what it must have taken for her to leave as she did. He missed her, wanted, he found, at odd times, to share things with her; wished with something fierce within him that she could see the walls of his house rising from the once neglected gardens that now had come alive once more.

On days when he could persuade her to escape from Grif and the demands of her family, his grief drove him to the arms of Matty, where he made love to her without love, without emotion, with little satisfaction.

Perhaps, he considered, riding home from Shannonbrook One in September, nearly eighteen months after the divorce scandal, perhaps I've grown out of the need for love. And a week later, he saw Berrima again.

The dreaded quarterly meeting of the board of Andrew Tweedie and Company usually met in Melbourne, but since Sydney now, in 1874, had equal the number of stores, and was the place of residence of more than half of the board of the Company, it was arranged that the quarterly meetings would alternate between the capital cities. This month it would be held in Sydney.

Aidan enjoyed the wrangling, knew of old the ambitious, the avaricious, liked to watch the sparring across the great mahogany table, and because he did not care, he often asked provocative questions of some directors, made statements that fell like rocks in still pools, and sometimes changed loyalties on a whim, and behaved, Andrew told him once, crossly, 'like everyone expects a damn' Irishman to behave, running with the fox and hunting with the hounds.'

753

'Shall I resign?' Aidan asked hopefully.

'No!' the Scotsman had growled, for Aidan's whims were more often than not intuitively correct, and Andrew, who preferred living in Melbourne, wanted to keep Aidan in as active a position within the Company as possible. For here in the Company Aidan had no ambitions, and here, as elsewhere, he could not be bought. Andrew was no fool; Aidan O'Brien was valuable to him.

For Andrew and his wife Marion, this time of the meeting was also an opportunity to socialize, and in their fondness for Aidan they shepherded him all over Sydney; to dinners, to exhibitions, the opera – and at last, on the afternoon before they were to leave to return home, to a garden party to honour one of the newly-acclaimed artists of the colony, who had been under the wing of Balbrook – 'Ye ken that young scapegrace Balbrook that was involved in the divorce scandal awhile back?' They were in the carriage driving along Old South Head Road. Aidan's mouth went dry, the palms of his hands were wet. 'Yes,' he managed to say.

'Quite a patron of the arts, was Balbrook – the lady concerned in the scandal had taken up photography and had a studio in the house we're going to . . .'

'We're going to Balbrook's house?'

'He's not there, now.' Marion's matter-of-fact voice, 'He gave *her* the house when he returned to England. His older brother was killed in a carriage accident, hadn't you heard? Mr Balbrook is now Lord Balbrook, and he's gone back to Warwickshire.'

'Leaving Mrs Ellis here in Sydney. With quite enough money to continue fostering the artistic side of Sydney life.'

Aidan looked a little askance at Andrew. He was sick with joy at the idea of seeing Berrima again, but couldn't help wondering about Andrew's attitude. 'What's the matter? Are you shocked that Marion and I would go to her house? Och, Aidan, lad, we're not snobs. Mrs Ellis is a fascinating woman – you'll like her, and she's quite well accepted in certain circles here in Sydney – not amongst the bourgoisie, perhaps – but any circle with any pretentions at enlightenment has forgiven her long ago.' Andrew's eyes twinkled. ''Tis reasonable enough to see, that while the mistress of a Baronet isn't the ideal acquaintance, the mistress of a Marquis – even his ex-mistress, if she's left a fortune – can still hold a little of her aura of respectability about her.'

Aidan was silent. He was wishing, suddenly, that he had not come. He was not ready for this, not now. 'I don't much care for the new school of painting,' Marion was lamenting. 'I look at Peter Ebley's work – he's the young man who's exhibition we're attending

754

– and I think I've forgotten to put my spectacles on. It's an unfinished style – like looking at a view through a foggy window.'

'Perhaps Mr Ebley needs glasses,' Andrew put in. The Tweedies discussed the merits of Peter Ebley's work until the carriage rolled up before the white-columned portico of a large house. A small orchestra was playing inside, and through the windows people could be seen moving about the large central hall.

Aidan thanked God that the Tweedie's knew nothing of his relationship with Mark and Berrima. As he entered the hall and handed his hat and cane to the manservant, he looked about with ambivalent suspense. But he knew no one here. There were several well-known names, a visiting Shakespearean actor, a Russian singer, whom Aidan had heard perform the evening before, several entrepreneurs, and great clutches of earnest young men who huddled in corners and discussed the 'depth', 'dormant power', and 'classical influences' of various writers and artists. The Tweedies seemed very much at home, greeted several people with 'My dear . . . !' and Aidan was struck by the fact that they had taken to Society with enthusiasm. Aidan flirted with Mademoiselle Babarovich, and tried to forget that Berrima might enter the room at any minute.

The afternoon passed, refreshments were served, then one of the entrepreneurs made a speech about the depth, dormant power, and pure classical lines of Peter Ebley's work. Afterwards, the guests milled about, some straying out onto the terrace and lawns with their view of the magnificence of Sydney Harbour. Aidan, too, wandered outside, raking the gardens with his eyes, but Berrima did not appear. He heard someone say that their hostess was called to the hospital, where one of her servants was ill (Nellie? Aidan found himself wondering) and by now he was almost glad that she was not present. He was debating what excuse to give the Tweedies that would enable him to leave the party and return to his hotel to pack, when his gaze was caught by a young man of about twenty-five, leaning against the balustrade, his arms folded. The man's hair was blonde and thick, the eyes blue and intent. He seemed to be watching Aidan. And, Aidan realized, now, had been watching him for some time. Aidan's puzzlement lasted only a few seconds, then he smiled. They were both smiling, moving towards each other. It was Berrima's younger brother, Richard Reynolds.

It was, Richard told him as they walked together in the garden, Nellie whom Berrima had taken to the hospital. She'd been helping move the photographic equipment, and had dropped one camera on her foot, breaking several bones. 'Poor Nellie,' Richard half-smiled. 'She's never approved of the photography – Ebley tells me she went off this morning in the carriage telling Berrima that she should see by this incident that "it's no 'obby for a lady".'

'Couldn't you have set her foot for her? You're qualified by now, aren't you, Richard?'

'Yes, but I was out at the time of the disaster.' He squinted back towards the house, looking very much like his father, Milton, 'I hung my little brass plate beneath my father's in Hobart Town for a year, but couldn't settle. I daresay I'll go back to it one day. But I've decided I rather like the vagabond life, you see.'

'You don't look like a vagabond.'

Richard touched the lapel of his well-tailored suit. 'No,' he laughed, 'but we were respectable vagabonds, remember.'

'No.' Aidan was gazing at him in interest, 'I know nothing of what you've been doing. I wrote to Berrima several times, but she never wrote back.'

Richard grew serious suddenly. 'Really? I'd thought . . . I presumed she'd invited you here today. And I was mightily pleased, I may add, to see you.'

'That's kind of you,' Aidan's smile was wry, 'but I arrived with my business partner and his wife. Berrima doesn't know I'm here.' And as Richard pursed his mouth, half-smiling, for a silent whistle of anticipation, he added, 'And I don't plan to stay. I didn't know, when we left, whose . . .'

'Mister O'Brien, forgive me, but if you cared enough to write to Berrima in that difficult time after the divorce, surely you care enough to wait to see her, now.'

'I doubt if she'd like to see me. If she'd have wished to, she'd have written, I'm thinking.'

Richard went to speak, then checked himself. They walked for a little distance, then the younger man stopped, faced Aidan with a frown. 'I'll have to beg your pardon for my presumption once more . . .'

Aidan was amused. 'Y' may as well stop apologizing, so. You always were presumptuous.'

Richard grinned. 'I was a spoilt young brat, was I not? In a way, we were all spoilt. I often wonder what Mother and Father back in South Hobart think of their eccentric progeny, now. But Mister O'Brien, I am in a position to discuss Berrima, and her welfare. You undoubtedly know only as much of her life these past few years as you've read in the newspaper after the divorce, or what you've gleaned from my parents. We've kept a great deal from them, too, I may tell you . . .' Richard swatted at the fronds of a willow they were passing, yanked a piece of trailing greenery down and toyed with it as they walked, 'The divorce wasn't the last we saw of Mark. It was one of the reasons Berrima decided to bring Nellie and travel with me – the photography was my hobby originally, you see.' He chewed his lip a little.

Aidan was trying to absorb what the boy was saying. 'Do you mean, that Mark was causing problems for Berrima?'

' "Problems", sir, is not the word. He's obsessed with her. Do you wonder why there are so many members of Sydney society here today? Berrima is accepted because no one in their right mind could have expected her to remain with Mark. Everybody knows – both here and in Melbourne. Even the police have been called to restrain him on four occasions, and you know what it takes for police to interfere in a domestic problem.' Richard was tearing leaves off the willow switch with almost savage intensity.

Aidan felt ill. 'You're after telling me that he . . . harmed her? Mark tried to harm her physically?'

'Not merely tried, Mister O'Brien. That, basically, although I don't wish her to know this, is why I gave up my practice. I've been with her two years now, since Balbrook left. She's tried to help Mark – and she's paid for it. Once he kept her in his house for three days and . . .' He stopped. 'You'll see the change in her.'

'She had only to write to me. She had only to come home.'

'I've wished that she would. She doesn't speak of you, but I'm no fool, I realize that there's something between you – no, don't protest! – I'm not about to pry, I have no right. But I'm glad you're here. Berrima's very happy at the moment. Mark's gone off, three weeks ago, and we haven't seen him. I hope I'm not being foolish in hoping that this is the last we'll hear of him.'

Aidan was silent, trying to cope with all this new information, this heavy battery of stimulus to emotions that had been dulled, now, for years. He said, and he could hear, unwillingly, the bitterness in his voice, 'She didn't come to me. Five years, and she never came to me.'

'I don't know why. I do know Mark hated you. Perhaps she was trying to protect you from Mark.'

Aidan gave a short laugh. 'No. She knows I can handle Mark.'

'Aidan,' the boy used his Christian name without realizing it, so intent was he on the words he was speaking, 'no one can "handle" Mark any longer.'

Aidan looked at him consideringly.

'Please,' Richard said, 'I have no right to be talking to you like this. Don't tell her I've spoken to you about it – I've told no one else. It's just that . . . Father often mentions you in his letters, and . . .

757

Aidan, please stay and see Berrima. Perhaps she'll be able to speak to you about it. I feel badly, discussing her affairs.'

'I can't stay. I'll not be forcing my presence on her . . .'

'You won't, I assure you . . .'

'I don't belong here, Richard.' He gazed at the young man kindly enough, but he was wishing, already, that he was away. The boy was as misguidedly romantic as all the Reynoldses, he could not see that Berrima cared nothing for him. Five years – and all this happening. She clung to her independence, in the face of any amount of horror, rather than claim his protection. She fought her way out of his grasp each time he reached for her.

The two men were now on the terrace once more. Aidan held out his hand to Richard, began his farewell. 'Aidan, for God's sake, will you trust her? I'm not speaking as her brother, now, but as a doctor. There's something very seriously wrong with Mark. It's not . . .' He stopped speaking a moment as a group of people passed and he was forced to return their greeting. When they had walked on he drew Aidan away a little from the crowds. 'It's not just the drinking, Aidan. I even approached Mark's family and asked if there was any hereditary insanity in their background. They were damn decent about it, said they'd tell me if there was – they too, want to find a reason for this – but there was nothing.'

'What?' Aidan studied the serious young face, 'Is it joking you are? Mark is . . .' he stopped.

'Mad? Say the word. Berrima and I have been forced to realize that it's the only reason for what's happened. His moods – wild with mirth one moment, black depression the next, or raging, violent. Yes, he's insane. If he hadn't left without trace, three weeks ago, I was going to have him committed. His family wished it, but Berrima held out against the idea for as long as possible – she still saw the old Mark within him. And I tell you, Aidan, she'd be the only person who could.' He paused, studied Aidan's face.

The Irishman felt an overwhelming sense of pity that he could not account for. He had hated Mark, there was no denying that. But the loss of that quick and clever mind, the winsome, amiable personality – to think that these had gone, and left only the shell of the man, was horrible to think on. And what if there were moments of lucidity, moments when Mark knew what had happened, what was happening?

'Do you understand?' Richard's voice cut in on his thoughts.

'Aye.' For he did. Berrima must love Mark, despite everything. Loved the memory of him, as he, Aidan, loved Anna's memory. 'It's a tragedy,' Aidan said. Then added grimly, 'But more for her than

758

him.'

Richard looked puzzled. 'Why do you say that?'

'To love someone in those circumstances – to see the implications, to suffer as much as she has already . . .' he was becoming angrier as he spoke, 'Sure, that's the tragedy. Mark doesn't know, much of the time – perhaps all the time. There's no escape for Berrima. Unless she chooses to escape.'

Richard gazed at him without speaking, and a sudden hum of voices from the drive made them turn. Berrima was stepping down from a carriage, was surrounded by people. Aidan caught only a glimpse of a figure in lavender silk, her hair invisible beneath a broad sun hat of straw, trimmed with lavender silk and velvet ribbon.

He caught one glimpse of her face, smiling as some man spoke to her, then she had turned to walk down the garden.

He had not realized that he had turned abruptly away, until he felt Richard's hand on his arm. 'Aidan, please. Let me tell her you're here.'

'No.' He smiled at the younger man suddenly. 'Sometimes a friendship can die as easily as a love affair, you know. You can reach the point where you do each other more harm than good. That's when it's best to leave.' His eyes sought Berrima, who now had her back to him, surrounded by people. He turned back to Richard, 'I doubt if there's anything worthwhile for your sister and myself to discuss.' He shook Richard's hand, went to find the Tweedies, asked them to excuse him, and left to call a cab.

72

'Strike a light! Floorboards!' Ben Halvorson came through the door of the new Shannonbrook Three shearers' quarters, and stopped dead in amazement. Behind him, his friend Snowy Butler ran into his back. 'Look, Snow, floorboards!'

'An' two stoves!' Snow, little more than a boy, possessing blonde hair of an almost white shade, bleached by the hot sun, went over to the large iron kitchen range and peered into the oven. He straightened, and turned to Aidan, standing just inside the door. 'You took pretty good care of your shearers before, Boss, but this is . . . it's . . . ' words seemed to fail him. He wandered over to the bunks, 'Proper bed ticks . . .' he was heard to murmur.

'Never seen nuthing like this before, Mister O'Brien.' Even the normally composed Ben seemed taken aback by the building. 'I gotta say this for you, you got the best reputation in the colony, I reckon, for coming up to scratch with wages . . . an' now this. Put me down for next season, hey?' he grinned. 'Once the blokes see this place they'll be bookin' in like it was a hotel.'

Snow was at the rear door, with his head stuck outside. He called back, 'Jeez, there's a dunny out here with a walkway to it. Crikeys!'

'Won't have to wet your feet when you go to splash your boots, mate.' Ben turned back to Aidan, 'Your boy – Liam, that's his name, isn't it? He back yet?'

'No,' Aidan said, 'I'd hoped he would be, but . . .' his voice trailed away. He had been thinking of Liam and Clemency all day, and with the arrival of the shearers was wishing Liam could be here to help him with the work at this important time.

'Still in Ireland, is he?' Ben swung his swag up on to a bunk, and began to unroll his blankets.

'Yes, he's at university.' And when the two men turned, 'He's a lawyer,' he said, and mingled with his pride in Liam was a slight regret, and a resentment that he had for some time been trying to dispel. It was creeping into the letters he wrote to his son, controlled reminders that the three Shannonbrook properties would be his, Liam's, when Aidan died. He told himself over and over that Liam's life was his own, but it worried him. What if Liam reversed the too-common occurrence of Irish sons leaving for newer lands, and never returning? What if Liam never returned?

The letters from Dublin finally arrived, within two days of each other, undoubtedly having travelled on the same ship.

Trinity College,
12th April, 1874.

My Dear Father,
   I am very sorry for the delay in writing to you, but I have been doing my very best to see at what time I could return to Australia.
   Unfortunately, I have commitments here, not only to the university itself, but to my students. It may be things will change, but I cannot see myself able to return to New South Wales within the next twelve months. Clemency understands the importance of my work, and will explain anything you don't understand.
   I look forward to seeing you next year, and miss you and the family, but there is little I can do at this stage.

760

Your obedient son,
Liam O'Brien.

The pompous little brat, Aidan thought, he wrote better letters when he was ten.

He brooded over the letter for two days, until Clemency's letter arrived, while he was at the mill, and he tore at the seal,

14 Rutland Square,
Dublin, Ireland.
10th April, 1874.

Dearest Papa,

It is very hard to explain, but I cannot come home to Australia at this stage. I miss you and Gran and Uncle Thomas – and I look forward to meeting my Aunt Ottilia and Cousins Corrie, Henry and Joe, very much.

But, Papa, sometimes greater things are at stake than mere personal feelings.

Liam understands, and believes I am doing the right thing. The Mitchells have been most kind. I am having a wonderful time, and am very happy. *Liam can explain things better than I can.*

Your loving daughter,
Clemency O'Brien.

'Arra, *fek*!'

Footsteps outside his office, and Thomas knocked and entered. 'Mrs Warwick is out there ordering timber, Aidan. It's fortunate she was talking at the time – what're y' like, roaring obscenities like that?'

'You were mad to have children, d' y' know that? Mad! They grow up to be perfect strangers, and horrible people, Thomas. I can honestly say that I wouldn't invite my ass of a son or my prig of a daughter to dinner – they'd bore me to death!'

He flung the letter from him.

Thomas picked it up with his usual calm, and read it. Aidan took Liam's letter from his pocket and handed that, too, to his brother.

Aidan watched his brother's face, and felt vindicated when even the mild Thomas scowled and looked up, one letter in each hand. 'Aye, 'tis a fierce cold tone Clemency's after using. Who are these Mitchells, again? Lawyers?'

'Anglo-Irish. Poets and musicians and a private income.'

'Mother of God, that's worse.'

There was a long pause. Thomas drifted to the window. Now even

Aidan could hear, above the whine of the saw, Helena Warwick's voice arguing with Fred Dent.

'Aidan?' Thomas said, without turning around, 'Your pardon was an unconditional one, was it not?'

'Aye. What makes you think of that?'

'You can return to Ireland, so.'

The two brothers stared at each other. Then Thomas said, gently, 'I think it's time, Aidan.'

Part 5
THE
HOMECOMING

Gone are the noble and stately halls,
Crumbled the pillars and tumbled the walls;
Weeds and nettles, bent and blown,
Grow where our pride was overthrown.
Gone: All is gone!

Translated from the Irish by EOIN NEESON

73

Why had he left it so long? he thought, so many times, during his first days in London. Why had he not come sooner?

The city filled him with delight; he spent far too much money, slept with two exceptionally beautiful women – introduced to him by one of Hedley Warwick's cousins, with whom he stayed for three days – visited the theatre and rode in Hyde Park, and felt mad and odd and not at all like himself and loved every minute of it.

He had a new wardrobe of clothes made by some of the finest tailors, including lightweight suits for the Australian summer. For the first time in his life he began to take a true delight in choosing his clothing, found he could care and even take pleasure in the different textures of wools and linens and silks.

He visited art dealers, and purchased paintings and bric-à-brac and a few excellent pieces of furniture, and sent it home in crates to Thomas, to be placed unopened by his incurious brother, within the spare room at Shannonbrook One.

If there was something frenetic about Aidan's spending, his desire to keep busy, to see and experience everything, he did not consciously acknowledge this. He was going to enjoy himself – for the first time in his life, he was going to enjoy himself!

And he decided, suddenly, at the beginning of his second week in London, that he would not go home immediately he had fetched the children – instead, he would take them on a tour of Europe. Yes, they would remain for a year, travelling the Continent. And he would buy things – they could help him choose – they would purchase things to have sent back to Shannonbrook Three, so that each of them would remember this year. Drapes and carpets and furniture – even a marble fireplace, begod! And when they reached home they could arrange things together, they would have the decorators in, and they would plan the house, like a real family once again!

He would lie awake at night, in his hotel above Hyde Park, and listen to the filtered sounds of the great city, and imagine his meeting with his children. They did not know he was coming – he was looking forward to surprising them, separately, seeing them against the backgrounds of the lives they had made for themselves.

And he would smile, for he realized he might have a difficult time convincing his children to leave Dublin and return with him. It was his own fault, he should not have let them remain away so long – but things had changed, things were different now. His position was secure, at last, he had more time for them. He would get to know them all over again, and they would be friends. Liam would help him run the properties, and Clemency, one day, would marry a New South Welshman. He would not object to her living in Sydney when she married, but, like Liam, she belonged in Australia. Close to home, close to him.

The Assistant Bursar of Trinity College crouched over the small coal fire. 'A clerk. Little better than a clerk,' he muttered to himself. He had not read Charles Dickens' works since they had first become popular thirty years before – but he was reminded, suddenly, of a scene in one of the novels now, as he thawed his chilblained thumb over the heat. He wore his mittens. Perhaps that was what made him feel so particularly Dickensian and depressed, but he suddenly saw his life as the central plot of a gloomy and Gothic tale. He glanced around at the tall ceiling and big narrow windows and the ancient oak panelling, and shivered at the suitability of the setting. It could not have a satisfactory ending.

To be Assistant Bursar at thirty had been remarkable. To be Assistant Bursar, still, at forty-eight, was a matter of perpetual reproach, from his wife, from his father-in-law, and mostly from himself. He totalled the success of his days in the perfection of petty tasks well done. On his tombstone, O'Fallon thought bitterly, noticing that the heat was sufficient to steam up his spectacles yet not to warm his hands, they will inscribe beneath his name, *Bernard O'Fallon, who lived between eighteen twenty-seven and such-and-such a date – a petty task well done.*

He moved to the window and stared out onto the Square. Deserted. Today Trinity played the Leinster Cricket Club at College Park, and it seemed as if there was not another human being in the University besides himself.

There was a knock at the door. O'Fallon turned towards it hostilely. He pulled his lips back from clenched teeth, lifted his shoulders, 'Go away,' he snarled beneath his breath, then dropped the pose abruptly. 'Come in,' he called in his normal voice, and moved towards his desk.

He would be officious, he decided. Really, today he was feeling very reckless. He sat down, not even bothering to pull off his mittens. He would be officious in mittens; it could be done.

The man who entered the room was not a wandering student. He was about O'Fallon's age, a powerfully built man of middle height, sharp-eyed, straight-backed, a man used to command. He was dressed in an expensive tailored suit and unfastened great-coat. A hat was held loosely in his hand, and his hair was dark, well-groomed, the skin swarthy, as if the man had some Mediterranean blood – but no, O'Fallon looked closely, his forehead was slightly paler. The man wore a hat, in a hot climate. India, perhaps, or the West Indies. The look of him bespoke an Englishman of the upper classes.

'Good day to you. I was told by a gentlemen down the hall that you could help me find my son. He's a tutor here.'

The voice was Irish, the accent not strong, but it was unmistakably that of a western county.

'I'm afraid you've come to the wrong office, sir. You'll find the Administration Office . . . '

'There was only the one bloke down there, and he hadn't heard of my son. He sent me up here, so.'

Bloke? 'Your son's name, sir?'

'Liam O'Brien – rather, William O' Brien.'

'Oh, dear.' Of course, it had to happen while O'Fallon was alone in the office, when Fitzwarren down in Administration was the only man there – and would he be the one to tell this man what had happened to his son? No, indeed.

'Would you sit down, Mr O'Brien?'

The man pulled up a chair. Even seated, he seemed to fill the room. O'Fallon toyed with his mittened hands, trying to think of some way of broaching the subject.

'Your son left the University staff two years ago, Mr O'Brien.'

'What?'

'Indeed. He . . . ' Leave it at that. 'He left.'

'I don't understand.'

'He's no longer here.'

The dark eyes narrowed. After a pause, the man leaned back in the chair. 'I hope that there was no . . . ill-feeling between my son and the College when he left?'

Oh. He could see why Fitzwarren had sent the man down here. Typical. O'Fallon tried to think of Liam O'Brien, stocky, and dark like the man before him. Angry. But it had been a small scandal, only. This was Trinity, after all. After the argument with the Dean, and the Chancellor, the young man had left without rancour. 'It was an amicable parting.'

But the father, a countryman originally. He had emigrated to Australia, he remembered, now. A man who had worked hard to have his son educated, who had now come half-way round the world to find him . . . He had fixed O'Fallon with his dark eyes, demanding more. 'Your son . . . ' carefully, now, 'your son was asked to resign from the Law School, Mr O'Brien, I must tell you. I do not remember the details of the case, I am only the Assistant Bursar, but I do remember that much.'

'What did he do?' It was not really a question. It was a half-growled threat, though whether directed at the son, or the College, O'Fallon did not know.

'There was . . . some disagreement with the Dean. Not a great matter. Teaching methods . . . something like that. Really, you should be speaking to the Dean about this . . . '

'The Dean . . . isn't here.'

'No. Well . . . '

'I don't particularly care why my son resigned, Mr . . . ?'

'O'Fallon. I'm sorry.' The two men shook hands. O'Fallon was becoming interested. Why didn't the father know that young O'Brien had resigned?

As Aidan settled back into his chair, he said, 'I've come from Australia to find my son, Mr O'Fallon, that's all. His academic career, or lack of it, is a matter of indifference to me. Would you be able to tell me the last address he left with you?'

'Of course.'

O'Fallon left the room and went down the hall to Administration. Looking up O'Brien's name, he found himself becoming intrigued. Why hadn't the boy written to his father? Why hadn't he given an address? He found it in the Register, but it was three years old, now. He copied the address onto a piece of paper.

'What are you doing?' Fitzwarren in the doorway.

'Helping Mr O'Brien with a query.' Even as O'Fallon stepped away, Fitzwarren had moved forward, shut the file and stood in front of it, protectively, almost aggressively.

'Tsk.' O'Fallon looked pityingly, reproachfully, at the administration clerk, glanced down at the address and up again, inferring as hard as he could, that this had been Fitzwarren's responsibility, and sauntered away.

'No,' Aidan gazed down at the paper, 'this is the address that I had. He left two years ago.'

'And you've heard nothing from him since?'

Aidan looked up. O'Fallon was a thin man, drained by the

768

hopelessness of his situation. But there was concern in his face, and genuine interest.

'Yes. Yes.' Aidan decided to tell the truth, it hardly mattered. 'I received a letter from him only four months ago. He used the University's address.'

O'Fallon mouthed an 'Oh', sat thinking hard. On the day that Trinity played Leinster, when only he and the pathetic Fitzwarren were left in the administration building, a real, a genuine Mystery walked through the doors. For he had no doubt that it was a Mystery. The young O'Brien had been a radical, and that would have been all very well, had he kept his political views outside his classes. And now he had disappeared and was writing lies to his father. A father of whom one would be wise to think twice before attempting to fool.

'Mr O'Brien,' this was none of O'Fallon's business, and yet . . . 'did you know that your son had Fenian sympathies?'

The shock on the man's face was genuine. 'A Fenian? *Liam?*'

'I am not telling you anything that was not general knowledge here at the time. Nor do I wish to distress you, but it was these political beliefs that were the cause of trouble with the Dean. Your son was a brilliant student, would have made a brilliant lecturer. But he was teaching History and Law from a rather one-eyed viewpoint. If he had been a rabid Loyalist, the result would have been the same. He was warned. Repeatedly. Everyone at the College could see the inevitable result. He was asked to leave.'

O'Brien had risen and moved to one of the tall narrow windows. O'Fallon felt awkward, wished to help, but did not know how he could. He had two sons himself. Quiet, dependable, uninteresting boys. But he placed himself in O'Brien's place, locked out of his child's confidence, searching for him . . .

Aidan was thinking, like bloody Seamus! It's the O'Donoghue in him. Seamus' altruism and his own, Aidan's, violence. He was mad for sending the boy to Ireland when he did.

And he knew, then, that Liam's assurances after 1867 had been lies. That year he had failed his studies, blaming it on the unsteady political climate, but it was a bad year for everyone, next year would be different . . . He had passed the following year, brilliantly, and had done very well since then.

Aidan felt ill. Liam had been living two lives, obviously. And managing remarkably well, until three years ago. Now he was lying through his teeth, in an effort to stay here, *and* be given financial help. So he was not working. Not, at least, at anything legal.

'We mustn't jump to conclusions.' It was as if O'Fallon had read his mind. Aidan turned to him. 'We could wait until tomorrow, and ask the members of the Law School if any of them have kept in contact with your son. Or . . . ' O'Fallon rubbed his nose.

'Or what?'

'I seem to remember an incident – your son was not alone in this escapade—' He hesitated. 'I don't wish to make a suggestion that might offend you.'

'Make it. I want my son.'

'He was arrested, Mr O'Brien. Oh, two years before he resigned. At some kind of political meeting. He was released immediately, but there may be some other names there, men more likely than university staff to have seen him since he left Trinity.' O'Fallon stood, moved out from behind his desk. O'Brien remained by the window, pale, somewhat shaken, O'Fallon thought. Why should his son's brief brush with the police upset him?

'Mr O'Brien?'

'I'm sorry. Yes?'

'Are you familiar with Dublin?'

'No. No, I come from Clare.'

'Then may I presume to suggest that I accompany you? I assume time is of the essence.'

'That's very kind of you, but I don't wish to impose . . . '

'No imposition. The Chancellor will understand.' He was feeling mad, quite mad. He took down his coat and hat and scarf, 'I'll just have a word with my associate.'

He found Fitzwarren addressing envelopes, and stood at the man's desk, looking down at him. 'The gentleman is a diplomat from Australia. Did he not tell you he was involved in Colonial Affairs?'

'No . . . ' Fitzwarren's two chins shook.

'It is unfortunate,' O'Fallon was pulling on his coat, 'that this had to happen when the Chancellor is unavailable. But it is a matter of urgency.' He placed his hat on his head, 'I have undertaken to assist Mr O'Brien. It is an international matter . . . ' He paused significantly.

'I thought his son . . . '

Wiith emphasis, 'His son, Fitzwarren, is connected with the Government. We are to make inquiries.' He wrapped his scarf about his throat, 'We must pull together, Fitzwarren, are you with me?'

'Certainly, O'Fallon.'

'Good lad. I shall be gone for the rest of the day.'

He walked away, thinking, my God, how will I explain, tomorrow? And wondered if this was to be the last time he stepped across the threshold.

Aidan liked O'Fallon. There was a humour that went oddly in harness with the man's gentleness of character. Aidan found himself telling O'Fallon the reasons behind his presence in Dublin. That he had been already, to the Mitchells' house in search of Clemency, and had been told by a servant that the entire Mitchell family had left for Paris two months ago. They would not be returning for another fortnight. In the meantime, Aidan had to find his son. And it was obviously not as easy as he had thought.

Yet it took only three hours to find Liam, would have taken less, but there were long waits at each department while uniformed policemen looked up records and files.

Aidan and O'Fallon became quieter and quieter. By the time they entered the hired cab that was to take them to Kilmainham Prison, Aidan's expression was black indeed. O'Fallon pitied him enormously, and was glad that he had come. For the first time in his years of labour in the Bursar's office he felt he was doing something worthwhile – and it had nothing to do with accounts.

To Aidan, the sight of Kilmainham filled him with horror; the arched gateways, the heavy iron gates, the grey slabs of stone walls towering massively up from the paved entrance yard, brought such memories back to him that he found it almost difficult to breathe.

He was thankful for O'Fallon's presence. The man had steered him adroitly through the maze of Dublin streets and government departments, and now, as they alighted from the carriage, tactfully offered to retire to an inn along the road a little. Aidan could meet him there when his interview was over.

Along a corridor, whitewashed, with a curved ceiling that brought back memories unwanted, unpleasant. The smell of carbolic, the faint noises of metal doors closing somewhere within the structure. And a waiting room, the identical British Colonial Prisons waiting room. White walls and barred window, small fire-place, table and two chairs . . .

The door opened. Liam was led into the room.

He seemed older than his twenty-eight years, Aidan was shocked to see, whether because of the drab prison uniform, or all that had happened, his father did not know. He could only stare at the younger man.

The guard positioned himself inside the door. Liam and Aidan gazed at each other. It was Aidan who stepped forward and embraced his son. And Liam began laughing, without humour.

'You old bastard,' he said, and it was odd to hear the strange accent, not English, not Irish, not American, something in between. 'You old bastard, why did you come? For God's sake, Father, why?'

'Liam . . . ' Aidan stood back and gazed at him, 'why didn't you tell me? I've had the devil of a time trying to find you . . . '

'Father, I wasn't in gaol when I wrote to you. This is my fourth visit here – they've no more proof now than they did any of the other times . . . '

Aidan was conscious of the guard at the door, and kept his rage in check, the rage that wanted to release itself in questions and accusations. It was obvious to him, as it was to the police, that Liam had been acting as a go-between within the now-underground Fenian movement. That much had been obvious from his police records.

'You're here for six months this time . . . '

'I've served three . . . '

'For possessing material of a seditious nature . . . '

'A few pamphlets . . . '

'And if I hadn't come back to Ireland?' Aidan barked suddenly. 'What then, Liam? What would have happened then, when you were released from here . . . ?'

'Why, Father, I've done nothing wrong.'

The elaborate innocence, his back to the guard, the eyes telling Aidan much more than the words, but a slight emphasis on the word 'wrong' – used instead of 'illegal' . . .

Aidan took a deep breath. 'I'll get you a lawyer . . . '

Mildly, 'My friends hired me a lawyer . . . '

'Your Boston friends.'

'Yes.' The note of warning in the word. 'I have an international circle of friends, Father. It's just that the past few years have made American affiliations a trifle suspect in the eyes of Her Majesty's representatives here.'

'I'll hire you a lawyer, and I'll find someone in Dublin Castle who'll see to it that . . . '

'Leave it alone, Father!'

The guard spoke up, 'Keep your voice down, lad.'

Both men glanced at him, then turned back, two antagonists, to gaze at each other.

Liam walked about the room, ran his hand through his hair in a kind of helpless, angry gesture, then whirled on his father. 'Can't you understand, I must see this through alone . . . ?'

'You've made a fool of yourself for long enough . . . '

'You've no right to draw conclusions like that . . . '

772

'I've had an officious little police officer telling me all you've been up to for the past five years – I don't need a pencil and paper to work out you've been a fierce eejit, Liam.'

'I can take care of myself . . . '

'Liam – men have hanged in this prison . . . some of your brave heroes . . . '

'I know! There's no need to go into details! You don't understand! They knew the risks they took. They thought it was worth it! They could have left Ireland to find a better life for themselves – but they chose to stay and fight. For their people and their country . . . '

Aidan's mind reeled. He had a feeling he had played this scene before. Time stood still and he was back in Killaloe, being berated by Martin and Tom-Joe Curran, Seamus and Thady, for his lack of interest in the Young Irelanders' plans. It was as if Seamus stood before him now, Seamus with his beautiful and glorious dreams that had led to his death – and Aidan could not bear it.

'You never cared for Ireland!' Liam was saying, tightly, his freckled face pale with his rage, 'You fought, all right, for yourself, Father. You turned your back on Ireland, and you fought only for yourself!'

They were on either side of the table. Aidan leaned across it, spoke in a low voice, but measured each word, flung each word into the boy's face. 'I was *exiled* from Ireland. At a time when there was no hope, no hope in the world, of a successful rebellion. And as for my motives in life – you self-centred young pup – I've fought hard, I have, sure – for you, y' great thick trawneen, for you and Clemency – so you wouldn't know what hunger is. I have a responsibility as a father before I have a responsibility as an Irishman. And you – with your words of patriotic loyalty – the country that had you grow up strong and healthy as you are, the country that gave me the money to educate you, is Australia, boyo!'

'I'm Irish!'

'You're Australian!'

'I make my own choice, Father! I'm free to make my own . . . '

'Y're not free! Y're rotting in an Irish prison just as I did!' A tense, terrible silence. When Aidan spoke again his voice was lower; it shook with the restraint of his emotions. 'And I'll not have it. I'll not have it, Liam.'

'I don't want your help, don't you understand that? Go home, Father. Let me lead my own life.'

'Not here.' Quietly, 'Not like this.'

Liam straightened, took in a long breath, said equally softly, 'You don't give up, do you? You have to control everything. Sure, you're

773

undoubtedly glad to find me in gaol so that you can pit yourself against Dublin Castle single-handed . . . '

He did not, of course. He had O'Fallon to advise him on procedure. And he had money to help him.

He hired the most capable firm of lawyers in Dublin, and his petition to the Lord-Lieutenant was attended to fairly promptly. He had several meetings with important persons in Dublin Castle, and in the end an amicable agreement was reached.

Liam could not fight this. He would dearly love to defy his father, but the idea of a further three months in Kilmainham would be more than he could bear. He was taken before the magistrate once more, bound over to keep the peace, in his father's care, on condition that he left Ireland within the month. Even without his training in law, Liam could read behind the carefully chosen words. He was not expected to return.

On the day he was released, Aidan took Liam and O'Fallon to dinner at his hotel on Saint Stephens Green.

Liam did his best not to appear surly before O'Fallon, but his rancour towards his father was hard to disguise. When Aidan began to talk of both of them journeying to Killaloe the following day, Liam looked up, glared, and refused.

'I'll stay at the hotel. I'm not chasing off to Killaloe. There's nothing for me there – I have friends in the city . . . '

'Friends that the police will be watching, y' young eejit! For God's sake, Liam! Do you want to land back in Kilmainham?'

'I'm not going back to Killaloe! It might have pleasant memories for you, Father, but all I remember is a damp cottage and a diet of fish and eels. I'll not be leaving Dublin for that!'

'Liam, you'll do as y'r . . . !'

'If I might make a suggestion . . . ' tentatively from O'Fallon, 'I live in a modest residence off Temple Lane. If you, Mr O'Brien,' addressing Liam, 'would care to stay with myself and my family, you would be more than welcome. I must agree with your father, however, that it would be madness to attempt to see any of your former acquaintances. It's quite possible that you, too, will be watched, until you're safely on the ship to Sydney. I leave the decision to you.'

'Well?' Aidan demanded, after a pause, 'What will it be? Killaloe with me, or Dublin at Mister O'Fallon's invitation – *with*, I hasten to add, your word that you'll not make contact with anyone.'

'What am I supposed to do while you're in Killaloe?'

'We have quite a library of books at home. My family are all keen readers,' O'Fallon put in.

774

Liam hesitated, then, 'Thank you. Yes, I'd like to stay.' And he reached across the table and shook O'Fallon's hand.

74

The Limerick, Castleconnell and Killaloe Railway – amazing him though it did with its very existence – did not convince him to travel on it. This was not a journey he wished to hurry. Instead, he took the fly boat up the canal to Portumna, then travelled by steamer down Lough Derg.

Despite the cold, he stood at the starboard rail for much of this last stretch of the journey, gazing as they passed, at the Holy Island, Inis Cealtra, with its tall tower and many deserted, overgrown monastery ruins. Beyond were the wild, wind-raked slopes of Slieve Bernagh, low, rounded hills, brown with heather, grey clouds trailing their ragged hems along the crests.

'I've come home . . . ' he told himself with suppressed excitement, over and over. Twenty-eight years to the very month that he had left Killaloe, he now returned.

There! There was the cottage, and beyond, O'Sullivans' – Minogues', now. The turf smoke from the holes in the thatched roofs blew over the water to him. His heart contracted. He wondered who was living in his own cottage, now. So small, so tiny, it was! And so many of his memories surrounded it!

And soon, soon . . . there were the tall pines, black amongst the naked birch trees . . .

He almost missed it, so thickly had the trees encroached upon what was once a clear view from the big house to the water. A bare patch of ground, it seemed, surrounded by the tall, ancient trees – but as the steamer moved abreast of the clearing, first the blackened walls of the stables became visible, then the low pile of rubble, bramble-covered, that marked where Tineranna had stood.

He had willed himself not to care, and he did not. He thought only of Corrie, breaking into the house to wring some sort of truth from Devlin Kelly. Corrie dying, and for nothing. No, he thought fiercely. No, even should William Kelly reproach him for ever in the after-life, he would not regret putting that house to the torch.

His hands were gripping the icy railing tightly, were aching with the cold and the stiffness of his grasp. He looked down at his hands as he flexed them, and paused. Calloused hands, still, but from holding reins, nothing more arduous. A heavy, expensive, gold signet ring on his hand, white linen cuffs, sleeves of a jacket made from the finest tweed by his tailor in London.

And he realized, suddenly, that he possessed enough money to buy Tineranna, and not only that, but half the town of Killaloe as well. Why, he thought, I'm richer than William Kelly and Robert Osborne put together.

He glanced back towards what had once been the big house. In a grisly chain of events, Corrie's death had not been for nothing. Had Aidan given himself up as he had promised Father McDonnagh, the magistrate might have been more lenient, Aidan might have been sentenced to seven years in Ennis Gaol, for his alleged participation in the raid on Killaloe had been his first offence. But Corrie had died, and Aidan had gone mad, and in burning Tineranna had proved he was a Terryalt and a violent man both. And his path had led only to Van Diemen's Land or death.

For the remainder of the journey, until the steamer docked in Killaloe, he was lost in retrospection. Would he have been happy coming from gaol in Ennis to eke out a living on an acre of potatoes? He would have had more children, God knows how many and Thomas would not have met 'Tillia, and he, Aidan, would not have met Berrima. He would still be married to Maura, who had only ever wanted this life; Maura would have been happy, and Corrie would still be alive . . .

He looked up as the gangplank went out with a roar and a rattle – looked up to see the Aille Vaun and its houses that were as picturesque and tiny to him, now, as if they had been Clemency's toys. And to his left, above the grey-roofed gables and drifting smoke from the fires, the square, ragged-topped turret of St Flannan's.

He had returned. And he was what he was, there was no point in imagining what might have been. The Famine had taken almost everything. But to a few – there were very few – it had been the means of escape, the beginning of a new and eventually better life.

The greatest loss had been Ireland itself. He knew there would be no permanent return to the land that had been his father's, and his father's before him. It was only standing here, on the deck, amongst the press of the crowd trying to move on to the gangplank, amid the cries and tears of welcome from the dock, that he realized that he, Aidan O'Brien of Tineranna, was a stranger here.

No one knew him in the streets. He stared at faces, looking for someone, anyone, familiar. But the faces were mostly younger faces,

776

the people who had been children when he had left Killaloe, or had not even been born at the time. He found he wanted to search, to look for a friend somewhere, anywhere. But later – it was madness, now, when he was tired. He went straight to the Royal Inn, and booked into a room, standing at the window, when the inn-keeper had left him, and gazing down at the river and the bridge, and Ballina opposite on the Tipperary shore. It was a different town, it was not the same.

But no, he thought suddenly, it's not Killaloe that's changed. It's I. I've changed.

He retired early, after a meal at the inn, and slept, only to be haunted by dreams of his childhood, of Devlin and the O'Donoghues, the Currans and Minogues – and Anna. Confused dreams, where nothing remarkable happened; they were simply alive again, together, not happy, not unhappy, simply living, as they had done. The simple, day-to-day play that had been their life. He woke before dawn with the knowledge that they were all gone. And he stared up at the ceiling for a long time before sleep claimed him once more.

He visited Father McDonnagh the following morning. The priest was in his late seventies now, but his back was straight, his brown eyes clear. They walked in the Presbytery garden, then down the street to the Aille Vaun. It was Father McDonnagh who was able to tell him that so many of his friends were gone. Many of the Minogues and O'Byrnes had emigrated to America, and even the O'Hagans, with their two remaining children, Deirdre and Eileen, had left, in the early 1850s, to emigrate to Boston.

It sobered them, the town seemed so quiet; the air of bustling activity, when Killaloe had been at the centre of the River Shannon trade, was gone, with the coming of the railway, for ever.

To brighten the mood, Daniel McDonnagh said, 'Can you still skip stones? You were very clever at that when you were a boy.' They were along the canal bank by now, near the pier head. Aidan laughed, bent and picked up a pebble. He threw it between the hulls of two boats moored at the pier. The water was fairly turbulent here, but still the stone skipped, three, four times across the water.

'Well done!' They were laughing.

'Better than I'd thought!'

'You never forget!'

'No. No . . . '

The laughter died out of them slowly, pushed out by the thought that claimed them both. When he was not smiling the priest's face was lined with the knowledge of sufferings, the face looked older than the man. 'Are you bitter?' The wind whipped his fine grey hair about his face.

'Arra, Father, I've a right.'

'I didn't ask you if you had a right. I asked you if you were.'

Aidan turned to scowl over the swift-flowing river. 'When I think about it. Corrie, Anna. Mostly it's Corrie and Anna. But I try not to think about it. I've been busy, made myself so.'

'You've done well, then? You look like a wealthy man.'

'Och, yes. I'm rollin' in the stuff.' He grinned at the priest, and he looked like a boy again. 'I know what you're asking. You're wanting to know if I hate Devlin Kelly. You're worried that I'll drop dead of a heart attack back in the Antipodes, and I'll go to Hell . . . '

'Something like that,' Daniel smiled, 'I worry about the state of your soul.'

'Someone should. I don't often remember to.'

'Do you hate him?'

'No. It was pitiful he was, looking back on it. And something I've never forgotten – Thady said Mrs Curran noticed how awful he looked. When he came back after Anna's death. Mrs Curran said he must have loved her. He must have, don't you think? To do what he did?'

The gentle eyes smiled into his, 'I'm sure he did.' Then he seemed to hesitate a moment, his eyes flickered, he glanced away across the river, scowled at the Arra Mountains. Aidan had the impression he was about to say something.

'What are you thinking, Father?'

Daniel's eyes came back to his face, seemed to study him, then he smiled once more. 'I was thinking of the hold the past can have over us. For good or evil. Don't let the past hold you, Aidan. You have a new life, now, don't let the past rule you.'

It was fair enough, Aidan supposed, for the older man to lecture him. Obviously Daniel McDonnagh, too, felt that he, Aidan, might have a right to be bitter. But the old priest was right. It would serve no purpose to brood about it.

As they walked on along the path, Daniel asked, 'And have you seen Liam?'

Aidan looked at him sharply. 'Aye. I've had him released. You did know he was in Kilmainham?' – seeing the look on the priest's face.

'What? Arra, Aidan, get away! *Liam?*'

'He's spent most of the past three years going back and forth to Boston.'

'*Liam?*'

'Amusing, is it not? Sins of the fathers . . . and uncles . . . '

778

Daniel was shaking his head, 'Take him home, lad. Take him back to Australia . . . '

'Aye, I'll do that, sure. I've business here though. And I've another nine days before Clemency returns.'

The priest's head came up. For a long moment he looked at Aidan. 'From where?'

'She's in Paris with the Mitchells.'

Again a pause. 'Who told you that?'

'Their housekeeper.'

'You asked specifically for Clemency?'

'Well, no. She's always gone with them on other trips – you don't think . . . '

'Aidan . . . has Clemency written to you, lately?'

'Four months ago . . . '

'Saying?'

'That she was very happy and that Liam would explain . . . '

'I dare say Liam wouldn't know what was happening, either,' the priest murmured. 'Clemency is how old, now?'

'Twenty-seven. What're you getting at, Father?'

Daniel was scowling at the ground thoughtfully. He looked up to say, 'I want you to remember, Aidan. That it's a wonderful thing. I want you to consider this not from your own point of view, but from a broader angle. What is best for Clemency. God's plan for Clemency.'

'She's married?' His heart gave a sudden leap, 'She's married some Dubliner and didn't want to tell me because . . . '

'She's joined the Sisters at Saint Theresa's Convent, as a novice, Aidan.'

Aidan realized he had been staring the priest in the face for half a minute. He could not gather his wits. First Liam, now Clemency . . . both determined to shock the bejaysus out of him.

He did not direct the words towards the priest, spoke rather to the river, the distant view. 'How could it happen?' The anger was in his voice. He could feel the edge of it and turned away a little, knowing that he must be careful before Father McDonnagh, who would have his own opinion on this. But the man must have known! Must have known for a long time. He stopped trying, stopped pretending. 'How long have you known?' It was an accusation, not a question.

The abrupt change of mood did not disturb the priest. He continued to study Aidan with the same tired, patient brown eyes. 'From the time she entered the convent. A year ago.'

'No one tells me! Why didn't she tell me! Dammit! You should see the letters I've received, from her and Liam both – frightened, immature little cowards that they are, each trying to pass the responsibility on to the other . . . '

'Aidan . . . '

'Why didn't she tell me? And Liam – smiling to himself – he knew! But no one tells me. I'll kill him. I'll kill her. My only daughter decides to become a nun and she doesn't so much as write to tell me . . . !'

'You'd have tried to dissuade her . . . '

'Of course I would! She doesn't belong in a convent any more than I belong in a monastery . . . '

'You'd have made a good priest,' McDonnagh grinned.

'Get away!' He stopped, glaring at the priest with eyes narrowed. 'You're going to defend her, aren't you? You think this is the right decision.' The priest looked down, took a deep breath and let it out in a sigh. 'Don't you?' Aidan pressed.

'I think Clemency must make her own decision.'

'It's the wrong one! I know her! She needs her freedom, she belongs in Australia! She needs . . . '

'Does she, Aidan? Are you thinking of what she needs? Or do you need her? Both your children are grown up. They don't need you any more.'

'What would you know . . . ?' he stopped, turned away, speechless for a moment, 'Dammit!' he roared back at the priest. 'You've ruined my day, you know that? You've made me angry with you, and I'm quarrelling with you just as I did that last day, twenty-eight years ago, and I didn't come here to quarrel with you, Father.'

'I had to tell you, Aidan. Because I'd rather you became used to the idea now. I'd rather you tried to intimidate me, rather than the Mother Superior.'

'Oh, so I'm about to bully the good Sisters now, am I?'

'Aidan, please . . . '

'Why!' he burst out. 'Just tell me that!'

'She felt she had a vocation – it's the Teaching Order, remember. Clemency is excellent in the classroom with the younger children . . . '

'But she's been so happy with the Mitchells . . . '

'Really, now, Aidan.' Something like reproach on Daniel's face. 'What sort of a life is that for a girl?'

With growing horror, 'I believe them to be a respectable family . . . '

'Och, they are! But very . . . sophisticated, Aidan. All that leisure – nothing to fill their time but music and travelling and . . . theatre.' Aidan had consciously to refrain from smiling. 'An

780

empty life it was, I believe. Yet Clemency enjoyed it for several years. Then, a year ago, it was as if she saw how empty it was. It was a purposeless existence . . . '

'She should have come home to Mittagong. I'd have given her plenty to fill her time.'

'It was something more than keeping busy.' Solemnly, 'God called her, Aidan. Those were her own words.'

'He wouldn't have told her to join a convent. He'd have told her to go home. She should clean her ears more thoroughly.'

'I'll have none of your blasphemy, Aidan! For Clemency's sake, accept it! Be happy for her sake!'

'No. Not until I hear it from her own lips. I don't believe she'll tell me.'

'She will.'

'I don't believe it.'

His day was ruined, as he said. He felt petulantly deprived of what had promised to be a pleasant visit with a dear friend. He had been confronting himself, feeling happier, he realized, as his time in Killaloe went on, to find how strong he'd become. There was nothing, he had thought, foolishly, that could happen to him that he could not face. But this!

'At least you won't have to wait ten days, now.' Daniel smiled. 'She's been in Dublin all along. You've only to go to the Convent.'

'Yes, I'll do that . . . ' But he raised his eyes to Craglea, thought of Finlea, and the main reason for his return to Killaloe, and murmured, 'I'll do that, sure. But there's something that must be done, first.'

It was a strange procession that rode through that misty afternoon along the road from Killaloe to Finlea.

Aidan rode the tall chestnut that he had hired from the stables in the village, and was followed by the glossy black hearse, the pride of the local undertaker.

At a previously assigned corner, Aidan met Roddy Minogue and his brother Gerry. They carried a shovel each, and much to the consternation of the undertaker, proceeded to climb up beside him on the hearse.

The ruined cottages lay just as Aidan remembered them, no one had rebuilt them, only black-faced sheep watched silently from a distance as Aidan dismounted and opened a creaking gate and the hearse drove into the field.

Brambles grew over the stones, and ivy clung close to each piece of fallen masonry, cementing it into its new order of place. But they managed to dislodge them. It took until well into the afternoon before Roddy cried, 'I've found him . . . '

It was Aidan who, carefully, raised the pathetic bleached bones and placed them in the coffin. All four men returned to Killaloe.

When Aidan left the village two days later, after spending most of that time with Father McDonnagh, the coffin had been buried in the Protestant churchyard of St Flannan's. Upon it rested a marble monument, simple in design, which bore the words:

> *Sacred to the Memory of*
> *NATHAN CAMERON*
> *Departed this Life*
> *December 15th 1846.*
> *An Honest Man and*
> *A Friend to the People of Tineranna.*

75

'But I'm certain Clemency wrote to you, Mr O'Brien. Even when an aspiring novice has already reached the age of twenty-one, we feel it most important that parents are notified – usually they are pleased to give their approval.'

The man seated opposite the Reverend Mother made no answer. His skin, a healthy tan, had paled slightly, and the look in his eyes – eyes that had been until just now direct, commanding – had the look of a creature hurt. She could tell, until that moment, that he had hoped there had, somehow, been some mistake.

The Reverend Mother's mouth compressed. It was obvious that the father had not ben told, it was not what she had expected of Clemency.

She surveyed the man for a moment from across her desk. He had been shaken, that was clear, but even now the beginnings of anger were becoming obvious in the set of his mouth and his narrowed eyes. He would be too well-mannered to make a scene, she knew; dealing for half a century with parents of pupils and novices alike, gave her the experience to judge this, but she needed to be careful all the same. He was a man of strong emotions, accustomed to his own way. He filled her bare little office with his presence. It was disturbing.

'Mr O'Brien,' she said smoothly, 'I want you to know that we love Clemency. Whether she became a nun or returned to Australia, or remained as companion to Mrs Mitchell, would, knowing she was happy, have delighted us. We're happier, of course, that she has chosen to join us, but the decision was hers, Mr O'Brien. We brought no pressure upon her at all.'

'I'm sure you didn't . . .'

'When she first went to live with the Mitchells we saw very little of her. They are great patrons of the arts here in Dublin, they entertain a good deal. Some of the people, foreigners, many of them, were not what I personally would want any daughter of mine to associate with – but the minds and the talent of the guests were of international renown. It was a marvellous time for her, I'm sure, and she received a great deal of encouragement with her own particular gift. The great Parnotti and Madame Mazzaran came to Dublin in 1870, and they gave a charity concert to aid the hospital. Clemency sang on the same programme. It was said that she could make a career upon the operatic stage, Mr O'Brien.' She paused again – surprise was upon his face. Reverend Mother realized that there was a great deal he did not know. She continued, 'That, of course, is out of the question, though Mrs Mitchell insists that the operatic stage is now a respectable profession. But Clemency gave several charity concerts under Mr Mitchell's guidance.'

'Who is Mitchell? What's he like?' He did not mean the questions to come out quite that way, abrupt, almost rude. And as he was afraid, they gave his thoughts away.

After a pause, the Mother Superior said quietly, 'Nicholas Mitchell, Mr O'Brien, possesses a reputation above reproach.'

'I didn't mean to suggest . . .'

'I know you did not, you have too much respect for your own daughter, I am sure, than to suspect there was anything more than respect and a love of the arts between herself and Mr Mitchell. There was no young man in Clemency's life. I questioned her closely about this, and I spoke to Mrs Mitchell. Clemency met many young men – some of them charming – but she treated even those most fond of her like a girl would treat her brothers.

'Mrs Mitchell has never really agreed with Clemency's decision to join our Order, but even she was not surprised. About two years ago Clemency began to come to morning mass occasionally here at the Convent. Soon she was coming every day. She grew closer to us, made friends once more among those pupils she had known who were now novices. She came back to Saint Theresa's as a novice herself about a year ago.'

There was a silence. Aidan nodded, was gazing at the desk before him, listening to the ticking of the clock upon the wall. He could not believe this story. There was something wrong. He could not imagine his daughter as the darling of the intellectual set any more than as the devout young girl drawn to the peace of the Convent. But the Mother Superior was not lying. Clemency had been, or was, both of these. Did he know her at all? Did he choose to remember her as she was, and refuse to concede her the potential to grow, to change?

He stood, a little too violently without meaning it, not noticing how the harsh screech of the chair legs made the Reverend Mother wince. He was at the window overlooking the garden. There was a bench outside, beneath a beech tree. A robin was perched on the back of the iron seat, hopping up and down the length of it, as if to keep himself warm. Aidan had a picture in his mind, suddenly, of Clemency, sunburnt, grass-seeds in her hair, running into the house from along the beach at Settlement Point, bringing the smell of the sea with her. The letters from home to him that spoke of Australia, of yellow pastures and blue skies . . . Could this Clemency choose to spend her life in grey corridors under grey Dublin sky and fog and . . .

'I realize how worried you are,' Reverend Mother was saying gently. 'I remember her when she came here, a turbulent little spirit she was, and a great deal of trouble she caused us. But first she learned the meaning of discipline, and then self-discipline, and all her more selfish yearnings to return to Australia, to have fine dresses, to be applauded for her singing – they passed away. She is happy now.'

'She was happy in Australia.' Clemency happy in this damp old building? And her selfish yearnings passed away?

'Let me say, rather, that she is content, Mr O'Brien. She is at peace.'

You talk as if she's dead, he thought. He was furious. 'I would like to speak to her, Reverend Mother.'

'Of course.'

Corridors of the same grey stone. The grey stone of Ireland; in twenty-eight years of the browns and reds of Australia he had forgotten the monochromatic coldness of the buildings. It should not have bothered him. On first arriving in Dublin, at Trinity, in Kilmainham, it had not bothered him to this extent. For he saw it as temporary. But these grey stones were claiming his daughter, and they were an enemy to him. As he followed the dark veiled figure of the Mother Superior, he felt panicked, helpless, he was losing. And there had not been a battle – could not be a battle, for this was Clemency's life, and he had loved her independence, could, in a way, blame himself for this. He hated the feeling, but there was nothing he could do. Decisions that affected him – she was *his* child, *his* – had been made years ago without consulting him. He had no part to play but that of letting her go, with good grace.

Another sparsely-furnished room overlooking another small square of lawn. No beech trees here, not even a shrub to break the severe lines of grey walls and rectangular mat of frost-bleached grass. He walked across the narrow space to the window, and gripped the ledge. *I can't bear it. Can't bear it.*

'Please wait here and I shall find her.' She left the room, her last sight of him standing at the window, handsome, powerful, and distressed. 'Oh, dear!' she muttered.

Aidan prowled up and down the room. A table, two chairs, a crucifix on the wall. The room was as bare as the view from the window. Dear God. What would he say to her? How to make her leave with him, come home? Mustn't shout, mustn't bellow, not at all. Calmness and control, sure, and loving interest.

He turned at the sound of the latch, and she was standing there. He said nothing at all. Could not speak.

She shut the door behind her, and came into the room. A stranger to him. Hair covered beneath a white veil, hands held in the broad sleeves of the grey gown. The face was the only visible part of her, a woman's face, the faintest lines on the forehead and about the eyes. A woman's face. Yet there were his own broad cheekbones and forehead, Maura's green eyes below the heavy russet brows. Freckles across the straight O'Donoghue nose, his mother's firm mouth and chin. But a woman's face. He had neglected to remind himself of this. Why had he expected an ignorant, innocent child, who had been somehow pressured into this?

'Good morning, Papa. God be with you.' Oh, the coldness, the distance! Twelve thousand miles stretched within those three yards between them. Twelve thousand miles and eleven years of bitterness. She had told him then she would never forgive him, and she had not.

'Hello, Clemency.' He was floundering in the coldness of her welcome, his own imagined picture of their reunion had gone from him, the words he had planned, gone from him. He could no more imagine himself crossing that space to hug her than he could have hugged the Mother Superior.

'I wanted . . . I was going to bring you home.'

Her eyes widened a fraction. 'All this way, Papa? There was no need.'

'Sure, I thought there was.' He felt the impatience creeping into his voice and checked it. 'There was no sense to be had from your letters.'

'But Liam. Liam said he'd explain . . . '

'Then I fear his courage deserted him at the last minute. His letter gave it that *you'd* explain.'

A silence. She had been gazing at him, but now lowered her eyes to the floor. 'I'm sorry, Papa. I haven't seen Liam for nearly six months.'

'I'm sure.' He was walking over to the window. 'You could hardly visit him in Kilmainham.'

'They caught . . . !' The words had burst from her. Aidan turned, but she was as before, gazing at the floor, as if the words hadn't come from her at all. He studied her for a long moment.

'Liam's coming home with me. I've arranged his release. I'd like to arrange yours.'

Her eyes met his. 'I'm not in prison, Papa.'

'No,' carefully, 'but you don't belong here, Clemency.'

'I do, Papa.'

'You don't.'

His facade was dropping fast. She could sense the dark rage in him from where she stood. She hated herself for being afraid, would she never feel she could conquer her awe of him? He did not belong here, was as out of place as a black bear in a neat parlour. She almost smiled. Patience. The bear would become bored and go away. One would not be wise to force it, take to it with a poker.

Her calmness, her little smile infuriated him. Once again he felt he was losing ground, and felt helpless in the face of decided events. His daughter was years from taking her final vows, but there she was, her mind committed to doing so. Out of his reach, beyond his control.

'Why did you decide on this?' he asked, and his voice was calm once more.

'I feel it's what God wants me to do.'

'What of you? What do *you* want to do?'

'I want what God wants.'

'But God's intentions are often open to interpretation,' he said, mildly. 'How can you be sure he's made Himself perfectly clear?'

And she laughed. She laughed a little, and it was his Clemency, his Rebel, and almost, he was about to cross to her, hold her . . .

'You don't understand, Papa. Just believe me. I must make my own decisions.'

His mind ran round about, looking for the right key, the way to find her again. She had laughed, then locked him out with her words.

'Clemency, I feel, as your father, that I must ask you this. Did you fall in love with Nicholas Mitchell?'

She had not expected this. She paled, but answered almost immediately, 'No, Papa. And you shouldn't even suggest it. He's a devout Christian, and devoted to his family.'

'I wasn't asking for a character reference, Clemency. I want to know . . . '

'I know what you wanted to know. I admired him a great deal, more than any other man I've ever known. I admire his intellect and his kindness and his talent as a musician.'

'How old is he?'

'What has that to do with it?' Her eyes were beginning to lose some of their tranquillity. Aidan correspondingly lowered his own voice, made his tone conversational, 'How old is he, Clemency?'

'Forty-two.'

'And his wife, how old is she?'

She hesitated. 'A little older. Seven or eight years older. But that has nothing to do with it. They love each other very much, they adore their children . . . '

'Four little girls, I think you said . . . '

'Yes.'

'And is she gifted, too, Mrs Mitchell?'

'She's a poet, and playwright. Her works have been performed in Belfast and London, as well as Dublin . . . '

'A very busy lady, no doubt. Reverend Mother tells me they entertained a great deal.'

'Yes . . . '

His voice was quiet, interested, he walked about the room a little, sometimes looked out the window. 'Mr Mitchell's interest was predominantly music, and his wife's, literature. Did you meet many young poets in their house?'

'Why, yes. James Carroll, and Bosco Lionard, and Charles St John Martin, and . . . '

'No young ladies?' A little surprise here, amusement.

'Well . . . No, not many, they were mostly young men. Mrs Mitchell didn't have many close female friends, she's a woman of very strong opinions about literature. She said women writers . . . '

''Twas an unfair prejudice, in her case, don't you think? The musical interests of the family were not so discriminated, I hope.'

'Mrs Mitchell is not like that, Papa. She has a particular personality that appeals to young men . . . ' She was floundering, beginning to blush. 'She has shown the greatest kindness to *me*, I'm her particular friend. But the young poets feel she is a type of . . . of . . . '

'Mother figure.'

'Yes. No!'

'Goddess?'

'No. Well . . . '

'At soirées they sit at her feet, gather about the chaise longue . . . And the little girls – do they see much of their mother?'

'Well, she's very busy, always writing. She needs peace in order to write . . . '

'So you would spend much of your time with the children.'

'Yes. The girls are very musical. We would spend a great deal of our time about the piano . . . '

'Clemency, your piano playing has always been execrable.'

A pause. Icily, 'It has improved, Papa.'

'With Mr Mitchell's help.'

'Yes.'

'And Mrs Mitchell did not mind. Indeed, encouraged you.'

'Yes.'

He strolled to the window, and looked out on to the blank walls and blank turf. Then he turned to face her, and said gently, 'Did Mitchell love you, Clemency?'

Her gaze came up to his, full of horror, 'No, Papa!'

'I wouldn't blame him if he did, with the life he led, with a more sophisticated wife who had long since become bored with him. Och, Clemency – I've spoken to Liam about it. He sensed that it was so. Though to be fair to Mitchell, I daresay you began as just another of his daughters.'

'Yes, he felt about me like that. Just like that.'

'But Mrs Mitchell gave you more and more responsibility, until you became a sort of surrogate wife.'

'No, Papa!' Her face had a touch of pink in her cheeks.

'But you must have understood him better than his wife did. You shared in his interests more than his wife did. And you loved his children, more than his wife did. And no doubt he told you these things.'

'Stop, Papa.' The pink in her cheeks deepened.

'Look at me. He did, didn't he?' His tone was still conversational, gentle. 'Don't lie to me, Clemency. I'm not angry with Mitchell. I can understand the man.'

'It didn't have any bearing on my coming here, Papa.'

'He was lonely, of course. And he turned to you quite innocently.'

788

'This was my own decision.' Her voice was trembling.

'You respected him a great deal, and it upset you to see his misery . . . '

'I'd been considering the Convent for some time . . . '

'And one day, without either of you knowing why, or how it happened, he put his arms around you, and he kissed you.'

The silence was deafening. When he looked at her, the calm hands were not hidden within the sleeves, but were clenched into fists at her sides. She was Maura, pure Maura.

'You are *vile*! You sully *everything*. He never touched me, you horrible crude man, he never touched me! It's so like you, just like you, who have no morals and no integrity, to accuse Nicholas Mitchell of such behaviour! How dare you!'

'I know more of life, more about men than you do, Clemency . . . '

'You know what *you're* like. You think that Nicholas has the same lack of respect for his wife that you showed towards Ma!'

'You know nothing about that . . . '

'I know you had other women! That's why Ma took us away from Port Davey – I heard her talking to you, before we left – she couldn't bear to stay with you!'

'Clemency, you're wrong . . . '

'You're a hypocrite, Papa! And I won't have you speaking of Nicholas in that way! You're not even to talk of him! He's worth ten of you!'

He was delighted. It was the child he remembered. He almost laughed, wanted to step forward, to hold her.

'You keep away from me! I hate you! I can't bear you to touch me! You killed Ma! You broke her heart, y' bastard! And I hate you! I hate what you did to her! To all of us! I've never forgiven you, and I never will!'

They remained where they were, only half-conscious of the door opening and closing again. Slowly, they became aware of Reverend Mother standing there. Each of the three were embarrassed, though none of them showed it. The control of years claimed each of them, and even Clemency, most appalled, composed herself in the silence that went on for a full minute. She knew with a dreadful certainty that the Reverend Mother had heard almost everything. Why, she, Clemency, had even sworn, or had she? Did she? She began to flush once more, ran all her words over again through her head, what had she said, what? And waited all the time for the Reverend Mother to speak.

Aidan's embarrassment was temporary. He was not sorry in the least, was abashed only that the Reverend Mother had so obviously seen through him. By the time he was out the front gate, perhaps out of this room, he would be over his embarrassment, and it would not bother him again. The Reverend Mother met his gaze. He tried to look apologetic. He did look respectful – but his eyes were glowing with a kind of triumph that he could not disguise.

The Reverend Mother knew that he was pleased, was congratulating himself, was telling himself that he had won. *The child was not a prize*, she wanted to tell him. *It was not a contest. We were not competing for your daughter*. But he would not believe that. This was a man who saw all of life in terms of winning or losing. A man accustomed to winning.

She turned to look at Clemency, and her expression softened a little. The girl, too, was ashamed, but though the humiliation of this moment would plague the girl for months, perhaps years, she would forget, eventually.

Reverend Mother would not forget. Her shame would always be with her. For she had been wrong. She had chosen to see Clemency's gentle smiles and quiet manner as contentment when in fact it was a mask of iron self-control, covering a deep unhappiness and a spirit as turbulent as it had ever been. She, the Mother Superior, had been wrong, she had wanted to believe Clemency had found the peace of the Lord at last. But you won't, her mind told the girl standing flushed and wretched before her, not until you have lived a long and eventful life and loved a man and borne children, and have known great happiness and great sorrow. Perhaps, at the end, you will have what I wished you to have. But I should have looked deeper, seen further. I should have known this before.

'I shall wait outside,' the father said. He had some sensitivity, at least.

And when the door shut behind him, Clemency was in Reverend Mother's arms. 'You'll make me go back with him, won't you?'

'Yes, my dear. The Lord will be with you, have no fear of that.'

'But I hate my father, Reverend Mother. I know it's a sin and I'll go to Confession directly, but I know it, all the feeling came back as soon as I saw him. I hate him!'

'Yes, my dear.' The older woman held her, one hand against the head upon her breast, 'But you also love him. You love him very much.'

76

'Sure I don't care if I never see the inside of a church again,' Liam said, then caught Clemency's reproachful glance, and added, 'except for Mass on Sundays. Honestly, Clemency, after twelve months I can't tell my Byzantine from my Baroque. They're all beginning to look alike.'

They came out of the chill of Saint Theodora's Cathedral to stand in the warm spring sunshine that flooded the square. Men in dark, drab clothing, swarthy-skinned, went back and forth about their business and eyed the three on the steps, particularly Clemency, with the cropped curls upswept beneath a small cream-coloured hat with its trailings of netting, and the tailored elegance of her cream-coloured dress with the ruffles of lace at the neck and cuffs.

'Let's go back to the hotel for lunch,' Liam suggested.

'It's not eleven yet.' Aidan glanced at his watch.

'We'll have an early lunch.'

Aidan sighed, took Clemency's arm and followed his son down the broad steps and across the square. They walked slowly up the street, but stopped at a shop in the harbour square. Aidan went inside while Clemency and Liam glanced at each other tellingly; they could hear him haggling over the price of a small bronze statue that he had admired in the window. The brother and sister strolled over beneath the trees that shaded the centre of the square, and Clemency sat down on a bench. They did not speak for several minutes, but gazed about them at the now familiar Corfu scene, and Liam sighed.

It would not be true to say that they were bored, rather they were restless, displaced. They had been uprooted abruptly from Dublin, yet they were not allowed to settle anywhere else. A year travelling about Europe had, for Liam and Clemency, been quite enough. They had other, more pressing problems to consider than whether they should stay for five days or eight on Corfu. They were worried at the changes to their lives that the return to Australia would bring.

Yet they did not speak of this. When Liam had been fetched from O'Fallon's house to the hotel where Aidan had arrived with Clemency, brother and sister had gazed at each other with understanding, for there had been no need for words, and they had no words to speak with; the thought, 'What will I do! What will I become?' was more terrifying when voiced aloud. Both knew the other would have no idea. They were each alone; alone with the ambitions of the man within the shop who was arguing, fighting, enjoying himself, on the trail of yet another object that he wished to possess. The only dependable thing in Liam and Clemency's life at that moment was the will of that man in the shop – and that will was no help, was something to be fought against, not to be relied upon.

'Are you sorry, Clem?'

She looked up, startled. It was the first time Liam had mentioned their past, or anything about their situation at all.

'I . . . I don't know. Are you?'

'I suppose it couldn't last.' Liam squinted out at the busy square, idly clutched at a falling Judas tree petal that floated down upon him with the slight breeze. 'All revolutionaries seem to run out of steam as they get older. Look what happened with Stephens and Colonel Kelly. They left the Rebellion too late – though maybe – arra, it's hard to say, now. Perhaps it would have been the same in '66 as '67. Perhaps Ireland wasn't ready. Perhaps it won't be, for a long time.' His voice had slowed, softened, then, more brightly, 'Yes, it's the truth, that revolution is a young man's game. I was useful, but I have to begin to think of the future, I suppose.'

An awkward silence ensued. They were on territory that was insecure, unknown to each of them.

Perhaps to change the subject, Clemency said, 'I wonder that Papa hasn't remarried.' It was Liam's turn to look surprised, 'If he had,' she continued, scowling, 'he wouldn't have come to fetch us home. I mean, what has he been doing all these years? He's good-looking and rich.'

'It's married to his work he is.'

'Yes. Perhaps that's it. And what about you?'

'I? What about me?' Liam looked a little suspicious, as if he already knew what the next question would be.

'Why haven't you married? How old are you, now, Liam?'

'Twenty-nine next month. I've been too busy, too.'

'Have you been in love?'

'I . . . no.'

'When we were in Rome and Paris you used to go out every night until very late. A few times you didn't come back till morning. I heard Papa taking you to task over it. Were you with women?'

He was scarlet, tried to glare at her, but was still too shocked. 'Jaysus, Clemency. Did they teach you about these things in the

792

Convent?'

She sat there, demurely, her hands on her reticule purse in her lap. 'A lady should still be aware of the facts of life,' she smiled.

'But she shouldn't talk about them, let alone ask impertinent questions in the middle of a public square.'

She laughed, 'Arra, you're as guilty as sin. You're very like Papa, you know that?'

'I'm not at all!'

'You are, and that's the truth. Handsome, heart-breaking divils of men. An I'm glad I'm the daughter and sister to you and know you so well. I'm immune to you at least, though I shall warn all my friends about you when we get to Mittagong.'

'And will you, to be sure.' He gazed at her with malicious humour. 'What about you? I bet Father has some bovine young farmer picked out for you to marry.'

'Get away . . . '

'Och. Clem, you're – what? Twenty-eight in August, are you not? You'll have to marry soon or your best breeding days will be over . . . '

'Don't be disgusting!' Suddenly she was really cross.

'You're the one who talks about facts of life. Father will want a liaison with one of the Pure Merino families, I'm sure,' Liam grinned. 'Some young bull in patent leather boots, or else some bespectacled, limp-haired, limp-wristed creature with a six-figure bank balance from Sydney . . . '

'Over my dead body. I've done with all . . . ' She stopped, was frowning out over the busy street.

Liam was intrigued. 'You've done with what?'

She looked at him sideways, smiled a little, without humour. 'You don't know me at all, really, do you? Certainly Papa doesn't, if he thinks he can push me into a marriage against my will . . . '

'What do you have against marriage?'

'It's a trap. Oh, not for a man – a man can go on with his life. But for a woman, it's the worst kind of dependence. Can you not remember Ma?' And her face, her voice, was bitter. Before Liam could form a reply, she had given a little, impatient shrug, as if even the thought made her feel constrained. 'I know what love is like. Marriage holds no mysteries for me – nor does it hold any appeal. I've attracted men by keeping my mouth shut and allowing them to believe me to be whatever they wish me to be. But give myself into one man's keeping forever? Sure and I'd be a fool, would I not, to do that?'

Liam studied her carefully. 'The Mitchells had a reputation for living a very unconventional lifestyle. I wonder if Father knows how unconventional?'

The green eyes snapped back to him. 'You keep your gob shut about that, Liam. You've done enough damage as it is. Let me get on with my own life – I plan to become a very eccentric, very contented old maid. And as such I'll have more freedom than you will, son and heir.' She had turned to the attack and pressed home, seeing his scowl. 'You'll have to toe the line, produce sons, carry on the family name – a prisoner in Papa's blueprint . . . '

'I'll be damned if I will!' He was angry that she had made him angry. 'I'll do as I please . . . '

'And so will I!'

Aidan was crossing the square towards them. They fell silent abruptly, but could not as readily change their hostile expressions.

'Are you quarrelling? Grown up as you are?'

They mumbled something and fell into step beside him. He carried the figurine in his arms in a paper parcel, and was very pleased with himself.

It was, Liam thought, as the months went by and the tour finally ended, as if he and his sister, for all their work and their enjoyment of their years in Ireland and overseas, had not built any real reserves within themselves. He would look at Clemency, sometimes, in the saloon of the ship, looking up from a book she had been reading, to gaze into space, and there was a lost quality about her, despite her words that day on Corfu, and he wondered if he appeared to her in the same light.

It was something to do with Australia, with the freedom of those early years in Tasmania. He did not understand what, exactly – it was not the acceptance of his play-fellows, for while Aidan had been in prison Liam had had to fight hard enough, and even when the family became wealthy, the knowledge was always there that others remembered his background. Life was easier in Dublin, easier still in Boston. Since he had left Australia he had involved himself totally in his studies, then in his teaching, then in his plotting and sub-plotting and the dangerous games within the Fenian movement. He had had goals that simply appeared, it was as if he did not even need to choose. For Clemency, within the convent, then caught up within the energy and enthusiasm of the Mitchell family, then back within the convent once more, he felt that it must have been the same. They had, both, embraced these self-consuming things to ward off their homesickness, hoping that what they followed would lead some-where . . . but it had not.

I am twenty-nine years old, Liam thought bitterly, yet I

know nothing, have achieved nothing. Letters after my name – what does that signify? And now I go home beneath the wing of this capable, loving despot, who has done it all . . . What is there for me to do?

He despised the black, self-pitying moods even as he had to endure them. He never spoke of them; indeed, to his father and sister he was optimistic, cheerful, steered clear of any talk that might lead to his betraying his sense of foreboding.

Clemency presumed that nothing worried Liam. To her, he appeared as he always had, kind, good-natured and amusing; to her he appeared carelessly confident, like her father in everything but his ambitions. Aidan had always possessed a direction; Liam, though always involved in something, somehow – was it that detached smile of his? His father never seemed detached – did not have that secure sense of direction. She was right in this; she was wrong only in believing that Liam did not mind.

Aidan, priding himself in accepting his children as they were, did not take it into consideration that they might not accept themselves. And because they loved him, and were a little afraid of him, they did not tell him. And what was there to say? It was all too esoteric; they both, Liam and Clemency, felt that they were too old to be complaining that they were afraid of the future, of this new country – which to them was the old country – of their ability to find a place within it.

The last letter Aidan had received from Thomas while in Europe had said that the roof of Shannonbrook Three had been finished, that the carpenters and plasterers were now at work on the interior.

He felt agitated, restless with excitement, as he sat in their carriage, a spanking new landau that he had had sent out from London to await them in Sydney. They had attended the horse sales and purchased two matching greys to pull it. Clemency said with a frown, 'They'll think we're fierce proud, Papa.'

'I'm bringing you home after twelve years,' he ruffled her short curls. 'I am proud of both of you.'

And it was strange, to return to Mittagong and feel a sense of homecoming. Enoch Wilkes came out the door of the *Argus* and called a welcome, and the farrier, Johnson, and Wally Sullivan, the owner-publican of the Hit-and-Miss hotel. They had to pull the carriage over to speak to Hal Peterson, who seemed very taken by Clemency – 'Despite your looking like a shorn sheep,' Liam murmured as they drove off. But they had to stop once more for Hedley Warwick, who called to them, from his own carriage, as they were

795

turning out of the township towards Shannonbrook Three. Helena was beside him, but even her tight-lipped face showed some semblance of interest this morning, as her eyes swept over the horses, the carriage, and Clemency's dress and bonnet. To Aidan's surprise, when Hedley invited the three of them to a dinner to welcome them back to Mittagong, his wife concurred with something like graciousness. Aidan agreed to the invitation, thanked them, and they drove on, Aidan shaking his head in amazement.

'We've arrived, my dears. I truly think, unless she's planning on poisoning us – that we have actually arrived in Mittagong society.'

''Tis Clemency. They want to pick her brains on the latest Paris fashions. You can tell them your short hair is all the rage, Clem. They'll be rushing home to hack their hair off with the kitchen scissors, to keep up with you in the latest style.'

She tried to smile at his teasing, but she did not share in the high spirits of her father and brother.

It had, she realized, been the simplicity of their lives in Tasmania that she had always thought of when she remembered Australia. In Tasmania their friends had been the simple, hard-working people of the Huon Valley and Port Davey. They had not known anyone like Mr and Mrs Warwick. And what's more, she thought with sudden mistrust, glancing at her father's back on the driver's seat before her, her father would not have wanted the friendship of people of that type, spoilt and rich. And though Mr Warwick seemed a gentleman, his wife was a positive horror, she could tell, looking over each of them as if she had a bad smell under her nose. Yet the dinner invitation had delighted her father. You've changed, she thought, and she hated the knowledge of how many times she had said that to him, in her mind, over the past twelve months.

What will happen? she wondered. Will I be happy here? I don't want to be a squatter's daughter – I want my freedom. And I can't tell him that, not for ages, or he'll look at me with that grim smile and those hard eyes, and remind me that I wouldn't have had even this much freedom, had he not dragged me out of that convent. I'm not going to let him know he was right. Not yet, damn him, not yet . . .

Past the stretch of Wingecarribee Swamp that the locals had nicknamed Henke's Marsh, for, on that side of the road, Henke's property bordered on to the low, boggy ground, and his round, quiet-moving figure could often be seen, invariably in long black waders, sketch book in hand, paddling gently about in the water after ibis or guinea hen. Now, for it had been a dry spring, the marsh was smaller in area, the grass green only at its edge, the native perennial trees forming a dull backdrop against the brilliant emerald foliage of the imported oaks and willows and chestnut trees planted closer to the road, and framing small farmhouses nestled in the crook of the hills.

And here were the gates that said, *Killaloe, T.P. O'Brien*, and here were the gates that were shadowed by the large hanging sign that read, *Shannonbrook Two mill, A.J. O'Brien, Prop.* and then a stretch of lichened stone wall, bringing memories of Ireland, and then green painted iron gates, wide open.

The grey slate roof and tall gables, the broad symmetry of the sandstone walls, appeared and reappeared between the trees and shrubbery as they went up the long driveway. 'Hell's outhouse . . . ' Liam muttered, while all Clemency could say, as a space between oak and pine would enable a broader view of the double-storeyed house, with its bay windows and broad, wrought-iron-lace trimmed verandah, was 'Oh, Papa . . . '

Aidan himself did not speak. For him it was as if all his life had been leading to this moment; all that he had ever worked for, suffered for, was embodied in those sandstone walls. This was the one tangible, this would not pass away.

The drive straightened out before it reached the circular section of gravel before the doors. Now that they were closer, they could see the unfinished rawness of it. The naked foundations rose from dried mud over which some hardy native grasses were already beginning to creep; not a flower, nor a vine softened the stone facade. The windows were blank and staring, without blinds or drapes, no smoke came from the tall chimneys, no chairs stood on the wide verandas. The only signs of life were the sounds of hammerings from within.

'Would that be Uncle Thomas, Papa? He won't be upset, will he, that we didn't tell him we'd arrived in Sydney . . . '

'Arra, he won't mind, he'll be grateful I saved him the torment of the visit to Sydney. You know he hates cities.'

Aidan pulled up in front of the steps. Liam jumped down, and stood staring up at the house. 'Mary, Mother of God, will you look at it, now.' He was laughing. He leaned his head against the side of the carriage and laughed. His hat fell off and he could not stop laughing long enough to retrieve it.

'What is it that you find so amusing?' Aidan glared at him. Then he glanced at Clemency, to find her, also, trying to suppress a grin.

'It's a lovely house, Papa. It's just so . . . grand, sure.'

'Are you after finding some fault with the design?' Aidan had turned back to the choking Liam, snarled the words at him.

'Nothing . . . Nothing, Father, I'm sorry.' Liam picked up his hat, and turned to gaze about the gardens, the broad sweep of lawn, the flagged paths that ran down between the trees. The laughter bubbled up within him once more. 'You didn't tell me!'

'Tell you what?' testily.

'That it was to be so damn *big*!'

'Watch y'r language!'

'It's a mansion, Father! You may as well be back in Killaloe – the new master of the big house. Y'r a squatter by adoption, Father! You wear the uniform!'

Aidan threw the horses' reins over to his son – but he threw too hard, and one of the straps of heavy new leather struck Liam's cheek. His laughter stopped abruptly.

Aidan's face was pale. He half-moved forward, stood his ground. 'I'm sorry, son. I . . . didn't mean that to . . . '

'It's all right.' The features, so like his father's, were stiff, unreadable, the voice calm.

'I wanted . . . I was going to ask you if you'd put the horses away – you might find Maurie or one of the lads out the back.'

'Aye, Father.'

Only a further infinitesimal pause, and Aidan had turned and walked up the steps into the house.

Clemency looked from her father's stiff back, to Liam, pale beneath his freckles. 'You hurt him, Liam. He's fierce proud of this house.' She went to climb from the carriage, he lifted her down almost roughly.

'He's too proud, and that's an end to it.'

She stood back, sought for something to say, but Liam was leading the two new horses and the carriage around the house in the direction of the stables. Clemency hesitated, then followed her father up the steps.

The clean, fresh smell of new wood warred with the smell of paints and varnish. She stood in the doorway and looked down a broad hall to where a staircase rose upwards. No furniture, just white plaster walls and bare floorboards. She moved forward. To her right, a small room, to her left, a large one – and she smiled, there was the largest of the marble fireplaces her father had purchased in Italy. Except for this, the room, sunny, the floor patterned by light through the two sets of french doors, was empty. She went to the fireplace, ran her hand over the cool, pale coral-coloured stone, looked around the room.

What sort of house will this be? Will it be a happy home? None of us are happy, not Liam, not Papa, not me. We're like this house, we're as empty as this house.

798

She did not see Mary in the hall doorway. She had come looking for Liam and Clemency, leaving Aidan to speak with Thomas in the kitchen. She paused, now, her small features and watchful dark eyes half-smiling with anticipation, then frowned slightly as she studied the girl.

Girl. She was a woman, now. The green eyes, bright green in the reflections of the emerald green travelling suit. So many folds and pleats and tucks in the full skirt, the enormous bustle, the train that had dragged along the floor and collected shavings that clung to the cloth. Very grand, very fashionable, Mary thought, but the body within the clothes was too thin, too angular. The mouth was held in a straight line that was neither natural nor flattering, and the eyes were narrowed as they traced the empty space of the room with something like bitterness.

Don't let her be like Maura, Mary prayed. Let her not have a narrow soul, dear Lord. Don't let the well-meaning Sisters have taken the life from her . . .

Clemency saw her. The green eyes opened wider, and the mouth, too, and all thoughts of Maura vanished.

Clemency was reminded, by Mary's thin, black-garbed, familiar presence, that all was not unknown, unsure. Gran was older, more stooped, but the smile was just as warm, the eyes just as loving and wise. And Clemency was running to her, 'Gran!' Yes, and tears in her eyes. 'I'm home, Gran! I'm home!'

77

It was typical, Liam thought, after the workmen had left and the whole family had gathered at Killaloe for dinner, that Aidan would begin working immediately. He locked himself away with Thomas in the office, and left Liam with Ottilia, Mary and Clemency – and all they could talk about were the children. The boys were grand, sure, and a new one had been born only ten months before, young Thomas junior, but it was a fierce boring way of spending one's first evening at home after twelve years away – especially when one knew nothing about one's surroundings. Why couldn't Father have left the business discussions until the morning, used what little daylight there was left to show Liam around the mills and the properties?

He glanced at Clemency. She had just come back from a walk with little Corrie, and she was laughing, and asking questions of him and his mother; Liam found himself almost resenting her ability to settle so quickly; really, it was out of character for her. He began to wonder if she were not secretly delighted with the opulence of Shannonbrook Three – she had already, that afternoon, claimed which bedroom would be hers, and was asking Ottilia how many hunts and horse shows were held in the district. So much, Liam thought, drily, for Poverty, Chastity and Humility – well, the former and the latter, anyway. Clemency was alive as he had not seen her for these past three years or more – he could think of nothing but the house that could have changed her so abruptly – for sure she knew what to expect, nothing else had changed.

But he had neglected to think of the effect of finding herself once more surrounded by her family, embraced within the circle of Mary, Thomas, 'Tillia and the four little boys, who seemed very taken with her already.

She lay awake that night on the couch in the Killaloe homestead, and wondered just what she had gained by the twelve years' absence from Australia. Liam, at least, had a law degree – if anyone would allow him to practice after his involvement with the Fenian movement. But I have nothing to show but a superficial knowledge of Latin and French and Italian and German. Really, I know nothing, have achieved nothing. And she thought with bitterness, *He should not have sent me away. He had no right. He should never have sent me away.*

It was the old litany, the old bitter litany of the time before the convent had opened its arms to her. She no longer felt safe, secure, she felt as savage, as vulnerable, as suspicious as she ever had. Her kin and her land – Tasmania, not this tame green countryside – they were what mattered to her. For twelve years she had been denied them. He had no right.

A horse whinnied from outside. She sat up, glancing at the clock on the mantelpiece. After midnight – she could just make out the hands of the clock in the moonlight. Again the whinny, and hoof-beats, now, slow, at walking pace, outside. She rose and went to the front door, glancing back along the hall to where light still showed from beneath the door of Uncle Thomas's study. She could hear the drone of the voices, Thomas's and her father's – business, business . . .

She opened the door, and stepped out into the cool of the night. 'Liam!' she called hoarsely to the fading shadow.

The figure stopped, turned, and came back, betraying itself as

800

Liam mounted on one of Thomas's horses, a fine dapple grey. 'That's Blue, isn't it? Where are you taking him?'

'Nowhere in a hurry, sure. It's like riding an elephant, being up here. Thomas bought the creature for Father – finest cob in the country they tell me. Draught horse, is more like it.'

Clemency came down the steps and stood at the grey's head. It had large, gentle eyes, turned to look at her, nuzzling her shoulder. 'He's a pet. You haven't told me why you're stealing him.'

'Just . . . ' He sighed, impatiently. 'I thought I'd ride into town for a few hours. Play cards, have a drink, you know.'

'Papa won't like it.'

His voice was tight, but even before he spoke, she told herself hers had been a tactless statement. 'Father doesn't own me.'

'Liam, you'll be back by morning, won't you? And don't let him find out – you know he doesn't like you going to brothels . . . '

'Jaysus!'

'Please, Liam . . . '

'Jaysus, Clemency! There wouldn't be one of those places in Mittagong, what're y' like!'

'You found them in Athens, and Barcelona and Trieste, and . . . '

'Look you, Clemency, stop lecturing me. Go back to bed or I'll climb down from this pachyderm and box y'r ears, so I will.'

'If he finds you gone in the morning . . . '

Abruptly, he began to dismount, and she took a step backwards. He laughed, retrieved his stirrup and turned the horse. 'I'll see you in the morning, Clem.'

'Liam . . . '

But the cob had broken into a canter, and was a pale shadow passing through the little orchard of young fruit trees Ottilia had planted.

Liam returned at six o'clock, managed to unsaddle the cob and creep, drunk, satiated and pleased with himself, into the spare bed in the boys' room, and had exactly a quarter of an hour's sleep before Corrie woke him by jumping on his chest and wanting to play.

Thereafter, even when the painting and wallpapering of Shannonbrook Three was completed, the furniture unpacked and all the belongings removed from Shannonbrook One, Liam was at home very little at night. Aidan questioned him about it, and he told his father he had made friends with Fitzroy Amberley and, to Aidan's secret disgust, Roger Pirie-Moxham's sons, Jeffrey and Laurie. They played poker, Liam said, and drank and argued a great deal. It was usually at Amberley's house that these meetings took place, and if, sometimes, Liam did not arrive home until the small hours, it was because sometimes they drank and argued too much, and forgot the time.

Aidan worried; wondered, sometimes, if he should go to visit Angie McGovern's residence and just see if the meetings with Amberley and the Pirie-Moxhams had perhaps adjourned there – but he did not like the thought that he would be spying on his son. Liam was – Good Lord, twenty-nine years old! He should not, even if he was a fierce fool, be accountable to his father any longer. And Aidan had other problems that occupied him, that kept him, too, away from home a great deal, at board meetings of Tweedie and Company, at one or the other of the mills, at work overseeing the improvements to the grazing stock of the three properties, or, lately, buying blood-stock at the Sydney horse sales.

The Southern Highlands Iron and Steel Company had finally been wound up, and Aidan had lost, altogether, about five thousand pounds. It was a loss he could live with – his position within the company had brought him contacts, friends and property, and he could not regret the experience. It gave him an interest in minerals, however, and he followed the news of the booms in tin and copper and iron until he died, but never again did he feel the compunction to invest. He would become annoyed, as an old man, when someone would speak of him as attempting to put the early iron industry on its feet. Some people said his losses in Southern Highlands Iron and Steel had embittered him against mining in general and the memory of his own investment in particular. But the more knowing ones, and certainly his own family, suspected that there was some slight embarrassment behind his reticence, that perhaps his one and only excursion into the field of mining shares had nothing, nothing at all, to do with what was *under* the ground.

There were some important developments, Thomas told Aidan, with regards to Donaldson's mill, while Aidan had been overseas.

'He's had a lot of trouble with equipment – the engine wasn't the best when he bought it – he's tried to cut corners at every turn and ended up back where he started from, watching us take most of the timber business in the Southern Highlands, while Donaldson himself is chasing his tail.'

'I like your turn of phrase, boyo, I do, sure.'

'In my opinion, Aidan, the only thing keeping Donaldson's mill going, is Sam Russell.'

'The overseer who came up from Goulburn? He's still here, then? Donaldson must be a good man to work for, perhaps.'

'Perhaps – or perhaps Sam Russell isn't the man who likes quitting.'

They were seated on the steps of Thomas's office at the Shannonbrook Two mill, in the gathering dusk. They both held mugs of strong tea that Fred Dent's wife had made them, and they sat wearily and watched the copper-beetles flying about, humming overhead, hearing the occasional soft thud as they hurled their hard little bodies against the lighted windows of the Dents' cottage, opposite.

'How do you come to know so much about the workings of Donaldson's mill?'

'I talk to the men, after Mass, in the pubs, wherever I meet them. Some of them are good workers, who really know timber. When I needed a few more men about eight months back, I approached three of them. Aidan, they wouldn't come. They wanted to keep working with Sam Russell.'

'You're coddin' me.'

'I'm not, and that's the truth. They're staying with the lower wages in order to work for Russell.'

'What is it about the man?'

'Arra, isn't it himself that runs that mill and not Donaldson? You were right about it, Donaldson's only motive in setting up that mill was revenge – there's rumours that Albertson and Pirie-Moxham and a few others who would have liked to see you slide gracefully down into bankruptcy helped him build it.

'But Sam Russell is somehow making that mill produce, and the men swear that he's fair, and a shrewd man and yet not an unfeeling one. Donaldson's crooked as a dog's hind leg, they tell me – but they'll defend Sam with their last breath.'

'We should buy Sam.'

'No, Aidan. I've approached him already. Even offered him a position as manager of both our mills. At twice the salary that Donaldson's paying him . . . '

'Y'r becoming precocious, my young brother . . . '

'I did what you'd have done.'

'Y'r right. What did he say?'

'He said no.'

'*What?*'

'He said – and you won't like this, so I'll quote verbatim and you can blame Russell, not me – "I work for Aidan O'Brien and I do things Aidan O'Brien's way. I work for Donaldson and I do things my own way." '

'The arrogant son-of-a-bitch.'

'You're very alike in a lot of ways,' Thomas grinned. Then, quickly, 'Fascinating, is it not, Aidan? Not all our money, nor our fine equipment and new workers' cottages can lure that man away from his leaking sheds and his croupy engines. And where he stays, his men stay.'

'He's crazy, and the men are bewitched. That's madness, Thomas.'

'There's more – young Neil, Sam's eldest boy, works with him, and they get along very well together. Bram, the youngest, is about nineteen, and as wild a lad as you'll find. He's fought not only with his father, but with Donaldson. It appears that Mrs Russell, Tessa, her name is, was hurt when part of the wall of their old cottage collapsed on her. The bricks were made more than fifty years ago – and we had a slight earth tremor here a few months back, that must have weakened the wall. Anyway, she was hurt, and Bram went with his father to see what Donaldson was going to do about it – and he said he'd do nothing at all. So Bram beat him up . . . '

'What? And his father let him . . . ?'

'Och, no – three blows was all it took, before Sam dragged him off – but it broke Donaldson's nose, and blacked his eye, and knocked him unconscious. This happened on the verandah of Donaldson's mansion, mind you – in full view of his daughters, who were playing croquet on the lawn . . . '

'Jaysus . . . '

'And Bram shook his father off, and headed for Sydney. But Donaldson's son called the police in, and they caught him stepping off the train. He's in gaol in Mittagong, now. I think we should find him a lawyer.'

'Do you, now?'

'Aye. Bram approached me about working for us a month ago. I said I'd consider it. I was going to agree because I like the lad. He reminds me of you at that age. A fierce hot-headed eejit. And besides, helping the son might just place the father on our side. I'd like that, Aidan. I'd like to see Donaldson left with nothing but a pile of toothpicks when Russell comes to work for us.'

'Arra, Tomás – y're diabolical.'

Thomas grinned his slow grin, their mother's smile. 'I can think up the diabolical schemes, but I don't like to put them into practice. I'll leave that to you. You have two weeks, by the way, that's when Bram goes up before Barrett, the magistrate.'

Aidan took a sip of his tea. It was cold. He asked, 'Wouldn't Russell be leaving Donaldson, now?'

'And if he did, wouldn't Donaldson be after closing the mill? And fifteen men out of work. I've spoken to them, they're begging Sam to stay on, to see this through. I've talked to Tessa, too. She's hoping that Donaldson might ask for leniency for Bram – if Sam quits now, Donaldson'll have the boy in Berrima Gaol for five years.'

Aidan sat silently for a moment, then sighed. 'I'd hoped to have a few quiet weeks settling in before throwing myself into something like this.'

'It's lying y'are. You never looked for a quiet day in your life. And it can't be now. If we help Bram, we're going to have to be prepared to be labelled radicals and Marxists and everything else short of murderers.'

'I'd yawn at that.'

Thomas grinned. 'Aye. So what shall we do?'

Aidan looked at his watch, tossed the contents of his mug onto the ground, and stood. 'We go to visit the Russells and offer our aid.'

'And if they ask why we're doing this, what do we say?'

'The truth. That we want to help Bram, employ them and drive Donaldson into a seizure. At the moment I don't think they'd be offended at that.'

Donaldson had not built new houses for his workers when his mill had opened. Instead they lived in the sprawling, long shearers' quarters, a converted barn, and a run down overseer's cottage on a corner of his estate that had once held the main homestead. This had long ago been pulled down and its stone used as the foundations for his large house half-a-mile further towards Mittagong.

They straggled down towards the creek, these old buildings, linked by tiny tracks that turned to slithery mud in wet weather. There was no well; the drinking water, washing water, was all drawn by bucket from the creek.

Someone in the Russell family had made an effort to paint the front door, and there were window boxes filled with white allysum, giving at least an air of comfort to the old building.

It was Tessa Russell who opened the door to them. The brothers liked her immediately, the direct grey eyes beneath glossy nut-brown hair, a smiling mouth. She looked young to be a mother of grown sons. A practical woman, and one who had seen hardship, yet she was outgoing and confident and not at all nonplussed by these visitors.

Russell was as dark and scowling as Aidan remembered him, and Neil looked like a younger version of his father. They all look Romany, Thomas thought, noticing their fine-boned faces, the narrow, arched noses that gave their faces such character.

Only Tessa seemed to welcome them immediately. It was three cups of tea and several scones with cheese later that Sam Russell began, at last, to unbend in his suspicion.

Even then, Aidan thought, I don't like you. Y'r an ungrateful, arrogant, know-it-all bastard, that you are. He smiled a little. Perhaps we are too much alike. The only thing I like about you is that you're honest and ambitious and I need men like you. As a friend, if I can't own you. Yes. As a friend. He gazed at the features that were even more dark and surly than his own. I shall make a friend of you if it kills us, he vowed to himself.

'I'll be paying you for this lawyer.' Sam's eyes went from Thomas to Aidan. 'I'll not be beholden to any man.'

Oh, God, Thomas groaned inwardly, he's going to be difficult. 'Of course,' Thomas murmured. 'But my nephew, Aidan's son, is a lawyer, though he's not practicing in the colony at the moment – he'll be able to find the best barrister for the job . . . '

'I'm not promising I'll come to work for you, O'Brien,' Sam turned to Aidan, 'you and I don't think the same.'

'Unfortunately, we do, but not at the same time, obviously. All I care about at the moment is keeping your son out of Berrima gaol – your son, as you'll remember, does wish to work for me.'

A pause, then, heavily, 'We don't . . . ' Sam's mouth tightened for a moment as he hesitated. 'We don't see eye to eye, Bramley and me – not like me and Neil. Bram won't listen to me. Thinks the sun shines out of you, though.' This was directed at Thomas. 'If you can get him out of this, he can go work where he likes. I don't want him in gaol – what he did was wrong, but he shouldn't be put in gaol for it.'

'It's often the way, with sons,' Thomas's gentle voice. 'They need to get away for a while, to find out who they are. Bram will be back with you within a few years.'

Tessa was smiling at him, from where she stood behind Sam's chair. Thomas flushed a little, felt that he was being trite. Tessa was thinking how good-looking he was, and, with amusement, that he did not know it, felt himself, undoubtedly, inferior in every way to the bear-shouldered, blunter-featured brother beside him. She did not know about Aidan O'Brien, he was too wealthy and too powerful to make her feel at ease. But she liked Thomas very much, and could see why Bram would turn to him for help. She had seen him in Mittagong, often, with the plump and good-humoured Ottilia and their children, and she had often wished to be friends with them.

Tessa had made up her mind. Whether or not she could trust Aidan, she trusted Thomas. They should accept the O'Brien's help.

806

She glanced down at Sam, and over at Neil, tight-faced, watchful. They were so proud, so cautious, so slow, sometimes! Often she amused herself with the thought that she was like the can of oil amongst the heavy machinery of this family; the cogs and wheels went grinding on, slowly, inexorably, not noticing how she went about, smoothing the way before them. If she disappeared, they would undoubtedly grind on, for a while, before they missed her. She knew this business of allowing Aidan O'Brien to interfere would keep them cogitating for days.

She squeezed Sam's shoulder. He looked up, and she looked back at him fixedly. She had very expressive eyes, and they told her husband a great deal. Go ahead. Say yes. We have no choice. I cannot bear it much longer. Say yes.

Sam scowled, turned back to Aidan, tried to cope with his envy of the man; Sam would have liked to have hated him, it would have been easier to have had cause to hate him. But, 'Yes. All right. We'll be grateful for your help.' Then, quickly, 'I wouldn't take it – but it's the boy. He's only nineteen. Too young to be in gaol. I'm doing this for the boy.'

Tessa served a good, plain meal for them, and the men remained talking together until four in the morning, long after Tessa had gone to bed. They found they had much in common, Aidan and Sam Russell, and they began to find these things in the long hours when facades are easier to lower and energy for aggression is at a low ebb. The first seeds of their friendship were sown that night, while Neil, his father's shadow, tried to follow the conversation and occasionally dozed in his chair.

78

Liam was bored and restless. Farmwork seemed senseless; like hauling buckets of water to the sea, or threading beads on to an unknotted string, the job was continuous, endless, and held no sense of satisfaction for him.

He had been asked by Maurie Templeton and Jim Chaffer to go drinking in Mittagong, and Fitzroy Amberley, who had his own establishment separate from his mother's on the road to Moss Vale, had implied that there was to be a rather wild party this evening to which he was invited. Jeff and Laurie Pirie-Moxham, and a few other young men of the neighbourhood would be attending, and a few ladies of their acquaintance, Amberley had winked tellingly.

Liam had made up his mind to accept both invitations, but in the meantime, he had three hours to fill before Maurie and Jim would be finished their chores. He saddled his horse, a pretty chestnut thoroughbred that Aidan claimed was too short in the back to be of any use but parade work, and rode out the gates of Shannonbrook Three. At first he rode aimlessly, but as he passed the road that led towards Burrawang, he turned his mount, deciding to visit Garth Ellis.

It was good to have wild, down-to-earth friends like Maurie and Jim, and clever, witty characters like the Pirie-Moxhams and Amberley to accompany to Big Angie McGovern's for a night out, but his best friend in the district would have to be Garth Ellis. In Garth he had found someone akin to himself, possessed of the same restlessness. They were both, Garth often said, trapped in Mittagong against their wishes, Garth by responsibilities, and Liam by his sense of duty. This afternoon, Liam felt, he needed someone with whom to share his thoughts, someone who'd understand.

He usually met Garth at one of the hotels or taverns in Mittagong, this was the first time Liam had visited Garth's home, and was surprised, even in view of the family that Garth mentioned he had, to find it a large, comfortable Georgian house, surrounded by well-groomed lawns and gardens. He wondered if Garth helped with the gardening here, then smiled – it was difficult to imagine Garth doing anything like cutting lawns or weeding flower beds.

He knocked on the front door, and finding no answer, walked around the house to the back entrance. It was while he did so that his gaze caught sight of a figure at some distance down the garden. It was a woman, on a ladder, pruning a very old rosebush that was trained up and over a trellis. 'Excuse me!' Liam called as he walked towards her.

The ground was soft, for it had been raining heavily the night before. The softness of the soil accounted for the quietness of Liam's approach, and the sudden sinking of one of the legs of the ladder as the woman started, shifted her weight.

The ladder was falling, and Liam sprang forward – they were both upon the ground – Liam was conscious of the fact that he had not managed to break much of the woman's fall. Her face, when she turned to him, was covered with blood, 'Jaysus, ma'am, you've . . .'

And he stopped, feeling the blood rush to his own face. The clear brown eyes that gazed up at him were alight with amusement. 'I've been giving people frights for years with this beauty spot, sir. Please don't feel embarrassed,' she said, and they climbed to their feet. She was quite small, he saw, now, with curling dark hair that, escaped from her chignon, formed wispy ringlets around her face.

'I'm Liam O'Brien, ma'am,' he said, trying not to look at the disfigurement, feeling his heart contract at the sight of the rest of her face, so perfect. The dark red stain made him almost angry; he wondered how she could smile so, for it was unfair, unfair . . .

At the mention of his name she had stiffened a little, the look she threw him was one of dubiety. But, 'I'm Mrs Ellis,' and her small hand was placed within his own.

Liam righted the ladder for her, and she was saying, 'I'm afraid Garth is in Campbelltown on business today, Mr O'Brien. His family's lawyers are situated there, and I think he may be staying the night with Mr and Mrs Charles Reynolds in Camden.'

'Ah, I see.' And did he mistake it, or was there an air about the woman that was unfriendly, now that she knew his name? He puzzled over it a moment, still trying to realize that this beautiful and most unusual woman was part of what Garth had lamentedly termed 'the responsibilities that keep me from my work'. He had somehow gained the impression – sure, nothing Garth had said, for he was obviously devoted to his family – that Victoria Ellis was a rather narrow-minded woman, someone who was not as well-educated as her husband, perhaps, someone who almost certainly resented the necessary time he spent with his poetry.

He realized he had been standing there too long, gazing at her, and that now Victoria was looking at him with an equally suspicious frown.

Jaysus, he thought, I wonder if she blames me for all those nights Garth and I would be drinking at the Hit-and-Miss? He knew, too, that on a few occasions Garth had visited Big Angie's establishment with Amberley. Hell's outhouse, and Liam began to flush a little, once more, she probably classifies me with Amberley and the Pirie-Moxhams, all after leading her husband into wickedness.

Victoria was very politely, very coolly, inviting him to stay for afternoon tea, and after a moment of confusion, Liam surprised both of them by accepting. At the same time, he could hear children's voices coming from the house.

'The children are awake from their naps,' Victoria said, as they walked towards the building. 'We usually have tea together on the verandah when the weather is warm enough. Do you mind children at the tea table, Mr O'Brien?'

She really was trying to frighten him away. 'I like children, Mrs Ellis,' he said, and just in time, as two little girls, aged about five or six, and a little boy of about two, in a white frock, came down the stairs and rushed to him.

He had always thought it strange that children should like him, for he could not bring himself to make silly faces at them, nor treat them any differently to a grown-up, except to be a little more patient, as one would with a dog or a horse, until they understood what one meant. Whatever his attitude, children seemed not to mind, and at the end of that peculiar afternoon, when he should have been bathing and changing ready to ride into the Hit-and-Miss for several hours' serious drinking, and already wondering which of the girls at Big Angie's would be sharing his bed that night, he was sitting at the tea table with the small boy on his lap, and talking about Boston and New York with Victoria Ellis.

As the weeks went by, he found he was visiting the house as much to see Victoria as Garth; indeed, sometimes he preferred Victoria's company, for she had a wealth of common sense that he had found, once, in Berrima Ellis when he had been a boy at Glenleigh – and found occasionally in Clemency, but not often – and in other females, not at all. They would have excellent discussions, Garth, Victoria and himself, and he took to meeting Garth more and more at his house instead of in Mittagong, for he actually enjoyed the addition of Victoria to their talks on literature and travel, politics and music.

It was after a particularly comfortable, amusing evening, that Garth walked Liam some way down the drive, and said, without a preamble, 'I think it would be best, old chap, if you don't come to the house *quite* so much. Of course, Victoria and I love to have you, but it makes it deucedly hard for me to escape on other nights. Do you see? If we met each other in town it would be that much easier for me. Could you manage it?'

Liam murmured, 'Of course,' while feeling as if he had been kicked in the stomach. What was there to say, but 'of course'? He could not very well say, 'No, I prefer your wife's company to yours.'

And Liam rode home very slowly, for the knowledge had come to him that he preferred precisely that.

He stabled his mare for the night, and went up to the house with his mind still reeling. His thoughts were all confusion, and he did not wish, particularly, to understand them. I'll go away for a while, he thought, riding up the drive and around the house to the stables, I'll go away for a while and think about this . . .

He came up the stairs on to the back verandah of Shannonbrook Three, nodded briefly to a boy leaning against one of the posts, went inside – and came out again immediately, allowing the screen door to slam behind him.

'Clemency?'

'You say one word, and I'll go for your throat, so help me.'

'What are you doing in trousers, tell me?'

'Go away and don't be such a Puritan.'

'Purit . . . Clemency, has Father seen them?'

'Why do you think I'm standing out here? I'm allowing him to settle down a bit before I go back and continue the argument.'

Liam dropped down to sit on the steps, staring up at his sister. She wore the trousers loose over her riding boots, and a blue shirt, as new as the trousers, was tucked into the waistband. Her hair was pulled back loosely at the nape of her neck.

'I bought them today. Six pairs of trousers and six shirts. Himself told me to take them back to the store, but I won't. He'll get over it. What's the point of having a spinster daughter, I told him, if she wasn't a little eccentric? He wasn't amused.' She looked at her brother narrowly, 'This shouldn't matter to you, Liam, so if you side with him, you'll be sorry. I'm very serious about this.'

'*Why*? Sure I know you spend all your time outdoors, but . . . '

'I was bitten by a snake today.'

'*What?*'

'A red-belly it was, too. Look at the tooth marks.' She pulled up the leg of her trousers and showed him four tiny puncture marks in the soft leather of her boot.

'My God . . . did it break the skin?'

'The teeniest little bit – I've felt pretty dreadful all day, but Doctor Lawler said I was lucky. I rode straight into town to see him, and on the way to the surgery I bought the shirts and trousers.'

'You're mad, Clemency,' he said with admiration.

'I was trailing through the scrub after this lamb that was caught in some bushes, and I felt the snake bite me before I saw it. It was *wrapped around my boot*, Liam.'

'Get away!'

'I swear before God. It all comes from trailing about in those bloody skirts.'

He had never before heard his sister swear, realized, now, how shaken she was. He told himself he should censure her behaviour – but it was always so hard to think of Clemency as a woman, one of those species who were impossible to understand, who flirted and were made for protecting and venerating, even when one was trying to seduce them into acquiescence. Even now, he was seeing this incident from Clemency's point of view. 'Skirts would be a fierce handicap in the scrub, I should think. But still,' he tried to speak firmly, 'you could stay at home in the house like other women.'

She sighed, and did not even bother to answer him. He did not expect her to. 'You should have been a boy,' he added. 'Then you could run this place.'

She turned on him. 'I'm a woman, and I like being a woman – and I could *still* run this place.'

He looked ahead of him at the pink-tinged clouds behind which the sun had disappeared. The clouds, too, were rolling slowly towards the west, and it looked as if sun and clouds both were being dragged down the sky against their will. One of the sheep dogs, a Queensland Red Heeler with a bright, inquisitive face, loped over to him and leaned its head on Liam's knee. 'I wish you could run the place.' And he looked up at Clemency to see that he had pleased her.

They smiled at each other. Then she said, 'And you? What do you plan to do – besides running this place, for you'll not escape it, himself will see to that.'

'Me?' he sighed, watched the pink sky falling beyond the roof of the stables. 'I'll go to Sydney, I'm thinking. Study at the university, catch up on the law as it's practiced here – stay away about a year, I suppose.'

'You'll practice, then?'

'I'm fit for little else, Clemency.'

'Och, stop, Liam. You have a better education than anyone else in our family – and you're a man, you can do whatever you like.'

Then, in a change of voice, she said, 'Papa will miss you.'

'Will he?' the words came out, heavy with irony, before he could prevent them.

'Yes,' Clemency said quietly. 'He's a very lonely man, Liam.'

He stared at her. He never considered their father, he realized, in terms of any basic emotions such as loneliness. And then he thought, bitterly, if he is lonely, then sure it's his own fault. He's too clever at pretending not to need anybody. And so well-practiced in it, that nowadays he probably doesn't need anyone, at that.

Clemency, in the way she sometimes had of tuning into his thoughts, said, 'If you stayed a while longer, you might get to know Papa better. Sure we've not seen much of each other, any of us. We're all strangers, in a way.'

'I won't rush off anywhere. I'll stay until after Bram's case, for certain, and I know himself will be hurt if I rush straight way. But I'll have to be gone by March.'

812

He felt pleased, now the decision was made to go. March was four months away. Plenty of time to accustom his father to the idea. Plenty of time, too, he hoped, to get over his feelings for Victoria Ellis.

Liam and Aidan managed to gain the services of a highly experienced barrister for Bram's case. The man came to the Southern Highlands from Sydney a few days before the event, and stayed with the O'Briens. At the courthouse in Berrima, where the case was held, the lawyer managed to present Bram's behaviour in the light of his worry over his mother, and stressed, with a number of witnesses, the poor standard of the housing that had caused the incidents, and pleaded leniency.

Even Donaldson, aware of the district's public support of the Russells, admitted grudgingly that perhaps he had been hasty in his dismissal of Bramley Russell's claims, perhaps the boy was simply young . . . Donaldson finished by intimating that he would, in the future, allow the matter to be forgotten.

It was not Frederick Lawrence who presided over the case, but John Barrett, a police magistrate of renowned integrity and remorseless adherence to the written law. Not for John Barrett the no-man's-land of mitigating circumstances; he quoted the cases that had gone before with an almost religious fervour, and his decisions were handed down with the solemnity of a latter day Moses coming down the mountainside to his people.

Following the precedent of several similar cases, going back to the colony's birth almost a hundred years before, Bram was found guilty, and sentenced to eighteen months' imprisonment in Berrima gaol.

'It could have been worse,' Liam admitted, morosely, to Sam and Neil and Tessa afterwards.

'*What*?'

'Aye. He could have got up to five years – as it is, Bram could be home in a year.' And as Sam and Neil were beginning to mutter to themselves, 'You'll have to keep him out of trouble, Sam – though perhaps the lad will learn himself, after this experience.'

He wished he could do more for the family, for he had come to like the rather taciturn Neil, and he respected Sam as much as Aidan and Thomas did. Still, the incident taught Liam that his legal knowledge could be put to some good use in Mittagong.

It was strange to find that he could regard the Southern Highlands as home. But then, where else could Home be? Clemency talked often of returning to Tasmania, but he knew that even she would not leave her family to live there alone.

Yes, home may as well be Mittagong, Liam thought, but something in him rebelled at this, all the same. It seemed to be yet another decision that Aidan had made; best for all of them, of course, but Aidan's decision nevertheless.

79

Mary was finding that being rich could be tedious. And to make matters worse, she was growing *old*, so that servants took cleaning implements from her hands, these days, not only because she was infringeing on their own tasks, but because they genuinely believed that she could not manage quite ordinary chores without some help.

There were people to dig the vegetable garden, people to make soap and candles. People to sweep and dust, and Charity had taken over the large kitchen of the new big house at Shannonbrook Three with all the might and arrogance of Brian Boru marching into Cashel.

Mary was bored. She hated to admit this character flaw to herself, let alone anyone else, barricaded the feeling out with a lot of little tasks, took an even more avid interest in her grandchildren and their plans and activities. For that reason she liked to be with 'Tillia and Thomas and the boys on Killaloe. Shannonbrook Three dwarfed her, made her feel lost. When staying there she spent much of her time sewing and mending, sitting, often, for it was a dry summer, in the shade of the trees in the garden, a broad hat on her head to shade her eyes from the glare. On a day when it was too hot, when no breeze stirred and it seemed the whole world was dying, shrivelling, she retreated to the cool of the house, and took it into her head to check Clemency's wardrobe of dresses for any that needed mending.

She was alone in the house that day, except for Charity, incanting over bubbling pots of jam in the kitchen, and no one disturbed Mary in the two hours that she spent in Clemency's room. For she had never spent more than a few minutes there at a time, noticed, only now, how odd it was that Clemency should have not one or two, but three wardrobes in her room.

They were filled with clothes; silks, cottons, woollens and every kind of combination, every style and colour. On top of the wardrobe were boxes, some with more dresses, obviously never yet worn, and some containing bonnets and hats. The large, deep-drawered

814

bureau, however, was filled with trousers, moleskins and denims, and boys' shirts – Clemency's everyday costume.

Mary dropped stiffly on to the bed and sat looking about her; she had left all the wardrobe doors open, the better to survey the scene. She placed her pince nez on her nose and from where she sat, made an effort to count how many dresses there were. There were at least ten times twenty, she calculated, working on the space it took to hang twenty dresses. What was ten times twenty? Two hundred? Och, no . . . !

And so many of them never worn, so many she had never seen on the girl. What a waste – Caroline Kelly, sure, had never had a wardrobe such as this. Mary stood to take a closer look – and found moth-holes in more than one of the dresses. Moth-holes were the major problem, there was not a worn hem nor cuff to be found in all that collection of finery. Mary pulled out the offending casualities of neglect, growing angrier by the minute, but was forced to stop when she had a bundle of eight dresses that needed her needle. She gathered them into her arms and struggled with them to the door.

Clemency was coming through the front door, Liam behind her, as she started down the stairs. 'Arra, *you!*'

At the sound of her grandmother's voice, Clemency looked up, but the girl's surprised face was almost the last thing that Mary remembered. There was that sickening feeling of helpless fright as her foot caught in a trailing hem and she spun a little, off-balance, down into space, reaching out with a hand to where she believed the banister to be, and finding nothing. Clemency or Liam called out and there was only this as the stairs seemed to strike her body with an overwhelming force.

Mary awoke two hours later, and to Edward Lawler's astonishment, waved him aside, called Clemency into the room and began scolding her as if the accident had not happened to interrupt her. A sprained shoulder and concussion, and bruises to most of her body, did not make any difference to the force of Mary's anger.

Clemency tried to point out that the pile of mending had helped to cushion her grandmother's fall, but this did little good; she should not have had to be carrying such a load in the first place. Sitting up in her bed, pale but bright-eyed, Mary castigated her granddaughter for her vanity and her wastefulness.

'If you *wore* them it would be bad enough, for no one needs so many clothes. But to buy them and never use them! Clemency, is it mad you are? Are you soft in the head?'

'No, Gran, you know I'm not. I like pretty things, that's all.'

'But you never wear them!'

'I might! One of these days. In the meantime, they're there. I can look at them. I look at them quite often. I like to be surrounded by pretty things – there's nothing wrong in that, is there? You only ever wear black, but your dresses are always in the latest style.'

'I don't have two hundred of them, Clemency.'

'I'll get round to wearing them, Gran, I will, sure.'

'When?'

'When . . . this season. I plan to go to a lot of balls and entertainments this season.'

'Oh, you do!'

'Yes. So don't you worry about it.' She kissed her grandmother. 'I'll sort out some of the dresses and give some away, too. It was wrong of me to keep so many.'

'Just wear them. And Clemency . . . ' as the young woman headed for the door, 'tell your father I wish to see him.'

Hell's outhouse . . . Clemency grimaced to a thoroughly amused Doctor Lawler as she headed out into the hall.

Yet the result of that day was not quite what she had expected. She did not receive a lecture from her father, rather he came downstairs from his interview with his mother looking rather shamefaced, took her into his office and told her that he only now realized that he had been very remiss as a father, not only to herself, but to Liam.

For some seconds Clemency did not understand, then gradually, as her father began looking through his wastepaper basket, pulling out various cards of different shapes and colours, her heart began to shrink within her.

'Stubborn people, these Southern Highlanders . . . ' her father was muttering, 'just as well they keep on sending us these things. Here's a picnic to Fitzroy Falls organized for the fifteenth – Mrs Helena Warwick. And here's a dance after a day of picnic races at Lambert's property out at Bundanoon – that's for the sixteenth. And this is an exhibition of watercolours. Well, you can go unescorted to that one . . . '

'Papa, what are you saying? You don't mean that you've let Gran talk you into going into society, have you?'

He looked up. 'Yes, Clemency, we are about to go into society. I think, *asthore*, it's about time.'

She began to laugh, flopped back into one of the chairs and laughed for some seconds, stopping only when she saw that he was not amused at all. His scowl deepened; he was studying her, taking in the blue shirt belted over moleskin trousers, and kneeboots. She was conscious that there were muddy marks on her clothes from where she had taken a fall while jumping her horse across brush that afternoon. She began to explain this to her father, but he interrupted, 'If you rode side-saddle, you wouldn't take so many tumbles.'

'I don't fall often,' she said hotly. 'And I don't believe in riding side-saddle – practically strapped on to the horse's back – no wonder one doesn't fall off – or out, one should say. But it's not fair on the horse, either, that disproportionate weight, and it throws him off . . . '

'I'm not interested in your horse's ability to cope with the side-saddle, and that bay was bought, I might remind you, because he was trained to it . . . '

'Papa . . . '

'I *am* talking about this family taking its place in the Southern Highlands, Clemency. About joining this community and not simply being on its periphery.'

'It's filled with . . . '

' . . . And criticizing people we've barely come to know, for all the years we've been here.'

'I didn't want to know them. I don't need them.'

He stopped, and looked long and hard at her.

No, she was right, she did not need them. She did not need people to any great extent at all. She had all the security she needed with her family – and because they were alone, for the most part, in their Irishness, amongst families that were still English to the core, Aidan had seen nothing circumspect in not mixing with the other wealthy people in the district.

'I've been very selfish,' he said now. 'I blame myself for this. It's not too late, though – we are, I'm telling you, about to launch ourselves into society, Clemency. Oddly enough, society wants us, and we shall not hold back and be coy any longer.'

'You want to marry me off, that's it, isn't it? You want me to find a husband from amongst one of the Pure Merino families. To hell with that, Papa!'

'That's enough! I don't care, Clemency, whether you marry or not. And if you don't learn to curb your tongue and your temper, I doubt there's a man in the Southern Highlands who'd have you!'

She had taken a step towards him, her mouth open with her ready reply, when Liam knocked at the door, entering without waiting to be invited.

'Charity and I can hear you in the kitchen, so undoubtedly Gran can hear you, upstairs. Could you keep your voices down?'

'It's all right, I'm thinking. We've finished shouting at each other.' Aidan's eyes held Clemency's with a challenge. She half-opened her mouth to protest, but changed her mind and excused herself, leaving the room.

Aidan was true to his word, and nearly all those invitations that arrived were now accepted. Clemency, who stayed home during the first few weeks of Aidan's campaign, gradually became bored, and at her grandmother's insistence, began pulling out the dresses from the wardrobes, and joining the family on these excursions.

Mary, secretly, was amused. Aidan tackled the challenge of being accepted into Southern Highlands society with the same determination that he set about doing anything in his life, but for all that, she wondered if he took any joy in it. Liam, who by now knew virtually everyone in the Mittagong district, nevertheless, sat through dinners and danced through dances with preoccupied and unapologetic impatience, bringing the hopes of many young debutantes and their mamas to frustration.

The only time he did enjoy these evenings was when Victoria Ellis attended them, and then she forced him to limit himself to two dances with her, and not to speak to her unless someone else was included in the conversation. These bitter-sweet evenings almost drove him mad. There seemed to be nothing between the mindless coupling with Violetta and the other girls at Big Angie's, and the sterile posturings of polite society.

And the more he saw of Victoria, the less content he was with this state of affairs.

Liam was changing, in his attitudes and his relationships. He found that he could no longer enjoy the company of Laurie and Jeffrey Pirie-Moxham, Fitzroy Amberley and Garth Ellis. Fitzroy was becoming even narrower in his outlook, with the increased responsibilities of business since his mother's death a few months before, and Liam could almost understand that. The Pirie-Moxhams, he began to realize, were not really interested in growing up – and Garth . . . Garth Ellis frightened him more than all the others. Garth had the brains, the talent, to do something constructive with his life, but seemed unable to do so.

The conversations that they used to have, over port wine and cigars, were now taken up as before, but there was something wrong. Liam gradually came to realize that it was within himself. He had changed, Garth had not. He had come to accept that he must adapt to his new surroundings, make a place for himself here. Garth seemed to take a vicarious pleasure in being the outsider. Statements

818

such as 'Life terrifies me . . . ' would once, Liam thought with a kind of shock, have made him appreciate Garth's uniqueness, his sensitivity. Now – how could he, Liam, change so quickly? – it seemed only to emphasize Garth's inability to cope with the reality around him.

And Victoria . . .

It was not long before he realized that she was the prime cause for his resentment of Garth. He had visited their house on the Burra-wang Road often enough to see that Victoria was forced to be both mother and father to the three children, Gemma, Honor and Kenelm. Even in their small faces – and pàrticularly Kenelm's, for he would have worshipped his father, had he been allowed to – Liam saw a confusion, a frightening knowledge that Garth was using his writing (he spent ten hours a day in his study) as a means of keeping his family from him.

'If he could only have another success such as *Songs of Nattai*,' Victoria admitted to Liam, when he called one day. Garth had appeared out of his office, smiled quickly and asked if Liam, like a good chap, would mind being entertained by Victoria and the children for an hour or two while he wrestled with a particularly stubborn phrase.

Liam said, 'But, sure, it's not as though that's his whole life.' Victoria looked up at him even while he was continuing. 'He has a private income, has he not? He's not like that poor wretch, Gordon, who relied solely on his verse to keep him alive.'

Victoria's smile was sad. 'My husband knew Adam Lindsay Gordon, the man had a great deal of worry – yes, far more than Garth has. Gordon's suicide affected Garth very badly – and it had to coincide with the failure of Garth's second book of verse. It stopped him writing for several years.'

'What's he been doing then?' An impatience in his voice that he would have bitten back if he could. Victoria's eyes – Liam did not know anyone with more expressive dark eyes – were raised to his with a faint reproach.

'He's been working on his third collection of verse. He has great hopes for this volume – it's all the better, he tells me, for having spent so much time perfecting it. His second volume, *Waratah*, appeared too soon after *Songs of Nattai*, he thinks.'

'Well,' they were walking in the garden, and Liam bent to pull at the head of a dandelion in the grass, 'I hope it brings him the success he wants. For your sake.'

He should not have said it. The dark eyes came up to his, once more, startled, and Liam flushed, wondering how to explain his concern when, really, this was no concern of his.

But he was saved from his embarrassment by the arrival of the children, young Kenelm trailing a little behind. The two little girls ran to Liam, but the boy toddled to his mother. 'Darling . . . ?' Victoria's arms went out to him, and she lifted him to her.

'Sick . . . ' Kenelm said, rubbing his eye with his fist.

'Still?' Victoria felt his forehead. 'Yes, you are still very hot, aren't you? I think I'll take you up to bed.'

'Not that sick . . . ' Kenelm began squirming to get down. 'Want a story . . . '

'I'll tell you a story when you're in bed . . . '

'Oh, no, Mama,' Gemma put in, 'for then Mr O'Brien won't be able to hear, and you like Mama's stories, too, don't you, Mr O'Brien?'

'I do, sure,' Liam smiled.

'There, Mama – let's sit down here . . . ' Honor was pulling Liam by the hand over to a bench in the shade, and came back to tug at her mother's arm. 'And after we've heard a story, then you can put Kenelm to bed!'

Victoria was laughing, 'My dears, I'm sure Mr O'Brien must be very bored with my tales by now . . . '

'Not at all,' Liam said, reaching out to lift the heavy and drowsy little boy from Victoria's slight arms. 'I'd love to hear another story – as long as you'll promise that it will have a happy ending.'

'My stories always have happy endings, Mr O'Brien,' she said, and the light of confidence that was in her eyes as she spoke both comforted Liam, and disturbed him.

Liam left without seeing Garth that day, for after two hours, he still had not reappeared. Two days later, when Liam again returned to the house, it was to find that Garth was gone.

'He left yesterday . . . ' The front door was open and Liam, after knocking, had entered the hall as Victoria was coming down the stairs. 'Garth left for Sydney yesterday. He said Kenelm's crying kept him from concentrating.'

'Victoria . . . ' Liam was frightened by the woman's pallor. Her hair was mussed, her dress crumpled, she looked as if she had not been to sleep the night before.

'Liam . . . ' It was the first time she had used his Christian name, 'I haven't been able to leave Kenelm to go for the doctor, and now Gemma is ill, too. Would you . . . '

She did not finish. Liam had to rush forward as she fell, fainting, down the stairs, and only just caught her.

820

Garth returned to his family only hours before Kenelm died. Gemma, Honor and Victoria herself were ill for weeks, but gradually recovered. 'There's always cases of diphtheria at this time of year,' Edward Lawler said grimly to Liam and Clemency, who had come to stay in the house and nurse the family. 'This year it's just much worse – this is the third child this fortnight.' He turned with a warning scowl to Clemency. 'You be careful to stay away from 'Tillia and the boys for a while, now, won't you, Clemency?'

'Of course.' She drew herself up. 'It's not a fool I am.'

Edward's face relaxed into a smile. 'I know that. This is very good of you.' His eyes, dark-circled, showing the strain of this past fortnight, took in Liam as well. 'Very good of both of you.'

It was the end of the friendship between Garth Ellis and Liam. Aidan often wondered about it, but other than Clemency's muttered comments, virtually inaudible, when she returned home, there was nothing but Aidan's instincts to tell him that Liam felt Garth had let his family down in his behaviour at that time.

Liam, returning from visiting the Ellis family, just after Christmas, was considering leaving for Sydney earlier than he had planned. He went into the parlour directly he entered the house, planning to tell his grandmother, first. She would be a powerful ally when he broke the news of his coming departure to his father.

But Mary was not in her usual chair by the French doors. Liam checked upstairs, but her room was empty. He went to the kitchen.

'Miz Mary? I haven't seen her these past two hours. She was in the parlour.' Charity washed her floury hands and dried them, then joined him on a search of the house.

The storm that had been gathering all day, broke at that moment, adding to their worry. Even on the ground floor they could hear the force of the rain drumming on to the iron roof and the curved iron sheets that roofed the broad verandahs. Aidan, writing letters in his office, had seen nothing of his mother for a few hours, but, worried, sent Liam to the men's quarters to ask Maurie and Jim to join him in a search of the grounds.

He returned with all seven of the stockmen and farmhands, all concerned for Mary's welfare. One of the men rode to Killaloe, in case Mary had taken it into her head to walk there, for her horse and little gig were still in the barn. The others gathered in the kitchen, received their orders and headed out into the gardens, each carrying a lantern.

Clemency had ridden to Killaloe earlier that afternoon; Aidan somehow hoped that Mary had decided to join her. Still, he walked over the grounds, Liam beside him. The rain was cold, despite the heat of that day. The lamplight shone yellow on the leaves and tree bark and half-hidden statuary, but there was no sign of Mary.

Aidan and Liam searched the stables, the barn, the carriage sheds, then hesitated, hearing the voices calling, 'Mrs O'Neill . . . ! Cooee! Mrs O'Neill . . . !' from, it seemed, all corners of Shannon-brook Three.

'Father?' Liam said, 'She wouldn't have gone back to the home-stead on Shannonbrook One? If she was a little . . . confused – could she have gone to Shannonbrook One?'

Aidan was walking down the slope behind the barn, shining his lamp over the fences into the small yards. 'No, I don't think so. I hope so – but I don't think so. Ma!' he shouted, his voice disappear-ing into the rain that swept across the valley, 'Ma . . . !'

Over the fence, and into the horse paddock, dark shapes of the mares and their offspring, coming up to blink at the lights, their eyeballs white in the glare. Aidan and Liam shooed them away, kept shouting, moving all the time down towards the creek.

'Hell's outhouse . . . !'

'What! What is it?' Aidan whirled on his son.

'Horseshit – just there. I trod smack in it . . . '

'F'r God's sake, Liam . . . '

'I damn near slipped over in it! Do you . . . '

But Aidan had turned away, and in doing so, the swing of light from his lamp caught a dark shape on the pale grass, further down the hill. 'Ma? Ma!' He was running forward, throwing himself down on his knees beside the still, crumpled figure. The rain had plastered the black silk dress to her thin little body, the face was colourless, the eyes closed.

'Ma?' his voice shook; he touched her face, ice-cold. Liam was just coming to a halt beside him. Aidan looked up, thrust the lamp towards his son. 'Carry this, I'll take her.'

She awoke as he lifted her, opening her eyes tiredly. 'No, no, son . . . '

'It's all right, Ma, you're all right, now . . . '

'No, no . . . ' The little fists were pushing at his chest weakly, 'Let *him* carry me, *asthore* – he wants to. Sure I'm as light as a child for him to carry. He's much stronger than you, Aidan. Let him carry me, I'm as light as a child in his arms . . . '

He had stopped walking, looking over at Liam, but Liam, of course, did not know.

'Does she mean me?' Liam asked, puzzled.

'No,' he said, and holding his mother closer, turned away towards the house, for he knew she had gone from them.

822

80

Clemency had been filled with guilt that she had brought the diphtheria to the house from Victoria and Garth's home; but Edward Lawler said, no, her grandmother had died of heart failure; no one was to blame.

Aidan spoke little of his grief, before or after the funeral. He rose in the mornings, worked punishingly long hours, and went to bed exhausted. Thomas worried about him; Liam and Clemency grieved openly, but Aidan's defiant individualism had locked him away from all comfort. Thomas had cried in Ottilia's arms. Who did Aidan have?

He could have gone to Matty, he knew. But he was seeing less and less of her, lately. He knew instinctively she would not understand. He could not speak, anyway; his grief and his guilt could not be put into words. What voice had his mother heard to take her out of the house to such a distance? Why had he not noticed she was gone?

Liam found his father even more grimly unapproachable during this time, and only a week after the funeral, in January of 1877, he left for Sydney, nearly six weeks earlier than he had planned. Aidan, who had his own suspicions that his son needed, above all else, to put distance between himself and Victoria, did not object.

Why is it, Aidan wondered, as he watched the train pull out of Mittagong station, that the Ellis name seems to conjure up nothing but problems for myself and my family?

Aidan met Matty, quite by accident in the street, two days after Liam left. He had not seen her for some time, had been loathe, in fact, to continue their relationship now that his overly-astute children were home, preferring instead to visit a young widow in Campbelltown, and two ladies in the city, when on business for Tweedie and Company.

He had no idea if Matty missed him, felt a little guilty at forgetting her so easily, especially during lunch, when they were laughing together, and finding again their shared sense of humour, their past. Or so Aidan thought, until she said:

'I've taken matters into me own hands. I've put in for back

wages.'

'What?' Aidan grinned, 'And from whom? Grif?'

'No, you.'

'Is this blackmail, madam?'

'Nah, not at all. But seriously, Aidan, I bin real good to you, don't you agree?'

He was very amused. 'Aye,' he said, slowly, 'You've been an excellent companion – a great deal of trouble, at times, but on the whole, you've not allowed my life to be dull. And now you feel that you should be presenting me with a bill?'

'Nah, nothing like that. I just want you to say "yes", Aidan.' And she leaned across the table and took his hand. 'Say yes, an' I'll be grateful for the rest of my life.'

'Yes to what? I'm becoming very suspicious of you, Matty . . . '

'We couldn't keep up the payments on the farm, Aidan. It was too big for us, anyway, and too far away from you. I . . . I want to be closer to you, Aidan. I was even goin' to ask you if you'd set me and the kids up in a house in Mittagong, an' that way you could visit on your way through from one of your properties to the other, you know? You got the rooms above the stores, and there's that house in Queen Street that the Ellises used to own . . . ' Something dangerous in his eyes made her change tack almost immediately. 'But I never asked you, even though I would have thought we'd known each other long enough for you to think about it. I got no life with Grif any more – you ought to know that. I haven't slept with him since Harry was born – and I don't want to sleep with him again. I want you, Aidan.'

The emotion on her face frightened him. Matty had a considerable will, and to find that it was suddenly directed at him, was unnerving.

'Matty,' he said, keeping his voice low, controlled, for now he was afraid, very afraid, that this could easily turn into a scene. 'Matty, it wouldn't work, us living together – no, not even on a temporary basis . . . '

'We're good for each other, you know we are . . . ' Her eyes told him more than her voice; and she was right, in this. Their love-making was good, he could not deny this any more than he could deny that should she leave, he would miss her greatly. But to set her up as his mistress, to have her in his life as a permanent fixture . . .

'No, Matty. You're better off with Grif, and you know it.'

There was a silence, and he watched, worriedly, as her eyes opened wider. They ignored their food. The couple at the table in the corner left, and they were alone in the room. Matty seemed to

824

take courage from the fact that they were alone.

'You got thousands of acres. Thousands. And in all that space, you can't find no place for me. Or is it just me?' She raised her eyebrows inquiringly. 'Is it my kids that you object to?'

'No, Matty. It's the fact that there's no room, no time in my life to have a real relationship with anyone. I don't want you to be waiting for me, Matty, for I can't always promise I'll come.'

'You think I don't know that? You think I haven't lain awake and waited for you? Not just for days, nor weeks, Aidan – sometimes for months, years. Well, I've done waiting, lad. I'm building a life for myself and my family, and don't you bloody dare complain, Aidan O'Brien, 'cause as far as I can see, you owe me plenty.'

'What're you talking about?'

Her face was pale, set. 'We cleared a few acres, Grif and me, by the creek in the eastern corner of your latest property. Shannonbrook Three, is that what you call it? Well, we got our house half-built. And when Grif's finished helping me with it, I'm gonna tell him to shoot through, 'cause he's more trouble than he's worth, that man.'

She stopped because Aidan had frozen, was staring at her, and the chill of his looks froze the force of her words, too, and froze the courage in her. She put back her head defiantly. 'Ten acres, that's all, Aidan. Ten acres in the middle of all your thousands. Jesus, you can spare that, can't you?'

'No, Matty.' Low, dangerous.

'No?' She tried to laugh, 'I tell you, we've nearly finished the house . . . '

'No, Matty.'

'Aidan, be reasonable – where else is there for us to go? You know what a lousy provider Grif is. An' we're so close to the big house, Aidan, once Grif's gone – an' he wants to go, believe me, he'll be grateful when I tell him – then you can come visit me any time you want to. I can even visit you at the house, on days when . . . '

'No!'

He had half-stood, his face white. His whole body told of a ferocious defensiveness, and it was all Matty could do not to pull back in the face of it.

'You owe it to me,' she hissed. 'You owe me, Aidan, for all you done to me and my family . . . '

'What *I've* done . . . '

'You was the one who destroyed Nat, and Ettie, an' I had to work and whore for years to get to keep the Barley Sheaf, and if I wasn't so tired, so bloody *tired*, Aidan, of trying to cope on my own, I'd never have married Grif. An' you think that he married me to take care of me? Not bloody likely! He wanted to get his hands on that tavern, that's all. We had to sell it, finally, to pay for Griffith's debts – an' I wouldn't have cared, Aidan,' as he tried to interrupt, 'I wouldn't have cared, 'cause I'm tough, and I always bounce back when I'm kicked to the floor. But not now. No. No, me lad, not now. I'm not gonna sink that low again, an' I'm not gonna play the whore for anybody any more, 'cause I got my kids to think about.'

'Matty, I'll help you all you like . . . '

'Then let us stay . . . !'

'Not there! No! Not on Shannonbrook Three! It's mine, Matty! Mine! And I'll not be after sharing it with someone like Griffith Rodgers, nor any man!'

'He'll be gone, Aidan!'

'He'll never be gone! He knows bloody well that I've been helping you with money all these years, and he'll not leave when he can find all he needs by simply staying with you and his children and having me pay the bills!'

She was scarlet. 'He'll go, I'll make him go . . . '

'You've no right to! You married him, he's the father of your children . . . '

'Listen to him! For the love of God, listen to him! You bloody hypocrite, Aidan! Don't you bloody dare talk to me about the sanctity of marriage when you were whoring 'round on your wife practically from the moment you married her! And as for Grif's kids – they could be yours! Any one of 'em could have been yours! It was only luck that they weren't! An' if I'd had my head screwed on prop'ly, lad, I'd have made sure you thought one of 'em was yours! Women 'ave done it before this!'

'Matty, stop shouting . . . !'

'I don't care who hears me! I don't! Why should I care about you? You used me, Aidan! You used me for years, an' I got nothing to show for it . . . !'

He was standing, walking towards the door – but she caught up to him there; from behind her nails caught in his neck and dragged, deeply, up towards his ear. He cried out with the pain, whirled and struck her hard across the face. When she still came at him, he pushed her violently and she fell back, hitting one of the tables and knocking it over before she struck the wall.

'You bastard! You . . . !'

She stopped, and Aidan froze at the same time. A crowd of people, Donaldson and Hedley Warwick among them, were standing in the doorway, staring.

'Yes! Go on! Take a good look! See what he done to me!' Her lip

826

was bleeding, she was sobbing heavily, her hair had come loose and fallen down her back; he felt no pity for her, hated her. 'I'll make sure every one knows. I'll make sure everyone in this district sees you as you are! I won't rest 'til I do!'

He pushed his way through the crowd, avoiding Donaldson's triumphant gaze, the troubled, horrified look on Hedley Warwick.

He went to an agent and found a cottage for lease on the outskirts of Moss Vale. He paid the first year's rent and took the key from the man, still white-faced, trembling with rage.

That afternoon, with several of his stockmen, he rode to the spot where Griffith Rodgers was building his house.

It was the first time Aidan had set eyes on the man, but he found only what he expected. Griffith was a thick-set man, running to fat now. The face had once been handsome, weak. It was now merely weak.

He began speaking to Aidan in an ingratiating tone, then became more and more abusive as, ignoring him, Aidan's men went about knocking down the tent, piling the furniture and goods pell-mell into the wagon.

Thomas was with them, and he hated what he was doing, it ran too close to the vein, reminded him too vividly of Clare evictions. All the men went about their tasks tight-lipped, silent, obeying an Aidan O'Brien they had never seen before.

It was Thomas and Maurie and Jim who held Rodgers back while Aidan soaked the new cottage walls with paraffin and set fire to it.

Thomas, when he went home to 'Tillia, vomited all night.

When Matty returned home to the clearing with the children, already having seen the smoke and believing the worst, she found her home in ashes, and Grif sitting on a stump, toying with the keys to the new house. He was drunk, and declared to her white, visibly shaken face, that it was just as well . . . He waved the key. 'I'm quite satisfied,' he declared. 'Would've meant a lot of work. We can go back to town, now. Won't that be grand? Matty? I can't rightly blame the man. Let's forget him. We'll forget it, eh, Mat? Eh, Matty?'

The story of Aidan O'Brien burning down the squatters' hut went all over the district. For a while the wife of the man made claims that O'Brien had seduced her, but she saw early, Helena Warwick told her friends, that this did as much to discredit herself as it did Aidan O'Brien – not that there mustn't be some grain of truth in the allegations. Truth or an attempt at revenge, Mrs Rodgers soon ceased to press her story.

But the district took the tale of eviction and arson to its hotel bars and dinner tables for months afterwards. It pointed out only too well what everyone had always said about Aidan O'Brien. A hard-headed, hard-hearted ruffian . . .

These were the tales that Thomas heard, moving about the countryside on his business. He did not relay the stories to Aidan, who, anyway, did not seem to mind what the district thought of him, and Thomas even noted that, if anything, people actually treated his brother with more respect, a fearful kind of courtesy, when they were faced with him.

But within a year, the incident was all but forgotten. Aidan occasionally saw Matty from a distance when business took him into Moss Vale, but they never approached each other, Matty always avoided him.

She grew thinner, he noticed, as the years passed, and grimmer. There was now, he thought, something of Maura about her. She no longer wore colourful clothes – it happened gradually, as if this late venture into motherhood was robbing her of her youth more quickly than it should have done. She was like an exotic bird that was losing the bright feathers of the mating season, she was becoming almost drab; nowadays he saw her only in browns and greys, and always surrounded by the group of thin, dark-haired children.

Griffith Rodgers was working, Thomas managed to discover, in a lawyer's office in Moss Vale. The solicitor was a friend of Rodgers' family. Such men as Griffith Rodgers, Aidan reflected drily, were seldom allowed to starve. He and Matty would survive somehow.

It bothered Aidan, however, that his relationship with Matty should deteriorate to this. He had never before had to live at close quarters with an implacable enemy. Even his relationship with Donaldson was civil, and their differences had been caused primarily by conflicting business interests.

Matty had loved him, as much as she could love anyone. Yet it had come to this. The vital, grasping, indomitable spirit had been buried under demure brown alpaca, and hemmed in by a circle of demanding children.

He could bear that, she had chosen the path that Griffiths Rodgers would lead her; what he found hard to take was that she could so easily learn to hate him.

She did not ruin him, as she had said she wished to. She could have caused much more trouble, he knew, if she had tried. But no revenge came. They simply no longer existed in each other's lives. In a kind of impoverished respectability there was little left of the Matty he knew, and this, to a certain extent, was his punishment.

Matty had always been there, he could not foresee any change in her. Yet she, too, had grown beyond her need of him. It was one more of those incidents that made him feel vulnerable, his world not at all the same place it had seemed, only a matter of years ago.

His work took up most of his time, and his interest. Occasionally, he would feel the need of a woman's companionship, a woman's body. At these times he missed Matty very much. But there were other women, in Sydney, and a certain establishment in Campbelltown where he would go when his loneliness overtook him But as time went on he found that he needed it less and less.

Liam spent more than a year studying at Sydney University, less to prepare himself for his profession in New South Wales as to bury his thoughts in legal problems and conundrums; study was second nature to him, he enjoyed it.

He came home to Mittagong several times, and visited the Ellis family when he felt sufficiently detached from them to believe he could bear seeing them – he returned to Shannonbrook Three, and to Sydney, after these visits, with his self-sufficiency shaken, attacked his studies once more, and wondered when he would ever be free of his terrible tenderness for Victoria. That she missed him was obvious, and made his confusion all the greater.

At the end of the year, he was offered a position as lecturer in Legal History for six months, while the holder of that position, whom Liam had come to know and like, was in England on sabbatical leave. Despite his father roaring at him that he was once more being dragged down 'into the mire of academic *rawmaish*', he accepted.

It was while he was walking in the quadrangle one lunch hour, two months before his tenure was to end, that he was approached by a small woman in grey. He had been wondering, now he had applied and been accepted to practice law in the colony, if it was really what he wanted . . . had turned to greet one of the law librarians and, when he turned back, the woman was standing before him – he almost knocked her over.

'I'm sorry . . . ' He tipped his hat and was about to walk on.

'Forgive me – I heard the gentleman call you Liam – you are Liam O'Brien?'

'Yes . . . ' He stared hard at the woman. She had a fresh, clear complexion with hardly a line on her face, but her hair was prematurely and heavily streaked grey, in fact, almost white, throwing into prominence a pair of large brown eyes. 'Berri? Berrima Ellis?'

'I'm spending a few days at the library here,' she told him, as they walked about the grounds. 'I'm researching early colonial buildings. I have a publisher, now, you see – based here in Sydney – and this is my third book. I illustrate them with sketches from my photographs.

'I did one on seashores of New South Wales, another on the outback – Sydney and Melbourne people are becoming very curious about the rest of this country – many are travelling – I suppose that's what I am, a travel writer.'

'It sounds a very exciting life,' Liam said with genuine envy.

'It is.' She smiled. 'But we've been vagabonds for so long, Richard and myself, that we're longing to put down roots.'

'Richard . . . ' Liam's heart sank, then he remembered. 'Your brother, of course. Isn't he a doctor?'

'He was – and is again. He has a practice at Darling Point, and we live on the premises. You must come and dine with us, Liam.'

'I'd love to.'

They made arrangements for that very night, and after exchanging addresses, and agreeing on a time for Liam to arrive, they separated.

Liam was buoyed up with delight. He had gleaned a little information from Thomas in the two years since he had returned from Ireland, and he felt he understood Aidan's growling disinterest at any mention of Berrima's name. Suddenly Liam could not wait to get back to Mittagong. Father, you old gurrier, you don't deserve her – warm, giving, delightful little woman that she is. But she's your only hope. I'll have you on her doorstep with roses in your fist if I have to beat you into sensibility.

The house that Berrima shared with Richard was a fine, delicate-looking structure, strung about on two storeys with intricate wrought-iron verandahs. With its sweeping gravel drive and ordered garden, the house looked very much as he would imagine Berrima's house to be.

Nellie, older, plumper, beamed at him as she welcomed him. 'Ooh, how you've grown, Master Liam – Mr O'Brien I mean.' She took his coat and hat, regarding the well-built young man before her with fondness. His red-brown hair and the unusual, russet-coloured eyes were striking, and he had inherited his father's broad features and wryly humorous mouth.

'I'm delighted to see you again, Nellie – it's been many years.'

'That it has, Mr O'Brien. And many the sorrow in between,' she said, soberly, leading the way into the large and comfortable parlour.

Liam was puzzled by her words, but had no time to question her. Berrima was coming towards him, in a lavender blue silk gown, a fine cashmere shawl over her shoulders. The nearly white hair in its rolls and ringlets gave her something of the look of a French countess of a century before, and Liam took her hand, kissed it, and told her so.

She laughed, and it set the atmosphere for a light-hearted evening that was even more improved, Liam thought, by Richard Reynolds being absent, at a patient's childbed. Liam had not liked young Reynolds much as a boy, a spoilt, introverted child with a cutting tongue.

The doorbell rang at ten, when they were once again seated in the parlour, looking at Berrima and Richard's photographs, and they presumed it was Richard returned. But when Nellie entered the parlour it was to announce that it was a gentleman to see Mr O'Brien.

Liam glanced at Berrima, puzzled, but excused himself and went out into the hall. Nellie took his arm the minute the door was shut.

'I had to say that, sir. Please – he's in Mr Richard's waiting room.' And as he followed her to the rooms on the lower floor, she added, 'The gentleman is from the police, sir. He doesn't want to distress Miss Berrima, wants to be sure there's someone with her. You'll stay until Mr Richard comes home, won't you, sir?'

Bemused, Liam promised that he would; Nellie opened the door to the surgery section of the house, and Liam was confronted by a large square man, who introduced himself as Sergeant Healey, and who told him, gently enough, that the police believed they had found the body of Mark Ellis.

From that moment the evening took on a nightmarish quality, but even so, Liam could not, afterwards, regret that he had been there. Berrima, when he broke the news to her, had the sergeant brought upstairs to the parlour, and sat white-faced as he told them both the facts.

The body of an unknown man had been found in a narrow lane in The Rocks area of Sydney, four days before. There had been no identification on the body, and no one had been able to identify him. Although there were signs that the man had been drinking, there was no evidence of any foul play. Then, late this afternoon, a housebreaker had been apprehended, and on his person had been found a wallet, tooled with the name, *Mark Shaw Ellis*. The sergeant took the wallet from his pocket and handed it to Berrima.

She reached out her hand slowly, took the wallet, and stared at the fine quality piece of work; she had given it to Mark on their fourth wedding anniversary. She nodded. 'Yes, it's Mark's.'

'Our housebreaker admitted he found the wallet on the body

discovered in the laneway. Swore he hadn't harmed the man, that he was already dead when he robbed the body. We believe him, in view of . . . '

'In view of what?' Liam asked.

'That he died of natural causes.'

'How can you be certain?' Berrima asked. Her voice was barely audible. Liam glanced at her, could see white lines about her mouth, and was afraid, suddenly, that she might faint.

'Well . . . ' the policeman shifted on his seat, 'I hate to bring you news like this, but . . . Mrs Ellis, when a body is found – and there are many in these rougher areas of the city – and there's no identification and all the signs that the man was a . . . well . . . '

'A vagrant.'

Sergeant Healey studied the floor, finding it difficult to meet those dark eyes, large with shock and grief. 'Yes, ma'am. When it seems like a man is that type. With no evidence to the contrary, no one to claim the body, it's handed over, often, to the University.'

Oh, God, Liam thought, and reached for Berrima, beside him on the sofa, and took her hand. She did not seem to notice. She said, her voice toneless, 'The School of Medicine. The anatomy laboratory.'

'Yes.' Healey looked at her in some surprise, then remembered her brother was a doctor.

'And the cause of death?' Berrima asked.

'I don't know exactly, ma'am. Natural causes, is all my superior told me. I . . . I've been asked to tell you that the University has been notified, they'll be awaiting your instruction as to what to do with the remains.'

The word hung in the air. Liam glared at the policeman, who looked himself as if he could have bitten off his tongue.

'If there's no more questions, ma'am . . . '

'No. No . . . ' She rose, and saw him to the door, placing a cold hand in his, and thanked him.

Liam and Berrima stood together in the hall when the front door had closed upon the sergeant. The gaslight fell softly on them, the large clock ticked. Liam said, 'I'd . . . rather not leave until Richard comes home.'

The brown eyes came up to his, gratefully. 'I'm glad.' She made an effort to smile. 'You're very like your father, you know.'

'In what way?' He did not like to be told he was like his father.

'You somehow manage to be there when I need you.'

He took her hand, and they returned to the parlour.

Liam spent the night in the guest room, listening to each striking of the hours by the downstairs clock, and praying that Richard would come home before morning. It should be Richard who went with Berrima to the University. Richard would know about these things . . .

He fell asleep sometime after four a.m., and when Nellie woke him with a hesitant knock at the door at eight, bearing coffee and toast on a tray, it was to tell him that Mister Richard was still in attendance at the delivery.

It did not occur to Liam to cry off at the plans for the day, though Berrima gave him ample opportunity. No, he said, he did not mind. If she would not wait for her brother, then he himself would accompany her.

Nellie had recently married, and her husband, John, was now working for Berrima and Richard as a gardener and coachman. It was John who drove them at nine that morning, through the narrow streets of East Sydney, to make arrangements at a funeral parlour, and then on to the University.

'To think . . . ' Berrima murmured, as the carriage came through the heavy wrought-iron gates and up the sweeping cobbled drive, 'Mark was lying here all the time. All the time . . . '

Liam did not know what to say. When they alighted at the School of Medicine, he stood close by Berrima, but allowed her, since she seemed to wish it, to question the Dean.

The man was sympathetic, kind; Liam began to think that the whole business would not be so unpleasant after all, when Berrima said, 'Of course, I must insist on viewing the body. I must be certain that the body is that of my husband.'

'The police gave you a detailed description, Mrs Ellis. Surely, if you agreed with it . . . It's a little late, once the autopsy has been performed, that's why they didn't insist on your identifying . . . '

'But I wish to.'

The man looked pained, hesitated, then called an assistant to fetch the lecturer in Anatomy.

The smell of formaldehyde, faint but noticeable, entered with the small, austere-looking man in his dark business suit. Liam had the feeling he had not been far away. Both medical men were attempting to dissuade Berrima from viewing the body, and Liam could not help but add his own opinion. 'You had a detailed description from Sergeant Healey, Berri . . . '

'You understand, surely, Mrs Ellis,' the lecturer was saying, 'that an extensive post-mortem . . . '

'The mask is intact?' Her voice was cool, definite.

'Well, yes, but . . . '

'Then I must insist.' She gazed at them, pale but stubborn. The

833

doctors looked at each other, then nodded. 'Could you wait in the corridor, please,' the Dean said.

Almost an hour later they were taken to a bare room at some distance along a passage. It was the worst moment of Liam's life, gazing at the waxen, sunken face amongst the carefully-placed sheets. He looked once and turned away to gaze at the well-scrubbed floorboards.

'Yes,' he heard the controlled little voice at his shoulder, 'Yes, that is my husband.'

They left the room, then, and returned to the broad entrance hall. Through the large glass doors the winter sun was shining, the bare trees moved in the breeze. Liam wanted to run screaming through those heavy timber and glass doors, run across the lawn and keep running, away from the horror of this place.

The Dean had shaken their hands and left them to return to his office. The lecturer in Anatomy trotted to the doors with them, was saying in reply to Berrima's query as to the cause of death, 'It was a massive stroke, as the Dean told you; death would have been almost instantaneous. There were other factors, acute kidney and liver damage, and the heart was weak, but it was the meningioma that was the direct cause of the clotting, of course. There was nothing anyone could have done, you can rest assured of that, so you mustn't blame yourself, my dear. No doubt there were severe personality changes, hm? And the drinking, of course . . . headaches, eyesight problems. Oh, yes, it all fits the pattern. Tragic in a man so young – and so hard to detect.'

'What are you saying?' Berrima had stopped, was staring at the man.

'Why, the Dean would have told you, of course . . . A temporal lobe meningioma, Mrs Ellis. A brain tumour. Your husband would have been suffering from it for a very long time – perhaps ten years. You must have remarked on the personality changes, sudden mood swings, rages, perhaps, it all . . . '

The world was white, blinding white light, and when it dulled to the cloudy consistency of a heavy fog, she was gazing at the grey ceiling of the School of Medicine, lying full-length on the row of hard seats she had noticed by the doors.

And Liam, Liam O'Brien, looking so like his father, the shoulders stretching the material of his well-tailored suit, his hair fallen in his eyes and the brown-red eyes blazing, was shaking the poor little anatomy lecturer by his lapels.

'You fekking idiot,' he was saying. 'You fekking, fekking idiot . . . '

81

Liam arrived back in Mittagong in August, 1878, eighteen months after he had left. The winter had been cold, and it was snowing the day that Aidan drove the landau into the railway station to meet his son.

The train arrived, rushing past him with a roaring and a hissing and the smell of hot metal and coal smoke, the escaping steam filling the cold air, making the white snowflakes disappear, lost in cloud.

He could not see Liam in the groups of people stepping down from the train and heading for the station exit. Aidan walked towards the engine, peering at the faces that appeared out of the trailing steam and the falling snow.

A couple stopped before him, and he looked up with a laugh into Liam's face, turned to the woman . . .

'Hello, Aidan,' Berrima said, and held out her hand.

She wore a black cloak about her shoulders, the collar trimmed with fur, a black hat, small, elegant, with a trace of netting that almost masked her eyes, and her hair. Her hair was pulled back into ringlets at the back of her head, and there was nothing to tell a stranger that her hair had been a rich brown, nothing to tell a stranger that this woman could ever have looked like Anna O'Hagan. The hair was almost completely white, and there were faint lines upon her face, beneath her eyes, about her mouth. She looked tired, and strained. When he took her hand, she held her body stiffly, standing at a little distance, as if afraid of him. There was no real warmth in her dark eyes.

'Hello, Berri. Welcome back.' And he had almost, almost said, *Welcome home*.

He turned with a sense of gratitude to welcome Liam, but his son was pumping his hand even while he was beginning to edge off down the station. 'Hello, Father, good to see you – do you have the carriage outside?'

'Yes, I . . . '

'Good, could you let me have it? I'd like to drive out to see Victoria and Garth . . . ' Berrima began to speak, but he cut across her, 'I have some presents for the children. Berrima has her own gig and a real *maicin* of a little mare she's brought with her – they'll be unloading them, now. Father, Berrima was going to stay with Victoria, but the house is so small – I've suggested she stay at Shannonbrook, is that all right? Grand! I'll see you at home in a few hours – I'll tell Victoria you'll be over tomorrow, Berri . . . !'

'Liam!' To Aidan, the tone of voice would have frozen any other man in his tracks, but Liam was gone, handing his ticket to the station attendant, disappearing down the corridor of the station house. Berrima was glaring after him with vicious reproach.

'Would it be so intolerable for you, to stay in my house?'

The brown eyes came up to his, almost startled. They looked so much darker, now, framed by the pale hair. 'No, Aidan, of course not – but it may be awkward – for you . . . '

'Nonsense,' he said, purposefully misinterpreting her, taking her arm and guiding her off down the platform. 'There are fourteen bedrooms in the house, and the redoubtable Charity at the head of an army of small, silent housemaids. You'll be no trouble at all. Where's Nellie, by the way?'

'She and her husband John are looking after Richard. We have a house in Darling Point. I thought it best she stay there until I return.'

'And that will be . . . ?'

'Victoria was expecting me for a month . . . '

'At least that. You look as if you're in need of a rest.' He was watching the unloading of the gig and the horse. He felt Berrima gazing at him, but kept his eyes before him, as he said, statement, not question, 'Mark is dead, isn't he.'

When she spoke, there were tears in her voice. 'Yes,' she said.

He did not need to look at her to read grief and heartbreak into that word. He was filled with rage against her. Mark had divorced her, dragged her name through the courts and made a public spectacle of her. And finally he had died, probably drunk, Aidan decided, and she could barely speak for the sense of loss. She was a fool, as well. Senseless, faithless, feckless little hoor . . .

The mare was a pretty little black hackney. Her name, Berrima said, was Penny. They talked of her breeding and temperament for the first few miles, while the snow swirled about them, blotting out the view of the eucalypt forest on either side of the road. The subject of Penny exhausted, they lapsed into silence for several miles.

At last, because he could not stop himself, he asked, 'Was Mark's illness a long one?'

She was suddenly tense, on her guard. She did not answer him immediately, and finally, Aidan said unwillingly, with as much

836

kindness as he could muster, 'We won't discuss it if you don't wish to.'

'I don't wish to.'

'Then we won't,' he said with gentle finality, and inwardly cursed his son all the way home to Shannonbrook Three.

As they turned up through the main gates, she said, 'You must be very proud of the children, Aidan. Liam, I know, is a fine man. He was a great help to me after we . . . after Mark's death.'

'They're grand, sure,' he said, carefully avoiding the subject of Mark, as he promised himself he would, for the duration of her stay. 'Though they're not what I'd have expected.'

'In what way?'

'I thought – I don't know why – ' he scowled ahead – 'that Liam would be more scholarly, rather bookish and shy. And I was afraid Clemency . . . Well, between the convent and the family of Nicholas Mitchell, I expected a frightened little mouse, or a hard, sophisticated woman.'

'Neither of them are like you'd expected . . . ?'

There was a note of perplexity in his voice. 'It's like they never left Port Davey. Clemency's the tomboy she always was, runs the farm like a man – and looking like one half the time. And Liam, sure he's not still a minute, here or in Sydney, interested in everything, and settling down to nothing. Life with Liam is a series of enthusiastic beginnings.'

And he stopped, suddenly angry, but as much with himself as with her. He had been talking to her as if they were friends, as if she had never been away. And it came to him with a kind of sweet anguish that it was easy, comfortably easy to talk with her. She was a witch, that's what it was. He smiled, grimly.

Berrima leaned forward, on seeing her first glimpse of Shannonbrook Three. 'The house – why, Aidan, it's beautiful . . . ' She kept her gaze on the warm sandstone walls appearing and disappearing between the trees.

I built it for you. For you. He clamped his jaw tight against the words, his rage, the years of his hurt.

Charity had heard the carriage and was waiting on the front verandah. She stared, her eyes widening, then was rushing forwards. 'Mrs Ellis! Welcome home!'

Aidan pretended not to hear. He helped Berrima from the carriage, and unloaded the luggage, watching Charity, who had decided, thankfully, to live up to her name, and was drawing Berrima into the house. At the door, Berrima turned back. 'Penny, Aidan – remember what I told you – she can be a little temperamental . . . '

'Girl,' he growled, 'I've been handling horses all my life, I can handle this little toy, I'm thinking.' She smiled at him, and followed Charity into the house.

He placed the pony in a stall beside Blue, and, preoccupied, was stunned when the neat little head whipped out and gave him a sharp bite on the shoulder.

'Arra, y'bitch! Just like y'r . . . !' He stopped, guiltily, glancing at the door of the barn, and left the loosebox with a final baleful look at the mare, now attempting to nip Blue on the muzzle, and stamped up to the house.

Charity was waiting in the kitchen as he came through the back door. She flew at him like a distressed black Orpington, clucking, 'Poor little soul, have you seen the like? Like a washed out rag . . . I've put her in Miz Mary's room, it's warmest – don't go sticking out your lower lip like that, Miz Mary liked that girl, she'd want it that way.

'And that devil of a husband of hers gone at last – and a good thing, too – may his soul rest in peace. Fetch the sherry from the cupboard, there, will you, sir, and go sit with her and stop scowling, you'll frighten the girl to death.' Charity bustled off, back towards the parlour.

He did not fetch the sherry, but left immediately for the mill, and returned only in time to sit silently through dinner. He could find no words to say. But Berrima and Liam and Clemency chatted away together, and scarcely seemed to notice that he concentrated mostly on his food, and left the table early. They were interested in her life, the photographs, the tales she had to tell of goldfields and mining camps, of opera stars and theatres, of politicians and famous socialites. She wore a gown of black lace that was cut low and betrayed her still magnificent shoulders and breasts. Her waist was still tiny. In the lamplight, in her animation as she talked of a life she had loved, she looked twenty-five, a girl again. But not the girl she had been. She was like an impostor. Age had changed her face, the high, broad cheek bones, the stubborn little chin were more visible now, and the eyes were confident, even bold. She did not retreat in the face of Liam's teasing. Liam was almost flirting with her, and she – she met his gaze and gave him full measure of her wit, and her charm. Aidan escaped to his office, bewildered by the fact that he was affected. He should not care, he should not.

Later, sitting in the half-gloom, he heard Berrima and Clemency strolling in the garden. He approached the windows and stood looking out. He could hear no words, but Clemency was speaking animatedly. She was wearing a cloak over a frock of pale blue watered silk, and Aidan had not had much of a struggle to talk the girl into wearing it. Clemency had always been fond of Berrima. Liam obviously found her interesting. Even Charity accepted her. And he knew, suddenly, that it would be more than three or four weeks that Berrima would be staying with them.

He took a glass and his decanter of whiskey and poured himself a large shot. Drained it, waiting as the heady warmth of it spread through him. He poured another glass and drained that, too.

He began to feel calmer. He sat down on the leather window seat and gazed out at the gardens. The two women had returned, entering the house through the front door.

He had no comprehension of the feelings that were possessing him. He could not, despite his resentment, his hurt and his wounded pride, ignore the insistent voice that whispered that they were both free; Maura and Mark were gone, and beyond caring; he and Berrima were free . . .

They would never be free. He thought of these last years when he had needed her, when he could have helped her, could have saved her – but she would not allow him to save her.

No, there was no hope for them, now. The woman in the garden aroused no feelings of tenderness, or warmth within him. It was not Anna, it was not the child-woman Berrima. It was as if a guest had arrived, whose past meant nothing to him.

He had drunk too much whiskey. He went upstairs with careful precision, undressed and fell into bed, the room reeling about him.

He dreamed of Maura, of Anna – but an odd thing happened. He dreamed of the Sidhe of Craglea, and though, when she walked towards him, up the hill, he could not see her face clearly, he felt certain, even in his dream-state, that it was Berrima. He awoke and lay there, his body perspiring, despite the chill of his room, of his bed. So the dream was still warning him; it must be the Celt in me, he thought, I'm a little fey.

He rose and went to the window , and stood looking out over a white landscape. He thought, suddenly, of one of Devlin Kelly's story books that he had borrowed as a child. It contained the fairy story about a Snow Queen – he couldn't remember what it was about, exactly, except that she wasn't a very pleasant character . . . She stole people away, that was it.

Infatuation is a kind of madness, he told himself, staring down into the white garden as if Berrima would appear in it any moment. I was right to avoid it all these years. And now I'm too old, he thought, with a kind of satisfaction. I'll take my pleasures somewhere else, I'll not risk entangling myself with Berrima again. She only wanted me when she couldn't have me, only wants Mark now he, too, is beyond her. He hoped he would still continue dreaming of the Woman in Black, she served to remind him that his peace of mind, his jealously-guarded emotions were in danger.

He found his hands were made into fists by his sides – sure this was no joke at all. He would have to spend more and more time away from the house, keep away from Berrima as much as possible. It was bad enough to be haunted in my dreams, he thought, but this white-haired witch will be haunting my days as well.

He decided to leave for a few days in Sydney, immediately after breakfast.

Berrima had been a long time falling asleep. It was nothing new, she had almost become accustomed to lying awake, staring at the darkness for hours on end, only falling into an exhausted slumber just before dawn.

She was asking herself, now, why she had come, what she had expected. To meet Aidan at Garth's, or in Mittagong, somewhere in neutral territory, and after some months. She had wanted to return to the house in Queen Street, where she had known her last happy memories. Now, thanks to Liam, she was catapulted almost to Aidan's feet; there was no way she could politely leave, not for a week or so, at least . . . And could she bring herself to leave, now she was here?

She was as naive as she ever was, she thought savagely, and her restlessness drove her to rise and walk to the window, shivering, but not knowing, in the darkness, where to put her hands on her wrap. She stared out at a garden white with snow, the driveway was only barely discernible between the paler shadows of the lawns. She wished she was out there, in her little gig, heading Penny away down that drive . . .

To where? Wherever she went, the memory of the past would follow, the memory of Mark, all those Marks that had comprised the man who had been her husband for fourteen years. The memories would follow her – and the nightmares.

She found she was holding hard to one of the braids of her hair – it was an unconscious gesture she often caught herself in – it was as if she subconsciously wished to rip the thick, pale stuff from her head. Her hair should be dark, dark . . . She had looked at Clemency's thick auburn hair that night at dinner, and thought, mine was like that, more gold than red, but . . . Senseless thoughts. Other than dyeing her hair there was nothing to be done but become accustomed to it. Mark's legacy. One among many.

There was a slight noise, and she started, turned to the door – it was locked, of course. But that had not stopped Mark . . . No further sound, and she relaxed. The house was quite new – it was settling with the cold, that was all. She could not have borne it if Aidan had broken in on her and . . .

Tears spilled down her face. Tears for Aidan, whom she had never been able to reach and to whom she could not even try to reach, now. Tears for Mark, as he had been, as he had become. Tears, she told herself angrily, trying to wipe them away with her hands, of indulgent self-pity.

Yet afterwards she felt calmer. The childish weakness released some of the emotions within her. She knew she would tell him what had happened.

If he wanted to know. If he cared to know.

Her eyes traced the shadowy dark patches of deciduous trees wrapped in winter-sleep. The shapes had an order to them, even under their blanket of snow; it was a deceptive informality that matched the deceptive informality of his life.

'All my life I've loved you,' she told him, thinking of him lying somewhere in the house behind her, the keen eyes closed, the demanding mind at peace for these few hours at least. 'All my life, I've loved you. And I never really knew you. You never allowed me to know you. I'm grown up, now, Aidan. I'm wise enough not to love a man who has no tenderness in him. You've given me everything, over the years – but you've never shared yourself with me. Not your thoughts, your feelings.'

She had to laugh at herself, for one hand clung once more to the silver braid of hair.

A bird called outside, a hesitant little whimpering whistle of a call, as if to test the sound on the still blue air. Against the paling sky, the shadow of a home-flying owl was caught in mid-flight, and the artist in her thrilled. Oh, damn – *when* will there be cameras that can capture that?

Her work. The book on the Southern Highlands she had promised her publishers.

Her heart lifted. There was always her work. She would make something, something worthwhile, and this would stand for always, long after the memory of herself and Mark and Aidan had gone.

Her hands gripped either side of the window; suddenly she understood Aidan's feelings for this house, for his land.

More birds were calling, now, down in the silvering garden. Yes, she thought, I could perhaps heal myself here. If he'll allow it.

If he'll leave me in peace. I love this place already. I care for his children – and I think they need me. Aidan . . . is another question.

She yawned, a shaky yawn that was interrupted by a shiver. She returned to her bed, and fell asleep, one hand unconsciously clutching one thick white braid of hair.

Part 6
KELLY

He never loved the frenzy of the sun
Nor the clear seas,
He came with hero's arms and bullock's eyes
Afraid of nothing but his nagging gods.

SIDNEY KEYES

. . . they got ropes tied my hands and feet and (Constable)
Hall beat me over the head with his six chambered
colts revolver nine stitches were put in some of the
cuts by Doctor Hastings and when Wild Wright and my
mother came they could trace us across the street
by the blood in the dust and which spoiled the lustre
of the paint on the gate-post of the Barracks . . .

NED KELLY
The Jerilderie Letter

82

It was an uneasy peace that existed between Aidan and Berrima, but so well did they account for their actions, so scrupulous were their manners, that the house, if anything, ran more smoothly than before. Charity and Clemency, busy within and without the homestead, respectively, had had little patience with visitors, with the niceties of entertaining. Berrima excelled at it. Even when Aidan insisted that she send for her photographic equipment, she seemed to find time to make friends and renew acquaintances in the district, and there were suddenly more horses and buggies outside the homestead than ever before. First in manners and curiosity, then in genuine friendship, women as diverse as Miss Penridge and Tessa Russell, Doctor Lawler's daughters, Meg and Sophie, and even the redoubtable Helena Warwick, came to sit at tea in the large parlour, or drift with Berrima like colourful, somnolent moths about the lawns in the spring dusk.

Aidan tried not to think of this state coming to an end, of Berrima leaving, and did not dare, in the face of an aloofness that bordered on coolness, to ask her to stay. All he knew was that the house he had built in his pride and ambition, was suddenly a home, and he wanted things to go on as they were, did not dare hint at change that might upset the delicate balance.

Sam Russell, a regular visitor to the house, now, arrived in February, 1879, six months after Berrima arrived, quietly angry, more agitated, than she or Aidan had ever seen him.

He sat with them over tea in the parlour, and told them that he had approached Beecham Donaldson with an offer of purchase for his mill, on behalf of himself and eight of his fellow workers.

'I was lucky,' he said morosely, 'to escape with my life, let alone my job. I thought he'd have a fit of apoplexy. "No!" he roared, "How dare you, Russell! The answer is no, and damn your insolence, sir!" ' He drooped a little in his chair, '*Why* won't he sell? Everyone knows he's running that mill at a loss. He does the bookwork, but we all know how things stand. *Why* won't he sell?'

He unconsciously brought his fist down on the arm of the chair, a spindly foreign thing with tapestry seat and back; he checked it quickly for damage, and looked rather sheepishly over at Berrima. 'Sorry, Mrs Ellis.'

Berrima had been thinking, while Sam was speaking, it's one of the things I admire in Aidan. Ambitious as he is, tempted as he may be to buy Donaldson out, he's standing back, to help his friend. How he must puzzle his enemies in the district, they can never be sure of him. And, she wondered, can anyone?

She smiled. 'I can understand your frustration, Mr Russell. Aidan?' She turned, to find Aidan glaring into his cup of tea. 'Aidan, what's the matter with Mr Donaldson? Is it just pique? It seems an unreasonable attitude to take, if the offer was a fair one.'

'Pique, fear, wounded pride, sure, all of these.' He turned to scowl consideringly over at Sam. 'Did you happen to see today's *Herald*? I was going to ride over tomorrow with it to show you.' He took the folded Sydney newspaper from the table, and handed it to Sam, who stared at it for some seconds.

'He's advertised. He's *trying* to sell it. Then *why*, for heaven's sake?' he burst out. 'Why won't the man let his own men continue to work there?'

'I'm sure he'd be delighted to have the men continue working there, but that's a different story to having them own the place,' Aidan pointed out.'

'If he gets his money . . . ' Sam began, hotly.

'You're dealing with a man who's tried desperately to super-impose an English lifestyle on an Australian landscape, Sam. If it hadn't been for the gold rushes – who knows? Australia might have been the rigidly divided society that Britain and Ireland are. But the gold was a great equalizer. Baronets and ex-convicts, all scrabbling after the same goal – and with equal chance of success.' Why did he say that? He did not quite realize what he was saying, until he felt Berrima stiffen, was struck with the silent emanations of her dumb anger. She would be after thinking he meant her – and he had not meant that . . . Or had he? He went on, smoothly, not daring to glance at Berrima, although he could feel her gaze boring into him. 'But men like Donaldson will continue to play the squire and expect his vassals to remain in their place for ever. Class will tell, they used to say – but here, now, that's not necessarily so . . . '

'No,' Berrima smiled at Sam. 'Why, some of the finest families in Australia have convict blood in their backgrounds. The most imposing mansion can have a well-polished ex-convict at the head of its table. With money and carefully-learnt good manners, no one could tell.'

Sam grinned. 'Funny if Donaldson was an emancipist, eh? Wouldn't put it past him to be. He's got all the cunning of a man who's seen the worst side of life – all the greed, too.'

They both laughed with him, concentrated their attention on Sam for the rest of the visit, and swallowed their rage until the unsuspecting man was out the door, and riding his horse down the drive.

Berrima shut the door with barely disguised impatience and whirled on Aidan. 'How dare you!' she hissed, 'How dare you speak about me like that! Baronets and ex-convicts!'

'He didn't think I meant you!'

'He'd have read about the divorce, it's common knowledge in the district, and you know it!'

'Even if you're right,' coldly, wandering back into the parlour, 'and I don't say you are, they might recognize the baronet, but who is the ex-convict?'

'You! You, you grubby-minded great oaf! You! And don't think they don't still suspect that we were having an affair while I was editor of the *Argus*, and Sam might have heard about that, too. You weren't being subtle at all, Aidan, it was beneath you.'

'Girl, very few things are beneath me,' Aidan said, calmly. 'And I can't see what you're upset about. If I was lusting after you all those years ago when you ran the *Argus* _ and I don't deny that I did once, before you became so scrawny and haggard with bad temper – no one has any proof of it.'

'You made it as obvious at the time as you possibly could, making me editor in the first place, perching yourself on the corner of my desk day after day like a trained galah, watching everything from your beady little bloodshot eyes . . . '

'What are y' like, exploding like this? I don't like it, Berrima, when you spring a fight on me without warning. I'll oblige you, but I think you're being an hysterical female. For the last time, Sam wouldn't have thought I meant you, and certainly he wouldn't believe that I was an emancipist . . . '

'Are you blind, Aidan? Are you deaf? They've hinted about the possibility for years, everyone whom you've bought out, wiped out or made jealous by your success. You're a pirate, Aidan, you're a positive brigand! You've stabbed half the business population of the Southern Highlands in the back, at one stage or another – sometimes you've stabbed them in front of their eyes. Garth told me that they called you The Van Demonian when you were on the board of

Southern Highlands Iron and Steel – and everyone knows that nearly all the men who came from Tasmania during the gold rushes were ex-convicts . . . '

'You, too, came from Hobart Town, madam. You it was, with your scandalous conduct that became more scandalous when you finally took yourself off and out from under my beady little blood-shot eyes. Perhaps Mittagong was wondering whether you'd learnt your mode of behaviour within the walls of the Female Factory.' He stabbed a finger at her as she made a sudden movement, 'Slap me and I'll slap you back!'

She had made only a faint, unconscious gesture, and lowered her hand to her side. 'I was not about to strike you. I wouldn't demean myself by doing so.'

Their gazes were locked, Aidan scowlingly studied her features, aware that his heart was pumping with a very satisfactory kind of excitement. It was good, this. Though he could not understand how or why it had happened, this quarrel was long overdue. For so very long they had lived amicably – or seemingly so – and all he had wanted was to find some way of breaking through that detached, mature calm that the woman had come to possess. Until he found the real Berrima, the old Berrima, beneath this capable, self-sufficient facade, he felt shut out from her, a kind of rejection, the worse for no words being said. Now, it seemed, their resentments were rushing down upon them with the force of a flash flood along a creek that had been glassy calm. Berrima was saying, her jaw held tightly, 'Did the town talk about me very much, after I left with Mark? Or are you merely trying to hurt me?'

She saw his eyes narrow, suddenly, consideringly. He was wondering whether to be kind. And then he decided that she did not deserve it. 'And isn't it a trifle late,' he murmured, 'to be lamenting over the remains of your reputation?'

'Don't bandy words about in that smug way, Aidan. Tell me plainly . . . '

'It was a long time ago,' he almost said. 'People have forgotten.' But the thought was pushed aside by the savage and bitter knowledge that he had not forgotten, that for all Mark had done, to each of them, she had chosen to go with him. He swallowed on the memory of the loneliness of those years, pulled his mind back from it. 'A long time ago,' he repeated, trying to believe it. 'Why don't you begin worrying about what folk are saying now? The ex-convict and the adulteress, cohabiting together.'

'We're not cohabiting.' Her eyes were wide in alarm.

He had to laugh at her. 'No one else knows that.'

'Do you think I should go? The house in Queen Street is empty, isn't it? I could rent it from you.'

That was a mistake. Aidan gritted his teeth against her reminding him of the house she had shared with Mark, against the memory that claimed him, of lying on their bed, that night they had left, of the scent of her that still clung to her pillow; that she wished to return to that house and its memories of Mark.

'No,' he said. 'I don't want you to go. I ask merely that you consider that your reputation is in just as much danger now as it ever was.'

He left the room, then, and did not turn, but she caught up with him as he was entering his office, and took his arm with both of hers, sufficiently hard that she managed to pull him back, a little off-balance. 'Woman, this is my inner sanctum! You're after running the rest of the house like Catherine the Great, but would you please leave me one place where I can go to get some peace!'

But when he roared like this she knew she was safe, and stood her ground, her hands still around his arm. 'Telling me that – about my reputation – is that your gentle way of saying you'd like me gone?'

'I just finished saying I want you to stay. What do I have to do? Seduce you, marry you?' She had dropped her hands from him, and he moved to her, not liking that she chose that time to withdraw. 'Lock you up in the attic and brick you in?'

She looked oddly unsure, but now smiled, and laughed softly. He glared at her, and she laughed the more. He realized, then, with sudden bitterness, that she considered him to be joking. She had dropped into a chair, sat smiling at him, a smile that to him, was combined with fondess and not a little condescension.

'I wondered, Aidan,' she said, 'that was all. I don't want to stay where I'm not wanted.'

'You are wanted. I told you. You're useful. Since you arrived my son doesn't put his feet on the furniture and my daughter wears women's clothing at least fifty per cent of the time.'

'Is that all?'

There was a low note in her voice, a kind of a promise in the voice, but when he looked up, hopefully, she was gazing at him with only interested inquiry.

Then he said, coolly, 'Do you wish to go?'

'I love this house. I love Clemency, and Liam, they've been very kind – I'd miss them if I left.'

He made an effort not to grind his teeth. 'Perhaps I should move out to the stables. Perhaps you'd prefer it if I wasn't here at all.'

'Perhaps. I've always liked this room.' She smiled about at the four walls, 'I could make it my morning room . . . '

'Watch it, Berrima . . . '

'But I'd miss you, Aidan. Your bellowing and bullying and bad manners.'

His smile faded a little; it was one thing to know these things to be true, another to have them pointed out to one. 'I don't have Mark's manners, is that it? I don't have his well-bred charm. Balbrook did, undoubtedly. I obviously don't have the necessary good breeding to make a fit husband for you – you'll simply use my house as a holiday home until some other baronet or marquis comes to savour the mountain air, and then you'll be off with him . . . '

She said, 'You should have been a priest, Aidan. Yes. In the Inquisition. They had real need of someone like you; hard, who could see the soul and not the suffering of the human before you. You'd have excelled at that.' She stood, and he moved back only one step, was firmly between herself and the door. 'It was a mistake to come here, there's too much . . . ' She stopped.

'Too much what?' He moved a little closer to her.

She looked up at the dark eyes, watchful, unreadable. 'Too much bitterness,' she said.

'Swallow it,' he said, brutally. 'I can. You can, too, so.'

'It's hard, Aidan, living here. All these years, nothing's really changed . . . '

'And nothing will. We'll go on as we are, if that's what you want.'

'It's not what I want! Can't you understand that?'

'Nothing's happened, nothing's going to happen. I'll not be frightening you again, I'll not be making a fool of myself again, don't worry. And for what? You can trust me, Berrima. I'm not the kind of man who can sleep three to a bed, and that's what it will be.'

'That's up to you!' She almost shouted.

'We Irish have strong imaginations, and we're sensitive souls . . . '

'Don't boast about it. You can't free yourself from the past, nor from your guilt, for all your patronizing lectures to me . . . '

'*I* can't free myself from the past! Who's been mourning Mark all this time, all these years . . . '

'Mark deserved it! I owed it to him!'

'Bullshit! Bullshit, woman!'

'Your marriage was a parody, Aidan! You've no right to criticize me! You're more haunted than I've ever been!'

He took her shoulders, but she pushed back against his chest,

850

hard, with all her weight, and it brought her away from him, falling back against the edge of the desk, and a container of pencils and his pipe stand fell over with a crash.

The sound seemed to sober them. Into the silence, Berrima said quietly, 'I think this scene has gone on long enough, don't you? I'm sorry I lost my temper. It won't happen again. I'll leave you, now.'

As she moved, he half-stepped towards her, but on seeing her body stiffen, the look on her face as she met his gaze, he stopped. Berrima left the room.

He made up his mind to apologize to her the following morning at breakfast, but when he arrived downstairs it was to find that Thomas had joined the family, and a heated discussion was already in progress regarding the latest exploits of the Kelly gang.

'It was the boldest thing, to ride into Euroa and hold up the bank,' Clemency was saying. 'You must admit, they showed great foresight and daring – and that was in December – they've been wise to lay low ever since.'

'Daring and bold they may be,' Thomas said soberly, 'but don't be forgetting they're murderers, girl. The death of Sergeant Kennedy, going back to shoot the man point-blank . . . '

'He was mortally wounded – Ned saved him from a lingering death . . . ' Clemency said. 'And the two constables were shot . . . '

'*Must* we?' Berrima put in, but Liam cut across her.

'The Kellys should have left the area before they set Kennedy on his tracks . . . '

Aidan placed his paper beside his plate as he seated himself. 'They've left, now. The front page has it they've been seen here in New South Wales, heading north.'

'*Rawmaish* – 'morning, Father – I saw a newspaper that said that they'd gone to New Zealand.' Liam tapped the table top with his knife handle for emphasis, turned his gaze to Clemency. 'You can defend them all you like, girl, but they're doomed, the lot of them, even if Euroa hadn't happened. Kill a policeman – let alone three of them – and the Government will have to track you down, hang you. They won't look at the fact that the Kellys were hounded into crime by a corrupt police force. They have to hang them, now, to make an example of them.'

Aidan looked up, and saw Berrima standing, excusing herself. She would go to her little studio at the rear of the house, Aidan was sure; but before he could decide to follow her, Thomas had brought the conversation about to the missing sheep in the large paddock to the east of Shannonbrook Three. 'Twenty gone, altogether, Maurie tells me. I must admit, I'm surprised the numbers are so great. How do you hide twenty Merino ewes about here? Heinrich Henke is missing his prize bullock, too.'

Clemency laughed into her tea cup. 'Perhaps the Kellys have come to New South Wales. They did a bit of cattle duffing early in their career, did they not?'

'It's no cause for amusement, miss.' Aidan was chagrined at the thought of a day spent tallying his herds and flocks and arranging extra guards for them, with no chance to spend a few hours with Berrima. He turned crossly on his daughter, 'I'm spending years building up a small flock whose fine wool is topping the sales in Sydney, and in a matter of days I've lost twenty of them – and all you can do is joke about the Kellys.'

'Now, now . . . ' Thomas began.

But Clemency had already flared. 'I do a hell of a lot more than that! Who found where they'd cut the fences, tell me? And every day this past week I've been riding the boundaries with a rifle on my saddle – I'm doing as much as any man on this property!'

'Too much,' Liam put in. He had meant it kindly, in support of her, but somehow she took it as further criticism, stood from the table and was half-way to the door before the men could more than half-rise from their seats.

They sat down again in silence, waiting for the wire-screen door of the kitchen to slam. When it did, Thomas sighed. 'So much like her mother,' he said. 'A fine woman – but hard to know how to approach.'

'Like a porcupine,' Aidan growled.

Liam excused himself from the table, 'I'll ride with her today . . . '

Aidan smiled at his son. Liam had opened his office in Mittagong, and was doing well, but true to his word he helped as much as he could on Shannonbrook Three in his spare time. This was a Saturday, and Aidan said, 'Good lad,' as Liam headed for the door, appreciating that Liam could stay to help on the property and not be off about his own business.

Aidan turned to Thomas, and forgot Clemency for the moment. Later, he would blame himself for the events of that day. It had been a simple matter to say 'Good lad' to Liam. Might he not have thought to say some brief word of acknowledgement to Clemency? A word of praise, of appreciation where it was due, and Clemency blossomed. He knew this, had watched the smile on her as a child when some gentle word of his had lifted the burden of Maura's disapprobation.

But the woman Clemency had become puzzled Aidan. He remembered Maura telling him how he was spoiling her, indulging her in her independence, her tomboy ways running wild with the Malone girls. He wondered how right his wife had been. Clemency did a man's work, as she said, but her interest in running the property – and more, in her competency – placed her outside the realm of women he knew and understood.

But then, he thought, saddling Blue to ride off with Thomas, was there ever a woman he had understood?

'Do you reckon he'll marry 'er?' Bram Russell asked.

There was a suitably serious pause, each man leaned his elbows on the bar and changed weight from one booted foot to another. They had ridden further afield on this Saturday afternoon, and were propped up against the bar of the Surveyor-General Inn in Berrima.

'He's had six months to ask 'er,' Maurie said, finally, 'and he hasn't done, that's all I know.'

'She's a real good looker, with them big eyes and all that fantastic hair – Jeez, I don't think I c'd be living in a house with a woman like that for six months and not . . . '

'You just got back, Bram,' Jim Chaffer put in, 'you don't know how it is. The boss has hardly been round the place these past six months – he's staying over at Shannonbrook One mill for days at a time, or he's off in Sydney or Melbourne on business trips . . . '

'If he got married,' Bram said, hopefully, 'he might stay on the place more often . . . And if Mrs Ellis was The Missus, then she could make Miss Clemency stop riding round the countryside like a hooligan.'

The two voices on either side of him spoke at the same time, 'What've you got against Miss Clemency?'

'Nuthin'! Nuthin'! I don't like takin' orders from a woman, that's all, specially one that looks like a boy!'

'She nearly got killed by a red-belly stompin' through scrub in a long skirt . . . '

'Her orders make sense – we taught 'er everything she knows, all of us on Shannonbrook – she never thought herself too uppity to learn . . . '

'Someone's gotta be there to make the final decisions – she's better'n any overseer I've ever heard of . . . You ask for an extra blanket in winter, or if she c'd write you a letter . . . '

853

'You get sick sometime and you'll see . . . '

'Orright, orright! Bloody oath, are you part of a union on Shannonbrook? All I said was . . . ' Bram stopped when Maurie put a hand on his arm, and turned in time to hear, at the other end of the bar:

'Could you tell me where in the district I'd find a man by the name of Aidan O'Brien?' The stranger addressed the barman.

Maurie, Bram, and Jim looked at each other.

'Aidan O'Brien?' Maurie queried.

The stranger turned, 'Yes,' he said, and moved down the bar towards them. He wore a black suit, well-cut but dusty from what appeared to be days on the track, and he sported a beard of a red-brown colour. His hair was dark brown and his eyes grey, keen eyes; they flicked over the three boys. 'Do you know him?'

'Ah, it all depends on which Aidan O'Brien you mean. This feller you're looking for, come here about ten years ago, did he?'

'Yes, from Tasmania. I heard that he'd taken up a selection in this area.'

Jim had started smiling, turned away. Maurie said, 'Yairs, he did that. You haven't seen 'im for some years, then?'

The stranger ignored the lead. 'His land is close to Berrima?'

Jim began, 'That depends on which . . . ' but Bram had dug him in the ribs.

'Haven't got a score to settle with O'Brien, have you, mate?'

The stranger smiled. 'No. I can see you're friends of his. I simply wanted to see if he was doing well. From what I know of him, he deserves it.'

'That's about right.' Bram considered the man. He did not look like a bad type, but then again, he was not the kind of man whom one would like to antagonize, either. The grey eyes were mild, but there were lines on the man's face that seemed to say that this might be deceptive. Still, this was a very quiet Saturday night, and he could feel the mischief brewing in Maurie; a glance at him told him his friend was ready for some fun. 'Yairs,' Bram drawled. 'Life's been hard for O'Brien, all right. About all he can do, to scrape a living out of his little bit of a farm.'

He glanced again at Maurie, who was so in tune that he did not meet the look, and said without pause, because he recognized a somewhat upper-class accent to the man's voice, 'Last year the bears got into the corn – terrible damage . . . '

'The bank nearly foreclosed 'is mortgage this year.' Jim was beginning to join in. 'But he's managed to talk them into waiting for the harvest. O' course,' he added, ''is drinking problem didn't help . . . '

'Wait on, Jim,' Maurie looked warningly, 'Don't get carried away . . . ' Even the barman was scowling at them. Jim shrugged.

'O'Brien's a good bloke,' Bram said. 'Give you the shirt off his back, and it's not that he'd have a spare. Yes, he's a good bloke – share his last bear steak with you, O'Brien would.'

'Could you tell me where I'd find his farm?'

Bram started to say something, but Maurie cut in, 'Well, just south of town is a road that takes you to Moss Vale. You go through Moss Vale village, and there's a road to your right that'll take you out towards Robertson. Go along there for a few miles, past Henke's place on the marsh – you'll see a ridge off to your left – cut up through the paddocks – an' make sure you close the slip rails after you – and at the top of the rise, well, you'll see O'Brien's selection. Down across the valley to a hill on the other side – that's where he's got his hut . . . '

'A few cows . . . '

'Had some sheep until the dingoes got 'em . . . '

'You can see what's left of the cornfield, there by the creek . . . '

'I see.' The stranger tossed off his drink, a glassful of a strange flat pale liquid, nodded to the stockmen, and headed out the door. They grinned after him and watched him leave.

Maurie and Bram burst into suppressed laughter. Jim turned to the bartender. 'What was he drinking? Some expensive whiskey, I'll bet.'

'I wouldn't bet if I were you. It was ginger beer.'

That stopped the laughter. All three gazed after the man in some awe. 'A bloke who dares walk into a bar and order that has got to be bloody sure of himself,' Maurie murmured.

A pause followed. Then Jim said with a faint grin, 'Jeez, I'd like to be up on the hill above Shannonbrook Three when that bloke catches sight of O'Brien's little hut.'

The Hereford herd ambled away from the yards, up the slope to where they had been grazing before their muster. The four stockmen still remaining swung themselves up into their saddles and waved a farewell to the two men on the hillside. Thomas and Aidan O'Brien returned the wave. 'Come back sober!' Thomas shouted, and the men laughed. One called, 'No sir!' before they were off at a gallop, back to their quarters, to bathe and change into their best clothes, pomade their hair and head for Mittagong.

Aidan was still gazing broodingly after the herd of cattle. Thomas studied his brother for some seconds, sighed, and tried to break the mood. 'Well . . . That's it, so.'

'Damn and blast . . . When I get my hands on Liam . . . '

'Now, don't go blaming the boy – he can't be everywhere at once . . . '

'He should make sure someone is. Three Hereford cows – and the pick of the herd, too.'

Thomas grinned, could not help himself. 'What'll you do now? Have to call Peterson in – and that means Barrett will be snooping about . . . '

Aidan gave him a deadly look, and urged his horse forward at a walk, down the hill in the direction the young stockmen had taken.

Thomas brought his horse level with his brother's, his face serious, 'Now, Aidan, there's no room for pride. That's the second lot of cattle gone in a fortnight. And I've lost four yearlings from my own beef herd.'

'You're as much use as a stockman as Liam.'

Thomas turned in his saddle, sensitive as always to Aidan's criticism. 'Now that's unfair, and you know it. More'n five of us in the district have lost stock. If I'm not looking after Shannonbrook Two to y'r liking, then you know what you can do with it . . . ! I got me own farm, and . . . '

'I'm sorry, Thomas, I am. I'm looking for something to snap at . . . '

'Look somewhere else.'

'You do a grand job with Shannonbrook Two – I wouldn't trust anyone else . . . '

'Then take my advice now, Aidan. Call Peterson in . . . '

'No, I'll not have the police tramping all over my land . . . '

'Aidan, they're on your side, boyo.'

'Hal Peterson perhaps. Barrett? Never. He'd be quite happy to see me inside Berrima gaol – or even better, with my head in a noose.'

'Barrett won't like it if he gets to hear that you're withholding information . . . '

'He has enough to do harassing folk – he won't bother me.'

'He hasn't forgotten that you hired that lawyer for young Russell . . . ' Thomas paused, for down the hill from the direction of the homestead, came Liam, riding hard, 'Jaysus, look at that boy – and down that slope! He'll break his neck, Aidan . . . '

They reined in and sat their horses, watching Liam's lathered bay approach. As he drew rein sharply before them, half-turning his horse with the forward propulsion of his flight, he said urgently, 'Father! You'd best come home – we think we've caught one of the sheep thieves – Clem and me – we were checking the flock in the fifty acre, an' there were five gone . . . '

'*What?*'

'We caught one of the thieves, lurkin' about up on the slope above the creek – hell, Father, come on! Doctor Lawler's with him now, he might die before we get back, I had to hit him pretty hard, he was threatening Clemency . . . '

Aidan and Thomas glanced at each other, then turned their horses, without another word, and followed Liam back down the slope.

83

It was a mixed blessing, Berrima thought, that Doctor Lawler had brought his two eldest daughters for a social visit on that particular afternoon.

Meg and Sophie were twenty-four; not yet old maids, but there was a desperate eagerness about them, a coyness that did not match the astonishing magnificence of their dress – for they were very fashion-conscious – and this tended to fill men, and most women, with a sense of unease. It would be two men in a million, Berrima thought, who could tolerate the Lawler girls' giggling feather-headedness. No country district in Australia, even with the veneer of wealth that the Southern Highlands had, would possess men who could afford a woman who was purposefully, wilfully, decorative only.

Edward Lawler himself worried Berrima. His wife had died eighteen months ago, and from the time Berrima had arrived back, Edward's kind, round face had been turned towards her with interest. He seemed impervious to the fact that she was living in Aidan's house. Worse, Aidan seemed impervious to the dreaming way Edward looked at her over the tea table when he came to call. Today, she was certain, he had brought the girls to show them off to her. Berrima poured tea for them, chatted to them, and could barely contain her yawns.

When the little cavalcade came up the drive, Liam and the three horses, Clemency driving Heinrich Henke's little sulky, Berrima almost welcomed the diversion.

But once the unconscious man on the carriage seat had been

carried, with difficulty up the stairs and settled in a bed in one of the spare rooms, Berrima knew that except for his medical knowledge, Edward Lawler – and worse, his daughters – were the very last witnesses they needed.

In the man's wallet there was quite a sum of money, eighty three pounds, but there were no other papers. There was a gun, a wicked-looking bluemetal American weapon, that the man had worn strapped in a special kind of harness about his chest. And there was the name, *Kelly*, tooled into the base of the gun's handle. In the saddle bags and the blanket roll attached to the saddle of the horse were tobacco and paper and matches, a change of shirt and under-wear, and nothing more.

The Lawlers left, filled with suppressed excitement, before Liam arrived back with Aidan and Thomas.

'You can imagine what they think,' Berrima said, as she stood between the two brothers in the guest room, gazing down at the pale, bearded face on the pillow. 'That latest rumour in the Sydney newspaper that you spoke of this morning, Aidan – of course Edward had read it. He said, as he was leaving, that he'll call and see Sergeant Peterson and Mister Barrett.' Aidan groaned. 'We tried to persuade him to wait, but there was nothing we could say in the face of their . . . well, it looked like glee.'

'I'm sure it was,' Thomas murmured, 'Fond as I am of Edward he can be a fierce fool at times.'

Berrima turned to Aidan, 'Can we have Maurie or Jim stay in the house tonight, Aidan, just in case?'

He looked over at her with a faint smile, 'In case this boyo is Ned Kelly?' She flushed a little, but before she could retort, 'Maurie and Jim and Bram have been working two weeks without a break, I've given them three days off. I don't think we're in any danger from this young man at least 'til the lads come back. What was it Lawler said our Mister Kelly was suffering from – two cracked ribs and concussion? He'll not be moving for a while, Berri.'

Berrima was unsure, but did not insist. She led the way out of the room and down the stairs. Liam and Clemency sat on the front veranda steps, still surrounded by the contents of the man's saddle bags. The house was warmer than the evening air, and Berrima, in her thin muslin dress shivered slightly. The cool southerly breeze that she would at any other time welcome, moved through the pines with a surly whispering. A few petals from a rose bush at the end of the verandah blew along the floorboards, across the scattered, pathe-tically few personal belongings. Her gaze caught the heavy hand-gun, lying by Clemency. It is this, she thought, more than anything else, that worries me. She started when Aidan said, abruptly, 'Clemency, I want to know exactly what that man said to you.'

Clemency looked a little startled, then uncomfortable. 'When?'

'When he jumped you up there in the hills.'

She was conscious that all four of them were gazing at her, waiting. 'Well . . . I didn't exactly wait for him to jump me. In fact, in a manner of speaking . . . ' She took a deep breath, 'I jumped him.'

'*What!*'

She talked quickly, defiantly, perhaps wary of the look on her father's face, 'I could tell by the look of him that he was up to no good, or why would he be up there in our hills? If he was visiting us, why didn't he come up the front drive like everyone else?'

'Am I to understand that you shot at him?' The voice was so calm, she almost shrivelled beneath the gathering threat of his tone.

'He . . . it was . . . there was . . . yes. I kept him bailed up till Liam . . . '

'And you – ' Aidan turned and hurled the words like an accusation at his son – 'did you stop to ask him his business?'

'Stop to . . . ! He had a gun trained on Clemency . . . '

'Em . . . no,' Clemency interrupted, 'He didn't have it in his hand when he caught me, he might have had when you saw him chasing me . . . But I found it in his shoulder holster when we put him in the carriage, remember?'

'Well . . . yes. Maybe. But he had the gun on you when he started after you, I saw it – and I wasn't going to wait to pass the time o' day with the man! I hit 'im with the butt of me shotgun.'

A silence followed. Aidan's gaze went from one to the other of his children, then he said in a voice that betrayed more amazement than anything else, 'It's to my shame that you don't have a brain between you.'

'Look you, Father . . . '

'Em, Aidan . . . ' Thomas edged off towards the verandah steps. 'I'll be leaving you, so. I'll call back early tomorrow morning before Mass, shall I? And let me know if you need any of my lads here in the meantime.'

They bade him goodbye, and he trotted gratefully down the steps to his horse.

Before he was out of sight down the drive, Liam had stood, was volunteering to spend the night with the two stockmen sent to guard the large flock in the east paddock. Aidan sighed and let him go into the house for an early dinner in the kitchen before riding out with blankets and ground sheets for an uncomfortable night's vigil.

Berrima was gathering up the scattered belongings of the man Kelly, and turned to carry them off into the house. Before he could follow her, Aidan glanced at Clemency. Something in the set of the narrow shoulders made him pause, and he lowered himself down onto the front step beside her.

'I've brought trouble on us, have I not?' She made it less a question than a statement of fact.

'He could be one of the men stealing the stock, Clemency.'

'I may have killed him.'

'Och, no. He'll live.'

'He's not Ned Kelly, Papa. I had him pinned down by firing close about him, and he took shelter behind a tree, called out and asked me if I was the police, or what was my quarrel with him – I didn't answer, for if he'd heard my voice he'd have known I was a woman. I didn't really notice the sound of his voice then, but when he rushed me – when my rifle ran of out of bullets – he tackled me and took the gun out of my grasp, and "Madam, I think there has been some slight misunderstanding . . . " he said. He didn't sound like any Irish-Australian I've ever heard. Educated – even upper-class English.'

'Anglo-Irish Kellys,' her father murmured, his gaze on the darkening gardens before him, the shadows under the pines between the rhododendrons. 'I seem to be haunted by Kellys. And none of the meetings are auspicious.'

'You were educated by a Kelly, were you not?'

'I was, I shouldn't forget that. All I am, I owe to that man.'

She watched her father's scowling face for a moment. 'Papa, what is it you're worried about? That Barrett might find out about your years in prison?'

'Aye, that bothers me – odd, is it not? I don't care what the world thinks of me, if Father Davis castigated me from the pulpit as a right gombeen man – there are enough of them about here. But to be known as an ex-convict . . . It's a stain that'll blacken not only myself, but you and Liam, and your children. When I first came here, I didn't care if people knew – now I do.'

'People knew in Tasmania . . . '

'They were more tolerant in Tasmania. I didn't know, when I came here, what kind of area this was – it's as if every wealthy family in Australia feels it has to own a piece of the Southern Highlands. Why, I don't know, but there it is. It's an agricultural Mayfair.' And as Clemency laughed softly, 'I've come a little higher up the social ladder than I meant to, Rebel. And now I'm here, I'm realizing what a long way it is to fall. I don't want to fall.'

'You won't,' she said, and her confidence made him grin.

'So,' he said, 'and you don't believe that we have Ned himself upstairs? You'd be world-famous if he should be.'

'Arra, stop. There'll be trouble in the next few days, though, for Doctor Lawler and his gaggle of daughters will have spread the rumour that he is Ned Kelly – it'll be all over the district.' As her father scowled, she added, 'It was stupid of me. I can't even blame Liam. I should have approached Kelly with the rifle pointed at him and demanded his business. It was the fact that he was laughing that enraged me, you see. He sat there on that great black brute of a horse, looking down over the creek to the house here, and *laughing*, as if he'd perpetrated some great practical joke. I presumed he was one of the sheep and cattle thieves, and I lost my temper,' she finished morosely.

'It's hard to think clearly sometimes.' Aidan's voice was calm. 'In an emergency, especially. I've made mistakes myself, placed myself in dangerous situations when I needn't have.' That winter's night in Killaloe, the lane that led to Reddan's barn, and Seamus's death . . .

'I give orders 'round the place like an overseer,' came the disgruntled little voice beside him, 'yet I can't keep my head myself. I should stay home with my needlework.'

'Nonsense. I couldn't do without you.'

Her head came up sharply, 'You don't mean that.'

'I do indeed.' And he was speaking truthfully, should have, he realized, long ago. 'There's no overseer on Shannonbrook – in the nature of things there's four of us. I suppose I'm the head of the place, but the men respect you as well as myself, Thomas or Liam. You do a grand job, Rebel, and I'm proud of you. You've learnt more than many a young man would about running an estate – you must learn, also, that you're not above making embarrassing mistakes. A man has that right, you have it, too. If you can't show understanding of your own weakness and drive yourself too hard, you'll have no understanding of your workers – and you'll be a hard mistress because of it.'

She had been watching him, drinking in his words, and now leaned forward impulsively and kissed his cheek.

He placed an arm about her, and they sat there in companionable silence for a while, watching the gathering dusk. The sun was setting behind them, at the rear of the house; the pines before them were washed with pink in its reflection. The pair of kookaburras who had raised their young in a nest in one of the oaks at the head of the drive, chortled in what seemed like hysterical delight in the evening, and the currawongs, winging in over the fields, sounded their *curra-curra-currawah* as some kind of entrance anthem for the night. Far off on the horizon lightning danced, silently, a false promise of rain, of relief to the dry earth that would not come, not yet.

Berrima made up a cot in the injured man's room, and despite Aidan's pressure that he be allowed to watch the man, Berrima insisted that she would be the better nurse, and in the end she had her way.

The man Kelly lay as if dead all night. Still Berrima could not sleep, rose a dozen times to check if the silence meant that his breath had left him. But he breathed quietly, and she would go back to her own small bed, tell herself that she was exhausted, she must sleep – but sleep would not come.

This was such a quiet house. Whether because it was new, or so sturdily built she could not guess, but she had never known a house to be so *silent*. She had noticed it in her own room but it seemed doubly eerie in this room, where she shared the space with another . . .

For the first time in . . . five years. The thought amused her. If the man was Ned Kelly, she could tell her grandchildren. No. She must stop that. The poor man – he was not Ned Kelly. And if he was a sheep thief he certainly did not dress in a practical manner. She glanced towards the wardrobe where she had hung the man's suit after she had cleaned the dust from it. The label inside the suit bore the trade name of one of the finest British tailors; the hat came from a men's hatters in New York. What kind of sheep thief was this?

The breeze through the open casements stirred the lace curtains, and the shadows caused by this made patterns across the man's bed. So still . . .

She rose and went to the bedside, lit the lamp, turning the wick down low, and gazed at his face. He was a handsome man, and from what she could tell, for the beard was heavy, he was thirty, to thirty-five years old. His hands lay on the coverlet; the fingers were long, sensitive, there were callouses from the reins, but he had done no hard manual work. She compared them with Liam's broad, capable palms, or Aidan's powerful, scarred hands. No, this man had done little labour in his life. He was very fit – she had helped Doctor Lawler undress him and wash him, and the man had a fine body, slim, broad-shouldered. He was a drifter, perhaps, spending most of his time in the saddle . . .

Then why the gun? Why that instrument of death that Liam had toyed with all evening before her reluctant gaze, commenting on the fact that the weapon was beautifully kept – and the holster that had been around the man's chest. What of that? So the revolver was within his reach, whenever he needed it.

She shivered, although the night was not cold, then turned down the lamp, and returned once again to her bed. She found she wanted Aidan. She found that she had been able to look upon this young man's body with clinical interest, it reminded her only of how long it had been – how very long . . . And it was Aidan she wanted. Aidan who lay a thousand miles from her, just along the corridor.

She fell asleep only as dawn was touching the sky outside the window, when the birds whose songs had become familiar to her over the past six months began to waken in the trees of the formal garden. And in the bed across the room, the stranger, too, slept on.

Aidan spent a restless night. He had been worrying about Sam's lack of success in persuading Donaldson to sell his mill, and he lay trying to think of ways of breaking down Donaldson's stubborn resistance. But in the middle of this problem, and his more personal problem of the missing stock, had come this stranger. And Barrett would soon follow, he knew it. The very drama of the situation was such that the magistrate would thrive on it.

In the fourteen months since Bram Russell's trial, John Barrett had earned a reputation for harsh punishments delivered from the bench, and for some interference in police matters to an extent unknown in the district for twenty years or more. Barrett belonged to an era when police rule was absolute. In some areas it still held sway; the Kellys were victims of it. But the Southern Highlands was puzzled, uneasy, about Barrett while being half-pleased that crime was kept so strictly in check in the district.

Aidan tossed in his bed, unhappily. And the scandal of it – that was part of it, the bloody scandal of a man suspected to be one of the Kellys, found on *his* land. The police over the border in Victoria were hounding the Irish settlers who were sympathetic to the Kellys. There were honest traps, sure. Peterson and young Foles were two – but the legacy of the police force in the Australian colonies was this, that many of their number were ex-convicts, or had trained, the younger ones, with men who had been the bullies of the prisons, who naturally gravitated on release to a job where they could continue to bully, now with the sanction of the law behind them.

He tried not to think of the fate of the man Kelly, if he were connected with some low dealings. What if he'd killed innocent women or children? Aidan would not feel sorry for him then, sure. *But he was caught on my land. If he hangs, it will be because he was kept prisoner in my house. I will have helped in his death.*

He told himself that he was a wealthy landowner, that he now held a position of some respect in the district, despite his prison background. He had joined the upper classes through his own hard work, through sacrificing his family's happiness, perhaps even Maura's life. He held all this now in the three tracts of land called Shannonbrook. He had become one of the landed gentry – some even called him a squatter, and he liked that, for it gave him a sense of permanence, a history that he would like to have believed he possessed. And now, belonging with these people, he must take his stand with them. The stranger was a threat to the order of things – so he would be judged amongst Aidan's circle of acquaintants. Kelly was a potential predator, with his killer's name and his killer's gun, and the powerful and the wealthy, with so very much to lose, must close ranks against him. Destroy him, or drive him out, he was not one of them. Aidan, admitted, and mostly accepted, within the pale, must show himself at one with his fellows. They would be watching him, would prefer it if he showed an even greater amount of zealousness than they. He should, after all; to prove that he was one of them.

Berrima awoke early, went briefly to her own room and changed her dress before returning to the sickroom. She sat with a book in a chair by the bed, but it was difficult to concentrate. The man Kelly was the only one who seemed relaxed in the entire house; there was tension to everyone, she had noted it last night at dinner. Aidan, particularly, seemed worried and preoccupied. As if he were threatened, as if his carefully-built castle were under siege. And all due to this man . . .

She looked up, then, and her heart stopped, changed beat, so eerie it was to find those grey eyes watching her, the face that she had bathed and worried over for fifteen hours suddenly alive, an entity, an intelligence that she knew nothing about, and watching her.

'You've been awake a while.' Her voice sounded calm, at least.

'I . . . ' he began, but stopped; his eyes, puzzled, studied her.

His breathing was shallow, now he was awake he was tensing, the pain in his ribs would be claiming him, and he must be frightened. She felt more confident at this thought, and felt pity for him once more. She leaned forward a little, and said gently, 'Can you tell me who you are?'

The grey eyes were calm; she noticed they were soft eyes, perhaps it was simply the dark lashes, but no. His face was lined, grim, but

864

the eyes held a gentleness that was completely at variance with the rest of him. He smiled, slowly, and said, 'I'd hoped you might tell me.'

'Who you are? I don't know you. Is your name Kelly?'

'Kelly? No. But it means something. Something . . . ' His eyes half-shut, then he opened them again, watching her as if he were waiting.

'You remember nothing?'

His voice was soft, well-spoken, the accent indeterminate, upper-class British with something – American? – over it. 'I didn't . . . panic too much. I thought . . . I hoped . . . ' The smile pulled again at the rather grim mouth, a mouth unused to smiling. 'I hoped this was home. A charming room. Comfortable. I hoped I knew you. Forgive me . . . for staring at you that way. I looked at the room . . . and at you . . . until I thought I knew you both. But I don't . . . '

'No.'

He gazed around the room, the eyes becoming unquiet, betraying his confusion; he turned away from her, and she waited, but after a few seconds it was obvious that he was sleeping, lightly, more shallowly than before.

Clemency was waiting outside the door when Berrima left the room to fetch warm water for the jug. 'Berri? He's awake, isn't he?'

Clemency, too, looked as if she had spent a restless night, there were shadows under her eyes. 'Yes,' Berrima said. 'He woke briefly just now, but . . . '

Clemency, still clad in only her nightdress, was headed for the door, and Berrima placed a hand on her arm. 'Clem, you can't go in there like that.'

'For heaven's sake, I'm covered from neck to toes! I must speak with him . . . '

'Later, when you're dressed. And Clemency . . . ' The younger woman had turned away towards her own door, and Berrima hesitated, 'Wear a dress, today, would you? For your father's sake. Mister Barrett and Sergeant Peterson may be here this morning.'

'Trail about in a dress just to impress a few policemen and a hairy, dirty bushranger? I'll not. I'll stay out of the house altogether rather than that.'

She did not wait for Berrima's reply, but turned away, returned to her own room, and closed the door behind her.

Across the room, Clemency's reflection in the full-length mirror stared back at her. White nightgown. She looked ridiculously young. She approached her reflection until close enough to see her own age in the glass. She thought of the mad years in Europe with the Mitchells before it had gone so wrong, become so ugly. Now, with the coming of this man, life had gone wrong all over again, she had sensed it, in the moment when they had stood close on the hillside the previous day, and the grey eyes had studied her face with the same interest she had seen in men before. In Europe, London, no not here. She moved closer to her twin in the glass and studied each wrinkle and line in her face, and wished one could lose one's naïveté with the years as easily as one lost one's skin tone. Growing older would have its compensations if one inherited wisdom automatically.

Barrett and Peterson arrived later that morning, questioned Clemency and an apparently uncooperative Kelly. She did not witness this latter exchange, but waited downstairs, thinking of the fuss the congregation had made of the family after Mass that morning, people questioning, commiserating, *congratulating* her, while all the time that man lay upstairs, injured, and perhaps innocent, and it was all her fault.

The tension between her father and Mr Barrett was obvious, and when Aidan refused to give the man up into police custody until Edward Lawler called and pronounced him fit to travel, Clemency and Berrima had gazed at each other and waited for Barrett to explode. An iron-grey man, hair, eyes, voice; hard and cold. He did not take lightly to being defied. Even Hal Peterson stood braced, it seemed, for some blistering emanation from Barrett that would land Peterson in the middle of a tug-o'-war between friendship and responsibility as a police officer. In the end, he suggested quietly that perhaps they could visit Thomas O'Brien and question him about his missing stock, thus giving the doctor time to arrive. Barrett left, with the young policeman, and the confrontation was, for the moment, diverted.

The man Kelly had dressed, Berrima told Clemency, when he knew he was to be held for questioning. Clemency approached her, now, in the kitchen, and asked to be allowed to take the man's dinner to him on a tray. Doctor Lawler had been sent for, but had not yet arrived, neither had Barrett and Peterson returned from Killaloe. Berrima was preoccupied and busy, helping Charity, it was obvious that they would have to invite Barrett and Peterson to stay for dinner. Clemency made a plate of cold chicken and salad and headed, with the tray, for the man's room.

She knocked briefly on the door and entered, balancing the tray with difficulty. She placed the tray on the dresser, shutting the door behind her, before she looked up.

866

Kelly surveyed her with a slight scowl from where he stood by the window. He was fully dressed in the black suit; had shaved his face, except for a moustache, and with his hair neatly combed, Clemency was taken aback by how attractive he was.

He said, 'I'm sorry. I didn't recognize you for a moment.' He was polite enough to add merely, 'You have your hair up.'

'Yes. I nearly didn't recognize you, either. I've brought your dinner, Mister Kelly.'

'Thank you.' He had not looked once at the tray. After a pause, he moved towards her slightly, 'I owe you an apology. I hope I didn't frighten you too much – our first meeting wasn't exactly auspicious.'

'You shouldn't have shot back at me – y'r lucky I didn't kill you.'

The man almost smiled. 'I'm glad you restrained yourself.'

Clemency was beginning to feel unsure of herself. She somehow suspected that sheep thieves would not use words like auspicious. Perhaps it was merely an act but her first impression of him seemed more and more to be the correct one, he seemed educated, he did seem like a gentleman. She said grudgingly, 'I shouldn't have been so hasty, I suppose – and I'm sorry, too, that Liam hit you as he did. He was only trying to protect me.'

'He does that. Zealously.'

There he went with the long words again. For all the books I've read and all the years with the Mitchells, I don't speak like that, she thought. 'It's our fault, too, I suppose, that you're in trouble, now. What with the stock that's been vanishing in the district, and that trouble in the south—'

'Trouble?'

'Everyone's so interested in . . . in the Kellys. They're even reporting their exploits in the London *Times*, I've heard. All the newspapers are full of conjectures about them . . . So y'see, whether you're a bushranger or not – you picked the wrong time to arouse supicion in Mittagong, Mr Kelly.'

As she turned back towards the door, he said, 'So you believe I'm Ned Kelly?'

She turned back to him, startled to find that he had moved closer to her. 'It's Mr Barrett's opinion that counts now. What I think doesn't matter . . . '

'It might to me. Mr Barrett seems to think that your brother interrupted me in an attempt upon your virtue . . . What do you think?'

'I have to go to dinner.'

As she turned to the door once more he had moved forward quickly, and the door slammed shut before she had opened it more

867

than a few inches. The move had put painful pressure on his ribcage, and he winced, but managed to smile down at her.

'Bushrangers are romantic creatures, aren't they? Half-bandit, half-knight errant – I'll bet your friends envy you for capturing one.'

'Get away from this door . . . '

'And of course, it wouldn't be the same thing if I didn't make an attempt upon your virtue – in fact, one might say, it's almost expected of me.' She moved away from him, along the door. He added helpfully, 'I hope I'm frightening you.'

For all his words the menace from him was not a physical one. He was playing with her. He was clever with words, this one, and he was a man of far greater experience than she had known. This was what she did not like. He was laughing at her, saw her as an hysterical female, was treating her as if she was an idiot like Sophie Lawler. 'You're mad. Let me open the door, or I'll scream so loud . . . '

'You disappoint me – what a very feminine reaction to an unpleasant situation. Or do you withdraw into these little female niceties when wearing a dress . . . ?' He touched her collar gently. 'I take it you must have changed for Mr Barrett's benefit. I'm sure you wouldn't bother, simply to impress a hairy, dirty bushranger.'

He had his reaction; her mouth opened and she began to flush, the scene outside his door early that morning coming back to her. 'Mr Kelly – you were eavesdropping.'

'Miss O'Brien, you have a loud voice.'

He had stepped back, opened the door. She watched him warily, then moved quickly to step through – he had taken her arm. 'Are you sure you wouldn't like me to kiss you? I'd hate to think that you left disappointed in me . . . '

Before she could pull away he drew her to him and his lips were on hers. It was too sudden – there was only the smell of soap, the almost forgotten feel of freshly-shaven skin – his mouth did not demand anything of her – she had broken away, and it was over. She stared at him, too shocked to speak, while he was saying, 'You may add that to whatever story of affronted virtue you have told to Mr Barrett.'

He was still smiling, that faint, mocking smile. *He thinks I told Barrett that he . . . He thinks I'll have him arrested for . . .* It was the unfairness of it, more than the kiss. It was not until later that she remembered to be angry about the kiss – what possessed her now was rage that she was regarded as a weak, melodramatic milksop, who went whining to her father and Barrett – she did not think, had punched him hard in the stomach with her left fist and just as hard to his mouth with her right. 'I hope they hang you!' she hissed, ignoring the man, almost doubled up with the pain from his ribs,

868

and stepping back, she slammed the door hard, only then, with a feeling of horror, realizing what she had done.

Lawler came, gave his pronouncement that the man could travel as long as it was in a buggy, and left after having a whiskey with the men in the parlour. As Berrima had suspected, Peterson and Barrett stayed to dinner, and the night took on an unreal quality, rather like dreaming of a party, the dream becoming a nightmare and one unable to quite wake up. Aidan left, at one stage, to fetch another bottle of port from the kitchen, and Clemency hissed ot him. 'If he dislikes you so much, why is he such a hypocrite that he stays to dinner?'

Aidan grinned, and looked back at Barratt, standing gazing up at the map of the Shannonbrook properties that hung on the wall, 'He's hoping he'll learn something new, something useful,' he said.

His confidence was for his daughter's benefit only. He stamped down the hallway towards the kitchen and the cellar door, hearing as the door closed behind him, Barrett's voice commenting on how very much land the O'Briens seemed to own . . .

'*Bastard* . . . ' Aidan muttered, 'Sell his mother for candle fat, so he would. Miserable old *gombeen* . . . '

Charity had finished for the night, and retired to her rooms above the stables. The kitchen was in darkness – Aidan bent to find the lamp, had pulled his matches from his pocket . . .

It came from the roof, he thought – but no. The verandah outside the kitchen, a scraping on the tin of the roof, a dull sound of something heavy landing in the shrubbery that grew outside the back porch.

So Kelly, the young fool, was trying to escape.

Aidan leaned in the doorway tiredly. It was the final straw, so it was. He went back along the hall, running softly on the thick carpet, went into his darkened office, found the revolver that he kept in his desk drawer, and headed once more for the back of the house.

When he entered the stables he found that Kelly had lit the lamp, though the flame was turned down low. The man was walking off down between the stalls, his saddle over his arm – whirled when he heard the faint squeak of the barn door, reached beneath his coat – he stopped. For the gun, of course, was somewhere within the house. He relaxed, slowly, and the two stood there, studying each other.

Aidan held the revolver at waist level. Kelly was not really pleased with the casualness of Aidan's stance, and Aidan noticed. *He's like a cornered animal*, he thought, *like a cornered tiger, he's looking for my weakness, hoping he's stronger than I am. He's really dangerous.* Yet he said, conversationally, 'I'm beginning to think, you're not to be trusted.'

Kelly opened his mouth to speak, paused, and exhaled slowly. 'That's . . . a reasonable judgement, I suppose.'

Aidan moved forward a little, until the light fell on both of them. He felt suddenly awkward, the reality of the situation dawning upon him. 'I often wondered, you know – what I'd do if I ever landed in this position – being responsible for someone who was running from the police.'

'You'd consider letting me go?'

'No. That's what bothers me. There was a time when I would have – but I've worked too hard to get where I am, Mr Kelly.' He smiled regretfully, gestured with the gun, 'Shall we go back to the house?' Kelly stepped towards him. 'Don't be thinking of jumping me. I've had five whiskeys, a lot of wine and a glass of port – my hand's unsteady enough an' my mood is belligerent enough to shoot you and regret it only much later.'

Kelly regarded him for a few seconds, then walked by him quietly enough. He replaced his saddle on one of the tack stands by the door.

'Will you consider telling me who you are?' Aidan asked, 'I could help you, you know. But unless you trust me . . . '

'It's not a matter of trust.' Aidan could not see the younger man's face, it was in shadows as he leaned on one of the tack stands. 'It was a mistake, my coming here, but telling you who I am won't solve anything. If you could only give me my gun, and my horse . . . '

'No, son. I'm sorry.' Aidan opened the doors. 'Shall we go?'

They stepped out into the warm night, Kelly walking slowly, Aidan following close, but not too close, behind him.

Aidan could tell the man was beginning to lose his, until now, cool manner. As they walked across the paved saddling yard, he said tightly, 'I've no one who knows me in this colony – they could keep me in gaol for months . . . '

'Lad, it's not me that called the law in, I don't want you in gaol . . . '

'You're assigning me to it with little enough compunction.'

Aidan came to a halt. After a step or two, Kelly did also, and turned to face the older man. 'I let you go, boyo, and Barrett will have me in gaol by the morning – it'd give him and a lot of other people a great deal of satisfaction.'

'You've got the money and position now to . . . '

'Damn the position! No amount of money can help my family live

870

it down if I'm dragged in front of a magistrate!' He gestured with the gun once more, and Kelly walked on. As they did so, Aidan continued, wondering at the same time why he was telling Kelly all this. Or was he rationalizing himself? 'I *own* this land. I worked me guts out logging Huon pine in the South-West of Tasmania to get the money for Shannonbrook One – bought it freehold – mortgaged it to the last tree stump to buy Shannonbrook Two – and that was nothing to what I had to go through to get this place! I'll not be risking it for any man.'

'You'll not lay a hand on any of our racehorses!' Men were coming from the back door of the house, Barrett's words came almost at the same time over Liam's, 'The man's escaped, O'Brien! In an emergency the law . . . '

Then all came to a halt on the top step of the verandah, and stood gazing down at the two men approaching across the yard.

'Well,' Barrett said, and even in the dim light from the lantern hung near the door, Aidan could see the smile begin to spread across his face. He came slowly down the stairs. 'We've been saved a great deal of trouble, gentlemen.'

They left soon afterwards, Kelly seated beside Barrett in his carriage, handcuffed to the armrest of the seat, and to make absolutely certain, his ankles tied together with rope.

The sergeant left at the same time. Oddly enough, as the carriage lights and the dark shape of Peterson on his horse all vanished into the darkness of the drive, there was not the feeling of relief that Berrima and the O'Briens had expected. They stood grouped on the steps while the summer moths fluttered around them, Berrima and Clemency holding their shawls about them against the coolness of the evening, and all watched the cavalcade long after the lights had reached the main road.

'Aidan?' Berrima spoke without turning, 'What do you think?'

'About Barrett? Y'd be washing me mouth out with soap.'

'About Mr Kelly.'

'I believe him. I can't say why. He's a man with a past, sure, but I think he's telling the truth in this. Clemency?'

She turned, thinking he wished to say something. When he did not speak, she realized he was asking for her opinion. She did not know how to put her intuitive feelings into words, made the mistake of beginning, 'He has nice eyes . . . ' then stopped, and scowled at Liam, who was shaking with silent laughter, 'Stop it. How do you see a man if not by his eyes? He scares me . . . But I don't think he's bad. At least,' she added, after a pause, 'not clean through.'

84

If the whole terrible business had any redeeming feature, Clemency told Berrima the following afternoon, it was that she at last managed to see the interior of a whorehouse. 'Of course, I've visited, and even stayed in, the house of many a *demi-mondaine*, but they don't have the same feeling of . . . trade I suppose, that permeates the average brothel.'

Berrima had been tidying her catalogue of photographic plates, and now looked over at the younger woman. 'I don't believe what I'm hearing. Clemency, do you speak like that to everybody?'

'Of course not, I'm not a complete eejit. But really, Berri, it was worth all the trouble just to see how awful it was.' She looked unsure. 'Don't tell me I've shocked you?'

'I'll reserve judgement. What happened?'

'Papa's been sending telegrams all day, to Sydney and Melbourne and Euroa, but no one's replied. He wants someone to come and tell Mister Barrett that our Mister Kelly *isn't* Ned.

'You know how Liam decided to go off to town late last night, and Papa told him to go directly to the gaol this morning and try to talk some sense into Kelly – but apparently Liam went off drinking with Hal Peterson last night. I went to the gaol while Papa was at the Post Office, and demanded of Hal where Liam was, and he told me – the establishment of Mrs Angela McGovern.'

'Big Angie's?' And she flushed, annoyed, when Clemency burst into laughter.

'And . . . and I went there after Liam – but they wouldn't let me in, at first, so I dodged them, Big Angie and that little weasely man, Alby, that she has as a bartender, and I ran upstairs. All the doors were locked – it was only about eight in the morning – I didn't know where to find Liam. So I bellowed, "Fire! Fire!" and then hid behind a potted palm – you should see the place, Berrima, all pink and red plush and chandeliers – 'tis the worst taste imaginable . . . '

'What happened when you yelled, "Fire! Fire!"?'

'Well, the occupants of the room all looked pink plush as well, as I saw them – they came running out of the rooms, clutching their clothes, clients and whores alike – and they collided with the mob coming up the stairs after me – and in the confusion I managed to find the room Liam was in and we got out over the balcony. What's more we made it to the gaol before Papa did, though he did wonder as he came in, where the fire wagon was heading . . . '

'Clemency . . . '

But Clemency could tell she was delighted. 'I don't know what it is about our Mr Kelly, but he's certainly brightened our drab lives, has he not?'

Aidan took a chance, and sent another telegram, that afternoon, to Frederick Lawrence, in Campbelltown. He had seen the man only a few times since they met at the saleyards in Camden some years before. He had been a hard man, but a fair one during his term as administrator of Brown's River Probation Station – and his attitude when he had met Aidan in Camden gave the Irishman some hope that there might be something that Lawrence could do. Kelly was now to be charged with attempted assault upon Mr Barrett – there had been some altercation during questioning that morning, about which Peterson would not speak; even when Aidan and Liam, furious, pointed out that Barrett had no right to be questioning the man in the first place.

For Aidan, the only good news that day came from Peterson, who waved to Aidan as he was about to ride home to Shannonbrook Three, and called him over to tell him, with some satisfaction, that the sheep thieves had been apprehended. 'We've found your twenty Merinos, a farmer up near Bundanoon was tempted to buy them because of the cheap price, but he became nervous, and called us in, instead. We'll get most of the stock back, I reckon. Six fellows involved – got them in the gaol now, next to your mate, Kelly.'

Aidan scowled, 'I take it from your reference to Kelly being "my mate" that he has no connection with the men who stole my sheep and cattle.'

'None at all. As a matter of fact, they'd read a copy of the Mittagong *Argus*, and they're beside themselves with excitement that it could be Ned Kelly in the next cell. They keep on yelling at him down the passage that he could tell *them*, at least, and if his brother Dan, and Joe Byrne come to break him out, not to forget and leave them behind in the rush.'

'You're codding me.'

'Does that mean am I pulling your leg? No, Mr O'Brien, and they weren't pulling Kelly's, they're dead serious. Kelly's so sick of their begging and pleading that he's asking Foles and me to gag them. Oh – and he's asking to see you, too, sir.'

Aidan considered. 'No. Not now. If he's decided to stop playing games then he can just wait for a while – this town has danced attendance on him quite enough.'

'You don't think he's Ned Kelly, do you?'

'No. But he's an arrogant son-of-a-bitch, whoever he is. I don't think another night in gaol is going to hurt him.' And at Peterson's scowl, he added, 'And beside, it's to you he should be talking, should he not?'

'Yes, that's right. We'll see you tomorrow then?'

'Aye. Tell Kelly I'll be back, then.'

'Right. And stop by the stables when you come to the station – I picked up my new colt while I was in Bowral – not a patch on Kelly's animal, but a fine creature. I'd like to see what you think of him.'

'I'll do that, sure.'

He was deep in thought as he rode up the driveway of Shannon-brook Three, and almost did not see Berrima, behind the black cloth and the spindly legs of her camera, aiming the round brass-rimmed eye at the house. He smiled, rode over the lawn to her, and stood watching until the photograph was taken, then, as the silver head of curls popped out from the cloth, 'Are you sure there's enough light?'

She started a little, turned and regarded him with a smile that took in the sweating Blue as well. 'How can a horse with such large feet be so quiet?'

''Tis yourself that's to blame,' he said, dismounting, 'pouring buckets of water on this lawn every day.'

She looked around the garden with satisfaction, 'It's my joy, this garden, these lawns. You're not sorry, are you?'

'No.' He had forgotten the subject, was gazing at her and wondering what she would do if he reached for her . . . But now she was fiddling with the insides of the infernal machine, her voice issuing once more from beneath the cloth, 'I've sent Liam and Clemency to the Donaldson's mill to ask Sam and Tessa and the boys to dinner on Saturday – is that all right? We haven't seen them for some time.'

'It's grand.' She was dismantling the camera and he stepped in and took the unwieldy object from her, held it carefully over his shoulder and headed for the house, slowly, Blue's reins over his arm, the great grey walking sedately, tiredly, behind them. 'A couple of the men from Donaldson's passed me on the road on the way home, come to think of it – they looked as if they wanted to speak to me, but I was a bit brusque – if one more person asks me if I captured Ned Kelly, I'll ring the man's neck, so help me.'

Berrima was frowning, 'Are you sure it was Kelly they wished to discuss? You should have checked, Aidan. Why would the men

874

from the mill be coming home at this hour?'

They had their answer an hour later, when a shaken Liam and Clemency arrived home. Aidan and Berrima were drinking iced tea on the verandah, and called out to the two who were about to continue on around the drive to the back of the house with only a wave. They looked at each other, and dismounted. There were dark smears on their shirts, but before Berrima or Aidan could speak, Clemency had said, trying to manage a small smile, 'We were going to clean up before we told you . . . '

'It's Sam, Father . . . '

'There was an accident,' Clemency said. 'It was . . . ' She had suddenly flung her horse's reins to Liam, and dived up the steps into the house. They heard her trip on the stairs, then the sound of the bathroom door slamming.

Liam continued stonily, 'She coped quite well when it happened. I blame myself – we were talking in Sam's smoko – he doesn't usually take a break, he said – but he made us tea, and . . . He got angrier and angrier the more he spoke to us – about Donaldson and his refusal to sell. He asked us to wait – and he went into Donaldson's office . . . '

'For God's sake, Liam, *what happened*?' Liam was so pale Aidan thought he would collapse, and took his son by the shoulders. Liam finished in a rush, dry sobs shaking him. 'He came out of the office, furious – I think he'd forgotten we were there – he went straight to that bloody engine – it was behaving erratically all day, he'd told us– one of the men was fussing about it . . . I think Sam pushed the pressure up – but I'm not sure – the other man was thrown clear – it exploded – the bloody engine exploded as Sam began to walk away – he fell against the saw.'

Aidan was holding Berrima, had barely realized that she had moved to him, reached for him, but he held her close, one arm about her.

'He's lost his right arm, Father. Clemency and I did what we could to stop the bleeding – that's why we look . . . Doctor Lawler's at the Russell's cottage, now. Sam's still unconscious.'

Berrima drove with Aidan to the cottages in the hollow. There was, even as they drew up outside Sam and Tessa's house, a tense feeling of waiting that hung about the little huddle of shabby buildings.

They're waiting for Donaldson, Aidan thought, seeing a few curtains move faintly at the windows. And he wondered if Donaldson had been to visit the Russell home. Wondered if he would come, at all.

The doctor had already left. Sam lay upon the bed in the main bedroom, his face the colour of wax. The bedclothes were drawn up to his chest, and one could not tell, Aidan thought, that he was not asleep, and had both his arms, still, beneath that coverlet, were it nor for the ghastly pallor of his skin behind the heavy moustache.

Tessa was seated by the bed, Berrima went to stand beside her. The two women held hands, as if Tessa could draw strength from Berrima's presence. 'It was Donaldson. All Donaldson's doing. We had the paper drawn up, explaining everything simply; how the men would each put in an eighth and buy the mill from him.

'But the answer was the same as last time. He wouldn't listen. Neil said Donaldson wouldn't even look at the paper. Pride. That's all it was. He'd rather have the mill go to some bloke from Sydney who doesn't understand timber – all because he can't bear to know that Sam succeeded where he failed. Neil said he kept telling Sam to "remember his place" – you can't blame a man for getting upset at treatment like that.'

She fell silent a moment, turned to gaze down at her husband's face. 'That machinery,' she said, 'he used to come home from work each day, cursing it. Always said if it wasn't for him it would've packed up years ago. He cared about that mill, you know.' She looked up at Aidan, and her eyes were filled with a kind of fear. 'How will he live, Aidan?'

'Tessa, don't worry – I'll see that you have everything you need, and there'll be a job at one of my mills – the offer for Sam to manage both of them still stands.'

'You're very good to us, but . . . I don't mean the money, security. You know him as well as anyone. He's a man who lives by his hands. He made that dresser, the bed – all this furniture. He's a working man, Aidan. He's lived for his work. How can I make him want to live, now?'

Aidan had no real answers for her, gazed down at Sam and wondered, what if it had been me? What if one of my saws had taken my arm – would I want to live? And a sick anger grew in him, as he tried to imagine it. No, dammit, he would not give in, even so. And Sam, Sam must not be allowed to give in, either.

'He still has his head on his shoulders.' His voice sounded harsh even to his own ears, and the two women looked up at him, almost startled. 'He was a fine carpenter and workman. But he was an even better overseer.' He almost glared at Tessa. 'When he wakes, tell him nothing's changed – and if he still wants that mill, dammit, he shall have it. Nothing's changed, do y' hear, Tessa? Tell him I said that nothing's changed.'

When they left the room, it was to find the two boys in the parlour. Young Bram was sitting white-faced by the clean-swept hearth, Neil was prowling up and down the room.

'Neil?' He stopped pacing at the sound of Aidan's voice. 'I know what you're thinking, Neil, and you'd be right. It's Donaldson's fault, and he'll pay for it. I'll be going to Sydney next week and I'll see my lawyers . . .'

'Lawyers! What will they do? Donaldson is as twisted as any lawyer you could find – and it won't depend on lawyers, Mr O'Brien, it's up to the magistrate – probably Barrett!'

'Not necessarily . . .'

Bram interrupted, quietly, 'It was a lawyer who got me a lighter sentence, mate. C'mon, Neil, Mr O'Brien's right. Shouting and blustering doesn't do any good, you'll only upset Ma if she thinks you're planning on getting even with Donaldson.'

Tessa was still within the other room. Aidan and Berrima turned to look at Neil, worriedly, and he glared at his younger brother before looking defiantly back at Aidan. 'I'm not having Donaldson get away with it – and the magistrate won't do anything!'

'He can, Neil, if a lawyer can make him see reason . . .'

'You don't know the law like we do. If you saw it from where we did, when Bram got into trouble, you'd talk differently, Mr O'Brien . . .'

'Neil, we'll sue Donaldson for damages – do you know what . . .'

'*We'll* sue? You mean you! We haven't got the money to hire lawyers from the big smoke! And Pa wouldn't want to be in debt to you again! What are you doing this for, anyway? That mill's been taking business from your own – you can't tell me that having the engine blow up and the overseer crippled isn't going to put money into your pockets!'

'Neil!'

It was Tessa, standing in the doorway to the bedroom. She went to step forward to her son, furious, but Aidan placed a hand on her shoulder. He did not take his eyes from Neil. He let the silence settle for a moment, controlling his own urge to slap the boy. He said, 'Why am I doing this? Because I've known Donaldson longer than you, boy, and I know what kind of man he is, and I'd like to step on him like the red-bellied snake he is. But more than this – I'm doing it for that man in there, who's going to have to learn to write, to eat, to work with one hand instead of two – a man who's worth ten of Donaldson and five of you! For all this time you've been thinking of revenge, and you haven't once thought of your father, how much he'll need your support – and a calm, sensible outlook on this. I'm going to make life so uncomfortable for Donaldson that he'll be glad to see the last of that mill – and the law is going to help me, Neil. What about you?'

Neil gazed at him sullenly. Aidan wondered that Liam could find anything worthwhile in the boy – surely he'd end badly with this infuriating habit he had of acting first and thinking second, if at all. But then, taking in Neil's belligerent stance, the black scowl on the face, he thought that, once, half Killaloe had undoubtedly thought the same of himself.

He was working at Shannonbrook Two mill later the following morning when he was interrupted by a brief knock at the door. It opened without him giving permission to enter, and presuming it was Thomas, Aidan kept writing. The letter before him was to the barrister who had represented Bram Russell, asking if he would contact Liam as soon as possible regarding representing Sam Russell in a case of damages against Beecham Donaldson.

Two men had entered the office. Aidan glanced up, noted Thomas and Liam's presence, murmured a greeting and kept writing.

'Father, it's about Kelly. Something has to be done.'

He was writing just that phrase in his letter, scowled and muttered, 'What?'

'Kelly,' said Thomas. 'The man in Mittagong gaol. Had you forgotten him? What are we going to do?'

'Let him rot.' Aidan kept writing, became aware, then, of Liam seating himself almost aggressively on the corner of the desk, folding his arms as if he was not about to leave in a hurry. Aidan finished the sentence he was writing and looked up into the obdurate face of his son.

'I was in town today, at the gaol,' Liam said, 'I must tell you, I almost came to blows with your friend Barrett . . . '

'Of all the . . . ' Aidan threw himself back in his chair.

'It's grand, now, it's grand, don't panic. We had quite a discussion. He even told me why he hates the Irish, Father – 'twas Clemency, yesterday, who pointed out to me how very many Irish were amongst the cases on which our friend Barrett has based his reputation. Apparently his young son was killed in a carriage accident in Cork city in '67. Barrett was stationed there, and he was sending his wife and son back to England for safety. They didn't reach the ship, were caught in a skirmish between Fenians and police and the horses bolted.'

'I didn't know that.' Aidan frowned, thoughtfully. 'So he

878

migrated to remove himself from the memory, did he? And trailed his hatred half-way round the world with him.'

'I finished by feeling sorry for him.'

'*What?*'

'He'd no sooner finished telling me that, than Frederick Lawrence, the magistrate from Campbelltown came in – we were in the police station, by the way. Lawrence had been sent ahead by the Superintendent of Police. They asked me to leave the room, so Foles showed me out back to Kelly's cell, but the conversation was too interesting. Poor Foles danced from one foot to another, but he didn't make a sound – I hovered by the grill in the door and heard everything that Barrett and Lawrence said to each other. Foles could, too, but he pretended otherwise.

'Barrett's finished, Father. Lawrence is a friend of his, and the Superintendent allowed him to break the news. Apparently Peterson wrote an unofficial report to the Superintendent, concerning Barrett's treatment of Kelly, he was goaded something fierce, it seemed. And the report was the final complaint amongst a great many. The Premier himself it was that sent the Superintendent down here to investigate, but the orders were clear, Barrett's to be offered an honourable retirement . . . '

'Jaysus, Mary and Joseph . . . '

'It's grand, is it not?' Thomas's eyes were alight.

'But you should have heard Lawrence. "John," he said, all earnestness and concern, "John, this colony is changing, your toughness may have been necessary once, but Australia, more than any other country in the world, has so much to make up for. We have an ugly past," he says, "and people here are trying to forget it, to build something worthwhile over it. They're becoming more conscious of the law – and of their rights," he says. "We're a free country now, John, not a penal settlement." And didn't I grab young Foles and dance him down the line of cells, and 'twas all I could do not to shout "Bravo!" and "Australia *go Bráth*!" Oh, it was a grand moment, sure.'

'And the newspapers from Sydney have it that Ned Kelly and his gang rode into the town of Jerilderie yesterday, held the whole town at gunpoint and emptied its pockets. So our man isn't Ned Kelly,' Thomas added, with satisfaction.

'That was what upset Barrett more than anything else – it was obvious that he'd been praying all night that he'd go down in history as the man who arrested Ned Kelly. And now,' Liam stood, confronted Aidan, 'what are we going to do about the man?'

Aidan glared at him. 'What's it got to do with me? Even if he's not

Ned Kelly, he's proved himself to be as obstinate and rash a young trawneen as I've ever come across . . . '

'I like him, Father. Oh, I admit, the few times I spoke to him, when he was at Shannonbrook Three, we didn't have much rapport,' Liam grinned. 'At one stage, Berrima had to get between us – but in the gaol we've both been a bit more reasonable – the atmosphere is sobering, you must admit. He still wants to see you, Father. I told him I'd ride home, pick up his money and return to the gaol – he's to be released on bail. Can I tell him you'll see him?'

Aidan sighed. 'Liam, I don't need any further complications – if the man wants a job . . . '

'I don't know that he does. He told me what he told Barrett, that he's English, a sailor working on an American line, for the most part. He claims his First Mate's papers are in Melbourne. I believe him. Can I bring him back to Shannonbrook Three this afternoon?'

'At least hear what the boy has to say, Aidan,' Thomas prompted.

'All right! But don't be thinking that I'll be putting him on the payroll, for I won't. We'll have enough trouble if Donaldson's mill goes out of business, finding jobs for his workers. Now – can we talk about Sam Russell and what the hell we're going to do to help him? *Without* ruffling that damnable pride of his.'

85

Liam had brought several books with him and closed his office for the day. The three men stayed in Aidan's office and discussed the law of damages and the pitifully few cases where an employee had won a case against his employer. Liam left the books with Aidan, finally, and rode on to Shannonbrook Three to fetch Kelly's bail money. Thomas drifted back to his own office, and Aidan was left, for the rest of the day, to pour over the heavy, beautifully-bound books with their small print and dry pages, their equally dry contents.

He was still brooding on the possible outcome of the court case, the possibly grim future that awaited Sam Russell, when he returned to Shannonbrook Three. He entered the house, seemingly deserted in the heavy oppressive heat of the afternoon, and headed for his office. A whiskey, that was what was needed – he'd take it upstairs and drink it in a cold bath . . .

880

William Kelly it was, standing by the windows where a faint breeze stirred the curtains, William turning his head in just such a way, the stance, the well-cut dark suit – Aidan had stopped, his hand on the door knob, affected, for a moment, by the illusion. He came into the room. Kelly faced him, watchful, an invisible tension emanating from him. Aidan realized the younger man had been waiting for some time.

'I'm sorry,' he lied, closing the door after him. 'I was held up at the mill.'

'Liam told me about your friend, Sam. You must be very worried.'

'I am that.' He seated himself behind his desk, gesturing, at the same time, that Kelly take a seat in an armchair across from him.

There was an uneasy pause, then, 'I would have told you everything, had you come to see me in the gaol. I wanted to, for I'd spoken to Peterson and young Foles and your son, and I realized how much I'd put you in jeopardy. I felt I owed it to you to tell you the truth, before I left Mittagong.'

'And how would you be placing me in jeopardy?'

'By making you confront a man who had the power to drag up your past against you, to destroy all you've built here. No one knows about your term in prison here, I realized, but since you hadn't changed your name, Barrett could have traced you through Convict Records. Liam's legal career would be damaged, your own place in society – I've seen enough of Australian society to know its attitude to emancipists. Doors would be closed to you. Yet you risked all that.'

'Less because I like you than because I hate Barrett.'

Kelly smiled. Aidan's face betrayed nothing, but his nerves were taut with his sense of danger. It was that odd sort of personal fear that overcame him whenever someone mentioned his past. The fear he had known when he had seen Frederick Lawrence again in Camden; when Hal Peterson had admitted to knowing of him. The fear for his children, that they must not have to suffer for his wrongs, the whispers behind gloved hands, the sniggers behind their backs. 'And from where did you get your information about my past?' His voice calm, hands clasped loosely on his desk top, mind already trying to feel the way ahead, watching Kelly's every gesture. Was this leading to blackmail, perhaps? Let the man tell the world, in that case, but I'll beat the tar out of him before he leaves.

'They told me in Killaloe. Father Daniel McDonnagh. He didn't want me to come to find you, said I was being foolish – but I had to come. I don't know why. Perhaps I felt I owed you something.

But . . . there's nothing I can do here. I thought I'd find you a struggling settler . . . ' He exhaled a little, sharp laugh as he looked about the room. 'You have so much – I don't mean merely material things. You have everything. My mother would be content to know that you've achieved all you have, that you're happy.'

In the dreadful pause that followed, Kelly wished he had not spoken, wished himself out the door and away. The man behind the desk had paled visibly beneath his tan, his face was closed, it gave nothing away, but the broad hands had unconsciously gripped the arms of his chair, the knuckles white. Kelly could not leave. He gazed at the man he had come twelve thousand miles to see, the man it had taken eleven years to find, and he knew that he needed some acknowledgement, some reaction, even if it were hostile.

Aidan spoke softly, his voice barely audible. He took in Kelly's face, feature by feature, and the proof was there, had been there all along – but it was impossible, impossible . . .

'You're Anna's son. You're Devlin and Anna's son.'

Michael Kelly told Aidan only the brief facts of his life, that he was born at Burnley Grange, near Biddestone, Wiltshire, in February, 1847, ten months after his parents arrived in England. He spoke of where he was educated, the change in the family's name and religion on Devlin's second marriage, and, when Aidan asked, he told of his career in the merchant navy.

They did not discuss Devlin. It was odd, until Kelly realized, later, that Aidan knew his father perhaps better than any man living, and there had been no need for explanations.

It was just as well. In this, the two men were alike; the early hurts and heartaches had been buried under the characters they had been forced to forge for themselves. Their early suspicion of each other, which began to thaw that night of Kelly's return to Shannonbrook, was caused by their own recognition of a remorseless self-sufficiency.

Never, to anyone, would Kelly speak of his earliest memories, of Burnley Grange and Aunt Celia, who loved him and gave him the only affection he was to experience in his life. Yet, quite unwittingly, Aunt Celia frightened him, in her well-meaning desire to see that Michael did not forget the memory of his real mother. There were several portraits and miniatures, and Aunt Celia would recount stories of his beautiful Mama who had loved him and who had died so tragically on the hunting field. It filled the child with a sense of loss, of unfairness, from which he never quite shook himself free, and a kind of guilt that Mama had gone away so soon after his own appearance in the world. Had she been displeased with him? When he was taken to see her grave – it was one of his most vivid memories – when he was two or three, he had had nightmares for weeks afterwards.

He decided very early in his life, indeed, could not remember a time when he thought otherwise, that he did not like his father very much. He liked him even less when he quarrelled with Aunt Celia. This did not happen very often, but sometimes, from behind a closed door, Michael could hear voices raised, and the terrible words were as terrifying as the waves of hate and suspicion that came even through the heavy woodwork and made him tremble.

His pleasure when his small sister, Caroline, was born, was as short-lived as the child herself, and then the little coffin was being lowered into the ground, not far away from his mother's resting place. And for a long time Aunt Celia was sad, and that made him afraid. If Aunt Celia became too unhappy, it might occur to her to leave as his Mama had done – and to go where? Between the horror of his golden-haired Mama and his small sister in boxes in the ground, and the splendour of Celia's declaration that Mama and little Caroline were with God's angels in heaven, was the despair that no one was telling him the truth. Mama had gone away. She had left him. And if Mama, who had been so gentle, so happy with Burnley Grange and Father's moodiness, should, one day, leave without a goodbye, how much more likely was Aunt Celia to go?

And Aunt Celia did leave. There was even talk of another sister – but the boy had only just accepted the idea of the new baby, named for Celia, when the news came that she, too, had gone away. Michael was six years old, and felt very alone.

Father brooded, snapped, bellowed at him or ignored him altogether. He was no help at all. The boy began to wonder if it was not Father, in his unpleasantness, who made women and small sisters take fright and leave home. He eyed his tall, handsome and unapproachable father, and thought that he could hardly blame them.

Really, the happiest times were when Father was away in London, and the boy went to stay with their neighbours, the Beresfords. They had no children of their own and spoilt him, and he always regretted the time when Lady Beresford would, herself, help him on with his coat and place his hat on his head, and admonish him to be a good boy for his Papa, and she would kiss his cheek, and Lord Beresford would bend down like a creaking oak and shake hands as if the boy were quite grown up, and the carriage would wheel him away. Away from the gaiety of Orwhitton, across the two miles and a world of difference, to the grey walls of Burnley once more.

One day, on an afternoon visit, he was told that Lady Beresford had recently given birth to a daughter, and he was taken upstairs by Lord Beresford, a very large, raw-boned man who always smelt pleasantly of pipe tobacco, to see the new baby.

It filled him with despair. Not only was it ugly, but he felt certain that with the nursery filled with the cries and demands of this black-haired monkey-like creature, there would no longer be room for him.

Coming home in the carriage with his father, he had cried. Looking back at the giddy, excessively-ornamental and well-loved facade of Orwhitton, he felt certain that things would never be the same again.

His father had been appalled by the tears. Had demanded to know what was the matter. The boy tried to think of words, but none would come. It had to do with leave-takings, the empty feeling when there was no one about to hug, and warm ladies who seemed never to stay when they were needed. It was to do with betrayal and the terrible power of babies, it had a great deal to do with the man who sat opposite him in the carriage, demanding that Michael stop that nonsense immediately. He was slapped. He was shaken. It made him sob the harder.

When they reached Burnley the boy was exhausted, and numbed into silence in the face of his father's displeasure. Nevertheless, he was dragged into the house by his wrist and told to go upstairs to his room at once.

Until that day, the boy had never broken down in front of his father. Until that day, his father informed him at dinner in the evening, he had had no idea that he had bred such a very wet excuse for a son. It was obvious, Father said, that the Beresfords' influence had been kindly meant, but staying with them had done little to prepare Michael for the realities of the world. The same was to be said for Statton, the gentle, bookish young tutor Devlin had engaged for Michael eighteen months previously.

At that time, the boy did not understand, heard his father murmuring, 'It won't do . . . It won't do . . . ' all through the meal, and studying his son as if each time he looked at him some new character fault showed upon his countenance.

There were discussions with his father, in the next few days, on the meaning of Being a Man, of Taking One's Place in the World, of Making One's Way. The boy, withdrawing into the studied control with which he always dealt with his father, tried to understand. Michael was all his father had; the future of his family, the future of

884

Burnley Grange, depended upon him. For Michael's own good, he must dispense with these moods of emotional self-indulgence, not hide behind books, nor waste his time in immature play. Michael was born with a certain position to uphold. He was a Gentleman. In a world, Father said solemnly, with a touch of bitterness, where not all men were Gentlemen. Life was Earnest, it was Difficult. True success came with being hardened to the worst, being able to meet other men on their own ground, never to allow the world to see one's weaknesses, and even better, not to have weaknesses at all.

The next week, Statton left Burnley Grange. The old woman who had been the boy's nursery maid was dismissed, the pretty young upstairs maid and the tweeny were dismissed, and older, grim, silent ladies in dark dresses took their places. Mrs Croker, who had been housekeeper at Burnley for thirty years, was retired, and replaced with a head butler. A footman appeared to wait on the table instead of the parlour maid. It was odd, but the feminine influence at Burnley was gradually being dispensed with.

Not one, but two new tutors arrived. A tall, bent scarecrow of a man whose dark clothes seemed to flap about him; this was Mr Barker, who took the boy for all subjects except geography. Michael often wondered why this was. For surely Mr Barker knew as much of the world as Mr Wells. But as it was, Wells took the boy for geography – and boxing, shooting, horsemanship and fencing. And, as it appeared to the boy as he grew older, Wells was watchdog as well.

Play, innocent, imaginative play – Cavaliers and Roundheads with the boys of the neighbouring estates and his cousins, Robert and George Du Buisson, who were somehow related to Aunt Celia's mama, were now a thing of the past. He did not miss Robert and George, who spoke fluent French behind his back and had no chins, but he missed his other friends.

When the boy was twelve, he left for school, withdrawn, quietly confident, self-sufficient. He did not cry with homesickness, he had no need of the passionate attachments that the other boys knew. He had no time. By that stage the message that his father, Barker and Wells had instilled for years had come to be second nature. Succeed. Depend on no one but oneself. When pushed, push back. But faster, harder than one's opponent.

He made no friends, and needed none, the competition was all. He won nearly every scholarship, every contest, every award. When he did not win, he was physically ill for days. But he hid this, too. And he remembered who had beaten him, and worked harder for the next confrontation.

885

He saw little of his father during these years; when they were brought face to face, the boy was questioned about his successes at school, on the playing field, asked how many birds he had brought down, if he had been shooting, and, if out hunting, how close behind the MFH he had been, and whether he had been close at the kill. His father rarely joined him in these pursuits, although he often came out to watch, to give advice. He seemed, on the whole, to be proud of the boy. It pleased Kelly to see this, and he tried all the harder. It would have been good, the boy thought sometimes, if his father shared in these pastimes, but it was the next best thing, knowing his father was interested enough to watch. Once, when his cousins visited, they were all three about fifteen or sixteen, they had quarrelled, and had fought. Despite the unfair odds, Kelly was more than holding his own. His father, discovering the scene of battle, had been delighted. Kelly remembered his father's face, smiling as he pulled him back from Robert and George. Later he overheard Devlin saying to a rather disapproving Lord Beresford, 'He has such a vicious temper, you see. Can't keep him out of scrapes. I was the same at his age. My father had the devil of a time with me. Boys will be boys, eh, Beresford? I learnt to harness my temper; Michael will, too, in time.' It was at that moment that Kelly realized that he hated his father. Had, in fact, hated him for years.

It was fortunate, he thought, as he grew older, that he was actually quite talented at the rough pursuits that his father encouraged him in. Though Barker and Wells left his father's employ, there were always tutors in boxing and fencing and pistol shooting, whenever he returned to Burnley for holidays. Devlin boasted amongst his friends of his son's skill, his marksmanship. Kelly was pleased that his father was pleased, but never understood why these things seemed to mean so much to his parent.

When he was twenty-one, reading Natural and Experimental Philosophy at Oxford, still preoccupied with winning, still proving himself constantly to himself, a letter had arrived from Lady Serena Beresford.

At first Kelly had thought that it meant his father was ill. But no. There was a note from Lady Beresford, only, and another letter, addressed to him in an unfamiliar hand.

The accompanying letter from Lady Beresford stated that she had been a close friend of Anna's, and in that capacity, had promised, in the last week before she died, that Anna's letter would be forwarded to him on reaching his majority . . .

It was a gentle letter, the handwriting light and uncertain. It spoke of no recriminations against his father, but reminded him – yet he had the feeling that she knew as she wrote it that he might have no knowledge of this at all – that his blood was Irish, that he was a Kelly, before he was a Retcliffe, that he had grandparents on the O'Hagan side, and two aunts, Dierdre and Eileen, in Killaloe. She begged him not to forget them, to take care of them.

'*Another matter of which I must speak concerns one of my dearest friends, Aidan O'Brien.*' The boy, to the end of his days, remembered these words. '*It is no disloyalty to your father to tell you that I was once betrothed to Mr O'Brien.*

'*In the Famine, terrible things happened; Michael, my brother, your uncle, whom your father graciously allowed me to call you after, died of typhoid. Many thousands died of starvation and disease. Many were driven to acts of violence when, in normal times, they would be peaceful people. I have read of these things happening in Ireland, and have sensed, from hearing your father speak of his business worries to friends, that things are very bad at Tineranna. I feel we shoud be there. It is Devlin's home; it is your home.*

'*I do not understand the full facts, so will not presume to try to explain. My son, I know that you will grow up to be a kind, honest, Christian man. You are before me as I write this, on the carpet by my bed, playing with the toy soldiers your father brought you back from London. I see strength in your face even now. That you possess a kind heart, my darling boy, I already know. I ask you, for the sake of the friendship between the O'Brien family and my own, to see that justice is done. I cannot explain any further; Father Daniel McDonnagh, of Killaloe, will help you, I am sure. I only ask you, in my place, to right any wrong that has been done.*

'*Your father is a good man, Michael. You may not always understand him, nor he you, for he had a lonely soul even as a child, and such men cannot reach out. Use understanding.*

'*I wish I could know you as a man. I feel, even now, that you will make me proud.*'

He had left for Burnley that same day, arriving very late at night. He had burst in on Devlin, who had been reading quietly in his study, and had demanded to know what the letter meant.

His father, coldly furious, admitted it. Their family name was Kelly. Devlin had changed it with the full approval of his uncle, Lord Hallswood; there was no secrecy, if Michael had shown any curiosity about his family background, Michael would have been told. It had been a matter of social expediency, that was all. To succeed here in England, the first step was to be English. Devlin made no effort to disguise his contempt for his son's reactions. The loss of a common Irish surname was a small price to pay for acceptance.

They had quarrelled. Devlin had demanded to see the letter – Michael, in his desire to lash out, to hurt, handed it to him.

Without reading it, Devlin had dropped it into the fire. 'There is no Michael Kelly. No past. I don't want it mentioned again.'

He did not remember attacking his father, came to himself only when the butler and footman were pulling him back, twisting his arms up behind his back in an effort to hold him.

Devlin's eye was half-closed with the contusion on his cheekbone, his lip was bleeding heavily. He pulled himself up from where he had fallen over his chair, waving away an offer of aid from the butler.

When the servants had gone, and the two were alone once more, 'I'm not angry with you, Michael,' Devlin said, calmly, 'I want you to know that, in case you're afterwards stricken by conscience. I've always hoped you'd grow up capable of putting your opinions across . . . forcibly. I think I've succeeded. After all,' he murmured, dabbing at his mouth with his handkerchief, 'if you can kill your own father, you can kill anyone . . .'

Kelly did not wait to hear any more. He left the room and went upstairs, and early the next morning, he left Burnley Grange. He never returned to Wiltshire.

With Kelly's brief story, and Aidan's knowledge of Devlin, the Irishman was able to piece together a picture, a broad, unhappy canvas of a young man living out Devlin's frustrated dreams for himself. With Michael Kelly's training and upbringing, ten years at sea would harden such a man to the point where the gun in its holster was not at all surprising, it was expected.

'There's something else that you should know. I've killed two men. One in San Francisco, one in Melbourne. A friend of mine was murdered by three sailors – I had one of them arrested, the other two escaped. One tried to kill me, later, but I was carrying the Colt by then . . . I didn't stay about to stand trial. The last man I tracked down myself, to Melbourne . . . you can check the story with the Victorian authorities – it was self-defence – there were witnesses.'

'I'm sure there were,' Aidan murmured. 'Did the man know you were coming? Did you give him plenty of time to become nervous? I suppose he came after you, did he, in the end?'

The thin face was closed, the grey eyes cool. Aidan wondered at the coldness of the man, wondered even more at his own empathy with him. He asked quietly, 'Why did the three men murder your friend?'

'He was the one chosen to replace the second mate when he died on a voyage out of Hong Kong to San Francisco. I was only a seaman then, and I was pleased for Japheth – he was a fine man and a brilliant seaman. He was also black, Mr O'Brien. When the police found his body, two days after we docked in San Francisco . . . the captain and I had to identify him – it was hard. They'd beaten him to death, then went off drinking, and boasting about it.'

In the silence that ensued, the only sound was the crickets and a sleepy sounding bobook owl, somewhere out in the darkened garden. Aidan became aware of how dark the room had become. He rose and drew the curtains, lit each of the lamps carefully, and knew, as he did so, that he believed the man.

Kelly had stood when Aidan had stood, was now standing by the empty fireplace, his gaze on the flame of the silver and crystal lamp on the mantelpiece, the prisms of its glass fringe minute and myriad bursts of colour.

'I saw Father McDonnagh four years ago,' Aidan said. 'He told me nothing about your visit . . . ' He frowned, 'But come to think of it, he did give me a little lecture on burying the past.'

The man's voice had a touch of bitterness to it. 'That's easy for Father McDonnagh to say. He delivered a little sermon to me, too – he felt I was wrong to leave my father as I did. When I said I felt I had to find you, he claimed he didn't know where in Tasmania you were. I thought he was lying to me, for my own good, but apparently you had lost touch in those years.

'I called myself Michael Williams while I was in Killaloe, Father McDonnagh was the only one to know who I was. I was able to speak to a great many people, learnt a lot about you, and your family. I saw Tineranna, or what remained of it. I think it was then that I decided I had to find you – it was almost as if my mother knew what was building between my father and yourself. The bitterness – it must go back a long way.'

'It does.'

He saw Kelly hesitate, and turned his back, then returned to his chair behind his desk, in an attempt to preclude any further questions. He would not speak of reasons, of causes, pushed back the memories of Anna being carried away, down the road in the great dark carriage, of Corrie O'Neill, of a long dead copper-coloured hunter called Chloe, and Samhradh . . . all the spiteful and malicious acts of revenge that was the sum total of his memories of Devlin Kelly, now Retcliffe.

Aidan looked over at the younger man. 'Do I call you Kelly or Retcliffe?' But he knew the answer before the man's jaw tightened.

'I haven't used Retcliffe since I found out the truth. I followed the O'Hagans to Boston and stayed with my Aunt Eileen; I converted to Roman Catholicism while I was there.'

'Hell's outhouse,' Aidan said mildly, 'You are taking your Irishness seriously.'

'And shouldn't I?'

'Don't be so defensive, boyo, you're not on trial, here.' He sighed and leaned back in his chair. 'What will you do now? Go back to sea?'

'I suppose I should. I'd like to avoid, if I could, having my father know of my whereabouts.'

'Has he tried to find you?'

Grimly, 'Yes. He wants me back in England. It's become something of an obsession for him.'

'He's hired private investigators, I suppose . . .'

'Among other methods. You can see why I didn't want Mr Wilkes to publish the story of that arrest.'

'Even the story of the false arrest is of enough interest to be in every newspaper in the country.'

'I suppose I should move on.' He chewed his lip for a few seconds. 'But I want to stay.' He looked over at Aidan.

Grey eyes. William's eyes. They held Aidan. He tried not to think that this should have been his son, not Devlin's . . . He shrugged, scowled. 'It's one thing to hire a drifter, even an out-of-work sailor, Kelly. To hire a man with a degree from Oxford to herd sheep and cattle . . .'

'I didn't stay to get my degree. But I know what you're saying. I'm over-qualified,' he smiled.

'You know damn well you are.'

'Perhaps I like herding cattle. In fact, I'm sure I will. I know a little about estate management, you know. Burnley covered two thousand acres, and I was being trained to take over the running of the estate one day.'

'You might end up running Shannonbrook.'

Their eyes held with a good-natured challenge. 'Yes,' Kelly said, 'I just might.'

It had been two in the morning when they had finished talking, and Aidan had taken a lantern and extra bedding to show Kelly his quarters.

He could, Aidan said, have the room off the barn that had been reserved for the overseer that had not, to date, been hired. But Kelly preferred to share accommodation with the other men. In the stockmen's quarters, a sleepy Bram and Jim had been the only ones to stir, lifting their heads to grin a welcome. Aidan shook Kelly's hand, and left him.

But it was too strange, too splendid a thing to allow him to sleep. The grand irony. Devlin Kelly's son. And the centre of Devlin's world – for while the boy felt only his father's strictures, his emotional detachment, Aidan could see the compulsive interest, the preoccupation with Kelly's success.

That was another irony, he thought, finally unable to lie still any longer and rising to stand at the open window and gaze down over the sleeping garden. Devlin had wanted a strong, independent, even a ruthless son – and he had one. A man who would not stay in England to follow whatever plans his father had undoubtedly made for him. Kelly had struck out on his own.

It was grand. He laughed to himself; it was wonderful, a glorious story – he longed to share it, could not wait to tell Berrima.

And then, of course, he must tell his children.

It was then, thinking of Clemency, that he realized that he did not want to tell her. Now Ma was gone, no one but Thomas knew the real details of his life in Killaloe and the events leading up to his transportation; Liam and Clemency had both betrayed curiousity, and Berrima, he knew, was prevented only by good manners from asking him – but he had told them very little. It did not bear thinking about, better to forget it, as much as he could.

He was gifted in this, the ability to put the past behind him. Ma has possessed it, even Thomas. Liam could, too, if the need arose. But not Clemency. He knew with a certainty born of his knowledge of his daughter that this news, at this time, might be all that was needed to turn her against Kelly. There was too much of Maura in her. Clemency, like Maura, could not free herself from the past. At least, he thought, reaching for his pipe and tobacco and scowling as he stood at the window and lit the pipe, at least, not yet a while.

He shook his head quickly. His mind was racing ahead. He did not like to think that he was that diabolical. No. Better not to think about the future. Let things happen as they may.

He had clawed and struggled and fought all his life to bend events to serve his own needs. Now, suddenly, this impossible thing had happened. He wanted to enjoy it. The boy was right, he thought, I have everything, now, that I need. I require nothing of anybody. I'm not even dissatisfied. Begod, I've even learnt to live with Berrima – or rather, without her.

He clasped his hands behind his back, rocking on his heels a little, enjoying this sense of almost childish delight. For, for the first time in his life, without trying, without doing anything at all – he had what Devlin Kelly wanted. Without even trying to hold it, he possessed it. He thought of Devlin, alone at Burnley Grange, twelve thousand miles away, and his son, sleeping in Aidan's stockmen's quarters because he wished to, and he began to laugh, half-choking, as he did so, on his pipe smoke.

86

The following morning Aidan was almost relieved to find that Clemency had breakfasted early and left the house. He would be able to explain to his daughter separately, later. With Liam and Berrima, however, he waited until the meal was nearly over, when they were sipping the last of their tea, and announced calmly, 'Kelly – Michael Kelly, that is – will be staying on for a while. I've hired him as a stockman.'

Only Liam looked surprised. Berrima watched Aidan, as if waiting for him to continue. He felt a little disappointed at her lack of reaction, but went on, speaking mostly to the grinning Liam, 'I discovered why he was loathe to give his name – he's related to the Kellys I knew in Killaloe.'

'Not Devlin Kelly's son?'

Aidan stared at Liam, who looked a little abashed. 'Sure and Father, you might have known I'd look up the records of the trial while I was at Law School. I read the newspaper reports, too. Between yourself and my uncles Thady and Seamus it's no surprise that I became a Fenian, is it?'

Aidan's eyes went to Berrima. She was gazing down at the table, her expression unreadable. Aidan glared at his son. 'Yes,' he said tightly, 'Michael Kelly is Devlin's son.'

'Does Clemency know?'

Begod, but this pup was becoming astute. The russet eyes were laughing at him. Liam knew exactly how things stood. 'Not yet,' Aidan said.

'Would you like me to tell her?'

'You'd like that, wouldn't you? And a heavy-handed job you'd make of it. No, thank you kindly, I feel it's up to me.'

'Suit yourself. Though the result's going to be the same whoever breaks the news.' Liam had stood, 'I'll go and welcome our new

892

stockman, so. 'Bye, Berri, Father – see you this evening.'

Liam left the room. A warm breeze billowed the light curtains at the windows as the door closed behind him. Aidan turned back to Berrima.

'Well,' he said. She was still gazing at the table. 'Is something wrong?'

'Oh, no.' After a few seconds, 'I take it Kelly's father had something to do with your being transported.'

It was his turn to look down, scowling. 'He had a great deal to do with it, yes. But it was mostly my fault. I behaved like an eejit.' There was nothing else to say, but, 'I'm trusting, however, that Kelly doesn't take after his father.'

Again the awkward silence, then Berrima said, 'Do you want to talk with me, Aidan? It's about time we talked, my dear, don't you think?'

'Och, no. There's nothing to discuss. It's all behind me. I don't think about it any more.'

She had turned to gaze out the window. Aidan was puzzled, wondering if he had somehow hurt her feelings, while knowing that he could not go back over the past, not even with her. He wished she would look at him. If she looked at him he might be able to read something in the dark eyes that would give him a clue to what she was thinking. But she kept her head averted.

Aidan was becoming uncomfortable. He smiled and changed the subject. 'Have you heard from your publishers?' he asked. 'Did they like the sketches?'

Then the eyes came up to his, held his with a strange look that was almost sadness. So strange was her expression that he nearly reached his hand across the table to hers and asked what the matter was, but—

'I had a letter two days ago,' she was saying impassively. 'They want the text broadened to include a description of the Wombeyan Caves, but everything else is fine. They like the sketches.'

'Grand,' he said, smiling at her. 'That's grand, now.'

She was standing, so he stood, also, and she was murmuring something about checking with Charity about some pies she was to take to Sam and Tessa – and before Aidan could think of anything to prevent her leaving, she was out of the room. He could hear the rustle of her petticoats along the thick green carpet of the hall.

Are her petticoats black, also? He discovered he was gripping his tea cup in his two hands only when the delicate handle came away in his grasp. He stood looking at the two pieces of china bemusedly, a sudden memory of the fine china set at the house in Queen Street,

893

shattering on the stone hearth – Berrima in his arms, his body within her body . . . Over so soon. Yet it was never over.

He placed the broken tea cup carefully in its saucer, the handle beside it. It rang a little, a tinkling sound.

Thomas was completely stunned at the news. 'Why?' He prowled about his office at Shannonbrook One mill. 'Mother of God, why would Devlin Kelly's son come here?' And in the end he had left the mill, ridden to Shannonbrook Three and, he told Aidan when he had returned, talked to the boy. Thomas was convinced, but still puzzled, perhaps always would be. But he liked Michael Kelly, he told his brother. He may be a decent fellow – he was Anna's boy, after all.

Aidan was late returning to the house that evening, and found Clemency coming around the house, headed towards the front steps, as he was riding Blue up the drive. She saw him, and made an effort to reach the steps quickly, but he had noticed her appearance, placed his heels to Blue's sides and manoeuvred the grey's considerable bulk between his daughter and the route of escape. She was wearing a riding habit, and somehow looked worse for it, for she was dripping wet. Her saturated hair clung to her back and the dark blue habit hug damply all around her, making a puddle in the dust where she stood.

'What in the name of all that's holy has happened to you?'

She glared up at him. The sun slanted over the roof of the house and she shielded her eyes with her hand. 'Liam and I had a slight difference of opinion, Papa. It finished with him pushing me into the horse trough. May I go inside, now?'

'And why,' very calmly, 'did Liam throw you in the horse trough?'

'Can we discuss this inside?'

'It's about eighty five degrees, Clemency, you can't tell me you're uncomfortable . . . '

She broke in over the top of him, determined to get it over with, 'He was teasing me. He was making odious comments because I told him Sophie Lawler has her cap set for him . . . '

'Does she?'

'Yes! And he started telling me he could court whom he wishes and that Sophie might be mistress of Shannonbrook one day, and – and I lost my temper and hit him. So he pushed me in the horse trough.'

She went to move, but so did Blue. 'Was it Sophie that started all this?' came the detached voice from above her.

894

Clemency's gaze lost some of its intensity. She looked away. 'Come, Clemency, you and Liam haven't brawled like this since you were children and you used to borrow his catapult. Something must have set you off . . . '

'He was making comments about Michael Kelly – Och, he was codding me, I suppose, but I didn't like it. I don't want Mr Kelly here, and I don't think you should have hired him without having asked the rest of us if we had any objections . . . '

'Perhaps you're right, but . . . '

'All I said was that I wouldn't have Liam laughing at me when all the district was talking about him visiting Victoria Ellis now her husband's left her and gone to Melbourne, and he said they were simply friends and that really, his heart was set on Sophie – oh, it was all too silly, and it just got out of hand, Papa, that's all . . . '

He had dismounted, was standing quietly listening to all this, but when she went to push past him she found a hand on her shoulder, and stopped. 'Both of you are mature adults, now. People could overhear you shouting to each other, servants, farm workers, had you thought of that?'

'Tell Liam . . . '

'I intend to, but I'll tell you first, since you're here. You won't keep people's respect if you behave like a termagant, Rebel.'

She knocked his grip from her shoulder with a vicious swipe of her hand. 'You'd best stop using that name for me, if you're after wanting me to conform. Perhaps the good sisters had the care of me too late to turn me into a lady, Papa. Maybe you should have got me out of your way years before.' She was moving past him, but he took her arm and swung her around to face him.

'It was your mother's wish, and you know it. I was trying to please your mother . . . '

'For the first and last time.'

They were gazing at each other with more anger than either of them had thought they possessed. Aidan breathed, 'It's the truth you're speaking – but I could slap your face for saying it.'

Her expression changed. A moment before it had been Maura's face gazing at him, Maura's eyes, narrowed to green and spiteful slits. Now the eyes were widening, softening with regret. 'I'm sorry, Papa. I'm sorry . . . '

They were in each other's arms, and he patted her shoulder, even while he thought, She'll never forgive me, never. I can't criticize her for her anger, for I've failed her, and she's right not to forgive me.

'Clemency?' he said, gently.

'Yes, Papa?'

'You are very *wet*.'

She pulled back, and they were laughing. Then, 'Why, Papa?' she was asking soberly. 'Why let Kelly stay on here when you disliked him so?'

'He's the son of the man I tried to kill, Clemency, the reason behind my being transported to this country.' His anger had drained him, the gentle phrases he had practised had deserted him. He watched her eyes grow wider. 'He came to see me to make some kind of amends – Bram called on me today and told me Kelly was looking for my homestead when you and Liam found him. I'm letting him stay for the sake of his grandfather, who meant a great deal to me, and because, like Liam, I feel I like the man on better acquaintance.'

'There are many fine men who're looking for jobs as stockmen.' The green eyes were narrowed again.

Hell's outhouse, but this was a complex girl. She would not retreat. She reminded him as much of Berrima as Maura, he thought, and then, *or is she like me?*

'I'm taking Kelly on,' he said clearly, 'because I'm curious, because I like to take chances, to tempt fate. Because the man wants to stay and because I wish to give him the chance to prove himself, because it's a grand thing that he wants to be here rather than with his bastard of a father, but mostly, *mostly*, girl, because capable as you are, I'm still the master of this house and these properties, and when I make a decision, you'll stand by it like everyone else on the place. Do I make myself clear?'

For a moment the eyes held his, then, 'Perfectly, Papa,' she said, and turned and marched up the stairs into the house, the dignity of her retreat marred only slightly by the squelching of her wet riding boots as she walked.

She stood naked in front of her mirror and towelled herself dry. She liked looking at herself, less in self-interest as in a kind of defiance. At school, and, later, as a novice, she and the other girls had had to bathe in cotton shifts. Ideally a woman did not, in her entire life, look on her own body. It might lead to impure thoughts. In the years between the schoolroom and the novitiate, there had been room aplenty for impure thoughts.

She felt a flush creep up her neck at the thought of those years in London, Paris, Florence, Brussells . . . Madness. It had been a time of utter madness. Christabel Mitchell and her lovers, her titled and eccentric friends and *their* lovers, and the romance, the intrigue, the danger . . .

896

If only the actual sex had not been so very boring.

Really, it was no wonder so many people wrote so much about the preludes to sexual intercourse. It was so vital a requirement to the continuation of the species that if people stopped writing and talking about it and simply did it, then the human race would probably die out within a generation.

Her mother had murmured to her when the dreadful bleeding had begun, when Clemency was thirteen, that this was God's way of telling her she was a woman. She had made her mother cross by commenting that surely the Mind that had created the universe could have thought of a better way. Her mother had turned her back and begun fussing with the kettle on the hob. With her back turned, Maura had said, 'There's worse, too. I may as well tell you, now. Your husband will do things to you when you're married. Nasty things, to do with your Private Parts. You have to put up with it, if you want children.'

The girl had gazed at her mother in shock. The only parts Clemency could think of that were Private were those between her legs. When she was unclothed she could see virtually everything else. What would a man want with her Private Parts?

Now, nearly eighteen years later, she smiled at her naivety. Sex with the three handsome young lovers she had chosen, at intervals of two or three years, had not been as nasty as her mother had promised. Neither had it been, as Christabel Mitchell had promised, 'Divine'. It was rather pleasant, time-consuming and messy. Afterwards, when one tried to explain that the relationship was over, it became Emotional.

Though, perhaps, she told herself, as she pulled on trousers and shirt and picked up her saturated riding habit to take it to Charity, it was her own fault for choosing a Frenchman, an Italian and a Russian Count. Their very nationalities seemed to connote passion of the most extreme order.

Of an evening, she usually took a carrot or a biscuit down to the stables and gave it to the pretty little bay gelding her father had bought for her when she arrived back in Australia. While Kelly had been ill, in the homestead, she had brought a treat for the black gelding – Lucian, Kelly called him – as well as her own horse. Lucian was a beautiful animal, and she would have asked to ride him, had the owner been anyone else but Michael Kelly.

Lucian was not in his loosebox when she entered the stables, and she was standing talking to her own horse when the large door at the front of the barn opened and Kelly led his mount and Aidan's Blue, down the passageway between the stalls. He paused on seeing Clemency, standing there twisting the remaining carrots in her hands. 'Miss O'Brien.' He nodded, led his own horse into the loose-box, then led Blue to his. Clemency approached the large black gelding with its alert, fine-boned head, and held out one of the small carrots on the palm of her hand.

'You'll be spoiling Lucian, Miss O'Brien,' Kelly said mildly, opening Blue's loosebox door. The big, intelligent grey moved forward of his own accord. Aidan had looped the reins through the throat lash, and the animal allowed Kelly to shut the door and attend, first, to the more temperamental Lucian.

Clemency stood back as he passed her, then moved forward and leaned on the loosebox door. 'So everything's worked itself out.'

Kelly removed the saddle and placed it on the half-door, making her step back. He smiled at her, turned back to the animal, and began to curry-comb the dry sweat from the coat.

'And you're going to stay on here?'

He did not pause in his brush strokes, but looked over at her, eyebrows raised. 'You don't believe I should?'

She had her hands in her trouser pockets, scowling, 'Papa seems to trust you – I don't. I think you'll bring us trouble, and I'd prefer it if you took it somewhere else.'

This stung him. Perhaps, he was able to consider later, because she had come quite close to the truth. And it hurt his pride that this little raggamuffin in her ill-fitting men's clothes could want him gone. He knew with an opinion born of long experience, that women found him attractive. Not many women disliked him, because he was sensitive to their desires. No woman, in his entire life, had ever come close to asking him to go away.

'Your father is an astute man,' he pointed out, politely. 'Why don't you trust his judgement?'

'I make up my own mind, Mr Kelly.'

'And you think,' he was saying gently, 'that I'm a bounder, a libertine, an unprincipled rogue . . . '

'Exactly. So why don't you do the gentlemanly thing and leave?'

He considered, or seemed to consider, then he said, 'The gentle-manly thing . . . would be to stay. And sometime in the course of our . . . long acquaintance – perhaps you'll change your mind about me.'

She gazed at him for a long moment, and he was amused to see that she was furious. 'Just why did you come here, Mr Kelly? Don't you have a home of your own?'

He had finished grooming Lucian, took the saddle and bridle to

898

the tack stands, and entered Blue's loosebox. Clemency followed him to the door.

'Of course I have a home of my own,' he said. 'I just don't choose to live there, that's all.'

'Shall I guess why? You've spent years, apparently, looking for my father – do you want to revenge yourself upon him, for something that's happened in the past?'

He grinned, removed the saddle from Blue and placed it over the half-door. 'No, Miss O'Brien. It was curiosity, only. Your father must have told you that he was engaged to my mother when she eloped with my father to England.' And from the look on the woman's face, she did not know. 'I'm sorry,' he said, sincerely, 'Perhaps I shouldn't have spoken.'

'Why not?' through stiff lips. 'It's about time somebody told me what happened. So. That's the reason, is it? My father could have been your father. Do you like my father better than your own, perhaps? What was that you said beyond in the house? "Bushrangers are romantic creatures"? So are Irish rebels, Mr Kelly, though I take the risk of disillusioning you by telling you that my father has fought more for himself than he ever did for Ireland.'

He watched the pale little freckled face, its pointed chin and Aidan's rather square jaw, and realized, on the heels of his anger, that the girl was undoubtedly right. Aidan O'Brien had assumed enormous proportions in Kelly's life since he first began to piece together a picture of the man, eleven years before. He had come, in the end, to be prepared for disappointment, almost expect it. The greatest shock of these past few days, perhaps, was to find that the man was everything Kelly, as a young, naive twenty-one-year-old fleeing from Burnley, had wanted him to be.

He tried to think of a way to turn the conversation on this infuriating young woman. He would not allow her to discomfit him. Her rage was disproportionate, and that in itself was intriguing. Perhaps she was not indifferent to him.

Not for the first time, he wondered why he found her so attractive when really, she was like nothing else he had met before. She was not unfeminine, despite the eccentricity of her trousers and shirt. She was quite pretty, and in a gown she had looked delightful. She did not, despite the rigours of the Australian climate, look to be thirty, only a year younger than himself, as Father McDonnagh had told him O'Brien's daughter was.

He had thought to find both O'Brien children married. Clemency would be a plump matron with three or four children. Instead he had been literally knocked from his saddle by a slim woman with masses

899

of auburn hair and direct green eyes, possessed, he knew, of a great deal of courage, if not a great deal of sense. She was the only one at Shannonbrook not to welcome him, and he was increasingly uneasy to discover that her regard was the one that mattered most.

He realized, suddenly, watching her scowling up at him from beyond the safety of the half-door, that it was her very independence and disregard for convention that drew him to her. She, unlike himself, seemed to have no need of competing amongst her sex. She had set herself outside all that. He envied her strength while he felt empathy, suddenly, for her solitariness. He wondered how much of their aloneness they had in common.

He said, carefully, as a first effort towards detente, 'Why do you resent me, Miss O'Brien? I promise you, I won't cause trouble, as you put it, for your family. My gun, by the way, is locked in your father's desk, and he tells me I'll have it back only when I leave his employ. Does that set your mind at rest?'

'Not very much, sure.'

He stepped to the door, so that despite the wooden partition they were fairly close. 'You've heard of Kismet, Miss O'Brien?'

'Persian for Fate,' she said, flatly, and he knew she wanted to step back, but did not want him to believe she was afraid of him.

'More poetic than Fate. I believe I was meant to come here. The situation is very strange, is it not?'

'Pishogue,' she said, rudely. 'You've got 'roos in your top paddock, that's why you're here.'

He had to put his head down in an effort not to laugh. 'God help the man who tries to seduce you, young woman,' he murmured, then looked up, worried that he might have affronted her, but she was looking at him, puzzled. He thought aloud, gazing at her suddenly, consideringly, 'I wonder what would have happened if our parents had stayed in Killaloe. No doubt we'd have grown up together on Tineranna, running barefoot by the shores of Lough Derg . . .'

'To hell with that!' Now she was affronted.

Gazing at her earnestly, speaking with candour, he said, 'And if that had been the case, wouldn't you expect me, as your landlord, with a great deal of power over you, to treat you with respect, and good manners?'

She was no fool. The green eyes narrowed to emerald slits and she did not need to speak to tell him that she knew exactly what he'd do, had he that much power. 'What I'm trying to say,' he said, feeling the ground going from under him as it had never done with a woman before, 'is that I'd like to expect the same good manners from you.

900

Might we be friends?'

The knowing eyes opened wider and studied him. Then a small brown hand was held out to him over the half-door. He took it in his own – and found the two carrots lying in his palm. 'Feed y'r own horse,' she said, and left the barn.

Berrima and Aidan walked in the garden, later that evening, and listened to Clemency practising the piano. She was feeling disturbed and it came through her playing, quite noticeably.

'Mr Kelly disturbs her, Aidan,' Berrima said. 'I wonder if you've thought of the possible effects of his staying here?'

'Arra, you're not going to tell me that Clemency'll fall in love with the man, are you? *Rawmaish*, Berri.'

'If she did, you'd be the last to know.'

'I know my daughter better than you, I'm thinking,' he growled.

And she stopped walking, turned to him, tilting her head a little. 'Aidan, I know you too well not to know what you're thinking. You can see that Kelly is handsome, charming, with just that air of mystery that would intrigue any woman, and you're quite happy that Clemency should find him attractive, flirt with him, break his heart, if she can – but she's your daughter, and therefore you assume that she has your cool control over the emotions.' His eyebrows shot up, and he was about to reply, but she went on, 'She may not be like you at all, not in this, Aidan. She may be much more like Maura – and Thomas – than you think. Clemency may be waiting for one great love of her life. Her disinterest in the men she has met to date may not be because she's aloof, but because she has extremely high expectations. She may be waiting for Prince Charming, Aidan – many an old maid is. And perhaps, in that rather enigmatic young man, she may believe she's found him . . . '

He was half-smiling, had his hands in his pockets, and was strolling about her almost happily. He looked up to gaze at her, 'Waiting for the magic, is she?'

The words struck a chord within her – not a pleasant one. Then the memory returned, they were words from her farewell letter to him, before she had run away with Mark. *Who is Berrima when she isn't waiting for the magic?* He was remorseless. She gazed at him, and for the first time in the six months she had lived in his house, she came close to hating him.

She said, 'I'm telling you only that you shouldn't play with people. Their emotions and reactions are capable of surprising even you.'

The broad mouth smiled at her, mockingly, 'I shall endeavour to remember your advice, Mrs Ellis.'

'Do that, Aidan.' And she walked away, back to the house, angry to find that she was shaking a little.

Kelly dined with the family that night. In the warm glow of the candlelight, he looked around at the faces of the family, and wondered at his feeling of pleasure and contentment. It was not simply relief that he was free of gaol, that he could, tomorrow, tonight, saddle Lucian and resume his travels. Suddenly that thought held no excitement for him at all, and what was more, he acknowledged reluctantly, it had been some time since it had.

He was welcomed here. It was very odd, but that seemed to be the cause for his good spirits; he sensed that he was welcome. Berrima Ellis, even Charity, who had been hovering solicitously over him all evening, as well as the O'Briens themselves, they all seemed to care, they had all tried to help him. He realized that they were caring people . . .

His gaze met Clemency's, who was seated opposite him at the table. Her eyes glowed a little, then the fire died as she lowered her eyes to her plate. Well, he smiled faintly, perhaps not everyone welcomed him.

He could hardly blame her; in his arrogance he had behaved badly, her attitude towards him had not thawed – and perhaps it would not. All through the meal he had tried to set her at ease, but it appeared that no amount of his present charm would atone for her first impression of him. Her stubbornness irritated him. He tried not to care that her responses were polite, automatic, that her face held no friendly interest when it was turned towards him. But he did care.

She intrigued him. When he had first discovered, up on the hill, that she was a woman, he had thought she might be simple; one of those poor creatures that even the most gifted families can spawn, who was allowed, for the sake of peace, to indulge in whatever little idiosyncracies she may wish. A harmless creature who had, on that particular day, managed to get her hands on a gun . . .

In the bedroom, when he had heard the exchange between Clemency and Berrima, and, later, when she had brought his dinner to him, he realized he had been wrong. She was not simple, she was obviously mad. Or at the least, eccentric.

Now, he was revising even that opinion. Dressed in an evening gown, contributing intelligently, sometimes precociously, to the conversation, he realized that there was much more to her.

At thirty years of age, she would be regarded by many as an

902

old maid. Not for the first time, he wondered why she had not married. She was not a cold woman – but she tried hard to be. Through the talk of politics, the inevitable dissection of the happenings of the past few days, Kelly felt himself drawn to studying the girl across the table. Her gown was of jade green taffeta; it made her eyes appear very green. She was not mad, and if eccentric, only sufficiently so to be interesting. He cursed his habit of making instant decisions about people – perhaps she was right to distrust him . . .

He dragged himself back to the discussion, tried to concentrate on Liam, who was declaring that the judiciary system of New South Wales needed a good shaking up.

I want to stay, Kelly thought, with a sudden sense of longing that he could not remember knowing since he had been very young. There was something about each of them, in their different ways, that drew him. If I stayed, he told himself, I could learn from them, I could help them, perhaps. Aidan obviously had many enemies . . . Kelly glanced up at the broad, hard features of the man at the head of the table. Young Constable Foles had spent quite a lot of time chatting to the prisoner, and was a wealth of information on the inhabitants of the Mittagong district. Kelly had a sketchy but sensational outline of Aidan's career since he had come to the Southern Highlands. Such men as Aidan O'Brien would always make enemies. All the more reason, Kelly decided, that he needed friends.

Aidan watched as the man became more and more preoccupied as the meal progressed. His gaze seemed to linger on each of them, and there was something in the dark grey eyes that spoke of concern.

Kelly's eyes, in that moment, found Clemency's, and her father half-smiled. This would be the danger, of course. Kelly was well-educated, polished, articulate. Clemency, who went through life with a practised indifference, was now pushing her food about her plate with the scowling concentration of a chess player trying various moves; she was not indifferent where Kelly was concerned.

Aidan glanced at Berrima. She, too, had seen, but she lowered her head after giving Aidan one brief glance. She had given him her opinion that afternoon, had warned Aidan not to toy with people – as if he were likely to do that, and his own daughter involved. Berrima had said that Kelly was dangerous; she could not forget the blue-metal Colt. The look she now threw him reminded him of this.

But Aidan liked the man. He could not say why. Perhaps it was the eyes; they were gentle eyes, oddly at variance with the rest of the man; the face, the body, spoke of a hard man who lived on his wits and his reflexes. He could, Aidan thought, be a good man to have about, should something go wrong.

He scowled, trying to shake off the feeling that something might go wrong; it was not only the fact that he had dreamed of the Woman in Black last night, though it did seem that she visited him whenever some conflict or danger was brewing. No, it was Sam, and the tension amongst the workers at the mills; it was the fact that Donaldson and young Amberley and Pirie-Moxham rode about, these days, with men on either side of them, or with guns prominently displayed on their saddles. There was no need, but the fear and suspicion bred more fear, more suspicion. Donaldson had taken what he saw as a stand in not paying any compensation to Sam Russell, not helping him in any way. Sam Russell was well-loved, and behind the thoughts of every working man in the district whose family's very lives depended on their health and strength, was the thought; what if it had been me?

87

Aidan was afraid, after the disagreement in the garden, that Berrima, in her strange mood of late, would take it into her head to leave. While feeling a little uncomfortable about the subterfuge, he even visited Sam and Tessa, to offer them the caretakership of the house in Queen Street, in case Berrima was planning, in truth, to remove herself there. He would explain to her later, sure; and besides, she could not be too angry with him, as Donaldson had served notice on the Russells to leave the cottage even before the rumour of the damages suit had reached him; men were calling to him on the streets, his former workers shouted insults at him, and the letter evicting the Russells had mentioned 'disloyalty to an employer and landlord in inflaming and inciting other workers against their rightful superior.' Tessa took the letter to Berrima at Shannonbrook Three, then burnt it, telling Sam, when he had sufficiently recovered, only the fact that they must leave.

To Aidan's surprise, both Sam and Tessa were adamant in their refusal to live in the Queen Street house. Tessa, privately, regarded the place as bad luck, and liking Berrima as a friend wanted her to have the place should she leave Shannonbrook, so the two women could visit each other. To Aidan, she merely stood by Sam's decision, and there was no way that Sam's pride could allow this further proof of his dependence on Aidan. 'Anyway,' he finished, the large, darkly handsome face scowling up at Aidan from the bed, 'though I thank you kindly, the house is too bloody grand by half.'

Aidan, determined now, found another tenant for the house, and at the agent's leased another, smaller sandstone cottage in the village. He made sure Berrima 'discovered' it and told Tessa. The Russells rented the cottage cheaply from the agent, and never knew who was behind it. Tessa had her suspicions, but she said nothing, went gratefully about the task of moving her belongings in, and keeping the restless spirits of her husband from sinking into bitterness.

There was little chance to talk to Berrima, and Aidan doubted if he wished to. She seemed content to remain at Shannonbrook, content to remain aloof from him. When he forgot himself, sometimes, and touched her shoulder, her hair, as he passed her, he could feel her tense. The bitter-sweet memory of the one time they had lain together haunted him in a way that held him back from her more than drew him to her body. He had vowed, once, and meant it, that he would not touch her until she wanted him – and then he had lost control, taken her by force, and she had obviously despised him for it ever since. He could not, it seemed, compete with Mark, whatever Mark was like between the sheets, for she had gone with Mark, despite everything.

Now Mark was dead and he was an even stronger adversary. Aidan had entered Berrima's room, once, when she was visiting 'Tillia and Thomas, and stayed in the room only long enough to gaze, for several seconds, appalled, at the two portraits, a painted miniature and an early photograph, of Mark that stood upon the dressing table. He had left the room immediately, and after that he no longer wondered why she stiffened at his touch, why there was sometimes a look of reproach in her gaze, why sometimes she flared into anger with him. The dressing table was not the only shrine to Mark Ellis, she carried one within herself, and Aidan pitied her even as he bitterly resented her.

He took his longing for her to other women's bodies, and he behaved towards Berrima with as much courtesy as he possessed. He had hopes that she might come to her senses. *All she has to say is that she wants me*, he told himself, lying alone in his bed at Shannonbrook or beside one of his female companions in Sydney, where he often amused them and enraged himself by murmuring the name of one of the colony's gaol towns at his moment of climax. *All she has to do is say she wants me. I won't demand that she sacrifice her* happiness, her life almost, as Mark did; I'll not demand her reputation and good name as Balbrook did. But I'll not follow on her haughty little heels and risk her spurning me again. I'll be damned if I will.

No one but the architect of Shannonbrook Three knew the original purpose of the little, windowless room that Berrima used as a darkroom. An extra pantry, or coolroom, perhaps. Berrima knew only that she was grateful for it. The studio itself, however, bothered her; the windows were narrow here, unlike the front of the house, and they did not allow much light into the room. She discussed it with Aidan, and without her needing to suggest anything to him, he told her that the obvious thing would be to make the windows larger.

It was one of those puzzling incidents that teased her brain, as the workmen arrived and half the wall in the studio was reduced to rubble, that his generosity reached such extents, while his feelings for her remained cool, aloof. The large panes of glass were fitted in the wall, from two feet above the floor, all the way to the ceiling, and light flooded the little room. When the workmen had cleaned the place and departed, Berrima spent much time standing at the window and wondering how long she herself would be kept in the dark. There were, she thought, no windows in Aidan's soul. Certainly not, as the poet said, his eyes, which ran over her with cool appraisal, and like as not drifted off from her almost in dismissal. Yet he blasted holes in his beloved house, simply so that she might amuse herself with what, she was sure, he felt were her toys. Perhaps she was unwise to allow him to do this, though she held the incident lose her. But perhaps she should have moved back to the house in Queen Street. It was let at the moment, but when the tenant left she could rent it from Aidan and live there – alone.

She leaned her hands on the wooden window frames, and scowled out over the view of pine trees and yellow paddocks dropping down the slope. Alone. No, not even her work could compensate for the loss of the maddening, beloved people who surrounded her here. She sighed, for she knew there would be no change forthcoming. Aidan must be accepted the way he was, there would be no point in making some wild declaration to him, embarrassing him, making him withdraw even further from her. Perhaps this was one of the prices one paid for growing older, she thought, smiling grimly. The thought of Aidan finally taking her in his arms and crying, 'If only I'd known sooner!' like the hero of her early *Miranda* stories was not worth the risk of destroying the friendship they had. And besides – she turned to gaze about the room – did she really want Aidan to take

906

her in his arms? She had been there before, and hard and strong those arms were. Hard and strong his kisses, also. They demanded something of her that she was afraid she no longer knew how to give. With Mark, love had turned into a nightmare, and the memory was still there, though she purposefully refused ever to think on it. 'I'm a coward,' she said softly to herself, leaning back against the window frame and looking at the little room that would form the centre of her world. 'I'm as much of a coward as Aidan. We live for what we build, for those things are sure, and safe.' And she realized that for all their friendship, Aidan did not represent safety to her. And what's more, and the thought made her smile, she undoubtedly did not represent safety to Aidan.

When she had the studio arranged the way she wished, she began to turn her mind to subjects. The entire family was coerced, separately, into standing or sitting stiffly in front of her cameras over the following weeks, and even Jim, Bram and Maurie were inveigled with promises of Charity's tea buns and apple pie if they would sit still, grouped around a corner of the stableyard, looking business-like, with a mock fire and branding irons. They escaped after a morning of this only when news came of a bushfire west of Bowral. It had been a dry summer, and the threat had hung in the air with the heat and the drone of the cicadas. Every man that could, as in every Australian community, had gone to aid the few settlers who were threatened. 'But in this case,' Berrima muttered to Clemency, as the boys raced off around the drive with whoops of exuberant relief, 'I think they go rather more willingly than usual.'

It was a good thing, perhaps, Liam and the barrister, Arthur Gold-man, both assured Aidan, that the court case was set so far ahead in August of that year, five months away. Aidan had been enraged, had railed against Donaldson and his influential friends who had obviously been behind the delaying tactics. But Sam would be completely well by then, Goldman suggested, and he would need all his strength for the ordeal of facing a defending barrister who would attempt to prove him incompetent, reckless, and possibly, a liar. Aidan grudgingly saw his point.

He was kept busy in those months, was able to come home to Shannonbrook only to eat and sleep, sometimes so late that the house was in darkness when he arrived. And every morning he was awake and dressed and breakfasted and out of the house by six.

With the extra orders that came flowing into the Shannonbrook mills, however, came the more sobering sight of men from

Donaldson's mill, looking for work. The doors of the mill had been closed despite the new engine that had been ordered, only six weeks after the accident. Donaldson cut his losses, explained privately to those who'd listen, and there were many who did, that underhand tactics from rival mills in the district was behind his inability to keep his mill running.

Aidan and Thomas managed to find work for many men. 'Too many,' Aidan grumbled to his younger brother, whose kind heart and memories of the Famine often warred with his business-sense.

But even those who could not gain work at the Shannonbrook mills bore the O'Briens no ill-will. All those who had worked for Donaldson knew, from the frequent sight of O'Brien horses or vehicles outside the Russells' cottage, of the friendship between the two families. And they waited, paying a stiff rental to stay in the cottages on Donaldson's property, to find out exactly what would happen.

The news soon spread that the district court list for August was to include *Russell vs Donaldson* – and the entire district erupted and divided. No one doubted, for all Sam's bitterness and anger, the dark malevolence that shone in his eyes and twisted the once firm mouth into a downward line, that the money, the real power and impetus behind this move, was Aidan O'Brien.

'Under the law of Torts,' Liam recited to Clemency as they stood in the centre of the exercise ring, lungeing one of the yearlings, 'a man can sue his employer for damages incurred while working at his job.' Liam scowled, 'But there've been very few successful cases.'

'Why?' Clemency demanded, 'if a man's asked to work outdated, dangerous machinery like poor Mr Russell, and the rotten gurrier who owns it won't have it fixed . . . Will the law be after siding with the rotten gurrier?'

Liam glanced across at his sister. 'Charles Dickens once said that the law is an ass. Be that as it may, Sam will have to prove that he was injured through no fault of his own.' The inexorable, detached lawyer's voice went on. He contemplated the lagging colt before him, chirped to him, let him see the long whip snake out. The colt's ears flicked and he lengthened his stride. Round and round them, the long lead unstrained, the neck arched, the yearling cantered, till the world beyond it, for both of them, seemed to blur.

Liam, who had been enjoying himself, did not mind Clemency coming to watch him work, for this was one of the horses that he himself had bred, had seen being born, and he was proud of the animal; but he did not like to be reminded, on this warm autumn afternoon, when the sun was so pleasant and the breeze cool, of the

908

problems building around them. Despite his academic ability, his pleasure in arguing points of law, slipping in and out the intricacies of a centuries-old legal system, there was something within Liam that called for action. When faced, as he had rarely been faced while studying within the womb that was Trinity, with injustice seen at first hand, he found it almost impossible to keep the necessary detachment. Sam's case brought his own conflict to the fore.

He glanced down at Clemency, beside him; she was scowling from beneath the brim of her hat, the freckled arms folded across her chest. She had made no effort to tie back her hair, let alone put it up, and it curled in long corkscrews out from beneath her hat. He wondered how much of the greater implications she saw in this suit for damages, but received an answer when she said:

'But that law seems to be weighted in favour of the employer. A man wouldn't want to stick his fingers under a butcher's blade, no woman in a mine wants the ore truck to run over her. The employer could say, "You should have been watching what you were doing." And the employee would say, "The blade slipped," or, "I didn't move out of the way fast enough when the truck ran backwards." An' the employer would say, "Ha! y' contributed to the accident by your own negligence".'

'That,' Liam said, 'is about it.'

'That's it? I'm playing Devil's advocate, Liam. I was expecting you to tell me I'm wrong – and you say that's *it*?'

'Aye. That's what happens. Something'd have to break, or the employer would have to be demanding something very difficult and dangerous of the employee – *above*,' as his sister went to interrupt, 'the danger normally inherent in the work the employee does, before a court would find that an accident was an employer's fault.'

'Well, Mr Russell will win, then,' Clemency said confidently. 'For Donaldson was asking the impossible for that machinery to keep going indefinitely. And something did break, did it not? Mister Russell will win, so.'

She waited for corroboration, but Liam, feeling the colt to have had enough, was calling 'Whoa . . . ' gently, and at the same time, drawing in the lungeing rope. Clemency heard him sigh, and her confidence sagged a little. Liam was a lawyer; Liam knew about these things; and it was dawning on her that Liam had his doubts about the outcome of this court case.

On Saturday and Sunday afternoons, when Clemency would often, in her riding habit for propriety's sake, ride out to visit Killaloe, or the Henkes' place, or Victoria Ellis, she was frequently accompanied by Michael Kelly.

The first time, they had been riding into Mittagong at the same time, quite by accident, but the following day, he asked if he could ride with her, and gradually it became a fairly common occurrence. She never went in search of him, but he seemed, at these times, always to be about, somehow.

This Sunday, when he had asked to join her, she agreed, though she had no destination in mind. He did not ask for one, and they ambled about the tracks by Fitzroy Falls for two hours before she said, finally, when they were on their way home:

'My father didn't order you to accompany me on these rides, did he?'

'No . . . But he did say that he was glad that I accompanied you. He worries about your safety; I think that's perfectly natural.'

Clemency scowled over at him. 'I've ridden about this country for years before you came here, Mr Kelly, and I keep a rifle on my saddle, you'll notice. Besides,' she could not help adding, for this was a man, she was finding, with whom it was difficult to argue, and even more difficult to defeat. 'Besides, if my father knew that you'd grabbed me y'rself in that insolent way, when you first came to Shannonbrook, I doubt if you'd be taking care of anything more important than poddy calves. If he didn't fire you outright.'

He sighed. When a piece of paper blew across before his horse's feet he controlled its sudden start and half-rear easily, before continuing, gently, 'But you didn't tell him. And I'd thought that by now you must have forgiven me for that. I was concussed, I remind you. In fact, the more I think about it, the less I remember the incident. What did happen?'

He turned to her with such a comic look of enquiry that when she began hotly to tell him of his misconduct, she realized how silly she sounded, and she smiled. 'I hate you when you make me laugh when I'm angry. I'm beginning to think you like my tempers, you always seem to put me into one . . . '

'My secret is out,' he lamented.

'You're codding me. No man likes a woman who's a shrew . . . '

'You're not a shrew. You're a woman of high mettle – and I like you very much.'

There, he did it again. She stared at the track before her horse's ears, and hoped she wasn't about to go pink, betray the fact that she had noticed his words. First he put her in a rage, then he laughed her out of it, then he said something kind, something complimentary, and she who could sense flattery and loathed it, did not know in this case, what to do. For she wanted to believe he was not sincere, and yet something, something in the grey eyes, told her that he was.

This afternoon she was saved from giving the man any reply. They had come out on to the road to Burrawang, and up the hill, amongst the trees, was the neat, two-storey house that Victoria Ellis now lived in, alone, with her two daughters. And as Clemency's gaze was caught by the picturesque look of the Georgian-styled building amongst its garden, she stopped herself only just in time from pointing it out to Kelly. For Liam's chestnut mare was tied to a tethering post by the front door.

How many times a week was he calling here after he finished at the office: three, four? Clemency liked Victoria very much, and knew that with the children in the house, nothing intimate would be taking place. They were talking about Liam's work, perhaps, or the children. Gemma and Honor were very fond of Liam, Clemency had seen that on the visits the little family had made to Shannonbrook. Yet all the same . . . I wish he'd find a girl of his own, she thought, for she often sensed a loneliness in Liam, something that told her that he did not like to be the only one amongst his friends who was not paying court to one special girl, if they weren't actually married, already. It was good that he had such a friend as Victoria Ellis, but where could that relationship lead? She hoped Liam didn't love Victoria, it would mean heartache, for both of them.

It was the wailing that broke into her thoughts. She looked up, thinking at first it was a lamb or a calf in pain, but no. There, off to the side of the road, seated on the grassy verge, his mouth open in a cry that was broken by sobs, was a very grubby small boy.

They both dismounted, but it was Kelly who reached the child first. 'Hello, what're you doing out here so late? Where do you live?' Only a thin and keening wail in reply.

'What's your name?' Clemency reached for the child, gathered him to her, and Kelly, half in surprise, watched the child's arms go about her neck.

'Dadda – want Dadda . . . !'

'What's your name, little one, and we'll take you to your Dadda . . .'

He sniffed and looked her in the face, studying it, and Kelly smiled to himself at the seriousness of the two. 'Harry,' he said.

Kelly, too, was down on one knee. 'And your last name, Harry?'

'Harry. I want me Dadda.'

'Where is he, son?' Kelly's voice was gentle, and Clemency looked up at the face beside her, the concern a new emotion, the whole a new Kelly she had not seen, no mockery, no cynicism. 'If you can tell us your Dadda's name, we'll take you home.'

'Dadda . . . ' a hiccup, ' . . . in Mel-bunn.'

'Oh, Lord,' Kelly lowered his head.

'And Mama? Where's Mama?' Clemency asked.

'Don't want Mama. Want Dadda.'

Kelly sighed. 'Would you like to ride on my horse, Harry? He's a very tall horse, and you might be able to see your home from up there. What do you think?'

A sudden smile, a wonderful smile, through a very wet, very dirty mask. Kelly was pulling his handkerchief from his pocket, was wiping the grubby face. 'You know, under the dirt and the moisture from eyes and nose, Harry, you're a very handsome boy. I'll bet your mama is very pretty, is she?'

'Yes,' proudly, climbing to his feet and walking unaided towards Kelly's mount.

When they were all mounted, the boy behind Kelly, and the horses moving, 'I'll bet that pretty mama of yours is crying right at this moment – I'll bet she's most upset at losing you . . . '

Gradually, through reasoning such as this, and various promptings along the way, they were able to find their way to a small, slab-built settler's cottage, set away amongst the trees. A cow grazed beside a thin chestnut horse in the small house paddock, chickens scratched about before the front of the house and a thin blue mongrel of a dog came rushing, snarling, from a hole beneath the verandah.

Several children came streaming out of the house, and stood in an excited semi-circle around the two horses. 'Harry, where you bin?' 'Harry, Mama's gonna beat you good and proper . . . !' 'Where you bin, Harry, we bin looking everywhere . . . !'

She came around from the rear of the house at a run, slowed when she saw the two horses, the woman in the well-tailored riding habit, lifting Harry down reluctantly from behind the tall man in the saddle. She walked forward without hurry, her eyes on the woman, while Kelly, too, dismounted, and they stood in the midst of the five children.

Harry hung back a little, then changed his tactics and ran to his mother, clinging to her skirt, 'I won't do it again – I won't – I won't – I won't . . . '

'Hush, Harry,' trying to pull her dress free of the little burr-like claws.

'You won't hit me with the razor strop, will you? Will you, Mama? Will you? You won't, will you?'

Her eyes on the younger woman. 'You found him?'

912

'Yes, he was quite a distance away, on the Burrawang Road . . . He was sincerely sorry for running away even then, I assure you . . . '

'He misses his Dad,' the woman said simply. She looked down at the curly fair head, now buried in her skirts. 'I . . . the house is a mess . . . I'd invite you in, but . . . you wouldn't be . . . '

'No, thank you all the same . . . ' Clemency and Kelly spoke the words at the same time, and exchanged a look, a grin, before the girl continued, 'We'd best be going home. I'm just glad he's safe.' The man helped her to mount her horse, for today she rode side-saddle, and when she was mounted, Clemency noted the sharp and considering look the woman was giving both Kelly and herself.

'Good evening, ma'am,' Kelly said, touching his hat a little, before mounting his own horse. Clemency murmured a goodbye, also. The woman said, 'Thank you for bringing the boy home safe, Miss O'Brien.' Still staring at them, taking in, it seemed, every detail of their faces. Even when they turned their horses, and for a while all the children ran down the track beside and behind them, calling goodbyes, Clemency knew the woman was gazing after them, unmoving.

It was not until they reached the bottom of the track, where it joined the road, that Clemency realized that none of them had exchanged names, and she wondered how the woman knew that she was an O'Brien.

She turned back to the children. 'What's your father's name?' she asked.

It was the eldest child, a pretty girl, brown as a gypsy, who answered, 'Griffith Rodgers.'

When she thought of Kelly, from that day on, it was always with the same look upon his face that he had shown the little boy, and in his voice, now, beneath the arrogant tone and the droll, sometimes gently barbed words, she heard the gentleness that he could betray, and it disturbed her even more, she found, than when he was an out-and-out villain. The more I see of him, she thought, the more I like him. Oh, damn him, damn him.

For it was becoming increasingly difficult to ignore Kelly. Clemency liked to work with her father, and for some reason, her father, since Kelly's arrival, had the man close much of the time, talking to him, explaining things, sometimes, Clemency noted, with more patience and in greater detail than her father would explain to Liam, were he interested in Shannonbrook – or to me, she thought somewhat bitterly, if I'd been a boy.

There was no avoiding each other, for as he had hinted on that ride during which they had found the errant Harry, her father did not like her riding alone on the great rambles that she took about the countryside on her bay. The very value of the horse, her father pointed out to her on more than one occasion, might prove too much of a temptation for some desperate character one of these days. So whether through her father's orders, or through Kelly's own inclinations, she was often in his company, and the uneasy feelings that his presence engendered did not fade, as she had thought they would, but grew stronger.

She liked to be with him, there was no denying this. She who did not need anyone, was made to laugh, often, and this was strange, and rather frightening, that a man she had known for such a short time seemed to understand her, and, what was more, be capable of drawing forth from her a humour that she did not believe she possessed. He liked to tease her, even to flirt with her, in a comic way; and when they disagreed, which was frequently – despite his seemingly easy-going nature – he could be stubborn, beneath it all, and sometimes there was no moving him. During these spats he nearly always came out ahead, for he had a deadly kind of logic that was worse than Liam's lawyer's dialectics; she would nearly always be forced into withdrawing into aloofness, like an uppity squatter's daughter would be likely to, more priggish than the Lawler girls, and she did not like that one bit.

Kelly showed no sign, as the months passed, of wanting to leave. On the contrary, he seemed to enjoy his work, often keeping late hours such as only Aidan did, sometimes neglecting to take a day off when it was due to him, and generally proving himself to be hard-working and reliable. More than this, he began to betray a surprising amount of knowledge of the running of a large property, and this, too, made Clemency suspicious. Somewhere, she speculated, Kelly had known a position of some trust and responsibility. Why, then, when he had first come to Shannonbrook, had he been drifting?

Liam was the first to notice that Kelly was watching them. He liked the man, their personalities complemented each other, and Liam found someone, at last, with whom he could commune at something like the same level that he had shared with friends in Dublin and Boston. Kelly knew too much, Liam found, about economics, points of law and British politics not to have had a damn' fine education. They would argue happily on these matters while herding sheep and cattle, digging fence posts or cutting fire breaks.

Kelly admitted, finally, to being educated at Oxford. It did not

914

surprise Liam, but served to puzzle him further. At the time of this revelation they were helping dig a dam in what Aidan termed the Killaloe paddock, thirty acres of Shannonbrook Two that adjoined Thomas's property, and Kelly, like all the men, was shirtless, despite the chill of the wind, for it was early autumn. Liam noticed the callouses on Kelly's hands, the shoulders now burnt brown from much work like this in the sun over the past months. Liam had studied Law at Trinity, he was here shovelling mud in Mittagong, New South Wales, because of his family. But Kelly?

Kelly looked up, at that moment, and caught Liam scowling at him. 'I wasn't suited to academic life,' he said, as if knowing what Liam was thinking.

'Y'r mad, boyo.'

'Perhaps.'

'You could have been independent, not taking orders from my father, nor anyone else. What in the name of all that's holy do we have here that you want?'

And even as he said it, it occurred to him that it might be Clemency. But he would not say that. He decided suddenly, with customary impetuosity, that he would like Kelly for a brother-in-law too much to risk the suggesting of it so soon.

Kelly was leaning on his pick handle. 'What do you have? You have a kind of . . . basic integrity. You're good people. Interesting, too, things are never dull. But basically, you're good. And you have guts. All of you – I include Mrs Ellis as well.'

'So you should,' Liam growled, and Kelly grinned, but said nothing. 'And that's our fascination?' Liam asked. 'We're decent and amusing and we've got guts?'

'Basically, yes.'

'And your own family – it wasn't like that?'

'No.' A definite sound, an end-to-that-line-of-questioning sound. Liam did not press the matter.

But, less preoccupied than the rest of the family, with his practice taking him away from the homestead much of the time and giving him a kind of perspective, he began to see other illustrations of Kelly's professed interest in the household. He followed Aidan like a shadow, was always the first to volunteer for any work that would mean accompanying Aidan; Liam would see Kelly watching his father, studying him when Aidan did not see. It was a little eerie. Kelly behaved towards Berrima with exquisite gallantry, and betrayed a great interest in the photography. On weekends and even sometimes during the week, when she could persuade Aidan to free him from his duties, Kelly accompanied Berrima on jaunts in the wagon, up into the hills, and helped her set up the heavy equipment.

And Clemency. Clemency he watched perhaps most of all, with a strange waiting quality that was similar to his preoccupation with Liam's father, but mixed, sometimes, with a hungry look that pleased Liam even while it brought out a good deal of his possessiveness. But he was never sure, for these looks were not common; most of the time there was affection there, and tolerance, and Liam would relax. No, there was no overtly sexual interest there; Liam could find very little about Clemency, in her out-sized trousers and men's shirts, for any man to find remotely sexual.

Liam began to believe, privately, that Kelly might have 'roos in the top paddock. 'A deprived childhood,' he thought, 'brought up by servants, and either no father, or a disinterested one. That would explain why he likes to borrow mine.'

Though happy with his own legal practice, he could not help the faint resentment of the place his friend was beginning to take in his father's estimation. After a small fire had broken out on Shannonbrook One, and was contained largely due to Kelly's handling of the men called to it, Aidan had named the man head stockman. And after that, or perhaps because of that, Kelly was invited more and more to the house, and was finally eating with the family three or four times a week.

It was not this that Liam objected to; rather it was the subtle way that his father had begun to trust Kelly, to ask his advice, to tend to discuss matters with Kelly rather than him. He told himself that it was unreasonable to do things any other way, considering his own life now revolved around his practice in Mittagong; but all the same, some touch of envy of his friend was creeping into their relationship which amused Liam even as it tormented him. 'Father never discusses the mills or the stock or the crops with me. When he makes plans, he does not consult me.' These thoughts occurred to him in his black moods, and he was not much encouraged by the memory that even before Kelly's arrival, he had not often been included in his father's decisions.

He complained, sometimes, to Victoria. Victoria understood. He came more and more to depend on her friendship, the empathy that shone in her eyes. He wished, as time went on, and he saw more of her and the children, that the vacant place in the household could be a place that he could fill. Once, when he was particularly depressed over a land deal that had gone badly for one of his clients, and when he had returned to Shannonbrook to find that Aidan and Kelly had gone off to visit Sam Russell and had not waited for him to return home, he had said something of the sort to Victoria.

916

'I wish I could stay,' he said. 'I wish it was myself who belonged here, who had the right to be here, and not Garth.'

And something rather terrifying had happened. Victoria had paled a little, had crossed the room, slowly, to sit beside him, and with the lovely dark eyes on his face, said, 'Liam, I'm tired of such words as "right" and "duty" and the entire fabrication. The ideal is all very well – but I'm living a reality, here, with the children, alone. I will not listen to thoughts of ideals and other comforting phrases. I want you here, isn't that enough?'

Her face had been very close to his, the tragic mark on her face was most pronounced, due to her pallor, her eyes were wide and questioning, asking . . . what?

'Aye, it is,' he had almost stammered in his surprise. 'You've been so good to me, I . . . I don't know what I'd be if I didn't have your friendship . . . '

He knew even then his words were not the right words, but he did not realize how very wrong they were until later, when he had time to think over those crucial minutes. Now, he saw only that Victoria's expression had frozen for a few seconds, then a small, very stiff smile had appeared on her lips. She did not immediately pull away, and Liam was left for a desperate interval with her face tantalizingly close to his, but with the knowledge that he was too frozen to move, and it was too late, the words could not be taken back. He rode home that night cursing himself for a fool.

He spent his next three nights at Big Angie's, and lay in the arms of a careless, unknown woman, and wondered what was wrong, why he could not accept or give affection to the one woman who genuinely cared for him.

He continued to visit Victoria and the children, and they were the gentle, good friends that they always were. That there were no recriminations, only Victoria's usual quiet dignity, only served, if anything, to make him feel worse.

To the rest of the family, there was nothing changed within Liam. Sometimes he disliked this ability in himself to hide his unease and his sense of insecurity. It was a legacy of his days at school in the Huon Valley, when he had had to affect cheerful unconcern for his peers' opinions on his convict father. He had, he realized now, and with some bitterness, almost perfected the art of cheerful unconcern.

It took a month, in which time he could not bring himself to seek solace, once more, at Big Angie's, and waited in his bed at night for some sort of answer to come to him. Only one did. He dressed one night at midnight, went to the stables and saddled his chestnut.

When she opened the front door, Victoria, in her wrap, said nothing, stood studying Liam's face, then reached for him, silently, wrapping her arms about his neck, as he buried his face in her hair.

88

Aidan was more unnerved than he would have thought possible, to open the door of his office at Shannonbrook Two mill, later that day, and find Matty seated there.

'The overseer – he let me in.'

'Ah.' And the silence between them competed with the din from the saws, until Aidan shut the door. And the silence was winning. He swallowed, sat down behind his desk. 'Well,' he said.

Matty seemed more confident than he. It was very odd the light in her eyes, her confidence.

She leaned forward. 'I don't see why I should, but I came to warn you. Not that it makes no difference to me. If they was to kill you I'd like as not dance on your coffin, lad. But I like what I seen of your kids. Your daughter brought my Harry home one day when he got lost, did you know that?'

'No.' Aidan regarded her coolly from his side of the desk.

'You ought to get her to wear dresses and behave like a lady, though. It shows at the moment, that she don't respect you. The Lord God says in Proverbs, 'Raise up a child in the way he should go; and when he is old he will not depart from it.'

Jaysus . . . He could hardly believe what he was hearing, tried to piece together all he had heard of Matty in the past years, and connect this with the woman before him.

'Matty, if I need someone to preach to me, I'll go to Mass, and have young Father Davis hurl fire and brimstone at me.'

She looked at him, narrowly. By pursing her mouth up, many small lines appeared around her lips. It looked as if she pursed her lips often, these days. He thought with a shock that she was now forty-three. Yet she looked much older. And it was not, he thought crossly, so much her skin, her figure or her hair. There was barely a touch of silver in the fair hair pulled severely back beneath her bonnet. She sat up straight in her chair, and he could see her full bosom and slim waist; had already noted that she moved with all her old grace. Rather, it was inside that Matty had changed. She looked out at the world with different eyes. It should not have come with her leaning toward religion, he thought. Perhaps the bitterness had begun to grow years before; and a brief, immediately-quashed sense of guilt claimed him with the memory of his refusal to help her family any further. He had had nothing further to do with her since paying the first year's rent on the Moss Vale cottage. Soon after that, her name began appearing in the newspaper, concerned with fund raising for a new chapel in Moss Vale. Matty served on committees, visited the sick with tureens of soup, decorated the chapel, when it was built, with flowers, and to Aidan's shock, in later years even taught Sunday school. There was no trace of his Matty in the woman who sat opposite him.

But sure he had thought that of Berrima, too. And he had found the middle-aged woman now holding sway at Shannonbrook to have lost none of her spark, her fire, and – now he had become used to the changes in her – to be more attractive, more desirable. He had found strengths in Berrima he had not thought possible, and while these new depths to her character terrified him, they drew him also.

Nothing about Matty now drew him. He realized that what had fascinated him all those years ago had been her earthiness, her basic equation of affection with sexual intercourse. Her lack of guilt or hypocrisy. And more than this, perhaps above all these things – she had loved him. Even the last time she had spoken to him, when she had screamed those terrible words at him, her rage had been born of her love for him.

She no longer loved him. And her feelings had been so dulled by the years of wasted, constant giving, to himself and to the wastrel Grif, that, quite understandably, she had no affection left to give.

She said now, 'I had a dream. Same dream every night or so for a fortnight. That someone knocks on the door of your fine house and you go to the door and open it, and someone shoots you.' He was smiling at her and it infuriated her. 'It's very real, Aidan! I see you crumple and try to speak but there's a hole in your chest, and lots of blood – but you look up at whoever it is like you're real puzzled, as if you know the person, maybe it's someone you trust. But you can't speak, and you fall, and you're lying on the floor dead and there's blood all over the green carpet . . . '

'Green?' His eyes narrowed, but still he smiled. 'The carpet was green?'

Yes. It was clear, it was real vivid, like I was there. 'Why' her eyes were alight, 'is the carpet green?'

'Yes,' he drawled, and leaned back to study her. 'How did you know, Matty?'

'*Know?* I don't know. No one's ever invited me to your precious Shannonbrook Three, specially not by the front door. It just goes to show, though, don't it? I really saw the scene like it could happen. You got to be careful, Aidan.'

He continued looking at her, the broad cynical mouth turned up a little at the corners. 'Matty, have you thought that the dream may mean that *you'd* like to shoot me and watch me die on my green carpet?'

Her eyes narrowed. 'Stop flattering yourself. I don't care that much about you. I pity you, because you're a Papist and you'll go to hell and damnation with all the other followers of Anti-Christ, but that's the extent of my feelings for you.'

He was gazing very hard at the desktop, and knowing him of old, she knew he was trying hard not to smile. 'You'll learn. You'll find out when it's too late.' For she saw that he was destined to go on repeating his mistakes. He was that sort of man. She found a sudden and welcome wave of tolerance sweep over her. She had found the truth, found a strength beyond her. Aidan O'Brien would go on until the day he died, trying to solve his problems alone. There was nothing anyone could do to save him.

'I don't want you dying a violent death, Aidan. For old times sake, I don't want to see you hurt. If the Lord has given me this sign that you're in danger – from someone you know – then I should tell you. I'm neglectful in my duty as a Christian if I don't.'

'I'm very grateful to you, Matty,' he said gently. 'I shall light a candle for you at Mass next Sunday.'

'No, thank you,' she said primly. 'Just watch out that no mongrels are plotting against you. That's the other reason I wanted to see you. I don't know whether anyone's told you or not, but every week Pirie-Moxham and Donaldson meet at Barrett's house. And any one of their servants or roustabouts can tell you that they don't mean you any good.'

'They might be meeting to play poker.' But his eyes held their old watchful look, and she knew he was aware of the danger.

'You know what it is, don't you?' she said abruptly. 'All these years you bin running with the fox and hunting with the hounds. You want the wealth and position you've earned, but you feel guilty about leaving your class behind. No use telling you you'll never please either the nobs or the slobs, as an American digger once told me. You already know that. But you're paying for it, now.'

Perhaps,' he said smoothly. 'But I'll have to take the risks. There

920

are risks in everything.'

'Your confidence in yourself can't carry you through all the time. You don't consider what other people are after. You make too many enemies, Aidan, and they're out to get you. My dreams are never wrong.' She stood, and Aidan rose to his feet. 'That's all I got to say to you.'

'Matty . . . how are things with you? Do you need anything?'

Again the lines appeared around her mouth. 'We got ourselves a little farm. We got all the friends we need among our brothers and sisters at the chapel. They don't have no selfish motives behind their offers of friendship.' And she left him.

He stood at the window and watched her walk across the yard to a battered little cart pulled by a thin, ewe-necked chestnut. Something inside him ached a little, and rather than put a name to it, he turned back to his desk; but for all that day, he felt restless, resented Matty for coming, for stirring feelings and fears he had considered long dead.

Riding through Mittagong that afternoon, on his way to Shannon-brook One, Aidan stopped at Hutchins' General Store to collect a copy of the Sydney morning paper. Preoccupied, in spite of himself, with Matty and her fears for him, he did not notice the group of men until he was about to step off the wooden footpath to the waiting Blue.

They stood off to the right, three of them, Donaldson, Pirie-Moxham and Amberley, standing to attention in their grey suits, looking portentous and, to Aidan's mind, rather comic.

He waited for one of them to speak, but each man merely scowled uncomfortably, and Aidan, finally, said, 'Well, is this a deputation?'

'No. That is, I suppose so. We all agreed that we should take a stand on this . . . ' young Amberley began.

But Donaldson had interrupted, his face already beginning to flush with suppressed anger, 'O'Brien, let's face it, you're as much a part of the business life of Mittagong as any of us. Hadn't you better decide where your loyalties lie?'

'If the three of you,' Aidan kept his voice calm, 'are trying to say that you speak for the businessmen of Mittagong, I'd call you liars . . . ' Donaldson went to retort – 'and just to get the record straight, gentlemen, I'm a farmer – and one who owes loyalty to no one.'

He turned and mounted his horse, but the three were determined to continue; Pirie-Moxham said, harshly, 'We want this business dropped, O'Brien. Russell is just one man, after all. This business has had repercussions right through the district . . . '

Donaldson added, 'We don't want the men thinking they can get money from us every time they have an accident . . . Your taking up this cause makes them think that compensation should come to them as a matter of course.'

Amberley growled. 'They're believing in rights that they just don't . . . '

Aidan said tightly, 'I don't think we have anything to discuss, gentlemen. If you'll excuse me, *I* have work to attend to.' And his emphasis on the word 'I' was not lost on them. He rode off; the three watched him stonily for a long time.

Two days later, when Aidan was in Mittagong visiting Sam and Tessa, two visitors arrived at Shannonbrook Three. It was Liam who opened the door to be greeted by two young men who introduced themselves as Robert and George Du Buisson, cousins of Michael Kelly's.

'Cousins . . . ' Clemency hung back to whisper to Liam as Berrima ushered the visitors, in bowler hats and frock coats, every inch gentlemen, into the parlour. 'They don't look like Kelly, that's sure.'

Liam grinned, 'They've no chins, did you notice? They'd look like twins were it not that one's six feet and the other a head shorter.'

'They can't help that, nor their chins . . . '

'Liam?' Berrima called from the parlour, 'Would you tell Mister Kelly that his cousins are here?'

'I will, sure.'

But Clemency had taken his arm. 'I'll go – until they arrived, Berrima was trying to talk me into going to a dance that her relatives in Camden are holding next week, so let me go, Liam. By the time I come back she'll have forgotten about it.'

She was conscious, as she walked to the stables, of a small regret that she was not wearing a dress that morning. It shouldn't matter, sure, but the sharp little dark eyes of the two brothers had flicked over her like a duster, she felt, before turning away to Berrima's obvious gentility and safe, bustled femininity. It was not as if she cared what the Du Buissons – could that be their real name? – felt about her. Yet it made her feel uncomfortable to think of them returning to England with reports of the fast daughter of the house, who wore men's clothing.

It was Saturday. Kelly had recently moved from the men's quarters to the little room off the tack end of the barn; Clemency suspected it was to remove himself from the boisterous company of

922

Ben Halvorson and young Snowy Butler, returned to Shannonbrook briefly for the harvesting. She was amused to see Kelly at the window, and she walked past him unnoticed; so intent was he on hanging what appeared to be curtains in the window.

As she entered the barn, she noticed that his door was open, so she stood for a moment, watching him. He was standing on the bed; the room smelt of carbolic, as if he had scrubbed the disused little room thoroughly, and it was then that she noticed that the curtains he was hanging were very damp.

'Kelly?' she said, and was immediately gratified as he spun around, tripped on the blankets, and finished seated on the bed with the damp curtains around him. 'What're y' like? Those curtains are still wet.'

'They'll dry as easily hanging here as outside.' He frowned at her. 'Good morning to you, Miss O'Brien. Do you usually enter a man's room without warning like that?'

She was trying not to laugh as he picked himself up out of the tangles of curtain and stood once more on the bed. She walked over to him, and stood watching as he struggled to attach the rod to its brackets. 'It's your cousins,' she informed him, 'Robert and George Du Buisson, they're up at the house waiting for you.'

They were quite close, and she could see the look of alarm, disbelief, in his eyes. Then he said, in a detached voice, 'Thank you for telling me.' And he had picked up his hat and was heading out the door.

She followed him outside, half-running to keep up with his long stride. 'Are they your cousins?'

'Yes.'

'Do you not like them?'

He looked down at her with one eyebrow raised. 'Have you met them?'

She had to hide a smile. 'Are they fools?'

'I could forgive them being fools. It's their stupid, shallow natures and their fathomless greed that I find so abominable.'

His jaw was clenched, and she realized that she saw him angry for perhaps the first time. And it was a cold anger, a deep and frightening anger. She had placed a hand on his arm before she realized she had made the gesture. 'Kelly? If you don't like them, and you really don't want to see them – sure I could have them thrown off the place.'

And he paused, his eyes studying her for a moment; she became aware that she still held his arm, and slowly lowered her hand to her side. Still he gazed at her, smiling a little. 'Thank you, Clemency,' he said, gently, 'but if they must be thrown off the place, I believe I can throw them further than you.'

They entered the house together, but Clemency did not stay. She heard the murmur of voices, could sense the tension that would ensue just from the way that Kelly marched into the parlour. She went upstairs to her room, and searched through her wardrobes. Why did Papa encourage her in having dresses made? It seemed that every time she donned a dress it was to wear it for the first time . . . she chose a pink-and-grey-striped woollen dress. It took longer to scrape her hair up, and it was only to find, on coming downstairs, that all the effort had been wasted. The Du Buissons, and Kelly, were nowhere to be seen.

Berrima was standing in the parlour by the windows, gazing down the drive. Behind her were the tea things on the small table, one of the cups fallen over in its saucer and liquid spilled all over the tray cloth. Clemency, puzzled, righted the cup, but before she could speak Berrima said, 'They've gone,' and turned a bemused face to the younger woman. 'I thought they were going to come to blows, Clemency. Kelly loathes them, and they were . . . Oh, I don't know what they wanted with him, but they were so ingratiating – "My dear Michael . . . !" and pumping his hand, while Kelly stood there as if he were made from marble. It's all very strange.'

'Did they go off together?'

'No. When I came back with the tea things, Kelly had one of them, the tall one, Robert, I think, by the collar. He let him go when I entered the room, but when his cousins began speaking about home – in Wiltshire, I gathered – Kelly stormed off. I'm disappointed in him.'

'Why?' Clemency suddenly felt defensive.

'It was immature, don't you think? Rather petulant. Though he did say that Aidan was expecting him at Shannonbrook Two this afternoon. And after he left, his cousins appeared very disappointed, and said, after a while, that they'd be taking the evening train to Sydney – they're sailing for England in three days time.'

Clemency took a slice of cake from the tea tray.

'Clemency?' She looked up when Berrima spoke to her again. 'What do you know of this?'

'Nothing,' through a mouthful of cake.

'My dear, something was very wrong with that meeting just now. Mr Kelly was white with rage. Why?'

'Sure and why should I be knowing what does or does not disturb Mr Kelly?'

'Don't be naive, Clemency. I think I have a right to know.'

924

Clemency felt a prickle of resentment. And why, she silently asked the older woman, do you have a right to know? You're a guest here, it's not your house. You're here because I asked Papa for you to stay. 'Kelly's told me nothing,' she said, truthfully enough.

'If he'd tell anyone, he'd tell you.'

'And why's that?' They were fencing now. Clemency was edging for space, did not want to hear, felt a peculiar sense of encroachment with Berrima's words.

'Clemency, I've been meaning to speak to you about this for some time, but you're certainly old enough to judge matters such as this for yourself, and so I've held back. My dear, it's plain to anyone with even moderate sensitivity that Kelly's been attempting to avoid falling in love with you – and after four months, even he's beginning to realize it. He must have spoken to you. I believe he'd want you to know about his background.'

Why should the girl be looking like that? – white-faced, her eyes filled with something that looked like terror. It was so strange that Berrima, already unnerved by the afternoon's almost farcical goings-on, laughed a little. And it was only then, seeing the girl actually flinch, that Berrima realized that Clemency had never thought of the possibility of Kelly caring deeply; and she knew, too, that Kelly had not spoken to her, not of his background, nor of his feelings.

'Clemency . . . ' She took a step towards the younger woman, seeing her own confusion, all those years ago, and filled with compassion – but the girl had stepped back.

'You're wrong. You're wrong. He doesn't feel towards me in that way at all. He doesn't. He treats me like a child – and one that's not very bright, at that. And I don't care. For I feel nothing for him. Nothing. Berri. I feel nothing for anybody, and I won't have you making suppositions like that, nor hinting to anyone else that there's anything between Mr Kelly and me.'

She was sorry the minute she said that, for Berrima looked as if she had been struck. 'I would have thought,' she breathed, 'that you'd know me better than to consider that I'd do such a thing. But I'm beginning to think your knowledge of human nature is very limited indeed, Clemency. Has it occurred to you that Kelly patronizes you because a facade of superiority is an excellent cloak behind which to hide his feelings. He's no more used to loving than your . . . than you – and unless one of you grows up, you'll never reach any understanding . . . '

'I don't want to talk about it!'

'And if he had begun to speak about his past – you wouldn't want to listen, would you? As far as his feelings are concerned, you don't

925

plan on giving him any encouragement at all.'

'No!'

There was a long silence. Finally, 'I'm glad, then,' Berrima said, quietly, 'for I was worried that he may hurt you. But if you care nothing for him . . . '

'Nothing at all.'

Berrima, after a pause, nodded seriously, then took up the tray, and left the room.

Clemency ran up the stairs to her room, changed once more into her trousers, and went to the stables to saddle her horse. She rode all that afternoon, out beyond Glenquarry to Avoca and Fitzroy Falls, and leaned on the railing and watched the tons of water cascading hundreds of feet into the valley floor.

She did not want to go home immediately, she found, and though she arrived back late, she turned her horse up the drive towards Shannonbrook Two. Since a mill fire, several years ago, when she and Liam had been in Ireland, her father usually rode to the mill each night to check on the security there; it was now almost dusk, and she felt certain she would find him there, or perhaps at Uncle Thomas's Killaloe.

She felt, somehow, that her father would know some way out of her confusion. Her father would advise her. She did not understand her own feelings, but she needed her father's presence, needed his strength, his capable good humour.

She almost collided her horse with Kelly's black gelding; she came upon him suddenly, around a sharp bend, and they only narrowly turned their horses to avoid each other.

His eyes ran over her little bay critically. 'You shouldn't be pushing him like that, he's exhausted.'

'I didn't – I've been walking him, I only cantered from the start of the drive.' There we go again, she thought, I feel like a schoolgirl. 'Why were you going so fast?' she threw back at him, 'Exorcising demons, Mr Kelly?'

He smiled a little, but did not answer. He appeared to be waiting, somehow. And she dismounted from her horse, then, and walked him over to the grassy bank of the creek, wondering as she did so, what she hoped to say to this man. There were too many unanswered questions, too many mysteries.

She did not glance behind her, but heard him sigh, heard the creak of saddle leather as he also dismounted, and after a few moments he was walking his horse beside hers. Her horse turned and rubbed its head against her, knocked her off-balance a little so she brushed against Kelly, and she was aware then, if she had not

926

been before, that the man's physical presence was unsettling. Drat Berrima, she thought, putting ideas in my head. *Or did Berri merely voice something I knew was true?*

'What's the matter, Clemency?' His gaze was curious, only, she noted, he doesn't look like a man in love. What could Berrima be thinking about? He didn't behave at all in the manner in which some of Mrs Mitchell's admirers had behaved. His eyes did not glow, his hands did not tremble. He did not follow her about and listen to her every word. He said he went riding with her because her father wished it, and sometimes he told her that she talked too much. No, Berrima was obviously of a far more romantic bent than Clemency had thought. The only time Kelly's gaze fell on her with any warmth was when he found her amusing. He found her amusing now.

'I think you ought to tell Papa,' she said, in an effort to wipe the tolerant humour from his face.

'Tell him what?'

'Everything. All the trouble you're in. And I know that you're in trouble.' She watched him struggle to keep that amused, rather condescending expression, but he could not. There was obviously some truth in her words, for they drove all humour from the grey eyes. She sat down on the ground beside him. 'What do they want?' she asked, and only then remembered that she was not supposed to care. 'They don't want to harm you, do they?'

'No. They want me alive and well. In England.'

'They can't make you go back there . . . '

'They've tried.' His mouth twisted a little, without humour.

'Why England?'

'My father is there. I stand to inherit quite a fortune and a large estate – and the reason Rozencrantz and Guildenstern back there are following me about, is to make sure I don't forget about it.'

She looked at him rather coldly. 'Why do you talk about your father only in terms of your inheritance?'

'Those are the terms he thinks in. Money, power, power and money. He has a simple philosophy on life.'

'But . . . I remember, when you first came here, the day you woke up and Mr Barrett was questioning you – you told them your parents were dead.'

'I lied. I do that, sometimes.'

'To hell with you!' Her eyes narrowed. 'And Rozencrantz and Guildenstern – they were spies, in Shakespeare's *Hamlet*.'

'And she knows her classics, too. Is there no end to your talents?'

But when she did not speak, he said, more seriously, 'My father is one of those men who believe children owe their parents absolute loyalty and obedience.'

'That's ridiculous. You have your own life to live. Do you mean to tell me that your father sent Rozencrantz and Guildenstern after you to persuade you to come home to England?'

'They can be very persuasive.' He spoke mildly, but Clemency sensed something was wrong.

Looking straight ahead, she said, 'You have to learn to trust somebody sometime.'

She felt, rather than saw his head come around towards her, was conscious of him studying her face. 'Yes,' he said. 'Yes, there comes a time when you have to learn to trust. But sometimes it's a long search, finding someone to trust.'

'Well, you have, now.'

His hand was on her shoulder, and she realized, even before the gentle pressure that turned her towards him, that she was deep into a misunderstanding. One swift look into those grey eyes, and she fixed her own gaze on the breast pocket of his blue shirt. 'You must tell Papa immediately. He'll understand, and he can help, no matter what the . . . '

He had stood, bringing her up with him with an iron grip on her shoulders that made her wince, forget whatever she was about to say. He did not speak, that was the worst of it, simply stared down into her face as if he'd like to slap her. His hands trembled on her arms as if he wished to shake her – and then she was free, standing alone, and he was turning to his horse, mounting to the saddle.

'Kelly . . . '

'It'll be dark soon, Miss O'Brien . . . '

'Kelly, I was speaking as I was, because . . . ' She stood at his stirrup and gazed up at him, and his face was hard, unreadable.

'Yes?' he prompted.

'Because I care about what happens to you. You . . . you wanted us to be friends, did you not?'

He smiled a little, and the smile was genuine, and she relaxed somewhat. 'Yes,' he said.

She turned to her own horse, and mounted, and they rode on, silently, for a few hundred yards before he said, 'I'm not the only person who needs to learn how to trust, you know.'

He did not look at her as he spoke, and she stared ahead, not knowing how to answer him, and in silence, they rode into the stable yard.

Thomas came to call a half hour later, to find Aidan standing on the front veranda of Shannonbrook Three, smoking his pipe, breathing in the cool air that seemed somehow fresher, as if rain – and there had been so little all that summer, all that autumn – might finally be on the way.

They stood beside each other in quiet companionship for several minutes and watched the clouds gather, bunching up towards the north, but rolling, rolling still from the south.

'Ah, sniff that!' Thomas said. 'And strange is it not, Aidan, for an Irishman to be sniffing the wind and anticipating the rain as we would a warm day in spring, were we back home. Aidan? Come down into the garden with me – I feel like a walk about. Sure if we're caught out in a downpour, I'll dance in it, so glad I'll be to see some rain!'

Aidan fell into step with his brother willingly enough; from here on the slopes of the gardens they could see the thoroughbred colts in their paddock, galloping about, their tails and manes flying, mad with excitement and the scent of change on the wind.

'What are you going to do about Michael Kelly?'

Ah. So that was it. Aidan looked over at Thomas's determined face and smiled.

'Arra, wipe that smug look off your face, Aidan O'Brien. I know how this pleases you. Great crack, is it not? I've been waiting all this time for you to speak of it, but you won't, it's clear. Too pleased with y'rself, I'm thinking.'

'Will you let me speak?'

'Oh, by all means, speak! What will you do, tell me?'

'Nothing, Thomas. This is Australia, not Ireland. We betray a healthy disinterest in a man's past here – and it's thankful I am that it's so.'

'Aidan, those two cousins of Kelly's called at Killaloe this morning, getting the names mixed, thinking Kelly worked on my place. You know what 'Tillia's like, insisted they stayed to lunch, and they did – and the strangest tale they told me.'

'Oh?'

'Devlin is ill, back in Wiltshire in England, and left to run a huge estate by himself, and Michael – wasn't he engaged to a fine girl, and an heiress to boot, and didn't he run off on his father without warning? All his father wants to do is see the boy again before he dies, Aidan, and that cold-hearted young man won't go home to England at all . . . '

'Thomas,' with deceptive mildness, 'I don't want to hear any gossip . . . '

'And when your own daughter is involved, Aidan?'

'Involved?' Aidan grinned, 'Och, no. I know they see a great deal of each other – but it's my thinking that it's because they've not met anyone like each other before. And they're both loners, both had unusual childhoods that have made them feel different to other people – it won't take them long to talk themselves out, then they'll forget each other. I doubt if Kelly will stay long.'

Thomas regarded him with patent scepticism. 'Is it only myself you're lying to, or are you so much of a trawneen that you're lying to yourself as well?' And as Aidan was about to protest, 'You've just given me a list of reasons that any fool could see would make any pair of young people fall in love with each other – and what would you do then, lad?'

'If they wanted to marry?' Aidan's smile was bland. He knew he was not hiding his satisfaction, but with Thomas he felt no need to hide his emotions. He grinned, 'Now, Tomás, would I be withholding my blessing from those two? They're not children, and to tell the truth, I'm pleased with Kelly. I like the man.'

'Aidan,' and Thomas's face was serious, he stopped walking and turned to his brother, 'Aidan, that boy is filled with hate. I don't think you see it, perhaps he's had no need to show it, for he feels safe here, it's obvious. But the hate is there, and such men, haunted as they are by their pasts, make poor husbands, Aidan. Their wives suffer even more than they themselves . . . '

The double edge to his words struck home to Thomas, and he paled with the realization of the pain he might have inflicted. Aidan had been walking a little ahead along the path, paused now, could have been looking at the view between the pines and not have heard. 'I . . . I'm sorry. I didn't mean to suggest . . . '

Aidan turned, smiling a little. 'I know – but what you say is the truth. Though Kelly isn't like me, Thomas, he's travelled and he's lived – perhaps too much. This won't be a boy making a foolish decision. He's a man, who knows what's in store for him.'

'His father.'

'Pardon?'

'His father, that's who it is that's in store for him. Aidan, do you honestly believe that Devlin Kelly will allow his only son to marry your daughter?'

Aidan laughed delightedly. 'Sure and what can Devlin Kelly do to prevent it? For a start, he's twelve thousand miles away – and for another, Kelly's way past his majority. Arra, by God,' his grin was suddenly malicious, the dark eyes sparked. 'I'd like him to try to stop it, sure I would. This isn't Killaloe, we'd be on my ground now . . . '

Thomas spoke earnestly, disliking the look on Aidan's face; there was a cunning and malevolence that had never been there when Aidan was a boy, and it always chilled Thomas.

'Listen to me, Aidan. You didn't come to know Devlin as a man. In fact, I doubt if you ever really knew him at all. You suffered at his hands as a boy, and you saw him only in terms of how he affected your life. Did you ever, ever once, in all those years, try to put yourself in his place, to feel what he must have felt, protected, isolated as he was at Tineranna, never taught how to approach people, how to make friendships, for his father was too busy and his mother was a fool.'

'I don't want to talk about him.'

'We will talk about him, for I'm the only one of your family who'll dare bring up your past to your face . . . ' Aidan had begun to march away a little, back in the direction of the house, but his brother hurried and kept pace with him, finally pulling on Aidan's arm.

'I tried,' Aidan burst out. 'Once or twice, when we were young, I tried to put myself in Devlin's place, for I felt a kind of pity for him. But it never lasted long, Thomas, it was more than I could bear. For in his place, I'd have grown up like William Kelly! With the education, the advantages, with Tineranna as my birthright, I'd have grown to be a man that William Kelly could have been proud to have as a son. And thinking that, I'd look at Devlin, the witless, gutless *maicin* that he is, and I'd see how he despised everything his father stood for . . . '

'Aidan, you're wrong. He loved his father more than you know.'

'He did not! F'r William lived for Tineranna, for helping his people. Devlin loathed the place – couldn't wait to sell it to some gombeen of an Englishman. Don't try to tell me otherwise, for I was there. I know.' Aidan's rage was a fever, a sickness, it possessed him to his very bones, and he knew he had not forgotten, he had forgotten nothing. He cursed himself for his lack of control, he cursed Thomas for stirring up these memories, and he knew, now, why he never turned his thoughts backwards, along that dark road to famine-torn Ireland and the man that he had been.

Thomas was saying, calmly – to Aidan the calmness of the voice only aggravated him further – 'Very well. Cling to your stubborn ideas of Devlin as a boy. But you left Killaloe in '47, Aidan. And Devlin returned, later, if you'll remember.

'He kept his son's existence a secret, for I suppose he didn't want the O'Hagans interfering, wanting to see the boy, to write to him. Devlin was already ambitious, but looking back on it, I don't think it was for himself, it was ambition for his son. Don't you see? Through

931

all his unhappiness, the sense of loneliness and displacement that kept him returning time after time to Tineranna, was the idea that his son wouldn't be torn between Ireland and England, as Devlin had been . . . '

'And I suppose that's why he changed his name? To help his son's prospects? *Rawmaish*, Thomas. Devlin was always ashamed of being Irish, he fled to his Englishness for his own sake, not the boy's.'

'Will you allow me to finish anything I begin to say?'

'Sorry.'

'Whatever his reasons, Devlin cares about the boy, you have to agree with that. I don't approve of the way Kelly was brought up, from the little he told me of life in Burnley Grange, it is a wonder he's not an extremely selfish and cold-blooded man. But Devlin thought he was doing the right thing, the boy is all he has.' Thomas spoke with emphasis.

'Thomas, where is all this leading to, if I'm not being ill-mannered? Are you after telling me that Kelly should go? Is that it?'

'I don't believe you'll send him away.' They looked at each other for some seconds. 'But take care, Aidan. I don't know why I feel so certain about this, but I don't believe Devlin will let Kelly go so easily.'

'What can he do about it? Chase after him? Wave his finger in the boy's face?'

'Chase after him? That's not an impossibility. You know Kelly's been followed all these years. That alone should tell you that Devlin is serious . . . '

Aidan burst into laughter, reeling away a little to swing by one arm around one of the garden lampposts. He was delighted, could not speak for laughing.

'So much of the boy in you, still.' Thomas was saying, severely, 'At fifty-four years old . . . '

'Fifty-five, Thomas.'

And Thomas scowled at him. Reluctantly he had to admit Aidan did not look anywhere near fifty-five. The lines on his face had been there from the time of the Famine, etched deeper, he was certain, by the years in prison. But for all that, and the grey hair at his temples, now, Aidan's skin was healthy and smooth, the light in his eyes, whether it smouldered or danced, as now, in amusement, was the light within the boy he had fought and played with all those long years ago. It was as if life, having marked him so early in his existence, had been easier with him, in compensation. Never able to be called handsome as a young man, in middle age Aidan O'Brien had come into his own. He looked, Thomas thought, to be in his forties. But, 'Fifty-five,' he said, 'all the more reason to grow up, Aidan. This isn't a game. If that's what it is to you, then it's time you took a closer look. Have you not thought of this – the Famine made you what you are, as it made Devlin what he is.'

'A murderer. A lying, gutless murderer.'

Thomas was momentarily shaken. If Aidan had said this with sudden hatred, with barely suppressed rage, his brother would have felt more at ease. But the smile was still on his mouth, and the eyes held something like a black humour. And Thomas, when he had recovered from his surprise, was afraid. He said, quietly, 'You'll kill him, won't you? For what he did to Corrie? If you find him again, you'll kill him.'

Aidan regarded him for a second too long, before he said, 'No, Thomas. I won't kill him. I promise you, I won't kill him.'

And before Thomas could speak, his brother had clapped him on the back, was guiding him back towards the house. 'You'll dine with us, of course. Berri will insist on it. And I've got port that Andrew has imported for me – wonderful stuff – you must try it with me.'

Thomas could think of no way to steer back into that dangerous moment, was not even sure, God forgive him, that he wanted to. He allowed his brother to steer him towards the lighted house.

89

'Victoria's been writing books,' Liam told Clemency two days later, when they were riding to Shannonbrook One to check the beef cattle that ran in the scrubby hill paddocks of the property. 'She's been writing down all the stories that she used to tell her children. *The Family at Allawah*, the first story was called – it was my idea that she write them down, it was just after Kenelm's death, and I thought it would help her. She liked writing – there are five books, now.' He looked over at his sister with a wry smile, 'She's just had the first accepted by a publisher in London.'

'But that's marvellous.'

'Aye, it is. But she's so delighted, you see, because they want the other four books as well. They've offered to pay her passage to England – and she's going to accept. That's why I've been feeling like a bear with a sore head all morning. I don't know what I'm going to do, Clem.'

There was no emotion in the voice, the words were stated simply, Liam gazing at the road before him, but Clemency's heart contracted at the stark sense of grief that was evident in her brother.

'Is she . . . Is she returning to Garth?'

'Och, no! He's living in Sydney. But she has relatives in London, she'll stay with them. She feels she should go, for the children's sake.'

Clemency tried to find words that would cheer him. Perhaps Victoria would come back, perhaps he could go to London and visit them . . . but it was useless, and she knew it. There was no consolation for Liam, his emotions were too deeply, too tragically entangled, and Clemency, while feeling pleased that her self-sufficient brother would confide in her, nevertheless felt her own inadequacies.

And anyway, she told herself at various times for the rest of that day, perhaps it's the best thing that could happen. And perhaps Victoria knows that, too.

Liam was extremely proud of the bridge over the creek. It had been his idea, and he had spent a great deal of his spare time looking at bridges about the district before he designed this one. The men had helped, of course, he could not have done it alone; but it had been his project, proof to himself, and, he hoped, to his father and Kelly, who was by dint of his sailing, clever with ropes and wood in a way that defied his languid, impeccably-dressed appearance. If he looks like a fop, he should act like one, Liam thought, and then became aware of the unfairness of that statement.

Kelly was beside him, now, helping to hammer down the last supports of the bridge's handrail, and was dressed almost identically to Liam, both wearing knee boots and moleskins and check shirts and the broad straight-brimmed hats. Yet Kelly could still look like a gentleman, and for all his being the hired man, this aura of being quality was with him whether dressed in his Sunday best for Mass, or covered with mud and stinking sheep dip. While me, Liam thought, I look like an Irish farmer, whatever manner I'm dressed; even should I go to the Bar, I'd look like an Irish farmer in me wig and gown. He sighed. It was fate, he supposed, it was that indefinable thing that Kelly had that he did not, that made the girls turn and follow the man with their eyes. One 'Good morning' from Kelly and they'd stop all day for a conversation, but should Liam try and they'd be telling him that their fathers were just inside the store and

934

wouldn't approve of them speaking to him like this. That was, when they answered him at all.

Liam scowled, then, 'Women!'

'Ah.' Kelly turned back to finish hammering in the nail before him, saying over the top of the din, 'What particular aspect bothers you? Too many, not enough, one you want who doesn't want you?'

Liam wished he had not spoken. What advice could Kelly – or any other man – give him? 'One I want, who wants me, but the situation's hopeless,' he murmured. Kelly looked over at him, and Liam grinned, shrugged, turned back to his work. 'What about you?' He decided to turn the conversation. 'I don't know anything about affairs of the heart, but it seems you're not having much success, either. You do have a bit of a *grä* for Clemency, do you not?' The look that Kelly gave him was black. 'All right,' Liam laughed. 'I'll be after minding my own buisness. But I'll just say this, don't give up. She's smart as a whip in some things, is Clemency – in others she's a fierce fool. You'll need to get her alone somehow, and away from here . . . '

'I thought you were the one who didn't know anything about affairs of the heart . . . '

'Rawmaish! I know my sister. She's wrapped herself in Shannon-brook Three like it was cotton wool – if I decide I don't want the place, I'll lay odds that she'll ask Father to leave it to her – aye. She wants it – she should have been a boy, she loves the place like a farmer born – and though I look the part, 'tis no farmer I am.' He looked a little embarrassed at having said so much, but went on, 'You should go to the Camden Show, since Father and I can't get away.'

Kelly had reached for another nail, was busy hammering.

'He'd like someone to keep an eye on Berrima and Clemency. Besides, you've hardly taken a day off in all the months you've been here . . . '

Kelly paused in his hammering. 'I'll ask Clemency,' he smiled. 'She might have some objections, we had a quarrel yesterday, over her handling of Erin's Boy at Saturday's hunt – she may not want me anywhere near her for a while.'

'She'll get over it – she always does, I'll say that for her. Arra, an' what's this?' Kelly looked up at him, then followed his gaze.

Clemency, in a lemon coloured dress and hat, was driving along the road from the homestead, in the small pony trap. She pulled Penny up beside the bridge.

Liam stood, smiling at the picture, and walked off the bridge towards her. 'Where have you been? To Mass on a Tuesday?'

935

'No, Penny's feeling her oats a bit – I'm taking her round the farm for a while, then I'm going into town. To do some shopping. For the fair on Saturday.'

'I hope you're not going to start on that again. You know I can't take you, Clem . . .'

'Not at all.' She stepped down from the trap. 'I'm going with Berrima – we shall probably have a wonderful time.' Kelly had gone back to his hammer and nails. Her voice was loud enough to be heard over the hammering. 'Liam, I think Penny's been favouring her off-side foreleg. Would you have a look at it for me?' And she lifted her skirt a little, for the ground was damp, here, and stepped on to the bridge.

Liam led Penny forward by the bridle. 'I can't see her favouring it . . .'

Clemency turned. 'Oh, I'm sure of it . . .'

Softly, 'But, Clem . . .'

Equally softly, 'I'm *sure* of it.'

As she walked off, he turned back to the horse, leading her forward again, and answered loudly, 'I see . . . Of course, *now* I see . . .' He lifted her off-side foreleg and studied the hoof with concentration.

'Good morning, Miss O'Brien.'

'Good morning, Mr Kelly.' Clemency strolled past him with elaborate casualness, and crossed to the opposite bank of the creek. She half-disappeared from his sight, walking beneath the willows.

She had planned to go up to him and come straight out with the request. But somehow her feet had carried her past him of their own volition. He had not seemed overly friendly, but then, she had aimed a blow at him with her riding crop yesterday – and why not, when he called her reckless and said she should be banned from the hunting field until she learned to control herself and her horse at a fence. It wasn't as if she had struck him with the crop, she hadn't even meant to, and he had stepped back out of the way, with that deftness of movement that always surprised her, and he had laughed at her, said, 'That's what I mean about your jumping, Miss O'Brien, you have no eye for distances,' and had gone off smiling. Could he have been more angry than he seemed? She had never really seen him angry, never heard him shout. Not like Papa and Liam, who bellowed and roared even when they were in high spirits . . .

'The edge of the creek is undercut, there. Don't go too close.' She stepped back, and turned to find him on the other side of the willow, holding back the fronds as if they were a curtain. 'I'd hate to see you fall in, when you've gone to so much trouble.' He had moved

936

towards her, easily, and she narrowed her eyes, checking his face for mockery. 'You don't usually wear a dress to go shopping in town . . . ' He leaned one hand against the bark of the tree. One huge branch was warped, bent low, and she sat down upon it.

'I . . . just . . . felt like it . . . '

'A creature of impulse . . . '

'Yes . . . no!' She scowled. She shouldn't have come, she should have known better than to think he had any manners in him, or that he had forgotten that swipe with the riding crop.

'Clemency . . . ' He sat down beside her on the branch, pulling at a piece of grass to place between his teeth, and chewed the end a little as he said, 'You didn't have to go to so much bother, you know.'

She studied his face. The firm mouth remained firm, but she had the feeling there was laughter behind his eyes. 'I don't know what you . . . '

'I'm sure you do.'

Again they paused, then she began to smile. 'Mr Kelly, I . . . '

'If you want me to escort you to the show at Camden, all you have to do is ask.'

She stared at him, a flush beginning to creep up her throat. 'That's absurd – I had no such intention . . . ' She stood up and went to walk off; quickly, Kelly, too, had stood, and being in her way, she went to step around him. Too close to the bank, it was crumbling beneath her – with a scream, she clutched at an overhanging branch – but Kelly reached out and grasped her, pulling her forward. He stood, holding her shoulders, and she gazed at the earth that now muddied the clear stream where she had stood a minute before. He shook her slightly, and there was laughter in his voice. 'I know you had no intention of asking me – you were giving me every opportunity to ask you myself.'

She turned to look up at him, then, realizing his proximity, she pulled back. She had had enough. In a low voice, she said, 'I do not care if you attend that fair or not, Mr Kelly – in fact, I would prefer it if you did not.'

Kelly withdrew into politeness. 'Then I'm disappointed, Miss O'Brien. For I was going to ask to accompany you – had you given me the opportunity.'

She gazed at him for a moment, then turned and walked towards the bridge – but she stopped before stepping on to it and turned to him, angry and close to tears.

'Why? Why did you have to do that?'

He answered a trifle awkwardly, as if he were already regretting a little. 'You were playing a game. I don't like playing games. I'm not

937

used to games . . . '

'Why couldn't you . . . pretend? Why couldn't you learn to pretend? Other people do . . . '

And he turned fully to her, said grimly, 'Not I. And not you, I'd hoped.'

She said in a low voice, 'It's a hurtful kind of honesty you subscribe to, Mr Kelly.' And she turned and walked on to the bridge.

Kelly was taken aback a little at her words, and started after her. She was almost at the other side of the bridge when she caught her dress on a nail; it was the one Kelly had not finished hammering into the upright. Clemency turned and began to tug at it, angrily.

'Let me help you . . . ' from behind her.

It was the final straw. She shouted at him, 'You stay away from me!'

A final tug at her dress, with all her weight behind it – it gave with a rip and she was overbalancing—

Even as Kelly rushed forward, she had lost her balance, made an attempt to clutch at the railing – but it did little good. The unsteady handrail gave with her weight, and handrail and Clemency fell backwards into the creek with a splash.

'Liam!' Kelly shouted. He had his hat and one boot off ready to leap into the water, when Clemency surfaced, spluttering, to stand in the water just above her waist.

'My bridge!' Liam bellowed, dropping a startled Penny's reins and charging down the slope. 'Look what you've done to my bridge . . . !'

The once pert hat was sitting soggily over one ear as she screamed at him, 'Damn y'r bridge! A pox on y'r bloody bridge . . . !'

Kelly pulled on his boot, took up his hat and pulled it down over his eyes, trying not to grin.

'Two days it took us, Clemency!' Liam shouted, 'Two days t' get that bloody handrail made . . . !'

'Help me out of here, Liam – I'm gonna kill y' . . . !'

It was too much for Kelly, who roared with laughter. Clemency turned on him furiously. 'How dare you . . . !'

She managed to struggle to the bank, but slipped on the mud in attempting to climb out. 'My dress . . . look at it! Oh, damn it – damn it!'

Liam, also grinning now, came to the edge of the creek and went down on one knee, holding his hand out to her, but the bank was steep and slippery, and the weight of her saturated gown made it difficult for her to gain a foothold. She kept sliding back, and each time the little yellow hat slipped further and further over her face –

Liam collapsed, finally, in a heap on the bank, and doubled over with laughter.

'I can see nothing amusing about this incident at all! I could have drowned, you miserable, misbegotten gurrier! Get me out of here, Liam! Get me out!'

Clemency and Berrima left for Camden and the residence of Uncle and Aunt Charlie escorted by Edward Lawler and his daughters.

Liam was conscious that Berrima was not pleased with Aidan for not attending, and Clemency's relationship with Kelly had cooled into frosty courtesy since the incident at the bridge.

He was glad when Kelly and Aidan decided, a few hours after the Lawlers' landau had disappeared down the drive, to go to Camden after all. That evening, Liam drove Victoria and the children to the station in Moss Vale, and put them on the train for Sydney. They would spend two days with Garth, then board the steamer for London.

There were no words that Liam could think to say, he had tried everything, every argument that his well-trained mind could devise, but Victoria would not divorce Garth, would not marry, nor live with Liam. Only as the train was pulling out did his calm give way. 'This is madness, Vicky! Can't you understand what you're doing to both of us?'

He held tight to her hand as the train moved a little faster. Her eyes filled with sudden tears, but she said, only, 'It's best for all of us . . . ' and she was pulling her hand from his. He stood still, watching the bright, excited faces of the little girls, the tear-stained face of Victoria, growing smaller, disappearing in the cloud of steam that blew backwards towards him, from the engine.

When he returned home, Shannonbrook Three was strangely quiet; except for his knowledge that Charity was in the kitchen it would seem that the house had been abandoned. He had brought work home from his office, but he could concentrate very little during those two days, and he drifted through the rooms, hating his own lack of resilience, angry that the feelings of loss should claim him so completely.

He was almost relieved when the family arrived home, though he could tell immediately that the weekend had not been a success.

'I went riding with Richard Reynolds early in the morning,' Clemency explained when they were mixing the feed for the year-lings, later that evening, 'And for some reason Berri's Aunt Charlotte became terribly incensed. I should have had a chaperone, apparently – and maybe she was right.' Clemency finished thoughtfully,

'Richard's a bit of a lad, nowadays. I don't want you to tell Berri, but I had a hard time defending my honour, Liam, on more than one occasion.'

She looked over at her brother, who was grinning. 'And what did Kelly have to say about Doctor Reynolds being so fresh with you?'

He was even more amused to see her colour, was delighted that Clemency, at least, had had some excitement. She deflected the question, murmuring, 'Richard's joined the army, he's not only Doctor Reynolds, he's Lieutenant Reynolds. The Lawler girls were very taken with him.' She stopped portioning the crushed oats into the buckets to smile at her brother. 'Richard's five years younger than me – he kept saying he likes mature women – arra, I'd be a liar if I said I didn't enjoy myself. But Kelly's cross with me.'

'Does that matter to you?' He looked her directly in the eye.

She lowered her head over the oats. 'I didn't think it would,' he heard her mutter.

'Clem, why haven't you married? I know you'd refuse Kelly, should he ask you. I'm not judging you, but I'd like to know why.'

She straightened, gazed at him with her mouth held firm. 'All right, I'll talk about it just this once, and then I won't speak of it again, and I don't want any questions.

'Falling in love is easy – I've done it lots of times, Liam, and I'm not one tenth as innocent as you probably believe me to be. But love doesn't last, and when it's over and you've made the mistake of marrying – then you're left with what Ma and Papa had – and that's another word for hell.'

'Clem, it doesn't have to . . . '

'I'm not taking that chance. I'm not placing myself near any risk that I'll end up like Ma, Liam. Dead inside, and hating the world – don't try to tell me it wasn't so! You don't know! You never saw Ma like I did!' She lowered her voice, as if annoyed with herself for losing her control. 'I'm a rich woman, and I'm a free woman – and I'll stay that way rather than risk it all for a prize that might not exist.'

'Real love that lasts?' he suggested.

'Sure, those are strange words from your lips . . . '

And he had to swallow against the constriction in his throat, the burning in his eyes. 'Maybe so,' he murmured, and he took his pair of feed buckets and went with them to the pump, leaving the conversation unfinished. He mixed water with the feed, then carried it down the yards to where the leggy young horses that he was training each morning, hung their heads over the fence and whickered to him.

940

'Shut y'r gobs,' he muttered at them. 'What have you lot got to complain about, I'd like to know.'

The court case had failed.

Aidan, Thomas and Liam stood beneath the stone portico of the Berrima court house and watched, through the light drizzle of rain, Donaldson's carriage lurch away. Men were running along side it, a young boy threw a stone, and the words, the shouted insults and even threats, came back to them.

Aidan sighed and looked around for Sam, but he and Tessa and Neil were nowhere in sight. 'Where're the Russells? They were beside me just now . . . '

Liam went off to look for the family, and Aidan, now that the focus of Donaldson had gone, found himself ringed by a group of anxious faces – What did he think would happen now? What would happen to the mill? Had he heard anything about it re-opening? What would happen to Sam? What could they do to help Sam?

Aidan caught sight of Goldman, the barrister, and headed for him, making some placating, and, he felt, inadequate replies to the men. The only thing he could say and mean, sincerely, was that the matter would not end here. He felt heavy with his sense of failure, that there was, in truth, no plans in his mind, he had not thought beyond this moment, had, despite Liam's and Goldman's caution, believed they would win.

They discussed the matter late into the night at Sam's house. The Russells had left the court even before Donaldson, and Aidan was determined to see Sam, to make sure he did not give up hope.

'You've got the job of overseer of my mills,' he told Sam, 'and I've decided we should appeal, too.' He turned to glare defiantly at Goldman and Liam. Goldman raised his eyebrows, Liam grinned. Aidan demanded, 'Are you two going to try to talk me out of it?'

It was Goldman who said, 'We'd wondered about the possibility months ago.' He and Liam exchanged glances. 'We both feel that an appeal would be a good idea. The case would be held in Sydney, and there'd be wider publicity for the matter . . . '

'No one's asked me,' Sam growled. The other three men turned to him. 'There's no point to it – Donaldson'll just stand up in court like he did this morning and lie, and the judges'll believe him. I'll not have you do it, Aidan.'

Goldman left for Sydney the following day, and it was only after a week of steady pressure from Aidan, Liam and Tessa that Sam was persuaded to allow the appeal to go ahead. 'The law has to change,' Liam pointed out, 'and it's outlaw cases like ours that turn the tide

941

– if you don't want to do this for yourself, think of the other poor bastards being killed and maimed all over the country, working faulty machinery and taking risks that shouldn't be demanded of them, all to keep their families alive.'

Sam growled his acquiescence.

When Ben Halvorson arrived with the other shearers over the next few weeks, he had already heard the tale. 'Grandest yarn I come by in years,' he grinned at Liam, the day he settled his belongings into the shearers' quarters, and the two men stood on the verandah in the shade. 'But I was worried, all the same. Just watch them blokes you're haulin' through the courts, mate. I know 'em, I know their kind, and if they can't get you in the open, they'll get you when your back's turned, if you know what I mean.'

Liam grinned. 'We'll be careful, Ben.' He looked around at the other men, lounging on the verandah, enjoying the cool of the evening, for the brief dusk was settling in. 'I can't see Snowy – is he not coming this season, then?'

Ben had just rolled and lit one of his sliver-thin cigarettes. He squinted through the smoke at Liam as if the words had hurt. 'Nah. He's not coming back.' He pulled the cigarette from his mouth and sighed, threw down the smoke into the dirt, and ground it into the soil with the heel of his boot. 'He's gone, mate. Ol' Snow. 'Bout a month ago, at Gulgong. Bloody shame, it was.'

'An accident? He was only . . . what? Twenty-four? Twenty-five?'

'Twenny-three. 'Is mum told me. I rode to Mudgee an' told 'er meself, 'bout what happened. Only twenny-three . . . '

Ben turned his head to spit out some strands of tobacco that had clung to his tongue.

'Snow wasn't real good when he arrived at the shed – y' c'd tell he was crook, and coughin' all the time. An' it wasn't helped by the barney we had with the squatter, neither – wanted us to take less than we did last season, an' we wouldn't do it, so 'e locked the gate on us, on all of us who wouldn't accept the cut. We camped there fer three days, them three days last months when it pissed with rain, an' we thought the drought was broke. An' the Ol' Man, 'e was gettin' 'is shearers anyway, they were too desperate for work, they wouldn't stick together. So we all gave up, eventually, and went to work for the lesser money.

'But it galled me, mate. I fell asleep in that leaky shed every night – y' c'd stick a finger through the gaps between the slabs on them walls, I'm not jokin', mate! – an' I'd dream of this place. But that shed – puddles in the dirt floor, mate. Y' come in the door an' ya fall

942

down five inches into a puddle – an' the fleas in them old ticks! That was bad enough, but the wind – the rain stopped but that wind kept blowing. We stuck up newspapers round Snow's bed, 'cause by then 'e was too sick to work – an' the Ol' Man, you think he'd send fer a doctor? "By the time he drives the thirty miles out here," 'e says, "the boy'll be back on his feet."

'Well, 'e wasn't. One night 'e was took so bad I stole – borrowed – the Ol' Man's favourite and rode inter town, dragged the doctor out of his bed.

'Snow died while we were on our way. The Ol' Man was fer having me gaoled fer horse-stealing, but that doctor took 'im to task with all these words I never heard before – but the long an' the short of it was, 'e said we was livin' like animals, and it wasn't the ploorisy nor newmonia that killed Snow, it was the shed, an' the pig-swill we was eating. 'E was bonzer, that bloke. I didn't get arrested, only because of him.

'So,' Ben finished, 'that's what happened to Snowy. He was a good boy, Snowy. We all pitched in and gave something to his mum. The Ol' Man said he'd done enough payin' for the funeral.'

The boy's death shook Liam. He shared Ben's anger with the owner of the station, but such conditions and attitudes were so common that there was very little redress. At the back of Liam's mind, over the next few months, was that Snowy, younger than he, just as healthy until this last illness, had had his life cut off so abruptly. Time began to matter to Liam, the mistakes that he had made began to matter, the future began to matter most of all.

He would be working in his Mittagong office, and come to himself to realize that he was not concentrating on the matter before him, at all. He would be wondering at his own stupidity, his lack of under-standing, cursing his precipitous temper, the fact that all his legal training did not help his own sense of proportion, give him a sense of perspective in the real world when his own feelings and desires were under threat. 'Tis all very well on paper, he thought, gloomily, years and years of studying every side of a question, impartial, unbiased, and when it comes down to it, I prefer to be in there, fists, boots and all.

He no longer had the haven that was Victoria's companionship, felt himself drifting like a storm-wracked ship at sea, and there was nothing, it seemed, to be done about it but wait, and hope the storm would pass. Riding home from his office one evening, through a biting, sleety rain, he decided he would write to her, just a friendly letter – he would share the writing space with Clemency, just to prove that it was just a letter from old family friends. He stabled his horse, and entered the house through the deserted kitchen, determining, now he had made up his mind, to find Clemency immediately, and ask her to begin the letter. She wouldn't mind. It had been she who had heard, through Sophie Lawler, that Garth Ellis had sailed for London only a week after Victoria and the children. Liam had felt ill at the thought of a reconciliation between the two; Victoria belonged to *him*, even the children, he felt, were more his than Garth's. Where had Garth been when the family had been ill, when young Kenelm had died?

'Clemency?' He called his sister's name as he came into the hall, less because he wanted her to appear suddenly as to disperse the rage in him when he thought of the mockery of Victoria's marriage.

No one in the parlour could have heard him calling, for they were making far too much noise themselves. His father sat in his chair by the fire, his newspaper lying ignored upon his lap, attempting to keep a serious face, while occasionally making an interjection – but Clemency and Charity were oblivious. Liam entered the room and stood still, seeing a pink-faced, very angry Charity, and Clemency standing with her back to the fireplace, almost defensively, holding a new-born lamb in her arms.

'I live here,' his sister was saying hotly, 'I've a right to make a simple request in my own home . . . '

'No you don't, miss, beggin' your pardon! No you don't, when it comes to bringin' dirty animals into my kitchen!'

'Charity,' Aidan said soothingly, 'I think what Miss Clemency means is . . . '

But Clemency was away, now. 'You think you run the whole damn house, Charity . . . '

'Clemency, would you mind not interrupting me . . . '

Charity's chin wobbled. 'I'll not be spoken to that way! I'm only thinking of the health of you lot, I am! And a fine lot of good you'll be to your precious livestock, Miss Clemency, if you catch some disease from that animal and drop off the twig yerself! Serve you right, I'll think! Expecting me to cook and clean in that kitchen and step around that bleating, smelly little . . . '

'Charity, if you'll . . . '

'Have you seen the mess out there, Mr O'Brien? *She* won't be the one who has to clean it up! Little black marbles all over my clean waxed floor – it's not good enough, Miss Clemency, it's just not!'

'Clemency, take the lamb down to Maurie and Jim, they'll . . . '

'I can't! They've got a dozen in their own quarters already – Ben told you when he arrived that you needed more shepherd's huts . . . '

944

'I'll thank you to leave the running of this property to me, girl, and . . . '

'I don't 'ave to put up with this! I may as well tell you right now, that Job Kirwin over at Mr Lambert's place has offered for me, an' he's got two rooms above the stables that we can have as soon as we're married.' She looked around at their stunned faces. 'So I don't have to stay here and trip over lamb pebbles, Miss Clemency, an' I'll thank you to remember it!'

Aidan had stood, was moving Clemency by the arm, past Liam in the doorway. 'Put that creature with the others in the men's quarters, or you'll *both* be sleeping outside tonight,' he said in a low voice as he manoeuvred his daughter out the door.

Liam followed his sister down to the kitchen, and watched, amused, as she took up a quart pot filled with hot water, in which were two feeding bottles of milk.

'Here,' Liam stepped to Clemency, 'I'll take it out to the boys . . . '

'All right,' grudgingly. 'But wait for a minute.' While he held the little creature she pulled the blue ribbon that held her hair back free, and tied it around the lamb's neck.

'Hell's outhouse, Clem, what's that for?'

'I don't want him to get mixed up with that other mob – this one's special. Just feel the fleece on him, Liam.'

'Fuzz,' said Liam.

'You wait, he'll be a champion, this one – he's from one of the ewes Papa bought from Mister Lawrence. His name is George.'

'Jaysus, Mary and Joseph, now I've heard everything. Why George?'

'He looks like a George.' She fondled the lamb's head, then pushed Liam towards the door. 'Put him under your coat as you cross the yard.'

'Arra, I'll make him a raincoat before we leave, and give him a shot of Father's brandy . . . '

He was half-way to the door when she called him back.

'Liam? Why not take him to Mr Kelly's quarters? He won't mind a few lamb's pebbles on the floor . . . '

'Have you seen what he's done to that room in the barn? Varnished the timber walls and hung hunting prints – he's got an armchair and a little square of carpet on the floor, now. He just might mind a few lamb's pebbles . . . Clem?'

She was grinning, taking the bleating George from his grasp, heading for the door.

'At least take your coat, it's—!' But she was gone, a dark shadow

945

leaping down the verandah steps and across the cobbled yard. Liam sighed, grinning to himself, and went back towards the sound of Charity's shrill voice, now definitely tearful, and the low murmur of his father's placating tones. A mediator was obviously needed; the letter to Victoria would have to wait.

Clemency's heart was thudding against the warmth of the little animal in her arms. Yet part of her mind stood off from the emotions she felt, and judged them.

Infatuation certainly made one feel more alive than at any other time. It could become like a drug; one could, if one wasn't careful, become addicted to it in the same way as an opiate. Michael Kelly was, it seemed, becoming a need in her life, and one that she was not altogether sure that she welcomed. He filled all her waking thoughts; the past few days he had been filling her dreams as well. She had not planned on any course of action, but the half-frozen, bleating George was a pleasant excuse to see the man's room, to be alone amongst surroundings more intimate than the paddocks of Shannonbrook or the homestead.

Only briefly did she wonder if she was placing herself in a situation that might lead to some problem more disagreeable than the confused longing that she knew now. It was better not to think, to give herself up to the moment, dangerous though it was.

He looked surprised to see her, but grinned when he saw her burden, and held his arms out for it. As he carried the lamb over to the fireplace, Clemency had time to glance about the room, to notice the warmth of the glow of firelight and lamplight on the timber walls, the bookcase, the sketches of clipper ships and hunting scenes in their frames.

The rug by the hearth was already occupied by a blue cattle dog puppy, very wet, about three months old. He stood up, wagging his tail, and approached the lamb. After examining it, he came over to Clemency.

Kelly took the quart pot of bottles from her. 'He was curled up outside the barn door, wet and frozen. He has a torn ear – one of the older dogs teaching him the pecking order, I suppose. Do you know his name?'

'Liam bought him from Mr Warwick. He's nameless.'

'Nameless? Here, Nameless!'

The puppy went to him. Kelly bent down on the rug, and Clemency, taking one of the bottles, bent to feed the lamb. 'I meant that he didn't have a name, yet. But Nameless has a certain appeal to it.' She grinned over at Kelly. 'I'll tell Liam you suggested it.'

946

'And who's this?' Kelly looked critically at the lamb. 'One of your father's merinos, isn't he? He'll be a prize one, too . . . ' He was feeling the short, curly fleece, and Clemency felt delighted to have her opinion vindicated. 'His name's George,' she said, seating herself on the rug, the better to steady herself against the lamb's hungry tugging at the bottle in her hand.

'After my cousin, George Du Buisson? This fellow looks as if he has more character in his face . . . '

'Don't be cruel. I called him George because it's a regal name, and one day he'll be king of the flock, won't you , George?' She looked up at Kelly. 'Do you mind him staying here for tonight? The lads below have their work cut out for them as it is.'

The grey eyes smiled into hers as he pulled Nameless, who was attempting to nudge George away from the teat to take it himself, back on to his lap. 'I don't mind.'

And it happened quite naturally, when the lamb had finished feeding and was curled quietly in her lap, and the puppy was asleep with its head on Kelly's knee, that the man leant across and kissed her. They disturbed the sleepy young animals only long enough to move closer together, then sat, contentedly, his arms about her, gazing into the fire. The rain on the tin roof beat a noisy but somehow comforting song, a promise of green grass and plenty, then it was softening to a sigh, a whisper along the corrugations, louder, softer, with the wind.

'It's snowing again,' Kelly said.

Clemency lifted her head to one side a little, the better to hear the difference in sound, and when Kelly's mouth had brushed her cheek, the line of her jaw, the sensitive place just beneath her ear, she forgot rain, snow, Shannonbrook, and the world became only sensation, his lips, his hands – they were kneeling, their bodies pressed close together, and he was saying, 'I've waited for you for so long, I've wanted you for so long . . . I must have you, Clemency, do you understand? I don't think I can live unless you're mine . . . *mine* . . . '

'I know . . . ' she murmured, giving herself up to him, already, in her mind, 'I know . . . '

He was still a moment, and she opened her eyes to find the grey eyes, dark lashes, close to her own; a glance that begged of her while it demanded of her, 'You'll say yes?'

'Yes, yes . . . ' she murmured, but he was not kissing her, he was holding her tightly to him, rocking her a little in his arms.

'When?' he spoke into her damp hair, his breath was warm against her scalp; she raised her head, wanting his mouth on her mouth.

'When, Clemency? I shall go mad, you little tease . . . '

'Now . . . Right now . . . '

He was laughing as he kissed her, 'And what priest will marry us if we drag him out of bed at this hour?'

He was so close to her, saw her face pale, then the blood rush to two spots on her cheeks. 'Priest?' The voice beginning low and rising almost to a squeak.

And she had torn herself from him, had risen, tripping over dog and lamb, and was on the other side of the room. 'Mr Kelly? Exactly what was it you just asked me to comply with?'

'You said yes.' He got to his feet, watching her narrowly.

'To what? To what?'

He stood gazing at her, and the grey of his eyes was no longer soft, nor tender, but held all the warmth of a sleety rain cloud. 'I'm more interested, Miss O'Brien, in what you thought my proposal was.' She did not answer him, her face becoming pinker. His voice lower, he said, 'I'm afraid I know.'

Clemency stood by the door, wishing the ground would swallow her up. Still he looked at her, in that cool, detached way of his, and she was forced, eventually, to look away. 'I suppose I've shocked you.'

'A little.'

She glanced at him, unsure. It was always so hard to tell if he were laughing at her. 'Well, you've shocked me, too. What would you gain by marrying me? I wouldn't have thought you were the marrying sort, Mr Kelly.'

'I wasn't. Until now.'

'You wouldn't be marrying me for money. I have a feeling that you're running away from a great deal of it.'

'Quite correct.'

'And it can't be for social position, for you know my father's an emancipist and at any time he may slither from the tenacious hold he has in society, should he be discovered . . . '

'You don't know me at all, if you think that bothers me. Have you not considered that I may wish to marry you because embarrassing as it is to say it in the face of your indifference, I happen to love you, Clemency?'

She was furious that the words could so affect her, to find that she had been standing there for some seconds, staring at him, unable to think, to formulate a reply. He walked towards her; the lamb stood on wobbly legs and came bleating after him. It would have been rather funny, if she wasn't so filled with resentment; his physical

948

proximity to her, only a short time ago a warm and glowing promise, was now an intimidation.

She scowled at him. 'I'm not what you think I am, Mr Kelly.'

'That's just been made clear to me. But it makes you even more intriguing. Are you usually so susceptible to a man's advances?'

The fist that she brought up towards his face was caught almost effortlessly in his. He held it as she tried to pull away. 'It's not only ridiculous but spiteful you are,' she hissed. 'I chose you in much the same manner that you chose me – that doesn't make me a hoor.' Her eyes narrowed. 'But neither am I the pure-minded virgin that you'd want to wed and bed – or was it to be the other way about?' For a second his grip on her fist almost tightened but he controlled himself. She spoke quickly, 'I'm a fallen woman, Mr Kelly, not once, but three times over. Is that the kind of woman that you want for a wife?'

He had not, as she was certain he would, let her go. Her bent fingers were still imprisoned within his, not exerting any pressure; her own pulling back away from him was stabbing her own fingernails into her palm. She lifted her other hand to prise his fingers loose and found that wrist imprisoned, her hands crossed, and pulled into his chest so that he could study her face more nearly.

'I want you for my wife. I want whatever woman you are, for my wife.'

'And you'd be my father's son, would you not? Assured of your place here. You'd have wanted to marry me if I had two heads, Michael Kelly – you're a man obsessed . . . '

He was shaking her, and she wondered if she had gone too far. 'If you weren't your father's daughter you wouldn't be the way you are, you little idiot. And if being obsessed is what I feel when I contemplate the warmth, the integrity and acceptance I've found here, then yes, I'm obsessed.' He continued, as she was about to spit some new maliciousness at him, 'And as for your virginity—' he shrugged, 'I've never made love to a virgin in my life, and I don't particularly wish to. My own memories of that state are a combination of guilt, dread and unreasonable expectations.'

There, he was doing it again, making her smile when she did not in the least wish to. She lowered her head, trying not to laugh. When she looked up, the soft expression was there once more upon his face, but he would not allow her to relax at all.

'Tell me this. Did you love the men concerned?'

She was startled. 'Did I say there was more than one?'

'You said you were a fallen woman three times over. Three lapses

949

of morality with one man would count as the one indiscretion, I should think. Who were they?'

She half looked over her shoulder at the door, found him manoeuvring her about until he had his back to it. She lowered her head and murmured their names.

'I beg your pardon?'

'I said, Jules, Vincenzo and Sergei.'

He seemed to consider. 'French, Italian and Russian? And where did you find them? No, never mind. What did they do for a living?'

'I can't see what this has to do with you!' But she sensed from the set of his mouth, the look in his eyes, that he was not about to let her go until the whole story was out. 'A poet, an operatic tenor, and nothing very much, as far as I could see. Sergei, that is. He was a count. Will you let me go, now?'

He did so, but still seemed comfortably settled against the door. 'Why didn't you marry one of them, Clemency? I can see you as a countess, oddly enough, more easily than as the wife of a poet or an Italian tenor. You'd drag Sergei back to Russia and turn his estate into a model of efficiency.'

She did not know whether to be pleased by this or not, and answered sulkily, 'I don't want to marry anyone.'

'But you're not happy as you are.'

'That's no guarantee that I'll be any happier married. Especially to you.' And she cursed herself inwardly for not thinking to deny, outright, that she was unhappy. 'And I am happy,' she added defiantly.

'Why did you enter the convent?'

Hell's outhouse. She marched back into the room, prowled up and down, trying to hold onto her temper, determined not to give way to her desire to scream and shriek at the man. Why had this meeting gone wrong? How could an encounter that had begun so well descend to this? She stood thumping her fist lightly on the back of the armchair, looking about the room that had suddenly taken on all the aspects of a prison.

'Were you running away from something?' Kelly asked.

She exploded, 'Does every nun who takes her vows have to be running away from the world? People with your simplistic, ignorant approach don't even consider those women with a genuine love of God, and a desire to pray for a mankind that can't or won't pray for itself . . . '

'I didn't ask about the majority of nuns. I asked about you.' His quiet tone, the clearness of his diction, cut across her words. He walked over to her, pulled her in front of the armchair and sat her

950

down by pressing on her shoulders.

'I wish I hadn't come here tonight. I wish I'd left George in the snow . . . '

'I'm very glad you came. Tell me about the Mitchells.' Kelly sat down on his neatly-made bed, still close enough to the door to reach it before she could.

The Mitchells . . .

She turned her face away, towards the fire, and she saw there Nicholas Mitchell's long, gentle, handsome face, the face that could be transformed when at the piano, or before an orchestra; a silent, lonely man, who came alive only with his music.

It had been a long time since she had thought of Nicholas. It dismayed her a little, that she could forget him when he had filled her life for so many years . . .

'Did you love him?' It was Kelly's voice, but she found no flaring of rage within her as she would have expected; it was as if he had timed this question for when she was, at last, ready to ask it of herself.

'I believe I did,' she said. 'I cared about him, his happiness, his career, quite deeply.'

'And did he love you?'

'Yes.' Wonderingly, still gazing into the fire. She knew that now, too. Admitted that. 'He told me, one day, that he wanted me to be his mistress. Very . . . very clumsily. I was frightened – I should have seen the inevitability of it – I shut my mind to it. To be with him, you see, was enough. He even said . . . he said Christabel wouldn't mind – he said his wife wouldn't mind, because there'd been others . . . But as long as he and Christabel stayed together . . . Appearances . . . ' Her voice trailed away. She suddenly realized to whom she was speaking and turned startled eyes to the man on the bed, but he was gazing at her quietly. He said, 'It must have rather appalled you.'

She smiled. 'It did, but it shouldn't have. I knew Christabel very well – I admired her, she lived life on her own terms. But it's as if our whole world, the style of life that we lived, then, left nothing over. I realized that we were all . . . burning ourselves out. And for no great purpose. Only self-amusement. The convent was a reaction to it – not a sensible one, I realize that, now.'

She turned to watch the man on the bed and wondered at his ability to draw forth her feelings. She stood, and he stood, with that quick grace of his. She said, 'May I leave now? And can we forget this entire embarrassing incident? I trust in your honour, Kelly, that you'll speak of this to no one.'

'Of course, that goes without saying. What does disturb me is that you found our discussion embarrassing. I'm afraid you'll try to forget it, in that case, and I don't want you to. I want you to remember it . . . ' He was standing very close to her, but there was no threat emanating from him. She felt a kind of sadness, and almost reached for him, but knew, now, she could not. 'I meant everything I said, Clemency. I want you to marry me. No, don't start protesting. Just remember, and consider it. Please.'

He stepped out of her way, and she moved to the door, opened it, and had to pause there, turn to him. 'How can you still say that, after all I told you?'

'About Jules, Vincenzo and Sergei?' He smiled a little. 'Because they never touched your life.'

'They . . . '

'They may have possessed you physically, but you'll be mine, as my wife, in a way that you were never possessed by any other man.' She was colouring once more, looked away. 'I think you know this,' he said, quietly, 'and that's what frightens you. Giving up your autonomy into someone else's hands. That takes trust. I trust you. You, however, obviously don't trust me. I'm disappointed, but I'm not disheartened. I'm a very patient man, and I think you'll be worth all the trouble you're putting us both through.'

'You could have . . . ' It was hard to find the right words. 'You could have seduced me easily. I wanted you to seduce me, and instead you're after talking of long-term plans as if you were training a colt. I won't be waited for.'

He was down on his heel, stirring the fire. 'Clemency, there's an uncomfortable draught coming through that door. George, Nameless and I would prefer it to be closed.'

'Tell me! Why are you insisting on marriage instead of a liaison – just tell me that!'

'No, I shan't,' he said calmly, prodding the coals into life, 'because you do not deserve to hear the very many admirable things I have to say about you. They'll fall on deaf ears. I'll wait until you're ready to listen.'

She waited for him to look up at her, but he did not. He said, 'Please close the door, Clemency. Goodnight, my dear.'

She slammed the door, and heard the young dog, Nameless, give a startled yelp.

She strode across to the verandah through the lightly falling snow – but changed her mind, and walked three times about the house before she felt calm enough to face the others.

The impossible, the terrifying, the unthinkable had, it seemed,

952

happened. She had fallen across a man who seemed to understand her completely, to accept her, and he was a man she wanted – yes, quite desperately. And he wanted her. Not just for one night, or several. But for ever.

And ever has it been that the more perfect a love seems to be, so correspondingly, is the fear of its loss. The greater the miracle, the more one wonders at one's worthiness to possess it. Clemency, who saw, she felt, only too clearly her own frailties, looked upon the love of this man as a burden upon her own inadequate soul. By the time she had finished her damp perambulations about the house, she had shrugged it off, rejected it.

It can't last. Then he'll be full of regrets; his bitterness will drive him away – like Papa, like Ma . . . She shivered, and not just from the cold.

Part 7
SHANNONBROOK
THREE

Will you be as hard,
Colleen, as you are quiet?
Will you be without pity
On me forever?

Listen to me, Noireen,
Listen aroon;
Put healing on me
From your quiet mouth.

I am in the little road
That is dark and narrow,
The little road that has led
Thousands to sleep.

DOUGLAS HYDE

90

Charity's marriage to Job Kirwin was the only light-hearted affair in those months. Job left Lambert's employ and came to work as groom and coachman at Shannonbrook Three, adding, Liam noted, his own dour air of gloom to an already gloomy house.

The letter to Victoria was written, and Liam turned back to his work, searching through his mail each morning as if the very writing of the letter might prompt Victoria to have posted her own. He would have to wait months, he told himself, but watched the mail with an obsessive longing that he hated even while he could not rationalize it.

The tension in the house was growing, too. Kelly and Clemency seemed to avoid each other, and Aidan and Berrima, despite Liam's hopes, had returned from Camden with no new warmth between them. Liam was disappointed, even attempted to talk to Berrima, to persuade her to tell Aidan of those last days in Sydney, of Mark's death. And there was more, he knew, that she was keeping to herself. She had the look, sometimes, of a woman who was haunted – and that, perhaps, was the literal truth.

'You're presuming I wish my friendship with your father to . . . deepen into something else, Liam.' She smiled a little. 'I can't honestly say that I wish that.' And as he began to speak, she placed a hand against his face, 'No, Liam, desist for my sake. Your father and I have a tolerant kind of friendship that we never knew, until now – I have my work, and he has his. In our busy lives there's little room for anything else.'

He had left her, dissatisfied, knowing in his heart there was no point in trying to talk to his father about Berri. He would meet with a wall of impenetrable silence, if not downright hostility for attempting to interfere. And besides, his father was rarely home; it almost seemed, these days, as if he were trying to avoid Shannonbrook Three, and Berrima.

He was with his father, one night in October, when Hedley Warwick had invited them to join himself and Lawler for drinks at the Hit-and-Miss. Thomas joined them 'for an hour', but at nine that night they were still there, the topic of conversation never ranging far from the matter of Sam Russell and Donaldson, and the appeal case scheduled for May the following year.

Kelly rode into Mittagong and found them still there at ten o'clock, the doors closed, and a heated discussion in progress. Wal, muttering about the threat of Hal Peterson making a check, nevertheless opened the door to Kelly, and he, too, was soon drawn into the discussion.

'I know we need trade unions in this country,' Thomas was saying. 'Have you read Jeremy Wilton's article in the *Herald*? He's made a study of these things, and his findings on poverty makes the idea of this being the land of golden opportunities for all just laughable.'

'Jeremy Wilton is an eccentric,' Edward Lawler put in. 'And when will poor workers banding together to make demands of the wealthy make any difference to the way of things? People take fright at such talk – look at the Chartists – everyone's afraid of another French Revolution. And the fear will make the rich push down even harder. It's a vicious circle.'

'Are you saying we should ignore what's happening?' Warwick asked, surprising the other men by his vehemence. 'What of the factories in Sydney where they're hiring children of eleven and twelve – of course they're not supposed to, but wages are so low and conditions so bad in some places, that there's no choice but to send the children out to work as soon as possible. And here in the country it's worse, if anything, for some. Whole families dependent on the money the husband makes as a shearer, and that's at the whim of the station owner.' He looked up. 'I'm excluding you from this, Mr O'Brien, you pay well, and your men know it. And that, come to think of it, is another reason why some of the other landowners hereabouts resent you.'

'The shearers should organize themselves,' Liam said, and they all noticed the trace of bitterness in his words. 'Trouble is, they're too bloody spread out – the size of this country will defeat the shearers.' And his thoughts were on Ben and Snowy as he swirled the last of the beer in his glass.

'And what happens when such men do organize? That's what's happened with Sam Russell and his friends. You couldn't get them more organized – a *co-operative*.' Warwick peered at each of them over his glasses. 'And ever since Marx's *Manifesto* in '49, all the factory owners have been so bloody sensitive about communism.'

'It's just a philosophy,' Edward waved his hand airily, 'it'll be like any other Utopian ideal – put power into *any* man's hands and he becomes a tyrant – then you'll have *another* revolution . . .'

'Now let's not be generalizing.' Aidan leaned across the table to

958

Warwick, 'You've obviously been watching the developments in this town very closely in your quiet way. What is it that's disturbing people? Is it just a change to the order of things? Do those with land here and factories in Sydney fear that there'll be repercussions . . . ?'

'That's about it.' Warwick nodded so violently that he had to push his glasses back up his nose.

Kelly interrupted then, 'Mister O'Brien, Wal's getting impatient to close, I think – it's past eleven . . . '

'Hush,' Liam jabbed him in the ribs. 'Hedley, you've got to be wrong. One little co-operative . . . '

'It's not just the co-operative, Liam. It's this worker's compensation business. Have you stopped to think how many accidents occur in factories? My uncle owned woollen mills in Yorkshire – I can remember visiting them when I was younger, seeing children of seven working ten hour shifts. Have you been inside one of the factories in Sydney or Melbourne and seen the conditions?'

And it was strange, Aidan thought, how easily, for once, Liam was vanquished. He began to colour, and sat back quietly. Later, Aidan would remember that he took no further part in the conversation, but listened, and appeared a little abstracted.

Hedley Warwick put in drily, 'According to Jeremy Wilton's figures, factory wages leave very little over for saving.'

'Maybe it's not economic organization that worries them – maybe it's something more violent . . . '

'Rawmaish, Edward!' Aidan stood up. He had drunk far too many whiskeys and the pressure of his bladder was by now too great to ignore. 'I'm going to the outhouse, this conversation'd give anyone . . . '

Warwick half-stood, leaned across the table to him. 'Donaldson went running to his . . . sympathetic friends, immediately after Russell's accident happened . . . ' It was as if he had waited a long time to speak of this.

'For advice, maybe . . . ' Aidan edged towards the door.

'He was badly frightened, they all are, because they see this co-operative as a threat to the monopolies of the wealthy in this district . . . '

'Augh . . . ' Aidan had to leave. He turned his back on the raised voices to wend a rather unsteady path between the deserted tables, out the back door of the hotel and down to the latrines.

The gentlemen's toilets were simply three partitioned cubicles, the platform of the toilet seats erected over a grave-shaped trench in the ground. Aidan relieved himself, nose wrinkling at the stench from the sewer, adjusted his clothing and left the little building.

959

He had almost reached the hotel verandah when the figure appeared from the shadows. Aidan, humming to himself, oblivious, bumped into the man. 'Oh – pardon . . .' He squinted up at the tall figure; in the darkness, and with a broad-brimmed hat pulled over the face, the stranger's features could not be made out. 'If you're lookin' for the outhouse,' Aidan said, helpfully, 'it's back . . .'

He had half-turned to point. The pain exploded in his lower stomach as the man's fist drove hard into his body, and he was bent double, unable to move, his mind screaming with the pain – and the others, the boots on the gravelly soil, the hard hands gripping his shoulders, his arms . . .

It would never end, it seemed as if it would never end – with no breath, no means of orienting himself, no opportunity to cry out for help, the fists rained down on his body while he was pinned, helpless, and only slowly did the almost welcome darkness claim him.

He awoke completely disoriented. The dirty yard looked unfamiliar, the darkened buildings and walls about him looked strange, threatening. From a horse yard over to his left, a pale shape whickered to him; Aidan stumbled to his feet, the familiarity of Blue the only comforting thing in the nightmare of nausea and pain that claimed him. He had to stop to vomit twice as he was unfastening the gate, but he had his horse free, unlooped the reins from where they were tied to the saddle, and somehow managed to mount the animal. Blue set off through the gateway at the rear of the cobbled yard. It was good, Aidan thought, that the horse seemed to know where to go.

It was Berrima who found him. Hearing one of the French doors banging loose in the wind, she came downstairs and found Aidan unconscious in the hall, the front doors wide open.

'She was right . . .' he murmured, through swollen lips, as she cradled his head, calling his name. 'She was right, the bitch. On the green carpet . . . the little bitch was right . . .'

'You idiot. Oh, you complete fool . . .'

He opened his eyes to Berrima, and the pain. Every breath an agony, a confused memory of Glenleigh . . .

No. The sunlight of early morning on the cream walls of his bedroom at Shannonbrook Three. And Berrima, in her nightgown, with a robe over it. She was pressing a cool cloth to his face, bending over from where she sat beside him on the bed. Even in the midst of

960

the pain that possessed him, his eyes were drawn to the open neck of her robe, the neckline of her nightdress, low, and lace at that. The cloth cooled his face, and her other hand, on his hair, was gentle; he tried to lie quietly, but could not take his eyes from her, and impossible though it was, he felt himself stirring, felt the blood pulsating painfully through his lower body. 'Jaysus . . . ' He half-laughed, felt his lip split open, tasted fresh blood in his mouth.

'Oh, Aidan, lie still.'

He muttered unintelligibly, trying to turn his face away from her touch, the maddeningly compassionate fingers that had the exact opposite effect of that of the soothing calm that she wished to instil in him.

'Aaaunngh . . . '

'Are you in great pain? Hush, lie still . . . '

'Jaysus, Mary and . . . '

'Hush, Aidan . . . '

'Woman, will you . . . will you come into bed this instant?' he gasped. 'Will you for God's sake come into this bed, or cover y'rself, for y' killin' me by degrees, Berrima Ellis. Do one thing or the other, but begod, do something.'

She looked down at herself, flushed a little, and pulled her robe about her. 'I'm sorry . . . ' she smiled.

'I'll not let you forget this, Berrima. I have a long memory . . . '

'I know,' she laughed. 'Aidan, don't try to talk . . . '

'Who brought me home?'

'You came home yourself, you foolish man. Thomas, Liam and Kelly were frantic, looking for you, but you'd disappeared.'

'Did they . . . ' He tasted bile in his mouth, had to swallow, 'Did they find who . . . '

'No, Aidan. Kelly and Liam rode back this morning, to tell Hal Peterson and to ask about the town, but they've found nothing. You didn't recognize the men responsible?'

'No. It was too dark, and they weren't after giving me much time . . . '

There was a faint knock at the door, and it opened, Clemency's head appearing around it. She smiled in relief when she saw him awake. 'Arra, Papa, you look awful.'

'Aye, insult me. Make the most of this time, Rebel, for in a short time you'd better be moving faster than I will.'

She grinned. 'I'll go and tell Liam and Kelly you're all right. They've been on the point of grabbing their . . . '

'Clemency,' Berrima interrupted, 'Kelly and Liam can see your father now, if they wish.' The two women looked at each other, Clemency's gaze strayed back to her father, and she smiled a little, nodded, and left.

'What's this about Liam and Kelly?'

She was adjusting his pillows. 'Oh, they were very worried and upset – once they see that you're all right . . . '

She stopped. They both heard the sound of horses' hoofs on the gravel outside, slow, steady, but at least three horses. Berrima rose and went to the window.

'Who is it?' Aidan went to roll over but could barely move. Placing one hand to his chest, he could feel the heavy bandages. He remained still, trying to calm his breathing and the pain, while Berrima's voice came calmly, 'Maurie. Only Maurie Templeton.' She turned back into the room, and smiled at him.

'Has Maurie taken up circus riding?'

She looked puzzled. 'I don't . . . '

'Since when has he taken to riding three or four horses at once?'

'I . . . ' and now she looked unsure. 'Just a moment, Aidan . . . ' She was heading for the door.

'Berrima!'

She was gone. He lay for a moment, then, as the voices began downstairs, tense, angry voices, he managed to push the bedclothes aside, to stand, reach for his robe and pull it on over his nightshirt.

He could see them from the head of the stairs, Liam, Kelly and Berrima, too angry to notice him as they came from the office.

'Your father wouldn't want you to do this . . . ' Berrima was saying.

Kelly was checking his revolver, placing it in his shoulder holster, pulling on his jacket. Liam was shoving the shells from a Winchester 44.40 into his pocket, trying to move past Berrima to the door, the rifle in his hand. 'If it was Father in the same circumstances . . . '

'You have no proof . . . !'

Kelly said, grimly, 'I saw a man with Donaldson today; I can't remember his name, but he comes from Melbourne, and his reputation isn't good.'

Berrima's face was white and the brown eyes blazed up into Kelly's face. 'And where did you meet such a man to know that, Mr Kelly?'

Kelly's discomfort lasted only a second or two, before he smiled a little, sheepishly, 'I'm afraid I can't remember. I've been in so many unsavoury places and dealt with so many unpleasant people, Mrs Ellis, that I must admit I often become confused.'

'Cut the talking. Try to understand, Berrima, and get out of our way, will you?' And as Liam moved Berrima gently but firmly out of the way—

'Stop . . . right . . . there.'

And they looked around to find Aidan on the stairs, battered but standing upright, gripping the banister for support, or perhaps in rage, anger in his voice as he said, 'Come inside, Liam – shut that door.'

Liam had only just begun to open it, and paused with his hand on the knob. 'Father, if we leave this up to Hal Peterson . . . '

'*Do as y'r told*!'

Liam shut the door. Stony-faced, he and Kelly moved past Berrima to the stairs. Aidan leaned over the banister to them. 'Now, I'll tell you this once, and there's an end to it. You don't know if it was Donaldson, or Pirie-Moxham or a syndicate of every businessman in Mittagong who's behind this. And you can't go beating them all up, nor waving guns in their faces. Whoever did this, did it for a purpose, and it's not going to work. That's all that concerns us, right now.'

Liam looked sullen. It was Kelly who looked up at Aidan uncomprehendingly. 'You're going to let them get away with it?'

'It's not your concern, boyo, what I'm going to do!' And to both, 'I don't need either of you to fight my battles for me . . . '

And as they both began to speak at once, he brought his fist down on the banister with a jolting effect that made him gasp. He saw a new Kelly, now, the man that Devlin had created, as mad and as bloody-minded as Liam was instinctively, as he himself had been. 'Set foot outside that door, either of you – and you needn't bother to come back.'

They gazed up at him, weighing his determination against their own. Then they glanced at each other – and Liam began to remove the bullets from the rifle, and Kelly was unfastening his jacket and unbuckling the shoulder holster.

Clemency burst in the front door, her eyes finding Liam. 'What's keeping you? Maurie's got the horses ready . . . ' She stopped on seeing their faces, and looked up, freezing as she saw her father at the stair railing.

'Oh,' she said.

Hal Peterson questioned Beecham Donaldson concerning the stranger who had been seen by Kelly. Charles Stoner was his new assistant and secretary, Donaldson insisted, and indeed, the immaculate Mr Stoner seemed to fit that description, a polite and handsome young man in a dark suit who answered all Peterson's questions willingly and civilly.

'Charlie Stoner is always civil,' Kelly told the police sergeant later, when Hal called at Shannonbrook Three. 'He'll be civil right up to the time he—'

'He what?' Peterson regarded Kelly narrowly. It was not like the man to so nearly lose control of his tongue – and the moment was over. 'Come, Kelly,' Peterson prompted, 'if you know anything about this character . . . '

'He's not to be trusted,' Kelly said, with his usual calm. 'Anything else, and I may be up for defamation of character.' He grinned, but Peterson was not amused. Kelly was too much like all the other O'Briens, too damn' independent for their own good.

The senior O'Brien was at that moment arguing with Thomas and Liam from his 'temporary office' upstairs. Berrima, who had had heated arguments with Aidan when he refused to allow her to nurse him, echoed the feelings of the entire family when she thought that Aidan, when not in control of his business and affairs, was more tyrannical than the healthy despot they had taken for granted.

She buried her rebellious thoughts in her work, and left Aidan to the ministerings of Clemency and Charity. If he wanted her, let him ask for her; in the meantime she had her own work to do.

It was while she was trying to think of new subjects for her camera that she struck upon the idea of the old iron mine. Lying idle for several years now, the deserted buildings and rusting machinery would make some excellent studies.

Though the equipment was heavy, she somehow managed by herself much of the time. Clemency would join her occasionally, and Kelly, who showed a surprising eye for composition, often went with her, and that was a help. But most of the time she preferred to work alone. It was one compensation, she thought, for having little or no reputation. One couldn't surprise people, and it was virtually impossible to shock them.

She finished with twenty-five photographs of the mine – the yawning hole of the shaft itself, some fine studies of chimney stacks against the dark, low hills with interesting cloud patterns above; a few morning shots of the strong light and shade patterns on the cranes and mysterious, abandoned machinery whose original purpose eluded her. She felt the power of the place, however. It had, by its presence, created the township of Mittagong. Even while it had despoilt the surroundings, it had, for a while, lived and breathed, an idol created by men; men worshipped it, gave their wealth and their lives to it. The soil here was red with iron. The little nearby stream ran red with it. The monster that the men created, that had ruined so

964

many of them, devouring fortunes and leaving no trace, now lay still, its metal rusted. And in the rain, it, too, bled. The rain washed the monster's blood back to the soil.

She would return to Shannonbrook, during this time, trailing skirts stained brown-red about the hems, with rust-coloured smudges on her face, smiling to herself, her mind already preoccupied with planning the next day's activities.

She was pleased with the photographs. It was early one evening that the last print was mounted on to cardboard and she gathered all twenty-five together and left the studio. Charity was in the kitchen, but merely grunted as Berrima showed her work. 'Who'd want to look at pitchers of the old mine I'd like to know.'

'They're already talking of pulling down some of the buildings for the stone, Charity. If they do, then there won't be any record of what the plant looked like.'

'So?'

'Well, it's important. Historically speaking.'

Charity sniffed. 'Never saw the point of history meself.'

Berrima gave up, gathered the photographs once more and was heading for the door, when Charity said, 'Oh, there's something else. That Miz Warwick called here today while you was out with that camera thing. She wants you to return her visit, she said, to discuss this ball you'd promised to hold here on the first day of summer. Which is – ' and Charity looked at Berrima with such accusing intensity that her eyes almost crossed – 'just two weeks away.'

'The first of December – of course. I'd forgotten to write it on the calendar . . .' Why had she promised this to Helena? Admittedly the proceeds from the evening would be going to a good cause, but there was enough trouble in the house . . .

'Thank you very much, Miz Ellis,' Charity was sniffing, 'and just what are we going to do about all these hordes of people who're going to descend on us, tell me that? And are Meggie Danaher and me going to have to do all the work here in the kitchen?'

'No, Charity, of course not. Tomorrow I'll sit down with you and you can tell me what you'll need for the catering, and I'll have more people hired for the evening, of course. You must remember, the ball is to raise funds for a hospital in the district, and we should do our part. I'll start planning immediately.'

She retreated to the door, shutting it on the petulant voice, ' . . . All very well . . . and him upstairs shouting and bellowing at a body . . . '

Berrima hesitated in the hall, and then on an impulse, took the photographs upstairs and knocked on the door of Aidan's room.

Liam and Thomas had gone, and Aidan was sitting up against pillows, surrounded by paperwork, writing a letter in his large, forward-thrusting hand. He stopped, however, when the door opened and she entered the room.

He looked up and smiled at her. There was still warmth in his eyes – even when she interrupted him, as she did now, when he was busy wrestling with the financial statements from Andrew Tweedie's emporiums. It was the side of his business interests that he liked the least; undoubtedly, Berrima thought privately, because it was the one over which he had the least control.

He pushed the paperwork aside, now, and seemed to welcome the diversion of the photographs, spreading them in two rows across the bed and studying them.

'Yes . . . ' he said softly, finally, 'you've captured it. The old men, the ones who began it, who loved the place – if they were here they'd say you captured it in all its splendour. It *was* splendid, you know.' He paused, frowning, and she watched him, surprised at his manner. 'Some of the board members, even while I was there, they loved it too, I'm thinking. Some of them. I was too busy thinking in terms of money to realize it at the time, but even in the last years there were a few members of the board who believed in that mine for its own sake. They must have left it in the evenings and seen the sun warm the stone walls as you have, here. They'd have seen the machinery fall silent with a stark feeling of grief. I know Hedley did. It wasn't just the fact that he lost money when the mine failed – he was immensely proud of the fact that this was the first iron mine in Australia. For that reason alone I believe that he'd have kept it going, if he could. As old Amberley would have done,' he added, quietly, his eyes still on the photographs. 'Sure, it's a shame, is it not? – I've not thought about it until now – but it's a shame the mine had to close.'

'Perhaps, one day, they may open it again . . . '

'Och, no, girl. We've no real deposits of coal nearby, we're too far from the sea . . . and I don't know whether there was all that much iron in the first place. No . . . ' and there was a trace of regret in his voice that surprised even himself, 'Mittagong will never be a New Sheffield, as they'd hoped. It's glad I am, so, that you've made these, for there'll soon be little enough left to mark the site, I'm thinking.'

Hedley Warwick . . . yes, the iron mine had been something that was his alone, that he did not have to explain to his rather overbearing wife. And its existence would have appealed to his sense of

966

public spirit. He had often spoken of Mittagong with pride, felt that it would take its place in Australia's memory in the same way that Eureka had possessed people's imaginations. Australia would become a country of great mineral wealth, and it was here in Mittagong that the first Australian steel had been forged.

I'll take the photographs to Hedley and Helena tomorrow, Berrima decided. Even Helena, who was never interested in the mine except as a means of establishing her position in Mittagong society as the wife of a member of the board, even she could not deny that these were fine photographs.

They were still bent over the prints when there was a knock at the bedroom door. One of the young housemaids bobbed a curtsey and told Berrima that a Mr Garth Ellis was waiting to see her in the parlour.

Garth had leased the comfortable and not insubstantial lodge that belonged to Pirie-Moxham's country estate, Summer Hill. Even the big house remained empty for much of the year, and Garth mentioned to Berrima, on that first visit to her, that Pirie-Moxham might consider selling up altogether and returning to Sydney to live permanently.

'Would you consider buying Summer Hill?' Berrima asked him. 'When Victoria returns with the children . . . '

'But she won't.' Garth's smile was wry, even bitter. 'I was in England, you'll remember. I didn't stay. Victoria welcomed me in the house, and the children are as fond of me as they can be, considering we hardly see each other, but she won't consider a reconciliation. And to tell the truth, I doubt if I really want one.'

'But Garth, you love her, I know you do.'

He stared at the floor before him for several seconds before answering. 'Perhaps. But too much has happened for us to go back to where we began.' They were drinking tea on the verandah, and as Garth reached out for his cup, Berrima realized what was so strange about his handling of the china. Garth's hands had always been long, slim-fingered; they were now swollen, the joints enlarged. 'Yes,' he said, 'It began about four years ago, just rheumaticky pains; but it's become worse, I find it hard to hold a pen, sometimes. And of course, my cricket and hunting days are at an end.'

'That must be very hard for you . . . ' And she knew, now, that the change in his appearance was not simply the grief over the end of his marriage, nor his difficulties in his work, but was caused by pain. Pain had caused the once-generous mouth to become twisted, held as it now was, pain and the knowledge that his weakened joints

967

would not enable him to lead the field, to excel at the sports in which he had taken so much pride.

To give him confidence, she tried to draw him out on his latest work, but found him strangely uncommunicative. It was at the publishers, it would be in British bookshops in a few weeks – but he did not know, he who once would not have doubted, whether it would be a success or not. From his manner of speaking, a stranger might believe that he did not care.

'And Victoria?' She almost hesitated, but he answered the question quite naturally.

'Victoria is well, and thriving on the hypocrisy and attention that follows a commercially successful author. She has the inestimable gift of being able to ignore the serious and knowledgeable critics and pay attention only to the mindless sycophants who praise her.' Then he looked across at Berrima's rather startled face. 'If I sound jealous, I undoubtedly am.' He smiled a little.

Berrima said, 'I'm sure your next book will be a success, Garth; it will put you back where you belong – you mustn't let a few bad reviews embitter you.'

'No, by all means. But with one first book praised by the critics, and the four subsequent ones denounced, which is the correct estimation? I wonder about that. I wonder a great deal. For if I thought it was the latter, I don't think I could live, Berri. I'm afraid I couldn't bear it.'

Berrima controlled a sigh, reflected on the tenuousness of Garth's self-confidence. It came only through his writing. In his efforts to surpass that first, intoxicating success, he had allowed Victoria and the children to drift away from him, so now, in truth, the writing was all that there was left.

He was saying that he would go back to England eventually. 'But I want to stay in Mittagong for a while, to try to recapture something of the atmosphere that I was able to place in *Songs of Nattai*. After all, this is where it all began.'

'Yes, it did.'

But, Berrima wondered, is it the right thing to go back? Was it Nattai that gave him the inspiration for the poetry, or was it Victoria herself?

Garth was standing, preparing to leave, and without thinking, as she rose, Berrima said, 'But won't you stay for dinner? Clemency and Liam will be home soon . . .'

Garth smiled, took her hand in both of his. 'Berri, you don't believe that anyone can hold resentments, do you? For you're too good, too generous yourself . . .'

968

'Garth, you're mad if you have that opinion of me!' But she sobered as she gazed into his face, knowing what he was trying to say. 'Was it Liam's friendship with Victoria that caused you and he to become estranged? I hope it wasn't, for it was entirely innocent, Garth.' And when he did not speak, 'Please, Garth, you must learn to trust people, you need your friends. Don't shut yourself away from us, like—'

She did not go on, and he said, gently, 'Like Mark.'

'We all care for you, Garth. Not just for your brilliance, but because of the kind of person you are.'

He gazed at her for some seconds, his face unreadable, then he had bent, kissed her on the cheek, a fond, tender kiss, and he left, without turning around.

Berrima stood, puzzled, for a long time, for Garth's breath, as he kissed her, had smelt sweet, vaguely familiar. Gin. Yes, that's what it was. She moved to the steps and stood looking after him, worriedly. It was odd that she should worry more about Garth now, when as a boy she had not liked him very much at all. And it came to her, watching the figure, sitting in the saddle like the superb horseman he was, vanishing from sight down the drive, that Garth was reminding her more and more of Mark. The same vulnerability, she thought, the same compelling vulnerability. And she understood, then, why Victoria would never have him back.

91

Her first evening out of mourning dress since Mark's death. She came downstairs a little nervously, wondering if Aidan would notice, what he would say . . .

'Tommy's got a stummick ache.'

She tried to tell herself she had heard incorrectly. She came down the last two stairs, holding the train of her lavender ball gown over her arm, and bent over to young Corrie. 'Pardon?'

'Tommy's got a stummick ache. We were eating plums all afternoon. Do you think that did it?' he repeated, patiently.

Thomas's three older boys stood solemnly in front of Berrima as she was about to join Aidan on the verandah. She glanced at each guilty face, and sighed. Looking up towards the open front door, she could see Thomas and Kelly flanking Aidan as he welcomed guests on the front steps, and beyond them, those guests who had already been greeted and were strolling about in the lighted gardens. The orchestra, on the verandah, was playing merrily; worried as she was, all seemed to be well. 'Where's Tommy now?'

'In the upstairs bathroom.' Young Henry, named for his grandfather, Heinrich, and already displaying that gentleman's sturdiness and scientific bent, added, '*I* think it's 'cause he ate the stones. We *did* tell him to spit them out. He's the only one of us who wouldn't, and he's the only one who's sick. He's going to the toilet all the time and he *pongs*. So it must be the stones.'

'Where's your Mama?'

'In the kitchen with Mrs Charity. We didn't want to tell her – she'd hit us with the wooden spoon. We thought we'd better tell you.'

'I think,' Berrima said, 'that you should tell Mama too. I'll go up to Tommy.'

She found him looking particularly white, half his face being covered with Aidan's shaving lather. Berrima gently but firmly took the razor from his grasp. 'I *am* sick,' he said plaintively, 'but I was bored, too.'

The three men downstairs on the verandah, in a lull between groups of guests arriving, bore vastly different expressions on their faces. Kelly watched the crowd on the lawns, guarded, as if, despite the relaxed and sociable scene before him, his senses warned of danger. Thomas looked disgruntled; he still could not see why Aidan had invited Donaldson here tonight. And not only Donaldson, but Pirie-Moxham and Lambert and Amberley and Barrett as well. *And* their plump and tight-mouthed wives whose gazes told clearly that they found fault everywhere they looked.

Aidan was the only one who appeared relaxed and happy. He rocked on his heels occasionally, Thomas noted, with something of the satisfaction he had shown as a boy when all went well with him. All these people came to admire his house, his food, to compliment him on all he had. That's what it is. He's in control, Thomas decided, or he thinks he is. He sighed, and Aidan turned to him impatiently. 'Will you stop that? You're like a calf with colic – what's the matter with you?'

'I think Liam's right – I think y're crazy. It's a farce, that's what is,' Thomas growled.

'The whole of Mittagong has been looking forward to this party. And the proceeds go towards the hospital – do you not remember that? I'll not cancel it because of Donaldson . . . '

970

Thomas was unconvinced. He scowled at Aidan's face, the signs of his beating still faintly visible. 'An' you look like you've been dragged backwards through a threshing machine . . . '

'Shut up, Tomás,' mildly. 'Just enjoy the evening, everyone else will.'

'Including those that have no right to. How you could serve up food and liquor to that . . . '

Kelly interrupted to say 'Maybe Donaldson won't come.'

'He'll come.' Aidan said with grim confidence, 'It'll look bad if he didn't.'

'But what'll you do if . . . '

'Thomas, nothing's going to happen.'

Thomas shifted a little, still uneasy. 'I wish you'd let me notify Constable Foles . . . '

'And what would that do? It was hard enough to convince Hal Peterson to take his leave, without throwing a scare into young Foles as well.'

'I wish Hal was here . . . '

'No police! I tell you, I'll find some way of getting at Donaldson . . . '

Kelly could not keep silent. 'Liam and I could've found out . . . '

Kelly was a few steps below Aidan. The older man turned to look down into his face, stonily. 'I've learnt something in these past thirty years. Violence isn't the only way to get what you want. I'll get Donaldson – where he'll least expect it and most resent it.'

'How?' Kelly scowled.

'In his pocket.'

He brushed aside Thomas's questions, and went down the steps, seeing Doctor Lawler and his daughters arriving.

When Berrima and 'Tillia had settled Tommy into bed, Berrima made her way at last down into the garden. By this time most of the guests had arrived. She found Helena Warwick, Sophie Lawler and Mrs Corbett surrounding Garth Ellis, and she paused when he smiled at her. Even as she joined the group, welcoming them, part of her mind was thinking back to the party Pirie-Moxham had given for Garth – could it have been thirteen years ago? It had been almost the same group of women about Garth, then. But a very different Garth. She realized with a shock that no one had not seen him since that night could see the handsome, confident, athletic-looking young man at the peak of his success, in this thin, stoop-shouldered, quiet man with the bitter mouth and the droll, dry wit that seemed to be drying with his body. Garth was ageing, Berrima saw, almost frighteningly fast. He looked at least forty-five, and he was only

971

thirty-three. The skin was too pale, and puffy under the eyes. It came to her that he might be drinking heavily.

'We were discussing Adam Lindsay Gordon's work,' he said now, to her. 'Which is your favourite of his works?'

Her smile was rather hesitant; even before all these women, it was not like him to be so formal. 'Why, I don't know . . . *The Sick Stockrider*, I think or *Ye Wearie Wayfarer*, perhaps.'

'Personally, I find your work far superior to Gordon's, Mr Ellis.' This from the wide-eyed Sophie, who was obviously completely beneath Garth's spell.

It was as if he had not heard her. His eyes still on Berrima, he said, 'My favourite of Gordon's is *Sunlight on the Sea*—' and he quoted,

> *'I miss the form of one I know—*
> *(The sunlight wanes upon the sea)*
> *'Tis not so very long ago;*
> *We drank his health with three-times-three,*
> *And we were gay when he was here;*
> *And he is gone – and we are gay . . . '*

Berrima was conscious only of the shock, was able to smile, and say, 'But the rest of that verse!—

> *Where has he gone, or far or near,*
> *Good sooth, 'twere somewhat hard to say.*

'I'm afraid it makes me feel that Mr Gordon couldn't find the energy to search for the good rhyme. Even the metre is a bit laboured, don't you think?'

He did not reply. Meg was saying, 'I think Berrima's right, his best poem is *Ye Wearie Wayfarer*—

> *'Life is mostly froth and bubble,*
> *Two things stand like stone,*
> *Kindness in another's trouble,*
> *Courage in your own.'*

They were all smiling at Megh, and Berrima took the chance to extricate herself, with apologies, in order to greet her other guests. Walking away, she forced herself not to turn around and glance back at Garth, to check if he were looking after her, with that bitter smile that had accompanied his quotation from Gordon's work. Even Helena and Mrs Corbett had stiffened, had suspected immediately, as Berrima had, that the words were a comment on her treatment of Mark. But no – she shook her head, Garth was above such malice. He did not blame her for all that happened to Mark, surely did not believe the rumours that Berrima and Aidan . . .

And we were gay when he was here;
And he is gone -- and we are gay.

Perhaps she was not the only person to be reminded of that night thirteen years ago, and of all that had changed since then. She shivered slightly, looking around at the glittering assembly. How polite we are, she thought. We are quality people, good solid upper-class Australians – with the gloss of British manners. But underneath? We still jostle for place, she thought. We still struggle, privately. This is not England, we can't relax. There will never be any standing order here, all is change and movement.

She saw Aidan, then, across the lawn. He was speaking to Clemency, looked as if he might be lecturing her, sotto voce, judging from the scowl on their faces, commanding on his, impatient, resentful on hers.

At the same time as Berrima moved toward him he looked up and saw her, spoke finally to Clemency with a smile, and began to move across the lawn to meet Berrima. She forgot her suspicions of Garth, forgot her uneasiness. The feeling of being isolated within the crowd left her and she moved towards him with a sudden sense of gladness that surprised her in its intensity.

Clemency, who had just been reprimanded by her father for remaining too long in the company of Richard Reynolds in their walk about the gardens, stood scowling after her father. As if she cared what people thought! And who was he to care what people thought? What a bore he was becoming, to be sure. Was it Berrima who had done this? Given him this hypocritical gloss of gentility that put boundaries and borders on her life? Suddenly, things were acceptable or not acceptable – and always it was *his* opinions, *his* judgements that mattered.

Richard was now speaking to Garth Ellis, and Clemency looked about for Kelly. As she had thought, he was still speaking to Genevieve Vallon, over by the fountain. Clemency stood, scowling with resentment at everything but the offending Kelly. If Aidan had only asked, or shown any respect for Clemency's wits and sensitivity, she would have told her father why it was she had gone walking with Richard. He was pleasant, and amusing, and he kept her mind from the memory that Kelly had remained close to Genevieve, a fair-haired, attractive girl whose family had only recently moved to the Highlands.

She tried to look unconcerned, tapped her foot to the music, was looking about and wondering which group to join when from behind her, a voice grew louder as its owner approached, ' . . . can't tell what may happen – stay close to me, and no drinking, you understand?'

Even the voice sounded over-rich, and it had a wheeze to it as if the words were forced out. It was unmistakably Donaldson's voice.

'Drinking doesn't affect my work.' A lighter voice, younger. Clemency turned, but the men had stopped walking and did not pass the thick trellis of flowering wisteria against which she stood.

'You've been drinking already – I want you to have your wits about you . . . and another thing – don't talk to *anybody* . . . '

'Some party this'll be . . . '

'Stoner, you weren't hired to enjoy yourself . . . I paid off Morris and Yates – I can let you go just as . . . '

'All right, all right . . . '

There was a pause, and the man Stoner must have been looking across at the tables laden with the supper, for he grunted, 'Food looks all right, anyway . . . '

Clemency edged slowly sideways, did not turn around; her heart was thudding hard against her stays, and she looked wildly about for her father – but he and Berrima had vanished. She had seen Liam, and approached him, coming up to him at the same time as Kelly on the other side.

'Donaldson's here . . . ' Clemency said.

Liam stiffened, his eyes going to the two men only now walking out from behind the trellis.

'So that's Stoner.' Liam scowled at the new man.

'I heard him talking – Donaldson – I heard him say he'd paid off Morris and Yates, and he could pay off this man, too. His name's Stoner. He's . . . Kelly? What's the matter?'

'Nothing!'

'Do you know him? You looked . . . '

'No. But he's obviously involved with what happened to your father.'

'By God, I'll bet he's one of the blokes who . . . ' Liam had taken only a step forward, when . . . 'Liam?'

Liam turned. His father was standing behind him.

'The music's started. Why don't you ask Genevieve to dance?'

Liam gazed at him grimly for a moment, perfect understanding between them, then Liam unwillingly walked off in search of Genevieve.

Kelly followed his progress across the lawn, and when Aidan next spoke it was from close beside him.

'Your gun is in my office.'

974

Kelly sighed. 'Yes, sir, I know.'

Aidan said, 'I'm telling you more. I put it in the gun cupboard and locked it. And I've locked the door.'

Kelly, expressionless, turned to gaze at him. Aidan returned the look. 'I don't want any trouble tonight.'

Kelly said grimly, 'It might not begin with Liam and me . . . '

'But you'll not contribute to it, either.'

He saw Miss Finchley arriving in the company of the newspaperman, Enoch Wilkes, then, and began to walk off to join Berrima in greeting them. 'Why don't you dance?' he said in parting. 'That's that new waltz from *Die Fledermous*, is it not? A pity to waste it.'

Kelly and Clemency were left frowning after him. When Kelly turned to her, she said, 'You don't have to dance with me, Mr Kelly.'

She was already being propelled firmly on to the wooden dancefloor. 'I know, Miss O'Brien. But since my employer wishes it . . . '

She faltered a little, stepped on his foot, and her flush deepened. ''Tis me you're dancing with, not my father. If I tell you you don't have to, you don't. You may lead me off the floor, Mr Kelly.' He was silent. He looked above her head, and she could tell he was searching the crowd for Donaldson and the man Stoner. Liam waltzed past with Genevieve in his arms, but Kelly did not seem to notice.

Some seconds passed in silence, and then he looked down at her. 'I'll be going away in a short while. As soon as this business of Sam and Donaldson is cleared up.'

She was not looking at him, and was thankful for that, for surely her feelings must be written on her face. She swallowed, and managed to say, 'Going away? For ever?'

His voice was harsh. 'Would it matter, Clemency?' And when she tried to find an answer, 'I don't think it would. But no, to put your mind at rest, for I'd hate to believe I left you pining at the casement like Tennyson's Mariana . . . '

'I'd not!' Fiercely.

'Then it's a matter of indifference to you that I'll be away two weeks.'

She studied his face. He was looking down at her, but there was no warmth in his eyes. Even his tone of voice was colder than it used to be. There was no feeling there. She should not ask, but she could not stop herself, 'Where are you going?'

'So many questions . . . ' with good-natured reproof. When she looked away, he said, 'I have business in the south. I'll be in Melbourne seeing to some matters I've left untended for a long time.'

975

'And then?'

'Then?' He raised one eyebrow.

'Will you . . . will you be coming back? Or are you going to go to sea once more?'

'I hadn't considered that.' The voice was cool. 'No doubt I'll consider these things while I'm away.'

He might not come back at all. He might leave, and never come back at all.

'You talked once of going home. To England, I mean. Burnley Grange, isn't it?'

He looked down at her. 'I would have returned to Burnley only because I felt my wife might like it. It's a beautiful building, the only drawback being my father's presence. But since that time I've grown out of any foolishness I might have been labouring under. Affections can wither and die for lack of encouragement, you know, rather like plants which aren't watered. So that strange humour that was upon me has passed away, thank God, and I've turned my mind to other things. No, I won't be returning to Burnley.'

She was hoping he wouldn't notice how often or how deeply she was flushing with embarrassment. He was thinking, no doubt, that she was bringing the conversation back to Burnley in order to taunt him with that scene in his quarters. She was sorry she had spoken. But she wanted to know what he was thinking; it was so hard to break through to him lately. It had happened gradually, over months, she realized now, but his humour had faded, the warmth in his eyes had given way to a coolness, and he had been, for weeks now, less a friend than an acquaintance. Very much her father's employee. Waltzing with her – and surely this must be the most beautiful waltz ever composed – and telling her he did so only because her father had ordered it. She bit her lip, waiting for him to make the next effort at conversation, but he did not. When she glanced up his gaze was no longer upon her; his body was held stiffly, away from her, and it was not imagination, she knew it with a certainty, he was thinking of something else. When the music ended, he escorted her to a bench where there was a seat beside Sophie Lawler, and with a bow, left her.

'Even if he isn't a bushranger,' Sophie's voice in her ear, 'he's still the handsomest man here.' Clemency turned to scowl at her, but Sophie was looking across the crowded lawn. 'Except for that young man – who is he, Clemency? The dark-haired young man – he looks like a Latin bandit – he's even more handsome than Mr Kelly, though he's a trifle thin and his mouth's very hard.' Clemency fol-followed her gaze. Sophie was looking with interest at Charles Stoner.

So, on the other side of the lawn, was Liam. It was an evening, Liam thought, when all their time would be spent in watching each other. Aidan was alert; for all his bonhomie, he did not drink very much. And Kelly was doing his usual sheep-dog tricks and following Aidan about. Liam wondered if he wore the colt strapped under the jacket of his dinner suit, and found himself hoping that he did.

The lights twinkled amongst the trees and the fountain reflected jewel colours in the drops that fell and melted in the pool. The music floated over them all. The women swept about the terraces and lawns; the tight-fitting skirts with the enormous bustles and the trains that swept along the ground, made Liam think of peacocks with their tail feathers folded. Yet they stalked and preened themselves, nevertheless – look at Genevieve, dancing with Richard Reynolds! – and the men bowed, and danced and flashed their best smiles, and were charming gentlemen all.

And at least five of us are wary as hell, he thought, waiting for the other to make a move.

Stoner had noticed Sophie, and at that moment was wondering how far he could safely proceed to flirt with any of the women here. Donaldson was watching him like a hawk – and so was Kelly . . . Stoner smiled to himself, and sipped the glass of punch in his hand. He liked this job – it was relatively clean after his last few contracts – and it was good to get out of Melbourne. He had been country-bred, and at times like this, particularly moving in such an obviously wealthy crowd, he began to wonder if he might not move out of the city permanently. If Donaldson could be kept at his present pitch of nervousness, he might decide he needed a body-guard permanently.

'Good evening!'

Stoner turned. It was the red-haired bloke, the Irishman's son. Stoner noted that he was a lot broader-shouldered up close. Or maybe the shoulders of his dinner jacket were padded. 'G'day,' he said briefly, turning back to survey the crowd and Sophie Lawler.

'I'm Liam O'Brien.' The voice seemed to wait for some kind of acknowledgement.

'Is that so?'

'You came with Donaldson.' Again the pause.

Stoner realized the man was not to be ignored and turned fully to him. 'Yeah,' he said.

'A friend of his?' The tone was conversational. The man's eyes were a funny colour, almost red, like a mad dog's. Stoner smiled to himself. He could sense the tension in O'Brien. This was good. He liked that. Maybe there would be trouble with the man, he would

977

like that even more. 'You ask a lot of questions . . . '

'Or are you an employee?' The tone was losing some of its friendliness. Stoner merely looked at the man, felt the adrenalin in his own body, considered the right attack for a man of O'Brien's weight and fitness. He looked like he could fight – but he was angry. Not unnatural, he had a stake in this. Stoner, who had never killed for love or revenge, nor in defence of any ideals, had a theory. It was that that very lack of emotional involvement in the jobs he was paid to do made him clear-headed. And this helped him to stay alive, he was sure, when other men, with more to lose, acted rashly.

'Where do you come from?' Liam asked, all pretence at good manners gone.

'Carrawobbity,' he answered, truthfully enough. Most people thought he made it up, and he liked to put them off their stride. 'But I been all over.'

'And where were you when my father was beaten up?'

Here we go! 'What're you talking about?'

'Where were you?'

Donaldson had said no trouble. But it would look even stranger if he did not react to an unfair allegation. 'If you're gonna accuse me of somethin', mate, I hope you got the proof – or the guts to back yourself up . . . '

'It was dark, my father said, and you didn't speak – didn't give him any warning, you and your two friends . . . I'm surprised you had the courage to come here alone.'

Stoner gave an elaborate sigh, gazing around at the treetops as if asking Providence for patience, then, 'This is your party, right?' and he reached out lazily with his cup of punch and poured the contents slowly over Liam's head.

Aidan was speaking with Berrima, Marion and Andrew Tweedie, and the latter, in the middle of a discussion on the plans for the new hospital, gave a gasp. Aidan and Berrima turned—

Liam was standing by the dinner tables, with the cherry-coloured punch running down his face on to his white shirt front – there was a piece of orange peel stuck to his hair.

Stoner was saying quietly, close to Liam, 'I don't like your punch – and I don't like you!'

'Excuse me while I reach for a napkin . . . ' Liam reached past the man for one of the napkins from the table.

'Liam!' Aidan's voice, a bark of warning, and both looked up.

'It's all right, Father,' Liam was wiping his face, 'I'm perfectly calm.'

It was the last thing that Stoner was to remember. Liam had spun suddenly, bringing his fist up with him, and hit Stoner between the eyes with such force that the man crashed backwards across the table, taking it with him. People gasped or screamed, moving back in fright, but it was all over in a second. Stoner lay still on the grass, surrounded by the debris of two days' cooking and salad-making in Shannonbrook's kitchen.

Aidan and Liam gazed at each other. 'I'll . . . go and change,' Liam said.

Tightly, 'That would be wise.' The crowd moved back for Liam, and he walked off, meeting Berrima's shocked face with an embarrassed grin, and went up to the verandah steps into the house.

Thomas had appeared, grinning, above Stoner's inert form. 'Well, we'd better haul him off to Donaldson's carriage, I guess . . . '

Aidan scowled at his brother. He was full of surprises, was Thomas. Why, he looked almost pleased that Liam had made a scene. Aidan glared around at the crowd. 'Where is Mr Donaldson . . . '

They heard it, then, from the other side of the lawn, raised voices, a woman's scream, and from the general confusion, a man's voice, pitched high with fear, 'O'Brien! O'Brien! . . . '

Aidan was off at a run, pushing people out of his way. He stopped at the inner circle of a crowd that was gathered around Donaldson and Sam Russell – gathered at a safe distance, for Sam was standing with a shotgun held to his chest with the stump of his left arm. The muzzle was pointed at Donaldson, who was gazing at him with rage mingled with terror.

'Put it down!' he was saying, 'Russell – for God's sake . . . '

Aidan was only barely conscious of Kelly to one side of him, Berrima on the other; he gestured for them to stand back, and he stepped forward. 'Sam? Sam, give me that, there's no need . . . '

'Keep back, Aidan! This is between Donaldson and me . . . !'

'All right! But put the gun down. We'll go into the house and talk . . . '

'No! I want to have it out *now*! I want the truth! You hear, Donaldson?' The wild gaze turned back to the frightened mill-owner. 'I want the truth told in front of all these people . . . '

Donaldson's voice became hard in the face of his embarrassment; a huge crowd was gathering, everyone he knew. For a second he forgot his fear. 'You're insane, Russell . . . '

'Whose responsibility was it to keep that machinery working safely? . . . *Whose*?'

'I . . . you're only making it worse for yourself, man . . . you threatening me won't help . . . '

Kelly spoke to Berrima, softly, said her name, and she turned startled eyes to gaze up at him. He was looking beyond her, she thought, at the two protagonists. 'Berrima, I want you to go back to the house and get my gun for me . . . '

'Kelly, Aidan said you weren't to . . . '

'Stoner's awake, Berrima.' She followed his gaze. Stoner was indeed awake and on his feet, circling slowly around the group, one hand moving slowly towards his coat.

Kelly's voice was urgent. 'Please, Berrima . . . he said he locked it in the gun . . . '

'I know where the keys are . . . ' With a final glance at him, she was pushing her way back through the crowd, towards the house.

Donaldson was gaining courage; red in the face, he began to threaten. 'You shoot me, and they'll hang you, Russell, you know that . . . '

'Please, Sam,' Aidan begged, 'let me have the gun . . . let's talk . . . ' But Sam's eyes were only for Donaldson. 'And what about O'Brien here – who had him beaten up?'

Donaldson's eyes flicked away from the deadly gun to Aidan. 'I don't know what you're . . . '

'He was the only one with the influence to stand up to you – so you had to stop him, didn't you?'

There was a dreadful silence. The townspeople were glancing at Aidan, back to Donaldson, then muttering amongst themselves. Donaldson could see their conjecture, their suspicion. His eyes flickered around at their faces; it was a bad thing, he would never live this down. People whispering, talking about him. 'I . . . I don't have to listen to your ravings . . . ' he said to Russell, 'You're lying, you know it . . . '

Stoner had his hand inside his coat, held it there; was waiting, Kelly knew, for the right moment. He would kill Sam, or Aidan, because he wanted to, and because he would feel that was what Donaldson would want. Kelly doubted this latter – Donaldson was ruthless, but he was no murderer. But there was no way to convey this to Stoner. He could not be stopped, he did not want to be stopped.

A movement in the crowd to the left – Liam was edging up behind Sam. And then Berrima was there, beside Kelly, and the Colt, the stock warm from her grasp, was placed in his hand.

Sam's voice was almost breaking on the emotion within him. For months the bitterness, the anger had built and built inside him, and now there was no going back.

'I'm not going to let go of this gun until you've owned up, Donaldson . . . You weren't man enough to admit that the mill was losing money . . . you weren't man enough to admit that we men could've made a go of it . . . !'

'Don't try to tell me that you're doing this for those mill workers!' Donaldson shouted, 'It's for yourself! You blame me for losing your arm . . . ' and as Sam tightened his grip on the gun, 'Listen . . . listen, Russell – let's do what O'Brien suggests – let's go inside and . . . '

It was then that Liam suddenly leapt forward, grabbing the muzzle of the shotgun and forcing it up and away from the crowd. It fired with an explosion that rang and roared around the garden's huge trees, rang and roared over them all. Branches, dislodged by the shot, fell over the four men, as Aidan joined Liam and wrested the gun from Sam's hand.

'Aidan!' It was Thomas's voice, but when Aidan whirled it was to see Stoner pulling a handgun from his jacket, aiming it at Aidan's chest—

And Kelly had stepped between them, facing Stoner, the Colt mysteriously in his hands. 'Kelly!' And the man's shoulders came back a little; Aidan knew in that moment that he had stopped him from shooting Stoner.

'Stoner, you fool, put that down!' shouted Donaldson. He had looked off, now, away to the side, his family had run to him, but Aidan, still holding Sam's shotgun did not look at him. Each time Stoner moved to get a clear view of Aidan or Sam, Kelly moved also.

'Get out of my way, mate . . . '

Aidan only barely heard Stoner's words, only just caught Kelly's reply.

'You want a fight, take it up with me.' Then, louder, to Aidan, 'Is this the man who beat you up?'

Aidan, scowling, 'I don't know . . . it's not important, Kelly. Both of you, put . . . '

'It's not . . . ? He'd have killed you just now!'

'Put the guns down!'

Kelly did not move. Aidan did not need to see his face to know that it was set, the fury within him barely contained.

'What's the matter, Kelly? Being a farm boy softened you up? Not like Port Melbourne, hey, Kelly?' Stoner gave a half-smile, 'You got witnesses, Kelly, it'd be self-defence this time, too . . . '

Aidan looked from one to the other, then said to Kelly, quietly, 'I'd have thought you'd had enough of killing, boy.'

The man did not move. Aidan had no idea if he had even heard through his rage. Kelly asked Stoner, 'Did you beat up Mr O'Brien?'

Stoner's smile deepened. 'What are you going to do about it? Shoot me?'

'Kelly, that's all we need! Now put the gun down!' Aidan spoke from desperation, saw for the first time what Devlin Kelly had tried to do, and how he had succeeded. The man was like a machine.

Kelly said, 'He tried to kill you . . . '

Aidan gazed at the inflexible back, searching around in his mind for something, anything, to pull the man back from whatever dark country his mind moved in.

'Boyo,' he said carefully, distinctly, 'either you put that gun down, or you can pack y'r swag and clear off Shannonbrook right now . . . ' The head came up, just a fraction. Slowly, very slowly, the shoulders relaxed their tension, the gun in Kelly's hand was lowered.

Stoner was furious. For the first time in his professional life he had lost control, he had botched this badly; he was searching for some way to goad Kelly into raising the gun once more, when he felt a hard pressure in the small of his back.

'Mr Stoner, what you feel is the . . . the barrel of Mr O'Brien's Merwin and Hulbert. It's loaded, and at this range I can't help but cause you considerable damage. Please put your gun down.'

Stoner, more from shock than any other emotion, remained transfixed. Was this O'Brien's wife? The pretty creature, fair and rather delicate-looking, who had welcomed them on arrival?

'Mr Stoner, I am a very frightened woman. What's more, I know very little about firearms. Mr O'Brien once told me that this particular weapon has a very good trigger action, very smooth. That, combined with my emotional state, could just mean that I might shoot you at any moment without really meaning to. I would advise you to put your gun down.'

Stoner lowered the gun, and Thomas stepped forward and took it from him.

92

Garth Ellis asked to join the discussion in Aidan's office. Liam scowled, but Aidan studied Ellis's face, and had a feeling that the man might have something to say.

Stoner, despite Donaldson's protests and his own, was locked in one of the loose boxes in the stable for the night, and the party went on, oddly enough, with more excitement and gaiety than before. The horses were raffled by Thomas and Kelly, and the cheers and groans of those participating in the draws could be heard from within the office, though all the men were too busy to pay attention.

'You sold the mill yesterday,' Aidan told Donaldson, 'to someone from Sydney.'

Donaldson's gaze came up to him. 'How did you know?'

Aidan did not answer. And after a time Donaldson said, softly, 'Through a Sydney agent . . . I should have checked . . . If I'd known it was you buying, I'd have burnt every last . . . '

Sam stood up, angry. 'Be damned!'

Aidan held up his hand. 'Now wait a minute . . . '

But Sam, who had begun to calm down, was furious once more. 'Playing the philanthropist now, are we? I don't want your bloody charity . . . '

'I'm no bloody philanthropist! I got me baser instincts! Besides helping you, I was out to get *him*!'

He jabbed his finger towards Donaldson, who stood up. 'Look here, O'Brien . . . !'

'Oh, sit down and shut up!'

A silence. Donaldson seated himself, glaring at the Irishman.

Liam said, 'Sam, you and the men can still buy the mill from Father . . . '

'I don't want his bloody charity!'

Aidan was stung. 'Ask me the price before you go talking about charity!'

'I'll fight this, O'Brien,' Donaldson was hissing. 'I swear to you, I'll fight this . . . '

'Mr Donaldson,' Garth Ellis spoke up for the first time, 'have you heard of Henry Kendall?'

'I don't want to talk about bloody poets now, Ellis.'

'Oh, but Kendall is more than a bloody poet, Mr Donaldson. For the past five years he's been working at Fagan's sawmills in Port Macquarie, on the north coast. He knows as much about timber as you do, Mr Donaldson.'

'What's this to do with me?'

'Only this. The Premier, Sir Henry Parkes, is a close friend of Kendall's. I've been to Government House and I've spoken to Sir Henry myself. It seems he, along with a lot of other people, are becoming worried about the decimation of the native trees – it's almost certain that Sir Henry is going to appoint Henry Kendall as Australia's first Inspector of Forests.'

Garth waited a little, allowing this to sink in. Liam, over by the window, watched his former friend's slightly flushed face, and thought, he's enjoying himself. And let him, begod, he's doing something that doesn't directly help himself for the first time since I've known him.

'I've thought of asking Kendall down here to stay for a few weeks – he's been ill with consumption and the air might do him good. I've told him a lot about the mills in the district – particularly yours, Mr Donaldson. He was most interested in yours.'

Donaldson stood, pale now, and started across the room to the glass doors. He paused only on the threshold to say, 'Don't bother to threaten me, Ellis. Threaten the new owner. You think he'll be any different to me? His replanting schemes are just token gestures – good for publicity. He'll be cutting corners with that mill as he does with his others.' He turned to leave, hesitated, then turned to Aidan, icily, 'I suppose you'll be reporting me to the police – about Stoner . . . '

'Aye.'

'You'll not prove anything.'

'Doubtless. But I'll try, Donaldson, I'll try.'

Donaldson's face suffused with colour, and he left, then, without another word.

'Sam?' Sam looked up. 'I'll go to see Donaldson tomorrow. We might be able to bargain with him. If we call off the Appeal case for damages, and I forget about my unofficial bout with Stoner, Donaldson might just forget what happened tonight. I think he'll see the advantages in the suggestion. And Sam,' in order to stop the frightening look of emotional relief on his friend's face –

'Yeah, what?' Sam was rubbing his eyes with the heel of his hand as if he were tired, and he glared up at Aidan.

'Go home and get Tessa and your boys. This party'll go on till dawn if I'm not mistaken.'

Liam walked out on to the verandah with Garth. 'That was good of you,' Liam said. 'You didn't have to say that. We appreciate it. Will you drink with me, Garth?'

Garth turned to look at the other man. 'No,' he said. 'This isn't going to be an excuse to let bygones be bygones, O'Brien. I did what I did inside there for Russell's sake. He's a fine man, and I've always had respect for him. But I've no respect for you. Nor will I ever have. I've tried to forget what's happened, God knows, but I can't.' And he went to turn away.

'It wasn't me that destroyed your marriage,' Liam said fiercely. 'I'll not bear all the blame – so don't go away clutching that excuse to yourself, Garth. Victoria loved you – she loved *you* – but you left her, long before you took yourself away physically. So wrapped up you were, in your own sense of failure that you let your marriage crumble around you. You abandoned Victoria, Garth – it's no wonder she turned to me. I cared about her more than you ever did in your preoccupation with yourself . . . '

The words were cut off, the twisted hands were at Liam's throat, hands surprisingly strong, and he was hauled forward by his shirt front. 'You admit it.' Garth's voice hoarse with rage, his face white, 'You admit it. You slept with her.'

Liam did not struggle, meeting the wild eyes so close to his own with calm contempt. He did not speak.

Garth waited, shook him a little. 'Did you?' Still no reply, but that contemptuous look seemed, of a sudden, to represent a thousand condescending, sneering faces. For a second, he almost punched the face before him, but he was too aware of his physical limitations, the destruction already wreaked upon his body. So he stepped back, instead, and his venom found another outlet.

'Pirie-Moxham has been approached about leasing Summer Hill; did you know that? I met the prospective tenant at the Moxhams' town house in Sydney last week.'

He was gratified at the look of puzzlement that flitted over Liam's belligerent face. He had been prepared for a fight. Well, he would have one, but on Garth's terms.

'What're y' talking about?'

'Devlin Retcliffe. Apparently he knew your father in Ireland. The Moxhams were very interested in that, but Mr Retcliffe is a true gentleman, related to Lord Hallswood, I believe, and he kept his secrets to himself.

'And there are secrets, aren't there, Liam? Mark told me a garbled tale, once, when he was very drunk, but I'd caught him out in so many lies I didn't believe anything he said about your father by that time. Is it true? What Mark said? Was your father transported to this country?'

Later Liam would look back on that moment as the first sign of self-restraint he had ever shown. But at the time he did not understand the feelings within him. Felt himself go pale, felt the blood leave his face with rage, and knew that he wanted, above all, to smash his fist into the spiteful face before him – and yet he did not. Something cool and hard at the back of his mind told him no; and he continued gazing at Ellis for some seconds before saying, 'You're pathetic, y' know that? You'll stop at nothing, will you? Get out of here, Garth. Get out of here before I tell Berrima what a creeping, gutless wonder you are, and destroy the illusions of perhaps the only person on this earth who has any respect left for you!'

He did not know how frightening he looked, nor how much like his father, despite the fair, freckled skin, the dark red hair. The face, the stance, was Aidan O'Brien, and that and the words, terrifying in their truth, had Garth backing away, along the verandah. He could feel already the effect of too much wine on a stomach empty for days of anything but his anger and resentment. He swallowed against the rising taste in his mouth, turned and jumped lightly from the verandah to the ground, and had soon disappeared around the house, in the darkness of the trees.

Liam stood for several minutes, leaning against the verandah post, only now realizing where he was, only now seeing the celebrations, for such they had become, going on down in the garden. Someone was singing 'For he's a jolly good fellow' but from where he stood, Liam could not see whether it was for his father or Sam Russell. His hands were shaking, and he tried to tell himself that he was over-reacting. He had suffered no ill-effects after the altercation with the man Stoner.

But that had been different. An open fight. For the first time in his life, with Garth Ellis's words, had come the realization that not all his fights were to be open fights. He straightened, and stood looking down the garden to where his father, Sam on one side and Berrima on the other, was drinking a very large glass of punch and laughing at something young Sean Danaher was saying.

'Perhaps this has made you as hard as you are,' he murmured aloud to the man. 'Perhaps years of threats from enemies you barely knew to be enemies, planning campaigns you could not hope to guess at – perhaps that has made you what you are.'

★

986

'Four hundred and fifty pounds . . . !' Thomas looked up from his auctioneers desk to Kelly and Clemency; he watched the last of the horses, a yearling filly by Chattawa being led away across the lawn by her new owners. 'Begod, they'll build an entire hospital out of this evening's doings.'

'And a free entertainment,' Kelly murmured, but only Clemency heard him.

'I'll take the money up to the house, put it in Aidan's safe.' And he had gathered up the cashbox and, joined by 'Tillia and Corrie, the only one of their boys still awake, they trooped up the slope towards the house.

Clemency was still regarding Kelly. 'You're very cool, aren't you? Stoner really wanted to kill you, and it would shake any other man. But . . .'

'I'm used to it.'

She was surprised. His tone was precise, matter-of-fact.

'We did speak of this before. I thought you understood.'

She searched his face, but no, no warmth there, no hint that he cared if she understood, or desired that she did.

Then he smiled. 'Berrima was rather wonderful, wasn't she? Who'd have thought she'd have it in her! I would have been less surprised if it had been you.'

She was glaring at him, mouth compressed. 'Why?' she demanded.

'Your nature is, shall we say, more reckless? Actually,' he continued, 'part of my mind was preoccupied, during that scene, with the worry that you'd dash out in front of Stoner and valiantly defend me. Or were you hoping, perhaps, that he'd shoot me? I'm sure Lieutenant Reynolds was.'

'I don't think that's amusing. But, for your information, I would have done something, but I was prevented.'

'By the chivalrous Lieutenant . . .'

'No, you great . . . you fool! By Uncle Thomas and 'Tillia – they had one of my arms each and they wouldn't let go, or I'd . . . Why are you laughing? Kelly? Stop laughing!'

He placed his arms around her, and lifted her off her feet, and when, still delighted with her, he went to let her go, he found her arms were about him.

'Kelly . . .'

'Oh, excuse me.' Richard Reynolds stood a little distance away, the smile on his face not touching his eyes. 'Berrima has asked me to find you, Miss Clemency, to ask if you'd help her serve the coffee.' He bowed, and strode away, quite briskly.

Clemency and Kelly stood apart. 'Well,' he said, 'that succeeded.'

She turned to him. 'What?'

'Lieutenant Reynolds was most put out. No doubt he'll go up to his room very shortly and spend a sleepless night gnashing his teeth and chewing his pillow. That was the point of that display, was it not?'

His smile held humour, but it was directed at her, it was not something to be shared. And there was something else, a condescension, in his voice.

'You think I planned . . . I didn't! I . . . '

'He approached from behind me. Please don't try to tell me you didn't see him.'

She was speechless, gazing into that set face, the cool grey eyes. She found she wanted to scream at him, *I saw only you. Only you.* But her anger overrode her. 'Get you gone to Melbourne, then, if your opinion of me is as low as that,' she hissed. 'Get you to hell and back for all I care, you blind, ignorant, arrogant Saxon swine!'

He looked taken aback; then, almost as if he had had second thoughts, went to take her arm. 'Clemency . . . ' but she moved too fast, was gone at a run up the slope of lawn. Her slippers tapped sharply across the now deserted dance floor, and across the flagged area by the fountain. He stood and watched her disappear into the house.

He stayed behind with the remaining guests, and when all but the O'Briens and their staff had gone, helped pack up the chairs, the benches, the trestle tables, and store them away in the barn.

Clemency, Berrima and 'Tillia had changed by then, into more practical day-dresses, with pinafores over them, and when they and Charity and Job and a few of the stockmen were finished, they all gathered in the kitchen for tea and the remainder of the cakes and sweets. 'What's left,' Thomas scowled at Liam, 'after you'd sent Stoner through the best of me wife's cooking.' He looked about with a mock scowl. 'And where's my brother, tell me? He's not been about helping us tidy up . . . '

'He's in the office,' Berrima answered. 'Mr Warwick and Jeremy Wilton and Andrew Tweedie are with him.'

'The *Honourable* Jeremy Wilton?' Liam looked up, startled and pleased. 'I didn't even know he was here tonight – did he come with Andrew?'

'He arrived later.' Berrima was looking a little concerned, though her smile tried to cover it. 'I don't know anything about the matter they're discussing.'

Liam made up his mind to find out. The idea of Jeremy Wilton at

Shannonbrook Three and no one had thought to tell him! Sure the man was one of the most powerful in the Labour movement, one of the richest men in New South Wales, originally trained as a minister in the Church of England, and a philanthropist whose works went as far afield as prison reform, educational scholarships for gifted children of poor families, and lately, an interest in seeing unions set up in those trades where men and women were exploited and sometimes brutalized. He had been into dingy workshops, down mines, into attic sweatshops where seamstresses worked in ill-lit discomfort. He agitated constantly, hounding politicians incessantly to do something about these conditions.

'Come in!' His father called, in answer to Liam's knock.

There were four men present; Hedley Warwick was seated in a chair between Andrew Tweedie and Jeremy Wilton. Liam was surprised and a little disappointed to see that this champion of the working class was no giant physically, but a small, narrow-shouldered individual whose eyes, set in a head that appeared too large for his body, looked out from behind horn-rimmed glasses. The hair was thin, the hands and feet small and neat, and on the whole, Liam thought, as his father introduced them, Wilton looked more like a bank clerk than the man that a former Governor had called 'a thorn in the flesh of this colony's business class'.

Yet the eyes were bright, keen with intelligence, and both they and the lines about the mouth told of a good humour, a face that smiled easily, for all the determination that the chin betrayed.

Liam felt, even in the time it took for Jeremy Wilton to shake his hand, that his face and his mind were being scanned. 'Good to meet you, O'Brien. You have an excellent name as a lawyer in the district.'

Liam felt himself flush, murmured something suitably self-deprecating and finished, 'The honour's mine, sir.'

Aidan was standing by the fireplace. There was only one vacant chair in the room, and that was behind Aidan's desk. 'Sit down, Liam.'

'Father? I'm fine standing.'

Impatiently, 'No, I'll stand. I need to prowl a bit – these three think they have my back against the wall. Anyway – I think better on my feet.' Aidan was scowling, but there was a smile there, too. The other three men were grinning.

As Liam sat down almost guiltily in his father's chair, Hedley Warwick was saying, 'Aidan, you've still given us no reason at all for your decision.'

'I've given you plenty. You simply ignore what I'm saying and

989

talk on as if I hadn't spoken . . . '

Jeremy Wilton's voice came drily. 'Perhaps your reasons don't satisfy us. Your brother and your son here, help you run the properties and the mills . . . '

'And ye'll not be telling me,' Andrew's heavy Scots accent cut across Wilton's voice, 'that your work on the Board of Tweedie and Company keeps ye busy night and day.'

'No,' Aidan grinned, 'I'd not attempt to do that. But . . . ' Aidan, to his son's amazement, was looking genuinely nonplussed, his customary confidence somehow shaken, 'it's just ridiculous, so it is. I swear to God, I've never considered it. And no, no, I won't consider it! What're you like, trying to tell me I'd be successful – me with more enemies than Cain. And if I was!' he shouted as the three voices were raised against him, 'Me, to stand up there in the Legislative Council in a starched collar, like a great jumped-up trawneen and try to talk rows of Saxon landowners into voting the way I tell 'em? Get away!'

'If Charles Gavan Duffy, one of the Young Irelanders, Father, could succeed in politics . . . '

'Now *you*,' his father was over by the window by now, and the other three had to screw themselves round to look at him, 'you know the way of these things – you've had the learning as a lawyer, y're young and can talk a blue streak when you wish it. And you have the confidence – you can move in any circle, all the men on Shannonbrook accept you as one of them. If anyone could get the votes and get these reforms passed, it'd be you.'

The other three turned back, and Liam found himself pinned by four pairs of eyes, all stripping his mind and soul bare, weighing him up as raw material. 'Ye-es,' Jeremy Wilton said slowly.

Liam had not felt so surrounded, so vulnerable, since the day he had stepped out of the Fenian meeting place in Dublin and had found himself surrounded by four plain clothes members of the Constabulary.

He felt the same panic now; his eyes went to the three men, then back to his father. To the end of his days, he wondered if Aidan had planned this. 'And how could I be doing that,' his father would say, 'when I wasn't to know you'd come busting in that door?'

And then, he realized that he was delighted. Aye, he was. For this was an honour, to be even considered, and dammit, all his father said was true. Why, he thought, with lifting heart, I'd be better at it than he would. Not even because of age, or background or education. Just him being him and me being me. He was made for his small empire – he created it for himself. And I . . . I was made for this. I don't need to talk about what should be done – Snowy dying in the cold of that Gulgong shed, Sam Russell and the accident that had taken his arm and his livelihood – now I can do something.

All these thoughts had been tumbling about in his head while the four men had been talking excitedly, over the top of each other. Liam came to himself to find them gazing at him, silent.

'Well?' Jeremy Wilton said.

'Pardon?'

'Well, will you stand, or not? Are you interested?'

'Yes. Yes, I am. I'll stand.'

'This needs a drink,' and Aidan was at the cabinet, and pouring glasses of his best whiskey.

With the small glass in his hand, still seated behind the heavy rosewood desk, Liam heard the Honourable Jeremy Wilton say, 'To William O'Brien – future Member of Parliament for the State of New South Wales.'

93

Two weeks later, Liam made his first speech to the group of men who had pledged their support to him. There were about three hundred men and women in the School of Arts, and Aidan, seated with Berrima half-way down the room, knew that many of these people had driven great distances to be here to meet their candidate. Liam spoke well, with hardly a trace of his brogue – which both saddened and satisfied Aidan. There were many things, he thought, that were about to be left behind.

And yet for Liam's sake, he was glad. This was a grand thing, to be sure. That an O'Brien of Killaloe would be a Member of Parliament – his son! The enormity of it shook him. Even the hair stood up on the back of his neck when he realized the magnitude of what was happening, this man on the stage before him, who held the crowd with his powerful voice and the open face and obvious sincerity of his beliefs, this man was the son of Aidan O'Brien, who had arrived in Van Diemen's Land and clanked in chains up the hill past the Government buildings where that Colony's policies were made. It could only happen here, he thought. Even the Americans aren't as mad as this.

He mentioned the subject of his past to Liam, wondering if it were not best to make some declaration to the public now, before the boy began his political career, rather than risk being exposed by some opponent who would try to use the fact of Aidan's background to discredit his son.

'Let them find out,' Liam shrugged. 'Why should we be acting as if it mattered? Agrarian outrages in Ireland have much less stigma attached than you'd think, Father. And it was the Famine, remember. Arra, I'm not ashamed of you – so there's no point being defensive about it. Not that I know many of the details, anyway.'

If he had hoped that this would elicit some response from his father, he was disappointed. Aidan appeared to be gratified by Liam's attitude, but he merely smiled, he did not volunteer any information. Liam, who had every possible report of Aidan's trial while he was in Ireland, could not connect the deeds with the man he knew. But Aidan would not, apparently, talk any more of it now than before.

And it occurred to Liam to mention the man Retcliffe, whom Garth Ellis had said was to be the new tenant at Summer Hill. He had his mouth open, ready to say, 'By the way, Garth Ellis told me . . . ' but he hesitated, paused. For Aidan to bring up the subject of his past, of his own volition, meant that he was very worried. And not for his own sake, Liam thought, with something like surprise, but for mine. And knowing this, Liam kept silent about Retcliffe. He might not come; or he might come and know nothing about Aidan O'Brien. Or, he might know, and come, and say nothing. There were too many imponderables. Aidan had enough worries, with the farms and the businesses, and the fact that Liam would not be able to run the small empire, in the face of his own career, should anything happen to Aidan.

Liam felt guilty about this, and was glad that his father made no remonstrances, accepted his son's decisions with good grace. More and more, Liam thought, watching Clemency moping about Shannonbrook Three in the weeks that Kelly was in Melbourne, it would seem as if Clemency would have her ambition of being mistress of Shannonbrook on her father's death. Liam, determined that he would eventually win, was equally sure that his sister would finally marry Michael Kelly. 'And everything will work out, so,' he told himself in a satisfied tone.

He was gaining confidence in every area of his life. It was as if this coming election had been the key that made all other components lock into place. The machinery worked, he saw some purpose in what had been, before, a confusing pattern of mystifying objects.

'I admire you very much for what you're doing,' Ottillia told him, once, on one of his visits to his uncle's farm. He looked up at her sharply, saw that she meant these words, and that she was a little puzzled. 'I've heard your speeches,' she said. 'I liked what you said, last week, about all of us having to forget that we're Germans, Englishmen, Irishmen, Italians, Chinese, and begin thinking that we're Australians first, that nothing can be done with this huge country until we give our loyalty to *it*, and not to the land of our birth. And it's true, that it's harder for us, than for Americans, or Canadians, for their countries are more hospitable than this – there's so little good farming land here – so much desert – the distances between our cities could defeat us . . . '

'Well, and here I was thinking you were dozing through that speech – and here it is repeated, word for word . . . !'

'Of course I heard every word! I also heard a lot of people muttering that you were a Republican – Mr Lambert, and Mr Ellis – and Fitzroy Amberley whispered to his wife that you were going to press for Federation. Are you?'

'I think I will,' he said carefully. ''Tis not just the Irish in me that resents having to stand at attention before the British flag. There's a lot of native-born Australians who don't like to see this grand country divided up on a map like a Surrey vegetable garden. One plot for apples – that's Tasmania, one plot for pineapples – that's Queensland . . . '

'Do they grow pineapples in Surrey?' His aunt's blue eyes laughed. But Liam only smiled in return.

'It's serious,' he said. 'At the moment there's no reality to the word "Australia", and there won't be, until we cease being New South Welshmen and Victorians and Western Australians, colonies only, all those places, and band together. I want to see the flag that those diggers raised at Eureka flying over all this land – all of it. The Southern Cross – aye! I'll stand up and salute that! I'll sing its praises till Kingdom come! But I'll be damned if I'll be kissing the foot that's on my neck.'

The morning sun flooded through the window of Berrima's studio. She was surrounded by scissors and cardboard and glue, making a kind of bound book in which to keep the photographs of the iron mine. The smell of the glue, combined with the warm sun was making her sleepy. Aidan had perched himself on the edge of her desk, then moved abruptly, going to sit on a chair against the wall. There was a column behind him, made of plaster-of-Paris, and an embroidered purple cloth that he had brought back from Greece lay

993

over the back of the chair and tumbled in folds down to the floor. Berrima had been taking photographs of Clemency, in the costume of a muse, a few days before; a very bored, sullen muse, who clutched her quill and scroll with aggression and glared out over Olympus's heights to the earthly fields below as if she could not get away fast enough – which was perfectly true.

Aidan now sat back in the chair with one arm loosely along the backrest, the other hand drumming on his knee, elbow resting on the chair's arm. The heavily-muscled legs in white moleskins were crossed negligently, one booted calf resting on his knee. Berrima studied him. He, too, was scowling out the window over the paddocks.

'You look like Caligula.'

He turned to her slowly with eyebrows raised. 'I'm resenting that. Why not Nero? Why that ratbag Caligula?'

'I don't know, it was the first thought that came into my head.'

He snorted. 'Your basic opinion of me is fairly low, then, I'm thinking.'

'Only half the time,' she murmured.

He sighed. When she looked up, he was scowling over his domain once more, and she knew that he had forgotten her. 'What are you thinking of?' she asked, gently.

'I'm watching the smoke over towards Burrawang. The last thing we need is a bushfire, here. It'll race through that dry undergrowth out Kangaloon way. We should have been burning off more these past few years.'

He glanced at her. Her hands were stilled at her work and she was watching him. He smiled at her, rose to his feet and left the room, to return to his work.

Berrima went back to her own, but found it difficult to concentrate. She rose and opened the window wider, but barely a breath of breeze stirred. The air was hot and dry, and there was no trace of cloud in the brilliant, clear, merciless blue of the sky.

It was the major threat to all of them, a danger inherent in the land they lived in. In the Highlands there had been no real threat for three or four years, but the next day, when Berrima woke, the scent of burning eucalypt was on the air, and from her window she could look directly at the sun; the smoke haze had turned it to a yellow ball that hung in a yellow sky. The entire garden, still, breathless, was bathed in the weird light.

As soon as they had breakfasted, Aidan and several men from Shannonbrook Two and Three rode off to investigate the fire.

It was burning on a wide front, and growing wider; they met

994

Garth Ellis and Doctor Lawler only just out of Glenquarry, and were told that they had been sent to fetch as many men as they could find.

Messages were sent back for wagons and water barrels, blankets and digging implements, the several draught horses that Aidan had bred on Shannonbrook Three, and to warn the other farmers in the area that they may be called upon to help.

Killaloe and Shannonbrook were in no danger, but there were great tracts of land to the south-east that were not yet cleared, or were partially-cleared, and small farms nestled in amongst the scrub, whole families that must be warned – and, as the morning went on and a dangerous southerly breeze sprang up, evacuated from their houses.

At odd times during that day, Aidan would think about Berrima, back at Shannonbrook Three, would think of the normality of his life; he found he had to do this, for he was becoming afraid, and all around him, as the flames grew hotter and they were covered in powdery ash as they worked to dig firebreaks, he could see the fear growing on each of the men's faces. He had fought bushfires before, but from nowhere, this violent, scarlet, devouring giant was consuming whole hills and valleys. Reports came from one of Henke's rousabouts, that the fire had swept around to the west and had cut the main road to Mittagong, had been stopped only by the Wingecarribee Marsh.

There were women here, setting up trestle tables, building fires and even rough ovens, cooking, baking, serving tea and cool water to the men as they came from their back-breaking toil to pause for a few minutes' rest. Berrima came, and Helena Warwick. Mrs Albertson swept majestically about, giving orders but working just as hard at the same time; even the Lawler girls went back and forth carrying buckets of water to the men. Often, he saw Genevieve Vallon, the flames giving a wild kind of beauty to the unusual planes of her face, and he noticed that she stood with Liam for some time, talking in low voices, before Liam rode off to evacuate several families to the west, whose farms were now in danger.

Aidan was asked to take charge of one section, working with men whom he knew, Kelly and Liam among them, but left the section in Heinrich Henke's charge, when the wind changed, to find Liam and help with the evacuations.

'He's having trouble!' Garth Ellis grinned at Aidan as they met, Garth driving a wagon with a load of belongings for an elderly man and woman who seemed to be in a state of shock. 'That road up there! The place at the end! They've got a gun, and they won't come out!' He drove the horse on, and Aidan had not returned his smile – lately there was something malicious to Garth Ellis's smile that Aidan did not like. He felt it was over Victoria – but begod, that was years ago, Garth shouldn't be coming back to Mittagong to wallow in his past if he couldn't take whatever that past told him of his own failures. He put his heels to Blue's sides and raced Thomas and Kelly up the long, rutted drive, winding between tall eucalypts, into a clearing on the top of the hill.

The house was a small, slab-built cottage of only two rooms. As Aidan, Thomas and Kelly rode up, they could see Hedley Warwick and Wal Sullivan, proprietor of the Hit-and-Miss, loading trussed and squawking chickens into a wagon already loaded with fodder, but pitifully few personal belongings. A red heeler snapped and snarled around the men's feet, further hampering their work; when it ran off to bark at the three horses, Hedley and Wal looked up in relief.

Another explosion from the shotgun went off in the house, and the three men looked startled. 'What's going on here?' Aidan asked. 'Will you tell me that? Is that my son shooting in there?'

For answer, there was the sound of furniture being knocked over within the house, a woman's voice raised to a screech. 'Leggo! Leggo of me!' And the sound of a child's wailing cry of fright.

And Liam's voice, even as Aidan, Thomas and Kelly had dismounted, thrown their reins to Wal, were heading for the house . . . 'Drop the gun . . . ! Drop it!' and over the screaming a shot exploded.

The child screamed the louder, the woman's harsh voice, 'Give it back! Give it to me . . . !'

Aidan froze, turned back to look inquiringly at Hedley Warwick; but before he could voice his question, the door to the cottage burst open, and Liam emerged, dragging Matty Rodgers by the hair, at the same time attempting to cover his face from the blows that she aimed at him. 'We don't need no help from you,' she shrieked. 'We never did! It's my house! Mine!'

'You want to get yourself burnt like a bloody baked possum?' Liam stopped only long enough to slap her face. 'If so, you'll not be taking your children to perdition with you! Use y'r sense!'

He was dragging her in the direction of the wagon, and it was only now that both looked up and saw Aidan, Matty ceasing her struggling so abruptly that Liam stumbled and almost fell.

'You.'

Hedley Warwick, who had once been witness to another scene between these two, swallowed hard, and glanced at Aidan's face.

There was nothing to be read on those stony features. He merely nodded, gravely. 'Mrs Rodgers.'

'I might've known. Expect you set the fire on purpose.'

'Liam,' Aidan kept his eyes on Matty as he spoke, 'get the children out of the house.'

'I'm not leavin'!'

'I'm sorry,' grimly, 'you have no choice, and very little time . . .'

'Again.'

A wave of guilt made him angry; he glared at Matty, pale hair fallen loose about her waist, face as defiant as ever, and he wanted to step to her, yes, even in front of these man and slap her face as Liam had done. Instead he said, 'You'd have valuables you'd want to collect. The wagon's there – one of the men will take you down to Finchley's place – you'll be safe there . . .'

'I'm not leaving!'

The ash was hailing on them faster, thicker now, and more than ash – there were sparks amongst some of the falling debris that was blown towards them on the hot wind. Liam had quietly moved back towards the house, and now came out the door carrying a screaming toddler of about eighteen months old, and a baby wrapped in a shawl. Several older children, wide-eyed, frightened, trailed after him. Wal stepped forward to Matty. 'C'mon, Mrs Rodgers, I'll help you fetch your things . . .' And he took her arm, gently enough.

Aidan had to leave. He turned away, took up Blue's reins, and was about to mount when Matty's shrill voice grated on his ears, 'You got no right! When will you leave us alone!' He gritted his teeth, mounted the horse, and gestured for Thomas, Kelly and Liam to follow him. 'You ain't God Almighty, Aidan O'Brien! That's who you think you are, but you ain't. You'll rot, you will, for all you done! God'll see to it! You'll rot! You ain't got no right to do this . . . !'

Perhaps it was the smoke, yes, it must be – the choking, dry smoke that clung to his lungs and wind pipe that made him ill; the nausea was a pain in his gut and he sat hunched in the saddle for miles, in silence, and tried not to think of the woman back there, the thin, too thin woman with her brood of brown-skinned, tinker-like children.

'All right.' Liam's horse was suddenly beside Blue. Liam was leaning on the pommel of his saddle, gazing at his father. 'What was all that about?'

Aidan did not answer, scowled ahead, but Thomas, on the other side of Liam looked over with as close to a look of active dislike that Aidan had ever seen. 'Tell him,' he said.

After a pause, Aidan said, 'She and her husband built a place on Shannonbrook Three.'

'What? When?'

'Years ago. You were in Sydney. They wouldn't move on. I gave them fair warning . . . '

'You didn't burn them out?' He waited for his father to say no, of course he did not. He waited, but all Aidan said was, 'They wouldn't move on.' His voice was little above a growl, his eyes on the road ahead.

And he led the men back to the firebreak, and from that moment there was no time to think, little time to look about; an occasional glance at the sky, at the ground covered, the ground yet to be covered, the faces of the men that surrounded him, the sweat running down their necks into shirts that were soaked with the stuff, stained with falling ash, blackened, burnt leaves that floated down on them. He was conscious that his hands hurt, for it had been years since he had wielded a spade, an axe, a pick, for as many hours as he now worked. Only when his hands began to slip from the bleeding blisters did he wrap his hands in bits of sacking, before going on.

'Mr O'Brien!'

The voice had called him twice before Aidan looked up. Beyond Bram Russell, whose voice he had heard, Ralph Lambert sat upon his restive horse. 'Mr Lambert wants you, Mr O'Brien!'

Lambert looked a little non-plussed. As Aidan walked over to him, he said, 'You're in charge of this section?' And as Aidan nodded, coolly, he added, 'I need three men, at least three men, O'Brien.'

'Y're joking . . . '

'We're further down the slope – I've got men who've been working since four this morning without a break.'

Aidan sighed, looked around at the men, who had slowed to listen. 'Liam – you and Bram and Maurie, go down the slope with Mr Lambert.'

And as he was about to turn back to his work, Liam was squinting up at Lambert through the grey perspiration, to demand, 'What's the big rush to save the timber down there? Wouldn't you be better off clearing the ground by the road?'

'That scrub backs on to my property, and Fitzroy Amberley's. We've got sheep in paddocks there – paddocks only half-cleared . . . '

'Lambert, you got my sympathy – but if this fire gets to the road, there's more'n forty properties that'll lose their entire crops and dwellings . . . '

'We've almost finished the fire break! My men are dropping with exhaustion – are you going to help us, or not?'

Liam turned, glanced at his father, then reluctantly walked over to the lines of horses, Maurie and Bram following.

The men ate in shifts, tin mugs of hot soup that the women had cooked at home, heated in huge cauldrons over camp fires. Aidan had time, watching them moving back and forth, their skirts pinned up to avoid the ash that was swirling like snow around their feet, to wonder how Berrima was, whether she was frightened. Sometimes, through the smoky haze, he caught sight of Matty, helping the other women, but she kept well away from him, and for this he was thankful.

'Might be good fortune.' Aidan looked over to where a begrimed Garth Ellis, a brandy flask in his hand, was smiling at the sky. Aidan realized then, that the other man had been speaking for some time. 'The wind's changed, Aidan. And it's brought some cloud, see?' The smile was turned to Aidan; then he held out the flask to him.

'No, thanks all the same, boyo.'

'But I've another three in my saddle bag.' Aidan shook his head, but Hedley Warwick and Heinrich Henke accepted the proffered flask.

'I think there's rain in them clouds . . . ' Wal Sullivan stared hopefully at the sky.

'God wouldn't be that good.' Garth stood. 'He wouldn't be that merciful . . . ' And he walked back to his spade and his work.

'That's a bitter young man,' Hedley Warwick said, walking beside Aidan back to their tools.

'Aye,' Aidan growled, 'and less than useless if he keeps drinking like that.' He looked around, scowling, then added, 'You had any news from Lambert's section?'

'No, not at all. They'd still be busy – that wind may not help in that gully, the way it's situated.'

'My son's been down there all day.'

And Aidan began to worry. Each wagon that rolled up with water barrels and equipment, each horseman that rode into the clearing, made him look up, hopefully. The sun was beginning to go down the sky like a clot of blood, and the wind was cold; then the sun vanished, and Aidan was still thinking of the gully, when the first heavy drops fell.

Beside him, Neil Russell dropped to the ground and burst into tears; men were shouting, running, women laughing, Hedley Warwick took Aidan's shoulders and whirled him around; everywhere people were sobbing with relief, weeping on each other's shoulders, hugging, dancing about, while the cool rain fell, more and more heavily.

Aidan made his way through the people that greeted him, grasped for him, slapping his back, pumping his hand; beyond them, at a distance, he saw Kelly approaching, rather eerily, through the smoke haze that was even now clearing.

'I've asked everyone who's come back from that section,' he said, when he drew close to Aidan, 'they haven't seen Liam or the boys . . . '

Aidan laid a hand on his arm, then walked past him, for he could see Lambert, shoulders slumped, riding an exhausted animal through the dancing crowds.

'Lambert!' Aidan had hold of the bridle. 'Where are my men? Where's my son?'

Lambert dismounted. 'We . . . we don't know.'

'*What?*'

'Donaldson's boy and young Ellis came back with me. I sent one of them down to warn the men in the gully – that was when the wind changed . . . I don't know what happened. The man came back . . . he mustn't have been able to get through . . . '

'Don't you *know*? What did he tell you?'

'He didn't! He didn't! How was I to know he was drunk? He didn't appear drunk! I couldn't get anything out of him – he didn't ride back to the firebreak, he went on, across timber like the devil was after him! It was Donaldson's son who told me he'd been drinking . . . '

'Ellis. Garth Ellis. You sent Garth Ellis to get my son out of that gully . . . '

'He's the finest horseman over rough ground that this colony has, O'Brien!' Lambert's face was white with his fear. 'I didn't know, I tell you! I didn't know that he wasn't in possession of himself . . . '

Aidan had gripped his shoulder hard, turned him towards his horse. 'Take me there – now.'

'You can't get through! We tried, man, don't you understand? It's gone under! All that section's gone under!'

It hissed and steamed and glowed, black and fiery gold and hot scarlet, like a scene from hell, and Aidan stood at the top of the rise and gazed down into the natural furnace, and thought of Liam, of Bram, of Maurie – but mostly of Liam . . .

They were pulling him back, but he had no recollection of stepping down that burning hillside, felt the rain on his face and his own

1000

sobs of fear, and they were dragging him away, his own voice screaming, screaming, '*Liam!! Lia-a-am!!*'

Later, nothing of that afternoon made sense, it was confused memories of Sam Russell's stricken face, seated there beside him at the camp fire as they waited for the rain to cool the scorching hot ground, waited for the search to begin.

Let him be alive, Aidan prayed. Take anything I've got – take me. Only let him be alive. Dear God, let him be alive . . .

'Drink this up . . . We'll be goin' in there, soon. We'll know, soon.' It was Thomas. He thrust a tin mug of tea into Aidan's hand. 'Drink it, boyo,' he ordered.

Aidan raised it to his lips, numbly, but half-choked on the strength of the brandy. He raised his eyes to Thomas, but before he could speak—

'Vengeance is mine, saith the Lord . . . '

Thomas was standing with his mouth slightly open, gazing across the fire. Matty stood there, her eyes on Aidan, hard, unnatural eyes. 'You destroyed our home, you broke my man's spirit . . . '

Thomas said, 'Woman, would you . . . '

'Our home is burnt again – everything's gone. The only farm to burn, on that road, and it was ours. But justice was done.' She nodded, slowly. 'I prayed to God to punish you . . . and now he has.'

Aidan, standing, his eyes tormented, took a step around the fire towards her, 'Will you hit me?' she cried, 'Hit me! I'm not afraid of you!'

And he stopped, for her next words were chilling in its toneless recitation, the way her tongue lingered on each word, '*As the fire burneth a wood, and as the flame setteth the mountains on fire, so the Lord persecutes the wicked . . .* ' She turned briefly to Sam Russell. 'Your son is alive. I see him walking in the ashes.' Then she turned to Aidan. 'But your son is dead. He lies under burning timber.'

Thomas looked at his brother, expecting a denial, anger – but Aidan looked like a cornered animal, as if the woman terrified him – and begod, she was enough to terrify anyone. 'Woman, y're mad,' Thomas breathed, but his voice held no scorn.

The woman's eyes had not left Aidan's face in all this time. 'Go home to your fine house,' she said, 'your land and your crops. God has spoken to me. Your son is dead.'

And she walked away, her dark dress and pale hair wavering in the smoke of the fire, the warping draughts of burning air.

'She's bitter because of her own home being destroyed. It's un-

hinged her. Don't mind her, Aidan. She's mad, poor woman . . . '
Aidan could not answer Thomas. He watched Matty until she had disappeared from sight.

Edward Lawler appeared beside Thomas. Aidan glanced at him, but did not greet him. It was too difficult, just now, to collect one's thoughts, to make any decision, however minute; the chilling numbness, where only his son's name, his face, claimed Aidan's thoughts, left no room for any other emotion but his fear.

They rode up to the campfire, and saw the procession with the stretchers, coming up the slope. The rain, which had lightened off for a little time, was falling fast and heavily once more, and Aidan knew, as instinctively as any other Southern Highlands man that day, that the drought had broken at last.

The irony became more tragic when he dismounted from Blue, and walked down to meet the exhausted men and their burdens. By now he was sick with his grief, and the nightmare day was a purgatory that seemed merely to go on and on. So he looked at the dark figures, only two stretchers, and was almost shaken to see that both were still alive.

'Maurie . . . ?' He walked along by the stretcher.

'Liam . . . he saved us, Mr O'Brien. Wasn't for him . . . Pointed the way we should go . . . If it hadn't been for him . . . ' the boy was sobbing, moaning with the pain of salt tears on scorched skin.

'All right, Maurie, all right, boyo . . . I know you did your best.'

He stood back a little, watched the other stretcher approach, young Bram, eyes closed, whimpering quietly. Sam, walking beside the stretcher, looked up at Aidan with such a look of thanksgiving that Aidan could hardly bear it.

'Father?'

At some distance down the hill, a dark spectre in a blackened blanket, flanked by Wal Sullivan and Ralph Lambert, moving amongst the equally dark skeletons of the trees; it came towards him, up the white, ash-covered slope, shoulders hunched, moving painfully, and 'Father?' it said, through a smoke-choked throat.

Aidan took one step, then two, and with a cry, he broke into a run. Sliding, tripping on the treacherous ground, he ran through the smoking remains, and the singed and blackened figure, coming to a halt and swaying with exhaustion, only just had time to open his arms to his father before the older man reached him, and their arms were about each other.

94

Several small homesteads were burnt, and a roadside inn, between Robertson and Glenquarry was found, when the owners returned, to be a smoking pile of ashes and blackened brickwork. Fortunately, there appeared to be no loss of life.

Aidan had the word spread amongst the firefighters and their families that he would be holding a party the following evening, to celebrate the fact that the danger had passed, to return some of the atmosphere of gladness to the Christmas season that was upon them, and almost forgotten in the past few days.

'We'll take up a collection, tomorrow night, too,' he told Thomas, 'for the victims of the bushfire.'

Thomas looked hard at him. 'Aye,' he said.

Kelly was invited to dinner that evening, was able to bathe and change in the bathroom of the homestead, and stayed late, talking to Liam and Aidan, after Berrima and Clemency had retired. When he returned to his room in the barn it was to find that the blue heeler, Nameless, had leapt through the open window and was asleep on his bed. Kelly tossed him off, good-naturedly, and opened first the door of his room, then the barn, to allow the dog out. Surprisingly, there was no hesitation. Nameless bounded forward, and it was only then that Kelly saw Clemency.

She stood in the middle of the wet yard, the rain falling softly about her in the darkness. He could make out that she was wearing the pale blue dress she had worn at dinner, with no coat or shawl.

'What are you doing?' He walked towards her and took her arm. 'Come inside . . . '

'No! No, we'd best talk out here.'

'Clemency, has it come to your attention that it's raining?'

'Good. It'll help me think more clearly. I . . . I went riding, today, past Summer Hill, the Pirie-Moxhams' old property.'

'And?' he prompted, when she paused.

'And I . . . '

He interrupted, 'It's nothing to do with Garth, is it? He hasn't been back to the lodge . . . '

'I don't know – it's nothing to do with Garth. I just . . . I simply

1003

decided, today, that it might be best if we did get married, after all. You see . . . '

She was pulled forward into his arms, startled by his reaction. 'Do you mean that?'

'Yes,' she answered, rather stiffly. 'That is, if you still want me.'

The rain had been gradually increasing, and now it was falling quite heavily; a roll of thunder moved across the sky above them. He studied her face in the dim light from his window and saw that she meant her words. He laughed, delighted, held her close to him and whirled her about the wet, cobbled yard. 'Say it again!' he cried, as if even the rain and thunder did not exist except for his amusement in this moment. 'Say it again, that you'll marry me!'

'I . . . I'll marry you – Kelly, it's pouring with rain . . . '

'Say it louder, so I'll believe you really mean it. Look me right in the face, and say it!'

'I'll marry you, I'll marry you . . . !' He began whirling her about once more, as if they were on a ballroom floor. 'Kelly, will you stop? I'm dizzy . . . !'

He stopped, pulled her damp body close, drew her face up to his and kissed her, possessing himself of her lips and her will in a way that no man had before. The world was still reeling for her, and the emotions engendered by his kiss did nothing to make her feel more secure. She was forced to cling to him; the darkness and the rain and the warmth of his lips were robbing her of her sense of place, her very substance.

It was Kelly who pulled away first. 'When?' he whispered.

'T . . . Tomorrow. As soon as possible.'

She could feel the warmth of his body, all of his body, through their saturated clothes. She thought he would tell her to be sensible, press for more preparation time, but he did not. It was the only time she regretted what she was doing; her heart betrayed her and pitied him when, 'I didn't believe in miracles, until now,' he murmured.

'Kelly, I . . . '

'Yes, tomorrow,' he said, his voice low, almost a growl. 'Tomorrow, and not a minute too soon . . . '

'And I don't want anyone else to know.'

'What?' And for the first time he was suspicious, pulled back from her. 'What is this, Clemency? What's the reason behind this elopement?'

'It's not an elopement. I just don't want a fuss, being pointed at for marrying at my age. Please, Kelly.' She wound her arms about his neck. 'Let's do it my way. Just this once.'

He watched her, narrow-eyed. Then she stiffened as he said,

1004

'What happened at Summer Hill?'

She tried not to look alarmed, smiled a little. 'That's where I had the idea, that's all. Perhaps I *am* a creature of impulse, as you once said.' She looked up and found him gazing at her sceptically. 'Oh, please, Kelly, marry me tomorrow and don't ask foolish questions. I promise that after tomorrow I'll do things your way. I will, truly. Whatever you say – it's grand with me. Only don't ask me to explain my feelings now, when I can't.'

He looked at her then, the shadowed grey eyes possessed of an intensity that she only met with every ounce of her will. Then he had smiled a little, and she was afraid. But the voice was gentle as he pulled her to him, and said over her shoulder, his breath warm on her damp hair, 'And will you really be an obedient wife, Clemency? It's worth marrying you just to see you try.'

She kissed him lightly, smiled up at him, 'Tomorrow?'

He sighed. 'Tomorrow.'

'And can I . . . can I spend the night with you?'

He hesitated. She went to kiss him again, but he held her back a little. 'No,' carefully, 'we'll wait for tomorrow night.'

'Oh, but—'

Each of his words clearly enunciated. 'But what?'

'Nothing. If you're sure . . . '

'I'm not. Go away.'

'But if you . . . '

'Go away *now*.' And she was turned about and slapped on the behind, hard enough to send her forward a few paces. When she looked back he had disappeared inside the barn, the door was shut and she heard the bolt fall into place.

The dog, who had been watching the odd behaviour of the humans, whined a little to see the man go, then started when Clemency hissed, 'You stupid *eejit* of a man!' and slunk off to the kennels, thinking she meant himself.

There was no single moment of decision, no sudden realization that it was over. Aidan would, perhaps, blame her parents' letter, thinking that their coming to stay with Aunt and Uncle Charlie in Camden and their promise to visit Berrima was behind her decision; an unwillingness for them to see her living in Aidan's house.

But even then, she thought, she was over-estimating his sensitivity. He was delighted that Milton and Margaret Reynolds would be coming that Christmas, did not think to ask Berrima how she felt, did not think, it seemed lately, of Berrima at all.

On the day following the fire, very early before the house had stirred, Berrima took the key to the house in Queen Street, Mittagong, harnessed Penny to her little buggy, and drove, through a freshly-washed morning, to the home she had shared with Mark.

Of course, it was Aidan's house now; he had bought it from the bank only a short time after she and Mark had left. It was odd, how many things that surrounded her life had been purchased by Aidan O'Brien. Glenleigh, the house next door to her parents; the *Derwent Chronicle*; the Mittagong *Argus*; the house in Queen Street – and Mark. Her photography was her own; but only because she had escaped him for those vital years. Her heart? He had had that for twenty odd years and never noticed. Her body? He had not bought that, he had taken it . . . No, she had given it, once, briefly – though she had always had the suspicion that had she protested, he would have taken her anyway. So long ago . . . here, in this house . . .

The front gate creaked open before her. Aidan had been too busy, and the tenant too careless to have the house maintained, and the paint on the windows and doors as well as the picket gate and fence, was peeling away. The front garden was neat enough, but ragged, the bushes unpruned, an air of abandonment about the place, even here.

Inside, it was better. Aidan had had carpets replaced, and the furniture, many pieces her own, that he had bought at the auction, had stood the years well.

She walked through the rooms, and each had memories, the sad restless spirit of Mark, Aidan's more turbulent presence, even her own, the girl she had been; all were here. She stood a long time in each room, and listened to it, and found within each, scenes of those years, the last years of her happiness with Mark, for it had been here that she had hoped that a new beginning could be made, it was here that she had seen that hope fade for ever.

Out through the kitchen to the back garden, and it was clear, in this place more than any other, of all that time could do. The lawn was overgrown, the rose bushes and flowerbeds choked with brambles, convolvulus and ivy. It was only the faint, warm wind on her cheeks that made her realize that she had tears running quietly, unchecked, down her face.

She turned her back on the view then, and looked back at the house, and tried to imagine what to do with all she saw before her, how best to cope, to make some kind of future on the foundations of the past.

'Berri?'

1006

Liam approached her as she came through the front door of Shannonbrook Three; he held a letter in his hand, was smiling, until he drew closer to her, and slowed his stride. 'What's the matter?'

'Nothing – why?' She was headed for the mirror above the hall table, was gazing at her red-eyed reflection even as he was saying, 'You look as if you've been crying.'

'Oh, the pollen in the air – I was sneezing coming past all the privet hedges. Are there any letters for me?'

'This one.' He handed her a business-like envelope. 'And this.' He placed in her hand an already-opened letter, addressed to Aidan, 'It is from Will and Cora Teloar – Father invited them to spend Christmas with us, and since business has brought Will to Sydney he's able to make it. Hope they're here for tonight – he's a bit vague about the date.'

She smiled a little. 'So everyone will be here. That's wonderful. May I?' She took the letter from Liam, and drifted off into the parlour to read it. She was glad when Liam did not follow her, but went off, whistling, about his own affairs.

The parlour was silent, unfamiliar, the furniture, the carpets gone; the polished floorboards could be seen, now, stretching between the folding doors, seventy feet to the end of the dining room. Every chair in Shannonbrook Three, it seemed, lined the walls. The Steinway stood in the corner on its heavily carved legs, polished until it gleamed deep gold.

Berrima sat on the piano stool and opened the letter from Will, and it was a delight to read his words, hear his voice, in her mind, after all these years. And it would be even better for Aidan, she thought soberly, folding the letter, that Will and Cora and their daughter, Olwyn, now fourteen, would be here when she had gone. It would help him over the worst of his sense of . . . loss? She smiled grimly – of inconvenience, more likely.

The second letter was from her publisher who, after reiterating his delight in her latest book, suggested that she might consider, for her next, a more detailed work on the islands of the Great Barrier Reef, off the Queensland coast; when she was next in Sydney, perhaps she could call to see him to discuss the idea, and the advance she would need in her travels . . .

And she realized, only then, how irrevocable this decision to leave this house had become. All things were conspiring to take her away. She sat amongst the strangeness of the ballroom, that had once been a cosy parlour, comfortable dining room. When the party was over, these rooms would appear again, as they had always been. But something would be changed; when she came to the house, it would be as a guest only, and that, not often. Anyway, she thought, as she stood and moved to the door, the sense of comfort had been illusory. She had no real place here. After tonight she would be gone, without regrets.

Still, the sense of a leave-taking followed her about as she gathered her clothes, the books, the few personal belongings she would need over the next few days. With the house full of servants bustling about, she had no difficulty in gathering the linen and blankets she needed from the closets. She wrapped all these things in paper parcels or boxes, tied them neatly with ribbon, and carried them down to her buggy as if she were about to deliver Christmas presents. She smiled to herself as she drove Penny down the drive and towards Mittagong once more. They are presents, she thought, presents to myself. *To Berrima, your independence, with love from Berrima, Christmas, 1879.*

'And about time, too,' she murmured, looking up and smiling at the blue sky. Penny was still fresh and spanked along; above them the dappling, meagre but fragrant leaves of the gum trees towering on either side seemed to flee backwards as she rushed forwards. 'It's about time.'

It was odd, Aidan thought, glancing at his watch, that so few people were here. One or two townsfolk who had helped with the fire, but no one from the area about Shannonbrook except Thomas and his family, and Heinrich Henke and his wife.

Everyone knew to come at about six, so there was plenty of daylight left for the younger children – but here it was half-past eight, and where the hell was the rest of the Southern Highlands? There was food enough for five hundred, he had had deliveries made from every bakery in Mittagong, Bowral, Moss Vale, Robertson and as far away as the township of Berrima, and sides of pork and beef were roasting on spits over coals on his precious front lawn, temporary shelters raised over them in case it should rain.

Where was everyone?

He prowled up and down the front verandah, stopped to tap his foot a little at the music issuing from about the beer kegs. The Danahers from Burrawang were here, at least, and there'd be music, grand Irish music, for they were a talented family, playing barawn, pipes, fiddle and flute. They swung, now, into *The Irish Washerwoman*, and Aidan hummed along, the music of his childhood comforting him somewhat in his agitation.

For he had decided, after watching Berrima withdrawing further and further from him in the past few weeks, that he could delay no longer. That morning, in his office, he had found the keys to the Queen Street house to be missing, and there was only one person in the house who would care enough to steal them. He ran an almost certain risk of having her laugh in his face, but tonight he would make his very last gambit, and propose to Berrima. Tomorrow was Christmas Eve, there was a feeling of goodwill in the air – or would be, when people turned up. He'd ply her with champagne, and put the question to her as a business proposition almost. Very coolly. And Will and Cora were arriving in the next few days, and Milton and Margaret Reynolds. He'd ask Berri to take a few days to consider – aye, that was it, would refuse to listen to a refusal until after Christmas – and hopefully her parents and the Treloars would persuade her to see the sense in his offer.

He tugged, irritated, at his stiff white collar. He felt absurdly nervous. The fifteen-years' gap in age between Berrima and himself still bothered him, but they were both older, now; Berri was now forty years old, hard though it was to grasp the fact. Besides, she had lived in his house for eighteen months now, and had shown no interest in any other man, though several had shown an interest in her. She had, until recently, seemed quite content here. Her short-ness with him lately might even be because – love aside – she felt he owed it to her to make her position here more tenable. He did owe it to her. He was foolish to have waited so long, for her to come to him. He would make up, in warmth and passion, for what she lacked, and he would spoil her, pamper her, treasure her, and she would forget Mark. In his, Aidan's arms, he would make her forget him. He leaned against the verandah rail and felt a warmth in his loins at the thought of it. Say yes, Berri, he pleaded with her in his mind. Forget the past, and say yes . . .

'Aidan?'

He turned, startled. She was standing in the open French doors that led to the parlour. The lamps that strung the verandah shone on the silver hair, the lustre of the turquoise satin gown, the colour matching the jewels at her neck and ears.

He found he had been holding his breath. She moved towards him. Her hair had been elaborately styled for this evening, and thick ringlets hung down her back and over her shoulder, past her breasts. He took her hand. 'You look like Marie Antoinette,' he murmured.

She laughed a little. 'Liam said something of the sort to me, once.'

'Oh? Discerning of him.'

'He told me I looked like an eighteenth-century French countess. It's more like you, however, to give me the mixed compliment of telling me I look like a doomed queen.'

1009

She had moved past him a little, and he was left wondering at her words, until she said, 'Have you seen Kelly and your children?'

'No. I suppose they're down in the garden.'

'Clemency looks lovely tonight, you'll be very proud of her. But Charity said she saw her and Liam climb into the landau beside Kelly, and they drove off – it was about two hours ago.'

'I hope they're not in any scrape,' he growled.

'I can't see what mischief they'd be up to in their formal dress. Perhaps they've gone to fetch some of their friends.'

They stood silently for a moment. Aidan checked his watch, more in nervousness than impatience, but Berrima was saying, 'I suppose a lot of people will be late – six was a little early, and there was so much to do after the fires. Many families will be only just settling back into their homes after the evacuations.'

He looked unconvinced, but said, 'Well, the weather's clear, and the garden looks grand, does it not?'

She looked down to where the lights twinkled amongst the trees; it was a fairy-like scene. Danaher's fiddle began a solo rendition of the wistful *Eileen Aroon*.

'Berri . . .' Aidan began, for there was a tension, a strong bond between them, at this moment; he could sense it, as if all her energy, all her thoughts were concentrated upon him in the same way that his thoughts were upon her.

'Aidan, I'm leaving tonight.'

He looked over at her, slowly, had not even assimilated her words when she continued, 'I've prepared the Queen Street house a little, I have nearly all I need there. I'll fetch my photographic equipment and the rest of my belongings over the next few days. I'd like you to tell me the purchase price of the house.' She added, 'I'll buy it back from you – or rent it from you, if . . .'

He took her wrist, quite gently, and she did not wrench it away, did not pull back at all as he drew her down the verandah and in at the French doors of his office. He closed them behind him and turned to her.

'What foolishness is this, tell me? Leaving? At Christmas? And what will your parents and the Treloars think when they arrive expecting to see you . . .'

'I'm going to Mittagong, Aidan, not New Zealand. They can visit me at the Queen Street house, or I can visit them here.' And as he began to speak, 'I've had a letter from my publishers, Aidan. I'll be leaving fairly soon for Queensland to research another book. I want to know I have my own home to return to.'

'You do. Here.'

'This isn't my house.'

'It is. It can be. You infuriating little eejit – I knew you were plotting something for the Mittagong house, but I didn't think you'd move so fast. I was going to . . . I was going to ask you to marry me, Berri. Tonight, very romantically, under the rose arbour, perhaps, with Danaher's violin playing in the background.' He smiled, 'Then you have to ruin my carefully laid plans.' He placed his hands on her shoulders, 'Say yes, anyway. Overlook the clumsiness of my approach and say yes, Berri.'

'You . . . were planning on proposing to me? Tonight?'

'I couldn't risk you leaving me.'

'No,' and her voice had lost its amazement, gained a considering tone. 'No, of course not.' She was laughing softly. 'Well, isn't that ironic – but quite typical of your perversity. When did you come to the decision that I had some value in your life?'

He felt as if she had struck him. No, worse than that, for she had struck him more than once during their quarrels, and his rage had always carried him beyond the blow – he never used to feel it. He felt this, keenly, and said, almost humbly, for him, 'You've always been valued in my life. Of all things, I've valued you the most.'

'At what price, Aidan?' And when he looked confused, 'Come, you must be able to place a figure to me – everything else in your life has a price ticket. How much have you spent on keeping me close to you? Fifty, seventy thousand pounds? Do you wish to marry me now, simply because you don't like to lose sight of your investment?'

'Begod, you've become a monster,' he breathed. 'You've become a bitter, hard woman, Berrima . . .'

'Aidan, you taught me all I know.'

He stared at the woman, and in the silence, from the garden, a haunting wail flowed into the strains of the lament, *Boulavogue*, played on the *uilleann* pipes. Aidan shivered and rubbed the back of his neck, for the sound brought his childhood very close, walking home down darkened boreens, leaving a cottage where still the piper Brogan played, the music floating out over darkened fields and hedgerows.

Berrima, too, looked disturbed, had moved away a little, and it prompted Aidan to say, gently, 'It's Mark, isn't it?'

She turned and looked at him rather intently for a few seconds. 'Did Liam ever talk to you about that? About Mark's death?'

'No. Should he have?'

'He gave his word he wouldn't. I'm glad he kept it.' She hesitated, then told him of meeting Liam at the university, of the news of Mark's body being found, of the visit to the School of Anatomy.

1011

During this, she had seated herself in one of the chairs, now looked up at Aidan, gazing at her, appalled. 'Mark died of a growth within his brain – a temporal lobe meningioma.' She gave an almost harsh laugh. 'There! I can even give you the correct name for it. I've said it over to myself often enough. That's what killed him. After robbing him of his strength, his character, his personality, after warping him until there was nothing left of the man I married – for more than eight years it had been growing, Aidan – the thing finally killed him.'

He could only stand and stare at her.

'All that he'd done to me, in those past years, the drinking, the beatings, the cruelty – they weren't Mark at all.' She stood up, moved about the room, twisting the rings on her finger a little; she stopped near the empty hearth, did not turn when she said, 'My hair is white, Aidan, because Mark once broke into the house I shared with Richard, when my brother was away. He tied me to a chair, and accused me of sleeping with you, with Richard, with my father, and every other man he could think of. He took a pair of scissors, and he cut my hair off, then he took a razor, and he shaved my head. Then he left me. Nellie returned from a three day holiday with friends, and found me. I'd been tied to the chair for two days, surviving by drinking the water from the vases . . . ' She gave a short and mirth-less laugh, and turned to Aidan.

'And you wondered – don't you tell me you didn't – why I began my affair with Balbrook? I never loved him – but he loved me – and I met him just as I was recovering from what Mark had done. Bal-brook knew – he offered me protection and security, and I spent years of my life allowing him to love me. I needed that, Aidan. He was uncomplicated, and affectionate, rather boring, and very safe. I needed that, at that time; not the sort of relationship that I would have had with you. To be caught between you and Mark was something more than I could bear.'

'Berri . . . '

'Shut up!' she said savagely. 'For once in your life, listen to me, Aidan. Don't just hear me, but try *listening*.

'When Balbrook's brother was killed, and he inherited the title, I told him immediately that I wouldn't marry him, that I was leaving him. I think he was relieved. It was Richard's idea to leave the cities behind and travel with the cameras – I could think of nothing that would be better.

'And after Mark died – I didn't want anybody. I couldn't forget Mark. I went over and over everything that happened, and I couldn't forgive myself for not realizing that no man, *no man*, can

1012

change so much. Perhaps he was always weak, and spoilt, but he was no demon. And he became a demon.

'I'm a good nurse, my father, my brother and sister are all fine doctors – I should have realized. I should have seen.'

Aidan was leaning on his desk, feeling more ill than he thought possible. 'My God . . . ' and the tears caught in his throat. He did not dare look up at her. 'My God . . . '

'I should have told you before, perhaps,' and the light voice, the distinctive voice that had haunted all his dreams these last twenty years, the girl who had grown up to womanhood and surpassed him in courage and maturity, sounded practical, almost apologetic. 'I don't mean to upset you now, you have guests coming – but it seems you had this night chosen for a climax to our little drama, and we may as well bare our souls completely and settle things once and for all.'

He stared at her, shook his head slowly. 'Jaysus, but you're cool, Berri.'

'Emotionless, you mean? That's quite correct, Aidan. There would, perhaps, have been some return of feeling, somewhere in these past eighteen months, if you'd reached for me even once with tenderness. Don't ask for emotions now, Aidan. I have none left.' And she had turned towards the French doors.

He shouted at her, his hands balled into fists with his impotence, his tearing pity for her. 'Berri, why didn't you tell me! *Why!*'

She stopped, did not turn. Calmly, 'Aidan, why didn't you ask?'

She opened the glass doors, and the music and laughter of the lighted garden struck them like the scene of a play as the curtain goes up. They both paused. The garden held much the same crowd as when they had entered the office, but Aidan's only concern, now, was the woman with her back to him, about to step out on to the verandah and down the steps to join those people, away from him. He had reached out his hand to take her arm, when a knock came on the office door. Both turned towards the sound. 'Come in,' Aidan said crossly.

The door opened to admit Charity, looking rather wide-eyed. 'A gentleman to see you, sir. Mr Devlin Retcliffe.'

Aidan's hand reached for Berrima, but she was gone, out the French doors. He stood, grasping the doorway, watching the small, slender figure in turquoise satin move away, down the green of the lawn, towards the lights.

Behind him, the door closed, and a man coughed, discreetly.

95

The two men stared at each other, and it was only when Aidan had closed the French doors that Devlin moved forward into the room.

'O'Brien.' A statement, slow, wondering, without, Aidan noticed, any patronization or hostility.

'Retcliffe.' Aidan decided to give him the benefit of this. His own heart was thumping hard, it was as if a ghost stood before him, and here, here in his office at Shannonbrook Three, the face of Devlin Kelly seemed a hundred times more disturbing. So he had come. Twelve thousand miles. For his boy. And Aidan felt a strange emotion – something like pity, or understanding, for there was a pain written in Devlin's eyes; those blue, mocking eyes that had looked on so much of Aidan's humiliation and grief, held something that Aidan had shared. He's like me, he thought, with something like wonder, and it swept aside Aidan's memory that this had been the man who killed Corrie O'Neill – he's like me, going to Kilmainham for Liam.

They were shaking hands, and it was not unpleasant, the touch of the man, the grip was dry and firm enough. Aidan could not prevent himself from studying him, thin, with white, receding hair, stooped shoulders and a face that was very lined, very tired. Aidan struggled to equate this elderly man with the boy who had ruined him. It was hard, for he realized that in his mind, Devlin had never changed. Aidan saw him as he had been in the courtroom in Ennis, the day of Aidan's trial, the last time he had seen him . . .

'You look well, O'Brien,' Devlin was saying.

'And you.'

Devlin smiled. 'No, that's kind of you, but I've been overworking and had a slight heart attack several months ago. When I greet myself in the mirror each morning the experience is written there.'

'Please,' Aidan said. 'Sit down. You'll have a whiskey?'

'Thank you.'

Thomas had been right, the young trawneen had been right, Devlin had come . . . Of course, the man must be mad. Aidan smiled to himself as he poured the drinks, then sobered. Hell's outhouse, why did this scene, in which he would take a fierce delight at any other time, have to occur when Berrima was slipping from his grasp? She would be down there in the garden now, upset by the memories he had made her stir, and yet he was not there to comfort her; he had had no time to comfort her. He could only pray that she would not really leave tonight – surely she would not leave without saying goodbye . . . Aidan wondered where Kelly was, and cursed the man for leaving at such a time.

They sat in two chairs on either side of the empty hearth, and studied each other. Again, Aidan could not help smiling a little; they were both of them so civilized, so calm.

It was Devlin who broke the silence to say, quietly, 'I had months, of course, on the voyage to Australia, anticipating this meeting.' He smiled a little. 'But nothing was gained by it. Seeing you again – you're the first person from Killaloe I've spoken to since Anna died, did you know that? Seeing you again, realizing all that's happened . . . ' he stopped, then went on, more firmly, 'It was good of you to see me, O'Brien.'

'I don't really know how I can help you. Your business is with your son – and I'm afraid he's not here at the moment. He'll be back shortly.'

'Yes, so your servant said. I felt I should, in the circumstances, pay my respects to you. I'm sorry that it seems to be an awkward time.' And this last came in a rather strained fashion. Aidan glanced up quickly. Devlin's gaze was upon his glass, but Aidan had the feeling, for the first time, that this interview was not as easy for Devlin as it seemed.

Aidan was silent, decided not to help him. And after a moment, Devlin stood, and moved about the room, studying the paintings, the furniture, critically. Aidan watched him, narrow-eyed, felt pleased with himself that the man would not be able to fault the room. Arra, it must gall you, all this, he thought.

His back to Aidan, Devlin said, 'I've written to Michael many times. Did you know?'

He had turned, but Aidan's face did not betray any surprise. 'No,' he said.

'He never replied to my letters. The only news I had of him came through his cousins, Robert and George.' Devlin smiled a little wryly. 'They've been my only contact with Michael for the past eleven years. My son feels rather bitter towards me.' He paused. 'In fact, I could go so far as to say, he sometimes gains some kind of vicarious pleasure from hurting me.'

'And why,' Aidan asked, his tone conversational, 'should your son show such an interest in me?'

Devlin laughed a little, fondly. To Aidan, it was an intensely aggravating sound. It reminded him of too many times that Devlin had laughed, too many things the man had found amusing. Not of itself unpleasant, the laugh was nevertheless unpleasant because of Devlin's arrogance, his insolent dismissal inherent in the sound. 'I'm sure Michael would have told you, O'Brien, about the Quest. That's what I've called it – it's provided me with a great deal of amusement over the years. And it's been very good for Michael – helped build his character. He expected you to be poor, you see, that he'd find you a broken man, and he was planning on making some kind of reparation, the foolish boy. But it proves he has a heart in him – I'm glad that he could show compassion to those less fortunate than himself, it's the mark of a gentleman, after all.' He looked around him. 'You've done very well, all things considered. I offer you my sincere congratulations.'

'How,' Aidan asked smoothly, 'did Kelly come to know about me?'

The face changed, contorted a little, and even Aidan was surprised when the silence went on and on.

'A letter, wasn't it?' Aidan prompted good-naturedly. He moved the whiskey in his glass round and about, smiling up at Devlin. 'Anna was always a tender-hearted creature. Loyal, too. How long were you married, now? A year?'

'Nineteen months.'

Devlin's face was an ugly shade of mottled pink. Aidan had the disturbing and rather exciting thought of him dropping dead on the rug, but then he remembered his guests on the lawn outside. 'Sit down, sit down, Retcliffe.' The word sounded strange in Aidan's mouth, but he liked the idea of it more and more. Michael was a Kelly, as his grandfather had been before him; Devlin was a bad seed, an accident of birth.

Devlin had not sat. 'Why are you looking at me like that?' There was almost an edge to the voice.

'I'm sorry. Old memories, I suppose. Are you after hearing the music outside? Takes you back, does it not?'

'I . . . ' Devlin hesitated. 'You were very fond of Anna, I know that. You must have worried about her, if she was happy . . . '

Aidan watched, and waited.

Devlin was drawing a slender leather notebook from his pocket, and from it he took a letter. He handed it to Aidan. The paper was soft from much handling, the folds had torn, in some places. 'Read it.' Devlin said, 'It's personal, but I'd like to share it with you. I feel she would have wished you to see it. It may put your mind at rest a little.'

And there it was, her handwriting, her words coming to him across the years, and he forgot Devlin, forgot Berrima, forgot, for a moment, that the words were written not to himself, but to another man.

17th November, 1847.

My Dearest Love,

 I want to write this, though I should tell you. You are before me now, asleep, and I do not wish to wake you.

 Some quarrels can be good things, many true words can be spoken in anger that, could one overlook the manner in which they are spoken, can lead to a greater understanding.

 I learnt last night, during our terrible quarrel, exactly how much you needed me, my love and my reassurance.

 My dear, they are yours, though I have been too self-conscious to be too open about my feelings, not knowing how they would be accepted.

 Please do not allow jealousy to ruin all we have. I want the following years to be a time when we are drawing closer to each other, not further apart. You are all that matters to me, the only man I ever loved. What occurred between Aidan O'Brien and myself was an innocent, childish affection that left me when you appeared in my life. I have been happier with you than I ever thought possible.

I should tell you this, I long to tell you this

So even in this he had been wrong. The only sure thing he had known in his life was proved to be as uncertain as everything else. There was no time to acknowledge what had occurred within him, to consider how things stood. Devlin was waiting for his wife's letter to be returned to him. Aidan kept his head bent until he felt sure of his self-control, but knew as he looked up that his eyes would still betray some moisture that he had not been able to blink back. Suspicious as he was of Devlin's motives, in this he had been right; Aidan's mind was more at rest; Anna had been happy, his tears had been his last gift to her.

'Thank you,' he said, handing the letter back. 'Thank you for showing this to me.'

Devlin looked at him, and did not appear smug, but rather startled, in fact. He held the letter, and fumbled a little as he put it away in his notebook. 'It means a lot to me, as you can imagine,' he muttered. 'She was the only fine thing ever to happen to me.'

And then, strangely enough, Aidan could think of no questions to ask. Even should Devlin decide to tell Aidan all the day-to-day details of his life with Anna it would mean nothing. Anna, through Devlin's eyes, was not the Anna Aidan had known. Nothing could bring that girl closer to him than she was already, that dream of his earliest feelings of love and tenderness. Aidan stood, moved to the French doors and opened them, for the room was uncomfortably warm. A faint cool breeze stirred, and Aidan noticed two facts about the scene before him that irritated him. One was that he could smell rain on the wind, could see where the stars were being swallowed one by one by the dark, invisible clouds; and second, the small group, for such it was, was now at the tables, eating. There could not be above thirty people in the group.

He stood gazing at the scene, yet spoke to the man behind him. 'Why are you here, Devlin? Can you really be thinking that you can make your boy return to England with you against his wishes?'

He turned, on this, and was in time to see Devlin's slow smile. 'No,' he replied. 'No, I don't really expect that I can persuade him to return with me. I wanted to see him. I . . . I miss him a great deal. I have no doubt that he'll return to England eventually. The place of one's birth always draws one, no matter what unhappiness it conjures up. Perhaps because the home of one's childhood is the only place where we actually believed that we could make the world into the place we wished it to be.'

Aidan stared at the man. 'And Tineranna did that for you?'

Devlin's mouth tightened a little. 'And why not? Did you think you were the only one with ambition in that schoolroom? Why do you think I worked so hard at my lessons? I wanted – though why I bother to tell you this, I don't know – to make my father proud of me. That's what I dreamed about through those interminable Latin and geography lessons, that my father would notice that I was excelling at something. You may think I failed my father, failed Tineranna. Yes, perhaps I did. But I did not plan to. The world as I wished it as a child had my father proud of me. That world rejected me before I could reject it. It's taken me until now, in my old age, to realize that I never could be what my father wished me to be.'

Aidan could almost have preferred the Devlin who spat bitter vituperative, for this man, owning to his weaknesses, was a disquieting spectacle. He growled, 'Then if you know how hard it is to live up to a father's demands, why the devil can't you leave Kelly alone to make his own choices?'

'His name,' Devlin said, mildly enough, 'is Michael.'

'He prefers Kelly. Will you not grant him that, at least? He's the one who has to walk about within his skin, answer to a name – let it

1018

be his choice – and he is a Kelly, as you are.'

Devlin had turned a little, made a gesture of dismissal. 'We won't quarrel about that.'

'By all means. I don't want to quarrel at all. It just seems a little strange, to me, that you're repeating the same pattern that you find so reprehensible in your father. One would have thought you'd be the first man to allow his son to find his own goals in life, make the most of what *he* feels to be his capabilities . . . '

'But in some things my father was right.' The blue eyes glowed as Devlin leaned forward to Aidan. 'Ah, yes, I'll admit that. My father was a strong man, capable of meeting any challenge in life. I was not strong, and I avoided confrontations. I took a cowardly approach to nearly every crisis of my life.' The voice was bitter, the man had forgotten Aidan, and was talking almost to himself. 'You know how pliant Anna was, how gentle – why even Celia, at the end, she'd stand up to me . . . But Anna – she never changed, she was always patient, kind . . . When she died, Serena Beresford said that she was a saint long before her death – and I do believe she was right.' The voice hardened. 'But there was a great deal of Anna in Michael. He had the disturbing ability of being able to shrug off slights, not that he was a coward, he was simply too . . . amenable. I had great plans for him, from the very beginning, and I saw, from my own experience, that such a nature, so like Anna's and with my own solitary inclinations – it wouldn't do. Do you understand?' His head came up for a sharp glance at Aidan, and before the latter could answer, 'No, I don't think you would understand. I arrived in Mittagong three days ago, and I've had your son pointed out to me. Just to look at him one could see that there was a boy who met life head on.' And oddly enough, the two men smiled at each other.

'Aye,' Aidan admitted, 'he does that. But that, too, brings problems. It may interest you to know, that there've been several times this past year when your son has pulled mine out of fights, helped him keep his head when he would have lost it.'

Devlin smiled grimly. 'That's his training,' he said, with a touch of satisfaction. 'I'm proud of the way that Michael has grown up. I've made a man of him, though many people criticized my methods. He was too soft as a child, too soft. If he's made fit for life, if he now succeeds at life, it's due to the man I've made him. It's like raw clay, you see; it must be fired, somehow. My success is due to the constant care I took with Michael as a child, to see that the process wasn't undermined by other people's good intentions. And you can see for yourself, that it worked. Yes, I can be very proud of Michael.' And only then did something like affection warm the voice.

Aidan was so taken aback by this speech that he could not immediately reply. His own children had brought themselves up, swinging in trees like 'possums at Port Davey, and though he and Maura admonished them, fed them and cared for them, he did not think either he or Maura regarded child-rearing as a process. He was still staring bemusedly at Devlin when there was a brief knock at the door.

When Aidan called out to enter, Berrima came into the room, stood there for a moment, glancing from one man to the other, trying to gauge something of the atmosphere, of what lay behind the tension between the two. 'If you're waiting for Kelly to come home – they may be a while – would you like some supper?'

Devlin smiled at Berrima, and it was a smile that bore all his old charm. 'Why, yes, thank you.'

Introductions were made, and the three walked down the lawn together. Aidan left Berrima with Devlin long enough to warn Thomas of their guest's identity, before bringing Devlin across to him. Aidan was able to pull back from the crowd a little, growled through clenched teeth, though only Berrima heard him, 'I'm gonna kill Kelly. I'm gonna kill 'im, I swear it . . . '

'Did Kelly lie about his name?' she asked. 'Is it really Retcliffe?'

'Arra, he didn't lie. He's a Kelly alright. Himself, there, he's the one who's changed his name.' He turned to look at Berrima. She was staring at him. 'I should have told you, I suppose – but how was I to know the man would really come all this way. Thomas said he would, of course. Did I . . . Did I ever tell you about Anna O'Hagan?'

'No,' Berrima breathed, not believing the calm tone of his voice, not believing whatever was happening.

'She was a girl in Killaloe. She's dead, now . . . '

'Maura told me about her,' Berrima interrupted, 'at Glenleigh, years ago. I thought . . . she said I looked like her.'

'Aye, you do, a little. I was betrothed to Anna, y'see, and the bastard seduced her, married her. She was Kelly's mother.'

And Berrima understood the incident at Glenleigh, now, remembered Maura's spite as she spoke of the dead girl. Now Berrima knew why.

Aidan was leaning back against a tree trunk with his arms folded. 'I married Maura to forget – that's why the marriage was doomed, I'm thinking. 'Twas a sin against God, and against Maura – and God and Maura knew.'

Berrima moved to him, as if sensing his distress. 'Maura loved you, Aidan. She was happy with you.'

1020

'Was she?' He was unconvinced. 'I never loved Maura. And it's to my shame that I could never make her believe that I did.'

So it was all becoming clear. And with a sense of horror, Berrima began to realize that she did not want to know. It was not a simple story of the past – for it was going on still. Kelly was part of Aidan's past, and even more so, the man speaking now to Thomas. Perhaps that was why Aidan did not speak of it. Perhaps it was more frightening than he could bear, and he had the knowledge, all these years, that it was not over. Perhaps it never would be.

He looked down at her, for she was so very quiet. She had paled a little, and when she spoke, 'Aidan?' her voice broke into a strange little squeak on his name, so that she had to repeat it. 'Aidan – Kelly . . . He's not . . . he's not your son, is he?'

He burst into laughter. He laughed and laughed, lifted her up and whirled her about then he set her down, but held her to him. 'Och, I love y'!' he grinned, all unconscious of the fact that this was the first time he had said these words, 'I love y', y' evil-minded little woman!'

When it began to rain, everyone adjourned to the house.

Berrima was relaxed enough, seated in the parlour-dining room, to make conversation with Devlin Retcliffe, asking him safe questions about Killaloe, and even Tineranna, and she learnt much, by this, of their backgrounds.

Aidan covered his confusion well, but he could not overcome his feeling that the past was being raked up within his own house, and by a man who had played such a culpable part in it. And yet he coped, for much of the conversation held no fear, no hurt and horror. It was possible, he saw with a shock, to find things that meant something to each of them, the christenings and weddings on the estate, the ceilis, the fairs in Killaloe and Limerick and Ennis. They chose the good things to discuss, and Aidan saw that this was due to Berrima, who seemed to sense the slightest tension, and steered the conversation to safe topics.

Aidan was surprised when Devlin half-stood, suddenly, and then he heard the sounds that the other man had obviously been waiting for, all evening.

There was much laughter from those gathered on the verandahs, and Liam's voice, 'Berri? Father?' He and Clemency entered the room, laughing, Clemency walking in with her shoulders hunched, in a great coat that came down to her heels, and a large black hat down over her eyes. Liam did not notice Devlin, 'Father McBride loaned her his hat – and the coat belonged to his great-grandfather – would you believe it . . . '

It was only then that something in the tension of their father and Berrima communicated itself to them; they became aware that the other guests had not clustered about their host but were keeping a distance, as if they sensed something was not quite right.

'Devlin Retcliffe – my son, Liam . . . my daughter, Clemency . . .'

Liam snatched the hat from Clemency's head before shaking hands with the man. Jaysus, Mary and Joseph, so here was trouble at last . . . He should have seen what was coming, should have connected the tenant of Summer Hill with that other Devlin of Aidan's youth. But it was too late.

'I've already met your daughter.' Devlin Retcliffe was smiling at the woman in the outsized greatcoat. All eyes turned to Clemency. She unbuttoned the greatcoat, and allowed Liam to help her free of it before she placed her hand in Devlin's.

Aidan watched her, in ivory coloured silk, a fine lace shawl over her shoulders; she wore a gold locket that had been one of Maura's few pieces of jewelry, bought when the family had begun to prosper. Aidan glanced at Berrima, and he smiled; she was right, he was very proud of Clemency tonight, not only for her looks but for her manners, just the right amount of coolness when she said, 'I'm delighted that you could come this evening, Mr Retcliffe. Michael will be so pleased.'

Kelly opened the barn doors with his mind still occupied with the thought of Clemency and the problems that lay ahead. He had made Clemency promise not to break the news to her father before he arrived at the house . . . He swung the doors back with more energy than he need have, scowling before him – and stopped.

The light from his own carriage lamps lit the inside of the barn and showed the strange carriage lying there. In the first loosebox a chestnut rolled white-rimmed eyes at him. A hired buggy, he judged, leading his own carriage horses into the barn.

He was just lighting the lamp when the voice spoke behind him. 'Ullo, Master Michael.'

Kelly whirled about, stood staring, felt the blood drain from his face.

The small, grey-haired man came from the opdm main doors. 'You'd remember me, maybe, I was your father's groom for a year or two before you left . . . He was kind enough to bring me as well as his valet . . . Dovey's the name.' Still Kelly did not move. 'I . . . I'm sorry I give you such a start.' He stepped forward. 'Ere, let me put the horses away for you . . .'

1022

'You leave the horses alone!' Kelly came to life, and Dovey froze. In a calmer voice, 'What are you doing here?' Dovey was silent, looking most unhappy. 'He's not here.' The little man shifted from one foot to another. 'He's not here. He can't be *here*.'

Dovey looked unhappier still. 'Yessir. Yessir, Mr Retcliffe is here – up at the house . . . ' His eyes were on the floor. This was a nasty business . . . He could not meet the younger man's eyes.

When the sound of the doors being closed came to their ears, they both turned quickly. Aidan stood there, still holding one of the doors partly open. Kelly stiffened, but the Irishman was looking at Dovey.

'I'm sorry we didn't think of you earlier – Mrs Kirwin has some supper for you in the kitchen.'

'Thank you, sir.' But he hesitated. 'I'll put the horses away first, sir.'

Kelly was still standing by the horses' heads. 'No, leave them.'

Dovey's sense of duty was overcoming his fear. 'I couldn't allow you to do that, sir. It's my job . . . '

'Go!'

'Yessir!'

He scuttled past Aidan, out the door, and Aidan closed it, firmly but gently, behind him.

For a long moment they gazed at each other, Kelly with troubled eyes. 'I did warn you. I offered to go.'

Aidan sighed. 'I know, lad. 'Tis not myself I'm worried about, now. 'Tis Liam's career, and my own fault it is for not making a clean breast of the matter when I first came here. Still – we'll face the problem when it comes . . . Finish there and come up to the house as soon as you can . . . '

'No!'

Aidan had half-turned, looked back now with a scowl at the pale, set face. 'No. I'm not going to the house while he's there.'

Aidan studied him for a moment, finding it difficult to understand; it was not like the man he had come to know; Kelly was tense, unapproachable, his whole stance that of unyielding stubbornness. Aidan said softly, 'You hate him that much?'

'I'll pack my things and go to stay in Mittagong until this is settled. Tell my father I'll see him at Summer Hill in the morning.' And he was marching off towards his room.

A roar, 'You come back here!!'

Kelly stopped, froze, body rigid with anger.

'Until I give you your pay, you're still working for me – now unharness those horses!'

Kelly turned slowly to gaze at him. For a second neither man moved, then Kelly walked to the steaming, restive animals and began to remove their harness.

Aidan watched him carefully for a while, then moved to one of the looseboxes and leaned against the door. After a pause, 'The trouble with you is that you've no staying power.' Kelly threw him a black look. 'You're running scared, aren't you?'

'I'm not running . . . '

'Y'are.'

'You don't know my . . . !' He stopped, bent his head to the harness straps.

Aidan was almost amused. 'You were about to say I don't know your father.'

'Yes.'

Aidan took out his pipe and lit it, replacing the match carefully in the box after extinguishing it; he felt calmer, had regained his self-control. 'I'm understanding a little of what's going on. He's baiting me, hoping I'll throw you out. On the one hand, I want to . . . ' Kelly looked over at him, Aidan meeting his look with equal grimness. 'But on the other hand, I don't want to give Devlin the satisfaction.'

For a moment he studied Kelly through the pipe smoke. 'What is it, do you think? Does he want you so badly? Or does he hate me so much?'

Kelly was out of sight behind the horses, but his voice came drily, 'You've just summed up the two driving forces in my father's life.'

Aidan raised his eyebrows. 'He hates me?' Hate was a strong word, one did not hate anything one did not respect, and fear. Aidan looked pleased. 'That's interesting,' he murmured.

Kelly had straightened, was gazing at him. 'Did Clemency tell you . . . ?'

'Tell me what?'

'Nothing. Sir, don't underestimate my father.'

'I did that once before.' Aidan's voice was hard. 'It cost me eight years of my life. I'm not about to do it again.'

'I was riding past Summer Hill yesterday and his carriage passed me coming in the gates,' Clemency said. 'He recognized me, it seemed, and asked to speak to me about Michael Kelly. So I had tea with him, and he made it clear he'd stop at nothing in order to cause trouble between Papa and Kelly. He thinks, then, that Papa will send Kelly away – and Kelly will go home to England. It's foolishness, but he hinted that he had enough information to ruin Papa.'

Liam growled. 'I don't see what all the fuss is about. The man might not say anything – and if he does, I don't see that it will make any difference. Richard Dry's father was an ex-convict – I never could work out why Father was so ashamed of it. I'll make an announcement to the papers, if that'll keep Father happy, break the news to the press before Retcliffe, or Kelly, or whatever he calls himself can make any trouble.'

'I don't think he's a vicious man,' Berrima murmured. The three of them sat in the office, waiting for Aidan to return with Kelly. Devlin had said he'd like to walk on the cool of the verandah until they returned. 'He's simply very hurt that Kelly can so easily turn his back on all he tried to do for him.'

Liam did not answer, but prowled up and down the room, and Berrima could tell that despite his confident manner, he was worried.

She thought, it's not just Liam. Aidan has made too many enemies in this town, no one will allow him to forget his past. And he's at a stage of his life when he'd like to believe he's achieved something. This would be an enormous set-back. He'd have to build a reputation all over again – and there are some who will never allow him to forget.

It was not until much later that Aidan discovered how Kelly and Clemency and Liam had spent their evening. Kelly remained with his father in the office for some time, and the O'Briens were able to spend some time with their guests. Afterwards, Kelly joined them on the verandah, stood beside Clemency, and told a startled Aidan that they had been married that evening, in the township of Berrima.

Aidan had embraced a rather apprehensive Clemency and shaken Kelly's hand, before the news had quite reached him in all its manifestations.

Kelly said, soberly, while the others were clustering about Clemency, 'And my father would like to speak to you, sir. He's in your office.' Aidan grinned, could not understand that Kelly could not see the humour in the situation. If his life was going to be one long farce, he told himself, walking quickly back down the verandah to his office doors, then, begod, he would enjoy it.

His humour left him after only two minutes with Devlin. There was little doubt that the man was emotionally as well as physically ill, that the news of the unsuitable marriage had driven him to the edge of hysteria.

1025

Aidan could not reach him; the garbled plans for an annulment, the man's desperation, stirred Aidan's pity even while it irritated him almost beyond endurance.

'Let him go!' he almost shouted at Devlin. 'This has been inevitable since those two set eyes on each other, can't you see that? They love each other and they're married! I don't know if I'm any more pleased about this than you are, but it's done. It's done, Devlin! Accept it, man!'

'It's reckless, irresponsible – no thought for anyone but himself—'

'Like you, when you eloped with Anna?'

The words acted as a kind of stunning blow to the other man. For several minutes he sat in his chair, and did not speak. Aidan could hear the little band, now in the ballroom, strike up a waltz. 'Devlin? Come join the celebrations. Take it with good grace, for your son's sake.'

Devlin lifted a greyish tinged face to him. 'No,' he said quietly. 'Show me the way to the stables. I'll see Michael at Summer Hill tomorrow.'

Aidan would have liked to have struck the man, so great was his exasperation with the man's selfishness. But there was no point. He stood, tired. 'Come,' he said, and led the way along the hall to the kitchen.

It was empty, and Aidan wondered where Charity and Job and Devlin's coachman, Dovey, were to be found – perhaps in the ballroom with the dancing, it was that kind of informal evening – but Aidan continued through the back door and out on to the rear verandah with the almost somnambulistic Devlin; he was not about to lead him into the middle of the festivities and risk a scene of recriminations for all his friends to witness.

The yard was silent, it was raining softly. The coolness of it, falling on his face seemed to revive Devlin. 'You're delighted at this, I daresay. I wouldn't put it past you to have suggested it to Michael.' Devlin stood in the rain, unmindful of it. 'You don't care if he ruins himself – you'd like that.'

Aidan kept walking. 'I don't know what y'r talking about – they surprised me as much as you . . . '

'And he'll stay here – you'll allow him to stay here. Do you have any idea what he's leaving behind in England? He has responsibilities, O'Brien.' And he took Aidan's arm, pulled at him a little. 'For God's sake. I'm begging you – don't allow him to do this! If we both fight them, we could press for an annulment . . . '

'Get away! Are y' mad?'

'There were plans – plans made years ago! The estate – what will become of that! How would you feel, O'Brien, if your son was lured away to waste his life on the other side of the world from you! If he left all this . . . ?'

'It'd be his decision! Don't you understand? When will you let go! He doesn't want your plans! He wants his own plans!'

'If you told him to go! If you told your daughter you won't allow this marriage. How can I make you see? Michael will be turning his back on a brilliant future – to stay here in Australia! He doesn't love your daughter, he's doing this to spite me! You can't allow this marriage! You can't!'

They had almost reached the corner of the house, the area had broadened into the stableyard. Aidan stopped, turning to stare at the other man, and squinted at him through the light rain. Softly, 'Y're crazy, Devlin. I've finally realized it. Y'r as mad as a March hare . . . '

He went to continue walking, but Devlin had taken his arm. 'You'll never understand, will you? You feel you can despise me because I want more for my son than you do for yours . . . '

'You want it for yourself! You always did!'

'I am an ambitious man! I'll not apologize for it . . . !'

'You sold out on everyone! Y'r father, y'r faith, Anna, y'r son . . . !'

'My father's ideals were not mine! When the Famine came, it was up to me to keep us from bankruptcy . . . '

'And y' did that! At the cost of everything William Kelly believed in!'

'You dare to talk like that! You who swore seditious oaths against the government . . . '

'The British government . . . !'

'Your all-consuming pride . . . I saw you there, in the dock receiving sentence. You were too arrogant even to plead innocent – you'd have murdered Hubert Osborne if you could! You'd have murdered me! It's your jealousy and your pride that gave you those eight years in prison, O'Brien. And what did it prove? At the end of it all, now that you've turned your back on Ireland and her struggle for independence, now that you've sold out yourself by coming here and living better on this soil than any Irish landlord could in Ireland – what did it all prove, all your heroics?'

Aidan smiled a little, but there was no humour in it. For the man was right in this, at least. 'Nothing,' he said. 'Eight years gone. But it's behind me. I have everything, now.'

Devlin's voice was low. 'Then give Michael back to me. He's all I have.'

'He goes where he wants!'

'He's nothing here! Before this business of his mother's letter, he was quite happy to settle at Burnley Grange, to marry a fine girl, Eleanor Beresford – he needs a wife like Eleanor, O'Brien. An English wife! For Michael is English, our land, our roots are in England – he belongs in England! He'll be grateful, someday, for these steps I'm taking. But don't stand in his way, O'Brien! For God's sake, don't use your influence against me! Don't take your hatred of me out on Michael . . . '

In the feeble light from the lamps outside the stables, Aidan could yet pick out every feature of Devlin's face. The rain ran down the hollows of his cheeks, and he looked old. The sunken features were almost frightening in their grim earnestness, the eyes burnt unnaturally. 'Admit it,' he said hoarsely, 'you hate me. Even as a boy you hated my wealth, my position . . . '

Aidan found his voice. 'I despised you, because you were a snivelling little coward – and y'r still a coward. Can't live y'r own life – can't face the future without y'r son – not for his sake – for yours.'

'Everything I've done has been for Michael! Everything!'

'Without Michael lording it at Burnley Grange you feel you've lived for nothing – achieved nothing worthwhile! And you'd be right, Devlin. You were a parasite from the day you were born – and now y'r a dried-up husk of a man. Y'r pathetic.'

'I married Anna.'

Aidan had turned away, but he stopped at the words . . .

'I married Anna. I gave her everything, rescued her from what would have been degradation and poverty. That was all you could have offered her!'

Oh, he was calm, so calm. Never had he felt so much in control of himself, his words. 'Don't try to bait me. Anna's dead. Even she has escaped you.' And he had begun to turn away again when the words were breathed behind him.

'And I had you transported.'

Aidan stopped dead, felt his heart stop. For a long moment the only sound was the rain all around them. Neither man noticed that they were becoming saturated. They had eyes only for each other, Aidan's face closed, expressionless, Devlin's teeth showing a little in a smile that was not a smile.

'Who do you think helped convince Osborne that you were at Ceelohg that night?'

Silence. Devlin shifted a little, moved back a little, watched Aidan warily, but could not stop himself, it seemed, from pouring out the dangerous words.

Or was there another motive? Despite his strong sense of self-preservation, his caution, Aidan was being pulled down into the old rage, the anger of the past, with each clipped phrase that Devlin spoke. 'I hardly need to have bothered, for look where your lunacy led you – to burn down Tineranna. What a fool you were! For you loved it more than I did. I used to watch you, as a child, running your hands over the furniture, touching the velvet of the drapes. It used to make me sick to see your grubby little peasant's hands on our belongings – but my mother said you were to be pitied, you and your family, with your genteel pretensions. We used to watch you and laugh . . . '

Aidan, stoney-faced, was moving forward, towards him a little. Devlin shifted back, but the movement brought his wandering mind back to the point. 'Didn't you wonder about that pardon? Old Osborne, there in Ceelohg like an old spider cocooned in his web – he lived to be eighty-six, O'Brien! Osborne and his conscience – sending for the Dean, who sent for the magistrate, Clarkson, so matters would be tidy when the old man died. He didn't mention me – I grant him that – but he sent for that priest, McDonnagh, and they all sat about and decided that you had been most unjustly treated. Osborne signed one of those fearfully boring death-bed confessions – then lived another four years amongst the threats of the populace and the disapprobation of his peers. When I found out that they'd granted you a pardon, I was past caring. You'd been in prison for eight years by then.'

Aidan was upon him, sobbing with rage; they went down rolling, Devlin struggling to reach the gun in his pocket, but Aidan forcing his hand away from the weapon, the other hand on Devlin's throat, pushing it back . . . It could not be a fair fight; though half a head taller, Devlin was no fighter. Aidan had picked him up, struck him hard, followed after the fallen figure, picked him up to strike him again – this time when Devlin fell, it was such a distance that, stunned as he was, some instinct for self-preservation had him groping for, and finding, the small revolver in his waistcoat.

Aidan paused, standing almost above Devlin, as the gun was pointed at his chest. Devlin edged backwards, used his free hand to help himself get to his knees, still kept moving backwards, ridding himself of the threatening presence that stood too close to him, but oblivious of the mud and the pools of water on the ground. His chest ached, he was dizzy, and knew he could not find his feet – but keep the gun on O'Brien, keep it upon him . . . 'And . . . and that's not all. You . . . you left them – your wife and children, your family . . . you left them to go off in chains with your pride – neighbours of

1029

theirs were evicted, or took to begging – unknown people were dying of starvation on the roadsides . . . but your family lived – you want to know why?'

Aidan stood, swaying slightly with exhaustion, his hands still itching to get at Devlin – but he was cool, still, he was not afraid of the gun, knew Devlin of old, knew he would not have the courage . . .

'Father McDonnagh helped them – they'd get no help from the likes of you, sure . . . '

'It was I.'

Aidan scoffed, 'Get away . . . '

'I gave them food, money . . . I kept them alive right through the Famine. The passage money to Australia – where do you think that came from?'

'Y'r lying!'

'In return for your wife.'

The man standing before him did not move. Devlin swallowed, sensing death in that stone-like figure, like . . . yes, like Corrie O'Neill . . .

Devlin's voice was low, but every word carried. He no longer cared what happened, he had lost everything. He would make sure that he left O'Brien, too, with nothing. 'I came back to Killaloe in 1853, I hired Maura to help me with my correspondence when I fell and broke my wrist – but she was more than a secretary, O'Brien. We were lovers, all through that spring . . . '

He stopped, for he thought, at first, that O'Brien was sobbing. But no, the broad shoulders were heaving with silent laughter.

'What do you find so amusing? That your wife was my mistress . . . ?'

The laughter was no longer silent, O'Brien roared his delight, and Devlin could only stare at the man as if he had gone mad. He gripped the gun tighter, wanting to shoot his adversary, standing there, mocking him, as he had always mocked him. 'Stop it . . . ' he hissed, 'it's the truth. Ask your brother – he'd know. Ask him, if you don't believe me. *Stop laughing!*'

Aidan, off-balance, stumbled backwards a little, came up against the side of the house, and leaned there, weak with laughter. Each time he looked at Devlin, his shaking hands holding the gun, his slack mouth casting slurs upon Maura's unassailable virtue, he laughed the wilder. 'Maura?' he managed to gasp, '*My* wife – and *you?*'

'It's true!' Almost a scream. 'I swear by Almighty God! It's true!'

1030

Aidan was unmoved by the oath; managed to control his mirth to the point where he could study Devlin, on his knees, oblivious to the mud. Mud coated the side of his face, the expensive suit and coat. Almost to himself, Aidan murmured, 'Eight years . . . It was almost worth it. Yes, by God – to see you here tonight, it was almost worth it.'

For a long moment, Devlin stared at him, then, slowly, slowly, his shoulders sagged a little; the gun came down slightly; Devlin's eyes had not left Aidan's face. 'You don't believe me.' And his voice was soft, as if he, too, spoke to himself. 'You're so . . . confident, aren't you? So . . . sure. I think that's what I've hated most about you. Always so sure.'

'There's the barn, there.' Aidan's voice was hard, his eyes were hard. 'Go get y'r carriage, Devlin.'

He walked over to the barn doors, thumped upon them briefly, and turned back towards the house without looking upon Devlin again.

'I'll kill you!' Devlin screamed, and he brought the pistol up once more, sighted down it at the broad back, 'I did have Maura! Do you hear me? Ask your family! Turn around, damn you! Ask your family! They knew! The whole village knew!'

He went to climb to his feet, but stumbled forward a little to his knees again – footsteps behind him, and Dovey was at his side, helping him up, attempting, gently, to take the gun.

'Mr Retcliffe, sir . . . '

Aidan paid no attention to the voices behind him. He was exhausted, weak with laughter, kept touching the side of the house – his house, his house, for support as he walked towards the back verandah, and Berrima waiting somewhere within. Behind him the voice kept screaming, above the servant's pleas,

'I did have her! I did! Do you hear me, O'Brien? I did!'

96

Aidan made his way up the steps and through the back door, thankful to find both the kitchen and the hallway deserted. He passed the hall mirror on his way to the stairs and almost laughed outright at the sight of himself; saturated with rain, patched indiscriminately with mud, and there was a cut on his forehead, made in the struggle with Devlin.

Aidan stood smiling at his bedraggled reflection, while the music from the dance floor waltzed over him. He was exhausted, yet elated, turned and climbed the stairs, wondering what suit to change into for the rest of this dramatic, though less than dignified, evening . . .

He was on the third stair from the top, hidden by the bend in the staircase, when he heard the voices in the hall below him. Two new arrivals, speaking in subdued voices as they looked about, but he could hear them, could see a little of a woman's dress as the rumble of her companion's voice became words.

' . . . all happening at once. Though disasters do, don't they?'

'Joe Danaher said he's hardly been seen all evening – Sam, he may be dreadfully upset . . . '

'If he is, he'll want to face it on his own, I know enough of Aidan O'Brien to realize that. Where were we supposed to put our coats?'

Sam and Tessa Russell headed towards the rear of the house, unattended, as all the staff had been drawn to the egalitarian festivities in the ballroom and on the front verandah. Aidan stood in the darkness of the stairs and waited, and as they returned, he heard, ' . . . could be just an act of spite – a lot of lies. For all the external sanctimoniousness – oh, there's a past there, mark my words . . . ' Outrage in Tessa's usually mild tones.

'Too many details, too many names – the probation station, the fact that Berrima's parents met him at Port Arthur – I know how you feel, Tessa, but it's true, all right.'

They passed beneath him. 'What will we say, Sam? What will we say to him to tell him that we don't care, that it makes no difference . . . ?'

'Ignore it altogether. No point in bringing it up – like you say, it makes no difference, so we won't point it out . . . '

Tessa had stopped. From where Aidan stood he could make out her brown hand gripping the newel post; she was facing away from him, towards the front doors. 'But everyone else?' Her voice was low, but it carried easily up the stairs to their silent host, 'Where are all Aidan's friends tonight, Sam? Compare tonight with the crowd who came the night of the hospital ball . . . '

'They'll come around, even if only from curiosity.' Sam's voice faded a little, Tessa followed. 'Let's go join them, Aidan might be back by . . . '

The voices were drowned in the strains of a polka as the door to the ballroom was opened, then closed, muting the sound of the celebrating once more.

Aidan, numbly, began climbing the remaining stairs. His chest ached, painfully, as if he had been kicked viciously and could not collect his wits nor his breath. It was not Devlin . . . his confused thoughts told him, Devlin would not play his trump card so soon. No, it had been earlier, early enough to circulate through every family in the Highlands, big house and shearer's hut, and damn his name before all of them.

He stopped at the head of the stairs. A vivid picture came to him of Matty – Matty who now had no home; Matty, through the smoke and heat haze of the campfire. The Woman in Black, purveyor of death . . . ? In her rage and her bitterness she had hoped for Liam's death in her vision of him being consumed by flames. She had been cheated of that – perhaps she had resorted, then, to the one weapon of vengeance that she still possessed. Was Matty his Woman in Black?

Aidan dragged tiredly to his room, and changed into clean clothes without any real memory, afterwards, of doing so. He descended the stairs, but did not turn towards that room where the floorboards shook with the beat of merry feet, where the sounds of a reel, and laughter and singing, came to him where he stood in the deserted hall. No. Not yet. He could not face the pity on his friends' faces, the calculated, quizzing of his enemies. Not just yet. He took his hat from the hallstand, left the house by the back door, and in the barn, saddled Blue. He rode off, directionless, down through the paddocks at the rear of the stables.

Clemency sat at her dressing table in her bedroom, still in her wedding gown, yanking out her hair pins from her elaborate coiffure with a perverse disregard for her own comfort, and cursing Devlin Retcliffe with all the considerable flair of a whaling and sealing man's vocabulary.

She had thought there would be time, days, weeks, perhaps, in order to explain to Kelly; but now, of course, everything was ruined. He would never see reason, now. He had gone through the evening with what that idiot Sophie Lawler called, 'the most *passionate* expression when he looks at you . . . ' Clemency had smiled, graciously, avoided looking at Kelly as much as possible, knowing the controlled hunger in his eyes was not born of a warm and tender longing. Except for my head on a platter, she thought, as the orchestra struck up the bridal waltz and her new and temporary husband swept her on to the floor.

She had escaped at ten, according to a pre-arranged agreement with Aidan and Liam, who were telling the guests that the young couple had escaped quietly and taken the late train to Sydney for a few days' honeymoon. That would avoid any practical jokes – the last thing she wanted was a hoolie.

The door of her room was locked. Ten minutes ago, Kelly had knocked, tried the handle, and when he could not gain admittance had called her name, softly, once or twice. He did not make a fuss. Clemency, seated on the edge of her chair, holding her breath, had been glad for that. He had gone away, then; one could not hear footsteps on the thick carpet, but she had heard the door of the green guest room, which a sickeningly coy Charity had prepared for them, open and close.

She felt very mean, pulled her brush through her tangle of curls and despised herself for not managing this matter more honestly, for being afraid, even now, of a confrontation with a man who was obviously genuinely fond of her. She would see him tomorrow morning – sure he was probably too angry to wish to speak with her tonight, anyway . . . Her hand slowed in her brush strokes and despite herself, she thought of Kelly alone in the large double bed in the green room. The furniture was a matching walnut suite, made by craftsmen in Melbourne. For a moment there was a warming vision of herself within that large walnut bed with Michael Kelly – it was her right, she told herself. But no. That would be closing the trap over her head. She had done what she had to do. Devlin Retcliffe, with the thought that exposing Aidan O'Brien would mean a slur on the name of any grandchildren he might have, had been vanquished, and her father's name was safe.

She smiled, remembering her last view of Devlin, leaving Aidan's office with her father; even then, something in Retcliffe's stooped shoulders told her she had won. It made up for having to sit through that travesty of a civilized tea ceremony at Summer Hill yesterday, when the clever, twisted old man had skimmed and danced with his Saxon rhetoric all about the fact that if Aidan did not tell Kelly to leave, 'Unfortunate memories may be stirred in the ensuing antagonisms . . . Old quarrels brought to life . . . your father's rather tragic recklessness . . . ' The old bastard had looked so regretful.

It was a pity Aidan would never know the truth, for she knew her father well enough to see that this sort of sacrifice would not have his respect let alone his approval. He would try to tell her his reputation did not mean that much to him, and yet hadn't he been boring herself and Liam to death for years, now, talking of respectability? It was the one area in which she felt her father to be a complete fool – but if he cared for his precious reputation, she would help him defend it. As long as he didn't allow his fondness for Kelly to stop her achieving that annulment.

In her mirror she had a clear view of the door, looked up at the slight sound, in time to see the key pop out of the lock and fall softly to the carpet. With barely a sound, the lock was betraying her, the handle turning – and Kelly was standing inside the door, closing it behind him. She stared at him. 'How did you do that?'

He held up a key. 'From Charity's collection.' The other hand held what appeared to be a thin rod of metal. 'From the kitchen drawer – a meat skewer.' The latter was laid carefully on her book case. The former was used to lock the door from the inside, then pocketed, along with its twin from the carpet.

There was nowhere to run. She sat there, stiffly, watching him approach with his easy and negligent grace, smiling just a little, and it was even more worrying that there was no sign of rage upon his face. He stood behind her, and they both, for the first time, studied themselves together, caught, in their finery, except for Clemency's tumbled curls, as if for a formal portrait. Then his hands were on her shoulders, moving gently to her neck, resting there, his long fingers at the hollows of her throat.

Her stays were far too tight, not only could she barely breath with the feel, the light, maddening touch of his hands on her, but she was aware that her breasts were pushed up into the bodice of the low-cut gown. When his eyes left the mirror and looked down at her, her palms, clutching the edge of the dressing table and her hairbrush, were damp with her terror and . . . no, not at all. *I feel nothing, nothing, nothing, nothing . . .*

'Let me help you.' His hands were lifting her heavy hair, reaching for the clasp of her locket. 'No,' he murmured, 'you'll have to hold your hair out of the way.' He looked at her in the mirror.

Why was it so hard to let go of the dressing table flange, to place the brush on its surface, to raise her arms? 'Clemency?' softly, almost encouragingly. 'Lift your hair.'

Slowly, she raised her arms, and held her hair away from the back of her neck. His eyes met hers in the mirror, then lowered themselves to the minute clasp of Maura's locket. It came away, she felt it, but he paused, and gazed at her for a moment, and she felt vulnerable, exposed, somehow, before the heavy locket had swung forward, brushing each of her breasts, and was before her. She snatched it, holding it in her fist as her hair fell forwards over her shoulders. 'I tried to tell you last night,' she said, her chin raised. 'But then I grew afraid. I thought you wouldn't have gone through with it, if you'd known what I was trying to do.'

'Oh, but I would have.'

Again the maddening hands on her shoulders, but she was puzzled, watched his smiling reflection warily, 'You would?'

'Yes, you do me an injustice, Clemency. I perfectly understand your desire to protect your father.'

'Oh. That's grand, so.'

'What I find so difficult to forgive is that you stooped to such low methods of achieving your ends.'

She scowled at him, turned on her chair and rose, moved across the room. 'You told me your father demanded to see the wedding certificate. We might have been able to fabricate the wedding, but we couldn't fabricate that.'

Kelly sat down on her dressing table chair after swinging it about a little, the better to watch her. 'And now you feel that my father will keep his silence.'

She approached him, tried to appeal to the man behind the implacably cool exterior, 'Kelly, I know I've hurt you, but won't you be generous and forgive me? We can sort this out amicably, sure. Once your father leaves Mittagong we can have the marriage annulled – your father won't know, he'll be on his way to England by then. Sure, he's probably so disgusted with you for marrying an O'Brien that he'll never bother you again with all that filial devotion pishoguery – I may have done you a favour.'

'There are compensations, then, you think?' Still his expression was unreadable. 'Plots within plots . . . ' She gazed at him, unsure. He sighed. 'So that was it. A brief marriage that is no marriage. You planned it very well.'

'I had to.' She tried to smile a little, testing; but there was no answering empathy in the man's face. 'Papa's become so socially conscious these past few years. He's worked so hard to build a new life here. *I* don't care if people know he's an emancipist. But *he* cares. I don't want him hurt.'

'Commendable.'

'If . . . if we're quiet, no one need know we're not sleeping in the same room.' She glided over to the door, was about to urge him to go, but stopped with her hand on the knob. She was startled to turn and find Kelly directly behind her. He grinned, suddenly, and leaned against the door.

'Do you have the feeling, Mrs Kelly, that we've played this scene before?'

'Give me the key. Go to the green room . . . '

'The green room,' he drawled, 'that's what they call the room in a

1036

theatre where actors meet after a performance – a place where they can wind down and relax the tensions of a demanding evening . . . '

'I'm not listening to this – *give me the bloody key.*'

' . . . and tonight you gave a magnificent performance, my dear.'

She had whirled away from his closeness. 'I'm tired, and I don't want to fight with you . . . '

'I, too, am tired, Mrs Kelly . . . '

She turned at the first note of menace in his voice, and found the look that had so fascinated Sophie to be there upon his face once more. No – she must be careful; men were strange creatures, too easily, for them, anger could be turned into desire. She moved a little further from him, still facing him, feeling her heart thudding against her stays and cursing herself for having Aunt Ottilia, who'd helped her dress, lace her so tight, with all her inherent strength upon the laces. She began to understand, now, why illustrations of women in perilous situations always had them with a hand clasped to their bosoms; it was a fact that she was only now discovering, that agitation and a crushing physical pressure on her ribs and lungs made one fragile indeed.

'Kelly, I feel quite ill,' she said truthfully enough. 'All the excitement of the past few days, running the property single-handed while you men were at the fire . . . '

'Poor pet,' he said gently, moving towards her.

'Kelly, I've treated you with a total lack of respect. I wouldn't blame you, sure, if you never spoke to me again. Tricking you into marrying me was a low, despicable subterfuge that could have ruined your life. It was beneath contempt . . . ' They moved about the room, Clemency backwards, facing him, as if involved in a dance where the partners do not touch, round and about the furniture. 'We have to stay calm, and not complicate things further, you see that, of course. A rash move – what I mean is . . . Begod, you wouldn't want to stay married to a woman such as myself, only think on it! Wearing trousers, berating you constantly, spending all your money – just look at those three wardrobes of clothes! – you couldn't afford me, Kelly, you must think very carefully before you allow one moment of blind lust to sweep away your reason and leave you . . . '

He had collapsed into a little armchair near the window, and for a moment she thought he was weeping – he was, but with laughter, his head in his hands. He could not speak for laughing, and she stood and watched him with her mouth slightly open, too taken aback to think. 'Oh, dear . . . Clemency . . . ' when he could finally find his voice, 'Please don't worry. Your virtue is safe, for I won't insist on consumating our marriage tonight.' He looked up at her with his eyes filled with amusement.

'Then you agree about the annulment,' she prompted, glad to see, though she did not like being the butt of it, that his amusement had dispersed his anger and his desire.

'Oh, no.' He was sobering very quickly, now. There was that familiar and unpleasantly steely look to the grey eyes. 'No annulment, Mrs Kelly. You see, I still want you as my wife. I don't have any regrets.'

Her ribs began to feel they were crossing each other like lattice-work; one hand to her chest, she tried to take calm breaths. 'When you've had a few days to consider . . . This is no basis for a marriage, deceit, and betrayal . . . '

His mouth turned up, slowly, the grey eyes studying her. 'I'll find it in my heart to forgive you, Clemency.'

'I don't want to be forgiven!' She stamped her foot. 'I want an annulment!'

'On what grounds?' the voice velvet.

'Why, non-consummation, of course . . . ' She began to blush a little, and turned away from him to walk to the other window. Vaguely, for it was open a little, came the sound of music from the ballroom. She wanted to open the window wider, but was afraid someone might hear if she and Kelly began to shout. She was feeling more and more light-headed, the room was so warm . . .

'Non-consummation . . . You had very little regard for my masculine pride in this matter, didn't you?' he said, mildly, and before she could retort, 'And just how, my darling, did you plan to prove the marriage was not consummated?'

'Sure, we . . . we tell the court, or sign affidavits, or – oh, why do you ask such silly questions? Liam will work it out.'

The face looked very grim. He had been leaning back in his chair, but looked, somehow, more dangerous, as if the negligence of his pose was deceptive. 'Judges have a tendency to ask silly questions just like that. And do you really believe that affidavits from two people who wish to be rid of each other will count for much?'

'Oh. Well, then – I suppose we have Doctor Lawler make some . . . embarrassing . . . medical examination . . . '

And the grey eyes were regarding her quietly, a touch of humour in their depths, in the curve of his mouth as he waited.

'No!' she squealed, and whirled away, almost losing her reasoning with the sudden knowledge of the ghastly truth. Jules was a name, and a vague memory of an afternoon spent in the bedroom of a townhouse in Paris. Jules suddenly loomed portentiously in her life in a way he never had during their brief liaison – there would be no proof of non-consummation. '*No, no, no . . . !*' She had no idea of her actions, heard the sound of china and glass crashing into the fireplace, found books beneath her hands and thrust them from her with all her force – losing her balance and reaching for the wall her hands came in contact with the drapes . . .

'No . . . ' She was murmuring the word aloud, came to herself lying on the floor, her head on her arms, realized she had fainted. On the floor, she felt a little better, her head was clearer, though it ached a little, and her heart still pounded. Kelly must be gone, and she could loosen the ridiculous stays . . .

He had not moved from his chair, but she surprised him in a look of pity as he gazed at her. 'Well,' he said calmly, 'I'm glad indeed to have witnessed that. I'll know, in future, what to remove from your vicinity in the order in which you reach for them; glassware and china first, followed by books and heavier ornaments, and finishing with the soft furnishings.'

She looked about her, slowly. The room was a disaster. It had always been so neat – white walls and only a few treasured ornaments – most of the latter lay shattered in the empty hearth. The white coverlet had been pulled from her little bed, the drapes lay on the floor. She sniffled; somewhere during that embarrassing scene she had begun to cry, but defiant, she turned to him. She was drained, too tired, too weak just yet, to raise herself from the floor, sat amidst the yards of the once spurious wedding gown and glared at the man she had married. 'You knew,' she accused the calm features, 'you knew all along I'd want an annulment . . .'

'I suspected,' he amended. 'Even you can't be so very impulsive about such a thing as marriage. I know it's a state that rather terrifies you.'

She looked up, about to argue, but his eyes held something that made her feel argument was useless, and besides, she was too tired. 'And you knew,' with bitter rancour, 'you knew I wouldn't be able to gain an annulment because of . . . There was no way to prove I was . . . Because I'd been . . . '

'Deflowered?' he put in helpfully. 'Yes, I have a great deal for which to thank Jules, Vincenzo and Sergei. If it hadn't been for them – or at least, one of them – we wouldn't be married at this moment.'

She wished she had the breath and the strength to rise gracefully and go to him, to slap his face very hard. She pressed her hand to her side and glared at him through her hair. 'We're trapped.' And the

1039

very word filled her with despair – the music that came through the window was a travesty, celebrating a change she wished no part in. 'Trapped . . . ' she murmured.

'That's a state of mind.' And she hated his gentle reasonableness more than anything else. 'You're trapped – *I* feel very happy, Mrs Kelly.'

'Stop calling me that!'

'Where shall we live, Clemency? Shall we buy a property here? Go back to England, or Ireland? I could buy Tineranna, if you'd like.' More soberly, 'I think I will buy Tineranna, anyway. I feel I should.'

'One more reason to spite your father?' she said, venomously.

He looked at her calmly. 'Your ability to speak the unadulterated truth is one of the main reasons why I adore you. You look a picture on that carpet,' he added, as she turned from him with a cry of frustration, 'but I'd prefer it if we could be seated on chairs and talk about our future like two adults.'

The pain in her side and the remorseless voice seemed the only, albeit unwelcome, realities. 'There's only one more thing I wish to speak with you about . . . '

'Go away!'

She felt his hand on her hair, realized with a shock that he was seated on the floor beside her. 'I'm going to be a faithful husband, Clemency. I spent most of the day considering it, and that's why I could stand up there in that church today and mean each and every one of those vows. It was comforting to know that at least one of us meant what they said.'

'Go away!'

'I'd like to know, merely to satisfy my curiosity, how long the affairs with Jules, Vincenzo and Sergei lasted.'

She tossed her hair back to regard him darkly. 'Are you going to throw them up at me for the rest of our lives?'

'No. And at least you have the good manners to remember your lovers' names. I've had too many and cared too little, I'm afraid, so there – I'm giving you some ammunition should we ever do battle on that score.'

He waited, and she sat up. 'Once with Jules and Vincenzo, twice with Sergei. Why are you looking at me like that?'

'Why twice with Sergei? He stirred the depth of your being such as no man had before?' And she did not like the turn of his mouth, as if he were trying not to smile.

'No,' she grated. 'He was more . . . persistent.'

'Yes,' consideringly, 'it's a trait I've admired in the Russians.'

His kind of madness was worse than hers, she decided, his

1040

tolerance bordered on the compulsive, and it weakened her; to fight him was like fighting a shadow. 'Kelly, divorce me on the grounds of adultery, on any . . . '

He had taken her face in his hands, kissed her gently, and then shook his head. 'No talk, not even a thought of adultery. I'm going to be a very tolerant husband, Clemency, more than you deserve. I shall give you rope enough to trip yourself with time and again. But adultery? No, my darling, that I will not tolerate. Cuckold me with any variations of Jules, Vincenzo or Sergei, no matter what the nationality, and I'll beat you so hard you won't be able to sit in a chair for a fortnight, let alone indulge in anything more athletic.'

'If you divorce me, I'll be your mistress, I'll even live in sin with you . . . '

'You can pretend to do that, my love. As for reality we have to think of the children . . . '

'Children! I loathe children!'

'Treat them like you treat puppies and lambs and they'll never know. Anyway, fortunately, I'm extremely rich. I can see our entourage will contain a whole tribe of nannies and nursery maids.'

'*Why do you want me!*' She pummelled at his chest until she had to stop for breath, then he kissed her, gently. 'No, Kelly,' pulling back, 'I'm too angry – and I'm afraid.'

He stood up, and thankfully, drew her up with him. 'So am I,' he said quietly.

And he was leaving. He paused at the door. 'Your little room is very charming, my darling. But you're my wife, and I love you, and I want you with me. Just down the hall, Clemency. A new life, if you want it, if you have the courage for it.'

And he was gone.

She was left looking about the wreckage of her room. Suddenly she saw it through his eyes. Clean, bare, colourless. Hell's outhouse, it looked just like Ma's room at Glenleigh!

She flopped down on to the bed, and gasped as her stays bit into her. She sat there, looking about her at what seemed to be the fragile defence she had built against the world. She was crying, gently, noiselessly, as she stood and began to struggle with the hooks of her gown.

In her nightdress, she studied her face in the mirror. Oddly enough, she looked pretty, there was colour in her cheeks and her eyes looked large, though it was deceptive – she was tired, so tired . . .

And still the tugging at her mind, at her body, and it led her, barefoot, to the door of her room, and she shut it behind her with only a brief look back at the years of her aloneness. Along the hall, and she opened the door of the green room, entered as if she had been pulled physically into the room.

She stood there, against the door, feeling the coolness of the woodwork through her thin nightdress. Her husband was reading a book. He looked up at her.

'If you say one word,' she said, 'I'll hit you.'

He did not speak, but opened his arms to her.

Tap. Tap-tap.

Aidan opened his eyes blearily, raised his head painfully from his arm, and tried to focus on the direction of the aggravating noise that had been going on for some time.

Tap-tap. Tap. Tap-tap.

A currawong, hard pale eyes intent, was stabbing with its cruel, steel-grey beak at his office window. A moth was caught within the room, it fluttered at the window not far from Aidan's face, and the currawong, on the window ledge outside, could not understand why his beak remained bruised but empty. Aidan made a slight move, and the bird took flight, left its irritatingly unavailable dinner and flew on black and white wings up into a tree, where it sat crowing its disgust, dancing along the branch.

Aidan's left arm was numb, his neck was stiff, and his head thumped as if one of the Danahers was playing the barawn within his skull. He groaned, looked out at the clear blue of the sky, then about his office desk at the three bottles of whiskey that comprised his entire month's supply here at Shannonbrook Two. There was half a bottle left. Jaysus, Mary and Joseph, it's a wonder he had not killed himself . . .

There was a small stove in the corner, and he lit it to heat water, made himself a cup of tea, and used the rest of the water to shave with the razor and soap he kept in a drawer. He then went outside, relieved himself, brought up the tea, and felt a little better.

His drunkenness had numbed his senses, but there were no answers for him this morning, no new sense of direction; nothing had changed from the confusion of the night before. He took Blue from the horse shelter, saddled him, and rode through the mill yard, wondering, as he did so, what had brought him here last night. Because here, with the timber, was where it had begun, his rise to wealth and social acceptance? Perhaps he had needed evidence of all he had built up, to strengthen himself for what lay ahead.

Matty must have a new home, no matter what had happened, no

matter what had been said. He owed her that. He would make sure it was in Moss Vale, near a school for the children, at a distance from him. And she was not to know he was behind it. He would arrange it as soon as possible.

And Clemency – he was absurdly aggrieved that she was married. He had had time to think, on that ride last night, in the hours in his office, drinking himself into unconsciousness – and though it irritated him, he was still aware of an unreasonable possessiveness. His little Rebel, Mrs Michael Kelly; even though she had married the man her father would have chosen for her, he disliked the manner in which she had gone about it. He had not wanted to spoil her wedding day with recriminations, but this morning he would tell her in no uncertain terms that she could at least have waited for a decent wedding and let him give her away.

Berri . . . There was no decision to be made there. Behind his need for action was the desire to anaesthetize his pain, the memory of her as she had been the night before, never more desirable to him, and never, as it turned out, further away from him.

The road here was steep, churned by carts over the past few days, and softened further by the rain of the night before. Twice, Blue's back hoofs slid with him. Aidan dismounted, then, and led the horse down the hill, walking, as much as possible, on the grassy verge. His thoughts were on the Queen Street house, and how often he would be allowed to call there – he smiled at a picture of himself with roses in his hand, nervously waiting on the doorstep. The smile became grim. Whatever it would take, begod. He would do whatever it would take to bring her home.

A bell bird called, off to his left, a pure, tinkling sound that was not often heard, now the Yarrawa scrub was being cleared and settled. Aidan glanced down the wooded slope towards the sound – and stopped, abruptly. Blue's nose bumped him between the shoulder blades. The horse stopped, stood close, breathing in the smell of its master, but Aidan was oblivious. He stood on the muddy track, feeling sick, faint, all his senses screaming at him. For there, drifting up the slope between ferns and tree trunks, in and out of the green shadows, was the Woman in Black.

The silver hair floated about her knees, it caught the sun and almost dazzled in its white light, cold, white and shining. Aidan stared, and wanted to run, but just as in the dreams, he could not move, could not, was imprisoned in his terror, frozen to the ground where he stood as the spectre floated towards him. All the deaths he had ever known came crowding upon him, the voices of the dead whispered to him . . . It was growing darker, darker . . .

He was clinging to the pommel of his saddle, his cheek against the warm leather, gasping for air, the spots that had crowded and darkened his vision were fading, he became aware of the smell of Blue's sweaty coat, the smell of the saddle leather, felt the horse stamp away the flies that were crawling on his legs, felt the soft muzzle come about to question at his jacket pocket, puzzled.

'Aidan?'

He did not move. The hair stood up on the back of his neck.

'Aidan, are you all right?'

It was Berrima. He recognized the voice, knew without looking up that it was Berrima. He still felt weak, his heart thudded alarmingly, but he raised his head and turned to look at her.

She still stood a little distance from him, down in the greenery. The morning sun through the leaves on the trees about them threw mottled patterns over her. She wore a black dress, one of her Mourning Mark dresses that had so irritated him, fold on fold of black silk and tafetta. The high collar held a brooch of silver and onyx. A black satin bonnet swung in one of her hands, and a black-beaded reticule purse in the other.

'Are you ill?' Concern on her face, in her low voice. She walked nearer to him.

'I . . . It's the heat. It's fierce hot, even now.' He swallowed with difficulty, stared at her face, at the incredible hair . . .

'I . . . I took my hair down. As you say, the heat . . . And I have a headache. I was going to put my hair up before I reached the mill.' She paused, as if it were his turn to speak.

'You came looking for me?'

She smiled, and she was lovely, and there was nothing, now, of Anna O'Hagan. Only Berrima, unreachable, there in the ferns. 'Everyone's asleep,' she said. 'I made them promise to wait until ten before they came searching for you – but I cheated, and left early. I had a feeling you'd come here – I don't know why. I left Penny and the carriage at the bottom of the slope when I realized how slippery it was.' He knew he was looking at her too intently, for she looked away, back down the slope through the trees. 'I saw some wild orchids, pink ones – do you see?'

He saw the pale pink blur amongst the shadows down the slope. 'No,' he said. 'Show me.'

And he tied Blue to a branch, and left him grazing, to follow Berrima down into the cool depths of shade. The bell bird called again, once, and from somewhere, invisible below them, a stream whispered. At a distance, in a drier part of the scrub, the cicadas were tuning up; by ten they would be a pulsing beat that would claim the bush, their song as harsh as the summer itself.

'Here,' she said.

The plant was attached to the V of a tree trunk, palest pink blossoms on delicate stems, each flower with a deeper pink centre, petals curled back, the colour almost throbbing amongst the cool greens of leaves and moss.

'Lovely,' he said. He studied it for a few minutes, then looked around them. There was something in the quiet of the place that reminded him of his glade at Port Davey, a sense of being at one with the earth, that the rest of civilization, resented at such a time, was thankfully, far away. He said, 'Will and I found a place like this, once.'

She smiled at him. 'You must bring him here. He and Cora and their daughter arrived on the late train last night. The party was just flagging, but it brightened after that . . . ' She watched him, and he saw something both questioning and knowledgeable in the brown eyes. 'You shouldn't have left so soon, Aidan. Father Davis arrived, and the Russells, and Hedley and Helena Warwick – so very many people, we had about three hundred there by eleven . . . '

'Why?' He regretted it, had almost barked the word.

She looked away, then brought her gaze back to his. 'Yes, everyone knew. The whole district knows. A woman called Matty Rodgers from near Glenquarry is telling everyone who'll listen . . . '

He had turned away, then felt her hand on his arm. 'It had to happen, Aidan. Clemency and Liam will be the first to tell you that. Both of them said this morning that they were relieved – Clemency, particularly, found it very amusing, for some reason. So don't be unhappy for their sakes.'

He turned to her, was about to speak, but the black dress annoyed him, he forgot what he was about to say, and growled, 'Why are you wearing black, Berri?'

Her face sober, 'It's Garth, Aidan. They went through the wreckage of the tavern that was burnt in the fire, looking for any valuables, and they found Garth's body. I can only hope he was unconscious when the fire reached the building. They found what remained of his horse in the burnt stables. The cigarette case that Mark gave Garth for his twenty-first birthday was found on the man's body – it was Garth. Hedley Warwick told us when he and Helena arrived last night – it was another reason why everyone was late arriving, the news of Garth, your past being exposed by that woman, and, as I suggested yesterday, so much for people to do, to help themselves, or relations or friends to clean up after the fires.'

1045

'I'm sorry about Garth,' Aidan said. 'He was a clever young man – 'twas a tragedy.'

'I won't wear mourning for long – I just feel . . . there's no one here who knew him closely, I was his only family here. I wrote to Victoria this morning. Liam added a short message. He let me read it. A gentle, tender message from a friend,' she smiled. 'But Victoria will understand, and I believe she'll come home to him.'

'Ah,' he said. 'And your parents?'

'I'm hoping they'll be in on the morning train. Liam's meeting it for me. They might be home when we get there.'

'Home,' he said heavily, gazing at her steadily.

She looked back at the orchids and touched one of the blossoms. 'I mean Shannonbrook Three, you know that.'

'I don't know what you mean. Last night you say you're leaving, then today you come looking for me. Why, Berri? Pity?'

'For you?' She laughed a little, did not even look at him. 'You'll cope, Aidan, with or without me. I was worried about you, that was all. I've been . . . resentful, you know, all these years, that you never shared any of your past with me. I felt your self-reliance was one of the things that drove a wedge between us. And then, last night, watching you when that man entered the house, realizing who he was and what you had been through because of him – I saw, then, that you weren't hiding things as much from me, as hiding them from yourself. I didn't want to leave,' and she was close to him, gazing up into his face, scanning his face, 'until I spoke to you. Can we talk, Aidan, when we get back to the house? Sometime, when we can be alone.'

'We can talk here,' he growled, for she was so very close . . .

But it would not do for Berrima. 'We can't stay here, Aidan. We have years to talk through. If you want to.'

'Yes,' he said, and he knew, now. 'Yes, I want to.'

She smiled, and turned away, up the slope, and he was filled with a childish rage that he gave way to without a second's hesitation, scooped her up in his arms, despite the protest of his stiff back, and looked about him. 'Aidan . . . !' He lowered her onto the ground, and leaned on her shoulders.

'Talk we will, as much as you like, but back at Shannonbrook Three are Kellys and Reynoldses and Treloars, and servants and more demands on you and I than I'm happy about right now.

'Now here,' as she was about to protest, 'we have leeches, in scrub like this. And bull ants, and snakes, and trap-door spiders . . . ' She gazed up at him with her eyes wide, yet even then, she refused to squirm and show she was afraid. 'And I'm going to hold you here as an unwilling prisoner until I . . . '

He did not manage to get any further, for she had reached up, placed her lips on his, her arms about his neck, and when she pulled back a little, 'Yes, Aidan.'

'I haven't asked you, yet. Do you still love me? Despite everything? For I love you, if it makes you feel better to hear me say it. Words won't make me any easier to live with though.'

'Yes,' she laughed.

'And – I'm mad to keep asking this bloody question – will you marry me, y' little hoor?'

'Yes.'

He stared at her, almost suspiciously. 'Begod, that was quick . . . No arguments? No rationalizations . . . ?'

She merely smiled up at him. Her hands were in his hair; he could feel the outline of her body beneath him, even through her heavy skirts. 'Berrima,' carefully, 'would you kick and scream and bellow, if I took you here and now?'

'Would it make any difference?'

'No. I just wondered if you'd kick and scream and bellow . . . ' Her lips were raised to his, reaching for his, and he leant to her, rolled over, lifting her with him, and the breeze whipped the silver hair around them, and the red lips were claiming him, the white arms were about him, and he gave himself to her – there was no past, no fear, there would be no more nightmares. Everything was right, *right* as he melted into her and knew he would never dream of the Woman in Black again for she would be beside him. Need never fear her again, for it was not Death that she had offered him.

She would not let him pluck the spray of tiny orchids for her, insisted they leave it growing. They walked together down the hill road, his arm about her, Blue following sedately behind them. They did not speak, for there was time and time for talking, and these were their last moments alone before the house opened its doors and its responsibilities to them.

Aidan tied Blue's reins to the back of the buggy and they drove home, Berrima seated beside him, her feet curled up on the seat beneath her skirts. He had taken off his coat, and she leaned her face against his shoulder, liked to feel the play of muscle along it as he drove. Once she looked up to find him gazing over Penny's ears with a dark and rather forbidding frown. 'What's the matter?' she asked gently.

He seemed to hesitate, glanced at her, then, 'Will we ever be able to get over it? Knowing we've wasted all these years?' She was very moved, and so surprised at his sudden desire to speak of his feelings that she could not, immediately, form a reply. And he had turned to her again, with all the longing of his soul upon his face, and said, 'Can we make . . . can we make an agreement? Not to hurt each other any more?'

She had no words, leaned forward to him, and he looped the reins over his arm before he drew her into his embrace.

'Aidan . . . ' through her tears, 'the reins . . . Penny . . . '

'Arra, she knows her way home.'

And this was true.

ABOUT THE AUTHOR

Veronica Geoghegan Sweeney was born in Paddington, New South Wales. After a year studying law at the University of Tasmania, she transferred to the New South Wales Conservatorium of Music, and began studying acting with Colleen Clifford and the Genesian Theatre. She has worked, variously, as singer, actress, playwright and script-writer. *The Emancipist* is her first novel. She is the great-great-granddaughter of Irish convicts, and the great-granddaughter of a bullock-driver who pioneered the north-west region of New South Wales. Her maternal grandfather was a horsebreaker and driver of mail coaches through the outback, and her father's family farmed in the New England Ranges until they lost their property in the Great Depression.

Her cultural links with Ireland remain strong, and she now, when her work allows, spends her time travelling between the three places she loves most, and to which *The Emancipist* is a tribute, Ireland, Tasmania, and the Southern Highlands of New South Wales.